A GRAMMAR OF CONTEMPORARY ENGLISH

RANDOLPH QUIRK

A GRAMMAR OF

SIDNEY GREENBAUM

CONTEMPORARY

GEOFFREY LEECH

ENGLISH

JAN SVARTVIK

ʃP

SEMINAR PRESS NEW YORK AND LONDON
A DIVISION OF HARCOURT BRACE JOVANOVICH, INC.

LONGMAN GROUP LIMITED LONDON
Associated companies, branches and representatives throughout the world

PUBLISHED IN THE UNITED STATES OF AMERICA BY

SEMINAR PRESS Inc. 111 Fifth Avenue, New York, N.Y. 10003

© **Longman Group Ltd 1972**

First published 1972
ISBN 0 582 52444 X
For Seminar Press Inc: ISBN 0 12 901250 5
Library of Congress Catalog Card Number 72 189941

Printed in Great Britain by
William Clowes & Sons, Limited,
London, Beccles and Colchester

CONTENTS

SYMBOLS AND TECHNICAL CONVENTIONS

Since our use of symbols, abbreviations, bracketing and the like follows the practice in most works of linguistics, all that we need here is a visual summary of the main types of convention with a brief explanation or a reference to where fuller information is given.

AmE, BrE:
American English, British English (*cf* Chapter 1.19 *ff*).

S, V, O, C, A, O_i etc:
See Chapter 2.3 *ff*, 3.9 *f*; when italicized, strings of these symbols refer to the clause types explained in Chapter 7.2 *ff*.

a BÈTter 'one:
Capitals in examples indicate *nuclear* syllables, and accents indicate the *intonation*, and verticals indicate *stress*: see Appendix II.3 *ff*, 12.

when DO is used:
Capitals in description indicate basic forms abstracted from the set of morphological variants ('we *do*', 'she *does*', 'they *did*', . . .)

*a more better one:
A preceding asterisk indicates an unacceptable structure.

?they seem fools:
A preceding question mark indicates doubtful acceptability; combined with an asterisk it suggests virtual unacceptability.

Help me (to) write:
Parentheses indicate optional items.

Help me with my work   [42]
Bracketed numerals appear after examples when required for cross-reference.

4.37; App I.12:
Cross-references to material other than examples are given by chapter (or appendix) and section number.

Bolinger (1971a):
References to other published work (see 2.27) are expanded in the Bibliography, *pp* 1085 *ff*.

He came $\begin{Bmatrix} \text{to} \\ \text{from} \end{Bmatrix} \begin{Bmatrix} \text{London} \\ \text{New York} \end{Bmatrix}$
Curved braces indicate free alternatives.

$\begin{bmatrix} \text{He} \\ \text{She} \end{bmatrix}$ does $\begin{bmatrix} \text{his} \\ \text{her} \end{bmatrix}$ best:

Square brackets indicate contingent alternatives; *eg* selection of the top one in the first pair entails selection of the top one in the second also.

{His [expensive (house insurance)]}:

Contrasting brackets can be used to give a linear indication of hierarchical structure.

[ɸju] 'phew':

Square brackets enclose phonetic symbols; the IPA conventions are followed (*cf* Jones (1969), *pp* xxxii *ff*).

/justə/ 'used to':

Slants enclose phonemic transcription, with conventions generally as in Jones (1969) and Kenyon and Knott (1953), but the following should be noted:

/e/ as in *best*, /ɪ/ *bid*, /i/ *beat*, /ɒ/ *hot*, /ɔ/ *law*, /ɑ/ *father*, /ʊ/ *full*, /u/ *fool*, /ɜ(r)/ *bird*, parentheses here denoting the possibility (*eg* in AmE) of 'postvocalic *r*'.

ONE
THE ENGLISH LANGUAGE

The importance of English
Criteria of 'importance'
1.1

English is the world's most important language. Even at a time when such a statement is taken as a long-standing truism, it is perhaps worthwhile to glance briefly at the basis on which it is made. There are, after all, thousands of different languages in the world, and it is in the nature of language that each one seems uniquely important to those who speak it as their native language – that is, their first (normally sole) tongue: the language they acquired at their mother's knee. But there are more objective standards of relative importance.

One criterion is the number of native speakers that a language happens to have. A second is the extent to which a language is geographically dispersed: in how many continents and countries is it used or is a knowledge of it necessary? A third is its 'vehicular load': to what extent is it a medium for a science or literature or other highly regarded cultural manifestation – including 'way of life'? A fourth is the economic and political influence of those who speak it as 'their own' language.

1.2

None of these is trivial but not all would unambiguously identify English. Indeed the first would make English a very poor second to Chinese (which has double the number of speakers) and would put English not appreciably in front of Hindi-Urdu. The second clearly makes English a front runner but also invites consideration of Hebrew, Latin and Arabic, for example, as languages used in major world religions, though only the last mentioned would be thought of in connection with the first criterion. By the third criterion, the great literatures of the Orient spring to mind, not to mention the languages of Tolstoy, Goethe, Cervantes and Racine. But in addition to being the language of the analogous Shakespeare, English scores as being the primary medium for twentieth-century science and technology. The fourth criterion invokes Japanese, Russian and German, for example, as languages of powerful, productive and influential communities. But English is the language of the United States which – to take one crude but objective measure – has a larger 'Gross National Product' (both in total and in relation to the population) than any other country in the world. Indeed the combined GNP of the USA, Canada and Britain is 50 per cent higher than that of the remaining OECD countries (broadly speaking, continental Europe plus Japan) put together: *cf* Organization for Economic Co-operation and Development, *Main Economic Indicators*, June 1971.

What emerges strikingly about English is that by any of the criteria it is prominent, by some it is pre-eminent, and by a combination of the four it is superlatively outstanding. Notice that no claim has been made for the importance of English on the grounds of its 'quality' as a language (the size of its vocabulary, the alleged flexibility of its syntax). It has been rightly said that the choice of an international language, or lingua franca, is never based on linguistic or aesthetic criteria but always on political, economic and demographic ones.

Native, second, and foreign language
1.3
English is the world's most widely used language. It is useful to distinguish three primary categories of use: as a *native* language, as a *second* language, and as a *foreign* language. English is spoken as a native language by nearly three hundred million people: in the United States, Britain, Ireland, Australia, New Zealand, Canada, the Caribbean and South Africa, without mentioning smaller countries or smaller pockets of native English speakers (for example in Rhodesia and Kenya). In several of these countries, English is not the sole language: the Quebec province of Canada is French-speaking, much of South Africa is Afrikaans-speaking, and for many Irish and Welsh people, English is not the native language. But for these Welsh, Irish, Québecois and Afrikaners, English will even so be a *second* language: that is, a language necessary for certain official, social, commercial or educational activities within their own country. This second-language function is more noteworthy, however, in a long list of countries where only a small proportion of the people have English as their native language: India, Pakistan, Nigeria, Kenya and many other Commonwealth countries and former British territories. Thus, a quarter of a century after independence, India maintains English as the medium of instruction for approximately half of its total higher education. English is the second language in countries of such divergent backgrounds as the Philippines and Ethiopia, while in numerous other countries (Burma, Thailand, South Korea and some Middle Eastern countries, for example) it has a second language status in respect of higher education. It is one of the two 'working' languages of the United Nations and of the two it is by far the more frequently used both in debate and in general conduct of UN business.

1.4
By *foreign* language we mean a language as used by someone for communication across frontiers or with people who are not his countrymen: listening to broadcasts, reading books or newspapers, commerce or travel, for example. No language is more widely studied or used as a

foreign language than English. The desire to learn it is immense and apparently insatiable. American organizations such as the United States Information Agency and the Voice of America have played a notable role in recent years, in close and amicable liaison with the British Council which provides support for English teaching both in the Commonwealth and in foreign countries throughout the world. The BBC, like the USIS, has notable radio and television facilities devoted to this purpose. Other English-speaking countries such as Australia also assume heavy responsibilities for teaching English as a foreign language. Taking the education systems of the world as a whole, one may say confidently (if perhaps ruefully) that more timetable hours are devoted to English than any other subject.

We shall look more closely in the next section at the kind and degree of demand, but meantime the reasons for the demand have surely become clear. To put it bluntly, English is a top requirement of those seeking good jobs – and is often the language in which much of the business of 'good jobs' is conducted. One needs it for access to at least one half of the world's scientific literature. It is thus intimately associated with technological and economic development and it is the principal language of international aid. Not only is it the universal language of international aviation, shipping and sport: it is to a considerable degree the universal language of literacy and public communication. Siegfried Muller (former Director of the Languages-of-the-World Archives in the US Department of Education) has estimated that about 60 per cent of the world's radio broadcasts and 70 per cent of the world's mail are in English. The great manufacturing countries Germany and Japan use English as their principal advertising and sales medium; it is the language of automation and computer technology.

The demand for English
1.5
The teaching of English
The role of chief foreign language that French occupied for two centuries from about 1700, therefore, has been undoubtedly assumed by English – except of course in the English-speaking countries themselves, where French is challenged only by Spanish as the foreign language most widely studied. Although patriotism obliges international organizations to devote far more resources to translation and interpreter services than reason would dictate, no senior post would be offered to a candidate deficient in English. The equivalent of the nineteenth-century European 'finishing school' in French now provides a liberal education in English, whether located in Sussex or in Switzerland. But a more general equivalent is perhaps the English-medium school organized through the state

education system, and such institutions seem to be even more numerous in the Soviet Union and other east European countries than in countries to the west. More general still, of course, is the language work in the ordinary schools, and in this connection the introduction at the primary (pre-*lycée*, pre-*Gymnasium*) level of foreign language teaching has meant a sharp but almost accidental increase in English teaching and in the demand for English teachers. That is, if a foreign language is to be taught at the primary level, what other language should the French or German schools teach but English? And if children already have some English before entering secondary education, what more obvious than to continue with this particular foreign language, making any other language at secondary level a lower priority option, learned to a less adequate degree?

To take France as an example, in the academic year 1968–69, English was being learned as first foreign language by 80 per cent of secondary school pupils, the nearest rival being German with 16 per cent. When we include those who study it as their second foreign language, we have a total of over two million teenagers studying English in France, a country with a tradition for teaching several other European languages – Spanish in the south-west, Italian in the south-east and German in the northeast.

1.6
A lingua franca in science and scholarship
We might refer also to an inquiry recently made into the use of foreign languages by the learned community in French-speaking territories. It transpired that 90 per cent found it necessary to use books in English – and this percentage included scholars whose research lay in the field of French literature. Perhaps even more significant: about 25 per cent preferred to publish their scholarly and scientific papers in English. The latter point is strikingly paralleled in Italy and Germany. About 1950, the Italian physics journal *Nuovo Cimento* decided to admit papers in languages other than Italian: in less than 20 years the proportion of papers published in Italian fell from 100 per cent to zero and the proportion of papers published in English rose from zero to 100 per cent. A German example: between 1962 and 1968 alone the proportion of articles published in English in *Physikalische Zeitschrift* rose from 2 per cent to 50 per cent. In both these cases, the change may in part be due to the editors' acceptance of papers by American, British and other English-speaking physicists, but for the most part one would surely be right in thinking that it reflects the European scientists' desire to share their research most efficiently with their colleagues all over the world by means of the twentieth-century lingua franca. Telling evidence of this is pro-

vided by the European journal *Astronomy and Astrophysics* in which two-thirds of the contributions by French scientists are in English, and by the official publication of the Agence Internationale de l'Énergie Atomique, *Nuclear Fusion*, where *all* articles are in English, despite the fact that the Agency is subsidized by the French Government.

1.7
International character of English

For the foregoing observations, we have deliberately drawn heavily on the work of an outstandingly qualified Frenchman, Denis Girard, Inspecteur Régional de l'Académie de Paris, in order to insure ourselves against the danger of overstating the importance of English, and to assure ourselves of seeing English measured in terms of international values. Not that one is tempted to do otherwise. English, which we have referred to as a lingua franca, is pre-eminently the most international of languages. Though the mention of the language may at once remind us of England, on the one hand, or cause association with the might of the United States on the other, it carries less implication of political or cultural specificity than any other living tongue (with French and Spanish also notable in this respect). At one and the same time, it serves the daily purposes of republics such as the United States and South Africa, sharply different in size, population, climate, economy and national philosophy; and it serves an ancient kingdom such as Britain, as well as her widely scattered Commonwealth partners, themselves as different from each other as they are from Britain herself.

But the cultural neutrality of English must not be pressed too far. The literal or metaphorical use of such expressions as *case law* throughout the English-speaking world reflects a common heritage in our legal system; and allusions to or quotations from Shakespeare, the Authorized Version, Gray's *Elegy*, Mark Twain, a sea shanty, a Negro spiritual or a Beatles song – wittingly or not – testify similarly to a shared culture. *The Continent* means 'continental Europe' as readily in America and even Australia and New Zealand as it does in Britain. At other times, English equally reflects the independent and distinct culture of one or other of the English-speaking communities. When an Australian speaks of *fossicking* something out (searching for something), the metaphor looks back to the desperate activity of reworking the diggings of someone else in the hope of finding gold that had been overlooked. When an American speaks of *not getting to first base* (not achieving even initial success), the metaphor concerns an equally culture-specific activity – the game of baseball. And when an Englishman says that something is *not cricket* (unfair), the allusion is also to a game that is by no means universal in the English-speaking countries,

Grammar and the study of language
Types of linguistic organization
1.8
Sounds and spellings

The claim is, therefore, that on the one hand there is a single 'English language' (the grammar of which is the concern of this book), but that on the other there are recognizable varieties. Since these varieties can have reflexes in any of the types of organization that the linguist distinguishes, this is the point at which we should outline these types of organization (or 'levels' as they are sometimes called), one of which is 'grammar'. When someone communicates with us by means of language, he normally does so by causing us to hear a stream of sounds. We hear the sounds not as indefinitely variable in acoustic quality (however much they may be so in actual physical fact). Rather, we hear them as each corresponding to one of a very small set (in English, /p/, /l/, /n/, /i/, /ð/, /s/ . . .) which can combine in certain ways and not others. For example, in English we have *spin* but not **psin*, our use of the asterisk here and elsewhere in this book denoting non-occurring or unacceptable forms. We similarly observe patterns of stress and pitch. The sounds made in a particular language and the rules for their organization are studied in the branch of linguistics known as PHONOLOGY, while their physical properties and their manner of articulation are studied in PHONETICS.

Another major method of linguistic communication is by visual signs, that is, writing; and for English as for many other languages there has been developed an alphabetic writing system with symbols basically related to the individual sounds used in the language. Here again there is a closely structured organization which regards certain differences in shape as irrelevant and others (for example capitals versus lower case, ascenders to the left or right of a circle – *b* versus *d*) as significant. The study of GRAPHOLOGY or ORTHOGRAPHY thus parallels the study of phonology in several obvious ways. Despite the notorious oddities of English spelling, there are important general principles: *eg* combinations of letters that English permits (*tch, qu, ss, oo*) and others that are disallowed (**pfx, *qi, *yy*) or have only restricted distribution (final *v* or *j* occurs only exceptionally as in *Raj, spiv*).

1.9
Lexicology, semantics, grammar

Just as the small set of arabic numerals can be combined to express in writing any natural numbers we like, however vast, so the small set of sounds and letters can be combined to express in speech or writing respectively an indefinitely large number of WORDS. These linguistic units enable people to refer to every object, action and quality that members of a society wish to distinguish: in English, *door, soap, indignation, find, stupefy, good, uncontrollable,* and so on to a total in the region of at least half a million. These units of language have a meaning and a structure (sometimes an obviously composite structure as in cases like *uncontrollable*) which relate them not only to the world outside language but to other words within the language (*good, bad, kind,* etc). The study of words is the business of LEXICOLOGY but the regularities in their formation are similar in kind to the regularities of grammar and are closely connected to them (*cf* App I.1 *ff*). Meaning relations as a whole are the business of SEMANTICS, the study of meaning, and this therefore has relevance equally within lexicology and within grammar.

There is one further type of organization. The words that have been identified by sound or spelling must be combined into larger units and it is the complex set of rules specifying such combination that we refer to as GRAMMAR. This word has various common meanings in English (as in other languages: *cf: grammaire, Grammatik*) and since it is the subject matter of this book some of its chief meanings should be explored.

The meanings of 'grammar'
1.10
Syntax and inflections

We shall be using 'grammar' to include both SYNTAX and the INFLECTIONS (or accidence) of MORPHOLOGY. The fact that the past tense of *buy* is *bought* (inflection) and the fact that the interrogative form of *He bought it* is *Did he buy it?* (syntax) are therefore both equally the province of grammar. There is nothing esoteric or technical about our usage in this respect: it corresponds to one of the common lay uses of the word in the English-speaking world. A teacher may comment

John uses good grammar but his spelling is awful

showing that spelling is excluded from grammar; and if John wrote *interloper* where the context demanded *interpreter*, the teacher would say that he had used the wrong word, not that he had made a mistake in grammar. So far so good. But in the education systems of the English-speaking countries, it is possible also to use the term 'grammar' loosely so as to include both spelling and lexicology, and we need to be on our guard so that we recognize when the word is used in so sharply different a way. A 'grammar lesson' for children may in fact be concerned with any aspect of the use, history, spelling or even pronunciation of words.

When *grammar* is prefixed to *school* (as it is in several English-speaking countries, though not always with reference to the same type of school), the term reflects the historical fact that certain schools concentrated at one time upon the teaching of Latin and Greek. This is the 'grammar' in their name. No serious ambiguity arises from this, though one sometimes comes upon the lay supposition that such schools do or should make a special effort to teach *English* grammar. But there is a further use of 'grammar' which springs indirectly from this educational tradition. It makes sense for the lay native speaker to say

Latin has a good deal of grammar, but English has hardly any

since the aspect of Latin grammar on which we have traditionally concentrated is the paradigms (model sets) of inflections. This in effect meant that grammar became identified with inflections or accidence, so that we can still speak of 'grammar and syntax' in this connection, tacitly excluding the latter from the former. And since all of the uses of 'grammar' so far illustrated might appear in the speech or writing of the same person, the possibilities of misunderstanding are very real.

1.11
Rules and the native speaker
Nor have we completed the inventory of meanings. The same native speaker, turning his attention from Latin, may comment:

French has a well-defined grammar, but in English we're free to speak as we like

Several points need to be made here. To begin with, it is clear that the speaker cannot now be intending to restrict 'grammar' to inflections: rather the converse; it would seem to be used as a virtual synonym of 'syntax'.

Secondly, the native speaker's comment probably owes a good deal to the fact that he does not feel the rules of his own language – rules that he has acquired unconsciously – to be at all constraining; and if ever he happens to be called on to explain one such rule to a foreigner he has very great difficulty. By contrast, the grammatical rules he learns for a foreign language seem much more rigid and they also seem clearer because they have been actually spelled out to him in the learning process.

But another important point is revealed in this sentence. The distinction refers to grammar not as the observed patterns in the use of French but to a codification of rules compiled by the French to show the French themselves how their language should be used. This is not grammar 'immanent' in a language (as our previous uses were, however much they differed in the types of pattern they referred to), but grammar as codified by grammarians: the Academy Grammar. There is no such

Academy for the English language and so (our naive native speaker imagines) the English speaker has more 'freedom' in his usage.

1.12
The codification of rules

The 'codification' sense of *grammar* is readily identified with the specific codification by a specific grammarian:

Jespersen wrote a good grammar, and so did Kruisinga

and this sense naturally leads to the concrete use as in

Did you bring your grammars?

and naturally, too, the codification may refer to grammar in any of the senses already mentioned. A French grammar will be devoted very largely to syntax, while accidents of intellectual history in the nineteenth century lead one to treat without surprise the fact that an Old High German grammar (or an Old English grammar) may well contain only *inflections* together with a detailed explanation of how the *phonological* system emerged.

The codification will also vary, however, according to the linguistic theory embraced by the author, his idea of the nature of grammar *per se* rather than his statement of the grammar of a particular language:

Shaumjan has devised a grammar interestingly different from Chomsky's

It is important to realize that, in the usage of many leading linguists, this last sense of grammar has returned to the catholicity that it had in the Greek tradition more than two thousand years ago, covering the whole field of language structure. Thus, in the framework of formal linguistics, contemporary generative grammarians will speak of 'the grammar' as embracing rules not only for syntax but for phonological, lexical and semantic specification as well.

1.13
Grammar and other types of organization

Progress towards a more explicit type of grammatical description is inevitably slow and the whole field of grammar is likely to remain an area of interesting controversy. While theoretical problems are not the concern of this book, our treatment cannot be neutral on the issues that enliven current discussion. For example, we would not wish to assert the total independence of grammar from phonology on the one hand and lexico-semantics on the other as was implied in the deliberate oversimplification of 1.8 *f*. Phonology is seen to have a bearing on grammar even in small points such as the association of initial /ð/ with demonstrativeness and conjunction (*this*, *then*, *though*, etc: 2.13). It is seen to bear on lexicology, for example, in the fact that numerous nouns and verbs differ only in the position of a stress (App I.43, App II.5):

That is an 'insult
They may in'sult me

But most obviously the interdependence of phonology and grammar is shown in focus processes (*cf* the connection between intonation and linear presentation: 14.2–7), and in the fact that by merely altering the phonology one can distinguish sets of sentences like those quoted in App II.20.

The interrelations of grammar, lexicology and semantics are still more pervasive. To take an obvious example, the set of sentences

John hated the shed
John painted the shed
Fear replaced indecision

have a great deal in common that must be described in terms of grammar. They have the same tense (past), the same structure (subject plus verb plus object), will permit the same syntactic operations as in

The shed was painted by John
Did John paint the shed?
It was John that painted the shed

Up to a point they will also permit the permutation of their parts so that the abstraction 'subject – verb – object' appears to be an adequate analysis:

John replaced the shed
John hated indecision

But by no means all permutations are possible:

*Fear painted the shed
*Fear hated indecision
*John replaced indecision

To what extent should the constraints disallowing such sentences be accounted for in the grammatical description? Questions of this kind will remain intensely controversial for a long time, and little guidance on the problems involved can be given in this book (*cf* however 7.37–38).

1.14
Grammar and generalization
Our general principle will be to regard grammar as accounting for constructions where greatest generalization is possible, assigning to lexi-

cology constructions on which least generalization can be formulated (which approach, that is, the idiosyncratic and idiomatic). The gradient of 'greatest' to 'least' in the previous sentence admits at once the unfortunate necessity for arbitrary decision. Confronted with the correspondences:

He spoke these words   ↔   The speaker of these words
He wrote these words   ↔   The writer of these words

we will wish to describe within grammar the way in which items in the first column can be transformed into the shape given them in the second. But this will leave us with second column items such as

∅   ↔   The author of these words

for which there is no first-column 'source'. This particular example, we may agree, raises no semantic problem: there is merely a lexicological gap in the language – no verb *auth*. But we have also first-column items for which there is no second-column transform:

He watched the play   ↔   ∅

Here we cannot account for the constraint in terms of a lexical gap, but we may be very uncertain as to whether it is a problem for lexicology or grammar (*cf* App I.24).

One further example:

He spattered the wall with oil
He smeared the wall with oil
He rubbed the wall with oil
He dirtied the wall with oil
*He poured the wall with oil

It is not easy to decide whether we should try to account within grammar for the imbalance in relating items from such a set to alternative predication forms (12.62 *f*):

He spattered oil on the wall
He smeared oil on the wall
He rubbed oil on the wall
*He dirtied oil on the wall
He poured oil on the wall

The question is not merely how minimally general must a rule be before it ceases to be worth presenting within grammar but one of much deeper theoretical concern: what, if anything, ultimately distinguishes a rule of grammar from a rule of semantics? Provided that we can remember at all times that such questions remain matters for debate, no harm is done by offering – as we do in this book – some provisional answers.

Varieties of English and classes of varieties
1.15
Having established, subject to these important qualifications, the extent
to which we may speak of different types of linguistic organization such
as phonology, lexicology and grammar, we may now return to the point
we had reached at the beginning of 1.8. What are the varieties of English
whose differing properties are realized through the several types of
linguistic organization?

A great deal has been written in recent years attempting to provide a
theoretical basis on which the varieties of any language can be described,
interrelated and studied: it is one of the prime concerns of the relatively
new branch of language study called SOCIOLINGUISTICS. The problem
is formidable, we are far from having complete answers, and all attempts
are in some degree an oversimplification. It may help now to consider
one such oversimplification for the purposes of this book. First, an
analogy. The properties of dog-ness can be seen in both terrier and alsa-
tian (and, we must presume, equally), yet no single variety of dog em-
bodies all the features present in all varieties of dog. In a somewhat
similar way, we need to see a common core or nucleus that we call
'English' being realized only in the different actual varieties of the language that we hear or read. Let us imagine six kinds of varieties ranged
as below and interrelated in ways we shall attempt to explain.

THE COMMON CORE OF ENGLISH

VARIETY CLASSES	VARIETIES WITHIN EACH CLASS
Region:	$R_1, R_2, R_3, R_4, \ldots$
Education and social standing:	$E_1, E_2, E_3, E_4, \ldots$
Subject matter:	$S_1, S_2, S_3, S_4, \ldots$
Medium:	$M_1, M_2, \ldots$
Attitude:	$A_1, A_2, A_3, A_4, \ldots$
Interference:	$I_1, I_2, I_3, I_4, \ldots$

The fact that in this figure the 'common core' dominates all the varieties means that, however esoteric or remote a variety may be, it has running through it a set of grammatical and other characteristics that are present in all others. It is presumably this fact that justifies the application of the name 'English' to all the varieties. From this initial point onwards, it will be noted that nothing resembling a noded tree structure is suggested: instead, it is claimed by the sets of braces that each variety class is related equally and at all points to each of the other variety classes. We shall however return and make qualifications to this claim. The classes themselves are arranged in a meaningful order and the justification will become clear in what follows.

Regional variation
1.16
Varieties according to region have a well-established label both in popular and technical use: 'dialects'. Geographical dispersion is in fact the classic basis for linguistic variation and in the course of time, with poor communications and relative remoteness, such dispersion results in dialects becoming so distinct that we regard them as different languages. This latter stage was long ago reached with the Germanic dialects that are now Dutch, English, German, Swedish, etc, but it has not been reached (and may not necessarily ever be reached, given the modern ease of communication) with the dialects of English that have resulted from the regional separation of communities within the British Isles and (since the voyages of exploration and settlement in Shakespeare's time) elsewhere in the world.

Regional variation seems to be realized predominantly in phonology. That is, we generally recognize a different dialect from a speaker's pronunciation or accent before we notice that his vocabulary (or lexicon) is also distinctive. Grammatical variation tends to be less extensive and certainly less obtrusive. But all types of linguistic organization can readily enough be involved. A Lancashire man may be recognized by a Yorkshireman because he pronounces an /r/ after vowels as in *stir* or *hurt*. A *middy* is an Australian measure for beer – but it refers to a considerably bigger measure in Sydney than it does in Perth. Instead of *I saw it*, a New Englander might say *I see it*, a Pennsylvanian *I seen it* and a Virginian either *I seen it* or *I seed it*, if they were speaking the natural dialect of their locality, and the same forms distinguish certain dialects within Britain too.

Note
The attitude of native speakers to other people's dialect varies greatly, but, in general, dialects of rural and agricultural communities are regarded as more pleasant than

dialects of large urban communities such as New York or Birmingham. This is connected, of course, with social attitudes and the association of city dialects with variation according to education and social standing (1.18) rather than region.

1.17

It is pointless to ask how many dialects of English there are: there are indefinitely many, depending solely on how detailed we wish to be in our observations. But they are of course more obviously numerous in the long-settled Britain than in the more recently settled North America or in the still more recently settled Australia and New Zealand. The degree of generality in our observation depends crucially upon our standpoint as well as upon our experience. An Englishman will hear an American Southerner primarily as an American and only as a Southerner in addition if further subclassification is called for and if his experience of American English dialects enables him to make it. To an American the same speaker will be heard first as a Southerner and then (subject to similar conditions) as, say, a Virginian, and then perhaps as a Piedmont Virginian. One might suggest some broad dialectal divisions which are rather generally recognized. Within North America, most people would be able to distinguish Canadian, New England, Midland, and Southern varieties of English. Within the British Isles, Irish, Scots, Northern, Midland, Welsh, South-western, and London varieties would be recognized with similar generality. Some of these – Irish and Scots for example – would be recognized as such by many Americans and Australians too, while in Britain many people could make subdivisions: Ulster and Southern might be distinguished within Irish, for example, and Yorkshire picked out as an important subdivision of northern speech. British people can also, of course, distinguish North Americans from all others (though not usually Canadians from Americans), South Africans from Australians and New Zealanders (though mistakes are frequent), but not usually Australians from New Zealanders.

1.18
Education and social standing

Within each of the dialect areas, there is considerable variation in speech according to education and social standing. There is an important polarity of uneducated and educated speech in which the former can be identified with the regional dialect most completely and the latter moves away from dialectal usage to a form of English that cuts across dialectal boundaries. To revert to an example given in a previous section, one would have to look rather hard (or be a skilled dialectologist) to find, as an outsider, a New Englander who said *see* for *saw*, a Pennsylvanian who said *seen*, and a Virginian who said *seed*. These are forms that tend to be replaced by *saw* with schooling, and in speaking to a stranger a dialect speaker would tend to use 'school' forms. On the other hand, there is no simple equation of dialectal and uneducated English. Just as educated English (*I saw*) cuts across dialectal boundaries, so do many features of uneducated use: a prominent example is the double negative as in *I don't want no cake* which has been outlawed from all educated English by the prescriptive grammar tradition for hundreds of years but which continues to thrive in uneducated speech wherever English is spoken.

Educated speech – by definition the language of education – naturally tends to be given the additional prestige of government agencies, the learned professions, the political parties, the press, the law court and the pulpit – any institution which must attempt to address itself to a public beyond the smallest dialectal community. The general acceptance of 'BBC English' for this purpose over almost half a century is paralleled by a similar designation for general educated idiom in the United States, 'network English'. By reason of the fact that educated English is thus accorded implicit social and political sanction, it comes to be referred to as Standard English, and provided we remember that this does not mean an English that has been formally standardized by official action, as weights and measures are standardized, the term is useful and appropriate. In contrast with Standard English, forms that are especially associated with uneducated (rather than dialectal) use are often called 'substandard'.

1.19
Standard English
The degree of acceptance of a single standard of English throughout the world, across a multiplicity of political and social systems, is a truly remarkable phenomenon: the more so since the extent of the uniformity involved has, if anything, increased in the present century. Uniformity is greatest in what is from most viewpoints the least important type of linguistic organization – the purely secondary one of orthography. Although printing houses in all English-speaking countries retain a tiny element of individual decision (*realize, -ise; judg(e)ment;* etc), there is basically a single, graphological spelling and punctuation system throughout: with two minor subsystems. The one is the subsystem with British orientation (used in all English-speaking countries except the United States) with distinctive forms in only a small class of words, *colour, centre, levelled,* etc. The other is the American subsystem: *color, center, leveled,* etc. In Canada, the British subsystem is used for the most part, but some publishers (especially of popular material) follow the American subsystem and some a mixture (*color* but *centre*). In the American Mid-West, some newspaper publishers (but not book publishers) use a few additional separate spellings such as *thru* for *through*. One minor

orthographic point is oddly capable of Anglo-American misunderstanding: the numerical form of dates. In British (and European) practice '7/11/72' would mean '7 November 1972', but in American practice it would mean 'July 11 1972'.

In grammar and vocabulary, Standard English presents somewhat less of a monolithic character, but even so the world-wide agreement is extraordinary and – as has been suggested earlier – seems actually to be increasing under the impact of closer world communication and the spread of identical material and non-material culture. The uniformity is especially close in neutral or formal styles (1.27) of written English (1.25) on subject matter (1.24) not of obviously localized interest: in such circumstances one can frequently go on for page after page without encountering a feature which would identify the English as belonging to one of the *national standards*.

National standards of English
1.20
British and American English

What we are calling national standards should be seen as distinct from the Standard English which we have been discussing and which we should think of as being 'supra-national', embracing what is common to all. Again, as with orthography, there are two national standards that are overwhelmingly predominant both in the number of distinctive usages and in the degree to which these distinctions are 'institutionalized': American English and British English. Grammatical differences are few and the most conspicuous are widely known to speakers of both national standards; the fact that AmE has two past participles for *get* and BrE only one (3.68), for example, and that in BrE the indefinite pronoun *one* is repeated in co-reference where AmE uses *he* (4.126) as in

$$\text{One cannot succeed at this unless} \begin{Bmatrix} \text{one} \\ \text{he} \end{Bmatrix} \text{tries hard}$$

Lexical examples are far more numerous, but many of these are also familiar to users of both standards: for example, *railway* (BrE), *railroad* (AmE); *tap* (BrE), *faucet* (AmE); *autumn* (BrE), *fall* (AmE). More recent lexical innovations in either area tend to spread rapidly to the other. Thus while radio sets have had *valves* in BrE but *tubes* in AmE, television sets have *tubes* in both, and *transistors* are likewise used in both standards.

The United States and Britain have been separate political entities for two centuries; for generations, thousands of books have been appearing annually; there is a long tradition of publishing descriptions of both AmE and BrE. These are important factors in establishing and institutionalizing the two national standards, and in the relative absence of such conditions other national standards are both less distinct (being more open to the influence of either AmE or BrE) and less institutionalized.

1.21
Scotland, Ireland, Canada
Scots, with ancient national and educational institutions, is perhaps nearest to the self-confident independence of BrE and AmE, though the differences in grammar and vocabulary are rather few. There is the preposition *outwith* 'except' and some other grammatical features, and such lexical items as *advocate* in the sense 'practising lawyer' or *bailie* 'municipal magistrate' and several others which, like this, refer to Scottish affairs. Orthography is identical with BrE though *burgh* corresponds closely to 'borough' in meaning and might almost be regarded as a spelling variant. But this refers only to official Scots usage. In the 'Lallans' Scots, which has some currency for literary purposes, we have a highly independent set of lexical, grammatical, phonological and orthographical conventions, all of which make it seem more like a separate language than a regional dialect.

Irish (or Hiberno-) English should also be regarded as a national standard for though we lack descriptions of this long-standing variety of English it is consciously and explicitly regarded as independent of BrE by educational and broadcasting services. The proximity of Britain, the easy movement of population, and like factors mean however that there is little room for the assertion and development of separate grammar and vocabulary. In fact it is probable that the influence of BrE (and even AmE) is so great on both Scots and Irish English that independent features will diminish rather than increase with time.

Canadian English is in a similar position in relation to AmE. Close economic, social and intellectual links along a 4000-mile frontier have naturally caused the larger community to have an enormous influence on the smaller, not least in language. Though in many respects (*zed* instead of *zee*, for example, as the name of the letter 'z'), Canadian English follows British rather than United States practice, and has a modest area of independent lexical use (*pogey* 'welfare payment', *riding* 'parliamentary constituency', *muskeg* 'kind of bog'), in many other respects it has approximated to AmE, and in the absence of strong institutionalizing forces it seems likely to continue in this direction.

1.22
South Africa, Australia, New Zealand
South Africa, Australia and New Zealand are in a very different position, remote from the direct day-to-day impact of either BrE or AmE. While in orthography and grammar the South African English in educated use

is virtually identical with BrE, rather considerable differences in vocabulary have developed, largely under the influence of the other official language of the country, Afrikaans. For example, *veld* 'open country', *koppie* 'hillock', *dorp* 'village', *konfyt* 'candied peel'. Because of the remoteness from Britain or America, few of these words have spread: an exception is *trek* 'journey'.

New Zealand English is more like BrE than any other non-European variety, though it has adopted quite a number of words from the indigenous Maoris (for example, *whare* 'hut' and of course *kiwi* and other names for fauna and flora) and over the past half century has come under the powerful influence of Australia and to a considerable extent of the United States.

Australian English is undoubtedly the dominant form of English in the Antipodes and by reason of Australia's increased wealth, population and influence in world affairs, this national standard (though still by no means fully institutionalized) is exerting an influence in the northern hemisphere, particularly in Britain. Much of what is distinctive in Australian English is confined to familiar use. This is especially so of grammatical features like adverbial *but* or the use of the feminine pronoun both anaphorically for an inanimate noun (*job . . . her*) and also impersonally and non-referentially for 'things in general':

The job's still not done; I'll finish her this arvo, but.
(. . . it this afternoon, however.)
'Are you feeling better?' 'Too right, mate; she'll be jake.'
('. . . Absolutely, old man; everything will be fine.')

But there are many lexical items that are to be regarded as fully standard: not merely the special fauna and flora (*kangaroo, gumtree, wattle,* etc) but special Australian uses of familiar words (*paddock* as a general word for 'field', *crook* 'ill', etc), and special Australian words (*bowyang* 'a trouser strap', *waddy* 'a bludgeon', etc).

1.23
Pronunciation and standard English
This list does not exhaust the regional or national variants that approximate to the status of a standard (the Caribbean might be mentioned, for example), but the important point to stress is that all of them are remarkable primarily in the tiny extent to which even the most firmly established, BrE and AmE, differ from each other in vocabulary, grammar and orthography. We have been careful, however, not to mention pronunciation in this connection. Pronunciation is a special case for several reasons. In the first place, it is the type of linguistic organization (1.8)

which distinguishes one national standard from another most immediately and completely and which links in a most obvious way the national standards to the regional varieties. Secondly (with an important exception to be noted), it is the least institutionalized aspect of Standard English, in the sense that, provided our grammar and lexical items conform to the appropriate national standard, it matters less that our pronunciation follows closely our individual regional pattern. This is doubtless because pronunciation is essentially gradient, a matter of 'more or less' rather than the discrete 'this or that' features of grammar and lexicon. Thirdly, norms of pronunciation are subject less to educational and national constraints than to social ones: this means, in effect, that some regional accents are less acceptable for 'network use' than others; cf 1.16 Note.

Connected with this is the exception referred to above. In BrE, one type of pronunciation comes close to enjoying the status of 'standard': it is the accent associated with the English public schools, 'Received Pronunciation' or 'RP'. Because this has traditionally been transmitted through a private education system based upon boarding schools insulated from the locality in which they happen to be situated, it is importantly non-regional, and this – together with the obvious prestige that the social importance of its speakers has conferred on it – has been one of its strengths as a lingua franca. But RP no longer has the unique authority it had in the first half of the twentieth century. It is now only one of the accents commonly used on the BBC and takes its place along with others which carry the unmistakable mark of regional origin – not least, an Australian or North American or Caribbean origin. Thus the rule that a specific type of pronunciation is relatively unimportant seems to be in the process of losing the notable exception that RP has constituted.

Note
The extreme variation that is tolerated in the pronunciation of English in various countries puts a great responsibility upon the largely uniform orthography (1.19) in preserving the intercomprehensibility of English throughout the world. A 'phonetic' spelling would probably allow existing differences to become greater whereas – through 'spelling pronunciation' with increased literacy – our conventional orthography not merely checks the divisiveness of pronunciation change but actually reduces it.

1.24
Varieties according to subject matter
Varieties according to the subject matter involved in a discourse have attracted linguists' attention a good deal in recent years. They are sometimes referred to as 'registers', though this term is applied to different types of linguistic variety by different linguists. The theoretical bases for

considering subject-matter varieties are highly debatable, but certain broad truths are clear enough. While one does not exclude the possibility that a given speaker may choose to speak in a national standard at one moment and in a regional dialect the next – and possibly even switch from one national standard to another – the presumption has been that an individual adopts one of the varieties so far discussed as his permanent form of English. With varieties according to subject matter, on the other hand, the presumption is rather that the same speaker has a repertoire of varieties and habitually switches to the appropriate one as occasion arises. Naturally, however, no speaker has a very large repertoire, and the number of varieties he commands depends crucially upon his specific profession, training, range of hobbies, etc.

Most typically, perhaps, the switch involves nothing more than turning to the particular set of lexical items habitually used for handling the topic in question. Thus, in connection with repairing a machine: *nut, bolt, wrench, thread, lever, finger-tight, balance, adjust, bearing, axle, pinion, split-pin,* and the like. 'I am of course using *thread* in the engineering sense, not as it is used in needlework', one says. But there are grammatical correlates to subject-matter variety as well. To take a simple example, the imperatives in cooking recipes: 'Pour the yolks into a bowl', not 'You should' or 'You must' or 'You might care to', still less 'The cook should . . .' More complex grammatical correlates are to be found in the language of technical and scientific description: the passive is common and clauses are often 'nominalized' (13.34*f*); thus not usually

You can rectify this fault if you insert a wedge . . .

but rather

Rectification of this fault is achieved by insertion of a wedge . . .

More radical grammatical changes are made in the language of legal documents:

Provided that such payment as aforesaid shall be a condition
precedent to the exercise of the option herein specified . . .

and the language of prayer:

Eternal God, Who dost call all men into unity with Thy Son . . .

It need hardly be emphasized that the type of language required by choice of subject matter would be roughly constant against the variables (dialect, national standard) already discussed. Some obvious contingent constraints are however emerging: the use of a specific variety of one class frequently presupposes the use of a specific variety of another. The use of a well-formed *legal* sentence, for example, presupposes an *educated* variety of English.

Note
Some subject matter (non-technical essays on humanistic topics, for example) invites linguistic usages that we shall refer to as *literary*; others (law, religion) involve usages that are otherwise *archaic*, though there is a strong trend away from such archaism in these fields. Poetry also frequently uses archaic features of English, while 'literary' English must sometimes be described as *poetic* if it shows features that are rare in prose. By contrast, technical or learned writing, in showing a close relation to a particular subject matter (psychology, electronics, or linguistics, for example), is often pejoratively referred to as *jargon*, especially when technical language is used too obtrusively or to all appearances unnecessarily.

Varieties according to medium
1.25
The only varieties according to medium that we need to consider are those conditioned by speaking and writing respectively. Since speech is the primary or natural medium for linguistic communication, it is reasonable to see the present issue as a statement of the differences imposed on language when it has to be couched in a graphic (and normally visual) medium instead. Most of these differences arise from two sources. One is situational: the use of a written medium normally presumes the absence of the person(s) to whom the piece of language is addressed. This imposes the necessity of a far greater explicitness: the careful and precise completion of a sentence, rather than the odd word, supported by gesture, and terminating when the speaker is assured by word or look that his hearer has understood. As a corollary, since the written sentence can be read and re-read, slowly and critically (whereas the spoken sentence is mercifully evanescent), the writer tends to anticipate criticism by writing more concisely as well as more carefully and elegantly than he may choose to speak.

The second source of difference is that many of the devices we use to transmit language by speech (stress, rhythm, intonation, tempo, for example) are impossible to represent with the crudely simple repertoire of conventional orthography. They are difficult enough to represent even with a special prosodic notation: *cf* App II.21. This means that the writer has often to reformulate his sentences if he is to convey fully and successfully what he wants to express within the orthographic system. Thus instead of the spoken sentence with a particular intonation nucleus on *John* (App II.14)

JŎHN didn't do it

one might have to write

It was not in fact John that did it.

Note
The advantages are not all on one side, however; the written medium has the valuable distinctions of paragraph, italics, quotation marks, etc, which have no clear analogue in speech (App III.1 *ff*).

1.26

As with varieties according to subject matter, we are here dealing with two varieties that are in principle at the disposal of any user of English as occasion may demand, irrespective of the variety of English he uses as a result of region and education. But again there are contingent constraints: we do not expect less educated speakers to perform in written English with the facility that educated speakers acquire. This indeed is what a great deal of education is about.

There are contingent constraints of another kind. Some subject-matter varieties of English (legal statutes especially) are difficult to compose except in writing and difficult to understand except by reading. Other varieties are comparably restricted to speech: the transcript of a (radio) commentary on a football match might have passages like this:

Gerson to Pelé; a brilliant pass, that. And the score still: Brazil 4,
    Italy 1. The ball in-field to – oh, but beautifully cut off, and . . .

On the other hand, a newspaper report of the same game would be phrased very differently.

Varieties according to attitude
1.27

Varieties according to attitude constitute, like subject-matter and medium varieties, a range of English any section of which is in principle available at will to any individual speaker of English, irrespective of the regional variant or national standard he may habitually use. This present class of varieties is often called 'stylistic', but 'style' like 'register' is a term which is used with several different meanings. We are here concerned with the choice of linguistic form that proceeds from our attitude to the hearer (or reader), to the subject matter, or to the purpose of our communication. And we postulate that the essential aspect of the non-linguistic component (that is, the attitude) is the gradient between stiff, formal, cold, impersonal on the one hand and relaxed, informal, warm, friendly on the other. The corresponding linguistic contrasts involve both grammar and vocabulary. For example:

Overtime emoluments are not available for employees who are
    non-resident . . .
Staff members who don't live in can't get paid overtime . . .

While many sentences like the foregoing can be rated 'more formal' or 'more informal' ('colloquial') in relation to each other, it is useful to pursue the notion of the 'common core' (1.15) here, so that we can acknowledge a median or unmarked variety of English (see 1.35 Note), bearing no obvious colouring that has been induced by attitude. As in

> This student's work is now much better and seems likely to go on
>   improving

and thousands of sentences like it. On each side of this normal and neutral English, we may usefully distinguish sentences containing features that are markedly formal or informal. In the present work, we shall for the most part confine ourselves to this three-term distinction, leaving the middle one unlabelled and specifying only usages that are relatively formal or informal.

Note
A further term, SLANG, is necessary to denote the frequently vivid or playful lexical usage that often occurs in casual discourse, usually indicating membership of a particular social group.

1.28
Mastery of such a range of attitudinal varieties seems a normal achievement for educated adults, but it is an acquisition that is not inevitable or even easy for either the native or the foreign learner of a language. It appears to require maturity, tact, sensitivity and adaptability – personality features which enable the individual to observe and imitate what others do, and to search the language's resources to find expression to suit his attitude. The young native speaker at the age of five or six has broadly speaking one form of English that is made to serve all purposes, whether he is talking to his mother, his pets, his friends or the aged president of his father's firm. And although even this can cause parents twinges of embarrassment, it is understood that the invariant language is a limitation that the child will grow out of.

The foreign learner is in a somewhat similar position. Until his skill in the language is really very advanced, it is attitudinally invariant, though the particular variety on which he is 'fixed' is much less predictable than that of the native child. If much of his practice in English has been obtained through textbooks specializing in commercial training, his habitual variety will be very different from that of the learner who has done vacation work helping on a farm. These are extreme examples, but it is a commonplace to notice an invariant literary, archaic flavour in the speech of foreign students, and even a Biblical strain in the students from some parts of the world. Better this no doubt than an excessively informal usage, but in any case just as the native child's youth protects him from criticism so does the overseas student's accent inform his listeners that there are respectable reasons for any inappropriateness in the language variety he uses.

1.29
The three-way contrast is not of course adequate to describe the full range of linguistic varieties that are evoked by differences of attitude. Martin Joos considers that we should at least add one category at each end of the scale to account for the extremely distant, rigid (he calls it 'frozen') variety of English sometimes found in written instructions, *eg*

Distinguished patrons are requested to ascend to the second floor

and to account also for the intimate, casual or hearty – often slangy – language used between very close friends (especially of similar age) or members of a family, or used when a speaker feels for any other reason that he does not need to bother what the listener (or reader) thinks of his choice of language. We might thus match the foregoing example with

Up you get, you fellows!

We are thus now in possession of a potential five-term distinction:

(rigid) – FORMAL – normal – INFORMAL – (familiar)

One final point on attitude varieties. As with the English dictated by subject matter and medium, there are contingency constraints in the normal selection of attitudinal variety. Just as statute drafting (subject matter) normally presupposes writing (medium), so also it presupposes a particular attitude variety: in this case 'rigid'. Similarly it would be hard to imagine an appropriate football commentary on the radio being other than informal, or a radio commentary on the funeral of a head of state being other than formal, though both are in the same medium (speech).

Varieties according to interference
1.30
Varieties according to interference should be seen as being on a very different basis from the other types of variety discussed. It is true that, theoretically, they need not be so sharply distinguished as this implies. We might think of the 'common core' (1.15) in native speakers being 'distorted' in one direction where a person is born in Ohio and in another direction if he is born in Yorkshire. The differences in their English might then be ascribed to the interference of Ohio speech and Yorkshire speech respectively on this common core.

But in more practical terms we apply 'interference' to the trace left by someone's native language upon the foreign language he has acquired. Indeed, to be still more severely practical, we apply it only to those traces of the first language that it is pedagogically desirable to identify and eradicate. Otherwise, we should be applying an identical classification to linguistic situations that are sharply different: on the one hand, the recognizable features of Indian English or West African English (undoubtedly inherited from one generation to another) which teachers may be trying to eradicate and replace with speech habits more resembling BrE or AmE; and on the other hand, the recognizable features of Irish English (many of which are the reflexes of Irish Celtic), which are also passed on from one generation to another but which are approved by teachers as fully acceptable in educated Irish use.

1.31
The important point to stress is that the English acquired by speakers of other languages, whether as a foreign or as a second language (1.3–4), varies not merely with the degree of proficiency attained (elementary, intermediate, advanced, let us say) but with the specific native language background. The Frenchman who says 'I am here since Thursday' is imposing a French grammatical usage on English; the Russian who says 'There are four assistants in our chair of mathematics' is imposing a Russian lexico-semantic usage on the English word 'chair'. Most obviously, we always tend to impose our native phonological pattern on any foreign language we learn. The practised linguist is able to detect the language background of his English pupil and this has obvious implications for language teaching in devising drills that will be directed to helping students with the problems that give them the greatest difficulty.

At the opposite extreme are interference varieties that are so widespread in a community and of such long standing that they may be thought stable and adequate enough to be institutionalized and regarded as varieties of English in their own right rather than stages on the way to a more native-like English. There is active debate on these issues in India, Pakistan and several African countries, where efficient and fairly stable varieties of English are prominent in educated use at the highest political and professional level.

1.32
Creole and Pidgin
At an extreme of a different kind, there are interference varieties which have traditionally been used chiefly by the less prosperous and privileged sections of a community but which have also been stable over several generations. Political, educational and sociolinguistic thought vacillates as to whether such creolized forms of English (as in Sierra Leone or the Caribbean) should be institutionalized or not. Would Creole speakers benefit from the self-assurance this might give, or (since

the élite in their society would still learn a more international English in addition) would the danger be that this would tend to perpetuate their underprivileged status? Here is a sample of Jamaican Creole in an orthography that already suggests partial institutionalization:

> Hin sed den, 'Ma, a we in lib?' Hie sie, 'Mi no nuo, mi pikini, bot
> duon luk fi hin niem hahd, ohr eni wie in a di wohld an yu kal
> di niem, hin hie unu.' Hin sed, 'Wel Ma, mi want im hie mi a nuo
> mi.' 'Lahd nuo, masa! Duo no kal di niem, hin wi kom kil yu.'
> Hin sie, 'Wel Ma, hin wi haf fi kil mi.'   [See Note *a*]

Creole is normally the principal or sole language of its speakers, being transmitted from parent to child like any other native language. Moreover, for all its evidence of interference from other languages, it is usually more like ordinary English than Pidgin is and gives less impression of being merely a drastic reduction of ordinary English.

Pidgin is technically distinguished from Creole by being essentially a 'second' language (1.3), used rather to replace a native language for restricted public (especially commercial) purposes than to conduct family affairs and talk to one's children. In New Guinea an attempt has been made to raise the status of Pidgin (and its speakers) by institutionalization as 'Neomelanesian'; a public press, local administration and some education both secular and religious are conducted in it. Here is a sample from the Neomelanesian version of St Mark's Gospel ('Gud Nius Mark i Raitim'), Chapter 13, verse 13:

> Na olman bai i bel nogud long yufela bilong nem bilong mi. Tasol
> man i stap strong oltaim i go i kamap long finis bilong em,
> disfela i ken stap gud oltaim.   [See Note *b*]

In this case (as distinct from the Creole example) it would be very difficult to spell the passage in conventional orthography, and this is an interesting indication that we are here beyond the limits where it is reasonable to speak of a variety of English.

Note

[*a*] He said then, 'Ma, and where does he live?' She says, 'I don't know, my child, but don't look hard for his name, or anywhere in all the world that you call the name, he will hear you.' He said, 'Well, Ma, I want him to hear me and know me.' 'Lord, no, master! Do not call the name: he will come and kill you.' He says, 'Well, Ma, he will have to kill me.'

[*b*] And everyone will feel badly towards you on account of my name. But anyone who stays strong right till the end, this person will remain in well-being for ever.

Relationship between variety classes
1.33

In presenting the table of varieties in a schematic relationship in 1.15, reference was made to each stratum of varieties being equally related to all others. In principle, this is so. A man may retain recognizable features of any regional English in habitually using a national standard; in his national standard, he will be able to discourse in English appropriate to his profession, his hobbies, a sport; he could handle these topics in English appropriate either to speech or writing; in either medium, he could adjust his discourse on any of these subjects according to the respect, friendliness or intimacy he felt for hearer or reader. And all of this would be true if he was proficient in English as a foreign or second language and his usage bore the marks of his native tongue. Clearly, as we review this example, we must see that the independence of the varieties is not solely a matter of principle but also, to a large extent, a matter of actual practice.

But to an at least equally large extent the independence does *not* hold in practice. We have drawn attention to contingent constraints at several points (for example, in 1.29). Let us attempt to see the types of interdependence as they affect the varieties system as a whole. To begin with, the regional varieties have been explicitly connected with the educational and standard varieties. Thus although there is 'independence' to the extent that a speaker of any regional variety may be placed anywhere on the scale of least to most educated, there is interdependence to the extent that the regional variety will determine (and hence it dominates in the table, 1.15) the educational variety: a person educated in Ohio will adopt educated AmE not BrE. There is an analogous connection between the interference variety and the regional and educational variety: someone learning English in Europe or India is likely to approach a standard with BrE orientation; if in Mexico or the Philippines, an AmE orientation.

1.34
Next, the subject-matter varieties. Certain fields of activity (farming and ship-building, for example) are associated with specific regions; clearly, it will be in the (especially uneducated) dialect of these regions and no others that the language of daily discourse on such activities will be thoroughly developed. In other fields (medicine, nuclear physics, philosophy) we will expect to find little use of uneducated English or the English of a particular region. In discussions of baseball, AmE will predominate but we will not expect to find the vocabulary or grammar specific to AmE in reports of cricket matches.

Since writing is an educated art, we shall not expect to find other than educated English of one or other national standard in this medium. Indeed, when we try on occasion to represent regional or uneducated English in writing, we realize acutely how narrowly geared to Standard

English are our graphic conventions. For the same reason there are subjects that can scarcely be handled in writing and others (we have mentioned legal statutes) that can scarcely be handled in speech.

Attitudinal varieties have a great deal of independence in relation to other varieties: it is possible to be formal or informal on biochemistry or politics in AmE or BrE, for example. But informal or casual language across an 'authority gap' or 'seniority gap' (a student talking to an archbishop) presents difficulties, and on certain topics (funerals) it would be unthinkably distasteful. An attempt at formal or rigid language when the subject is courtship or football would seem comic at best.

1.35
Finally, the interference varieties. At the extremes of Creole and Pidgin there is especial interdependence between the form of language and the occasion and purposes of use: indeed the very name *Pidgin* (from 'business') should remind us that it is of its nature inclined to be restricted to a few practical subjects. Creole is usually more varied but again it tends to be used of limited subject matter (local, practical and family affairs). As to English taught at an advanced intellectual level as a second or foreign language, our constant concern must be that enough proficiency will be achieved to allow the user the flexibility he needs in handling (let us say) public administration, a learned discipline such as medicine with its supporting scientific literature, and informal social intercourse. The drawback with much traditional English teaching was that it left the foreign learner more able to discourse on Shakespeare than on machinery – and chiefly in writing at that. A swing towards a more 'modern' approach is hardly welcome if it concentrates on colloquial chit-chat, idioms and last year's slang. Attempts to teach a 'restricted' language ('English for engineers') too often ignore the danger in so doing of trying to climb a ladder which is sinking in mud: it is no use trying to approach a point on the upper rungs if there is no foundation.

Our approach in this book is to keep our sights firmly fixed on the COMMON CORE which constitutes the major part of any variety of English, however specialized, and without which fluency in any variety at a higher than parrot level is impossible. What was said in 1.27 about an unmarked variety in respect of attitude applies also to the varieties conditioned by the other factors such as medium, subject matter and interference. Only at points where a grammatical form is being discussed which is associated with a specific variety will mention be made of the fact that the form is no longer of the common core. The varieties chiefly involved on such occasions will be AmE and BrE; speech and writing; **formal and informal.**

Note
The distinction between 'marked' and 'unmarked' relates to the differing degrees of inclusiveness, specificity and neutrality that two related linguistic forms may have. For example, while *he* and *she* are opposed as masculine and feminine respectively, the former can be regarded as unmarked in comparison with the latter since *he* can include 'feminine' more readily than *she* can include 'masculine' (as in 'Ask anyone and *he* will tell you').

Varieties within a variety
1.36
Two final points need to be made. First, the various conditioning factors (region, medium, attitude, for example) have no *absolute* effect: one should not expect a consistent all-or-nothing response to the demands of informality or whatever the factor may be. The conditioning is real but relative and variable. Secondly, when we have done all we can to account for the choice of one rather than another linguistic form, we are still left with a margin of variation that cannot with certainty be explained in terms of the parameters set forth in 1.15 and discussed in subsequent paragraphs.

For example, we can say (or write)

He stayed a week	*or*	He stayed for a week
Two fishes	*or*	Two fish
Had I known	*or*	If I had known

without either member of such pairs being necessarily linked to any of the varieties that we have specified. We may sometimes have a clear impression that one member seems rarer than another, or relatively old-fashioned, but although a rare or archaic form is likelier in relatively formal rather than in relatively informal English, we cannot always make such an identification. It might be true for the plural *cacti* as opposed to *cactuses*, but it would hardly be true for *beer enough* as opposed to *enough beer*, where the former is rarer but probably more used in informal (or dialectal) speech.

1.37
It may help to see variation in terms of the relationships depicted opposite, where both the verticals represent a 'more-or-less' opposition. The upper pole of the first vertical corresponds to the features of greatest uniformity, such as the invariable past tense of *bring* in the *educated* variety of English, or the many features characterizing the main stable *common core* of the language, such as the position of the article in a noun phrase. The lower pole of the first vertical corresponds to the area of fluctuation illustrated in 1.36. The second vertical represents the situation in which, on the other hand, an individual may indulge in such a

fluctuation (*I wonder whether* one moment and *I wonder if* a little later), and on the other hand, there may be fluctuation within the community as a whole (one member appearing to have a preference for *He didn't dare ask* and another a preference for *He didn't dare to ask: cf* 3.21). This appears to be a natural state of affairs in language. All societies are constantly changing their languages with the result that there are always coexistent forms, the one relatively new, the other relatively old; and some members of a society will be temperamentally disposed to use the new (perhaps by their youth) while others are comparably inclined to the old (perhaps by their age). But many of us will not be consistent either in our choice or in our temperamental disposition. Perhaps English may

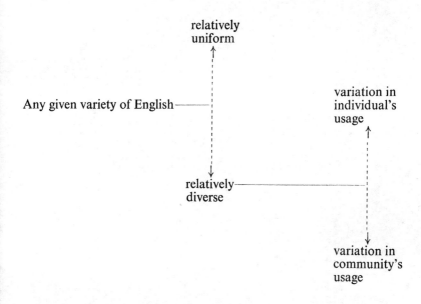

give rise to such fluctuation more than some other languages because of its patently mixed nature: a basic Germanic wordstock, stress pattern, word-formation, inflection and syntax overlaid with a classical and Romance wordstock, stress pattern (App II.4), word-formation (App I.3) – and even inflection and syntax. The extent to which even highly educated people will treat the Latin and Greek plurals in *data* and *criteria* as singulars or will use *different to* and *averse to* rather than *different from* and *averse from* – and face objections from other native speakers of English – testifies to the variable acknowledgement that classical patterns of inflection and syntax ('differre *ab*', 'aversus *ab*') apply within English grammar. It is another sense in which English is to be regarded as 'the most international of languages' (1.7) and certainly adds noticeably to the variation in English usage with which a grammar must come to terms.

Bibliographical note

On English in relation to other languages, see British Council (1969), *pp* 7–22; Girard (1970); Halls (1969); Muller (1964).

On linguistics and the teaching of English, see Lyons (1968); Halliday, McIntosh and Strevens (1964); Nickel (1971).

On varieties of English, see Avis (1967); Branford (1970); Crystal and Davy (1969); Hall (1966); Joos (1967); McDavid-Mencken (1963); Quirk (1972); Spencer (1971); Turner (1966).

THE SENTENCE: A PRELIMINARY VIEW

Parts of the sentence

2.1

Subject and predicate

In order to state general rules about the construction of sentences, it is constantly necessary to refer to smaller units than the sentence itself. Our first task must therefore be to explain what these smaller units are that we need to distinguish, confining our attention for the present to a few sentences which, though showing considerable variety, are all of fairly elementary structure.

Traditionally, there is a primary distinction between SUBJECT and PREDICATE:

John	carefully searched the room	[1]
The girl	is now a student at a large university	[2]
His brother	grew happier gradually	[3]
It	rained steadily all day	[4]
He	had given the girl an apple	[5]
They	make him the chairman every year	[6]

Although such a division obviously results in parts which are (in these examples) very unequal in size and dissimilar in content, it is of course by no means arbitrary. As will be seen in 14.10 f, the subject of the sentence has a close general relation to 'what is being discussed', the 'theme' of the sentence, with the normal implication that something new (the predicate) is being said about a 'subject' that has already been introduced in an earlier sentence. This is of course a general characteristic and not a defining feature: it is patently absurd in relation to sentence [4], for example. Another point is that the subject determines concord. That is, with those parts of the verb that permit a distinction between singular and plural (3.54 ff), the form selected depends on whether the subject is singular as in [2], *the girl is*, or plural as in [6], *they make*.

Furthermore, it is important to distinguish the subject since it is the part of the sentence that changes its position as we go from statement to question (*cf* 2.18 ff, 7.55 ff):

Did *John* carefully search the room?	[1q]
Did *his brother* grow happier gradually?	[3q]
Did *it* rain steadily all day?	[4q]
Had *he* given the girl an apple?	[5q]

2.2

Operator, auxiliary, and predication

In contrast with the subject, there are few generalizations that we can usefully make about the predicate since – as [1–6] already make clear – it tends to be a more complex and heterogeneous unit. We need to subdivide it into its constituents. One division has already been suggested in [1q], [3q], [4q] and [5q]; this distinguishes AUXILIARY as OPERATOR (as in [5q]) and the special operator-auxiliary DO (as in [1q], [3q], [4q]) on the one hand from what we may call the PREDICATION on the other. The distinctions may be illustrated as follows:

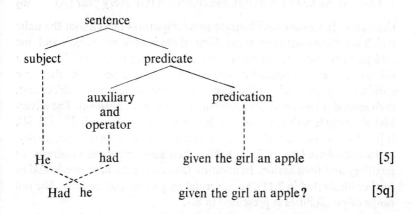

This particular division of the sentence is especially important for understanding how interrogative and negative forms of sentences are formed (2.18 ff, 7.41 f, 7.56), how certain adjuncts are positioned (8.7), and how certain types of emphasis are achieved (14.7, 14.25), for example. Since the verb phrase may have several auxiliaries (in which case the first is the operator) or none, as in [1], [3], [4], [6] (in which case DO is introduced when an operator is required), and since moreover the verb BE – and frequently also (especially in BrE) HAVE – can act as operator, it is best to defer further discussion of the roles and relationship of operator and auxiliary to 3.5 ff.

Verb, complement, object, adverbial
2.3
Instead, we shall turn to an alternative division of predicate into four important and for the most part obviously distinct units. We shall ignore the further possibility of regarding them rather as divisions of the predication, and – more importantly – we shall for the present ignore the fact that some adverbials should be regarded as having a relationship with the whole sentence rather than with a part such as the predicate; see 8.2–6 on disjuncts and conjuncts.

The four units are VERB, COMPLEMENT, OBJECT, and ADVERBIAL,

here abbreviated as V, C, O, A; together with the SUBJECT (S), they constitute the ELEMENTS of sentence (and clause) structure:

John (S) carefully (A) searched (V) the room (O)	[1]
The girl (S) is (V) now (A) a student (C) at a large university (A)	[2]
His brother (S) grew (V) happier (C) gradually (A)	[3]
It (S) rained (V) steadily (A) all day (A)	[4]
He (S) had given (V) the girl (O) an apple (O)	[5]
They (S) make (V) him (O) the chairman (C) every year (A)	[6]

Even these few examples illustrate some important facts about the units which are distinguished in them. First, there is only one *subject* and one *verb* in each sentence, whereas there can be more than one *object* as in [5], and more than one *adverbial*, as in [2] and [4]. Secondly, there are striking regularities about the relative position of elements: subject first, verb second, object and complement in a post-verb position. The adverbial is clearly less tied: we see that it can appear finally, as in [2], [3], [4], [6]; between *subject* and *verb* as in [1]; [2] shows a further possibility, and we shall see later (8.7) that this is best seen as between operator or auxiliary and predication. In addition (as in the present sentence and as further illustrated in 2.11), an adverbial may be placed initially. The full range of possibilities is presented in 8.7.

When we come to examine (2.11) the kinds of structure that can function as one of these elements of sentence structure, we shall see that considerable variety is possible in each case. Already however we might notice that there is particularly great heterogeneity about S, O, C, and A (though S and O appear to have the same range of possibilities). The variety can of course be much greater even than has been illustrated thus far. Indeed S, O and A can themselves readily have the internal constituents of sentences:

She (S) saw (V) that [*it* (S) *rained* (V) *all day* (A)] (O)	[7]
His brother (S) grew (V) happier (C) when [*his friend* (S) *arrived* (V)] (A)	[8]
That [*she* (S) *answered* (V) *the question* (O) *correctly* (A)] (S) pleased (V) him (O) enormously (A)	[9]

The italicizing is intended to emphasize the similarity between subordinate (or dependent) clauses and independent sentences. At the same time this and the bracketing can interestingly suggest that *when* in [8] and *that* in [7] and [9] operate as A, O, and S respectively (though this is only partly true) while more importantly being themselves 'expanded' by the dependent clauses. We shall in fact treat such items as part of the dependent clauses when we come in 11.8–12 to examine the whole problem of subordinating clauses within other clauses.

2.4

Complements and objects

Quite apart, however, from the differences in internal structure between one element and another, there are other differences already illustrated in [1–9] that must concern us immediately. For example, the relation between *the room* in [1] and the other elements in that sentence is very different from the relation between *the girl* in [5] and its fellow elements, though both are labelled 'object'. Even more obviously, perhaps, the two elements labelled 'object' in [5] play sharply distinct roles in this sentence. We need in fact to distinguish two types of object and two types of complement in the sentences so far illustrated:

$$\text{object} \begin{cases} \text{direct object } (O_d) \\ \text{indirect object } (O_i) \end{cases}$$

$$\text{complement} \begin{cases} \text{subject complement } (C_s) \\ \text{object complement } (C_o) \end{cases}$$

The direct object is illustrated in

John carefully searched *the room* (O_d)   [1]
He had given the girl *an apple* (O_d)   [5]

and in 7.14 and 7.19 we shall attempt semantic generalizations characterizing the function of the direct object. Meantime it should be understood that the direct object is by far the more frequent kind of object, and that with most ditransitive verbs (2.5) it must always be present if there is an indirect object in the sentence. Example [5] illustrates also the indirect object:

He had given *the girl* (O_i) an apple   [5]

As here, the indirect object almost always precedes the direct object; it is characteristically (though by no means always) a noun referring to a person, and the semantic relationship is often such that it is appropriate to use the term 'receptive'. Loosely, one might say in most cases that something (the direct object) tends to be done for (or received by) the indirect object.

Turning to complements, we may illustrate first the subject complement:

The girl is now *a student* (C_s) at a large university   [2]
His brother grew *happier* (C_s) gradually   [3]

Here the complements have a straightforward relation to the subjects of their respective sentences such that the subject of [2] is understood as being a 'girl student' and the subject of [3] a 'happier brother'. The 'object complement' can be explained as having a similar relation to a direct object (which it follows) as the subject complement has to a subject:

They make him *the chairman* (C$_o$) every year   [6]

That is to say, the direct object and object complement in this example, 'him the chairman', correspond to a sentence like [2] having a subject and a subject complement:

He is *the chairman* (C$_s$)

The parallel between object complement and subject complement holds also in that the former can often be realized by the same range of units as the latter:

They made him *happier* (C$_o$)
He is *happier* (C$_s$)

Note
On the replacement of the indirect object by a prepositional phrase, see 6.37, 7.6, 14.40.

Categories of verb
2.5
There are different types of verb corresponding closely to the different types of object and complement. Sentences such as [2] and [3], which have subject complements, have INTENSIVE verbs and all other sentences have EXTENSIVE verbs. The latter are INTRANSITIVE if as in

It rained steadily all day   [4]

they do not permit any of the four object and complement types so far distinguished (see Note *a*). Extensive verbs are otherwise TRANSITIVE. All transitive verbs take a direct object; some in addition permit an indirect object, and these will be distinguished as DITRANSITIVE. A few verbs take an object complement as in [6] and these will be referred to as COMPLEX-TRANSITIVE. It is necessary to make this additional terminological distinction for a number of reasons. In the first place, as we saw in 2.4, the relation holding between direct and indirect object is very different from that between direct object and object complement, the latter relation being identical to the 'intensiveness' holding between subject and subject complement. Secondly, although the relations between verb and direct object are identical whether the verb is transitive or ditransitive, the relations between a complex-transitive verb and its direct object are usually very different. This may be illustrated with the verb *make* which will allow all three possibilities, transitive, ditransitive, and complex-transitive:

She made a cake	[10]
She made him a cake	[11]
She made him a hero	[12]

Between [10] and [11] where *made* is transitive and ditransitive respectively, the relation with *a cake* is constant irrespective of the indirect object *him* introduced in [11]. In [12], where *a hero* is object complement, the relation between *made* and its direct object *him* is quite different from that obtaining between *made* and the direct object *a cake* in [10] and [11].

Note

[a] The verb *rain* permits a 'cognate object' (7.19): 'It's raining *big drops*'; also metaphorically, 'He rained *blows* on his opponent'.

[b] The difference is further illustrated by the fact that [12] permits variants as follows, with identical meaning: 'She made him into a hero', 'She made a hero out of him', whereas [11] is susceptible of variation in a quite different way: 'She made a cake for him'.

2.6

But distinctions between verbs need to be drawn not only in relation to object- and complement-types but also in relation to whether they themselves admit the aspectual contrast of 'progressive' and 'non-progressive' (see 3.39 *ff*). Thus it is possible to say

John carefully *searched* the room	[1]
or John *was* carefully *searching* the room	
His brother *grew* happier gradually	[3]
or His brother *was growing* happier gradually	
It *rained* steadily all day	[4]
or It *was raining* steadily all day	

But it is not possible to use the progressive in

The girl *is* now a student at a large university	[2]
*The girl *is* now *being* a student ...	
She *saw* that it rained all day	[7]
*She *was seeing* that it rained ...	
John *knew* the answer	[13]
*John *was knowing* the answer	

When verbs (either habitually or in certain uses) will not admit the progressive, as in [2], [7], [13], they are called STATIVE. When they will admit it, as in [1], [3], [4], they are called DYNAMIC. It is normal for verbs to be dynamic and even the minority that are almost always stative can usually be given a dynamic use on occasion. See further, 2.16.

We may now sum up the verb distinctions that have been drawn so far, leaving further elaboration till later (7.2–7):

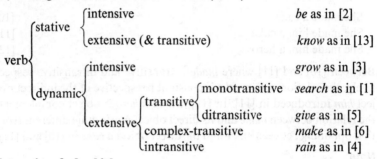

Categories of adverbial
2.7

Next we may take a preliminary look at adverbials. This is an extremely complex area of English grammar and a proper treatment must be deferred to Chapter 8. Here we need be concerned only with such distinctions as are necessary to explain some of the chief restrictions in constructing the simplest sentences. We may begin by looking at [2] again, which has two adverbials:

> The girl is *now* a student *at a large university*   [2]

We can omit elements from this and continue to have grammatical sentences:

> The girl is a student *at a large university*   [2i]
> The girl is a student   [2ii]
> The girl is *now* a student   [2iii]
> The girl is *at a large university*   [2iv]

but not if we leave only

> *The girl is *now*   [2v]

On this evidence we may say that the adverbials *now* and *at a large university* belong to different classes and it seems natural to label them 'time' and 'place' respectively. But we must not be misled into thinking of this distinction as referring in simple literal terms to time and place. By a process of metaphor, language allows us to map abstract notions on to outlines otherwise concerned with the physical world. In neither *at a disadvantage* nor *at nine o'clock* is there any question of being 'at' a place, but on the basis of [2iv] and [2v] we may class the former as 'place' and the latter as 'time', since

> She is at a disadvantage

is a grammatical sentence while

> *She is at nine o'clock

is not. Such subclasses of adverbial will however be considered in more detail in 8.10 *ff*.

2.8

Consider now the fact that the adverbial *carefully* in [1] could be replaced by many others, making acceptable sentences in each case:

John searched the room {
carefully
slowly
noisily
sternly
without delay
}

But if these same adverbials were inserted in sentences which had stative verbs, the sentences would become unacceptable:

The girl is now a student . . .
She saw this . . .
John knew the answer . . . {
*carefully
*slowly
*noisily
*sternly
*without delay
}

It is clear that we again have a subclass of adverbials. Because the verbs with which they can occur allow the progressive, the aspect of on-going activity, it is appropriate to refer to them as 'process'.

We should note further that there is a class of adverbials like *completely* which are permissible before the verb in some sentences but not in others; for example

He *completely* searched the room

but not

*She *completely* made a cake

We may call these 'amplifying intensifiers' in contrast to adverbials like *certainly* which can be inserted in all sentences; for example

He *certainly* searched the room
She *certainly* made a cake

Adverbials of this latter type may be called 'emphasizing intensifiers'. Leaving aside as 'other' those that we have not yet characterized, we have so far distinguished the following types of adverbial:

adverbial {
place
time
process
intensifier {amplifying
emphasizing}
other
}

2.9
Some types of subject

Consideration of subtypes of *subject* must be left until 7.14–18, but it will have been noticed already that in the illustrative sentences several sharply different kinds of subject have been encountered and that some of them are obviously tied to the type of verb or type of sentence as a whole. For example, we have seen the 'impersonal' subject in [4] and should note that sentences about the weather containing verbs like *rain* or *snow* are virtually restricted to having *it* as subject. Again, if we compare the unacceptability of such sentences as (a) with the acceptability of (b):

$$
\text{(a)} \left\{ \begin{array}{l} \text{*The girl} \\ \text{*His brother} \\ \text{*The university} \end{array} \right\} \quad \text{is} \left\{ \begin{array}{l} \text{tomorrow} \\ \text{next week} \\ \text{at two o'clock} \end{array} \right.
$$

$$
\text{(b)} \left\{ \begin{array}{l} \text{The play} \\ \text{His marriage} \\ \text{The examination} \end{array} \right.
$$

we must recognize in (b) a subclass of 'eventive' nouns as subject.

2.10
Types of sentence structure

Additional distinctions like those made in 2.8–9 need serve for the present only to help us bear in mind at the outset that the summary of sentence-structure rules that now follows is a deliberate oversimplification which ignores not only many of the important qualifications to be described in later chapters but also some of the distinctions already glimpsed in the present one. Each line constitutes a pattern which is illustrated by means of a correspondingly numbered example which contains just those obligatory and optional (parenthesized) elements that are specified in the formula.

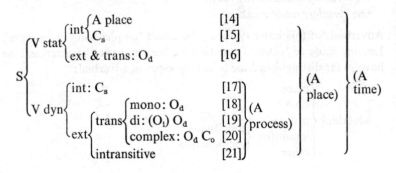

| She is in London (now) | [14] |
| She is a student (in London) (now) | [15] |

John heard the explosion (from his office) (when he was
locking the door)   [16]

Universities (gradually) became famous (in Europe) (during
the Middle Ages)   [17]

They ate the meat (hungrily) (in their hut) (that night)   [18]

He offered (her) some chocolates (politely) (outside the hall)
(before the concert)   [19]

They elected him chairman (without argument) (in
Washington) (this morning)   [20]

The train had arrived (quietly) (at the station) (before we
noticed it)   [21]

Note

Among the less important patterns ignored in this formula are V stative as ditrans
(*He owes me some money*) and as complex-trans (*She thinks him brilliant*) and the
obligatory A with V dynamic intrans (*He lives in London*) and trans (*She put the vase
on the table*). See 7.2 *ff*.

2.11
Element realization types

We noted in 2.3 that these functional elements in sentences could be
realized by linguistic structures of very different form. The structures
realizing the verb element are in some ways the most straightforward
since here it is a question always of a *verb phrase*. There is however considerable variety and complication even here. The verb phrase may, as
in all the examples used so far, be 'finite' (showing tense, mood,
aspect and voice) or 'non-finite' (not showing tense or mood but still
capable of indicating aspect and voice): *cf* 3.10. Consider the following
initial adverbial which takes the form of a clause with non-finite verb,
having been challenged:

Having been challenged rudely in the street, John was angry   [22]

Whether finite or non-finite, the verb phrase can consist of one word, as
in [1] and most other illustrative sentences so far, or of more than one
word, in which case the phrase consists of a 'head verb' preceded by one
or more 'auxiliary verbs' as with the non-finite verb phrase in [22] and
the finite verb phrases in the following:

He *had given* the girl an apple
He *has been challenged* rudely
He *may be growing* happier

The subject of a sentence may consist of a 'clause' as in [9], but usually of a 'noun phrase', a variable and potentially highly complex unit which will be examined further in Chapters 4 and 13. It may consist of a pronoun, as in [4] and [5], for example, or of a single common or proper noun as in [17] and [16] respectively. But it may be an indeterminately long structure having a noun as head, preceded by other words such as an article, an adjective, or another noun, and followed by a prepositional phrase or by a relative clause; it is by no means uncommon to find all such items present in a noun phrase:

> *The new gas stove in the kitchen which I bought last month* has a
>   very efficient oven

Again, a subject may be a nominal relative (11.20).

Subject complements, direct objects and object complements may be realized by the same range of structures as subjects, but subject and object complements have the additional possibility of being realized by adjectival phrases (having an adjective as head), as in [3] and

> She made him *very much happier*

Indirect objects, on the other hand, have fewer possibilities than subjects, and their realizations are chiefly noun phrases, as in [5] and [19]; unlike direct objects and subjects (*cf* [7] and [9] respectively) they cannot be realized by *that*-clauses.

Finally, adverbials can be realized by adverbial phrases (having an adverb as head) as in [1], [4]; by noun phrases as in [4] and [6], *all day* and *every year*; by prepositional phrases – that is, structures consisting of a noun phrase dominated by a preposition – as in [2], *at a large university*; and by clauses as in [8], where we have a finite-verb clause as adverbial, or [22], where we have an adverbial non-finite-verb clause.

Parts of speech
2.12

It will have become clear from the preceding section that the structures realizing sentence elements are composed of units which can be referred to as *parts of speech*, a traditional scheme in terms of which members of the Indo-European group of languages have been analysed since classical times. It may be helpful to present some examples of the parts of speech or 'form classes' as they are commonly distinguished in English:

(a) *noun* – John, room, answer, play
   adjective – happy, steady, new, large, round
   adverb – steadily, completely, really, very, then
   verb – search, grow, play, be, have, do

(b) *article* – the, a(n)
   demonstrative – that, this
   pronoun – he, they, anybody, one, which
   preposition – of, at, in, without, in spite of
   conjunction – and, that, when, although
   interjection – oh, ah, ugh, phew

Even so short a list of examples raises several important questions. First, we should notice that the examples are listed as *words* (see Note), in their 'dictionary form' and not as they often appear in sentences when they function as constituents of phrases: thus the singular *room* and not the plural *rooms*, the simple *happy* and not the comparative *happier*, the infinitive (or uninflected) *grow* and not the past *grew*, the subject form *he* and not the object form *him*.

Note

From even the few examples given, it can be seen that a part-of-speech item may consist of more than a single word. This is especially common in the case of complex prepositions (6.5), such as *in spite of*, *out of*, etc and phrasal verbs (12.19 *ff*), such as *look at*, *stand out* (compare the related adjective *outstanding*, again one part of speech but this time one word also). Equally, however, we may look upon a part of speech as being downgraded to become less than a word: for example, the adverb *out* in the adjective *outstanding*, the adjective *black* in the noun *blackbird*, or (from this viewpoint) the noun *spite* and the prepositions *in* and *of* in the preposition *in spite of*. Despite the uncertainty as to what constitutes a compound (App I.44 *ff*) and despite the lack of universal correspondence between the orthographic word, the 'grammatical' word, and the 'lexical item', parts of speech are frequently called 'word-classes'.

2.13

Secondly, some of the examples appear as more than one part of speech (*play* as noun and verb, *that* as demonstrative and conjunction) and more of them could have been given additional entries in this way (*round* can be noun, verb, adjective, adverb and preposition). This is a highly important feature of English, and further attention will be drawn to it in App I. 31–43. Similarly, we should notice a direct correspondence between most adjectives and adverbs, the latter usually consisting of the former plus *-ly*. Less obviously, there is an important correspondence between all words beginning /ð/ (*the*, *that*, *then*, for example) and many of those beginning *wh-* (*which*, *when*, for example): basically the former are relater or indicator words and the latter interrogative words, but the secondary functions cannot be summarized so easily (*cf* especially 4.28 *ff*, 5.48, 10.63 *ff*).

Thirdly, though this book cannot be concerned with English phonology, it must be pointed out that interjections frequently involve the use of sounds that do not otherwise occur in English words. Thus *ugh* is the spelling of an exclamation often pronounced something like [ʌx] or [əx] and *whew* or *phew* is pronounced [ɸju] or even [ɸːɔ] though the 'ach-laut' /x/ and the bilabial fricative /ɸ/ are not phonemes in standard AmE or BrE. This observation is not without significance in considering the general status of interjections which though meaningful are integrated within neither the grammatical structure nor the lexicon of the language.

2.14
Closed-system items
The parts of speech in 2.12 were listed in two groups, (a) and (b), and this introduces a distinction of very great significance. Set (b) comprises what are called 'closed-system' items. That is, the sets of items are *closed* in the sense that they cannot normally be extended by the creation of additional members: a moment's reflection is enough for us to realize how rarely in a language we invent or adopt a new or additional pronoun. It requires no great effort to list all the members in a closed system, and to be reasonably sure that one has in fact made an exhaustive inventory (especially, of course, where the membership is so extremely small as in the case of the *article*).

The items are said to constitute a *system* in being (i) reciprocally exclusive: the decision to use one item in a given structure excludes the possibility of using any other (thus one can have *the book* or *a book* but not **a the book*); and (ii) reciprocally defining: it is less easy to state the meaning of any individual item than to define it in relation to the rest of the system. This may be clearer with a non-linguistic analogy. If we are told that a student came *third* in an examination, the 'meaning' that we attach to 'third' will depend on knowing how many candidates took the examination: 'third' in a set of four has a very different meaning from 'third' in a set of 30.

2.15
Open-class items
By contrast, set (a) comprises 'open classes'. Items belong to a class in that they have the same grammatical properties and structural possibilities as other members of the class (that is, as other nouns or verbs or adjectives or adverbs respectively), but the class is 'open' in the sense that it is indefinitely extendable. New items are constantly being created and no one could make an inventory of all the nouns in English (for example) and be confident that it was complete. This inevitably affects the way in which we attempt to define any item in an open class: while it would obviously be valuable to relate the meaning of *room* to other nouns with which it has semantic affinity (*chamber, hall, house, . . .*) one could not define it as 'not *house*, not *box*, not *plate*, not *indignation, . . .*', as one might define a closed system item like *this* as 'not *that*'.

Of course, in any one phrase or sentence the decision to select a particular word at one place in the structure obviously imposes great constraints on what can be selected at another. But it is essential to see that in an arrangement like the following there is in principle a sharp difference between the number of possibilities in columns *i*, *iii*, and *iv* ('closed') and the number in *ii* and *v* ('open'):

	i	*ii*	*iii*	*iv*	*v*
(John)	may	sit	by	this	fountain
	will	stare	at	that	tree
	must	read	from		window
	:	hurry	along		blackboard
		:	on		girl
			:		path
					:

The distinction between 'open' and 'closed' parts of speech must be treated cautiously, however. On the one hand, we must not exaggerate the ease with which we create new words (*cf* App I.1 *f*): we certainly do not make up new nouns as a necessary part of speaking in the way that making up new sentences is necessary. On the other hand, we must not exaggerate the extent to which parts of speech in set (b) of 2.12 are 'closed': new prepositions (usually of the form 'prep + noun + prep' like *by way of*) are by no means impossible.

But there is a yet more important caveat. Although they have deceptively specific labels, the parts of speech tend in fact to be rather heterogeneous. The adverb and the verb are perhaps especially mixed classes, each having small and fairly well-defined groups of closed-system items alongside the indefinitely large open-class items. So far as the verb is concerned, the closed-system subgroup is known by the well-established term 'auxiliary', though as we shall see in Chapter 3, auxiliaries themselves are of sharply different types. With the adverb, one may draw the distinction broadly between those in *-ly* that correspond to adjectives (*complete-ly*) and those that do not (*now, there, forward, very*, for example). But this is an oversimplification and in any case the latter items, the closed-system ones, comprise several subsets with overlapping membership and there is little by way of a well-established framework within which to describe them; discussion must therefore be deferred until Chapters 5 and 8.

2.16
Stative and dynamic

The open classes have some notable general characteristics. We have just seen that adverbs of the productive class are in a one-to-one relation with adjectives. We shall see in App I.23 *ff*, I.34 *ff* that there are

regular word-formation processes giving a comparable one-for-one relation between nouns and adjectives and between nouns and verbs. For
the rest, it is useful to see nouns, adjectives and verbs in connection with
the opposition of stative and dynamic introduced in 2.6. Broadly speaking, nouns can be characterized naturally as 'stative' in that they refer
to entities that are regarded as stable, whether these are concrete
(physical) like *house, table, paper,* or abstract (of the mind) like *hope,
botany, length.* At the opposite pole, verbs can be equally naturally
characterized as 'dynamic': they are fitted (by their capacity to show
tense and aspect, for example) to indicate action, activity and temporary
or changing conditions. These relations between the open classes can be
summarized thus:

STATIVE   noun ⟷ adjective

DYNAMIC   verb   adverb

But we saw in 2.6 that there were some verbs such as *know* which could
not normally be used with the progressive (**he is knowing*): that is,
which could not be seen as referring to something that was in progress.
Verbs so used we called 'stative', and they should be seen as exceptions
within the class of verbs. There are exceptions in the other direction
among the nouns, not all of which need be stative. For example, a child
may be well-behaved one minute and *a nuisance* the next. The situation
is similar when we turn to the remaining open word-class, adjectives.
Although they are predominantly stative (*tall, red, old*), some adjectives
can resemble verbs in referring on occasion to transitory conditions of
behaviour or activity such as *naughty* or *insolent.* And since *to be* must
be used to make predications having any noun or adjective as complement, we must qualify the statement made in 2.6 that this is a stative
verb: it can also be used dynamically, in the progressive, when the complement is dynamic:

He is being $\begin{Bmatrix} \text{a nuisance} \\ \text{naughty} \end{Bmatrix}$ again

Indeed, it is essential to realize that these primary distinctions are
in the nature of general characteristics rather than immutable truths. No
small part of language's value lies in its flexibility. Thus we can take a
normally dynamic item (say the verb in 'He *wrote* the book') and
'nominalize it' it ('The *writing* of the book') pretending – as it were – to
see the action as a static 'thing'. So also the verb *tax* beside the noun
taxation. Again, the name 'participle' reflects the fact that such a form
participates in the features both of the *verb* ('The girl is sitting there')
and of the *adjective* ('The sitting girl'). See further 3.39 *ff,* 5.13, 5.38.

2.17
Pro-forms
The names of the parts of speech are traditional, however, and neither
in themselves nor in relation to each other do these names give a safe
guide to their meaning which instead is best understood in terms of
their grammatical properties. 'Adverb' is a classic instance (5.42 *ff*). We
have seen some justification in the previous section for 'participle',
and of course the 'pronoun' is an even clearer exception in correctly
suggesting that it can serve as a replacement for a noun:

John searched the big *room* and the small *one*   [23]

More usually, however, pronouns replace noun phrases rather than nouns:

The man invited *the little Swedish girl* because *he* liked *her*   [24]

There are pro-forms also for place, time, and other adverbials under
certain circumstances:

Mary is *in London* and John is *there* too   [25]
Mary arrived *on Tuesday* and John arrived *then* too   [26]
John searched the big room very *carefully* and the small one
    less *so*   [27]

In older English and still sometimes in very formal English, we find *thus*
or *so* used more generally than in ordinary modern English as pro-forms
for adverbials:

He often behaved *prudently* but he did not always behave $\begin{cases} thus \\ so \end{cases}$

But *so* has a more important pro-function in modern usage, namely, to
replace – along with the 'pro-verb' DO – a predication (*cf* 2.2):

She hoped that he would search *the room carefully before
    her arrival* but he didn't do so   [28]

Here *so* replaces all the italicized portion and *do* replaces the head verb
search as is shown below; see also 9.80, 10.54 *ff*.

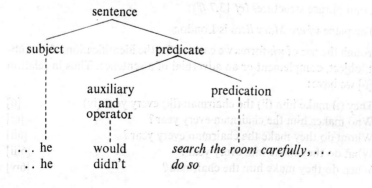

Frequently however the pro-predication is achieved by the operator alone or sometimes by adding (especially in BrE) a relevant form of the pro-verb DO after it:

A: 'He didn't *give her an apple*'   B: 'Yes, he *did*'   [29]
They suspected that he had *given her an apple* and he
    had (*done*)   [30]

Finally, it may be briefly observed that the use of the pro-forms greatly facilitates sentence connection as in [29], the conjoining of sentences to form 'compound sentences' as in [25] or [30], and the subordination of one sentence within another to form 'complex sentences' as in [24]. These sentence developments will be examined in Chapters 10 and 11.80–86.

Sentence processes
Questions
2.18
Wh-questions

The pro-forms we have been considering may be regarded as having the general meaning 'We know what this item refers to, so I need not state it in full'. In 2.13 attention was drawn to correspondences of the *then-when* type, and we may now consider the *wh*-words of English (see Note *b*) as a special set of pro-forms diametrically opposed to the others in having the general meaning 'It has not been known what this item refers to and so it needs to be stated in full'. This informal statement will account for the use of *wh*-forms in questions:

Mary is *in London*
Mary is *there*
Where is Mary?

But the paraphrase of the *wh*-forms is broad enough to help explain also their use in subordinate clauses such as the relative clause postmodifiers in noun phrase structures (*cf* 13.7 *ff*):

The place *where Mary lives* is London

Through the use of *wh*-forms we can ask for the identification of the subject, object, complement or an adverbial of a sentence. Thus in relation to [6] we have:

They (i) make him (ii) the chairman (iii) every year (iv)   [6]
Who makes him the chairman every year?   [6i]
Whom do they make the chairman every year?   [6ii]
What do they make him every year?   [6iii]
When do they make him the chairman?   [6iv]

It will be noticed that in each case the *wh*-form is placed in first position
and that unless this is questioning the subject, as in [6i], when the verb
follows in its normal second position (2.3), the *wh*-form is followed by
the operator (2.2, 2.17) which in turn is followed by the subject and predication. The full rules for *wh*-questions will however be given in 7.63–67
when it will also be explained for instance why the form *what* (rather
than *whom*) is used in [6iii]. For the present, we should point out that
not all subjects, objects, complements or adverbials can be elicited by
wh-questions (and even [6iv] above would be unusual in relation to [6]):

It rained steadily all day	[4]

*{ Q: What rained steadily all day?
{ A: It

His brother grew happier gradually	[3]

*{ Q: What did his brother grow gradually?
{ A: Happier

John carefully searched the room	[1]

?{ Q: How did John search the room?
{ A: Carefully

Nor can the verb element be so elicited:

They make him the chairman every year	[6]

*{ Q: What do they him the chairman every year?
{ A: Make

We can however elicit the predication (2.2):

He had given the girl an apple	[5]

{ Q: What had he done?
{ A: Given the girl an apple

They make him the chairman every year	[6]

{ Q: What do they do?
{ A: Make him the chairman every year

Finally, just as some *wh*-questions are impossible, so there are *wh*-
questions for which there is no corresponding statement form, notably
the greeting 'How do you do?'

Note

[a] Despite the fact that the answer to [6i] would be a plural subject, the question
here (as normally) poses the 'unmarked' singular: *Who makes . . .?* (On 'marking', see 1.35 Note).

[b] The *wh*-forms include not only *which, when, why, where,* etc but also, less obviously, a few items pronounced with initial /h/, some having *wh*- in spelling (*who,
whose, whom*), and one not (*how*).

[c] Interrogation involving 'echo questions' has few of the restrictions exemplified here (cf 7.81 ff). Thus:

'His brother is WHÁT?' 'Happy'.

and even:

'It WHÁT yesterday?' 'Rained'.

2.19
Yes-no questions

Beside wh-questions, which elicit information on particular parts of a sentence, there are questions which seek a yes or no response in relation to the validity of (normally) an entire predication:

Did John search the room?

Such questions normally open with an operator which is then followed by the subject and the predication (2.2). The only alternative is to retain the statement organization of the sentence and to mark it as a question by intonation (App II.13) or punctuation, according as one is speaking or writing:

John searched the room?

Yes-no questions may however be focused upon some part of the sentence, and this may be achieved by a grammatical focus process (14.18) or prosodically (by stress and intonation):

Was it John that searched the room?
Was it the room that John searched?
Did JÓHN search the room?

The fact that such alternatives exist indicates the possibility of ambiguity in the normal yes-no question, particularly in writing, where there is no prosody to guide us. Clearly, the validity of

John carefully searched the room   [1]

is destroyed for the sentence as a whole as soon as any part of it is questioned. Is it the case that someone carefully searched the room, but that it was not John? Or that John searched the room, but not carefully? Or that John carefully searched something, but not the room? Or that John did something carefully to the room but did not search it? Moreover, the validity may be destroyed in respect of more than one part: someone searched the room, but not carefully, and it was not John.

2.20
The focus of a question

In fact the first illustrative question in this chapter,

Did John carefully search the room?   [1q]

would be unlikely to occur for two reasons. First, if we did not know whether John had searched the room, we would not try to find out in the same breath whether he had searched it carefully. Second, if a *yes-no* question were to be asked with all the elements of [1q] in it, the adverbial *carefully* would be placed finally:

Did John search the room carefully?

This would carry the implication that only the degree of care was being questioned. (On the 'focus' of interrogation, see also 7.56 Note *b*.)

Our examples have led up to some important general truths about *yes-no* questions. To avoid ambiguity in locating the basis of challenged validity, questions are *either* kept short, introducing one factor at a time,

Is this the room?
Did anyone search it?
Was it John?
Did he do it carefully?

or they are made unambiguous by grammatical or prosodic focusing, as in

Is this the room that John searched carefully?
Did John search THÍS room carefully?

or they are presumed to challenge the predication as a whole or the final element of the sentence, as in

Did John search the room?
Did John search the room carefully?
Did John search the room carefully last week?

Negation
Assertion and non-assertion
2.21

There are close analogies to the foregoing discussion when we turn to *negation*. While a *yes-no* question normally challenges the validity of a predication as a whole, negation rejects it. And like *yes-no* questions, negative sentences involve the operator, requiring the insertion of *not* (or the affixal contraction *-n't*) between the operator and the predication:

John did not search the room
The girl isn't a student

As with *yes-no* questions, too, ambiguity may arise about the basis of the disclaimed validity if one merely introduces the negative particle into a sentence with as many elements as [2],

The girl isn't now a student at a large university

unless one uses prosodic or grammatical focus to resolve the ambiguity. The girl was a student at one time but not now; she is still at a large university but is not a student there; she is at a university but it isn't large. More simply, we keep negations (like *yes-no* questions) short or accept the presumption that if the negation does not apply to the predication as a whole it applies to the last element. Thus

John didn't search the room carefully

would be presumed to deny only that his searching the room was not careful. On this issue of 'scope', see 7.49.

There is a yet more important similarity between questions and negations, a semantic one which brings further grammatical links in its train. A sentence such as

He offered her some chocolates   [31]

is an *assertion*. Now a sentence can become non-assertive in one of two ways: by becoming negative or by becoming a question. We do not therefore have two independent systems

positive : negative
declarative : interrogative

but rather an interrelated system in which *assertion* involves both 'positive' and 'declarative' while *non-assertion* has a subsystem either 'negative' or 'interrogative'. The relationship may be diagrammed thus:

$$
\text{sentence}
\begin{cases}
\text{assertion – positive and declarative} \\[1ex]
\text{non-assertion}
\begin{cases}
\text{interrogative}
\begin{cases}
\text{positive} \\
\text{negative}
\end{cases} \\[2ex]
\text{negative}
\end{cases}
\end{cases}
$$

Note
This is of course a special technical use of 'assertion'; in ordinary speech, negative sentences can be regarded as assertions:

'I did not steal it' was his constant assertion.

2.22
While it is right to show 'interrogative' as lying between the upper extreme 'positive and declarative' and the lower extreme 'negative', it is important to recognize that 'interrogative' has a closer relationship to 'negative' in springing like it from the 'non-assertion' node. Evidence for this is not difficult to find. As compared with the *some* of the positive-declarative [31], we find *any* in the corresponding question and negation:

Did he offer her any chocolates?   [31q]
He didn't offer her any chocolates   [31n]

This discussion (like the diagram in 2.21) ignores, however, the type of negation which is a denial or contradiction of the positive; in such a case, *some* could be retained:

He did NÒT offer her some chocolates

Note
The contrast between assertive and non-assertive forms can be realized in other grammatical relations than here illustrated (*cf* 7.44). For example, 'He *needs to* take the exam' (*'He *need* take the exam') beside the non-assertive '*Need* he take the exam?', 'He *need* not take the exam'. It can also be realized lexically; compare:

I *agree* that he offered her *some* chocolates
I *deny* that he offered her *any* chocolates

2.23
Negation and question
Questions, like statements, can be positive or negative; to [31], [31q] and [31n], we can add

Didn't he offer her any chocolates?   [31qn]

But since, as we saw in 2.21, interrogative is not in an equal relation to both positive-declarative and negative, we should not expect positive and negative questions to contrast identically to positive and negative statements. This could not be so because the interrogative in [31q] must cancel out or neutralize the positive in [31] in being non-assertive as opposed to assertive. The result is that a 'positive' question like [31q] is neutral as to the answer that is expected: it may be 'yes' or 'no' with equal probability. But equally the interrogative in [31qn] neutralizes the negative in [31n] with the result that this question form has been developed in English as a way of showing a speaker's surprise that the context has implied that the answer is 'no'. See further 7.58, but *cf* also 2.26 where the negative *yes-no* question is related to exclamation.

From the special way in which the imbalance between positive and negative works in *yes-no* questions, it may come as no surprise to realize that there are severe restrictions on the use of *wh*-questions with negatives at all (see 7.65 Note). Compare

Where is Mary?
*Where isn't Mary?

At the end of 2.18, we noted the non-occurrence of a statement corresponding to 'How do you do?' *Yes-no* questions beginning 'Would you mind...?', used as polite requests, likewise have no assertion form – though (a final point of parallel between negative and interrogative) they have a corresponding negative statement form, used as a tentative expression of desire:

> I wouldn't mind a cup of coffee. Shall we stop at the next village?
> (*I would mind a cup of coffee. Let's drive on.)

Note
Of course, rebuttal or echo utterances can derive pungency from flouting linguistic restrictions:

> 'Where's Mary?' 'Where ìsn'T Mary! In Chicago last week, Paris now, . . .'
> 'Would you mind closing the window?' 'Yes I wòuld mind!'

2.24
Other processes

Interrogation and negation may be thought of as 'sentence processes': they are ways in which we may think of ourselves as taking a ready-made statement (and even a question like 'Who is John?' presupposes a statement 'John is X') and giving it a different dimension of meaning largely by replacing or adding constituents. There are other such processes though hardly of such general application. The element 'object' (direct or indirect) may be permuted to become 'subject' in a focus-shifting process involving the *passive* voice (3.12 f, 12.1–18, 14.8f). Thus beside:

> John carefully searched the room   [1]

we can have:

> The room was (carefully) searched (by John)

Beside:

> He had given the girl an apple   [5]

we can have

> An apple had been given (the girl) (by him)

or

> The girl had been given an apple (by him)

And beside:

> They make him the chairman every year   [6]

we can have:

> He is made the chairman (every year) (by them)

In all of these examples, parentheses as usual mark optional items. We cannot, however, make the object complement or the adverbials the subject of a passive sentence:

*The chairman is made him (every year) (by them)
*Every year is made him the chairman (by them)

Limitations of a different kind arise in relation to the process which relates a statement to a command by the use of the *imperative* (7.72–77):

Search the room!
Give the girl an apple!
Don't give the girl an apple!

Although, as we see, the imperative can be positive or negative, it is restricted – unlike the other sentence processes – to present tense verbs and to sentences whose subject, usually unexpressed, is *you* (but see 7.73):

(You) give the girl an apple!
*(We) give the girl an apple!
*Gave the girl an apple!

There are also restrictions on the use of the imperative with verbs that are normally stative (2.6):

*Know the answer!

Exclamation
2.25
Out of context, examples like 'Search the room!', 'Give the girl an apple!' could be parts of a sentence echoed exclamatorily, in which case no restrictions on person or tense apply:

A: John gave the girl an apple
B: *Gave the girl an apple!* How kind he is!   [32]

The last part of [32] introduces us, however, to a more tightly organized type of exclamation involving *wh*-forms in a way not dissimilar to their role in questions (2.18). Corresponding to the exclamation at the end of [32] there must be the sentence

He is (very) kind   [33]

where the parenthesized *very* reminds us that the adjective phrase expressing the subject complement allows an indication of degree to be stated. It is this 'indicating' part that is replaced by *how* in [32] when the adjective phrase is moved to initial position much as it would be in a question

How kind is he?   [34]

except that the declarative word-order is retained:

How kind he is!

There is a further important difference. As a positive question (*cf* 2.22), example [34] is neutral as to whether a high or a low degree of kindness is involved; the exclamatory use of *wh*-forms always indicates that the degree is *high* of whatever is the variable quality. These exclamations resemble the corresponding *wh*-questions, however, in virtually disallowing negation (*cf* 2.23):

   *How kind he isn't!

2.26
A further interesting relation between question and exclamation is to be observed in the fact that the negative *yes-no* question can be used exclamatorily:

   Isn't he kind!

Unlike the actual corresponding *yes-no* question (which would be expressing surprise at the anticipated answer 'No'), this exclamation has a falling nuclear tone (App II.12) on *kind*, is confident of agreement in the form of a confirmatory 'Yes', and – as with *How kind* – implies a high degree of the adjective quality.

It will be clear from the discussion so far that the exclamation process is essentially concerned with degree and we must defer fuller discussion to 7.78 *f* when we can make use of the grammar and semantics of gradability which will be studied in Chapter 5. In the meantime, we may merely ponder the implications of

| What a present he had given the girl! | [35] |
| *What the girl he had given a present! | [35a] |

Since [35] would be as unacceptable as [35a] if it began 'What the present . . .', we see that a noun phrase needs 'indefiniteness' (4.30) if it is to permit exclamation: in other words, that indefiniteness in the noun phrase corresponds to degree potential in the adjective phrase. The indefiniteness, moreover, leaves open for the context alone to make clear what the variable quality is whose high degree is being exclaimed. Thus, according to context, [35] could mean 'What a *very good* present . . .' or 'What a *very bad* present he had given the girl'.

2.27
Relation to later chapters
The purpose of this chapter has been to explore the structure of the English sentence in such a way as to provide, as it were, a small-scale map of the topics to be explored in some detail in the main body of the book. As with any small-scale map, most of the details have had to be ignored and complicated contours have been smoothed out and simplified. But to

compensate for the disadvantages in this degree of distortion, the chapter is intended to have the advantages of the geographical analogue as well. In other words, it is hoped that the details which have not been ignored are more important for English grammar as a whole than those that have. And the possibility of achieving at the outset an overview of the major features of English grammar (to which the reader will doubtless wish to return from time to time during his study of subsequent chapters) will make it easier to understand the larger-scale exposition of individual features that will now preoccupy us.

Before returning to consider the sentence in more detail in Chapter 7, we must study the special characteristics of the separate units which can enter sentence structure as elements. Thus, Chapter 3 presents the grammar and semantics of the verb phrase and Chapter 4 examines nouns, pronouns, and the basic structure of the noun phrase. Chapter 5 studies the grammar and semantics of adjectives and adverbs, while Chapter 6 is devoted to the relations expressed by prepositions and prepositional phrases.

In the light of these detailed studies, Chapter 7 then re-examines the structure of the simple sentence and its processes, as they affect all elements except the adverbial. The complex matter of adverbials, however, requires separate treatment, and Chapter 8 is devoted to it. Chapter 9 moves into a different dimension, in presenting topics – ellipsis, coordination, and apposition – which affect units of widely ranging degrees of complexity. Their study leads naturally to the links which relate one sentence to another (Chapter 10) and to the subordination of one or more sentences within another (Chapter 11).

Chapter 12 follows up Chapter 3 with more attention to the verb phrase, and to special classes of verb, together with problems relating to voice, phrasal and prepositional verbs, and complementation. Similarly, Chapter 13 follows up Chapter 4 in exploring the full complexity that is possible for the noun phrase to attain in taking within itself the structures separately examined in earlier chapters. Chapter 14 also involves a knowledge of the whole grammar as described in preceding chapters, but this time with a view to presenting the various ways in which individual parts of a sentence can be arranged for focus, emphasis, and thematic presentation.

The three Appendices deal with aspects of English which, though strictly peripheral to grammar, nevertheless impinge upon it at various points necessitating frequent reference in the body of the book to the topics concerned. They are word-formation (App I); stress, rhythm, and intonation (App II); and finally, the system of punctuation (App III).

Each of the chapters and appendices ends with a bibliographical note giving guidance on further reading relevant to the material just presented. We concentrate in such notes on references to recent contributions, particularly by way of learned monographs and articles. This means that we assume, normally without further recommendation, that the reader will consult the major grammarians of the past, whose works are of course cited in the general Bibliography, *pp* 1085 *ff*: for example, the compendious studies by Curme, Jespersen, Kruisinga, Poutsma, Sweet, Visser, and others, to which (as well as to the bibliography by Scheurweghs, 1963–8) all succeeding grammarians are heavily indebted.

Bibliographical note
Some recent contributions of particular relevance to the outline of grammar presented in Chapter 2: Gleason (1965), especially Part Two; Lyons (1968), especially Chapters 4 and 5; Schopf (1969), especially Chapter 3. An earlier work providing an introductory study of great interest is Sapir (1921), especially Chapters 4 and 5.

THREE
THE VERB PHRASE

Verb classes

3.1

Sentences consist of subject and predicate, and the predicate consists of auxiliary and predication (*cf* 2.1 *ff*):

> *He* (S) *will* (auxiliary) *give the girl an apple* (predication)

We will now take a closer look at the auxiliary verb and that part of the predication which constitutes the verb phrase. Let us begin by examining the following sentences:

He *should see* the play	[1]
He *had seen* the play	[2]
He *was seeing* the play	[3]
He *saw* the play	[4]
He *happened to see* the play	[5]
He *expected to see* the play	[6]
He *expected that he would see* the play	[7]
He *expected to have to be forced to see* the play	[8]

We will subject the first six sentences to a few tests in order to see how they behave in various grammatical environments.

Some operational tests

3.2

The normal question forms would be these:

Should he *see* the play?	[1q]
Had he *seen* the play?	[2q]
Was he *seeing* the play?	[3q]
Did he *see* the play?	[4q]
Did he *happen to see* the play?	[5q]
Did he *expect to see* the play?	[6q]

Sentences 1–3 have INVERSION, *ie* the subject and the first verb of the predicate change places. Sentences 4–6 have a periphrasis with DO where DO is introduced to act as a 'dummy' first verb in the verb phrase.

3.3

The second test is NEGATION with *not*:

He *shouldn't see* the play	[1n]
He *hadn't seen* the play	[2n]
He *wasn't seeing* the play	[3n]
He *didn't see* the play	[4n]
He *didn't happen to see* the play	[5n]
He *didn't expect to see* the play	[6n]

Again, sentences 1–3 differ from the remaining three in having an enclitic negation, *n't* (a contracted form of the negative word *not*), affixed to the first element of the original verb phrase. As in questions, sentences 4–6 take DO-periphrasis.

Note

Whereas there is no negative sentence such as

   *He *saw not* the play

we do have an acceptable negative sentence

   He *expected not to see* the play

(though with no contracted form **expectedn't*). This negation, however, is associated with *to see* rather than with the preceding verb. This is obvious from the natural periphrasis with a *that*-clause as object:

   He *expected that he wouldn't see* the play

which is not synonymous with

   He *didn't expect that he would see* the play

Furthermore, the natural syntactic break occurs before *not:*

   He *expected* in fact *not to see* the play
   *He *expected not* in fact *to see* the play

By contrast, whereas

   *He *saw not* the play

was rejected above,

   He *saw not* the play but the film

is acceptable. The reason is that the negation goes with the noun phrase rather than with the verb:

   ~ It was not the play but the film that he saw.

3.4

Thirdly, consider how the verb is replaced by a PRO-FORM with *so:*

He *should see* the play		*should* she		[1pro]
He *had seen* the play		*had* she		[2pro]
He *was seeing* the play	and so	*was* she		[3pro]
He *saw* the play			*did* she	[4pro]
He *happened to see* the play			*did* she	[5pro]
He *expected to see* the play			*did* she	[6pro]

Sentences 1–3 have their original first verb as pro-form, whereas sentences 4–6 require a form of DO (see 9.80, 10.52 *ff*).

3.5
Auxiliaries

These tests give the same results and indicate that the verb phrases in sentences 1–3 are radically different from the verb phrases in sentences

4–6. *Should, had,* and *was* represent the class of AUXILIARY VERBS. They are, as the name implies, 'helping verbs', *ie* they have no independent existence as verb phrases, but only help to make up verb phrases, which consist of one or more other verbs, one of which is a LEXICAL VERB. The auxiliaries make different contributions to the verb phrase: DO is only an empty carrier in certain sentence processes, whereas BE and HAVE contribute aspect, and the modal auxiliaries contribute modality (expressing such concepts as volition, probability, and insistence). Note that DO, BE, and HAVE can also be used as lexical verbs, *eg: Do it!* Auxiliaries will be discussed in 3.17 *ff*.

3.6
Operators

Although the auxiliaries have different functions in the verb phrase, they have one important syntactic function in common when they occur initially in the finite verb phrase (3.10):

Will he ask any questions?
Is he asking any questions?
Is he asked any questions?
Has he asked any questions?
Has he been asking any questions?
Will he have been asked any questions?

The first auxiliary of the verb phrase is isolated from the rest of the predicate no matter how complex the verb phrase is. For this purely syntactic function of the auxiliaries we will use the generic term OPERATOR. Since the lexical verbs BE and (sometimes in BrE) HAVE also take

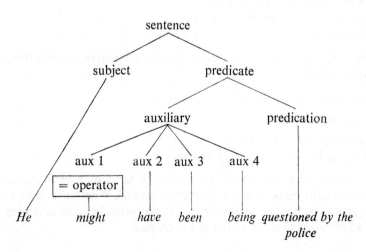

inversion without DO-periphrasis, the term operator will also be used for them:

> *Is* she a pretty girl?
> *Has* she any money? (BrE)

(The variant constructions with HAVE are discussed in 3.18.) The complex verb phrase of *He might have been being questioned by the police* (3.13) is thus analysed, within its sentence, as shown in the diagram, *p* 65.

Semi-auxiliaries and lexical verbs
3.7

Sentences 4–6 reveal differences under VOICE TRANSFORMATION, where active sentences are transformed into passive sentences (with the same or at least very nearly the same meaning; see 12.2).

> The play *was seen*   ⎫   [4pass]
> The play *happened to be seen* ⎬(by him)   [5pass]
> *The play *expected to be seen* ⎭   [6pass]

It is clear that the verb phrase in sentence [4pass] consists of an auxiliary (*was*) and a lexical verb (*see*). Under voice transformation, [5] and [6] are differentiated, the first verb in [5] being shown by this test to be similar to an auxiliary. Unlike EXPECT (which is a lexical verb), HAPPEN belongs to the class of SEMI-AUXILIARIES. It is sufficiently subordinate to the head of the verb phrase (*see*) to admit its object (*the play*) to become the subject of a passive construction. There are of course perfectly acceptable passive sentences with EXPECT:

> The play *was expected to be seen* by him
> He *was expected to see* the play
> It *was expected of him to see* the play
> It *was expected that he would see* the play

These passive sentences, however, are entirely different in meaning from the original sentence

> He *expected to see* the play

whereas the two sentences

> He *happened to see* the play
> The play *happened to be seen* by him

are close in meaning. EXPECT is in fact the head of a verb phrase which has as its object another verb phrase (*to see*). What we have here, then, is not one but two predications. The difference between sentences 6–8 which we gave at the outset of the chapter

He *expected to see* the play [6]
He *expected that he would see* the play [7]
He *expected to have to be forced to see* the play [8]

is only to be found in the different realizations of the object clause: in [6] and [8] it is non-finite (a *to*-infinitive clause), in [7] finite (a *that*-clause).

The object-function of the infinitive clause of [6] is also manifest from the fact that it has a pro-form with *it*. Compare [5] and [6] in this respect:

*He *happened* it [5pro/*it*]
He *expected* it. [6pro/*it*]

3.8

SEMI-AUXILIARIES, for example HAPPEN (as in sentence 5), are like lexical verbs (such as EXPECT in sentence 6) in that they do not take inversion or negation with *not* without DO-periphrasis; nor do they have *so* pro-form without DO (*cf* however the concatenative subset below):

Should the boy *see* the play?
Did the boy *happen to see* the play?
Did the boy *expect to see* the play?

The boy *shouldn't see* the play
The boy *didn't happen to see* the play
The boy *didn't expect to see* the play

The boy should see the play and *so should* his parents
The boy happened to see the play and *so did* his parents
The boy expected to see the play and *so did* his parents

Semi-auxiliaries are like auxiliaries in that they form a unit with the infinitive (*ie* their head) which is sufficiently close to admit of the transformation from active to passive in the head:

The play *should be seen* by the boy
The play *happened to be seen* by the boy

Auxiliary and semi-auxiliary verbs allow the passive only in the non-finite head, and cannot be made passive themselves:

The play *wasn't* $\begin{Bmatrix} *should \\ *happened\ to \\ expected\ to \end{Bmatrix}$ *be seen* by the boy

(*Should*, of course, could not in any case be made passive, since it has no past participle form, see 3.22.)

In the class of semi-auxiliaries there is, however, a subset of 'conca-tenative' verbs with BE or HAVE as a first element: BE GOING TO, HAVE TO, etc. Since BE, and sometimes HAVE (in BrE especially), share the charac-teristics of auxiliaries whether they are auxiliaries proper (as in *Is he coming tonight?*) or lexical verbs (as in *Is he your favourite?*), semi-auxiliaries whose first element is one of these verbs admit of inversion, negative with *not*, and *so* pro-form without DO:

Is the boy *going to see* the play?
The boy *isn't going to see* the play
The boy *is going to see* the play, and *so are* his parents

There are however certain restrictions on the use of some verbs in this subset (see Note below).

Among the semi-auxiliaries we can distinguish two subclasses depend-ing on whether they can appear in an equivalent cleft-sentence (Subclass ii) or not (Subclass i):

The boy $\left\{\begin{array}{l}\text{tended}\\\text{seemed}\end{array}\right\}$ to be late

$\sim$ It $\left\{\begin{array}{l}\text{*tended}\\\text{seemed}\end{array}\right\}$ that the boy was late

SEMI-AUXILIARIES

Subclass i	Subclass ii
BE ABOUT TO	BE CERTAIN TO
BE APT TO	BE (UN)LIKELY TO
BE BOUND TO[a]	APPEAR TO
BE GOING TO	HAPPEN TO
BE LIABLE TO	SEEM TO
BE SURE TO	TURN OUT TO, etc
BE TO[b]	
had/'d better/best[c]	
HAVE TO[b]	
HAVE GOT TO[b]	
COME TO ('happen to')	
FAIL TO	
GET TO	
TEND TO, etc	

The three classes, auxiliary verbs, semi-auxiliary verbs, and lexical verbs, are shown in *Fig* 3:1. The auxiliaries are further discussed in 3.17–22. For the morphology of the semi-auxiliary set which includes one of the primary auxiliaries BE and HAVE, see 3.18–19. The morphology of the

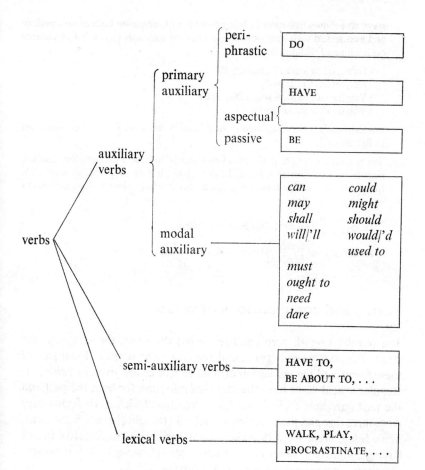

Fig 3:1 Verb classes

other semi-auxiliary verbs is the same as that of lexical verbs (see 3.9, 3.54 *ff*).

Note

[a] The (apparent) passive form of BE BOUND TO has no active analogue:

He was bound to be a failure
*Somebody bound him to be a failure

[b] Unlike HAVE TO, BE ABOUT TO, etc, the semi-auxiliary verbs BE TO and HAVE GOT TO exist only in simple forms; they have, for example, no infinitives (*cf* 3.29, 3.33, 3.34):

The children may {have to / be about to / *be to / *have got to} go to bed now

HAVE TO behaves like HAVE in being capable of functioning both as an auxiliary and as a lexical verb in questions and negative sentences (3.18). It has variants both with and without DO-periphrasis:

⎰Have you to leave? (especially BrE)
⎱Do you have to leave?
⎰You haven't to leave (especially BrE)
⎱You don't have to leave

DO-periphrasis is normally used in AmE, and is the more frequent construction in BrE as well.

[c] The normal spoken form of *You'd better stay* is /ju betə(r) steɪ/ and the standard negative is *You'd better not stay*. In this respect it is like *He'd rather stay, He'd rather not stay*, which however is not a semi-auxiliary since it does not accept voice transformation:

He'd $\begin{Bmatrix} \text{better} \\ \text{rather} \end{Bmatrix}$ eat breakfast before 9 o'clock

Breakfast had $\begin{Bmatrix} \text{better} \\ \text{*rather} \end{Bmatrix}$ be eaten before 9 o'clock.

Forms and combinations of verbs

3.9

The normal English verb has five forms: the BASE, the -S FORM, the PAST, the -ING PARTICIPLE, and the -ED PARTICIPLE. Examples of these forms and the indication of their functions are given in *Table* 3:1. Regular lexical verbs have the same -*ed* inflection for both the past and the past participle (*called*, see 3.57). Irregular lexical verb forms vary from three (*eg: put, puts, putting*, see 3.63 *ff*) to eight (*be, am, is, are, was, were, being, been*, see 3.19). The modal auxiliaries are defective in not having infinitive (**to may*), -*ing* participle (**maying*), -*ed* participle (**mayed*), or imperative (**may!*). See further 3.20 *ff*.

Table 3:1
VERB FORMS

FORM	SYMBOL	EXAMPLE	FUNCTIONS
(1) base	V	*call* *drink* *put*	(a) all the present tense except 3rd person singular[a]: I/you/we/they *call* (b) imperative: *Call* at once! (c) subjunctive: He demanded that she *call* him (d) infinitive; the bare infinitive: He may *call*; and the *to*-infinitive: He wants her *to call*

Table 3:1 *continued*

FORM	SYMBOL	EXAMPLE	FUNCTIONS
(2) -*s* form (3rd person singular present)	V-*s*	*calls* *drinks* *puts*	3rd person singular present tense: He/she/it *calls*
(3) past	V-*ed*$_1$	*called* *drank* *put*	past tense: He *called* yesterday
(4) -*ing* participle (present participle)	V-*ing*	*calling* *drinking* *putting*	(a) progressive aspect (BE + V-*ing*)[b]: He's *calling* you (b) non-finite -*ing* clauses: *Calling* a spade a spade
(5) -*ed* participle (past participle)	V-*ed*$_2$	*called* *drunk* *put*	(a) perfective aspect (HAVE + V-*ed*$_2$): He *has drunk* the water (b) passive voice (BE + V-*ed*$_2$)[c]: He *is called*

Note

[a] For '1st, 2nd, 3rd person', see 4.108.

[b] KEEP, KEEP ON, GO ON, GO ON AND ON may also be considered progressive auxiliaries (3.39 *ff*):

  He *keeps asking* questions all the time

[c] GET may also be used as a passive auxiliary (*cf* 12.3):

  He *got killed* in the war.

3.10
Finite and non-finite verb phrases compared

The verb forms operate in finite and non-finite verb phrases, which are distinguished as follows:

(1) Finite verb phrases have tense distinction, *ie* present and past tense to express grammatical time relations (see 3.23 *ff*):

$$\text{He}\left\{\begin{array}{l}\textit{studies}\\\textit{studied}\end{array}\right\}\text{English}$$

(2) Finite verb phrases can occur as the verb phrase of a main clause. There is person and number concord between the subject and the finite verb (*cf* 7.23 and 7.31).

  Concord is particularly 'overt' with BE (*cf* 3.19):

$$\left.\begin{array}{l}\text{I }\textit{am}\\\text{You }\textit{are}\\\text{He }\textit{is}\\\text{We }\textit{are}\end{array}\right\}\text{here}$$

With most lexical verbs overt concord is restricted to a contrast between 3rd and non-3rd person singular present (3.54 *ff*):

He *reads* ⎱
They *read* ⎰ the paper every morning

With the modal auxiliaries there is, however, no overt concord:

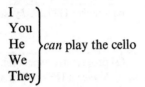

I ⎫
You ⎪
He ⎬ *can* play the cello
We ⎪
They ⎭

(3) Finite verb phrases have mood, which indicates the speaker's attitude to the predication. In contrast to the 'unmarked' INDICATIVE mood, we distinguish the 'marked' moods IMPERATIVE, to express a command (see 7.72 *ff*), and SUBJUNCTIVE, to express a wish, recommendation, and so forth (see 3.16). Both the imperative and the present subjunctive consist of the base form of the verb:

Come here at once!
The committee suggests that he *come* in tie and jacket

(4) Finite verb phrases have a finite verb form, *ie* either an operator or a simple present or past tense form.

The infinitive ((*to*) *call*), the *-ing* participle (*calling*), and the *-ed* participle (*called*) are the non-finite forms of the verb. In main clauses, they can occur only where a finite verb is first element in the verb phrase. However, they can occur in other elements in the main clause, such as subject and object. Compare these two sets:

FINITE VERB PHRASES	NON-FINITE VERB PHRASES
He *smokes*	*To smoke* like that must be dangerous
He *is smoking*	I hate him *smoking*
Smoke!	He entered the office, *smoking* a big cigar.

3.11
Simple finite verb phrases
The finite verb phrase is SIMPLE when it consists of only one verb, which may be imperative (see 7.72 *ff*), present, or past (see 3.16, 3.24 *ff*):

Work harder!
He *works* hard
He *worked* hard

The verb phrase is COMPLEX when it consists of two or more verbs, as in

John *has worked* hard
John *may work* hard
John *may have been working* hard

Note
BEWARE is used in the imperative and in complex verb phrases with modal auxiliary:

Beware of the dog!
You should beware of pickpockets here

Thus it is not used in simple declarative or interrogative sentences:

*We beware of girls
*Do you beware of girls?

Complex finite verb phrases
3.12
These are of four basic types:

Type A (MODAL/PERIPHRASTIC) consists of a modal or periphrastic
auxiliary + the base of the verb-phrase head. For example: He *must examine.*

Type B (PERFECTIVE) consists of the auxiliary HAVE + the *-ed* participle of the verb-phrase head. For example: He *has examined.*

Type C (PROGRESSIVE) consists of the auxiliary BE + the *-ing* participle of the verb-phrase head. For example: He *is examining.*

Type D (PASSIVE) consists of the auxiliary BE + the *-ed* participle of the verb-phrase head. For example: He *is examined.*

3.13
These four verb types can also enter into various combinations with each other:

AB: He *may have examined*
AC: He *may be examining*
AD: He *may be examined*
BC: He *has been examining*
BD: He *has been examined*
CD: He *is being examined*
ABC: He *may have been examining*
ABD: He *may have been examined*
ACD: He *may be being examined*
BCD: He *has been being examined*
ABCD: He *may have been being examined*

In these strings the different complex verb phrase types are 'telescoped' into one another. This means that combinations of the basic types form structures where the head of the first also functions as auxiliary of the second, and so forth. For example, ABD has the following structure:

A, consisting of the auxiliary *may* + the base *have*, +

B, consisting of the auxiliary *have* + the *-ed* participle *been*, +

D, consisting of the auxiliary *be* + the *-ed* participle *examined*, where *have* is shared by A and B and *be(en)* is shared by B and D.

The order in which the four types can form combinations is indicated by the alphabetical symbols (A, B, C, D) which label them. A cannot follow B, B cannot follow C or D, etc, but gaps are allowed: AC, AD, ACD, BD, etc. *Fig* 3:2 gives a graphic representation of how the finite verb phrase (simple or complex) is built up in a left-to-right progression.

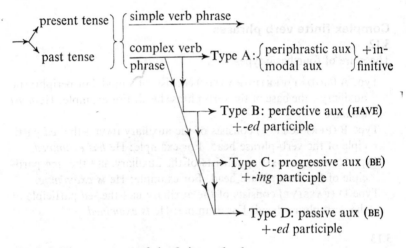

Fig 3:2 The structure of the finite verb phrase

First, the selection of present or past tense for the first element; then the selection of none, one, two, three, or four of the complex verb phrase types as indicated by the direction of the arrows. This outline of the structure of complex verb phrases is an oversimplification, which does not account for all the linguistic facts. It does not, for example, cover *He may be about to be getting fed*, but such phrases can, as we shall see in 3.14, be related to these basic types.

Some of the types of complex verb phrase are uncommon but grammatical; thus while

They *might have been being examined*

is very unlikely to be used, it has a structure that is undoubtedly acceptable in a way that is not the case with, for example,

*They *have may being being examined.*

3.14

There are long strings of verbs that do not fit our analysis of the complex verb phrase into the four types A, B, C, and D. For example, a string like *would seem to have been eating* cannot be analysed as AABC. One defining criterion of modal auxiliaries was that they cannot co-occur with one another in the verb phrase. However, there is no such restriction for semi-auxiliaries (3.8). This means that they can combine freely with auxiliaries (including modal auxiliaries) or other semi-auxiliaries into long concatenated verb phrases, for example:

Your wife *might have happened to call* you up
The sampling volume *would have to be increasing*
This problem *seems to have to be dealt with.*

3.15
Non-finite verb phrases
Unlike finite verb phrases (see 3.10), non-finite verb phrases have no tense distinction or imperative mood, and cannot occur in construction with a subject of a main clause (*cf* 11.5):

*He to do it easily

But:

He did it easily
It was easy for him to do it

Since modal auxiliaries have no non-finite forms (infinitive or participle) they cannot occur in non-finite verb phrases. However, the aspect and voice auxiliaries HAVE (Type B) and BE (Types C and D) have no such restriction. If we relate the structure of the non-finite verb phrase to that of the finite verb phrase (3.13), we can tabulate them as follows:

		INFINITIVES	PARTICIPLES
simple		*to examine*	*examining*
complex	B	*to have examined*	*having examined*
	C	*to be examining*	*being examining*[a]
	D	*to be examined*	*being examined*
	BC	*to have been examining*	*having been examining*
	BD	*to have been examined*	*having been examined*
	CD	*to be being examined*	*being being examined*[a]
	BCD	? *to have been being examined*[b]	? *having been being examined*[b]

Note

[a] *Examining* is used for the unacceptable **being examining* and *being examined* for
  **being being examined*.

[b] The last two non-finite verb phrases *to have been being examined* and *having been being examined* are felt by speakers to be awkward.

3.16
The subjunctive

The subjunctive is not an important category in contemporary English and is normally replaced by other constructions. It can be described in three separate statements:

(a) The MANDATIVE SUBJUNCTIVE in *that*-clauses has only one form, the base (V); this means there is lack of the regular indicative concord between subject and finite verb in the 3rd person singular present, and the present and past tenses are indistinguishable. This subjunctive is productive, to the extent that it can be used with any verb in subordinate *that*-clauses when the main clause contains an expression of recommendation, resolution, demand, surprise, and so on (*We demand, require, move, insist, suggest, ask*, etc *that*...). The use of this subjunctive occurs chiefly in formal style (and especially in AmE) where in less formal contexts one would rather make use of other stylistic devices, such as *to*-infinitive or *should*+infinitive. In each of the following pairs the more formal subjunctive construction is given first.

> We ask that the individual citizen *watch* closely any
>   developments in this matter
> We ask the individual citizen to watch closely any
>   developments in this matter

> It is necessary that every member *inform* himself of these
>   rules
> It is necessary that every member should inform himself of
>   these rules

> There was a suggestion that Brown *be* dropped from the
>   team
> There was a suggestion to drop Brown from the team

(b) The FORMULAIC SUBJUNCTIVE also consists of the base (V) but is only used in clauses in certain set expressions which have to be learnt as wholes (see 7.86):

> *Come* what may, we will go ahead
> God *save* the Queen!
> So *be* it then!
> *Suffice* it to say that ...

Be that as it may, . . .
Heaven *forbid* that . . .

(c) The *WERE*-SUBJUNCTIVE is hypothetical in meaning and is used in conditional and concessive clauses and in subordinate clauses after optative verbs like *wish* (see 11.69). This subjunctive is restricted to one form: *were*. It occurs in the 1st and 3rd person singular present of the verb BE, matching the indicative *was*, which is the more common in less formal style:

If I $\begin{Bmatrix} were \\ was \end{Bmatrix}$ rich, . . .

If she $\begin{Bmatrix} were \\ was \end{Bmatrix}$ to do something like that, . . .

He spoke to me as if I $\begin{Bmatrix} were \\ was \end{Bmatrix}$ deaf

I wish I $\begin{Bmatrix} were \\ was \end{Bmatrix}$ dead

Note
Only *were* is acceptable in 'As it were' (=so to speak); *were* is usual in 'If I were you'.

Auxiliaries
The primary auxiliaries (*do, have,* and *be*)
3.17
Do

The PERIPHRASTIC AUXILIARY DO is the most neutral or 'auxiliary-like' of all the auxiliaries. It has no individual meaning but serves as a 'dummy' operator (3.6) in sentence processes such as those described in 2.18 (see further pro-forms in 10.52). The auxiliary DO has the following forms:

	NON-NEGATIVE	UNCONTRACTED NEGATIVE	CONTRACTED NEGATIVE
present	*do* /du/ *does* /dʌz/	*do not* *does not*	*don't* /doʊnt/ *doesn't*
past	*did*	*did not*	*didn't*

There is also a lexical verb DO ('perform', etc) which has the full range of forms, including the present participle *doing* and the past participle *done* (see 3.70):

What have you been *doing* today?
I haven't *done* much, I'm afraid

Table 3 : 2
DO-PERIPHRASIS
(The modal auxiliary *can* is given for comparison with DO)

	positive	negative	interrogative	negative-interrogative	tags	emphatic or persuasive
imperative	*Wait!*	*Don't wait!*				*Do wait!*
present	*He waits*	*He doesn't wait*	*Does he wait?*	*Doesn't he wait?*	*He waits, doesn't he?* / *He doesn't wait, does he?*	*He does wait*
	He can wait	*He can't wait*	*Can he wait?*	*Can't he wait?*	*He can wait, can't he?* / *He can't wait, can he?*	*He can wait*
past	*He waited*	*He didn't wait*	*Did he wait?*	*Didn't he wait?*	*He waited, didn't he?* / *He didn't wait, did he?*	*He did wait*
	He could wait	*He couldn't wait*	*Could he wait?*	*Couldn't he wait?*	*He could wait, couldn't he?* / *He couldn't wait, could he?*	*He could wait*

DO-periphrasis is required in the following cases (see *Table* 3:2; for HAVE and BE, see 3.18 and 3.19):

(a) In sentences negated by *not* where the verb is imperative (7.76), simple present, or simple past:

He *didn't like* mathematics

However, there is no DO-periphrasis in non-finite verb phrases:

Not *liking*
Doing not *liking*
}mathematics, he gave it up

Not *to go*
To do not *go*
}would be shameful

(b) In questions involving inversion where the verb is in the simple present or past tense (7.56, 7.63):

Did he *stay* long?
What *did* he *say*?

There is no DO-periphrasis

(i) in positive *wh*-questions beginning with the subject:

What *happened*?
Who *came* first?

(ii) in *yes-no* questions without inversion:

He *said* that?

(c) In tag questions and substitute clauses where the verb is simple present or past tense (see 7.59 *ff* and 10.52 *ff*):

He knows how to drive a car, *doesn't* he?

(d) In emphatic or persuasive constructions where the verb is simple present, simple past, or imperative (7.77, 14.7, 14.47):

He *did* say he would be here at nine, didn't he?
Do sit down!

(e) In sentences with inversion caused by certain introductory words such as the negative adverbs *never*, *hardly*, etc when the verb is in the simple present or past tense (see 8.18, 8.66, 14.16):

Never *did* he *think* that the book would be finished

3.18
Have

The aspect auxiliary HAVE combines with past participles to form perfective complex verb phrases (Type B, 3.12). The auxiliary HAVE has the following forms:

	NON-NEGATIVE	UNCONTRACTED NEGATIVE	CONTRACTED NEGATIVE
base	*have, 've*	*have not, 've not*	*haven't*
-*s* form	*has, 's*	*has not, 's not*	*hasn't*
past	*had, 'd*	*had not, 'd not*	*hadn't*
-*ing* form	*having*	*not having*	
-*ed* participle	*had*		

Note

There is also a transitive lexical verb HAVE which in some uses can be constructed either as an auxiliary (without DO-periphrasis) or as a lexical verb (with DO-periphrasis). In the stative sense (3.40) of possession HAVE is often (especially in BrE) constructed as an auxiliary. AmE prefers the DO-construction:

I $\left\{ \begin{array}{l} \textit{haven't} \\ \textit{don't have} \end{array} \right\}$ any books

In dynamic senses (*receive, take, experience*, etc) HAVE in both AmE and BrE normally has DO-periphrasis:

Does he *have* coffee with his breakfast?
Did you *have* any difficulty getting here?

The DO-construction is required in such expressions as

Did you *have* a good time?

There is also the informal HAVE GOT, where HAVE is constructed as an auxiliary, which is frequently preferred (especially in BrE) as an alternative to HAVE. It is particularly common in negative and interrogative sentences. As a further alternative for expressing negation, we have the negative determiner *no:*

I *have no* books
I *haven't got* any books.

3.19
Be

The auxiliary BE has two functions: as ASPECT AUXILIARY Type C, and as PASSIVE AUXILIARY Type D (see 3.12). BE is unique among English verbs in having eight different forms:

		NON-NEGATIVE	UNCONTRACTED NEGATIVE	CONTRACTED NEGATIVE
base		*be*		
present	1st person singular present	*am*[a], *'m*	*am not, 'm not*	(*aren't, ain't*)[b]
	3rd person singular present	*is, 's*	*is not, 's not*	*isn't*
	2nd person present, 1st and 3rd person plural present	*are, 're*	*are not, 're not*	*aren't*
past	1st and 3rd person singular past	*was*[a]	*was not*	*wasn't*
	2nd person past, 1st and 3rd person plural past	*were*[a]	*were not*	*weren't*
-ing form		*being*	*not being*	
-ed participle		*been*		

Note

[a] BE is the only verb in English to have a special form for the 1st person singular of the present (*am*) and two distinct past forms (*was, were*). In the subjunctive (see 3.16) the 1st and 3rd person singular past forms are the same as in the plural (*were, were not, weren't*).

[b] *Aren't I* is widely used in BrE, but there is no generally acceptable contracted form for *am not* in declarative sentences. *Ain't* (AmE) is considered by many to be substandard; as well as serving as a contracted *am not*, it is used also for *isn't*, *aren't*, *hasn't*, and *haven't*.

[c] For the aspectual functions of BE and HAVE, see 3.37 *ff*, and for the passive construction with BE, see 12.2.

[d] Lexical verb BE may have DO-periphrasis in persuasive imperative sentences:

   Do be quiet!

and regularly has the periphrasis with negative imperatives:

   Don't be silly!

But DO-periphrasis does not occur elsewhere with BE:

   He isn't lazy   ~ *He doesn't be lazy
   Is she a student? ~ *Does she be a student?

The modal auxiliaries
3.20
The modal auxiliaries are the following:

NON-NEGATIVE	UNCONTRACTED NEGATIVE	CONTRACTED NEGATIVE
can	*cannot, can not*	*can't*
could	*could not*	*couldn't*
may	*may not*	*(mayn't)*[a]
might	*might not*	*mightn't*
shall	*shall not*	*shan't*[b]
should	*should not*	*shouldn't*
will	*will not*	*won't*
'll	*'ll not*	—[c]
would	*would not*	*wouldn't*
'd	*'d not*	—[c]
must	*must not*	*mustn't* /mʌsnt/
ought to	*ought not to*	*oughtn't to*[d]
used to	*used not to*	*usedn't to* /jusnt/
		(*didn't use to*)
(need)[e]	*need not*	*needn't*
(dare)[e]	*dare not*	*(daren't)*

Note

[a] *Mayn't* is restricted to BrE, where it is rare.

[b] *Shan't* is rare in AmE.

[c] There are no contracted negative forms of *'ll* and *'d* since they are themselves contractions. These forms are braced with *will* and *would* because *'ll* and *'d* can always be expanded to *will* and *would* (except, of course, when *'d=had*, see 3.18).

[d] *Ought* regularly has the *to*-infinitive, but AmE occasionally has the bare infinitive in negative sentences and in questions (although *should* is commoner in both cases):

> You oughtn't smoke so much
> Ought you smoke so much?

[e] DARE and NEED as non-negative auxiliaries occur chiefly with inversion (see 3.21).

3.21
Marginal modal auxiliaries
USED /just/ always takes the *to*-infinitive and occurs only in the past tense. It may take DO-periphrasis, in which case the spellings *didn't used to* and *didn't use to* both occur. The interrogative construction *used he to* is especially BrE; *did he used to* is preferred in both AmE and BrE.

DARE and NEED can be constructed either as modal auxiliaries (with bare infinitive and without inflected -*s* form or past tense) or as lexical verbs (with *to*-infinitive, -*s* inflection and past forms). The modal verb construction is restricted to non-assertive contexts (see 2.21), *ie* mainly negative and interrogative sentences, whereas the lexical verb construction can always be used and is in fact the more common. DARE and NEED as auxiliaries are probably rarer in AmE than in BrE.

	MODAL AUXILIARY CONSTRUCTION	LEXICAL VERB CONSTRUCTION
positive		He *needs to* go now
negative	He *needn't* go now	He *doesn't need to* go now
interrogative	*Need* he go now?	*Does* he *need to* go now?
negative-interrogative	*Needn't* he go now?	*Doesn't* he *need to* go now?

Note

[*a*] 'Non-assertive contexts' are not confined to overtly negative and/or interrogative sentences but can also be present in adverbials, *eg: He need do it only under these circumstances, He need do it but once;* in determiners, *eg: He need have no fear, No soldier dare disobey;* in pronouns, *eg: Nobody would dare predict . . .;* or even implicitly, *eg: All you need do is, . . .* ('You need do no more than . . .').

[*b*] Blends between the two constructions occur and seem to be widely acceptable in the case of DARE:

> We do not dare speak

[*c*] The passive raises problems with some auxiliaries. For example, DARE does not accept the voice transformation (3.7):

> {The boy daren't leave the car
> {*The car daren't be left by the boy

However, this does not mean that DARE cannot occur in passive verb phrases:

> I dare not be seen with her

but only that there is no direct active-passive clause relation (12.2 *ff*), as there is with most auxiliaries:

> {The boy shouldn't leave the car
> {The car shouldn't be left by the boy

Sometimes there are shifts in their range of meaning (see 3.43 *ff*) as in:

> {John could drive the car (ability or possibility)
> {The car could be driven by John (possibility only)
> {I shall read the book tonight (future or speaker's volition)
> {The book shall be read tonight (speaker's volition only)

3.22

The three criteria we have used to define auxiliaries are inversion, negation, and the use of pro-forms (see 3.2–4). However, modal auxiliaries, as distinct from the primary auxiliaries DO, HAVE, and BE, have some additional morphological and syntactic characteristics.

(1) Modal auxiliaries are all followed by the infinitive, which is bare except with *ought* and *used:*

>You *ought to* comb your hair sometime
>He *used to* read for hours on end

(2) Modal auxiliaries can only occur as the first (finite) element of the verb phrase but not in non-finite functions, *ie* as infinitives or participles:

MODAL AUXILIARY	PRIMARY AUXILIARY	LEXICAL VERB
*to may	*to have* (*eaten*)	*to eat*
*(is) maying	(*is*) *being* (*eaten*)	*eating*
*(is) mayed	(*has*) *been* (*eaten*)	*eaten*

(3) Modal auxiliaries are not inflected in the 3rd person singular of the present tense (where lexical verbs have the *-s* form, see 3.55):

>You⎫
>He ⎭*may* write   You *like*⎫to write
>   He *likes* ⎭

(4) Both the present and past forms of the modal auxiliaries can be used in present tense sequence (*cf* 3.52):

>I think he⎰*may* ⎱stay now
>   ⎱*might*⎰

>I think he⎰*has to* ⎱stay now
>   ⎱**had to*⎰

Time, tense, and aspect
3.23
Time is a universal concept with three divisions:

PAST TIME   PRESENT TIME   FUTURE TIME

The concept is universal in that the units of time are extra-linguistic: they exist independently of the grammar of any particular language. In our use of language, however, we make linguistic reference to these extra-linguistic realities by means of the language-specific category of tense.

Tense
3.24
English has two tenses: PRESENT TENSE and PAST TENSE. As the names imply, the present tense normally refers to present time and past tense to past time:

She *is* quite well today
Yesterday she *was* sick.

3.25
Simple present
The simple present and past tenses have various uses.

(1) PRESENT WITHOUT REFERENCE TO SPECIFIC TIME is used where there is no limitation on the extension of the state through the present into the past and future time. This category includes 'eternal truths', which do not refer specifically to the present but are general timeless statements. We may distinguish two related types (see the figure below):

(a) Universal time statements, particularly associated with stative verbs (see 3.40):

Two and two *make* four
The albatross *is* a big bird
Onions *smell*

(b) Habitual time statements, particularly associated with dynamic verbs (see 3.40). They often have adverbs like *every day*, etc:

We *go* to France every year
He *loves* going to the theatre

In fact, however, it is possible to have stative or dynamic verbs with both (a) and (b); dynamic verbs, used in either of these ways, imply repetition of the event.

STATIVE	DYNAMIC	
Two and two *make* four	The sun *sets* in the west	UNIVERSAL TIME
John *knows* the answer	We *cycle* to work every day	HABITUAL TIME

This is by far the most important group of uses of the present tense.

(2) The INSTANTANEOUS SIMPLE PRESENT is used only with dynamic verbs which signify an event simultaneous with the present moment. Some typical uses are the following:

commentaries: Moore *passes* the ball to Charlton
demonstrations: I now *place* the turkey in the oven
exclamations: Here *comes* the winner!
performative declarations: We *acknowledge* your letter

(3) SIMPLE PRESENT WITH FUTURE TIME REFERENCE (*cf* 3.31)
can be used

(a) when there is a temporal adverbial in the clause:

The plane *leaves* for Chicago at eight o'clock

(b) in conditional and temporal clauses introduced by *if, unless,
after, before, as soon as, when,* etc (see 11.68):

He'll do it if you *pay* him
I'll let you know as soon as I *hear* from him

(4) SIMPLE PRESENT WITH PAST TIME REFERENCE is used with,
for example, the 'communication verbs' *tell, hear, learn, write,* etc
to express the persistence in the present of the effect of a past
communication:

John *tells* me that you have been abroad (roughly = '... has
told ...')

3.26
Simple past

The basic meaning of the simple past tense is to denote definite past time,
ie what took place at a given time or in a given period before the present
moment. It is found with adverbs referring to past time: *I spoke to him
last week.* There are, however, some exceptional cases in which the past
tense does not have to refer to past time.

(1) In INDIRECT (REPORTED) SPEECH past tense in the reporting
verb tends to make the verb of the subordinate clause past, too.
This phenomenon is called back-shift (see 11.74).

Direct speech:	I *am* here	You *look* well
Indirect speech:	You *say* you *are* here	I *think* you *look* well
	You *said* you *were* here	I *thought* you *looked* well

(2) ATTITUDINAL PAST is related to the attitudes of the speaker
rather than to time. In the following pairs, the past tense is more
polite than the present tense:

${Do \atop Did}$ you want to see me now?

I ${wonder \atop wondered}$ if you could help me

(3) HYPOTHETICAL PAST is used in some subordinate clauses,
especially *if*-clauses:

If I *were* you, ...

If I$\begin{Bmatrix} was \\ were \end{Bmatrix}$an opera singer, ...

If you *loved* me, you wouldn't say that.

Note

If I were an opera singer (see 3.16) is considered preferable by many speakers.

Some means of expressing future time
3.27

There is no obvious future tense in English corresponding to the time/tense parallel for present and past. Instead there are a number of possibilities of denoting future time. Futurity, modality, and aspect are closely related, and future time is rendered by means of modal auxiliaries or semi-auxiliaries, or by simple present or progressive forms.

3.28

Auxiliary verb construction

SHALL + infinitive (in 1st person only; chiefly BrE).
WILL or 'LL + infinitive in all persons, including 1st person.

I$\begin{Bmatrix} shall \\ will \end{Bmatrix}$*try* to do my best

He *will be* here in half an hour
I'*ll do* it for you

The future and modal functions of these auxiliaries can hardly be separated (*cf* 3.46 *f*). Although *shall* and, particularly, *will*, are the closest approximation to a colourless, neutral future, they do not form a future tense comparable to the present and past tenses. *Shall* in the sense of future is restricted to the 1st person in Standard BrE, whereas *will* can be used in the same sense in all persons throughout the English-speaking world. Prescriptive usage has exerted considerable influence in the direction of using *shall*.

The auxiliary construction is also used to refer to a statement seen in the past from a point of orientation in the future:

They *will have finished* their book by next year.

3.29

Be going to + infinitive

This construction denotes future and intention (*cf* 3.46). Its general meaning is 'future fulfilment of the present'. Looked at more carefully,

BE GOING TO has two more specific meanings, of which one, 'future of present intention', is used chiefly with personal subjects:

> When *are* you *going to get married?*

The other meaning is 'future of present cause', which is found with both personal and non-personal subjects:

> She'*s going to have* a baby
> It'*s going to rain*

Both these suggest that the event is already 'on the way'. BE GOING TO is not generally used in the main clause of conditional sentences, *will*/*'ll* or *shall* being preferred instead:

> If you leave now, you'*ll* never *regret* it
> *If you leave now, you *are* never *going to regret* it.

3.30
Present progressive
The present progressive refers to a future happening anticipated in the present. Its basic meaning is 'fixed arrangement, plan, or programme':

> The orchestra *is playing* Mozart

Since the progressive is used to denote present as well as future, a time adverbial is often used to clarify in which meaning the verb is being used:

> They *are washing* the dishes$\begin{cases} now \\ later \end{cases}$

The present progressive is especially frequent with transitional dynamic verbs like *arrive, come, go, land, start, stop*, etc, which refer to a transition between two states or positions:

> The plane *is taking off* at 5.20
> The President *is coming* to the UN this week.

3.31
Simple present
The simple present is regularly used in subordinate clauses that are conditional (introduced by *if, unless*, etc) or temporal (introduced by *as soon as, before, when*, etc; see 11.68):

> What will you say if I *marry* my boss?
> The guests will be drunk, before they *leave*

The use of the simple present in main clauses may be said to represent a marked future aspect of unusual definiteness, in that it attributes to the future the same degree of certainty one normally associates with present and past events. It is used for statements about the calendar:

Yesterday was Monday, today is Tuesday, and tomorrow *is* Wednesday

and to describe immutable events or 'fixtures':

When *is* high tide?
What time *is* the football match?

Both the simple present and the progressive (3.30) are often used with dynamic transitional verbs: *arrive, come, leave*, etc, both having the meaning of 'plan' or 'programme':

The train$\begin{cases} leaves \\ is\ leaving \end{cases}$tonight from Chicago.

3.32
Auxiliary verb construction + progressive

The auxiliary verb construction (3.28) can be used together with the progressive infinitive to denote a 'future-as-a-matter-of-course': *will/shall* + BE + V-*ing*. The use of this combination avoids the interpretation (to which *will, shall*, and BE GOING TO are liable) of volition, insistence, etc:

He'*ll do* his best (future or volitional interpretation possible)
He'*ll be doing* his best (future interpretation only)

This complex construction can be used to convey greater tact and consideration than the simple auxiliary construction does:

When *will* you$\begin{cases} put\ on \\ be\ putting\ on \end{cases}$another performance?

When *will* you$\begin{cases} come? \\ be\ coming? \end{cases}$

3.33
Be about to + infinitive

This construction expresses near future, *ie* imminent fulfilment:

We *are* (just) *about to leave.*

3.34
Be to + infinitive

This expresses (a) arrangement, (b) command, or (c) pre-destined future:

(a) We *are to be married* soon
There'*s to be* an investigation

(b) You *are to be* back by 10 o'clock
(c) If he*'s to succeed* in his new profession, . . .

3.35
Future time in the past

Some of the future constructions just discussed can be used in the past tense to express time which is in the future when seen from a viewpoint in the past.

(1) AUXILIARY VERB CONSTRUCTION with *would* (rare; literary narrative style)

The time was not far off when he *would regret* this decision

(2) BE GOING TO + INFINITIVE (often with the sense of 'unfulfilled intention')

You *were going to give* me your address

(3) PAST PROGRESSIVE

I *was meeting* him in Bordeaux the next day

(4) BE TO + INFINITIVE (formal = 'was destined to' or 'arrangement')

He *was* later *to regret* his decision
The meeting *was to be held* the following week

(5) BE ABOUT TO ('on the point of')

He *was about to hit* me.

Aspect
3.36

Aspect refers to the manner in which the verb action is regarded or experienced. The choice of aspect is a comment on or a particular view of the action. English has two sets of aspectual contrasts: PERFECTIVE/NON-PERFECTIVE and PROGRESSIVE/NON-PROGRESSIVE.

The tense and aspect categories can be combined in various ways, so that we get the following system of contrasts in the complex verb phrase:

SYMBOL	NAME	EXAMPLE
Type B	present perfect	he *has examined*
	past perfect	he *had examined*
Type C	present progressive	he *is examining*
	past progressive	he *was examining*
Type BC	present perfect progressive	he *has been examining*
	past perfect progressive	he *had been examining*

Perfective
3.37
Present perfect
The present perfect indicates a period of time stretching backwards into some earlier time. It is past with 'current relevance':

> simple past: John *lived* in Paris for ten years
> present perfect: John *has lived* in Paris for ten years

The simple past of the first sentence indicates that the period of residence in Paris has come to a close. The perfective aspect here denotes that John still lives there at the moment of speaking (although there is no implication that his residence there will continue). Compare also the following pairs of sentences:

> His sister *has been* an invalid all her life (*ie* she is still alive)
> His sister *was* an invalid all her life (*ie* she is now dead)

> For generations, Nepal *has produced* the world's greatest soldiers
>   (*ie* the nation of Nepal must still exist)
> For generations, Sparta *produced* Greece's greatest warriors
>   (*ie* the state of Sparta may no longer exist)

> Peter *has injured* his ankle and it's still bad
> *Peter *has injured* his ankle but now it's better

The choice of perfective aspect is associated with time-orientation and consequently also with various time-indicators (*lately, since, so far*, etc). It is therefore helpful to consider these two together. Here are some examples:

ADVERBIALS WITH SIMPLE PAST (refer to a period now past)		ADVERBIALS WITH PRESENT PERFECT (refer to a period stretching up to the present)	
I *saw* him	yesterday (evening)	I *haven't* *seen* him	so far
	a week ago		hitherto
	earlier this week		up to now
	last Monday		since Monday
	the other day		since last week
	at four o'clock		since I met you
	in the morning		lately
	on Tuesday		

ADVERBIALS WITH EITHER
SIMPLE PAST OR PRESENT PERFECT

$$I\begin{Bmatrix}saw\\have\ seen\end{Bmatrix}him\begin{cases}today\\this\ month\\this\ year\\recently\end{cases}$$

There is also a difference statable in terms of definiteness (4.28 *ff*). In the following examples the past implies definite reference and the perfect indefinite reference:

Did you *hear* Segovia play? ('on a certain occasion')
Have you *heard* Segovia play? ('at any time')

3.38
Past perfect
The past perfect has the meaning of past-in-the-past:

John *had lived* in Paris for ten years (when I met him)

In some contexts the simple past and the past perfect are interchangeable, *eg:*

I ate my lunch after my wife$\begin{Bmatrix}came\\had\ come\end{Bmatrix}$home from her shopping

Here the conjunction *after* is sufficient specification to indicate that the arrival from the shopping expedition had taken place before the eating, so that the extra time indication by means of the past perfect becomes redundant.

The perfect can be combined with the progressive (see 3.39) into present perfect progressive (*has been examining*) and past perfect progressive (*had been examining*).

Progressive
3.39
Progressive aspect indicates temporariness – an action in progress instead of the occurrence of an action or the existence of a state:

simple present: Joan *sings* well
present progressive: Joan *is singing* well

These two sentences have the same tense but different aspect. Notice the meaning difference between them: *Joan sings well* refers to Joan's competence as a singer, that she has a good voice; *Joan is singing well* refers to her performance, that she is singing well on a particular occasion. The simple/progressive aspectual contrast also applies in the past tense:

simple past: Joan *sang* well
past progressive: Joan *was singing* well

In addition to process and continuation, there are a number of other concomitant meanings or overtones that go with the progressive aspect, such as limited duration, incompletion, simultaneity, vividness of description, emotional colouring, and emphasis. Compare the following contrastive pairs of sentences:

John *plays* the banjo	INDEFINITE TIME
John *is playing* the banjo	TEMPORARINESS: 'John's activity at this particular moment is playing the banjo'
The professor *types* his own letters (and always has)	HABITUAL ACTIVITY of the professor
The professor *is typing* his own letters (these days)	LIMITED DURATION: the progressive suggests that the professor's activity is of limited duration
John always *comes* late	CHARACTERISTIC ACTIVITY, allows an objective tone
John'*s* always *coming* late	CHARACTERISTIC ACTIVITY, necessarily occurring with adverbs like *always* and *continually*. It imparts a subjective, emotionally coloured tone.
I *read* a book that evening	COMPLETION: the speaker reached the end of the book before the end of the evening
I *was reading* a book that evening	INCOMPLETION: there is no implication that the reading was completed in the course of the evening

Note

Besides the regular progressive auxiliary BE, the verbs KEEP (ON), GO ON, etc have a similar function:

John $\begin{Bmatrix} keeps \\ goes\ on \end{Bmatrix}$ asking silly questions.

3.40

Dynamic and stative verbs

In 2.6 it was noted that some verbs can occur with progressive aspect (*He was writing a letter*) but that others cannot do so (**He was knowing* *the answer*). The distinction between verbs in dynamic use (as with WRITE) and stative use (as with KNOW) is a fundamental one in English grammar, and it is also reflected in a number of other ways than in the progressive. For verb categories, we may mention the imperative (7.72 *ff*), the 'pseudo-cleft sentence' (see 14.21 *f*) with DO pro-form, and the causative construction (see 12.52 *ff*); for adverbial categories we may mention manner adverbs requiring an animate subject (such as *reluctantly*, see 8.42) and the *for . . . sake* construction. Although the classes of adjectives will be discussed in detail in 5.37 *ff*, we will here draw attention to the parallel dynamic/stative distinction that also holds for adjectives. The table below shows the verbs LEARN and KNOW and the adjectives *careful* and *tall* as complements of the copula BE.

GRAMMATICAL FEATURE	DYNAMIC	STATIVE
progressive	I'm learning the language I'm being careful	*I'm knowing the language *I'm being tall
imperative	Learn the language! Be careful!	*Know the language! *Be tall!
pseudo-cleft sentence with a DO pro-form	What I did was (to) learn the language What I did was to be careful	*What I did was (to) know the language *What I did was to be tall
causative construction	I persuaded her to learn the language I persuaded her to be careful	*I persuaded her to know the language *I persuaded her to be tall
manner adverb requiring an animate subject	I learned the language only reluctantly I was careful only reluctantly	*I knew the language only reluctantly *I was tall only reluctantly
for . . . sake construction	I learned the language for my fiancée's sake I was careful for my fiancée's sake	*I knew the language for my fiancée's sake *I was tall for my fiancée's sake

3.41
Classes of lexical verbs
Although it is convenient to speak of 'dynamic' and 'stative' verbs, it is important to note that it would be more accurate to speak of 'dynamic'

and 'stative' uses of verbs. HAVE and BE, for example, can be used either way – with the expected consequences, such as aspectual constraints:

John $\begin{cases} is\ having\ \text{a good time ('is experiencing')} \\ *is\ having \\ has \end{cases}$ a good car ('possesses')

Mary $\begin{cases} is\ being\ \text{a good girl today ('is behaving well')} \\ is\ \text{a good girl ('is by nature a good girl')} \end{cases}$

The progressive aspect will be related to seven subclasses of verbs: A1–5 are dynamic and B1–2 are stative verb uses. Starting with the classes that are most likely to occur in the progressive, we have:

[A] DYNAMIC VERBS

[A1] *ACTIVITY VERBS:* ABANDON, ASK, BEG, CALL, DRINK, EAT, HELP, LEARN, LISTEN, LOOK AT, PLAY, RAIN, REMIND, READ, SAY, SLICE, THROW, WHISPER, WORK, WRITE, etc.

$\begin{cases} \text{The guests } were\ playing \text{ cards round the dining-room} \\ \quad \text{table} \\ \text{The guests always } played \text{ cards after dinner} \end{cases}$

[A2] *PROCESS VERBS:* CHANGE, DETERIORATE, GROW, MATURE, SLOW DOWN, WIDEN, etc. Both activity and process verbs are frequently used in progressive aspect to indicate incomplete events in progress.

$\begin{cases} \text{We } ate \text{ dinner (together every day)} \\ \text{We } were\ eating \text{ dinner (when my friend arrived)} \end{cases}$
$\begin{cases} \text{The weather } changed \text{ (overnight)} \\ \text{The weather } was\ changing \text{ (as I woke up)} \end{cases}$

[A3] *VERBS OF BODILY SENSATION* (ACHE, FEEL, HURT, ITCH, etc) can have either simple or progressive aspect with little difference in meaning.

John $\begin{cases} felt \\ was\ feeling \end{cases}$ better and decided to go to work

[A4] *TRANSITIONAL EVENT VERBS* (ARRIVE, DIE, FALL, LAND, LEAVE, LOSE, etc) occur in the progressive but with a change of meaning compared with simple aspect. The progressive implies inception, *ie* only the approach to the transition. Compare the following pairs:

The train $\begin{cases} arrived \\ was\ arriving \end{cases}$

The old man $\begin{cases} died \\ was\ dying \end{cases}$

[A5] *MOMENTARY VERBS* (HIT, JUMP, KICK, KNOCK, NOD, TAP, etc) have little duration, and thus the progressive aspect powerfully suggests repetition.

$$\text{The child}\begin{cases} jumped\ (=\text{once}) \\ was\ jumping\ (=\text{several times}) \end{cases}\text{for joy}$$

Of course, the progressive aspect does not always imply repetition with these verbs, *eg*

> The man *was jumping* off the bus when the policeman caught him

[B] STATIVE VERBS

[B1] *VERBS OF INERT PERCEPTION AND COGNITION:* ABHOR, ADORE, ASTONISH, BELIEVE, DESIRE, DETEST, DISLIKE, DOUBT, FEEL, FORGIVE, GUESS, HATE, HEAR, IMAGINE, IMPRESS, INTEND, KNOW, LIKE, LOVE, MEAN, MIND, PERCEIVE, PLEASE, PREFER, PRESUPPOSE, REALIZE, RECALL, RECOGNIZE, REGARD, REMEMBER, SATISFY, SEE, SMELL, SUPPOSE, TASTE, THINK, UNDERSTAND, WANT, WISH, etc. Verbs of this class characteristically occur with *that-* or *wh*-clauses and do not normally occur in progressive aspect. (*Cf* non-agentive subject, 7.16 *f.*)

$$\text{I}\begin{cases} understand \\ *am\ understanding \end{cases}\text{that she is coming}$$

The same verbs with other uses belong of course to other classes, *eg*

> I *am thinking* of her all the time (activity verb)

> $\begin{cases} \text{I } see \text{ ('understand') what you mean} \\ \text{I } am\ seeing \text{ ('pay a visit to', activity verb) the doctor today} \end{cases}$

> $\begin{cases} \text{I (can) } smell \text{ perfume} \\ \text{I } am\ smelling \text{ the perfume (activity verb)} \end{cases}$

[B2] *RELATIONAL VERBS:* APPLY TO (everyone), BE, BELONG TO, CONCERN, CONSIST OF, CONTAIN, COST, DEPEND ON, DESERVE, EQUAL, FIT, HAVE, INCLUDE, INVOLVE, LACK, MATTER, NEED, OWE, OWN, POSSESS, REMAIN (a bachelor), REQUIRE, RESEMBLE, SEEM, SOUND, SUFFICE, TEND, etc. These verbs are usually impossible in progressive aspect.

> $\begin{cases} \text{He } owns \text{ a big car} \\ \text{*He } is\ owning \text{ a big car} \end{cases}$

> $\begin{cases} \text{His actions } deserve \text{ some comment} \\ \text{*His actions } are\ deserving \text{ some comment} \end{cases}$

{ This book *belongs* to my wife
{ *This book *is belonging* to my wife

3.42
Perfect progressive
The perfect progressive denotes a temporary situation leading up to the present moment. The progressive overtones of incompletion and emotional colouring can also be found.

simple perfect: John *has lived* in New York since 1970
perfect progressive: John *has been living* in New York since 1970

The meaning difference is slight, but the use of the progressive indicates that the speaker considers John's residence in New York to be temporary. Compare also:

Who'*s eaten* my dinner? (*ie* there is nothing left of it)
Who'*s been eating* my dinner? (*ie* there is some left; also more readily suggests disapproval)

The meanings of the modal auxiliaries
3.43
So far the modal auxiliaries have been considered only in respect of their syntactic and morphological properties. We will now make a schematic survey of their chief meanings. (For the meanings of the modals in negative and interrogative sentences, see 7.52 and 7.62.)

3.44
Can/could
CAN

(1) Ability = *be able to* = *be capable of* = *know how to*	He can speak English but he can't write it very well ('He is able to speak/ capable of speaking . . .')
(2) Permission = *be allowed to* = *be permitted to* (*Can* is less formal than *may* in this sense)	Can } May } I smoke in here? ('Am I allowed to smoke in here?')
(3) Possibility = *it is possible that/to* (theoretical possibility; *cf: may* = factual possibility)	Anybody can make mistakes The road can be blocked ('It is possible to block the road') The road may be blocked ('It is possible that the road is blocked')

COULD

(1) Ability	I could never play the banjo
(2) Permission	Could I smoke in here?
(3) Possibility (theoretical or factual, *cf: might*)	That could be my train The road could be blocked

Note

Ability can bring in the implication of willingness (especially in spoken English):

$\left. \begin{array}{l} \text{Can} \\ \text{Could} \end{array} \right\}$ you do me a favour?

3.45
May/might

MAY

(1) Permission = *be allowed to* = *be permitted to* In this sense *may* is more formal than *can*. Instead of *may not* or rare *mayn't*, *mustn't* is often used in the negative to express prohibition.	You may borrow my car if you like You $\left\{ \begin{array}{l} \text{mustn't} \\ \text{are not allowed to} \\ \text{may not} \end{array} \right\}$ borrow my car
(2) Possibility = *it is possible that/to* *May* = factual possibility (*cf: can* = theoretical possibility)	He may never succeed ('It is possible that he will never succeed')

MIGHT

(1) Permission (rare; *cf* 3.52)	Might I smoke in here?
(2) Possibility	What you say might be true

Note

[a] *May* (='possibility') is replaced by *can* in questions, and normally also in negative sentences. Note the difference in meaning between:

This may be true   ~ Can this really be true?
                          ~ This can't be true

He may not be serious   ~ He can't be serious ('It is not possible that he
('It is possible that he   is serious')
is not serious')

[b] There is a rare use of *may* as a 'quasi-subjunctive' auxiliary, *eg* to express wish,
normally in positive sentences (*cf* 7.86, 11.72 Note *b*):

> May the best man win!
> May he never set foot in this house again!

3.46
Shall/should
SHALL (volitional use; *cf* 3.27 *ff*)

(1) Willingness on the part of the speaker in 2nd and 3rd person ('weak volition'). Restricted use.	He shall get his money You shall do exactly as you wish
(2) Intention on the part of the speaker, only in 1st person ('intermediate volition'). Especially BrE.	I shan't be long We shall let you know our decision We shall overcome
(3) *a* Insistence ('strong volition'). Restricted use. *b* Legal and quasi-legal	You shall do as I say He shall be punished The vendor shall maintain the equipment in good repair

Of these three meanings it is only the one of intention ('intermediate
volition') that is widely used today. *Shall* is, on the whole and especially
outside BrE, an infrequent auxiliary with restricted use compared with
should, will and *would*. It is only in the first person singular of questions
that it cannot be replaced by *will*:

$$\left.\begin{matrix}\text{Shall}\\ \text{*Will}\end{matrix}\right\}\text{I come at once?}$$

In the first person plural, *eg*

$$\text{What}\left\{\begin{matrix}\text{shall}\\ \text{will}\end{matrix}\right\}\text{we drink?}$$

shall asks for instructions, and *will* is non-volitional future (especially in
AmE). *Will I/we* has become increasingly common not only in contexts
of non-volitional futurity (*Will I see you later ?*), but also in sentences expressing helplessness, perplexity, etc:

> What will I do?

How will I get there?
Which will I take?

This usage is predominantly AmE but examples may be found in BrE too. A similar meaning is also conveyed by BE GOING TO:

What are we going to do?

SHOULD

(1) Obligation and logical necessity (= *ought to*)	You should do as he says They should be home by now
(2) 'Putative' use after certain expressions, *eg: it is a pity that, I am surprised that* (see 11.72, 12.35 ff)	It is odd that you should say this to me I am sorry that this should have happened
(3) Hypothetical use (1st person only and especially BrE) in the main clause with a conditional subclause (= *would*)	We $\begin{Bmatrix} \text{should} \\ \text{would} \end{Bmatrix}$ love to go abroad if we had the chance
(4) Tentative condition in conditional clauses	If you should change your mind, please let us know

3.47
Will/would
WILL (*cf* 3.27 ff)

(1) Willingness ('weak volition') unstressed, especially 2nd person. 'Downtoners' like *please* may be used to soften the tone in requests	He'll help you if you ask him Will you have another cup of coffee? Will you (please, kindly, etc) open the window?
(2) Intention ('intermediate volition'). Usually contracted '*ll*; mainly 1st person	I'll write as soon as I can We won't stay longer than two hours
(3) Insistence ('strong volition' = *insist on*). Stressed, hence no '*ll* contraction. An uncommon meaning	He ˈwill do it, whatever you say ('He insists on doing it . . .') (*Cf* He ˈshall do it, whatever you say = 'I insist on his doing it')

(4) Prediction
Cf the similar meanings of other expressions for logical necessity and habitual present. The contracted form 'll is common

(a) Specific prediction:

The game $\begin{Bmatrix} \text{will} \\ \text{must} \\ \text{should} \end{Bmatrix}$ be finished by now

(b) Timeless prediction:

Oil $\begin{Bmatrix} \text{will float} \\ \text{floats} \end{Bmatrix}$ on water

(c) Habitual prediction:
He'll (always) talk for hours if you give him the chance

WOULD

(1) Willingness ('weak volition')	Would you excuse me?
(2) Insistence ('strong volition')	It's your own fault; you ˈwould take the baby with you
(3) Characteristic activity	Every morning he would go for a long walk (*ie* it was customary) John ˈwould make a mess of it (informal = it was typical)
(4) Hypothetical meaning in main clauses	He would smoke too much if I didn't stop him
(5) Probability	That would be his mother

3.48
Must

(1) Obligation or compulsion in the present tense (= BE OBLIGED TO, HAVE TO); except in reported speech, only *had to* (not *must*) is used in the past. In negative sentences *needn't*, *don't have to*, *not be obliged to* are used (but not *must not*, *mustn't* which = *not be allowed to*). See 3.21, 3.45, 7.52

You must be back by 10 o'clock
Yesterday you had to be back by 10 o'clock
Yesterday you said you $\begin{Bmatrix} \text{had to} \\ \text{must} \end{Bmatrix}$ be back by 10 o'clock
You $\begin{Bmatrix} \text{needn't} \\ \text{don't have to} \\ \text{are not obliged to} \end{Bmatrix}$ be back by 10 o'clock

(2) (Logical) necessity
Must is not used in sentences with negative or interrogative meanings, *can* being used instead

There$\left\{\begin{array}{l}\text{must} \\ \text{has to}\end{array}\right\}$be a mistake

but: There cannot be a mistake

Must can occur in superficially interrogative but answer-assuming sentences

Mustn't there be another reason for his behaviour?

3.49
Ought to
Obligation and logical necessity

You ought to start at once
They ought to be here by now

Note
Ought to and *should* both denote obligation and logical necessity, but are less categorical than *must* and HAVE TO. *Ought to* is often felt to be awkward in questions involving inversion, and *should* is preferred.

3.50
Used to /juːstə/
A state or habit that existed in the past but has ceased (*cf: would*, and *formerly* or *once* + past)

He used to fish for hours
He used to be
He was formerly $\left.\right\}$an excellent golfer
He was once

The modal auxiliaries in relation to tense and aspect
3.51
Future time
Since modal auxiliaries cannot combine with other modal auxiliaries, they cannot be used with *will/shall* to denote future (see 3.28):

*He will may leave tomorrow

In many contexts, the modal auxiliaries have inherent future reference, both in their present and past forms:

He$\left\{\begin{array}{l}\text{may} \\ \text{might}\end{array}\right\}$leave tomorrow

Compare this with the use of the present (but not the past) form of lexical verbs to denote future time:

He$\left\{\begin{array}{l}\text{leaves} \\ \text{*left}\end{array}\right\}$tomorrow

3.52
Present and past tenses
Only some of the modals have parallel uses in the present and past tenses:

PRESENT	PAST
can	*could*
may	*could* (*might*)
shall	*should*
will/*'ll*	*would*/*'d*
must	(*had to*)
–	*used to*
ought to	–
need	–
dare	*dared*

He can speak English now	He couldn't come yesterday
He'll do anything for money	He wouldn't come when I asked him yesterday

The usual past tense of *may* denoting permission is *could*:

Today, we $\begin{Bmatrix} can \\ may \end{Bmatrix}$ stay the whole afternoon

Yesterday, we $\begin{Bmatrix} could \\ ?might \end{Bmatrix}$ only stay for a few minutes

The following modals are not used in the past tense except in reported speech: *must, ought to,* and *need* (but *cf* 3.21). *Had to* serves as the past of both *must* and *have to*:

He $\begin{Bmatrix} must \\ has\ to \end{Bmatrix}$ leave now

He $\begin{Bmatrix} *must \\ had\ to \end{Bmatrix}$ leave in a hurry yesterday

Yesterday the children $\begin{Bmatrix} *must \\ *ought\ to \\ *needn't \\ ?daren't \\ dared\ not \\ did\ not\ dare \end{Bmatrix}$ go out and play

He said the children $\begin{Bmatrix} must \\ ought\ to \\ needn't \\ daren't \\ dared\ not \\ didn't\ dare \end{Bmatrix}$ go out and play

In fact, all the past tense forms are used with verbs of reporting in the past tense (11.77):

He said
$\begin{cases} \text{the guests would be late} \\ \text{the road might be blocked} \\ \text{the children could go out and play} \end{cases}$

In addition to their regular past tense function, the past forms of the modal auxiliaries occur in present tense environments with meanings that differ somewhat from those of the present forms. There is a difference between the first and second member of the following pairs:

'ability' $\begin{cases} Can \\ Could \end{cases}$ you recommend a good book?

'permission' $\begin{cases} May \\ Might \end{cases}$ I ask you to speak up?

'volition' $\begin{cases} Will \\ Would \end{cases}$ you be good enough to come and see me as soon as you can?

'possibility'   It $\begin{cases} may \\ might \end{cases}$ start raining tomorrow

In these cases the past forms do not express past time but greater consideration, politeness, or tentativeness than the corresponding present forms. This is an example of the HYPOTHETICAL use of the auxiliaries (cf the hypothetical past in 3.26).

3.53
Perfective and progressive aspects
The perfective and progressive aspects are normally excluded when the modals express 'ability' or 'permission' and also when *shall* or *will* express volition. These aspects are freely used, however, with other modal meanings; eg

'possibility'   He may have missed the train
                 He can't be swimming all day
'necessity'   He must have left his umbrella on the bus
                 You must be dreaming
'prediction'   The guests will have arrived by now
                 John will still be reading his paper

The morphology of lexical verbs
3.54
We will consider lexical verbs under two heads: regular (such as CALL) and irregular (such as DRINK). What they have in common is the five forms BASE, -S FORM, -ING PARTICIPLE, PAST, and -ED PARTICIPLE

(see *Table* 3:1 in 3.9). The distinction between regular and irregular verbs is based on the extent to which the last two forms are predictable from the base.

3.55
-s and -ing forms of all lexical verbs

Two of the forms, the *-s* form and the *-ing* form, are predictable from the base (V) of both regular and irregular lexical verbs except modal auxiliaries (which are not inflected in the 3rd person singular present and lack both participles; see 3.22). The *-ing* form of both regular and irregular verbs is formed by adding *-ing* /ɪŋ/ to the base.

BASE	-ING FORM
agree	*agreeing*
pass	*passing*
push	*pushing*
weep	*weeping*

The *-s* form of both regular and irregular verbs (sometimes spelled *-es*, *cf* 3.62) is also predictable from the base. It has three spoken realizations: /ɪz/, /z/, and /s/; so also, the contracted forms of *has* and *is* (3.18 *f*).

/ɪz/ after bases ending in voiced or voiceless sibilants, *eg*

	BASE	-S FORM
-/s/	*pass*	*passes*
-/z/	*buzz*	*buzzes*
-/tʃ/	*catch*	*catches*
-/dʒ/	*budge*	*budges*
-/ʃ/	*push*	*pushes*
-/ʒ/	*camouflage*	*camouflages*

/z/ after bases ending in other voiced sounds, *eg*

-/l/	*call*	*calls*
-/b/	*rob*	*robs*
-/aɪ/	*try*	*tries*

Exceptional forms are:

do	/du/	*does*	/dʌz/
have		*has*	
say	/seɪ/	*says*	/sez/

/s/ after bases ending in other voiceless sounds, *eg*

-/t/	*cut*	*cuts*
-/k/	*lock*	*locks*
-/p/	*sap*	*saps*

Regular lexical verbs
3.56
Regular lexical verbs have only four different forms:

(V)	BASE	*call*	*like*	*try*
(V-*ing*)	-*ING* PARTICIPLE	*calling*	*liking*	*trying*
(V-*s*)	-*S* FORM	*calls*	*likes*	*tries*
(V-*ed*)	PAST/-*ED* PARTICIPLE	*called*	*liked*	*tried*

The reason why they are called regular is that we can predict what all the other three forms are if we know the base of such a verb. This is a very powerful rule, since the base is the form listed in dictionaries and the vast majority of English verbs belong to this regular class. Furthermore, all new verbs that are coined or borrowed from other languages adopt the regular pattern, *eg*

xerox ~ xeroxing ~ xeroxes ~ xeroxed

Note

[a] The assimilation process is less marked in the case of nouns, where foreign plurals are often kept, sometimes with an alternative native ending (see 4.74):

> *antenna ~ antennae/antennas*
> *cherub ~ cherubim/cherubs*

[b] Both regular and irregular verbs have, as we have seen, predictable -*ing* participles and -*s* forms. The difference between regular and irregular verbs is therefore restricted to V-*ed*. As the past (V-*ed*$_1$) and the -*ed* participle (V-*ed*$_2$) are identical in all regular verbs, it will be convenient to refer to them as the -*ed* form (V-*ed*) without subscripts.

3.57
The past and the -*ed* participle
The past and the -*ed* participle (V-*ed*) of regular verbs have three realizations:

/ɪd/ after bases ending in the alveolar stops /d/ and /t/, *eg*

	BASE	V-*ed*
-/d/	*pad*	*padded*
-/t/	*pat*	*patted*

/d/ after bases in voiced sounds other than /d/, *eg*

	BASE	V-*ed*
-/oʊ/	*mow*	*mowed*
-/z/	*buzz*	*buzzed*
-/dʒ/	*budge*	*budged*

/t/ after bases ending in voiceless sounds other than /t/, *eg*

	BASE	V-*ed*
-/s/	*pass*	*passed*
-/k/	*pack*	*packed*

The spelling of regular verb inflections
3.58

The regularity accounted for so far applies only to the pronunciation of lexical verbs. The following rules apply to the spelling of the inflections:

GENERAL RULE:
> The -*s* form is written *s:*   *look ~ looks*
> The -*ing* form is written *ing: look ~ looking*
> The -*ed* form is written *ed: look ~ looked*

EXCEPTIONS: There are four types of exception to these rules, result-ing in doubling of consonant, treatment of -*y*, deletion of an *e*, and addition of an *e*.

3.59
Doubling of consonant

(a) Final base consonants are doubled before -*ing* and -*ed* when the preceding vowel is stressed and spelled with a single letter.

bar	*barring*	*barred*
beg	*begging*	*begged*
permit	*permitting*	*permitted*
prefer	*preferring*	*preferred*
occur	*occurring*	*occurred*

There is no doubling when the vowel is unstressed or written with two letters (as a digraph):

enter	*entering*	*entered*
visit	*visiting*	*visited*
dread	*dreading*	*dreaded*

(b) Bases ending in certain consonants are doubled also after single unstressed vowels:

humbug	*humbugging*	*humbugged*	-*g* → -*gg*-
traffic	*trafficking*	*trafficked*	-*c* → -*ck*-

BrE, as distinct from AmE, breaks the main rule also with respect to certain other consonants:

signal	*signalling*	*signalled*	(BrE)
signal	*signaling*	*signaled*	(AmE)
travel	*travelling*	*travelled*	(BrE)
travel	*traveling*	*traveled*	(AmE)

$-l \rightarrow -ll-$

program(me)	*programming*	*programmed*	(BrE)
program	*programing*	*programed*	(AmE)

$-m \rightarrow -mm-$

worship	*worshipping*	*worshipped*	(BrE)
worship	*worshiping*	*worshiped*	(AmE)

$-p \rightarrow -pp-$

Most verbs ending in -*p*, however, have the regular spellings in both BrE and AmE, *eg:*

develop	*developing*	*developed*
envelop	*enveloping*	*enveloped*
gallop	*galloping*	*galloped*
gossip	*gossiping*	*gossiped*

Note
In computer technology AmE usually has *programmed.*

3.60
Treatment of -*y*

(a) In bases ending in a consonant + *y*, the following changes occur before the -*s* and -*ed* inflections:

$$(\text{consonant} +) \text{-}y \rightarrow \begin{cases} \text{-}ie \text{ before -}s\text{:} & carry \sim carries \\ \text{-}i \text{ before -}ed\text{:} & carry \sim carried \end{cases}$$

The past of the following two verbs has a change -*y* → -*i* also after a vowel:

lay ~ *laid*
pay ~ *paid*

Contrast:

play ~ *played*
stay ~ *stayed*, etc

Say ~ *said* has the same change of spelling but, in addition, a change of vowel /eɪ/ → /e/, which makes it an irregular verb (see 3.66).

(b) In bases ending in -*ie*, the following change occurs before the -*ing* inflection:

$$\text{-}ie \rightarrow \text{-}y \text{ before -}ing\text{:} \begin{cases} die \sim dying \\ lie \sim lying \end{cases}$$

3.61

Deletion of -e

If the base ends in a mute -e, it is regularly dropped before the -ing and -ed inflections:

> abate   abating   abated
> create   creating   created
> shave   shaving   shaved

Verbs with bases in -ee, -ye, and -oe are exceptions to this rule in that they do not drop the -e before -ing; but they do drop it before -ed, as do also forms in -ie (tie ~ tied):

> -ee: agree   agreeing   agreed
> -ye: dye   dyeing   dyed
> -oe: hoe   hoeing   hoed
> Also: singe   singeing   singed

Note

Compare dye ~ dyeing with die ~ dying and singe ~ singeing /sɪndʒɪŋ/ with sing ~ singing /sɪŋɪŋ/.

3.62

Addition of -e

The addition of -e occurs in bases ending in sibilants in the following cases:

(a) Unless the base is already spelled with a final mute -e, the -s suffix is spelled -es

> refuse   ~ refuses
> fish   ~ fishes

(b) An -e is added in two irregular verbs ending in -o, DO and GO, before the -s suffix (note also the change in the pronunciation of the vowel in does)

> do /du/ ~ does /dʌz/
> go   ~ goes

Irregular lexical verbs
3.63

Irregular lexical verbs are like regular verbs in having -s forms and -ing forms predictable from the base (see 3.10 ff). But they differ from regular verbs in the following ways:

(a) Irregular verbs either do not have the predictable -ed inflection (find ~ found ~ found) or, if there is an alveolar suffix, break the rule in 3.57 for a voiced suffix (eg: mean ~ meant /t/, in contrast to *clean ~ cleaned* /d/; *burn ~ burnt* /t/, which is in variation with the regular *burned* /d/).

(b) Irregular verbs typically, but not necessarily, have variation in their base vowel. The reason for this phenomenon, called 'gradation' or 'ablaut', is historical, and it is a characteristic of Indo-European languages in general:

find   found   found
choose   chose   chosen
write   wrote   written

(c) Irregular verbs have a varying number of distinct forms. Since the *-s* form and the *-ing* form are predictable for regular and irregular verbs alike, the only forms that need be listed for irregular verbs are the base (V), the past ($V\text{-}ed_1$), and the past participle ($V\text{-}ed_2$). These are traditionally called 'the principal parts' of a verb. Most irregular verbs have, like regular verbs, only one common form for the past and the *-ed* participle, but there is considerable variation in this respect, as the table shows:

	BASE	$V\text{-}ed_1$	$V\text{-}ed_2$
all alike	*cut*	*cut*	*cut*
$V\text{-}ed_1 = V\text{-}ed_2$	*meet*	*met*	*met*
$V = V\text{-}ed_2$	*come*	*came*	*come*
all different	*speak*	*spoke*	*spoken*

Irregular verb classes
3.64

The 200-odd irregular English verbs can be classified on the basis of criteria derived from these characteristics. Since it is impractical to account for both pronunciation and spelling together, only pronunciation will be considered in setting up the classes of irregular verbs. The criteria to be used are the following:

(a) V-*ed* identity: $V\text{-}ed_1 = V\text{-}ed_2$, *eg: met*
(b) suffixation in $V\text{-}ed_1$ and/or $V\text{-}ed_2$, including not only alveolar suffixes (*dreamt*) but also nasal suffixes (*shaken*)
(c) vowel identity: the base vowel is kept unchanged in the other principal parts, *eg: put*

Table 3:3 shows that these three criteria divide irregular verbs into seven classes:

Class 1 has three pluses, which indicates that a verb like BURN is very close to a regular verb. The only difference is that *burned* has an irregular variant *burnt* with a voiceless suffix after a voiced sound.

Table 3:3

IRREGULAR VERB CLASSES

CLASS	EXAMPLE	V-*ed* IDENTITY	SUFFIXATION	VOWEL IDENTITY
Class 1 (3.65)	BURN	+	+	+
Class 2 (3.66)	BRING	+	+	−
Class 3 (3.67)	CUT	+	−	+
Class 4 (3.68)	MEET	+	−	−
Class 5 (3.69)	MOW	±	+	±
Class 6 (3.70)	KNOW	−	+	±
Class 7 (3.71)	SWIM	−	−	−

Class 2 has no vowel identity, *eg: teach ~ taught*. Many of the verbs in these two classes manifest some differences between BrE and AmE. For example, in Class 1a (3.65), AmE prefers the regular /d/ variants and BrE the /t/ variants of *burned/burnt, learned/learnt*, etc. Similarly, in Class 2, AmE favours the regular *dreamed* and BrE the irregular *dreamt* with vowel change and voiceless suffix.

Class 3 has all principal parts identical (as in *hit*).

Class 4 has V-*ed* identical with change of base vowel without suffixation (*strike ~ struck*).

Class 5 has a past suffix in *-ed* and two past participle suffixes, one alveolar and the other nasal (*sawed* and *sawn*). Most verbs have vowel identity.

Class 6 has three different principal parts, usually with a nasal V-*ed*$_2$ suffix (*break ~ broke ~ broken*).

Class 7 is the class of irregular verbs that is the most irregular: V-*ed*$_1$ and V-*ed*$_2$ are different; there is no suffixation but change of the base vowel (*come ~ came ~ come*). Most remote of all is *go ~ went ~ gone* which has an altogether different V-*ed*$_1$ root.

Although we will not further define the differences among the verbs of each class, the verbs will be grouped together as (a), (b), (c), etc for mnemonic reasons. Parentheses, for example (*dwelled*), are used around less common forms. 'R' denotes the existence also of regular variants.

Note

[a] The variation between /d/ and /t/ in Classes 1 and 2 applies to verbal uses; AmE has, for example, *burnt toast, burnt umber. All the burnt wood* would mean 'wood with a burnt appearance'; *all the burned wood* would mean 'wood that has been consumed'.

[b] The following list contains most of the irregular verbs in present-day English, but is not meant to be exhaustive. For example, it does not include very unusual or archaic verbs like *gird*, or verbs with irregular forms that have very restricted use and hence are better dealt with in the dictionary, for example *proven* for *proved*, as in *a proven record* and *not proven* (used as a legal term); *shaven* in adjectival uses (*a shaven chin*) but otherwise regularly *shaved* (*He has shaved*).

3.65

Class 1 (*burn*, etc)
Characteristics:
   V-*ed*$_1$ is identical with V-*ed*$_2$
   Suffixation is used but voicing is variable
   Vowel identity in all the parts

	V	V-*ed*		COMMENTS
1a	*burn*	*burnt*		For Class 1a verbs, the regular
		burned	(R)	/d/-form is especially AmE
	dwell	*dwelt*		and the /t/-form especially
		(dwelled)	(R)	BrE
	learn	*learnt*		
		learned	(R)	*a learned* /ɪd/ *man* (adj)
	smell	*smelt*		
		smelled	(R)	
	spell	*spelt*		
		spelled	(R)	
	spill	*spilt*		
		spilled	(R)	
	spoil	*spoilt*		
		spoiled	(R)	
1b	*bend*	*bent*		Also *unbend*
	build	*built*		
	lend	*lent*		
	rend	*rent*		restricted use
	send	*sent*		
	spend	*spent*		
1c	*have*	*had*		-*s* form: *has*
	make	*made*		

Note
There is a tendency to associate -*t* forms in Class 1a more with V-*ed*$_2$ than with V-*ed*$_1$, and with V-*ed*$_1$ when there is least implication of duration:

   He *spelt* it/has *spelt* it like this on only one occasion.

3.66

Class 2 (*bring*, etc)
Characteristics:
   V-*ed*$_1$ is identical with V-*ed*$_2$
   Suffixation is used but voicing is variable
   Change of base vowel

V	V-*ed*	COMMENTS
2a *bereave*	$\begin{cases}\textit{bereft} \\ \textit{(bereaved)} \quad \text{(R)}\end{cases}$	V-*ed*$_2$ *bereaved* usually = 'left desolate'
cleave	*cleft*	Also V-*ed*$_1$ = *clove* and V-*ed*$_2$ = *cloven*
creep	*crept*	
deal	*dealt* /e/	
dream	$\begin{cases}\textit{dreamt} \text{ /e/} \\ \textit{dreamed} \text{ /i/ (R)}\end{cases}$	especially BrE especially AmE
feel	*felt*	
flee	*fled*	
keep	*kept*	
kneel	$\begin{cases}\textit{knelt} \\ \textit{(kneeled)} \quad \text{(R)}\end{cases}$	R especially AmE
lean	$\begin{cases}\textit{leant} \text{ /e/} \\ \textit{leaned} \text{ /i/} \quad \text{(R)}\end{cases}$	especially BrE especially AmE
leap	$\begin{cases}\textit{leapt} \text{ /e/} \\ \textit{leaped} \text{ /i/} \quad \text{(R)}\end{cases}$	especially AmE
leave	*left*	
mean	*meant* /e/	
sleep	*slept*	
sweep	*swept*	
weep	*wept*	
2b *beseech*	*besought*	restricted use
bring	*brought*	
buy	*bought*	
catch	*caught*	
seek	*sought*	
teach	*taught*	
think	*thought*	
2c *lose* /u/	*lost*	
2d *sell*	*sold* /oʊ/	
tell	*told* /oʊ/	
2e *hear*	*heard* /ɜ(r)/	
2f *say* /eɪ/	*said* /e/	-*s* form: *says* /e/

3.67

Class 3 (*cut*, etc)

Characteristics:

    All three parts V, V-*ed*₁, and V-*ed*₂ are identical

    No suffix or change of the base vowel

V and V-*ed*	COMMENTS
bet	Also in BrE: *betted* (R)
bid (Also V-*ed*₁ = *bade*, V-*ed*₂ = *bidden*)	Also *overbid*, *underbid*, etc
burst	
cast	Also *broadcast*, *forecast* (both sometimes also R)
cost	*cost* (trans) is R = 'estimate the cost of'
cut	
hit	
hurt	
knit	Usually R: *knitted*
let	
put	
quit	Also R: *quitted*
rid	Also R: *ridded*
set	Also *upset*
shed	R = 'put in a shed'
shit	Not in polite use
shut	
slit	
split	
spread /e/	
sweat /e/	Also R: *sweated*
thrust	
wed	Also R: *wedded*
wet	Also R: *wetted*

3.68

Class 4 (*meet*, etc)

Characteristics:

    V-*ed*₁ is identical with V-*ed*₂

    No suffixation

    Change of base vowel

	V	V-*ed*	COMMENTS
4a	*bleed*	*bled*	
	breed	*bred*	
	feed	*fed*	Also *overfeed*, etc
	hold	*held*	Also *behold, uphold, withhold,* etc
	lead	*led*	Also *mislead*
	meet	*met*	
	read /i/	*read* /e/	
	speed	*sped*	Also R: *speeded*
4b	*cling*	*clung*	
	dig	*dug*	
	fling	*flung*	
	hang	*hung*	Also *overhang.* Also R (*hanged*) when = 'put to death'
	sling	*slung*	
	slink	*slunk*	
	spin	*spun*	Archaic *span* as V-*ed*$_1$
	stick	*stuck*	
	sting	*stung*	
	strike	*struck*	Literal = 'hit'; for metaphorical *strike* see Class 6 Ca
	string	*strung*	
	swing	*swung*	
	win	*won*	
	wring	*wrung*	
4c	*bind*	*bound*	Also *unbind*
	find	*found*	
	grind	*ground*	
	wind	*wound*	Also *rewind, unwind*
4d	*light*	*lit* / *lighted* (R)	
	slide	*slid*	
4e	*sit*	*sat*	
	spit	*spat*	AmE also V-*ed* = *spit*
4f	*get*	*got*	AmE also *gotten* for V-*ed*$_2$ in certain senses of the word, *eg* 'acquire', 'cause', 'come'
	shine	*shone*	Also R when = 'polish' (especially AmE)
	shoot	*shot*	Also *overshoot*

	V	V-*ed*	COMMENTS
4g	*fight*	*fought*	
4h	*stand*	*stood*	Also *misunderstand, understand, withstand*, etc
4i	*stride*	*strode*	V-*ed*$_2$ *strid(den)* rare; also *bestride*

3.69

Class 5 (*mow*, etc)

Characteristics:

V-*ed*$_2$ has two suffixes, one alveolar which is identical with V-*ed*$_1$, the other nasal

No change of the base vowel for V-*ed*$_1$

V	V-*ed*$_1$	V-*ed*$_2$		COMMENTS
hew	*hewed*	*hewn* / *hewed*	(R)	
mow	*mowed*	*mown* / *mowed*	(R)	
saw	*sawed*	*sawn* / *sawed*	(R)	
sew /oʊ/	*sewed*	*sewn* / *sewed*	(R)	
shear	*sheared*	*shorn* / *sheared*	(R)	
show	*showed*	*shown* / *(showed)*	(R)	Sometimes spelled *shew, shewed, shewn*
sow /oʊ/	*sowed*	*sown* / *sowed*	(R)	
strew /u/	*strewed*	*strewn* / *strewed*	(R)	
swell	*swelled*	*swollen* / *swelled*	(R)	a swollen head (person is ill) a swelled head (person is conceited)

3.70

Class 6 (*know*, etc)

Characteristics:

V-*ed*$_1$ and V-*ed*$_2$ are different. In all but two verbs, the latter has a nasal suffix

There is a range of base vowel changes and the verbs have been ordered according to vowel patterning:

in A, V-ed_1 and V-ed_2 have the same vowel
in B, V and V-ed_2 have the same vowel
in C, all three parts have different vowels
in D, all three parts have the same vowel
in E, V-ed_1 and V-ed_2 have different vowels

	V	V-ed_1	V-ed_2	COMMENTS
6Aa	break	broke	broken	
	choose	chose	chosen	
	freeze	froze	frozen	
	speak	spoke	spoken	
	steal	stole	stolen	
	(a)wake(n)	{ (a)woke / (a)wak(en)ed (R)	{ (a)woken / (a)wak(en)ed (R)	wake usually Class 6: woke ~ woken; awaken usually R
	weave	wove	woven	
6Ab	bear	bore	borne	She has borne six children (But: He was born in 1955) Also forbear
	swear	swore	sworn	Also forswear
	tear	tore	torn	
	wear	wore	worn	
6Ac	bite	bit	bitten	V-ed_2 sometimes = bit
	chide	chid	{ chidden / chid	Also R = chided
	hide	hid	{ hidden / (hid)	
6Ad	forget	forgot	forgotten	Also beget
	tread	trod	trodden	
6Ae	lie	lay	lain	= 'be horizontal'
6Ba	blow	blew	blown	
	grow	grew	grown	Also outgrow
	know	knew	known	
	throw	threw	thrown	Also overthrow
6Bb	forsake	forsook	forsaken	
	shake	shook	shaken	
	take	took	taken	Also mistake, overtake, undertake
6Bc	forbid	{ forbade / forbad	forbidden	
	give	gave	given	Also forgive
6Bd	draw	drew	drawn	Also withdraw

	V	V-*ed*$_1$	V-*ed*$_2$	COMMENTS
6Be	*fall*	*fell*	*fallen*	Also *befall*
6Bf	*eat*	*ate* $\begin{cases} \text{BrE } /e/ \\ \text{AmE } /eɪ/ \end{cases}$	*eaten*	
6Bg	*see*	*saw*	*seen*	
6Bh	*slay*	*slew*	*slain*	
6Ca	*drive*	*drove*	*driven*	
	ride	*rode*	*ridden*	Also *override*
	rise	*rose*	*risen*	Also *arise*, which is rare except when metaphorical: *The question arose . . .*
	smite	*smote*	*smitten*	Archaic except metaphorical in V-*ed*$_2$, *eg: smitten with her charms*
	strike	*struck*	*stricken*	*Stricken* virtually only in passive and as metaphorical adj (*stricken by arthritis*); see Class 4b
	strive	*strove*	*striven*	Also R = *strived*
	write	*wrote*	*written*	Also *underwrite*
6Cb	*fly*	*flew*	*flown*	
6Cc	*do*	*did*	*done*	Also *outdo, overdo, undo*, etc
6D	*beat*	*beat*	*beaten*	
6E	*dive*	$\begin{cases} \textit{dived (R)} \\ \textit{dove} \end{cases}$	*dived*	V-*ed*$_1$ *dove* is AmE only; the verb is R in BrE and often in AmE
	thrive	*throve*	*thrived*	Normal forms in both AmE and BrE; also R, especially in AmE

3.71
Class 7 (*swim*, etc)
Characteristics:
V-*ed*$_1$ and V-*ed*$_2$ are different
No suffixation
Change of base vowel

	V	V-ed_1	V-ed_2	COMMENTS
7a	*begin*	*began*	*begun*	
	drink	*drank*	*drunk*	*drunken*, adj
	ring	*rang*	*rung*	
	shrink	$\begin{cases} shrank \\ shrunk \end{cases}$	*shrunk*	*shrunken*, adj
	sing	*sang*	*sung*	
	sink	*sank*	*sunk*	*sunken*, adj
	spring	*sprang*	*sprung*	V-ed_1 also *sprung* in AmE
	stink	*stank*	*stunk*	Occasionally V-ed_1 = *stunk*
	swim	*swam*	*swum*	
7b	*come*	*came*	*come*	Also *become, overcome*
	run	*ran*	*run*	Also *overrun*
7c	*go*	*went*	*gone*	Also *undergo*

3.72
Irregular verbs: alphabetical order

verb	class	page	verb	class	page
DREAM	2a	113	LEAVE	2a	113
DRINK	7a	119	LEND	1b	112
DRIVE	6Ca	118	LET	3	114
DWELL	1a	112	LIE	6Ae	117
EAT	6Bf	118	LIGHT	4d	115
FALL	6Be	118	LOSE	2c	113
FEED	4a	115	MAKE	1c	112
FEEL	2a	113	MAY	aux	98
FIGHT	4g	116	MEAN	2a	113
FIND	4c	115	MEET	4a	115
FLEE	2a	113	MISLEAD	4a	115
FLING	4b	115	MISTAKE	6Bb	117
FLY	6Cb	118	MISUNDERSTAND	4h	116
FORBEAR	6Ab	117	MOW	5	116
FORBID	6Bc	117	OUTDO	6Cc	118
FORECAST	3	114	OUTGROW	6Ba	117
FORGET	6Ad	117	OVERBID	3	114
FORGIVE	6Bc	117	OVERCOME	7b	119
FORSAKE	6Bb	117	OVERDO	6Cc	118
FREEZE	6Aa	117	OVERFEED	4a	115
GET	4f	115	OVERRIDE	6Ca	118
GIVE	6Bc	117	OVERRUN	7b	119
GO	7c	119	OVERTAKE	6Bb	117
GRIND	4c	115	PUT	3	114
GROW	6Ba	117	QUIT	3	114
HANG	4b	115	READ	4a	115
HAVE	1c	112	REND	1b	112
HEAR	2e	113	REWIND	4c	115
HEW	5	116	RID	3	114
HIDE	6Ac	117	RIDE	6Ca	118
HIT	3	114	RING	7a	119
HOLD	4a	115	RISE	6Ca	118
HURT	3	114	RUN	7b	119
KEEP	2a	113	SAW	5	116
KNEEL	2a	113	SAY	2f	113
KNIT	3	114	SEE	6Bg	118
KNOW	6Ba	117	SEEK	2b	113
LEAD	4a	115	SELL	2d	113
LEAN	2a	113	SEND	1b	112
LEAP	2a	113	SET	3	114
LEARN	1a	112	SEW	5	116

verb	class	page	verb	class	page
SHAKE	6Bb	117	STRING	4b	115
SHALL	aux	99	STRIVE	6Ca	118
SHEAR	5	116	SWEAR	6Ab	117
SHED	3	114	SWEAT	3	114
SHINE	4f	115	SWEEP	2a	113
SHIT	3	114	SWELL	5	116
SHOOT	4f	115	SWIM	7a	119
SHOW	5	116	SWING	4b	115
SHRINK	7a	119	TAKE	6Bb	117
SHUT	3	114	TEACH	2b	113
SING	7a	119	TEAR	6Ab	117
SINK	7a	119	TELL	2d	113
SIT	4e	115	THINK	2b	113
SLAY	6Bh	118	THRIVE	6E	118
SLEEP	2a	113	THROW	6Ba	117
SLIDE	4d	115	THRUST	3	114
SLING	4b	115	TREAD	6Ad	117
SLINK	4b	115	UNBEND	1b	112
SLIT	3	114	UNBIND	4c	115
SMELL	1a	112	UNDERBID	3	114
SMITE	6Ca	118	UNDERGO	7c	119
SOW	5	116	UNDERSTAND	4h	116
SPEAK	6Aa	117	UNDERTAKE	6Bb	117
SPEED	4a	115	UNDO	6Cc	118
SPELL	1a	112	UNWIND	4c	115
SPEND	1b	112	UPHOLD	4a	115
SPILL	1a	112	UPSET	3	114
SPIN	4b	115	WAKE	6Aa	117
SPIT	4e	115	WEAR	6Ab	117
SPLIT	3	114	WEAVE	6Aa	117
SPOIL	1a	112	WED	3	114
SPREAD	3	114	WEEP	2a	113
SPRING	7a	119	WET	3	114
STAND	4h	116	WILL	aux	100
STEAL	6Aa	117	WIN	4b	115
STICK	4b	115	WIND	4c	115
STING	4b	115	WITHDRAW	6Bd	117
STINK	7a	119	WITHHOLD	4a	115
STREW	5	116	WITHSTAND	4h	116
STRIDE	4i	116	WRING	4b	115
STRIKE	4b/	115	WRITE	6Ca	118
	6Ca	118			

Bibliographical note

See Jespersen (1909–49), especially Parts IV, and VI, Chapters 2–5; Palmer (1965); Poutsma (1926–29), especially Part II.2.

On verb classes and forms and combinations of verbs, see Kajita (1968); Khlebnikova (1965); Strang (1968), especially Chapter 9; Svartvik (1966), especially Chapter 2; Twaddell (1960).

On tense and aspect, see Allen (1966); Close (1970); Closs and Waterhouse (1969); Crystal (1966); Diver (1963); G. Lakoff (1966); McCawley (1970); McIntosh (1966); Ota (1963); Quirk (1970).

On the meanings of the modal auxiliaries, see Boyd and Thorne (1969); Ehrman (1966); Leech (1969a, 1972); and Huddleston (1971), Chapter 7.

On the morphology of lexical verbs, see Kingdon (1957).

FOUR
NOUNS, PRONOUNS, AND THE BASIC
NOUN PHRASE

4.1
'Basic noun phrase' defined

The noun phrase is that element in the sentence which typically functions as subject, object, and complement (7.8 *ff*). Consider the subject in the following sentences:

(a) The girl
(b) The pretty girl
(c) The pretty girl in the corner $\Big\rangle$ is my sister
(d) The pretty girl who is standing in the corner
(e) She

Sentences (a–d) are alike in having the same noun (*girl*) as noun-phrase head. In (a) it has the simplest structure, consisting of only the definite article and the head; in (b) it has a premodifying adjective (*pretty*); in (c) it has, in addition, a postmodifying prepositional phrase (*in the corner*); in (d) it consists of a premodifying adjective, a head and a postmodifying relative clause (*who is standing in the corner*); in (e) it consists of only one word (*she*), which is one of a closed set of grammatical words called personal pronouns. Such pronouns can 'replace' nouns, or rather noun phrases, since they cannot occur with determiners such as the definite article, premodification, or (normally, *cf* 13.5 Note *a*) postmodification:

*The pretty she
?She in the corner

Since noun phrases of the types illustrated in (b–d) include elements that will be dealt with later in this book (adjectives, prepositional phrases, clauses, etc), it will be convenient to reserve until Chapter 13 the treatment of the noun phrase incorporating such items. The present chapter will be restricted to 'basic noun phrases' consisting of pronouns and numerals (4.106–129) and of nouns with articles or other closed-system items that can occur before the noun head including predeterminers like *all*, determiners like *these*, 'ordinals' like *last*, and quantifiers like *few* (4.13–27):

All these last few days

Nouns
Noun classes
4.2
Proper/common, count/mass nouns
Nouns have certain characteristics that set them apart from other word-

classes. For example, they can form plurals (*book ~ books*) and take articles (*the book ~ a book*). However, this is not true of all nouns: there are no forms **educations* or **homeworks*, or **a harm* or **a chess*. It is important, both for semantic and grammatical reasons, to distinguish between different subclasses of nouns. Consider the possibilities of the nouns *cake, bottle, bread,* and *John* in a sentence such as *I like ...* occurring with the following determiners and the plural:

zero (or no) article:	*cake*	**bottle*	*bread*	*John*
definite article:	*the cake*	*the bottle*	*the bread*	**the John*
indefinite article:	*a cake*	*a bottle*	**a bread*	**a John*
indefinite quantitative:	*some cake*	**some bottle*	*some bread*	**some John*
plural:	*cakes*	*bottles*	**breads*	**Johns*

Nouns like *John, Paris, Mississippi* are PROPER NOUNS. They do not have the full range of determiners and lack article contrast (*Paris ~ *The Paris, The Hague ~ *Hague, The Andes ~ *An Ande*). Proper nouns will be further discussed in 4.40 *ff*. The remaining words in the table are all COMMON NOUNS. *Bottle*, which takes definite and indefinite articles and admits a plural form, is an example of a COUNT NOUN. *Bread*, which takes zero article as well as definite article and indefinite quantifier, but does not have a plural form, is a MASS NOUN. *Cake* combines the properties of *bottle* and *bread*, and is consequently both a count and a mass noun.

Note

[a] A mass noun like *bread* can be 'reclassified' as a count noun involving a semantic shift so as to denote quality: 'kind of', 'type of', as in *What breads have you got today?* (see 4.5, App I.40).

[b] Although in sentences such as *I like cake, I like John*, the two nouns look superficially alike in terms of article usage, we will say that *cake* has 'zero article' but that *John* has 'no article'. The label 'zero' is appropriate in the case of common nouns which have article contrast (*cake* as opposed to *a cake* and *the cake*). Proper nouns have no article contrast if we disregard cases like *the John I mean is tall* (see 4.36(b)), and will therefore be said to have 'no article'.

4.3

Nouns with dual membership

The distinction according to countability into count nouns and mass nouns is basic in English. Yet, the language makes it possible to look upon some objects from the point of view of both count and mass, as in the case of *cake*:

I'd like $\begin{cases} \text{a cake, two cakes, several cakes, } \ldots \\ \text{some cake, another piece of cake, } \ldots \end{cases}$

There are many such nouns with dual class membership. Often they have considerable difference in meaning in the two classes.

COUNT NOUNS	MASS NOUNS
have pleasant *experiences*	have a great deal of *experience*
read an evening *paper*	wrap up a present in brown *paper*
She was a *beauty* ('a beautiful woman')	*Beauty* is to be admired
have confidential *talks*	dislike idle *talk*
hear an irritating *sound* ('noise')	travel faster than *sound*
see two little *lambs*	eat New Zealand *lamb*
press clothes with an *iron*	use tools made of *iron*

The same meaning distinction that exists between the count noun *lamb* (the animal) and the mass noun *lamb* (the meat) is achieved by lexical means in a few other pairs, for example:

see a nice little *pig*	buy Danish *pork*
eat two large *loaves*	buy some French *bread*
chop trees in the *wood*	import Canadian *timber*
saw (many) *sheep* in the field	hasn't (much) *mutton* for dinner

The distinction between count and mass can be paralleled by a similar distinction in abstract nouns:

Will they have much *difficulty* in their new jobs?
They have had very few *difficulties* so far

Cutting across the grammatical count/mass distinction we have then a semantic division into concrete (material) and abstract (immaterial) nouns (see *Fig* 4:1), though concrete nouns are mainly count and abstract mainly mass.

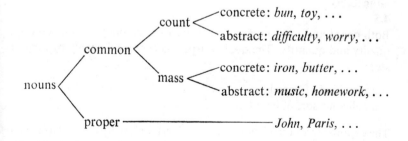

Fig 4:1 Noun classes

4.4
Countability

We have noted that mass nouns do not have a plural. It is, however, more accurate to say that they are invariable and lack number contrast:

Music is
*Musics are $\Big\}$ my favourite hobby

As the term 'mass' implies, the notion of countability (of 'one' as opposed to 'more than one') does not apply to mass nouns. Count nouns, which can be counted (*one pig, two pigs, several pigs, ...*), show the speaker as able to distinguish these items as separable entities. Mass nouns, on the other hand, are seen as continuous entities (*much pork, *one pork, *few pork, ...*) and show the speaker as regarding these substances or concepts as having no natural bounds. They are subject to division only by means of certain 'gradability expressions'.

Note

[a] It may be noted that, apart from a tendency for concrete nouns to be count and abstract nouns to be mass, there is no obvious logical reason for the assignment of various English nouns to the count or mass noun class. In some languages, nouns like *applause* and *information* are count nouns. We list a few that are grammatically different in some languages:

> Your *behaviour* leaves much to be desired
> I dislike *homework* on Sundays
> The workmen are making slow *progress*
> What lovely *sunshine* we are having today!

Also: *anger, applause, chaos, chess, conduct, courage, dancing, education, harm, hospitality, leisure, melancholy, moonlight, parking, photography, poetry, publicity, research* (as in *do some research*), *resistance, safety, shopping, smoking, violence, weather,* etc.

[b] It can be argued that *weather* is neither count (**a weather*) nor mass (**a lot of weather*). Yet we have *a lot of good weather, some bad weather.*

Gradability
4.5

Both count and mass nouns are subject to gradability in two respects: quality and quantity. The quality aspect is expressed chiefly by *kind* or *sort:*

> a new kind of pencil
> a delicious sort of bread

The expression of quantity by means of certain 'partitives' (*a piece of, a bit of, a loaf of,* etc) is different and should be seen as being imposed subsequently:

two loaves of bread
two kinds of loaves of bread

There are three types of 'partitives' which are used to express quantity of mass nouns: measures, typical partitives, and general partitives.

4.6
Measures

The measure partitives relate to precise quantities. (Suitable mass nouns are given in brackets.)

length: a foot of (water)
a yard of (cloth)
a mile of (cable)
area: an acre of (land)
volume: a pint of (beer)
a gallon of $\begin{cases} \text{(petrol, BrE)} \\ \text{(gas, AmE)} \end{cases}$
a quart of (milk)
weight: an ounce of (tobacco)
a pound of (butter)
a ton of (coal)

4.7
Typical partitives

With many nouns, there is a typical partitive appropriate to each specific case. In the tables, the typical partitive is preceded by one of the more general partitives discussed in 4.8. Nouns which can also be count nouns are denoted by 'C'.

(a) Concrete mass nouns

(heavy) armour	a $\begin{cases} \text{piece} \\ \text{suit} \end{cases}$ of armour
(Danish) bacon	a $\begin{cases} \text{piece} \\ \text{slice} \end{cases}$ of bacon
(brown) bread	a $\begin{cases} \text{piece} \\ \text{loaf} \end{cases}$ of bread
(Christmas) cake (C)	a $\begin{cases} \text{piece} \\ \text{slice} \end{cases}$ of cake
(white) chalk (C)	a $\begin{cases} \text{piece} \\ \text{stick} \end{cases}$ of chalk

Concrete mass nouns *continued*

(nut) chocolate (C)	a {piece / bar} of chocolate
(brown) coal (C)	a {piece / lump} of coal
(antique) furniture	{a piece / an article} of furniture
(green) grass	a {bit / blade} of grass
(dry) ice (C)	a {piece / block} of ice
(arid) land (C)	a {piece / strip} of land
(prime) meat	a {piece / roast} of meat
(Swedish) paper (C)	a {piece / sheet} of paper
(long) rice	a {bit / grain} of rice
(just) rubbish (also abstract)	a {pile / heap} of rubbish
(brown) sugar	a {piece / lump} of sugar

(b) Abstract mass nouns

abuse ('insult')	a word of abuse	C = 'misuse'
advice	a {piece / word} of advice	
business ('commerce')	{an item / a bit} of business	C = 'shop'
information	{a piece / an item} of information	
interest (finance)	{a bit / an amount} of interest	C = 'hobby'
news	{a piece / an item} of news	NB: *news* is singular (see 4.52)
work ('job')	a {piece / bit} of work	C = 'product'
evidence	a piece of evidence	
fever	an attack of fever	
passion	a fit of passion	also C
research	a piece of research	

4.8
General partitives
These are not, like typical partitives, restricted to specific lexical items.
They have been illustrated together with the typical partitives in 4.7.

> *a piece of* chalk/coal/advice, ... (the 'unmarked' and most widely
>   used partitive)
> *a bit of* grass/trouble, ...
> *an item of* information/news, ... (chiefly with abstract nouns)

Note
It is manifest from the placing of premodifiers in noun phrases consisting of a
partitive + *of* + mass noun that some 'typical' partitives are felt to form a closer
unit with the mass noun than 'measure' and 'general' partitives (*cf* 13.72): *a hot
cup of coffee*; *a good stroke of luck*; *a large pair of gloves*; *a nice glass of whisky*.

Words in -*ing:* a survey
4.9
Reference was made in 2.13 to the way one part of speech could share
features with another. It is important to realize that between the pure
noun in *We found some paintings* and the pure verb in *Brown painted his
daughter*, there is a gradient which merits careful study:

Some paintings of Brown's (*ie* some paintings that Brown owns)   [1]
Brown's paintings of his daughter (*ie* paintings owned by Brown,
   depicting his daughter but painted by someone else)   [2]
Brown's paintings of his daughter (*ie* they depict his daughter
   and were painted by him)   [3]
The painting of Brown is as skilful as that of Gainsborough
   (*ie* Brown's (a) finished product, *or* (b) technique of
   painting, *or* (c) action of painting)   [4]
Brown's deft painting of his daughter is a delight to watch
   (*ie* it is a delight to watch while Brown deftly paints his
   daughter)   [5]
Brown's deftly painting his daughter is a delight to watch
   (=[4c], [5] in meaning)   [6]
I dislike Brown's painting his daughter (*ie* I dislike *either*
   (a) the fact *or* (b) the way Brown does it)   [7]
I dislike Brown painting his daughter (=[7a])   [8]
I watched Brown painting his daughter (*ie: either* I watched
   Brown as he painted *or* I watched the process of Brown('s)
   painting his daughter)   [9]
Brown deftly painting his daughter is a delight to watch
   (=[4c], [5])   [10]

Painting his daughter, Brown noticed that his hand was
shaking (*ie* while he was painting) [11]
Brown painting his daughter that day, I decided to go for a
walk (*ie* since Brown was painting) [12]
The man painting the girl is Brown (*ie* who is painting) [13]
The silently painting man is Brown (*ie* who is silently
painting) [14]
He is painting his daughter [15]

4.10

Deverbal nouns
In [1], [2] and [3], we could replace *paintings* by *pictures* or *photographs;*
it is thus a perfectly regular concrete count noun (4.2), related only to
the verb *paint* by word-formation (App I.21). We shall refer to such
nouns as DEVERBAL.

4.11

Verbal nouns
In [4] and [5] *painting* is also a noun as can be seen by the definite article
in [4] and not only by the genitive premodifier in [5] but by the adjective
premodifier *deft* (as compared with *deftly* in [6]). But it is an abstract
mass noun (4.2) of the kind that can be formed from any verb by adding
-ing and inserting *of* before the noun phrase that corresponds to subject
if the object is not expressed:

Brown paints ~ the painting of Brown

or before the noun phrase that corresponds to object if this is expressed:

They polish the furniture ~ their polishing of the furniture

We shall refer to such forms as VERBAL NOUNS. We shall examine further in 4.93 *ff*, 13.27 *ff*, and 13.64 the important correspondence between the *-s* and *of*-genitives and the relations of possession, subject and
object, among others. Thus *the painting of Brown* can have at least three
meanings: a picture representing Brown; Brown's work or skill as a
painter; and the process of painting Brown by someone else. It should
be noted that we could not replace *painting* in [4] or [5] by *picture* or
photograph.

Note
One expects the name in [4] to be that of an artist of some reputation if the *of*-phrase
is to be used; otherwise the *-s* genitive would be more natural to convey this meaning:

Jack's painting is nearly as impressive as Gainsborough's

4.12

Participles

In [6] and [7], the genitive premodifier *Brown's* is used, but in place of the adjective in [5] we have the adverb *deftly*, and in place of the *of*-phrase we have the noun phrase *his daughter* directly following *painting* just as though it was the object of a finite verb phrase as in [15]. Traditionally this mixture of nominal and verbal characteristics has been given the name 'gerund', while the uses of *painting* in [8–15] have been distinguished as those of the '(present) participle'. This traditional distinction is made, irrespective of whether the structure in which the *-ing* item occurs is operating in the nominal function of [8] and [9], in which 'gerunds' also operate, as in [6] and [7], or in the adverbial function of [11] and [12], where 'gerunds' cannot operate; that is to say, where a genitive premodifier is unacceptable:

*Brown's painting his daughter that day, I decided to go for a walk

Where no premodifier appears, genitive or otherwise, the traditional view held *painting* to be gerund in

Painting a child is difficult

where the item is in a structure functioning nominally (in this case, as subject), but it was considered a participle if the same structure functioned adverbially as in

Painting a child, I quite forgot the time

No such categorial distinction however was made between

To paint a child is pleasant

and

To paint a child, I bought a new canvas

where the italicized item was traditionally regarded as an 'infinitive' in both.

In this book we shall disregard the distinction between gerund and participle, classing the *-ing* items in [6–15] as PARTICIPLES. In [6–13], the participle is in each case the non-finite verb or a non-finite clause; in [14] the participle is a premodifier in a noun phrase (13.44 *ff*); in [15] it is the head of a finite verb phrase (3.10 *ff*). The simplification in terminology, however, must not let us ignore the complexity of the different participial expressions as we move along the gradient to the 'most verbal' end at [15].

Determiners
4.13

We have seen that different classes and forms of nouns require different articles. If we consider the articles in relation to the count noun *pen* and the mass noun *ink*, we have this situation:

	COUNT	MASS
SINGULAR	*the pen* *a pen*	*the ink* *ink*
PLURAL	*the pens* *pens*	

Note

The forms of the definite and indefinite articles depend on the initial sound of the following word. There is one unstressed and one stressed set.

(i) The unstressed definite article is always written *the* but is pronounced /ðə/ before consonants and /ðɪ/ before vowels. The indefinite article is *a* /ə/ before consonants and *an* /ən/ before vowels. Note that it is the pronunciation, not the spelling, of the following word that determines their form:

the /ðə/ } boy, car, ...   the /ðɪ/ } ant, hour, ...
a /ə/   an /ən/

There is divided usage before some words that are written with initial *h*, depending on whether *h* is pronounced or not:

a(n) { hotel
       historical novel

(ii) The stressed forms are often italicized in print. In speech the distinction with regard to the quality of the following sound is neutralized for the definite article:

the /ði/ } boy, car, ...   *the* /ði/ } ant, hour, ...
a /eɪ/   *an* /æn/

The stressed definite article is often used to indicate excellence or superiority in some respect, as in

He would be *the* man for you to know
The demonstration will be *the* event this week.

4.14

The use of the articles is not the only possibility for 'determining' nouns:

the
a
no
what† } *pen*
this
every
each
either

† This *what* is the interrogative, as in *What book do you want?* As intensifier, *what* may co-occur with the indefinite article: *What a book!* Compare *such*: 5.57, 13.68.

These words, and some others, are called determiners. They form a set of closed-system items (see 2.14 *f*) that are mutually exclusive with each other, *ie* there cannot be more than one occurring before the noun head. Both **a the boy* and **a some boy* are ungrammatical. The determiners are in a 'choice relation', *ie* they occur one instead of another. In this respect they are unlike *all, many* and *pretty* which are in a 'chain relation', *ie* occurring one after another:

All the many pretty houses

The articles are central to the class of determiners in that they have no function independent of the noun they precede. Other determiners (like *some*) are also independent pronouns:

$$\text{I want} \begin{cases} \text{the ink} \\ \text{some ink} \end{cases} \qquad \text{Here is} \begin{cases} \text{*the} \\ \text{some} \end{cases}$$

Furthermore, the articles have no lexical meaning but solely contribute definite or indefinite status to the nouns they determine. Yet the dependence is not unilateral. A count noun like *boy*, for example, is, on its own, only a lexical item. It requires an 'overt' determiner of some kind to assume grammatical status. The articles will be discussed in 4.28–47 and the other determiners in the sections dealing with the pronouns (4.106–128).

Note

[*a*] There are two exceptions to the rule that count nouns cannot occur without a determiner.

   (i) Parallel structures: Man or boy, I don't like him (*cf* 4.38)
   (ii) Vocatives: Come here, boy!

[*b*] Coordinated noun-phrase heads can share a determiner placed before the first head:

   the boys and girls
   the radios, tape-recorders and television sets in this shop

[*c*] The indefinite article *a*(*n*) may be described as an unstressed numeral parallel to stressed *one* (4.126) in

$$\text{I want} \begin{cases} \text{a} \\ \text{one} \end{cases} \text{cigar}$$

[*d*] *A*(*n*) means 'a certain', 'a person giving his name as' in

   A Mr Johnson came to see you last night.

4.15

Just as we have noted in 4.13 that there are certain co-occurrence restrictions between articles and nouns, we will find additional restrictions when we consider determiners as a whole. The definite article can occur with all three noun classes but the zero and indefinite articles cannot. Similarly, for the other determiners, we have, for example,

$$no \begin{cases} pen \\ pens \\ ink \end{cases}$$

but no complete paradigms for

$$this \begin{cases} pen \\ *pens \\ ink \end{cases}$$

$$either \begin{cases} pen \\ *pens \\ *ink \end{cases}$$

$$enough \begin{cases} *pen \\ pens \\ ink \end{cases}$$

4.16
The following figures show that there are six classes of determiners with respect to their co-occurrence with the noun classes singular count (such as *pen*), plural count (such as *pens*), and mass nouns (such as *ink*).

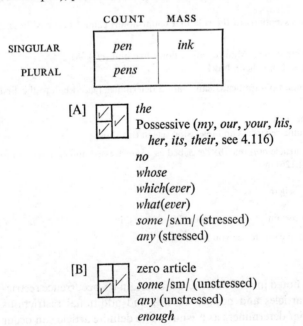

	COUNT	MASS
SINGULAR	*pen*	*ink*
PLURAL	*pens*	

[A]   *the*
Possessive (*my, our, your, his, her, its, their*, see 4.116)
no
whose
which(ever)
what(ever)
some /sʌm/ (stressed)
any (stressed)

[B]   zero article
some /sm/ (unstressed)
any (unstressed)
enough

[C] 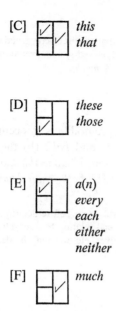 *this*
that

[D] *these*
those

[E] *a(n)*
every
each
either
neither

[F] *much*

Note
Many of the determiners have alternative *of*-constructions (*cf* 4.19):

Enough (of the) cake was left to satisfy her

Any
Some } (of the) books will do

Each
Either } of the books
Each
Either } book } will do

Closed-system premodifiers
4.17
The articles have been shown to be intimately connected with the nouns
they determine, and the class of determiner has been defined as a set of
closed-system items that are mutually exclusive with the articles. In addition to determiners, there is a large number of other closed-system items
that occur before the head of the noun phrase. These items, which will be
referred to as closed-system premodifiers, form three classes (predeterminers, ordinals, and quantifiers) which have been set up on the basis of
the possible positions that they can have in relation to determiners and
to each other. Within each of the three classes, we will make distinctions
according to their patterning with the classes of singular count, plural
count, and mass nouns (4.2 *ff*).

Note

We will also include here some premodifiers that consist of constructions with open-class items and commute to some extent with closed-system premodifiers, *eg: three times* (*cf:* archaic *thrice*), *a large quantity of* (*cf: much*).

Predeterminers
4.18

Predeterminers are unique among the premodifiers in occurring before the determiners. They are (a) *all, both,* and *half;* (b) the multipliers *double, twice, three times,* etc; and fractions like *one-third, one-fifth,* etc. Predeterminers are mutually exclusive: **all both, *half double.*

Note

'Restrictives' like *just, only, especially,* etc also occur before determiners (*Only the best cars are exported*), but they have no special relation to noun-phrase structure, since they can also modify verbs and adjectives, etc and may be dealt with more suitably in 8.13 *ff:*

$$He's\ just \begin{cases} \text{a boy} \\ \text{feeling sick} \\ \text{a little sick} \\ \text{sleepy} \end{cases}$$

4.19

All, both, half

These have restrictions on co-occurrence with determiners and noun heads, as is shown in *Fig 4:2.*

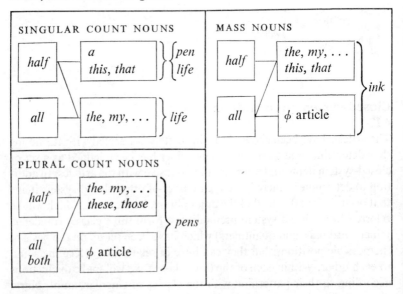

Fig 4:2 All, both, half

These predeterminers can thus occur only before articles or demonstratives but, for obvious semantic reasons, none of them can occur with the following 'quantitative' determiners: *every, (n)either, each, some, any, no, enough* (but see Note).

All, both, and *half* have *of*-constructions, which are optional with nouns and obligatory with personal pronouns:

all (of) the meat all of it
both (of) the students both of them
half (of) the time half of it

With a quantifier following, the *of*-construction is preferred (especially in AmE):

all of the many boys

All three can be independent nominals:

All ⎫
Both ⎬ passed their exams
Half ⎭

All and *both* (but not *half*) can occur after the head. With pronouns this is the only possible position (in addition to the prepositional construction):

The students ⎱ ⎰ all ⎱
They ⎰ ⎱ both ⎰ passed their exams

The zero article is used for generic reference (4.33 *f*):

All men are created equal (generic reference)
All the men in the mine wore helmets (specific reference)

The predeterminer *both* and the determiners *either* and *neither* are not plural proper but 'dual', *ie* they can only refer to two. Compared with the numeral *two, both* is emphatic:

Both (the) ⎱
The two ⎰ students were excellent

All is rare with concrete count nouns: *?I haven't used all the pencil* though it is less rare with contrastive stress: *I haven't read ÀLL the book,* where *book* is treated as a kind of divisible mass noun. The normal constructions would be *all of the book* or *the whole book.*

Before certain temporal nouns, *all* is used with the zero article in variation with the definite article: *all (the) day/morning/night.* The zero construction is normal in negative contexts: *I haven't seen him all day.*

Note

There is an adverbial use of *half* in emphatic negation where it can precede *enough:*

He hasn't $\left\{ \begin{array}{l} \text{half} \\ \text{nearly} \end{array} \right\}$ enough money!

4.20

Double, twice, three, four, . . . times

The second type of predeterminer includes *double, twice, three times,* etc, which occur with plural count and mass nouns and with singular count nouns denoting number, amount, etc:

>   double their salaries
>   twice his strength
>   three times this amount

Three, four, etc *times* consists of the open-class item *times,* and is thus not a proper closed-category premodifier. *Double, twice, three times,* etc have no analogue with *of*-construction:

>   *double of the amount

Furthermore, unlike *all* and *both,* these predeterminers cannot occur after the noun head:

>   *The amount double is what he asked for

Three, four, etc *times* as well as *once* can co-occur with the determiners *a, every,* and *each* and (less commonly *per*) to form 'distributive' expressions with a temporal noun as head:

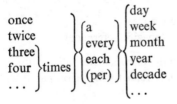

Sometimes (at least in AmE) *the* occurs in other distributive expressions:

>   five dollars the head

4.21

One-third, two-fifths, etc

The fractions *one-third, two-fifths, three-quarters,* etc, can also be followed by determiners, and have the alternative *of*-construction:

>   He did it in one-third (of) the time it took me

Note

All is not mutually exclusive with fractions when it serves as a mass modifier:

'They cut out two-thirds of it.' 'All two-thirds of it?'

4.22
Ordinals
Ordinals include the ordinal numbers (*first, second, third*, etc; see 4.129) as well as (*an*)*other, next*, and *last*. These words are 'post-determiners', *ie* they must follow determiners in noun-phrase structure, but they precede quantifiers (see below 4.25 *f*) and adjectives (see 5.41 (b)).

There appear to be two kinds of patterning (see *Fig* 4:3). *First, next, last*, and *another* ('in addition') can, optionally, co-occur with ordinal numerals and *few* before plural count nouns, whereas *second, third*, and the other ordinals which cannot be followed by any quantifiers modify singular count nouns.

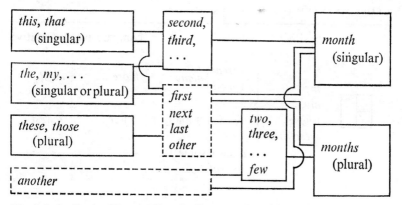

Fig 4:3 Ordinals. (Dotted lines indicate optional items).

Cardinal numbers and quantifiers
4.23
Cardinal numbers and quantifiers are mutually exclusive, *ie* we cannot have, for example, **five many* or **three plenty* – they follow determiners but precede adjectives.

4.24
Cardinal numbers
Cardinal numbers are *one* (with singular count nouns) and *two, three, four*, etc (with plural count nouns) (see 4.2, 4.129):

Give me just one good reason for your decision
All (the) four brothers are sailors

Quantifiers
4.25
CLOSED-SYSTEM QUANTIFIERS

The closed-system quantifiers are *many* (with the comparatives *more* and *most*), *few* (*fewer, fewest*), *little* (*less, least*), and *several* (*cf* 4.123–125).

There are too many mistakes in your essay

He is a man of few words

He took $\begin{Bmatrix} \text{little ('not much')} \\ \text{only a little ('some')} \end{Bmatrix}$ butter

One group of quantifiers modifies plural count nouns, the others mass nouns (*Table* 4:1). The quantifier *several* usually occurs with zero article: *several charming fisherman's cottages*. There is also a homonymous adjective ('separate', 'distinct') as in *the several members of the Board*.

Table 4:1
CLOSED-SYSTEM QUANTIFIERS

	positive		comparative	superlative
☑	*a* *the* *my, . . .* *whose* *these/those*	$\begin{Bmatrix} great \\ good \end{Bmatrix}$*many*	*more*	*most*
		few ('not many')	*fewer*	*fewest*
	a few ('some') *several*		— —	— —
☑	*the* *my, . . .* *whose* *this/that*	*little* ('not much')	*less*	*least*
	a little ('some')		*more*	*most*

Note

[a] The quantifier *little* should be distinguished from the homonymous adjective *little* ('small') which has no co-occurrence restrictions with numerals or count nouns: *five little girls*.

[b] *Much* can never occur with articles and is therefore a determiner (*cf* 4.13 *ff*).

[c] *Many* and *few* can also be used predicatively: *his few friends* ~ *his friends who are few* (in number).

[d] *A few* and *a little*, as in *a few friends* and *a little music*, cannot be analysed as consisting of the indefinite article *a* plus the quantifiers *few* and *little*, since the indefinite article does not occur with plural count and mass nouns (**a friends*, **a music*). There is also a semantic difference: *few* and *little* are negative, *a few* and *a little* positive (or at least neutral) terms:

He has few ('not many') friends and little ('not much') money
He has a few ('some') friends and a little ('some') money.

4.26

OPEN-CLASS QUANTIFIERS

Open-class quantifiers constitute three groups according to their patterning with noun classes (see *Table* 4:2).

Open-class quantifiers consist of heads like *lot, deal,* and *number* with an *of*-phrase as postmodification. The reason for including them here after closed-system quantifiers is to draw attention to semantic and syntactic similarities between the two classes. Quantitative expressions, whether they are determiners, or closed-system quantifiers, or open-class quantifiers, are mutually exclusive:

$$\text{John got}\begin{cases}\text{much} \\ \text{plenty of} \\ \text{a great deal of}\end{cases}\text{sympathy but little help}$$

Furthermore, the superficial quantitative head of the noun phrase which includes an open-class quantifier may show signs of subordination to the noun of the *of*-phrase, manifested by violation of strict concord (see 7.30):

$$\text{A lot of people}\begin{cases}\text{*was} \\ \text{were}\end{cases}$$
$$\text{A large number of people}\begin{cases}\text{?was} \\ \text{were}\end{cases}\text{here last night}$$

Table 4:2

OPEN-CLASS QUANTIFIERS

⊞ (bottom-left marked)	$\begin{rcases}\textit{plenty} \\ \textit{a lot} \\ \textit{lots}\end{rcases}of\begin{cases}\textit{students} \\ \textit{money}\end{cases}$ (all informal)
⊞ (top-right marked)	$a\begin{Bmatrix}\textit{great} \\ \textit{good}\end{Bmatrix}\textit{deal}$ $\begin{rcases}a \\ the \\ my, \dots \\ this/that \\ some\end{rcases}\begin{Bmatrix}\textit{large} \\ \textit{small}\end{Bmatrix}\begin{cases}\textit{quantity} \\ \textit{amount}\end{cases}$ $of\ money$
⊞ (bottom-left marked)	$\begin{rcases}a \\ the \\ my, \dots \\ this/that\end{rcases}\begin{Bmatrix}\textit{great} \\ \textit{large} \\ \textit{good}\end{Bmatrix}\textit{number of students}$

The open-class quantifiers that occur with mass nouns have both structural and semantic relations with the partitives that have been discussed in 4.5 *ff* in connection with gradability of mass nouns:

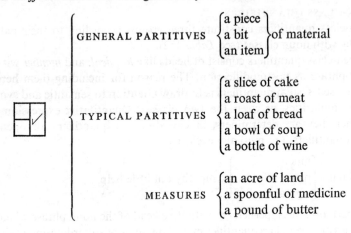

Where:

GENERAL PARTITIVES
$\begin{cases} \text{a piece} \\ \text{a bit} \\ \text{an item} \end{cases}$ of material

TYPICAL PARTITIVES
$\begin{cases} \text{a slice of cake} \\ \text{a roast of meat} \\ \text{a loaf of bread} \\ \text{a bowl of soup} \\ \text{a bottle of wine} \end{cases}$

MEASURES
$\begin{cases} \text{an acre of land} \\ \text{a spoonful of medicine} \\ \text{a pound of butter} \end{cases}$

4.27
Premodification structures

The classification of the predeterminers according to their relative position and patterning with noun classes allows us to construct rather complex structures of premodification, as for example:

SUBJECT						PREDICATE
predeter- miner	deter- miner	ordinal	cardinal/ quanti- fier	open-class premodi- fier	head	
Half	*my*	*first*		*new*	*salary*	*is spent*
Both	*these*	*last*	*two*		*days*	*were hectic*
All	*the*		*little*	*Danish*	*butter I had*	*is gone*

Examples such as these which are constructed to illustrate the possibilities that are available will tend to seem rather strained. Here, as in so many other fields of English grammar, the language provides a range of possibilities, not all of which are normally made use of to the theoretical limit.

Premodification by means of open-class items (adjectives, participles, inflected genitives, nouns, adverbial phrases, and sentences) will be discussed in 13.44 *ff*, where they can be related to all types of modification in the complex noun phrase.

Reference and the articles
Specific/generic reference
4.28

In discussing the use of the articles, it is essential to make a distinction between specific and generic reference. If we say

A lion and two tigers are sleeping in the cage

the reference is specific, since we have in mind specific specimens of the class 'tiger'. If, on the other hand, we say

Tigers are dangerous animals

the reference is generic, since we are thinking of the class 'tiger' without special reference to specific tigers.

We have noted in 3.39 *ff* that dynamic verbs admit of the aspectual simple/progressive contrast depending on the manner in which the action of the predication is viewed:

John always *sings* in the shower (habitual activity)
John *is singing* in the shower now (temporary activity)

With stative verbs, however, the aspectual contrast does not apply:

$$\text{John} \begin{Bmatrix} \text{knows} \\ \text{*is knowing} \end{Bmatrix} \text{Russian}$$

Similarly in the noun, the distinctions that are important for count nouns with specific reference between definite and indefinite and between singular and plural disappear with generic reference. This is so because generic reference is used to denote what is normal or typical for members of a class. Consequently, the distinctions of number and definiteness are neutralized since they are no longer relevant for the generic concept. Singular or plural, definite or indefinite can sometimes be used without change in the generic meaning (*cf* 4.33):

$$\begin{Bmatrix} \text{The German} \\ \text{A German} \end{Bmatrix} \text{is a good musician}$$

$$\begin{Bmatrix} \text{The Germans} \\ \text{Germans} \end{Bmatrix} \text{are good musicians}$$

At least the following three forms of *tiger* can be used generically:

$$\begin{Bmatrix} \text{The tiger} \\ \text{A tiger} \end{Bmatrix} \text{is a dangerous animal}$$

Tigers are dangerous animals

Note

However, there may be a difference in presupposition denoted by the articles in generic use. We may compare the following four sentences:

Dwarfs are a popular theme in literature
Hobgoblins are a popular theme in literature
The dwarf is a popular theme in literature
?The hobgoblin is a popular theme in literature

The indefinite form here seems to imply 'if they exist', while the definite form implies 'extant'.

4.29

The connection between the dynamic/stative dichotomy and the specific/generic dichotomy is not just one of parallelism but of interdependence, as appears in the following examples:

generic reference/simple aspect   *The tiger lives* in the jungle

specific reference ⎰ simple aspect   *The tiger* at this circus *performs* twice a day

⎱ progressive aspect   *The tiger is sleeping* in the cage

generic reference/simple aspect   *The English drink* beer in pubs

specific reference ⎰ simple aspect   *The Englishmen* (who live here) *drink* beer in the garden every day

⎱ progressive aspect   *The Englishmen are* just now *drinking* beer in the garden

4.30

Number, aspect, and definiteness compared

Generalizing the points that have been made above about the parallelism between certain verb and noun categories, we can best display this parallelism by using diagrams of the same type as we used for noun classes:

1a	2
1b	

Cell 1a seems in all cases to be the 'unmarked', and 1b the 'marked' term for the gradable systems: singular/plural, simple/progressive, indefinite/definite form. Cell 2 symbolizes the neutralization of the unmarked and marked distinction in the left-hand column. *Figs* 4:4–6 show, respectively, the situation for number (see further 4.48 *ff*), aspect (see further 3.36 *ff*) and definiteness (see further 4.35 *ff*).

count nouns: singular number	*mass nouns:* singular number
count nouns: plural number	

Fig 4:4
Number

dynamic verbs: simple aspect	*stative verbs:* simple aspect
dynamic verbs: progressive aspect	

Fig 4:5
Aspect

specific reference: indefinite form	*generic reference:* indefinite, zero, or definite article
specific reference: definite form	

Fig 4:6
Definiteness

4.31
Systems of article usage
After this consideration of some general grammatical relationships in the noun and the verb, we may now return to the problems of the articles by setting up two different systems of article use depending on the type of reference. *Cf: Fig* 4:7 with *Figs* 4:4 and 4:6.

	DEFINITE		INDEFINITE	
SPECIFIC REFERENCE	the tiger	the ink	a tiger	(some) ink
	the tigers		(some) tigers	

GENERIC REFERENCE	the tiger a tiger tigers	ink

Fig 4:7 Type of reference

With definite specific reference, the definite article is used for all noun classes:

> Where is the pen ⎫
> Where are the pens ⎬ I bought?
> Where is the ink ⎭

With indefinite specific reference, singular count nouns take the indefinite article *a(n)*, while plural count nouns and mass nouns take zero article or, usually, the 'light quantitative article' *some* (and *any* in non-assertive contexts, see 4.127): *I want a pen/some pens/some ink.* With generic reference, the distinctions for number and definiteness are neutralized with count nouns. With mass nouns, only the zero article is possible:

> The tiger is ⎫
> A tiger is ⎪
> Tigers are ⎬ beautiful
> Music is ⎭

4.32
Generic, specific, and unique reference
In addition to the two types of reference with common nouns (specific and generic), we have a third type with proper nouns: unique reference. Generic reference will be dealt with in 4.33–34, specific reference in 4.35–39 (see further 10.65 *ff*), and unique reference in 4.40–47.

Generic reference
4.33
Nationality words and adjectives as head
In the second set of examples in 4.29 there is a lexical change from *the English* (generic reference) to *the Englishmen* (specific reference). *The English* belongs to a class of noun phrases with adjectives as head (see 5.20 *ff*) that have generic reference. There are two kinds of adjectives that can act as noun-phrase head (see the discussion of 'conversion', App I.33):

(a) PLURAL PERSONAL (*the French = the French nation; the rich = those who are rich*), for example,

the Chinese	the blind
the French	the poor
the Japanese	the rich

(b) SINGULAR NON-PERSONAL ABSTRACT (*the evil = that which is evil*), for example,

the evil	the unusual
the good	the useful

The lexical variation in a number of nationality words, as between *an Englishman/several Englishmen/the English*, depending on type of reference, appears from *Table* 4:3.

Where nationality words have no double form (like *English, Englishman*), *the* + plural can be both generic and specific:

The Finns are industrious
The Finns that I know are industrious

Table 4:3
NATIONALITY WORDS

name of country or continent	adjective	specific reference		generic reference
		singular	plural (*two*, . . .)	plural
China	Chinese	a Chinese[a]	Chinese	the Chinese
Japan	Japanese	a Japanese	Japanese	the Japanese
Portugal	Portuguese	a Portuguese	Portuguese	the Portuguese
Switzerland	Swiss	a Swiss	Swiss	the Swiss
Vietnam	Vietnamese	a Vietnamese	Vietnamese	the Vietnamese
Israel	Israeli	an Israeli	Israelis	the Israelis
Pakistan	Pakistani	a Pakistani	Pakistanis	the Pakistanis
Africa	African	an African	Africans	the Africans
America	American	an American	Americans	the Americans
Asia	Asian	an Asian	Asians	the Asians
Australia	Australian	an Australian	Australians	the Australians
Italy	Italian	an Italian	Italians	the Italians
Russia	Russian	a Russian	Russians	the Russians
Belgium	Belgian	a Belgian	Belgians	the Belgians
Brazil	Brazilian	a Brazilian	Brazilians	the Brazilians
Europe	European	a European	Europeans	the Europeans
Germany	German	a German	Germans	the Germans[b]
Greece	Greek[c]	a Greek	Greeks	the Greeks
Hungary	Hungarian	a Hungarian	Hungarians	the Hungarians
Norway	Norwegian	a Norwegian	Norwegians	the Norwegians

Table 4:3 *continued*

NATIONALITY WORDS

| name of country or continent | adjective | specific reference | | generic reference |
		singular	plural (two, . . .)	plural
Denmark	Danish	a Dane	Danes	the Danes/ (Danish)
Finland	Finnish	a Finn	Finns	the Finns/ (Finnish)
Poland	Polish	a Pole	Poles	the Poles/(Polish)
Spain	Spanish	a Spaniard	Spaniards	the Spaniards/ (Spanish)
Sweden	Swedish	a Swede	Swedes	the Swedes/ (Swedish)
Arabia	Arabic[d]	an Arab	Arabs	the Arabs
England	English	an Englishman	Englishmen	{ Englishmen / the English
France	French	a Frenchman	Frenchmen	{ Frenchmen / the French
Holland the Netherlands }	Dutch	a Dutchman	Dutchmen	{ Dutchmen / the Dutch
Ireland	Irish	an Irishman	Irishmen	{ Irishmen / the Irish
Wales	Welsh	a Welshman	Welshmen	{ Welshmen / the Welsh
Britain	British	a Briton[e]	Britons	{ Britons / the British
Scotland	{ Scots / Scottish / (Scotch)[f]	a Scotsman / a Scot / (a Scotchman)	Scotsmen / Scots / (Scotchmen)	Scotsmen / the Scots / (Scotchmen) / (the Scotch)

Note

[a] *Chinaman* is used in a humorous and condescending way.

[b] The segment *-man* in *German* is not a masculine gender suffix (as in *Englishman*); there are no **Germen* or **Gerwomen*.

[c] *Grecian* refers chiefly to ancient Greece: *a Grecian urn*.

[d] *Arabic* is used in *Arabic numerals* (as opposed to *Roman numerals*) and in *the Arabic language; he speaks Arabic fluently*. But *Arabian brown, an Arabian camel, an Arab(ian) horse*.

[e] *A Britisher* is a colloquial (especially AmE) variant of *Briton*.

[f] The inhabitants themselves prefer *Scots* and *Scottish* to *Scotch*, which however is commonly used in such phrases as *Scotch terrier, Scotch whisky, Scotch plaid, Scotch eggs, Scotch pancakes*, etc. But *the Scottish universities, the Scottish Highlands, a Scottish accent*, etc, for denoting nationality rather than type.

4.34

Mass nouns and plural count nouns

When they have generic reference, both concrete and abstract mass nouns, and usually also plural count nouns, are used with the zero article:

He likes
$\begin{cases}\text{wine, wood, cream cheese, ...} \\ \text{music, chess, literature, history, skiing, ...} \\ \text{lakes, games, long walks, ...}\end{cases}$

Prepositional postmodification by an *of*-phrase usually requires the definite article with a head noun which thus has limited generic reference:

He likes
$\begin{cases}\text{the wine(s)} \\ \text{the music} \\ \text{the lakes}\end{cases}$ of France

Similarly, *the wines of this shop* is an instance of limited generic reference, in the sense that it does not refer to any particular wines at any one time. Note that the postmodification with an *of*-phrase is more restrictive than with other prepositions:

Mrs Nelson adores
$\begin{cases}\text{Venetian glass} \\ \text{the glass of Venice} \\ \text{*glass of Venice} \\ \text{the glass from Venice} \\ \text{glass from Venice}\end{cases}$

This type of postmodification structure should be compared to the frequent alternative with an adjectival premodification. In comparison with some other languages English tends to make a liberal interpretation of the concept 'generic' in such cases, so that the zero article is used also where the reference of the noun head is restricted by premodification.

MASS NOUNS	Canadian paper	the paper of Canada / paper from Canada
	Chinese history	the history of China
	Trotskyite politics	the politics of Trotsky
	American literature	the literature of America
	Restoration comedy	the comedy of the Restoration
PLURAL COUNT NOUNS	Japanese cameras	(the) cameras from Japan
	Oriental women	the women of the Orient

The zero article is also used with other plural nouns that are not unambiguously generic:

Appearances can be deceptive

Circumstances are always changing
Events have proved wrong
Matters have gone from bad to worse
Prices are always rising
Things aren't what they used to be.

Specific reference
4.35
Indefinite/definite reference
The indefinite form is taken to be the 'unmarked' term in the system of definiteness because it is natural to consider indefinite as being basic to definiteness. Definite can be shown to be secondary to indefinite in sentences like

John bought a TV, a tape-recorder, and a radio, but returned *the radio*

The definite article with *radio* is dependent on the earlier mention of *a radio*. Similarly, the sentence

The radio John bought is Japanese

where the noun-phrase head *radio* has a postmodifying relative clause, can be related to the following two sentences:

John bought *a radio* + *The radio* is Japanese

The indefinite article is not normal if the relative clause is restrictive.

?A radio John bought is Japanese

The indefinite article is, however, by no means unusual in sentences such as the following:

A cat John bought was ill when he got it
A book I want has been acquired by the library
A girl who makes me weak in the knees has just come into the room

On the other hand, no indefinite form is needed in the italicized phrases of the following sentences despite the fact that the nouns have not been mentioned before:

John came home from work. First he read *the paper* for a while, then he got up from *the chair* and turned on *the radio*.

There is no need to state that John had bought a paper and that there were a chair and a radio in his sitting-room. These things are part of the

cultural situation and can be taken for granted. We can thus make a
distinction between linguistic and situation reference.

4.36

Linguistic reference: anaphoric/cataphoric *the*

Linguistic reference is anaphoric or cataphoric (*cf* 10.63 *ff*).

(a) The anaphoric determiner is bound to an earlier mention of the same
noun. Thus the noun with the determiner has backward reference to
this antecedent, and there is co-reference between the two nouns. If
we say

> John ordered *a book* and *the book* has just arrived

the two occurrences of *book* refer to the same book. This is not the
natural interpretation of

> John ordered *a book* and *a book* has just arrived

which implies non-identity between the two occurrences of *book*. It is
only in the former case, where there is co-reference, that the pronoun *it* can replace the second noun phrase. Like anaphoric *the*, the
referential personal pronouns are definite forms. (Note however
non-referential pronouns such as *one;* see 4.126, 10.65.)

(b) The cataphoric determiner has forward reference to a postmodifying
prepositional phrase or relative clause, for example,

$$\text{The wines} \begin{cases} \text{of France} \\ \text{that France produces} \end{cases}$$

The interdependence between the determiner and the relative clause
is particularly obvious with names (which do not normally have a
determiner in isolation):

> *The Philadelphia* which Mr Johnson knows so well is a heritage
> of colonial times

can be seen as derived from

> *Philadelphia* is (in part *or* in a certain aspect) a heritage of
> colonial times
> Mr Johnson knows (this part *or* aspect of) *Philadelphia* so well

4.37

Situational reference

Situational reference involves the use of *the* with nouns whose reference is
immediately understood by the users of the language. When we talk of

the moon the presupposition is that, in our experience or field of interest, there is only one moon. We may call this use of the article the INDEX-ICAL *THE*. It may be seen as relatable to the cataphoric *the* by ellipsis (*the moon* ~ *the moon of the Earth, the stars* ~ *the stars that are visible*) where the postmodification is so obvious as to be superfluous, but naturally there is no reason to postulate such an elliptic process underlying each occurrence of indexical *the*.

One type of indexical *the* includes *the sun, the moon, the earth, the sky, the air*, which are concepts common to mankind as a whole. Because of this uniqueness they are very close to proper nouns based on count nouns (which however require capital initial letter): *The Bible, the Lord, the United States*, etc (4.46).

Another type of indexical *the* is more specific, being restricted to a particular society, nation or other locative expression. *The climate* may refer to the climate of a meteorological area, *the press* to the press of a country, etc. This type includes

the ballad	the press
the drama	the radio
the film	the telephone

Situational reference may be seen as involving both concrete and abstract uses of the nouns. In the sentences

He turned on the radio
What's on the radio tonight?

the first use of *radio* is concrete and the second abstract. In the case of *television* the abstraction normally involves the zero article. Compare

He turned on $\left\{\begin{array}{l}\text{the television}\\ \text{*television}\end{array}\right.$

What's on $\left\{\begin{array}{l}\text{the television}\\ \text{television}\end{array}\right\}$ tonight?

4.38
Common nouns with zero article
There are a number of count nouns that take the zero article in abstract, or rather specialized use, chiefly in certain idiomatic expressions (with verbs like BE and GO and with prepositions like *at, by*, etc):

go by car	sit in/look at, . . . the car
be in bed	make/sit on, . . . the bed

go to school (an institution)	go into/take a look at, . . . the school (a building)	

The following list gives a number of expressions with zero article in the left-hand column; for comparison, the right-hand column shows some of the nouns used with the definite article.

SEASONS	spring summer ⎰autumn ⎱fall winter	the spring the summer the autumn (BrE) the fall (AmE) the winter

SOME
'INSTITUTIONS'
(often with
at, in, to, etc,
cf 6.15)
	be in⎱
	go to⎰
		bed
		church
		prison
		
		hospital
		  (especially
		  BrE)
		class
		  (especially
		  AmE)
			lie down on the bed
			admire the church
			walk round the
			  prison
			redecorate the
			  hospital

	be at⎱
	go to⎰
		school
		college
		sea
		
		university
			drive past the school
			
			look out towards the
			  sea
			be at/go to/study at the
			  university
			  (preferred by many,
			  especially in AmE)

	be at/go home be in/leave town		approach the town
MEANS OF TRANSPORT (with *by*)	travel⎱ leave ⎬by come ⎰	bicycle bus car boat train plane	sit on the bicycle be on the bus sleep in the car sit in the boat take the/a train be on the plane

TIMES OF THE DAY AND NIGHT (particularly with *at, by, after, before*)	at dawn/daybreak, when day breaks	during the day
	at sunrise/sunset	admire the sunrise/sunset
	at/around noon/midnight	in the afternoon
	at dusk/twilight	see nothing in the dusk
	at/by night	wake up in the night
	(by) day and night	in the daytime
	before morning came } evening came } (rather on } formal after night fell } style)	in/during the morning in the evening in the night

MEALS		breakfast	the breakfast was good
		brunch (especially AmE)	
	have } before } at } after } stay for }	lunch tea (especially BrE) cocktails (especially AmE)	he poured the tea himself
		dinner	prepare (the) dinner
		supper	
	dinner will be served at 6.30	the dinner given in honour of the guests was magnificent

| ILLNESSES | appendicitis
anaemia
diabetes
influenza | the plague
(the) flu
(the) measles
(the) mumps |

PARALLEL STRUCTURES	arm in arm	he took her by the arm
	hand in hand	What have you got in your hand?
	day by day teaspoonful by teaspoonful	

man to man
face to face
from dawn to dusk

from beginning to end	from the beginning of the day to the end of it
from right to left	keep to the right
from west to north	he lives in the north

husband and wife
whether you are mason
or businessman
makes no difference

4.39

Article usage with common nouns in an intensive relation

Unlike many other languages, English requires the definite or indefinite article with the count noun complement in an intensive relation (see 7.2 *f*, 12.30 *ff*, 12.67 *ff*; *cf*: *That was fun*, etc, 5.11).

With indefinite reference, the indefinite article is used:

(i) intensive complementation ⎬ John { was / became / remained } { a mason / a businessman / a micro-biologist }

(ii) complex-transitive complementation (active verb) ⎬ Mary { found John / considered John to be / regarded John as } { a fool / a genius / an intellectual }

(iii) complex-transitive complementation (passive verb) ⎬ John { was looked upon as / was taken to be / was taken for } { a scientist / a scholar / a linguist }

The complement of TURN, however, has zero article:

John started out a music student before he turned linguist.

Definite reference requires the definite article:

(i) John was
(ii) Mary considered John ⎬ the genius of the family
(iii) John was looked upon as

However, the zero (or definite) article is used with the noun complement after copulas and 'naming verbs', such as APPOINT, DECLARE, ELECT, when the noun designates a unique office or task:

(i) John is (the) captain of the team
(ii) They elected Kennedy⎱
(iii) Kennedy was elected⎰(the) President of the United States

Note
There is hardly any meaning difference between the following two examples, the latter having an adjective complement:

I took him⎰for ⎱ ⎰an American ('as being an American citizen')
⎰to be⎰ ⎰American ('as being of American nationality')

Unique reference: proper nouns
4.40
Proper nouns are names of specific people (*Shakespeare*), places (*Milwaukee*), countries (*Australia*), months (*September*), days (*Thursday*), holidays (*Christmas*), magazines (*Vogue*), and so forth. Names have 'unique' reference, and (as we have seen in 4.2) do not share the characteristics of common nouns. In particular, they lack articles, or rather article contrast (*Paris* ~ **The Paris, The Hague* ~ *Hague ~ *A Hague). Proper nouns are written with initial capital letters. So also, frequently, are a number of common nouns with unique reference, which are therefore close to proper nouns, *eg: fate, fortune, heaven, hell, nature, paradise*.

However, when the names have restrictive modification to give a partitive meaning to the name (*cf* 4.36), proper nouns take the (cataphoric) definite article.

UNIQUE MEANING	PARTITIVE MEANING
during Easter	during the Easter of that year
in Elizabethan England	in the England of Queen Elizabeth
in Denmark	in the Denmark of today
Chicago	the Chicago I like (= 'the aspect of Chicago')
Shakespeare	the young Shakespeare

Proper names can be reclassified as common nouns, in which case they assume the characteristics of count nouns, *ie* take articles and plural number:

Shakespeare (the author)   ⎰a Shakespeare ('an author like S.')
⎰Shakespeares ('authors like S.')

There are also some other cases of proper nouns with article (4.46–47) but we will first consider some regular examples.

Proper nouns with no article
4.41
The following list exemplifies the main classes of proper nouns that take no article in accordance with the main rule (4.40):

Personal names (with or without titles; 4.42)

Temporal names (4.43)

(a) Festivals
(b) Months and days of the week

Geographical names (4.44)

(a) Continents
(b) Countries, counties, states, etc
(c) Cities, towns, etc
(d) Lakes
(e) Mountains

Name + common noun (4.45)

4.42
PERSONAL NAMES
Personal names with or without titles (*cf* apposition, 9.160 *ff*):

Dr Brown	Lady Churchill
President Kennedy	Cardinal Spellman
Mr and Mrs Johnson	General MacArthur
Professor and Mrs Smith	Captain O'Connor
Private Walker	Inspector Harris
Lord Nelson	Judge Darling (mainly AmE)

Note the following exceptions:

the Emperor Napoleon	the Lord (God)
(but: Emperor Haile Selassie)	(the) Czar Alexander
the Duke of Wellington	(the) Rev Smith

The article may also precede other titles, including *Lord* and *Lady* in formal use. Family relations with unique reference behave like proper nouns:

Father (Daddy, Dad, familiar) is here
Mother (Mummy, Mum, familiar) is out
Uncle will come on Saturday

Compare:

The father was the tallest in the family

4.43

TEMPORAL NAMES

(a) Names of festivals:

Christmas (Day)	Independence Day
Easter (Sunday)	Whit(sun) (mainly BrE)
Good Friday	Passover

(b) Names of the months and the days of the week:

January, February, ...
Monday, Tuesday, ...

Note that the days of the week have plurals (*I hate Mondays*); along with *next* and *last* + a noun, they have zero article when they are connected with a point of time implicit in the linguistic or situational context. Compare:

We'll leave $\begin{cases} \text{on Sunday} \\ \text{next month} \end{cases}$

He left $\begin{cases} \text{on the next Sunday} \\ \text{the} \begin{cases} \text{next} \\ \text{following} \end{cases} \text{month} \end{cases}$

Cf He left on a Sunday (without reference to a particular Sunday)

4.44

GEOGRAPHICAL NAMES
(*Cf* apposition, 9.162)

(a) Names of continents (normally no article also with premodifying adjective)

(North) America	(Medieval) Europe
(Central) Australia	(East) Africa

Note *Antarctica* but *the Antarctic*, like *the Arctic*

(b) Names of countries, counties, states, etc (normally no article with premodifying adjective)

(Elizabethan) England	(French) Canada
(modern) Brazil	(industrial) Staffordshire
(west) Scotland	(northern) Arkansas

Note *Argentina* but *the Argentine, the Ruhr, the Saar, the Sahara, the Ukraine, the Crimea, (the) Lebanon, (the) Congo; the Midwest; the Everglades* (and other plural names, see 4.47).

(c) Cities and towns (normally no article with premodifying word)

(downtown) Boston	(central) Brussels
(ancient) Rome	(suburban) London

Note *The Hague; the Bronx; the City, the West End, the East End (of London)*

(d) Lakes

Lake Windermere	(Lake) Ladoga
Lake Michigan	Silver Lake

(e) Mountains

Mount Everest	(Mount) Snowdon
Mount Vernon	Vesuvius
Mont Blanc	Ben Nevis

Note *the Mount of Olives*

4.45
NAME+COMMON NOUN
Name+common noun denoting buildings, streets, bridges, etc.

Hampstead Heath	Windsor Castle
Oxford Street	Buckingham Palace
Madison Avenue	Westminster Abbey
Park Lane	Canterbury Cathedral
Portland Place	Kennedy Airport
Bredon Hill	Paddington Station
Piccadilly Circus	Epping Forest
Leicester Square	Hampton Court
Westminster Bridge	Scotland Yard

Note *the Albert Hall, the Mansion House; the Haymarket, the Strand, the Mall* (street names in London); *the Merrit Parkway, the Pennsylvania Turnpike; (the) Oxford Road* as a proper name but only *the Oxford road* to denote 'the road leading to Oxford'.

Note
Names of universities where the first part is a place-name can usually have two forms: *the University of London* (which is the official name) and *London University*. Universities named after a person have only the latter form: *Yale University, Brown University*, etc.

Proper nouns with definite article
4.46
Most of the proper nouns which take the definite article turn out to be only apparent exceptions to the main rule if we consider them in relation

to the rules of English noun-phrase structure as a whole. Many proper nouns are common nouns with unique reference. *The New York Times, the Suez Canal, the British Museum,* etc are perfectly regular in taking the definite article, since they are basically premodified count nouns (*cf the long canal, the interesting museum,* etc). The difference between an ordinary common noun and a common noun turned name is that the unique reference of the name has been institutionalized, as is made overt in writing by initial capital letter. The following structural classification illustrates the use of such proper nouns with the definite article:

WITHOUT MODIFICATION

The Guardian   *The Times*

WITH PREMODIFICATION

the Suez Canal   *The Washington Post*
the English Channel   the Brains Trust
the National Gallery   the American Civil War
the Socialist Bookshop   the Ohio University Press
the Ford Foundation   the British Broadcasting
                                              Corporation (the BBC)

WITH POSTMODIFICATION

the House of Commons   the Cambridge College of Arts
the Institute of Psychiatry   and Technology
the Bay of Fundy   the District of Columbia

ELLIPTED ELEMENTS

The original structure of a proper noun is sometimes unclear when one element has been dropped and the elliptic form has become institutionalized as the full name:

the Tate (Gallery)   the Mermaid (Theatre)
the Atlantic (Ocean)   the (River) Thames
the Mediterranean (Sea)   the Majestic (Hotel)

4.47

The following classes of proper nouns are used with the definite article:

(a) Plural names (in general)

      the Wilsons (='the Wilson family')
      the Netherlands
      the Midlands

the Hebrides, the Shetlands, the Canaries (or the Canary
  Islands), the Bahamas
the Himalayas, the Alps, the Rockies (or the Rocky
  Mountains), the Pyrenees

Note *Kensington Gardens, Burnham Beeches*

(b) Geographical names

Rivers: the Avon, the Danube, the Euphrates,
        the Potomac, the Rhine, the Thames
Seas: the Pacific (Ocean), the Baltic, the Kattegatt
Canals: the Panama Canal, the Erie Canal

(c) Public institutions, facilities, etc

Hotels and restaurants:

the Grand (Hotel), the Waldorf Astoria, the Savoy

Theatres, cinemas, clubs, etc:

the Criterion, the Globe, the Athenaeum

Museums, libraries, etc:

the Tate, the British Museum

Note *Drury Lane, Covent Garden*

(d) Newspapers: *The Economist, The New York Times, The Observer,*
The Providence Journal

After genitives and possessives the article is dropped: *today's New*
York Times.

But note that magazines and periodicals normally have the zero
article: *Language, Life, Time, Punch, English Language Teaching,*
New Scientist.

Number
4.48

The English number system has two terms: SINGULAR, which denotes
'one', and PLURAL, which denotes 'more than one'. There is number
concord between subjects and finite verbs, *ie* a singular subject requires
a singular verb and a plural subject requires a plural verb: *the bird is*
flying/the birds are flying (3.10, 7.23). INVARIABLES cannot change
their number but are either singular (*gold*) or plural (*cattle*). The singular category includes common mass nouns (4.2) and proper nouns
(4.40 *ff*). Count nouns are VARIABLE NOUNS and can occur with
either singular or plural number (*boy~boys*).

invariable	*singular invariables*	mass nouns: concrete	gold	(4.49)
		mass nouns: abstract	music	(4.50)
		proper nouns	Henry	(4.51)
		some nouns ending in *-s*	news	(4.52)
		abstract adjectival heads	the beautiful	(4.53)
	plural invariables	summation plurals	scissors	(4.54)
		other pluralia tantum in *-s*	thanks	(4.55)
		some proper nouns	the Netherlands	(4.56)
		unmarked plural nouns	cattle	(4.57)
		personal adjectival heads	the rich	(4.58)

▶

variable	*regular plurals*	+ /ɪz/ horse horses		
		+ /z/ boy boys		(4.60–63)
		+ /s/ cat cats		

irregular plurals

VOICING
- /θ/ → /ð/ + /z/   bath   baths
- /f/ → /v/ + /z/   calf   calves   (4.65)
- /s/ → /z/ + /ɪz/   house   houses

MUTATION ——————— foot   feet   (4.66)

-EN PLURAL ——————— ox   oxen   (4.67)

ZERO ———————
- sheep   sheep
- Chinese   Chinese   (4.68–73)
- series   series

FOREIGN
-us →	*-i*	radius	radii	
	-ora	corpus	corpora	(4.75)
	-era	genus	genera	
-a → *-ae*		larva	larvae	(4.76)
-um → *-a*		stratum	strata	(4.77)
-ex / *-ix* → *-ices*		matrix	matrices	(4.78)
-is → *-es*		thesis	theses	(4.79)
-on → *-a*		criterion	criteria	(4.80)
-eau → *-eaux*		tableau	tableaux	(4.81)
zero (spelling only)		corps	corps	(4.82)
-o → *-i*		tempo	tempi	(4.83)
base + *-im*		cherub	cherubim	(4.84)

Fig 4:8 Number classes

Fig 4:8 gives an overview of the different number categories and their relationships. The numbers on the right-hand side indicate the section where the particular type is discussed.

Note

[a] In addition to singular and plural number, we may distinguish dual number in the case of *both*, *either*, and *neither* (4.13 *ff*, 4.127 *f*) since they can only be used with reference to two. Compare

Number of people

1	One	⎫
2	Both	⎬ of the students passed
3, 4, ...	All	⎭

[b] Unlike some languages where plural implies 'two or more', English makes the division after 'more than one' (*cf* 13.71):

I can stay only ⎰ one day
one and a half days
two days
one or two days

But:

I'll buy a pound and a half
I'll stay a day or two

Singular invariable nouns
4.49
Concrete mass nouns

Concrete mass nouns have no plural: *gold, silver, uranium*, etc. Reclassifications of mass nouns as count nouns have specific meanings, for example *butters* ('kinds of butter') and *a beer* ('a glass or can of beer'). (See 4.2 Note *a*, App I.40.)

4.50
Abstract mass nouns

These also have no plural: *music, dirt, homework*, etc. See, however, *injustices*, etc (4.3, App I.40).

4.51
Proper nouns

These take a singular verb and are typically invariable: *Henry, the Thames*, etc (4.40 *ff*).

4.52
Invariable nouns ending in *-s*

Note the following classes which take a singular verb, except where otherwise mentioned:

(a) *news:* Here is the 10 o'clock news

(b) SOME DISEASES: *measles, German measles, mumps, rickets, shingles*. Some speakers also accept a plural verb with words like *mumps*.

(c) SUBJECT NAMES IN *-ICS* (usually with singular verb): *classics, linguistics, mathematics, phonetics*
Similarly: *athletics, ceramics, ethics, gymnastics, politics, tactics* (*tactics requires/require concentration of troops*)

(d) SOME GAMES: *billiards, bowls* (especially BrE), *darts, dominoes, draughts* (BrE), *checkers* (AmE), *fives, ninepins*
But: *a billiard-table, a bowling-alley, a dart-board, a draught-board*

(e) SOME PROPER NOUNS: *Algiers, Athens, Brussels, Flanders, Marseilles, Naples, Wales; the United Nations* and *the United States* have a singular verb when considered as units.

4.53
Abstract adjectival heads
Abstract adjectival heads take a singular verb (*the beautiful* = *that which is beautiful;* see 4.33): *the beautiful, the evil, the good*.

Plural invariable nouns
4.54
Summation plurals
Tools and articles of dress consisting of two equal parts which are joined constitute summation plurals. The noun of which they are head can be made singular and countable by means of *a pair of: a pair of scissors*.

bellows	braces (BrE)
binoculars	flannels
pincers	knickers
pliers	pants
scales ('a balance')	pyjamas, pajamas (AmE) (*but* a
scissors	pyjama cord)
shears	shorts
tongs	suspenders (*but* a suspender belt)
tweezers	tights
glasses ('spectacles')	trousers (*but* a trouser leg)
spectacles (*but* a spectacle case)	

Note

[a] *Pyjamas/pajamas* is the only garment here with a separate top and bottom.

[b] Many of the 'summation plurals' can take the indefinite article, especially with premodification: *a garden shears, a curling-tongs*, etc (*cf* zero plurals, 4.68 *ff*).

4.55

Other 'pluralia tantum' in -*s*

Among other 'pluralia tantum' (*ie* nouns that only occur in the plural), the following nouns end in -*s*. In many cases, however, there are forms without -*s*, sometimes with change of meaning and sometimes merely in premodification.

the Middle Ages	
amends (make every/all possible amends)	
annals	
the antipodes	
archives	
arms ('weapons', an arms depot)	
arrears	
ashes (burn to ashes)	cigarette ash, ash-tray, Ash Wednesday
auspices	
banns (of marriage)	
bowels	bowel-movement
brain(s) ('the intellect', he's got good brains, *besides* a good brain)	
clothes /kloʊz/	cloths /klɒθs/ *which is the plural of* cloth
the Commons (the House of Commons)	
contents	the silver content of a coin
customs (customs duty, customs house)	
dregs (coffee dregs)	
earnings	
entrails	
fireworks (*also fig:* there were plenty of fireworks at the staff meeting)	
funds ('money', for lack of funds)	*regular homonym:* a relief fund ('a sum of money for a particular purpose')
goods (a goods train)	
greens	
guts ('bowels'; *also familiar:* he's got the guts to do it)	*regular mass noun in* cat-gut
heads (heads or tails?)	
holidays (summer holidays, BrE)	a holiday camp

letters (a man of letters)

lodgings (a lodgings bureau) · a lodging house, a poor lodging

looks (he has good looks) · give somebody a hard look

the Lords (the House of Lords)

manners

means (man of means, a means test)

minutes (the minutes of a meeting) · *but* 'I have a question about minute No 54'; *regular homonym:* in a minute (= 60 seconds)

oats · oatmeal; oatcake (*especially Scots*)

odds (in betting)

outskirts

pains (take pains, be at pains) · *regular homonym:* bodily pain

particulars (take down the particulars)

premises ('building' *in official style:* 'There is a suspect on the premises') · premise (in logic)

quarters, headquarters · *but* the Latin quarter ('district')

regards · win the regard of all

remains

riches

savings (a savings bank, a savings account)

spirits ('mood': to be in good spirits) · He showed a kindly spirit

spirits ('alcohol': to drink spirits) · Alcohol is a spirit

stairs (a flight of stairs) · staircase, stairway

suds

surroundings

sweepstake(s) · a sweepstake-ticket

tails (heads or tails?)

thanks

troops · a troop carrier, troop movement; *regular homonym:* a troop of scouts

tropics · the Tropic of Cancer

valuables

wages (to earn high wages) · a wage-earner, a wage-packet (BrE), a living wage, a good/poor/high wage

| wits (live by one's wits) | *homonyms, count:* He is a great wit; *mass singular:* His speech had wit |

4.56
Some proper nouns
(On the definite article, see 4.46 *f*)

ITEMS	EXCEPTIONS
the East/West Indies	
the Hebrides (*also in* 'the Hebrides Overture')	
the Highlands	a Highland terrier/fling/ character
the Midlands	the Midland region
the Netherlands (the Netherlands government)	

4.57
Invariable unmarked plurals

ITEMS	EXCEPTIONS
cattle	
clergy	*sometimes singular:* The clergy is to blame for the birth control problem
gentry	
people	*homonym count:* the English-speaking peoples
police	
vermin	
youth (the youth of a nation)	*homonym count:* The police arrested two youths (4.65)

4.58
Personal adjectival heads
Personal adjectival heads take a plural verb (*the rich = those who are rich*, 4.33)

the helpless   the (very) rich
the needy   the sick
the poor   the weary, etc

Variable nouns
4.59
Variable nouns have two forms: one singular and one plural. The singular is the unmarked form that is listed in dictionaries. For the vast majority of variable nouns, the plural is fully predictable from the singular, *ie*
they form the regular plural. If the plural cannot be predicted from the
singular, it is an irregular plural.

Regular plurals
4.60
The regular plural is formed by means of an *-s* suffix (the '*-s* plural').
The realization of this *-s* noun suffix in speech and writing follows the
same rules as the 3rd person singular verb suffix *-s* and, in speech, as
the contracted forms of *is* and *has* (3.18*f*) as well as the genitive
(4.96): see 3.55.

4.61
THE PRONUNCIATION OF THE REGULAR PLURAL
In speech, the regular plural has three different pronunciations (/ɪz/, /z/,
/s/) depending on the final sound of the base.

/ɪz/ after bases ending in sibilants:

/s/	horse	→ horses	/ʒ/	mirage	→ mirages
/z/	size	→ sizes	/tʃ/	church	→ churches
/ʃ/	rush	→ rushes	/dʒ/	language	→ languages

/z/ after bases ending in vowels and voiced sounds other than /z/, /ʒ/, /dʒ/:

bed → beds   hero → heroes

/s/ after bases ending in voiceless sounds other than /s/, /ʃ/, /tʃ/:

bet → bets   month → months

4.62
THE SPELLING OF THE REGULAR PLURAL
The *-s* suffix is written *-s* after most nouns including nouns ending in
silent *e* (*college ∼ colleges*).

There are several classes of exceptions:

(a) ADDITION OF *E*. The ending is spelled *-es* after nouns ending in sibilants, unless the noun is written with a silent *e:*

-s	gas	→ gases	*-ch*	porch	→ porches
-z	buzz	→ buzzes	*-sh*	bush	→ bushes
-x	box	→ boxes	*-ze*	size	→ sizes

(b) TREATMENT OF *- Y*

$$-y \rightarrow \begin{cases} -ys \begin{cases} \text{after vowel: } days \text{ (but nouns in } \textit{-quy}/\text{kwɪ}/ \text{ have } \textit{-quies)} \\ \text{in proper nouns: } the \ two \ Germanys, \ the \ Kennedys \\ \text{in } stand\text{-}bys, \ lay\text{-}bys, \text{ and } drys \text{ (informal AmE} \\ \quad \text{`prohibitionists')} \end{cases} \\ \textit{-ies} \text{ otherwise after consonant: } spy \rightarrow spies \end{cases}$$

(c) DOUBLING OF CONSONANT in a few words

fez → fezzes
quiz → quizzes
bus → busses (AmE, *besides* buses)

Doubling also occurs in some abbreviations:

p   → pp (pages)
l   → ll (lines)
MS → MSS (manuscripts)

(d) APOSTROPHE (*'s*) in some cases:

letters:	*dot your i's*
numerals:	*in the 1890's* or *1890s*
abbreviations:	*two MP's* or *MPs*
	three PhD's or *PhDs*

The variant without apostrophe is on the increase.

The regular plural suffix of nouns in *-o* has two spellings: *-os* and *-oes*. In the following cases the spelling is *-os:*

(a) after a vowel: *bamboos, embryos, folios, kangaroos, radios, studios, zoos;* exceptions are *goes* and *noes*
(b) in proper names: *Filipinos, Neros, Romeos, Eskimos, cf* 4.70 Note
(c) in abbreviations: *kilos* (<*kilogramme*), *photos* (<*photograph*), *pros* (<*professional*); *cf* also *pianos* and *taxis*, though these are scarcely regarded any longer as abbreviations

In other cases there is considerable vacillation, as the following sample shows. Less common forms are parenthesized.

	-os	*-oes*
concerto	concertos	
dynamo	dynamos	
quarto	quartos	
solo	solos (*cf* 4.83, soli)	
soprano	sopranos	
tango	tangos	
tobacco	tobaccos	
archipelago	archipelagos	archipelagoes
banjo	banjos	banjoes
buffalo	buffalos	buffaloes
cargo	cargos	cargoes
commando	commandos	commandoes
Dago	Dagos	Dagoes
flamingo	flamingos	(flamingoes)
halo	halos	haloes
motto	(mottos)	mottoes
tornado	tornados	tornadoes
volcano	volcanos	volcanoes
echo		echoes
embargo		embargoes
hero		heroes
Negro		Negroes
potato		potatoes
tomato		tomatoes
torpedo		torpedoes
veto		vetoes

4.63
COMPOUNDS
Compounds form the plural in different ways.

(a) PLURAL IN FIRST ELEMENT

attorney general	attorneys general (more usually as (c) below)
notary public (especially AmE)	notaries public
passer-by	passers-by
mother-in-law	mothers-in-law (also as (c) informally)
grant-in-aid	grants-in-aid
man-of-war	men-of-war
coat of mail	coats of mail

(b) PLURAL IN BOTH FIRST AND LAST ELEMENT

gentleman farmer	gentlemen farmers
manservant	menservants
woman doctor	women doctors

(c) PLURAL IN LAST ELEMENT (*ie* normal)

assistant director	assistant directors
boy friend	boy friends
fountain pen	fountain pens
woman-hater	woman-haters
breakdown	breakdowns
close-up	close-ups
grown-up	grown-ups
sit-in	sit-ins
lay-by (BrE)	lay-bys (NB: spelling)
stand-by	stand-bys (NB: spelling)
take-off	take-offs
gin-and-tonic	gin-and-tonics
forget-me-not	forget-me-nots
mouthful	{ mouthfuls / mouthsful }
spoonful	{ spoonfuls / spoonsful }

Irregular plurals

4.64

Irregular plurals are by definition unpredictable. Whereas the plurals /ɪz/ in *horses*, /z/ in *dogs*, and /s/ in *cats* can be inferred from the final sound in the singular of the nouns, there is no indication in the written or spoken forms of, say, *ox*, *sheep*, and *analysis* to suggest that their plurals are *oxen*, *sheep*, and *analyses*. The particular plurals of these nouns have to be learned as individual lexical units. In many cases where foreign words are involved, it is of course helpful to know about pluralization in the relevant languages, particularly Latin and Greek. On the pattern of

analysis → analyses

we can infer the correct plurals:

axis	→ axes
basis	→ bases
crisis	→ crises, etc

But we cannot rely on etymological criteria: plurals like *areas* and *villas*, for example, do not conform to the Latin pattern (*areae, villae*). See 4.76.

4.65

VOICING+-*S* PLURAL

Some nouns which in the singular end in the final voiceless fricatives /θ/, /f/, and /s/ have voicing to /ð/, /v/, and /z/, respectively:

(a) -*th* /θ/   → -*ths* /ðz/   bath   baths
(b) -*f(e)* /f/   → -*ves* /vz/   calf   calves
(c) -*s* /s/   → -*ses* /zɪz/   house   houses

The voicing of -*s* words occurs only in *house*. There is considerable indeterminacy between voicing and non-voicing in many words ending in -*th* and -*f(e)*:

(a) NOUNS IN -*th* /θ/	SINGULAR	PLURAL	
		/θs/	/ðz/
regular plural is normal after a consonant+*th:*	berth	berths	
	birth	births	
	earth	earths	
	hearth	hearths	
	length	lengths	
regular plural often occurs also after a vowel+*th:*	cloth	cloths	
	death	deaths	
	faith	faiths	
	heath	heaths	
	moth	moths	
	sloth	sloths	
double forms in:	oath	oaths	oaths
	sheath	sheaths	sheaths
	truth	truths	truths
	wreath	wreaths	wreaths
only voicing+-*s* plural in:	bath		baths
	mouth		mouths
	path		paths
	youth		youths

(b) NOUNS IN -*f(e)* /f/ :

	SINGULAR	PLURAL /fs/	/vz/
regular plural is normal:	belief	beliefs	
	chief	chiefs	
	cliff	cliffs	
	proof	proofs	
	roof	roofs	
	safe	safes	
double forms in:	dwarf	dwarfs	dwarves
	handker-chief	handker-chiefs	handker-chieves
	hoof	hoofs	hooves
	scarf	scarfs	scarves
	wharf	wharfs	wharves
only voicing + -*s* plural in:	calf		calves
	elf		elves
	half		halves
	knife		knives
	leaf		leaves
	life		lives
	loaf		loaves
	self		selves
	sheaf		sheaves
	shelf		shelves
	thief		thieves
	wife		wives
	wolf		wolves

Note
The painting term *still life* has a regular plural: *still lifes*.

4.66
MUTATION
Mutation involves a change of the medial vowel in the following seven nouns:

foot	feet	also *forefeet*
tooth	teeth	
goose	geese	

louse	lice	
mouse	mice	
man	men	*menservants* but *man-eaters* (see 4.63)
woman	women	

Note

[a] *Postman/postmen* and *Englishman/Englishmen* have no distinction in speech between singular and plural.

[b] *Mongoose* and *German* are not related to *goose* and *man*, respectively, and have regular plurals: *mongooses, Germans*.

4.67

THE -*EN* PLURAL

This occurs in three nouns:

brother	brethren	*brethren* (with mutation) = 'fellow members of a religious society'; otherwise regular *brothers*
child	children	(with vowel change /aɪ/ → /ɪ/)
ox	oxen	

Note

Penny $\begin{cases} \text{pence (irregular) in British currency: } \textit{Here is ten pence} \\ \text{pennies (regular) for individual coins: } \textit{Here are ten pennies} \end{cases}$

ZERO PLURAL

4.68

Some nouns have the same spoken and written form in both singular and plural. Note the difference here between, on the one hand, invariable nouns, which are either singular (*This music is too loud*) or plural (*All the cattle are grazing in the field*), and, on the other, zero plural nouns, which are variable in taking both singular and plural verb (*This sheep looks small, All those sheep are mine*).

4.69

Animal names

Animal names often have zero plurals. They tend to be used partly by people who are especially concerned with animals, partly when the animals are referred to in mass as food or game. With animal names that have two plurals, the zero plural is the more common to denote hunting quarries, eg: *We caught only a few fish*, whereas the regular plural is used to denote different individuals, species, etc: *the fishes of the Mediterranean*. When usage is variable, this has been indicated in the lists below, where minority forms are parenthesized.

	SINGULAR	PLURAL	
		regular	*zero*

Animal names that have the regular plural include the following:	bird cow dog eagle hawk hen lark monkey rabbit sparrow	birds cows dogs eagles hawks hens larks monkeys rabbits sparrows	
The following may have both plurals:	elk crab antelope duck reindeer fish flounder herring pike trout carp deer moose	elks crabs antelopes ducks (*farm-yard*) reindeers fishes flounders herrings (pikes) (trouts) (carps) (deers) (mooses)	(elk) (crab) antelope duck (*wild*) reindeer fish flounder herring pike trout carp deer moose
The following have only the zero plural:	grouse sheep plaice salmon		grouse sheep plaice salmon

4.70

Nationality names

Zero plurals occur with names in -*ese:*

Ceylonese	Lebanese
Chinese	Portuguese
Japanese	Vietnamese

Also: Sioux

Note
Certain nationality and tribal names are sometimes used without -s:

Bedouin(s), Eskimo(s), Navaho(s)

4.71
Some quantitative and partitive nouns
Preceded by a numeral or other indication of number, these frequently have zero plurals. In general, the zero forms are relatively informal except as premodifiers (*two hundred books*), when there is usually no alternative form (see Note).

	ZERO PLURALS	REGULAR PLURALS
two	{dozen glasses {dozen of these glasses	dozens of glasses
several	{hundred books {hundred of these books	hundreds of books
many	thousand insects	thousands of insects
five	{million people {million	millions of people five millions
a few	billion stars	billions of stars
eight	ton of coal	eight tons of coal
two	brace of partridges	
several	head of cattle	
ten	yoke of oxen	
five	hundredweight (of coal) (especially BrE)	
ten	gross of nails	
ten	stone (BrE weight)	
five	foot two ⎫(normal if	five feet
six	pound fifty ⎭ numeral follows)	six pounds

Note
Nouns denoting measure, quantity, etc, normally have zero plural when they are pre-modifiers in noun phrases, *eg*:

a ten-pound note	a five-second pause
a five-dollar bill	a ten-minute conversation
a twelve-inch ruler	a two-hour exam
a four-foot ladder	a sixty-acre farm
a six-mile walk	a five-yard space
a six-lane highway	a six-cylinder car

4.72

Nouns in -s

The following nouns invariably end in -*s:*

alms (*rare except in* live on alms, an alms-house)
barracks (an army barracks)
gallows (a/two gallows)
headquarters (a busy headquarters, the headquarters is/are here)
innings (a long innings, two innings, *BrE in cricket; AmE has the
    regular* an inning ~ two innings *in baseball*)
links ('grassy land near the sea': a golf-links; *the normal term is*
    a golf course)
means (language is a means of communication)
works (a gasworks, an ironworks, several waterworks)

Note

Die (in the expression *the die is cast*) is no longer recognized as being connected with *dice*, which also belongs here: *one dice/two dice*, or perhaps *one of the dice* for the singular. (*Die* 'engraved stamp for coining, etc') has the regular plural *dies*.)

4.73

Nouns in -es

A few nouns in -*es* /iz/ or /ɪz/, for example, *series, species*, have the same form in singular and plural: *this series is . . . , the two species are. . .* Although historically foreign, these zero plurals are probably not felt to be 'foreign' in the same way as, for instance, *basis ~ bases.*

FOREIGN PLURALS
4.74

Foreign plurals often occur in variation with regular plurals. The arrangement in 4.75 *ff* is not intended to serve as a guide to the plural formation of all such problematic words. For this a dictionary must be consulted. One rule-of-thumb is that foreign plurals often occur in technical usage, whereas the -*s* plural is the most natural in everyday language; *cf: formulas* (general) ~ *formulae* (in mathematics), *antennas* (general and in electronics) ~ *antennae* (in biology).

Our aim here will be to survey systematically the main types of foreign plurals that are used in present-day English and to consider the extent to which a particular plural form is obligatory or optional. For practical purposes, the lists are general and are not restricted to words that originate from the languages mentioned in the headings.

For the various noun endings, the order will be to start with the native plural, then list words with both native and foreign plurals, and end with words that have only foreign plurals. This will display the scale character of the language: the most open and the most closed types of plural formation occur as poles with the mixed types in between. This classification also seems realistic in view of frequent lack of agreement on the plural formation of many words. Within each of the three classes, the nouns have been listed in alphabetical order.

4.75

Nouns in -us /əs/ → $\begin{Bmatrix} \text{-i /aɪ/} \\ \text{-ora} \\ \text{-era} \end{Bmatrix}$ /ərə/ $\Big\}$ (*Latin*)

	REGULAR (*-uses*)	FOREIGN
bonus	bonuses	
bus	buses; busses (especially AmE)	
campus	campuses	
chorus	choruses	
circus	circuses	
genius	geniuses	
ignoramus	ignoramuses	
impetus	impetuses	
minus	minuses	
prospectus	prospectuses	
virus	viruses	
cactus	cactuses	cacti
crocus	crocuses	croci
focus	focuses	foci
fungus	funguses	fungi
isthmus	isthmuses	isthmi
nucleus	nucleuses	nuclei
radius	radiuses	radii
stylus	styluses	styli
syllabus	syllabuses	syllabi
terminus	terminuses	termini
corpus	(corpuses)	corpora
alumnus		alumni
bacillus		bacilli
locus		loci /-s-/
stimulus		stimuli
genus		genera

4.76
Nouns in -a /ə/ → -ae /i/ (*Latin*)

	REGULAR (-*as*)	FOREIGN (-*ae* /i/)
area	areas	
arena	arenas	
dilemma	dilemmas	
diploma	diplomas	
drama	dramas	
encyclopedia	encyclopedias	
era	eras	
idea	ideas	
panacea	panaceas	
panorama	panoramas	
quota	quotas	
retina	retinas	
sofa	sofas	
sonata	sonatas	
umbrella	umbrellas	
villa	villas	
antenna	antennas	antennae
formula	formulas	formulae
nebula	nebulas	nebulae
vertebra	vertebras	vertebrae
alga		algae
alumna		alumnae
larva		larvae

4.77
Nouns in -um /əm/ → -a /ə/ (*Latin*)

	REGULAR (-*ums*)	FOREIGN (-*a*)
album	albums	
asylum	asylums	
chrysanthemum	chrysanthemums	
museum	museums	
aquarium	aquariums	aquaria
curriculum	(curriculums)	curricula
forum	forums	(fora)
medium	mediums	media

Nouns in -um /əm/ → -a /ə/ (*Latin*) *continued*

	REGULAR (-*ums*)	FOREIGN (-*a*)
memorandum	memorandums	memoranda
moratorium	moratoriums	moratoria
stadium	stadiums	(stadia)
symposium	symposiums	symposia
ultimatum	ultimatums	(ultimata)
addendum		addenda
bacterium		bacteria
corrigendum		corrigenda
desideratum		desiderata
erratum		errata
ovum		ova
stratum		strata

Note

Datum is much less common than its original Latin plural *data* ('information, especially information organized for analysis'), which in English is usually constructed as a plural (*These data are inconclusive*), but often also as a singular, especially in scientific contexts (*This data is inconclusive*). The regular English plural *datums* occurs in the sense of 'a point', etc used as a reference in surveying.

4.78

Nouns in $\left\{\begin{array}{l}\text{-ex}\\\text{-ix}\end{array}\right\}$ → -ices /ısiz/ (*Latin*)

	REGULAR $\left\{\begin{array}{l}(\text{-}exes)\\(\text{-}ixes)\end{array}\right\}$	FOREIGN (-*ices*)
apex	apexes	apices
index	indexes	indices
vortex	vortexes	vortices
appendix	appendixes (anatomical)	appendices (in books)
matrix	matrixes	matrices
codex		codices

4.79
Nouns in -is /ɪs/ → -es /iz/ (*Greek*)

	REGULAR (*-ises*)	FOREIGN (*-es*)
metropolis	metropolises	
analysis		analyses
axis		axes
basis		bases
crisis		crises
diagnosis		diagnoses
ellipsis		ellipses
hypothesis		hypotheses
oasis		oases
parenthesis		parentheses
synopsis		synopses
thesis		theses

Note
Bases can be either the plural of *base* (pronounced / 'beɪsɪz/ or the plural of *basis* (pronounced /'beɪˌsiz/).

4.80
Nouns in -on /ən/ → -a /ə/ (*Greek*)

	REGULAR (*-ons*)	FOREIGN (*-a*)
demon	demons	
electron	electrons	
neutron	neutrons	
proton	protons	
automaton	automatons	automata
ganglion	ganglions	(ganglia)
criterion		criteria
phenomenon		phenomena

4.81

Nouns in -eau /oʊ/ → -eaux /oʊz/ (French; only the spelling is irregular in English.)

	REGULAR (-*eaus*)	FOREIGN (-*eaux*)
trousseau /usoʊ/	trousseaus	trousseaux
plateau	plateaus	plateaux
portmanteau (rather rare)	portmanteaus	portmanteaux
bureau	bureaus	bureaux
tableau	(tableaus)	tableaux
cf also		
adieu /ju/	adieus	adieux

4.82

Some nouns in -s and -x have zero (French; the zero plural is restricted to writing. The plural is regular in speech.)

chamois /ˈʃæmwɑ/
chassis /ˈʃæsɪ/
corps /kə(r)/
faux pas /pɑ/
patois /ˈpætwɑ/

4.83

Nouns in -o /oʊ/ → -i /ɪ/ (Italian)

	REGULAR (-*os*)	FOREIGN (-*i*)
soprano	sopranos	
virtuoso	virtuosos	(virtuosi)
libretto	librettos	(libretti)
solo	solos	(soli)
tempo	tempos	(tempi)
(graffito)		graffiti [usually plural]

For the spelling of the regular /z/-suffix, see below.

Note

Confetti (from Italian *confetto*, which is not used in English) takes a singular verb.

4.84
Nouns with -im plurals (Hebrew)

	REGULAR (-s)	FOREIGN (-im)
cherub	cherubs	(cherubim)
seraph	seraphs	(seraphim)
kibbutz		kibbutzim

Gender
4.85
In the same way as we have 'time' in nature and 'tense' in the grammar of the verb (3.23), we have a similar relation between 'sex' and the 'gender' of the noun. English makes very few gender distinctions. Where they are made, the connection between the biological category 'sex' and the grammatical category 'gender' is very close, in so far as natural sex distinctions determine English gender distinctions. (Compare this with, for example, the neuter gender for 'girl' in German: *das Mädchen*.)

It is further typical of English that special suffixes are not generally used to mark gender distinctions. For example, English *cousin* corresponds to both the French masculine *cousin* and the feminine *cousine*. Nor are gender distinctions made in the article. (Compare *the* with Ger-

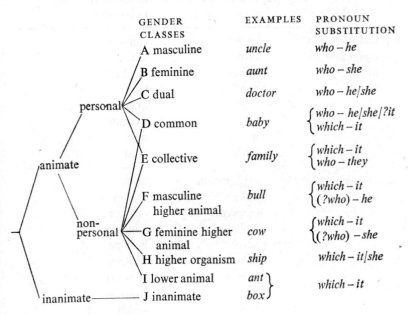

Fig 4:9 Gender classes

man *der/die/das* or French *le/la*.) English gender is, however, reflected in the *he/she/it* set of 3rd person personal pronouns. English gender may be generally described as COVERT in contrast to the OVERT gender system of many languages.

Some pronouns are gender-sensitive (the personal *he*, *she*, *it* and the relative *who*, *which*) but others are not (*some*, *these*, etc; see 4.109). The combinations of gender-sensitive pronouns (and, in addition, *they*) that substitute for singular nouns give us a set of ten gender classes as illustrated in *Fig* 4:9.

Note

If number of invariable nouns was also taken into account, additional classes would have to be set up for nouns like *people* (*they* – *who*), *dirt* (*it* – *which*), etc.

4.86
[A/B] Personal masculine/feminine nouns

These nouns are of two types. Type (i) has no overt marking that suggests morphological correspondence between masculine and feminine, whereas in Type (ii) the two gender forms have a derivational relationship. The derivational suffixes are not productive, however. We cannot except jocularly, for example, form *clerk/*clerkess* on the *host/hostess* pattern (*cf* App I.22).

	[A] PERSONAL MASCULINE	[B] PERSONAL FEMININE
(*i*) *morphologically unmarked for gender*	bachelor	spinster
	brother	sister
	father	mother
	gentleman	lady
	king	queen
	man	woman
	monk	nun
	uncle	aunt
(*ii*) *morphologically marked for gender*	bridegroom	bride
	duke	duchess
	emperor	empress
	god	goddess
	hero	heroine
	host	hostess
	steward	stewardess
	waiter	waitress
	widower	widow

Some masculine/feminine pairs denoting kinship have common (dual) generic terms, for example, *parent* for *father/mother*, and *child* for *son/ daughter* as well as for *boy/girl*. Some optional feminine forms (*poetess, authoress*, etc) are no longer in normal use, being replaced by the dual gender forms (*poet, author*, etc).

4.87
[C] Personal dual gender
This is a large class including, for example, the following:

artist	friend	person
chairman	guest	professor
cook	inhabitant	servant
criminal	librarian	speaker
doctor	musician	student
enemy	neighbour	teacher
fool	novelist	writer
foreigner	parent	etc

For clarity, it is sometimes necessary to use a 'gender marker':

boy friend	girl friend
man servant	woman servant
male student	female student

The dual class is on the increase as more and more positions in society are opened up to both sexes. For example, *engineer* and *nurse* are now dual gender, but were not formerly. With reference to the 'marked' sex, it is, however, still necessary to use a gender marker:

a male nurse	a nurse
an engineer	a female engineer

No rational rules can be given for whether a noun should have dual gender distinction or not. It seems, for example, quite arbitrary that *guest* and *servant* should be dual in contrast to *host/hostess* and *waiter/ waitress*.

4.88
[D] Common gender
Common gender nouns are intermediate between personal and non-personal. The wide selection of pronouns (*who–he/she/it*) should not be understood to mean that all these are possible for all nouns in all contexts. A mother is not likely to refer to her baby as *it*, but it would be

quite possible for somebody who is emotionally unrelated to the child or is ignorant of or indifferent to its sex.

4.89
[E] Collective nouns
These differ from other nouns in taking as pronoun substitutes either singular (*it*) or plural (*they*) without change of number in the noun (*the army: it/they; cf: the armies: they*) (*cf* 7.25). Consequently, the verb may be in the plural after a singular noun:

The committee $\begin{cases} \text{was} \\ \text{were} \end{cases}$ discussing the proposal

$\begin{matrix} \text{It} \\ \text{They} \end{matrix}$ decided to reject the proposal by a vote of five to two

There are nuances in meaning between the different substitution choices. The singular and plural choices are by no means in complete free variation. The distinction made within collective nouns may appear to be one of number rather than gender. However, it also involves gender, since the difference in substitution reflects a difference in attitude: the singular stresses the non-personal collectivity of the group and the plural the personal individuality within the group. English gives the speaker many such choices to express his attitude to the content of his message.

We may distinguish three subclasses of collective nouns: (a) specific, (b) generic, and (c) unique (see 4.32).

(a) SPECIFIC	(b) GENERIC	(c) UNIQUE
army	the aristocracy	the Arab League
clan	the bourgeoisie	(the) Congress
class	the clergy	the Kremlin
club	the élite	the Papacy
committee	the gentry	Parliament
crew	the intelligentsia	the United Nations
crowd	the laity	the United States
family	the proletariat	the Vatican
flock	the public	
gang		
government		
group		
herd		
jury		
majority		
minority		

4.90
[F/G] Higher animals
These are divided into masculine/feminine:

[F] MASCULINE ANIMAL	[G] FEMININE ANIMAL
buck	doe
bull	cow
cock	hen
dog	bitch
gander	goose
lion	lioness
stallion	mare
tiger	tigress

A further class might be set up, 'common higher animals', patterning with *which – it*, (?*who*) – *he/she*, to account for *horse, cat, tiger*, etc when no sex distinction is made or known. (In such cases, *he* is more common than *she*.)

4.91
[H] Higher organisms
These include ships, countries, and other entities towards which an affectionate attitude is expressed by a personal substitute:

'What a lovely ship.' 'What is *she* called?'

The proud owner of a sports car may refer to it as *she* (or perhaps as *he* if the owner is female).

Note
Names of countries have different gender depending on their use. (i) As geographical units they are treated as neuter: 'Looking at the map we see France here. *It is* one of the largest countries of Europe.' (ii) As political/economic units the names of countries are often feminine: 'France *has* been able to increase *her* exports by 10 per cent over the last six months.' 'England *is* proud of *her* poets.' (iii) In sports, the teams representing countries can be referred to as *they* (*cf* collective nouns, 4.89): 'France *have* improved *their* chance of winning the cup.'

4.92
[I/J] Lower animals and inanimate nouns
Lower animals do not differ from inanimate nouns in terms of our present linguistic criteria, *ie* both *snake* and *box* have *which* and *it* as pronouns. Still, sex differences *can* be indicated by a range of gender markers for any animate noun where they are felt to be relevant:

male frog	female frog
he-goat	she-goat
dog-otter	bitch-otter
cock-pheasant	hen-pheasant

We make no claim for the categories 'higher/lower animals' to parallel the biological classification. Some animals require finer gender distinctions in the language than others. This can be attributed to a number of factors. The layman normally has no knowledge about the sex of animals like *ant, herring, snake, spider;* or, even if he does, it may not be a fact that he wants or needs to indicate. This is only likely to happen with the animals that man, 'the speaking animal', has the closest connections with (in particular the domesticated animals).

Case
4.93
Common/genitive case
Case is a grammatical category that can express a number of different relationships between nominal elements. English nouns have a two-case system: the unmarked COMMON CASE (*boy*) and the marked GENITIVE CASE (*boy's*); six pronouns have in addition an objective case, thus presenting a three-case system, where common case is replaced by SUBJECTIVE and OBJECTIVE CASE (*he ~ him, cf* 4.107).

The 'central' but far from the only use of the genitive is to express possession. The construction is indeed sometimes called the 'possessive' case and the traditional name of the pronouns with genitive function is 'possessive' pronouns. We may compare

The children's toys⎫
Their toys   ⎬are new
                  ⎭

While it seems useful to retain the term 'possessive' for this set of closed-system words, it should be borne in mind that the label does not adequately apply to all uses of them. Possessive pronouns will be dealt with in 4.116.

4.94
The meanings of the genitive
The genitive constructions in 4.93 are related to the same basic sentence structure:

The children⎫
They   ⎬have new toys
            ⎭

The meanings of the genitive can best be shown by such sentential or phrasal analogues. The following include the more common meanings of the genitive, and we add, for comparison, a corresponding use of the *of*-genitive where this is possible.

GENITIVES	ANALOGUES
(a) *possessive genitive (cf* 13.27)	
my son's wife	my son has a wife
Mrs Johnson's passport	Mrs Johnson has a passport
my money	I have money
cf the gravity of the earth	the earth has gravity
(b) *subjective genitive*	
the boy's application	the boy applied
his parents' consent	his parents consented
my departure	I departed
cf the dip of the compass needle	the compass needle dipped
(c) *genitive of origin*	
the girl's story	the girl told a story
the general's letter	the general wrote a letter
your telegram	you sent a telegram
(d) *objective genitive*	
the family's support	(. . .) supports the family
the boy's release	(. . .) released the boy
her promotion	(. . .) promoted her
cf a statement of the facts	(. . .) stated the facts
(e) *descriptive genitive*	
a women's college	a college for women
a summer's day	a summer day/a day in the summer
a doctor's degree	a doctoral degree/ a doctorate
cow's milk	milk from cows
cf an absence of ten days	the absence lasted ten days

Note
In the 'appositive genitive', where the two noun phrases are equated denotatively, the -*s* genitive is now archaic: *Dublin's fair city*. The *of*-genitive is generally used (*cf* 13.27):

the City of York ~ York is a city
the pleasure of meeting you ~ meeting you is a pleasure

4.95
The -*s* and *of*-genitives
As we have seen in 4.94, it is reasonable to regard the genitive as having two forms:

(a) THE INFLECTED GENITIVE ('the -*s* GENITIVE') indicated in writing by apostrophe+*s* suffix or apostrophe only, after the modifying noun: modifying noun phrase+'*s*+head noun-phrase.

> the children's toys
> somebody's fault
> the body's temperature

(b) THE PERIPHRASTIC GENITIVE ('the *OF*-GENITIVE') consisting of the modifying noun phrase in a prepositional phrase after the head noun phrase: head noun phrase+*of*+modifying noun phrase.

> the toys of the (youngest) children
> the fault of somebody (or other)
> the temperature of the body

We speak here of 'noun phrases' rather than of 'nouns' since both the modifier and head may have modification:

> the naughty children's beautiful toys
> the beautiful toys of the naughty children
> the Museum of Modern Art's new Director

The last example illustrates the 'group genitive' (4.102, 13.64) where the inflection is added to the last word of the postmodification instead of the head (*Museum*). It is, however, the noun head that determines the choice of genitive. In the following sentences, only those with the personal noun head (4.85) can take the -*s* genitive irrespective of modification:

> The director's books
> *The bookshelf's books
> The director of the museum's books
> *The bookshelf of the museum's books

It will therefore be both convenient and relevant to discuss the genitive in terms of nouns rather than noun phrases.

The -*s* genitive must clearly be included in a discussion of 'case'. However, it is not obvious that the *of*-phrase should be included here, since the *of*-genitive is not an inflection but a structure of postmodification.

premodification: The Administration's policy

postmodification: The policy $\begin{cases} \text{of the Administration} \\ \text{that the Administration} \\ \quad \text{has adopted} \\ \text{adopted by the} \\ \quad \text{Administration} \end{cases}$ is mistaken

It seems, however, useful to highlight the functional similarity of the *-s* form and the *of*-phrase by calling them both 'genitives'. *Of* has become conventionalized as the chief preposition of the periphrastic genitive, which accounts for the name '*of*-genitive' (*cf* 6.45). Other prepositions can be used in a similar function:

the Ambassador's secretary

the secretary $\begin{cases} \text{of} \\ \text{to} \end{cases}$ the Ambassador

the door $\begin{cases} \text{of} \\ \text{to} \end{cases}$ his dressing-room

Further discussion of the genitive is deferred to the chapter on the complex noun phrases (13.27 *ff*), where the periphrastic genitive will be seen in relation to other types of postmodification.

4.96
The forms of the *-s* genitive
The *-s* genitive has different realizations in the two media. In writing there are two forms: one with apostrophe plus *s* (*boy's*) and the other with apostrophe only (*boys'*). In speech there are four forms: /ɪz/, /z/, /s/, and zero. See *Fig* 4:10.

Since the genitive inflection has the same speech form as the regular plural, it is necessary to make a distinction between those modifying nouns that have the *-s* plural and those that do not, *ie* singular nouns and irregular plurals not ending in *s* (*eg: children*, see 4.67). Regular *-s* plurals have the zero genitive (written with apostrophe only: *dogs'*, *cats', horses'*). Other nouns regularly take /ɪz/ if they end in sibilants (*horse's*), /z/ if they end in other voiced sounds (*dog's*), and /s/ if they end in other voiceless sounds (*cat's*). (See Note.)

The zero form is also used with other than plural nouns:

(a) With Greek names of more than one syllable:

Socrates' /-tiz/ wife
Xerxes' /-siz/ army
Euripides' /-diz/ plays

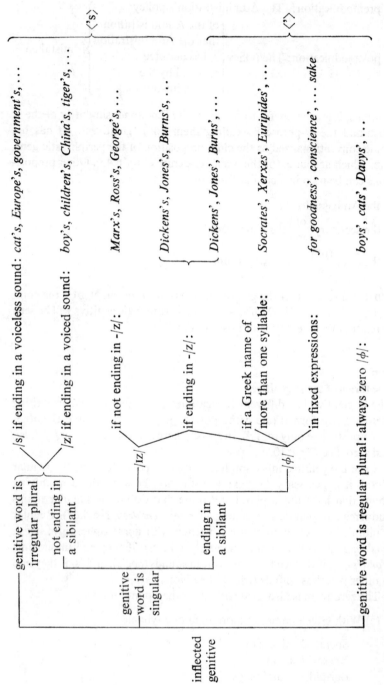

Fig 4:10 The forms of the inflected genitive

(b) In many other names ending in the voiced sibilant /z/ where, in speech, zero is a (less common) variant of the regular /ɪz/ genitive. There is vacillation (to say the least) both in the pronunciation and spelling of these names, as well as inconsistencies between the two media. The normal pronunciation appears to be the /ɪz/ form, but the normal spelling with apostrophe only. (The minority forms are given in parenthesis.)

WRITTEN FORMS	SPOKEN FORMS
Burns' (Burns's) poems	/(bɜnz) ˈbɜnzɪz/
Dickens' (Dickens's) novels	/(ˈdɪkɪnz) ˈdɪkɪnzɪz/
Jones' (Jones's) car	/(dʒoʊnz) ˈdʒoʊnzɪz/

Jesus and *Moses* normally have the zero form of the spoken genitive but are written *Jesus'* and *Moses'* (as well as *Jesus's* and *Moses's*).

Names ending in other sibilants than -/z/ have the regular /ɪz/ genitive:

Ross's /-sɪz/ theories

(c) In fixed expressions with *for . . . sake* where zero is used for euphony:

for goodness' sake
for conscience' sake

It will be seen that the rules for the pronunciation of the genitive *-s* suffix as /ɪz/, /z/ and /s/ are identical with the rules for the pronunciation of the -*s* suffix in the plural of nouns (4.61) and in the 3rd person

		REGULAR -*S* PLURAL			IRREGULAR PLURAL	
		singular	*plural*		*singular*	*plural*
SPOKEN	*common*	/bɒɪ/		*common*	/tʃaɪld/	/tʃɪldrən/
SPOKEN	*genitive*	/bɒɪz/		*genitive*	/tʃaɪldz/	/tʃɪldrənz/
		singular	*plural*		*singular*	*plural*
WRITTEN	*common*	boy	boys	*common*	child	children
WRITTEN	*genitive*	boy's	boys'	*genitive*	child's	children's

Fig 4:11 The inflected genitive in speech and writing

singular present of verbs (3.55). The effect of this syncretism is that, for example, /bɔɪz/ can correspond to any one of the following three written forms (see *Fig* 4:11):

(i) *Boys*, *ie* plural number/common case
(ii) *Boy's*, *ie* singular number/genitive case
(iii) *Boys'*, *ie* plural number/genitive case

Note
There is a difference between the genitive, where the ending is added to the last word of the noun phrase, and the plural, where the ending is added to the head (see further 4.102):

the King of Denmark's
the Kings of Denmark

Choice of the -*s* genitive
4.97
Selection of the -*s* genitive can best be described in relation to the gender classes represented by the noun which takes the -*s* suffix. Generally speaking, the -*s* genitive is favoured by the classes that are highest on the gender scale (see 4.85), *ie* animate nouns, in particular persons and animals with personal gender characteristics. Although we can say either *the youngest children's toys* or *the toys of the youngest children*, the two forms of the genitive are not normally in free variation. We cannot say, for example, **the roof's cost* or **the hat of John*. The main factor governing the choice of the one or the other genitive form is the animate, or rather personal quality of the modifying noun. Nouns denoting persons, whether proper names (*John's car*) or ordinary count nouns (*the student's car*), can always take the inflected genitive. It can also be used with animals. The rule-of-thumb here is that the higher animals are more likely to have the -*s* genitive than the lower animals (see 4.90).

the moth's wings   the wings of the moth
the dog's life   the life of the dog

4.98
The following four animate noun classes normally take the -*s* genitive, but the *of*-genitive is also possible in most cases; see 4.100.

(a) PERSONAL NAMES: Segovia's pupil
                                    George Washington's statue

(b) PERSONAL NOUNS: the boy's new shirt
                                     my sister-in-law's pencil

(c) COLLECTIVE NOUNS: the Administration's policy
the government's conviction
the majority's platform
the party's elder statesmen
the company's working capital
the nation's social security

(d) HIGHER ANIMALS: the horse's neck
the farm dog's bark
the lion's tail
the tiger's stripes

The inflected genitive is also used with certain kinds of inanimate nouns:

(e) GEOGRAPHICAL NAMES:

continents: Europe's future
countries: China's development
the United States' attitude
states: Minnesota's immigrants
Maryland's Democratic Senator
Rhode Island's colonial period
cities/towns: Hollywood's studios
London's water supply
universities: Harvard's Linguistics Department

(f) 'LOCATIVE NOUNS' denote regions, heavenly bodies, institutions, etc. They can be very similar to geographical names, and are often written with initial capital letter.

the earth's interior
the world's economic organization
the nation's chief waterways
the Club's pianist
the Gallery's rotunda fountain
the school's history

the Church's mission
the hotel's entrance
the hall's open window
a country's population
the city's cosmopolitan atmosphere
the town's taxpayers

(g) TEMPORAL NOUNS

the decade's events
a day's work
a week's holiday
a moment's thought

this year's sales
today's business
the theatre season's first big event

(h) NOUNS OF 'SPECIAL INTEREST TO HUMAN ACTIVITY'

the brain's total solid weight
the mind's general development

the game's history
the concerto's final movement

the body's needs
science's influence on our
    society
my life's aim
in freedom's name
the strike's end
the treaty's ratification
duty's call
the poll's results
love's spirit

the play's philosophy
the book's true importance
the novel's structure
a word's function
the car's performance on
    the road
the ship's surgeon
television's future
the wine's character
the machine's construction

Note

It seems that genitives other than possessive (see 4.94) have greater restrictions on the 'personal' quality of the modifying noun than the possessive genitive has. Compare:

The man's   ⎫
*The cow's ⎬ noticing it was unexpected
       ⎭
The man's hanging
*The dog's butchering

4.99

So far, the -s genitive constructions have been identified by reference to certain classes of the modifying noun: personal, collective, temporal, etc. There are some constructions with the inflected genitive which can best be described in terms of specific lexical noun heads. These include the following, of which the set (a) permit *of* while the examples with *length, reach, throw,* and *worth* in (b) are 'idiomatized' and do not permit an *of*-genitive:

    (a) (He stood at) the edge of the water

but

    (b) *(People don't get) the worth of their money

    (a)   *edge:* the water's edge
                the river's edge
         end: at his journey's end
                at his wits' end
     surface: the water's surface
  for . . . sake: for charity's sake
                for God's sake

    (b)   *length:* at arm's length
        reach: within arm's reach
       throw: at a stone's throw
       worth: their money's worth

Choice of the *of*-genitive
4.100
The *of*-genitive is chiefly used with nouns that belong to the bottom part of the gender scale (4.85), *ie* with nouns denoting lower animals and with inanimate nouns. Inanimate nouns regularly take the *of*-genitive, but, as we have noted (4.97–98), a great many occur with the *-s* genitive. This is the case with, for example, geographical names (*China's history*), locative nouns (*the city's traffic problems*), and temporal nouns (*this week's events*). In addition, there are numerous other inanimate nouns which can often take the *-s* genitive. They may be characterized as 'being of special interest to human activity', denoting parts of the body (*brain, mind*, etc), cultural activities (*orchestra, play*, etc), means of transport (*ship, radio*, etc), and so forth.

4.101
What we have said does not mean, however, that such inanimate nouns cannot be constructed with the *of*-genitive. The following nouns, for example, will equally well admit both genitive constructions:

the car's engine	the engine of the car
the book's title	the title of the book
the town's population	the population of the town
the earth's interior	the interior of the earth

The *-s* genitive is hardly acceptable in the following phrases:

?the wheel's hub	the hub of the wheel
?the house's windows	the windows of the house
?the ditch's depth	the depth of the ditch

But while the *-s* genitive is not fully acceptable with these nouns, it frequently is with the corresponding pronoun: *the depth of the ditch ~ its depth, the windows of the house ~ its windows*.

There is considerable overlap in the uses of the two genitives. Although either may be possible in a given context, one of them is, however, generally preferred by native speakers for reasons of euphony, rhythm, emphasis, or implied relationship between the nouns.

The use of the *-s* genitive is very common in headlines, where brevity is essential. Furthermore, the *-s* genitive gives prominence to the modifying noun. Compare:

HOLLYWOOD'S STUDIOS EMPTY
THE STUDIOS OF HOLLYWOOD EMPTY

The first makes a better headline, since it is not only shorter but also gives prominence to *Hollywood*. Similarly, of the following two genitives, the second has a more 'natural' balance than the first:

the excellent performance of the car on the road
the car's excellent performance on the road

4.102
The group genitive
This is the name of a construction where the *s* suffix is added to the last element of a noun phrase consisting of a postmodified or coordinated noun head (see 4.95 (b), 13.64):

my son-in-law's bicycle	the University of Minnesota's
somebody else's car	President
in a month or two's time	the Museum of Modern Art's
Beaumont and Fletcher's plays	Director
the King of Denmark's court	an hour and a half's talk

With coordinated noun phrases, a distinction is made between the coordinated genitive of (a) and the group genitive of (b):

(a) John's and Mary's books (some are John's and some are Mary's)
(b) John and Mary's books (all are jointly owned)

With one or both heads a pronoun, ambiguity can arise (*cf* 9.104 *f*), even where the coordinations are acceptable:

*John and her books
?John's and her books ⎫
His and her books   ⎬ (ambiguous as between (a) and (b))
*Her and his books
His books and hers (unambiguously (a))

4.103
The elliptic genitive
In this construction, the head is not expressed but it is explicit or implicit in the context:

My bicycle is better than John's
My car is faster than John's
His memory is like an elephant's
John's is a nice car, too.

4.104
The local genitive
This is restricted to certain institutionalized expressions where no head needs to be mentioned. It is used in the following three cases:

(a) For normal residence:

my aunt's
the Johnsons'

(b) For institutions such as public buildings (where the genitive is usually a saint's name):

St Paul's (Cathedral)
St James's (Palace)

(c) For a place where business is conducted:

the barber's   the chemist's (BrE)
the butcher's   the druggist's (AmE)
the grocer's

Note
In some cases the institutionalization is carried so far that the apostrophe is dropped and with it any connection with the genitive construction (*cf* 13.27*ff*): *Selfridges*, *Harrods*. With the disappearance of the small shopkeeper, the genitive of type (c) is frequently confused with the plural: *They took the rug to the cleaners*.

4.105
The double genitive
The double genitive consists of the combined inflected and periphrastic genitives, usually with a partitive meaning (13.30). The postmodifier must be definite and personal:

a work of Milton's ('one of   this great nation of ours
   Milton's works')   several pupils of mine
a friend of his father's   a friend of my parents'

Pronouns
Characteristics of pronouns
4.106
Pronouns share several characteristics, most of which are absent from nouns. As their name implies, they 'replace' nouns, or rather whole noun phrases, since they cannot generally occur with determiners such as the definite article or premodification (see further, however, 4.126 *ff*, 13.5 Note *a*):

the men   *the they
tall men   *tall they

The main differences between pronouns and nouns are the following:

(1) Pronouns constitute a closed system, whereas nouns form an open class. (For the 'closed system'/'open class' distinction, see 2.14 *f*).
(2) Many pronouns have certain morphological characteristics that nouns do not have:
   (a) Case-contrast for subjective/objective case, for example *I/me*, *he/him*, *who/whom* (see 4.107).
   (b) Person-distinction: 1st/2nd/3rd person, as in *I/you/he* (see 4.108).
   (c) Overt gender-contrast: masculine/feminine/neuter in the 3rd person, as in *he/she/it* (see 4.109).
   (d) Morphologically unrelated number forms, as in *I/we*, *he/they* (compared with the typical regularity of nouns: *boy ~ boys*, etc).

In addition, pronouns have a number system different from that of nouns (4.110). Before dealing with the different subclasses of pronouns, we will discuss common characteristics in relation to the categories case, person, gender, and number.

4.107
Case

Nouns and most pronouns in English have only two cases: COMMON CASE (*children*, *somebody*) and GENITIVE CASE (*children's*, *somebody's*, see 4.93 *ff*). However, six pronouns have an objective case, thus presenting a three-case system, where 'common' case is replaced by SUBJECTIVE and OBJECTIVE CASE. There is identity between genitive and objective *her* and partial overlap between subjective *who* and objective *who* (see 4.118 *f*). The genitives of personal pronouns are, in accordance with grammatical tradition, called 'possessive pronouns'.

subjective	*I*	*we*	*he*	*she*	*they*	*who*
objective	*me*	*us*	*him*	*her*	*them*	*who(m)*
genitive	*my*	*our*	*his*	*her*	*their*	*whose*

4.108
Person

Personal, possessive, and reflexive pronouns have, unlike nouns, distinctions of person (see *Table* 4:5).

1st person = the speaker (singular *I*/ plural *we*, etc)
2nd person = the person(s) addressed (*you*, etc)
3rd person = 'the rest', *ie* one or more persons or things mentioned,
    etc (singular *he*/*she*/*it*, plural *they*, etc).

English makes no difference between singular and plural number in the
2nd person except for reflexive pronouns:

Richard, you ought to be ashamed of *yourself*
Children, you ought to be ashamed of *yourselves*

2nd person *you* is also used in the indefinite sense of 'one', and 3rd person plural *they* in the sense of 'people in general' (*cf* 4.126 (c)):

You can never hear what he's saying
They've had no serious accidents this year.

4.109
Gender
The 3rd person singular of personal, reflexive, and possessive pronouns
is further distinguished by overt (natural) gender (see 4.85 *ff*): masculine *he*/*him*/*himself*/*his*, feminine *she*/*her*/*herself*/*hers*, neuter *it*/*itself*/*its*
(see *Table* 4:5). Relative pronouns also manifest a distinction between
personal (*who*, *whom*) and non-personal (*which*) (see 4.118).

4.110
Number
The number system of pronouns is different from that of nouns (see
4.48 *ff*). The personal pronoun *we* in the first person does not denote
'more than *I*' (*cf*: *the boy ∼ the boys*) but '*I* plus one or more others'.
Table 4:4 indicates some combinations. The following bundles of
two or three features of person occur: 1st + 2nd ('inclusive *we*' = *I* and
you), 1st + 3rd ('exclusive *we*' = *I* and *he*, etc), 1st + 2nd + 3rd, and
2nd + 3rd. In such cases the reflexive pronoun selection is determined by
person order in the bundle, *ie* 1st person takes precedence over 2nd
and/or 3rd, and 2nd takes precedence over 3rd.

Note, however, that the sequential order of subject items makes no
difference to the choice of reflexive pronoun:

You and I and John ⎫
John and I and you ⎬ will never give *ourselves* up
John and you and I ⎭

Table 4:4

DISTINCTIONS OF NUMBER AND PERSON IN PRONOUNS

In feature bundles of more than one person, the superordinate feature which selects the reflexive pronoun is circled.

	person 1st	2nd	3rd	*examples with reflexive pronouns*
singular number	+	−	−	*I* gave *myself* up
	−	+	−	*You* ought to be ashamed of *yourself*, Richard!
	−	−	+	*He* hurt *himself* / *She* hurt *herself* / *It* hurt *itself*
plural number	−	+	−	*You* ought to be ashamed of *yourselves*, children!
	⊕	+	−	*We* complimented *ourselves* too soon, John ('inclusive *we*')
	⊕	−	+	*We* shave *ourselves* with electric razors, John and I ('exclusive *we*')
	⊕	+	+	*You, John* and *I* worked *ourselves* to death while he played golf
	−	⊕	+	*You* and *John* shouldn't bother *yourselves* about it
	−	−	+	*They* helped *themselves* to coffee and cakes

4.111
Subclasses of pronouns

The class of 'pronouns' includes a number of heterogeneous items, many of which do not share all the above features. For example, *somebody* has no person-distinction (no 1st and 2nd person); no subjective/objective case contrast; and no overt gender-contrast for person (masculine/feminine). Yet it is included among our pronouns, since it does not occur with determiners and is a closed-system item. The point we want to make here is that all the characteristic features which single out the pronoun class from the noun class are not shared by all its members.

Personal, possessive, and reflexive pronouns may be called the 'central' pronouns, since they share those features we have mentioned as characteristic of pronouns as compared with nouns: in particular, they manifest person and gender contrast. Although these 'central' pronouns fill different syntactic functions, they have obvious morphological characteristics in common. This is also the reason why the possessives like *my*, *your*, etc have been given in the table, although they are determiners and cannot function alone instead of nouns, but only together with nouns (see 4.13 *ff*). *Fig* 4:12 shows the different subclasses of pronouns and gives references to sections where they are discussed.

Many pronouns have the double function of determiners and nominals

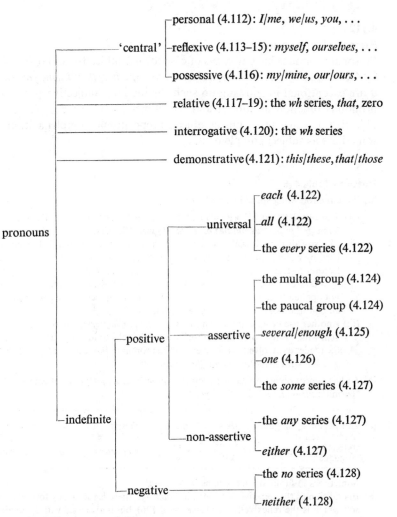

Fig 4:12 Pronoun subclasses

(which may be either fully independent or in construction with an *of*-phrase), for example,

Which bus goes
Which is the bus   ⎬ to Chicago?
Which of these buses goes

It will be convenient to deal with all such closed-system items with both determiner and nominal functions in the following sections on pronouns.

4.112
Personal pronouns

Personal pronouns have two sets of case forms: subjective and objective (*cf* 4.107 and *Table* 4:5): *I/me, we/us, he/him, she/her, they/them; you* and *it* are exceptional in showing no such distinction. Subjective personal pronouns function as subject and sometimes as subject complement; objective personal pronouns as object, prepositional complement, and sometimes as subject complement.

Notes to Table 4:5

[a] Note the following special uses of *we:*

  (i) The obsolete 'royal' *we* (=*I*) used by a single person, as in *We are not interested in the possibilities of defeat* (Queen Victoria).

  (ii) The so-called 'editorial' *we*, now formal and somewhat old-fashioned, is used by a single individual, as in *As we showed a moment ago, . . .* said by a lecturer instead of *As I showed a moment ago, . . .* This use of *we* is prompted by a desire to avoid *I*, which is felt to be a little egotistic. ('Editorial' here is not applied to the fully justified use of *we* with reference to the consensus of an editorial board or other collective body.)

  (iii) Another use of *we* can be seen in *As we saw in Chapter 3*, where *we* replaces *you*, which is felt to be too authoritative. *We* seeks to identify the writer and the reader as involved in a joint enterprise: compare *We now turn to a different problem* with *Let's turn to a different problem*.

[b] *Us* has almost obligatory contraction to *'s* in *let's* (*Let's go!*) but not where *let*= 'permit': *Please let us go without you!*

[c] 2nd person in restricted (religious) language		*thou*	*thee*	*thyself*	*thy*	*thine*
	singular	*thou*	*thee*	*thyself*	*thy*	*thine*
	plural	*ye /ji/ you*	*you (ye)*	*yourselves*	*your*	*yours*

[d] Sometimes in familiar use: *'em*, as in *Kill 'em!*

[e] In addition to the reflexive pronouns in *Table* 4:5 there is the chiefly formal *one-self* which is the reflexive form of *one* (see 4.126), but is also used with indefinite reference in non-finite clauses, *eg: To starve oneself is suicide.*

Table 4:5
PERSONAL, REFLEXIVE, POSSESSIVE PRONOUNS

			PERSONAL PRONOUNS		REFLEXIVE PRONOUNS[e]	POSSESSIVE PRONOUNS	
			subjective case	objective case		determiner function	nominal function
1st person		singular	*I*	*me*	*myself*	*my*	*mine*
		plural	*we*[a]	*us*[b]	*ourselves*	*our*	*ours*
2nd person[c]		singular	*you*		*yourself*	*your*	*yours*
		plural			*yourselves*		
3rd person	singular	masculine	*he*	*him*	*himself*	*my* ... *his*	*his*
		feminine	*she*	*her*	*herself*	*her*	*hers*
		neutral	*it*		*itself*	*its*	
		plural	*they*	*them*[d]	*themselves*	*their*	*theirs*

FUNCTION	SUBJECTIVE CASE	OBJECTIVE CASE
subject	*He* was late	
subject complement	It was *he*	It was *him*
object		I saw *him* at the station
prepositional complement		We cannot manage without *him*

As *Table* 4:5 shows, both subjective and objective case forms can be used for subject complement. Although the prescriptive grammar tradition stipulates the subjective case form, the objective case form is normally felt to be the natural one, particularly in informal style. However, the choice occurs chiefly in this restricted and infrequent construction with final pronouns, *ie* in 'object territory'. In the more natural construction with anticipatory *it*, the subjective case form normally occurs:

It was he who came

The objective case form is preferred in familiar style in verbless sentences, *eg*

'Who's there?' – 'Me'

After words which are indisputably prepositions, like *without, over, at,* etc, there is no question about using any other case form than the objective (but see Note below and 6.4):

We couldn't manage without $\begin{cases} \text{him} \\ \text{*he} \end{cases}$

After *but, except, than,* and *as,* however, there is vacillation (*cf* 4.114 (e)):

Nobody $\begin{cases} \text{but} \\ \text{except} \end{cases}$ $\begin{cases} \text{him} \\ \text{?he} \end{cases}$ can solve our problems

He is $\begin{cases} \text{more intelligent than} \\ \text{as intelligent as} \end{cases}$ $\begin{cases} \text{she} \\ \text{her} \end{cases}$

The reason for the vacillation is that *than* and *as* can be analysed either as prepositions, which require the objective case forms, or as conjunctions with ellipted predicates, which require the subjective case forms, as becomes apparent when no ellipsis occurs:

He is $\begin{cases} \text{more intelligent than she is.} \\ \text{as intelligent as she is.} \end{cases}$

Note

The prescriptive bias for the subjective forms may account for hypercorrect uses of them, as in *between you and I*. Another reason is that *you and I* is felt to be a unit, which can remain unchanged, particularly with the distance between the preposition and *I*. *Cf* also *Let you and I do it! He says she saw you and I last night*, which are not uncommon in informal conversation.

Reflexive pronouns
4.113

Reflexive pronouns end in *-self* (singular) and *-selves* (plural). These suffixes are added to the determiner possessives (*myself, ourselves; yourself, yourselves*), objective case personal pronouns (*himself, itself, themselves*) or their joint form (*herself*). See *Table* 4:5.

As the name implies, these pronouns 'reflect' another nominal element of the sentence, usually the subject, with which it is in co-referential relation (*cf* 7.34):

subject and object	*He* shaved *himself*
subject and indirect object	*He* allowed *himself* no rest
subject and subject complement	*He* is always *himself*
subject and prepositional complement	*He* looked at *himself*
subject and apposition	{ *He* couldn't come *himself* { *He himself* couldn't come

Reflexive pronouns have two distinct uses: non-emphatic and emphatic.

4.114
Non-emphatic use

Non-emphatic use of the reflexive pronouns occurs in the following cases:

(a) With obligatorily reflexive verbs, *ie* verbs which always require reflexive object, such as *absent oneself* (*from*), *avail oneself* (*of*), *betake oneself, pride oneself* (*on*):

She always prides *herself* on her academic background

Also *behave* virtually belongs to this set since it can take no other than a reflexive object: *Behave* (*yourselves*) *now!*

(b) With optionally reflexive verbs, *ie* verbs where the reflexive pronoun may be left out with little or no change in meaning, such as *adjust* (*oneself*), *dress* (*oneself*), *prove* (*oneself to be competent*), *shave* (*oneself*), *wash* (*oneself*)

(c) With 'non-reflexive verbs' where the reflexive pronouns are used to denote co-reference in contrast with non-co-referential objects:

He saw { *himself*
 { *him* } in the mirror

Here, *himself* is co-referent with the subject *he*, whereas *him* must refer to another person.

(d) The reflexive pronouns are also used as prepositional complements, where there is a close connection between the verb and the prepositional phrase (*cf* 12.19 *ff*); for example:

Mary could stand for hours looking at *herself* in the mirror
Do look after *yourself!*
She did not know what to do with *herself*
He thinks too much of *himself*
He takes too much upon *himself*

In prepositional adverbial phrases expressing spatial relationship, usually between concretes, the objective personal pronouns are used despite co-reference with the subject:

He looked about *him*
Have you any money on *you?*
She had her fiancé beside *her*
They placed their papers in front of *them*
They held firecrackers behind *them*
We have the whole day before *us*

But reflexive pronouns are often preferred when the reference is emotionally to a person's self. In such cases, the spatial relationship is often expressed by *within, inside,* etc:

He winced inside *himself*
She was beside *herself* with rage (reflexive obligatory)

These rules do not, however, account for all the data. There is considerable vacillation in this area, as the following examples show:

She's built a wall of Russian books around *her(self)*
Holding her new yellow bathrobe around *her(self)* with both arms, she walked up to him
Mason stepped back, gently closed the door behind *him(self)*, turned and walked down the corridor
They left the apartment, switching out the lights, and pulling the spring lock shut behind *them*

(e) In a further non-emphatic use the reflexives, in variation with personal pronouns, occur after *as, like, but, except* and elements of coordinated noun phrases (*cf* 4.112):

For somebody like $\left\{ {me \atop myself} \right\}$ this is a big surprise

$$\text{My brother and} \begin{Bmatrix} \text{I} \\ \text{myself} \end{Bmatrix} \text{went sailing yesterday}$$

Note

In the last example, the use of *myself* is felt by many speakers to be a hyperurbanism, a genteel evasion of *I*.

4.115

Emphatic use

Reflexive pronouns in emphatic use occur in apposition, have heavy stress and, unlike reflexive pronouns in non-emphatic use, have greater positional mobility:

I wouldn't kiss her *myself*
I *myself* wouldn't kiss her
Myself, I wouldn't kiss her

Of course, reflexive pronouns in reflexive use can also have emphatic stress:

He thinks of himSELF but not of ME

4.116

Possessive pronouns

These consist traditionally of two series: the attributive (*my, your*, etc) and the predicative, nominal (*mine, yours*, etc). (For coordination of possessive pronouns, see 4.102, 9.104 *f*.) In our classification, however, the former series belongs to the determiners, since they are mutually exclusive with the articles (see 4.13). They have been included in *Table* 4:5 for a convenient summary statement of related forms. Compare the two types of possessives with the genitive of nouns which is identical in the two functions:

$$\begin{matrix} \text{Mary's} \\ \text{my daughter's} \\ \text{her} \end{matrix} \Bigg\} \text{book} \qquad \text{the book is} \begin{Bmatrix} \text{Mary's} \\ \text{my daughter's} \\ \text{hers} \end{Bmatrix}$$

Unlike many other languages, English uses possessives to denote parts of the body and personal belongings, as well as in several other expressions:

He stood at the door with *his* hat in *his* hand
Mary has broken *her* leg
Don't lose *your* balance!
They have changed *their* minds again!

The definite article is, however, usual in prepositional phrases concerned with the object, or, in passive constructions, the subject:

She took me by *the* hand
Somebody must have hit me on *the* head with a hammer
I must have been hit on *the* head with a hammer.

Relative pronouns
4.117
Relative pronouns introduce relative clauses postmodifying nominal heads. Compare the three different types of noun-phrase postmodification: relative clause, participial clause, and prepositional phrase (which will be discussed in 13.5).

$$\text{The book} \begin{cases} \text{which is lying on the table} \\ \text{lying on the table} \\ \text{on the table} \end{cases} \text{is Mary's}$$

The relative pronoun *which* has anaphoric reference to the noun phrase (the antecedent) *the book*, which is postmodified by the entire relative clause.

4.118
There are two types of relative clauses: restrictive and non-restrictive. Restrictive relative clauses are closely connected with their heads prosodically and denote a limitation on the reference of the antecedents. Non-restrictive clauses are parenthetic comments (indicated by separate tone units in speech and by commas in writing) which do not further define the antecedent.

Restrictive relative clauses:

This is not something *that would disturb me anyway*
John was the best student *I ever had*

Non-restrictive relative clauses:

It's all based on violence, *which I hate*
They operate like politicians, *who notoriously have no sense of humour at all*

The difference between restrictive and non-restrictive relative clauses will be further discussed in 13.3, 13.8 *ff.* For the present, we only need to mention this difference in relative clause function and indicate that it affects the choice of relative pronoun, as appears in *Table* 4:6.

Table 4:6
RELATIVE PRONOUNS

	restrictive and non-restrictive		restrictive only
	personal	*non-personal*	*personal and non-personal*
subjective case	*who*	*which*	*that*
objective case	*whom*		*that*, zero
genitive case	*whose*	*of which*	
preposition + relative pronoun	prep + *whom*	prep + *which*	
relative pronoun ... preposition	*who/m/* ... prep	*which* ... prep	$\begin{cases} that \ldots \text{prep} \\ \text{zero} \ldots \text{prep} \end{cases}$

4.119
Relative pronouns include two series: *wh*-pronouns (*who, whom, whose, which,* and *what*), and *that* or zero. Compare:

I'd like to see the car $\begin{cases} \text{which} \\ \text{that} \\ \underline{} \end{cases}$ you bought last week

Neither series has number or person contrast. However, the *wh*-series has gender contrast for *who/which* (personal/non-personal, respectively), and case contrast for *who/whom/whose* (subjective/objective/genitive, respectively).

As *Table* 4:6 shows, *whose*, unlike *who* and *whom*, has both personal and non-personal reference. The distribution of *who* overlaps with that of *whom* in certain functions. *Whom* is the obligatory relative pronoun as complement immediately following a preposition. *Who* is quite frequent in familiar use in variation with *whom* as object and as prepositional complement when the preposition is end-placed and thus separated from the relative pronoun. Compare:

This is a man $\begin{cases} \text{whom} \\ \text{who} \\ \text{that} \\ \underline{} \end{cases}$ you should know

This is the man
$$\begin{cases} \text{to whom you spoke} \\ \left.\begin{matrix}\text{whom} \\ \text{who}\end{matrix}\right\} \text{you spoke to} \\ \left.\begin{matrix}\text{that} \\ \underline{\quad}\end{matrix}\right\} \text{you spoke to} \end{cases}$$

What differs from the other relative pronouns in that it 'contains' its antecedent (= *that which*):

What I mean is this . . .

It also has determiner function:

I'll do what little I can
Cf I'll do the little (that) I can.

4.120
Interrogative pronouns

These are formally identical with the *wh*-series of relative pronouns, but are functionally different. They have either attributive, determiner function (*which*, *what*, and *whose*, see 4.16) or nominal function (*who*, *whom*, *whose*, *which*, *what*). *Who*, *whose*, and *whom* have only personal reference. The case distinctions are the same as those of relative pronouns, except that the objective use of *who* is much more general. Unlike relative pronouns, however, *which* and attributive *what* may have both personal and non-personal reference (see further 7.63).

Who is missing?
Which is your car?
What is your opinion?
Whose is this car?
Who(m) did you stay with?
With whom did you travel? (formal)

Which and *what* have different uses: *which* is used with both personal and non-personal nouns but is selective, in that it has anaphoric or cataphoric definite reference (*cf* 4.36), whereas *what* has indefinite reference:

$$\left.\begin{matrix}\text{Which} \\ \text{What}\end{matrix}\right\} \left.\begin{matrix}\text{girls} \\ \text{books}\end{matrix}\right\} \text{do you like best?}$$

Which here implies that the choice is made from a limited number of known girls or books, whereas *what* implies 'what kind of'. Like many other determiners (*eg: both* and *all*), *which* has an alternative *of*-phrase construction:

$$\text{Which (of the)}\left\{\begin{matrix}\text{girls} \\ \text{books}\end{matrix}\right\}\text{do you like best?}$$

4.121
Demonstrative pronouns

Demonstrative pronouns have number contrast and both determiner and nominal function. The general meanings of the two sets can be stated as 'near' and 'distant' reference (*cf* 10.65 *ff*):

	singular	plural
'near' reference:	*this*	*these*
'distant' reference:	*that*	*those*

Demonstrative pronouns have several uses. In (a), (b), and (c) below the two sets *this/these* and *that/those* are contrastive; in (d) and (e) there is no such contrast, and only one of the sets is used in either.

(a) Anaphoric reference (*cf* 4.36) with optional *one/ones* (although the plural *ones* is rarer than the singular *one*):

Of all the books, I preferred
$$\begin{cases} \text{this (one)} \\ \text{that (one)} \\ \text{these (ones)} \\ \text{those (ones)} \end{cases}$$

(b) Deictic ('pointing') use (*cf: here* ~ *there, now* ~ *then, today* ~ *yesterday/tomorrow*, etc):

$$\left.\begin{array}{l} \text{This} \\ \text{That} \end{array}\right\} \text{is my friend Charlie Brown}$$

But as object or complement, the demonstratives can only have non-personal reference. Compare these two pairs:

$$\left.\begin{array}{l} \text{That} \\ \text{He} \end{array}\right\} \text{is the chairman}$$

$$\text{They made} \left\{\begin{array}{l} \text{*that} \\ \text{him} \end{array}\right\} \text{the chairman}$$

(c) Discourse reference (*cf* 10.63):

This is what I mean . . . (with either anaphoric or cataphoric reference, but especially the latter)
That is what I mean . . . (with only anaphoric reference)

(d) Determinative use (only *that/those*, which is non-contrastive):

$$\left.\begin{array}{l} \text{That which} \\ \text{What} \end{array}\right\} \text{upsets me most is his manners}$$

Those who are lazy will never pass

That which is very formal. There is no personal singular *that who where, instead, other constructions are used. For example:

$$\left.\begin{array}{l}\text{Anyone}\\\text{Anybody}\\\text{The person}\end{array}\right\}\text{who is} \dots$$

People who are . . .

Note that *He who* . . . is archaic.

(e) Emotive use of *this* in informal style (sometimes with a presupposition of familiarity 'we both know'):

Don't mention this wretched business again!
You know this fellow Johnson . . .
It gives you this great feeling of open spaces and clean air
Then I saw this girl . . .
Then I got this letter from Grace . . .

In very familiar style, *this* can occur entirely cataphorically as determiner:

Well, I'll tell you a story. There was this inventor . . .

4.122
Universal pronouns
These comprise *each*, *all*, and the *every* series (*Table* 4:7).

Table 4:7
UNIVERSAL PRONOUNS

		COUNT		MASS
		personal	non-personal	
singular	nominal	*everyone* *everybody* *every one* *each*	*everything* *every one* *each*	*all* (*the*) *ink*
	determiner	*every* *each* }*boy/pen*		
plural	nominal/ determiner	*all* (*the*) *boys/pens*		

There are two -*s* genitives: *everyone's* and *everybody's*. *Every* and combinations with *every* refer to three or more, and have collective reference.

Each refers to two or more, *ie* it can be dual or plural, and has individual reference. Thus:

There were two boys who called and I gave an apple to $\begin{cases} \text{each} \\ \text{*everybody} \end{cases}$

There were three boys who called and I gave an apple to $\begin{cases} \text{each} \\ \text{everybody} \end{cases}$

There is, however, a meaning difference between *each* and *everybody*. *Each* entails reference to something in the context, whereas *everybody* does not:

I walked into the room and gave an apple to $\begin{cases} \text{*each} \\ \text{everybody} \end{cases}$

Every one, each (one), and *all* have *of*-constructions. *Every* and *each* can have a singular or plural pronoun for co-reference:

$\left.\begin{matrix} \text{Every one} \\ \text{Each} \\ \text{Each one} \end{matrix}\right\}$ of the students should have $\begin{cases} \text{their} \\ \text{his} \end{cases}$ own books

Every can also be used with plural expressions such as *every two weeks, every few months.*

All has been said to have 'determiner function' since it can occur immediately before a noun. As we have seen in 4.19, however, it is actually a predeterminer, since it can be followed by determiners. Compare the different possible uses of *all*:

$\left.\begin{matrix} \text{All boys} \\ \text{All the boys} \\ \text{All of the boys} \\ \text{All} \end{matrix}\right\}$ want to become football players

Note
Like *each (one)* and *every one* above, *everyone* and *everybody* are often taken as plural (see 7.36).
   It would be easier for all if everybody minded his/their own business.

Assertive pronouns
4.123
Assertive pronouns consist of five groups: the multal group (*much, many, more, most*); the paucal group (*little, less, least; few, fewer, fewest*); the *several/enough* group; *one;* and the *some* group (*some, somebody, someone, something*).

4.124

Multal and paucal groups

The multal and paucal groups can be seen as antonyms with similar distributions (*Table* 4:8).

Table 4:8

MULTAL AND PAUCAL GROUPS

	MULTAL PRONOUNS		PAUCAL PRONOUNS	
	count	mass	count	mass
singular		*much*⎫ *more* ⎬*ink* *most* ⎭		*(the)*⎫ *(a)* ⎬*little* ⎫ *less* ⎬*ink* *(the) least* ⎭
plural	*many*⎫ *more* ⎬*pens* *most* ⎭		*(the)*⎫ *(a)* ⎬*few* ⎫ *fewer* ⎬*pens* *(the) fewest* ⎭	

Besides the regular *fewer chances* (with count nouns) and *less noise* (with mass nouns), *less* also occurs (despite prescriptive pressure) with plurals, eg: *This roof has fewer/less leaks than our old one, You have fewer/less marbles than me.* Only *less* is used in expressions denoting periods of time, sums, etc:

less than two weeks
less than $1000

4.125

Several **and** *enough*

Several and *enough* have both determiner and nominal function. They can take the *of*-construction. *Several* occurs only with plural count function. As determiner, *enough* may have either pre- or post-nominal position. The distribution is shown in *Table* 4:9.

Table 4:9

SEVERAL AND *ENOUGH*

	COUNT	MASS
singular		*enough*
plural	*several* *enough*	

John has made several mistakes in his essay

Have you got $\left\{\begin{array}{l}\text{enough food/books?}\\ \text{food/books enough?}\end{array}\right.$

Yes, we have enough

4.126
One

One has several different uses.

(a) NUMERICAL *ONE* when used with animate and inanimate singular count nouns is a stressed variant of the indefinite article *a(n)*, which is unstressed and has only determiner function. It is in contrast with the dual *two* and *both* and the plural numerals *three, four*, etc; *several;* and indefinite *some* (*Table* 4:10).

Table 4:10

NUMERICAL *ONE* AND CONTRASTS

	COUNT
singular	(*the*) *one* [stressed] *a(n)* [unstressed]
dual	*both* (*the*) [stressed] (*the*) *two*
plural	(*the*) *three, four,* ... *several* *some* [unstressed]

DETERMINER FUNCTION	NOMINAL FUNCTION
(the) one a $\Big\}$ boy/pen	one of the boys/pens
both (the) (the) two $\Big\}$ boys/pens	both two $\Big\}$ of the boys/pens
(the) three some $\Big\}$ boys/pens	three some $\Big\}$ of the boys/pens

(*The*) *one* is also in contrast with *the other* in the correlative construction:

One went this way, the other that way

Note that there is a somewhat formal or old-fashioned use of *one* meaning 'a certain' before personal proper names:

I remember one Charlie Brown at school

(b) REPLACIVE *ONE* (*cf* 10.46) is used as an anaphoric substitute for a singular or plural count noun. It has the singular form *one* and the plural *ones*. Replacive *one* can take determiners (*the, this, my, which, each,* etc) and premodifiers (*Table* 4:11).

Table 4:11
REPLACIVE *ONE*

	COUNT
singular	(*the*) *one*
plural	(*the*) *ones*

'I am looking for a particular book on syntax.' –
  'Is this the one you mean?'
'Yes, I'd like a drink, but just a small one.' –
  'I thought you preferred large ones.'

(c) INDEFINITE *ONE* means 'people in general', in particular with reference to the speaker. This use of *one* is chiefly formal and is often replaced by the more informal *you:*

$$\left.\begin{array}{l}\text{One would}\\ \text{You'd}\end{array}\right\} \text{think they would run a later bus than that!}$$

Indefinite *one* has the genitive *one's* and the reflexive *oneself* (see *Table* 4:5, Note *e*). In AmE repetition of co-referential *one* is characteristically formal, *he* or (informally) *you* being preferred instead:

$$\text{One should always be careful in talking about} \left\{\begin{array}{l}\text{one's}\\ \text{his}\end{array}\right\} \text{finances}$$

$$\text{One can't be too careful, can} \left\{\begin{array}{l}\text{one?}\\ \text{you?}\end{array}\right.$$

4.127
The *some/any* series and *either*
It is convenient to treat the assertive *some* series together with the non-assertive *any* series and *either*. The distributions are given in *Table* 4:12.
  Some, any, and *either* can have both determiner and nominal function and take the *of*-construction; the others have only nominal function.

Table 4:12

THE *SOME/ANY* SERIES AND *EITHER*

	ASSERTIVE			NON-ASSERTIVE		
	count		mass	count		mass
	personal	non-personal		personal	non-personal	
singular	*somebody* *someone* *either*	*something* *either*		*anybody* *anyone* *either*	*anything* *either*	
plural	*some*		*some*	*any* (see 4.127 Note *b*)		*any*

With reference to the distinction made in 2.21 *f* between assertion and non-assertion, we can see that there is parallel distribution between assertive *some* and non-assertive *any:*

assertive	*John bought some apples*
non-assertive/interrogative/positive	*Did John buy any apples?*
non-assertive/interrogative/negative	*Didn't John buy any apples?*
non-assertive/negative	*John didn't buy any apples*

Besides *not*, the negative context which brings about non-assertion may consist of:

(a) the negatives *never, no, neither, nor*
(b) the 'incomplete negatives' *hardly, nearly, almost, little, few, least, but, only, seldom*, etc
(c) the 'implied negatives' *just, before; fail, prevent; reluctant, hard, difficult*, etc; and comparisons with *too*

Compare the following assertive/non-assertive sentences:

(a) { John will always manage to do something useful
     { John will never manage to do anything useful

(b) { There was a good chance somebody would come
     { There was little chance anybody would come

(c) { John was eager to read something about the war
     { John was reluctant to read anything about the war
     { John was too lazy to read anything about the war

Although the main 'superficial' markers of non-assertion are negative, interrogative, and conditional clauses, it is the 'deep', basic meaning of the whole sentence which ultimately conditions the choice of the *some* or the *any* series. See further 7.44. For example, in the sentence

> Freud probably contributed more than anyone to the
> understanding of dreams

the basic meaning is negative and non-assertive, as appears in the para-
phase

> Nobody contributed more to the understanding of dreams than
> Freud

Conversely, *some* is often used in negative, interrogative, or conditional sentences, when the basic meaning is assertive ('positive orientation', see 7.57):

$$\text{Did} \begin{Bmatrix} \text{somebody} \\ \text{anybody} \end{Bmatrix} \text{telephone last night?}$$

The difference between these last two can be explained in terms of
different presuppositions: *somebody* rather suggests that the speaker
expected a telephone call, whereas *anybody* does not. In making an invitation or an offer, it is for the same reason polite to presuppose an
acceptance:

> Would you like some wine?

The following examples further illustrate the use of the *some* series in
superficially non-assertive contexts:

> If someone were to drop a match here, the house would be on
> fire in two minutes
> But what if somebody decides to break the rules?
> Will somebody please open the door?
> Why don't you ask something else?

Conversely, the *any* series is used with stress in superficially assertive
sentences with the special meaning of 'no matter who, no matter what':

> He will eat anything
> Anyone interested in addressing the meeting should let us know
> Any offer would be better than this.

Note

[a] *Somebody, someone, anybody, anyone* often occur with *their* in co-reference
(*cf* 7.36):

> *Somebody* lost *his/their* raincoat

[b] It should be noted that *any* can also be singular count:

> How *does any of us* know you are telling the truth?
> ANY *dog* might bite a child if teased.

4.128
Negative pronouns
These include the *no* series and *neither* (but *cf* also *little* and *few*). *Neither*
has both determiner and nominal function; *no* has determiner function;
the rest only nominal function (see *Table* 4:13; for concord, see 7.36).

Nobody ⎫
No one ⎬ has ⎫
None ⎭ ⎬ come yet
None have ⎭

None of the students {has / have} failed

Neither {of the (two) students / student} has failed

Nothing has happened yet
Nothing of this has come about!

Neither {of the accusations / accusation} is true

That's none of your business!

Table 4:13
NEGATIVE PRONOUNS

	COUNT		MASS
	personal	non-personal	
singular	*no* *no one* *nobody* *neither (of)* *none (of)*	*nothing (of)* *neither (of)* *none (of)*	*no* *none (of)*
plural	*no* *none (of)*		

4.129
Numerals
The numerals consist of CARDINAL numbers (*one*, *two*, *three*, etc)
and ORDINAL numbers (*first*, *second*, *third*, etc). They are given in
Table 4:14, which has been arranged to bring out the systematic nature
of the English numerals.

The typographical distinctions in *Table* 4:14 draw attention to the fact that cardinal numbers for 1 to 13, 15, 20, 30, 50, 100, 1000, etc are unsystematic and have to be learnt as individual items. Cardinal numbers from 14 to 99 are largely systematic, since they are formed by adding endings to the other numbers. There are two sets of such derivative numbers: 14 to 19 are formed by the ending *-teen;* 40, 50, 60, 70, 80, 90 are formed by the ending *-ty*. Compare the series:

four	~ fourteen	~ forty (Note *ou* ~ *o* shift)
five	~ fifteen	~ fifty (Note *v* ~ *f* shift)
six	~ sixteen	~ sixty
seven	~ seventeen	~ seventy, etc

Ordinal numbers for 1 to 3 are unsystematic (*first, second, third*). The rest are formed by adding *-th* to the cardinal numbers. Cardinal numbers ending in *-y* change to *-ie* before *-th:*

four ~ fourth	fourteen ~ fourteenth	forty ~ fortieth
five ~ fifth	fifteen ~ fifteenth	fifty ~ fiftieth
six ~ sixth	sixteen ~ sixteenth	sixty ~ sixtieth

Table 4:14

NUMERALS

0	nought		
1	one	1st	first
2	two	2nd	second
3	three	3rd	third
4	four	4th	fourth
5	five	5th	fifth
6	six	6th	sixth
7	seven	7th	seventh
8	eight	8th	eighth
9	nine	9th	ninth
10	ten	10th	tenth
11	eleven	11th	eleventh
12	twelve	12th	twelfth
13	thirteen	13th	thirteenth
14	fourteen	14th	fourteenth
15	fifteen	15th	fifteenth
16	sixteen	16th	sixteenth
17	seventeen	17th	seventeenth
18	eighteen	18th	eighteenth
19	nineteen	19th	nineteenth
20	twenty	20th	twentieth
21	twenty-one	21st	twenty-first
22	twenty-two	22nd	twenty-second
23	twenty-three	23rd	twenty-third
24	twenty-four	24th	twenty-fourth

Table 4:14 *continued*

NUMERALS

25	twenty-five		25th	twenty-fifth
26	twenty-six		26th	twenty-sixth
27	twenty-seven		27th	twenty-seventh
28	twenty-eight		28th	twenty-eighth
29	twenty-nine		29th	twenty-ninth
30	**thirty**		30th	thirtieth
40	forty		40th	fortieth
50	fifty		50th	fiftieth
60	sixty		60th	sixtieth
70	seventy		70th	seventieth
80	eighty		80th	eightieth
90	ninety		90th	ninetieth
100	one **hundred**		100th	(one) hundredth
101	one hundred and one		101st	(one) hundred and first
102	one hundred and two, etc		102nd	(one) hundred and second
1,000	one **thousand**		1,000th	(one) thousandth
1,001	one thousand (and) one, etc		1,001st	(one) thousand and first
2,000	two thousand		2,000th	two thousandth
10,000	ten thousand		10,000th	ten thousandth
100,000	one hundred thousand		100,000th	(one) hundred thousandth
1,000,000	one **million**		1,000,000th	(one) millionth

	BRITISH SYSTEM	AMERICAN SYSTEM
1,000,000,000	one thousand million	one **billion**
1,000,000,000,000	one **billion**	one **trillion**
1,000,000,000,000,000	one thousand billions	one **quadrillion**
1 + 18 zeros	one **trillion**	one **quintillion**
1 + 24 zeros	one **quadrillion**	one **septillion**
1 + 30 zeros	one **quintillion**	one **nonillion**

Note

[a] The symbol '0' has different spoken forms:

nought, naught /nɔt/, *cipher* /saɪfə/, *eg*

the figure nought (in mathematics)
.03 = 'point nought three'

zero /'zɪ(ə)roʊ/ (in mathematics and for temperature), *eg*

It's five degrees below zero

o /oʊ/, *eg*

Dial 7050 /sevn oʊ faɪv oʊ/ and ask for extension 90 /naɪn oʊ/ (in telephone numbers)
603.09 = /sɪks oʊ θri pɔɪnt oʊ naɪn/

nil /nɪl/, *nothing*, *eg*

The result of the match was 4–0 (four (goals to) nil; especially BrE)
Brazil won 4–0 (four (to) nothing).

love (in tennis), *eg*

Norway leads by 30–0 (thirty love) in the first game of the second set

[*b*]   With *hundred, thousand*, etc, *one* has an unstressed variant *a:*

$$\left.\begin{array}{l} one \\ a \end{array}\right\} hundred$$

[*c*]   Unlike the *y* → *ie(s)* change in nouns and verbs (4.62, 3.60), this change *y* → *ie(th)* adds a syllable. Compare:

the sixties /sɪkstɪz/
the sixtieth /sɪkstiɪθ/

[*d*]   The numerals *trillion, quadrillion*, etc are rare, and they tend to be known only by specialists in relevant fields.

Bibliographical note

See Jespersen (1909–49), especially Part II, Chapters 2–9; Kruisinga (1931–32), especially Part II.2; Poutsma (1926–29), especially Part II.1A, 1B; Strang (1968), especially Chapters 7 and 8.

On noun classes, see Bolinger (1969).

On reference and the articles, see Christophersen (1939); Powell (1967); Robbins (1968); Sloat (1969); Smith (1964); Sørensen (1958a and b).

On gender, see Kanekiyo (1965).

On pronouns, see Dušková (1965); Jackendoff (1969); Jacobsson (1968a and b); R. Lakoff (1969a); Postal (1966).

ADJECTIVES AND ADVERBS

5.1
Introduction

The *adjective* and the *adverb* have traditionally been considered parts of speech and these terms are currently used to denote English word-classes, although grammars may vary to some extent in what is to be included under each of the terms. Because of their general currency, it is convenient to continue to refer to adjectives and adverbs as English word-classes, but we must be aware that they do not constitute well-defined classes and, moreover, that neither class is homogeneous.

Characteristics of the adjective
5.2

Since we wish the class of adjectives to comprise items that have a similar syntactic function, rather than merely a resemblance in form, we cannot tell whether a word is an adjective by looking at it in isolation. We cannot do so because the form of a word does not necessarily indicate its syntactic function. As we have pointed out (2.13), an item may belong to more than one class, the classic example being *round* as in *a round of golf* (noun), *They round the corner* (verb), *a round object* (adjective), *He came round to see us* (adverb), *They sat round the table* (preposition). Some suffixes are indeed found only with adjectives, *eg: -ous* (App I.28), but many common adjectives are like *round* in having no identifying shape, *eg: good, hot, little, young, fat.* Nor can we identify a word as an adjective merely by considering its potentialities for inflection or affixation. It is true that many adjectives inflect for the comparative and superlative, *eg: great, greater, greatest.* But many do not allow inflected forms, *eg: disastrous, *disastrouser, *disastrousest* (5.74). Moreover, a few adverbs can be similarly inflected, *eg: (He worked) hard, harder, hardest* (5.76). It is also true that many adjectives provide the base from which adverbs are derived by means of an *-ly* suffix, *eg:* adjective *happy*, adverb *happily* (App I.30). Nevertheless, some do not allow this derivational process; for example, there is no adverb **oldly* derived from the adjective *old.* And there are a few adjectives that are themselves derived from an adjective base in this way, *eg: kindly,* an item functioning also as an adverb.

5.3

Four features are generally considered to be characteristic of adjectives:

(1) They can freely occur in attributive position (5.17), *ie* they can premodify a noun, *eg: happy* in *the happy children.*

(2) They can freely occur in predicative position (5.17), *ie* they can function as subject complement, *eg: old* in *The man seemed old,* or as object complement, *eg: ugly* in *He thought the painting ugly* (2.4).

(3) They can be premodified by the intensifier *very, eg: The children are very happy* (5.51).

(4) They can take comparative and superlative forms whether inflectionally, *eg: The children are happier now, They are the happiest people I know,* or by the addition of the premodifiers *more* and *most* (periphrastic comparison), *eg: These students are more intelligent, They are the most beautiful paintings I have ever seen* (5.68).

5.4

However, not all words that are traditionally regarded as adjectives possess all of these four features. Moreover, some of the features apply to words that are generally considered to belong to other classes. Let us look at a few examples of different types of adjectives, including some borderline cases, and at the same time extend our treatment to take account of words that are generally assigned to the traditional classes of adverb and noun. For this purpose, we have selected eight words, to each of which we apply five criteria. The first four of the criteria are an exploration of the four features that are considered characteristic of adjectives, while the fifth criterion introduces a feature that is characteristic of nouns. Since words can belong to more than one class, we place them in the context of a sentence, so that it should be clear which use of the words is being tested.

(a) John is *hungry*
(b) The universe is *infinite*
(c) Bob is an *utter* fool
(d) His reply was *tantamount* to an ultimatum
(e) Their house is *ablaze*
(f) Peter is *abroad*
(g) The meeting is *soon*
(h) His favourite meat is *lamb*

Note that while an attempt has been made to provide sentences that are similar syntactically, some differences are unavoidable. For example, *utter* in (c) could not be placed predicatively.

The five criteria:

(1) The item can function in ATTRIBUTIVE position: *the . . . N.*

(2) The item can function in PREDICATIVE position following the intensive verb SEEM: *The N seemed* . . . .

(3) The item can be premodified by the intensifier *very*.

(4) The item can accept COMPARISON, *ie* the comparative and superlative forms, whether inflected or periphrastic.

(5) The item can function as DIRECT OBJECT, *eg: I like* . . . or *I like a(n)*. . . . For this criterion to apply, either the indefinite article or the zero article must be available.

5.5

The results of the application of the criteria are displayed in *Table* 5:1.

Table 5:1

CRITERIA FOR ESTABLISHING ADJECTIVE CLASSES

	attributive	predicative with SEEM	VERY	comparison	direct object
(a) *hungry*	+	+	+	+	−
(b) *infinite*	+	+	−	−	−
(c) *utter*	+	−	−	−	−
(d) *tantamount*	−	+	−	−	−
(e) *ablaze*	−	+	−	−	−
(f) *abroad*	−	−	−	−	−
(g) *soon*	−	−	+	+	−
(h) *lamb*	+	−	−	−	+

The first four words in the leftmost column of *Table* 5:1 would be regarded by all grammarians as adjectives: *hungry, infinite, utter, tantamount,* while *abroad* and *soon* would be unhesitatingly assigned to the adverb class, and *lamb* to the noun class. However, *ablaze* is on the borderline between the adjective and adverb classes. If we examine the four undoubted adjectives in relation to the five criteria, we see what distinguishes them from the words that are assigned to other classes:

(i) Adjectives can function attributively (criterion 1) and/or predicatively after SEEM (criterion 2).

(ii) Adjectives cannot function as direct object if they are required to take the indefinite article or the zero article (criterion 5).

We can therefore include *ablaze* in the adjective class, since we can have

Their house seemed *ablaze*

where *ablaze* is functioning predicatively after SEEM, and we cannot have *ablaze* as direct object:

*I like *ablaze*

or

*I like an *ablaze*

We can see from *Table* 5:1 that criteria 3 and 4 – acceptance of pre-modification by *very* and the ability to take comparison – have no diagnostic value for the present purpose. These two features generally coincide for a particular word, and are determined by a semantic feature, the gradability of an item. Gradability is a semantic feature that cuts across word-classes. Many adjectives are gradable, just as many adverbs are gradable. And these two classes use the same features to realize the gradability of an item, in particular premodification by *very* and comparison (5.70 *ff*). Hence, these two features neither distinguish adjectives from adverbs, nor are found in all adjectives.

On the other hand, adjectives are distinguished positively by their ability to function attributively and/or their ability to function predicatively after intensive verbs, including SEEM. It is reasonable to suggest that those that function both attributively and predicatively are central to the class of adjectives, while those that are limited to one or other function are peripheral adjectives. Therefore, of the five adjectives given in *Table* 5:1, *hungry* and *infinite* are central adjectives, while *utter*, *tantamount*, and *ablaze* are peripheral adjectives.

Note

[a] Adjectives can function as direct object if they take a definite determiner:

> He will feed the hungry

but not otherwise:

> *He will feed a hungry
> *He will feed hungry

Under the same condition they can also function as subject, indirect object, and complement of a preposition (5.20–23). For convenience in framing the criterion, only one of the functions – direct object – is mentioned in criterion 5. But see 5.20 Note *f*.

[b] The attributive use of the noun *lamb* is exemplified in *lamb chops*. Nouns are commonly used attributively (5.11, 13.57 *f*, App I.44 *ff*). The apparent exceptions to the test for adjective status – attributive nouns and nouns appearing predicatively after SEEM – are discussed in 5.11.

The adjective and other word-classes
5.6

We now consider briefly some examples of overlapping between the adjective class and other word-classes. The overlapping may be due to syntactic features central to other classes but displayed by some adjectives, or to features central to the adjective class but displayed by some members of other classes. The three relevant word-classes are adverbs, nouns and participles.

Adjective and adverb
5.7

We have referred above (5.5) to *ablaze* as a borderline case between the adjective and adverb classes. Certain words beginning with *a-* have constituted a problem in classification for grammarians, some assigning them to the adjective class and others to the adverb class. These *a-* words function predicatively, but only a few can be freely used attributively. As we can see from *Table* 5:1, adverbs like *abroad* and *soon* can also be used predicatively. In actual fact, only a relatively small number of adverbs can function predicatively, namely, certain place and time adverbs (8.46, 8.73). But even these adverbs are used predicatively only after BE, while adjectives can be used with other intensive verbs as well. Hence, we specifically insisted on the intensive verb SEEM in criterion 2 for *Table* 5:1. With respect to their ability to be used predicatively with both BE and another intensive verb such as SEEM, we can therefore contrast the *a-* adjective *asleep* and the adjective *subject*, on the one hand, with the *a-* adverb *abroad* and the adverb *there*, on the other:

$$\text{The patient was} \begin{cases} \textit{asleep} \\ \textit{subject to fits} \\ \textit{abroad} \\ \textit{there} \end{cases}$$

$$\text{The patient seemed} \begin{cases} \textit{asleep} \\ \textit{subject to fits} \\ \textit{*abroad} \\ \textit{*there} \end{cases}$$

Notice the contrast between the *a-* adverbs in

$$\text{He went} \begin{cases} \textit{aboard} \\ \textit{abroad} \\ \textit{around} \\ \textit{away} \end{cases}$$

and the *a-* adjectives in the same sentence-frame:

$$\text{He went} \begin{cases} \textit{*afraid} \\ \textit{*alert} \\ \textit{*asleep} \\ \textit{*awake} \end{cases}$$

A- adjectives are unacceptable as part of the predication after verbs of motion. *A-* adverbs, however, are acceptable and denote direction after such verbs. The sentences with *a-* adjectives are acceptable insofar as the adjectives can be interpreted not as part of the predication but as supplementive adjective clauses (5.24). For example, we might be able to interpret *He went afraid* as 'He was afraid as he went'.

Common *a-* adjectives are

> *ablaze, afloat, afraid, aghast, alert, alike, alive, alone, aloof,*
> *ashamed, asleep, averse, awake, aware*

Alert and *aloof* are freely used attributively. Some of the other *a-* adjectives occasionally function attributively, though normally only when they are modified: *the half-asleep children, the fully awake patient, a somewhat afraid soldier, a really alive student* ('lively'), *a very ashamed girl.*

Note

[a] The acceptable alternative for adverbs to the unacceptable SEEM construction requires *to be* after SEEM. It is also available for adjectives:

$$\text{The patient seemed to be} \begin{cases} asleep \\ subject\ to\ fits \\ abroad \\ there \end{cases}$$

[b] Like the adverbs in *He was downstairs* and *He was outside, abroad* can be recalled by a question introduced by the interrogative adverb *where: Where is he? – Abroad.* Others among the *a-* adverbs, *eg: around* and *away,* are less likely to be the sole response of a *where* question, though they can supply the information requested by *where:*

$$\text{Where is he? He is} \begin{cases} around \\ away \end{cases}$$

[c] Notice the contrast between the *a-* adjective in

> They looked *asleep*

and the *a-* adverb in

> They looked *away*

With *asleep, looked* is an intensive verb, synonymous with *seemed.* With *away,* it is an intransitive verb, similar in meaning and use to *glanced.*

[d] *Alike* requires reference to conjoined noun phrases or to a plural noun phrase: *John and Mary are alike, He thought them alike.*

[e] Some *a-* adjectives freely take premodification by *very* and comparison, *eg: afraid, alert, alike, aloof, ashamed,* and *averse.* Others do so marginally, *eg: asleep* and *awake. Alive to* in the sense 'aware of' can be premodified by *very* and compared. Some of the *a-* adjectives can also be premodified by *very much* (particularly *afraid, alike, ashamed, aware*), and *aware* can be premodified by *(very) well* too. These modifiers are characteristically taken by many verbs (*cf* 5.15 Note, 5.36).

[f] *Alone* is perhaps a marginal adjective. Unlike the *a-* adverbs, it does not denote position or direction. When it is synonymous with *solitary* ('without companionship') rather than with *by . . . -self*, it is acceptable to at least some speakers with *seem* and *very* (*He seemed alone, He is very alone*).

5.8

Certain items that function as adjectives are also used to define in some way the process denoted by the verb, which is a typical use of adverbs (8.34). An example is *quick* in *He came back quick*. If in its adverbial use the item is not restricted to a position after the verb or (if present) the object, it undoubtedly belongs to both the adjective and adverb classes. For example, *long* and *still*, which commonly function as adjectives, are in pre-verb position in the following sentences and must therefore be adverbs:

Such animals have *long* had to defend themselves
They *still* can't make up their minds whether to go or not

Furthermore, the item clearly represents two different words if there is a semantic difference between the words in the two uses, as with *long* and *still*. But in a number of other cases, neither difference applies.

In many such cases, the adjective form and a corresponding *-ly* adverb form can be used interchangeably, with little or no semantic difference, except that some people prefer the adverb form:

He spoke $\begin{cases} \textit{loud} \text{ and } \textit{clear} \\ \textit{loudly} \text{ and } \textit{clearly} \end{cases}$ [1]

He drove the car $\begin{cases} \textit{slow} \text{ (especially AmE)} \\ \textit{slowly} \end{cases}$ [2]

She buys her clothes $\begin{cases} \textit{cheap} \\ \textit{cheaply} \end{cases}$ [3]

He came back $\begin{cases} \textit{quick} \\ \textit{quickly} \end{cases}$ [4]

In other cases there is no corresponding adverb form of the same lexical item, so that only the adjective form is available:

He always talks *big* (informal) [5]
They are running *fast*
They are working *late*
We finished *early* today
They will come *round* afterwards (replaced by *around* in AmE)

The adverbs *lately* and *roundly* do not correspond to the adjective forms *late* and *round* in the above sentences. Only a limited number of adjectives have adverbial uses. Contrast with sentences marked [1–5]:

*He spoke *brief* and *frank*	[1a]
*He drove the car *clever*	[2a]
*She buys her clothes *careful*	[3a]
*He came back *sudden*	[4a]
*He always talks *arrogant*	[5a]

Adjective forms like *slow* differ from the corresponding adverb forms in several ways:

(i) The adjective form, if admissible at all, is restricted to a position after the verb or (if present) the object:

> He *slowly* drove the car into the garage
> He drove the car *slowly* into the garage
> *He *slow* drove the car into the garage
> (?)He drove the car *slow* into the garage

It is similarly restricted in a nominalization realized by a participle clause containing a direct object:

> John's *slowly* driving the car annoyed his wife
> John's driving the car *slowly* annoyed his wife
> *John's *slow* driving the car annoyed his wife
> (?)John's driving the car *slow* annoyed his wife

(ii) The adjective form cannot be the focus of a cleft sentence, though this is possible for some corresponding adverbs:

> It was *slowly* that he drove the car into the garage
> *It was *slow* that he drove the car into the garage

But if the adjective forms are coordinated, they can sometimes (and for some speakers) be the focus of a cleft sentence:

> It was *loud and clear* that he spoke.

Note

[a] For the use of adjectives to express the result of the process denoted by the verb, *eg: That powder washed the clothes white*, see 5.17.

[b] For the use of adjectives as the sole realization of a verbless clause, *eg: Nervous, the man opened the letter*, see 5.24–27.

[c] In certain uses of SMELL and FEEL there is considerable idiolectal variation, and perhaps also fluctuation in the usage of the same individual, between the adjective and adverb forms:

> The flowers smell $\begin{cases} \text{beautiful} \\ \text{?beautifully} \end{cases}$

> He felt $\begin{cases} \text{bad} \\ \text{?badly} \end{cases}$ ('health' or 'guilty'/'unhappy' sense)

With SMELL, the variation depends on the particular item:

The flowers smell $\begin{cases} \text{good} \\ \text{*well} \\ \text{sweet} \\ \text{?sweetly} \end{cases}$

There are prescriptive objections to the adverb form for these items with SMELL with 'recipient' meaning (7.16) and to *badly* with FEEL. With FEEL and SMELL, the adverb form is used to express intensity of feelings:

He felt $\begin{cases} \text{strongly} \\ \text{deeply} \\ \text{keenly} \end{cases}$ about it

It smells strongly of garlic

The adjective *keen* has the different sense of 'enthusiastic' when it can also complement BE:

He $\begin{cases} \text{felt} \\ \text{was} \end{cases}$ keen about it

Notice the physical sense of *strong* in

He $\begin{cases} \text{felt} \\ \text{was} \end{cases}$ strong

The use of adverb forms after 'recipient' TASTE seems much less common and would be unacceptable to many speakers:

The food tastes $\begin{cases} \text{good} \\ \text{?well} \\ \text{marvellous} \\ \text{?marvellously} \end{cases}$

After 'recipient' LOOK and SOUND, it is normal to use adjective forms. There is a distinction in meaning between the adjectives *good* and *well* (5.35) after 'recipient' LOOK:

He looks good   ('He has a good appearance')
He looks well   ('It looks as if he is well')

5.9

A few items that normally function as adverbs can also be used attributively, like adjectives, *eg: the then chairman.* More such items are available to postmodify noun phrases, *eg: the sentence below.* Since only a relatively few adverbs are involved, it is simplest to list the adverbs with these potentialities. (See 5.61*ff.*) Alternatively, we can analyse *then* in *the then chairman* as a peripheral adjective like *utter* (5.4 *f*, *Table* 5:1), and consider *then* and other adverbs used attributively as belonging to both the adverb and adjective classes.

Adjective and noun
5.10

Some items can be both adjectives and nouns. For example, *criminal* is an adjective in that

(a) it can be used attributively: *a criminal attack*
(b) it can be used predicatively: *The attack seemed criminal to us*

But *criminal* also has all the characteristics of a noun, since it can be

(a) subject of a clause: *The criminal pleaded guilty to all charges*
(b) subject complement: *He is probably a criminal*
(c) object: *They have arrested the criminal*
(d) inflected for number: *one criminal, several criminals*
(e) inflected for the genitive case: *the criminal's sentence, the criminals' views*
(f) preceded by articles and other determiners: *a criminal, that criminal*
(g) premodified by an adjective: *a violent criminal*

We must therefore say that *criminal* is both an adjective and a noun, and the relationship between the adjective *criminal* and the noun *criminal* is that of conversion (App I.35). The italicized nouns in the following sentences are like *criminal* in this respect, since they often function as adjectives:

There was only one *black* in my class
He is investigating the *ancients'* conception of the universe
The *Almighty's* ways are often strange
The king greeted his *nobles*
You won't find many *classics* in our library

We need to distinguish the above instances of conversion, where the items are fully nouns, from adjectives functioning as the heads of noun phrases (5.20–23).

Note

In *His attack was criminal, criminal* is undoubtedly an adjective, since there is no article contrast (**His attack was a criminal,* **His attack was the criminal*) or number contrast. In *a criminal attack,* it also appears to be an adjective (roughly 'a brutal attack') and is not equivalent to (say) 'an attack by a criminal' (*cf* 5.11). It is presumably also an adjective in *criminal law* ('law relating to crime', *cf: civil law, commercial law*) and in both senses of *criminal lawyer* ('a lawyer specializing in criminal law' and 'a lawyer who is criminal'). See 5.34.

5.11

Nouns commonly function attributively, as premodifiers of other nouns (13.57 *f*):

the city council	a love poem
a stone wall	August weather

In this function, the attributive nouns resemble adjectives. However, the basically nominal character of these premodifiers is shown by their correspondence to prepositional phrases with the noun as complement:

the council of the city   a poem about love
a wall (made) of stone   weather (usual) in August

Such a correspondence is not available for attributive adjectives:

the urban council   a long poem
a thick wall   hot weather

though we can sometimes use a postmodifying prepositional phrase with a related noun as complement, *eg: a long poem* ∼ *a poem of considerable length.*

Like adjectives, nouns can function predicatively after intensive verbs, in particular after BE:

That man is a fool
The noise you heard was thunder
She became a nurse
He turned traitor

Some nouns can even function both attributively and predicatively. Moreover, these nouns are like adjectives in that they do not take number variation. The nouns denote material from which things are made or style (*cf* the corresponding classes of adjective, 5.41):

that concrete floor ∼ that floor is concrete
those pork pies ∼ ?those pies are pork
Worcester porcelain ∼ this porcelain is Worcester

It can be argued that these nouns have been converted to adjectives (App I.38).

Some nouns can also appear predicatively after SEEM, one of the diagnostic criteria for adjectives:

He seems a fool
His friend seems very much an Englishman
Your remark seems nonsense to me
My stay there seemed sheer bliss

These are indeed very close semantically to adjectives (*foolish, English, nonsensical, blissful*). The closeness is of course greatest for mass nouns such as *nonsense, fun* and *bliss*, since, like adjectives, they do not take number variation. Moreover, they can appear without an overt determiner. On the other hand, unlike adjectives functioning as heads of noun phrases (5.20 *ff*), these mass nouns take the zero article when they function (say) as direct object:

I like *nonsense*
He experienced *bliss.*

Note

[a] Attributive nouns can be coordinated with adjectives, *eg: weekly and morning newspapers, city and suburban houses,* but it seems that such conjoinings are normally only possible when there is an elliptical head ('weekly newspapers and morning newspapers', 'city houses and suburban houses'), but not otherwise (**a* city and pleasant house), cf* 9.100 *f.* Where both premodifiers are nouns, ellipsis need not be involved, *eg: a glass and concrete house* ('a house made of glass and concrete'), *a cheese and cucumber sandwich* ('a sandwich containing cheese and cucumber'). These become ambiguous in the plural (9.121), *eg: cheese and cucumber sandwiches* ('each of the sandwiches contains cheese and cucumber' *or* 'cheese sandwiches and cucumber sandwiches').

[b] The nouns that can most easily appear predicatively after SEEM are those that are gradable, that is to say the nouns that can be intensified by intensifying adjectives (5.31). However, some speakers, while accepting in this function mass nouns and singular count nouns, find plural nouns dubious:

?They seem fools
?His friends seem very much Englishmen

Material nouns, which are not gradable, are also dubious after SEEM:

?That floor seems concrete
?Those pies seem pork

[c] In informal usage (especially AmE), *fun* seems to have been fully converted into an adjective and can even accept *very* as premodifier:

That was a very fun party.

Adjective and participle
5.12

There are many adjectives that have the same form as participles in *-ing* or *-ed* (or the variants of *-ed*):

His views were very *surprising*
The man seemed very *offended*

They include forms that have no corresponding verbs:

The results were *unexpected*
His children must be *downhearted*
All his friends are *talented*
His lung is *diseased*

These adjectives can also be attributive:

his *surprising* views
the *offended* man
the *unexpected* results
his *downhearted* children
his *talented* friends
his *diseased* lung

When there are no corresponding verbs (*unexpect, *downheart, *talent, *disease), the forms are obviously not participles.

In some cases there are corresponding verbs but the -ed participle is not interpreted as passive. The passive interpretation is excluded, of course, if the corresponding verb can be used only intransitively:

the *escaped* prisoner   ('the prisoner who has escaped')
the *departed* guests   ('the guests who have departed')

But even in other instances, the passive interpretation is virtually impossible or is not obligatory:

a *grown* boy   ('a boy who has grown (up)')
the *faded* curtains   ('the curtains which have faded')
the *retired* manager   ('the manager who has retired' or 'the manager who has been retired')

Only with some of these is the predicative use allowed:

The curtains are *faded*
Her father is now *retired*
Her son is *grown* (dubious in BrE, but *full-grown* or *grown-up* is fully acceptable)
*The guests are *departed* (cf the reverse in *The guests are gone* ~ *the gone guests*)
*The prisoner is *escaped*

Sometimes there is a corresponding verb, but it has a different meaning. We can therefore have ambiguous sentences where the ambiguity depends on whether we have a participle or an adjective:

She is (very) *calculating* (But her husband is frank) – adjective
She is *calculating* (Don't disturb her while she is doing the arithmetic) – participle
They were (very) *relieved* (to find her at home) – adjective
They were *relieved* (by the next group of sentries) – participle

Notice that we can replace BE by SEEM only with the adjectives.

Note
Unexpected corresponds to the -ed participle of *expect* plus the negative particle:

unexpected ~ *not expected*

However, unlike *expected*, *unexpected* can be premodified by *very*, so that we can argue that the morphological change has introduced a semantic/syntactic change. The situation is less clear for the morphologically negative forms *unwritten* (eg: *unwritten law*) and *unbroken* (eg: *unbroken succession*), which resemble the positive forms in not accepting *very*. But see 5.15 Note.

5.13

Often the difference between the adjective and the participle is not clear-cut, and lies in the verbal force retained by the latter. The verbal force is explicit for the *-ing* form when a direct object is present. Hence, the following *-ing* forms are participles that constitute a verb phrase with the preceding auxiliary (3.12):

> His views were *alarming* his audience
> You are *frightening* the children
> They are *insulting* us

Similarly, the verbal force is explicit for the *-ed* form when a *by* agentive phrase with a personal agent (6.41, 12.14 *f*) is present, indicating the correspondence to the active form of the sentence:

> The man was *offended* by the policeman
> We are *appreciated* by our students
> She was *misunderstood* by her parents

For both participle forms, modification by the intensifier *very* is an explicit indication that the forms have achieved adjective status:

> His views were very *alarming*
> You are very *frightening*
> The man was very *offended*
> ?We are very *appreciated*

We might therefore expect that the presence of *very* together with an explicit indicator of verbal force would produce an unacceptable sentence. This is certainly so for the *-ing* participle form:

> *His views were very *alarming* his audience

However, with the *-ed* participle form, there appears to be divided usage, with increasing acceptance of the co-occurrence of *very* with a *by* agentive phrase containing a personal agent:

> ?The man was very *offended* by the policeman

In the absence of any explicit indicator, the status of the participle form is indeterminate. For the *-ed* form in

> The man was *offended*

the participle interpretation focuses on the process, while the adjective interpretation focuses on the state resulting from the process. For the *-ing* form the difference is perhaps clearer. If in the sentence

> John is *insulting*

the participle interpretation is selected, then the sentence expresses that John is in the process of giving insults and we expect an object, while in the adjective interpretation, the sentence points to a characteristic of John, *cf: John is rude.*

A participle interpretation is unlikely for some *-ing* forms if an object is absent, because the verb is normally transitive:

He is *surprising*   (*?He surprises*)
He is *interesting*   (*?He interests*)
It is *exciting*   (*?It excites*)
It is *tempting*   (*?It tempts*)

Note

[a] *-ed* participle forms accepting *very* can generally retain *very* when they co-occur with a *by*-agentive phrase containing a non-personal agent (12.14*f*):

I'm very disturbed by your attitude
We were very pleased by his behaviour

[b] If the adjective is used dynamically (5.38, 2.16, 3.40), it also focuses on the process, *eg:*

John is being *rude*
Don't be *rude.*

5.14

The participle sometimes reaches full adjective status when it is compounded with another element, which sometimes results in a sharp difference of meaning:

He is *looking* (at a painting)   He is (very) *good-looking*
The eggs are *boiled* hard   The eggs are (very) *hard-boiled*
He was *bitten* (by a snake)   He was (very) *frost-bitten*
It is *breaking* (his heart)   It is (very) *heart-breaking*

When an adjective or adverb is the first element of the compound, the intensifier can be interpreted as related to the first element rather than to the compound as a whole.

Note

Sometimes the passive participle cannot be used in environments where the compound adjective is admitted. For example, the verb *speak* does not allow a personal noun such as *man* as direct object, and hence we cannot have in the passive

*The man was *spoken*

But we can have *well-spoken* in place of *spoken:*

The man was *well-spoken*

Similarly, the verb *behave* does not take a direct object (except the reflexive) and therefore we cannot have a passive:

*The boy was *behaved*

But we can have an adjective compound:

The boy was *well-behaved.*

5.15

It is not only participles allowing the intensifier *very* that can be attributive (13.51 *ff*), as the following examples show:

her crying children	the married couple
the winning team	his published work
the boiling water	the captured prisoner

Note

Very intensifies gradable adjectives and gradable adverbs. Gradable verbs are intensified by other intensifying adverbs (8.19 *ff*), though these are often themselves premodified by *very*, *eg*: *very much, very well*. The relevance of the test on whether the participle forms accept *very* depends on whether the words are gradable, since, as we have seen (5.5), not all adjectives are gradable. Hence, if the corresponding verb allows (say) *very much* while the participle form disallows *very*, we have a good indication that the form in question is a participle rather than an adjective:

> She loved him *very much*
> He was *very much* loved (by her)
> He was loved *very much* (by her)
> *He was *very* loved.

5.16

A few adjectives are differentiated from participles by taking the *-en* suffix where participles with the same base have the *-ed* suffix (*shaved*) or are without a suffix (*drunk, shrunk*):

> *shaven, drunken, shrunken*

For a few others, mostly ending in a voiceless consonant, there is no difference between adjective and participle in spelling, but there is in pronunciation. Whereas the vowel of the participle suffix *-ed* is not pronounced, the suffix is treated in the adjective as a separate syllable pronounced /ɪd/:

> *blessed, crooked, dogged, learned, ragged*

Note

The suffix of *aged* is pronounced as a separate syllable, /ɪd/, when the word is predicated of a personal noun or modifies it (*The man is aged, an aged man*), but not, for example, in *an aged wine*.

Syntactic functions of adjectives
5.17
Attributive and predicative
The major syntactic functions of adjectives are attributive and predicative. These are termed the major syntactic functions, since a word that cannot function either attributively or predicatively is not recognized as an adjective (5.5).

Adjectives are attributive when they premodify nouns. Attributive adjectives appear betweeen the determiner (4.13 *ff*) and the head of the noun phrase:

the *beautiful* painting
a *mere* child
his *main* argument

Predicative adjectives can be

(a) subject complement: there is co-reference between subject and subject complement, the two being in an intensive relationship (7.6):

> Your daughter is *pretty*
> He is *careless*

(b) object complement: there is co-reference between direct object and object complement, the two being in an intensive relationship:

> I consider him *foolish*
> He made his wife *happy*

They are not only subject complement to noun phrases, but also to clauses. They can be complement when the subject is a finite clause:

That he needs it is *obvious*
Whether he will resign is *uncertain*

or non-finite clause:

To drive a car is *dangerous*
To play so hard is *foolish*
Driving a bus isn't *easy*
Playing chess is *enjoyable*

Similarly, adjectives can be object complement to clauses:

I consider $\begin{cases}\text{what he did} \\ \text{playing so hard}\end{cases}$ *foolish*

The adjective functioning as object complement often expresses the result of the process denoted by the verb (7.14):

He pulled his belt *tight*	[6]
He pushed the window *open*	[7]
He writes his letters *large*	[8]

The result of the process can be stated for each sentence:

His belt is tight	[6a]
The window is open	[7a]
His letters are large	[8a]

Note

The verbs in [6]–[8] have a causative meaning. For example, [6] can be paraphrased

He caused his belt to be tight by pulling it

Some verbs used in this type of construction primarily express cause:

She made him *happy* ('She caused him to be happy')
The news turned his hair *white* ('The news caused his hair to be white')

The analogy with adverbs can be seen in the resultative effect of an adverb such as *out* in

He pushed the window *out* ('He caused the window to be out by pushing it')

Compare this sentence with [7] above.

Postpositive
5.18

Adjectives can sometimes be postpositive, *ie* they can sometimes follow the noun or pronoun they modify. A postposed adjective (together with any complementation it may have, *cf* 5.19) can usually be regarded as a reduced relative clause.

Complex indefinite pronouns ending in *-body, -one, -thing, -where* (4.122, 13.37) can be modified only postpositively:

Anyone (who is) *intelligent* can do it
I want to try on something (that is) *larger*

Of course, adjectives that can occur only attributively (5.30 *ff*) are excluded:

*something (which is) *main*
*somebody (who is) *mere*

Postposition is obligatory for a few adjectives, which have a different sense when they occur attributively or predicatively. The most common are probably *elect* ('soon to take office') and *proper* ('as strictly defined'), as in

the president *elect*
the City of London *proper*

In several compounds (mostly legal or quasi-legal) the adjective is postposed, the most common being

court *martial*   body *politic*
attorney *general*   postmaster *general*
heir *apparent*   notary *public* (AmE)

Postposition (in preference to attributive position) is usual for a few *a-* adjectives (5.7) and for the four adjectives *absent, present, concerned, involved,* which normally do not occur attributively in the relevant sense:

The house (which is) *ablaze* is next door to mine
The boats (which were) *afloat* were not seen by the bandits
The men (who were) *present* were his supporters
The people (who were) *involved* were not found

Some postposed adjectives, especially those ending in *-able* or *-ible,* retain the basic meaning they have in attributive position but convey the implication that what they are denoting has only a temporary application. Thus, *the stars visible* refers to stars that are visible at a time specified or implied, while *the visible stars* refers to a category of stars that can (at appropriate times) be seen. We have a similar distinction between the temporary and the permanent in *rivers navigable* and *navigable rivers, actors suitable* and *suitable actors.* With a singular noun, postposition is common in a construction with *only: the only actor suitable.*

Note
Attributive *present* has the same sense as postposed *present* in the stereotyped expression *present company excluded* (where perhaps it has been transposed from its usual position because the participle has occupied that position) and in expressions that seem to be based on it (*eg: excluding present company, if we exclude present company*). In AmE, attributive and postposed *involved* and *concerned* have the same sense if the head of the noun phrase is *party* or *parties: the involved party, the concerned parties.*

5.19
For most adjectives postposition is possible if there is complementation of the adjective:

The boys (who were) *easiest to teach* were in my class   [9]
They have a house (which is) *larger than yours*   [10]
I know the actor (who is) *suitable for the part*   [11]
Students (who are) *brave enough to attempt the course* deserve to
succeed   [12]
There are many men there (who are) *not old enough to be your*
father   [13]

On the other hand, if the adjective is alone or merely premodified by an intensifier, postposition is not normally allowed:

*The soldiers (*rather*) *timid* approached their officer

However, if the noun phrase is generic and indefinite, coordinated adjectives or adjectives with some clause element added can be postposed, though such constructions are not very frequent:

Soldiers *timid or cowardly* don't fight well

> Soldiers *normally timid* don't fight well
> A man *usually honest* will sometimes cheat

The more usual forms are

> Timid or cowardly soldiers
> Soldiers who are timid or cowardly } don't fight well
> Soldiers who are normally timid don't fight well
> A man who is usually honest will sometimes cheat

The adjective of an adjective phrase can often be preposed, leaving its complementation in postposition. Thus, equivalent to sentences marked [9] and [10] are

> The *easiest* boys *to teach* were in my class   [9a]
> They have a *larger* house *than yours*   [10a]

If there is no complementation of the adjective and the adjective is modified by such adverbs as *enough* or *too*, the adjective with its modifier may be preposed:

> *Brave enough* students deserve to succeed
> A *brave enough* student deserves to succeed

On the other hand, if there is complementation and the adjective has such a modifier, preposing of the adjective and its modifier is often excluded:

> *Brave enough* students *to attempt the course* deserve to succeed
> *A *brave enough* student *to attempt the course* deserves to succeed

But the adjective and its modifier may even then be preposed if they are placed before the indefinite article, though this construction seems possible only if the adjective phrase is part of the subject complement:

> He is (not) { *too timid* / *brave enough* } a student *to attempt the course.*

Note

[a] A few set phrases allow both attributive and postpositive positions with little or no semantic difference, perhaps the most common being *positive proof – proof positive*. Postposition is more usual in the set phrase *the answer pure and simple* and obligatory for the set phrase *from time immemorial*.

[b] We find the postposition of adjectives in poetry in cases where attributive position is the norm elsewhere in the language.

[c] *Galore* and (AmE) *aplenty* are postposed obligatorily:

> There were presents *galore*

Both are restricted to informal speech.

Head of a noun phrase
5.20
Adjectives can function as heads of noun phrases (4.53, 4.58), and (like all noun phrases) can be subject of the sentence, complement, object, and complement of a preposition. Adjectives as noun-phrase heads do not inflect for number or for the genitive case and they must take a definite determiner. Three types of adjectives function as noun-phrase heads.

[A] All adjectives qualifying personal nouns can be noun-phrase heads:

> *The poor* are causing the nation's leaders great concern
> There is a lack of communication between *the young* and *the old*
> *The innocent* are often deceived by *the unscrupulous*
> *The extremely old* need a great deal of attention
> We will nurse *your sick*, clothe *your naked*, and feed *your hungry*
> *The young in spirit* enjoy life
> *The rich* will help only *the humble poor*
> *The very wise* avoid such temptations
> *The wise* look to *the wiser* for advice
> *The old who resist change* can expect violence

These adjectives have generic reference and take plural concord. Hence, *the poor* cannot denote one person. (In contrast, *the noble* and *the black*, when used as nouns, can have singular reference: 5.10.) It is often possible to add a general word for human beings such as *people* and retain the generic reference, in which case the definite determiner is normally omitted, but the use of the adjective as head of the noun phrase is probably more common. The adjective can itself be modified, usually by restrictive modification (13.3).

Note
[a] We must distinguish these from cases of contextually-determined ellipsis (9.89, 10.79):

> The young students found the course difficult, *the older* found it easy

Here, *the older* is elliptical for *the older students*.

[b] Some of the above sentences illustrate the modification of the adjective. Premodification by adverbs (*the extremely old, the very wise*) seems to be easier than premodification by adjectives (*the humble poor*). Postmodification by relative clauses (*the old who resist change*) seems easier than postmodification by prepositional phrases (*the young in spirit*). Notice also that inflected comparison forms of the adjective are possible (*the wiser*). Inflection for comparison and modification by adverbs are indications of the adjective status of these noun-phrase heads, while modification by adjectives is more typical of nouns and modification by relative clauses is normally an indication of noun status. Avoidance of modifica-

tion by adjectives is probably related to the fact that this type of adjective as noun-phrase head tends to accept only restrictive modification. Premodifying adjectives with this noun-phrase head are normally interpreted as non-restrictive. For example, *the wretched poor* would not normally be taken as a subclass of poor people, whereas with its premodifying adverb *the wretchedly poor* would be so taken.

[c] In *the young in spirit* it is clear that the adjective itself is postmodified by a prepositional phrase, since the general noun cannot be postmodified by *in spirit* (*the people in spirit who are young*). On the other hand, in *the young of London* it is arguable that the prepositional phrase is postmodifying a general noun that has been ellipted, since we can say *the people of London who are young*. Similarly, we can argue that the relative clause in *the old who resist change* is postmodifying an ellipted general noun (*the people who resist change who are old*). Since *people* is is not the only noun we can supply (for example we could insert *persons* instead), such ellipsis must be weak ellipsis (9.7).

[d] The determiner *the* with these adjectives is the generic *the* (4.28 *ff*).

[e] Adjectives functioning as heads of noun phrases should be distinguished from nouns that are converted from adjectives, *eg: criminal* (5.10). The latter can be inflected for number and for the genitive and can usually take indefinite determiners.

[f] Although adjectives functioning as noun-phrase heads generally require a definite determiner, they can function as such without a determiner if they are conjoined:

*He is acceptable to *old*
*He is acceptable to *young*
He is acceptable to *both old and young*.

5.21

[B] Some adjectives denoting nationalities (4.33) can be noun-phrase heads:

You British and *you French* ought to be allies
The clever Swiss have preserved their neutrality for centuries
The industrious Dutch are admired by their neighbours

The adjectives in question are virtually restricted to words ending in *-(i)sh* (*British, Cornish, Danish, English, Irish, Spanish, Turkish, Welsh*), *-ch* (*Dutch, French*) and *-ese* (*Chinese, Japanese, Maltese, Portuguese*), with *Swiss* as an exception in not belonging to any of these groups. The adjectives refer to the nations. As with type [A] in 5.20, these noun phrases have generic reference and take plural concord. Unlike type [A], these cannot be modified by adverbs. They can be modified by adjectives, which are normally non-restrictive, *ie: the industrious Dutch* is interpreted as *the Dutch, who are industrious,* . . . (13.3, 13.46).

Note

[a] Some names of nations appear with or without an uninflected plural (4.70 Note), *eg: Eskimo, Navaho, Bantu*. The uninflected form is used as the head of a noun phrase.

[*b*] Postmodifying prepositional phrases and relative clauses can be either restrictive or non-restrictive:

> *The Irish* (*who live*) *in America* retain sentimental links with Ireland
> *The Polish, who are very rebellious,* resisted strongly

[*c*] These adjectives are sometimes used not to refer to the nation as a whole but to some part of it, for example, troops or tourists:

> *The French* invaded England in 1066
> *The British* retain control of the bridge
> *The Chinese* are staying in the hotel opposite

Except for the type exemplified in the last sentence the reference is to the power of the nation.

[*d*] *You British* and *you French* can also be analysed as having *you* as head and the names of the nationalities as noun phrases in restrictive apposition (9.160 *ff*).

5.22

Names of languages (some of them identical with the adjectives listed in 5.21) are used as full nouns. They can take possessive pronouns and a restricted range of adjectives:

> He doesn't know *much English*
> *Russian* is a difficult language
> He speaks *excellent English*
> *My Spanish* is very poor   ('My knowledge of the Spanish language is very poor')
> I can't understand *his difficult German*   ('the difficult German that he is speaking')

5.23

[C] Some adjectives have abstract reference when they function as noun-phrase heads. They include, in particular, superlatives, in which case we can sometimes insert *thing* in its abstract sense:

> *The latest* (thing, news) is that he is going to run for election
> *The very best* (thing) is yet to come
> He ventured into *the unknown*
> He admires *the mystical*
> He went from *the extremely sublime* to *the extremely ridiculous*

These take singular concord. A few are modifiable by adverbs.

Note
There are a number of set phrases in which an adjective with abstract reference is complement of a preposition (6.1 Note), *eg:* (*He left*) *for good,* (*He enjoyed it*) *to the full, in short.*

Supplementive adjective clause
5.24

Adjectives can function as the sole realization of a verbless clause or as the head of an adjective phrase realizing the clause. One such type of verbless clause is the supplementive adjective clause (11.48 *f*):

Nervous, the man opened the letter	[14a]
The man, *nervous*, opened the letter	[14b]
The man opened the letter, *nervous*	[14c]

As the above examples demonstrate, the supplementive adjective clause is mobile, though (partly to avoid ambiguity) it usually precedes or (less usually) follows the subject of the superordinate clause. When it follows the subject, as in [14b], it is in some respects like a non-restrictive relative clause (13.14 *f*):

The man, *who was nervous*, opened the letter

But the adjective clause suggests that the man's nervousness was shown, whereas the relative clause does not convey that implication. The difference is because the adjective clause is related to the predication as well as to the subject (5.25). Furthermore, unlike the relative clause, the adjective clause is mobile and (with the exception discussed below) its implied subject is the subject of the sentence. Thus, while we have

The man restrained the woman, *who was aggressive*

we do not have as its equivalent

*The man restrained the woman, *aggressive*

However, if the supplementive adjective clause contains additional clause constituents, its implied subject can be a noun phrase other than the subject of the sentence:

She glanced with disgust at the cat, $\begin{cases} \textit{quiet (now) in her daughter's lap} \\ \textit{now quiet} \\ \textit{*quiet} \end{cases}$

Other examples of supplementive adjective clauses:

Long and untidy, his hair played in the breeze	[15]
The man, *quietly assertive*, spoke to the assembled workers	[16]
Unhappy, she returned to work	[17]
Glad to accept, the boy nodded his agreement	[18]
Anxious for a quick decision, the chairman called for a vote	[19]

Note

In the case of participles, the implied subject can be other than the subject of the sentence:

She glanced with disgust at the cat, $\begin{cases} \textit{dead.} \\ \textit{mewing.} \end{cases}$

5.25

Under certain conditions an adverb may replace, with little change of semantic force, an adjective functioning as a supplementive adjective clause. Thus, instead of [14a] we might have

Nervously, the man opened the letter

Like the adjective, an adverb with this function (8.41 *ff*) refers to the subject, though it normally does so specifically in relationship to the action that he is performing. The adjective refers to the subject without explicit reference to the action, but unless otherwise stated, the characterization is only temporary in its application. For example, *nervous* in [14a] does not imply that the man is characteristically nervous. But an explicit time indicator can be introduced and in that case the semantic neutralization between adjective and adverb does not take effect:

Always nervous,
Always nervously, }the man opened the letters

With the adjective, the man's nervousness is generalized; with the adverb, it is stated only with respect to his opening of letters.

Note
An adverb cannot be substituted under certain conditions:

(i) if (obviously) there is no corresponding adverb, *eg: long* in [15].
(ii) if the adjective takes complementation or modification not allowed for the adverb, *eg* [16], [18], [19].

The more likely interpretation of *unhappily* if it replaced *unhappy* in [17] – 'it was sad that' – makes the adjective a preferable choice.

5.26

The implied subject of a supplementive adjective clause can be the whole of the superordinate clause:

Strange, it was she who initiated divorce proceedings	[20]
Most important, his report offered prospects of a great profit	[21]
More remarkable still, he is in charge of the project	[22]

For example, [20] is semantically equivalent to: *That it was she who initiated divorce proceedings is strange*. These clauses relate to the superordinate clause like comment clauses introduced by *what* (11.65). For example, for [20]:

What is strange, it was she who initiated divorce proceedings

The few adjectives that can be used for this purpose convey the attitude that what is being said is in some measure strange, *eg: curious, funny, odd, strange, surprising*. A few others seem possible if they are premodified by *more* or *most*, as in [21] and [22]. This type of adjective clause must precede its superordinate clause.

Note

A corresponding adverb can be substituted for the adjective with little or no difference in effect as with *strangely* for *strange* in [20]:

> *Strangely*, it was she who initiated divorce proceedings

The adjective, unlike the adverb, allows a *that-* or *how-* clause to follow:

> *Strange* $\begin{cases} \text{that it turned out that way} \\ \text{how she still likes him} \end{cases}$
>
> **Strangely,* $\begin{cases} \text{that it turned out that way} \\ \text{how she still likes him} \end{cases}$

This is because the adjective is elliptical for an extraposed construction (14.36 *ff*) or perhaps a pseudo-cleft construction (14.21):

> *It is strange* how she still likes him
> *What is strange is* how she still likes him

The adverb is more mobile than the adjective, though the adjective can be transposed from initial to end position if there is a sufficient pause:

> He even lied to his wife. *Strange!*

But in that case it seems as if it must be an exclamation ('How strange!') and constitutes a separate sentence.

5.27
Contingent adjective clause

A special type of supplementive adjective clause is the contingent adjective clause, which expresses the circumstance or condition under which what is said in the superordinate clause applies:

> *Enthusiastic*, they make good students (= When enthusiastic, . . .)
> [23]
> *Whether right or wrong*, he always comes off worst in an argument
>   because of his inability to speak coherently [24]
> *When ripe*, these apples are sweet [25]

As with the supplementive adjective clause that we have described earlier (5.24 *ff*), the implied subject of the contingent adjective clause is normally the subject of the superordinate clause, but the clause is not equivalent to a non-restrictive relative clause. A subordinator is often present, as in [24] and [25], but it is sometimes omitted, so that instead of [25] we can have

> *Ripe*, these apples are sweet

When the implied subject is the subject of the superordinate clause, it is normal to put the adjective initially, as in [25a], but it is not uncommon to put it finally in spoken English. If a subordinator is present, there is no problem in positioning the clause finally even in written English:

These apples are sweet *when ripe*   [25a]

The implied subject of the contingent clause can also be the object of the superordinate clause, though only a few adjectives are available for this use:

He sells them *new*   [26]
We can drink it *hot*   [27]
You must eat it *when fresh*   [28]

The adjective then usually comes finally and could be regarded as a complement (*cf* 7.2 Note *a*). A subordinator is also often present, as in [28]. If the subject of the superordinate clause is passive, the adjective normally appears finally:

*Ripe, the apples were picked
The apples were picked ripe

just as it normally does in an active form of the sentence, where the implied subject is the object of the superordinate clause:

*Ripe, they picked the apples
They picked the apples ripe

In informal spoken English, an adjective clause whose implied subject is the object of the superordinate clause can occur initially, though the position would be avoided if ambiguity resulted:

Hot, I can't drink coffee

The implied subject can also be the whole of the superordinate clause (which would be realized in the subordinate clause by the pro-form *it*):

If (it is) *possible*, the dog should be washed every day
When (it is) *necessary*, he can be taken to the doctor

But the subordinator cannot then be omitted.

See 11.44 *ff* for further discussion of adjective clauses and other verb-less clauses, as well as of non-finite clauses that require similar treatment.

Note

[a] Corresponding adverbs cannot replace adjectives in contingent adjective clauses. [24] is ambiguous between the more probable interpretation of the adjective clause as conditional and the other possibility that it is a non-contingent supple-mentive clause with the superordinate clause as its implied subject (5.26). In the latter interpretation, adverbs – *whether rightly or wrongly* – can replace the adjectives.

[*b*] The contingent clause is elliptical (9.9), with ellipsis of the subject or object (implied from the superordinate clause) and of an appropriate form of BE, and (if not present) of the subordinator.

5.28
Exclamatory adjective sentences

Adjectives that can be complement when the subject is a finite clause (5.17) can alone or as head of an adjective phrase be exclamations:

How good of you!
How wonderful!
Excellent!

These need not be dependent on any previous linguistic context, but may be a comment on some object or activity in the situational context (*cf* 7.79, 7.88).

Note

Since 'missing' elements cannot be uniquely recovered, there is no need to regard these exclamations as elliptical. See 9.18 *ff* for exclamations that are to be considered elliptical, though the ellipsis is not dependent on the linguistic context, *eg: Sorry!*

Subclassification of adjectives
According to syntactic function
5.29

One important way in which adjectives can be subclassified is according to the syntactic function they can perform. (For a morphological subclassification, see App I.27 *ff*.) The two main syntactic functions of adjectives are their use as attributives and as predicatives. Thus, adjectives can be subclassified according to whether they can function as:

(1) both attributive and predicative, *eg*
   a *hungry* man ~ the man is *hungry*
(2) attributive only, *eg*
   an *utter* fool ~ *the fool is *utter*
(3) predicative only, *eg*
   *a *loath* woman ~ the woman is *loath* to admit it

This would be a very simple subclassification, requiring the listing of all adjectives in three separate subclasses, if only each item had just one value. However, many items have more than one syntactic and/or semantic value. These syntactic-semantic homonyms complicate the task of separating adjectives into these three subclasses.

Most adjectives can be both attributive and predicative. They constitute the central adjectives (5.5) and no more need be said about them.

We turn now to consider the characteristics of the peripheral adjectives, those that are restricted to attributive or to predicative use. The restrictions are not always absolute, and sometimes vary with individual speakers.

Attributive only
5.30
In general, adjectives that are restricted to attributive position or that occur predominantly in attributive position do not characterize the referent of the the noun directly. For example, *old* can be either a central adjective or an adjective restricted to attributive position. In *that old man* (the opposite of *that young man*), *old* is a central adjective, and we can say *That man is old*. On the other hand, in the usual sense of *an old friend of mine* (a friend of old, a longstanding friend), *old* is restricted to attributive position and cannot be related to *My friend is old*. In this case *old* is the opposite of *new* (recently acquired). The person referred to is not being identified as old: it is his friendship that is old. Similarly, the attributive adjective in the *wrong candidate* does not refer to the wrongness of the person but to the mistake in identifying the person as a candidate. Adjectives that characterize the referent of the noun directly are termed INHERENT, those that do not are termed NON-INHERENT.

However, some non-inherent adjectives occur also predicatively. In part, non-inherent adjectives appear to be excluded from predicative position because of pressure from homonyms that commonly occupy that position, as with *old*. But the reasons for the restriction are not always clear. For example, both *a new student* and *a new friend* are non-inherent, yet only the former can be used predicatively:

That student is new
*My friend is new

Some of the factors that are involved in the restriction will emerge in the course of an identification of the types of adjective that are restricted to attributive position.

Note
A few words with strongly emotive value which will not be further discussed are restricted to attributive position, though the scope of the adjective clearly extends to the person referred to by the noun, *eg: you poor man, my dear lady, that wretched woman*. These all involve non-restrictive modification (13.3, 13.50).

5.31
Intensifying adjectives
Some adjectives have a heightening effect on the noun they modify or

the reverse, a lowering effect. At least three semantic subclasses of intensifying adjectives can be distinguished (*cf* 8.19 *ff*):

emphasizers
amplifiers
downtoners

Emphasizers have a general heightening effect; amplifiers scale upwards from an assumed norm; downtoners have a lowering effect, usually scaling downwards from an assumed norm.

DOWNTONERS, of which there are relatively few (*eg: slight* in *a slight effort, feeble* in *a feeble joke*), can be ignored for our present purpose, since they are generally central adjectives.

EMPHASIZERS are generally attributive only. Examples include:

a certain winner	pure ('sheer') fabrication
a clear failure	a real ('undoubted') hero
a definite loss	sheer arrogance
mere repetition	the simple truth
an outright lie	a sure sign
plain nonsense	a true scholar

The situation is more complicated for AMPLIFIERS. They are central adjectives if they are inherent and denote a high or extreme degree:

a complete victory ~ the victory was complete
great destruction ~ the destruction was great

On the other hand, they are attributive only

(a) when they are non-inherent:

a complete fool ~ *the fool is complete
a firm friend ~ *the friend is firm (asterisked in the relevant
  sense)

Complete refers to the completeness of the folly, and *firm* to the firmness of the friendship.

(b) when they are used as emphasizers, conveying principally emphasis rather than degree. For example, *total* in *total nonsense* is emphatic, while in *total destruction* it has a literal application ('the destruction of everything'). Hence the contrast:

total nonsense ~ *the nonsense was total
total destruction ~ the destruction was total

Examples of adjectives as amplifiers that are attributive only:

the absolute limit	a great supporter
a close friend	a perfect idiot

a complete fool	a strong opponent
an extreme enemy	total nonsense
his entire salary	utter folly
a firm friend	the very end

Many intensifying adjectives can be related to intensifying adverbs (8.19 *ff*):

It is utter folly to do that $\sim$ It is utterly folly to do that
It was a clear failure $\sim$ It was clearly a failure
He is a true scholar $\sim$ He is truly a scholar

Notice that several of them have homonyms that can occur both attributively and predicatively, *eg*

I drank some pure ('clean') water $\sim$ The water is pure
Those are real flowers $\sim$ Those flowers are real, not artificial

Examples of intensifying adjectives occurring predicatively include:

The disaster was *complete*
His condemnation was *extreme*
His folly was *great*
The earthquake was *strong*
Their victory is *certain*

Some intensifying adjectives are not found predicatively: *mere, sheer, utter.*

Note
Many adjectives can be used as intensifiers, usually with severe restrictions on the nouns they modify, *eg: a great fool* ('very foolish'), *a great baby* ('very babyish'), *a great friend* ('very friendly'), *a big fool* ('very foolish'), *a big baby* ('very babyish'), but not **a big friend* ('very friendly'). These are also restricted to attributive position.

5.32
Restrictive adjectives
Restrictive adjectives restrict the reference of the noun exclusively, particularly or chiefly. Examples, within noun phrases, include:

a certain person	the precise reason
his chief excuse	the principal objection
the exact answer	the same student
the main reason	the sole argument
the only occasion	the specific point
a particular child	the very man

Again, some of these have homonyms. For example, *certain* in *a certain person* is a restrictive (equivalent to 'a particular person'), while in *a certain winner* it is, as we saw in 5.31, an intensifier (equivalent to 'a sure winner'). In *John is certain that she will take it*, it is semantically related to the intensifier, but it is equivalent to *sure* in the sense of 'confident' and is limited to predicative position.

Some restrictive adjectives can be related to restrictive adverbs (8.13 *ff*):

> That was the precise reason ~ That was precisely the reason
> It is the main reason ~ It is mainly the reason

Note
Notice the use of *very* as a restrictive adjective rather than as a degree intensifier adverb:

> You are the *very* man I want

Compare with restrictive adverbs:

> You are *precisely* (*exactly*) the man I want

Very as an intensifying adjective is exemplified in 5.31.

5.33
Related to adverbials
Some adjectives that are attributive only can be related to adverbials but do not fall within the two types that have been discussed. These non-inherent adjectives include:

> my *former* friend ~ formerly my friend
> an *old* friend ~ a friend of old
> *past* students ~ students in the past
> a *possible* friend ~ possibly a friend
> the *present* king ~ the king at present
> an *occasional* visitor ~ occasionally a visitor
> an *apparent* defeat ~ apparently a defeat

Some require implications additional to the adverbial:

> the *late* president ~ till lately the president (now dead)
> the *former* reason ~ the reason stated formerly

If the adjectives premodify agentive nouns, the latter suggest as well a relationship to the verb base or to an associated verb:

> a *hard* worker ~ someone who works hard
> a *big* eater ~ someone who eats a lot
> a *good* thief ~ someone who thieves well
> an *excellent* pianist ~ someone who plays the piano excellently

Many of these adjectives have a temporal meaning. We might include with them *acting* ('for the time being') as in *the acting chairman.*

Note

Not all instances like *good thief* involve a restriction to attributive position. Possible conflict with homonyms seems a contributory factor. Thus *a good thief* is analogous to *a good writer*, *a good student*, or *a good detective* in that in all four instances *good* refers to the ability of the person in respect of the reference of the noun – good as a thief, good as a writer, etc. However, the last three instances of *good* can be used predicatively in the same sense:

    That writer is good
    That student is good
    That detective is good

and similarly:

    That writer is bad
    That student is weak
    That detective is bad

Nevertheless, we normally cannot use these adjectives predicatively in the intended sense when the noun is pejorative:

    a good thief ~ *that thief is good
    a poor liar ~ *that liar is poor
    a bad liar ~ *that liar is bad

On the other hand, one thief might well say of another *That thief is good*, but in that case he is not using *thief* pejoratively. *Cf: He is good at stealing, but bad at lying.*

5.34
Denominal adjectives

Some adjectives derived from nouns are restricted to attributive position. They include:

    a *criminal* lawyer ~ a lawyer specializing in criminal law
    an *atomic* scientist ~ a scientist specializing in atomic science
    a *woollen* dress ~ a dress made of wool

The first two examples contain agentive nouns with a denominal adjective (non-inherent) referring to the activity of the agent, while the third example contains an adjective denoting material. The same item may also be a central adjective. For example, *a criminal lawyer* can be a lawyer who is criminal, in which case *criminal* is a central adjective (5.10).

Predicative only
5.35

Adjectives that are restricted or virtually restricted to predicative position are most like verbs and adverbs. They tend to refer to a (possibly temporary) condition rather than to characterize. Perhaps the most common are those referring to the health or lack of health of an animate being:

    faint   ill (especially BrE)
    well   unwell

However, some people use *ill* and (to a lesser extent) *unwell* as attributives too.

Note

Sick (especially in AmE) is the exception among these 'health' adjectives in that its attributive use is very common:

the sick woman ~ the woman is sick

5.36

A larger group comprises adjectives that can take complementation (12.34 *ff*). Among them are

able (to)	fond (of)
afraid (that, of, about)	glad (that, to, about, of)
answerable (to)	happy (that, to, with, about)
averse (to, from)	loath (to)
aware (that, of)	subject (to)
conscious (that, of)	tantamount (to)

Some of these adjectives must take complementation and many normally do.

Many of these adjectives closely resemble verbs semantically:

He is *afraid* to do it ~ He *fears* to do it
They are *fond* of her ~ They *like* her
That is *tantamount* to an ultimatum ~ That *amounts* to an
ultimatum

Able to is equivalent to the modal auxiliary *can* in the ability sense (3.44).

Some of these adjectives that are restricted to attributive position have homonyms that can occur both predicatively and attributively, *eg: the conscious patient ~ the patient is conscious*. With others, the semantic distinction between the restricted item and its homonym is more subtle, *eg: The man is happy ~ a happy man* compared with *The man is happy to do it*, where *happy* is closer to *glad* or *pleased* than to its homonym. With some adjectives that take complementation there appears to be no semantic distinction, and we must say that they can freely occur in both positions, *eg: eager, indignant, surprised.*

Note

[a] Most of the *a*- adjectives are predicative only (5.7). As can be seen, several of them can take complementation.

[b] It is not usually possible for the adjective to be complement if the subject is undefined, and hence the oddness of

*A street is wide (cf 14.27)

The exception is with the generic use of the indefinite article (4.28 *ff*):

A tiger is dangerous.

Semantic subclassification
5.37
Some of the semantic distinctions that we are about to make have already been mentioned because they have syntactic correlates.

Three semantic scales are applicable to adjectives. It is important to realize that we are dealing with scales rather than with a feature that is present or absent. That is to say, not all the realizations of a feature are available in each case. Furthermore, there may be idiolectal variations in the recognition of a feature or in the acceptability of its realizations.

5.38
[I] Stative/dynamic
Adjectives are characteristically stative. Many adjectives, however, can be seen as dynamic (2.16, 3.40). In particular, most adjectives that are susceptible to subjective measurement (5.41) are capable of being dynamic. Stative and dynamic adjectives differ in a number of ways. For example, a stative adjective such as *tall* cannot be used with the progressive aspect or with the imperative: **He's being tall, *Be tall.* On the other hand, we can use *careful* as a dynamic adjective: *He's being careful, Be careful.* (For other differences see 3.40.)

Adjectives that can be used dynamically include:

> *abusive, adorable, ambitious, awkward, brave, calm, careful, careless,
> cheerful, clever, complacent, conceited, cruel, disagreeable, dull,
> enthusiastic, extravagant, faithful, foolish, friendly, funny, generous,
> gentle, good, greedy, hasty, helpful, impatient, impudent, irritable,
> irritating, jealous, kind, lenient, loyal, mischievous, naughty, nice,
> noisy, obstinate, patient, playful, reasonable, rude, sensible, serious,
> shy, slow, spiteful, stubborn, stupid, suspicious, tactful, talkative,
> thoughtful, tidy, timid, troublesome, unfaithful, unscrupulous, untidy,
> vain, vicious, vulgar, wicked, witty.*

5.39
[II] Gradable/non-gradable
Most adjectives are gradable, that is to say, can be modified by adverbs which convey the degree of intensity of the adjective. Gradability includes comparison:

tall   taller   tallest
beautiful   more beautiful   most beautiful

and other forms of intensification:

> *very* young
> *so* plain
> *extremely* useful

Because gradability applies to adverbs as well as adjectives, the subject is considered below in relation to both classes (5.70 *f*).

All dynamic adjectives are gradable. Most stative adjectives (*tall, old*) are gradable; some (principally 'technical adjectives' like *atomic scientist* and *hydrochloric acid* and adjectives denoting provenance, *eg: British*) are non-gradable (*cf* 5.41, 5.70).

5.40
[III] Inherent/non-inherent

The distinction between inherent and non-inherent adjectives has been discussed above (5.30). Most adjectives are inherent, that is to say, characterize the referent of the noun directly. For example, the inherent adjective in *a wooden cross* applies to the referent of the object directly: a wooden cross is also a wooden object. On the other hand, in *a wooden actor* the adjective is non-inherent: a wooden actor is not (presumably) a wooden man.

Gradable adjectives are either inherent, as in *a black coat*, or non-inherent, as in *a new friend*. Dynamic adjectives are generally inherent, though there are exceptions; for example, *wooden* in *The actor is being wooden* is both dynamic and non-inherent.

Table 5:2 gives examples of adjectives that illustrate the various possibilities with respect to the three semantic distinctions that we have been discussing.

Table 5:2

SEMANTIC SUBCLASSIFICATION OF ADJECTIVES

stative	gradable	inherent	
−	+	+	brave (man)
+	+	+	black (coat) NORMAL ADJECTIVE TYPE
+	+	−	new (friend)
+	−	+	British (citizen)

Note

In *a dull teacher*, the adjective *dull* is non-inherent, since a dull teacher is not necessarily a dull man. However, in the following sentence *dull* is being used dynamically and is now inherent:

The teacher is being *dull*

In this case the process of being dull is ascribed to the teacher, but the truth-value of what is said applies if we replace *the teacher* by another designation for the person:

That man ⎱ is being *dull*.
Mr Jones ⎰

5.41

Semantic sets and adjectival order

Apart from the semantic distinctions discussed in 5.38–40, semantic sets have been proposed to account for the usual order of adjectives and for their co-occurrence (13.65 *ff*):

(a) intensifying adjectives (5.31), *eg: a real hero, a perfect idiot*
(b) post-determiners (4.22 *ff*), including restrictive adjectives (5.32),
     eg: the fourth student, the only occasion
(c) general adjectives susceptible to subjective measure, *eg: careful,*
     naughty, lovely
(d) general adjectives susceptible to objective measure, including
     those denoting size or shape, *eg: wealthy, large, square*
(e) adjectives denoting age, *eg: young, old, new*
(f) adjectives denoting colour, *eg: red, black*
(g) denominal adjectives denoting material (5.34), *eg: a silken*
     handkerchief, a metallic substance, and denoting resemblance to a
     material, *eg: metallic voice, silken hair, cat-like stealth*
(h) denominal adjectives denoting provenance or style, *eg: a British*
     ship, a Parisian dress

Characteristics of the adverb

5.42

Because of its great heterogeneity, the adverb class is the least satisfactory of the traditional parts of speech. Indeed, it is tempting to say simply that the adverb is an item that does not fit the definitions for other parts of speech. As a consequence, some grammarians have removed certain types of items from the class entirely and established several additional classes rather than retain these as subsets within a single adverb class.

The most common characteristic of the adverb is morphological: the majority of adverbs have the derivational suffix *-ly*. Both the *-ly* suffix and the less common *-wise* suffix (*clockwise, moneywise*) are productive suffixes by means of which new adverbs are created from adjectives (and to a minor extent from participles) and from nouns respectively. But as we noted (5.2), some adjectives have an *-ly* suffix, while many words that we would undoubtedly wish to place in the traditional adverb class (*eg: often, here, well, now*) lack this termination. (For adverb suffixes, see App I.30.)

There are two types of syntactic functions that characterize the traditional adverbs, but an adverb need have only one of these:

(1) clause constituent
(2) modifier of adjective and adverb

Clause constituent
5.43

An adverb may function in the clause itself as adverbial, as a constituent distinct from subject, verb, object, and complement (2.3). As such it is usually an optional element and hence peripheral to the structure of the clause (7.4):

John *always* loses his pencils
I spoke to him *outside*
Perhaps my suggestion will be accepted
They may *well* complain about his appearance
I *quite* forgot about it
He may *nevertheless* refuse to accept our excuse

There are, of course, differences between the adverbs in the above sentences, most obviously the differences in their position and in their relationship to other constituents of the sentence. For example, *quite* is normally restricted to the position given to it in its sentence.

Note
The adverb may itself be modified, in which case the adverb phrase as a whole functions as adverbial:

John *nearly always* loses his pencils
They may *very well* complain about his appearance.

5.44

Adjuncts, disjuncts, conjuncts
The functions of the adverb as a clause element are examined in Chapter 8. For the present we merely outline the three classes that are discussed in that chapter:

adjuncts
disjuncts
conjuncts

ADJUNCTS are integrated within the structure of the clause to at least some extent. An adverb demonstrates its integration within clause structure, and hence that it is an adjunct, if it conforms to *at least one* of the following conditions (see further, 8.3):

(1) If it cannot appear initially in a negative declarative clause marked off from the rest of the clause by comma punctuation or its intonational equivalents (App III.9 *f*, App II.12 *ff*). The more mobile an adverb is, the less it is tied to the structure of the clause. Its independence is demonstrated if it can appear initially set off from the rest of the clause, and particularly if its position is not affected by the clause process of negation.

(2) If it can be contrasted with another adverbial in alternative interrogation, since this shows that it can be the focus of clause interrogation (7.68 *f*):

Are they waiting *outside* or are they waiting *inside?*

(3) If it can be contrasted with another adverbial in alternative negation, since this shows that it can be the focus of clause negation (7.51):

I didn't see him *beforehand,* but I did see him *afterwards.*

Examples of adjuncts:

They are waiting *outside*
We haven't *yet* finished it
Proudly, he showed his diploma to his parents
I can *now* understand it
He spoke to me about it *briefly*

DISJUNCTS and CONJUNCTS, on the other hand, are not integrated within the clause. What has been said about adjuncts applies to them in reverse:

(1) They can appear initially in a negative declarative clause marked off from the clause by punctuation or its intonational equivalents:

Frankly, he isn't tired.

(2) They cannot be contrasted with another adverbial in alternative interrogation:

*Is he tired *probably* or is he tired *possibly?*

(3) They cannot be contrasted with another adverbial in alternative negation:

*He isn't tired *probably,* but he is tired *possibly.*

Semantically, DISJUNCTS express an evaluation of what is being said either with respect to the form of the communication or to its content. Examples of disjuncts:

Briefly, there is nothing more I can do about it

Frankly, I am tired
Fortunately, no one complained
They are *probably* at home
She *wisely* didn't attempt to apologize

Semantically, CONJUNCTS have a connective function. They indicate the connection between what is being said and what was said before.

Examples of conjuncts:

We have complained several times about the noise, and *yet* he does nothing about it
All our friends are going to Paris this summer. We, *however,* are going to London
I have not looked into his qualifications yet. He seems very intelligent, *though*
If they open all the windows, *then* I'm leaving
I didn't invite her. She wouldn't have come, *anyway.*

5.45
Modifier

An adverb may function as a modifier of an adjective or of another adverb:

They are VERY *happy*	[29]
He is *stupid* ENOUGH to do it	[30]
It was a REMARKABLY *good* show	[31]
She drives TOO *quickly*	[32]
They play SO *very* well	[33]
He gave a FAR *more* easily intelligible explanation	[34]

In this function, the adverb premodifies except for *enough,* which (as adverb) can only postmodify, as in [30]. The item being modified may itself function as a modifier. For example, the adjective *good* premodifies the noun *show* in [31], while the adverb *far* premodifies the adverb *more* in [34] and the adverb *very* the adverb *well* in [33]. In both [31] and [34] the adverb is within a noun phrase. The structure of the noun phrase in [34] is the more complicated of the two, with a hierarchy of modification that can best be displayed by a tree diagram:

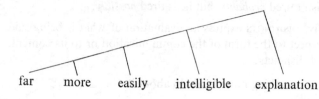

far   more   easily   intelligible   explanation

This second characteristic function of adverbs will receive detailed attention later in this chapter (5.51 *ff*), though it should be immediately pointed out that not all adverbs that modify adjectives will also modify adverbs (*cf* 5.54), and furthermore some adverbs may modify phrases – noun phrases and prepositional phrases.

The most conspicuous example of an adverb that functions only as a modifier of adjectives and adverbs and not as a sentence element is *very*.

Note
For *very* as an adjective, see 5.31 *f*.

The adverb and other word-classes
5.46
We now briefly consider some examples of overlapping between the adverb class and other word-classes. Similarities between adverbs and adjectives have been discussed earlier (5.7 *ff*). The other relevant word-classes are conjunctions and prepositions. We also take into account certain words (other than conjunctions and some conjuncts) that must be positioned initially, but these are not traditionally recognized as separate word-classes.

5.47
Conjunct and conjunction
A few conjuncts, *eg: so, yet*, resemble coordinators (coordinating conjunctions) both in being connectives and in certain syntactic features (*cf* 9.29 *ff*). In particular, these conjuncts cannot be transposed with their clause in front of the preceding clause. Thus, the order of the following two clauses (with the conjunct *so* in the second clause) is fixed:

We paid him a very large sum. *So* he kept quiet about what he saw.

If we invert the order of the clauses, the relationship between the two clauses is changed and *so* must now refer to some preceding clause:

So he kept quiet about what he saw. We paid him a very large sum.

However, the conjuncts differ from coordinators in that they can be preceded by a coordinator:

We paid him a very large sum, *and so* he kept quiet about what he saw.

The restriction on the order of clauses distinguishes the conjuncts from subordinators, which are also connectives. For example, a clause introduced by the subordinator *because* can precede or follow the superordinate clause without disturbing the relationship between the two clauses:

He will help us *because* we offered to pay him.
Because we offered to pay him, he will help us.

For further treatment of conjuncts, see 8.89 *ff*.

5.48
Adjunct and conjunction

A few subordinators can be seen to be a fusion of conjunction and pro-adjunct, in particular *where* (place at or place to), *when* (time), *how* (manner), *why* (reason).

Where and *when* introduce adverbial clauses (11.27 *f*):

He saw them $\begin{Bmatrix} \text{when} \\ \text{at the time(s) at which} \end{Bmatrix}$ they were in New York

I'll go $\begin{Bmatrix} \text{where} \\ \text{to the place(s) to which} \end{Bmatrix}$ they go

We'll go $\begin{Bmatrix} \text{where} \\ \text{to the place(s) at which} \end{Bmatrix}$ the food is good

He'll stay $\begin{Bmatrix} \text{where} \\ \text{at the place(s) at which} \end{Bmatrix}$ it is comfortable

Where and *when*, and to a lesser extent *why*, are also used as relatives (13.7, 13.14):

the place $\begin{Bmatrix} \text{where} \\ \text{at which} \end{Bmatrix}$ he is staying

the time $\begin{Bmatrix} \text{when} \\ \text{at which} \end{Bmatrix}$ he was here

the reason $\begin{Bmatrix} \text{why} \\ \text{for which} \end{Bmatrix}$ he did it

Where, *when*, *why*, and *how* are all used to introduce nominal clauses (11.18, 11.20):

I know $\begin{Bmatrix} \text{where} \\ \text{at which place} \end{Bmatrix}$ he is staying

I wonder $\begin{Bmatrix} \text{when} \\ \text{at which time} \end{Bmatrix}$ he was here

I realize $\begin{Bmatrix} \text{why} \\ \text{the reason for which} \end{Bmatrix}$ he did it

That was $\begin{Bmatrix} \text{how} \\ \text{the way in which} \end{Bmatrix}$ they treated her

These four *wh-* words are also used as interrogative pro-adjuncts (7.63 *ff*):

Where
At what place } is he staying?

When
At what time } was he here?

Why
For what reason } did he do it?

How
In what way } did they treat her?

The function of *where*, *when*, and *how* as pro-forms for adjuncts is clearly demonstrated in the few cases where a verb requires complementation by an adjunct:

*She put it	[35]
*He lived	[36]
*They treated her (unacceptable in the sense 'behaved towards her')	[37]

These sentences become acceptable if an adjunct of the appropriate type is added:

She put it *there*	[35a]
He lived *then*	[36a]
They treated her *well*	[37a]

But complementation can also be provided by the appropriate subordinators, evidence that they are functioning as pro-adjuncts:

He found it *where* she put it	[35b]
I wonder *when* he lived	[36b]
I saw *how* they treated her	[37b]

In a sentence such as

I put it *where* he could find it

one could argue that *where* is functioning as an adjunct in both clauses, which have been made to overlap by the subordinator:

I put it *there*
        there he could find it

On the other hand, it is equally possible to argue that the obligatory complementation of a place adjunct is satisfied by the whole clause of place rather than by *where*. The same reasoning applies to the obligatory complementation for TREAT provided by manner and comparison clauses (11.41):

$$\text{She treated him}\begin{cases}\text{as he deserved}\\\text{as though he were a stranger}\end{cases}$$

Note

[a] Most of the other *wh-* words are pro-forms for noun phrases, which can clearly function as clause constituents: *who, whom, which* (7.63*f*).

[b] There do not appear to be any verbs which require complementation that would be satisfied by *why*.

5.49
Reaction signal and initiator

Apart from conjunctions and some conjuncts, certain other items must be positioned initially. They are important because of their high frequency in spoken English and some are restricted to the spoken language. These can be assigned to two small classes:

(1) *reaction* signals (7.88), *eg: no, yes* (including variants such as *yeah* or *yep*), *m* (including variants such as *hm, mhm*)
(2) *initiators* (7.89), *eg: well, oh, ah*

These can be distinguished from disjuncts since the latter are mobile. They can be distinguished from conjuncts because they can serve as response utterances. Reaction signals normally serve only as response utterances. Initiators can serve both as reponse utterances and as initiators of conversations.

5.50
Adjunct and preposition

There are several different types of combinations of verbs plus particles (12.19 *ff*). If the verb is intransitive, we can recognize the particle as a prepositional adverb (*cf* 6.9 *f*) functioning as adjunct, *eg*

The men looked *away*
She is growing *up* quickly
The airliner has taken *off*
The prisoner broke *down* after many hours of interrogation

When a noun phrase follows the particle, it sometimes appears as if we have a prepositional phrase, with the particle as preposition:

He took *in* the dog   [38a]

However, the adverbial nature of the particle in such phrasal verbs (12.24) is generally shown by its mobility, its ability to follow the noun phrase:

He took the dog *in*   [38b]

Similarly,

They turned *down* the suggestion	[39a]
They turned the suggestion *down*	[39b]
They turned *on* the light	[40a]
They turned the light *on*	[40b]

In contrast, the preposition must be followed by its complement:

They took *to* John quickly	[41a]
*They took John *to* quickly	[41b]
He is relying *on* our help	[42a]
*He is relying our help *on*	[42b]
He believed *in* their promises	[43a]
*He believed their promises *in*	[43b]

The instances we have mentioned so far are not to be confused with examples like

He walked *past*	[44a]
He walked *past the car*	[44b]
*He walked *the car past*	[44c]
He was moving *about*	[45a]
He was moving *about* the town	[45b]
*He was moving *the town about*	[45c]

It is possible to regard *past* in [44a] and *about* in [45a] as prepositions with some generalized ellipsis of the noun phrase (6.9*f*).

Adverb as modifier
Modifier of adjective
5.51
An adverb may premodify an adjective:

That was a VERY *funny* film
He is QUITE *right*
It is EXTREMELY *good* of you
He made the examination EXTRAORDINARILY *easy*
There was a SOMEWHAT *uneasy* silence as we waited
She has a REALLY *beautiful* face

One adverb – *enough* – postmodifies adjectives:

His salary wasn't *high* ENOUGH.

Most commonly, the modifying adverb is an intensifier (*cf* 5.31, 8.19*ff*), whether an emphasizer, conveying primarily emphasis and not scaling (*eg: really*), or an amplifier, denoting a high degree (*eg: very*), or a downtoner, suggesting an incomplete or low degree (*eg: somewhat*). The most frequently used modifier, both of adjectives and of adverbs, is *very*.

Other intensifiers include:

so large	*terribly* awkward
pretty good	*quite* wrong
rather quiet	*unbelievably* fat
unusually tall	*amazingly* calm

Many intensifiers are restricted to a small set of lexical items, *eg: deeply* (anxious), *highly* (intelligent), *strikingly* (handsome), *sharply* (critical).

Many intensifiers can modify adjectives, adverbs, and verbs alike.

Note

In informal speech, *kind of* and *sort of* are used as downtoners for premodification of various parts of speech, including (especially AmE) adjectives and adverbs:

He is KIND *of clever*
He spoke SORT *of proudly*.

5.52

Adjuncts (5.44, 8.8 *ff*) when made premodifiers tend to retain their general meaning:

an *EASILY debatable* proposition (= a proposition that can be easily debated)
his *QUIETLY assertive* manner

On the other hand, disjuncts (8.78 *ff*) tend to become intensifiers, *eg: surprisingly good, unnaturally long, incredibly beautiful, unusually easy.* Thus *surprisingly good in*

He made a *surprisingly good* speech

can be paraphrased as 'He made a speech that was good to a surprising extent'.

Note

We need to distinguish the adverb as premodifier of adjective from the adjunct constructed with a verb-participle. For example, *a surprisingly worded letter* is 'a letter that is worded in a surprising manner' since *worded* is a passive participle and not an adjective. Ambiguity arises when the form can be either a participle or an adjective. Thus, *his peculiarly disturbed friend* can be either 'his friend who has been disturbed in a peculiar manner', in which case *disturbed* is verbal and *peculiarly* an adjunct, or 'his friend who is disturbed to a peculiar extent', in which case *disturbed* is adjectival and *peculiarly* its premodifier. *Cf* the difference in aspect and implied 'permanence' (13.53).

5.53

Apart from intensifiers, adverb premodifiers may be 'viewpoint' (*cf* 8.11 *f*), *eg*

> *POLITICALLY expedient* ('expedient from a political point of view')
> *ARTISTICALLY justifiable*
> *THEORETICALLY sound*
> *TECHNICALLY possible*
> *ECONOMICALLY weak*
> *ETHICALLY wrong*

Adjectives are premodified by a few other adverbs that cannot easily be categorized, though they too seem often to have some intensifying effect (but *cf: easily* in 5.52):

> *OPENLY hostile*
> *EASILY justifiable*
> *READILY available*

They tend to modify deverbal adjectives, *ie* adjectives derived from verbs (App I.29).

Note
There does not seem to be justification for setting up a class of 'viewpoint adjectives' analogous to the class of viewpoint adverbs. The viewpoint semantic element in the sentences below comes from the noun that the adjective modifies:

> It doesn't make *economic sense*
> His *financial position is precarious*
> My *personal point of view* hasn't been taken into account.

5.54
Modifier of adverb
An adverb may premodify another adverb:

> They are smoking *VERY heavily*
> They didn't injure him *THAT severely*
> I have seen *SO very* many letters like that one
> He spoke *EXTREMELY quickly*
> He played *SURPRISINGLY well*
> I expect them *PRETTY soon*

As with adjectives, the only postmodifier is *enough:*

> He spoke *cleverly ENOUGH*

Adverbs modifying other adverbs can only be intensifiers. Thus, though we have the manner modification by *quietly* in *quietly assertive* we cannot have it in

> *He spoke *QUIETLY assertively*

And, similarly, the modification by a viewpoint adverb (5.53) in *theoretically sound* does not have a corresponding *theoretically soundly:*

*He reasoned *THEORETICALLY soundly*

Notice that this is not merely a stylistic objection to the juxtaposition of two words ending in *-ly,* since

He reasoned *extremely soundly*

is acceptable, where *extremely* is an intensifier.

A similar set of intensifiers is used for both adjectives and adverbs.

A few intensifying adverbs, particularly *right* and *well,* premodify particles in phrasal verbs:

He knocked the man *RIGHT out*
They left him *WELL behind.*

Note

The intensifier *ever* forms a compound with *wh-* words, *eg: wherever, whenever, however.* It also intensifies *wh-* words that have no adverbial function.

5.55
Modifier of preposition

The few intensifying adverbs that can premodify particles in phrasal verbs (5.54) can also premodify prepositions or (perhaps rather) prepositional phrases (6.55):

The nail went *RIGHT through* the wall
His parents are *DEAD against* the trip
He made his application *WELL within* the time.

5.56
Modifier of determiner, predeterminer, postdeterminer

Intensifying adverbs (including downtoners) can premodify indefinite pronouns (4.122, 127), predeterminers (4.18 *ff*), and cardinal numerals (4.24):

NEARLY everybody came to our party
They recovered *ROUGHLY half* their equipment
He received *ABOUT double* the amount he expected
VIRTUALLY all the students participated in the discussion
They will stay *FULLY ten* weeks ('for ten full weeks')
OVER two hundred deaths were reported
I paid *MORE THAN ten* pounds for it

The indefinite article can be intensified when it is equivalent to the un-stressed cardinal *one*:

> I didn't have *MORE THAN a* dollar on me
> They will stay for *ABOUT a* week
> *ALMOST a* thousand demonstrators attended the meeting

With the ordinals and superlatives, a definite determiner is obligatory for premodification:

> We counted *APPROXIMATELY the first* thousand votes
> She gave me *ALMOST the largest* piece of cake.

Note

We might add here the premodification of *the same*:

> They did it in *MUCH the same* way.

Modifier of noun phrase
5.57

In informal style, a few intensifiers may premodify noun phrases and precede the determiner in doing so. The most common of these among adverbs are *quite* and (especially BrE) *rather*. Though not adverbs, *such* and *what* are included for comparison (13.68).

> He had *QUITE a party*
> He was *QUITE some player*
> They were *QUITE some players*
> They will be here for *QUITE some time*
> He is *SUCH a fool*
> They are *SUCH thieves*
> *WHAT a mess* they made
> *WHAT babies* they are
> It was *RATHER a mess*.

Note

[a] Others may be interpreted as not specifically modifying the noun phrase, since they are mobile. For example in

> He was *really* some player

transposition of *really* to pre-verb position does not seem to affect the meaning, provided that the appropriate intonation pattern is given. Transposition of *quite* is not possible.

[b] For many people, plural noun phrases are not premodified by *rather*:

> He is *rather a fool*
> ?*They are *rather* fools.

[c] If the noun is not gradable, then *rather* cannot be used unless a gradable adjective is present. And in that case *rather* is intensifying the adjective. Positions before

the adjective and before the determiner are both possible, with little or no semantic difference:

*It is rather a table
It is rather a big table
It is a rather big table.

[d] For the relationship between adverbs like *only* and *also* and noun phrases, see 8.13 *ff*.

5.58

Kind of and *sort of* (both informal) can precede or follow the determiner, though more usually the latter:

He gave SORT OF *a laugh*
He gave a SORT OF *laugh*

Other *of* phrases precede the determiner, if present:

I had A BIT OF *a shock*
They asked A HECK OF *a lot* (familiar)
They gave me A HELL OF *a time*. (familiar)

Note

In familiar style, the *wh-* words as interrogatives can be postmodified by certain set prepositional phrases, *eg:*

who ⎱ ⎧ *on earth*
what ⎬ ⎨ *(in) the heck*
where ⎰ ⎩ *(in) the hell*

Omission of the preposition in the last two examples is preferred by some and obligatory for others.

5.59

Some disjuncts and conjuncts (5.44) occasionally appear within the noun phrase, not modifying the noun phrase but related to a modifying adjective phrase:

A cure has now been found for this FORTUNATELY *very rare* disease
   ('a disease that is fortunately very rare')
He wrote an OTHERWISE *extremely good* paper ('a paper that is
   otherwise extremely good')

Similarly, the viewpoint adjuncts (5.53) that appear after the noun phrase are related to the premodifying adjective within the phrase:

A *good* paper EDITORIALLY can also be a *good* paper COMMERCIALLY

The more usual form for the sentence is

An EDITORIALLY *good* paper can also be a COMMERCIALLY *good* paper.

5.60

The noun phrase is perhaps postmodified by an adjective or adverb in a number of phrases of measure:

John is *ten years OLD* ('of age')
Peter is *five feet TALL* ('in height')
They stayed up *all night LONG*
The lake is *two miles ACROSS*
The sun shines in our country *all the year ROUND*
They dug *ten feet DOWN*

But it is arguable that at least in some cases the converse is true, that is to say the adjective or adverb is premodified by the noun phrase. For example:

I met him $\begin{Bmatrix} \text{a week ago} \\ \text{a week before} \end{Bmatrix}$ (=earlier by a week)

Contrast with these

I met him the week before (=the previous week)

where *before* seems to be a postmodifier (5.61). Analysing the noun phrase as premodifier is supported for some of the instances given above by the fact that the noun phrases can be evoked as responses to questions with premodifying pro-form *How:*

How old is John? Ten (years)
How tall is Peter? Five feet

On the other hand, only the adverb can be omitted in some cases, a fact that indicates it is the modifier in those cases:

The sun shines in our country *all the year* (round).

Note
All the year round and *the whole year round* are fixed expressions. We cannot, for example, have **all the month round* or **the whole month round*.

5.61

Some adverbs signifying place or time postmodify noun phrases (13.36):

PLACE: *the way ahead, the direction back, the hall downstairs, the noise backstage, his trip abroad, his journey home, the sentence below, the photo above, your friend here, that man there, his return home, the neighbour upstairs.*

TIME: *the meeting yesterday, the meal afterwards, the day before, their stay overnight.*

The time adverbs appear to be limited to those denoting a point of time or a period of time (*cf* 8.56 *ff*).

In some of the phrases the adverb can also be used as a premodifier (5.63):

> *the downstairs hall, the backstage noise, his home journey, the above photo, the upstairs neighbour*

Note

Many of these postmodifying adverbs can be used predicatively with BE, *eg: The noise is backstage, The sentence is below, The meeting was yesterday, The meal was afterwards.*

5.62

Indefinite pronouns, *wh-* pronouns, and *wh-* adverbs are postmodified by *else: someone else, all else, who else. Else* also postmodifies compounds with *where: somewhere, anywhere, everywhere, nowhere.*

5.63
Premodifier of noun

A very few adverbs premodify nouns within the noun phrase (13.45): *the away games, the then president, the above sentence, in after years. Then* and *above* are probably the most common. The occasional use of other adverbs is felt as ad hoc: *the now generation, the now cigarette.*

Note

In such expressions as *inside information* and *outside door*, the premodifiers are probably felt to be full adjectives, converted from adverbs. See also 5.9.

5.64
Adverb as complement of preposition

A number of adverbs signifying time and place function as complement of a preposition. Of the place adverbs, *here* and *there* take the most prepositions: *along, around, down, from, in, near, on, out (of), over, round, through, under, up. Home* can be the object of the prepositions *at, from, near, toward(s).* The other place adverbs are restricted to the preposition *from:*

$$
from \begin{cases} above \\ abroad \\ below \\ downstairs \\ indoors \end{cases}
$$

$$\text{from} \begin{cases} \text{inside} \\ \text{outdoors} \\ \text{outside} \\ \text{upstairs} \\ \text{within} \\ \text{without} \end{cases}$$

Time adverbs most commonly taking prepositions are shown below.

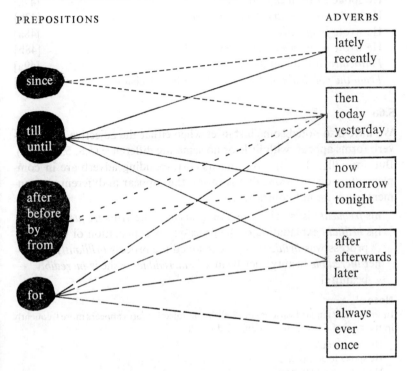

PREPOSITIONS   ADVERBS

Note

[a] The preposition *of* sometimes occurs with *now* and *late*.

[b] The expression *for ever and ever* is typical of Biblical and liturgical styles of English. It is curious that analogous reduplicated phrases are virtually restricted to informal use: *for months and months, for years and years.*

Correspondence between adjective and adverb

5.65

We have earlier observed (5.42) that adverbs are regularly, though not invariably, derived from adjectives by suffixation. There is another sense in which adjectives and adverbs are related, apart from the morphological relationship. A correspondence often exists between constructions containing adjectives and constructions containing the corresponding adverbs. The simplest illustration is with adverbs equivalent to prepositional phrases containing a noun or noun phrase that is a generic term (10.5) and the corresponding adjective as premodifier:

He liked Mary *considerably*	[46a]
He liked Mary *to a considerable extent*	[46b]
He spoke to John *sharply*	[47a]
He spoke to John *in a sharp manner*	[47b]
He wrote *frequently*	[48a]
He wrote *on frequent occasions*	[48b]
Politically, it is a bad decision	[49a]
From the political point of view, it is a bad decision.	[49b]

5.66

We have also noted some instances when either the adjective or the adverb forms appear, with little or no semantic difference (5.8, 5.25, 5.26). But normally, the adjective and its corresponding adverb are in complementary distribution; that is to say, they appear in different environments and are not contrastive:

his *frequent* visits: his visits are *frequent* ∼ he visits *frequently*
his *brilliant* explanation of the process: his explanation of the
    process was *brilliant* ∼ he explained the process *brilliantly*
her *incredible* beauty: her beauty is *incredible* ∼ she is *incredibly*
    beautiful

Note

In some non-standard varieties of English, the adjective form appears more frequently in the type of construction exemplified in 5.8:

He doesn't talk *proper*
He spoke to John *sharp*
He comes here *frequent*

However, these are unacceptable in Standard English.

5.67

There are many cases where a construction with the adverb form seems basic to an understanding of the corresponding construction with the adjective form (*cf* 13.49).

(1) The adjective-noun sequence may imply a process or a time relationship, with a corresponding clause containing an adverb. We can point to differences in grammar and meaning in the interpretation of *a beautiful dancer*:

    a beautiful dancer ∼ a dancer who is beautiful

a beautiful dancer ~ a person who dances beautifully (who
does a beautiful dance or beautiful dances)

In the second interpretation the adjective refers to the process part
of an agentive noun. Other examples are:

a hard worker
an eventual loser
a frequent visitor
a heavy eater
a light sleeper

We should include here cases where the agentive noun lacks an
agentive suffix: *a former student, a good thief*. Similarly, there are
instances where the noun normally lacks a corresponding verb, but
where the reference is to the process part of the noun's meaning:

a good soldier (one who acts well in his role as a soldier)
a poor mother
the present mayor
an apparent enemy

Many of these adjectives can occur only attributively in this use.
They belong to the class of adjectives that were referred to earlier
as non-inherent (5.30, 5.33).

(2) Analogous correspondences do not have this restriction to attributive position:

He loved her *deeply* ~ his *deep* love for her
He writes *legibly* ~ his *legible* writing
He will *probably* apply for it ~ his *probable* application for it
Surprisingly, he decided to leave ~ his *surprising* decision to
leave

Whereas in the sentential construction we have the adverb, in the
nominalization we have the adjective.

(3) The adjective may refer to an implied process associated with a
concrete object:

a fast car (a car that one drives fast)
a fast road
a good typewriter

(4) Most intensifying adjectives (*cf* 5.31) can be seen as related to adverbs:

total nonsense ~ it is totally nonsense
a clear failure ~ it is clearly a failure

a true scholar ~ he is truly a scholar
a real idiot ~ he is really an idiot

Many of these can occur only attributively in this use.

(5) Many restrictive adjectives (*cf* 5.32) can be seen as related to adverbs:

the main reason ~ it was mainly the reason
the precise argument ~ it was precisely the argument

Most of these can occur only attributively.

Comparison and intensification
5.68
Comparison refers to

(1) the inflected forms in *-er* and *-est* (5.73),
(2) their periphrastic equivalents in *more* and *most*,
(3) the similar, lesser and least degrees of comparison for which there are no inflected forms available and for which we most commonly use the premodifiers *as*, *less*, *least*.

The potentiality for inflections gives us three forms for many adjectives and for a few adverbs, as exemplified by the adjective *young*:

ABSOLUTE	COMPARATIVE	SUPERLATIVE
young	younger	youngest

The comparative is used for a comparison between two, while the superlative is required where more than two are involved. The superlative is sometimes used for a comparison between two, 'He is the youngest (of the two brothers)', but this use is considered loose and informal by many.

Too in the sense 'more than enough' might also be mentioned here:

It's too long ('longer than it should be')
He speaks too quickly ('more quickly than he should speak')

Note

[a] *More* and *most* have other uses in which they are not equivalent to the comparison inflections. Notice the paraphrases in the following two uses of *more*:

He is more than happy about it (=He is happy about it to a degree that is not adequately expressed by the word *happy*)

He is more good than bad (=It is more accurate to say that he is good than that he is bad)

The uninflected form cannot be substituted in this function:

*He is better than bad

(But *cf*: *It is worse than useless, He is worse than bad.*)
Most in

> She is most beautiful

is not the superlative in BrE, though it can be in AmE. In BrE, the sentence can only mean she is extremely beautiful and not that she is more beautiful than all others. This absolute sense of *most* is common in AmE too. Absolute *most* is restricted as to the adjectives with which it occurs, perhaps premodifying only those expressing subjective rather than objective attitudes (5.41):

> She is most *unhappy*
> *She is most *tall*

In BrE *most* is a superlative only when preceded by the definite article:

> She is *the most beautiful* (*woman*)

or when the basis of comparison (5.69) is made explicit by a postmodifying prepositional phrase, *eg*:

> (that) most beautiful *of women*

In both AmE and BrE there is a tendency to use absolute *most* with a preceding definite article to express an even higher degree:

> Isn't she the most beautiful woman? ('an extremely, extremely beautiful woman')

as compared with '*a* most beautiful woman'.

[b] In Australian English, *too* is common in the sense 'absolutely' in responses:

> A: He's clever.
> B: Too right, he is. (=That is absolutely true)

Too can be a synonym of *extremely* in informal (perhaps even gushy) speech:

> It's too kind of you
> That's too true

It is also commonly used (especially in AmE) as a synonym of *very* in negative sentences:

> I don't like it too much
> I don't feel too good.

5.69

Basis of comparison
We can make the basis of comparison explicit. The most common ways of doing so include correlative constructions introduced by *than* (correlative to *more, less*) and by *as* (correlative to *as*), and prepositional phrases with *of*:

John is $\begin{Bmatrix} \text{more} \\ \text{less} \end{Bmatrix}$ stupid *than Bob* (*is*) [50a]

John behaves $\begin{Bmatrix} \text{more} \\ \text{less} \end{Bmatrix}$ politely *than Bob* (*does*) [50b]

John is as stupid *as Bob* (*is*) [51a]

John behaves as politely *as Bob* (*does*) [51b]
John is the more stupid *of the* (*two*) *boys* [52a]
Of the (*two*) *boys,* John behaves the more politely [52b]
John is the most stupid *of the* (*three*) *boys* [53a]
Of the (*three*) *boys,* John behaves the most politely [53b]

The basis of comparison can also be shown by the noun which the adjective premodifies:

John is the more stupid *boy* (formal; more commonly 'John is
more stupid than the other boy') [54a]
John is the most stupid *boy* [54b]

For comparative constructions, see 11.53 *ff.*

Note

[a] The prepositional phrases in [52] and [53] can be either initial or final. Final
position is more frequent, especially when the construction contains the adjective.
[b] Note the obligatory presence of *the* before *more* and *most* in [52] and [53].
[c] Some standard of comparison may be implicit in the use of the absolute form of
the adjective, and in such cases the basis of comparison can also be made explicit:

He is stupid *for a child of his age.*

See also 5.33 Note.

Gradability
5.70
The types of intensifiers modifying adjectives and adverbs have been mentioned earlier (5.51, 5.52, 5.54). Here we are concerned with restrictions on their use analogous to those for comparison. In general, amplifiers and comparatives are allowed by the same range of adjectives and adverbs, those that are gradable (5.39). The range for emphasizers and those downtoners not expressing degree (*eg: virtually*) is much wider, as we can see from their co-occurrence with a non-gradable adjective such as *non-Christian:*

$$\text{He is}\begin{cases}\text{definitely}\\\text{virtually}\\\text{*more}\\\text{*very}\end{cases}\text{non-Christian}$$

There are also restrictions on the use of particular intensifiers, and these can sometimes be stated in semantic terms:

$$\text{most}\begin{cases}\text{happy ('subjective', } cf \text{ 5.41)}\\\text{*tall ('objective', } cf \text{ 5.41)}\end{cases}$$

$$\text{utterly}\begin{cases}\text{wrong ('negative')}\\\text{*right ('positive')}\end{cases}$$

$$\text{perfectly}\begin{cases}\text{natural ('positive')}\\ *\text{unnatural ('negative')}\end{cases}$$

Amplifiers and comparatives are available for adjectives that refer to a quality that is thought of as having values on a scale. They are also available for adverbs that refer to a manner or to a time that is thought of in terms of a scale. Thus, in

John is *English*

the adjective *English* does not allow amplifiers or comparatives if it refers to John's nationality, which is not a quality of John. However, if *English* refers to the way he behaves, they are admitted:

$$\text{John is}\begin{cases}\text{very English}\\ \text{more English than the English}\end{cases}$$

Similarly, *original* cannot normally be intensified or compared in *the original manuscript*: it does not refer to a quality and there can be only one original manuscript. On the other hand, if *original* refers to the quality of the work, it may be intensified or compared: *a more original book*. We may compare the two uses with that of the corresponding adverb:

He always writes *very originally*
*He came from Cleveland *very originally*

The time adjunct *originally* cannot be intensified or compared, since it refers to a point of time.

Note

[a] There are exceptions to the co-occurrence of a particular intensifier with a semantic class of adjectives. For example, though *utterly* tends to co-occur with 'negative' adjectives, *utterly reliable* and *utterly delightful* are common. People vary in the exceptions they allow.

[b] *This is the more original manuscript* is a possible sentence. The sentence has broadened the qualitative range of *original* to include qualities that relate to manuscript sources; for example, to suggest that the manuscript belongs to a series that is closer to the original than other series.

5.71

Certain types of adjectives and adverbs that generally do not accept intensification or comparison are listed:

(1) Conjuncts (5.44, 8.89 *ff*): *very therefore, *more nevertheless*.
(2) Some intensifiers (for adjectives, 5.31; for adverbs, 5.51, 5.52, 5.54 *ff*, 8.19 *ff*): *very really, *very utter folly, *more somewhat*.
(3) Restrictives (for adjectives 5.32; for adverbs, 8.13 *ff*): *extremely only, *the very main reason*.

(4) Additives (for adverbs, 8.13 *ff*): **very additional, *more also.*

(5) Adjectives denoting provenance (5.41) but not when they refer to style: **a very British army, *a more Parisian citizen (cf: a very British attitude).*

(6) Most adjectives or adverbs referring to time *when* (for adverbs, 8.57 *ff*): **the extremely present occasion, *very then.*

(7) Adjectives or adverbs referring to definite frequency of time (for adverbs, 8.61 *ff*): **very daily, *more once.*

(8) Most adjectives or adverbs indicating time relationship (for adverbs, 8.68 *f*): **very previous, *extremely already.*

(9) Most adjectives or adverbs referring to place (for adverbs, 8.45 *ff*): **very here, *more below.* But there are exceptions. The adjectives *bottom* and *top* may take degree intensifiers including *very.* Some place adjectives and adverbs may take degree intensifiers but not *very: extreme right, due east, far south.*

(10) Some adjectives and adverbs expressing an extreme degree never take intensifiers or comparison: **more utter(ly).* But others are in divided usage (8.24): *?very complete(ly), ?more perfect(ly).*

5.72
Unmarked term in 'How' questions and measure phrases
How is used as a pro-form for degree intensifiers of the adjective or adverb in questions and exclamations:

How *efficient* is he?   How *efficiently* does he work?
How *beautiful* she is!   How *beautifully* she dances!

'Measure' adjectives that cover a scale of measurement and have two terms for opposite extremes of the scale use the upper extreme as the 'unmarked' term in *How* questions and with the measurements. That is to say, the use of the upper extreme does not assume that the upper extreme is applicable:

A: How old is your son?   B: He's three months (old).

How old is he? is equivalent to *What is his age?*, while *He's three months old* is equivalent to *His age is three months.*

Adjectives that are used as the unmarked term in *How* questions and with measurements are listed, with the marked term given in parenthesis:

old (young)	deep (shallow)
tall (short)	high (low)
wide (narrow)	thick (thin)
long (short)	

Other adjectives are used as the unmarked term for premodification by interrogative *How* but are not used with measurements. They include:

fat (thin)	strong (weak)
big (small)	bright (dim)
large (little)	heavy (light)
far (near)	

Some adverbs also use an unmarked term in *How* questions. They include the italicized words in:

How *much* does she like him?
How *often* did they complain?
How *quickly* does he do his homework?
How *far* did he drive?

Note

[a] If we use the marked term, as in *How young is John?* we are asking a question that presupposes that John is young, whereas the unmarked term in *How old is John?* does not presuppose that John is old. Notice that neither term is neutral in exclamations:

How young he is! ('He is extremely young')
How old he is! ('He is extremely old')

[b] *Full* and *empty* can be used equally, although *How full* is commoner than *How empty: half full ~ half empty; three-quarters full ~ three-quarters empty.*

Inflection of adjectives for comparison
5.73

The inflectional suffixes are *-er* for the comparative and *-est* for the superlative:

wide ~ wider ~ widest
young ~ younger ~ youngest
low ~ lower ~ lowest

A small group of highly frequent adjectives have their corresponding comparatives and superlatives formed from different stems:

good ~ better ~ best
bad ~ worse ~ worst
far ~ { further ~ furthest
      { farther ~ farthest

Old is regularly inflected as *older, oldest,* but in a specialized use, restricted to human beings in family relationships, the irregular forms *elder, eldest* are normally substituted:

My *elder brother* is an artist
His *eldest son* is still at school

However, *older than* is used rather than **elder than.*

With adjectives taking the regular inflections, certain regular changes in spelling or pronunciation may be introduced in the base of the adjective when the suffixes are added.

CHANGES IN SPELLING

(1) Final base consonants are doubled when the preceding vowel is stressed and spelled with a single letter (*cf* 3.59):

> *big* ~ *bigger* ~ *biggest*
> *sad* ~ *sadder* ~ *saddest*

(2) In bases ending in a consonant + *y*, final *y* is changed to *i* (3.60):

> *angry* ~ *angrier* ~ *angriest*
> *early* ~ *earlier* ~ *earliest*

(3) If the base ends in a mute -*e*, it is dropped before the inflectional suffix (3.61):

> *pure* ~ *purer* ~ *purest*
> *brave* ~ *braver* ~ *bravest*

The same applies if the base ends in -*ee* (*cf* 3.61):

> *free* ~ *freer* ~ *freest*

CHANGES IN PRONUNCIATION

(1) A disyllabic base ending in /l/ normally loses its second syllable before the inflection:

> *simple:* /sɪmpl/ ~ /sɪmplə(r)/ ~ /sɪmplɪst/
> *humble:* /hʌmbl/ ~ /hʌmblə(r)/ ~ /hʌmblɪst/

(2) For speakers that do not give consonantal value to a final *r* in spelling, the /r/ is pronounced before the inflection:

> *rare:* /rɛə/ ~ /rɛərə/ ~ /rɛərɪst/

Note

[a] *Well* ('in good health') and *ill* ('in bad health', especially BrE) are inflected like *good* and *bad* respectively for the comparative:

$$He\ feels\begin{cases}better\\worse\end{cases}$$

But people may associate *better* and *worse* solely with *good* and *bad* respectively in the health sense. Thus, *He is better* is equivalent to *He is well again*.

[b] *Elder* in *elder statesman* is not a comparative. In this use of *elder* there is no corresponding *old* or *eldest*.

5.74

Monosyllabic adjectives that are commonly used can freely form their comparison by inflection. Many disyllabic adjectives can also do so, though like most monosyllabic adjectives they have the alternative of the periphrastic forms:

His children are
{ politer
  politest
  more polite
  the most polite }

My jokes are
{ funnier
  funniest
  more funny
  the most funny }

Other adjectives can only take periphrastic forms:

We are
{ *reluctanter
  *reluctantest
  more reluctant
  the most reluctant (of all) }
to say anything

Her dress is
{ *beautifuller
  *beautifullest
  more beautiful
  the most beautiful }

Common disyllabic adjectives that can take inflected forms are those ending in an unstressed vowel, /ļ/ or /ə(r)/:

(1) -y: funny, noisy, wealthy, friendly
(2) -ow: hollow, narrow, shallow
(3) -le: gentle, feeble, noble
(4) -er, -ure: clever, mature, obscure

Common adjectives outside these four categories that can take inflectional forms include:

common, handsome, polite, quiet, wicked

Note
Disyllabic participle forms ending in -ing or -ed do not take inflections:

*tiringer, *woundeder

5.75

Most adjectives that are inflected for comparison can also take the periphrastic forms with *more* and *most*. With *more*, they seem to do so more easily when they are predicative and are followed by a *than* clause:

John is *more mad* than Bob is

It would be difficult to find a man *more brave* than he is
He is *more* wealthy than I thought

Periphrastic forms are, however, abnormal with a number of mono-syllabic adjectives, including those listed above as forming their comparison irregularly:

bad	good	small
big	great	thick
black	hard (physically)	thin
clean	high	tight
fair (in colour)	low	well
far	old	wide
fast	quick	young

Note

There seems to be no problem in using the periphrastic forms with any adjective in the comparative construction formed with the correlative *the:*

The more old he is, the more wise he becomes

Good and *bad*, however, appear to require inflected forms.

5.76
Inflection of adverbs for comparison

For a small number of adverbs (none of them formed by adding *-ly*, with the exception of *badly*), the inflected forms used for comparison are the same as those for adjectives (5.73). As with adjectives, there is a small group with comparatives and superlatives formed from different stems. The comparatives and superlatives are identical with those for the corresponding adjectives (5.73), for the determiner *much* (4.16), and the quantifier *little* (4.25):

well ~ better ~ best
badly ~ worse ~ worst
little ~ less ~ least
much ~ more ~ most
far ~ $\begin{cases} \text{further} \sim \text{furthest} \\ \text{farther} \sim \text{farthest} \end{cases}$

Adverbs that are identical in form with adjectives take inflections, following the same spelling and phonetic rules as for adjectives, *eg: early, late, hard, slow, fast, quick, long.* *Soon*, which has no corresponding adjective, is frequently used in the comparative (*sooner*), but is not common in the superlative (*soonest*). Some find the superlative unacceptable or at least very informal, but it seems perfectly acceptable as a pre-modifier of certain adjectives, *eg:*

the soonest possible date, the soonest available time

Note
Badly is not an exception in the most important respect. The inflections are not added
to the *-ly* form of *badly* but to a substituted stem.

5.77
Premodification of comparatives and superlatives
The comparatives of both adjectives and adverbs, whether inflected or
periphrastic, can themselves be premodified by amplifying intensifiers
(*cf* 5.54, 8.19, 8.23 *ff*), the words in parenthesis being additional intensifiers of these intensifiers:

$$
\left.
\begin{array}{l}
\left.
\begin{array}{l}
\text{that} \\
\text{(so) (very)}
\end{array}
\right\} \text{much} \\
\qquad \text{(all) the} \\
\qquad\qquad \text{far} \\
\qquad\qquad \text{a lot} \\
\qquad\qquad \text{lots}
\end{array}
\right\}
\begin{array}{l}
\text{better} \\
\text{sooner} \\
\left.
\begin{array}{l}
\text{more} \\
\text{less}
\end{array}
\right\}
\begin{array}{l}
\text{careful} \\
\text{carefully}
\end{array}
\end{array}
$$

Some of these intensifiers can be repeated indefinitely for emphasis:

very very . . . much sooner
much much . . . more careful
far far . . . more carefully
so so . . . much better (repeated *so* in BrE only)
so very very . . . much better

Generally, however, the repetition is permissible only if the repeated
items come first or follow *so:*

so very very much . . . better
*very much much . . . better

A number of noun phrases (most of them informal) are also available
for the degree intensification of comparatives:

$$
\left.
\begin{array}{l}
\text{a hell of a lot (familiar)} \\
\text{a heck of a lot (familiar)} \\
\text{a damn sight (familiar)} \\
\text{a good deal} \\
\text{a great deal} \\
\text{a good bit}
\end{array}
\right\}
\begin{array}{l}
\text{better} \\
\text{sooner} \\
\left.
\begin{array}{l}
\text{more} \\
\text{less}
\end{array}
\right\}
\begin{array}{l}
\text{careful} \\
\text{carefully}
\end{array}
\end{array}
$$

Similarly, many downtoners (*cf* 5.51, 8.19, 8.29 *ff*) may premodify the
comparatives:

$$
\left.
\begin{array}{l}
\text{rather} \\
\text{somewhat} \\
\text{scarcely} \\
\text{hardly} \\
\text{a little} \\
\text{a (little) bit}
\end{array}
\right\}
\begin{array}{l}
\text{better} \\
\text{sooner} \\
\left.
\begin{array}{l}
\text{more} \\
\text{less}
\end{array}
\right\}
\begin{array}{l}
\text{careful} \\
\text{carefully}
\end{array}
\end{array}
$$

The inflectional superlative may be premodified by the degree intensifier *very: the very best, the very least.* If *very* premodifies the superlative, a determiner is obligatory:

She put on *her very best* dress
They are working *the very least* they can

The analytic superlative is not normally premodified by the intensifier *very: *the very most careful man.*

Bibliographical note

Some recent contributions of relevance to adjectives in general: Bolinger (1961); Bolinger (1965) *pp* 139–180; Halliday (1967–68); Lees (1960b); Teyssier (1968); Vendler (1968).

On the position of adjectives, see particularly Bolinger (1967b); Jacobsson (1961); on stative and dynamic adjectives, see Schopf (1969); on the comparison of adjectives, see Bolinger (1967c); on the intensification of adjectives and adverbs, see Bolinger (1971a); on adverbs in general, see Chapter 8 below.

SIX
PREPOSITIONS AND PREPOSITIONAL PHRASES

Prepositional phrase

6.1

Preposition and prepositional complement

A prepositional phrase (see 2.11 *f*) consists of a preposition followed by a prepositional complement, which is characteristically either a noun phrase or a clause (*wh*-clause or V-*ing* clause) in nominal function:

PREPOSITION	PREPOSITIONAL COMPLEMENT
with	certainty
at	the bus-stop
from	what he said
by	signing a peace treaty

Note

Exceptionally (mainly in idioms), an adverb (5.64) or an adjective may function as prepositional complement: *at once, before long, in there, until now, since when, at least, at worst, in brief.* In addition, even prepositional phrases can on occasion act as prepositional complements (6.8 Note).

6.2

That-clauses and infinitive clauses

That-clauses and infinitive clauses, although they frequently have a nominal function in other respects, do not occur as prepositional complements. Alternations between the presence and absence of a preposition are observed in cases like:

⎧ He was surprised *at* her attitude
⎪ He was surprised *at* what he saw
⎨ He was surprised that she noticed him
⎩ He was surprised to see her

⎧ They persuaded him *of* the need for more troops
⎪ They persuaded him *of* how many troops they needed
⎨ They persuaded him that they needed more troops
⎩ They persuaded him to send for more troops

Such alternations show that the preposition which normally follows certain verbs and adjectives is omitted before a *that*-clause or infinitive clause (see 12.34 *ff*). Further examples of verbs and adjectives which can have either prepositions or *that*-clauses are:

> *ask (for), conceive (of), decide (on), convince (of), inform (of), insist (on), remind (of/about), tell (of/about), be afraid (of), be ashamed (of), be aware (of), be sorry (about), be sure (of)*: see also **5.36**.

Note

[a] This restriction on the use of *that*-clauses can frequently be bypassed, if necessary, by the construction *the fact that:*

> I gather, from *the fact that* he hasn't written for more money, that he has found a job
> They persuaded him of *the fact that* they needed more troops

[b] Combinations such as *except that*, *but that* (=*except that*), and *in that* are considered compound conjunctions, not combinations of prep+*that* (11.9).

6.3
Postposed prepositions

Normally a preposition must be followed by its complement; but there are some circumstances in which this does not happen, because the complement has to take first position in the clause, or else is absent through ellipsis:

> WH-QUESTIONS: Which house did you leave it *at*? (7.63)
> RELATIVE CLAUSES: The old house which I was telling you *about* is empty (13.8 *f*)
> WH-CLAUSES: What I'm convinced *of* is that the world's population will grow to an unforeseen extent (11.18, 11.20)
> EXCLAMATIONS: What a mess he's got *into!* (7.78 *f*)
> PASSIVES: She was sought *after* by all the leading impresarios of the day (14.8)
> INFINITIVE CLAUSES: He's impossible to work *with* (14.23)

As the examples show, the preposition in such cases frequently takes a final position in the clause, a position much criticized in the past as contrary to 'good grammar'. A prejudice against such postposed prepositions remains in formal English, which offers (for relative clauses and for direct or indirect questions) the alternative of an initial preposition:

> It was a situation *from which* no escape was possible

This construction is often felt, however, to be stilted and awkward in informal English, especially in speech, and indeed in some cases (7.63 Note *c*) the postposed preposition has no preposed alternative.

Simple and complex prepositions
6.4
Simple prepositions

Most of the common English prepositions, such as *at*, *in* and *for*, are simple, *ie* consist of one word. Other prepositions, consisting of more than one word, are called complex. The following is a comprehensive list of simple prepositions (F = formal):

> *aboard, about, above, across, after, against, along, alongside, amid* (F) (or *amidst* F), *among* (or *amongst* rare), *apropos* (*of*), *around, as, at, atop* (AmE, F), *before, behind, below, beneath, beside, besides, between, beyond, but, by, despite, down, during, for, from, in, inside, minus, notwithstanding, of, off, on* (or *upon* F), *opposite, out* (AmE), *outside, outwith* (Scots = *except*), *over, past, per, plus, round, since, than, through, throughout, to, toward* (AmE), *towards* (BrE), *under, underneath, until* (or *till*), *up, via, with, within, without.*

In addition to this list, there are a few words which behave in many ways like prepositions, although they have affinities with verbs or adjectives:

> *except, excepting, bar, barring, concerning* (F), *considering, following, including, granted, pending* (F), *less, like, near, save* (archaic), *unlike, worth*

He gave us all *bar* (= 'except') three of the sketches
Granted his obsequious manner, I still think he's ambitious enough to do the job
Two gold-hilted swords, each *worth* £10,000, were sold at Sotheby's last Monday.

6.5
Complex prepositions

Most complex prepositions are placeable, according to their form, into one of three categories:

> [A] ADVERB+PREP: *along with, apart from* (BrE), *aside from* (AmE), *as for, as to, away from, into* (*cf* 6.7), *off of* (AmE), *on to* (or *onto*), *out of, together with, up to,* etc.
> [B] VERB/ADJECTIVE/CONJUNCTION/etc+PREP: *except for, owing to, due to, but for, because of,* etc.
> [C] PREP$_1$+NOUN+PREP$_2$: *by means of, in comparison with, instead of,* etc.

In C, which is by far the most numerous category, the noun in some complex prepositions is preceded by a definite or indefinite article:

> in *the* light of; as *a* result of

This category may be further subdivided according to which prepositions function as Prep$_1$ and Prep$_2$:

> *IN*+NOUN+*OF*: *in case of, in charge of, in view of, in need of, in*

> *spite of, in front of, in lieu of, in favour of, in place of, in face of, in aid of, in quest of, in respect of, in search of,* etc
>
> IN+NOUN+*WITH*: *in contact with, in common with, in line with, in accordance with,* etc
>
> B Y+NOUN+*OF*: *by means of, by way of, by virtue of, by dint of,* etc
>
> ON+NOUN+*OF*: *on account of, on behalf of, on top of, on pain of, on the strength of,* etc
>
> OTHER TYPES: *at variance with, in exchange for, in return for, in addition to, in relation to, at the expense of, for the sake of, in/with regard to, with respect to, at the hands of,* etc

Note

Monosyllabic simple prepositions are normally unstressed; polysyllabic prepositions (whether simple or complex) are normally stressed. In complex prepositions, the stress falls on the word (adverb, noun, etc) preceding the final preposition.

6.6
'Cohesiveness' of complex prepositions

Strictly speaking, a complex preposition is a sequence that is indivisible both in terms of syntax and in terms of meaning. However, there is no absolute distinction between complex prepositions and constructions which can be varied, abbreviated and extended according to the normal rules of syntax. Rather, there is a scale of 'cohesiveness' running from a sequence which behaves in every way like a simple preposition (*eg: in spite of* [*the weather*]), to one which behaves in every way like a set of grammatically separate units (*eg: on the shelf by* [*the door*]). Nine indicators of syntactic separateness are listed below.

(a) Prep$_2$ can be varied

 on the shelf at [*the door*] but not *eg: *in spite for,* etc

(b) The noun can be varied as between singular and plural

 on the shelves by [*the door*] but not **in spites of*

(c) The noun can be varied in respect to determiners

 on shelves by [*the door*] but not **in a/the spite of*

(d) Prep$_1$ can be varied

 under the shelf by [*the door*] but not **for spite of*

(e) Prep$_2$+complement can be replaced by a genitive

 $\left.\begin{array}{l}\textit{on the surface}\\ \textit{in spite}\end{array}\right\}$ *of the table* ~ *on its surface* but not **in its spite*

(f) Prep$_2$+complement can be omitted

 on the shelf but not **in spite*

(g) Prep$_2$+complement can be replaced by a demonstrative

 on that shelf but not **in that spite*

(h) The noun can be replaced by nouns of related meaning

  on the ledge by [*the door*] but not *in malice of

(i) The noun can be freely premodified by adjectives

  on the low shelf by [*the door*] but not **in evident spite of*

In all these respects, *in spite of* 'qualifies' as a complex preposition, whereas *on the shelf by* does not.

As examples of sequences which lie between these two poles, we may take *in quest of*, *in search of*, *in comparison with*, and *in defence of* as showing progressively less of the character of a preposition and more of the character of a free syntactic construction.

In quest of is slightly less cohesive than *in spite of* in that it has property (h) (*cf: in search of*).

In search of is less cohesive still, in having property (f) (*cf: in search*) as well as property (h) (*cf: in quest of*).

In comparison with goes further, in that it has property (d) (*cf: by/ through comparison with*) as well as properties (f) (*cf: in comparison*) and (h) (*cf: in common with*).

In defence of goes yet further, having four of the properties of a free construction, *viz:* (c) (*cf: in the defence of*), (e) (*cf: in her defence*), (h) (*cf: in support of*), and (i) (*in keen/stubborn/bold/etc defence of*).

On the other hand, all these types might reasonably be considered 'complex prepositions', in that they have more in common with *in spite of* than with *on the shelf by*.

6.7
Boundary between simple and complex prepositions

The boundary between simple and complex prepositions is also an uncertain one. Orthographic separation is the easiest test to apply, but anomalies such as writing *into* as one word and *out of* as two merely emphasize the arbitrariness of the distinction between one and more than one word.

A test that can be applied to most cases is that a preposition when simple is identical in form to its corresponding prepositional adverb (*by* ~ *by*, etc: 6.9–10); a complex preposition, on the other hand, loses its final element when transferred to the function of adverb (*apart from* ~ *apart:* 6.10 Note).

As the remainder of this chapter will chiefly illustrate simple prepositions, it may be valuable to give here a few instances of the use of complex prepositions:

In terms of money, her loss was small.

Two men were interviewed at Bow Street Police Station *in connection with* a theft from an Oxford Street store.

How many delegates are *in favour of* this motion?

His biography of Eisenhower is in many places *at variance with* the official reports.

In line with latest trends in fashion, many dress designers have been sacrificing elegance to audacity.

Legal English is notable for complex prepositions, the following being among those found mainly in legalistic or bureaucratic usage: *in case of*, *in default of*, *in lieu of*, *on pain of*, *in respect of*.

6.8
Syntactic function of prepositional phrases

Prepositional phrases may function as:

(a) *Adjunct (6.34 ff)*:

The people were singing *on the bus*

(b) *Postmodifier in a noun phrase (13.25 ff)*:

The people *on the bus* were singing

(c) *Complementation of a verb (6.51–54)*:

We were looking *at his awful paintings*

In this and the following function, the preposition is more closely related to the preceding word, which determines its choice, than to the prepositional complement.

(d) *Complementation of an adjective (6.51–54)*:

I am sorry *for his parents*

(e) *Disjunct (6.47–50)*:

He did, *in all fairness*, try to phone the police

(f) *Conjunct (6.47–50)*:

On the other hand, he made no attempt to help the victim or apprehend her attacker

Of these functions, those of adjunct and postmodifier are the most common. As conjuncts, prepositional phrases are largely limited to idiomatic or stereotyped phrases: *of course, in a word, with respect, in conclusion, at any rate*, etc.

Note

Like adverbs (5.64), prepositional phrases may occasionally take a nominal function, *eg* as subject of a clause, or even as prepositional complement:

> *Between six and seven* will suit me
> He crawled out from *under the table.*

Prepositions and prepositional adverbs
6.9

A prepositional adverb (5.50) is a particle which shares the form, but not the syntactic status, of a preposition. It is capable of standing alone as an adjunct, disjunct, conjunct, postmodifier, etc without the addition of a prepositional complement:

> A car drove past the door (*past* is a preposition)
> A car drove past (*past* is a prepositional adverb)

In the examples below, the adverb is respectively (a) an adjunct, (b) a postmodifier:

> (a) Despite the fine weather, we stayed *in* all day
> (b) The day *before*, I had spoken to him in the street

The following is a full list of (simple) prepositional adverbs:

> *aboard, about, above, across, after, against†, along, alongside, apart, around, before, behind, below, beneath, besides, between, beyond, by, down, for†, in, inside, near, notwithstanding, off, on, opposite, over, outside, past, round, since, through, throughout, to* (in a few idioms such as *to and fro*), *under, underneath, up, within, without*
> (†only in phrases such as *votes for and against*)

All, with the exception of *without* and the conjuncts *besides* and *notwithstanding*, are primarily adjuncts of time or place.

Both prepositions and adverbs commonly appear in idiomatic combinations with a preceding verb; *eg: make for, make up, make up for.* Here, however, we shall pay attention only to their meaning and syntactic behaviour as individual items, idiomatic usage being a concern of the dictionary rather than of the grammar. Discussion of phrasal verbs (*ie* combinations of verb and adverb which behave syntactically or semantically as a single unit) is postponed to 12.19 *ff.*

Note

Adverbs normally receive stress, whereas simple prepositions (especially monosyllables) normally do not: *He thrust 'in his hand* (*in*=adverb) is thus distinct from *He swam in the lake* (*in*=unstressed prep). Similarly:

> Which prisoner did they march 'in? (where *in* is adverb)
> Which uniform did they march in? (where *in* is preposition)

6.10

Usually a prepositional adverb can be explained as a prepositional phrase from which the complement, having a definite understood meaning, has been deleted (*cf* 5.50, 8.57 Note *d*):

Is Mary *around*? (='around the house/building, etc')
There's a bus *behind* (='behind us/the car/house, etc')
Poor George nearly fell *off* (='off the horse/bus/roof, etc')
I haven't seen him *since* (='since that day/time, etc')

However, adverbs do not always correspond to equivalent prepositional usages: *eg* there is no equivalent preposition for the adverbs *over* and *off* in

At last the war's *over*
He's going *off* on his travels again.

Note

If it corresponds to a complex preposition, an adverb is not identical in form to the preposition, being without the final word: *out of* ~ *out*; *away from* ~ *away*, etc. There is also a category of 'complex adverb', since prepositional phrases such as *in favour*, *on top*, and *in return* have the role of adverb in relation to the complex prepositions *in avour of*, *on top of*, *in return for*, etc.

Prepositional meanings

6.11

In the most general terms, a preposition expresses a relation between two entities, one being that represented by the prepositional complement. Of the various types of relational meaning, those of PLACE and TIME are the most prominent and easy to identify. Other relationships such as INSTRUMENT and CAUSE may also be recognized although it is difficult to describe prepositional meanings systematically in terms of such labels. Some prepositional uses may be elucidated best by seeing a preposition as related to a clause; *eg: The man with the red beard* (6.46) ~ *The man who has the red beard; my knowledge of Hindi* (13.28*f*) ~ *I know Hindi*.

In the survey of prepositional meanings to which most of this chapter is devoted, place and time relations will be dealt with first, and will be followed by a more cursory exemplification of other relations such as 'cause', 'goal' and 'origin'. So varied are prepositional meanings that no more than a presentation of the most notable semantic similarities and contrasts can be attempted here.

Place
6.12

Prepositional phrases of place are typically either adjuncts (relating an event or state of affairs to a location) or postmodifiers (relating some 'object' to a location); they may also act as obligatory 'predicative' adjuncts following the verb BE, as in *Maggy is in the kitchen* (see 2.10).

Fig 6:1 indicates relations of meaning between a number of prominent prepositions of place.

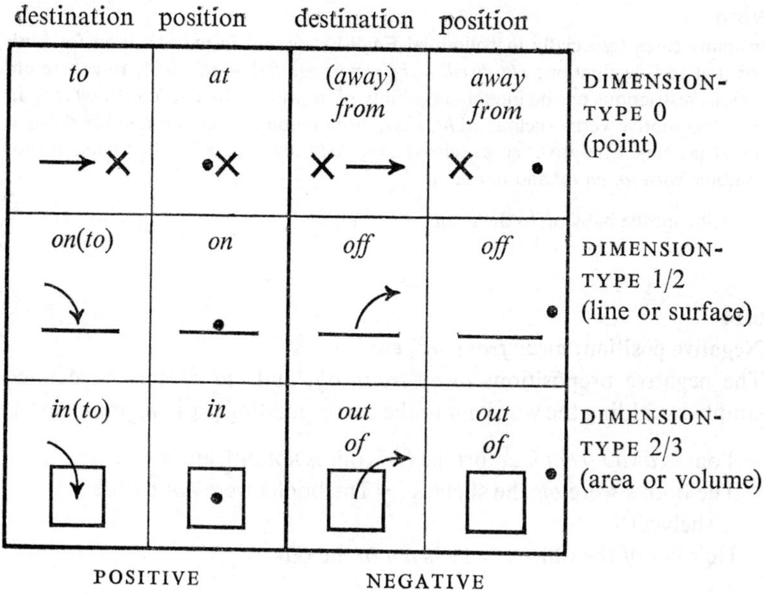

destination	position	destination	position	
to →X	*at* •X	*(away)* *from* X→	*away* *from* X •	DIMENSION- TYPE 0 (point)
on(to)	*on*	*off*	*off*	DIMENSION- TYPE 1/2 (line or surface)
in(to)	*in*	*out* *of*	*out* *of*	DIMENSION- TYPE 2/3 (area or volume)

POSITIVE   NEGATIVE

Fig 6:1 Some prepositions of place

Note

[a] Some of the prepositions in the above diagram can be replaced by other prepositions with the same meaning: *upon* is a formal equivalent of *on; inside* and *within* can substitute for *in*, and *outside* for *out of*.

[b] *On to* is of restricted use in AmE; it is sometimes spelt as a single word: *onto*.

6.13
Simple position and destination: *at, to*, etc

Between the notions of simple position (or static location) and destination (movement with respect to an intended location) a cause-and-effect relationship obtains:

DESTINATION	POSITION
Tom went *to* Cambridge.	*as a result:* Tom was *at* Cambridge
Tom fell *on(to)* the floor.	*as a result:* Tom was *on* the floor
Tom dived *in(to)* the water.	*as a result:* Tom was *in* the water

A prepositional phrase of 'position' can accompany any verb, although this meaning is particularly associated with verbs of STATIVE meaning (2.6, 3.40), such as *be, stand, live*, etc; the meaning of 'destination' generally (but by no means always – see 6.22) accompanies a verb of DYNAMIC 'motional' meaning, such as *go, move, fly*, etc.

Note
In many cases (especially in colloquial English), *on* and *in* may be used for both position and destination: *He dived in the water*; *He fell on the floor*. But there are various restrictions on the interchangeability of *on* with *on to* and *in* with *into*: eg in BrE, locomotive verbs such as *walk, slide, swim* require *on to* and *into* for destinational meaning. Causative verbs such as *place, stand, lay, sit*, on the other hand, do not combine with *to, on to*, and *into* at all:

$\begin{cases} \text{*She sat the baby on to the chair} \\ \text{She sat the baby on the chair} \end{cases}$

6.14
Negative position: *away from, off*, etc
The negative prepositions *away from, off*, and *out of* may be defined simply by adding the word *not* to the corresponding positive preposition:

Tom is *away from* Cambridge (=Tom is *not at* Cambridge)
The books were *off* the shelves (=The books were *not on* the shelves)
He's *out of* the office (= He's *not in* the office)

6.15
Dimension-types: *at~on~in*, etc
The dimension-type of a preposition is the dimensional property ascribed, subjectively speaking, to the location denoted by the prepositional complement.

One may compare the three phrases *at the door, on the door*, and *in the door*. In the phrase *at the door*, the door is envisaged as a dimensionless location, a vague 'point on the map', and no details concerning its shape or size come into focus. This is dimension-type 0. The phrase *on the door*, on the other hand, makes us see the door as a two-dimensional thing, ie a surface. *On*, in fact, can indicate a location of either one or two dimensions (a line or a surface). This is therefore dimension-type 1/2. With *in the door*, the door is seen as a three-dimensional object, an object having volume. *In* can also be applied to two-dimensional locations which are seen as 'areas' (typically enclosed or bordered pieces of territory) rather than 'surfaces'. (This, like the other distinctions involving dimension-types, is psychological or perceptual, rather than 'real'.) *In*, therefore, belongs to dimension-type 2/3.

It is clear from the foregoing that the same object can be viewed in terms of any of three dimension-types:

> The manager stood *at* the door
> There was a new coat of paint *on* the door
> There was woodworm *in* the door

Further examples of each type are:

DIMENSION-TYPE 0:
| at the shop | at the North Pole |
| at the bus-stop | at the end of the road |

DIMENSION-TYPE 1/2:
line: (The city is situated)	*surface:* (A notice was pasted)
on the River Thames	on the wall
on the boundary	on the ceiling
on the coast	on my back

DIMENSION-TYPE 2/3:
area: in the world	*volume:* in a box
in the village	in the bathroom
in the park	in the cathedral

The contrast between *on* (='surface') and *in* (='area') has various implications according to context, as these examples show:

{ on the window: The frost made patterns on the window
                                  (window = glass surface)
{ in the window/mirror: A face appeared in the window/mirror
                                  (window, mirror = framed area)

{ on the field: The players were practising on the field
                                  (field = surface for sports)
{ in the field: Cows were grazing in the field
                                  (field = enclosed area of land)

{ on the island: He was marooned on a desert island
                                  (viewed as a mere space)
{ in the island: He was born in Long Island (viewed
                                  as an inhabited interior)

The opposition between *at* (dimension-type 0) and *in* (dimension-type

2/3) can also cause difficulty. *In* is used for continents, countries, provinces, and sizeable territories of any kind; but for towns, villages, etc, either *at* or *in* is appropriate, according to point of view: *at/in Stratford-upon-Avon*. A very large city, such as New York, London, or Tokyo, is generally treated as an area: *He works in London, but lives in the country*. But one could treat it as a point on the map if global distances were in mind: *Our plane refuelled at London on its way from New York to Moscow*.

With buildings, also, both *at* and *in* can be used. The difference here is that *at* refers to a building in its institutional or functional aspect, whereas *in* refers to it as a three-dimensional structure:

He's $\begin{cases} \text{at school (BrE)} \\ \text{in school (AmE)} \end{cases}$ (='He attends/is attending school')

He's in school (=(in BrE) 'He's actually inside the building – not,
   eg on the playing fields')

So too *at/in Oxford; at home* but *in the house*.

Note

[a] On the zero article in *at school* etc, see 4.38.

[b] In some cases it may be more difficult to explain the use of a preposition in terms of dimension-type: *at the seaside* (*cf: on the coast*); *in the world* (*cf: on (the) earth*). Even here, however, the implications of *at, on*, and *in* are felt to be different. *At the seaside* suggests a point of contact with the sea, rather than a one-dimensional coastline. *On the earth* sees the world as a surface (*eg* as a geologist might see it) rather than as a place where people live.

[c] When a place is being regarded as a destination rather than a position, it is more natural to see it vaguely as a geographical point than as an area. Hence the more frequent use of *to* than of *into* in reference to countries etc: *The gypsies came to England in the fifteenth century* (contrast *The gypsies were in England*).

[d] In addition to the prepositions mentioned, *against, about*, and *around* are commonly used as prepositions of simple position or destination: *against* in the sense 'touching the side surface of' (*He's leaning against the wall*); *about* and *around* in the sense of 'in the vicinity of' (*He's been snooping about/around the place all day*).

[e] Two additional meanings of *on* as a preposition of position are 'hanging from'

   The apples are still *on* the tree

and 'on top of'

   Humpty Dumpty sat *on* the wall

We may see these as extending the basic meaning of *on* to include the most obvious static relationship of contiguity between a smaller and a larger object.

6.16

Relative position: *by, over, under*, etc

Apart from simple position, prepositions may express the RELATIVE POSITION of two objects or groups of objects:

He was standing *by* his brother (='at the side of')

I left the keys *with* my wallet (= 'in the same place as')

Above, below, over, under, on top of, underneath, beneath express relative position in a VERTICAL DIRECTION, whereas *in front of* and *behind* represent it in a HORIZONTAL DIRECTION. *Fig* 6:2 depicts the relations expressed by '*X is above Y*', '*Z is behind Y*', etc. The antonyms

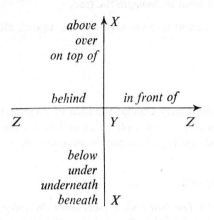

Fig 6:2 Vertical and horizontal direction

above and *below*, *over* and *under*, *in front of* and *behind* are not positive and negative, but converse opposites:

The picture is *above* the mantelpiece = The mantelpiece is *below* the
   picture
The bus is *in front of* the car = The car is *behind* the bus

Over and *under* as place prepositions are roughly synonymous with *above* and *below* respectively. The main differences are that *over* and *under* tend to indicate a direct vertical relationship and/or spatial proximity, while *above* and *below* may indicate simply 'on a higher/lower level than':

The castle stands on a hill above (*rather than* over) the valley
The doctor and the policeman were leaning over (*rather than* above)
   the body when we arrived

Underneath and *beneath* are less common substitutes for *under; beneath* is formal in style. *Underneath,* like *on top of,* generally indicates a contiguous relation.

Note
Other prepositions of relative position are *beside, near (to), between, amid(st), among(st).*

6.17
Relative destination: *by, over, under,* **etc**
As well as relative position, the prepositions listed in 6.16 (but not, generally, *above* and *below*) can express relative destination:

The bush was the only conceivable hiding-place, so I dashed *behind* it
When it started to rain, we all went *underneath* the trees

This use is distinct from that denoting PASSAGE behind, under, etc (6.18).

6.18
Passage: *by, over, under,* **etc**
With verbs of motion, prepositions may express the idea of PASSAGE (*ie* movement towards and then away from a place) as well as destination. With the prepositions listed in 6.16, this occurs in sentences like:

He jumped *over* a ditch
Someone ran *behind* the goal-posts

In sentences like the last, or like *The ball rolled underneath the table,* there is an ambiguity: we can supply either the meaning of 'passage' (='the ball passed under the table on the way to some other destination') or the meaning of 'destination' (='the ball rolled under the table and stayed there').

Note
A triple ambiguity may in fact arise with the above sentences, or more clearly with *A mouse scuttled behind the curtain,* which may be interpreted not only in the senses of 'passage' and 'destination', but also in the static sense, implying that the mouse stayed (scuttling back and forth) behind the curtain all the time.

6.19
Passage: *across, through, past*
The sense of 'passage' is the primary locative meaning attached to *across* (dimension-type 1/2), *through* (dimension-type 2/3) and *past* (the 'passage' equivalent of *by* which may also, however, be substituted for *past* in a 'passage' sense). Note the parallel between *across* and *on, through* and *in* in *Fig 6:3*.

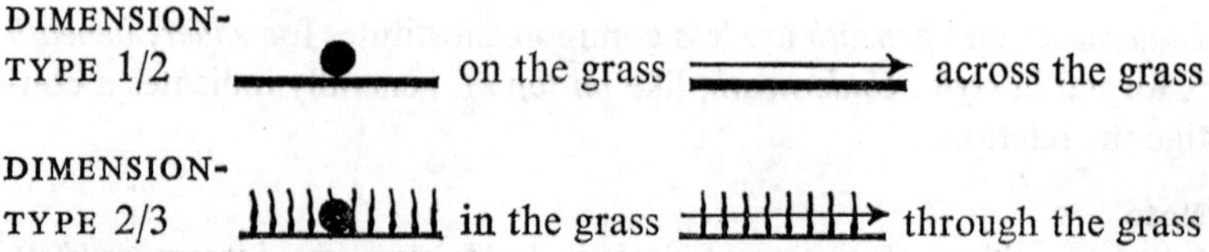

DIMENSION-
TYPE 1/2   ●────── on the grass ══════▶ across the grass

DIMENSION-
TYPE 2/3   )))))●(((((in the grass ⫲⫲⫲⫲⫲⫲▶ through the grass

Fig 6:3 *On* and *across, in* and *through*

The upper pair treat the grass as a surface, and therefore suggest short grass; the lower pair, by treating the grass as a volume, suggest that it has height as well as length and breadth – that is, that the grass is long. There is a meaning of *over* corresponding to *across* in this sense: *The ball rolled over/across the lawn.*

6.20
Movement with reference to a directional path: *up, down, along,* etc
Up, down, along, across (in a slightly different sense from that of 6.19), and *(a)round*, with verbs of motion, make up a group of prepositions expressing movement with reference to an axis or directional path. *Up* and *down* contrast in terms of vertical direction, while *along* (= 'from one end towards the other') contrasts with *across* (= 'from one side to another') in terms of a horizontal axis.

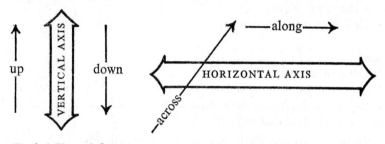

Fig 6:4 *Up* and *down*   *Fig* 6:5 *Along* and *across*

But *up* and *down* are also used idiomatically in reference to a horizontal axis:

He lives {down the road
          {up the coast

I walked up and down the platform

Up and *down* here express the notion of 'along', and need not have any vertical implications.

With *(a)round*, the directional path is an angle or a curve:

We ran up the hill
We ran (a)round the corner

Toward(s) is in a category of its own, having the meaning 'in the direction of'.

6.21
Orientation: *beyond, over, past,* etc
Most prepositions listed in 6.16 and 6.20 can be used in a static sense of orientation. This brings in a third factor apart from the two things being

spatially related: *viz* a 'point of orientation', at which (in reality or imagination) the speaker is standing. *Beyond* (= 'on the far side of') is a preposition whose primary meaning is one of orientation; furthermore, *over*, *past*, *across*, and *through* can combine the meaning of 'beyond' with more specific information of dimension-type etc on the lines described in 6.19:

> He lives *across* the moors (*ie* 'from here')
> The village *past* the bus-stop/*through* the wood, etc

Up, *down*, *along*, *across*, and *(a)round* (see 6.20) are used orientationally with reference to an axis in

> The shop *down* the road (*ie* towards the bottom end of . . .)
> His office is *up*/*down* the stairs (*ie* at (or towards) the top of . . .)
> There's a hotel *across*/*along* the road (*ie* on the other side/towards the other end of . . .)
> He lives *(a)round* the corner.

6.22
Resultative meaning
When combined with the verb BE, all prepositions which have motional meaning can also have a static resultative meaning indicating *the state of having reached* the destination:

> The horses are *over* the fence (= 'have got(ten) over')
> At last we are *out of* the forest (= 'have got(ten) out')

Resultative meaning is not always distinguishable out of context from other static meanings; its presence is often signalled, however, by certain adverbs (*already*, *just*, *at last*, (*not*) *yet*, etc), and it is characteristically found with negative prepositions *from*, *out of*, etc or with prepositions of 'passage' such as *across*, *through*, and *past*.

6.23
Pervasive meaning: *all over, throughout,* etc
Over (dimension-type 1/2) and *through* (dimension-type 2/3), especially when preceded by *all*, have pervasive meaning (either static or motional):

> That child was running *all over* the flower borders
> Chaos reigned *all through* the house

Throughout, substitutable for *all through*, is the only preposition whose primary meaning is 'pervasive'. Occasionally the 'axis' type prepositions of 6.20 are also used in a pervasive sense:

> There were crowds (all) *along* the route
> They put flowers (all) *around* the statue.

6.24

Seven senses of *over*

Let us now see how one preposition (*over*) may be used in most of the senses discussed:

POSITION: A lamp hung over the door
DESTINATION: They threw a blanket over her
PASSAGE: They climbed over the wall
ORIENTATION: They live over (='on the far side of') the road
RESULTATIVE: At last we were over the crest of the hill
PERVASIVE (STATIC): Leaves lay thick (all) over the ground
PERVASIVE (MOTION): They splashed water (all) over me.

6.25

Verbs incorporating prepositional meaning

When a verb contains within its own meaning the meaning of a following preposition, it is often possible to omit the preposition; the verb then becomes transitive, and the prepositional complement becomes a direct object:

climb (up) a mountain   pass (by) the house
jump (over) a fence   pierce (through) the defences
flee (from) the country   turn (round) a corner

6.26

Metaphorical or abstract use of place prepositions

Many place prepositions have abstract meanings which are clearly related, through metaphorical connection, to their locative uses. Very often prepositions so used keep the groupings (in terms of similarity or contrast of meaning) that they have when used in literal reference to place.

One may perceive a stage-by-stage extension of metaphorical usage in such a series as:

(i) in shallow water (purely literal)
(ii) in deep water (also metaphorical='in trouble')
(iii) in difficulties (the noun is not metaphorical, but the preposition is)
(iv) in a spot (='in a difficult situation': the preposition is analogous to that of (iii), but another locative metaphor is introduced by the noun. The result is a phrase that could not occur in a literal sense, because *at a spot* (dimension-type 0) would be appropriate instead.)

Examples in relation to the literal meanings are:

IN/OUT OF; AMID (rare)/AMIDST

   position → state, condition:

   in/out of danger; in difficulties; to keep out of trouble; amidst
   a mass of troubles

   enclosure → abstract inclusion:

   in books/plays; in a group/party; in/out of the race

ABOVE/BELOW/BENEATH

   vertical direction → abstract level:

   to be above/below someone on a list; above/below one's income;
   such behaviour is beneath (not *below*) *him; he's above such*
   behaviour

UNDER

   vertical direction → subjection, subordination:

   under suspicion/orders/compulsion; he has a hundred
   people working under him

UP/DOWN

   movement on vertical axis → movement on list or scale:

   up/down the scale; up/down the social ladder

TO/FROM

   starting point/destination → originator/recipient:

   a letter/present from Browning to his wife (6.39–40)

BEYOND/PAST/OVER

   resultative meaning; physical → abstract:

   beyond/past endurance; beyond/past hope; beyond/past
   recovery; we're over the worst

BETWEEN/AMONG(ST)

   relative position → abstract relation between participants:

   a fight/match between . . .; quarrel/agree among(st) ourselves;
   relationship/contrast/affinity between two things

Note

[a] *Over* and *under* act as intensifiers, rather than as prepositions, with the meanings 'more than' and 'less than' in expressions of measure: *The car was travelling* (*at*) *over/under sixty miles per hour.*

[b] A few prepositions (chiefly *in* and *out of*) can operate in an apparently converse relationship. For example:

   The horse is *in* foal (= The foal is *in* the horse['s womb])
   The office is *out of* envelopes (= There are *no* envelopes *in* the office)

   Cf also *out of breath.*

Time
6.27

A prepositional phrase of time usually occurs as adjunct or postmodifier, but it can occasionally be itself the complement of a temporal preposition (cf 6.8 Note): *a voice from out of the past*. The temporal uses of prepositions frequently suggest metaphorical extensions from the sphere of place similar to the metaphorical extensions discussed in 6.26.

6.28
Time *when: at, on, in*
Thus *at, on*, and *in* as prepositions of 'time *when*' are to some extent parallel to the same items as positive prepositions of position (6.12), although in the time sphere there are only two 'dimension-types', *viz* 'point of time' and 'period of time'.

At is used for points of time (chiefly clock-time) (*at ten o'clock, at 6.30 pm, at noon*, etc); also, idiomatically, for holiday seasons (*at the weekend* (BrE), *at Christmas, at Easter* – referring to the season of Christmas/Easter, not the day itself); and for the phrases *at night, at the/that time*, etc).

On is used with phrases referring to days (*on Monday, on the following day, on New Year's Day*); otherwise *in* or, less commonly, *during* is used to indicate periods of time: *in the evening, during Holy Week, in August, in the months that followed, in summer, in 1969, in the eighteenth century*, etc.

Note
On Monday morning, on Saturday afternoon, on the following evening, etc illustrate an exceptional use of *on* with a complement referring to a *part* of a day, rather than a *whole* day. This use also extends to other cases where the time segment is a part of a day which is actually mentioned: *on the morning of 1st June*, etc. But with phrases like *early morning, late afternoon* it is normal to use *in: in the late afternoon of 15th September*.

6.29
Duration: *for*, etc
Duration is expressed by *for:*

> We camped there *for* the summer (*ie* from the beginning to the end of the summer)

Contrast:

> We camped there *in* the summer (*ie* probably not for the whole summer)

Frequently-used idiomatic phrases of this kind are *for now, for ever* and *for good* 'for ever'.

Also, *over, (all) through*, and *throughout* have a durational meaning parallel to their pervasive meaning in reference to place (6.23):

> We camped there *over* the holiday
> We camped there *through(out)* the summer

Over normally accompanies noun phrases denoting special occasions (such as holidays and festivals), and so generally refers to a shorter period of time than *through(out)*.

From ... to is another pair of prepositions whose locative meaning is transferred to duration. The American alternative expression (*from*) ... *through* is useful in avoiding the ambiguity as to whether the period mentioned second is included in the total span of time:

> We camped there (*from*) June *through* September (AmE)
>   (=up to and including September)
> We camped there *from* June *to* (or *till*) September (BrE)
>   (=up to [?and including] September)

6.30
Before, after, since, and until/till
These are conjunctions as well as prepositions (see 11.27). As prepositions, they occur almost exclusively as prepositions of time, and are followed by either (a) a temporal noun phrase (*eg: before next week*), (b) a subjectless V-*ing* clause (*eg: since leaving school*), or (c) a noun phrase with a deverbal noun (App I.24, 34) or some other noun phrase interpreted as equivalent to a clause:

> until the fall of Rome (='until Rome fell')
> before the war (='before the war started or took place')
> since electricity (='since electricity was invented')

Informally, *until* is sometimes preceded by *up: up until last week.*

6.31
Between, by, and up to
Other prepositions of time are *between, by*, and *up to:*

> I'll phone you *between* lunch and three o'clock
> *By* the time we'd walked five miles, he was exhausted
> *Up to* last week, I hadn't received a reply.

Absence of prepositions of time
6.32

In many cases, a preposition of time is absent, so that the temporal adjunct takes the form of a noun phrase instead of a prepositional phrase (see 8.57 *ff*):

> I saw him *last Thursday*
> I'll mention it *next time I see him*
> *This year*, plums are more plentiful than in any year I can remember
> *Every summer* she returns to her childhood home

Prepositions of time *when* are always absent immediately before the deictic (or 'pointing' – *cf* 4.121b) words *last*, *next*, *this*, and *that;* and the quantifying words *some* and *every;* also before nouns which have 'last', 'next', or 'this' as an element of their meaning: *I saw him yesterday/today; I'll see him tomorrow evening.*

The omission of the preposition is optional with deictic phrases referring to times at more than one remove from the present, such as (*on*) *Monday week* (BrE), (*in*) *the January before last* (in AmE the *in* has to be omitted here), (*on*) *the day before yesterday;* also with phrases which identify a time before or after a given time in the past or future: (*in*) *the previous spring*, (*at*) *the following weekend*, (*on*) *the next day*. Thus, both the following alternatives are acceptable:

> $\begin{cases} \text{We met on the following day} \\ \text{We met the following day} \end{cases}$
> $\begin{cases} \text{We met on that day} \\ \text{We met that day} \end{cases}$

On the whole, the sentence without the preposition tends to be more informal and more usual. Non-deictic phrases containing *the* must have the preposition: *We met on the day/in the spring.*

Note

[a] In AmE and in very informal BrE, the omission of the temporal preposition goes further; one frequently hears sentences such as *I'll see you Sunday*, in in which the preposition *on* is omitted before a day of the week standing on its own. Another type of omission (characteristic of AmE) is in initial position preceding a plural noun phrase:

> *Sundays* we go into the country

[b] The preposition is generally not omitted before the BrE inverted word-order phrases (*on*) *Sunday next,* (*in*) *January last,* etc.

6.33

In addition, the preposition *for* is often omitted in phrases of duration:

> We stayed there (*for*) three months

The snowy weather lasted (for) the whole time we were there
(For) a lot of the time we just lay on the beach

The omission almost invariably takes place with phrases which begin with *all*, such as *all day, all (the) week:*

We stayed there all week (*not* *for all week)

In other cases, however, the omission is impossible: for example, with many 'event' verbs: *I haven't spoken to him for three months* (not **I haven't spoken to him three months*). Initial position in the clause also seems to discourage omission: *For 600 years, the cross lay unnoticed.*

Note

[a] When they occur initially, the phrases *for ages, for days, for years*, etc cannot be abbreviated by omission of the preposition: * *Years we've waited.*

[b] Temporal phrases such as *a month ago, all the year round, all (the) night long* end with an adverb, and in form they are more like phrases of measure (*cf: 10,000 feet up; 3 miles across:* 5.60) than prepositional phrases. There is thus no question here of an omitted preposition.

Other meanings: prepositional phrase chiefly as adjunct
6.34
Ranges of meaning

There follows now a survey of the more important prepositional usages apart from those of time and place. Meanings are elucidated by paraphrase, by antonymy, or grammatical transformation. Fields of meaning are classified according to whether they chiefly involve the prepositional phrase as adjunct, postmodifier, disjunct, or complementation to verbs or adjectives. Fields of prepositional meaning are notoriously difficult to classify, and in some cases it is better to think of a range or spectrum of meaning first as a single category, then as broken up into separate overlapping sections. First, therefore, we deal with two important spectra which may be visualized as follows:

$$
(6.35\text{--}38)
\begin{array}{l}
\uparrow\text{cause} \\
\text{reason} \\
\text{motive} \\
\text{purpose} \\
\text{destination} \\
\downarrow\text{target}
\end{array}
\left.\begin{array}{l} \\ \\ \end{array}\right\} \begin{array}{l} for \\ why \end{array}
\qquad
(6.39\text{--}42)
\begin{array}{l}
\uparrow\text{manner} \\
\text{means} \\
\text{instrument} \\
\text{agentive} \\
\downarrow\text{stimulus}
\end{array}
\left.\begin{array}{l} \\ \\ \end{array}\right\} \begin{array}{l} with \\ how \end{array}
$$

We may refer to these spectra, for brevity, as CAUSE~PURPOSE and MEANS~AGENTIVE respectively. In part, our reason for putting various meanings under a single heading is that some of them have, as a linking element, association with particular prepositions and *wh*-words: *for* and *why* in the first case, *with* and *how* in the second.

After these important areas of meaning, we turn to lesser areas which are not so easily brought together under general headings.

Cause~purpose
6.35
Cause, reason, motive: *because of,* etc

At one end of the spectrum of cause ~ purpose, we have prepositions expressing either the material cause or the psychological cause (motive) for a happening:

Because of the drought, the price of bread was high that year.
Richard and Ben, *on account of their wide experience in climbing,* were voted leaders of the expedition.
I hid the money, *for fear of what my parents would say.*
The survivors were weak *from exposure and lack of food.*
Some support charities *out of duty,* some *out of a sense of guilt;* rarely is human compassion the chief motive.
He said it *for fun,* but they took him seriously.

On account of is a more formal alternative to *because of* as an expression of cause or reason. The other three prepositions are mainly restricted to the expression of motive, *ie* psychological cause: *from gratitude/kindness, out of gratitude/kindness,* etc. *For* is found with a relatively small number of expressions: *for fear/love/want (of)/joy/sorrow,* etc.

Phrases of cause, reason and motive answer the question 'Why . . . ?'

6.36
Purpose, intended destination: *for*

He'll do anything *for money*
Everyone ran *for safety*
For the journey, they packed three large picnic baskets of food
He died *for his country*

The uses of *for* illustrated above have in common a notion of 'purpose', as we see from the possibility of paraphrasing them by a clause (*in order*) *to* . . . (see 11.39): *for money* = 'in order to gain money', *for safety* = 'in order to reach safety', etc. To express intended destination, *for* is used with verbs such as *run, start, head, leave,* and *set out: He set out for London,* etc.

Phrases of purpose or destination answer the questions 'Why . . . ?', 'What . . . for?', 'Where . . . for?', or 'Who . . . for?'. They frequently occur as postmodifiers, as well as adverbials: *the scenery for the play,* etc.

6.37

Recipient, goal, target: *for, to, at*

When *for* is followed by noun phrases denoting persons or animals, the meaning is rather one of 'intended recipient':

> He laid a trap *for his enemies*
> He made a beautiful doll *for his daughter*

So used, the *for* phrase can often be equated with an indirect object (see 7.6, 12.60 *f*): *He made his daughter a beautiful doll; She cooked him a dinner.*

In contrast to the notion of '*intended* recipient' expressed by *for*, the preposition *to* expresses 'actual recipient' in sentences such as:

> He sold the car *to his next-door neighbour*

Here again there is a transformational relationship with the indirect-object construction (7.6):

$$
\text{I}\begin{Bmatrix}\text{gave}\\\text{lent}\\\text{sold}\end{Bmatrix}\text{the book to my friend} \leftrightarrow \text{I}\begin{Bmatrix}\text{gave}\\\text{lent}\\\text{sold}\end{Bmatrix}\text{my friend the book}
$$

At, in combinations such as *aim at* (where the prepositional phrase is complementary to the verb), expresses INTENDED GOAL or TARGET:

> After aiming carefully *at the bird*, he missed it completely
> A vicious mongrel was snapping *at his ankles*

As the first sentence shows, the intended goal need not be achieved. A contrast in many cases (*kick at, swipe at, charge at, bite at, catch at, shoot at, chew at*) may be drawn between this use of *at*, in which some idea of 'aim' is implied, and the direct object construction, which indicates attainment of the goal or consummation of the action as planned. *He shot at the Commander-in-Chief* means something very different from *He shot the Commander-in-Chief*: to the first one could add 'but missed him', whereas one could not to the second. In other cases, where the verb is intransitive, *to* must be used if the attainment of the goal is to be stressed: *He ran at me/He ran to me.*

Note

There is a significant difference between *at* and *to* when combined with verbs of utterance such as *roar, bellow, shout, mutter, growl: He shouted at me* suggests that I am being treated merely as a target (*eg* of abuse), while *He shouted to me* implies that the shouter is communicating with me, *ie* that I am the recipient of the message. *At* here usually suggests hostility.

6.38

Source, origin: *from*

The converse of *to* (='goal') is *from* (='source'):

Bill lent the book *to me* ↔ I borrowed the book *from Bill*

From is also used with reference to 'place of origin':

He comes from Austria (=he is Austrian)
I'm from Madrid

This type of prepositional phrase occurs not only as an adjunct, but as a postmodifier: *the man from Mars; a friend of mine from London.*

Means~agentive
6.39

Manner: *with, in . . . manner, like*

We were received *with the utmost courtesy*
The task was done *in a workmanlike manner*
Like a pestilence, the army swept through the city, leaving nothing
but desolation behind (*ie* 'In the manner of a pestilence . . .')

Note that *like* can have the meaning of 'manner' with extensive verbs (2.5); with intensive verbs, its meaning is purely that of 'resemblance': *Life is like a dream*. This meaning is common with disjuncts (8.78 *ff*) in sentences whose main verb may be extensive; contrast:

He writes poetry like his brother (manner)
Like his brother, he writes poetry (resemblance)

Manner phrases, like manner adverbs, can sometimes be evoked by the question 'How . . . ?', especially if the sense of 'means' is effectively excluded:

A: How did he speak? B: He spoke $\begin{cases}\text{competently.} \\ \text{with great skill.}\end{cases}$

6.40

Means, instrument: *by, with, without*

By can express the meaning 'by means of':

I usually go to work *by bus/train/car/boat*
The thief must have entered and left the house *by the back door*
By working the pumps, we kept the ship afloat for another 40 hours

Phrases of means answer the question 'How . . . ?'.

With, on the other hand, expresses instrumental meaning:

He caught the ball *with his left hand*   [1]
Someone had broken the window *with a stone*   [2]

There is a correspondence between these sentences (which normally require a human subject and a direct object) and sentences containing the verb *use*: *He used his left hand to catch the ball; Someone had used a stone to break the window*. There is also an alternative construction in which the noun phrase denoting the instrument becomes a subject: *His left hand caught the ball; A stone has broken the window*. (On 'instrumental' subjects, see 7.15.)

For most senses of *with*, including that of instrument, *without* expresses the equivalent negative meaning: *I drew it without a ruler* (*ie* 'I did not use a ruler to draw it').

Phrases of instrument, like those of means, answer the question 'How . . . ?'.

A: How did he do it?   B: With an axe.

Note

[a] Mode of transport is expressed by *on* as well as *by*: *on the bus/the train/a ship/a plane* are not purely locative phrases (location in such cases would be expressed by *in* rather than *on* – see 6.15), but rather indicate the condition of being 'in transit'. Thus, *I go to work on the bus* is an alternative to *I go to work by bus*. But although one can say *I met Peter on the bus*, one cannot say **I met Peter by bus*: the meaning 'by means of' is here inappropriate. *On* is used instead of *by* in the phrases *on foot*, *on horseback*. Notice the absence of the article in these phrases, as well as in *by bus*, etc (see 4.38).

[b] *Of* is used with the verb *die* in *He died of hunger* etc. This meaning is poised between 'cause' and 'means': on the one hand, one speaks of the 'cause of death' (*cf: He was suffering from hunger*); on the other hand, this type of phrase would be evoked by the question *How did he die?* (or *What did he die of?*) rather than *Why did he die?*

6.41

Instrument, agentive: *with, by*

Converting now the sentences with instrumental subject ([1] and [2] above, *cf* 7.15) into the passive, we obtain:

The ball was caught *with/by his left hand*
The window has been broken *by a stone*

In the passive, that is, the instrument may be expressed by a *by*-phrase, and is thus treated as parallel to an agentive (7.14).

While the 'instrument' is the inert and normally inanimate cause of an action, the 'agentive' is its animate (normally human) initiating cause. Where either of these could occur as subject of an active sentence, there is a corresponding passive sentence, in which the agentive or instrument is expressed by a *by*-phrase:

We were observed by a passing stranger
   (↔ A passing stranger observed us)

The crops have been ruined by frost
   (↔ Frost has ruined the crops)

The difference between instrumental phrases containing *with* and *by* is a fine one:

He was killed *by an arrow*
He was killed *with an arrow*

Either of these sentences could describe the same incident. The difference is that the *with* phrase always implies an agentive: ('Someone killed him with an arrow'), whereas a *by*-phrase does not. This follows from the fact that the *by*-phrase corresponds, in transformational terms, to the subject of an active sentence. One could say *We were driven indoors by the rain*, but not **We were driven indoors with the rain*, as there is no conceivable agentive (except God) for the action in the second sentence.

The agentive *by*-phrase also occurs as a postmodifier to signify authorship: *a picture by Degas, a novel by Tolstoy*, etc.

Note

[a] More generally, both the 'instrumental' and 'agentive' *by*-phrase are said to express the 'agent' (as they are in 12.2 *ff*). One of the reasons why we distinguish them here is that they cannot be coordinated, or collapsed, by coordination, into a single prepositional phrase: **He was killed by a man and (by) an arrow*. If however different processes are involved, coordination is possible:

   The area was ravaged by floods and by guerrilla forces

[b] Outside the passive clause proper, agentive and instrumental *by*-phrases can occur after adjectives which are past-participial in form and passive in meaning:

   I was very alarmed by the news he brought
   The child was unwanted by its parents

The intensifier *very* and the prefix *un-* here are indicators of the adjectival status of the participle (5.13).

[c] The *by*-phrase may indicate either 'means' or 'instrument' in a sentence such as *The news was confirmed by a telegram* (either 'Someone confirmed it by means of a telegram' or 'A telegram confirmed it'). Since the instrumental sense is tied to a passive verb phrase, only the 'means' interpretation is possible with active verbs:

   The news came *by telegram*.

6.42
Stimulus: *at*

The relation between an emotion and its stimulus (normally an abstract stimulus) can often be expressed by *at:*

   I was alarmed at his behaviour

This may be compared with the instrumental use of *by:*

   I was alarmed by his behaviour

Both of these can be treated as passive equivalents of *His behaviour alarmed me,* and the noun phrase following *at* may be treated as a 'quasi-agent'. Further exemplification of this use of *at* is given in 6.54 and 12.16.

Note
A number of other prepositions may introduce 'quasi-agents' after certain participles:

I'm worried *about this* (*cf* This worries me)
He's interested *in history* (*cf* History interests him)
His plans were known *to everyone* (*cf* Everyone knew his plans)

6.43
Accompaniment: *with*
Especially when followed by an animate complement, *with* has the meaning 'in company with' or 'together with':

I'm so glad you're coming *with us*
Jock, *with several of his noisy friends,* was drinking and playing
    poker till after 2 am

In the second sentence, the *with* phrase serves a function very close to coordination with *and:* 'Jock and several of his noisy friends were . . .'.
    An example of a phrase of accompaniment occurring as postmodifier is:

Curry *with rice* is my favourite dish

In this sense, as in most other senses, *without* is the negative of *with: They're going without us; You never see him without* (*ie* 'unaccompanied by') *his dog.*

6.44
Support, opposition: *for, with, against*

Are you *for* or *against the plan?* (*ie* Do you support or oppose the
    plan?)
Remember that every one of us is *with you* (= 'on your side')
It is prudent to go *with* rather than *against the tide of public opinion*

For conveys the idea of support, *with* that of solidarity or movement in sympathy; *against* conveys the contrary idea of opposition. In this use, there is no negative *without* contrasting with *with.*

Other meanings: prepositional phrase chiefly as postmodifier of noun phrase
6.45
Genitive *of*
The most common English preposition, *of,* occurs chiefly as a post-

modifying genitive in noun phrases, and is most conveniently discussed in the chapter on the complex noun phrase (13.27–29). The relation of the genitive *of*-phrase to the *-s* genitive (or inflected genitive) is explained in 4.94 *ff*. Here we merely give some exemplification of the extremely varied uses of *of*, with analogous sentences or phrases:

a typewriter of my father's   (my father has a typewriter)
the courage of the man   (the man has courage)
the envy of the world   (the world envies . . .)
the trial of the conspirators   (. . . tries the conspirators)
the virtue of thrift   (thrift is a virtue)
a flock of sheep   (sheep make up the flock)
a glass of water   (the glass contains water)
seven of my friends   (. . . amounting to seven)
people of the Middle Ages   (people who lived in the Middle Ages)
the house of my dreams   (the house which I see in my dreams)

6.46
'Having': *of, with, without*
In the case of the second example above, the relationship of 'having' can be in the opposite direction:

the courage of the man ∼ a man of courage
the tremendous force of the wind ∼ a wind of tremendous force
the distinction of the performance ∼ a performance of distinction

In the right-hand examples, it is the notional subject of HAVE, not its notional object, that is the head of the noun phrase. This way round, *of* is limited to the expression of abstract attributes, and the notion of 'having' is more generally expressed by *with:*

a man *with a red nose* ('who has a red nose')
an industrialist *with a house on the Costa Brava* ('who has a house . . .')
a woman *with a large family*
a box *with a carved lid*

As elsewhere, the negative of *with* is *without:*

a play *without any faults* ('a play with no faults')
women *without children* ('childless women')
the house *without a porch* ('. . . which has no porch')

The correspondence between phrases with *with* or *without* and relative clauses with *have* applies also to clauses in which *have* is followed by a quasi-clausal object (14.31 *ff*):

the girl *with a boy friend in the navy* (↔ . . . who has a boy friend in the navy)
the factory *with its chimney smoking*
a room *with its door open*

The above phrases with quasi-clausal complements are unlike any other kind of prepositional phrase, and could reasonably be regarded as verb-less or non-finite clauses (11.4 *ff*), *with* and *without* thereby being treated as conjunctions rather than prepositions. *With* and *without* followed by quasi-clausal complements may occur as adjunct as well as postmodifier:

He wandered in *without shoes or socks on*
With so many essays to write, I doubt if I shall have time to visit you

Here, the fuller clausal equivalent is a participial adverbial clause (11.48 *ff*), not a relative clause:

Having so many essays to write, I doubt if I shall have time to visit you.

Other meanings: prepositional phrase chiefly as disjunct or conjunct
6.47
Concession: *in spite of, despite, for+all, with+all, notwithstanding*

I admire him, *in spite of his faults.*
Despite strong pressure from the government, the unions have refused to order a return to work.

$\left.\begin{array}{l}With\\For\end{array}\right\}$ *all his boasting and ostentatious training*, he was knocked out in the first round by a man lighter than himself.
Thomas Carlyle, *notwithstanding his tedious rhetoric*, is a master of the sublime in prose style.

In spite of is a general-purpose preposition of concession; *despite* is rather more formal, and *for/with all* more colloquial. The combinations *for all* and *with all* (*all* being an obligatory predeterminer with this meaning) are rather restricted in their use. *Notwithstanding* is formal and rather legalistic in style.

6.48
Reference: *with regard to, with reference to* (formal), *as to, as for*

With reference to your letter of April 29th, I confirm my Directors' agreement to advance a further sum of £200.

With regard to education, it's one of the most backward places in
   the country.
As for the burglar, he escaped through the attic window.

As to and *as for* (='returning to the question of . . .') are less formal
than the other complex prepositions in this group. *As to* and *with regard
to* can be used in postmodifying phrases as well as in disjuncts: *I'd like
to know your opinion as to/with regard to the burglar's behaviour.*
   Other prepositions within the same general area of meaning are *regarding, in regard to, with respect to, in respect of,* and *on the matter of.*

6.49
Exception: *except for, with the exception of, apart from, excepting, except, but, bar, barring*

We had a very pleasant time, *except for the weather.*
With the exception of James, none of us had any money.
The worst period of my life, *apart from the war,* was when I was
   out of work.
They were all rescued *except(ing) the captain,* who stayed behind
   to safeguard the vessel.
Finally, we had packed everything *but the typewriter.*

Except for, with the exception of, and *apart from* are used primarily in
disjuncts. *Except, excepting,* and *but,* on the other hand, function
generally (in the case of *but* exclusively) in postmodifying phrases: *all
except two; any time but now;* etc. Thus *but* cannot occur initially as a
preposition: **But me, everyone was tired.* The prepositional phrase, in
such constructions, is often separated from its noun head, and postposed to the end of the clause (*cf* 14.41):

Everyone *but me* was tired ~ Everyone was tired *but me*

Further, the noun phrase must contain a determiner or indefinite pronoun of absolute meaning (positive or negative): *no, any, every, each,
nobody, anywhere, everything,* etc. Hence one may say *all but one,* but
not, *eg:* **some but one,* or **many but one.*
   Bar and *barring* are rarer substitutes for *except* and *excepting.*

Note
[a] Prepositions of exception quite often have a clause or prepositional phrase as
   complement (*cf* 6.8 Note):

   except *in the south-east*
   apart from *when I last spoke to you*
   in addition to trying to swim
   except for what I ordered

This is an indication of their marginal status as prepositions: they are in some ways parallel to the quasi-prepositional words of comparison *as* and *than: cf: more than in the south-east; as recently as when I last spoke to you.*

[b] The combination *all but* is used colloquially as an intensifier:

He *all but* (='very nearly') *strangled me*

[c] *But* as a preposition has to be distinguished from *but* as a conjunction (9.28 *ff*). Both the resemblance and the contrast between the two functions are brought out in:

$$\left\{\begin{array}{l}\text{Everyone had a good time } but \text{ John}\\ \text{The students had a good time}\left\{\begin{array}{l}but\ not \text{ John}\\ but \text{ John } did\ not\end{array}\right.\end{array}\right.$$

6.50
Negative condition: *but for*

It is to be noted that *but for* is not used in the sense of exception, but rather that of 'negative condition': *But for Gordon, we should have lost the match* (*ie* 'If it hadn't been for Gordon . . .', 'If Gordon hadn't played as he did . . .', etc).

Other meanings: prepositional phrase chiefly as complementation of verb or adjective
6.51
Subject matter: *about, on*

He told me *about his adventures*
He's lecturing *on new techniques of management*

With the meaning 'on the subject of, concerning', *about* and *on* can combine with a considerable range of verbs and adjectives (12.34), including:

speak about/on	teach (someone) about
argue about/on	read about
hold forth about/on	hear about
lecture about/on	quarrel about
preach about/on	keep quiet about
confer about/on	tell (someone) about
write about/on	inform (someone) about
communicate about/on	find out about
be knowledgeable about/on	be reasonable about
learn about	

On is reserved for deliberate, formal linguistic communication (speaking, lecturing, writing, etc), and is therefore inappropriate for verbs like *read, quarrel,* and *teach*, which do not necessarily involve the subject of the sentence in using language; also for verbs like *chat* (informal) and *gossip* (informal), which denote the inconsequential use of language. Thus *He spoke on butterflies* would suggest he was making a formal speech: *He spoke about butterflies* would probably refer to an informal conversation or casual allusion.

This difference of meaning occurs also with postmodifying phrases, in which *on* and *about* (= 'on the subject of') are quite extensively used:

a book about/on butterflies	a story about a princess
a talk about/on antiques	ignorance about sex
a discussion about/on drugs	the facts about Suez
a word about/on the garden	a fuss about nothing

These two prepositions are used similarly introducing adverbials following the verb BE:

This book is $\begin{Bmatrix} \text{on} \\ \text{about} \end{Bmatrix}$ stamps.

Note

[a] *Of* is a somewhat rarer and more literary alternative to *about* in *tell . . . of; speak of; talk of; inform . . . of;* etc. Both *about* and *of* are possible with *think*, but with a difference of meaning: *He thought about the problem* = 'He pondered/considered the problem'; *He thought of the problem* = 'He brought the problem to his mind'.

[b] A less usual alternative to *about* and *on* is *concerning*, which is formal to the point of being rather stilted: *a dispute concerning land rights*.

6.52

Ingredient, material: *with, of, out of*

After verbs of 'making', *with* indicates an ingredient, whereas *of* and *out of* signify the material or constituency of the whole thing:

You make a cake *with eggs* (*ie* 'eggs are one of the ingredients')
He made the frame (*out*) *of wood* (*ie* 'wood was the only material')

The same contrast of meaning is seen with *build* and *construct*:

The terminal was built/constructed *with reinforced concrete*
The terminal was built/constructed (*out*) *of reinforced concrete*

With also enters into expressions such as *paved with brick, filled with water, loaded with hay*.

Of (used with nouns denoting 'material') is found in a postmodifying function as well as in adverbials: *a bracelet of solid gold, a table of polished oak* (*ie* 'made/consisting of polished oak'); here it may also be used metaphorically: *a man of steel; a heart of stone*.

6.53
Respect, standard: *at, for*
Just as we saw in 5.68 *f* that we could not say *This boy is bigger* without relating the comparative adjective explicitly or implicitly to a standard of comparison, so a gradable adjective without the comparative form implies some standard or norm: *big* means something different in *This elephant is big, This cat is big*, since 'big for an elephant' presupposes a larger scale, and a larger norm, than 'big for a cat'. We can make the norm explicit by a *for* phrase:

> He's not *bad for a youngster* (*ie* considering he is a youngster)
> That dog is long-legged *for a terrier*

A further way in which a prepositional phrase may specify the meaning of a gradable adjective is to use *at* to introduce the respect in which the adjective is appropriate to its noun phrase (see 12.34):

> He's good/clever/brilliant *at organizing things*
> He's bad/hopeless/terrible *at games*

These two prepositional uses are not restricted to adjectival complementation: they occur also in a number of other grammatical roles, as the following examples show:

> I'm a complete dunce *at mathematics*
> She's getting on very well *at her job*
> *For an Englishman*, he speaks foreign languages remarkably well
> It's a dreadfully expensive toy *for what it is.*

6.54
Reaction: *at, to*
A sentence such as *Their rejection of the offer surprised me* presents, by means of a straightforward subject-verb-object construction, the relationship between an event, an emotional reaction, and the person who undergoes the reaction. The same relationship can be expressed by the passive: *I was surprised by their rejection of the offer* or, alternatively, by the passive with the preposition *at* replacing the agentive preposition *by: I was surprised at their rejection of the offer.* Here *at* (as we saw in 6.42) signals the relation between the emotive reaction and its STIMULUS. *Surprised* in this context is a participial adjective (note that it can be preceded by *very*, see 5.13), and it is with such adjectival forms that *at* (= 'stimulus') characteristically combines (see 12.34):

alarmed at	disgusted at
amused at	delighted at

Less commonly, verbs and non-participial adjectives have this construction:

laugh at   be angry at
rejoice at   be glad at

Another way to state the same idea is to let the main clause represent the event acting as a 'stimulus', and to let the REACTION be expressed by the preposition *to* followed by an abstract noun of emotion: *To my annoyance, they rejected the offer. To my annoyance* in this context is an attitudinal disjunct, comparable with adverbs such as *surprisingly* (8.82–85).

Yet another way of putting it is to use a *to*-phrase to identify the PERSON REACTING: *To me, their rejection of the offer was a surprise.* In this last sense, *to* is not limited to emotive reactions; it applies equally to intellectual or perceptual responses:

To a mind based in common sense, his ideas are utterly
   incomprehensible
It looked *to me* like a vast chasm

In this last case the *to*-phrase is not a disjunct, but an adjunct.

Note

[a] The idea of 'stimulus' is sometimes expressed by other prepositions, in place of *at: resentful of, disappointed with, sorry about, worried about,* etc. *At* has, moreover, a common alternative in *about: annoyed at/about, pleased at/about,* etc.

[b] In BrE, *with* rather than *at* is used when the 'stimulus' is a person or object rather than an event: *I was furious with* (not *at*) *John; I was delighted with* (not *at*) *the present.* But in AmE, *I was furious/angry/livid at John* is quite usual. With eventive nouns (2.9), *at* is generally acceptable: *I was furious at John's behaviour.*

6.55
Modification of prepositional phrases

It is worth noting that prepositional meanings (particularly of time and place) are subject to modification as regards degree and measure, and that prepositions may therefore (like many adjectives and adverbs) be preceded by intensifiers (5.55). The following are representative examples:

I left it *just* (= 'a little way') inside the garage
He had wandered *right* (= 'completely') off the path
Now their footsteps could be heard *directly* above my head
I'm *all* (= 'thoroughly') in a muddle
She's *badly* out of sorts
Few people are *completely* against public ownership

There is doubt in such cases as to whether the intensifier should be treated as applying to the whole prepositional phrase, or to the preposition alone. Occasionally, the possibility of placing the intensifier after the whole phrase suggests that it is the phrase as a whole that is qualified:

Few people are against public ownership *completely*.

Position of prepositional phrases
6.56
Position of adverbial prepositional phrases

To conclude the chapter, something will be said about the position of prepositional phrases, though their position as adverbials is further discussed in Chapter 8.

In most cases apart from adverbials, the syntactic function of a prepositional phrase virtually determines its position. A postmodifying phrase, for example, normally follows directly the element it postmodifies (although discontinuous postmodification sometimes occurs – 13.72 *ff*).

As an adverbial, however, the prepositional phrase is mobile, and for convenience, one may distinguish its three major positions in the sentence as INITIAL, MEDIAL, and FINAL or END position (8.7).

For the adjunct, end position (*ie* after the verb and complement/object if any) is the most frequent, but initial position is also quite commonly assumed, especially with phrases of time:

I saw him again on Friday ∼ On Friday, I saw him again

Initial position (before the subject) is unusual, however, for phrases having a close connection with the verb, *eg* phrases of destination following a verb of motion:

Into the room he strode

Such unusual orderings, where they occur, are to be treated as instances of 'marked theme' (14.11), and may be recognized as such by the fact that a comma cannot be inserted between the prepositional phrase and the subject: **Into the room, he strode*.

With disjuncts and conjuncts, the priority is in the opposite direction; the more common position is before the subject, though both are acceptable:

In my opinion, the wrong decision was made
The wrong decision was made, *in my opinion*

For adverbial prepositional phrases in general, the medial or parenthetical position is the least usual; it is likely to be used only with short phrases, or where factors such as focus and the complexity of the sentence make the other positions undesirable or impossible:

She could, *of course*, have phoned from the office
They arrived at a village from which the inhabitants, *for fear of enemy reprisals*, had fled in panic

The most acceptable medial positions are after the subject; after the operator; between verb and complement or object; between indirect and direct object; between object and object complement:

His sister *at that time* was studying medicine
His sister was *at that time* studying medicine
His sister became, *in time*, a qualified doctor
She found the work, *on the whole*, satisfying and enjoyable

To these we may add the position between conjunction and subject in coordinate or subordinate clauses, since although they precede the subject, adverbials in this position have the character of a parenthesis, and may be treated as medial:

The airliner was preparing to land when, *to everyone's horror*, a man with a gun rushed to the front of the plane, waving his arms and shouting.

6.57
Relative position of prepositional phrases
A set of prepositional phrases with the same function may occur in sequence, notably as adverbials or as postmodifiers:

I spoke to him in secret in the corridor after dinner for a very good reason
The father of three in the corner with the blue jacket has been trying to catch your eye for some time

The structure of the first sentence can be elucidated by bracketing as follows:

⟨{[(I spoke to him) in secret] in the corridor} after dinner⟩ for a very good reason

That is, generally speaking, the phrases are placed in order of close relationship to the verb, those forming the complementation of the verb coming first, and conjuncts or disjuncts coming last. As the bracketing shows, the adverbial phrase applies to everything in the preceding subject or predicate, including any preceding adverbials. Since an initial adverbial generally applies to the whole of the sentence that follows it, it would be natural, in a re-ordering of the sentence, to transfer the final adverbial rather than any other to initial position:

> For a very good reason, I spoke to him in secret in the corridor after dinner

Similarly, successively deleting the outermost prepositional phrase, we might re-order as follows:

> After dinner, I spoke to him in secret in the corridor
> In the corridor, I spoke to him in secret
> In secret, I spoke to him

With postmodifying phrases, an analogous general principle holds: phrases are placed in order of their closeness of relationship to the head (13.39 *ff*). On the whole, *of*-phrases precede other phrases, *eg* those introduced by prepositions of place.

Note
In a noun phrase, a sequence of phrases modifying the same head must be distinguished from a successive embedding of phrases such that one is a postmodifier within the prepositional complement of another (see 13.39c). Both analyses are possible for:

> (i) [(The girl in the armchair) with the pretty legs]
> (ii) [The girl in (the armchair with the pretty legs)]

where (i) means 'The girl who is in the armchair and who has the pretty legs'; and (ii) means 'The girl who is in the armchair which has the pretty legs'.

6.58
Exceptions
Where there is no significant difference in the closeness of two prepositional phrases to the verb or to the noun head, the ordering often does not matter. Thus

> the man in the corner with the blue jacket

could be re-ordered with no difficulty or change of meaning as

> the man with the blue jacket in the corner

The ordering from 'logically innermost' to 'logically outermost' is sometimes violated; but if this happens, the phrase placed in an abnormally early or late position is usually marked off by intonation or punctuation as a parenthesis or afterthought:

> I spoke to him for a very good RÈASON, after DÍNNer.

Bibliographical note

Detailed documentation of English prepositional usage is to be found in Aksenenko (1956); Hill (1968); Poutsma (1926–9), Part II.2, Chapter 60.

Theoretical treatments of the roles of prepositions are provided by Bennett (1968); Bugarski (1969); Fillmore (1969); Rosenbaum (1967a), especially *pp* 81–99, on the function of prepositions in clausal complementation.

The following are studies of more limited aspects of English prepositions: Leech (1969a), Chapter 8, on prepositions of place; Lindkvist (1950), on the locative uses of *in*, *at*, *on*, and *to;* Quirk and Mulholland (1964), on complex prepositions; Jacobson (1964), on the position of prepositional phrases.

Clause patterns

7.1

Simple and complex sentences

We return now to the theme of 2.1–10: the structure of the simple sentence. Sentences are either simple (containing just one clause) or complex (containing more than one clause), a CLAUSE being a unit that can be analysed into the elements S(ubject), V(erb), C(omplement), O(bject) and A(dverbial) identified in 2.1 and 2.3. Thus a complex sentence containing two clauses can be analysed twice over into such elements, once for the independent clause (11.3) and once for the dependent clause included within the main clause:

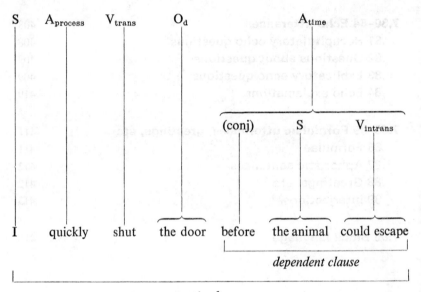

Further discussion of complex sentences is deferred to Chapter 11; it is advisable at this stage, however, to become used to the distinction between a sentence and a clause, so that it is seen that S, V, O, C, and A are elements of clause structure rather than elements of sentence structure.

The present chapter is restricted not only to the simple sentence, but also to those aspects of the simple sentence chiefly involving S, V, O, and C. The adverbial, as a clause element more detachable and more mobile than the others, will be considered separately in Chapter 8.

7.2
Clause types
At this stage we need a restatement in more detail of the clause patterns of 2.10, ignoring the stative/dynamic distinction of the verb (3.40 *ff*) and excluding from consideration complementation by a clause

I want *him to go,* I know *that he's there,* etc

which is to be dealt with in 12.47 *ff*. This account of clause types also has a rather different emphasis from that in 2.10, in that we are interested only in elements which (in a certain sense explained in 7.3 below) are obligatory following a given type of verb.

The clause types in their simple declarative form are:

(1) Type *SVC*   S $V_{intensive}$ $C_{subject\text{-}comp}$

Mary   is $\begin{cases} \text{kind} \\ \text{a nurse} \end{cases}$

(2) Type *SVA*   S $V_{intensive}$ A_{place}

Mary   is $\begin{cases} \text{here} \\ \text{in the house} \end{cases}$

(3) Type *SV*   S $V_{intrans}$
The child   was laughing

(4) Type *SVO*   S $V_{monotrans}$ O_{direct}
Somebody   caught   the ball

(5) Type *SVOC*   S $V_{complex\text{-}trans}$ O_{direct} $C_{object\text{-}comp}$

We   have proved   him $\begin{cases} \text{wrong} \\ \text{a fool} \end{cases}$

(6) Type *SVOA*   S $V_{complex\text{-}trans}$ O_{direct} A_{place}
I   put   the plate   on the table

(7) Type *SVOO*   S $V_{ditrans}$ $O_{indirect}$ O_{direct}
She   gives   me   expensive presents

The general picture is quite simple; there are:

a two-element pattern SV

three three-element patterns $SV + \begin{cases} C \\ A \\ O \end{cases}$

three four-element patterns $SVO + \begin{cases} C \\ A \\ O \end{cases}$

Cutting across this sevenfold division are the main verb classes: INTRANSITIVE (followed by no obligatory element); INTENSIVE (followed by C_s or A_{place}); and TRANSITIVE (followed by O_d). Subcategories of S, V, C, and A are defined in 2.3 *ff;* abbreviations commonly used in this chapter are O_d (direct object), O_i (indirect object), C_s (subject complement), and C_o (object complement).

Note

[a] It is possible to have a clause with the structure S V O_i O_d C_o, but the C_o in such cases is always optional: *She gave us our coffee black; I sold him the car almost new.* We may therefore treat these as belonging to Type *SVOO*, and there is no need to add an eighth clause-type *SVOOC*. A similar optional C_o can occur after an *SVOA* pattern: *They dragged him home blind drunk.* (See 5.27.)

[b] C_o and A_{place} sometimes precede O_d in Types *SVOC* and *SVOA*: *We have proved wrong the Prime Minister himself; He took from his pocket a handful of gleaming coins.* (See 14.39.)

[c] Most obligatory adjuncts are A_{place}, but there are quite a number of cases to which the term 'place', even in a broad metaphorical sense, does not apply:

He is *without a job*
We kept him *off cigarettes*
They treated him *kindly.*

[d] There is also a rare clause pattern S V O_i C_s: *John made Mary a good husband* (ie 'John was a good husband to Mary').

7.3
Complementation

The elements O_d, C, and A in the above patterns are *obligatory* elements of clause structure in the sense that they are required for the complementation of the verb. By this we mean that, given the use of a particular verb in a particular sense, the sentence is incomplete if one of these elements is omitted *eg: *I put the book* (Type *SVOA*) and **He resembled* (Type *SVO*) are unacceptable. In some cases, certainly, a direct object or object complement in one of these patterns may be considered grammatically optional:

He's eating – *cf* He's eating an apple (Type *SVO*)
He made her career – *cf* He made her career a success (Type *SVOC*)

Many grammarians treat such cases as the first above in terms of the omission or deletion of the object with a transitive verb. Our approach, however, will be to regard this as a case of conversion (App I.31), whereby a word such as *eat* is transferred from the transitive to the intransitive category. Thus *He's eating* is an instance of clause-type *SV* rather than of *SVO* (with optional deletion of the object).

Note

[a] To justify treating object-omission as a matter of conversion, we may notice that it is idiosyncratic, in the sense that it applies to some transitive verbs but not to others:

They're hunting deer – They're hunting
but   They're chasing cats – *They're chasing

Also, one can find 'nonce' object-omissions, which again points to a word-formation process (App I.1, App I.2 Note *a*) rather than a syntactic process. Thus (*) *John is licking today* is a highly improbable sentence for which one could (as with all nonce-formations) think up an interpretation if one tried hard enough (*eg* a situation in which two people are alternately employed in licking and sticking stamps on letters). Conversions from one verb category to another, including from transitive to intransitive verbs, are exemplified in App I.41.

[*b*] A similar approach may be made to cases where the indirect object is omissible:

She gives expensive presents – *cf* She gives her friends expensive presents
(Type *SVOO*)

But here the case for conversion is not so strong, and one may regard the indirect object with many verbs as an optional element similar in status to an optional adverbial.

[*c*] With LIVE in the sense 'reside' there is an obligatory adverbial of place, while with LIVE in the sense 'be alive' there is a virtually obligatory adverbial of time:

He lives in China
He lived in the nineteenth century

LIVE is therefore an intensive verb, rather than an intransitive verb.

7.4
Optional adverbials

The patterns of 7.2 can be expanded by the addition of various optional adverbials. For example (optional adverbials are bracketed):

Type *SV:*   (A)   S   V   (A)
             (Sometimes) she sings (beautifully)

Type *SVA:*   (A)   S   V   (A)   A
             (In America) narrow ties are (currently) out of fashion.

Type *SVOO:* S   v   (A)   V   O   O
             She has (kindly) sent us some photographs

Sometimes, as in the last example, an adverbial intervenes between two parts of the verb phrase (8.7).

7.5
Transformational relations

One way of distinguishing the various clause types is by means of 'transformational' relations, or relations of grammatical paraphrase.

Semantically, Types *SV*, *SVC*, and *SVA* are close, as is shown by occasional equivalences of the following kind:

S V ↔ S V C_s
The baby is sleeping ↔ The baby is asleep
Two loaves will suffice ↔ Two loaves will be sufficient

$$S V C_s \leftrightarrow S V A$$

He is jobless $\leftrightarrow$ He is without a job

On the whole (14.45), English prefers to avoid the plain *SV* pattern where alternatives are available.

Clauses containing a noun phrase as object are distinguished by their ability to be converted into passive clauses, the object noun phrase assuming the function of subject (V_{pass} = passive verb phrase):

Type *SVO:*
> A number of people saw the accident (S V O_d) $\leftrightarrow$ The accident was seen by a number of people (S V_{pass} [A])

Type *SVOC:*
> Queen Victoria considered him a genius (S V O_d C_o) $\leftrightarrow$ He was considered a genius by Queen Victoria (S V_{pass} C_s [A])

Type *SVOA:*
> An intruder must have placed the ladder there (S V O_d A_{loc}) $\leftrightarrow$ The ladder must have been placed there by an intruder (S V_{pass} A_{loc} [A])

Type *SVOO:*
> My father gave me this watch (S V O_i O_d) $\leftrightarrow$
> $\begin{cases} \text{I was given this watch by my father (S } V_{pass} \; O_d \; [A]) \\ \text{This watch was given me by my father (S } V_{pass} \; O_i \; [A]) \end{cases}$

As Type *SVOO* clauses have two objects, they often have two passive forms, as shown above – one in which the direct object becomes subject, and another (more common) in which the indirect object becomes subject. Further discussion of the active-passive relationship is found in 12.2 *ff*.

As the formulae show, the passive transformation converts clauses of types with an object into equivalent types without the object (or, in the case of *SVOO*, without one of the objects). Thus the passive *He was considered a genius* of *SVOC They considered him a genius* is closely parallel to *SVC* (*He seemed a genius*), except for the passive verb phrase. In all passive clause types, the agentive *by*-phrase (6.41), incorporating the subject of the corresponding active clause, has the status of optional adverbial. (It is marked [A] in the above examples.)

7.6
Intensive relationship

An *SVOC* clause is often equivalent to a clause with an infinitive or *that*-clause (12.47 *ff*):

> I imagined *her beautiful* $\leftrightarrow$ $\begin{cases} \text{I imagined } her \; to \; be \; beautiful \\ \text{I imagined } that \; she \; was \; beautiful \end{cases}$

This equivalence shows that the O and the C of an *SVOC* clause are in the same relation to one another as the S and C of an *SVC* clause. This relation is expressed, wherever it is expressed at all, by an intensive verb, and we may therefore call it, for further reference, an INTENSIVE RELATIONSHIP. The intensive relationship is important in other aspects of grammar apart from clause patterns. It underlies, for example, relations of apposition (9.130 *ff*).

Further, we may extend the concept of 'intensive relationship' to the relation of subject to adverbial and object to adverbial in *SVA* and *SVOA* patterns respectively. (For *SVOA* patterns, see 8.54, 8.73.)

SVOO clauses can be transformed into *SVOA* clauses by the substitution of a prepositional phrase following the direct object for the indirect object preceding it (12.62):

> She sent *Jim* a card ↔ She sent a card *to Jim*
> She left *Jim* a card ↔ She left a card *for Jim*

To and *for*, in their recipient senses (6.37), are the prepositions chiefly involved, but others, such as *with* and *of*, are occasionally found:

> I'll play *you* a game of chess ↔ I'll play a game of chess *with/*
> *against you*
> She asked *Jim* a favour ↔ She asked a favour *of Jim*

Note

[a] There are some exceptions to the passive transformation with Type *SVO;* eg:

> John had the book ↔ *The book was had by John (7.16, 12.5).

[b] More acceptable than the second passive transformation of Type *SVOO* is the equivalent transformation of *SVOA:*

> Some flowers had been brought *him*

is less natural than

> Some flowers had been brought *for him*

In some cases the former type seems quite unacceptable:

> *Some fish had been caught/bought/cooked *us*

[c] There are, however, some recipient *to*-phrases and *for*-phrases which cannot be transformed into indirect objects: *He suggested the idea to Bill; He reviews books for The Guardian;* etc. A borderline case is: *Tactfully he would explain him what was what* (Malamud).

7.7
Multiple class membership of verbs

It must be borne in mind that one verb can belong, in various senses, to a number of different classes (App I.41), and hence enter into a number of different clause types. The verb *get* is a particularly versatile one, being excluded only from Type *SV:*

Type *SVC:*   He's getting angry
Type *SVA:*   He got through the window
Type *SVO:*   You'll get a surprise
Type *SVOC:* He got his shoes and socks wet
Type *SVOA:* He got himself into trouble
Type *SVOO:* He got her a splendid present

Through the multiple class membership of verbs, ambiguities can arise: *I found her an entertaining partner*, like *She called him a steward*, could be interpreted either as *SVOC* or as *SVOO*.

Clause elements syntactically defined
7.8
For a fuller appreciation of the clause patterns just outlined, we need to know, of course, on what grounds the elements subject, verb, complement, object, and adverbial, are to be identified. The identification of the verbal element presents no problem, as this is the only function in which a finite verb phrase can occur. For the other elements, the following criteria should be of use.

7.9
Subject
A subject

(a) is a noun phrase (4.1 *ff*) or a clause with nominal function (11.14);
(b) occurs before the verb phrase in declarative clauses, and immediately after the operator (2.2, 3.6) in question clauses;
(c) has number and person concord, where applicable (7.23, 7.31), with the verb phrase.

Note
Exceptions to (b), *viz: wh*-questions without inversion and declarative clauses with inversion, are discussed in 7.64 and 14.14–16.

7.10
Object
An object (direct or indirect)

(a) like a subject, is a noun phrase or clause with nominal function;
(b) normally follows the subject and the verb phrase;
(c) by the passive transformation, assumes the status of subject (7.5).

An INDIRECT OBJECT, where both objects are present, precedes the DIRECT OBJECT, and is semantically equivalent to a prepositional phrase (7.6); a direct object may occur without an indirect object, but not vice versa (except in the second passive transformation of *SVOO* clauses).

Note

[a] Thematic objects (14.11) are an exception to (b), as are *wh*-objects in questions and exclamations (7.64, 7.78).
[b] Exceptions to (c) are considered in 12.4 *ff*.

7.11
Complement
A complement (subject or object)

- (a) is a noun phrase, an adjective phrase, or a clause with nominal function;
- (b) follows the subject, verb phrase, and (if one is present) object;
- (c) does not become subject through the passive transformation.

Note

Exceptions to (b) are noted in 7.64, 14.11, and 14.39.

7.12
Adverbial
An adverbial (see 8.1)

- (a) is an adverb, adverb phrase, adverbial clause, noun phrase, or pre-positional phrase;
- (b) is generally mobile, *ie* is capable of occurring in more than one position in the clause;
- (c) is generally optional, *ie* may be added to or removed from a sentence without affecting its acceptability.

Note

An exception to (c), the obligatory adverbial of the *SVA* and *SVOA* patterns, is mentioned in 7.2 *f*.

Clause elements semantically considered
7.13
Participants
In terms of meaning, every clause describes an event or state in which a number of participants (normally one, two or three) are involved. For example, the clause *A boy stole the apple* contains a verb phrase describ-

ing the nature of the action itself, a subject denoting an AGENTIVE participant (or 'doer'), and a direct object denoting an AFFECTED participant (or 'victim'). As it is the S, O, and C elements of the clause that mainly express these participant roles, the meanings of verb and adverbial will not be studied in this section; (the semantics of adverbials is given fuller attention in Chapter 8).

Note
We are not concerned with clausal subjects and objects in 7.13–22.

7.14
Agentive, affected, recipient, attribute
The most typical semantic role of a subject is AGENTIVE: that is, the animate being instigating or causing the happening denoted by the verb:

> *John* opened his eyes

The most typical function of the direct object is that of the AFFECTED participant: a participant (animate or inanimate) which does not cause the happening denoted by the verb, but is directly involved in some other way:

> Many M.P.s criticized *the Prime Minister*
> I've broken *a plate*

The most typical function of the indirect object is that of RECIPIENT (or 'dative' participant); *ie* of animate being passively implicated by the happening or state:

> I've found *you* a place

It may be observed that although *I've found a place for the magnolia tree* and *I've found a place for Mrs Jones* appear to be equivalent utterances, only the second can be transformed into a clause with indirect object: *I've found Mrs Jones a place*, not **I've found the magnolia tree a place*. This is because *the magnolia tree* is not animate and therefore does not qualify for the recipient role.

The role of the subject complement is that of attribute of the subject, whether a current or existing attribute (with stative verbs) or one resulting from the event described by the verb (with dynamic verbs).

> CURRENT ATTRIBUTE: He's *my brother;* He seems *unhappy;*
>   We lay *quiet;* We felt *cold;* She remained *silent;* It reads *clear.*
> RESULTING ATTRIBUTE: He became *restless;* He turned *traitor;*
>   He fell *ill;* The clothes washed *clean* (12.31 *ff*).

The role of the object complement is that of attribute of the object, again either a current or resulting attribute:

CURRENT ATTRIBUTE: I ate the meat *cold;* I prefer coffee *black;* I imagined him *dead;* I got the truck home *safe;* I judged him *a fool.*

RESULTING ATTRIBUTE: They elected him *President;* He knocked me *senseless;* He drove me *mad;* He painted the wall *blue;* She's growing her hair *long;* The heat turned the milk *sour* (12.67 *ff*).

Note

[a] An object complement, as its name implies, cannot refer to an attribute of the subject. It follows, therefore, that the final element of each of these three sentences is something other than an object complement:

He ran the shop *single-handed*
He drove the damaged car home *completely undismayed*
He was educated *a Protestant*

In fact, the elements in italics are best classified as verbless adverbial clauses consisting only of a noun phrase or adjective phrase (see 11.51). Their adverbial status is shown (i) by the possibility of omitting them without rendering the clauses unacceptable, and (ii) by the possibility (in the first two examples) of preposing them:

Single-handed, he ran the shop.

[b] With quite a number of verbs (see 12.68), a complement noun phrase may be converted into an *as*-phrase of the same meaning by the insertion of *as:*

I count him *as* my best friend.

Some verbs, like *regard,* allow only the *as* construction. Thus the following sentences illustrate three possibilities: *as* necessary, *as* impossible, and *as* possible:

I regard him as my friend (*not* *I regard him my friend)
I think him my friend (*not* *I think him as my friend)
I count him my friend (*or* I count him as my friend)

[c] There is a parallel, in meaning, between a complement and the obligatory 'predicative' adverbial of the *SVA* and *SVOA* patterns. *I prefer my chicken in wine* and *I imagined myself in long trousers* are close to *I prefer my chicken cold* and *I imagined myself happy.*

7.15
Agentive and instrumental subject

Although it is possible to state, as in 7.14, the *typical* role of a clause element, the elements S and O are more versatile in meaning than has generally been considered. Accordingly, we turn now to lesser (but nevertheless important) functions of these two elements.

Apart from its agentive function, the subject frequently has an instrumental role; that is, it expresses the unwitting (generally inanimate) material cause of an event:

The avalanche destroyed several houses

With intransitive verbs, the subject also frequently has the AFFECTED role elsewhere typical of the object:

Jack fell down
The pencil was lying on the table

We may also extend this latter function (although the name AFFECTED is not ideal for the purpose) to subjects of intensive verbs:

The pencil was on the table

It is now possible to see a regular relation, in terms of clause function, between adjectives or intransitive verbs and the corresponding transitive verbs expressing CAUSATIVE meaning:

$S_{affected}$ V	$S_{agent/instr}$ V $O_{affected}$
[I] The door opened	John/The key opened the door
The dam blew up	Terrorists blew up the dam
My roses are growing	I am growing my roses
[II] The tree has fallen	Someone has felled the tree
The flowers have died	The frost has killed the flowers
An arm rose	Someone raised an arm

$S_{affected}$ V C	$S_{agent/instr}$ V $O_{affected}$
[III] The road became narrower	They narrowed the road
I got angry	His manner angered me
He (almost) went blind	The sun (almost) blinded him

$S_{agentive}$ V	$S_{agentive}$ V $O_{affected}$
[IV] The soldiers marched (home)	They marched the soldiers (home)
My dog was walking	I was walking my dog
Joe stood (against the wall)	They stood Joe (against the wall)

While in many cases (Group I) the identical verb performs both transitive and intransitive roles without a change of form, in other cases (Group II) the intransitive verb has to be replaced by another verb, which may resemble it in spelling and pronunciation. In Group III, an adjective X is matched by a causative verb (of the same, or slightly different, form) with the meaning 'cause to be X'. Group IV, on the other hand, shows that the subject of an intransitive verb may itself be agentive, in which case the switch to a causative construction entails changing that element into an 'affected' one; thus we understand from *They stood Joe against the wall* that Joe reached that position without the help of his own volition.

Note

[a] One of the reasons for separating agentive from instrumental subjects is that the

two cannot be coordinated. We can say *The gamekeeper wounded him* and *A gun wounded him* but not *The gamekeeper and a gun wounded him* (*cf* 6.41 Note *a*).

[*b*] The boundary between agentive and affected subjects is not clear, except on the grounds of whether an element of causation or volition is present. Some verbs allow both interpretations: *Suddenly he jumped* might suggest an involuntary action (*eg* after being stung by a wasp) or a deliberate one. A phrase of purpose (*eg: in order to attract attention*) can be added only to the agentive type.

[*c*] There are quite a few triplets showing a combination of the relations in Groups I and III; *eg: open* (adj); *open* (intrans verb)='become open'; *open* (trans verb)= 'cause to be open'.

7.16
Recipient subject

The subject may also have a recipient (or 'dative') role with verbs such as *have*, *own*, *possess*, *benefit* (*from*), as is indicated by the following relation:

Mr Smith has bought/given/sold his son a radio → So now his
    son has/owns/possesses the radio

The perceptual verbs *see* and *hear* also require a 'recipient' subject, in contrast to *look at* and *listen to*, which are agentive. The other perceptual verbs *taste*, *smell*, and *feel* have both an 'agentive' meaning corresponding to *look at* and a 'recipient' meaning corresponding to *see:*

Foolishly, he tasted the soup
*Foolishly, he tasted the pepper in the soup

The adverb *foolishly* requires the agentive; hence the second sentence, which can only be understood in a non-agentive manner, does not make sense.

Verbs indicating a mental state may also require a 'recipient' subject:

I thought you were mistaken (*cf* It seemed to me . . .)
I liked the play (*cf* The play pleased me/gave me pleasure)

Normally 'recipient' subjects go with stative verbs (2.6, 3.40 *ff*). Some of them (notably *have* and *possess*) have no passive form:

They have a beautiful house ↔ *A beautiful house is had by them

Note
A passive form of HAVE occasionally occurs in idioms: *A good time was had by all; Have you ever been had?* (colloquial) (=tricked; also with sexual meaning). *Possess* has a passive in the rare biblical sense of *He was possessed by devils.*

7.17
Locative and temporal subject

In other clauses, the subject has the locative function of designating the place of the state or action, or the temporal function of designating its time:

London is foggy ('It's foggy in London')   [1]
My tent sleeps four people ('Four people can sleep in my tent')   [2]
This path is swarming with ants ('Ants are swarming all over
      this path')   [3]
This jar contains coffee ('There's coffee in this jar')   [4]
Yesterday was a holiday ('It was a holiday yesterday')   [5]

Again, verbs following locative subjects normally have no passive or progressive form:

The bag holds seven pounds ↔ *Seven pounds are held by the bag
                                      ↔ *The bag is holding seven pounds

One may distinguish temporal subjects from 'eventive nouns' mentioned in 2.9:

The match is tomorrow, etc.

7.18
Empty *it* subject

Finally, a subject may lack semantic content altogether, and consist only of the meaningless 'prop' word *it:*

It's raining/snowing/drizzling, etc
It's getting dark
It's cold in here
It was sunny/fine/cool/stormy, etc yesterday ('Yesterday was
      sunny', etc)
It's Sunday tomorrow (='Tomorrow is Sunday')

These are clauses in which no participant is required for the completion of the verb's or adjective's meaning; there is accordingly no participant role for the subject to perform, except where optionally, the subject position is assumed by a locative or temporal phrase. In such cases, the clause with 'prop' subject is an alternative to some of the clauses, such as [1] and [5], under 7.17. The 'prop' subject occurs mostly in clauses concerning time or weather.

Note
On *it* as a personal pronoun, see 4.112. The 'prop' subject *it* as discussed here must be distinguished from the 'anticipatory' *it* of sentences like *It was nice seeing you* (14.36), where the 'prop' subject is a replacement for a postponed clausal subject (= *Seeing you was nice*).

Locative and effected object
7.19

We turn now to roles of the DIRECT OBJECT. Apart from the AFFECTED OBJECT (7.14), semantic types of direct object are the LOCATIVE OBJECT and the EFFECTED OBJECT. Examples of the 'locative object' are:

> We walked the streets ('We walked *along/through* the streets')
> He swam the river ('He swam *across* the river')
> He passed the notice ('He passed *by* the notice')
> The horse jumped the fence ('. . . jumped *over* the fence')

There are similar uses of such verbs as *turn, leave, reach, surround, penetrate, mount, cross, climb* (see further examples in 6.25). Superficially, these objects may look like adverbials with an omitted preposition (*cf: We stayed three days*, etc, 6.32 *f*). In most cases their status as objects is clear, however, from their ability to assume subject role in a corresponding passive clause: *The fence was jumped by the horse*, etc.

An effected object is one that refers to something which exists only by virtue of the activity indicated by the verb:

> Baird invented television
> John has painted a new picture
> I'm writing a letter

With agentive subject and an affected object, one may always capture part of the meaning of a clause (*eg: X destroyed Y*) by saying 'X did something to Y'; but this does not apply to an effected object – *Baird invented television* does not imply 'Baird did something to television'.

One may include in this category also the type of object (sometimes called 'cognate') which repeats, partially or wholly, the meaning of the verb:

. . . sing a song	. . . think some unkind thoughts
. . . act a part	. . . fight a good fight
. . . dream a dream	. . . die a miserable death

The object of *ran a race* might also be classed as a cognate 'effected' object, although it is like a locative object in being replaceable by a prepositional phrase: *ran in a race*. In expressions of this kind, the prepositional alternative is preferable, if not obligatory, if some other element intervenes after the verb:

> He ran the 100 metres   *but:*   He ran well *in* the 100 metres
> He played the piano   *but:*   He played jazz *on* the piano.

Note

[a] There are rare cases in which it is the meaning of the subject, rather than of the

object, that is presupposed by the verb: *The frost froze hard; The sun was setting; His eye winked at me.* In such cases one may speak of a 'cognate subject'.

[b] A more dubious category of object consists of phrases of extent or measure, as in

> He ran a *mile*
> It costs *ten dollars*
> He weighs *almost a ton*

As these clauses do not generally permit the passive transformation, there is reason to analyse them as *SVA* rather than *SVO*. However, the final element behaves at least marginally like a direct object, as is shown by question forms with *What* alongside *How much:*

> What does it weigh? How much does it weigh?

The ambiguity of sentences such as *We ate a lot*, which may be *SVO* or *SVA*, is discussed in 8.33.

7.20

A third type of effected object takes the form of a verbal noun preceded by a common verb of general meaning, such as *do, make, have, take, give.* This construction is often more idiomatic, especially in colloquial English, than an equivalent construction with an intransitive verb (see further 14.45):

> He did little work that day ('He worked little that day')
> He made several attempts to contact me ('He attempted several times to contact me')
> The prisoner made no comment
> He's having a bath/a holiday (BrE)/a smoke
> He took a rest/a vacation (AmE)/a dislike to her/a dive into the water
> He gave a jump/a yell, etc
> The car gave a jolt/a bang/a lurch

Have and *take* in these examples have agentive subjects (*have* being the typical British, and *take* the typical American form), while *give* usually has an involuntary force and therefore accompanies an 'affected' subject. *He gave a jump* contrasts with *He took a jump* in suggesting that he could not help the action. (*Take,* however, has an 'affected'subject in *He took a fall/a beating,* etc.)

7.21
Effected indirect object

There is only one exception to the rule that the indirect object has the role of 'recipient': this is when *give* (or sometimes related verbs like *pay, owe*) has an 'effected' object as direct object and an 'affected' object as indirect object:

> I gave the door three kicks ('I kicked the door three times')
> I paid her a visit ('I visited her')
> I owe you a treat ('I ought to treat you')

These clauses, as the paraphrases make clear, are equivalent to clauses with a direct object as 'affected' object.

Note
The use of *give* etc above may be compared with the use of *receive, get,* and *have* in a parallel passive sense: *I had/got/received a shock; The table had/got/received a wipe.* There is also an interesting equivalence of *They gave/shot each other glances* and *They exchanged glances* ('They glanced at each other').

7.22
Summary

As a summary of these functions, we finally present in *Table* 7:1 the chief participant functions for each clause type, with example sentences. Although, as the table shows, the semantic functions of the elements (particularly S and O) are quite varied, there are certain clear restrictions, such as that the object cannot be 'agentive' or 'instrument'; that a subject (except in the passive) cannot be 'effected'; that an indirect object can have only two functions – those of 'effected' and 'recipient'. The assignment of a function to the subject seems to have the following system of priorities:

> If there is an 'agentive', it is S; if not,
> If there is an 'instrument', it is S; if not,
> If there is an 'affected', it is S; if not,
> If there is a 'temporal' or 'locative', it may be S; if not,
> The prop word *it* is S.

Naturally, where the passive transformation applies, it transfers the role of the direct or indirect object to the subject.

Note
The above treatment of sentence elements does not include discussion of clauses as S and C.

Table 7:1

PARTICIPANT FUNCTIONS

Type	S	V	O₁	Od	Cs	Co	A	example
SVC	aff	inten			curr			She's happy.
	aff	inten			result			He became a man.
	agent	inten			curr			He sat tight.
	agent	inten			result			He turned traitor.
	loc	inten			curr			The Sahara is hot.
	temp	inten			curr			Last night was warm.
	it	inten			curr			It's windy.
SVA	aff	inten					loc	He was at school.
	agent	inten					loc	He kept out of trouble.
SV	agent	intr						He was working.
	aff	intr						The curtains disappeared.
	it	intr						It's raining.
SVO	agent	mono		aff				He caught the ball.
	instr	mono		aff				The stone hit me.
	rec	mono		aff				He has a car.
	agent	mono		rec				We rewarded John.
	instr	mono		rec				The will benefits us all.
	agent	mono		loc				He climbed a mountain.
	loc	mono		aff				The bus seats thirty.
	agent	mono		eff				I took a bite.
	aff	mono		eff				I gave a gasp.
SVOC	agent	comp		aff		curr		He declared me a criminal.
	agent	comp		aff		result		I made her my secretary.
	instr	comp		aff		result		The sun dries it yellow.
	rec	comp		aff		curr		I found it strange.
	agent	comp		eff		curr		I took a swim naked.
SVOA	agent	comp		aff			loc	He placed it on the shelf.
	instr	comp		aff			loc	A car knocked it down.
	rec	comp		aff			loc	I prefer them on toast.
SVOO	agent	ditr	rec	aff				I bought her a gift.
	agent	ditr	aff	eff				She gave her hair a brush(ing).
[*SVOOC*]	agent	ditr	rec	aff		curr		I bought him those fresh.
	agent	ditr	aff	eff		result		I gave it a wipe clean.

[*Abbreviations:* S(ubject); V(erb); O₁ (indirect object); Od (direct object); Cs (subject complement); Co (object complement); A(dverbial); agent(ive); instr(ument); aff(ected); eff(ected); loc(ative); temp(oral); rec(ipient); intr(ansitive); inten(sive); mono(transitive); comp(lex transitive); ditr(ansitive); curr(ent attribute); result(ing attribute)]

Subject-verb concord
7.23
Concord

Concord can be broadly defined as the relationship between two grammatical elements such that if one of them contains a particular feature (*eg* plurality) then the other also has to have that feature. The most important type of concord in English is concord of number between subject and verb. The normally observed rule is very simple:

> A singular subject requires a singular verb
> A plural subject requires a plural verb

On number in the verb phrase and noun phrase, see 3.10 and 4.48 *ff;* the English verb inflections (except for the verb BE) only make a distinction of number in the 3rd person present. Hence sentences (1) and (2) are grammatical, while (3) and (4) are not:

(1) The window is open	(3) *The window are open
(sing + sing)	(sing + plur)
(2) The windows are open	(4) *The windows is open
(plur + plur)	(plur + sing)

A clause in the position of subject counts as singular for purposes of concord: *How you got there doesn't concern me; To treat them as hostages is criminal.* The same is true of prepositional phrases, etc acting as subject: *After the meeting is the time to speak,* etc. Nominal relative clauses on the other hand, since they are equivalent to noun phrases (11.14), may have plural as well as singular concord: *What were once human dwellings are now nothing but piles of rubble.*

Note

[a] In fact, it is possible to generalize the rule of concord to 'A subject which is not definitely marked for plural requires a singular verb'; that is, to treat singular as the 'unmarked' form, to be used in neutral circumstances, where no positive indication of plurality is present. This would explain, in addition to clausal and adverbial subjects, the tendency in informal speech for *is/was* to follow the pseudo-subject *There* in existential sentences such as

> There's hundreds of people on the waiting list (14.26).

[b] Apparent exceptions to the concord rule arise with singular nouns ending with the -*s* of the plural inflection (*measles, billiards, mathematics,* etc 4.52), or conversely plural nouns lacking the inflection (*cattle, people, clergy,* etc 4.57):

> Measles *is* sometimes serious
> Our people *are* complaining

[c] Plural words and phrases (including coordinate phrases, see 7.26) count as singular if they are used as names, titles, quotations, etc (see further 9.164):

> *Crime and Punishment* is perhaps the best-constructed of Dostoyevsky's novels; but *The Brothers Karamazov* is undoubtedly his masterpiece.

'The Cedars' has a huge garden.
'Senior Citizens' means, in common parlance, people over sixty.

(The titles of some works which are collections of stories, etc, however, hover between singular and plural: *The Canterbury Tales exist/exists in many manuscripts*.) Such noun phrases can be regarded as appositional structures with a deleted singular head: *The book 'Crime and Punishment', The expression 'Senior Citizens'*, etc.

7.24
Principles of grammatical concord, notional concord, and proximity

The rule (7.23) that the verb matches its subject in number may be called the principle of GRAMMATICAL CONCORD. Difficulties over concord arise through conflict between this and two other principles (or, if a weaker term is preferred, 'tendencies'), the principle of NOTIONAL concord and the principle of PROXIMITY. 'Notional concord' is agreement of verb with subject according to the *idea* of number rather than the actual presence of the grammatical marker for that idea. Thus *the government* is treated as a plural idea in *The government have broken all their promises* (BrE), as is shown not only by the plural verb *have*, but also by the pronoun *their*. The principle of 'proximity' denotes agreement of the verb with whatever noun or pronoun closely precedes it, sometimes in preference to agreement with the headword of the subject:

No one except his own supporters *agree* with him
One in ten *take* drugs

These principles and their interaction will be illustrated below in three areas where concord causes some problems: where the subject contains (a) a collective noun head (4.89); (b) coordination; and (c) an indefinite expression of amount.

English speakers are often uncertain about the rules of concord. School grammarians have insisted rather rigidly on grammatical concord, with the result that people often carry in their minds a conflict between this rule and the rule of notional concord, which tends to prevail over it in colloquial English.

7.25
With collective nouns

In BrE, collective nouns, notionally plural but grammatically singular, obey notional concord in examples such as:

The public are tired of demonstrations   [6]
The audience were enjoying every minute of it   [7]

The Crown have a good case (legal)   [8]
Our Planning Committee have considered your request   [9]

Although singular and plural verbs are more or less interchangeable in
these contexts, the choice is based, if on anything, on whether the group
is being considered as a single undivided body, or as a collection of
individuals. Thus plural is more likely than singular in [7], because consideration is being given to the individual reactions of members of the
audience. Contrastingly, singular has to be used in sentences like:

The public consists of you and me   [10]
The audience was enormous   [11]
The crowd has been dispersed   [12]
My company is opening a new factory   [13]

In contrast to [11], *The audience were enormous*, if it occurred, would
refer to an audience of enormous people. On the whole, the plural is
more popular in speech, whereas in the more inhibited medium of writing the singular is probably preferred. It is generally safest for a foreign
learner, when in doubt, to obey 'grammatical concord'.

In AmE, in contrast, collective noun subjects almost always go with
a singular verb. But even in AmE, a plural verb may be preferred when
a plural seems obligatory elsewhere in the sentence:

The audience are raising *their hands* to signify their approval.

Note

[a] An incidental point: when a noun referring to a collection of people has plural
concord, it antecedes *who/whom/they/them* rather than *which/it. Cf:*

a family *who* quarrel amongst *themselves*
a family *which* dates back to the Norman Conquest

[b] Naturally, when a collective noun subject occurs in the plural, plural concord is
unavoidable: *The audiences were enormous.*

With coordinated subject
7.26

When a subject consists of two or more noun phrases coordinated by
and, a distinction has to be made between appositional (*cf* 9.96) and
non-appositional coordination.

Under non-appositional coordination we include cases that can be
treated as an implied reduction of two clauses. These have a verb in the
plural:

Tom and Mary *are* now ready (↔ Tom is now ready and Mary is
now ready)
What I say and what I think *are* my own affair (↔ What I say
is . . . and what I think is . . .)

Conjoinings expressing a mutual relationship, even though they can only indirectly be treated as reductions of clauses in this way, also take a plural verb:

> Your problem and mine *are* similar (↔ Your problem is similar
> to mine and mine is similar to yours)

With the less common APPOSITIONAL COORDINATION, however, no such reduction is possible at all, for the coordinated structures refer to the same thing. Hence a singular verb is used:

> This temple of ugliness and memorial to Victorian bad taste was
> erected at the Queen's express wish and under her supervision

The two opening noun phrases here both refer to one object (say the Albert Memorial in London). The following example, however, is ambiguous, and could have either a singular or plural verb:

> His aged servant and the subsequent editor of his collected papers
> $\begin{Bmatrix} \text{was} \\ \text{were} \end{Bmatrix}$ with him at his death-bed

The question is: are the servant and the editor the same person, or two different people?

Some latitude is allowed in the interpretation of abstract nouns:

> Your fairness and impartiality $\begin{Bmatrix} \text{has} \\ \text{have} \end{Bmatrix}$ been much appreciated

There is doubt whether the fairness and impartiality represent two qualities or one. Invoking the principle of notional concord, we may use either singular or plural, depending on whether unity or separateness is uppermost in the mind.

Note

[a] The correlatives *both ... and ...* (9.123) occur only in non-appositional coordination: *Both your fairness and your impartiality have been appreciated.* (But *cf* 9.100).

[b] The principle of 'notional concord' also explains:

> The hammer and sickle was flying from the flagpole
> Danish bacon and eggs makes a good solid English breakfast
> The Bat and Ball sells good beer

where, despite coordination, the subject names a single flag, a single meal, and a single pub respectively. See also 9.121.

[c] Arithmetical sums provide further instances of phrasal coordination with the possibility of a singular verb: *Two and two make/makes four.* Cf other numerical expressions: *Ten times five is fifty; sixty people means a huge party.* The practice is different, however, with *Two fives are ten.*

7.27

Returning now to non-appositional coordination, we note that even a single noun head with coordinate modifiers may imply two separate sentences (*cf* 9.100), with the result that a plural verb may follow a singular mass noun subject quite legitimately:

Good and bad taste are inculcated by example
(↔ Good taste is . . . and bad taste is . . .)
American and Dutch beer are both much lighter than British
(↔ American beer is . . . and Dutch beer is . . .)

If the noun head is countable, of course, a plural form is expected:

Rodriguez' and Bristow's cars were badly damaged
(↔ Rodriguez' car was . . . and Bristow's car was . . .)

A similar collapsing of coordinate subjects into a single structure is observed when the subject is a clause:

What I say and think are no business of yours
(= What I say is . . . and what I think is . . .)

Alongside this there is the equivalent sentence with a singular verb:

What I say and think is no business of yours

In this case, the coordination belongs solely to the subordinate clause
(= 'That which I say and think . . .').

7.28

The rules are different for subject phrases coordinated with (*either* . . .) *or*:

Either the Mayor or his deputy is bound to come	[14]
What I say or what I think is no business of yours	[15]
Either the strikers or the bosses have misunderstood the claim	[16]
Either your brakes or your eyesight is at fault	[17]
Either your eyesight or your brakes are at fault	[18]

All these are instances of clausal coordination but, because of the disjunctive meaning of *or*, the verb form appropriate to one of the coordinate members on its own is chosen. With two singular subject phrases, as in [14] and [15], the verb is singular. With two plural subject phrases [16], the verb is plural. A dilemma arises with examples [17] and [18], where one phrase is singular and the other is plural; but this is generally solved by recourse to the principle of 'proximity', *ie* whichever phrase comes last determines the number of the verb.

Note

[a] The negative correlatives *neither . . . nor*, although disjunctive in meaning, behave in colloquial speech more like *and* than like *or* as regards concord:

> Neither he nor his wife *have* arrived

is more natural in spoken idiom than

> Neither he nor his wife *has* arrived,

the form recommended by traditional grammar. This preference is probably connected with the use of the plural verb with *neither* as a determiner or pronoun (7.29); but it may also reflect notional concord in that logically 'neither X nor Y' can be interpreted as a union of negatives: 'both (not-X) and (not-Y)'.

[b] Sometimes in speech the preposition *with* is treated as if it were a conjunction like *and*, giving rise to plural concord:

> One man with his wife, both looking very anxious, were pleading with a guard to let them through

This kind of mistake (for it would generally be classed as such) is natural in view of the similarity of meaning between this sentence and the equivalent sentence with *and*. Here the tendency towards notional concord (the *idea* of plurality in the subject is transferred to the verb) prevails over strict grammatical concord.

[c] The quasi-coordinators *as well as, rather than, more than*, and *as much as* (9.129), behave like prepositions rather than conjunctions when they occur in the subject:

> The Minister, as well as/rather than/more than/as much as the trades unions, is responsible for the present impasse

As with *with* (7.28 Note *b*), however, there may be occasional counter-instances in which notional concord prevails.

[d] In contrast, the coordinating correlatives *not . . . but* and *not only . . . but* (9.59) behave like *or;* the latter of the two subject noun-phrases determines the concord:

> Not (only) one, but all, of us are hoping to be there.

[e] The mixed expressions *one or two* and *between one and two* follow the principle of proximity in having plural concord. Grammatical concord is usually obeyed for *more than:*

> More than a thousand inhabitants *have* signed the petition
> More than one person *has* protested against the proposal

Thus although *more than one person* is notionally plural, a singular verb is preferred because (*one*) *person* operates as head of a singular noun phrase.

With indefinite expressions of amount
7.29

Another area of ambivalence, with regard to subject-verb concord, is that of indefinite expressions of amount, especially the determiners *no* and *any* and the matching indefinite pronouns.

It has been seen (4.127*f*) that *no* and *any* have both a mass and a countable use:

> MASS: So far no money has been spent on repairs
> COUNTABLE: No person of that name lives here

In both these cases the verb is singular. But the second sentence can be made plural, in which case a plural verb is required:

COUNTABLE: No people of that name live here
Any more odds and ends you can find are welcome

Any and *none* used as pronouns likewise have singular and plural meanings:

MASS: I've ordered the cement, but none (of it) has yet
arrived
COUNTABLE: I've ordered the shrubs, but none (of them) have/has
yet arrived

In the latter sentence, grammatical concord (or at least that version of it enshrined in prescriptive grammars) insists that *none* is singular; but notional concord (since the shrubs would scarcely have arrived singly) invites a plural verb. *Has* is therefore more conventionally 'correct', but *have* is more idiomatic in speech. These comments may be extended to *neither* and *either* as indefinite pronouns:

I sent cards to Mavis and Margery but neither (of them) has/have
replied; in fact, I doubt if either (of them) is/are coming

If a prepositional phrase with a plural complement follows the indefinite construction, a plural verb is favoured not only because of notional concord but because of the proximity rule:

none of *them* are . . . either of *the girls* are . . .; etc.

7.30

The same proximity principle may lead to plural concord even with the indefinites *each, every, everybody, anybody,* and *nobody,* which are otherwise unambivalently singular:

Nobody, not even the teachers, were listening
Every member of that vast crowd of 50,000 people were pleased to
see him

Although these sentences might well be uttered in casual speech, or inadvertently written down, most people would probably regard them as ungrammatical, because they flatly contradict grammatical concord. For such cases, where the proximity principle overrules grammatical concord, the term ATTRACTION is often used.

Other, more acceptable, instances of attraction arise with singular nouns of kind and quantity ([19] and [22] only informal):

Those kind/sort/type of parties are dangerous   [19]

A large number⎫
Plenty   ⎬ of people have applied for the job   [20]

The majority of them are Moslems   [21]

Loads/heaps/lots/gallons of the stuff is going to waste   [22]

[19] illustrates an idiomatic anomaly: there is lack of number concord
between the noun and the determiner *those*, as well as with the verb. This
awkwardness can be avoided by rephrasing *Parties of that kind* ... etc.
[20] and [21] show the nominally singular phrases *a large number of*, etc
being treated as plural and as equivalent to *many* and *most*. (*A large number* ... *has applied* would be a very pedantic adherence to grammatical
concord.) The opposite phenomenon, singular attraction, is observed in
[22], where phrases like *lots of* are treated as if equivalent to singular
much. Relevant aspects of noun-phrase structures are discussed in 4.26,
where the possibility of regarding locutions such as *a number of* as premodifiers is noted.

Note

[a] Although *each* is singular when a head or premodifier

> Each child *has* an ice-cream

it can be postposed to plural noun phrases:

> The children each *have* an ice-cream

(See 9.123.)

[b] The proximity principle, if taken to mean that agreement is determined by whatever immediately precedes the verb, can explain a singular verb in cases of inversion or of an adverbial quasi-subject: *Where's the scissors?; Here's John and Mary;
There's several bags missing* (7.63*f*, 14.15, 14.26). As what precedes the subject here
is not marked for plural (7.23 Note *a*), the singular verb follows by attraction.
These are colloquial examples; in formal English *are* would be substituted.

7.31
Concord of person

As well as concord of number, there is concord of person (3.10, 3.19,
4.108) between subject and verb:

> I am your friend (1st PERSON SINGULAR CONCORD)

> He is ready   ⎫
> He knows you⎬(3rd PERSON SINGULAR CONCORD)

Following the principle of proximity, the last noun phrase of a coordinate subject (where the coordinator is *or, either* ... *or*, or *neither* ... *nor*)
determines the person of the verb:

> Neither you, nor I, nor anyone else knows the answer
> Either my wife or I am going

Because of the awkwardness of this device, a speaker may avoid it by using a modal auxiliary which is invariable for person, *eg: Either my wife or I will be going.*

Note

[a] There is also concord of 2nd person singular pronouns and verbs (4.112 Note *c*) in archaic English: *Thou, Lord, hast redeemed us.*

[b] Some speakers feel that *Either you or I are going* is more natural than *Either you or I am going.*

[c] In cleft sentences (14.18), a relative pronoun subject is usually followed by a verb in agreement with its antecedent: *It is I who am to blame.* But 3rd person concord prevails (in informal English) where the objective case pronoun *me* is used: *It's me who's to blame.*

7.32
Summary

It is difficult to summarize the system of subject-verb concord in English, but one may risk the following generalizations:

[A] The principle of GRAMMATICAL CONCORD is the safest one to follow in formal usage, as it has the sanction of teaching tradition and authority.

[B] The principle of NOTIONAL CONCORD is that which is most natural to colloquial English.

[C] The principle of PROXIMITY, despite its minor decisive role in cases where the other two provide no guidance, is generally felt to lack validity on its own, and has more of an auxiliary role in supporting notional concord in colloquial speech.

Grammatical and notional concord generally work in harmony together; it is only in the few difficult cases that the rules-of-thumb above need to be invoked.

Other types of concord
7.33
Subject-complement concord

Subject-complement concord of number (but not of person) exists between S and C in clauses of type *SVC* (7.2); thus [23] and [24] are grammatical, whereas [25] and [26] are not:

The child was an angel	[23]	*The child was angels	[25]
The children were angels	[24]	*The children were an angel	[26]

This type of concord arises naturally from the denotative equivalence of subject and subject complement. There are, however, exceptions:

What we need most is books   [27]

That man is nuts/crackers ('mad', *slang*–especially BrE)   [28]
Good manners are a rarity these days   [29]
Those chairs are reproduction (especially BrE)   [30]
The next few bars are pure Tchaikovsky   [31]

Children can be $\begin{cases} \text{fun} \\ \text{a nuisance} \\ \text{good company} \\ \text{an investment} \end{cases}$ [32]

All these sentences except the first (where *what* is ambivalent with respect to number) contain a subject complement which, although nominal in form, has a function closer to that of an adjective than of a noun (*cf* 5.11). There is often no singular/plural contrast; for example, *Those men are crackers* does not have a singular form **That man is a cracker*.

There is an equivalent type of concord between object and object complement in *SVOC* clauses: *eg, He thinks children angels* is acceptable, but not **He thinks children an angel*.

This type of concord is, in fact, common to all cases of 'intensive' relationship (7.6).

Note

[a] For [27] and (in BrE) for [29] above there are variants in which the number of the verb is in agreement with the complement: *What we need most are books; Good manners is a rarity these days*. These are probably ascribable to the workings of notional concord, the idea of plurality being dominant in the first and that of singularity in the second. One could argue, from the apparent 'anticipatory concord', that such sentences are instances of inversion (14.15), and should be analysed C_s V S rather than S V C_s. This argument is difficult to sustain, however, since inversion does not take place in parallel circumstances elsewhere: **The committee are we* and **Us is the committee* are both deviant sentences.

[b] There can be failure of subject-complement concord in BrE when the subject is a singular collective noun (*cf* 7.25): *The Bennett family were remarkable musicians.*

7.34
Subject-object concord

Subject-object concord of number, person and gender is necessary, as well as subject-complement concord, where the second element is a reflexive pronoun (4.113 *ff*):

He injured himself in the leg (*but not:* **She injured himself in the leg*)

He hasn't been himself for weeks (*ie* 'He hasn't felt well') (*but not:* **She hasn't been yourself for weeks*)

The same concord relation holds when the reflexive pronoun occurs in other functions (*eg* as prepositional complement), or when the reflexive genitive *his own*, etc is used:

She's making a sweater for herself
They're ruining their own chances.

Note
In BrE, collective noun subjects permit, as one might expect, plural concord: *The navy congratulated themselves on, if not a victory, at least an avoidance of defeat;* similarly *everybody* and *everyone*: *Everybody crossed themselves.*

Pronoun concord
7.35
The relation between the reflexive pronoun object and its subject may be seen as a special case of the concord between a pronoun and its antecedent, *ie* the noun phrase for which it may be regarded as a substitute (see further 10.43). This type of concord may extend beyond clause boundaries. Thus the relative pronouns *who, whom* and *which* agree with their antecedent in the superordinate clause in gender, the first two being personal, and the last non-personal (4.117 *ff*):

The bag which I saw ...	[33]
The man who(m) I saw ...	[34]

Whose can be used with either animate or inanimate antecedents:

The house whose rafters were burnt ...	[35]
The man whose purse he stole ...	[36]

There is a feeling, however, that *whose* is more appropriate to personal antecedents, and some speakers cannot use an expression such as [35] without some feeling of uneasiness.

3rd person personal pronouns agree with their antecedents both in number and (in the case of the 3rd person singular pronouns *he, she,* and *it*) in gender:

John hurt his foot	[37]
Beatrice hurt her foot	[38]
John and Beatrice hurt their feet	[39]
The climbers hurt their feet	[40]

The violation of concord in the case of non-reflexive personal pronoun substitutes does not lead (as it does in the case of reflexive pronouns) to an unacceptable sentence, but to a different interpretation. One may compare [37] and [38] with:

John hurt her foot	[41]

where the suggestion is that John hurt someone else's foot (the someone else having been previously mentioned). That is, in [41], *her* cannot be a substitute for *John* but may be one for some other noun phrase.

7.36

English has no sex-neutral third person singular pronoun (*ie* one that expresses the common meaning of *he* and *she*), and so the plural pronoun *they* is often used informally (especially in BrE), in defiance of number concord, as a substitute for the indefinite pronouns *everyone, everybody, someone, somebody, anyone, anybody, no one, nobody*.

> *Everyone* thinks *they* have the answer   [42]
> Has *anybody* brought *their* camera?   [43]
> *No one* could have blamed *themselves* for that   [44]

The plural pronoun is a convenient means of avoiding the dilemma of whether to use the *he* or *she* form. The same dilemma can arise with co-ordinate subjects and with some indefinite noun phrase subjects, but here, resort to the evasive device of the plural pronoun is perhaps not so acceptable:

> ? *Either he or his wife* is going to have to change *their* attitude
> ? *Not every drug addict* can solve *their* problem so easily

The use of *they* in sentences like [42–44] is frowned upon in formal English, where the tendency is to use *he* as the 'unmarked' form when the sex of the antecedent is not determined. The formal equivalent of [42] is therefore:

> *Everyone* thinks *he* has the answer   [42a]

The same choice is made in referring back to a singular noun phrase with a personal noun of indeterminate gender as head:

> Every student has to make up *his* own mind   [45]

Although this use of *he* often sounds pedantic, there is no obvious alternative to it, in formal English, except the rather cumbersome device of conjoining both male and female pronouns:

> Every student has to make up *his or her* own mind   [45a]

We have noted (7.25) that singular collective nouns have plural subject-verb concord in cases where the speaker thinks of the group as made up of separate individuals. The same principle extends to pronoun concord:

> The government are cutting *their* losses (BrE)   [46]
> The government is cutting *its* losses   [47]

Although there is no number contrast in relative pronouns, this distinction can be expressed by the choice of *who* (personal, *ie* the group thought of as a set of individuals) as opposed to *which* (non-personal, *ie* the group as an indivisible abstraction).

Thus corresponding to [46] and [47], we may have:

The government, *who* are cutting *their* losses (BrE)	[46a]
The government, *which* is cutting *its* losses	[47a]

(*but not:* *The government, who is cutting their losses)

Selection restrictions
7.37
Apart from concord, there are other ways in which the choice of one element within a sentence may affect the choice of another.

The men scattered	*not*	*The man scattered
Police dispersed the rioters	*not*	*Police dispersed the rioter
The cars collided	*not*	*The car collided

Each of the above pairs shows how a particular verb requires a particular type of subject or object: *collide* (unless accompanied by a *with*-phrase) requires a plural subject; *scatter* and *disperse* require a plural 'affected' participant (7.14) – *ie* a plural subject when used intransitively or a plural object when used transitively.

Rules governing the kind of subject, object, or prepositional complement occurring with a particular verb come under the heading of selection restrictions. They differ from rules of concord, in that they do not involve two elements *sharing* the same feature, but one element *projecting on to* another a feature which is necessary for its meaningful use. That it is 'plurality' as a semantic feature rather than as a strictly grammatical feature that is in question here is shown by the possibility of substituting a collective singular for the plural noun: *The crowd scattered* and *The police dispersed the mob* are acceptable sentences.

Other features commonly entering into selection restrictions are:

'concrete' vs 'abstract': { The glass contains water / *The glass contains kindness

'animate' vs 'inanimate': { A pedestrian saw me / *A lampshade saw me

'human' vs 'non-human': { Finally we got married / *Finally the snakes got married

These restrictions are frequently violated in poetry and in other imaginative uses of language. The incongruity, in such cases, indicates that the speaker/writer intends us to make sense of his words at some deeper level, *eg* by metaphorical interpretation. In poetry, *leaves* may *dance*, *stars* may *bless*, *fears* may *lurk* or *linger*.

Selection restrictions apply not only to verbs, but to other word-classes, notably adjectives and prepositions. The oddity of *The music is too green* is explained by the requirement that *green* should be in an intensive relationship with a concrete noun. That of **until the town* is accounted for by a rule that *until* requires a temporal prepositional complement.

7.38

In spite of their importance in explaining what makes a 'correct English sentence', there is no need to dwell further here on selection restrictions, as they are more a matter of meaning than of syntax. Also, one may assume that similar restrictions on the semantic level occur in all languages, and therefore do not need to be stated specifically for English.

There is one type of selection restriction, however, which is specific to a particular word in a particular language, and helps to distinguish that word from its close synonyms. The two verbs *eat* and *feed*, used intransitively, tend to require personal and non-personal subjects respectively. Thus *Janet and Joe are eating* implies that Janet and Joe are 'persons'; whereas *Janet and Joe are feeding* implies that they are babies or animals. Details of such restrictions are to be sought (although they are not always found) in dictionaries, and in particular in dictionaries of synonyms.

The vocative
7.39

A vocative is a nominal element added to a sentence or clause optionally, denoting the one or more people to whom it is addressed, and signalling the fact that it is addressed to them:

JŎHN, I WÀNT you (voc S V O$_d$)
It's a lovely DÀY, Mrs JÓHNson (S V Cs voc)
And YOÙ, my FRÍENDS, will have to work HÀRDer (& S voc V A)

(On the intonation markings, see App II.12 *ff*.)

These three sentences show how a vocative may take an initial, medial, or final position in the sentence; in its optionality and freedom of position, it is more like an adverbial (or, more precisely, like a disjunct – see 5.44) than any other element of clause structure.

Intonationally, the vocative is set off from the rest of the clause either by constituting a separate tone-unit or by forming the 'tail' or post-nuclear part of a tone unit (App II.12). The most characteristic intonations are shown above: fall-rise for an initial vocative; rise for a medial or final vocative.

7.40
In form a vocative may be

(1) a single name with or without title (9.166 *ff*): *John, Mrs Johnson, Dr Smith,* etc.
(2) The personal pronoun *you; eg: Behave yourself, you.* (This is markedly impolite.) Or an indefinite pronoun; *eg: Get me a pen, somebody.*
(3) Standard appellatives, usually nouns without pre- or postmodification (not even the possessive pronoun):

> FAMILY RELATIONSHIPS: *mother, father, uncle:* or more familiar forms like *mom(my)* (AmE), *mum(my)* (BrE), *dad(dy), auntie*
>
> ENDEARMENTS: (*my) darling/dear/love/honey* (AmE), etc
>
> TITLES OF RESPECT: *sir, madam, My Lord, Your Excellency, Your Majesty, ladies and gentlemen,* etc
>
> MARKERS OF PROFESSION OR STATUS: *doctor; Mr/Madam Chairman; Mr President; (Mr) Prime Minister; Father* (for priest); *Bishop,* etc

These are also used as titles of respect.
(4) A nominal clause (very occasionally): *Whoever said that, come out here.*
(5) Items under (1), (2), or (3) above with the addition of modifiers or appositive elements of various kinds:

> (1) *My dear Mrs Johnson; young John*
> (2) *You with the red hair; you over there.* Less impolite and more jocular in tone are appositives like *you boys; you (young) fellows* (familiar); *you guys* (familiar AmE)
> (3) *Old man/fellow* (familiar); *young man/woman*

One obvious function of a vocative in English is to seek the attention of the person addressed, and especially to single him out from others who may be within hearing. A second function, less obvious but certainly no less important, is to express the attitude of the speaker towards the addressee.

Vocatives are generally used as a positive mark of attitude, to signal either respectful distance or familiarity (varying from mild friendliness to intimacy).

In addressing someone one knows by name, last name preceded by title (*Mr Jones, Miss Smith, Dr Robinson*, etc) is a politely formal manner of address, while first name (*John, Mary*, etc) indicates friendly familiarity. It is now much easier to be 'on Christian name terms' (BrE) or 'on a first name basis' (AmE) than formerly; address by family name alone (which used to indicate friendly male comradeship, as in *Holmes* and *Watson*) is rarely heard today, except in special situations (armed forces, school).

Forms of address to strangers in English are limited. *Sir* and especially *Madam* are too formal to be used other than to someone clearly senior or superior to oneself in age, status, etc. As isolated vocatives, *Mister* and *Missis* are substandard, and *Miss* is little better in BrE, although it is somewhat more generally used in AmE. Professional vocatives are also used sparingly nowadays and are generally reserved for people of highly respected status (*eg* doctors, clergy). In BrE, for example, there is a large variety of familiar (not necessarily disrespectful) vocatives for strangers, varying from the bus conductress's *dear, duck* or *love* to the transport-driver's *mate, skip* or *jock;* but these are not in educated use. It is worth bearing in mind, therefore, that there is a whole area of neutral interchange where no vocative is used or felt to be necessary.

Note
To gain the attention of a stranger, a speaker of English often relies on *Excuse me* (BrE) or *I beg your pardon* (AmE) rather than a vocative.

Negation
Negation with operator and *do*-periphrasis
7.41
The negation of a simple sentence is accomplished by inserting the word *not* between the operator and the predication (2.2, 3.6):

POSITIVE	NEGATIVE
The attempt has succeeded	~ The attempt has not succeeded
We may win the match	~ We may not win the match
I'm coming	~ I'm not coming
We have been defeated	~ We have not been defeated

What is meant by 'operator' here (as for questions) is either the first auxiliary verb of the verb phrase or BE as a main verb or (in BrE) HAVE as a main verb. Thus the negation of *I'm thirsty* is *I'm not thirsty;* one BrE negation of *He has a car* is *He hasn't a car* (3.18 Note). In colloquial English, the negator occurs in an enclitic contracted form *-n't*. Contracted negative forms of auxiliaries are listed in 3.20.

Note

[a] Some positive clauses have no negation; for example, *He is sure to succeed*~*He isn't sure to succeed* (cf: *He is bound to succeed*~*He isn't bound to succeed*).

[b] This chapter discusses negation as a syntactic process within the clause, rather than a process of word-formation. Negative affixes (*un-, in-, non-, a-, -less*), despite some affinities with the clause negator *not* (*eg: That is not true – That is untrue*), are dealt with in App I.11.

7.42

A problem arises with the negation of a clause which contains no auxiliary; *ie* a clause whose verb is a simple present or past tense form (apart from BE) like *give, gives,* or *gave*. English overcomes this problem by introducing the substitute or 'dummy' auxiliary DO, which, like modal auxiliaries, is followed by the bare infinitive:

> She sees me every week ~ She doesn't see me every week
> They understand my problem ~ They don't understand my
> problem
> The stranger sat down ~ The stranger didn't sit down

DO-periphrasis is discussed in more detail in 3.17.

7.43

Abbreviated negation

In circumstances where it is possible to abbreviate the operator by the use of a contracted form enclitic to the subject (3.17 *ff*), two colloquial forms of negation are possible:

> Someone's not coming ~ Someone isn't coming
> We're not ready ~ We aren't ready
> They've not caught him ~ They haven't caught him
> Sam'll not miss us ~ Sam won't miss us
> He'd not notice anything ~ He wouldn't notice anything

Note

[a] As there is no contracted form of *am not*, *I'm not coming* has no alternative of the kind given in the right-hand column above. Another consequence of this gap is that there is no universally accepted colloquial question form corresponding to the stiltedly formal *Am I not beautiful?* The contraction *aren't* is sometimes substituted (especially in BrE), but with some feeling of awkwardness: *Aren't I beautiful?* In AmE, *ain't* has considerable currency in both declarative and interrogative use.

[b] Restrictions on certain negative forms, especially *mayn't, mustn't, oughtn't, daren't* and *needn't*, are noted in 3.20 and 7.52.

7.44
Non-assertive forms and negative forms

The negative particle *not* or *-n't* is frequently followed (not necessarily directly) by one or more of the non-assertive items listed in the third column below (non-assertive pronouns are discussed in 4.127; see also 2.21).

SYNTACTIC CLASS	ASSERTIVE	NON-ASSERTIVE	NEGATIVE
(1) determiner	*some*	*any*	*no*
(2) determiner	(*one or the other*)	*either*	*neither*
(3) pronoun	*some*	*any*	*none*
(4) pronoun	(*one or the other*)	*either*	*neither*
(5) pronoun	*something*	*anything*	*nothing*
(6) pronoun	*somebody*	*anybody*	*nobody*
(7) pronoun	*someone*	*anyone*	*no one*
(8) process adverb	*somehow*	(*in any way*)	(*in no way*)
(9) place adverb	*somewhere* (informal AmE – *someplace*)	*anywhere* (informal AmE – *anyplace*)	*nowhere*
(10) time adverb	*sometime(s)*	*ever* (informal AmE – *anytime*)	*never*
(11) time adverb	*already*	*yet*	—
(12) time adverb	*still*	*any more/longer*	*no more/longer*
(13) extent adverb	(*to some extent*)	*at all*	—
(14) intensifier	*somewhat*	*any (the)*	*no, none the*
(15) additive adverb (8.13 *ff*)	*as well, too*	*either*	(See 7.44 Note)

The combination of *not* with a non-assertive form can be replaced, in most instances, by the negative word in the right-hand column; there are consequently two negative equivalents of each positive sentence:

(1) We've had some lunch ~ { We haven't had any lunch / We've had no lunch

(2) He saw one man or the other ~ { He didn't see either man / He saw neither man (*unusual*)

(3) We've had some ~ { We haven't had any / We've had none

(4) He saw one or other of the men ~ { He didn't see either of the men / He saw neither of the men

(5) I've bought something for you $\sim$ $\begin{cases} \text{I haven't bought anything} \\ \quad \text{for you} \\ \text{I've bought nothing for you} \end{cases}$

(6) I was speaking to somebody $\sim$ $\begin{cases} \text{I wasn't speaking to} \\ \quad \text{anybody} \\ \text{I was speaking to nobody} \end{cases}$

(7) I was speaking to someone $\sim$ $\begin{cases} \text{I wasn't speaking to} \\ \quad \text{anyone} \\ \text{I was speaking to no one} \end{cases}$

(8) I was somehow surprised $\sim$ $\begin{cases} \text{I wasn't in any way} \\ \quad \text{surprised} \\ \text{I was in no way surprised} \end{cases}$

(9) I've seen them somewhere $\sim$ $\begin{cases} \text{I haven't seen them} \\ \quad \text{anywhere} \\ \text{I've seen them nowhere} \\ \quad (\textit{unusual}) \end{cases}$

(10) He sometimes visits us $\sim$ $\begin{cases} \text{He doesn't ever visit us} \\ \text{He never visits us} \end{cases}$

(11) They've arrived already $\sim$ They haven't arrived yet

(12) He's still at school $\sim$ $\begin{cases} \text{He's not at} \\ \qquad \text{school any} \begin{cases} \text{longer} \\ \text{more} \end{cases} \\ \text{He's at school no longer} \\ \quad (\textit{unusual}) \end{cases}$

(13) I can help (to some extent) $\sim$ I can't help at all

(14) I'm (somewhat) wiser now $\sim$ $\begin{cases} \text{I'm not any (the) wiser now} \\ \text{I'm} \begin{cases} \text{no} \\ \text{none the} \end{cases} \text{wiser now} \end{cases}$

(15) Her mother's coming, too $\sim$ Her mother's not coming either

In all cases (except possibly that of *never*), the combination of *not* (*-n't*) and the non-assertive word is more colloquial and idiomatic than the negative variant. The absence of a negative word for *yet*, *at all*, and *either* means that there is only one negative version in examples 11, 12, and 15.

Note
It is not quite true to say that there is no negative word corresponding to the adverb *either; neither* and *nor* both occur as negative additive adjuncts, but only in an initial position with negative inversion (14.16):

He couldn't speak, (and) *neither* could he walk
He couldn't speak, *nor* could he walk
He couldn't speak, and he couldn't walk *either*

All these sentences mean the same, but the first two are somewhat literary in tone, while the last is decidedly colloquial.

7.45
Negative intensification
There are various ways of giving emotive intensification to a negative. For example, *by any means* and (informally) *a bit* are common alternatives to *at all* as non-assertive expressions of extent. Negative determiners and pronouns are given emphasis by *at all*, *whatever: I found nothing at all the matter with him; You have no excuse whatever. Never* is repeated for emphasis, or else combined with an intensifying phrase such as *in (all) his/her etc life: I'll never, never go there again; I've never in all my life seen such a crowd.* The combinations *not one* and *not a (single)* are emphatic alternatives to *no* as a countable determiner (see 7.50 Note). Other familiar and emotively coloured expressions of negation are exemplified by

> I didn't sleep *a wink*
> He didn't give me *a thing*
> I don't care *a damn* whether we win or lose.

7.46
Initial negative element
The non-assertive form associated with negation cannot precede *not* in the sentence; therefore there is no alternative construction to the simple negative form when that form occurs in a subject or initial adjunct.

> NEGATIVE SUBJECT
> No one listens to me   (?*Anyone doesn't listen to me)
> Nothing came of it   (?*Anything didn't come of it)
> None of us were ready   (?*Any of us weren't ready)
> Not one bottle was left

(Negative subjects can also be formed with the word *not* as a predeterminer, in the combinations *not all, not every, not everyone, not much, not many*, etc: *Not all economists agree with you*.)

> NEGATIVE ADJUNCT (in rather formal or literary style)
> Never will I make that mistake again
> Nowhere have we seen the results more clearly than in Europe
> Not until yesterday did he change his mind

These examples illustrate the inversion (reversal of subject and operator) that occurs with an initial negative element (14.16). The unacceptability of the normal clause order (*Never I will make . . . etc) should be noted.

Note

[a] The sequences *not a little/few, not infrequently,* (*a*) *not unattractive* (*woman*), etc do not form negative subjects or adjuncts in the sense discussed here. The effect of *not* here is merely a local one (7.50 Note), reversing the already negative force of the following expression. Such 'double negative' phrases are devices of understatement; *I was not a little worried* means, in fact, 'I was quite worried'.

[b] *Not yet* does not occur initially with a finite verb, and *no longer* and *no more* do so only in highly literary style: **Not yet have I seen him.*

[c] If *any, anyone* etc is postmodified, it can precede *not* in the sentence. For example:

Anyone who does that isn't honest.

7.47
More than one non-assertive form

If a clause contains a negative element, it is usually negative throughout, from the occurrence of the negative to the end, or at least until the beginning of a final adjunct. This means that after a negative, the non-assertive forms must normally be used in place of *every* assertive form that would have occurred in the corresponding positive clause:

I've never travelled *anywhere* by air *yet*
I haven't *ever* been on *any* of the big liners, *either*
No one has *ever* said *anything* to *either* of us
Not many of the refugees have *anywhere* to live *yet*

The non-assertive forms even occur in positive subordinate clauses following a negative in the main clause:

Nobody has promised that *any* of you will be released *yet*
That wouldn't deter anyone who had *any* courage

Assertive forms, however, are equally likely in such cases; and more generally, assertive forms do occur following a negative, so long as they fall outside the scope of negation (7.49).

Note

[a] Occasionally two negatives occur in the same clause: *I can't not obey* ('I have to obey'); *Not many people have nowhere to live* ('Most people have somewhere to live'); *No one has nothing to offer to society* ('Everyone has something to offer to society'). These sentences are somewhat like the 'double negative' of logic, in that each negator has its separate value and it is possible to find paraphrases, like those just given, which cancel out each negative, leaving an entirely positive sentence.

[b] In substandard English, however, there is an entirely different kind of 'multiple negation', where more than one negative form is used, but the meaning is that of a single negative: *No one never said nothing* (Standard English *No one ever said anything*). The explanation of this construction is that substandard English chooses a negative word wherever Standard English would choose a non-assertive word after a negative.

7.48

Seldom, rarely, etc

In addition to the negative words discussed so far, there are several words which are negative in meaning, but not in appearance. They include

> *seldom* and *rarely* (adverbs meaning 'not often' – 8.61)
> *scarcely* and *hardly* (adverbs meaning 'almost . . . not/no' – 8.29 *f*)
> *little* and *few* (determiners or adverbs meaning 'not much' and 'not many' respectively – in contrast, *a little* and *a few* are positive – 4.25 Note *d*)
> *only* (determiner or adverb meaning 'no more/other than' – 8.13 *ff*)
> *barely* (adverb meaning 'only just' – 8.29 *f*)

For three reasons these are treated as negative forms:

(1) They are followed by non-assertive rather than assertive forms:

> I seldom get *any* sleep
> I've spoken to hardly *anyone* who disagrees with me
> Few changes in government have *ever* taken so many people by surprise
> Only two of us had *any* experience at sailing

(2) When in pre-subject position, they normally cause subject-operator inversion:

> Rarely does crime pay so well as Mr Benn seems to think
> Scarcely ever has the British nation suffered so much obloquy
> Little need I dwell upon the joy of that reunion

> The inversion, as before, is literary or rhetorical in tone.

(3) They are followed by positive rather than negative tag-questions (7.59–60):

> She scarcely seems to care, does she?

Note

[a] *Seldom* and *rarely*, unlike the other negative words mentioned here, may themselves come under the scope of another negative:

> He doesn't visit us rarely
> ('It isn't rarely that he visits us')

[b] In addition to the words discussed, verbs, adjectives, or prepositions with negative meaning can govern non-assertive forms:

> He *denies* I ever told him
> I *forgot* to ask for any change
> *Unaware* of any hostility
> *Without* any delay
> *Against* any changes

Non-assertive forms may also be used in putative clauses (11.72):

> It's odd that he should ever notice it.

7.49
Scope of negation

Now let us consider more carefully the relation between negative words and the non-assertive words that they govern.

A negative form may be said to govern (or determine the occurrence of) a non-assertive form only if the latter is within the SCOPE of the negation, *ie* within the stretch of language over which the negative meaning operates. The scope of the negation normally extends from the negative word itself to the end of the clause, or to the beginning of a final adjunct. The subject, and any adjuncts occurring before the predication, normally lie outside it. (The operator is sometimes within, and sometimes outside, the scope – see 7.52 below.) There is thus a contrast between:

I definitely didn't speak to him ('It's definite that I did not')

I didn't definitely speak to him ('It's not definite that I did')

(The scope is marked by the horizontal bracket.) When an adverbial is final, however, it may or may not lie outside the scope (*cf* 8.8):

I wasn't LÌstening all the TÌME	[48]
I wasn't listening all the TÌME	[49]

The difference of scope, which is here marked by intonation, reflects an important difference of meaning: [48] means 'For the whole time, I wasn't listening', and [49] means 'It is not true that I was listening all the time'.

If an assertive form is used, it must lie outside the scope; therefore [50] and [51] below parallel [48] and [49]:

I didn't listen to some of the speakers	[50]
I didn't listen to any of the speakers	[51]

As we have seen (7.47), the scope can sometimes extend into a subordinate clause: *I didn't know that anyone was coming.*

7.50
Clause, local, and phrasal negation

One may distinguish clause negation discussed above from local negation, where the scope of the negation does not extend beyond a particular word or phrase. The difference is illustrated in the following:

CLAUSE NEG: Nothing agrees with me more than oysters
  (*ie* 'Oysters agree with me as much as – indeed, more than – anything else')

LOCAL NEG: Nothing agrees with me more than oysters
(*ie* 'Eating nothing agrees with me more than eating oysters')

Local negation may possibly be explained as negation of a clause condensed into a phrase; here, for instance, *nothing* can be interpreted 'eating nothing'. Strictly, the second sentence is not a negative sentence at all, but a positive sentence containing a negative word: this we see from the possibility of adding a negative tag question (7.59): *Nothing agrees with me more than oysters, doesn't it.* The type of negative phrase already noted in 7.46 Note *a* (*eg: a not unattractive woman; his not very handsome face*) may also be classed as local negation.

Note
Yet another minor type of negation, PHRASAL NEGATION, must be allowed for. This is the type which is grammatically restricted to a single phrase, but semantically applies to a whole clause. It is thus the opposite of local negation, which is grammatically similar to but semantically unlike clausal negation:

Not a word came from his lips (*cf* No word . . .)
He gave me *not even a moment* to collect my thoughts
Not five men survived the journey

Not here functions as a predeterminer in the italicized noun phrases; but it has the effect of negating the whole clause. Phrasal negation, which has emphatic meaning, is often combined with negative inversion (14.16).

7.51
Focus of negation
In describing negative clauses, it is important to identify not only the scope of negation, but the INFORMATION FOCUS. Marked information focus (14.3) applies to negative clauses in a special way: a special or contrastive nuclear stress falling on a particular part of the clause indicates not only that the contrast of meaning implicit in the negation is located in that spot, but that by implication the rest of the clause can be understood in a positive sense:

HÀRry didn't attack the Labour GÓvernment
(*ie:* '*Someone* attacked . . ., but it wasn't Harry')
Harry didn't *atTÀCK* the Labour GÓvernment
(*ie:* 'He did *something* to the Labour Government but he didn't attack it')
Harry didn't attack the LÀBour GÓvernment
(*ie:* 'He attacked *some* government, but it wasn't the Labour one')

(The typical intonation of such clauses is the contrastive fall + rise.) The scope and focus are interrelated in such a way that *the scope must include the focus.* From this it follows that one way of signalling the extent of the scope is by the position of the focus. Indeed, since the scope of the negation is often not unambiguously signalled at all, placing the information focus in a special position is a primary way of indicating that a special extension of the scope of negation has been made. One example of this is when, atypically, the scope of the negation is extended to include a subordinate clause of reason:

I didn't leave HÓME, because I was afraid of my FÀther   [52]

I didn't leave home because I was afraid of my FǍther   [53]

With more usual intonation, [52] allots a separate tone unit to each clause, and so places the *because*-clause outside the scope of the negative. (This interpretation can also be singled out by a comma in writing.) But [53] extends a single tone unit over both, and places a contrastive fall + rise on *father*. The effect of this is to place negative focus on the *because*-clause, so that the main clause is understood positively. The meanings are entirely different:

'Because I was afraid of my father, I didn't leave home'   [52]
'I left home, but it wasn't because of my father that I did so'   [53]

Intonation may be crucial also in marking the extension of the scope backwards to include the subject: an atypical phenomenon found in subjects which contain one of the 'universal' items *all* or *every*:

All cats don't like WÀTER (*ie* 'All cats dislike water')   [54]

ǍLL cats don't like WÁTER (*ie* 'Not all cats like water')   [55]

[54] has the normal negative scope, while [55] has contrastive (fall + rise) information focus on the subject, signalling its inclusion within the scope. The construction of [54] is, in fact, unusual: more common is the paraphrase with a negative subject: *No cat likes water*.

Note
When the negative word *not* itself has the focus, the scope may be restricted to that word, as in the denial sentence:

I did NÒT offer her some chocolates

('It is not true that I offered her . . .')

The same effect is achieved by focus on a negative operator (14.7):

I DÌDn't offer her some chocolates.

7.52
Negation of modal auxiliaries
The negation of modal auxiliaries requires some attention, in that here the scope of the negation may or may not include the meaning of the

auxiliary itself. We therefore distinguish between AUXILIARY NEGA-
TION and MAIN VERB NEGATION:

AUXILIARY NEGATION:
may not (='permission')
   You may not go swimming ('You are not allowed . . .')

cannot, can't (in all senses);
   You can't be serious ('It is not possible that . . .')

   You can't go swimming ('You are not allowed . . .')

   She can't ride a bicycle ('She is not able to . . .')

need not, needn't
   You needn't pay that fine ('You are not obliged . . .')

   It needn't always be my fault ('It is not necessary that . . .')

MAIN VERB NEGATION:
may not (='possibility')
   They may not bother to come if it's wet ('It is possible that they
   will not bother to come . . .')
will not, won't (all senses)
   Don't worry, I won't interfere ('I'm willing not to interfere')

   He won't do what he's told ('He insists on not doing . . .')

   They won't have arrived yet ('I predict that they've not arrived
                                                                    yet')
shall not, shan't (all senses)
   Don't worry, you shan't lose your reward ('I'm willing to see
   that you don't lose your reward')
   I shan't know you when you return ('I predict that I will not
                                                              know . . .')
must not, mustn't (='obligation')
   You mustn't keep us all waiting ('You'll oblige me by not
   keeping us waiting')
ought not, oughtn't (both senses)
   You oughtn't to keep us waiting ('obligation')

   He oughtn't to be long ('necessity')

Certain auxiliaries (*can* and *need*) follow the pattern of auxiliary negation, while others (*will, shall, must*) follow that of main verb negation. *May* belongs to the former group in its 'permission' sense, but to the latter group in the sense of 'possibility'. *Mustn't* is not used at all (and *must not* only rarely) in the 'necessity' sense; the gap is filled by *can't* in the sense of 'impossibility'. Thus the negation of

You *must* be telling lies

is

You *can't* be telling lies

The auxiliary negation of *must* is *needn't*, which has the two meanings of non-obligation and non-necessity:

A: Must we pack now? B: No, we needn't till tomorrow.

Because of the diametric opposition of meaning between 'permission' and 'obligation', an odd-seeming equivalence exists between *may not* ('non-permission') and *mustn't* ('obligation-not-to'):

$=\begin{cases}\text{You mustn't go swimming today} \\ \text{You may not go swimming today}\end{cases}$

On the whole, the past tense negative auxiliaries (*mightn't, couldn't, wouldn't, shouldn't*) follow the same negative pattern as their present tense equivalents, subject to the provisions described in 3.43 *ff*.

Note

As the above list shows, it is not normal for the same auxiliary to be used in the same meaning with two different kinds of negation. Occasionally, however, one meets an ambiguity which resides solely in the interpretation of the scope of negation. With a special emphatic pause before *not*, one might say *You may 'not go swimming*, meaning 'I permit you not to go' rather than 'I do not permit you'. From this possibility of unorthodox interpretation, acceptable instances of two negators in the same clause sometimes arise: *You can't not admire him* ('It is impossible not to admire him') is a sentence containing both auxiliary and main verb negation. More natural ways of expressing the same idea would be *You can't (help) but admire him* or *You can't help admiring him*.

Statements, questions, commands, exclamations

7.53
Formal classification

Simple sentences may be divided into four major syntactic classes, whose use correlates with different communicative functions:

    (1) STATEMENTS are sentences in which the subject is always present and generally precedes the verb:

John will speak to the boss today

On exceptional statements not containing a subject, see 9.19 *f.*

(2) QUESTIONS are sentences marked by one or more of these three criteria:

(a) the placing of the operator in front of the subject:

Will John speak to the boss today?

(b) the initial positioning of an interrogative or *wh*-element:

Who will you speak to?

(c) rising 'question' intonation:

You will speak to the BÓSS?

(3) COMMANDS are sentences which normally have no overt grammatical subject, and whose verb is in the imperative mood (3.10):

Speak to the boss today

(4) EXCLAMATIONS are sentences which have an initial phrase introduced by *what* or *how*, without inversion of subject and operator:

What a noise they are making!

Of these classes, the statement is by far the most important, and the exclamation the least important. When referring not to sentences but to clauses (which at this stage means 'main clauses'), we use the adjectives corresponding to these four types: (1) DECLARATIVE, (2) INTERROGATIVE, (3) IMPERATIVE, and (4) EXCLAMATORY.

There are also some minor sentence types, which will be considered in 7.85 *ff.*

7.54
Functions of discourse

The functions of discourse associated with these four classes are:

(1) STATEMENTS are primarily used to convey information.
(2) QUESTIONS are primarily used to express lack of information on a specific point, and (usually) to request the listener to supply this information verbally.
(3) COMMANDS are primarily used to instruct somebody to do something.
(4) EXCLAMATIONS are primarily for expressing the speaker's own feelings.

Two factors mar the neatness of the above account of the relations between sentence classes and discourse functions. First, the functions overlap: for example, the single sentence *I'd love a cup of tea* not only
conveys information, but expresses a feeling and even (by implication)
urges action on the listener. Secondly, the syntactic classes do not by
any means correspond one-to-one with the discourse functions: *What on
earth are you doing!* is a question as regards form, but an exclamation as
regards function; *I wonder if you'd kindly open the window?* is a statement according to form, but a command according to function. It is as
well to bear such discrepancies in mind, since the sentence classes as
considered in this chapter are defined grammatically rather than contextually.

Up to this point, the sentences discussed have been mainly statements.
The remainder of the chapter will be devoted to questions, commands,
and exclamations, as well as to a number of residual classes of minor
utterance.

Questions: *yes-no* type
7.55
Questions can be divided into three major classes according to the type
of answer they expect. Those that expect the answer *yes* or *no*, such as
Have you been to Paris?, are *yes-no* questions; those that contain a 'wh-
element' (*who? what? how?* etc) and expect a reply supplying the missing information posited by that element are *wh*-questions: *What is your
name?* A third type of lesser importance is the alternative question,
which expects as an answer one of two or more alternatives mentioned in the question: *Would you like STÉAK or CHÌCKen?* (7.68 *f*).

7.56
Yes-no questions
Yes-no questions, which we will consider first, are usually formed by
placing the operator (2.2, 2.18 *f*) before the subject, and using 'question
intonation' (rise or fall + rise, see App II.13–15):

STATEMENT	QUESTION
(S – Op – predication)	(Op – S – predication)
Frank is writing a BÒOK	Is Frank writing a BÓOK?
The boat has LÈFT	Has the boat LÉFT?
Our team was BÈATen	Was our team BÉATen?
He could have broken his LÈG	Could he have broken his LÉG?
I'll be WÀITing for you	Will you be WÁITing for me?

If a statement contains a straightforward present tense or past tense verb without an operator, the same applies here as in the case of negation (7.42), *ie* DO-periphrasis (3.17) is introduced:

STATEMENT	QUESTION
(S – predication)	(Op DO – S – predication)
The bus arrived late	Did the bus arrive late?
His methods bring success	Do his methods bring success?
He likes Dickens	Does he like Dickens?

Again, BE and sometimes HAVE (in BrE only) count as operator even when they occur without a following main verb, so that the whole verb is placed in front of the subject:

The Joneses are late again ~ Are the Joneses late again?
I have the exact change ~ Have you the exact change?

The American form of this last question (also current in BrE) is: *Do you have the exact change?* (see 3.18 Note).

Obviously, 1st and 2nd person pronouns are exchanged for one another when a question is converted into an equivalent statement:

Do *you* like it?   Yes *I* do.

Note

[*a*] Declarative questions (7.61) are exceptional in not requiring subject-operator inversion.

[*b*] By placing the nuclear stress in a particular part of a *yes-no* question, we are able to 'focus' the interrogation on a particular item of information which, unlike the rest of the sentence, is assumed to be unknown (*cf* focus of negation, 7.51). Thus the focus falls in different places in the following otherwise identical questions:

Was he a famous actor in THÓSE days?
    ('I know he was once a famous actor – but was it then or later?')
Was he a FÁMOUS actor in those days?
    ('I know he was an actor in those days – but was he a famous one?')

7.57

Positive orientation

Another typical characteristic of *yes-no* questions (except of declarative questions) is the use of the non-assertive forms *any, ever*, etc that we have already seen in operation in negative statements:

STATEMENT	QUESTION
Someone called last night	Did *anyone* call last night?
The boat has left *already*	Has the boat left *yet?*
I live *somewhere* near Dover	Do you live *anywhere* near Dover?
I suppose *some* of the class will ask *some* boring questions	Do you suppose *any* of the class will ask *any* boring questions?

Non-assertive forms, like the DO auxiliary, point to common ground between questions and negative statements. This ground is not hard to explain: clearly a question has neutral polarity, in the sense that it leaves open whether the answer is positive or negative. Hence questions like negatives belong to the class of 'non-assertions' (2.21).

On the other hand, a question may be presented in a form which is biased towards a positive or negative answer. A question has positive orientation, for example, if it uses (as sometimes happens) assertive forms in preference to non-assertive forms:

Did *someone* call last night? ('Is it true that someone called last night')

Has the boat left *already?*

Do you live *somewhere* near Dover?

These questions indicate that the speaker has reason to believe that the answer is yes: he merely asks for confirmation of that assumption. They are frequently used in making an offer: *Would you like some cake?*

7.58
Negative orientation
The opposite case of negative orientation is found in questions which contain a negative form of one kind or another:

Can't you give us any hope of success? ('Is it really true
     that you can't . . .?')   [56]
Isn't your car working?   [57]
Does no one believe me?   [58]

Negative orientation is complicated, however, by an element of surprise or disbelief which adds implications of positive meaning. Thus [57] means 'Do you really mean that your car isn't working? I had assumed that it was.' Here there is a combining of a positive and a negative attitude, which one may distinguish as the OLD ASSUMPTION (positive) and NEW ASSUMPTION (negative). Because the old assumption tends to be identified with the speaker's hopes or wishes, negative orientated questions often express disappointment or annoyance:

Can't you drive straight? ('I'd have thought you'd be able to, but
     apparently you can't')
Aren't you ashamed of yourself? ('You ought to be, but it appears
     you're not')
Hasn't the boat left yet? ('I'd hoped it would have left by now,
     but it seems that it hasn't')

A second type of negative question combines *not* (the formal signal of negative orientation) with the assertive items which are the formal signals of positive orientation:

> Didn't someone call last night?   [59]
> Hasn't the boat left already?   [60]

Such questions are similar in effect to type [I] tag questions (7.59), or alternatively to statements showing disbelief: 'Surely someone called last night!'

A different ordering obtains in negative questions according to whether the full or enclitic negative particle is employed; *-n't* precedes the subject, whereas *not* follows it:

> Didn't they warn you?
> Did they not warn you?

As the second construction is rather formal, however, the enclitic negative particle is usually preferred in informal spoken English.

Note

[a] The exclamatory negative question (*eg:* Isn't she CLÈVER!) is discussed in 7.70.

[b] The adjunct *either* only occurs in questions in the company of a negative:

$$\begin{Bmatrix} *\text{Did} \\ \text{Didn't} \end{Bmatrix} \text{he recognize you either?}$$

[c] Although a negative subject of a statement cannot be replaced by *not*+nonassertive form (7.46), the same restriction does not apply to negative questions, where the subject follows the clause negator *not*. Two question forms therefore correspond to the single positive form *No one believes me: Does no one believe me?* and *Doesn't anyone believe me?*

Tag questions
7.59

A further type of question which conveys positive or negative orientation is the tag question appended to a statement:

> The boat has already left, hasn't it?
> You aren't throwing these shoes away, are you?

The rules for forming the most common type of tag question are:

(1) The tag question consists of operator+subject (an enclitic negative particle preceding the subject, a full particle following it) in that order: *is he? isn't he? can't I? will you? could you not? did they not?*

(2) The operator is the same as the operator of the preceding statement:

> I *haven't* met you, *have* I?

(Where the statement contains no operator, use is made of *do/ does/did*, as for question formation in general: *He knows you, doesn't he?*)

(3) The subject of the tag is a pronoun which either repeats, or appropriately substitutes for, the subject of the statement.

(4) If the statement is positive, the tag is negative, and vice versa.

(5) The nuclear tone of the tag occurs on the auxiliary, and is either rising or falling.

Four main types of tag question emerge from the observance of these rules:

	RISING TONE	FALLING TONE
	[I]	[III]
POSITIVE+NEGATIVE	He likes his JÒB, DÓESN't he?	He likes his JÒB DÒESN't he?
	[II]	[IV]
NEGATIVE+POSITIVE	He doesn't like his JÒB, DÓES he?	He doesn't like his JÒB, DÒES he?

The meanings of these sentences, like their forms, involve a statement and a question; each of them, that is, asserts something then invites the listener's response to it. Sentence [I], for example, can be rendered 'I assume he likes his job; am I right?'. [II] means the opposite: 'I assume he doesn't like his job; am I right?'. Clearly these sentences have a positive and a negative orientation respectively. A similar contrast exists between [III] and [IV]. But it is important, again, to separate two factors: an ASSUMPTION (expressed by the statement) and an EXPECTATION (expressed by the question). On this principle, we may distinguish the four types as:

[I] Positive assumption + neutral expectation
[II] Negative assumption + neutral expectation
[III] Positive assumption + positive expectation
[IV] Negative assumption + negative expectation

The tag with the falling tone, it will be noted, invites confirmation of the statement, and has the force of an exclamation rather than a genuine question. In this, it is like (though perhaps not so emphatic as) exclamatory *yes-no* questions with a falling tone (7.70): *Isn't it gorgeous WÈATHer!* etc.

Note

The tag normally mirrors the subject and auxiliary of the independent clause of a complex sentence. There are exceptions, however, with verbs like *suppose* when they are introduced by a 1st person subject and followed by a *that*-clause:

I suppose you're not serious, are you?
(*not* *I suppose you're not serious, don't I?)

A further stage of irregularity is introduced in cases of transferred negation (11.79): *I don't suppose he's serious,i he?* Here, the subject of the tag is taken from the *that*-clause, but the absence of negation from the tag is explained with reference to the negative particle of the independent clause, which applies *semantically* to the *that*-clause.

7.60

There is a further, less common, type of tag question in which both statement and question are positive:

> Your car is outsÌDE, ís it?
> You've had an ÀCCIDENT, HÁVE you?

The tag always has a rising nucleus, and the situation is characteristically preceded by *oh* or *so*, indicating the speaker's arrival at a conclusion by inference, or by recalling what has already been said. The tone may sometimes be one of sarcastic suspicion:

> So THÀT's your little game, ís it?

Very occasionally, one encounters an equivalent type of tag question in which both statement and tag are negative:

> Oh, so you haven't touched a drop for YÈARS, HÁVEn't you?

We may thus add two further, less usual, types of tag question to the earlier four types:

POSITIVE+POSITIVE   [V]   So he likes his JÒB, DÓES he?
NEGATIVE+NEGATIVE   [VI]   So he doesn't like his JÒB, DÓEsn't he?

7.61
Declarative questions
Not all *yes-no* questions have subject-operator inversion. The declarative question is a type of question which is identical in form to a statement, except for the final rising question intonation:

> You've got the EXPLÓSIVE?
> They've spoken to the AMBÁSSADOR, of course?
> You realize what the RÍSKS are?
> Boris will be THÉRE, I suppose?
> He didn't finish the RÁCE?

Declarative questions have 'positive orientation' (or 'negative orientation'), as is observed from the necessity of using assertive or negative forms:

> The guests have had $\left\{ \begin{matrix} \text{nothing} \\ \text{something} \end{matrix} \right\}$ to eat?

not non-assertive forms:

*The guests have had anything to eat?

They are similar in force to type [I] or type [III] tag questions, except for a rather casual tone, which suggests that the speaker takes the answer *yes* (or *no*) as a foregone conclusion.

Note

[*a*] A second interrogative use of the statement construction is for echo questions (7.81–83).

[*b*] A tag question may be added to a declarative question:

You've got the EXPLÓSIVE, have you?

Only the rising tone on *explosive* distinguishes this from type [V] tag questions.

7.62
Yes-no questions with modal auxiliaries

The formation of *yes-no* questions with modal auxiliaries is subject to certain limitations and shifts of meaning. The modals of 'permission' (*may* especially BrE, and *can*) and of 'obligation' (*must*, especially BrE, and *have to*) involve the speaker's authority in statements and the listener's authority in questions:

A: ${May \atop Can}$I leave now?　('Will *you* permit me . . .')

　B: Yes, you${may \atop can}$.　('*I* will permit you . . .')

A: ${Must\ I \atop Do\ I\ have\ to}$leave now?　('Are *you* telling me . . .')

　B: Yes, you${must \atop have\ to}$.　('*I* am telling you . . .')

This means the question form anticipates the form appropriate for the answer.

A similar switch from listener to speaker takes place with *shall* ('volition') which (especially in BrE) implicates the speaker's will in statements, but the listener's will in questions:

You shall suffer for this! ('*I* intend to make you suffer . . .!')

Shall I switch off the television? ('Do *you* want me to . . .?')

The direct-question use of *shall*, however, is virtually restricted to first person subjects. With *we*, it has both exclusive and inclusive senses:

Shall we carry your suitcases? ('Would you like us to . . .?')

Shall we have dinner? ('Would you like us [including you] to . . .?')

May ('possibility') is not employed at all in questions; *can* (or more commonly, in AmE, *could*) takes its place:

A: $\begin{Bmatrix} \text{Can} \\ \text{Could} \end{Bmatrix}$ they have missed the bus?   B: Yes, they $\begin{Bmatrix} \text{may have.} \\ \text{might have.} \end{Bmatrix}$

Need (in BrE) is a non-assertive auxiliary in clauses where the corresponding positive form is *must*. Hence in questions:

A: (BrE) Need it happen? (*cf* AmE/BrE: Does it $\begin{Bmatrix} \text{need to} \\ \text{have to} \end{Bmatrix}$ happen?)

B: Yes, it $\begin{Bmatrix} \text{must.} \\ \text{has to.} \end{Bmatrix}$

If, on the other hand, *must* had occurred in A's question, it would have had 'positive orientation': 'Is it a fact that it must happen?'. Compare *Need it ever happen?* with *Must it always happen?*, where the assertive form has to be retained.

Questions: *wh*-type
Wh-questions
7.63

The second major category of question to be considered is the *wh*-question.

Wh-questions are formed with the aid of one of the following simple interrogative words (or Q-words):

who/whom/whose, what, which (4.120)
when, where, how, why (5.48)

As a rule,

(1) the Q-element (*ie* clause element containing the Q-word) comes first in the sentence (apart from some conjuncts and disjuncts);
(2) the Q-word itself, moreover, takes first position in the Q-element.

The only exception to the second principle is when the Q-word occurs in a prepositional complement. Here English provides a choice between two constructions, one formal and the other colloquial. In formal style, the preposition precedes the complement, whereas in colloquial style, the complement comes first and the preposition is left 'trailing' at the end of the sentence:

On what did you base your prediction? (formal)
What did you base your prediction *on*? (colloquial)

We may perhaps express this difference more neatly by saying that colloquial English insists that the Q-word comes first, while formal English insists that the Q-element as a whole comes first.

Note

[a] There is also a group of informal intensificatory Q-words *whoever, whatever, whichever, whenever, wherever,* and *however.* These are more usually, however, spelled as two separate words: *who ever,* etc (and so are distinguished from the subordinating *wh*-words *whenever, whoever,* etc – 11.12). The two parts of *why ever* are never run together as a single word: *Why ever didn't he tell me?* Various other ways exist of intensifying the emotive effect of a *wh*-question:

> Who *on earth* opened my letter?
> Who *the hell* are you?
> What *in heaven's name* do you think you're doing?

The last two examples illustrate the impolite use of intensification.

[b] On factors affecting the choice between *who* and *whom,* see 4.119 f, 13.12.

[c] The final preposition construction is less desirable when the preposition is remote from its complement, or when it is syntactically closer bound to the complement than to the verb. Awkward sentences like *What time did you tell him to meet us at?* are generally avoided. The awkwardness reaches comic proportions when combined with other constructions involving final particles (6.3, 6.9–10): *What did you bring this book to be read out of up for?*

7.64

The following are sentences in which the Q-element operates in various clause functions:

> *Who ever* opened my LÈTter?　(Q-element: S)　　　　　　　　[61]
> *Which books* have you LÈNT him?　(Q-element: O_d)　　　　[62]
> *Whose beautiful anTÌQUES* are these?　(Q-element: C_s)　　[63]
> *How wide* did they make the BÒOKcase?　(Q-element: C_o)　[64]
> *When* will you come BÀCK?　(Q-element: A_{time})　　　　　[65]
> *Where* shall I put the GLÀSses?　(Q-element: A_{place})　　[66]
> *Why* are they always comPLÀINing?　(Q-element: A_{reason})　[67]
> *How* did you MÈND it?　(Q-element: $A_{process}$)　　　　　[68]
> *How much* does he CÀRE?　(Q-element: $A_{intensification}$)　[69]
> *How long* have you been WÀITing?　(Q-element: $A_{duration}$)　[70]
> *How often* do you visit New YÒRK?　(Q-element: $A_{frequency}$)　[71]

As the examples indicate, falling intonation, not rising intonation, is characteristic for *wh*-questions: see App II.12.

We see above that normal statement order of elements is upset in *wh*-questions not only by the initial placing of the Q-element, but by the inversion of subject and operator in all cases except that in which the Q-element is subject, where the rule of initial Q-placement takes precedence over the rule of inversion.

Subject-operator inversion is the same in its application to *wh*-questions as in its application to *yes-no* questions: if there is no operator in the equivalent statement, DO is introduced as substitute operator in the question. BE (and sometimes, in BrE, HAVE) counts as an operator even when a main verb: *How are you?*

Note

[a] Adjuncts of instrument, reason, and purpose are normally questioned by the pre-positional constructions:

> *What* shall I mend it *with?*
> *What* did you do that *for?*

Although the latter of these questions could be replaced by *Why ...?*, it has no alternative with a preposed preposition: **For what did you do that?* In this respect it is like informal questions with BE followed by a final preposition: *What was it like?* (but not **Like what was it?*).

[b] Abbreviated questions consisting of Q-word and final preposition (which in this construction, unusually, bears nuclear stress) *Where to? What for/with? Who with/by?* are as popular in colloquial speech as questions consisting of the Q-word only: *Where? Who? Why?*. There is a common abbreviated negative question *Why not?* (10.61).

[c] Although there is no verbal Q-word for English, the content of the verbal element can be questioned by *what* as the object of the generalized agentive verb DO, or as subject of HAPPEN:

> A: What are you doing?   B: I'm reading.
> A: What have you done to/with my book?   B: I've hidden it.
> A: What's happening?   B: It's snowing.

[d] An indirect object cannot act as Q-element: instead of **Who(m) did you give the present?*, the equivalent prepositional complement construction is used: *Who(m) did you give the present to?* or *To whom did you give the present?*

[e] In *wh*-questions of the *SVC* pattern, it is possible to distinguish between noun phrases as S and C by signals of case and concord, where these apply: *Which is me?* (Q-element as S – said, for example, when looking at a photograph) contrasts with *Which am I?* (Q-element as C).

7.65
Presuppositions

Every *wh*-question may be matched with a statement called its presupposition. This is a statement which, in place of the Q-element, contains an indefinite expression such as *somebody*. The presupposition, which is assumed to be true by whoever uses the question, preserves of course normal statement ordering. Hence, if we list the presuppositions corresponding to some of questions [61–71] above, it will clarify the syntactic ordering of *wh*-questions in relation to statements:

PRESUPPOSITIONS

Someone opened my letter	[61a]
You have lent him *some of the books*	[62a]
You will come back *sometime*	[65a]
You mended it *somehow*	[68a]
You visit New York *sometimes*	[71a]

Note

The relation between a *wh*-question and its presupposition shows why negative questions of this type (except for *why* questions) are rare. While there is an acceptable presupposition for *why* questions:

Why didn't he do it? ~ He didn't do it for some reason

there is no such correspondence with other question words:

*Where didn't he do it? ~ *He didn't do it somewhere

The reason for the oddity of this last sentence is that *somewhere* is normally replaced by *anywhere* following a negative (see 7.44). On the other hand, *for some reason* is accepted following a negative because it is a disjunct, and therefore normally outside the scope of negation.

7.66
Pushdown Q-element

In the questions with a postposed preposition we have already studied, the Q-element is a part of the main clause only indirectly, being a prepositional complement, which is part of an adjunct, which in turn is part of the main clause. Here are other instances where the Q-element is embedded further down in the constituent structure of the sentence:

(1) Q-element as prepositional complement within noun phrase (in informal English):

{ *Which professor* did he marry the daughter of?
{ The daughter of *which professor* did he marry?

(2) Q-element as element of nominal object clause:

{ *What* would you like me to buy?
{ *How long* did he tell you he waited?

The phenomenon illustrated by (1) and (2) can occur not only in direct questions, but in other circumstances where an element is fronted (7.78, 11.55, 14.12 Note *a*, 14.19). We call the initial element in such cases a PUSHDOWN element.

Q-elements combining the embedding Types (1) and (2) are also possible:

Which mountain do they say they tried to climb to the top of?

It is also possible to repeat the same type of embedding a number of times; in the following example, the Q-element is a prepositional complement in a prepositional complement in a prepositional complement in a prepositional complement:

Which professor did he marry the daughter of the stepson of the former wife of?

Improbable as such a sentence is, it seems to be acceptable by the rules of English. On the other hand, there are clear and apparently arbitrary limits to what can be a Q-element. Elements of indirect questions, for example, are debarred this function; likewise elements of relative and adverbial clauses:

> How long can you be sure they waited? (Q in indirect statement)
> *How long can you be sure whether they waited? (Q in indirect question)
> *How many teams are you glad because we beat? (Q in adverbial clause)
> *Which park did we listen to the man who was speaking in? (Q in relative clause)

Note

[a] A type of sentence quite often heard in impromptu speech is one of the 'forbidden' types of relative clause above, with a pronoun inserted to stand proxy for the Q-element at the point in the dependent clause where, in statement order, it would occur:

> *Who else* did you notice whether *they* passed the exam?

Though ungrammatical by ordinary rules of *wh*-question formation, these sentences are obviously found useful in filling in the gaps left by starred sentences such as those above.

[b] When a Q-element is the subject of an indirect statement, the omission of the normally optional introductory *that* is obligatory:

> Who do you think did it?

not

> *Who do you think *that* did it?

7.67

More than one Q-element

There can be more than one Q-element in the same simple sentence: *Who said what to whom?* In such sentences, only one Q-element is moved to the front, the others remaining in their normal position. There is a choice, however, as to which Q-element is fronted, and this means that the same question can be put in more than one way. From the presupposition

> You have hidden something somewhere   [72]

we can move to either of these questions:

> What have you hidden where?   [73]
> Where have you hidden what?   [74]

[72] could also form the presupposition of a question containing only one Q-word. In that case, the other indefinite expression would remain in its assertive form:

Where have you hidden something?   [75]

Another (rare) possibility would be the substitution of the non-assertive form:

Where have you hidden anything?   [76]

which would mean 'I don't know whether you've hidden anything, but if you have, where is it?'. Both types of wh-question illustrated by [75] and [76] are unusual, as are also wh-questions containing a negative, except where the Q-word is why: Why don't you speak?

Alternative questions
7.68
The alternative question has already been defined in 7.55. There are two types, of which the first resembles a yes-no question, and the second a wh-question:

Would you like CHÓcolate, vaNÍLla or STRÀwberry (ice-cream)?   [77]
Which ice-cream would you LÌKE? CHÓcolate, vaNÍLla or
  STRÀwberry?   [78]

The first type differs from a yes-no question only in intonation: instead of the final rising tone, it contains a separate nucleus for each alternative: a rise occurs on each item in the list, except the last, on which there is a fall, indicating that the list is complete. The difference of intonation between alternative and yes-no questions is important, in that ignoring it can lead to misunderstanding – as the contrast between these replies indicates:

alternative: A: Shall we go by BÚS or TRÀIN?   B: By BÙS.
yes-no: A: Shall we go by bus or TRÁIN?   B: No, let's take
                                                    the CÀR.

The second type of alternative question is really a compound of two separate questions: a wh-question followed by an elliptical alternative question. Thus [78] might be taken as a reduced version of:

Which ice-cream would you LÌKE? Would you like CHÓcolate,
  vaNÍLla or STRÀwberry?

Any positive yes-no question can be converted into an alternative question by the addition of or not? or of a matching negative clause:

yes-no: Are you CÓMing?   [79]
alternative: {Are you CÓMing or NÒT?   [80a]
             {Are you CÓMing or ÀREn't you (coming)?   [80b]

The alternative variant, by spelling out the negative aspect of the question, is rather petulant in tone, but is otherwise indistinguishable in meaning from the *yes-no* question.

7.69
The structure of alternative *yes-no* questions follows the pattern of clausal coordination (9.61 *ff*); that is, two or more separate questions are collapsed together, wherever convenient, by ellipsis:

Did Íraly win the World Cup or (did) Brazìl (win the World Cup)?

(Brackets here enclose ellipted elements.) Often the remaining part of a second or subsequent alternative question is fronted to the appropriate position in the first question:

Did Íraly or Brazìl win the World Cup?

This type of fronting is also possible for the vacuous negative alternative in [80] above:

Áre you or Àren't you coming?

Where there is no repeated structure, no ellipsis is possible, and so the second question appears in its full form:

Is it RÁIning or has it STÒPped?

Minor types of question
7.70
Exclamatory question
We turn now to two minor question types: the exclamatory question, and the rhetorical question. ('Echo questions', which in fact need not be questions in form, will be described later in 7.81–83.)

First, we consider the exclamatory question, which is a question in form, but is functionally like an exclamation (7.78 *f*).

The most characteristic exclamatory question is a negative *yes-no* question with a final falling instead of rising tone:

Hasn't she GRÒWN!
Wasn't it a marvellous CÒNCERT!

These invite the listener's agreement to something on which the speaker has strong feelings. The meaning, contrary to appearances, is vigorously positive.

A positive *yes-no* question, also with a falling tone, is another (but less common) way of expressing a strong positive conviction:

ˈAm ˈI HÙNgry!   ˈDid ˈhe look anNÒYED!   ˈHas ˈshe GRÒWN!

Both operator and subject usually receive emphatic stress.

Here we meet the oddity of pairs of sentences which contrast in terms of negation, but which have roughly the same effect: *Has she grown!* *Hasn't she grown!* There is, however, a slight difference: the negative question has, as a feature of its meaning, an appeal for the listener's agreement; it is therefore inappropriate for cases like *Am I hungry!*, where the experience reported is not shared by the listener. The meanings of each type are roughly represented by these paraphrases:

> Wasn't it a marvellous CÒNcert! – 'What a marvellous CÒNcert it was!'
> Has she GRÒWN! – 'She HÀS grown!'

Note

[a] Exclamatory questions of this kind sometimes occur as elliptical replies, in which a speaker affirms his agreement with what another speaker has just said:

> A: Her performance in Rigoletto was outstanding.
> B: Yes, wÀsn't it.

[b] In AmE an exclamatory question can be pronounced with a rising tone:

> Wasn't the concert terRÍfic?

But in this case, a reply is expected.

7.71
Rhetorical question

Just as the exclamatory question is a question which has the effect of an exclamation, so the rhetorical question is a question which functions as a forceful statement. More precisely, a *positive* rhetorical question is like a strong *negative* assertion, while a *negative* question is like a strong *positive* one.

POSITIVE:

> Is that a reason for desPÁIR? ('Surely that is not a reason . . .')
> Can anyone doubt the wísdom of this action? ('Surely no one can doubt . . .')

NEGATIVE:

> Is no one going to deFÉND me? ('Surely someone is going to defend me')

Unlike exclamatory questions, these rhetorical questions have the normal rising intonation of a *yes-no* question, and are distinguished phonologically only by the unusually low or high starting-point of the rise.

There is also a rhetorical *wh*-question, which is equivalent to a statement in which the Q-element is replaced by a negative element:

> Who KNÔWS/CÂRES? ('Nobody knows/cares')
> What DÎFference does it make? ('It makes no difference')

Again, the intonation is that of an ordinary *wh*-question, except that a rise-fall tone is likely.

Commands
7.72
Commands without a subject

We begin with the most common category of command, that which differs from a statement in that

(1) it has no subject,
(2) it has an imperative finite verb (the base form of the verb, without endings for number or tense).

Otherwise, the clause patterns of commands show the same range and ordering of elements as statements:

Type *SV:* Jump (V)
Type *SVC:* Be reasonable (V C)
Type *SVOA:* Put it on the table (V O_d A_{place})
etc

The imperative verb, however, is severely restricted as to tense, aspect, voice, and modality. There is no tense distinction or perfect aspect, and only very rarely does the progressive form occur:

Be preparing the dinner when he comes in

A passive is equally rare and, except when the auxiliary is some verb other than BE, as in *Get washed,* is restricted to a few set commands:

Be prepared
Be seated
Be reassured by me

These restrictions are connected with the understandable incongruity of combining an imperative with a stative non-agentive verb: **Sound louder!* Modal auxiliaries do not occur at all in imperative sentences.

Commands are apt to sound abrupt unless toned down by markers of politeness such as *please: Please eat up your dinner; Shut the door, please.* Even this only achieves a minimum degree of ceremony; a more tactful form of request can only be arrived at if one changes the command into a question or a statement: *Will you shut the door, please? I wonder if you would kindly shut the door; I wonder whether you would mind shutting the door;* etc.

Note

Stative verbs can be interpreted as dynamic, however, in special contexts: *Know the answer by tomorrow!* (= 'Get to know . . .', 'Learn . . .').

7.73

Commands with a subject

It is implied in the meaning of a command that the omitted subject of the imperative verb is the 2nd person pronoun *you*. This is intuitively clear, but is also confirmed by the occurrence of *you* as subject of a following tag question (*Be quiet, will you*), and by the occurrence of *yourself* and of no other reflexive pronoun as object: *Behave yourself*, not **Behave himself*, etc.

There is, however, a type of command in which the subject *you* is retained:

> *You* be quiet!
> *You* mind your own business, and leave this to me!

These commands are usually admonitory or 'finger-wagging' in tone, and frequently express strong irritation. As such, they cannot naturally be combined with markers of politeness, such as *please*: **Please, you be quiet!* They may be used, however, in another way, to single out (by pointing) two or more distinct addressees: *You come here, Jack, and you go over there, Mary.* A 3rd person subject is also possible:

> *Somebody* open this door
> *Everybody* shut their eyes
> *Jack and Susan* stand over there

It is easy to confuse the subject, in these commands, with a vocative noun phrase (7.39). Whereas the subject always precedes the verb, however, the vocative (as we saw earlier) is an element that can occur in final and medial, as well as initial, positions in the sentence. Another difference is that the vocative, when initially placed, has a separate tone-unit (typically fall-rise); the subject merely receives ordinary word-stress:

> VOCATIVE: MĂRY, play on MỲ side
> Play on MỲ side, MÁRY
> SUBJECT: |Mary play on MỲ side

The distinctness of vocative and imperative subject is confirmed by the possibility of their co-occurrence: *JŎHN, |you listen to MÈ!*

Note

[a] Apart from *will you?*, other tag questions heard with an imperative are *can you? won't you? can't you?* Also the familiar *wh*-question *why don't you* is sometimes appended: *Take a rest, why don't you?*

[b] There is uncertainty about the person of a reflexive pronoun after a 3rd person subject: *Everyone behave themselves* and *Everyone behave yourselves* both seem acceptable (on the use of a plural substitute pronoun for *everyone*, see 7.36). With a vocative, in contrast, only the 2nd person reflexive, in agreement with the understood subject, is allowable: *Behave yourselves, everybody.*

[c] Another confusion easily made is that between a command with *you* as subject, and a statement with *you* as subject as used, for example, in giving street directions: *You go up there until you reach the bridge, then you turn right . . ..* It is the unstressed subject of the statement that distinguishes it formally from the command, since the subject of a command is always stressed, even if a pronoun: '*You go up there.* Needless to say, the admonitory tone of the command would be quite unsuitable in giving street directions.

7.74
Commands with *let*

First person imperatives can be formed by preposing the verb *let* followed by a subject in the objective case:

Let us all work hard
Let me have a look

The same applies to 3rd person subjects:

Let each man decide for himself
If anyone shrinks from this action, let him speak now

Except for the *let me* type, all these are rather archaic and elevated in tone. A colloquial alternative to *let us*, however, is the common abbreviated form *let's:*

Let's have a party
Let's enjoy ourselves

In very colloquial English, *let's* is sometimes used for a 1st person singular imperative as well: *Let's give you a hand.* There are no 2nd person imperatives with *let: *Let you have a look.*

Note
This type of imperative, in which *let* is no more than an introductory particle, should be kept separate from the ordinary 2nd person imperative of *let* as a transitive verb (12.57). That they are distinct is shown by the fact that *Let us go* in the sense 'Permit us to go' cannot be abbreviated to *Let's go.*

7.75
Summary

At this stage, structural types of command may be summarized as follows:

		1st PERSON	2nd PERSON	3rd PERSON
without subject		—	[I] Open the door	—
with subject	without *let*	—	[II] You open the door	[III] Someone open the door
	with *let*	[IV] Let me open the door Let's open the door	—	[V] Let someone open the door

By far the most common type is the subjectless 2nd person command (Class I).

7.76
Negative commands
To negate the first three classes of command, one simply adds an initial *Don't*, replacing assertive by non-assertive forms where necessary:

[I] Open the door   *Don't* open the door
[II] You open the door   *Don't* you open the door
[III] Someone open the door   *Don't* *anyone* open the door

1st person imperatives, on the other hand, are generally negated by the insertion of *not* after the pronoun following *let*:

[IV] $\left\{\begin{array}{l}\text{Let's}\\\text{Let us}\end{array}\right\}$ not open the door

Informally, however, the negation with *Don't* is frequently heard:

[IV] Don't let's open the door

and the same construction is available for Class V:

[V] Don't let anyone fool himself that he can get away with it.

Note
[a] The more formal full form *do not* can replace *don't* in a negation of Class I: *Do not open the door*. It is a curious feature of negations in other classes, however, that the uncontracted form cannot be used: **Do not you open the door; *Do not anyone open the door*. This suggests that *don't*, like *let*, is more of an invariable introductory formula, in commands, than an auxiliary verb.

[b] Negative commands are seldom followed by tags. The only tag operator that seems possible is the positive auxiliary *will: Don't make a noise, WÌLL you*. The tag has a falling tone.

7.77
Persuasive imperatives
A persuasive or insistent imperative is created by the addition of *do* (with a nuclear tone) before the main verb:

> Do have some more sherry
> Do let's go to the theatre

This construction only applies to Classes I and IV.

Note
[a] *Do*, like *don't* and *let's*, acts as an introductory imperative marker, and is not identical with the emphatic *do* of statements (14.47). To see this, notice that neither *do* nor *don't* in commands fulfils the strict conditions of *do*-periphrasis (3.17); they are not introduced to make good the lack of an operator, but indeed are added to the front of an operator if one is present: *Do be seated; Don't be silly*. (Contrast the unacceptability of **He does be silly!*) This peculiarity of imperative *do* is also found in the quasi-imperative *Why don't you* construction: *Why don't you be careful.*

[b] *Do, don't*, and *let's* are used in isolation as elliptical commands:

> A: Shall I open the door?   B: $\begin{cases} \text{Yes, do.} \\ \text{No, don't.} \end{cases}$
> A: Shall we watch the game?   B: Yes, let's.

Exclamations
7.78
In discussing exclamations as a formal category of sentence, we restrict our attention to the type of exclamatory utterance introduced by *what* or *how*.

Exclamations resemble *wh*-questions in involving the initial placement of an exclamatory *wh*-element, which may be called the X-element. The syntactic order is therefore upset to the extent that the X-element (which may be object, complement, or adverbial as well as subject) may be taken from its usual (statement) position and put into a position of initial prominence. On the other hand, in contrast to *wh*-questions, there is generally no subject-operator inversion:

X-element as subject: *What an enormous crowd* came! (S V)   [81]
X-element as object: *What a time* we've had today! (O_d S V A)   [82]
X-element as complement: *How delightful* her manners
are! (C_s S V)   [83]

X-element as adverbial: $\begin{cases} \textit{How I used to hate geography!} \\ \text{(A S V } O_d) \\ \textit{What a long time we've been} \\ \text{waiting! (A S V)} \end{cases}$
    [84a]
    [84b]

In addition, the X-element, like the Q-element of the *wh*-question, can act as prepositional complement:

> What a mess we're in!

and can even occur as a pushdown element of an indirect statement (again like the Q-element, 7.66), although the structure is rare:

> What a girl I thought I was going to marry!

It is possible (but again rare) for the prepositional phrase as a whole to occur initially as X-element:

> For how many years have I waited!

This example also illustrates the occasional inversion of subject and operator in literary English, particularly with the A S V and O S V patterns.

7.79
The range of *wh*-words and their functions that can be used in exclamations is far less wide than that available in *wh*-questions. In fact, it is restricted to *what* functioning as pre-determiner in a noun phrase, and *how* functioning as intensifier (of an adjective, adverb, or clause); *cf* [82], [83], and [84a]. The limitation to these three functions is not surprising when one realizes that the X-word indicates an extreme position on some scale of value, and therefore can only appear at points in the sentence where an expression of degree is possible. Exactly the same functions are fulfilled (especially in women's speech) by the emphatic degree items *such* (as a determiner) and *so* (as intensifier) in statements and questions (14.48):

> We've had *such* a time
> Her manners are *so* delightful
> Why did you use to hate geography *so*?

Wh-exclamations are very frequently indeed reduced by ellipsis to the single X-element: *What a terrible wind! How encouraging!*

Note
How is like *so* (in exclamatory utterances) in that when it is an intensifier, it cannot modify an adjective which itself has a premodifying function. Instead of

> *a *how/so* noisy party

we must say

> *what/such* a noisy party.

Echo utterances

7.80

Echo utterances are utterances which repeat as a whole or in part what
has been said by another speaker. They may take the form of any
utterance or partial utterance in the language, and to that extent cut
right across the division of sentences into statements, questions, commands, and exclamations. On the other hand, all echo utterances are
either interrogative or exclamatory in function. Moreover, interrogative
echoes bear some of the marks of question classification, in that they can
be divided into *yes-no* and *wh*-types, the former invariably having rising
question intonation. There is little harm, therefore, in simplifying terminology by calling these echo utterances 'echo questions' and 'echo
exclamations', so long as we bear in mind that 'question' and 'exclamation' here are contextual rather than formal labels. There are two types
of echo question: the recapitulatory echo question and the explicatory
echo question.

7.81

Recapitulatory echo questions

A recapitulatory echo question is simply a question which repeats part
or all of a message, as a way of having its content confirmed. The simplest type is a *yes-no* question which merely repeats, with question intonation, what has just been said:

> A: I didn't like that meal.   B: You didn't LÍKE it?
> A: The Browns are emigrating.   B: émigrating?
> A: Switch the light off, please.   B: Switch the LÍGHT off?

To make the meaning explicit, one could prefix to each of these questions
the words 'Did you say . . . ?'. Sometimes, indeed, a tag clause . . . (*did*)
you say? is added: *Switch the LÍGHT off, (did) you say?*

There is also a *wh-* echo question which indicates, by the Q-word,
which part of the previous utterance the speaker did not hear:

> A: It cost five dollars.   B: HÓW much did it cost?
> A: He's a dermatologist.   B: WHÁT is he?
> A: We're leaving him here.   B: WHÁT are you doing with him?

In this case, '. . . did you say?' could be supplied immediately after the
Q-element: *HÓW much did you say it cost?* These *wh-* echo questions, as
we see above, have a characteristic intonation pattern: a rising intonation with the nucleus on the Q-word itself.

In the examples above, the Q-element is fronted as in normal *wh-*
questions. But in a variant type of *wh-* echo question, the statement
order is retained:

A: We saw the Marianskis yesterday. B: You saw (the) WHÓ?

The order where no fronting takes place is obligatory for commands:

A: Switch the light off. B: Switch WHÁT off?

Although recapitulatory echo questions are ostensibly requests for the repetition of information, they frequently have other functions, such as to express incredulity, or merely to fill in a conversational gap. They are familiar, or even impolite, in implication unless accompanied by an apology: *Sorry,* WHÁT *was his job?*

Note

[a] The generalized recapitulatory *wh*-question WHÁT *did you say?* is sometimes truncated to the familiar or impolite monosyllable WHÁT?, just as the alternative formula *I beg your pardon?* can be reduced simply to *Pardon?* Other abbreviated requests for repetition are *Pardon me?* (AmE), *Excuse me?* (AmE), and *Sorry?* (BrE).

[b] *What?* on its own can also express general incredulity:

A: I paid £1000 for that picture. B: WHÁT? You must be mad.

7.82
Questions about questions

Since an echo question can refer back to any type of utterance, a special case of it is a question about a question, sometimes called 'a question raised to the second power':

A: Have you borrowed my PÉN? B: (Have I) borrowed your PÉN?

This is a *yes-no* question about a *yes-no* question; but in fact, in addition to this there are theoretically three further possible types, all of which do occur:

Yes-no QUESTION ABOUT *wh*-QUESTION:
A: What do you think of the picture?
B: What do I THÍNK of it?

Wh-QUESTION ABOUT *yes-no* QUESTION:
A: Have you ever been to Valladolid?
B: (Have I ever been) WHÉRE?

Wh-QUESTION ABOUT *wh*-QUESTION:
A: How did you enjoy the carnival?
B: How did I enjoy WHÁT?

7.83
Explicatory echo questions

The second main category of echo question is the explicatory echo question, which asks for the clarification, rather than the repetition, of something just said. It is always a *wh*-question, and is identical to the recapitulatory *wh*-question, except for the substitution of a falling tone for the rising tone on the Q-word:

A: Take a look at this!   B: Take a look at WHÀT?
A: He's missed the bus again.   B: WHÒ's missed the bus?
A: Oh dear, I've lost the letter.   B: WHÌCH letter have you lost?

The last example could be paraphrased 'Which letter do you *mean* (rather than 'did you say') you have lost?'. The Q-word replaces some item of definite meaning (*eg* a personal pronoun) whose reference is unclear in the context.

Note
There are abbreviated forms of these as of other *wh*- echo questions – A: *Look over there!* B: *WHÈRE?* The general explicatory echo question WHÀT may also be noted. Its meaning is roughly 'What do you want?' – A: *John!* B: *WHÀT?*

7.84
Echo exclamations
The echo exclamation, like the echo question, repeats part or all of a preceding utterance; but in contrast to the rising tone of the echo question, it is characterized by a rising-falling (or high falling) tone. The utterance to be repeated may be a statement, question, command or, for that matter, exclamation:

A: I'm **going** to London for a holiday.
  B: *To LÔNdon!* That's not my idea of a rest.
A: Have you been to Paris?
  B: *Been to PÂris!* I'll say I have!
A: Open the door, please.
  B: *Open the DÔor!* Do you take me for the doorman?
A: What a beautiful day!
  B: *What a beautiful DÂY!* You must be joking.

Such exclamations, expressing astonishment at what has been said, are very similar in role to the incredulous type of echo question. Indeed, the repetitions italicized above could be spoken either with an exclamatory falling nucleus, or with the rising tone of the echo question.

Either in the echo question or the echo exclamation, one could repeat the earlier utterance with varying degrees of completeness. Thus, rather than *To London!* in the first example, one could have said *You're going to London! Going to London!* or simply *London!* Some irregular subject-predicate constructions are produced in these exchanges:

A: I hear you're a linguist.
  B: *I/me a linguist!*

A: Ted's going to write the music.

B: Ted write the music? What a splendid idea!

Formulaic utterances, greetings, etc
7.85

After examining the four major classes of utterance, we are left with a residue of minor categories which, unavoidably, must be presented as something of a museum of oddments.

7.86

Formulae

Many of these remaining types are formulae in the sense that although they may have the appearance of belonging to one of the major classes, they enter into few of the relations of substitutability that are common to members of those classes. For instance, the greeting formula (appropriate to a first meeting) *How do you do?* cannot be subordinated as an indirect question (*They asked him how he did*) or answered in equivalent statement form (*I do very well*). Two slightly less restricted kinds of *wh*-question are the question without an auxiliary *why* (+*not*)+ predication:

Why get so upset?   Why not enjoy yourself?

and the *how/what about* type of question:

What about the house?   How about joining us?

These are not formulaic in the previous sense, but are irregular in that they lack some of the elements normally found in a *wh*-question.

There are also patterns which are defective in terms of regular clause or sentence structure, such as the verbless imperatives:

Off with the lid!   Out with it!   Down with him!

To this we may add a number of exclamatory types:

If only I'd listened to my parents!
To think I was once a millionaire!
Oh for a drink!   Oh to be free! (archaic except when jocular)
You and your statistics!
Now for some fun!

Apart from such cases, we must notice sentences which contain fossilized elements no longer productively used in present-day English. The old optative subjunctive survives, combined with inversion, in

Far be it from me to spoil the fun
Suffice it to say we lost
Long live anarchy! (archaic except when jocular)

and without inversion in

God save the Queen!   Bless you!

Equally, the greeting formula *How goes it?* (familiar) enshrines an isolated instance of the old subject-verb inversion without DO-periphrasis.

A slightly less archaic formula for expressing a wish is *may* + subject + predication: *May the best man win! May you be happy!*

Note
Certain archaic patterns, such as those marked, tend to survive only in jocular use.

7.87
Aphoristic sentences
Among other minor sentence types is the aphoristic sentence structure found in many proverbs:

The more, the merrier	[85]
Least said, soonest mended	[86]
Handsome is as handsome does	[87]
Easy come, easy go	[88]

These all have one structural feature in common: the balancing of two equivalent constructions against each other. Yet they must all be considered to some extent anomalous; thus in [87] *handsome* is used on two occasions as if it were a noun; in examples [85] and [86] there is no main verb. Example [85] may be taken as an ellipsis for something like *The more there are of us, the merrier we are,* a pattern which, although still on the aphoristic model, is at once more explicit and more productive than those of any of the quoted proverbs. This pattern will be dealt with under proportional clauses (11.42).

7.88
Greetings, etc
We turn now to greetings and other formulae used for stereotyped communicative situations. Most of these are either grammatically irregular, or grammatically defective, in the sense that only in a very limited way can they be grammatically analysed (*eg* they cannot be broken down into clause elements S, V, C, A). In the following list we give a few examples of the major types:

GREETINGS: Good morning/evening (formal); Hello; Hi (very familiar)

FAREWELLS: Goodbye; Cheerio (familiar, BrE); Cheers (very familiar); See you (very familiar); Bye(-bye) (very familiar); So long (very familiar)

INTRODUCTIONS: How do you do? How are you? Glad to meet you

REACTION SIGNALS:
   (a) *assent, agreement:* Yes; Yeah ([jɛ:]); All right; OK (familiar); Certainly; Absolutely; Right
   (b) *denial:* No; Certainly/definitely not; Not likely

THANKS: Thank you/thanks (very much); Many thanks; Ta (BrE slang)

TOASTS: Good health! (formal); Your health! (formal); Cheers! (familiar); Here's to you/your new job/the future

SEASONAL GREETINGS: Merry Christmas; Happy New Year; Happy birthday; Many happy returns (of your birthday)

SLOGANS: Down with/Up with the Scottish Nationalists; Nixon out; Nixon for ever

ALARM CALLS: Help! Fire!

WARNINGS: Mind; (Be) careful; Watch out/it; Look out!

APOLOGIES: (I'm) sorry; (I beg your) pardon

IMPRECATIONS (very familiar; graded in order from mild blasphemy to indecency): Blast (you/it)! Oh hell! Damn (you/it)! Go to hell! Bugger (it/off)! (BrE) Fuck (you/it/off)!

EXPLETIVES (very familiar; likewise in order of increasing strength): My! Gosh! (By) Golly! (Good) Heavens! (Good) God! Good Lord! Christ Almighty!

MISCELLANEOUS EXCLAMATIONS (familiar):
   Faster! Not so fast! Goal! Success! Good! Excellent!
   You lucky girl/boy; Well, well; Oh dear; (What a) pity!
   Shame! Poor John; Silly boy!

Note

Some imprecations are imperative in form, but they do not have the structural potentialities of commands. For instance, there are no negative forms *Don't blast you! *Don't bugger it, and no indefinite object such as *some students* is possible: *Blast some students!

7.89
Interjections

Interjections are purely emotive words which have no referential content. Some of them have phonological features which lie outside the regular system of the language. *Whew,* for instance, contains a bilabial fricative ([ɸiu], [ɸ:]); *tut-tut* consists of a series of alveolar clicks, [ʇ]. Other indications of pronunciation are supplied below as necessary.

Oh (surprise); *Ah* (satisfaction, recognition, etc); *Oho* (jubilant surprise); *Wow* (great surprise); *Yippee* (excitement, delight); *Aha* (jubilant satisfaction, recognition); *Ouch* [autʃ], *Ow* [au] (pain); *Ugh* [ʌx] (disgust); *Ooh* (pleasure, pain); *tut-tut* (mild regret, disapproval); *Alas* (archaic: sorrow); *Uh-huh* ('Yes'); *Mm* (Casual 'Yes'); *Hey* (call for attention); *Eh?* [ei] (impolite request for repetition)

Note

Interjections are sometimes used to initiate utterances: *Oh, what a nuisance; Ah, that's perfect*, etc.

7.90
Block language

We have considered in 7.86–89 many utterances which do not permit or require analysis into elements of clause structure. Apart from formulae of colloquial conversation, however, there is a whole realm of usage where, because of its rudimentary communicative role, language is structured in terms of single words and phrases, rather than in terms of the more highly organized units of the clause.

Language so used may be termed block language. It appears in such functions as labels, titles, headings, notices, and advertisements. Simple block-language messages most often consist of a noun or noun phrase or nominal clause in isolation: no verb is needed, because all else necessary to the understanding of the message is furnished by context. Examples are:

ENTRANCE	ENGLISH DEPARTMENT	DANGER: FALLING ROCKS
PURE LEMON JUICE	FRESH TODAY	HIGHLY RECOMMENDED
A GRAMMAR OF CONTEMPORARY ENGLISH		WHERE TO GO IN LONDON
HOW TO WIN FRIENDS AND INFLUENCE PEOPLE	THE FIRST LUXURY BOUND COLLECTOR'S EDITION OF AGATHA CHRISTIE'S WORK TO BE AVAILABLE IN THIS COUNTRY	

On a slightly higher communicative level, block language (especially in newspaper headlines) develops its own abbreviated clause structures:

(1) FILM-STAR MARRIES EX-PRIEST (S V O_d)
(2) ELECTION A LANDSLIDE FOR SOCIALISTS (S C_s)

(3) NIXON TO MEET ASIAN PREMIERS (S V O$_d$)
(4) SHARE PRICES NOW HIGHER THAN EVER (S A C$_s$)
(5) JACKLIN BEATEN BY BONALLACK (S V A)
(6) CHANCES OF MIDDLE-EAST PEACE IMPROVING (S V)

These differ from orthodox clause structures in omitting closed-category words of low information value, such as the articles and the finite forms of the verb BE. (For instance, in ordinary discursive English, (2) would read *The election is a landslide for the Socialists*.) Obviously, the purpose of the omissions is to reduce the length of the message to the smallest number of words compatible with comprehensibility.

Note
Prohibitions on notice boards often assume the special block-language form of a noun phrase introduced by *No: No smoking; No entry; No unauthorized entry after dark*.

Bibliographical note
The grammar of the simple sentence has been one of the chief concerns of modern grammatical studies. Outlines from the viewpoint of transformational grammar appear, for example, in Chomsky (1965), especially Chapter 2; Jacobs and Rosenbaum (1968), especially Chapters 6 and 10; Langendoen (1970).

Recent contributions on specific topics include:

[A] CLAUSE PATTERNS
Bach (1967); Gleason (1965), especially Chapter 13; Halliday (1967-68).
[B] CLAUSE ELEMENTS SEMANTICALLY CONSIDERED
Anderson (1968); Fillmore (1968) and (1969); Halliday (1967-68); Lyons (1968), especially Chapter 8; Nickel (1968) and Olsson (1961) with reference to what is here termed 'effected object' (7.19 *f*).
[C] NEGATION
Jackendoff (1969); Jespersen (1917); Klima (1964).
[D] QUESTIONS
Bolinger (1957); Katz (1968); Malone (1967). On the intonation of questions see Kingdon (1958), §§103 *ff*.
[E] COMMANDS
Bolinger (1967a); Thorne (1969).
[F] BLOCK LANGUAGE (7.90)
Leech (1963); Straumann (1935).

Introduction

8.1
Units realizing adverbial functions

This chapter is concerned with the adverbial, an element in clause structure (2.3, 2.7–8, 7.1, 7.12). Adverbial functions are realized by:

(1) Adverbs (including adverb phrases, *ie* phrases with adverbs as
their heads):

> Peter was playing *as WELL as he could*
> They *very OFTEN* praised Tom
> We'll stay *THERE*

(2) Noun phrases (less common):

> Peter was playing *LAST WEEK*
> They praised Tom *MANY TIMES*
> We'll stay *NEXT DOOR*

(3) Prepositional phrases:

> Peter was playing *WITH GREAT SKILL*
> They praised Tom *FOR HIS GENEROSITY*
> We'll stay *AT A HOTEL*

(4) Finite verb clauses:

> Peter was playing *ALTHOUGH HE WAS VERY TIRED*
> *WHEN THEY SAW THE REPORT*, they praised Tom
> We'll stay *WHERE IT IS CONVENIENT*

(5) Non-finite verb clauses, in which the verb is

    (a) infinitive:
> Peter was playing *TO WIN*

    (b) *-ing* participle:
> *MAKING A LOT OF NOISE* they praised Tom

    (c) *-ed* participle:
> *IF URGED BY OUR FRIENDS*, we'll stay

(6) Verbless clauses:

> Peter was playing, *UNAWARE THAT HIS WIFE WAS IN THE*
> *AUDIENCE*
> *GRATEFUL FOR HIS HELP*, they praised Tom
> *WHILE IN LONDON*, we'll stay at a hotel

Although it is true that some adverbial functions can be realized by
the whole range of structures, others are chiefly realized by only certain
structures. For example, connection between clauses is usually effected

by adverbs and prepositional phrases. Prepositional phrases are handled in Chapter 6 and clauses in Chapter 11, while in this chapter we concentrate on adverbial functions realized by adverbs.

Note

For adverbs realizing functions other than those of adverbial, see 5.45, 5.51 *ff*.

8.2
Classes of adverbials

Adverbials can be divided into two classes, distinguished by whether or not they are integrated to some extent into the structure of the clause. Those that are *integrated* to some extent are termed ADJUNCTS. Those that are *peripheral* to clause structure are subdivided into DISJUNCTS or CONJUNCTS, the distinction between these two being that conjuncts have primarily a connective function. *Fig* 8:1 summarizes the distinctions we have just made.

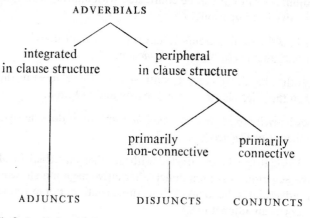

Fig 8:1   Adverbials

8.3
Criteria for adjuncts

An adverbial is integrated to some extent in clause structure if it is affected by clausal processes. Three criteria have been selected as diagnostic for adjuncts, that is as evidence that an adverbial is affected by clausal processes and is therefore an adjunct. If an adverbial satisfies *one or more* of the criteria it is an adjunct.

(1) If an adverbial cannot appear initially in a negative declarative clause, it is an adjunct. For example, although *quickly* can appear initially in a positive clause, as in

    Quickly they left for home

it cannot do so if the clause is negative (with the negative particle *not* or *-n't*):

>*Quickly they didn't leave for home

Hence, *quickly* is an adjunct. On the other hand, *perhaps* is unaffected by whether the clause is positive or negative:

>*Perhaps* they left for home
>*Perhaps* they didn't leave for home

(2) If an adverbial can be contrasted with another adverbial in alternative interrogation, it is an adjunct, alternative interrogation showing that the adverbial is the focus of clause interrogation. For example, the adverbial clause in

>He writes to his parents *because he wants to*

is an adjunct because it can be contrasted with another adverbial in alternative interrogation:

>Does he write to his parents *because he wants to* or does he write to them *because he needs money?*

On the other hand, we cannot contrast two *since*-clauses in this way when the *since*-clauses express reason and not time:

>*Does he write to his parents *since he wants to* or does he write to them *since he needs money?*

(3) If an adverbial can be contrasted with another adverbial in alternative negation, it is an adjunct, alternative negation showing that the adverbial is the focus of the clause negation. For example, *on Monday* is an adjunct in

>We went to Chicago *on Monday*

because it can be contrasted with another adverbial in alternative negation:

>We didn't go to Chicago *on Monday*, but we did go there *on Tuesday*

On the other hand, we cannot contrast the two prepositional phrases in

>*We didn't go to Chicago, *to John's amazement*, but we did go there, *to Mary's amazement*.

Note

[a] Criterion 1 does not apply to an adverbial clause that is sequentially fixed in rela-

tion to the superordinate clause (9.31) and therefore cannot appear initially even in a positive clause. For example a clause introduced by resultative *so that*

He spent very little, *so that he had plenty of money*

cannot be transposed to initial position:

**So that he had plenty of money*, he spent very little

The immobility of the *so that* clause is not an indication of its integration in the superordinate clause (as would be the immobility of an adverb). *So that* clauses are usually separated intonationally from the preceding clause.

[b] Criterion 1 should in fact be amplified. If the adverbial cannot appear before a negative clause *in an independent tone unit with a falling-rising nucleus*, it is an adjunct. For example, the adjunct *again* ('another time') can appear initially before a negative clause, but it would usually carry a falling nucleus and it would usually not be in an independent tone unit:

A|GÀIN he didn't say anything|

On the other hand, the conjunct *again* ('I tell you again') usually appears in this position in an independent tone unit with falling-rising nucleus:

A|GǍIN| he|didn't say ÀNything|

The conjunct *again* is separated by comma punctuation when it occurs initially (App III.10).

[c] Criterion 1 does not apply to negative clauses with subject-operator inversion. In such cases an initial negative adjunct such as *never* (*cf* 8.66) itself affects a clausal process and hence demonstrates a measure of integration in clause structure.

8.4
Criteria for disjuncts and conjuncts

Disjuncts and conjuncts satisfy none of the above three criteria. That is to say, the following three statements can be made for both disjuncts and conjuncts:

(1) They can appear initially before a negative clause. Disjunct clauses that are sequentially fixed in relation to superordinate clauses (9.31) are an exception: they cannot, of course, appear initially before even a positive clause.

(2) They cannot be contrasted with another adverbial in alternative interrogation.

(3) They cannot be contrasted with another adverbial in alternative negation.

8.5
Distinction between disjuncts and conjuncts

Conjuncts are distinguished from disjuncts because they have primarily a connective function. As an index of their connective function, conjuncts cannot serve as a response to a question, whether a *wh*-question or a *yes–no* question, even when they are accompanied by *yes* or *no*. On the other hand, disjuncts can serve as response to a *yes–no* question, though usually they require to be accompanied by *yes* or *no*. For example, *probably* in

He will *probably* be there tomorrow

is a disjunct, since it can be a response:

A: Will he be there?   B: Yes, *probably*.

In contrast, *therefore* in

I sent him a personal invitation. He will *therefore* be there tomorrow.

is a conjunct. We cannot use *therefore* in a response:

A: Will he be there tomorrow?   B: *Yes, *therefore*.

8.6
Syntactic homonyms

It is important to realize that items can belong to more than one class and even to more than one subclass within a class. For example, *like his brother* is a postmodifying phrase (13.25) in

I once met a man *like his brother* ('Who resembles')

an adjunct in

He writes *like his brother* ('He writes in the same way as his brother')

and a disjunct in

He is an author, *like his brother* ('He is like his brother in that he is an author')

It is particularly obvious that many adverbs are syntactic homonyms, that is to say they belong to more than one class or subclass. If we say that an adverb is a disjunct of a certain subclass, we are referring to the adverb in a particular function and ignoring its homonyms. For example, *naturally* is a disjunct in

Naturally, they are behaving ('of course')

and an adjunct in

They are behaving *naturally* ('in a natural manner')

Similarly, *yet* is a conjunct in

I've been waiting outside his door the whole day. *Yet* I haven't seen him. ('nevertheless')   [1]

and an adjunct in

I've been waiting outside his door the whole day. I haven't seen him *yet*. ('so far')   [2]

We know that the two instances of *naturally* and the two instances of *yet* are different because, in the first place, we understand differently the sentences within each set of sentences.

We can also demonstrate that they are syntactically different and are therefore to be regarded as homonyms. Thus *yet* ('so far') in [2] is a non-assertive form (7.44 ff, 7.57) and therefore cannot appear in a declarative positive clause:

*I have seen him *yet*   [2a]

On the other hand, it can be moved to another position:

I haven't *yet* seen him   [2b]

though not to a position before the negative particle:

*I have *yet* not seen him   [2c]

In contrast, *yet* ('nevertheless') in [1] appears before the negative particle. Moreover, the sentence can be made positive:

Yet I have seen him   [1a]

However, it is immobile in initial position and cannot be transposed:

*I *yet* have seen him   [1b]
*I have seen him *yet*   [1c]

Our discussion of the two instances of *yet* demonstrates that we *identify* an item as a conjunct, disjunct or adjunct (or member of a subclass of these) both by the syntactic features present in its environment and also by the features that are potential to it. And these potential features may be either positive (its ability to accept these features) or negative (its inability to accept these features). When we *characterize* an item in isolation as a member of a particular class or subclass, we do so on the basis of its potential syntactic features.

Note

When the term *homonym* is used in this chapter, it is used in the sense of syntactic homonym. Our examples show homonymy between an adjunct and a conjunct or disjunct. There appear to be no instances of homonymy between a conjunct and a disjunct.

8.7
Definitions of positional terms

We distinguish four positions of adverbials, in particular for the declarative form of the clause:

> *I* – initial position (*ie* before the subject)
>
> *M1* – medial position *1*: (a) immediately before the operator, or (b) between two auxiliaries
>
> *M2* – medial position *2*: (a) immediately before the verb, or (b) before the complement in intensive BE clauses
>
> *E* – end position: (a) after an intransitive verb (b) after an object or complement

Clauses and most prepositional phrases normally occur in *E*, though *I* is not uncommon. *M* positions are rare for clauses and most prepositional phrases, and when they appear in those positions they are regarded as parenthetic. Mobility (the ability to appear in a range of optional positions) is highest for adverbs and short prepositional phrases (in certain functions), and *M1* tends to be restricted to these.

If there are no auxiliaries present, *M1* and *M2* are neutralized:

> They sometimes watch television

If the subject is ellipted, *I* and *M1* (or both *M*) positions are neutralized:

> I've been waiting outside his door the whole day and *yet* haven't seen him
>
> They are bored with television and *yet* watch it

E includes any position between clause elements after the stated elements, *eg:*

> I paid *immediately* for the book
>
> I paid for the book *immediately*.

Adjuncts
Syntactic features of adjuncts
8.8

Certain syntactic features are general to adjuncts. Exceptions to these features are noted when subclasses of adjuncts are treated.

(1) Adjuncts can come within the scope of clause interrogation and can be the focus of the question. Because of their ability to be the focus of the question, they can be contrasted with one another in alternative interrogation:

> Did you see him *yesterday* or did you see him *today?*

Alternative interrogation is diagnostic criterion (2) for the class of adjuncts (8.3).

(2) Adjuncts can come within the scope of clause negation and can be the focus of the negation (7.49, 7.51). Because of their ability to be the focus of clause negation, they can be contrasted with another item in alternative negation:

> They didn't treat him *politely*, but they did treat him *fairly*

Alternative negation is diagnostic criterion (3) for the class of adjuncts (8.3).

(3) Adjuncts can come within the scope of predication pro-forms or predication ellipsis (10.52 *ff*). For example, in

> John *greatly* admires Bob, and *so does* Mary

the pro-form in the second clause includes the adjunct of the first clause, the sentence being synonymous with

> John *greatly* admires Bob, and Mary *greatly* admires Bob.

Similarly, these two sentences are synonymous:

> Peter will pay back the loan *when he gets his salary at the end of the month*, but George *won't*.
>
> Peter will pay back the loan *when he gets his salary at the end of the month*, but George won't pay back the loan *when he gets his salary at the end of the month*.

(4) Adjuncts can be the focus of restrictive adverbials such as *only* (8.13 *ff*):

> They only want the car *for an* HÒUR

Only will normally be interpreted as referring specifically to *for an hour*. That is to say, the sentence is interpreted as meaning that they want the car for an hour and not for longer. If *only* and the focused adjunct are positioned initially, subject-operator inversion usually takes place:

> Only *afterwards* did he explain why he did it

(5) Adjuncts can be the focus of additive adverbials such as *also* (8.13 *ff*):

> They will also meet ÀF*terwards*

Also will normally be interpreted as referring specifically to *afterwards*, the sentence implying that they will meet afterwards in addition to some other time previously mentioned or implied.

(6) Adjuncts can be the focus of a cleft sentence (14.18):

> It was *when we were in Paris* that I first saw John

(7) Adjuncts can occur in all types of dependent clauses (*cf* Chapter 11):

> He wanted them *to pay IN LONDON*
> They started *shooting RAPIDLY*
> *Interpreted STRICTLY*, the regulation could not be enforced
> He warned his customers that the clothes were import rejects
>   *to avoid any complaints AFTER THEY HAD TAKEN THEIR*
>   *PURCHASES HOME.*

8.9
Adverbs as adjuncts

Certain additional features apply mostly to adjuncts realized by adverbs:

(8) Adverb adjuncts can be the focus of clause comparison:

> John writes more *clearly* than his brother does
> Mary held the baby as *expertly* as her mother did

(9) Adverb adjuncts can be premodified by *however* to form the opening of a dependent adverbial clause:

> However *strongly* you feel about it, you should be careful what you say

(10) Adverb adjuncts can be premodified by *How*, a pro-form for degree intensifiers, when it introduces a question or exclamation:

> How *often* does he drink beer?
> How *cautiously* he drives!

(11) Adverb adjuncts can be premodified by *so* followed by subject-operator inversion and a correlative clause:

> So *monotonously* did he speak that everyone left.

8.10
Subclassification of adjuncts

It is convenient to discuss adjuncts under classes that are essentially semantic. The disadvantage in doing so is obvious: we may obscure the syntactic similarities between adjuncts that differ semantically. However, the semantic classes have a mnemonical value and most of the terms applied to them are either in current use or are self-explanatory. *Fig* 8:2 gives the classes and their subclasses. They will be discussed in the order shown in the figure.

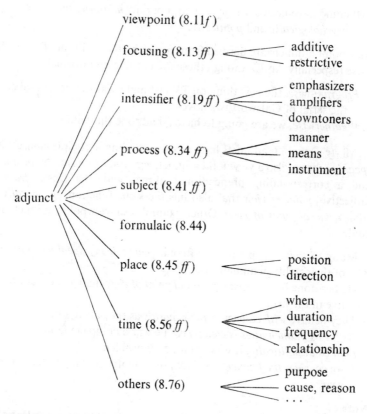

Fig 8:2 Adjuncts

Viewpoint adjuncts
8.11
Viewpoint adjuncts can be roughly paraphrased by 'if we consider what we are saying from a [adjective] point of view' or 'if we consider what we are saying from the point of view of [noun phrase]'.

Adverbs realizing viewpoint adjuncts are most commonly derived from adjectives by the addition of an *-ly* suffix. Examples are:

Visually, it was a powerful play.
Morally, politically, and economically, it is urgent that the government should act more effectively on aid to developing countries.
Geographically, ethnically, and linguistically, these islands are closer to the mainland than to their neighbouring islands.
To tap a private telephone line is not *technically* a very difficult operation.

It could have been a serious defeat, not only *militarily* but *psychologically* and *politically*.

Viewpoint adjuncts are derived from nouns by the addition of the suffix -*wise* (especially AmE), though these are considered informal:

Program-wise, the new thing on TV last night was the first number of the serial of Galsworthy's novel.
Weatherwise, we are going to have a bad time this winter.

All -*ly* viewpoint adjuncts have a corresponding participle clause with *speaking* that is also a viewpoint adjunct, *eg: visually ~ visually speaking*, and a corresponding prepositional phrase with the frame *from a* [adjective] *point of view* that also has the same function, *eg: morally ~ from a moral point of view*. Other examples of viewpoint adjuncts include

Many of these people have suffered, *economically speaking*, because of their political affiliations.
He has done better *from a personal point of view* than any other executive in the firm.
They behave *with respect to their morals* as they always have done.
As far as mathematics is concerned, he was a complete failure.
Looked at politically, it was not an easy problem.
If we consider the financial position, the country is going to have a bad year.

Note

[a] The corresponding clause with *speaking* resembles one of the correspondences for style disjuncts (8.80 *f*). However, the other correspondences for style disjuncts do not constitute correspondences for viewpoint adjuncts. For example, *to speak morally* does not correspond to the viewpoint adjuncts *morally* and *morally speaking*.

[b] Most viewpoint adjuncts in -*wise* are now written without hyphens.

8.12

Viewpoint adjuncts, whatever their structure, favour *I* position (*cf* 8.7). They allow the features general to adjuncts (8.8), except that adverbs functioning as viewpoint adjuncts cannot be modified:

Morally, they have won a victory
**Very morally*, they have won a victory

Hence they do not accept clause comparison or the modification possible for many other adverb adjuncts (8.9).

Focusing adjuncts
8.13

Focusing adjuncts make explicit either that what is being communicated is restricted to a part that is focused, in which case they are called RE-STRICTIVE ADJUNCTS, or that a focused part is an addition, in which case they are called ADDITIVE ADJUNCTS.

Focusing adjuncts constitute a fairly limited set of items, mostly adverbs, but also some prepositional phrases. Common items are listed below. Restrictive adjuncts are subdivided into EXCLUSIVES and PARTICULARIZERS.

RESTRICTIVES

(a) EXCLUSIVES restrict the application of the communication exclusively to the part focused:

> *alone, exactly, exclusively, just, merely, only, precisely, purely, simply, solely*

(b) PARTICULARIZERS restrict the application of the communication particularly or mainly to the part focused:

> *chiefly, especially, largely, mainly, mostly, notably, particularly, primarily, principally, specifically; at least, in particular*

ADDITIVES

> *again, also, either, equally, even, further, likewise, neither, nor, similarly, too; as well, in addition*

Examples of the use of focusing adjuncts with an indication of the part that is focused:

> You can get a B grade *JUST for that answer*
> *ONLY the extremely wealthy customers* could afford to buy those
> I *am SIMPLY asking the time*
> We judge them *PURELY on the final examination*
> *AT LEAST ten workers* reported sick yesterday
> *ESPECIALLY the girls* objected to his manners
> The workers, *IN PARTICULAR*, are dissatisfied with the government
> We bought *some beer AS WELL*
> John, *LIKEWISE*, has refused to become a member
> *EVEN Bob* was there

We have not analysed focusing adjuncts as part of the noun phrase in sentences such as

ONLY the extremely wealthy customers could afford to buy those
ESPECIALLY the girls objected to his manners

There is strong justification for not doing so:

(1) Focusing adjuncts can focus on pronouns and proper names which otherwise do not accept restrictive modification (*cf* 13.3):

$$ONLY \begin{Bmatrix} John \\ they \end{Bmatrix} \text{could afford} \ldots$$

(2) Focusing adjuncts can focus on a noun phrase to which they are not juxtaposed (8.14*f*):

I don't want any beer. I *ONLY* want *some water*.

(3) Even with the subject of the clause, when the focusing adjunct is juxtaposed to the noun phrase, most focusing adjuncts can either precede or follow the noun phrase (8.16), though the latter position tends to be restricted for most adjuncts to spoken English:

ONLY the extremely wealthy customers could afford to buy those.
The extremely wealthy customers ONLY could afford to buy those.

(4) The focusing process seems to be the same whether the focus is on a noun phrase or on some other unit, as can be seen from the examples of sentences with focusing adjuncts given above in this section as well as from those that will be given in the immediately following sections. Focusing from a distance applies also to units other than noun phrases:

Hurry up with the water. I *PARTICULARLY* want some *now*.

Note

The clausal negative particle *not* could be regarded as a negative restrictive adjunct, excluding the part of the clause that is focused. For clausal negation, see 7.41–52.

Position and focus
8.14

In spoken English, most focusing adjuncts when positioned between the subject and predicate can usually focus on more than one part of the sentence, the part focused being intonationally marked.

For example, the focus of the restrictive adjunct *only* in

John *only* phoned Mary today   [3]

varies with the intonation we give the sentence:

|John ŏNly||phoned MÀry today| [3a]
  = Nobody but John phoned Mary today

|John only PHÒNEd Mary today| [3b]
  = John did nothing else with respect to Mary but phone her
|John only phoned MÀry today| [3c]
  = John phoned Mary today but nobody else
|John only phoned Mary toDÀY| [3d]
  = John phoned Mary today but not at any other time

Similarly, the focus of the additive adjunct *also* in

John *also* phoned Mary today   [4]

varies with the intonation we give the sentence:

|John ÀLSO phoned Mary today| [4a]
  = John as well as somebody else phoned Mary today
|John also PHÒNEd Mary today| [4b]
  = John phoned Mary today in addition to something else he did
    with respect to Mary today
|John also phoned MÀry today| [4c]
  = John phoned Mary as well as somebody else today
|John also phoned Mary toDÀY| [4d]
  = John phoned Mary today as well as at some other time(s)

8.15

Formal written English is influenced by the traditional teaching that urges the placing of restrictive and additive adjuncts in positions that will avoid ambiguity. The positions of *only* in written sentences such as [3a′] convey unambiguously the interpretations of the corresponding spoken forms in 8.14 such as [3a]:

ONLY John phoned Mary today   [3a′]
  = Nobody but John phoned Mary today
John phoned *ONLY Mary* today   [3c′]
  = John phoned Mary today but nobody else
John phoned Mary $\begin{cases} ONLY\ today \\ today\ ONLY \end{cases}$ [3d′]
  = John phoned Mary today but not at any other time

And similarly for *also:*

John, ALSO, phoned Mary today   [4a′]
  = John as well as somebody else phoned Mary today
John phoned *ALSO Mary* today   [4c′]
  = John phoned Mary as well as somebody else today

$$\text{John phoned Mary}\begin{cases} \textit{ALSO today} \\ \textit{today ALSO} \end{cases}\qquad\qquad [4d']$$

= John phoned Mary today as well as at some other time(s)

Provided the nucleus is on the focused part, these positions carry the same interpretation in spoken English.

In the written form, the position between the subject and lexical verb results in a triple ambiguity for the sentences:

John *only* phoned Mary today   [3']
John *also* phoned Mary today   [4']

The adjunct can focus on any of the three elements that follow it. Hence, [3'] can be synonymous with any of the spoken forms [3b], [3c], and [3d], and similarly [4'] can be synonymous with any of the spoken forms [4b], [4c], and [4d]. Moreover, since commas are sometimes omitted from [4a'], [4'] can also be synonymous with [4a']. However, in practice the context usually makes it clear which interpretation is required. In written English, especially in informal varieties, focusing adjuncts are commonly positioned before the verb when they focus on some part of the predicate other than the verb. But ambiguity in written English can be avoided if they are placed immediately before the element in the predicate on which they focus. If that element is at the very end of the predicate then they can be positioned finally. If the focused element is the subject, then an unambiguous written form will depend on the focusing adjunct. Some, like *only*, can precede the subject, and that position is unambiguous. Others, like *also*, must normally follow the subject. If these adjuncts are separated by commas, as in [4a'],they unambiguously focus on the subject.

Note

[a] The focus can be on part of the clause element, *eg* on the adjective *orange* rather than on the whole noun phrase *orange juice* in

I don't like most fruit juices. I *ONLY* like *orange* juice

In speech, *orange* would usually receive extra prosodic prominence.

[b] When the focus is on time *when* adjuncts like *today*, [3] can be taken in two senses with certain restrictives like *only*: (i) John phoned Mary today and at no other time; (ii) John phoned Mary as recently as today.

8.16
Positions of restrictive adjuncts (*cf* 8.7)

Most restrictive adjuncts can either precede or follow the part on which they are focused, though it is more usual for them to precede. *Just*, *merely*, *purely*, and *simply* normally must precede, and hence final position in the clause is unacceptable or dubious for them:

You can get a B grade *for that answer* $\left\{\begin{array}{l} *JUST \\ *MERELY \\ ?*PURELY \\ *SIMPLY \end{array}\right.$

They all would have to be preposed:

You can get a B grade $\left\{\begin{array}{l} JUST \\ MERELY \\ PURELY \\ SIMPLY \end{array}\right\}$ *for that answer*

On the other hand, *alone* normally must follow the part on which it is focused:

You can get a B grade *for that answer ALONE*

and hence *alone* as a restrictive adjunct normally does not occur in *I* position:

ALONE ten workers reported sick yesterday

though the virtually synonymous *only* can take either position:

$\left\{\begin{array}{l} ONLY \text{ ten workers} \\ Ten \text{ workers } ONLY \end{array}\right\}$ reported sick yesterday.

Note

[a] *In particular* favours a position after the focused part.

[b] *Exactly* commonly focuses on *wh*-interrogatives, and *precisely* does so too, but less commonly:

    EXACTLY who is asking for me?
    What EXACTLY do you mean?
    I know *EXACTLY where* to find him.

Otherwise, *exactly* does not precede the subject unless it premodifies a noun phrase with a quantifier, fraction, multiplier, or cardinal numeral:

    EXACTLY ten people were present.

Just also focuses on *wh*-interrogatives, but can only precede them:

    JUST why do you want it?

Just can also focus on *exactly* and *precisely*:

    JUST exactly what do you expect?

or on a *wh*-word also focused by *exactly* or *precisely*:

    JUST who EXACTLY are you?
    JUST where PRECISELY do you want to go?

[c] The restrictive adjunct *only* is to be distinguished from the concessive conjunct *only* (8.89, 8.90).

[d] The restrictives *just, merely, simply* can freely appear in front of imperative sentences:

You don't have to be present. $\left\{\begin{array}{l} Just \\ Merely \\ Simply \end{array}\right\}$ send a letter of explanation.

Nor and *neither* can too, when they are used correlatively:

Neither speak to them *nor* write to them.

8.17
Positions of additive adjuncts (*cf* 8.7)

The following additive adjuncts normally precede a focused part in the predicate but follow a focused subject:

again, also, equally, similarly, in addition

On the other hand, *too* and *as well* normally follow a focused part, wherever in the clause it may be, while *even* normally precedes:

I know your family has expressed its support. We $\begin{Bmatrix} TOO \\ AS\ WELL \end{Bmatrix}$ will do what we can for you.

Yesterday the Robinsons were here with their new baby. They brought their other children $\begin{cases} TOO. \\ AS\ WELL. \end{cases}$

The whole town came out to welcome him home. *EVEN his animals* seemed happy to see him again.

My father won't give me the money. He won't *EVEN lend* it to me.

Neither and *nor* are restricted to *I* position and *either* to *E* position, on whichever part they may be focusing:

His father wouldn't give him any money, and $\begin{Bmatrix} NEITHER \\ NOR \end{Bmatrix}$ would he *lend* him any.

His father wouldn't give him any money, and he wouldn't *lend* him any *EITHER*.

Further seems to be restricted to focusing on the predicate or part of it, and normally precedes:

He argued that men were best for the job. He *FURTHER* argued that *some women would be physically harmed by the work*.

Compare the use of *again* for focusing on the subject (and *cf: also*, 8.14 *f*):

We can argue that the social sciences should be given priority. *THIS, again*, follows from what I said before.

Note
[a] For further examples of additive adjuncts, see 10.22; they should be distinguished from additive conjuncts (8.89).
[b] *Even* is both additive and concessive (*cf* 10.37).
[c] *Neither* and *nor* require subject-operator inversion. See 10.22 and 9.55–56.
[d] There is an additive adjunct *besides*, which is not often used (*cf* 10.22).

8.18

Syntactic features of focusing adjuncts

Focusing adjuncts differ syntactically in several respects from adjuncts in general. The differences are briefly stated, with a number in parenthesis denoting the numbered feature in 8.8 and 8.9. Focusing adjuncts normally cannot be the focus of other focusing adjuncts (4, 5). They cannot be the focus of a cleft sentence (6) or of clause comparison (8), nor can they be premodified by *however, how,* or *so* (9–11). While some focusing adjuncts can come within the scope of both interrogation and negation and be the focus of both the question and negation, it usually does not seem possible to frame alternative interrogation or negation with focusing adjuncts (1, 2).

Other syntactic features applying to focusing adjuncts:

(1) They cannot be modified: *very only, *extremely also

(2) Most of them cannot be coordinated: *just and exactly, *equally and likewise. But we have one cliché coordination:

> He is making the suggestion PURELY AND SIMPLY for your benefit

Focusing adjuncts are the focus of the question in

> Did she see him óNly once?
> Will they release *the major as WÉLL?*

and of negation in

> They won't punish MÈREly John
> They won't release *the major as WÈLL*

But most additive adjuncts cannot be the focus of negation. Indeed, *too* cannot even be within the scope of negation while *neither* and *nor* themselves effect the negation (*cf* 10.22).

Examples of alternative interrogation with restrictive adjuncts:

> Did she see him *only once* or did she see him *more than once?*
> Did she invite *merely girls* or did she invite *also boys?*

Alternative interrogation does not seem plausible with most additive adjuncts, and alternative negation seems implausible with both types of focusing adjuncts.

Certain restrictives can be the focus of an initial *not* with consequent subject-operator inversion. Besides the normal

> He *not only* protested: he (also) refused to pay his taxes

we can also have

> *Not only* did he protest: he (also) refused to pay his taxes

Restrictives allowing this subject-operator inversion are

just, merely, only, simply

of which *only* and *merely* do so most commonly. The construction implies a correlative clause, with (*but*) *also* as common correlatives for the second clause. *Not only* can appear initially in this construction without subject-operator inversion, with focus on the subject:

NOT ONLY he protested: . . .

Not even can also occur initially, but without subject-operator inversion:

NOT EVEN John protested.

Focusing adjuncts can appear within the focal clause of a cleft sentence to focus an item:

It was $\begin{cases} only \\ particularly \\ also \\ even \end{cases}$ John who protested.

We should distinguish the cleft sentence from a correlative structure which it resembles but from which it differs prosodically:

It was *not* that John protested; it was *merely* that he was rude.

In the above sentences the adjuncts are functioning within the superordinate clause to which the *that*-clause is complement. Restrictives, additives and some disjuncts (*eg: possibly, probably*) commonly occur in this correlative structure. Other examples:

It's *partly* that she's good-looking, it's *partly* that she's clever.
It's *not* that they object to him; it's *more probably* that they have no
    interest in him.
It's *not just* that he's young; it's *surely* that he's inexperienced.

Note
Exactly and *precisely* are used as comment utterances on a previous declarative sentence:

A: He has no business to be there.

B: $\begin{cases} Exactly. \\ Precisely. \end{cases}$

But these seem to be related to some implied sentence, such as 'That is *exactly* (*precisely*) what I feel'. *Quite* ('I quite agree') is used in the same way in BrE. In AmE *right* is used to express agreement, and is more common than *exactly* or *precisely*.

Intensifiers
8.19
Intensifiers have in common a heightening or lowering effect on some unit in the sentence. In this chapter we are concerned with their effect

on the force of the predicate in part or in whole, and particularly on the force of the verb. The intensifiers can be divided into three semantic classes:

(1) emphasizers
(2) amplifiers
(3) downtoners

It must be noted that *intensifiers* are not limited to indicating an 'intensification'; they indicate a point on the intensity scale which may be high or low. Emphasizers have a general heightening effect; amplifiers scale upwards from an assumed norm; downtoners have a lowering effect, usually scaling downwards from an assumed norm. Scaling is possible only when the verb is gradable. The three classes are shown with their subclasses in *Fig* 8:3. The classification is merely a rough

INTENSIFIERS
— EMPHASIZERS (*eg: definitely*)

AMPLIFIERS [maximizers (*eg: completely*)
boosters (*eg: very much*)]

DOWNTONERS [compromisers (*eg: kind of*)
diminishers (*eg: partly*)
minimizers (*eg: hardly*)
approximators (*eg: almost*)]

Fig 8:3 Classification of intensifiers

guide to semantic distinctions. This is because (a) the varying effects of intensifiers represent a semantic gradient, which is obscured by a clear-cut division into classes; (b) some intensifiers are sometimes used for different effects; and (c) speakers vary in their use of intensifiers.

Most of the common intensifiers are adverbs, but there are also some noun phrases and a few prepositional phrases.

Note
[a] For intensifying adjectives, see 5.31. For modifying adverbs as intensifiers, see 5.51 *f*, 5.54–58.
[b] For gradability with reference to adjectives and adverbs, see 5.39, 5.70*f*.

Emphasizers
8.20
Common emphasizers include:

[A] *actually, certainly, clearly, definitely, indeed, obviously, plainly, really, surely; for certain, for sure, of course*
[B] *frankly, honestly, literally, simply; fairly* (BrE), *just*

Group A consists mainly of items that can also function as attitudinal disjuncts expressing the comment that what is being said is true (8.82). Group B consists mainly of items that can also function as style disjuncts conveying the speaker's assertion that he is speaking the unvarnished truth (8.80 *f*). Since it is normally expected that a person intends his hearer to accept what he says as true, the addition of the comment or assertion emphasizes the truth of the communication. When these emphasizers are positioned next to a part of the communication, without being separated intonationally or by punctuation, their effect is often to emphasize that part alone, though there may be ambivalence as to whether the emphasis is on the part or on the whole.

Examples of the use of emphasizers:

> She *plainly* likes the dress
> I *honestly* don't know what he wants
> I can't *really* believe him
> He *actually* sat next to her
> I *just* can't understand it
> They will *surely* object to his intervention
> They *literally* tore his arguments to pieces
> They *obviously* don't want it
> He *fairly* jumped for joy (BrE)
> I *simply* don't believe it
> They will warn us *for sure*.

Note

In Group A, *for certain* and *for sure* cannot function as attitudinal disjuncts (among other things, they cannot be positioned initially) but are obviously related to *certainly* and *surely* respectively in their intensifier uses. In Group B, *fairly* (BrE) and *just* cannot function as style disjuncts. However, *fairly* can be related to the set of style disjuncts *to be fair, to put it fairly*, etc, for which there happens to be no corresponding adverb, while an association can be seen between *simply* (*simply*, style disjunct; *I am speaking simply*, process adjunct 'in a simple manner'; *I simply say*, restrictive (8.13) 'merely', 'only', 'just') and *just* (*I just say* – restrictive).

8.21
Co-occurrence restrictions on emphasizers

While emphasizers in Group A seem to be free to co-occur with any verb or predication, those in Group B tend to be restricted. For example, *fairly* (BrE) requires some suggestion of exaggeration in the predication:

> In her anger, she *fairly* screamed at him (BrE)
> *In her anger, she *fairly* spoke to him

On the other hand, *honestly* tends to co-occur with verbs expressing attitude or cognition:

They *honestly* admire her courage
He *honestly* believes their accusation
?*In her anger, she *honestly* screamed at him

When some emphasizers are used with gradable verbs they may also
have a scaling effect akin to that of boosters (8.23):

He *really* likes her ('He likes her *very much*')
I *indeed* appreciate your help ('I *greatly* appreciate your help')
He *definitely* impressed them ('He impressed them *greatly*')

But unlike the boosters, these have a heightening effect with non-
gradable verbs too:

He *really* was there
She *indeed* sat next to them
We *definitely* saw it

Other emphasizers tend to have a scaling effect more readily with
gradable words that are adjectives and nouns (5.51 *ff*):

He was *certainly* funny ('He was *very* funny')
I am *frankly* appalled at his attitude ('I am *extremely* appalled . . .')
He's *obviously* a fool ('He's a *big* fool')
He's *clearly* a dangerous man ('He's a *very* dangerous man')

The scaling effect of *really* and *indeed* is more obvious with adjectives:

It was *really* funny
He's dangerous *indeed*

Really is exceptional in its ability to come within the noun phrase:

He's a *really* dangerous man

Truly is like *really* in this and other respects, but it is formal and much
rarer. For some speakers it sounds slightly archaic.
    Speakers may vary in the extent to which they feel that all or some of
these emphasizers have a scaling effect.

8.22
Syntactic features of emphasizers
Most emphasizers normally precede the item they emphasize (*M1* or *M2*
positions for verb phrases, *cf* 8.7), but *for certain* and *for sure* are exceptional in being postposed. Emphasizers are adjuncts because they
cannot appear initially (8.3). However, they differ from many other
adjuncts in several ways. With reference to the numbered features in 8.8
and 8.9, emphasizers cannot be contrasted with one another in alterna-

tive interrogation (1) or alternative negation (2); they cannot be the focus of focusing adjuncts (4, 5) or of a cleft sentence (6), nor (in the case of the adverbs) can they be the focus of clause comparison (8) or be premodified by *however, how* or *so* (9–11). They can, however, come within the scope of predication pro-forms or ellipsis (3).

As several of the examples in 8.20 show, most emphasizers can precede a negated verb phrase, except for *fairly* (BrE):

> They *fairly* danced for joy at the news (BrE)
> *They *fairly* didn't dance for joy at the news

Since *for certain* and *for sure* do not precede the verb anyway, they cannot precede clausal negation. Several intensifiers tend to co-occur with clausal negation and precede the verb phrase in such a case, in particular *honestly, just, simply*.

Five emphasizers can lie within the scope of clause negation:

> *actually, definitely, really, for certain, for sure*

All of them can become the focus of negation:

> I don't RĔALly know him
> He didn't ĂCtually sit next to her
> They don't DĔfinitely want it
> They don't know *for* CĔRtain
> I can't tell yet *for* SŬRE

Since *actually, definitely,* and *really* can also lie outside the scope of clause negation, we have a contrast between the two possibilities, the scope of negation being marked by the horizontal bracket (7.49):

> { I really don't know him ('The real truth is that I don't know him')
> { I don't really know him ('It's not the real truth that I know him')

> { He actually didn't sit next to her ('The actual fact is that he didn't sit next to her')
> { He didn't actually sit next to her ('It's not an actual fact that he sat next to her')

> { They definitely don't want it ('It's definite that they don't want it')
> { They don't definitely want it ('It's not definite that they want it')

All the emphasizers except *certainly* and *surely* (and probably *fairly* too) can appear in a question. We can therefore contrast

$$\text{Do they} \begin{cases} *certainly \\ *surely \\ definitely \\ really \end{cases} \text{want him to be elected?}$$

In general, the emphasizers do not appear with imperatives, but some people use *actually*, *definitely*, and *really* with imperatives:

Don't *actually* hate him for it – it wasn't really his fault.
Definitely buy one now.
Make an effort this time. But *really* make an effort.

The emphasizers cannot be modified or are unlikely to be modified, with the exception of *definitely*, which is sometimes premodified by *very*.

Certain emphasizers not listed in 8.20 appear in restricted environments.

(1) *always* when preceded by *can* or *could* in a positive declarative clause:

> You *can always* sleep on the FLŎOR ('You can certainly . . .')

The possibility of adding to this sentence an adverbial referring to a specific future time such as *tonight* rules out the temporal meaning of *always*.

(2) *well* when preceded by *can, could, may, or might* in a positive declarative clause:

$$\text{It} \begin{cases} may \\ might \\ can \\ could \end{cases} well \text{ be true that he beat her}$$

('It may indeed be true . . .')

With some verbs, only certain of these auxiliaries are admitted:

$$\text{He} \begin{cases} may \\ might \\ *can \\ could \end{cases} well \text{ play for his school}$$

('It is very possible that he will . . .')

(3) *Realistically* when co-occurring with *can, could,* or *might* is close to being an emphasizer:

> They *can realistically* be expected to cause trouble (?'can really')

(4) *needs* (rare, literary) when preceded or followed by *must* in a declarative or interrogative clause. The clause must be positive:

That *must needs* be their intention ('must inevitably')

(5) *necessarily* when preceded by *must*:

A school teacher who wishes to be honest *must necessarily* prepare his lessons ('must inevitably')

Necessarily otherwise is not a pure emphasizer. It tends to co-occur with the clausal negative particle:

That doesn't *necessarily* follow ('That doesn't have to follow')

Note

[a] *Indeed* can be postposed:

I appreciate your help *indeed*

This is more common with adjectives (particularly if they are modified by another intensifier) and nouns:

He was very tired *indeed*
It was a sacrifice *indeed*

[b] *Readily, easily, with ease,* and *comfortably* (especially when in *M* positions) come close to being emphasizers. *Easily* tends to co-occur with the modal auxiliaries.

They *readily* admitted their guilt
They might *easily* have been arrested
We will *comfortably* finish on time

Contrast these with the manner adjunct *easily* and the manner/result adjunct *comfortably* in

He writes *easily* ('in an easy style')
They furnished the place *comfortably* ('in such a way that it was comfortable')

Amplifiers
8.23
Amplifiers scale upwards. They are divided into (a) MAXIMIZERS, which can denote the upper extreme of the scale, and (b) BOOSTERS, which denote a high degree, a high point on the scale. Boosters are very much an open class, and new expressions are frequently created to replace older ones whose impact has grown stale.

Most amplifiers can be contrasted in alternative negation with *to some extent*, and this ability is a semantic test for their inclusion in the class of amplifiers:

He didn't ignore my request *completely*, but he did ignore it *to some extent*.

They don't admire his music *greatly*, but they do admire it *to some extent*.

On the other hand, emphasizers cannot be so used:

*He didn't *really* ignore my request, but he did ignore it *to some extent*.
*They don't *definitely* admire his music, but they do admire it *to some extent*.

Common amplifiers, within these two subclasses, include:

MAXIMIZERS
absolutely, altogether, completely, entirely, extremely, fully, perfectly, quite, thoroughly, totally, utterly; in all respects;
the superlative *most*

eg They *fully* appreciate our problems
They *thoroughly* disapprove of his methods
They *totally* believed in the leader's integrity
He *completely* ignored my request
I can *perfectly* see why you are anxious about it
He *entirely* agrees with you
We *utterly* deplore his tactics
I enjoyed the play *extremely*
I *absolutely* refuse to listen to your grumbling
He *altogether* rejects such views
I *quite* forgot about her birthday
He paid for the damage *fully*
She hasn't closed the door *completely*

BOOSTERS
badly, bitterly, deeply, enormously, far, greatly, heartily, highly, intensely, much, severely, so, strongly, terribly, violently, well; a great deal, a good deal, a lot, by far;
exclamatory *how;*
the comparative *more*

eg They *greatly* admire his music
I need a drink *badly*
They like her *very much*
They resent him *deeply*
He *bitterly* regretted his mistake
I *much* prefer the old methods
I *so* wanted to see her ('I wanted to see her so much')
His results *far* exceeded my expectations

We all know him *well*
They annoy me *a great deal*
We miss our old friends *a lot*
How they suffered! ('How very much they suffered!')

The distinction between maximizers and boosters is not an absolute one. In particular, when maximizers are in *M2* position they often express a very high degree, whereas when they are in *E* position they are more likely to convey their literal meaning of an extreme degree. For example, many speakers may see very little difference in force between the maximizer *utterly* and the booster *violently* when these are in *M2* position:

They $\begin{Bmatrix} utterly \\ violently \end{Bmatrix}$ detested him

Speakers vary in whether they give a literal reading to the maximizer, and the tendency to use the maximizer for merely a high degree is greater for attitudinal verbs such as *detest*.

8.24
Modification and comparison of maximizers

If the maximizers are interpreted literally as expressing the extreme on a scale, they cannot themselves be modified or compared for degree. Modification and comparison is inapplicable to prepositional phrases and most adverbs not ending in *-ly* (*altogether, quite, most*). With the other adverbs there is considerable variation in usage, with the semantic class of verb as a further variable. We exemplify the variation by taking the first nine sentences in 8.23 that illustrate the use of maximizers and testing the maximizers in them for modification and comparison. We consider four possibilities:

[I] premodification of the maximizer by *how*, introducing a question or exclamation, *eg:*

How thoroughly do they disapprove of his methods?
How utterly we deplore his tactics!

[II] premodification of the maximizer by *however* to form the opening of a dependent adverbial clause, *eg:*

However totally they believed in the leader's integrity, they were prepared to examine his actions dispassionately.

[III] the maximizer as the focus of clause comparison, *eg:*

He ignored my request *more completely than she did*

[IV] premodification of the maximizer by *very, eg:*

They *very fully* appreciate our problems

Table 8:1
MODIFICATION AND COMPARISON OF MAXIMIZERS

	I HOW	II HOWEVER	III MORE THAN	IV VERY
fully	+	+	+	+
thoroughly	+	+	+	+
totally	+	+	+	?
completely	+	+	+	?
perfectly	+	+	?	?
entirely	+	+	?	—
utterly	+	+	—	—
extremely	?	?	—	—
absolutely	—	—	—	—

Table 8:1 gives the results of the testing. As can be seen from the table, it is possible to use *fully* and *thoroughly* to denote a very high point on the scale. The queries in the table indicate an area of divided usage. There is a prescriptive tradition forbidding the use of *very* or the comparative with *completely* and *perfectly* and with their respective adjective forms.

Indeed, similar restrictions on modification and comparison apply to the adjective bases of these adverbs, though they are not identical. *Table* 8:2 lists these adjective bases and shows the results of tests on them for modification by *more* and by *very*. Modification by *how* and *however* coincides with that for *more*.

Table 8:2
MODIFICATION AND COMPARISON OF ADJECTIVE
BASES OF MAXIMIZERS

	MORE	VERY
full	+	+
thorough	+	+
total	?	—
complete	?	?
perfect	?	?
entire	—	—
utter	?	—
extreme	?	?
absolute	?	—

The queries represent in part divided usage. But the acceptability of the modifiers with these intensifying adjectives (5.31) also depends on the noun. If the noun is abstract and derived from a verb, it seems more acceptable to modify the adjective by *more* or *very*. Contrast

I have never seen a more complete $\begin{cases} \textit{?investigation} \\ \textit{?*fool} \end{cases}$

He has a very perfect $\begin{cases} \textit{?understanding} \text{ of the problem} \\ \textit{?*right} \text{ to do what he likes} \end{cases}$

The item may have a homonym that is not an intensifying adjective and there need not then be any problem of modification:

He expressed *very extreme* views
His views on the subject are *more extreme* $\left.\begin{array}{c} \\ \\ \end{array}\right\}$ (*extreme* = radical)
  than mine

Co-occurrence restrictions on amplifiers
8.25
Certain amplifiers tend to co-occur predominantly with certain verbs, for example:

I entirely + agree
I badly + need, want
I completely + forget
They greatly + admire, enjoy

In other cases the amplifiers select a semantic class of verbs, for example *greatly* with verbs having a favourable implication and *utterly* with verbs having an unfavourable implication. Or some intensifiers, such as *deeply*, select the class of 'emotive' verbs:

They wounded him *deeply* (emotional wounding)
They wounded him *badly* (physical wounding)

Even when there is an item-class selectivity, the amplifier may be unable to select all the items in the class. We have

deeply + hate, dislike, admire, love, value

but not

*deeply like

Further investigation may also show that semantically-definable classes of amplifiers tend to co-occur with semantically-definable classes of verbs.

But the situation can be even more complicated. Sometimes there are syntactic conditions for certain types of lexical co-occurrence. *Much* is largely used in non-assertives, unless premodified:

*I like him *much*

I like him $\left\{\begin{array}{l} very \\ so \\ too \end{array}\right\}$ *much*

Do you like him *much*?
I don't like him *much*

Yet with some verbs, unpremodified *much* can be used, but only in *M2* position:

We *much* $\left\{\begin{array}{l} \text{prefer his offer} \\ \text{admire your technique} \\ \text{appreciate your invitation} \\ \text{regret the inconvenience} \end{array}\right.$

*We $\left\{\begin{array}{l} \text{prefer his offer} \\ \text{admire your technique} \\ \text{appreciate your invitation} \\ \text{regret the inconvenience} \end{array}\right\}$ *much*

Note

Very much miss is another example of the selection of the gradable sense of a verb. While

They missed her

is ambiguous between the 'emotive' sense ('feel sorry or unhappy at the loss or absence of') and the sense of 'arriving too late for', the addition of *very much* allows only the emotive sense:

They *very much* missed her
They missed her *very much*

Where the emotive sense would not be normal, *very much* cannot be added:

*They got up late, and so they $\left\{\begin{array}{l} very\ much\ \text{missed the bus} \\ \text{missed the bus}\ very\ much \end{array}\right.$

Non-emotive *miss* is non-gradable.

8.26

Amplifiers co-occur only with gradable verbs. Emphasizers can co-occur with non-gradable verbs such as DRINK or JUDGE:

He *really* drinks beer
He will *definitely* judge us

When amplifier items co-occur with non-gradable verbs they do not function as amplifiers, but as quantifiers, duratives or frequentatives (8.33) or process adjuncts (8.34 *ff*):

> He drinks beer *a lot* ('often')
> He will judge us *severely* ('in a severe manner')

However, a non-gradable verb can become gradable when the focus is on the result of the process rather than on the process itself. For example, if the perfective particle *up* is added to DRINK or the perfective aspect of the verb is used, the focus is on the result and an amplifier such as *completely* can co-occur with DRINK:

> He *completely* drank up his beer
> He has *completely* drunk his beer

Similarly, while JUDGE is non-gradable, MISJUDGE is gradable, since MISJUDGE is concerned with the result of the judging:

> $*$He $\left\{\begin{array}{l}\text{very much}\\ \text{badly}\end{array}\right\}$ judged the situation
>
> He $\left\{\begin{array}{l}\text{very much}\\ \text{badly}\end{array}\right\}$ misjudged the situation

And if *badly* is used with JUDGE, it is interpreted as a process adjunct (perhaps expressing a blend of process with result) and must be put in *E* position:

> He judged the situation *badly* ('in a way that was bad and with bad results')

Note

The gradable/non-gradable distinction between JUDGE and MISJUDGE is found in other morphologically-related verbs:

NON-GRADABLE	GRADABLE
calculate	miscalculate
estimate	overestimate, underestimate
rate	overrate, underrate
represent	misrepresent
behave]	misbehave
manage	mismanage

8.27
Positions of amplifiers (*cf* 8.7)

M2 and *E* positions are open to most adverbs that are amplifiers; noun phrases and prepositional phrases are restricted to *E* position. In positive declarative clauses, *M2* position is favoured for both boosters and maximizers when we want to express a scaling upwards, but *E* position is preferred for maximizers when we want to denote literally the upper extreme of the scale. Hence, the effect of the maximizer *completely* in *M2* position in

He *completely* denied it

is close to that of the booster *strongly* or the emphasizer *really*, which can have a scaling effect similar to that of boosters (8.21):

$$He \begin{Bmatrix} strongly \\ really \end{Bmatrix} denied\ it$$

On the other hand, when *completely* is in *E* position:

He denied it *completely*

the intention seems to be closer to

He denied *all of it*

Where the literal meaning is expected, some people find only *E* position acceptable:

?He *completely* dissected the animal
?They *completely* shared the apartment

He dissected the animal *completely* ('into all the prescribed parts')
They shared the apartment *completely* ('the whole of the apartment')

We can also contrast the probable interpretations of *violently* in the two positions shown in

They *violently* attacked him
They attacked him *violently*

In *M* position, *violently* is likely to be interpreted as a booster (= *greatly*) and, *attacked* will then be equivalent to 'condemned', a verbal assault. On the other hand, when *violently* is in *E* position, we are likely to interpret it literally (= with violence) as a manner process adjunct (8.34 *ff*), with *attacked* now referring to physical assault.

In negative, interrogative, and imperative clauses, *E* position is normal in all cases.

Note

[a] The adverbs *extremely*, *most*, and (when no comparative clause follows) *more* are restricted to *E* position. Exclamatory *how*, of course, appears only at the beginning of the sentence.

[b] Some adverb boosters (including *well*) occasionally appear in *M1* position, usually (but not necessarily) when they are themselves intensified or before an emphatic auxiliary:

I *very much* would prefer to see you tomorrow
I *so* did want to meet them
I *well* can understand your problem

M1 position is common for *very much* in *very much would like*, though some find it odd:

?I *very much* would like to speak to you some time today.

8.28
Syntactic features of amplifiers

With reference to the numbered features in 8.8 and 8.9, amplifiers can be contrasted with other intensifiers in alternative interrogation and negation (1, 2) and can come within the scope of predication pro-forms or ellipsis (3). On the other hand, they cannot be the focus of a cleft sentence (6):

*It was *completely* that he ignored your request

But for some people, they can be the focus of a cleft sentence if they are modified or if the focal clause is interrogative or negative (*cf* 8.31, 8.39, 8.64):

?Was it *completely* that he ignored your request?

?I know that it wasn't *entirely* that he agreed with us

?I wonder how *fully* it was that they appreciated your problems

Most boosters accept comparison and modification (8–11), but maximizers vary in this respect (8.24).

Amplifiers do not usually serve as a response to a *How* question, unlike some process adjuncts (8.34 *ff*):

*How do they admire his music? (They admire it) $\begin{cases} \textit{Very much.} \\ \textit{Greatly.} \end{cases}$

How do you like it? (I like it) $\begin{cases} \textit{Very much.} \\ \textit{?Greatly.} \end{cases}$

They can often be evoked by *How much*:

How much do they admire his music? (They admire it) *Greatly.*

Downtoners
8.29

Downtoners have a lowering effect on the force of the verb and many of them scale gradable verbs. Downtoners can be divided into four groups:

(a) COMPROMISERS have only a slight lowering effect

(b) DIMINISHERS $\Big\}$ scale downwards considerably
(c) MINIMIZERS

(d) APPROXIMATORS serve to express an approximation to the force of the verb, while indicating its non-application

The four groups represent semantic distinctions among downtoners,

but the assignment of individual downtoners to particular groups is not
beyond dispute. Common downtoners include

(a) COMPROMISERS

kind of ⎫
sort of ⎬ (informal, especially AmE)

quite ⎫
rather ⎬ (especially BrE)

enough, sufficiently, more or less

eg I *kind of* like him (informal, especially AmE)
   As he was walking along, he *sort of* stopped and fell flat on
   his face (informal, especially AmE)
   I *quite* enjoyed the party, but I've been to better ones (especi-
   ally BrE)
   I'm sure you'll like her *well enough*
   He *more or less* resented their interference

(b) DIMINISHERS

mildly, moderately, partially, partly, slightly, somewhat;
in part, in some respects, to some extent;
a little, least (of all)

eg The incident *somewhat* influenced his actions in later life
   We know them *slightly*
   I *partly* agree with you
   They have always *mildly* disliked him
   They *moderately* prefer coffee to tea
   I can admire his courage *to some extent*

(c) MINIMIZERS

a bit
negatives (7.48): *barely, hardly, little, scarcely;*
non-assertives (7.45): *in the least, in the slightest, at all*

eg I can *scarcely* ignore his views
   I didn't enjoy it *in the least*
   He *little* realizes what trouble he has caused
   They don't support him *at all*
   I don't like his attitude *a bit*
   We don't mind *in the slightest*

(d) APPROXIMATORS

almost, nearly, practically (informal), *virtually, as good as, all but*

eg I *almost* resigned
   He *virtually* dictated the terms of the settlement

> They *practically* forced him to resign
> They *as good as* ruined the school
> She *all but* kissed us

There are a number of noun phases that can be minimizers only in negative clauses, *eg*

> I didn't sleep *a wink* last night
> I don't owe you *a thing*

See 7.45 for other examples.

Note

[a] For the distinction between *little* and *a little*, see 4.25 Note *d*.

[b] Some speakers use *kind of* and *sort of* as approximators with non-gradable verbs:

> He *sort of* smiled at us (= You could almost say he smiled at us)
> He *kind of* fell down (= You could almost say he fell down)

When they are used as approximators, we can say (*cf* 8.30):

> He *sort of* smiled at us, but in fact he didn't smile at us
> He *kind of* fell down, but in fact he didn't fall down

For other speakers, they are always nearer to *more or less* than to *almost*. Both uses are very informal and especially common in AmE.

8.30

Approximators differ from most other downtoners in that they imply a denial of the truth-value of what is denoted by the verb. Hence we can say, with the approximator *almost,*

> I *almost* resigned, but in fact I didn't resign

But we cannot deny in this way the truth-value of what is said when we use most other downtoners:

> *I *kind of* like him, but in fact I don't like him
> *We know them *slightly*, but in fact we don't know them

The negative minimizers differ from both approximators and other downtoners in allowing for a revision that is intended to be a version that is more strictly true rather than to be a denial of the truth-value of what has been said:

> I can $\begin{Bmatrix} scarcely \\ hardly \end{Bmatrix}$ ignore his views; in fact I can't ignore his views.
> I can *barely* understand him; in fact I can't understand him.
> He *little* realizes the trouble he has caused; in fact he doesn't realize it.

In each case, the second clause carries the partial denial in the first clause to a full denial,

Compromisers reach out towards an assumed norm but at the same time reduce the force of the verb. If we say

I *kind of* like him (informal, especially AmE)

or

I *rather* like him (especially BrE)

we do not deny liking him. But we seem to be deprecating what we are saying, 'I might go as far as to say I like him'.

The difference between diminishers and minimizers is not the nearness to the bottom of the scale, though most minimizers are indeed near the bottom. They are distinguished in their behaviour with respect to negation. Diminishers are not usually the focus of negation, but when they are, the effect is to push the scaling towards the top. For example, with fall-rise nuclei:

They didn't praise him SLĬGHTly ('They praised him a lot')
We don't like it *a* LĬTtle ('We like it a lot')

On the other hand, the effect of negation on those minimizers that accept negation is to deny the truth-value of what is denoted by the verb (with falling nuclei):

They didn't praise him *in the* SLĬGHTest ('They didn't praise him')
We don't like it *a* BĬT ('We don't like it')

Four of the minimizers – *barely, hardly, little, scarcely* – form a subgroup. They are themselves negative (7.48) and cannot be negated (*cf* 8.66). On the rare occasions when they are positioned initially, there is subject-operator inversion. Of these four, *hardly, scarcely,* and *barely* can co-occur with non-assertives or with minimizers like *a wink* or *a thing*:

They $\left\{\begin{array}{l}scarcely\\hardly\\barely\end{array}\right\}$ need $\left\{\begin{array}{l}\text{it } at\ all\\a\ thing\end{array}\right.$

I *scarcely* slept *a wink*

For some people, the co-occurrence of these non-assertives or minimizers is marginally acceptable with *barely*.

Certain minimizers not listed above appear in restricted environments (*cf* 8.22):

(1) *possibly* and *conceivably* when they co-occur with *can* or *could* in a non-assertive clause:

They *can't possibly* leave now ('They can't under any circumstances leave now')
Can he *conceivably* want it? ('Can he in any way want it?')

This use of *possibly* and *conceivably* is to be distinguished from their use as disjuncts (8.82 *ff*). Contrast:

> They can't *possibly* leave now (minimizer)
> They *possibly* can't leave now (disjunct – 'It's possible that they can't leave now')

(2) *never* is a negative minimizer in

> You will *never* catch the train tonight ('You will not under any circumstances catch the train tonight')

The presence of an adverbial referring to a specific future time such as *tonight* rules out the temporal meaning of *never* (*cf: always* in 8.22). In non-assertive clauses *ever* can replace *never* as minimizer:

$$\text{Will he} \left\{ \begin{array}{l} ever \\ never \end{array} \right\} \text{catch the train tonight?}$$

8.31
Syntactic features of downtoners

With reference to the numbered features in 8.8 and 8.9, some downtoners can lie within the scope of clause interrogation and negation (1, 2). Exceptions include the compromisers *kind of, sort of, rather, more or less;* the minimizer negatives; and most approximators. The focus of clause negation can be on the compromiser *quite,* the diminishers, and the approximators *almost* and *nearly,* but only when the negation is a denial of a previous assertion. Contrast in alternative interrogation or negation seems possible only for the compromisers *enough* and *sufficiently,* for the diminishers, and for the approximators *almost* and *nearly.*

Downtoners come within the scope of predication pro-forms or ellipsis (3). Some downtoners can be focused by *only* (4). These include all the diminishers (excluding *least*), and the minimizers *barely* and *a bit.* The same downtoners can be the focus of a cleft sentence (6) under the same conditions as for amplifiers (8.28). None of the downtoners can be the focus of *also* (5). Only diminisher adverbs and the minimizer *little* can be the focus of clause comparison or be premodified (8–11). For example:

$$\text{compromisers} \left\{ \begin{array}{l} kind\ of \\ sort\ of \end{array} \right.$$

$$\text{diminishers} \left\{ \begin{array}{l} partly \\ in\ part \\ in\ some\ respects \\ to\ some\ extent \end{array} \right.$$

approximators $\begin{cases} almost \\ nearly \end{cases}$

A few downtoners can precede a negative verb phrase:

I *almost* didn't meet him
He *sort of* didn't want to say anything about it (informal, especially, AmE)

Many downtoners can serve as the response to a question introduced by *how much*. Exceptions include most compromisers (except *enough* and *sufficiently*), the non-assertive minimizers (unless preceded by *not*), and all the approximators.

Note

In informal style (especially BrE) *rather* can be a response to a *yes-no* question, but it then equals an enthusiastic *yes:*

A: Will you come with me? B: RÁther.

Quite (especially BrE) can be a comment on a previous statement, synonymous with *exactly* and *precisely* (8.18 Note):

A: He has no right to object. B: QUÌTE.

8.32
Positions of downtoners (*cf* 8.7)
Most downtoners favour *M2* position but can also occur in *E*. Some are restricted to *M2:*

quite, rather, as good as, all but

Others tend to be restricted either to *M2* or to *M1*(b), the latter being the position between two auxiliaries:

barely, hardly, scarcely, practically, virtually

Hence we may have

He could *hardly* be described as an expert
He will *virtually* have finished by the time they arrive

On the other hand, *M1*(a), the position immediately before the operator, is unacceptable to many:

?He *hardly* could be described as an expert
?He *virtually* will have finished by the time they arrive

A few are restricted to *M2* in a positive clause, but can precede a negative phrase in *M1* (8.31):

kind of, sort of, almost, nearly

A few others favour *E* position:

  a bit, at all

or are restricted to *E:*

  enough, a little

On the other hand, a few diminishers can occupy even *I:*

  partly, in part, in some respects, to some extent

8.33
Homonyms of intensifiers: quantifiers, frequentatives, duratives
It is convenient to mention at this point that many items that are intensifiers are also used to denote a measure of quantity or of duration or frequency in time. These intensifiers include

  all the minimizers
  the compromisers *enough, sufficiently*
  the boosters *much, a lot, a good deal, a great deal*
  the diminishers *a little, least, somewhat, to some extent*

We can therefore contrast several uses of (say) *a lot:*

  I like them *a lot* ('to a great extent' – booster intensifier)
  I paid him *a lot* for his work ('a large amount' – quantifier)
  I see him *a lot* ('often' – frequentative)
  I slept *a lot* last night ('a long time' – durative)

In all of these uses, *a lot* can be evoked as an answer to the question *how much?* but in addition the frequentative can be a response to a *how often* question ('How often do you see him?'), and the durative to a *how long* question ('How long did you sleep last night?').

There can be ambiguities as a result of more than one of these uses being allowed in a given instance:

  He doesn't drink *very much* ('a very large amount' – quantifier, or
    'very often' – frequentative)
  She suffered *very little* ('to a small extent' – diminisher intensifier,
    or 'rarely' – frequentative)
  They *scarcely* disagreed with him ('to a minimal extent' – minimizer
    intensifier, or 'rarely' – frequentative)
  He irritated me *enough* last night ('to a sufficient extent' – booster
    intensifier, or 'sufficiently often' – frequentative, or 'for a
    sufficiently long time' – durative)

Some of the quantifiers must be analysed as direct objects rather than as adjuncts, because they can be made the subject of the passive form of the sentence:

> I paid him *a lot* for his work ↔ *A lot* was paid him (by me) for his work
> He drank *enough* ↔ *Enough* was drunk (by him)
> They wrote *a bit* about conditions in their city ↔ *A bit* was written (by them) about conditions in their city

Others cannot be made subject:

> I *scarcely* paid him for his work ~ **Scarcely* was paid (by me) for his work
> He drank *sufficiently* ~ **Sufficiently* was drunk (by him)
> They wrote *somewhat* about conditions in their city ~ **Somewhat* was written (by them) about conditions in their city

Those that can be made subject can also be evoked by a *what* question. They can be the head of a noun phrase postmodified by a prepositional phrase:

> very little ⎤
> enough ⎟
> a lot ⎬ of the work
> a bit ⎟
> a good deal ⎦

Note

[a] For the relationship between quantifiers and frequentatives see 8.67.

[b] Many intensifiers, particularly boosters, have homonymous process adjuncts (8.34 *ff*):

> He *bitterly* regretted his mistake (booster intensifier)
> He spoke *bitterly* about the way he had been treated ('in a bitter manner' – manner process adjunct)

See also 8.37 for the possibility of a blend of intensifier with process adjunct.

Process adjuncts
8.34

Process adjuncts define in some way the process denoted by the verb. They can be divided into at least three semantic subclasses:

(a) MANNER
(b) MEANS
(c) INSTRUMENT

Manner adjuncts constitute by far the largest group to be realized by adverbs. For common pro-forms for process adjuncts (particularly (*in*) *that way*, *like that*), see 10.51.

8.35
Manner adjuncts

EXAMPLES OF THE USE OF MANNER ADJUNCTS:

She spoke to him *coldly*

They sprayed tear gas *indiscriminately* on the protesters

They were *categorically* told that no more oil would come from the wreck

Nixon spoke *Johnson-style* at the press conference

They are deluded if they think *otherwise*

Her influence showed itself *more obviously* in the colours of the furniture and curtains

They began arguing *loudly*

He failed to question the witness *thoroughly*

He repaired the house *like an expert*

She replied to questions *with great courtesy*

He spoke *in a way that reminded me of his father*

They played the game (*in*) *a different way*

She dances (*in*) *the same way as I do*

They cook ((*in*) *the*) *French style*

He always writes *in a carefree manner*

They walked (*in*) *single file*

You should write *as I tell you to*

Manner adjuncts are realized most commonly by adverbs and prepositional phrases (6.39) and less commonly by noun phrases and clauses (11.41).

Noun phrases with *way*, *manner*, and *style* as head tend to have the definite article:

$$\text{She cooks chicken} \begin{cases} \textit{the} \text{ way I like} \\ \text{in} \begin{Bmatrix} \textit{the} \\ \textit{a} \end{Bmatrix} \text{way I like} \end{cases}$$

As the above example illustrates, we can regard such noun phrases as having omitted the preposition *in* (cf 6.32 f, 8.36, 8.37).

An adverb manner adjunct can usually be paraphrased by *in a ... manner* or *in a ... way* with its adjective base in the vacant position. Where an adverb form exists, it is usually preferred over a corresponding prepositional phrase with *manner* or *way*. Hence,

He always writes *carelessly*

is more usual than

$$\text{He always writes } \textit{in a careless} \begin{cases} \textit{manner} \\ \textit{way} \end{cases}$$

On the other hand, there is probably no difference in frequency with other types of corresponding prepositional phrases:

He prayed $\begin{cases} \textit{fervently} \\ \textit{with fervour} \end{cases}$

She spoke $\begin{cases} \textit{animatedly} \\ \textit{with animation} \end{cases}$

Adverbs as manner adjuncts can often serve as the response to a *How* question (*cf* 8.28, 8.36):

A: *How* did Nixon speak at the press conference?
  B: Johnson-style.

But other units as manner adjuncts can more easily serve as responses:

A: *How* does she dance?   B: *The same way as I do.*
A: *How* should I write to him?   B: *As a friend would write.*
A: *How* do they cook?   B: *In the French style.*

The main method of forming manner adverbs is by adding an *-ly* suffix to an adjective. Three minor methods are by adding *-wise, -style,* or *-fashion* to a noun:

snake-wise	French-style	schoolboy-fashion
Indian-wise	cowboy-style	peasant-fashion

With these forms the prepositional paraphrase would include post-modification:

in the manner of $\begin{cases} \text{a snake} \\ \text{an Indian} \\ \text{the French} \\ \text{cowboys} \\ \text{schoolboys} \\ \text{peasants} \end{cases}$

See App I.30.

8.36
Means and instrument adjuncts

EXAMPLES OF THE USE OF MEANS ADJUNCTS:
  These linguistic units were separated *intonationally*
  He decided to treat the patient *surgically*
  I go to school *by car*
  He gained entry into the building *by means of a bribe to the guard*
  You can best influence them *by your own example*
  You can stop the machine *by pressing this button*

EXAMPLES OF THE USE OF INSTRUMENT ADJUNCTS:
> He examined the specimen *microscopically*
> You can cut the bread *with that knife*
> He was killed *with a bullet*

Most means and instrument adjuncts are prepositional phrases (*cf* 6.40 *f*). Like manner adjuncts, these adjuncts can serve as a response to a *How* question.

Some noun phrases function as means adjuncts. We can consider them as related to prepositional phrases (*cf* 8.35):

> He sent it (*by*) *air mail*
>
> Fly $\left(\begin{Bmatrix} with \\ by \end{Bmatrix} \right)$ *Air France*
>
> He travelled to Washington (*by*) *first class*.

Note
The adjunct in

> He examined the specimen *microscopically*

can be either instrumental ('with a microscope') or manner ('in microscopic detail'). It is also possible to interpret it as expressing means ('by means of a microscope').

8.37
Semantic blends
Some adjuncts express a blend of manner with some other effect.

(1) MANNER WITH RESULT, AND SOMETIMES INTENSIFICATION:
> He fixed it *perfectly* ('in such a way that it was perfect' – manner and result)
> He plays football *well* ('in such a way that the results are good' – manner and result)
> The soldiers wounded him *badly* ('in such a way and to such an extent that it resulted in his being in a bad condition' – manner, booster intensifier, result)

(2) MANNER WITH TIME DURATION (*cf* 8.60):
> He's walking *slowly* ('in a way that is slow in time')
> He stopped the car *suddenly* ('in a way that took a very short time')
> They broke the news to him *gradually* ('in a way that was spread over a period of time')

Such items are more fully time adjuncts when they appear in *I* or *M2* positions:

> *Suddenly*, I felt free again ('it suddenly happened')

My brother *quickly* despised his school ('soon'; 'My brother quickly
   came to despise')
We *gradually* appreciated his contribution to society ('We gradually
   came to appreciate')

Noun phrases and prepositional phrases that seem at first sight to be
equivalent to adverbs may be less flexible than the adverbs in this
respect:

All of a sudden, I felt free again ('it suddenly happened')
?He stopped the car *all of a sudden* ('in a way that took a very short
   time')
He is now going (*at*) *full speed* ('in a way that is very quick in
   time'; cf 8.35 for the omission of prepositions)
*At full speed my brother despised his school.

Note
There are some adverbials that seem to be process adjuncts, but do not fit into any of
the descriptions that we have given, *eg*

They approved the contract *generally* [or *in general*], but objected to a few clauses
She directed the work *personally* [or *in person*]
'It's empty,' he announced *superfluously*
These proposals come *strangely* from someone in his position
He bought it *cheaply*

In the last example, *cheaply* is regarded by some as a hypercorrection and is often replaced by the adjective form *cheap*. See also 8.57 Note *e*.

8.38
Co-occurrence restrictions on process adjuncts
Process adjuncts co-occur with dynamic verbs, but do not co-occur with
stative verbs (3.40 *f*). Hence, adverbials that function only as process
adjuncts cannot co-occur with stative verbs:

He likes them ⎫ ⎧ *skilfully
He owns it ⎭ ⎩ *awkwardly

Process adjuncts, of course, cannot be used as adverbials with intensive
verbs:

He is a teacher ⎫ ⎧ *skilfully
They seem happy ⎬ ⎨ *awkwardly
She looks angry ⎭ ⎩

8.39
Syntactic features of process adjuncts
With reference to the numbered features in 8.8 and 8.9, process adjuncts
can be contrasted with one another in alternative interrogation and

negation (1, 2) and can come within the scope of predication pro-forms or predication ellipsis (3). They can be the focus of *also* (5) and of *only* (4). Normally, manner adjuncts cannot be the focus of a cleft sentence (6) but their acceptability seems to increase for some people if they are modified or if the focal clause is interrogative or negative (*cf* 8.28, 8.31, 8.64):

> *It was *categorically* that they were told that no more oil would come from the wreck
> Was it *categorically* that they were told that no more oil would come from the wreck?
> ?It's *in the French style* that they cook
> It isn't *in the French style* that they cook
> ?It was *loudly* that they argued
> It was *so very loudly* that they argued

On the other hand, means and instrument adjuncts can readily become the focus of a cleft sentence:

> It was *intonationally* that these linguistic units were separated
> It was *by a bullet* that he was killed

Adverbs that are manner adjuncts can be the focus of clause comparison and can be premodified by *however*, *how* and *so* (8–11). Adverbs expressing means or instrument do not allow these features, since they cannot be modified at all. Hence, *microscopically* in

> He examined the specimen *very microscopically*

can only be a manner adjunct ('in microscopic detail'), although without the premodifier *very* it can be a means or instrument adjunct (*cf* 8.36). The inability of means and instrument adverbs to be modified presumably relates to their derivation from non-gradable nouns.

8.40
Positions of process adjuncts (*cf* 8.7)

Process adjuncts favour *E* position, since they usually receive the information focus. Indeed, no other position is likely if the process adjunct is obligatory for the verb and, therefore, the meaning of the verb is completed by the adjunct:

> { They live *frugally*
> { *They *frugally* live

> { They treated his friend *badly*
> { *They *badly* treated his friend

Since the passive is often used when the need is felt to focus attention on the verb, process adjuncts are commonly placed in *M2* rather than in *E* when the verb is in the passive:

Discussions were *formally* opened today on the question of
  international disarmament
Tear gas was *indiscriminately* sprayed on the protesters

Contrast also

He put the point *well*
*He *well* put the point
The point was put *well*
The point was *well* put

However, *M2* is odd for means and instrument adverbs even in the passive, presumably because they normally receive the information focus:

?*These linguistic units were *intonationally* separated
*The specimen was *microscopically* examined (asterisked in the
  relevant senses)

Manner adverbs occasionally appear in *I:*

Loudly they began arguing

Process adjuncts realized by other units can occur more easily in *I*, that position being preferred if the focus of information is required on another part of the sentence:

With great courtesy she replied to my questions
By pressing this button you can stop the machine.

Note
M position is also possible for process adjuncts that are not adverbs, but it is rare for them to appear in that position:

She, *with great courtesy*, replied to my questions
You can, *by pressing this button*, stop the machine

See further 6.56, 11.26.

Subject adjuncts
8.41
Subject adjuncts characterize the referent of the subject with respect to the process or state denoted by the verb. Most are homonyms of manner adjuncts, and all are either adverbs or prepositional phrases. Subject adjuncts relate to the person of the subject as well as to the process or state. Two groups can be distinguished: [A] a general group, and [B] a volitional group.

466 Adjuncts, disjuncts, conjuncts

Group A: GENERAL GROUP
    Group A appears to be an open class.

      eg: *Resentfully*, the workers have stood by their leaders ('The workers have stood by their leaders and were resentful about it')

          With great pride, he accepted the award ('He was very proud to accept . . .')

          For once, they have *frankly* admitted their mistakes ('It was frank of them to . . .')

          Manfully, they insisted the situation was not too bad ('It was manful of them to . . .')

          He has *consistently* overruled the lawyer's objections ('He has been consistent in . . .')

          Bitterly, he buried his children ('He was bitter when he . . .')

          Sadly, he roamed the streets ('He was sad when he . . .')

          With great unease, they elected him as their leader ('They were very uneasy when they . . .')

Group B: VOLITIONAL GROUP
    Common volitional subject adjuncts include:

      deliberately, (un)intentionally, purposely, reluctantly, voluntarily, wilfully, (un)willingly

      without intention, on purpose, with reluctance

      eg: *Intentionally*, they said nothing to him about the matter ('It was their intention not to . . .')

          On purpose, he left his proposals vague ('It was his purpose to . . .')

          He *deliberately* misled us ('He was being deliberate when he . . .')

          With great reluctance, she called the police to arrest her guest ('Though she was very reluctant to do so . . .')

8.42

Many of the subject adjuncts, particularly those in Group A, show their relationship to the subject by the paraphrase they allow in which their adjective stem is in predicative relationship to the subject. For example, we must provide a different paraphrase for the subject adjunct *bitterly* from its homonyms as manner adjunct and booster intensifier:

    Bitterly, he buried his children ('He was bitter when he . . .')

    He spoke *bitterly* about the treatment he received ('He spoke in a bitter way . . .')

    He *bitterly* regretted their departure ('He very much regretted . . .')

And similarly for an example from Group B:

He refrained *deliberately* from joining the party ('He was being
deliberate when he . . .')
He spoke slowly and *deliberately* ('in a deliberate manner')

Volitional subject adjuncts differ from other subject adjuncts in
several respects:

(1) Volitional adjuncts have in common that they express the subject's
intention or willingness, or the reverse.

(2) Volitional adjuncts can often occur with intensive verbs if (a) the
adjective complement is being used dynamically or (b) if the noun-
phrase complement implies activity or (c) if there is a locative
adjunct:

> *Intentionally*, he is being foolish
> *Deliberately*, he is being a nuisance
> *Reluctantly*, he was in London

Contrast:

> $*$*Intentionally*, he is $\begin{cases}\text{wealthy}\\\text{foolish}\end{cases}$
> $*$*Deliberately*, he is an adult

On the other hand, general subject adjuncts cannot co-occur with
intensive verbs:

> $*$*Proudly*, he was in London
> $*$*Sadly*, he is being foolish (asterisked as subject adjunct, 'He is
> sad when he is. . .', *cf: sadly* as attitudinal disjunct, 8.82 *ff*)

(3) Volitional adjuncts can more easily appear before clause negation
than other subject adjuncts:

> *Intentionally*, he didn't write to them about it
> *Deliberately*, they didn't send him the money
> ?*Proudly*, he didn't write to them about it
> ?*Resentfully*, they didn't send him the money

Subject adjuncts cannot co-occur with an inanimate subject:

> *The rain *deliberately* fell
> *The rain fell *deliberately*
> *The water is *resentfully* boiling
> *The water is boiling *resentfully*

However, in the passive form it is the agent (whether present or not) that
must be animate:

> The show was *deliberately* stopped (by X)
> Their luggage was *resentfully* packed (by X)

The presence or implication of an animate agent does not in itself en-
sure acceptability of a subject adjunct. For example, the sentence

   *The house was *resentfully* built last year

is odd, presumably because building a house takes too long for resentment to be maintained. Contrast

   The house was *resentfully* sold last year.

Note

The analogue of restrictive and non-restrictive adjectives or clauses (13.3) provides
another way of looking at the distinction between process adjuncts and subject
adjuncts. The subject adjunct in, for example,

   Bitterly, he buried his children

can be paraphrased

   He buried his children *and I tell you that he was bitter when he did so*

The non-restrictive relative clause can similarly be paraphrased by a coordinate
clause:

   Alan, *who is my teacher*, has joined the army ('Alan has joined the army and I tell
   you that he is my teacher')

8.43
Syntactic features of subject adjuncts

Subject adjuncts do not accept most of the numbered features for
adjuncts in 8.8 and 8.9. Those in Group A tend not to precede clause
negation (8.3):

   *Sadly, he didn't roam the streets (asterisked in the sense 'He was
      sad when he . . .')
   ?*With great unease*, they didn't elect him as leader

Similarly, those in Group A tend not to precede a negative subject:

   **With great unease*, nobody elected him as leader

However, if we can interpret the negated sentence as conveying the
meaning of a volitional action, we can sometimes add a subject adjunct
of Group A. For example, though

   ?**Proudly*, he didn't accept the award

is odd, the sentence

   Proudly, he wouldn't accept the award

is acceptable, because 'wouldn't accept' means 'refused', and a refusal
can be done with pride.

The volitional subject adjuncts allow alternative interrogation (8.8 (1)):

> Did he leave his proposals vague *on purpose* or did he do so
> *unintentionally?*

Adjuncts from both groups can come within the scope of predication pro-forms or ellipsis (8.8(3)):

> He has *consistently* overruled the lawyer's objections and *so has* she
> (consistently overruled the lawyer's objections)
> He *deliberately* misled us and *so did* she (deliberately mislead us)

Unlike most other adjuncts, subject adjuncts often cannot appear with imperatives:

> **Uneasily* elect him as your leader
> **Sadly* tell them about it

In such cases it is equally odd to say

> *Elect him as your leader *and be uneasy when you do so*
> *Tell them about it *and be sad when you do so*

(If *be* is interpreted as equivalent to *seem* or *pretend to be*, the sentences are not odd.)

On the other hand, we can have

> *Gladly* reveal what you know
> *With full confidence in your success*, make your views known to them

just as we can have

> Reveal what you know *and be glad when you do so*
> Make your views known to them *and have full confidence in your*
> *success when you do so*

Subject adjuncts, like process adjuncts, do not seem to be able to precede an emphatic auxiliary:

> **Proudly*, he *did* accept the award
> **On purpose*, he *did* leave the proposals vague

In this respect they can be contrasted with subject disjuncts such as *wisely* and *rightly* (8.82 *ff*):

> *Wisely*, he *did* accept the award
> *Rightly*, he *did* leave the proposals vague

Subject adjuncts tend to occur in *I* and *M* positions (*cf* 8.7). *M2* is probably preferred.

8.44

Formulaic adjuncts

Formulaic adjuncts (*cf* 13.50 for formulaic adjectives) generally resemble subject adjuncts of Group A, except that they tend to be restricted to *M2* position (excluding *please*). They are a small group of adverbs used as markers of courtesy. The most common are exemplified below:

He *kindly* offered me a ride
We *cordially* invite you to our party
She announced that she will *graciously* consent to our request
He *humbly* offered his apologies
Take a seat *please*

Formulaic adjuncts require the active subject or the passive agent (whether present or implied) to be personal nouns.

The formulaic adjuncts can appear in questions that constitute a request. There are therefore restrictions on the number of the person of the subject in questions (normally first for *cordially* and *humbly*, second for *kindly* and *graciously*):

May we *cordially* invite you to our party?
May I *humbly* offer my apologies?
Will you *kindly* take a seat?
Will you *graciously* consent to our request?

Please, however, allows all persons:

May I *please* explain my reasons?
Will $\left\{\begin{matrix} \text{John} \\ \text{you} \end{matrix}\right\}$*please* move to one side?

Kindly and *please* are the only formulaic adjuncts to appear freely before imperatives, though *graciously* occasionally does so too:

Graciously accept this gift from your admirers

Kindly is restricted to *I* position in imperatives:

Kindly leave the room
Kindly don't tell him what I said

Please, however, is mobile in imperatives:

Please leave the room
Ask him *please* what he wants
Open the door *please*

Unlike *kindly* and the other formulaic adjuncts, *please* is normally limited to sentences containing an imperative, or having the function of a command, or containing a reported command, or constituting a request. With non-imperative sentences, it appears before the verb or in *E* position:

Will you *please* leave the room?
You will *please* leave the room.
I wonder whether you would mind leaving the room *please*.
I asked him whether he would *please* leave the room.
May I *please* have my book back?

Please and (to a lesser extent) *kindly* are very commonly used to tone down the abruptness of a command.

Please cannot be modified. The others can be modified by *very*. However, *kindly* is not modified by *very* in questions and commands (whether grammatically imperatives or semantically commands):

?Will you *very kindly* take a seat?
*Very kindly leave the room.
?You will *very kindly* leave the room.

The first and last of the above sentences are perhaps possible with *very kindly* when they are said in a tone of exasperation.

We can paraphrase the formulaic adjuncts, in most cases as we did the subject adjuncts. For example, for the first set of sentences in 8.44:

He was kind enough to . . .
We express our cordiality by . . .
. . . she will be gracious enough to . . .
He was humble enough to . . .
Please me by . . .

Place adjuncts
8.45
Most place adjuncts are prepositional phrases (6.12–25) or, less frequently, clauses (11.28). Since these are discussed, as indicated, in the relevant chapters, we shall not deal with them here in detail.

Adverbs that are place adjuncts are a closed class and a comprehensive list can be given. Most can be used for both position and direction:

aboard, about, above, abroad, across, ahead, alongside, anywhere, around, ashore, astern, away, back, behind, below, beneath, between, beyond, down, downhill, downstairs, downstream, east, eastward(s) and other directions with *-ward(s)* as suffix, *elsewhere, everywhere, far, here, hereabouts, home, in, indoors, inland, inshore, inside, locally, near, nearby, north, nowhere, off, on, opposite, out, outdoors, outside, overboard, overhead, overland, overseas, somewhere, south, there,*

through, throughout, under, underfoot, underground, underneath, up,
uphill, upstairs, upstream, west, within

Where in its various uses (*cf* 5.48) can be added to this list. For *here* and
there as pro-forms for place adjuncts, see 10.50.

A few place adjuncts denote direction only:

after, along, aside, before, by, downward(s), forward, inward(s), left,
outward(s), over, past, right, round, sideways, skyward, upward(s)

A few noun-phrase heads can also be used in place adjuncts denoting
both position and direction:

He lives *a long WAY from here* ⎫
The house is only *a short DISTANCE away*⎬position
He has come *a long WAY* ⎫
They have moved *a fair DISTANCE from us*⎬direction

They include noun phrases of measurement:

He is *ten MILES from here*
They stood only *two FEET from us*
He threw it *about ten YARDS.*

Note

[a] The compass points used for both position and direction can be compounded,
eg: northwest, east-north-west.

[b] There are some nautical terms used for both position and direction that are
normally part of a technical vocabulary, but are found in literature dealing with
the sea, *eg: aft, larboard, port, starboard.*

[c] For *here, above,* and *below* as signals in discourse reference, see 10.64.

8.46

Co-occurrence restrictions on place adjuncts

When place adjuncts are used to denote position, we term them
POSITION ADJUNCTS, and when they are used to denote direction, we
term them DIRECTION ADJUNCTS. Direction adjuncts can be used
only with verbs of motion or with other dynamic verbs (3.41) that allow
a directional meaning:

I think you should now turn *left* ('to the left')
He jumped *over the fence*
He kicked the ball *into the goal*
She was whispering softly *into the microphone*

On the other hand, position adjuncts can be used with all verbs, including stative verbs (3.41):

stative:
$$\begin{cases} \text{I heard about it } \textit{in London} \\ \text{I have the key } \textit{here} \\ \text{The ground seems very soft } \textit{locally} \end{cases}$$

Position adjuncts can also be used with the intensive verb BE:

It's much warmer *inland*

Indeed, they can be used as predicative adjuncts with the intensive verb BE, even if the subject is concrete:

The birthday party is *in the next room*
All our men are *aboard*
The meeting will be *upstairs*
The house you want is *on the other side of the street*

But the progressive is excluded (*cf* 8.73):

*The birthday party *is being in the next room*

Contrast:

The birthday party *is being held in the next room*

Some direction adjuncts can also be used with BE, but with a static resultative meaning, indicating the state of having reached the destination (6.22):

They are *past* by now ('have got(ten) past')
The men will be *along* soon ('will have got(ten) along')
We will soon be *over the border* ('have got(ten) over the border')
I've never been *to London* ('never got(ten) to London')

Some place adjuncts can be obligatory adjuncts, providing verb complementation to verbs other than BE:

We don't *live here*

direction:
$$\begin{cases} \text{I'll } \textit{get below} \\ \text{You should } \textit{set} \text{ that dish } \textit{in the middle} \\ \text{I'll } \textit{put} \text{ the kettle } \textit{on the stove} \end{cases}$$

Some place adjuncts are used non-literally in phrasal verbs:

The light is *on* ('is shining')
When John heard what happened, he *blew up* ('became very angry')

Up and *down* are used as intensifiers or perfectives:

You must *drink up* quickly ('finish drinking')

For phrasal verbs, see 12.19 *ff*. For the transferred or abstract use of place prepositions, see 6.26.

Note

[a] Many place adjuncts can be explained as truncated prepositional phrases (6.10).

[b] Place adjuncts cannot be predicative adjuncts with intensive verbs other than BE (5.7).

8.47
Wh-questions

Position adjuncts can normally be evoked as a response to a *where* question:

A: Where is he staying? B: *In a hotel.*
A: Where's Alan? B: *Outside.*

The appropriate question for direction adjuncts is *where* plus the relevant directional particle, except that for 'direction towards' the particle *to* is commonly omitted:

A: *Where* are you going (*to*)? B: (*To*) *the park.*
A: *Where* have you come *from?* B: (*From*) *the supermarket.*

The direction particle as adjunct is more likely to serve as a response to a *where* question if a destination is implied:

A: Where are you going? B: $\begin{cases} Out(side) \\ In(side) \\ Back \\ Ahead \\ ?Away \\ ?Off \\ *About \\ *By \\ *Round \end{cases}$

Place adjuncts that are used abstractly cannot, of course, be questioned:

He is *in trouble.*
*A: Where is he? B: *In trouble.*
He turned the light *out.*
*A: Where did he turn the light? B: *Out.*

8.48
Ambiguity between position and direction adjuncts

Since position adjuncts can co-occur with dynamic verbs allowing directional meaning, ambiguities can arise between positional and directional interpretations of the adjunct (*cf* 6.13 Note):

He is allowed to run *outside*
The baby was crawling *upstairs*

The more probable interpretation for these adjuncts is that they are directional, but a positional interpretation

'When he is outside he is allowed to run'
'When he was upstairs the baby was crawling'

can be given in speech, for example by putting the adjuncts in a separate intonation unit. In writing, transposition to *I* will favour a positional interpretation.

Note
For potential differences in position and intonation between position and direction adjuncts, see 8.52.

8.49
Position and direction adjuncts in the same clause
Position and direction adjuncts can co-occur, with the position adjunct normally following the direction adjunct in *E:*

The children are running *around upstairs*
He was thrown *overboard near the shore*

With two prepositional phrases there is often a structural ambiguity in the status of the second phrase, which might be either an adverbial of the clause or a postmodifier of the noun head in the first phrase:

Some of the children are walking *to the lake in the park*
('are walking to the lake and are walking in the park' or 'are walking to the lake which is in the park')
People move to *a new house in America* every few years
('People move to a new house every few years; they do so in America' or the improbable 'People move every few years to a new house which is in America')

The position adjunct can be put in *I* position to avoid giving it end-focus (14.2 *ff*):

Upstairs the children are running *around*

It can appear in that position when it co-occurs with a direction adjunct, thus avoiding any ambiguity in the case of prepositional phrases:

In the park some of the children are walking *to the lake*
In America people move *to a new house* every few years

Depending on the structure of the sentence, there are other ways of avoiding such ambiguities, *eg*

Some of the children are *in the park* and walking *to the lake*
People move *in America to a new house* every few years

The fact that position adjuncts normally appear further from the verb suggests that they are less closely related to the verb than direction adjuncts. *Cf* also 13.32.

Note
If a position adjunct is obligatory, it is of course closely related to the verb (8.46).

8.50
Hierarchical relationship
Two position adjuncts can co-occur in hierarchical relationship:

Many people eat *in restaurants in London*

Only the superordinate position adjunct can be transposed to *I:*

In London many people eat *in restaurants*
*In restaurants many people eat *in London*

Two direction adjuncts can also co-occur in hierarchical relationship:

He came   *to London*   *from Rome*
He went   *from Rome*   *to London*

The normal order of these direction adjuncts when they are juxtaposed accords with the interpretation of the verb. *Come* denotes destination, and therefore the destination (*to London*) is normally mentioned before the point of departure (*from Rome*), whereas *go* denotes departure and therefore the reverse order is normal. Nevertheless, the adjunct denoting point of departure is superordinate in both cases, since it alone can be in *I:*

From Rome he $\left\{ \begin{array}{l} \text{came} \\ \text{went} \end{array} \right\}$ *to London*

The normal order of juxtaposed direction adjuncts otherwise follows the same order as the events described:

They drove   *down the hill*   *to the village*
He flew   *over the city*   *towards the airport*

If one of the adjuncts is an adverb, it normally comes before a prepositional phrase (*cf* 8.77):

Many people eat   *here*   *in restaurants*
They drove   *downhill*   *to the village*
He flew   *overhead*   *towards the airport*
He flew   *west*   *over the city*

8.51

Coordination

Two position adjuncts can be coordinated:

Soldiers were on guard *inside and outside*
We can wait for you *here or in the car*

and so can two direction adjuncts:

They went *up the hill and into the station*
They ran *across the field and past the farmhouse*

But a position and a direction adjunct normally cannot be coordinated. Hence in

The baby was crawling *upstairs and into his parents' bedroom*

upstairs can be interpreted only as a direction adjunct (*cf* 8.48), since it is coordinated with a prepositional phrase that has only a directional function.

8.52

Positions of place adjuncts

The relative positions of direction and position adjuncts have been discussed earlier (8.49 and 8.50). Both types of adjuncts favour *E:*

position $\begin{cases} \text{I'll meet you } downstairs \\ \text{We're eating } in\ the\ kitchen \\ \text{You'll find the sugar } where\ the\ coffee\ is \end{cases}$

direction $\begin{cases} \text{I'll go } downstairs \\ \text{We're moving some new furniture } into\ the\ kitchen \\ \text{I'm going (to) } where\ there's\ a\ warmer\ climate \end{cases}$

Position adjuncts, particularly prepositional phrases, often appear in *I*. They may be put there to avoid end-focus (14.2 *ff*), or to avoid ambiguity (*cf* 8.48), or to avoid a clustering of adjuncts at *E*, though it is not usually possible to isolate any one reason.

On the tree there were some very large oranges
Outside children were jumping and skipping
In the nursery the children were playing happily but noisily
On the stage men were fighting, and *in the body of the hall* women were screaming

The expressions *Here* ... BE and *There* ... BE with a pronoun as subject and the verb in the simple present are commonly used to draw attention to the presence of somebody or something:

Here it is

Here I am
There she is
There you are

Speakers sometimes put position adjuncts in *M2* and more rarely in *M1:*

Life is *everywhere* so frustrating
We are *here* enjoying a different kind of existence
They *there* noticed a very curious statue

M positions are occupied by a few position adverbs, the most common being *here*, *there* and compounds with *-where* (*elsewhere*, *everywhere*, *nowhere*, *somewhere*).

M positions are not normally open to direction adjuncts:

*They are $\begin{cases} there \\ into\ the\ kitchen \end{cases}$ moving some new furniture

But they can take the position between verb and object if the object is long:

They moved *into the kitchen* every stick of furniture they possessed

Occasionally, however, some direction adjuncts occupy *I*. In that position, they have a dramatic impact and a rhetorical flavour and normally co-occur with a verb in the simple present or simple past:

Down they flew
Away he goes
On they marched

If the subject is not a pronoun but a noun (and therefore has greater information value), subject-verb inversion is normal when either a direction adjunct or a position adjunct is in *I* (14.15):

Down flew the jets
Away goes the servant
Along the road roll the wagons
Over the bridge marched the soldiers
Ahead sat an old man
Below is a restaurant
In the doorway stood my brother
On the very top of the hill lives a hermit

Here BE and *there* BE with the verb in the simple present are common in speech:

Here are the tools
There's your brother

Direction adjuncts are put in *I* virtually only in literary English and in children's literature (stories, poems, and nursery rhymes). A few exceptions occur in informal speech, mainly with *go, come,* and *get* in either the imperative with the retained subject *you* (7.73) or in the simple present:

$$
\left.\begin{array}{l}
\text{Up (the hill)} \\
\text{Down (the stairs)} \\
\text{In (the bath)} \\
\text{Out (of the water)} \\
\text{Off (the table)} \\
\text{Over (the fence)} \\
\text{On (the horse)} \\
\text{Under (the bridge)}
\end{array}\right\} \text{you} \left\{\begin{array}{l} \text{come} \\ \text{go} \\ \text{get} \end{array}\right.
$$

$$
\left.\begin{array}{l}
\text{On} \\
\text{Under} \\
\text{Round}
\end{array}\right\} \text{you go} \qquad \text{There they} \left\{\begin{array}{l} \text{go} \\ \text{come} \end{array}\right. \qquad \text{Here} \left\{\begin{array}{l} \text{I} \\ \text{we} \end{array}\right\} \text{go}
$$

Here he comes

Note

[a] Particles in phrasal verbs (12.24) cannot be in *I*:

Down the car broke
Up cracked the soldier

[b] There are some idiomatic expressions with *here* and *there*:

$\left.\begin{array}{l} \textit{Here} \\ \textit{There} \end{array}\right\} \textit{you are}$ = This is for you

Here we are = We've arrived at the expected place
There you are = That supports or proves what I've said

[c] For *here* as time indicator, see 10.12 Note *b*. For the use of *here* in discourse reference, see 10.64.

8.53
Syntactic features of place adjuncts

Place adjuncts can generally accept all the features listed for adjuncts in 8.8, but since most adverbs that function as place adjuncts cannot take comparison or modification by *however, how* and *so*, they do not accept the features listed in 8.9.

Normally a direction adjunct is the focus of negation in a negative sentence and therefore it normally does not precede clausal negation:

Across the park he didn't walk
Towards the fort the soldiers did not march

On the other hand, it is normal for position adjuncts to do so:

Indoors the people are not eating
Nearby there aren't any soldiers

Most place adjuncts, including prepositional phrases, accept intensification (5.54 *f*, 6.55):

> They drove *due EAST*
> He went *right INTO THE HOUSE*
> He turned *sharp LEFT*
> He went *a long way UP* (*THE MOUNTAIN*)
> They are staying *far INLAND*

A type of clause comparison can be achieved by the use of $\begin{Bmatrix} further \\ farther \end{Bmatrix}$ ...
than:

> They are $\begin{Bmatrix} further \\ farther \end{Bmatrix} \begin{Bmatrix} AHEAD \\ DOWNSTREAM \end{Bmatrix}$ *than we are*
> He went $\begin{Bmatrix} further \\ farther \end{Bmatrix}$ *UP THE MOUNTAIN than I did*

Many accept questioning with *How far:*

> *How far ACROSS are they?*

while *here* and *there* accept questioning with *How near* instead:

> *How near HERE are they?*

The following place adverbs do not allow premodification by *far:*

> *here, there;* the compounds in *-where; about, around, between, hereabouts, locally, opposite, throughout.*

But *cf* the common expression *few and far between.*

Note
Two place adjuncts are inflected for comparison, *near* and *far*, and can be the focus of clause comparison. These together with *nearby* can be premodified by *very* and by the premodifiers in the three clause processes listed in 8.9 (9–11).

8.54
Position adjuncts in relation to subject and object
Position adjuncts normally indicate the place of the referent of the subject and (if present) of the object, and usually the place is the same for both referents:

> I met John *on a bus.* (This implies that John and I were on the bus.)

But sometimes the places can be different:

> I saw John *on a bus.* (John was on the bus but I need not have been on the bus.)

With certain verbs the reference is always to the place of the object and normally that will differ from the place of the subject (*cf* 8.73). These verbs denote having or placing:

$$I\begin{Bmatrix} have \\ keep \\ put \\ park \\ shelter \end{Bmatrix} \text{my car } in\ a\ garage$$

With certain verbs, position adjuncts are resultative and are like predicative adjuncts of the direct object:

I want *my car IN THE GARAGE* ('to be in the garage')
I expected *a leak IN THAT PIPE* ('to be in that pipe')

The verbs are verbs of saying, arranging, expecting, or wanting where the object has future reference. Not all such constructions allow an expansion simply by *to be:*

I expected a *riot IN THE CITY* ('there to be a riot in the city')
They threatened *a riot SOMEWHERE*
He urged *a picnic ON THE ISLAND*
They plan *a meeting AT MY HOUSE*

But these allow a replacement of the object by a *that*-clause:

that a riot would be in the city; that a riot would be somewhere; that a picnic be (held) on the island; that there should be a meeting at my house.

In some cases HAVE rather than BE is implied:

They offered *a barbecue NEARBY* ('to have a barbecue nearby')
I like *my dinner IN THE KITCHEN* ('to have my dinner in the kitchen')

In all such cases, the position adjunct is restricted to *E*.
The position adjunct may sometimes refer to the object in a conditional relationship:

We ought to condemn *such activities HERE*
I only like *barbecues OUTDOORS*

These can be paraphrased by clauses with *if* or *when: such activities if they take place here; barbecues when they are held outdoors.* These adjuncts are also restricted to *E*.

8.55
Direction adjuncts as imperatives

Certain direction adjuncts are commonly used as imperatives, with an implied verb of motion:

> *Out(side)!, In(side)!, (Over) Here!, (Over) There!, (Right) Back!,*
> *Down!, Off!, Up!, Under!, Left!, Right!, Away!*
> *Up the stairs!, Out of the house!, To bed!*

Note

[a] This applies also to some other adjuncts, *eg: Quickly!, Slowly!, Carefully!*

[b] *I must away* is sometimes used in BrE with an implied verb of motion ('I must go away').

Time adjuncts
8.56

Time adjuncts that are clauses (11.27, 11.68, 11.70) or prepositional phrases (6.27–31) or noun phrases (6.32–33) are discussed elsewhere, as indicated, and therefore we shall not deal with them here in detail.

Adverbs as time adjuncts are a relatively closed class, though a fairly large one. They can be divided into four semantic classes, but some items belong to more than one class. The four classes and their subclasses are shown in *Fig* 8:4.

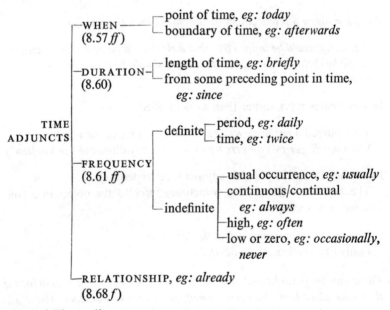

Fig 8:4 Time adjuncts

Time *when* adjuncts
8.57
Most time *when* adjuncts can serve as a response to a *when* question:

A: When did he arrive? B: $\begin{cases} \textit{Quite recently} \\ \textit{Last night} \\ \textit{At five o'clock} \\ \textit{While you were at the library} \end{cases}$

When in its various uses (*cf* 5.48) is in part pro-form for the time adjuncts in this class. For *then* as a pro-form for these time adjuncts, see 10.49.

Time *when* adverbs can be divided into

[A] those denoting a point of time
[B] those denoting a point of time but also implying the point from which that time is measured

Common adverbs in these two groups include:

Group A
again ('on another occasion'), *early* ('at an early time'), *just* ('at this very moment'), *late* ('at a late time'), *now* ('at this time'), *nowadays* ('at the present time'), *presently* ('at the present time', especially AmE), *simultaneously* ('at the same time'), *then* ('at that time'); *today, tomorrow, tonight, yesterday*

Group B
afterwards, before, earlier ('before'), *eventually* ('in the end'), *finally* ('in the end'), *first* ('before all else', 'before that', 'at first'), *formerly, immediately* ('at once', 'within a very short time'), *initially* ('in the beginning', 'at first'), *instantly* ('at once'), *just* ('a very short time ago'), *last* ('after all else', 'in the end'), *lately* ('a short time ago'), *later* ('afterwards'), *momentarily* ('in a moment', AmE), *next* ('after that'), *once* ('at some time in the past'), *originally* ('in the beginning', 'at first'), *previously* ('before'), *presently* ('soon'), *recently* ('a short time ago'), *shortly* ('soon'), *since* ('after that'), *soon, subsequently, then* ('after that')

Examples of the use of time *when* adjuncts:

Group A
They lived in London for the first few years of their marriage and were *then* very happy
Come and see us *again*
I was in New York *last year* and am *now* living in Baltimore
I'm *just* finishing my homework

Does he want us to be here *early tonight?*
The meeting starts *tomorrow at eight o'clock*
I was awarded my Bachelor of Arts degree *in 1970*
I suggest that we see him *tomorrow night* or at the very latest *on Sunday*
I'll tell you all the news *when I get back home*

Group B

He's going to the barber but will be back here *later*
I went into my room and *immediately* started to work
I haven't got any time at the moment but I'll see you *soon*
She *once* owned a dog
I've *just* heard that you are leaving us
Take a drink and *then* go to bed
He *recently* had an accident
A preliminary investigation seemed to indicate that he was implicated in the fraud, but a fuller investigation has *since* proved beyond all doubt that he was innocent
I left the factory *before the strike*
Will you be there *after lunch?*
He owed me a lot of money and wouldn't pay me back until I got my lawyer to write to him. He has paid me back in full *since then*
The appointment was made *a month ago* ⎫
I wrote to him about it *a (good) while back*⎬(cf 5.60)
She left him *after he struck her*
The Prime Minister announced his resignation *before the votes were counted fully*

Most time *when* adjuncts in Group A normally occur at *E*, but *just* is restricted to *M2* while *nowadays* and *presently* commonly occur in *I* (cf 8.7). Those in Group B commonly occur at *I* or *M2* (cf 8.58). *M1* position is open to most of Group B and to *now*, *nowadays*, and *then* in A.

Note

[a] *Earlier* and *later* are synonymous with *before* (*that*) and *afterwards* respectively:

He remembered the many insults that he had *earlier* experienced
He handed in his resignation, and *later* regretted his hasty action

They are not the comparatives of *early* and *late* respectively. We cannot substitute *early* and *late* for them in the above sentences:

*He remembered the many insults that he had *early* experienced
*He handed in his resignation and *late* regretted his hasty action

The true comparatives of *early* and *late* are exemplified in

We are eating ⎰*late* ⎱today
                ⎱*later*⎰

Today we'll be leaving home $\begin{cases} early \\ earlier \end{cases}$

[b] *Presently* is synonymous with *soon* where there is a modal auxiliary or (for some) when the verb in the past:

They $\begin{cases} \text{will } presently \text{ call on him} \\ presently \text{ called on him} \end{cases}$

(Some find *presently* unacceptable when it co-occurs with a verb in the past.)

On the other hand, when the verb is in the present, it is synonymous with *at present* (especially AmE):

They $\begin{cases} \text{are } presently \text{ in London} \\ \text{are } presently \text{ calling on him} \end{cases}$

[c] *After* is less commonly used than its synonym *afterwards*.

[d] *After, before,* and *since* are prepositions (6.30) and conjunctions (11.27) as well as adverbs. When used as adverbs, they could be regarded as prepositions in truncated prepositional phrases:

A preliminary investigation seemed to indicate . . ., but a fuller investigation has *since* (that time) proved . . .

He has been unhappy for a long time, but I've never seen him so unhappy *before* (this time).

The meeting is at six. I'm leaving now, but I'll see you *after* (the meeting).

Since does not normally serve as a response to a *when* question:

A: *When* have you been to England? B: **Since*.

Since prepositional phrases and clauses require *since when* in the question:

A: *Since when* have you given the orders?
B: *Since* the manager made me foreman.

[e] Some adjuncts seem to be a blend of time *when* with manner and perhaps also place (*cf* 8.37):

He told them *secretly* of his intention to resign ('when they were by themselves')

They criticized him *publicly* ('in a public place', 'when they were in public')

He mentioned it to them *privately* ('in a private place', 'when they were in private')

But in all the cases the communication could be made in writing, and no place would then be involved.

8.58

Most of the adverbs in Group B can be used as correlatives to denote a temporal sequence:

First they petitioned the Governor, but heard nothing from him. *Then* they wrote to the President, and received a polite but vague reply from some official. They *next* organized a peaceful demonstration. And *finally* they picketed all Federal buildings in the city.

I think this first day of our vacation is going to be very enjoyable for us. We'll probably *first* play a game of tennis. *Afterwards* we'll take a shower because we usually put a lot of effort into the game. *Then* we'll do some sun-bathing on the beach. *Eventually*, we'll take a walk into town.

When they are correlatives, they tend to occur in *I* or *M* positions.

Note
For the use of many adjuncts in Group B for time relationship, see 8.68.

8.59

Time *when* adjuncts can be in a hierarchical relationship:

> They were here *late last night*
> I'll see you *at nine on Monday*
> I spoke to her *earlier today*
> We'll meet *tonight after the show*

The order of the adjuncts at *E* depends in part on information focus (14.2 *ff*), but the tendency is for the superordinate adjunct (the one denoting the more extended period) to come last. However, the order may be reversed if the other adjunct is considerably longer:

> I was in New York *last year before the first snow fell*
> They became drunk *today within a very short time*

It appears that only the superordinate adjunct can occur in *I* (8.50, 8.62):

> *On Monday* I'll see you *at nine*
> *At nine I'll see you *on Monday*

8.60
Time duration adjuncts

Time *duration* adjuncts can be divided into two groups:

> [A] those denoting *length of time*
> [B] those denoting *duration from some preceding point of time*

Time *duration* adjuncts in Group A can serve as a response to a *how long* or *for how long* question:

A: (For) How long are you staying?   B:
> *Not very long*
> *Permanently*
> *A very short time*
> *(For) About a month*
> *Till I can get my car repaired*

Adverbs in Group B cannot serve as a response to such a question though other units in the group can:

A: (For) How long have you been collecting stamps?

B: $\begin{cases} *Since \\ *Recently \\ Since\ last\ month \\ Since\ I\ was\ a\ child \end{cases}$

Common adverbs in the two groups include:

Group A
> *always, awhile, briefly, indefinitely, long, momentarily* ('for a
> moment'), *permanently, temporarily*

Group B
> $\left.\begin{array}{l} lately \\ recently \end{array}\right\}$('during a recent period')
> *since* ('from some time in the past')

Those in Group B co-occur with perfect aspect (*cf* 11.70):

His studies $\begin{Bmatrix} \text{haven't been} \\ \text{*weren't} \end{Bmatrix}$ improving $\begin{cases} lately \\ recently \\ since \end{cases}$

But *lately* sometimes co-occurs with the simple present tense when it is
used for habitual time (3.25):

> He used to visit Chicago every two or three months, but *lately* he *goes*
> there about once a week.

Examples of the use of time *duration* adjuncts:

Group A
> I imagine he'll want to stay *awhile*
> I have *always* lived here
> He is *temporarily* out of work
> We always have to wait *so long*
> He was *momentarily* stunned by the impact of the explosion
> I'll be in California *for the summer*
> We slept (*for*) *a long time*
> Was it noisy *the whole night*?
> They are on duty *all night long*
> You can buy fresh fruit here *the whole year round* (*cf* 5.60)
> The office is open *Mondays through Saturdays* (AmE)
> There was no trouble *while we were there*
> *Until I saw the building* I had no idea how ugly it was
> They will keep the trophy *until summer*

Group B
> I have *recently* been collecting stamps

He insulted me last year and I haven't spoken to him *since*
He arrived this morning and he has been complaining (*ever*) *since*
We quarrelled in our last year at school and I have never seen her
   since
Things haven't become any better *lately*
I have seen her only once *since last Saturday*
I have been waiting for the books to be delivered (*ever*) *since I came
   to this apartment*

Time *duration* adjuncts are normally positioned at E, except for three adverbs normally positioned at $M2$ (*cf* 8.7):

momentarily, permanently, temporarily

Note

[a] When *lately* and *recently* are time *when* adjuncts (8.57), they can co-occur with simple past as well:

He $\begin{Bmatrix} lately \\ recently \end{Bmatrix}$ moved into a new apartment

Since requires perfect aspect even when it is a time *when* adjunct:

He $\begin{Bmatrix} \text{has since moved} \\ \text{*since moved} \end{Bmatrix}$ into a new apartment

[b] Uninflected *long* is normally a non-assertive form and positioned at E:

?He stayed long (*cf* He stayed *a long time*)
He didn't stay *long*
Did he stay *long*?

Inflected or modified *long* is assertive and also positioned at E:

He stayed $\begin{Bmatrix} longer \\ too\ long \end{Bmatrix}$

Uninflected *long* can be an assertive form when it co-occurs with certain verbs and is then usually positioned at $M2$. The verbs seem to be mainly verbs of belief or assumption (11.79), attitudinal verbs, and some verbs of speaking:

He has *long* admired my style of writing
I have *long* thought of retiring at the age of 55
The merits of the scheme will be *long* discussed

Long behaves like *much* in many respects (8.25).

[c] We should add to Group A the intensifiers that can also function as duratives (8.33):

I have spoken to him *enough* this morning ('long enough', 'a long enough
   time')
We played cards *a little* last night ('for a short time')
We always have to wait *a lot* when we go to see the doctor ('a long time')

[d] Notice that a prepositional phrase introduced by *during* can refer to time *when*. For example, the prepositional phrase in

I spoke to him *during last week*

would probably be interpreted as a reference to some point of time, and in that case would be no different from

I spoke to him *last week*

or

I spoke to him *on Monday*.

Time frequency adjuncts
8.61

Most time *frequency* adjuncts can serve as a response to a *how often* question:

A: How often do you wash your car? B:
$$\begin{cases} \textit{Rarely} \\ \textit{Monthly} \\ \textit{Once a week} \\ \textit{Every Sunday} \\ \textit{From time to time} \\ \textit{Whenever I find a spare} \\ \quad \textit{half-hour} \end{cases}$$

Adverbs and noun phrases are most commonly used for time *frequency*.

Adverbs expressing time *frequency* can be divided semantically into two major subclasses:

[I] those naming explicitly the times by which the frequency is measured: DEFINITE FREQUENCY

[II] those not doing so: INDEFINITE FREQUENCY

Each of these subclasses can in turn be subdivided. Common adverbs are listed for each subclass.

[I] DEFINITE FREQUENCY
    [A] PERIOD FREQUENCY
        hourly, daily, nightly, weekly, fortnightly (BrE), *monthly, quarterly, annually, yearly, biannually, semi-annually*

    [B] TIME FREQUENCY
        again ('another time'), *once* ('one time only'), *twice;* otherwise noun phrases or prepositional phrases, *eg: three times, on five occasions*

[II] INDEFINITE FREQUENCY
    [C] USUAL OCCURRENCE
        commonly, customarily, generally, habitually, invariably, normally, ordinarily, usually

    [D] CONTINUOUS/CONTINUAL FREQUENCY
        always, constantly, continually, continuously, ever ('always'), *incessantly, permanently, perpetually*

[E] HIGH FREQUENCY
frequently, often; regularly, repeatedly

[F] LOW OR ZERO FREQUENCY
infrequently, irregularly, occasionally, periodically ('from time to time'), *rarely, seldom, sometimes; never, ever* ('at any time')

Examples of the use of time *frequency* adjuncts:

[I] DEFINITE FREQUENCY
  [A] PERIOD FREQUENCY
  Committee meetings take place *weekly*
  I shall be in my office *every other day*
  Each summer I spend my vacation in Bermuda
  Come here *twice A WEEK*
  If so desired, rent can be paid *per week* instead of *per month*

  [B] TIME FREQUENCY
  I have been in Singapore *ÒNCE* (only)
  He *again* demanded a refund ('for a second time')
  Bob phoned *twice* today
  I visit England *THREE TIMES a year*
  I perform operations *THREE DAYS each week*
  On the average, I see them *ONCE every three weeks*

[II] INDEFINITE FREQUENCY
  [C] USUAL OCCURRENCE
  He *generally* leaves home at seven
  We *normally* don't go to bed before midnight
  As a rule it's very quiet here during the day
  As usual, nobody asked anything at the end of the lecture
  For the most part, we play tennis on Sunday morning

  [D] CONTINUOUS/CONTINUAL FREQUENCY
  Does she *always* dress well?
  He is *continually* complaining about the noise
  She *incessantly* asks for more money
  They are *perpetually* in debt

  [E] HIGH FREQUENCY
  I have *often* told them to relax more
  They *regularly* take their dog for a walk in the evening
  Have you been drunk *many times?*
  She leaves the door unlocked *time after time*
  They explained *again and again* that they couldn't help it, but he didn't believe them

[F] LOW OR ZERO FREQUENCY

We are *occasionally* invited to their house for a party
I *sometimes* think she doesn't know what she's talking about
He has *never* been in Singapore
They *seldom* watch television during the day
They haven't *ever* seen my wife
I have driven *a few times*
You should phone them *now and again* ('occasionally')
Do you visit your parents *from time to time?* ('occasionally')
We play cards *off and on* ('occasionally', informal)
I have been in his office *on several occasions*

Most time *frequency* adjuncts are normally positioned at *E* (*cf* 8.7). However, adverbs of indefinite frequency (Groups C-F) are normally positioned at *M2*, but are often found at *M1*, while prepositional phrases denoting usual occurrence (Group C) are normally positioned at *I*.

Note

[a] We should add to Groups E and F items that are used as intensifiers (8.33):

[E] *much, a lot, a good deal, a great deal* (all equivalent to *often* or *very often*)
[F] *a little* ('very occasionally'), *little* ('hardly at any time'), *less* ('less frequently'), *least* ('least frequently'), *a bit* ('occasionally'); *barely, hardly, scarcely*

Enough and *sufficiently* as frequentatives denote a sufficient number of times and therefore do not fit into either of these groups. Alternatively, we can say that they can fit into both groups. As frequentatives, *hardly*, and *scarcely* tend to co-occur with non-assertive *ever* ('at any time'):

I $\begin{Bmatrix} hardly \\ scarcely \end{Bmatrix}$ever go there

Barely is rare as a frequentative.

[b] Assertive *ever* is used much less frequently than non-assertive *ever:*

I am *ever* open to new ideas ('always', formal)

8.62

Adjuncts of definite frequency in Group A denote the period of time by which the frequency is measured, while those in [B] express the measurement in number of times (*cf* 4.20). Items from each group can co-occur, normally with the item from [B] coming first:

You should take the medicine *twice* [B] *daily* [A]

Those in [A] can also co-occur with each other in a hierarchical relationship:

She felt his pulse $\begin{cases} hourly \text{ [A] } each \, day \text{ [A]} \\ each \, hour \text{ [A] } daily \text{ [A]} \end{cases}$

The order of the adjuncts in E depends in part on information focus (14.2 *ff*), but only the one denoting the longer period can occur in I (*cf* 8.50, 8.59):

$$\begin{bmatrix} Each\ day \\ Daily \end{bmatrix} \text{she felt his pulse} \begin{bmatrix} hourly \\ each\ hour \end{bmatrix}$$

$$* \begin{bmatrix} Hourly \\ Each\ hour \end{bmatrix} \text{she felt his pulse} \begin{bmatrix} each\ day \\ daily \end{bmatrix}$$

Co-occurrence of the adverb forms, however, is odd even if the one denoting the longer period is in I:

?She felt his pulse *hourly daily*
?*Daily* she felt his pulse *hourly*

Those in [B] can likewise co-occur with each other in a hierarchical relationship, where the subordinate adjunct denotes the number of times for each of the times denoted by the superordinate adjunct. The verb must be a momentary verb (3.41):

I hit him *twice on two occasions* ('two times on each of two occasions')

The superordinate adjunct tends to follow the subordinate adjunct and can be in I position:

On two occasions I hit him *twice*
?*Twice* I hit him *on two occasions*

While the adverbs and the noun phrases X *times* are ambiguous between superordinate and subordinate function in such a hierarchy, the prepositional phrases *on X occasions* are unambiguously superordinate.

Adjuncts in [B] can often be the response to the question *How many times?* The question is used to elicit the adjunct when only one item from [B] is involved, but it can also elicit the subordinate or superordinate adjunct when two items from [B] are involved:

A: How many times did you hit him?   B: *Twice.*
A: How many times did you hit him on the two occasions?   B: *Twice.*
A: How many times did you hit him twice?

B: $\begin{cases} On\ two\ occasions. \\ Twice. \end{cases}$

Adjuncts of definite frequency can also co-occur with items from each of the subclasses of adjuncts of indefinite frequency:

You should $\begin{cases} normally\ [C] \\ always\ [D] \\ often\ [E] \\ seldom\ [F] \end{cases}$ take the medicine *twice* [B] *daily* [A]

Note

In the hierarchical relationship, repetition of the same adverb is avoided for stylistic reasons:

?I hit him *twice twice*
?*Twice* I hit him *twice*.

8.63

Adjuncts of indefinite frequency in Group C denote usual occurrence. They differ from most of the other adjuncts of indefinite frequency in that they can precede the clausal negative, in which case they express that it is normal for something *not* to occur:

Generally,
Normally, }he doesn't take medicine
Usually,

They differ from those in [E] and [F] that can precede negation in that it is a contradiction to assert both that it is normal for something to occur and also that it is normal for it not to occur:

**Generally,*   *generally,*
**Normally,* }he doesn't take medicine, but{ *normally,* }he does (take
**Usually,*   *usually,*   medicine)

On the other hand, those in [E] and [F] that precede negation express a high or low frequency. It is not contradictory to assert that it is frequent (or infrequent) for something to occur and at the same time that it is frequent (or infrequent) for it not to occur:

[*Often*   ] he doesn't take medicine, but [*often*   ] he does
[*Occasionally*]   [*occasionally*]
                                                                (take medicine)

We can see from this example that *often* does not necessarily imply the majority of times, and the same is true for *frequently*. However, those in [C], like *generally*, do imply the majority of times. Most in [C] allow for exceptions. We can therefore say, for example:

Generally,
Normally, }he doesn't take medicine, but *sometimes* he does (take
Usually,   medicine)

Note

[a] *Invariably* is the only one in [C] that denies the possibility of exceptions:

**Invariably,* he doesn't take medicine, but *sometimes* he does (take medicine).

[b] *Generally speaking* and (occasionally) *normally speaking* are used as frequency adjuncts corresponding to *generally* and *normally* respectively (*cf* 8.81).

8.64

Frequency adjuncts like *usually* in [C] as well as *often* and *frequently* in [E] can be the focus of negation:

$$\text{He doesn't} \begin{cases} \check{U}\text{sually} \\ \check{O}\text{Ften} \\ \text{FR}\check{E}\text{quently} \end{cases} \text{speak from notes}$$

But for those in [C], apart from the special case of *invariably* (8.63 Note *a*), there is as a general rule no logical difference resulting from whether the adjunct is within the scope of negation or not (7.49, 7.51). Somebody agreeing with a previous speaker could remove a frequency adjunct of [C] from the scope of negation:

A: He doesn't *ǔsually* speak from notes.
  B: That's true. He *usually* DÒESn't (speak from notes).

To take the paraphrase of *usually*, there is no logical difference between the two sentences:

It's usual for him *not* to speak from notes
It's not usual for him to speak from notes

On the other hand, there is a logical difference between positioning *often* or *frequently* within the scope of negation and positioning them outside of it. Whereas, as we saw in 8.63, we can say

Often he doesn't take medicine, but *often* he does

we cannot say

*He doesn't *ǒFten* take medicine, but *often* he does (take medicine)

because when *often* or *frequently* come within the scope of negation we deny the frequency, and we cannot then assert it.

If frequency adjuncts in [C] co-occur with duration adjuncts (8.60), there can be a difference according to whether the frequency adjunct is within the scope of negation or not:

|*ǔsually*| he doesn't sleep for two days at a time
  ('The usual thing is for him to go without sleep for two days at a time')
He doesn't *ǔsually* sleep for two days at a time
  ('It's rare for him to sleep as long as two days at a time')

The same distinction applies for *often* and *frequently*.

Often and *frequently* can be the focus of a cleft sentence, particularly if they are modified or in a negated or interrogated focal clause (*cf* 8.28, 8.31, 8.39):

It's *very frequently* that he loses money
It's *not often* that I have a chance to speak to him
Is it *often* that she drives alone?

But they cannot be the focus if the sentence is negative:

$$*\text{It's}\begin{Bmatrix}frequently\\often\end{Bmatrix}\text{that she doesn't speak to him}$$

though this is possible for some speakers if there is modification of the adjunct:

It's *all too frequently* that people don't offer to help
Is it *very often* that she doesn't speak to him?
It isn't *very often* that she doesn't speak to him
It's *not often* that he doesn't help

Rarely and *seldom* of Group F, *cf* 8.61, can also be the focus of a cleft sentence:

$$\text{It's}\begin{Bmatrix}rarely\\seldom\end{Bmatrix}\begin{Bmatrix}\text{that he loses any money}\\\text{that people don't offer to help}\end{Bmatrix}$$

8.65

Indefinite frequency adjuncts can co-occur with each other in a hierarchical relationship (*cf* 8.50, 8.59, 8.62):

Normally [C], committee meetings are held *infrequently* [F]
Usually [C], he *constantly* [D] complains of headaches when he is assigned a responsible task
They *seldom* [F] put on plays *again and again* [E]
I have *often* [E] telephoned him *a few times* [F] on the same day

Even some adjuncts in the same group can co-occur if we use momentary verbs (3.41):

They have *often* [E] pressed his bell *repeatedly* [E] without getting an answer
I have *rarely* [F] knocked on his door (*only*) *a few times* [F]

It is not clear what all the conditions are for co-occurrence. Contrast with the above examples:

?They have *often* [E] beaten him *frequently* [E]

Non-assertive *ever* ('at any time') is commonly used with the negative forms *hardly, rarely, scarcely* in [F]; *cf* 8.66. Its use with *never* is considered substandard by some speakers:

?I *never ever* go there.

8.66

Whereas frequency adjuncts in [C], such as *usually*, can precede negation (8.63), those in [D] normally cannot:

$$*\text{He} \begin{Bmatrix} always \\ constantly \end{Bmatrix} \text{doesn't pay his debts on time}$$

$$*\text{He} \begin{Bmatrix} continually \\ incessantly \end{Bmatrix} \text{didn't drink whiskey}$$

Instead we use *never, not . . . ever*, or *not . . . at all:*

$$\text{He} \begin{Bmatrix} never \text{ pays} \\ \text{did}n't \text{ }ever \text{ pay} \end{Bmatrix} \text{his debts on time}$$

He did*n't* drink whiskey *at all*

Those in [E], such as *frequently* and *repeatedly*, denote a high frequency and those in [F], such as *occasionally* and *never*, denote a low or zero frequency.

Several in [F] are negative forms (7.48):

barely, hardly, little, never, rarely, scarcely, seldom

When these are in *I* position, they cause subject-operator inversion, such usage being literary or rhetorical in tone.

Note

[a] The following in [E] and [F] don't precede negation:

　　[E] *regularly*
　　[F] *infrequently, irregularly;* the negative forms; the non-assertives, *eg: ever*

In addition, none of the frequentatives that are used as intensifiers (8.61 Note *a*) can precede negation, *eg: much, enough, least.*

[b] *Regularly* normally denotes high frequency as well as 'at regular intervals'.

8.67

Time frequency adjuncts and quantifiers

If the subject is generic (4.28 *ff*), many adjuncts of indefinite frequency, particularly when positioned at *I* or *M*, are equivalent to certain predeterminers (4.18 *ff*) or to certain quantifiers (4.25) in the noun phrase of the subject. For example, in

Sailors drink rum *often* ('on many occasions')

often is included in the predication and refers to the frequency of the drinking of rum. However, the effect of either of the versions

$$\begin{matrix} \text{Often sailors} \\ \text{Sailors often} \end{matrix} \Big\} \text{drink rum ('it often happens that . . .')}$$

is very similar to

Many sailors drink rum

Other examples:

Good novels are *always* worth buying
   = All good novels are worth buying
Policemen are *usually* unarmed in Britain
   = *Most* policemen are unarmed in Britain
Universities *often* have linguistics departments
   = *Many* universities have linguistics departments
A dog is *sometimes* a dangerous animal
   = *Some* dogs are dangerous animals
Students *occasionally* fail this course
   = *A few* students fail this course
Englishmen *rarely* talk to strangers in trains
   = *Few* Englishmen talk to strangers in trains
Officers *never* get drunk while on duty
   = *No* officers get drunk while on duty

If the direct object is generic, the adjunct may be equivalent to a pre-determiner or quantifier in the noun phrase of the direct object:

Our university *always* expels riotous students
   = Our university expels *all* riotous students
Soldiers *often* guard government buildings
   = Soldiers guard *many* government buildings

Note
Two of the above sentences have alternative interpretations to those given above:

Policemen are *usually* unarmed in Britain
   = It is usual for all policemen to be unarmed in Britain, but all are sometimes armed
Englishmen *rarely* talk to strangers in trains
   = On rare occasions all Englishmen talk to strangers in trains

Time relationship adjuncts
8.68
Time adjuncts included here do not find a place in other semantic sub-classes. They all express some relationship in time. Common adverbs in this subclass can be divided into three groups:

Group A
   many of those denoting temporal sequence, also used for time *when* (8.57 *f*):

   *afterwards, before, eventually, finally, first, later, next,
   originally, previously, subsequently, then*

Group B

$\left.\begin{array}{l} \textit{already} \\ \textit{yet} \end{array}\right\}$('by or before a given or implied time')

still ('(even) up to this time', '(even) up to that time')

Group C

again ('as before')

Examples of the use of time *relationship* adjuncts:

Group A

Did she *first* see him when he was a child?

I've been considering what to do since he *last* discussed with me his problems

She broke her leg *for the first time* while she was skiing in Switzerland

These techniques were *originally* used in the Second World War

It wasn't until the end of the party that I was *finally* introduced to her

Group B

By the time I arrived they had *already* left

We haven't *yet* eaten

We *still* don't know where we are going to live

I have *so far* bought two shirts and a pair of shoes

They have finished their work *by now*

I don't want it *any more*

Group C

I feel better *again*

Put it together *again* ('as before')

It will never be the same *again* in our home.

8.69

Time *relationship* adjuncts in [A] tend to co-occur with a time *when* adjunct (8.57 *ff*). If they are adverbs, they normally appear in *M2*. *Again* in [C] normally occurs at *E*.

Of the adverbs in [B], *already* and *still* normally occur in *M2*, and *yet* in *M2* or *E*. These three adverbs differ in their behaviour with respect to negation and other sentence processes normally requiring non-assertives (7.44, 7.57*f*). *Yet* is usually a non-assertive form (7.44), but it can occur in an assertive HAVE *to* construction:

I have *yet* to find out what he wants

Yet can also be used as an assertive form when it is closer in meaning to *still*:

$\left\{\begin{array}{l}\text{I can see him } \textit{yet}\\ \text{I can } \textit{still} \text{ see him}\end{array}\right.$
$\left\{\begin{array}{l}\text{There's plenty of time } \textit{yet}\\ \text{There's } \textit{still} \text{ plenty of time}\end{array}\right.$

Still can precede negation, but normally cannot lie within the scope of clause negation (7.49) except in questions. By contrast, *already* can never come within the scope of clause negation except in questions, and it normally cannot precede negation. The possibilities for the three adverbs in declarative, negative, and interrogative sentences are given below, where the paraphrases or suggestions for context indicate semantic similarities and differences between the adverbs:

DECLARATIVE POSITIVE
I *already* like him' ('I have by this time come to like him')
*I *yet* like him
I *still* like him ('I continue to like him')

DECLARATIVE NEGATIVE (adverb preceding negation)
*I *already* haven't spoken to him
*I *yet* haven't spoken to him
I *still* haven't spoken to him ('I haven't spoken to him so far')

DECLARATIVE NEGATIVE (adverb following negation)
*He can't *already* drive
He can't drive *yet* ('He can't drive up to this time')
?He can't *still* drive ('He can't continue to drive')

INTERROGATIVE POSITIVE
Have you *already* seen him? (That was quick)
Have you seen him *yet*? (You've been here ages)
Do you *still* see him? ('Do you continue to see him?')

INTERROGATIVE NEGATIVE
Haven't you seen him *already*? ⎫ ('Haven't you by this time seen
Haven't you seen him *yet*?   ⎭ him?')
Don't you *still* see him? ('Don't you continue to see him?')

For the non-assertives *any more* and *any longer* and the negative *no more*, see 7.44.

Note
[a] The difference between *already* and *yet* in questions is that *already* expects an affirmative answer whereas *yet* leaves open whether the answer is negative or positive (7.57f).
[b] *Yet* and *still* come close in meaning in the HAVE *to* construction:
   I have *yet* to meet him
   I have *still* to meet him

Both of the sentences mean 'It remains for me to meet him', but the sentence with *still* implies an obligation that remains to be fulfilled and that is likely to be fulfilled.

[c] *Still* often blends concessive and temporal meanings. For example, in

It's very late and he's *still* working

the effect of *still* is to express not only the continuance of the action but also to suggest that the continuance is surprising ('He's continuing even so to work'). See also the concessive conjunct *still* (8.89).

8.70
Relative positions of time adjuncts

In the previous sections we have frequently referred to the normal positions of time adjuncts in the various subclasses. We now turn to the relative positions of adjuncts from the three major subclasses that can co-occur at E position: time *when* (8.57 *ff*), time *duration* (8.60), and time *frequency* (8.61 *ff*). These tend to occur in the order

time *duration* (D) – time *frequency* (F) – time *when* (W)

The following sentences exemplify the normal order (but *cf* 8.77):

I was there *for a short while* (D) *every couple of hours* (F) *on Monday* (W)
He played with us *very frequently* (F) *last week* (W)
I'm paying my rent *monthly* (F) *this year* (W)
Our electricity was cut off *briefly* (D) *today* (W)
We'll discuss the matter *during lunch* (D) *tomorrow afternoon* (W)
He'll be staying here *for the summer* (D) *every year* (F)
He does exercises *for several hours* (D) *every weekend* (F)

8.71
Coordination

Time adjuncts in the same subclass can be coordinated:

TIME *WHEN*
   today and tomorrow
   now or later
   before or after
   in 1970 and (in) 1971
   when we were there and afterwards

TIME *DURATION*
   permanently or temporarily
   during the summer and (during the) winter
   for the week or (for the) month

TIME *FREQUENCY*
    once or twice
    often and regularly
    each day and (each) night
    a few times or many (times)

Note

Now and then and *now and again* are common coordinated expressions used for time frequency ('from time to time', 'occasionally'). Similarly, *again and again* and *over and over* are used to denote frequent repetition and not just two repetitions.

8.72
Time adjuncts and time reference

Time adjuncts play a part in specifying the time reference of the verb auxiliaries. Thus, it is the time adjuncts that determine that the reference in

    He is playing *now*

is present, whereas that in

    He is playing *tomorrow*

is future. Because of their time significance, some time adjuncts cannot co-occur with particular forms of the verb group. Thus, *tomorrow* does not co-occur with the simple past:

    *He played *tomorrow*

and *yesterday* does not co-occur with the present nor (normally) with the modal auxiliaries:

$$*\text{He} \begin{cases} \text{may} \\ \text{will} \\ \text{should} \end{cases} \text{play } yesterday$$

For further discussion of this topic, see 3.23 *ff* (in particular sections 25, 26, 30 *f*, 37 *f*); 8.57 Note *b*; 8.60; 8.75; 11.68; 11.70.

Note

An apparent exception is with verbs of saying, arranging, expecting, or wanting where the object has future reference (8.54, 8.73). In such cases, though the expressed verb is in the past, there may be a time adjunct with future reference, since the adjunct's reference is to the object:

    He called for a meeting *next week* (=He called for a meeting to be held next week)
    She wanted the book *tomorrow* (=She wanted to have the book tomorrow)
    They predicted a crisis *next month* (=They predicted that there would be a crisis next month)

There can also be an adjunct with past reference that relates to the verb in the past:

    As far back as March, they predicted a crisis *next month* (*ie* their prediction of a crisis next month was made as far back as March).

8.73

Time adjuncts as predicative adjuncts with *be*

Time adjuncts can co-occur with all verbs, including BE:

It's much warmer *now*

Many of them can also be used as predicative adjuncts with BE:

TIME *WHEN*
   The meeting will be *tomorrow*

TIME *DURATION*
   I'm afraid the noise will be *for the whole summer*
   The show is *from nine till twelve*

TIME *FREQUENCY*
   Interviews are *every hour*
   Guided tours around the museum are *twice a day*

BE in such cases is equivalent to TAKE PLACE, and the subject must either be an abstract event noun or an eventive noun. For example in

The opera will be *tonight*

the opera is interpreted as 'the performance of the opera'.

The progressive is excluded when time adjuncts are used as predicative adjuncts with BE (*cf* 8.46):

*Interviews *are being every hour*

Contrast

Interviews *are being held every hour*

Some adverbials cannot be predicative adjuncts, including time *frequency* adjuncts in [C], *eg: as a rule*, and in [D], *eg: always* (8.61).

We saw that with certain verbs the reference of the place adjunct may be to the place of the object rather than to that of the subject (8.54). Similarly, the reference of the time adjunct may be to the object. We can sometimes express the relationship by a sentence in which the object of the original sentence is subject and the time adjunct is predicative with BE. There are two types of such references to the object, as with the place adjuncts:

(1) The verbs denote the placing or movement of the object, and a place adjunct is present indicating the resulting place of the action. The time adjuncts denote time *duration*.

   They threw him in prison *for life* ('He will be in prison for life')
   He's moving the family into a hotel *temporarily* ('The family will be in a hotel temporarily')

We're sending her to London *for the summer* ('She will be in
London for the summer')

They left the car in the street *for an hour* ('The car was in
the street for an hour')

(2) The verbs are verbs of saying, arranging, expecting, or wanting
where the object has future reference. The time adjuncts denote
time *when*, time *duration*, and time *frequency*.

TIME *WHEN*

He expected the guests *next week* ('that the guests would
come next week')

They arranged the meeting *for later today* ('that the meeting
would be held later today')

He set the alarm *for seven o'clock* ('so that the alarm
would go off at seven o'clock')

TIME *DURATION*

He predicts a state of tension *for a long time* ('that there
will be a state of tension for a long time')

They offered us the house *for the summer* ('that we could
use the house for the summer')

TIME *FREQUENCY*

They promised her a party *every Saturday night* ('that she
would have a party every Saturday night')

I suggest an informal discussion *occasionally* ('that there
should be an informal discussion occasionally')

Note

Where the time adjunct can also refer to the action of the verb, there may be ambiguity. For example, the sentence

They promised her a party *every Saturday night*

can also mean that the promise was made every Saturday night. If the adjunct is
moved from *E* position, this interpretation is the normal one:

Every Saturday night they promised her a party.

Syntactic features of time adjuncts
8.74

There are differences between time adjuncts with respect to the numbered
syntactic features in 8.8 and 8.9. Most time adjuncts allow features that
are general to adverbials. However, time *frequency* adjuncts in [C], *eg:
usually, as a rule,* allow only the first three of the features listed in 8.8:
they can be the focus of a question, they can be the focus of negation,
and they can come within the scope of predication pro-forms or predication ellipsis.

Most time adverbs do not allow the features of modification listed for adverbs in 8.9. Such adverbs cannot be premodified by *very*. Time adjuncts allowing modification are:

TIME *WHEN*: *early, late, recently*
TIME *DURATION*: *long, briefly, recently*
TIME *FREQUENCY*: *commonly* [C], *constantly* [D], *incessantly* [D]; Group E; several in Group F: *infrequently, irregularly, little, rarely, seldom*

Some adverbs that cannot be premodified by *very* can be premodified by other intensifiers:

$$\left.\begin{array}{l}\text{(very) much}\\ \text{somewhat}\\ \text{a lot}\\ \text{a little}\end{array}\right\}\left\{\begin{array}{l}\textit{after}\\ \textit{afterwards}\\ \textit{later (`afterwards')}\\ \textit{before}\\ \textit{earlier (`before')}\end{array}\right.$$

Others in the same semantic group do not seem to allow at least some of these intensifiers:

$$\left.\begin{array}{l}\text{*(very) much}\\ \text{?somewhat}\\ \text{?a lot}\\ \text{?a little}\end{array}\right\}\textit{previously}$$

$$\left.\begin{array}{l}\text{*(very) much}\\ \text{*somewhat}\\ \text{?*a lot}\\ \text{?*a little}\end{array}\right\}\textit{subsequently}$$

Note

[a] *Still, already,* and *yet* allow none of the features in 8.8 and 8.9 except that they come within the scope of predication pro-forms or predication ellipsis (3) and they can occur in dependent clauses (7). As time adverbials, none of these three adverbs can appear initially in an independent tone unit before a negative sentence. Hence they fall within our definition of adjunct.

[b] With respect to ability to be focused by a cleft sentence, by *only*, or by *also*, some general statements can be made for frequency adjuncts in [D], *eg: constantly,* [E], *eg: often,* and [F], *eg: occasionally*. None of the three groups allow focusing by *also*, [D] and [E] cannot be focused by *only*, and [D] cannot be focused by a cleft sentence. There are also individual differences within the groups. For example, in [F] *never* and *ever* cannot be focused by a cleft sentence, though others in [F], *eg: seldom,* can be. And acceptability in a cleft sentence is often improved if the item is modified or the focal clause is interrogative or negative (*cf* 8.28, 8.31, 8.39, 8.64).

[c] *Again, last,* and *instantly* cannot be the focus of *only* or of a cleft sentence, and, except *again*, none of them can be the focus of *also*.

8.75

Many time adjuncts do not co-occur with imperatives. This restriction applies to time *when* adjuncts (8.57) that cannot co-occur with future reference (*cf* 8.72). We cannot, therefore, say

*Go there $\left.\right\}$ $\begin{cases} yesterday \\ at\ a\ former\ time \\ not\ long\ ago \end{cases}$
*Let's go there

just as we cannot say

*I order you to go there $\left.\right\}$ $\begin{cases} yesterday \\ at\ a\ former\ time \\ not\ long\ ago \end{cases}$
*He will go there

Similarly, we cannot use with imperatives those time *duration* adjuncts (8.60) that refer to a duration from some preceding point of time or to a duration ending at some point in the past:

*Stay $\left.\right\}$ $\begin{cases} recently \\ until\ last\ week \\ since\ I\ came\ here \end{cases}$
*Let's stay

Time *frequency* adjuncts of Group C denoting usual occurrence (8.61), *eg: usually, generally, normally,* are unlikely to co-occur with imperatives.

Note
While we can say

Go there *now* ('at this time')

it is odd to say

?*Go there *presently* ('at the present time' though acceptable in the sense 'soon')

just as the prepositional phrase *at the present time* is odd with imperatives. When *just* is used with an imperative, it is a restrictive adjunct synonymous with *merely* (8.13, 8.16 Note *d*):

Just go there.

8.76
Other classes of adjuncts
Some classes of adjuncts are realized by prepositional phrases or clauses and either rarely or not at all by adverbs. For example, there are prepositional phrases and clauses expressing purpose (6.36, 11.39), but there are few adverbs used in this way. (See Note *b* below.) Other classes of adjuncts are realized by prepositional phrases only; for example, adjuncts expressing source or origin (6.38), as in

He took the book *from me*
I come *from London*

Furthermore, the nearest equivalent among adverbs to an adjunct prepositional phrase or clause may not be an adjunct. The conjunction *because* and the preposition *because of* can both introduce adjuncts of cause or reason (11.37, 6.35):

> *Because he made a mistake*, several people died
> *Because of his mistake*, several people died

However, the adverbs referring to reason or cause are not adjuncts but conjuncts (8.89), since they do not themselves convey the reason or cause but refer back to some previous mention of it:

He made a mistake and $\begin{Bmatrix} so \\ therefore \end{Bmatrix}$ several people died.

Note

[a] On a similar relationship between disjunct clause and conjunct, see 8.78.

[b] Perhaps *symbolically* ('for a symbolic purpose', 'as a symbol') and *experimentally* ('for an experimental purpose', 'as an experiment') in the following sentences are instances of adverbs used to denote purpose:

> They *symbolically* buried the car as a protest against pollution
> The teacher *experimentally* called the students by their first names.

8.77
Relative positions of adjuncts
In the appropriate sections, we have outlined the positions of adjuncts that belong to a particular class and also the positions of adjuncts relative to those in the same class. There remains the question of the positions of adjuncts relative to those in other classes. Three general principles must first be stated, and these apply to relative order whether within a class or between classes:

(1) The normal relative order can be changed to suit the desire for end-focus (14.3.).

(2) A clause normally comes after other structures, since otherwise these would be interpreted as adjuncts of the clause:

> We stood talking *for a very long time where the fire had been*

(3) Longer adjuncts tend to follow shorter adjuncts:

> I was studying *earlier in the university library*

This principle often coincides with the preceding one.
Where adjuncts cluster in *E* position, the normal order is

process – place – time

This order is exemplified in

> He was working *with his shears* (process) *in the garden* (place)
> *the whole morning* (time).

Adjuncts that can occur in *I* are often put in that position for reasons of information focus, but also to avoid having too many adjuncts at *E*. We might, therefore, have moved the time adjunct in the above sentence to *I:*

> *The whole morning* he was working *with his shears in the garden*

It is not usual for more than one adjunct to be in *I*, but time and place adjuncts sometimes co-occur there:

> *In London, after the war*, damaged buildings were quickly demolished and replaced by new buildings that were the admiration of architects from all over the world.

Viewpoint adjuncts also co-occur with other adjuncts at *I:*

> *Economically, in this century* our country has suffered many crises.

Note

[a] On positions of prepositional phrases as adjuncts, see 6.56 *f*. On positions of clauses as adjuncts, see 11.26 *ff*.

[b] As many as three adverbs can co-occur at *E:*

> Children are writing *badly now everywhere*

But, if they are all *-ly* adverbs, the result is odd:

> ?Children are writing *badly locally lately*

Of course, the adverbs can themselves be modified:

> Children are writing *very badly now almost everywhere.*

[c] With prepositional verbs (12.23), it is normal for adjuncts to follow the complementation, even though insertion of an adjunct is allowed.

Disjuncts
8.78

Most disjuncts (8.2–5) are prepositional phrases or clauses. The nearest equivalent among adverbs to a disjunct prepositional phrase or a disjunct clause may be a conjunct. For example, clauses of reason or cause introduced by *since* (11.37) are disjuncts:

> *Since we live near the sea*, we enjoy a healthy climate

On the other hand, the corresponding adverbs are conjuncts (8.89). The adverbs merely indicate the logical relationship with what preceded. They do not convey the reason or cause themselves, but refer back to some previous mention of it:

We live near the sea and $\left\{ \begin{matrix} so \\ therefore \end{matrix} \right\}$ we enjoy a healthy climate

For disjunct prepositional phrases, see 6.47 *ff*. For disjunct clauses, see 11.29, 11.37, 11.52, 11.65–66.

Note

The *since* clause is a disjunct because it cannot be contrasted with other adverbials in alternative interrogation or in alternative negation (8.3). Whether a clause is a disjunct or adjunct does not depend solely on which conjunction introduces it. For example, most *because* clauses are adjuncts, but a final *because* clause may be a disjunct (*cf* 9.23, 11.37):

He's drunk, *because I saw him staggering.*

8.79

Adverbs as disjuncts can be divided into two main classes: STYLE DISJUNCTS (by far the smaller class) and ATTITUDINAL DISJUNCTS. Style disjuncts convey the speaker's comment on the form of what he is saying, defining in some way under what conditions he is speaking. Attitudinal disjuncts, on the other hand, comment on the content of the communication. These two classes and their subclasses are displayed in *Fig* 8:5.

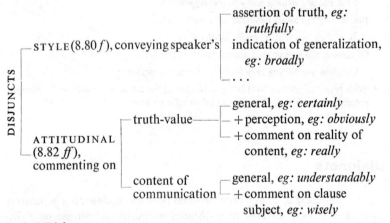

Fig 8:5 Disjuncts

Style disjuncts
8.80

The relationship between the adverb as style disjunct and the clause to which it is attached can be expressed by a clause in which a homonym of the style disjunct is a process adjunct (8.34 *ff*), the subject is the *I* of the speaker, and there is a verb of speaking. Thus, *frankly* in

> *Frankly,* I am tired

is equivalent to *I tell you frankly* or *I say frankly.* If the clause is a question, the conjunct may be ambiguous:

> *Frankly,* is he tired?

Frankly in the question may correspond to *I ask you frankly* or to the more probable *Tell me frankly.*

Common adverbs as style disjuncts include:

Group A
> *bluntly, candidly, flatly, frankly, honestly, seriously, strictly, truly, truthfully*

Group B
> *approximately, briefly, broadly, crudely, generally, roughly, simply*

Others
> *confidentially, literally, metaphorically, personally*

Those in Group A express the speaker's assertion that he is being truthful in what he is saying, while those in Group B indicate that the speaker is making a generalization.

Examples of the use of style disjuncts:

> *Briefly,* there is nothing more I can do about it
> I don't want the money, *confidentially*
> *Seriously,* do you intend to resign?
> *Personally,* I don't approve of her
> You ask me what he wants. *Quite simply,* he wants to move to a
>   better climate
> *Strictly speaking,* nobody is allowed in here
> *Putting it at its lowest terms,* he has little market-value
> There were twelve people present, *to be precise*
> *With respect,* none of them is competent to give an opinion on the
>   matter
> *In short,* she is mad but happy
> *If I may say so,* that dress doesn't suit you

Note
Many conjuncts also correspond to a construction with a verb of speaking (8.90).

8.81
For some adverbs as style disjuncts, we have a series corresponding to them in other structures. For example, in place of *frankly* in

> *Frankly,* he hasn't a chance

we could put:

> prepositional phrase – *in all frankness*
> infinitive clause – *to be frank, to speak frankly, to put it frankly*
> -*ing* participle clause – *frankly speaking, putting it frankly*
> -*ed* participle clause – *put frankly*
> finite verb clause – *if I may be frank, if I can speak frankly, if I can put it frankly*

Not every style disjunct will allow the full range. Thus, we have *in all fairness* but not the style disjunct *fairly; in short* but not *shortly*. Similarly we have *flatly*, but not *flatly speaking*.

But for almost all of the adverbs listed in 8.80 corresponding participle constructions with *speaking* are available as style disjuncts, *eg: frankly ~ frankly speaking, seriously ~ seriously speaking*. Many have infinitive clauses of the form *to be* plus the stem adjective, *eg: bluntly ~ to be blunt, personally ~ to be personal*. Those allowing such infinitive clauses have a corresponding finite clause with *if, eg: if I may be blunt, if I may be personal*.

Note

[a] The order of adjunct and verb in the participle construction with *speaking* is more or less stereotyped. *Speaking frankly* is far less likely than *frankly speaking*. On the other hand, *speaking generally* is the participle construction equivalent to the adverb style disjunct *generally*. The style disjunct *generally* (with its corresponding prepositional phrase *in general*) is to be distinguished from the time adjunct *generally*, synonymous with *normally* or *usually* (8.61, 8.63 Note *b*). The style disjunct is exemplified in

> The committee interviewed the two writers. *Generally*, the writers were against censorship.

Since the time adjunct has a corresponding participle clause *generally speaking*, the inverted form *speaking generally* is sometimes used for the disjunct.

[b] The style disjunct *personally* is to be distinguished from the intensifier *personally*, which is synonymous with the appropriate reflexive form of the pronoun:

> I $\left\{ \begin{array}{l} personally \\ myself \end{array} \right\}$ have never been to New York

These are both to be distinguished from the adjunct *personally* that is synonymous with *in person:*

> He signed the document *personally*.

[c] *Truly* has been included among style disjuncts. It corresponds both to *I tell you truly* and in many environments also to *It is true (that)*, the latter type of correspondence being common to many attitudinal disjuncts (8.83). However, unlike such attitudinal disjuncts but like other style disjuncts, it can appear before a question:

> I think he has no right to be there. *Truly*, what is your opinion?

Neither *It is true* nor *Is it true* can replace *truly* here.

Attitudinal disjuncts
8.82
Adverbs as attitudinal disjuncts convey the speaker's comment on the content of what he is saying. Two major groups can be distinguished, which can in turn be subdivided.

Group I
These disjuncts present a comment on the truth-value of what is said, expressing the extent to which the speaker believes that what he is saying is true. Group I seems to be a closed class of adverbs and most instances are given.

(a) For adverbs this is the largest subgroup of disjuncts in Group I and differs from the other two subgroups in that the disjuncts neither imply a perception of the truth of what is being said nor indicate the sense in which the truth-value is being judged.
Those expressing conviction (*cf* 8.82 Note *d*):

admittedly, assuredly (rare, formal), *avowedly* (formal), *certainly, decidedly* (rare, formal), *definitely, incontestably* (rare, formal), *incontrovertibly* (formal), *indeed, indisputably* (formal), *indubitably* (rare, formal), *surely, unarguably* (rare, formal), *undeniably, undoubtedly, unquestionably*

Those expressing some degree of doubt:

arguably, allegedly, conceivably, doubtless, quite (etc) *likely, maybe* (informal), *perhaps, possibly, presumably, purportedly* (formal), *reportedly, reputedly* (formal), *supposedly*

(b) These convey the view that one can perceive the truth of what is said. The perception is usually a mental rather than a physical perception.
Those expressing conviction:

clearly, evidently, manifestly (rare, formal), *obviously, patently* (rare, formal), *plainly*

Those expressing some degree of doubt:

apparently, seemingly (rare, formal)

(c) These state the sense in which the speaker judges what he says to be true or false. There is usually a reference to the reality or lack of reality in what is said (*cf* 10.36).
Those asserting the reality of what is said:

actually, really, factually (rare, formal)

Those expressing a contrast with reality:

only apparently, formally, hypothetically, ideally, nominally, officially, ostensibly (formal), *outwardly, superficially, technically, theoretically*

Those expressing that what is being said is true in principle:

basically, essentially, fundamentally

Group II

Disjuncts in this group convey some attitude towards what is said. Only the more common adverbs are included. Those with a participle stem in *-ing, eg: surprisingly*, are the most productive class of adverbs as attitudinal disjuncts.

(a) These do not normally express the view that the speaker's judgment applies also to the subject of the clause to which the disjunct is attached.

What is said is judged to be strange or unexpected:

amazingly, astonishingly, curiously, funnily enough (enough usual in BrE, obligatory in AmE), *incredibly, ironically, oddly, remarkably, strangely, suspiciously, unexpectedly*

What is said is judged to be appropriate or expected:

appropriately, inevitably, naturally, not unnaturally, predictably, typically, understandably

What is said is judged to cause satisfaction or the reverse:

annoyingly, delightfully, disappointingly, disturbingly, refreshingly, regrettably

What is said is judged to be fortunate or unfortunate:

fortunately, unfortunately, happily (formal), *unhappily* (formal), *luckily, unluckily, sadly* (formal), *tragically*

Other judgments:

amusingly, conveniently, hopefully (especially AmE), *mercifully, preferably, significantly, thankfully*

(b) These express a judgment on what is being said as a whole and normally apply the same judgment simultaneously to the subject of the clause.

Judgment is passed on whether what is said is right or wrong:

correctly, incorrectly, justly, unjustly, rightly, wrongly

Judgment is passed on the wisdom or skill of what is described:

> *artfully, cleverly, cunningly, foolishly, prudently, reasonably, unreasonably, sensibly, shrewdly, wisely, unwisely.*

Examples of adverbs as attitudinal disjuncts and of other adverbial structures with similar semantic force (*cf* 6.54, 11.52, 11.65–66):

Certainly, he had very little reason to fear their competition.
Obviously, nobody expected us to be here today.
Really, the public does not have much choice in the matter.
Understandably, we were all extremely annoyed when we received the letter.
He is *wisely* staying at home today.
To my regret, he did not accept our offer.
They arrived, *to our surprise*, before we did.
With justice, they have assumed their place among the nation's heroes.
To the great admiration of all the onlookers, he plunged into the water and rescued the struggling child.
On paper, he ought to have won, but *in fact* he lost.
Of course, nobody imagines that he will repay what he borrowed.
It was *no doubt* clever of him to offer his resignation at that point in the proceedings.
To be sure, we have heard many such promises before.
Even more important, he has control over the finances of the party.
They are not going to buy the house, *which is not surprising in view of its exorbitant price.*
What is even more remarkable, he manages to inspire confidence in the most suspicious people.

Note

[a] Several adverbs with *-ed* participle stems in [Ia] and [Ib] usually imply that the view of others is being quoted: *allegedly, reportedly, reputedly, supposedly.*

[b] *Doubtless* in [Ia] is not synonymous with 'without doubt'. Like *no doubt*, it in fact implies some doubt and is synonymous with 'very probably'. *Undoubtedly*, on the other hand, expresses conviction. *Apparently* in [Ib] is equivalent to 'it appears' or 'it seems', which do not express certainty. However, this is not true for some speakers who equate *apparently* with 'it is evident'. *Admittedly* and *certainly* imply concession as well as certainty (*cf* 10.35).

[c] Just as the verb SEE can be used for both physical and mental perception (*cf: I see* (*ie* realize) *what you mean*), so the adverbs in [Ib] can be used for both types of perception. In

> *Obviously*, he doesn't want us to help him

the speaker's conviction may well be based on what the person has said rather than anything that has been perceived visually. On the other hand, in

Obviously, he is in very poor health

it may be based largely on the person's appearance.

[*d*] Style disjuncts such as *truthfully* and *honestly* (8.80) and attitudinal disjuncts such as *certainly* and *definitely* both express conviction about what is said. But the style disjuncts assert the veracity of the speaker while the attitudinal disjuncts assert the truth of what is said.

8.83

We have seen that adverbs as style disjuncts correspond to a clause with a verb of speaking (8.80). Many adverbs as attitudinal disjuncts, though not all, also correspond to other structures. They may, indeed, correspond to more than one structure. When we give the set of correspondences for adverbs in particular groups, we mean that the set applies to adverbs in those groups and not to adverbs in other groups. We do not claim, however, that all adverbs in the groups allow the correspondences. For example, many adverbs in Group I (8.82), such as *certainly*, correspond to the structures exemplified in

It is certain (that) he doesn't object
That he doesn't object *is certain*

But these correspondences do not apply to (say) *perhaps*. To avoid repetition, we use only the variants with extraposition and anticipatory *it* (14.36). Hence, we give the correspondence for *certainly* in Group I as

It is certain that he doesn't object.

8.84

The semantic distinction between adverbs in Groups I (*eg: certainly, clearly*) and II (*eg: fortunately, wisely*) is reflected in the fact that it is possible to use putative *should* (3.46, 11.72, 12.35) in the correspondences of Group II. If *should* is inserted in correspondences of Group I, it conveys obligation (3.46) and alters the meaning of the sentence radically.

Group I

$\begin{bmatrix} Certainly, \\ Clearly, \end{bmatrix}$ he is behaving well

$\neq$ It is $\begin{bmatrix} certain \\ clear \end{bmatrix}$ *that* he *should* be behaving well ('ought to be behaving well')

Group II

$\begin{bmatrix} Fortunately, \\ Wisely, \end{bmatrix}$ he is behaving well

$=$ *It is* $\begin{bmatrix} fortunate \\ wise \end{bmatrix}$ *that* he *should* be behaving well

Putative *should* is excluded from Group I correspondences, where the factual basis of what is said is asserted or questioned, whereas it is admitted in Group II correspondences, where an opinion is expressed.

Most of the adverbs in Group II allow also a correspondence with an infinitive clause:

$$\begin{bmatrix} Fortunately, \\ Wisely, \end{bmatrix} \text{ he is behaving well}$$

$$= It\ is\ \begin{bmatrix} fortunate \\ wise \end{bmatrix} \textit{for}\ \text{him to be behaving well}$$

This type of infinitive clause is a common replacement for a *that*-clause with *should* (11.72).

Note

[a] *Assuredly* and *decidedly* are roughly synonymous with *surely* and *undoubtedly* respectively. They do not correspond to the structures

$$It\ is \begin{Bmatrix} assured \\ decided \end{Bmatrix} that \ldots$$

$$\begin{Bmatrix} I\ am \\ One\ has \end{Bmatrix} \begin{Bmatrix} assured \\ decided \end{Bmatrix} that \ldots$$

Surely is commonly used to invite agreement from the person or persons addressed.

[b] *Naturally* and the equivalent understatement, *not unnaturally*, are paraphrasable by 'as might have been expected' or 'of course'. They do not correspond to *it is natural* or *it is not unnatural*.

8.85

The semantic distinction between Subgroups IIa (*eg: surprisingly, understandably*) and IIb (*eg: rightly, wisely*) is reflected in the fact that only in the latter group is it normal to have a correspondence in which the judgment is predicated of the subject.

Subgroup IIa

$$\begin{bmatrix} Surprisingly, \\ Understandably, \end{bmatrix} \text{ John returned the money}$$

$$\neq *\text{John was} \begin{bmatrix} surprising \\ understandable \end{bmatrix} \text{ to return the money}$$

Subgroup IIb

$$\begin{bmatrix} Rightly, \\ Wisely, \end{bmatrix} \text{ John returned the money}$$

$$= \text{John was} \begin{bmatrix} right \\ wise \end{bmatrix} \text{ to return the money}$$

The predication automatically applies to the subject in an active sentence and to the agent in a passive sentence, whether the latter is present or recoverable or indefinite (12.11). Hence, we can still set up these correspondences for items in Subgroup IIb in the following instances:

$$\begin{bmatrix} Rightly, \\ Wisely, \end{bmatrix}$$ the money was returned by John

$$= \text{John was } \begin{bmatrix} right \\ wise \end{bmatrix} \text{ to return the money}$$

$$\begin{bmatrix} Rightly, \\ Wisely, \end{bmatrix}$$ the money was returned

$$= \text{Someone was } \begin{bmatrix} right \\ wise \end{bmatrix} \text{ to return the money}$$

These adverbs can be used wherever a human agent is implied, though it may not always be possible to state the correspondences as systematically as in the above instances:

$$\begin{bmatrix} Rightly, \\ Wisely, \end{bmatrix}$$ the meeting *ended* early today

$$= \text{X} \begin{Bmatrix} was \\ were \end{Bmatrix} \begin{bmatrix} right \\ wise \end{bmatrix} \text{ to end the meeting early today}$$

$$\begin{bmatrix} Rightly, \\ Wisely, \end{bmatrix}$$ the book costs only five dollars

$$= \text{X} \begin{Bmatrix} was \\ were \end{Bmatrix} \begin{bmatrix} right \\ wise \end{bmatrix} \text{ to fix the price of the book at only five dollars}$$

$$\begin{bmatrix} Rightly, \\ Wisely, \end{bmatrix}$$ his car is in a garage overnight throughout the winter

$$= \text{He is } \begin{bmatrix} right \\ wise \end{bmatrix} \text{ to keep his car in a garage overnight throughout}$$
$$\text{the winter}$$

Note

Some adverbs in [II] allow correspondences with a personal subject, either the *I* of the speaker or indefinite *one*:

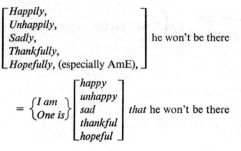

Syntactic features of disjuncts
8.86
In general, disjuncts – whether style or attitudinal – do not allow any of the syntactic features listed for adjuncts in 8.3, 8.8, and 8.9 (*cf* also 8.4). Other features applying to disjuncts include:

(1) Most attitudinal disjuncts cannot appear in any position in a question (*cf* Note *a*, below):

> *Does he *fortunately* know about it?

On the other hand, most style disjuncts can appear in a question, even initially:

> *Frankly*, does he know about it?

But *cf*

> **Personally*, is she very clever?

(2) Most attitudinal disjuncts cannot appear in an indirect question (*cf* Note *a*, below):

> *He asked whether, *fortunately*, they knew anything about it.

Style disjuncts can appear in an indirect question:

> They want to know whether, *strictly speaking*, they're trespassing.

(3) Most attitudinal disjuncts cannot appear with imperatives:

> **Fortunately*, don't tell him.

But *cf*

> Perhaps tell him now.

On the other hand, some style disjuncts (including most in Group A, 8.80) can do so, even in *I* position:

> *Frankly*, don't tell him.

(4) While disjuncts can appear in almost any position, the normal position for most disjuncts is *I*. However, some attitudinal disjuncts in [Ia], *eg: probably, possibly*, and all in [IIb], *eg: rightly, wisely*, normally occur at *M2*, and often at *M1* (*cf* 8.7).

(5) Disjuncts appear with some difficulty in dependent finite clauses, but do so more freely than conjuncts (8.94):

> He was a man who, *unaccountably*, had few friends.
> What, *interestingly enough*, pleased them most was her enthusiasm.

> Though he was *quite rightly* dismissed, he was given six months' salary.

Note

[*a*] Certain attitudinal disjuncts in Group Ia (8.82) expressing some doubt (*eg: perhaps, possibly, conceivably*) are marginally acceptable in direct and indirect questions, but not at *I* position. Some in [Ic] (8.82) are acceptable in questions perhaps even initially, *eg: basically, essentially, fundamentally, ideally*.

[*b*] It seems that attitudinal disjuncts can appear within a clause that is loosely attached to a question:

> Did they refuse the first offer, expecting, *naturally*, a better offer?

[*c*] Some attitudinal disjuncts can be used as a comment on a previous statement, usually accompanied by *yes* or *no:*

> A: They have returned to San Francisco.
> B: *Very wisely.* ('They were very wise to do so')
> A: They won't be coming back.
> B: *Unfortunately*, no. ('It's unfortunate that they won't')

A few style disjuncts (*honestly, literally, seriously, truly, truthfully*) are used as verbless questions:

> A: I'm going to resign.
> B: *Seriously?* ('Were you speaking seriously when you said that?')

The attitudinal disjunct *really* is commonly used in this way:

> A: I'm going to resign.   B: *Really?* ('Is that so?')

8.87

Most disjuncts can be modified. Common premodifiers are *very* and *quite*. For some attitudinal disjuncts in [IIa] (8.82), the postmodifier *enough* is common, particularly for those evaluating the communication as odd (*bizarrely, curiously, eerily, funnily, oddly*):

> *Oddly enough*, he hasn't said anything about it

Several can be premodified by *not*, in particular *surprisingly* and some with negative prefixes (*unexpectedly, unreasonably, unwisely, unusually*):

> *Not surprisingly*, he protested strongly about it
> *Not unreasonably*, she refused him

Other common premodifiers include the comparatives *more, most, less, least*:

> *Strangely*, he has not been here lately. *Even more strangely*, he has not phoned.
> *More amusingly than wisely*, he kept on insisting on his right to speak.

Note

[*a*] Attitudinal disjuncts with *-ed* participle stems, *eg: undoubtedly, allegedly*, cannot be modified.

[b] *Enough* as a modifier of disjuncts does not mean 'sufficiently'. For example the phrase *oddly enough* is paraphrasable by 'odd though it may seem'.

[c] Item-negation of the disjunct can co-occur with clause negation:

Not surprisingly, they were *not* happy with their results.

8.88

A specification of range can be added for attitudinal disjuncts in [IIa] (8.82), normally a prepositional phrase introduced by *for:*

Luckily for John, the gun was not loaded ('John was lucky that . . .')

For John specifies that *luckily* is not to be generalized, but applies specifically to John. Specification can also be made by *from X's point of view* or *from the point of view of X:*

Understandably enough from his point of view, he does not want the news to reach his family before he tells them himself.

An equivalent effect is obtained in prepositional phrases as attitudinal disjuncts, where the noun phrase in the genitive or in the *of*-prepositional phrase specifies the range, *eg: to my regret, to his annoyance, to their disappointment, to John's surprise, to the delight of all present*. Adverbs in [IIa] with participle stem in *-ing, eg: annoyingly*, generally have a corresponding prepositional phrase in this form. The prepositional phrases are more commonly used than the adverbs.

We can achieve the same effect by sentential relative clauses (11.52, 13.15), *eg: which surprised John* or *which I regret*, or by comment clauses (11.65), *what delighted all present* or *what disappoints them*. Sentential relative clauses are probably used most commonly of all.

Note

[a] *Surprisingly* and its synonyms can only take a *for-* specification that refers to a noun or pronoun co-referential with a noun phrase later in the clause:

Surprisingly for him [*ie* for John], the altitude affected John adversely
Surprisingly for him [*ie* for John], John failed the exam
**Surprisingly for his father*, John failed the exam

Contrast the last sentence with

Annoyingly for his father, John failed the exam

Whereas *surprisingly for him* means others are surprised about him, *annoyingly for his father* means his father is annoyed.

This distinction does not apply to the corresponding prepositional phrases. *To my surprise* is equivalent to 'I am (or 'was') surprised'.

[b Corresponding sentential relative clauses can be found for attitudinal disjuncts in all groups having corresponding '*it is* adj *that* . . .' clauses except [Ia] (8.82):

$$\begin{bmatrix} \textit{Certainly,} \\ \textit{Obviously,} \\ \textit{Understandably,} \\ \textit{Wisely,} \end{bmatrix}$$ he didn't want to have anything to do with them

He didn't want to have anything to do with them, which was
$$\left[\begin{array}{l} \text{*certain} \\ (painfully) \\ obvious \\ understandable \\ wise \end{array}\right]$$

On the other hand, all have corresponding comment clauses, though often a modifier such as *very* or *more* is required. Hence, we can have

> *What was even more certain*, he didn't speak at the meeting.

[c] Adverbs in [IIa] that express an opinion as to whether a statement is fortunate or not (*eg: fortunately, luckily*) allow the interpretation that the subject is fortunate or the reverse. But this is not a necessary implication of their use. For example,

> *Fortunately*, John keeps his car in a garage overnight during the winter.

does not necessarily mean that John is fortunate, though out of context this sentence conveys that implication strongly. But we can add to the sentence in such a way as to make it clear that the intention is that someone else is fortunate:

> *Fortunately*, John keeps his car in a garage overnight during the winter. Bob was therefore able to start the car very easily when he needed to borrow it in a hurry early this morning.

From this context, it is clear that it is Bob who is fortunate. Compare also:

> *Fortunately for me* (= I am fortunate that) John keeps his car in a garage overnight during the winter.

In contrast, adverbs in [IIb], such as *rightly* or *wisely*, do not allow *for-* prepositional phrases specifying the range of the adverb.

Conjuncts
8.89
Most conjuncts (8.2–5) are adverbs or prepositional phrases (*cf* 8.76, 8.78). The part that conjuncts play in clause and sentence connection is

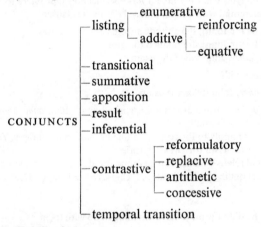

Fig 8:6 Conjuncts

discussed elsewhere (10.17 *ff*). For the distinction between conjuncts and conjunctions, see 9.29 *ff*. *Fig* 8:6 displays the semantic subclasses of conjuncts as defined by their role in clause and sentence connection.

Conjuncts are listed below according to their subclasses. Except for enumerative conjuncts, which are an open class, all adverbs are given, as well as some common prepositional phrases and noun phrases. References are to the sections in Chapter 10 where the conjuncts are discussed.

ENUMERATIVE (10.19)
first, second, third . . .
first(ly), secondly, thirdly . . .
one, two, three (especially in learned and technical use)
a, b, c (especially in learned and technical use)
next, then
finally, last, lastly
in the first place, in the second place . . .
for one thing . . . *(and) for another (thing)*
for a start
to begin with, to start with
to conclude

REINFORCING (10.21)
again (formal), *also, further* (formal), *furthermore, more* (rare, formal), *moreover, then* (informal, especially spoken), *too* (rare, AmE), *in addition, above all, on top of it all, to top it (all), to cap it (all), what is more*

EQUATIVE (10.21)
correspondingly (formal), *equally, likewise, similarly, in the same way, by the same token*

TRANSITIONAL (10.24)
incidentally, now (informal)
by the way, by the by(e)

SUMMATIVE (10.25)
altogether, overall, then, therefore, thus (formal), *(all) in all, in conclusion, in sum, to conclude, to sum up, to summarize*

APPOSITION (10.26, *cf* also 9.138)
namely (often abbreviated to *viz* in formal written English), *thus; in other words, for example* (often abbreviated to *e.g.* or *eg* in written English and sometimes spoken as /i dʒi/), *for instance that is* (often abbreviated to *i.e.* or *ie* in specialized written English and sometimes spoken as /aɪ i/), *that is to say*

RESULT (10.27)
accordingly, consequently, hence (formal), *now, so* (informal),

therefore, thus (formal), *as a consequence, in consequence, as a result*
[*somehow* ('for some reason or other')]

INFERENTIAL (10.28)
else, otherwise, then
in other words
in that case

REFORMULATORY (10.30)
better, rather
in other words

REPLACIVE (10.31)
again, alternatively, rather
better, worse
on the other hand

ANTITHETIC (10.33)
contrariwise (formal), *contrastingly* (formal), *conversely* (formal)
instead (blend of antithetic with replacive)
oppositely (rare), *then*
on the contrary, in contrast, by contrast, by way of contrast
in comparison, by comparison, by way of comparison
(on the one hand . . .) on the other hand

CONCESSIVE (10.34)
anyhow (informal), *anyway* (informal), *besides* (blend of reinforcing with concessive), *else, however, nevertheless, nonetheless* (formal, also spelled *none the less*), *notwithstanding* (formal), *only* (informal), *still, though, yet, in any case, in any event* (formal), *at any rate, at all events, for all that, in spite of that, in spite of it all, after all, at the same time, on the other hand, all the same*

TEMPORAL TRANSITION (10.12)
meantime, meanwhile, in the meantime, in the meanwhile

Examples of conjuncts:

I'd like you to do two things for me. *First*, phone the office and tell them I'll be late. *Secondly*, order a taxi to be here in about half an hour.

You can tell him from me that I'm not going to put up with his complaints any longer. *What's more*, I'm going to tell him that myself when I see him tomorrow.

I see that you've given him an excellent report. You're satisfied with his work *then*, are you?

I took him to the zoo early this morning and then we went to see a circus. *All in all,* he's had a very good time today.

If you want to come here tomorrow, I'll make an appointment. Or *rather,* I'll ask my secretary to do so.

It was a very difficult examination. *Nevertheless,* he passed it with distinction.

He doesn't need any money from us. *On the contrary,* we should be going to him for a loan.

Note

[a] The cardinal and ordinal numbers may be represented in writing by their symbols in the various systems:

1, 2, 3 . . .
I, II, III . . .
i, ii, iii . . .

Similarly, the alphabetic letters may be represented either as minuscules $(a, b, c . . .)$ or as majuscules $(A, B, C . . .)$. These different systems allow the writer to choose a hierarchy of listings and sublistings. In general, no clear conventions have been established for which sets of symbols are to be subordinate to other sets, and the writer is therefore free to choose a hierarchy of sets for his own purpose.

[b] *Too* as reinforcing conjunct (rare, AmE) occupies *I* position.

[c] *Somehow* has been included among conjuncts because it fits the criteria for the class (8.2 *ff*), and it is listed with result conjuncts because it is closest to them semantically. It differs from all other conjuncts in not indicating a relationship between its clause and what precedes:

Somehow I don't trust him ('for some reason or other')

Somehow is in fact used when the reason is not made explicit in the preceding context. In contrast, other result conjuncts (*eg: therefore* – 'for that reason') require the reason or cause to be given in the preceding context. Hence the clause to which they are attached states the result or consequence.

[d] An example of the antithetic conjunct *oppositely* (rare):

Any normal person is depressed when given proper cause for depression.
Oppositely, normal people become very excited when, for example, they have won a big prize.

[e] *On the other* is an alternative form of *on the other hand* when it is a correlative with *on the one hand.*

8.90

As with disjuncts (8.80 *f,* 8.83 *ff*), many conjuncts correspond to other structures. Almost all of these, indeed, are like style disjuncts in that the correspondence incorporates a verb of speaking and usually the subject is the speaker (8.80). The conjunct is normally represented lexically in the correspondence by a homonymous adjunct. We therefore consider the correspondences according to the class of homonymous adjunct.

[I] TIME AND PLACE ADJUNCTS

The succession in time or place conveyed by the adjuncts is converted into the logical succession of discourse when there is the implication of a verb of speaking. The correspondence has as its subject the speaker, but it is sometimes possible to use an indefinite pronoun instead (*eg* indefinite *one*, *we*, or *you*). The correspondence can usually be given the form

$$\left.\begin{array}{l} \textit{One} \text{ (etc) } \textit{can} \\ \textit{I will} \end{array}\right\} \textit{say} + \text{homonymous adjunct}$$

We can include here most listing adjuncts, the conjuncts *now* and *then* (whatever their subclass), and a few conjuncts scattered through other subclasses, *eg: by the way, yet, still, after all, at the same time.*

Examples:

There are two things that the Government can do: *First* ('I will say' +*first*), it can cut spending on defence; *second* ('I will say' + *second*), it can reduce the number of civil servants.

If astronauts have landed on the moon, *then* ('one can say' + *then*) there is no reason why they can't land on Venus.

[II] ADDITIVE ADJUNCTS

Here, too, the correspondence incorporates a verb of speaking and usually the subject is the speaker. We can include here the additive conjuncts.

Examples:

Most of us see no reason why capital punishment should not be abolished. *Further* ('I will further say'), the arguments in favour of corporal punishment seem trivial to most of us.

The acts of a parish council must be confirmed by the parish meeting. *In addition* ('I will tell you in addition'), decisions of a parish meeting must be confirmed by a referendum of all the electors in the parish.

These additive adjuncts (*cf* 8.13 *ff*) have themselves homonymous time, place or process adjuncts.

[III] PROCESS ADJUNCTS

The same type of correspondence can be established here. The conjuncts involved are scattered through the various subclasses of conjuncts.

Examples:

> *Incidentally* ('I tell you' + *incidentally*), he didn't want the book
> *To conclude* ('I tell you' + (*in order*) *to conclude*), it was a great success

Some conjuncts have correspondences that do not fit into the three categories we have set up:

(1) the enumerative conjuncts that are cardinal numbers and alphabetic letters:

$$\text{'I will say'} + \begin{cases} one,\ two,\ \ldots \\ a,\ b,\ \ldots \end{cases}$$

(2) the conjunct *only:*

> I intended to read the book, *only* ('I would *only* say') I felt too tired.

(3) the conjunct *rather:*

> What unites the party is the absence of a policy. Or *rather* ('I should *rather* say'), there is a policy but it has not been properly formulated.

(4) reformulatory *better:*

> In the example given for *rather* in (3) above, *rather* could be replaced by *better* in the sense 'It would be *better* for me to say'.

(5) replacive conjuncts *better* and *worse:*

> You can write to him about it. *Better still* ('This would be *better still*'), write to his father.

(6) concessive conjunct *however:*

> He didn't like the food. *However* ('*However* true that may be'), he didn't complain about it.

(7) The conjunct *though* is related to the conjunction *though*. Often it is an informal equivalent to an abbreviated subordinate clause with the conjunction *though* as subordinator:

> His food is rather a problem. He looks fit, *though*.

The sentence is interpreted as

His food is rather a problem. He looks fit, *though* his food is
rather a problem.

The implied subordinate clause need not be identical with the
content of a previous clause:

Singapore must now be one of the best-defended cities in the
world. There is no reason, *though*, to suppose that the people
of Singapore would want to spend as much money on
defence as Britain has spent.

The implied subordinate clause represented by the conjunct could
be something like '*though* the people of Singapore are pleased to
have one of the best-defended cities in the world'. See also 8.91
Note *b*.

Note

[*a*] Some conjunctions, *eg: while, since, as*, are used for both temporal and logical
relation.

[*b*] For some conjuncts it is difficult to find a correspondence accounting for the
homonymous adjunct, *eg: so, otherwise, at any rate*. Others have no homonymous
adjuncts, *eg: furthermore, moreover, namely, nevertheless, consequently, meanwhile*.
But some of these are compounds with an element that functions as an additive,
time or place adjunct, *eg: furthermore, moreover, nevertheless*.

8.91

Positions of conjuncts (*cf* 8.7)

The normal position for most conjuncts is *I*. In that position they are
usually separated from what follows by a tone unit boundary in speech or
a comma in writing. In other positions, they are in an independent tone
unit or enclosed in commas if these devices either prevent confusion with
homonyms or contribute towards the indication of information focus
(14.2 *ff*).

Some conjuncts are restricted, or virtually restricted, to *I* position:

again	*more*
also	*only*
altogether	*overall*
besides	*similarly*
better	*so*
else	*still*
equally	*then* (antithetic)
further	*too* (rare, AmE)
hence	*yet*
likewise	

M positions are rare for most conjuncts, and *E* rarer still. Those that readily occur at *E* include

> *anyhow*
> *anyway*
> *otherwise*
> *though* (particularly common) $\Big\}$ (frequent also at *M*)

Note

[a] *So*, *yet*, *only*, and *else* are distinguished by the punctuation convention that allows them to be separated from the previous clause by a comma where other conjuncts would require a more major mark of punctuation (App III.16). However, *else* is normally preceded by the coordinator *or*.

    So, *yet*, and *else* usually occur without intonation or punctuation separation from what follows. However, when *so* signals a general inference from the previous linguistic context and might be paraphrased by 'it follows from what we have said', it is often marked by punctuation and intonation separation:

> *So*, you think you know best (informal)

For *so* and *yet* in relation to coordinators, see 9.29 *ff.*

[b] The concessive conjunct *though* is a marginal case. We have earlier pointed out that *though* is often equivalent to a subordinate clause with the subordinator *though* (8.90). The problem arises when *though* is in *I* position and meaning is preserved if it is transposed elsewhere in the clause. In such cases, there is normally a major pause or punctuation mark between the two clauses. For example,

> He is poor – *though* he is satisfied with his condition.

is equivalent to

> He is poor. He is satisfied with his condition, *though*. (more informal)

In speech a special kind of intonation is required for such a clause, normally a falling-rising nuclear tone:

> he is |pòor| – though he |is sătisfied with his condition|

Notice that the sentences are not equivalent to

> *Though* he is satisfied with his condition, he is poor.

but to

> *Though* he is poor, he is satisfied with his condition.

Although can be used in the same way:

> He is poor. He is satisfied with his condition, *though*.
> $= \begin{cases} \text{he is |pòor| – } \textit{although} \text{ he is |sătisfied with his condition|} \\ \textit{Although} \text{ he is poor, he is satisfied with his condition.} \end{cases}$

But, unlike *though*, *although* is not a conjunct, and it cannot be transposed elsewhere in the clause:

> He is poor. *He is satisfied with his condition, *although*.

Final *though* and *although* clauses can be regarded as implying some claim of the speaker, *eg*:

> He is poor – (I maintain that this is true)
> $\begin{cases} \text{although} \\ \text{though} \end{cases}$ he is satisfied with his condition.

Cf final *because* clauses functioning as a disjunct of reason (8.78 Note, 9.23, 11.37).

[c] An example where comma punctuation might avoid ambiguity is given with inferential *then:*

> Well, what did you want, *then?*

Without the preceding comma, *then* would probably be interpreted as a time adjunct (probably 'after that') rather than as the inferential conjunct ('in that case').

8.92
Conjuncts as correlatives

Some conjuncts can correlate with the subordinator of a previous clause to reinforce the logical relationship between the clauses. This is because a similar logical relationship is effected by both the subordinator and the conjunct, except that the conjunct must always have anaphoric reference whereas often a subordinate clause can either precede or follow its superordinate clause. For example, the following sentences are similar in meaning to some extent:

> *Though* he is poor, he is satisfied with his situation
> He is poor, *yet* he is satisfied with his situation

The major difference is that the second states his poverty as a fact, whereas in the first his poverty is presupposed as given information (*cf* 14.5). We can combine both subordinator and conjunct in one sentence:

> *Though* he is poor, *yet* he is satisfied with his situation

Indeed, with concessives we can reinforce the concession by having more than one concessive conjunct in the second clause:

> *Though* he is poor, *yet* he is *nevertheless* satisfied with his situation.

The conjuncts that reinforce particular subordinators (*cf* 11.10) are shown below. It should be noted, however, that it is more usual to reinforce condition and concession subordinators than cause and time subordinators.

condition: if . . . . then

concession: although
(even) though
while
granted (that)
even if

yet
still
however
nevertheless
nonetheless
notwithstanding
anyway
anyhow

cause:	because seeing (that)	$\left\{\begin{array}{l}\text{therefore}\\\text{hence}\\\text{accordingly}\\\text{consequently}\end{array}\right.$
time:	while	$\left\{\begin{array}{l}\text{meanwhile}\\\text{meantime}\end{array}\right.$

Note

[a] The two instances of *while* listed above are different. *While* in the concessive list of subordinators is synonymous with the subordinator *though*, and the other *while* is equivalent to 'during the time that'.

[b] Certain other expressions with concessive force may correlate with a concessive conjunct, for example, *true, clearly,* or *certainly, cf* 10.35.

8.93

Conjunctions for clauses with conjuncts

A clause containing a conjunct may be linked to a preceding clause by one of the coordinators (*and, or, but*) but not all the conjuncts admit each coordinator. The following conjuncts seem to be limited to the specified coordinators:

and so

but $\left\{\begin{array}{l}\textit{however}\\\textit{then}\ (\text{antithetic})\\\textit{though}\end{array}\right.$

or $\left\{\begin{array}{l}\textit{else}\\\textit{again}\ (\text{replacive})\end{array}\right.$

$\left.\begin{array}{l}\textit{and}\\\textit{but}\end{array}\right|\left\{\begin{array}{l}\textit{besides}\\\textit{still}\\\textit{yet}\\\textit{nevertheless}\end{array}\right.$

Two of these conjuncts – *however* and *though* – cannot follow the conjunction immediately. That is to say, if *but* links their clause to the preceding clause, *however* and *though* cannot be initial, although they can be if there is no conjunction in front of them. We can therefore have:

He doesn't eat very much, *but* he looks healthy, *though.*

He doesn't eat very much. *Though* he looks healthy, doesn't he?

You can phone the doctor if you like, *but* I very much doubt, *however,* whether you will get him to come out on a Saturday night.

You can phone the doctor if you like. *However,* I very much doubt whether you will get him to come out on a Saturday night.

On the other hand, we cannot have

> *He doesn't eat very much, *but though* he looks healthy.
> *You can phone the doctor if you like, *but, however,* I very much
> doubt whether you will get him to come out on a Saturday night.

So, only, yet, replacive *again*, and antithetic *then* cannot be preceded by
subordinators. There do not appear to be such restrictions on the disjuncts.

Note

The concessive conjunct *only* (informal) is a marginal case. Some speakers allow the
coordinator *but* to precede it:

> ?I intended to go, but *only* I didn't feel well

For those who do not allow *but, only* has a status similar to that of the subordinators
for and resultative *so that* (9.37–38).

8.94
Syntactic features of conjuncts

In general, conjuncts (like disjuncts, *cf* 8.86) do not allow any of the syntactic features listed for adjuncts in 8.3, 8.8, and 8.9 (*cf* also 8.4).
Features applying to conjuncts include:

(1) Virtually all conjuncts can appear with questions:

> *Anyway,* do you know the answer?
> *Also,* why should he pay for the damage?
> Will you *therefore* resign?

Most can readily appear in *I* position with questions. The conjuncts *only* and *somehow* (and perhaps also *too* in its rare conjunct
use) are exceptional in that they cannot appear with questions.

(2) Conjuncts restricted to *I* position are unacceptable in indirect
questions:

$$\text{*He asked whether} \begin{Bmatrix} yet \\ so \\ hence \end{Bmatrix} \text{they would stay}$$

Some mobile conjuncts are acceptable:

$$\text{He asked whether} \begin{Bmatrix} instead \\ anyway \\ as\ a\ result \\ nevertheless \\ ,\ on\ the\ other\ hand, \\ therefore \end{Bmatrix} \text{they would stay}$$

(3) Unlike most disjuncts, most conjuncts can appear with imperatives, whether positive or negative:

Moreover,
Incidentally,
Nevertheless, } (explain the situation to them
Otherwise, } (don't explain the situation to them
What's more,
All the same,)

(4) Unlike disjuncts, adverbs as conjuncts do not accept modification:

*very incidentally, *accordingly enough

(5) Conjuncts are not usually coordinated. Enumerative and additive conjuncts are exceptional in readily taking appositional coordination, *eg: fifthly and finally, first and most important.*

(6) Conjuncts occasionally occur in dependent finite clauses (*cf* 8.86):

(a) ADVERBIAL CLAUSES:
I saw him, because *otherwise* he would have complained.
I met him in the park, when, *however*, it was raining heavily.
I saw him when he was very busy and when, *moreover*, his workers were threatening to strike.

(b) RESTRICTIVE RELATIVE CLAUSES:
He was generally considered a man who might *anyway* break his promise.
He was a supporter of the government, but he made a speech that constituted, *however*, an attack on the Prime Minister.

(c) NON-RESTRICTIVE RELATIVE CLAUSES:
I'm inviting Peter, who is a student, and who *therefore* cannot afford to spend too much money.
I spoke angrily to Bill, who *consequently* strode away without answering me.

Notice that in the example in (a) with *otherwise* we can transpose the clauses with the conjunct remaining in its subordinate clause:

Because *otherwise* he would have complained, I saw him.

This is an exception (applying only to some conjuncts and only when they are in subordinate clauses) to the general rule that a conjunct has anaphoric reference (8.92). In some instances a conjunct does not function in the subordinate clause in which it appears, but must instead apply to the superordinate clause:

I can explain it orally. If, *however*, you insist, I'll put it in writing.
= I can explain it orally. *However*, I'll put it in writing, if you insist.

In such a case, the subordinate clause cannot be transposed together with the conjunct. The conjunct can be transposed to the beginning of the sentence or to some position within the superordinate clause.

Note
[a] The conjuncts *better* and *worse* can be modified, *eg: better still, even worse.*
[b] For appositional coordination, see 9.175.

Bibliographical note
Some recent contributions on adverbs: Bolinger (1971a); Crystal (1966); Fraser (1971); Greenbaum (1969a) and (1970); Jacobson (1964).

9.1
Introduction

This chapter is devoted primarily to coordination and apposition. But since these phenomena often involve the device of ellipsis, we begin with a consideration of the nature of ellipsis. It seems convenient to bring together here cases of ellipsis not dealt with under coordination or apposition (later in this chapter), sentence connection (10.53 *ff*, 10.74 *ff*) or comparison (11.56). We shall also indicate some constructions where there appears to be no reason to posit ellipsis.

Ellipsis
Nature of ellipsis
9.2

Ellipsis is purely a surface phenomenon. In the sentence

> She might sing, but I don't think she will (sing)   [1]

the word *sing* is ellipted. In a strict sense of ellipsis, words are ellipted only if they are uniquely recoverable, *ie* there is no doubt as to what words are to be supplied, and it is possible to add the recovered words to the sentence. Therefore, *sing* is ellipted also in

> She rarely sings, so I don't think she will (sing) tonight   [2]

The expansion in [2] is not a mere repetition of the form of the verb as given earlier in the sentence, since the use of the modal auxiliary involves a consequent morphological change. It remains true that *sing* in [2] is uniquely recoverable and can be added to the sentence.

What is uniquely recoverable depends on the context. The examples we have given involve ellipsis that is dependent on what is present in a previous clause within the same sentence. In a larger context, across sentences, the ellipsis might be different. For example, given the sentence

> She can't sing tonight, so she won't (sing)

we assume that *sing* is ellipted, as indicated. However, different items are ellipted when this same sentence is in a context such as the following:

A: She always bores our company when she sings. I hope she won't bore them tonight.
B: She can't sing tonight, so she won't (bore them tonight).

In contrast to these instances where there is undoubtedly ellipsis, in the common response

> Thanks

it is not clear what missing elements are left unexpressed. We could expand the sentence in various ways, for example:

I owe you my thanks
I give you thanks

Thanks is therefore not elliptical in the strict definition of the term. Indeed, it may be argued that no elements are left unexpressed, and that *Thanks* is no different from *Hello* in this respect (for further examples, see 7.86, 7.88).

9.3

Ellipsis is not to be confused with the concept of deletion postulated in some theories of grammar, notably that of transformational grammar. To take a simple example, if we compare the sentences

John wants Mary to read   [3]
John wants to read   [4]

it is clear that [4] requires us to understand that John is the subject of *to read*. Our knowledge that John is the subject reflects an important semantic implication of the type of construction exemplified in [4]. But for all this, *John* is not ellipted, since (in the intended co-referential sense) the insertion of *John* produces an unacceptable sentence:

*John wants John to read.

Note
Ellipsis may coincide, however, with some cases of optional deletion as formulated in such theories of grammar.

9.4
Motivation for ellipsis

Ellipsis is most commonly an abbreviating device that reduces redundancy. A major use of ellipsis is the avoidance of repetition, and in this respect it is like substitution (10.39 *ff*), which can often be used instead of ellipsis. For example, we can avoid the repetition of *sing* not only by ellipsis of the word:

She might sing, but I don't think she will (sing)   [1]

but also by the substitution of a pro-form:

She might sing, but I don't think she will *do so*   [1a]

Repetition is often avoided for stylistic reasons. Where avoidance of repetition is a motivating factor, ellipsis is usually anaphoric, as in [1]. But occasionally it is cataphoric:

John doesn't want to (apologize), but clearly he must, apologize.

However, redundancy need not relate to words that can be implied from the linguistic context. The ellipted words may be obvious from the situation:

(Do you) Want some?

Such forms of ellipsis are restricted to familiar style (9.18 *ff*).

There is another important motivation for ellipsis. By omitting items that are shared, attention is focused on the new material, as in the dialogue below:

A: Have you spoken to him?   B: (I have) Not yet (spoken to him).

Note
In addition, repetition can sometimes be avoided by the substitution of co-referential expressions (10.4 *ff*):

Peter Sand denied he ever struck his students. *The teacher* claimed that the school administration had a grudge against him.

Ellipsis dependent on linguistic context
Adverbial finite clause
9.5
In adverbial finite clauses the whole of the predication or part of it can be omitted, except that we cannot ellipt merely the object; *cf* (5) below. See also 9.69, 9.83.

(1) WHOLE OF PREDICATION (*cf* 9.82)
John will play the guitar at the party *if Tom will* (*play the guitar at the party*)
Because Alice won't (*dust the furniture*), Mary is dusting the furniture

(2) SUBJECT COMPLEMENT ONLY (*cf* 9.84)
I'm happy *if you are* (*happy*)
You must also be a member of the party, *since he is* (*a member of the party*)

but not if the verb in the subordinate clause is other than BE:

*He became a member, since she became (a member)

(3) ADJUNCT ONLY (*cf* 9.85 *ff*)
Tom was at Oxford *when his brother was* (*at Oxford*)
I'll write to the committee *if you'll write* (*to the committee*) *too*

(4) LEXICAL VERB ONLY (*cf* 9.72)
John is playing Peter *though Tom won't* (*play*) *Paul*
I'll pay for the hotel *if you will* (*pay*) *for the food*

but not

(5) OBJECT ONLY (*cf* 9.84)

> *He took the money *because she wouldn't take* (*the money*)
> *I'll open an account *if you'll open* (*an account*)

We can avoid repetition of the object by using pro-forms (10.43 *ff*):

> He took the money because she wouldn't take *it*
> I'll open an account if you'll open *one*

The elliptical adverbial clause normally follows its superordinate clause. If only the lexical verb is ellipted and does not itself comprise the whole of the predication, the adverbial clause must follow. If the ellipted lexical verb comprises the whole of the predication, then the adverbial clause may precede:

> Since Tom can't (play the guitar), John will play the guitar
> Only if you will (go), will I go

A superordinate clause can only be elliptical if it follows the adverbial clause on which the ellipsis is dependent:

> If Tom resigns, *John may* (*resign*)
> **John may* (*resign*), if Tom resigns.

Note

[*a*] As elsewhere, for example with coordination (9.71), an auxiliary in its reduced form cannot precede ellipsis:

> *I'm happy if you're.

[*b*] We cannot ellipt only the auxiliary:

> *Tom will play the guitar, if Mary (will) sing

nor can we ellipt the entire verb phrase:

> *Susan was happy when Alice (was) miserable
> *George will carry the cases if Bob (will carry) the parcels

But the entire predicate can be ellipted in an *if*-clause when the subject is *anyone*, *no one*, or a similar pronoun (4.127 *f*):

> If anyone (knows), he knows.

9.6

Just as with coordination (9.76 *ff*), most co-occurrences of auxiliaries in the two clauses are allowed. For this purpose, the ellipsis of an adverbial clause is equivalent to the ellipsis of the second conjoin (the second of the coordinated clauses, *cf* 9.39), and this is so whether the adverbial clause precedes or follows. Thus, the heads of the verb phrases need not be identical in the two clauses:

> *Because Alice won't* (*dust the furniture*), Mary is dusting the furniture.

Identical possibilities of co-occurrence are available to the ellipted superordinate clause, though as we have observed (9.5) this must follow the other clause:

Because Tom has resigned, *John may (resign)*.

Abbreviated clause: non-finite (*cf* 11.26)
9.7
The subject (co-referential with that of the superordinate clause) and an appropriate form of BE are ellipted in:

Although (he was) tired, he kept on working   [5]
If (they are) punished, they will not cooperate   [6]

If the subordinator is not present, there is not ellipsis in the strict sense, since more than one subordinator can be supplied (*cf* 11.47):

$$
\left.
\begin{array}{l}
(\textit{Although}) \\
(\textit{Even though}) \\
(\textit{Though})
\end{array}
\right\}
\textit{(he was) tired,} \text{ he kept on working} \qquad [5a]
$$

$$
\left.
\begin{array}{l}
(\textit{If}) \\
(\textit{When})
\end{array}
\right\}
\textit{(they are) punished,} \text{ they will not cooperate} \qquad [6a]
$$

Since the conjunctions are synonymous or partially so, and form a severely limited set of alternatives, we might consider this as a weak form of ellipsis, which we shall term *weak ellipsis*.

9.8
With adverbial *-ing* clauses, there are additional complications in identifying ellipsis:

(1) Stative verbs (3.40) do not normally allow the progressive form in finite clauses, and hence BE cannot be added:

Although knowing French, he attended the course   [7a]
**Although he was knowing French,* he attended the course [7b]

With dynamic verbs, BE can be added, but several interpretations involving tense and aspect are possible (*cf* 13.18):

Although living many miles away, he attended the course [7c]

$$
\text{Although he}
\left\{
\begin{array}{l}
\text{is living} \\
\text{was living} \\
\text{lives} \\
\text{lived}
\end{array}
\right\}
\text{many miles away, he attended the}
$$
                                                              course

(2) *Having* in the *-ing* clause does not allow the addition of the subordinator and subject:

> *Having watched Bob play,* John left the stadium   [8a]
> **After he having watched Bob play,* John left the stadium   [8b]

although either the subordinator or subject can be added:

> *After having watched Bob play,* John left the stadium   [8c]
> *John having watched Bob play,* he left the stadium.   [8d]

Note

[a] The *-ing* form does not convey progressive aspect in [7a], [7c], [8a], [8c], or [8d], *cf* 3.15, 3.39.

[b] In a construction of the type exemplified by [8d], a pronoun would normally be used in the second clause if subjects of the two clauses are co-referential. Type [8d] is rarely used.

9.9
Abbreviated clause: verbless

Ellipsis of subject and BE is also involved in verbless clauses introduced by a subordinator (5.27, 11.7):

> *While (he was) at Oxford,* he was active in the dramatic society.
> *Whether (he is) right or wrong,* Bob always loses in an argument.
> *Though (she was) already middle-aged,* she was very pretty.

9.10
Postmodifying *-ed* participle clause

It is possible to regard *-ed* participle postmodifying clauses (13.18 *ff*) as reduced relative clauses, with ellipsis of the relative and BE:

> Houses *(which are) owned by absentee landlords* will be confiscated
> The police rounded up men *(who are) known to have been in the building at that time*

There is not strict ellipsis because there is a choice of relatives: the *wh-* words in these sentences could both be replaced by *that*. Furthermore, in some cases the choice of tense for BE is not fully determined. For example, in the second sentence *were* could satisfactorily replace *are*.

9.11
Postmodifying *-ing* participle clause

As with the adverbial *-ing* clause (9.8), there is less justification for regarding the postmodifying *-ing* clause as reduced from a finite clause. Here too, BE cannot be inserted when a stative verb is used:

> The man *owning that car* will be fined for illegal parking   [9a]
> *The man *who is owning that car* will be fined for illegal parking   [9b]

9.12
Postmodifying adjective phrase

Postmodifying adjective phrases (5.18*f*), including those consisting only of an adjective, can normally be considered elliptical relative clauses, with ellipsis of the relative and BE:

No one (*who is*) *honest* will accept such a job.
The men (*who were*) *responsible for the administration of the school* refused to consider the matter.

As with the postmodifying participle clauses (9.10), there is not strict ellipsis, since the *wh-* words could be replaced by *that* and in some cases (for example, the second of the above sentences) the tense of BE is not fully determined.

Note

The mobility of the supplementive adjective clause (5.24), which can appear initially, as in

Nervous, the man opened the letter

precludes it from being regarded as an elliptical non-restrictive relative clause.

9.13
Postmodifying prepositional phrase

Weak ellipsis (under the same conditions as in 9.12) can be equally posited for many postmodifying prepositional phrases (13.25 *ff*), especially those denoting place, which can be treated as reduced relative clauses:

We have already tested the students (*who are*) *in that class.*
They sell cars (*that are*) *for handicapped drivers.*

But phrases which cannot be treated in this way are probably more numerous:

At the end *of the century*, the world population will have more
than doubled [10a]
*At the end *which is of the century*, the world population will
have more than doubled [10b]
A deciding factor *in the election result* was the television
campaign conducted by both candidates [11a]
*A deciding factor *which was in the election result* was the
television campaign conducted by both candidates [11b]

Note

A relatively small number of adverbs signifying place or time postmodify noun phrases (5.61) and some of the place adverbs in this function can be seen as reduced relative clauses:

the sentence (that is) below
the hall (that is) downstairs

But most cannot be expanded in this way, particularly those denoting direction:

the journey back ~ *the journey that is back
his return home ~ *his return that is home

9.14
Adjective as head of noun phrase

Adjectives functioning as heads of personal noun phrases (5.20, 5.21) can be regarded as elliptical in a weak sense, with some general noun such as *people* ellipted:

> *The poor* (*people*) need more help

However, if there is postmodification by a prepositional phrase, the general noun may have to be inserted before the adjective (5.20):

> *The poor in spirit* need more help   [12a]
> **The poor people in spirit* need more help   [12b]
> *The people poor in spirit* need more help   [12c]

But with prepositional phrases that can be seen as reduced relative clauses, the general noun can only appear after the adjective:

> *The poor* (*people*) *in the ghettos* need more help

While *in spirit* postmodifies *poor, in the ghettos* postmodifies *poor* (*people*).

9.15
Supplementing clause

A supplementing clause can be regarded as an elliptical clause (usually parenthetic or an afterthought) for which the *whole* of the preceding or interrupted clause constitutes the ellipsis:

> He told them (*presumably with his tongue in his cheek*) how he
>   came to be late.   [13]
> I caught the train – *just*.   [14]

These two sentences presuppose that two separate assertions are being made. The usual form for [14] is

> I just caught the train

[14] presupposes

> I caught the train – I just caught the train.

The same analysis applies if the items added as afterthought are in their normal order:

> I caught the train – *in time*.

Coordination is often possible, as with the appended clause (9.16).

9.16
Appended clause

An appended clause is similar to a supplementing clause except that only *part* of the preceding or interrupted clause constitutes the ellipsis, and an additional clause constituent is present:

They are meant to wound, *perhaps to kill.*

They are meant, which is present in the first clause, is ellipted in the second clause, and the additional clause constituent is *perhaps. To wound* and *to kill* have identical functions in their respective clauses.

Other examples are:

He is playful, *even mischievous.*

His performance will be judged by his superiors – *and even more importantly* – *by his colleagues.*

Note

A clause involving quantifiers interestingly illustrates the appended clause. The appended clause

They visit many schools, *sometimes in an official car*

does not mean the same as

They *sometimes* visit many schools *in an official car*

Rather, it presupposes two assertions:

They visit many schools
They sometimes visit schools in an official car

Notice that the second assertion does not necessarily imply that they visit many schools.

9.17
Miscellaneous

Further types of ellipsis are found in other chapters and reference should be made to the sections where they are discussed:

(1) the elliptic genitive (4.103):

His memory is like an elephant's (memory)

(2) in comparative constructions (4.112, 11.56):

James enjoys the theatre more than Susan (enjoys the theatre)

(3) across sentences (10.53 *ff*, 10.74 *ff*):

A: Did you speak to John about it?
B: No, (I spoke) to Peter (about it).

Ellipsis not dependent on linguistic context
9.18

Some types of ellipsis are not dependent on the adjacent linguistic context for their interpretation. They may, however, be dependent on the situational context. For example, *Told you so* can be expanded to *I told you so* or to *We told you so*. The more probable interpretation may be obvious from the situational context, though even then there may be indeterminacy. These forms of ellipsis are restricted to familiar English. In most cases of non-dependent ellipsis, it is the initial words of a sentence that are ellipted. The ellipted items are those that normally occur before the onset in a tone unit, and hence have light stress and are on a low pitch (App II.12). It may therefore be more accurate to ascribe the omission to subaudibility rather than to ellipsis (*cf* 13.8 Note).

Commands without a subject can hardly be included among the types of non-dependent ellipsis. The omitted subject of the imperative verb is *you* (7.73), but absence of the subject is the norm with imperatives, and is frequent in all levels of formality. It seems better to treat the omitted *you* in commands as implied rather than ellipted (9.3, 9.23).

Declarative sentences are best treated separately from questions, because an operator is obligatory in questions.

Initial word of sentence ellipted
9.19
Declarative sentence
[A] SUBJECT ALONE ELLIPTED

Either no auxiliary is possible (*eg: Serves you right!*) or one is included (*eg: Can't see*). The element ellipted can be:

(1) the 1st person pronoun, normally *I:*

> Beg your pardon
> Told you so
> Wonder what they're doing
> Hope he's there
> Don't know what to say
> Think I'll go now

Most of the verbs in such an elliptical construction can take a clause complement.

(2) the 2nd person pronoun:

> Had a good time, did you?
> Want a drink, do you?
> Had a good time?
> Want a drink?

The 2nd person pronoun is only ellipted in statements if a tag question is added. It is also ellipted, as in the last two examples above, in declarative questions (7.61). (The last example can be interpreted as an ordinary (non-declarative) question with *Do you* ellipted, *cf* 9.20.)

(3) the 3rd person pronouns:

> (He/She) Doesn't look too well
> (He/She/They) Can't play at all

(4) *it:*

> Serves you right
> Doesn't matter
> Looks like rain
> Must be hot in Panama

The ellipted *it* in the first two of the preceding examples is the anticipatory *it* (14.36) found in such sentences as *It serves you right that you fell*, while in the last two sentences it is the 'prop word' *it* in sentences like *It is cold* (7.18). These ellipted sentences could refer directly to an action in the situational context, for example *Serves you right* might be said to a child immediately after he fell, if he had been warned not to act in a dangerous way. On the other hand, *it* in the following examples is the pro-form *it*, but again may refer directly to an object in the situational context:

> Seems full
> Makes too much noise
> Boils too quickly

Some expressions may be interpreted out of context as having ellipsis of either type of *it:*

> Sounds fine to me
> Won't be any use

(5) *there:*

> Ought to be some coffee in the pot
> Must be somebody waiting for you
> May be some children outside
> Appears to be a big crowd in the hall

This is the existential subject *there*, as distinct from the true subject following the verb. The elliptical construction is likely to contain a modal other than *will*, but *won't* is common:

> (There) Won't be any food left for supper

[B] SUBJECT PLUS OPERATOR ELLIPTED

If lexical BE has been ellipted, the elliptical construction begins with what would be a subject complement in the full form.

(1) the 1st person pronoun (particularly *I*) plus BE:

> (Am) Sorry I couldn't be there
> (Am) Afraid not
> (We are) Afraid not

We alone cannot be ellipted, *eg: *Are afraid not.* For some speakers, the same applies to the singular pronoun *I;* for them *Afraid not* is acceptable, but not *Am afraid not.*

(2) *it* plus BE:

> Good to see you
> Odd he won't help us
> No wonder he's late
> (A) Shame they won't be there

The ellipted *it* is the anticipatory *it* noticed above in, *eg: Serves you right.* A type of empty *it* is exemplified in the ellipsis in

> (It's) Not that he is right

Elliptical sentences with ellipted *I* or *we* occur with ellipsis of operators other than BE:

> (I'll) See you later
> (We've) Got to go now.

Note

[a] The common elliptical phrases (*I've*) *got to* and (*I'm*) *going to* have acquired semi-institutionalized spellings, *gotta* and *gonna* respectively: *Gotta go now; Gonna go now.*

[b] *Had* is commonly ellipted in spoken English in the semi-auxiliary *had better* (3.8): *You better try it again.* The subject can then be ellipted as well: *Better try it again.*

9.20

Interrogative sentence

[A] SUBJECT PLUS OPERATOR ELLIPTED

If the elliptical construction begins with a verb, an auxiliary (HAVE, DO, or BE) has been ellipted and not lexical BE. In questions, the ellipted subject is usually *you:*

> (Do you) Want some?
> (Are you) Looking for anybody?
> (Have you) Got any chocolate?

If the construction in its elliptical form begins with what would be a subject complement or an adjunct in the full form, then BE is ellipted as well as the pronoun realizing the subject:

(Are you) Happy?
(Are you) Afraid of him?
(Are you) Hot?
(Are you) In trouble?
(Is it) Hot?
(Are they) Torn?
Why can't he get up? (Is he) Too weak?

[B] OPERATOR ELLIPTED

If the operator alone is ellipted, a subject is supplied. If there is a subject complement, it is BE that is ellipted:

(Is) Anything the matter?
(Are) You hungry?
(Is) That John?

If there is a verb, an auxiliary (HAVE, DO, or BE) is ellipted:

(Does) Anybody need a lift?
(Has) John done his homework?

A determiner in the subject noun phrase may be ellipted as well:

Why isn't he here today? (Is his) Car still not working?

9.21

Other general cases

Determiners, operators, and pronouns are commonly omitted in block language (7.90), *eg* in headlines, titles, notices. They are also commonly omitted in personal letters, in familiar style, in notes (*eg* of lectures), diaries, and (very drastically) in telegrams.

9.22

Non-productive cases

There are several other types of ellipsis not dependent on the linguistic context, but they are not productive. The lexical items or parts of lexical items that may be ellipted must be known individually. All the instances are restricted to familiar style. Subaudibility rather than ellipsis may be the factor that applies to most cases (*cf* 9.18).

[A] ELLIPSIS OF AN ARTICLE:

(The) Trouble is there's nothing we can do about it
(The) Fact is we don't know what to do
(A) Friend of mine told me about it

The omission of the indefinite article is common in the construction '*a(n)*+noun phrase+*of* prepositional phrase', as in (*a*) *friend of mine.* This may be combined with other ellipses:

(It is a) Pity he won't help
(It is a) Shame they won't be there

[B] ELLIPSIS OF A PREPOSITION:
(Of) Course he's there

[C] ELLIPSIS OF PART OF A WORD, OR CLIPPING:
He did it 'cause he wanted to

(where the apostrophe points to an ellipsis, and in BrE there is the semi-institutionalized spelling '*cos*);

'Fraid I won't be there

(where the ellipsis of part of the word is combined with the ellipsis of subject and *am: I am afraid I won't be there.*) The spelling '*Fraid* is semi-institutionalized.

In contrast to the two examples in [C], there are many instances of clipping that have become institutionalized (even in spelling) and where the clipped form may be used in all but the most formal styles (App I.59):

(tele)phone
(air)
(aero) }plane
photo(graph)
exam(ination)
(in)flu(enza)

9.23
Semantic implication and ellipsis
We have referred earlier (9.3) to semantic implication as distinct from ellipsis. It may be more convenient to consider cases of weak ellipsis as involving semantic implication rather than ellipsis. For semantic implication there is no necessity that items understood be uniquely recoverable, or that it be possible to add understood items to the clause without changing the form of the clause. Two illustrations are given to clarify this point. In

Frankly, he is very stupid

the disjunct *frankly* implies a comment of the speaker on the way he is speaking (8.80*f*). But there is no one set of missing items that can be supplied. We can expand *frankly* to (among many forms) *I am speaking* *frankly when I say* or *If I may put it frankly I would tell you.* Similarly, in

He's drunk, *because I saw him staggering*

there is an implication (*cf* 11.37) that might be expressed by

He's drunk, *AND I CLAIM THAT because I saw him staggering.*

But equally we can give the implication other forms, such as *and I know, and I am sure of it, and I am convinced of it, and the proof is.*

Coordination
9.24
Syndetic and asyndetic coordination
The term coordination is used by some grammarians for both syndetic coordination – when explicit indicators of coordination are present – and asyndetic coordination – when the relationship of coordination is not marked overtly. Sentence [15a] exemplifies syndetic coordination, with *and* as explicit indicator, while in [15b] we have asyndetic coordination with *and* omitted:

Slowly and stealthily, he crept towards his victim   [15a]
Slowly, stealthily, he crept towards his victim   [15b]

Explicit indicators of coordination are termed COORDINATING CON-JUNCTIONS, or (more simply) COORDINATORS. Not all juxtaposed words, phrases or clauses are manifestations of asyndetic coordination. The possibility of inserting the coordinator *and* is evidence that the construction is asyndetic coordination. For this reason, we shall generally exemplify coordination with a coordinator present.

Coordination and subordination
9.25
Explicit indicators of subordination are termed subordinating conjunctions or subordinators (more fully discussed in 11.9 *ff*). Both coordination and subordination (*cf* 11.2) involve the linking of units, but in co-ordination the units are constituents of the same level whereas in subordination they are on different levels. Thus (to take an example within a phrase, *cf* 13.60 *f*), in *his first and best novel* the coordinated adjectival phrase *first and best* functions as a premodifier of *novel*, and in that phrase *first* and *best* are equal constituents. On the other hand, in *his first good novel* the adjective *first* does not modify *novel* directly; it modifies *good novel* and *good* in turn modifies *novel*. Thus, there is a hierarchy in relationships and *first good* are not coordinated. One further example

with adjectives will be brought, this time without a coordinator. In *an elderly, foolish man*, the two adjectives are coordinated, each premodifying *man*, the head of the noun phrase. By contrast, *foolish old* in *a foolish old man* is not coordinated, since *foolish* modifies *old man* and not *man*. Notice that in the former expression we can insert *and* without changing the relationship between *elderly* and *foolish*.

9.26

A major difference between coordination and subordination of clauses is that the information in subordinate clauses is not asserted, but presupposed as given (*cf* 8.92, 14.5). Similar semantic relationships may be found in both types of constructions:

He has quarrelled with the chairman *and* has resigned   [16a]
Because he has quarrelled with the chairman he has resigned   [16b]
He tried hard, *but* he failed   [17a]
Although he tried hard, he failed   [17b]

The cause–result relationship between the contents of the two clauses is the same in [16a] and [16b], while the concessive–result relationship is the same for [17a] and [17b], though the ordering of the relationships is reversed with the subordinate clauses of [16b] and [17b]. Moreover, the same semantic relationship between the clauses may be indicated overtly by a conjunct (8.89 *ff*). Thus, the conjunct *yet* in [17c] has a very similar force to *but* in [17a]:

He tried hard, *yet* he failed   [17c]

Sentence [17c] is an asyndetic coordination with the conjunct *yet* in the second clause. Notice that this conjunct can be added to [17a], where *but* is the coordinator:

He tried hard, *but yet* he failed   [17d]

Although the pairs of sentences [16a–16b] and [17a–17b] are similar semantically, they are very different grammatically, since [16b] and [17b] are adverbial in clause structure. Adverbial clauses and their subordinators are treated in 11.9 *ff*, 11.26 *ff*; here we shall merely point out the grammatical differences between coordinators and subordinators.

9.27

It is sometimes said that an important difference between coordination and subordination is that only in the former can the order of the two linguistic units be changed without a consequent change in the semantic relationships of the units. It is true that the order can be reversed in certain sets of coordinated units:

Mary studies at a university *and* John works at a factory   [18a]
John works at a factory *and* Mary studies at a university   [18b]

But this potentiality is dependent on many factors, one of which is the relationship of meaning between the coordinated units, which may also have syntactic consequences (*cf* 9.40 *ff*). For example, if a cause–result relationship is implicit, the order of the coordinated clauses cannot be reversed without changing the relationship. Sentences [19a] and [19b] are obviously not synonymous:

He died and he was buried in the cemetery   [19a]
He was buried in the cemetery and he died   [19b]

Coordinators
9.28
Coordinators identified

We regard three conjunctions as coordinators: *and, or, but. And* and *or* are the central coordinators from which *but* differs in some respects. On the gradient between the 'pure' coordinators and the 'pure' subordinators are *for* and *so that* (meaning in this chapter, unless otherwise stated, 'with the result that'). *For*, indeed, is often classed as a coordinator. *Nor* is not a pure coordinator since it can be preceded by another coordinator (a potentiality not available to coordinators, as we shall see) and it contains a negative feature, which introduces some syntactic differences (9.55). *Both, either*, and *neither* are used as the first in a correlative pair with *and, or*, and *nor* respectively. These anticipatory elements are optional. They are not themselves coordinators, since, like *nor*, they can be preceded by another coordinator.

Syntactic features of coordinators
9.29

We shall now consider the syntactic features that apply to *and* and *or*, the central coordinators. With each feature, we note whether it is applicable to items that resemble coordinators in some respects: subordinators, conjuncts, and *but, for* and *so that*. At this stage we restrict our attention to the role of coordinators as clause-linkers.

9.30
Restricted to initial position

As clause coordinators, *and* and *or* are restricted to initial position in the clause:

John plays the guitar, *and* his sister plays the piano   [20a]
*John plays the guitar; his sister *and* plays the piano   [20b]

This is generally true of conjunctions and also of some conjuncts (notably *yet* and *so*), but it is not true of most conjuncts, *eg: moreover:*

John plays the guitar; his sister, *moreover*, plays the piano   [20c]

The conjunctions *though, as,* and *that* are exceptional in appearing non-initially in certain circumstances (11.34):

Though he is poor, he is happy	[21a]
Poor *though* he is, he is happy	[21b]
As I am unaccustomed to public speaking, I beg your indulgence for my few inelegant words	[22a]
Unaccustomed *as* I am to public speaking, I beg your indulgence for my few inelegant words	[22b]
Fool *that* he is, he immediately dived into the water	[23]

Though and *as* allow both positions, though initial position is normal. In the construction exemplified in [23] the position after the complement is obligatory:

*That he is fool, he immediately dived into the water   [23a]

Note

[a] *Although*, unlike *though*, is immobile:

**Poor *although* he is, he is happy.

[b] Sentence [22b] may be analysed as elliptical:

As unaccustomed *as* I am to public speaking, . . .

It is possible that *that* in [23] is a relative ('the fool that he is'), but it cannot be replaced by a *wh*-form.

Coordinated clauses sequentially fixed
9.31
Clauses beginning with *and* or *or* are sequentially fixed in relation to the previous clause and therefore cannot be transposed without producing unacceptable sentences or at least changing the relationships of the clauses:

They are living in England *or* they are spending a vacation there	[24a]
*Or they are spending a vacation there, they are living in England	[24b]

This is true for conjuncts, but not for most subordinators. Contrast the unacceptability of [25a], containing the conjunct *nevertheless*, with the acceptability of [25b], containing the subordinator *although*:

*Nevertheless John gave it away; Mary wanted it	[25a]
Although Mary wanted it, John gave it away	[25b]

However, clauses introduced by *but*, *for*, and *so that* are also positionally fixed. Contrast:

> *For he was unhappy, he asked to be transferred   [26a]
> *Because* he was unhappy, he asked to be transferred   [26b]

and resultative *so that* in [27] with purposive *so that* in [28]:

> *So that we weren't able to undo it, the whole thing was tied up
>   in knots   [27]
> *So that* he could buy a car, he saved a lot of money.   [28]

9.32

Presumably related to the fixed position of the clauses is the fact that when clauses are linked by the coordinators *and*, *or*, and *but* (also by *for* and *so that*), a pronoun in the first clause cannot have cataphoric (*ie* forward) reference to a noun in the second clause. For example, *she* in [29a] and [29b] cannot refer to *Mary:*

> *She* was unhappy, *and Mary* stayed the whole evening   [29a]
> *She* was unhappy, *but Mary* stayed the whole evening   [29b]

On the other hand, the pronoun can (but need not) have cataphoric reference when the clauses are joined by a subordinator:

> *Although she* was unhappy, *Mary* stayed the whole evening   [29c]

The most common position for a subordinate clause is final, in which case the pronoun is anaphoric:

> *Mary* stayed the whole evening, *although she* was unhappy   [29d]

Note

While the pronoun *she* in the first clause of [29a] and [29b] must have anaphoric reference to a previously-mentioned noun phrase, it is possible for the noun phrase in the second clause to have the same reference if it contains a general noun (and hence is like a pronoun) or if it characterizes the person referred to:

> *She* was unhappy, but { the girl / the idiot / your foolish daughter } stayed the whole evening.

9.33

Not preceded by conjunction

And and *or* do not allow another conjunction to precede them. This is also true for *but*, *for*, and *so that*. On the other hand, subordinators as well as conjuncts can be preceded by conjunctions. In [30] two clauses linked by the conjunct *yet* are also linked by *and*, which precedes the conjunct:

> He was unhappy about it, *and yet* he did what he was told   [30]

In [31] and [32] two subordinate clauses are linked by *and*, which precedes the second subordinator *because* and the second subordinator *so that* (with purposive meaning):

> He asked to be transferred, *because* he was unhappy *and*
> *because* he saw no prospect of promotion [31]
> He saved money *so that* he could buy a house *and so that* he
> would have enough for his old age [32]

By contrast, the conjunctions *but, for* and resultative *so that* cannot be preceded by *and:*

> *He was unhappy about it, *and but* he did what he was told [30a]
> *He asked to be transferred, *for* he was unhappy and *for* he
> saw no possibility of promotion [31a]
> *He saved money *so that* he was able to buy a house *and so*
> *that* he had enough for his old age [32a]

Note

A subordinate clause is not usually coordinated with its superordinate clause, but this occasionally happens when it is treated as an afterthought (9.15):

> He wouldn't do it – *and (all) because I didn't ask him in person.*

9.34

Ellipsis of subject

And and *or* allow ellipsis of the subject of the clause they introduce if the subject is co-referential with that of the preceding linked clause:

> I may see you tomorrow *or* (I) may phone later in the day [33]

This feature also applies, though somewhat less frequently, to *but:*

> They may complain, *but* (they) haven't said anything yet [34]

However, it does not apply to *for* and *so that:*

> *He did not want it, *for* was obstinate [35]
> *He did not spend very much, *so that* could afford a trip
> abroad [36]

nor does it apply to other conjunctions or to most conjuncts. But it does not seem to be unacceptable for the conjunct *yet* and (to a lesser extent, at least in informal spoken English) for the conjunct *so* and the temporal anaphoric adjunct *then* (meaning 'after that'):

> They didn't like it, *yet* (they) said nothing [37]
> They were tired, *so* (they) left early [38]
> They went home, *then* (they) went straight to bed [39]

A subordinator does not allow ellipsis even when its clause is linked by a coordinator:

> *She didn't say anything about it *because* he was new *and*
> *because* looked unwell   [40]

If the second subordinator in [40] is omitted, ellipsis is possible:

> She didn't say anything about it *because* he was new and (he)
> looked unwell   [40a]

On the other hand, conjuncts otherwise not allowing ellipsis will do so if preceded by a coordinator:

> *He went to bed early, *nevertheless* felt tired   [41a]
> He went to bed early, and (he) nevertheless felt tired   [41b]

9.35
Linking of subordinate clauses

As well as linking two main clauses, *and* and *or* can link subordinate clauses:

> He asked to be transferred, *because* he was unhappy *and* (*because*)
> he saw no prospect of promotion, *and* (*because*) conditions were
> far better at the other office.
> I wonder *whether* you should go and see him *or* (*whether*) it is
> better to write to him.

In each case, the second and subsequent subordinators may be ellipted. Such linking is not possible for conjuncts or for the other conjunctions except *but*. *But*, however, is restricted to linking a maximum of two clauses (*cf* 9.36):

> He said *that* John would take them by car *but* (*that*) they might
> be late.

Even so, *but* can only link certain types of subordinate clauses:

(a) *That*-clauses (11.17), as above; only in the case of *that*-clauses can the second subordinator, the one following *but*, be omitted.

(b) Temporal adverbial clauses:

> I spoke to him after the conference was over, *but before* he
> started work.

(c) Clauses introduced by the same conjunctions, which might be *wh*-words, *in order that*, purposive *so that*, or *because*. In such cases the first part of the sentence is negative, and contrasts with the part that follows *but*:

> She didn't see *who* MĔT the ambassador, *but who* took him
> away.

He didn't save *so that* he could go to school, but *so that* he could buy a new car.

But cannot link most other subordinate clauses:

?*They won't help you *if* you pay them, *but if* you promise to help them in return.

*They didn't stay *although* they were unhappy, but *although* they were bored.

However, if the negation is outside the verb phrase, *but* can more easily link *if*-clauses:

It might have turned out all right *not if* he had been more forceful *but if* he had been more tactful.

Note

[a] With *or*, certain verbs or adjectives in the superordinate clause allow (or, in some cases, require) that the subordinator *that* be replaced by *whether* or *if*:

He doesn't know *whether* Mary will pay for the dress *or* (*whether*) her mother will give it to her.
He's not sure *if* he should write to her *or* (*if*) she will phone him of her own accord.

[b] Speakers vary considerably as to the acceptability of various types of *if*-clauses linked by *but*.

9.36
Linking of more than two clauses

And and *or* can link more than two clauses, and when this is done all but the final instance of these two conjunctions can be omitted. Thus

John might take them by car, Mary might go with them by bus, *or* I might order a taxi for them.   [42a]

is interpreted as

John might take them by car, *or* Mary might go with them by bus, *or* I might order a taxi for them.   [42b]

In this respect, *and* and *or* differ from subordinators and conjuncts and even *but*. While it is possible (though unusual) to construct a sentence such as

John played football, Mary played tennis, *but* Alice stayed at home.   [43a]

such a sentence is interpreted as if the first two clauses had been linked by *and*:

John played football, *and* Mary played tennis, *but* Alice stayed at home.   [43b]

An indefinite number of clauses can be linked by *and* and *or*. Furthermore, some of the clauses may be linked by *and* and others by *or*. In such combinations, the coordinator is usually omitted in all but the final instance when the same coordinator links more than two clauses:

> Attend all the lectures, (and) write full notes on them, *and* read the prescribed books, *or* you'll be in trouble at the examination.

When several clauses are coordinated they may be on the same level of coordination or one set (consisting of one or more clauses) may be coordinated to a set of the others (*cf* 9.112). For example, in the following sentence X, Y, and Z symbolize the three clauses:

> [X] I'll pay for the meal *and* [Y] you pay for the taxi, *or* [Z] perhaps I'll pay for both.

The relationship between the clauses can be represented in a tree diagram:

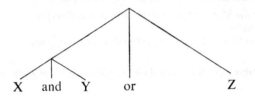

On the other hand, in the sentence

> [X] His parents live in New York *and* [Y] he writes to them from time to time *or* [Z] (he) phones them.

The probable relationship is represented by a very different diagram:

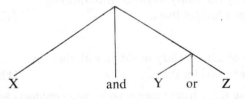

Coordination – subordination gradient
9.37
Table 9:1 displays the gradient from the central coordinators *and* and *or* to subordinators like *if* and *because*, with *but*, *for*, and *so that* on the gradient. The conjuncts *yet* and *so* are added to the table, because they have been considered by some to be coordinators. The six features of *and* and *or* have provided the basis for the six criteria used in constructing the matrix. If an item satisfies a criterion, this is indicated by a ' + ' in the cell at which the horizontal level of the item and the vertical column

of the criterion meet. If it fails to satisfy the criterion, a ' − ' is entered. The combination ' ± ' takes account of cases, explained in the previous discussion, where the item satisfies the criterion only under certain conditions. The six criteria applied to each item or set of items are:

(1) It is immobile in front of its clause.
(2) A clause beginning with it is sequentially fixed in relation to the previous clause and hence cannot be moved to a position in front of that clause.
(3) It does not allow a conjunction to precede it.
(4) It allows ellipsis of the subject of the clause if the subject is co-referential with that of the preceding linked clause.
(5) It can link subordinate clauses.
(6) It can link more than two clauses and when it does all but the final instance of the linking item can be omitted.

Table 9:1

COORDINATION − SUBORDINATION GRADIENT

		1	2	3	4	5	6
coordinators	*and, or*	+	+	+	+	+	+
	but	+	+	+	+	±	−
subordinators	*for, so that*	+	+	+	−	−	−
	if, because	+	±	−	−	−	−
conjuncts	*yet, so*	+	+	−	+	−	−

Note
When *because* introduces a disjunct clause (8.78 Note, 11.37), it resembles *for* and resultative *so that:*

He paid for the book, *because I saw him.*

9.38
We can justify the traditional inclusion of *but* among the coordinators and the exclusion of *for* and *so that* by pointing to two facts about *but* that distinguish it from the other two conjunctions: (a) the possibility of ellipsis of the subject under certain conditions when *but* introduces the clause and (b) the ability of *but* to link two subordinate clauses. The latter ability, in particular, reflects its status as a coordinator in that it links constituents at the same level. The inability of *for* and *so that* to link two clauses in this way is sufficient justification for excluding them from the class of coordinators. The conjuncts *yet* and *so* are anyway excluded

because they can be preceded by another conjunction. Nevertheless, both *for* and *so that* and conjuncts such as *yet* and *so* show some resemblance to the coordinators, which distinguishes them respectively from the subordinators and from conjuncts such as *nevertheless* and *therefore*. And, as we have seen, *but* also differs from *and* and *or* in certain respects.

Coordination of clauses
9.39
We first consider the coordination of clauses, with *and*, *or* and *but* as coordinators. The two or more clauses that may be coordinated (or conjoined) are termed here CONJOINS. Of the three coordinators, *and* is the least restricted in its role as coordinator of clauses and *but* the most restricted.

Note
[a] Conjoins are called CONJUNCTS by some grammarians, but the term CONJUNCT is used in this book for a class of adverbials used in linking.
[b] A sentence constructed from two or more conjoins is traditionally termed a COMPOUND SENTENCE.

Semantic implications of coordination by *and*
9.40
And denotes merely a relation between the clauses. The only restriction is the semantic one that the contents of the clauses should have sufficient in common to justify their combination. Thus, [44] is odd simply because it would be difficult to find any connection between the semantic content of the clauses to motivate their combination:

> *The people went to a dance *and* the equator is equally distant from the two poles. [44]

The implications of the combination vary and they depend on our presuppositions and our knowledge of the world. However, the semantic relationship can usually be made explicit by the addition of an adverbial. With each exemplification of a relationship that we give in the following sections we insert in parenthesis (wherever possible) an adverbial that would make the relationship explicit. For the sake of simplicity, we illustrate the types of implications with sentences containing just two clauses.

Of the eight types of semantic implication, in only three – (3), (7), (8) – can the sequence of clauses perhaps be reversed without changing the semantic relationship between the clauses. Even so, the sequence is rarely random.

9.41

(1) The second clause is a consequence or result of the first. This entails that the order of the clauses also reflects chronological sequence:

He heard an explosion *and* he (therefore) phoned the police.

9.42

(2) The second clause is chronologically sequent to the first, but without any implication of a cause–result relationship:

She washed the dishes *and* (then) she dried them.

Note

There can be no implication of chronological sequence if the clauses are given in a sequence contrary to that of chronological sequence. Thus, if the second clause is tense-marked to indicate that its content is prior chronologically, coordination of the two clauses is unacceptable in the intended meaning:

*She dried the dishes *and* she had washed them

This of course also applies when there is the additional implication of a cause–effect relationship:

*He phoned the police *and* he had heard an explosion

Notice, however, that these sequences are acceptable without linking by *and:*

She dried the dishes; she had washed them
He phoned the police; he had heard an explosion.

9.43

(3) The second clause introduces a contrast. *And* could be replaced by *but* when this implication is present:

Robert was secretive *and* (in contrast) David is candid.

9.44

(4) The second clause is a comment on the first:

They disliked John – and that's not surprising.

Note

If the first clause is sufficiently long, the second is sometimes inserted parenthetically within it. This is not an institutionalized device and gives the impression of being an *ad hoc* or unplanned interpolation:

Many students at our university – *and it is difficult to explain this* – reject the proposed reforms in university administration.

9.45

(5) The second clause is felt to be surprising in view of the first, so that the first clause has concessive force:

He tried hard *and* (yet) he failed

Here too, *but* could replace *and*. The use of *and* creates a special rhetorical effect, enhancing the impression that the second clause is unexpected.

9.46

(6) The first clause is a condition of the second:

Give me some money *and* (then) I'll help you escape.
Let's give him some money *and* (then) he won't tell anybody what we did.
We should give him some money *and* (then) he won't tell anybody what we did.

The implication in the first of the sentences is shown by the paraphrase:

Give me some money. If you give me some money (then) I'll help you escape.

A condition–consequence relationship is implicit between what is suggested in the first clause and the expected consequence contained in the second clause.
For the conditional implication to apply, it is usual that

(a) The second clause has a modal auxiliary (3.20 *ff*).
(b) The verb of the first clause is an imperative (7.72 *ff*) or contains a modal auxiliary.

Note
There are exceptions to both generalizations about the verb phrases in which the conditional implication can apply. The second clause can have the simple present with future reference:

Give me the bribe and you *get* the job

For some speakers the first clause can have the simple present with future reference:

He *makes* a move and I'll hit him.

9.47

(7) The second clause makes a point similar to the first:

A trade agreement should be no problem, *and* (similarly) a cultural exchange could be arranged.

9.48

(8) The second clause is a 'pure' addition to the first, the only implication being that the two statements are congruent:

He has long hair *and* (also) he wears jeans.

Semantic implications of coordination by *or*
9.49
Or usually denotes an alternative. As with *and* (9.40), the contents of the two clauses must have sufficient in common to motivate their justification as alternatives. Hence, the sentence illustrating this point for *and* is also odd if *or* is substituted:

> *The people went to a dance *or* the equator is equally distant from
> the two poles.   [44a]

9.50
Usually *or* is EXCLUSIVE, excluding the possibility of a realization of all but one of the alternatives:

> You can sleep on the couch in the lounge *or* you can go to a
> hotel.   [45]

The preferred alternative tends to be put first.

The content of some conjoinings excludes the possibility of both alternatives, as in [45]. But even when both alternatives are possible, as in

> You can boil yourself an egg *or* you can make some cheese
> sandwiches.   [46]

or is normally interpreted as exclusive. The addition of *either* to the first clause is more explicit in excluding the combination of both alternatives:

> You can *either* boil yourself an egg, *or* you can make some
> cheese sandwiches.   [46a]

However, even if *either* is used, a third clause can be added which explicitly allows both alternatives:

> You can *either* boil yourself an egg, *or* you can make some
> cheese sandwiches, *or* you can do both.   [46b[

For some speakers, the construction with *either* exemplified in [46b] is avoided, because of prescriptive teaching that insists that *either* should accompany only two alternatives.

Note
[a] The prescriptive teaching is partly based on the use of *either* as pronoun or determiner to refer to two only. Also, *either . . . or* is seen as related to *both . . . and*, which is more usually restricted to two.
[b] On *or* in alternative questions (where there is a closed set of options), see 7.68 *f*. The use of the correlatives *whether . . . or* and *if . . . or* in indirect alternative questions is discussed in 11.19.

9.51

When the content of the clauses allows it, *or* can be interpreted as INCLUSIVE, allowing the realization of a combination of the alternatives, as in

You can boil yourself an egg *or* you can make some cheese
sandwiches.   [46]

We can explicitly include the third possibility by a third clause:

You can boil yourself an egg, *or* you can make some cheese
sandwiches, *or* you can do both.   [46c]

In special varieties of the language requiring precision, particularly in the written form, the third possibility can be explicitly included by a combination of coordinators, *and/or:*

If the appliance is defective, write directly to the manufacturer
and/or complain to your local consumer protection service.   [47]

9.52

The alternative expressed by *or* may be a restatement, a correction of what is said in the first conjoin:

They are enjoying themselves, *or* at least they appear to be
enjoying themselves.

9.53

In addition to indicating an alternative, *or* may imply a negative condition. Thus in

Give me some money *or* I'll shoot   [48]

the implication can be paraphrased by the negative conditional clause *if you don't give me some money:*

Give me some money. *If you don't give me some money* I'll
shoot.   [48a]

This use of *or* is the negative analogue of one use of *and* (9.46), except that *and* generally requires an imperative or modal auxiliary in the first clause, whereas that is not a general requirement for *or*:

They liked the apartment *or* they wouldn't have stayed so long.

9.54

Semantic implications of coordination by *but*

But denotes a contrast. The contrast may be in the unexpectedness of what is said in the second conjoin in view of the content of the first conjoin:

John is poor, *but* he is happy

The sentence implies that his happiness is unexpected in view of his poverty. The unexpectedness depends on our presuppositions and our knowledge of the world. It would be equally possible to say

John is rich, *but* he is happy

if we considered wealth a source of unhappiness. However, the contrast may be a restatement in affirmative terms of what has been said or implied negatively in the first conjoin:

John didn't waste his time in the week before the exam, *but* studied hard every evening.

With this relationship, it is normal to ellipt the repeated subject in the second clause (*cf* 9.93). Notice that we cannot here insert conjuncts such as *yet* or *nevertheless*, but we can insert *on the contrary* (*cf* 10.33).

Correlatives
9.55
Nor, neither

Nor and *neither* can be used without being a correlative pair. They generally presuppose that a previous clause is negative or contains a negative word or a negative implication:

He did *not* receive any assistance from the authorities, *nor* did he believe their assurance that action would soon be taken.

Many people are *only* dimly aware of the ways in which the environment can be protected. *Nor* have governments made sufficient effort to educate them.

All the students were obviously very *miserable*. *Nor* were the teachers satisfied with conditions at the school.

Notice that *nor* is not the equivalent of *or* plus *not*, as might be thought from its morphological composition. Rather, it is nearer to being the equivalent of *and* plus *not*. Thus,

They *never* forgave him for the insult, *nor* could he rid himself of feelings of guilt for having spoken that way.   [49a]

is semantically equivalent to

They *never* forgave him for the insult, *and* he could *not* rid himself of feelings of guilt for having spoken that way *either*.   [49b]

In all these sentences, *neither* can replace *nor*. Both *neither* and *nor* can be linked to preceding sentences by *and* or *but*:

They *never* forgave him for the insult, $\left\{ {and \atop but} \right\} \left\{ {neither \atop nor} \right\}$ could he rid himself of feelings of guilt for having spoken that way.   [49c]

This possibility excludes them from the class of pure coordinators (9.33, 9.37–38). Moreover, *neither* and *nor* require subject-operator inversion in their clause, a feature suggesting a measure of integration within clause structure and one they share with some negative adjuncts when they appear initially (8.66, 14.16).

Note
In highly formal and archaic style, *nor* is occasionally found after an affirmative clause:

> It was hoped that all would be agreeable to that proposal. *Nor* was this hope disappointed.

Neither ... nor
9.56

Neither ... nor often constitute a correlative pair, negating two clauses conjoined by *and*. For example, the two clauses

> David loves Joan *and* wants to marry her

can be negated either by the negative particle *not* in each clause:

> David does *not* love Joan and does *not* want to marry her

or by the correlatives *neither ... nor:*

> David *neither* loves Joan *nor* wants to marry her

The correlatives emphasize that the negation applies to both clauses.

Correlative *neither* is mobile, its position reflecting the scope of negation (7.49):

> John *neither* has long hair, *nor* does he wear jeans
> Mary was *neither* happy, *nor* was she sad

Correlative *neither* does not entail subject-operator inversion, even when it occurs initially, though for non-correlative *neither* it is obligatory (9.55). *Nor* is usually followed by subject-operator inversion when both subject and operator are present:

> *Neither* Peter wanted the responsibility, *nor* did his wife

though if the predicates in the two clauses are identical, the more usual form would be:

> *Neither Peter nor his wife* wanted the responsibility

However, the inversion is not obligatory:

> *Neither* ten of the reasons they offered are acceptable *nor* even five of them will do

But when subject and/or operator are not present, there can be no inversion:

Bob has *neither* replied to my letters *nor* answered my
   telephone calls

John *neither* has long hair *nor* wears jeans

Notice that in the last example the form of the verb is *wears,* while in
the corresponding full form of the sentence, with inversion given above,
we find (*does . . .*) *wear.*

Note

[a] The correlatives *neither . . . nor* cannot be used when in the positive the second
clause is a comment on the first (9.44) or when the first is a condition of the second
(9.46).

[b] For some speakers, the rules for *neither . . . nor* are identical with those for *both . . .
and* (9.58), *ie* some kind of ellipsis is required.

9.57

A clause with correlative *neither* can be preceded by a coordinator, as
with non-correlative *neither* and *nor* (9.55). Correlative *nor,* however,
cannot be preceded by any conjunction:

*John *neither* has long hair, *and nor* does he wear jeans

This rule applies in general to correlatives. For example, *although* and
nevertheless are correlative in

Although John is poor, he is *nevertheless* happy

A coordinator cannot therefore be inserted:

*Although John is poor, *and* he is *nevertheless* happy

Without the initial subordinator, *nevertheless* is not a correlative, and
hence its clause can be linked by *and* or *but:*

John is poor, $\begin{Bmatrix} and \\ but \end{Bmatrix}$ he is *nevertheless* happy.

Other correlatives
9.58

The correlatives *either . . . or* (and *whether . . . or,* the corresponding
pair in indirect questions) have been mentioned earlier (9.50). At first
sight, the correlative pair *both . . . and* appears to stand in the same
relationship to *and* as *either . . . or* does to *or.* But, in fact, *both . . . and*
is not admissible in clause coordination unless there is a kind of ellipsis.
Hence, while we can have

Mary washed the dishes *and* Peter dried them

we cannot have

*Both Mary washed the dishes *and* Peter dried them

On the other hand, *both* can be inserted if the predications in the two clauses are directly linked:

Mary *both* washed the dishes *and* dried them
Mary will *both* wash the dishes *and* dry them

and with phrasal coordination (9.123), *eg*

Both Mary *and* Peter washed the dishes.

Note
With *both* there is not ellipsis in the strict sense, since ellipted items cannot be supplied (*cf* 9.98).

9.59
Common correlatives with *but* are *not* (and enclitic *-n't*) and *not only:*

He did*n't* come to help, *but* to hinder us.
They *not only* broke into his office and stole his books, *but* they (*also*) tore up his manuscripts.

With *not only*, the content of both clauses is felt to be surprising but the second clause, often reinforced by *also*, is felt to be the more surprising. A more dramatic effect is achieved by positioning *not only* initially, with consequent subject-operator inversion:

Not only did they break into his office and steal his books, *but* they *also* tore up his manuscripts.

9.60
The correlatives *just as . . . so* are used where one of the semantic implications of clauses conjoined by *and* applies, namely, where the second clause makes a point similar to the first:

Just as they must put aside their prejudices, *so* we must be prepared to accept their good faith.

For correlatives with subordinators, see 8.92, 11.10.

Ellipsis in coordination of clauses
9.61
Clausal and phrasal coordination
When two or more clauses are coordinated, certain clause constituents are often ellipted from all but one of the clauses. If, when we supply the ellipted items, the resultant sentence is semantically equivalent to the original elliptical sentence, then we have an instance of strict ellipsis:

We can go for a walk or watch television
=We can go for a walk or *we can* watch television

When two or more phrases are coordinated, we shall not regard such coordination as involving clausal coordination with ellipsis of all other constituents, even if in some cases the resultant sentence is semantically equivalent under some interpretations. This is because beyond a certain point it becomes more economical to discuss coordination in terms of what elements are realized rather than what elements are missing. (But see 9.96 for another reason.) For example, in

You and your brother can watch television now

the coordinated phrase *you and your brother* is not considered elliptical, despite the equivalence of

You *can watch television now* and your brother can watch television now.

Such coordination is regarded here as phrasal coordination. Within phrasal coordination, however, there can be ellipsis, for example of a determiner:

He telephoned his wife and (his) child

Phrasal coordination and ellipsis within it are separately dealt with later (9.99 *ff*).

On the other hand, we find it more convenient to treat under clause coordination cases of coordination of auxiliaries, of lexical verbs, or of verb phrases (9.67 *ff*).

Note

In effect, every case of ellipsis involves some semantic difference, since it suggests a closer connection than would be felt if the forms occurred in full (*cf* 9.92 *ff*).

Ellipted and realized items
9.62

Ellipsis in coordination is a means of avoiding repetition (9.4). But the ellipted items need not be identical in all respects with the realized items on which the ellipsis is dependent (*cf* 9.2). Three kinds of identity are found in elliptical coordinated clauses:

(1) The ellipted and realized items are identical lexical items and are co-referential:

John likes Mary, but (John) hates Susan

The two instances of *John* are identical lexical items and are co-referential.

(2) The ellipted and realized items are identical lexical items and refer to manifestations of the same type:

Bob will *buy a house*, and Peter might (buy a house) too

The two instances of *buy a house* constitute identical lexical items and the same type of transaction is referred to.

(3) The ellipted and realized items are identical lexical items but have different grammatical forms:

He has *complained*, and he will (complain) again

Type 3 applies chiefly to cases of ellipsis of the lexical verb where the elliptical clause contains an auxiliary requiring a different form of the lexical verb from that in the realized item (but *cf* 9.101). In contrast, the ellipted and realized items do not have different grammatical forms in

He may *complain*, and he probably will (complain).

9.63

If items have formal identity but are different lexical items, their conjoining is odd:

?She *made up* her mind and afterwards she *made up* her face.

Ellipsis makes the conjoining even odder:

*She *made up* her mind and her face.

The conjoining and ellipsis would be accepted as a linguistic joke.

Note
It is similarly odd if one of the clauses is subordinate:

*She *made up* her mind *after* (she *made up*) her face.

Simple and complex ellipsis
9.64

Ellipsis may be simple or complex. In simple ellipsis, either the ellipsis occurs in only one of the conjoined clauses:

They were married in 1960 and (they were) divorced in 1970

or identical items (*cf* 9.62) are ellipted in two or more conjoined clauses:

They were married in 1960, (they were) divorced in 1970, and (they were) reconciled in 1972

Bill felt severe pains in his chest, (Bill) decided to see his doctor, (Bill) drove at great speed to the surgery, (Bill) crashed into another car, and (Bill) was dead before he was taken out of the wreckage.

(The excessive repetition of *Bill* in the last sentence would of course compel resort to ellipsis for stylistic reasons.)

Simple ellipsis is usually anaphoric, with the realized items in the first of a series of clauses, as in the above examples, but it can be cataphoric, with the realized items in the last of the series, as in

John can (pass the examination), and Bob certainly will, *pass the examination.*

Tom is (playing for the school), Peter will be (playing for the school), and Harold might be, *playing for the school.*

Compare also

Married in 1960, *they were* divorced in 1970.

In simple ellipsis, the ellipsis normally occurs at one point in the clause, but if the subject is one of the ellipted items, more than one point can be affected:

My brother is *using the car* this morning and (my brother) will be (using the car) this afternoon.

The subject can be ellipted if it is present as a realized item in the first clause.

9.65

In COMPLEX ELLIPSIS, items are ellipted both anaphorically and cataphorically in the same sentence. The subject and (optionally) the auxiliary are ellipted in clauses after the first. Items ellipted in the first clause are realized in the last clause:

Bob is (unhappy), and (Bob) always will be, *unhappy*

If more than two clauses are conjoined with complex ellipsis, the middle clause or clauses may share the ellipsis of both the first and the last clauses:

My friend owns (paintings), (my friend) admires (paintings), and (my friend) often looks at, *paintings.*

(The commas after *will be* and *looks at* are acceptable only when the parenthesized items are omitted; cf App III.12, III.22.) If the operator is retained in the last clause, we may have the realized predication in the middle clause, so that it is the last clause that shares the ellipsis of the preceding clauses:

They can (pay the full fee) and (they) should *pay the full fee*, but (they) won't (pay the full fee).

In that case, we in effect have complex ellipsis in the first two clauses:

They can (pay the full fee) and (they) should *pay the full fee.*

and simple ellipsis in the last clause:

They can/should *pay the full fee*, but (they) won't (pay the full fee).

9.66

Table 9:2 indicates, with exemplification, the elements that can be ellipted in coordinated clauses.

Table 9:2

ELLIPSIS: COORDINATED CLAUSES

section(s)	element ellipted	ellipted in:	
		1st clause	last clause
9.67	SUBJECT		+
9.68, 9.70	AUXILIARY		+
9.72–78	1st PART OF PREDICATION (*often with ellipsis of auxiliary*)		+
9.76–78, 9.82–83	WHOLE OF PREDICATION		+
		+	
9.84	DIRECT OBJECT	+	
	SUBJECT COMPLEMENT	+	
			+
9.85–88	ADVERBIAL	+	
			+
9.89	HEAD OF NOUN PHRASE		+
9.90	COMPLEMENT OF PREPOSITIONAL PHRASE	+	

SIMPLE ELLIPSIS		COMPLEX ELLIPSIS
without ellipsis of subject	*with ellipsis of subject*	*ellipsis of subject* *(+ auxiliary) in last clause*
	Peter ate the fruit and (Peter) drank the beer	
John must clean the shed and Peter (must) read his book	Peter must have taken the course and (Peter must have) passed the examination	
Paul likes Mary, but Peter (likes) Joan	She is writing to her parents and (she) will be (writing) to her brother	
John has written a poem and Bob (has written) a short story	Paul is flying to Madrid to-night and (Paul is flying) to Athens next week	
John was the winner in 1970 and Bob (was the winner) in 1971	It's cold in December in England, but (it's cold) in July in New Zealand	
Joan will cook the meals today and Barbara (will cook the meals) tomorrow	My elder brother bought a house in London two years ago and (my elder brother bought a house) in the country this year	
George will take the course and Bob might (take the course)	They can pay the full fee, but (they) won't (pay the full fee)	
George will (take the course), and Bob might, take the course		They can (pay the full fee), but (they) won't, pay the full fee
John likes (Mary), and Peter hates, Mary		She washed (the shirts) and (she) ironed the shirts
George was (angry), and Bob certainly seemed, angry		They seem (happy), and indeed (they) must be, happy
Bob seemed angry, and George certainly was (angry)	Sarah became a member ten years ago, and (Sarah) still is (a member)	
Bob works (in London), and Peter lives, in London		Bill drinks (sparingly), and (Bill) smokes, sparingly
Tom was at Oxford, but his brother wasn't (at Oxford)	She paid for the tickets last week and (she) will pay (for the tickets) tonight	
We wanted fried fish, but they gave us boiled (fish)	We wanted fried fish, but (we) got boiled (fish)	
Bob is bored with (music), but Peter enjoys, music		He walked up (the hill) and (he) ran down, the hill

The table notes

(a) whether the subject of the clause is ellipted too
(b) whether the ellipsis is simple or complex
(c) whether the ellipsis takes place in the 'first' or 'last' clause.

An entry in the 'first' column means the ellipsis can apply to all conjoined clauses except the last, while an entry in the 'last' column means that the ellipsis can apply to all except the first clause.

The table also indicates in which sections of this chapter the types of ellipsis are discussed.

Ellipted elements
9.67
Ellipsis of subject

If the subjects of coordinated clauses are identical, it is common for occurrences subsequent to the first to be ellipted:

> *Peter* ate the fruit and (Peter) drank the beer
> *Mary* skipped and (Mary) jumped
> *John* read the book or (John) saw the film

Both the full forms and the pro-forms would be less common, particularly the former. However, if identical auxiliaries are present, then the pro-form is as normal as ellipsis:

> John has read the book or *he* has seen the film
> John has read the book or (John) has seen the film

But if the auxiliaries are different, ellipsis is more normal:

> Mary has washed the dishes and (Mary) will dry them
> Mary has washed the dishes and she will dry them

If more than two clauses with identical auxiliaries are coordinated, then the pro-form is probably more normal than ellipsis of subject alone:

> *Mary* has washed the dishes, *she* has dried them, and *she* has put them in the cupboard.
> *Mary* has washed the dishes, (Mary) has dried them, and (Mary) has put them in the cupboard.

The most normal of all is the ellipsis of both subject and auxiliaries (9.68):

> Mary has washed the dishes, dried them, and put them in the cupboard.

9.68

Ellipsis of subject and auxiliaries

If both subject and auxiliaries are identical, it is normal for both to be ellipted. There may be only one auxiliary:

Alice is washing and (Alice is) dressing

or more than one:

Peter must have broken in and (Peter must have) stolen the
  papers   [50]

Ellipsis is only possible in clauses subsequent to the first clause.

If both subject and auxiliaries are identical, repetition of the subject or substitution of a pro-form for the subject is allowed only when the auxiliaries are retained. Thus, we can have the full forms and pro-forms in [50a] and [50b] respectively, though these are less common than ellipsis:

Peter must have broken in and *Peter must have* stolen the
  papers   [50a]
Peter must have broken in and *he must have* stolen the papers   [50b]

On the other hand, we cannot have the full form or the pro-form if the auxiliaries are ellipted:

*Peter must have broken in and *Peter* stolen the papers   [50c]
*Peter must have broken in and *he* stolen the papers   [50d]

9.69

Repeated subject and auxiliaries in subordination

It is instructive to contrast coordination and subordination with respect to ellipsis of subject and auxiliaries. In subordinate clauses, ellipsis of subject alone or of subject with auxiliaries is generally not allowed:

Jack was looking well although *he had* slept little   [51]
*Jack was looking well although (had) slept little
Susan has looked after the baby while *she has* stayed with us   [52]
*Susan has looked after the baby while stayed with us
John told Alice that *he* loved her   [53]
*John told Alice that loved her
Mary must go to the supermarket today, because *she must* buy
  some groceries   [54]
*Mary must go to the supermarket today, because buy some
  groceries

If the auxiliary is BE, we can omit both subject and auxiliary in the subordinate abbreviated clause (9.7 *ff*, 11.26), though not one of the elements alone. But for this to happen, BE need not appear in the super-ordinate clause:

Jack was looking well although (he was) working hard
Bob will not cooperate if (he is) punished

Repetition of the full form of the subject is not allowed in most sub-ordinate clauses. Thus, the following sentences are unacceptable, if the subjects are co-referential:

John told Alice that *John* loved her	[53a]
Mary will watch television when *Mary* feels bored	[55a]

(They would be regarded as odd even if the subjects were intended to refer to different referents.) The normal way of dealing with repeated subjects in subordinate clauses is to substitute a pro-form:

John told Alice that *he* loved her	[53b]
Mary will watch television when *she* feels bored	[55b]

However, the subject might be repeated in an appropriate context as a stylistic device to show wilfulness:

Mary will watch television when *Mary* damn well feels like watching television

If the subordinate clause is positioned initially, it can contain a pro-form that refers forward to the full form in the superordinate clause:

That *he* loved her was conveyed to Alice by *John*	[53c]
When *she* feels bored, *Mary* will watch television	[55c]

Repetition of the full form is also possible, though very unusual:

That *John* loved her was conveyed to Alice by *John*	[53d]
When *Mary* feels bored, *Mary* will watch television	[55d]
Since *Mary* has been in New York, *Mary* has been in trouble	[56]

With a disjunct clause (8.78), the full form is possible (though again un-usual), whatever the position of the clause:

Mary has not been in trouble, although *Mary* has been in New York
Since *Mary* feels bored, *Mary* will not be allowed to watch television

When subordinate clauses follow their superordinate clause, sub-stitution is allowed only in the subordinate clause. Hence, the subjects cannot be co-referential in the following sentences, where the super-ordinate clause has the pro-form:

He told Alice that *John* loved her [53e]

She will watch television when *Mary* feels bored [55e]

On the other hand, when the subordinate clause precedes, substitution is allowed both in the subordinate clause and in the superordinate clause. Hence, it is possible in [53f] and [53c] to interpret the italicized items as co-referential, and natural so to interpret those in [55f] and [55c]:

That *John* loved her was conveyed to Alice by *him* [53f]

That *he* loved her was conveyed to Alice by *John* [53c]

When *Mary* feels bored, *she* will watch television [55f]

When *she* feels bored, *Mary* will watch television [55c]

9.70
Ellipsis of auxiliary

If only the auxiliary is ellipted, the realized items must be present in the first clause. The ellipsis is possible under certain conditions:

(1) The auxiliary cannot be ellipted if the subjects are identical or co-referential, and the subject is not ellipted as well. Hence, the unacceptability of

*Peter *will be* taking the course and $\left\{ \begin{array}{l} \text{Peter} \\ \text{he} \end{array} \right\}$ (will be) passing the examination.

In such instances, either the subject is ellipted or both subject and auxiliary are ellipted (9.67, 9.68).

(2) If the subjects are different, ellipsis of only the auxiliary is allowed:

John *must* clean the shed and Peter (must) read his book.

If there is more than one auxiliary element, it is normal for all to be ellipted:

John *will be* playing the guitar and Mary (will be) preparing the supper.

If the verbs in both clauses are identical, ellipsis of only the auxiliary is normally not allowed:

*John *will take* the French course and Peter (will) *take* the German course.

except that it is admissible for some speakers if there is subject-operator inversion:

?*Will* John *take* the French course and (will) Peter *take* the German course?

?*Did* John *explain* or (did) Bob *explain*?

Ellipsis of predication
9.71
Ellipsis of a part of the predication or of the whole of it can be treated
under four headings:

(1) ellipsis of the first part of the predication, which includes the
lexical verb
(2) ellipsis of the whole of the predication
(3) ellipsis of a subject complement or direct object
(4) ellipsis of an adverbial

In some cases the subject and/or auxiliary can be ellipted as well. If the
auxiliary is retained and the ellipsis is immediately following it, then the
auxiliary cannot be given in its reduced form. For example, the auxiliary
will is reduced in both instances to *'ll* in

She'll write to her parents and he'll write to his sister   [57]

But if the repeated *write* is ellipted, only the unreduced form of the
auxiliary is admissible:

She'll write to her parents and he *will* to his sister.   [57a]

Ellipsis of first part of predication
9.72
If only the first part of the predication, including the lexical verb, is
ellipted, the realized items are in the first clause and the ellipsis is in clauses
subsequent to the first. Some examples are given of ellipsis of the predication which leaves part of the predication following the ellipsis. If the
subject is retained, the ellipsis constitutes a gap in the clause.

(1) LEXICAL VERB ONLY
She has *written* to her parents and he may (write) to his
sister   [58]
Sylvia will *prepare* lunch and Alice might (prepare)
supper   [59]
Alice *was* happy and Susan (was) miserable   [60]
Paul *likes* Mary, but Peter (likes) Joan   [61]
I *work* in a factory, and my brother (works) on a farm   [62]

This ellipsis is not common, and some find it unacceptable if
identical auxiliaries are retained:

?Sylvia *must prepare* lunch and Alice *must* (prepare)
supper   [59a]

The subject too can be ellipted in the second clause:

> *She* is *writing* to her parents and (she) will be (writing) to her brother.
> *John made* his first wife happy, but (John made) his second wife miserable.

9.73

(2) VERB, INCLUDING AUXILIARY

> John *has written* a poem and Bob (has written) a short story.
> John *was given* a railway set, and Sue (was given) a doll.

The subject too can be ellipted in the second clause:

> *Paul is flying* to Madrid tonight and (Paul is flying) to Athens next week.

Ellipsis of the entire verb phrase or of only the lexical verb can take place in clauses containing an object and an object complement, but the subject must then be ellipted as well (*cf* 9.70):

> *He has promised* John a book, (he has promised) Bill a watch, and (he has promised) Mary a doll.
> *He has promised John a book, *he* (*has*) Bill a watch, and *he* (*has*) Mary a doll.
> *He made* John happy, but (he made) Mary angry.
> *He made John happy, but *he* Mary angry.

9.74

(3) VERB AND SUBJECT COMPLEMENT

> John *was the winner* in 1970 and Bob (was the winner) in 1971.
> The administration *seems obstinate* in our school and the teachers (seem obstinate) in your school.

And with ellipsis of subject:

> *It's cold* in December in England, but (it's cold) in July in New Zealand.

9.75

(4) VERB AND OBJECT

> Joan *will cook the meals* today and Barbara (will cook the meals) tomorrow.
> Peter *is playing football* for his school and Paul (is playing football) for his club.

And with ellipsis of subject, though this is perhaps rare:

> *My elder brother bought a house* in London two years ago
> and (my elder brother bought a house) in the country
> this year.

Notice that in certain contexts there can be ambiguity as to whether the subject and verb are ellipted or the verb and object are ellipted. For example, the sentence

> Bob will interview some candidates this morning and Peter
> this afternoon.

can be interpreted as having either of these two kinds of ellipsis:

> *Bob will interview* some candidates this morning and (he will
> interview) Peter this afternoon.
> Bob *will interview some candidates* this morning and Peter
> (will interview some candidates) this afternoon.

Auxiliaries in predication ellipsis
9.76
It will be observed that the ellipted form of the auxiliary or lexical verb sometimes varies from that of the realized form. The form of the verb or auxiliary is different when one is 3rd person singular present and the other is not:

> I *work* in a factory and my brother (work*s*) on a farm.
> Mary *is* going to Paris and her sisters (*are* going) to Rome.

9.77
The possible variation in forms of the auxiliaries is the same whether the whole or only part of the predication is ellipted, provided that in the former case the ellipsis does not take place in the first clause (*cf* 9.82). We therefore draw on both types to illustrate the variations. Of course, where the head of the verb phrase is the same, there is no variation:

> John needn't *stay* here, but George MÙST (*stay* here).
> Paul has *apologized*, and Bob SHÒULD have (*apologized*) by now.

In general, most co-occurrences of auxiliaries are allowed, for example:

(1) PRESENT AND MODAL
> John *understands* the situation and surely Peter should
> (*understand* the situation).
> His friends already *belong* to the club and he will (*belong* to
> the club) soon.

(2) PAST AND MODAL

> Bob *entered* the competition and Paul may (*enter* the competition).

(3) PERFECT AND MODAL

> John hasn't *met* my brother yet, but (he) will (*meet* my brother) soon.

(4) PROGRESSIVE AND MODAL

> Peter is *complaining* about the noise, but John won't (*complain* about the noise).

(5) PROGRESSIVE AND PERFECT

> John is *questioning* our motives, and Bill has (*questioned*) our results.
>
> John may be *questioning* our motives, but Peter hasn't (*questioned* our motives).

(6) PAST AND PERFECT

> Peter saw your parents last week, but (he) hasn't (*seen* your parents) since.
>
> Paul *apologized*, but Bob won't have (*apologized*).

9.78

One major exception is that an ellipted passive does not co-occur with any of the other forms. Though (as in the last example in 9.77) the past and perfect can co-occur with ellipsis of the head of the latter, the passive head cannot be ellipted despite its formal identity with a preceding past or perfect head:

> Paul *denied* the charge, but the charge wasn't *denied* by his friends.
> *Paul *denied* the charge, but the charge wasn't by his friends.
> John had *observed* many of the enemy's soldiers but hadn't been *observed* by them.
> *John had *observed* many of the enemy's soldiers but hadn't been by them.

One other co-occurrence seems dubious, that of modal followed by progressive:

> John won't *enter* the competition, but Peter is *entering* the competition.
> ?*John won't *enter* the competition, but Peter is.

Predication substitutes
9.79
The equivalent of the auxiliary for simple present and past in such

elliptical constructions is the operator DO. But DO is a pro-form not only for tense but, together with DO-phrases such as *do so* and *do it* (*cf* 10.52 *ff*), is a pro-form for the whole or part of the predication:

> I *like cheese*, and my family *does* too
> I *saw the play* on Friday and my wife *did* on Saturday
> Mary wouldn't *take the money*, but Susan *did*

The DO items must be regarded as pro-forms, since 'missing items' cannot be supplied:

> *I like cheese, and my family *does like cheese* too

However, it is certainly possible to regard the negative, interrogative, and emphatic forms as involving ellipsis in such constructions, since missing items can be supplied:

> I *like cheese*, but my family *doesn't* (like cheese).
> I *like cheese*, but *does* my family (like cheese)? No!
> I don't *like cheese* now, but I *did* (like cheese) when I was a child.

At all events, for ellipsis of predication, there is an obvious and systematic similarity in the part played by all the operators, including DO:

> My wife didn't play tennis, but I did
> My wife doesn't play tennis, but I do
> My wife can't play tennis, but I can
> My wife won't play tennis, but I will
> My wife wasn't playing tennis, but I was
> My wife isn't a good tennis-player, but I am
> My wife hasn't played tennis, but I have.

9.80

The most common pro-form for predication is *so* when used together with the pro-form DO or an operator in subject-operator inversion (10.54 *ff*):

> Mary wants a cup of coffee and so does Joan   [63]
> We have had enough to eat, and so have they   [64]
> Our city is noisy and dirty, and so is yours   [65]

Not can be a pro-form for the predicate (10.61), since it does not require an operator:

> Mary wants a cup of coffee, but not Joan   [63a]

The second clause of [63a] is a negative counterpart of the second clause of [63]. An alternative for [63a] allows the use of operator as well, but we then have ellipsis of the predication:

Mary wants a cup of coffee, but Joan does not (want a cup of
coffee) [63b]

9.81

To can be regarded as a pro-form for an infinitive clause in predication,
or as allowing ellipsis of the infinitive clause (10.58). Compare

I asked him to pay the rent immediately,

but he$\begin{cases} \textit{wouldn't} \\ \textit{didn't want to} \end{cases}$ (pay the rent immediately)

The realized items need not constitute an infinitive clause:

I saw him *riding his bicycle in the park*, and I told him not to (ride
his bicycle in the park).
I intended that they should *stay till the next day*, but they refused
to (stay till the next day).
He *left Paris this morning*, but he didn't want to (leave Paris this
morning).

9.82

Ellipsis of whole of predication

If the predication is ellipted completely, there is a choice between having
the realized items in the first clause or in the last (*cf*. 9.64 *f*):

George will *take the course* and Bob might (take the course) [65a]
George will (take the course), and Bob might, *take the course* [65b]

It is more common to have the realized items in the first clause, as in
[65a]. As we have noted (9.72), if the first part of the predication only is
ellipted, the realized items must be in the first clause:

John will *write* a poem and Bob might (write) a short story [66a]
*John will (write) a poem, and Bob might *write* a short story [66b]

When the predication is ellipted completely, the subject can also be
ellipted, but only in clauses subsequent to the first:

They can *pay the full fee*, and (they) certainly should (pay the full
fee), but (they) probably won't (pay the full fee). [67]

When the realized subject is in the first clause and the realized predication is elsewhere, we have complex ellipsis (9.65):

They no doubt can (pay the full fee), and (they) certainly should
(pay the full fee), but (they) probably won't, *pay the full fee*. [67a]
They can (pay the full fee) and (they) should *pay the full fee*,
but (they) won't (pay the full fee). [67b]

Other examples of predication ellipsis illustrating the alternatives:

John might have been *writing letters*, and Peter certainly was
 (writing letters).   [68a]
John might have been (writing letters), and Peter certainly
 was, *writing letters*.   [68b]
Alice may have *eaten*, and Sylvia certainly has (eaten).   [69a]
Alice may have (eaten), and Sylvia certainly has, *eaten*.   [69b]
Bob is *playing for the school*, and George may be (playing for
 the school).   [70a]
Bob is (playing for the school), and George may be, *playing for
 the school*.   [70b]
John could have been *watching television*, but (John) wasn't
 (watching television).   [71a]
John could have been (watching television), but (John) wasn't,
 watching television.   [71b]
He can *demand repayment*, and (he) will (demand repayment). [72a]
He can (demand repayment) and (he) will *demand repayment*.   [72b]

The co-occurrence of auxiliaries with predication ellipsis is the same
as when only the first part of the predication is ellipted ($9.77 f$),
provided that the realized predication is in the first clause. However, if
the realized predication is in the last clause, then only auxiliaries that take
the same head of the verb phrase will normally co-occur, as in the *b* set
in [65] and [68–72]. Thus, the following are dubious, though they may
occasionally appear in informal use:

?*Peter has (apologized), and John may, *apologize*
?*Bob is (reading), but Peter won't, *read*
?**Sally* has (seen them), and (Sally) may again, *see them*

Occasionally one or more of the auxiliaries is also ellipted, provided
again that the ellipted auxiliaries are identical with the realized ones:

The document could have (been signed), and (the document)
 should have, *been signed*.
They could (have saved more), and (they) should, *have saved more*.
John could (have been punished), and (John) should, *have been
 punished*.

Commas before the realized items in clauses after the first clause are
acceptable only when the parenthesized items are omitted (*cf* App III.12,
III.22).

9.83
Ellipsis involving both coordination and subordination
A set of coordinated clauses, one or more of which is elliptical, can be

subordinated to another clause. This need not affect the potentiality for ellipsis:

> *Peter must have* broken in and (Peter must have) stolen the papers.
> *I'm sure that Peter must have* broken in and (Peter must have) stolen the papers.

However, if only one of the clauses is subordinated, there cannot be ellipsis of the subject and/or of the auxiliaries:

> *Peter must have* broken in and stolen the papers.
> **Peter must have* broken in and *I'm sure that* stolen the papers.
>   (ellipsis of subject and auxiliaries)
> *Peter* ate the fruit and drank the beer.
> **Peter* ate the fruit and I think that drank the beer. (ellipsis of subject)
> John *must* clean the shed and Peter read his book.
> **John *must* clean the shed and it seems that Peter read his book.
>   (ellipsis of operator)

Instead, we normally use the appropriate pronoun as subject and repeat the auxiliaries:

> Peter must have broken in and I'm sure that *he must have* stolen the papers.
> Peter ate the fruit and I think that *he* drank the beer.
> John must clean the shed and it seems that Peter *must* read his book.

There can be ellipsis of the whole of the predication or of part of it in such cases, provided that the operator is retained, or, if there is no operator, at least the verb is retained:

> I told him to *go*, but he wouldn't (go).
> I thought she could *swim* and it seems that she can (swim).
> George will *take the course* and I believe that Bob might (take the course).
> George will (take the course), and I believe that Bob might, *take the course*.
> Bob seemed (angry), and I know that George was, *angry*.

However, if the operator is not retained, there cannot be ellipsis of the predication. Thus, though from

> Paul likes Mary and Peter *likes* Joan

we may ellipt the verb in the second clause:

> Paul likes Mary and Peter Joan

we cannot do so if we embed the second clause:

*Paul likes Mary and I know that Peter Joan.

Note
If instead of subordinating the clause, we insert a comment clause (11.65 *f*) the ellipsis is often not affected, because the comment clause is only loosely attached to the clause:

> *Peter* ate the fruit and *I think* drank the beer.
> *Bob will be* supervising the examination and, *it seems*, grading the papers.

9.84
Ellipsis of direct object or subject complement
If the direct object is elliptad, the realized items must be in the last clause:

> Mary washed (the shirts), Jane ironed (the shirts), and Alice
>   folded, the *shirts*.
> John likes (Mary), and Peter hates, *Mary*.

If the subject complement is ellipted, the potentialities for ellipsis depend on the verb in the last clause. When the verb in the last clause is other than BE, the rule is the same as for the direct object, *ie* the realized items must be in the last clause:

> George was (angry), and Bob certainly seemed, *angry*.
> *George was *angry*, and Bob certainly seemed (angry).

When the verb in the last clause is BE, the realized items can be either in the first clause or in the last clause:

> Bob seemed *angry*, and George certainly was (angry).
> John has recently become (a very hardworking student), and his
>   brother always was, *a very hardworking student*.

With ellipsis of the subject in clauses subsequent to the first, we have complex ellipsis (9.65):

> *Mary* washed (the shirts), (Mary) ironed (the shirts), and (Mary)
>   folded, *the shirts*.
> *John* felt (hungry), and (John) was, *hungry*.

The commas in the last clauses in the examples are acceptable only when the parenthesized items are omitted (*cf* App III.12, III.22).

Ellipsis of adverbial
9.85
It is often more satisfactory to say that the scope of the adverbial is extended to subsequent clauses than to say that it is ellipted. This is

particularly so when the adverbial is positioned initially, though it applies to restrictives (9.88) regardless of their position. For example, *unfortunately* in

> *Unfortunately*, John is not at home and Sally is too busy to see you.

appears to apply to a combination of the circumstances described in the two clauses rather than separately to each circumstance.

Conjuncts (8.89 *ff*), disjuncts (8.78 *ff*), and viewpoint (8.11 *f*), time (8.56 *ff*), and place adjuncts (8.45 *ff*) commonly have extended scope. Examples are:

CONJUNCT

> If John is a member, *then* we should call on him and (we
>   should) ask him to take us along.   [73]
> David hasn't any money of his own. *However*, he can ask his
>   parents for some, and he might be able to borrow a small
>   amount from his sister.   [74]

DISJUNCT

> *Perhaps* Joan is shopping and the children are at school.   [75]
> *To my surprise*, they didn't appoint him, and they didn't even
>   interview him.   [76]

VIEWPOINT ADJUNCT

> *Theoretically*, I have no objections to his proposal and nor
>   have any of my colleagues.   [77]
> *Politically*, he is very naive and he is at a considerable dis-
>   advantage in fighting the other more experienced
>   candidates.   [78]

TIME ADJUNCT

> *This afternoon* Mary intends to take the children to the beach,
>   but I am going to wash my car.   [79]
> *In the next few years* we shall have to deal effectively with the
>   pollution of the environment or life will come to a stop on
>   this planet.   [80]

PLACE ADJUNCT

> *In Britain* there is a great deal of apathy about politics, and
>   people fail to see much difference between the only two
>   parties that could form a government.   [81]
> *In our school* students and teachers get on well together, but
>   this harmony is comparatively recent.   [82]

9.86

Initial position of these adverbials is usually interpreted as implying an extension of scope to subsequent coordinated (or for that matter, subordinated) clauses, unless there is an indication to the contrary. For example, the addition of another disjunct to the second clause of [76] limits the scope of the first disjunct to the first clause:

> *To my surprise*, they didn't appoint him, and *to my horror*, they
> didn't even interview him.   [76a]

In some cases there is ambiguity. For example, in [80] the end of life on this planet is forecast either for some time in the next few years (with extension of the scope of the adjunct) or for some time in the more distant future.

If these adverbials are in the middle of the clause or at the end of any but the last clause, they are generally interpreted as applying to their particular clause only:

> Joan is *perhaps* shopping and the children are at school   [75a]
> Joan is shopping, *perhaps*, and the children are at school   [75b]
> Joan is shopping, and the children are *perhaps* at school   [75c]

However, if there is an ellipsis that links the two clauses more closely, the scope of the adverbial is extended to the second clause:

> Mary is *perhaps* inside the supermarket and John outside.

Adverbials in end-position that apply to both clauses seem to involve strict ellipsis, because the ellipted items can be added without any awkwardness. The realized adverbial may be in the first clause:

> Tom was *at Oxford*, but his brother wasn't (at Oxford).
> I shall certainly object *if they show the slides again* and you should
>   object (if they show the slides again) too.
> Brian wrote *to his parents* yesterday and (Brian) will be writing
>   again (to his parents) today.

Place and time adverbials at the end of the last clause can be interpreted as applying to both clauses if the clauses are short:

> Bob works (in London), and Peter lives, *in London.*
> They were married (in 1970) and (they were) divorced *in 1970.*
> John has driven (to Chicago), and Bill will drive, *to Chicago.*

Where there are different subjects for the clauses, there is normally an intonation break or comma punctuation before the adverbial in the final clause. The commas in the second clauses of the above examples are acceptable only when the parenthesized items are omitted (*cf* App III.12, III.22).

Note
In most of the sentences cited, repetition of the adverbial is either awkward or

changes the meaning. Sentence [75] is perhaps the only one where repetition of the adverbial produces a normal sentence that is roughly synonymous with the original:

Perhaps Joan is shopping and *perhaps* the children are at school.

9.87

Process adjuncts (8.34 *ff*) are occasionally ellipted, with the realized items present in the last clause:

Mary spoke (rudely), and John answered, *rudely*.
Bill drinks (sparingly), and Peter smokes, *sparingly*.

With ellipsis of the subject, we have complex ellipsis:

Bill drinks (sparingly), and (Bill) smokes, *sparingly*.

Once again, the commas in the second clauses are acceptable only when the parenthesized items are omitted (*cf* App III.12, III.22).

Notice that if there is an intonation break or comma between the clauses but not before the adverb, the adverb is understood to apply only to the second clause:

Mary spoke, and John answered *rudely*.

9.88

The scope of restrictives (8.13 *ff*), including the clausal negative particle *not*, is often dependent on the ellipsis of subject and auxiliary. If these adjuncts are positioned somewhere before the lexical verb in the first clause they are interpreted as extending their scope to subsequent clauses in which the auxiliary is ellipted. This normally applies only if

(a) the coordinator is *and* or *or;*
(b) an identical subject or an identical lexical verb is also ellipted.

Examples are:

Peter will *rarely* smoke or drink
David does *not* read books and see plays
John can*not* play the guitar or Bob the piano
Mary can *only* stay till Monday and Alice till Tuesday

If there is no auxiliary in the first clause, then the scope of the restrictive is always carried over if the coordinator is *or:*

Peter *never* smoked cigarettes or drank alcohol
John *only* eats or sleeps

With *and*, the scope can be interpreted as extended to subsequent clauses or not, though the content of particular instances may influence the interpretation one way or the other. For example, the scope of *only* will be understood as extended to the next clause in

> John *only* eats and sleeps

though not in

> John *only* smoked cigarettes and asked his parents to send him some more.

Note

[a] The conjoinings with *or* do not contain strict ellipsis, since elliptied items cannot be supplied.

[b] If the coordinator is *but* the scope of the adjunct is rarely extended and then only with the negative particle (*cf* 9.93):

> Bob did*n't* break the window but refuse to apologize for his action.

Even so, *and* would more commonly be used in place of *but*, with little or no semantic difference:

> Bob didn't break the window and refuse to apologize for his action.

[c] The scope of the negative particle is sometimes extended when neither subjects nor lexical verbs are identical, particularly if the coordinator is *or:*

> Mary *can't* sing or Joan dance.

9.89

Ellipsis of head of noun phrase

The head of a noun phrase can be ellipted, normally with the realized head in the first clause. The ellipted noun phrase can have various functions in the clause:

We wanted fried *fish*, but they gave us boiled (fish)	[83]
She wore the red *dress*, but the blue (dress) suits her better	[84]
He prefers Dutch *cheese* and I prefer Danish (cheese)	[85]

The ellipted noun phrase is object in [83] and [85], and subject in [84]. Notice that the noun phrases need not have the same function in both clauses: in [84] *the red dress* is object and *the blue* (*dress*) is subject.

This type of ellipsis is not limited to coordination:

> He prefers Dutch *cheese* to Danish (cheese).

> Although we asked for fried *fish*, they gave us boiled (fish).

Note

The substitute *one* is normally used when the head is a count noun that is not defined (*cf* 10.46):

> She wore a red dress, but a blue *one* suits her better.

9.90

Ellipsis of complement of prepositional phrase

The complement of a prepositional phrase can be ellipted, with the realized object in the second clause:

Bob is bored with (music), but Peter enjoys, *music*.
John crawled under (the fence), but Bill climbed over, *the fence*.

With ellipsis of the subject (and operator or auxiliary), we have complex ellipsis:

He walked up (the hill), and (he) ran down, *the hill*.
She will drive to (London), but (she will) fly back from, *London*.
He was a friend to (the party leader), and (he was) a strong
supporter of, *the party leader*.

At any point where a structure is incomplete and followed by a co-ordinator, the listener or reader searches for elements in the following clause that both grammatically and semantically complete it. Although [86] is awkward, we would have little difficulty in interpreting it as elliptical for [87]:

He went to, and after some time found the book in, the library. [86]
He went to *the library* and after some time *he* found the book in
the library.   [87]

9.91
Intonation and punctuation marking of ellipsis
The point where ellipsis has taken place is often marked in speech by an intonation break, that is to say, it co-occurs with the end of an into-nation unit (App II.12). The intonation break is sometimes accompanied by a pause. In written English comma punctuation is often used at the same point (App III.7 *ff*). Of course, if the ellipsis is at the end of the sentence there would anyway normally be an intonation break and sen-tence punctuation would be used.

When the ellipsis is in the second and subsequent clauses there is no intonation or punctuation marking for the ellipsis of the subject, or of the subject and immediately following elements:

Peter cooks his own meals and (Peter) washes his own clothes.
Mary will look after the children and (Mary will) take
telephone messages.
John will pay the electricity bill this week and (John will pay) the
gas bill next week.

It appears that a 'gap' is not felt when the ellipsis immediately follows the coordinator. In contrast, intonation marking is usually present in other cases of ellipsis, though punctuation marking is frequently absent (but *cf* App III.12):

Paul is writing to his parents and (Paul) will be (writing) to his
sister.

John likes Mary, and Peter (likes) Susan.
The men were drinking and the women (were) eating.

When the ellipsis is in the first clause, subsequent clauses usually have intonation or punctuation marking both at the point of ellipsis and the point corresponding to the beginning of the ellipsis in the first clause (App III.22):

George will (take the course), and Bob might, take the course.
Gerald likes (Sylvia), but Peter hates, Sylvia.
Tom always has been (my favourite), and always will be, my favourite.
He looked (tired), and (he) indeed was, tired.

However, intonation and punctuation marking may be absent if the ellipsis results in the linking of two lexical verbs:

Mary washed (the clothes) and (Mary) ironed the clothes.
Susan will sing and (Susan will) dance.

Semantic effect of ellipsis in coordinated clauses
9.92
Often the effect of ellipsis is no more than to suggest a closer connection between the content of the clauses, but sometimes the effect is to indicate that there is a combined process rather than two separate processes (*cf* 9.119 *ff*). This combinatory effect is common when the coordinated clauses are direct or indirect questions or subordinate to another clause, or when negation is involved. Thus in

Did Peter tell lies and hurt his friends?   [88]

the effect of the ellipsis is to imply that Peter's telling lies had the result that he hurt his friends. The sentence in [88] is one question, and may be answered by *yes* or *no*. There is no such implication in

Did Peter tell lies, and did he hurt his friends?   [89]

where Peter's telling lies and his hurting his friends are regarded as two separate processes and there are two separate questions. Sometimes, intonation may also be a factor. For example,

Did John play football or go for a wÁlk?

will probably be taken as one question, to be answered by *yes* or *no*. On the other hand,

Did John play FÓOTball or go for a wÀLK?
Did John play FÓOTball or did he go for a wÀLK?

would both be taken as alternative questions requiring as an answer that John played football or that he went for a walk (*cf* 7.68 *f*). Similarly, in

Did John break the window but refuse to pay for it?   [90]

the implications are that his refusal follows chronologically his breaking of the window and also that it is surprising in view of his breaking of the window. With *but*, a non-elliptical form is unacceptable:

*Did John break the window but did he refuse to pay for it?   [90a]

Note
In [90] it is probably more common to use *and* in place of *but*.

9.93

There may also be a combined process when the first conjoin is negated (*cf* 9.88). For example,

John DÌDN't break the window but refuse to pay for it   [91]

is a denial of the statement

John broke the window but refused to pay for it   [92]

As a negation of a combined process, [91] could evoke the retort *Yes, he did*. On the other hand, there are two separate processes in [93] and [94], and the scope of negation (7.49) in the first conjoin does not extend to the second conjoin:

John didn't break the window, but he offered to pay for it   [93]
John didn't break the window, but he didn't offer to pay for it, either   [94]

Neither the somewhat odd sentence in [92a] nor [92b] are semantically equivalent to [91]:

John didn't break the window, but he refused to pay for it   [92a]
John didn't break the window, but he didn't refuse to pay for it, (either)   [92b]

Note
Cf the effect of negation in *Don't drink and drive*, where the intention is not to prohibit either activity as such but only both in combination.

9.94

Negation in the first conjoin can similarly affect clauses coordinated by *or*. Thus,

John doesn't take a bus or go by train   [95]

can be the negative equivalent of

John takes a bus or goes by train   [96] which (*cf* 9.51) can be synonymous with one interpretation of

> John takes a bus and goes by train   [97]

when the combinatory possibility in the alternative is included. That is to say, [95] denies both possibilities, and hence the sentence is synonymous with [95a], [95b], and [95c]:

> John doesn't take a bus and doesn't go by train   [95a]
> John doesn't take a bus and he doesn't go by train   [95b]
> John doesn't take a bus nor does he go by train   [95c]

But [95] is not synonymous with

> John doesn't take a bus or he doesn't go by train   [95d]

This is because [95d] denies the truth of the statement in one of the conjoins, but not, as does [95], the truth of the statements in both the conjoins.

Note
The other interpretation of [97] is sequential (9.42), *ie* that John first takes a bus and then continues the journey by train. Another interpretation of [95] denies the possibility that only one alternative applies ('It is not true that John either takes a bus or goes by train'). It allows that John uses both methods of transport or neither method.

Coordination other than clausal
9.95
We have found it convenient to suggest that there is ellipsis of the rest of the clause when the verb phrases or parts of them – the auxiliaries or the lexical verb – are directly linked (9.67 *f*, 9.82 *ff*, 9.86 *ff*, 9.90 *f*). When other phrases are directly conjoined by *and* and *or*, we shall not attempt to posit ellipsis of the rest of the clause, though there may be ellipsis within the phrases. For example,

> *Peter and John* played football   [98a]

is not regarded as elliptical for

> Peter played football and John played football   [98b]

though, of course, in at least one interpretation, [98a] is synonymous with [98b], and [98b] then conveys the semantic implication of [98a], *cf* 9.3, 9.23. Instead we regard *Peter and John* as a coordinated plural phrase functioning as subject of the sentence, analogous to *the boys* or the pro-form *they*. This type of coordination is phrasal coordination.

Note
Most subordinators cannot be used to link phrases, but two – *if* and *though* – are used quite freely, as is the conjunct *yet*, in the linking of adjectives:

a pleasant *if* talkative child
a shabby *though* comfortable armchair
a simple *yet* devout prayer

and in the linking of adverbs:

He looked at me kindly *if* (somewhat) sceptically
He spoke firmly *though* pleasantly
He drove quickly *yet* safely

The formal and somewhat archaic *albeit* ('even though') is exceptional in that it is normally used to link phrases rather than clauses:

an intelligent *albeit* rash leader
He spoke firmly *albeit* pleasantly.

9.96

One reason for regarding *Peter and John* in 9.95 as analogous to *the boys* or *they* is that all of these require plural concord of the verb phrase:

Peter and John ⎤
The boys   ⎬ *are* my friends
They   ⎦

As a consequence, in some cases of phrasal coordination, we cannot even supply any ellipted elements. (See also 9.119 *ff.*) For example, if in place of the past in [98a] we use the present:

Peter and John play football   [98c]

the insertion of the verb and direct object after *Peter* results in wrong number concord:

*Peter play football and John play football   [98d]

In the relevant interpretation [98c] is equivalent to

Peter plays football and John plays football   [98e]

That is to say, the conversion of [98e] to [98c] involves a change in number concord.
    Furthermore, in

Bob and George are admired by their students   [99a]

one interpretation (made explicit if the prepositional phrase is expanded to *by their respective students*) is expressed by

Bob is admired by *his* [Bob's] students and George is admired
by *his* [George's] students   [99b]

and not by

*Bob *are* admired by *their* students and George *are* admired by
their students   [99c]

In appositional coordination (7.26) too, no ellipsis can be posited. For example, in the sentence

This temple of ugliness and memorial to Victorian bad taste was
erected at the Queen's express wish.

the two noun phrases in the subject refer to the same monument; they are in apposition, and hence a singular verb is used. If we expand the sentence to

This temple of ugliness was erected at the Queen's express wish
and *this memorial to Victorian bad taste* was erected at the
Queen's express wish.

we indicate that we are referring to two different monuments.

9.97

When the phrases are not directly conjoined, but an additional clause constituent is present, we can consider that there is clause coordination with ellipsis (or substitution – for *not, cf* 9.80, 10.61):

Peter, *and perhaps John*, plays football	[100]
Peter, *but not John*, plays football	[101]
Peter plays football, *and certainly basketball*	[102]
Joan plays many games, *and even tennis*	[103]

The elliptical clauses are appended clauses (*cf* 9.16). Instead of being in parenthetical juxtaposition to the subject, the appended clauses in [100] and [101] can be positioned finally:

Peter plays football, *and perhaps John*	[100a]
Peter plays football, *but not John*	[101a]

This would be the normal position.

If there is no constituent apart from the subject, the elliptical clause is often felt to be an afterthought and the construction tends to be restricted to informal and spoken English:

John writes extremely well – *and Peter*
Sally must clean the room – *or Joan*

But the elliptical clause need not be set off by intonation or punctuation, and would not be if *either* were used as an anticipatory element:

Either Sally must clean the room *or* Joan.

Note
Notice the singular number concord in [100] and [101] as opposed to the plural in [98c]. Some speakers would, however, feel uneasy over using either the singular or the plural and perhaps for that reason prefer the position of [100a] and [101a].

9.98

We cannot add ellipted elements in certain other cases. For example, even if we ignore for the moment the presence of *respective* in

My colleague failed, and I passed, our respective
examinations   [104a]

we cannot expand the sentence to

My colleague failed our examinations and I passed our
examinations   [104b]

Instead, [104a] implies

My colleague failed his examination and I passed my
examination   [104c]

Both (9.58), *respectively*, and *respective* cannot be retained if we expand the clauses. For example, we cannot expand

John *both* composed the music and wrote the words   [105a]

into

*John both composed the music and$\left\{\begin{matrix} \text{John} \\ \text{he} \end{matrix}\right\}$wrote the words   [105b]

Nor can we expand

John and Peter *respectively* composed the music and wrote
the words   [106a]

without reordering the elements and omitting *respectively*, as in

John composed the music and Peter wrote the words   [106b]

On *both*, *respectively*, and *respective*, see 9.123 *ff*.

Phrasal coordination
Noun phrases
9.99

Noun phrases are commonly conjoined (13.61, 13.69 *ff*):

Peter and John were there
Mary and I approved of the plan
They bought *illustrated magazines or books that contained beautiful
art-work*
I spoke to *the old men and the old women*

If the pronouns *you* or *I*, or their case variants, realize one of the conjoins, conventions of politeness require that *you* should always appear first and *I* last:

you or I	you or me
my friend and I	my friend and me
you or they	you or them
you, John, and I	you, John, and me

Note
Noun phrases with different participant roles are normally not conjoined (7.15 Note *a*).

9.100
Within the noun phrase there may be ellipsis of the head (*cf* 9.106). For example, in

> *Old and young men* were invited   [107a]

some of the men are said to be old and some are said to be young, [107a] being elliptical for

> *Old men and young men* were invited   [107b]

Hence in *old and young men* we have conjoined noun phrases with ellipsis of the head of the first noun phrase, and *old and young* are not conjoined adjectives. In contrast, there is no ellipsis, for the normal interpretation, in

> *Honest and clever students* always succeed   [108]

where the same students are both honest and clever. *Honest and clever* are therefore conjoined adjectives. Similarly, there is no ellipsis of the noun head with appositional coordination (7.26, 9.96), as in

> I like teaching *a studious or hard-working undergraduate*

On the other hand, *undergraduate* is ellipted after the first adjective in the following sentence, where two types of undergraduates are differentiated:

> I don't care whether he is *a studious or lazy undergraduate*

The addition of *both* is possible in [107a], but not in [108] in the proposed interpretation:

> Both old (men) and young men were invited
> *Both honest and clever students always succeed

Notice that when the adjectives are predicative, the converse applies, *ie* *both* can be added only when the adjectives jointly refer to the same noun phrases:

*Men who are both young and old were invited
Students who are both honest and clever always succeed

If the adjective phrase is postpositive (5.18 *f*), *both* is possible with either type, but with ellipsis there is marked pitch movement (App II.17):

Men both ↑ young and ↓ old were invited
Students both honest and clever always succeed

If merely two adjectives are conjoined, the coordinator *and* can be omitted with non-elliptical premodified adjectives only. Contrast

*Old, young men were invited
Honest, clever students always succeed

With a series of adjectives, the final *and* is occasionally omitted even in cases of ellipsis:

Old, young, wise, foolish, tall, (and) short men were invited
without distinction.

9.101

Ellipsis of the head of the noun phrase can occur with modifiers other than adjectives. For example, in

He has *workers from Ireland and from France* in his factory

workers is ellipted before *from France*. The ellipsis can also occur with numerals:

I know *three (poems) or four poems* by heart

Notice that the ellipted head need not have the same number as the realized head, whether the ellipsis is in the first conjoin or in the second conjoin (9.106). We can have

one (story) or two stories
one (reason) or more reasons
one dancer or two (dancers)
an old car or two (old cars)

A(n) can only be used instead of *one* if the ellipsis is in the second conjoin (*cf* 9.107). See also 13.70 *f*.
The ellipsis sometimes occurs in both conjoins:

The difference between *the tax on earned* (income) *and* (the tax)
on unearned income is enormous   [109]

In the first conjoin of [109] the head of the noun phrase in the post-modifying prepositional phrase is ellipted while in the second conjoin the head of the whole noun phrase is ellipted. We can also find the pre-position ellipted in the second conjoin:

the tax on earned (income) and (the tax on) unearned income

If the expanded sentence is felt to be unsatisfactory, there may be objections to the ellipsis. For example, ellipsis of the head as found in

We are now encountering *an equally serious or more serious*
situation than before   [110]

would be avoided by many because an additional ellipsis of a post-modifying prepositional phrase has to be understood and the resultant expansion is awkward:

?We are now encountering *an equally serious (situation to the one*
before) or (a) more serious situation than before   [110a]

Contrast with the previous examples

The bus for the Houses of Parliament and (for) Westminster Abbey
will soon be here   .   [111]

In this case, the closeness of these two places suggests that the same bus goes to both of them and if that is the intention, there is no ellipsis of *the bus* in the second conjoin. It is one bus that is being characterized.

9.102
A plural in the noun phrase sometimes replaces a construction with an elliptical singular. For example, instead of

The difference between *the tax on earned* (income) *and* (the tax)
on unearned income is enormous   [109]

we might have

The difference between *the taxes on earned* (income) *and on unearned*
income is enormous   [109a]

Assuming that there is only one tax for each type of income, there is no ellipsis of *taxes* in the second conjoin. Compare the ambiguity of

the meetings on Monday and on Tuesday   [112]

If there was only one meeting on each day there is no ellipsis and [112] is equivalent to

the meeting on Monday and the meeting on Tuesday   [112a]

On the other hand, if there was more than one meeting on each day, there is potential ellipsis and [112] is equivalent to

the meetings on Monday and the meetings on Tuesday   [112b]

But [112] could represent two further possibilities:

the meetings on Monday and the meeting on Tuesday
the meeting on Monday and the meetings on Tuesday

To take one further example:

the bills for gas and (for) electricity

can be interpreted in any of four ways, only one of which involves ellipsis:

the bills for gas and ((the bills) for) electricity
the bill for gas and the bill for electricity
the bill for gas and the bills for electricity
the bills for gas and the bill for electricity

There is in fact one further interpretation: the bills with combined accounts for gas and electricity. The same company may supply both gas and electricity and put both accounts on the same bill. Here, too, no ellipsis is involved.

9.103

Demonstratives linked with each other or with other determiners in the noun phrase appear to involve ellipsis of the head of the noun phrase:

this (book) and that book
these (chairs) and those chairs
these (students) and other students
that (reason) and some other reason

But in fact, the first demonstrative is a pro-form for a noun phrase, as will become clearer in 9.104 and 9.105. The singular forms of the demonstratives are normally not linked with their corresponding plurals.

9.104

Possessive pronouns are not normally linked:

*her or his friends
*our and my work

However, such linking is acceptable if *his* is the first member:

his or her friends
his and my work

This exception reflects the fact that of the possessive pronouns *his* alone is used attributively, predicatively, and with 'ellipsis' of a noun phrase head:

ATTRIBUTIVE: *his* friends
PREDICATIVE: Those friends are *his*
with 'ELLIPSIS': They both have friends, but *his* (friends) are the
                         more loyal.
                I know her friends, but I don't know *his* (friends).

On the other hand, with other possessive pronouns, a different form is used for attributive and for other uses, for example, *her* and *hers:*

ATTRIBUTIVE: *her* friends
PREDICATIVE: Those friends are *hers*
PRO-FORM: They both have friends, but *hers* are the more loyal
               I know his friends, but I don't know *hers*

In fact, the distribution of *her/hers* shows that *his* is really a pro-form for a noun phrase when it is not attributive, although neutralization of forms allows us to posit ellipsis of the noun head in certain cases. Notice that a head could not be supplied for *hers* in the same environment:

*They both have friends, but *hers friends* are the most loyal

In *his and her friends, his* can be interpreted as a pro-form without ellipsis. Compare the similar acceptability of

John's and Harry's friends
John's and my friends

The form *John's* is attributive like *her* and a pro-form like *hers:*

John's friends
Those friends are *John's*
They both have friends, but *John's* are the more loyal
I know his friends, but I don't know *John's*

For at least some people the predicative forms of the other possessive pronouns are more acceptable as the first item in premodified linking than the normal premodifying forms, particularly if both items end in -*s:*

?hers or his friends
?yours and Mary's neighbours

In informal speech we sometimes find the coordination of a set of possessive pronouns that echo the conventions for polite order (9.99):

Your, his, and my reports are all here
Those are *your and my* books.

9.105

The converse of what has been described in 9.103 and 9.104 is available
with the pro-form in the second conjoin:

this book and those	that method and the other
his friends and mine	your proposals and others
your work and his	many guests or few
her idea and John's	much satisfaction or little
his son and hers	

Only determiner-type items that can function as pro-forms for noun
phrases are normally admissible in this construction. Hence, we do
not have

*these students and other

*his son and her ('his son and her son')

Note

Three common frames should be noted:

one N or another: *eg* one way or another
some N or other: *eg* some reason or other
one or (the) other N: *eg* one or (the) other method

Only in the first can *or* be replaced by *and*, though far less frequently: *one way or another*
is a stereotyped expression.

9.106

The head of the noun phrase is very occasionally ellipted in the second
conjoin when an adjective is present:

old men and young (men)

the strong nations and the weak (nations)

See 9.100 for the more usual ellipsis in the first conjoin.

9.107

Articles cannot be linked with ellipsis of a noun-phrase head:

*the (book) and a book

*a (girl) and the girl

Nor can two noun phrases be conjoined if the only difference between
them is in the article:

*I read the book and a book

*I saw a girl and the girl.

Note

These restrictions do not apply to metalinguistic formulations (*cf* also 9.174 Note),
as in definitions. For example, *when* can be defined as

at the or a time at which
at the time or a time at which

9.108

An article realized in the first conjoin of a noun phrase is often ellipted in the second conjoin:

> a boy or (a) girl   the butter and (the) milk
>
> the boy or (the) girl   the boys and (the) girls
>
> the house and (the) gardens the shoes and (the) hat

The ellipsis of the article can be combined with ellipsis of a modifier (*cf* 9.110):

> a young boy or (a young) girl
>
> the cows (on our farm) and (the) bulls on our farm

When premodifiers are present, it can also co-occur with ellipsis of the head of the noun phrase in the first conjoin:

> the old (men) and (the) young men
>
> the lazy (students) or (the) industrious students

9.109

Other determiners can also be ellipted in the second conjoin:

> that boy or (that) girl
>
> my brother or (my) sister
>
> some butter and (some) milk
>
> other boys and (other) girls

They can also co-occur with ellipsis of a modifier:

> that young boy or (that young) girl
>
> some boys (studying at this school) and (some) girls studying at this school

9.110

In the ellipsis of premodifiers, the item is realized in the first conjoin and ellipted in subsequent conjoins:

> juicy plums, (juicy) peaches, and (juicy) oranges
>
> young boys and (young) girls
>
> fresh milk and (fresh) butter

When the parenthesized items are omitted, the examples are ambiguous. They can be interpreted as either involving ellipsis or not. If we wish to prevent the premodifier applying to subsequent conjoins we have to place the premodified noun phrase last:

> peaches, oranges, and juicy plums

If the noun phrase in the first conjoin has a determiner and we wish to ellipt the premodifier in subsequent conjoins, we have to ellipt the determiner with it:

the juicy plums, (the juicy) peaches, and (the juicy) oranges
a young boy or (a young) girl
some fresh milk and (some fresh) butter

These examples too are ambiguous. To prevent the premodifier (and sometimes the determiner) applying to subsequent conjoins we have to place the premodified noun phrase last:

peaches, oranges, and the juicy plums
a girl or a young boy

If we retain the determiner in subsequent conjoins, we prevent the ellipsis of the premodifier. Hence,

the juicy plums, the peaches, and the oranges

does not convey the information that the peaches or the oranges are juicy.

A postmodifier can likewise be ellipted, but it must be realized in the last conjoin and ellipted in previous conjoins:

cows (on our farm), bulls (on our farm) and pigs on our farm
boys (studying at this school) and girls studying at this school
men (who work hard) and women who work hard

To prevent the postmodifier applying to previous conjoins we place the postmodified conjoin first:

women who work hard and men

If a determiner is present in the first conjoin, it can either be ellipted or retained in subsequent conjoins:

the boys (studying at this school) and (the) girls studying at this school

Even if the determiners differ, ellipsis can take place:

many boys (studying at this school) and some girls studying at this school

We can prevent the postmodifier applying to the first conjoin by reversing the order of the conjoins:

some girls studying at this school and many boys

It is also possible to combine ellipsis of premodifier and postmodifier. For example, in place of

honest men who work hard and honest women who work hard

we can have either

> honest men and honest women who work hard

with ellipsis of the postmodifier alone, or

> honest men and women who work hard

with ellipsis of both premodifier and postmodifier. Both forms are ambiguous, since they can be interpreted as either full or elliptical forms. We can prevent the elliptical interpretation by reversing the order of the conjoins:

> honest women who work hard and honest men
> women who work hard and honest men

9.111
As we have already seen, the potentiality for ellipsis of modifiers in conjoined noun phrases is a fruitful source of ambiguity, since it is often possible to interpret the conjoined noun phrases as either with or without ellipsis.

Two examples of such ambiguity are given below, with the interpretations demonstrating methods for removing the ambiguity:

> *the old men and women*
>
> (1) the old men and the old women
> (2) the old men and the women
> (3) (some) women and the old men
>
> *simple books and magazines for children*
>
> (1) simple books for children and simple magazines for children
> (2) magazines for children and simple books
> (3) simple books for children and magazines for children
> (4) simple magazines for children and simple books

9.112
When three noun phrases are coordinated, the three may be on the same level of coordination or one may be coordinated to a coordination of the other two (*cf.* 9.36). Thus, in

> We thanked *John and Peter and Robert*

the intention may be (a) that we thanked John and also Peter and Robert, or (b) that we thanked John and Peter and also Robert, or (c) that we thanked all three. Each of the three types of relationship can be presented in a tree diagram:

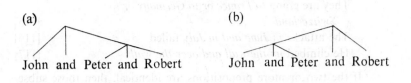

John and Peter and Robert   John and Peter and Robert

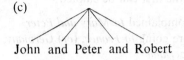

John and Peter and Robert

The same three types of relationships can be found if the coordinator is
or:

John *or* Peter *or* Robert

However, if only the second instance of the coordinator is present:

John, Peter, *and* Robert
John, Peter, *or* Robert

the relationship can only be that illustrated in diagram (c), all three noun
phrases being on the same level. And if there are two different
coordinators:

John *and* Peter *or* Robert

there are only two types of relationship – (a) and (b) – because a change
of conjunction prevents all three conjoins being on the same level:

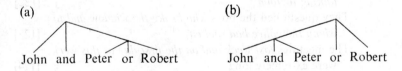

Analogous hierarchical relationships apply if there are more than three
nouns or noun phrases.

Units other than noun phrases
9.113
Other types of coordination will be briefly mentioned.

(1) PREPOSITIONAL PHRASES
    He spoke *for the first motion and against the second
    motion*   [113]
    John complained *to Mary and to Peter*   [114]

They are going *to France or to Germany or to Switzerland*   [115]

The attacks *in June and in July* failed   [116]

He climbed *up the wall and over the wall*   [117]

If the two or more prepositions are identical, then those subsequent to the first can be ellipted:

John complained *to Mary and Peter*   [114a]

They are going *to France, (or) Germany, or Switzerland*   [115a]

The attacks *in June and July* failed   [116a]

There are further possibilities of ellipsis:

He spoke *for the first and against the second motion*   [113a]

He spoke *for the first motion and against the second*   [113b]

He climbed *up and over the wall*   [117a]

He climbed *up the wall and over*   [117b]

9.114

(2) OTHER ADVERBIALS AND DEPENDENT CLAUSES

They came *quickly and with great force*   [118]

You can wash it *manually or by using a machine*   [119]

They can call *this week or whenever they wish*   [120]

They played *when the sun came out and when their parents were asleep*   [121]

I approached the girl *who was in the corner and who was talking to John*   [122]

They questioned the boys *who broke the window and to whom the police had spoken*   [123]

The meetings *last week and on the first day of this week* were extremely long   [124]

I prefer the sentences *below and on the next page*   [125]

But in some cases of postmodification there may be ellipsis of the noun-phrase head and therefore we in fact have coordination of noun phrases rather than of post modifiers. For example, both [124] and [125] have an elliptical noun-phrase head in one interpretation of the sentences, *the meetings* and *the sentences* respectively.

9.115

If two or more conjunctions are identical, those subsequent to the first can be ellipted:

I noticed *how Mary talked to them and* (*how*) *they answered her.* [126]

They admired a man *who could make up his mind quickly and* (*who*) *would keep his word.* [127]

If I can find the letter and (*if*) *you are interested in it,* I'll let you have it. [128]

On the other hand, if two clauses are identical except for their conjunctions, one of the clauses can be ellipted, normally the first, so that two conjunctions are linked:

I am prepared to meet them *when* (*they like*) *and where they like.* [129]

They will be arriving either *before* (*the show begins*) *or after the show begins.* [130]

Sometimes the second clause is ellipted:

They will be arriving *before the show begins or after* (*the show begins*). [130a]

With relative clauses introduced by a preposition and *whom*, ellipsis of the rest of the first clause is not uncommon:

I want to know *by whom* (*it was ordered*) *and for whom it was ordered.* [131]

Note

[a] In philosophical and mathematical discourse, *if and only if* is a common combination with ellipsis of the first clause.

[b] *If and when* is a stereotyped expression conveying a strong possibility that the condition in the clause will be realized:

If and when he buys the car, I'll try to persuade him to buy the insurance from me.

With *if and when* ellipsis may be disregarded, since *if and when* has become a unit. Other institutionalized conjoinings of conjunctions are:

as and when
unless and until

9.116

(3) ADJECTIVES

Adjectives can be conjoined when they are predicative:

She is *young and beautiful*

or attributive:

His *clear and forceful* delivery impressed the audience

With conjoined adjectives in attributive position, the coordinator *and* is often omitted:

His *clear, forceful* delivery impressed the audience

No ellipsis is involved in the conjoining of predicative adjectives as such, but there can be ellipsis of a premodifier or of complementation (5.36):

very cheap and (very) gaudy
I am loath (to do it) and afraid to do it

Notice in which conjoin the ellipsis occurs, *cf* 9.110.

Note
[a] For linked adjectives with an elliptical noun-phrase head, see 9.100.
[b] Attributive nouns can also occasionally be conjoined (5.11 Note *a*, 9.121):

a cheese and cucumber sandwich

9.117

(4) DERIVATIONAL PREFIXES AND ELEMENTS OF A COMPOUND
Some derivational prefixes that tend to be contrasted can be conjoined with ellipsis of the base of the word, *eg: ante-* (or *pre-*) *and post-natal care* or *pro- and anti-establishment, sub- and super-human.* The affixes concerned are the more loosely attached ones. Tightly attached affixes do not permit coordination, *eg: *im- and ex-ports.*
    Similarly, constituents of a compound can be linked with ellipsis of the last constituent, *eg: factory- and office-workers, sons- and daughters-in-law, hand-made and -packed, out- and in-patients, psycho- and socio-linguistics.* Once again, these constituents are loosely attached, and we do not have linking in the more cohesive compounds *toothache* and *headache: *tooth- and head-aches.*

9.118
Order in phrasal coordination
There is a relatively fixed order for subclasses of adjectives in asyndetic coordination (9.24), but when a coordinator is present the order is relatively free (*cf* 13.66). Apart from the special case of adjectives, the order of conjoined words can be influenced by a tendency for the shorter word to come first, *eg: big and ugly, cup and saucer.* There are also stereotyped coordinations where the conjoins are in virtually irreversible order, *eg: odds and ends; bread and butter; law and order; by hook or by crook; through thick and thin; knife, fork, and spoon.*

Combinatory and segregatory coordination
9.119

When conjoined phrases function in the clause, they may involve combinatory or segregatory coordination (*cf* 7.26 *ff*, 9.92 *ff*). The distinction applies to various types of conjoined phrases, but is perhaps clearest with noun phrases. When the coordination is combinatory, we can paraphrase the original sentence with two or more coordinated clauses. For example,

> *John and Mary* have a cold

is equivalent to

> John has a cold and Mary has a cold

But no analogous paraphrase is available for

> *John and Mary* make a pleasant couple

We cannot say

> *John makes a pleasant couple and Mary makes a pleasant couple

since the subject complement *a pleasant couple* requires the subject to be two conjoined singular noun phrases or a plural noun phrase, and it must be possible to interpret the plural noun phrase as having reference to two people (say, *they*, or *those two*, and not *the group* or *the trio*).

Here are some more examples where conjoined noun phrases represent combinatory coordination:

> He gave all his books to *Tom and Alice*
> *Peter and Bob* separated
> *Bill and Paul* look alike
> *John and Peter* are different from each other
> *Mary and Susan* are sisters
> *Bob, Peter, and George* constitute the opposition.

9.120

Other conjoined phrases too may involve combinatory coordination. Among adjectives, colour adjectives in particular allow a 'particoloured' interpretation:

> Our flag is *red, white, and blue* ('partly red, partly white, and partly blue')

In

> He painted the cars *black and white*

there is a combined process if each car is painted black and white, and separate processes if some cars are painted black and others white.

Similarly, there is a combined process with the conjoined adverbials in

We spent our vacation this year *in Paris and in Amsterdam.*
They renewed his contract *because he had worked well in the past year and in return for a promise that he would make a greater effort in the coming year.*

9.121

Sometimes there may be ambiguity as to whether we have a combined process or separate process, as with the conjoined adjectives in

He painted the cars *black and white*

In the sentence

John and Mary are married

there is a combined process if they are married to each other and there are separate processes if each is married to another person. Similarly,

John and Mary won the prize

is ambiguous: either they won the prize between them or they each won the prize on separate occasions. A very general difference in interpretation can be found in a sentence cited earlier (9.95),

Peter and John played football

where the intention could be that each played football separately or that they played together. Compare also

Bob and Ann went to Paris

where again there could either be a combined process or two separate processes.

Notice the use of singular number concord (*cf* 7.26 Note *b*) with some conjoins functioning as subject when they represent combinatory coordination:

Fish and chips is my favourite food ($\neq$ Fish is my favourite food and chips are my favourite food)
Bread and butter is better for you than cake ($\neq$ Bread is better for you than cake and butter is better for you than cake)
A ball and chain was suspended from the edge ($\neq$ A ball was suspended from the edge and a chain was suspended from the edge)

Contrast also the two interpretations of *cheese and cucumber sandwiches:*

> 'cheese sandwiches and cucumber sandwiches' – segregatory coordination with ellipsis of *sandwiches*
> 'sandwiches each containing both cheese and cucumber' – combinatory coordination

9.122

The distinction between combined and separate processes applies not only to conjoined noun phrases, but also to plural or collective noun phrases. Hence, we find combined process in

> *They* look alike
> *That group* constitutes the opposition

and separate processes in

> *They* are feverish
> *The children* have a cold

while there is ambiguity in

> *They* are married
> He painted the cars with *two colours.*

9.123

Certain markers explicitly indicate that the coordination is segregatory:

both	respective
each	respectively
neither . . . nor	apiece

Respective and *respectively* are not normally used in informal or familiar style.

While

John and Mary have won a prize	[132]

is ambiguous, we are left in no doubt that two prizes were won in

John and Mary each have won a prize	[132a]
John and Mary have *each* won a prize	[132b]
John and Mary have won a prize *each*	[132c]
Both John and Mary have won a prize	[132d]
John and Mary both have won a prize	[132e]
John and Mary have *both* won a prize	[132f]

Similarly, if the conjoined noun phrases are replaced by a plural noun phrase:

They each have won a prize	[132a1]
They have *each* won a prize	[132b1]
They have won a prize *each*	[132c1]
They both have won a prize	[132e1]
They have *both* won a prize	[132f1]

The equivalent for [132d] with the plural noun phrase is

Both of them have won a prize

A similar construction is also available as an alternative equivalent for [132a]:

Each of them has won a prize

The correlatives *neither ... nor* are the negative counterparts of *both ... and* (9.55 *f*). While

John and Mary did*n't* win a prize

is ambiguous, the sentence

Neither John nor Mary won a prize

makes it clear that two prizes are involved.

Apiece is also used as an indicator of segregatory coordination but is normally placed finally after a direct object:

John and Mary have won a prize *apiece*

It is restricted to clauses with an object and indicates that there are two or more referents of the object which are separately involved in what is described. Contrast:

John and Mary are *both* in New York
*John and Mary are in New York *apiece*.

Note
Both, but not *each*, is also used as a correlative with *and* in linked predications (9.58).

9.124

Respective is used as a premodifier in a plural noun phrase to indicate separate processes involving the referents of a coordinate noun phrase or another plural noun phrase in the sentence. For example,

John and Bob visited their uncles

could mean:

(a) John visited his uncle(s) and Bob visited his uncle(s)
(b) John and Bob together visited the uncles they have in common
(c) John and Bob together visited John's uncle(s) and also Bob's uncle(s).

On the other hand,

John and Bob visited *their respective uncles*

can only mean that John visited his uncle or uncles and that Bob visited his uncle or uncles. The use of *respective* does not help us distinguish the number of uncles since we cannot use *respective* with a singular noun-phrase head:

*John and Bob visited *their respective uncle*

If we wish to make the distinction we have to resort to clause coordination with or without ellipsis of the verb (9.72):

John visited his uncle, and Bob (visited) his uncle
John visited his uncles, and Bob (visited) his uncles
John visited his uncles, and Bob (visited) his uncle
John visited his uncle, and Bob (visited) his uncles

Separate processes are similarly indicated if the subject is a plural noun phrase:

$\begin{Bmatrix} \textit{The boys} \\ \textit{They} \end{Bmatrix}$ visited *their respective uncles*

The related noun phrases need not be in subject–object relationship:

John and Bob were telephoned by *their respective wives.*
Mary and Susan went to *their respective homes.*
Our respective parents are going to see the principal about the complaints made against *Bob and me.*

The related noun phrases can even be in different clauses or in different sentences:

Bob and I have had some serious trouble at school lately. *Our respective parents* are going to see the principal about the complaints.

9.125
Respectively is used to indicate which constituents go with which in the separate processes, the order of one linked set corresponding to the order of the other linked set. Some illustrations follow.

(1) LINKED SUBJECTS AND LINKED OBJECTS
John, Peter, and Robert play football, basketball, and baseball *respectively*.
= John plays football, Peter plays basketball, and Robert plays baseball.

(2) LINKED SUBJECTS AND LINKED PREDICATES
John and Peter work and study *respectively*.
= John works and Peter studies.

(3) LINKED SUBJECTS PLUS VERBS AND LINKED OBJECTS
John speaks, and Peter writes, French and German *respectively*.
= John speaks French and Peter writes German.

(4) LINKED SUBJECTS AND LINKED ADVERBIALS
John and Peter are going to Paris and to Amsterdam *respectively*.
= John is going to Paris and Peter is going to Amsterdam.

(5) LINKED OBJECTS AND LINKED ADVERBIALS
She found the handbag and the purse in the car and in the garage *respectively*.
= She found the handbag in the car and she found the purse in the garage.

Some of these uses of *respectively* are uncommon, particularly (3).

Some special uses of coordination
9.126

Members of a small class of verbs functioning as first conjoin in a set of coordinated verbs may be very similar to semi-auxiliaries (3.7 *f*). Thus,

I'll *try and come* tomorrow

is equivalent to

I'll *try to come* tomorrow

and

They *sat and talked* about the good old times

to

They *sat talking* about the good old times

Other examples include

Don't just *stand there and grin* ('stand there grinning')

He *went and complained* about us
Run and tell him to come here at once

Like *try* in being followed by a *to*-infinitive in the corresponding form
are *stop, go, come, hurry up*, and *run*. Like *sit* are *stand* and (positional)
lie.

Note

[*a*] The quasi-auxiliary use of a coordinated *try* appears to be limited to the simple
stem. Contrast the acceptability of

Try and see us tomorrow
He will *try and see* us tomorrow
He may *try and see* us tomorrow
They *try and see* us every day

with

*He *tried and saw* us yesterday
*He has *tried and seen* us
*They are *trying and seeing* us tomorrow
*He *tries and sees* us every day

Instead of coordination we must use the *to*-infinitive:

He *tried to see* us yesterday
He has *tried to see* us
They are *trying to see* us tomorrow
He *tries to see* us every day

Be sure and *be certain* can also be used like *try*, but appear to be limited to imperatives, *eg*: (*You*) *be sure and see us tomorrow*, corresponding to (*You*) *be sure to
see us tomorrow*.

[*b*] In familiar speech we also find

He$\begin{Bmatrix} up \\ upped \end{Bmatrix}$*and hit* me.

9.127

In informal speech, members of a small class of commendatory adjectives functioning as first conjoin can be very similar in meaning to intensifiers of the adjective in the second conjoin. The most common is
nice (*cf* 13.68):

This room is *nice and warm* ('warm to just the right degree')

Other examples include

His speech was *nice and short*
It was *lovely and cool* in there ('comfortably cool')

Some speakers use *good* in the same way, even when the adjective
form in the second conjoin is used like an adverb:

That road is *good and long*

> I hit him *good and hard*
> He drove *good and fast*.

Note

Notice also the informal use of the stereotyped conjoined adverbs *well and truly* for intensification, as in

> He is well and truly drunk.

9.128

Identical items may be conjoined an indefinite number of times. With comparative forms of adjectives and adverbs, the effect is to express a continuing increase in degree. The comparative particles *more* and *less*, or else the inflected comparative forms, are often coordinated:

> He felt *more and more angry* } = He felt increasingly angry
> He felt *angrier and angrier* }
>
> He drove *more and more slowly* } = He drove increasingly slowly
> He drove *slower and slower* }

However, the inflected forms cannot be coordinated with the periphrastic forms:

> *He felt *angrier and more angry*
> *He drove *more slowly and slower*

With verbs and the absolute forms of adverbs, the effect of coordination of identical items is to express a continuing or repetitive process:

> He *talked and talked and talked* (= He talked for a very long time)
> They *knocked and knocked* (= They knocked repeatedly)
> He talked *on and on and on* (= He talked on continuously)
> They went *up and up* (= They went continuously up)
> They hit him *again and again* (= They hit him repeatedly)

If a noun is repeated once, the effect may be to suggest that different types can be distinguished:

> There are *teachers and teachers* (= There are good and bad teachers)
> You can find *doctors and doctors* (= You can find good and bad
>   doctors)

However, if the noun is repeated more than once, the effect is to suggest a large number:

> There were *dogs and dogs and dogs* all over the place.

Note

[a] The stereotyped coordination in *out and out* (= thorough-going, utter) has an intensifying effect in premodification of nouns, *eg: He is an out and out liar.*

[*b*] Somewhat similar to the intensifying effect of some coordination is the effect of repetition of attributive adjectives when they are absolute (5.68) and of degree intensifiers:

> an *old, old* man = a *very old* man
> *very, very* good = *extremely* good

For degree intensifiers that can be repeated, see 5.77.

[*c*] In informal speech, expressions like *yes, no, OK, all right* are often repeated for emphasis. (See 14.49 on repetition.)

9.129
Structures relating to coordination

There are several QUASI-COORDINATORS which behave sometimes like coordinators and at other times (without any change of meaning) like subordinators or prepositions. The most prominent of them are clearly related to comparative forms (11.53–64):

> *as well as, as much as, rather than, more than*

In the following examples, they do not introduce noun phrases or clauses, and therefore resemble coordinators:

> He publishes *as well as* prints his own books.
> The speech was addressed to the employers *as much as* to the strikers.
> It was his tone *more than* what he actually said that discouraged me.
> He was pitied *rather than* disliked.

In other sentences, however, they clearly have a prepositional or subordinating role:

> *As well as* printing the books, he publishes them.
> *Rather than* cause trouble, I'm going to forget the whole affair.
> (see 11.43)

Another reason for not treating them as fully coordinative is that in subject position they do not normally bring about plural concord unless the first noun phrase is plural:

> John, *as much as* his brothers, was responsible for the loss.

They therefore resemble in this respect prepositions such as *with* or *in addition to* rather than coordinators such as *and*:

> John, *with* his brothers, was responsible for the loss.

Non-restrictive relative clauses have been considered as semantically equivalent to coordinate clauses. Such an assignment seems reasonable when the relative clause has the superordinate clause as its antecedent (11.52). Thus,

> John didn't go to the show, *which is a pity*.

is semantically equivalent to

John didn't go to the show, *and that is a pity.*

Note

[a] Another quasi-coordinator is the informal *let alone* ('still less'), which is preceded by a negative:

I've not even read the first chapter, *let alone* finished the book.

[b] Non-restrictive relative clauses can also be seen as appositives (9.180).

[c] *Etc* (*et cetera*) is used as an abbreviating device at the end of a series of conjoined phrases to indicate that the series has not been exhaustively given:

He packed his clothes, his books, his papers, *etc.*

And so on and *and so forth* (and their combination *and so on and so forth*) are used in the same way, but are restricted to informal contexts. *Et al* is used as an abbreviating device for a list of names. It is most common in legal documents and in scholarly writing, in the latter case to avoid repeating a list of collaborators:

J. C. Brown *et al.*

Apposition
Nature of apposition
9.130

Apposition resembles coordination in that typically the two or more units in apposition are constituents of the same level (*cf* 9.25), and indeed the central coordinators *and* and *or* are occasionally used as explicit markers of coordination. But for units to be *appositives*, *ie* in apposition, they must normally be identical in reference or else the reference of one must be included in the reference of the other. For example, in

Paul Jones, the distinguished art critic, died in his sleep last
night   [133]

Paul Jones and the *distinguished art critic* refer to the same person. Similarly, in

A neighbour, Fred Brick, is on the telephone   [134]

a neighbour is identified as *Fred Brick*. The relationship underlying apposition is therefore an intensive relationship (7.6):

Paul Jones is *the distinguished art critic*   [133a]
Fred Brick is *a neighbour*   [134a]

Note

There are co-referential relationships that do not seem to have been considered appositional, since the units fulfil distinctly different syntactic functions:

John washed *himself*
Jane likes *her* own hat best
Susan does whatever *she* wants.

9.131
Full and partial apposition

Grammarians vary in the liberality with which they apply the term *apposition*. Some apply it only to such cases as [133] and [134]. In those cases (a) each of the appositives can be separately omitted without affecting the acceptability of the sentence, (b) each fulfils the same syntactic function in the resultant sentences, and (c) there is no difference between the original sentence and either of the resultant sentences in extralinguistic reference. For example, by omitting each appositive in turn from [134] we obtain the two sentences:

A neighbour is on the telephone	[134b]
Fred Brick is on the telephone	[134c]

The apposition in [134] meets the three conditions: (a) the resultant sentences are acceptable; (b) both noun phrases are subject of their sentence; (c) *Fred Brick* and *a neighbour* are co-referential in the original sentence and hence we can assume the reference of the two resultant sentences to be the same. Apposition meeting these three conditions we term FULL APPOSITION.

On the other hand, we term apposition not meeting all three conditions PARTIAL APPOSITION. If condition (a) alone is not met, the difference between full and partial apposition is comparatively trivial. For example, from

An unusual present was given to him for his birthday, *a book on ethics*   [135]

only the second appositive can be omitted:

An unusual present was given to him for his birthday   [135a]

However, the first appositive cannot be omitted:

*Was given to him for his birthday, *a book on ethics*   [135b]

unless we re-position it initially:

A book on ethics was given to him for his birthday   [135c]

The type of partial apposition where the position of the appositive is the sole difference might be considered discontinuous full apposition.

Condition (b) is not met in

Norman Jones, at that time a student, wrote several best-
 sellers   [136]

Norman Jones is subject in

Norman Jones wrote several best-sellers   [136a]

but *at that time a student* cannot be subject in

At that time a student wrote several best-sellers   [136b]

Finally, condition (c) is not met in

*The reason he gave, that he didn't notice the car till too
 late,* is unsatisfactory.   [137]

We can omit each of the appositives in turn and each fulfils the function of subject in the resultant sentences:

The reason he gave is unsatisfactory   [137a]
That he didn't notice the car till too late is unsatisfactory   [137b]

However, [137b] is different from both [137] and [137a] since it does
not assert that a particular reason is unsatisfactory but that a particular
fact is unsatisfactory:

(*The fact*) *That he didn't notice the car till too late* is
 unsatisfactory.

9.132
Strict and weak apposition
The appositives may belong to the same general syntactic class, as in

Football, his only interest in life, has brought him many friends.

In such a case we term the construction STRICT APPOSITION. Other
examples of strict apposition have been given above in [133], [134], and
[135]. On the other hand, appositives from different syntactic classes
are said to be in WEAK APPOSITION. For example, the participle
clause and the noun phrase in

Playing football, his only interest in life, has brought him many
 friends.

Non-restrictive and restrictive apposition
9.133
Apposition may be NON-RESTRICTIVE or RESTRICTIVE (*cf* 13.16 *f*).
The appositives in non-restrictive apposition are in different information

units, and this fact is indicated in speech by their inclusion in separate tone units and in writing by commas or more weighty punctuation. For example, the apposition is non-restrictive in all the examples in 9.130–132 and in

Mr Campbell, the lawyer, was here last night

while it is restrictive in

Mr Campbell the lawyer was here last night (*ie* Mr Campbell the lawyer as opposed to any other Mr Campbell we know)

In non-restrictive apposition the two appositives have different information value, with one of the appositives having a subordinate role in the distribution of information. Its subordinate role is reflected in the fact that it is marked as parenthetic by intonation or punctuation. In

While *the President of the United States, Richard Nixon,*
    addressed the nation last night, there were violent
    demonstrations in the streets of Washington.   [138a]

the President of the United States is superordinate and *Richard Nixon* subordinate. On the other hand, in

While *Richard Nixon, the President of the United States,*
    addressed the nation last night, there were violent
    demonstrations in Washington.   [138b]

it is *Richard Nixon* that is superordinate, with *the President of the United States* constituting a separate and subordinate information unit.

Note
Subordinate appositives are not the same as exclamatory asides (*cf* 14.50 Note). An aside such as *the utter fool* in

John (the utter fool) insisted on staying with them

is an irregular insertion and can come anywhere in the sentence. Compare

John (can you believe it) insisted on staying with them

The difference between the two constructions is highlighted in the ambiguity of

John and Mary (*the idiots*) lost their way

In one interpretation, *the idiots* is intended as a clinical term and is appositive to *John and Mary*. In the other interpretation, it is synonymous with 'the fools' and is an exclamatory aside. The two interpretations can be distinguished intonationally, but there are differences between AmE and BrE in this respect. The normal intonations are given below:

APPOSITION – AmE and BrE
    John and MĂry (the Ìdiots) lost their way

EXCLAMATORY ASIDE – AmE
    John and MĂry (the Ídiots) lost their way

John and MÀry (the ídiots) lost their way

In AmE the aside is marked primarily by a lowering of its pitch relative to that of the rest of the sentence, though it would be usual for the terminal rise of *Mary* to be echoed in the aside, as shown above.

9.134
When restrictive apposition is also full, it is not clear which of the appositives is subordinate:

My friend Peter was here last night (full/strict)
The question whether to confess or not troubled the girl (full/weak)

In partial restrictive apposition, on the other hand, one of the appositives is modifier of the other. In

Next Saturday, *financial expert Tom Timber* will begin writing a
   weekly column on the national economy (partial/strict)
The explanation that he couldn't see it is unsatisfactory (partial/
   weak)

the modifiers are respectively

financial expert
that he couldn't see it

The syntactically subordinate role of one of the appositives is clear with partial apposition, since only the modifier can be omitted (9.131).

9.135
Combinations of appositional types
The three types of distinction we have made apply simultaneously. They are displayed in *Fig 9:1*. The possible combinations are illustrated below.

(1) FULL, STRICT, NON-RESTRICTIVE
   Paul Jones, the distinguished art critic, died in his sleep last
      night

(2) FULL, WEAK, NON-RESTRICTIVE
   Playing football, his only interest in life, has brought him
      many friends

(3) FULL, STRICT, RESTRICTIVE
   My friend Peter was here last night

(4) FULL, WEAK, RESTRICTIVE
   The question whether to confess or not troubled the girl

(5) PARTIAL, STRICT, NON-RESTRICTIVE
> *An unusual present* was given to him for his birthday, *a book on ethics*

(6) PARTIAL, WEAK, NON-RESTRICTIVE
> *His explanation, that he couldn't see it,* is unsatisfactory

(7) PARTIAL, STRICT, RESTRICTIVE
> Next Saturday, *financial expert Tom Timber* will begin writing a weekly column on the national economy

(8) PARTIAL, WEAK, RESTRICTIVE
> *The explanation that he couldn't see it* is unsatisfactory

APPOSITION
- $\begin{cases} full \text{ (either omissible)} \\ partial \text{ (only one omissible)} \end{cases}$
- $\begin{cases} strict \text{ (same syntactic class)} \\ weak \text{ (different syntactic class)} \end{cases}$
- $\begin{cases} non\text{-}restrictive \text{ (different information unit)} \\ restrictive \text{ (same information unit)} \end{cases}$

Fig 9:1 Combinations of appositional types

9.136
More than two units

Though we have found it convenient to exemplify apposition with merely two appositives, we have indicated earlier (9.130) that occasionally there may be more than two units in apposition, as in

> They returned to *their birthplace, their place of residence, the country of which they were citizens.*

There seems to be no motivation for combining any two of the noun phrases as one unit in the appositional relationship. On the other hand, we often find cases in which two or more units function as an appositive:

> She had *a splendid vacation: a Mediterranean cruise and a trip to the Bahamas*

In this case the coordinated noun phrases are together appositive to *a splendid vacation*, a general term in relation to which *a Mediterranean cruise* and *a trip to the Bahamas* are the particulars. But the units functioning as an appositive need not be coordinated by *and*:

> We have *everything we need: land, brains, wealth, technology*

Here the second appositive is a series of juxtaposed units which taken together are included under the general first appositive *everything we need*. There is yet another possibility: a hierarchy of appositional relationships, indicated by the various types of bracketing:

> We now find (*a new type of student*: [*the revolutionary* – {*the radical bent on changing the system and the anarchist bent on destroying it*}])

A new type of student is the first appositive, while all that follows it in the sentence constitutes the second appositive. But within the second appositive there is further apposition: *the revolutionary* is the first appositive, while what follows in the sentence is appositive to it.

9.137
Ambiguity between apposition and other constructions

We have earlier (9.133) noted the use of intonation and punctuation separation for the subordinate appositive in non-restrictive apposition. Where the lexical items allow for potential ambiguity, intonation or punctuation separation usually resolves the ambiguity in favour of an appositional interpretation. The pair of noun phrases in

> They sent *Joan a waitress from the hotel*

is interpreted as indirect object and direct object respectively, synonymous with

> They sent a waitress from the hotel to Joan

On the other hand, the pair in

> They considered *Miss Hartley a very good teacher*

is interpreted as direct object and object complement respectively, synonymous with

> They considered Miss Hartley to be a very good teacher

However, if the second noun phrase in each sentence is separated from what precedes by a tone unit boundary in spoken English or by a comma in written English, then the interpretation is weighted in favour of taking the first noun phrase as direct object with the second noun phrase as apposition to it.

A sentence such as

> They called *Susan a waitress*

is triply ambiguous, the three relationships being

(1) indirect object + direct object:

They called a waitress for Susan

(2) direct object + object complement

They said Susan was a waitress

(3) direct object + appositive:

They called Susan, who $\begin{Bmatrix} \text{is} \\ \text{was} \end{Bmatrix}$ a waitress

With the apposition interpretation, intonation and punctuation marking are obligatory.

9.138
Explicit indicators of apposition

A number of expressions are available for explicitly indicating apposition. They can be inserted between appositives, for example *namely* in

The passenger plane of the 1980s, namely *the supersonic jet*, will transform relations between peoples of the world.

It seems reasonable to say that if we add an explicit indicator we do not change full apposition into partial apposition, even though the presence of the indicator may affect the ability of the construction to meet the conditions for full apposition (9.131).

The indicators express certain semantic relationships between the appositives and therefore cannot be used for all cases of apposition. Some, however, have the same semantic function, though they may be restricted to different varieties of the language. Common indicators are listed below, those marking the same or similar relationship being grouped together.

that is to say, that is, ie (formal and written)
namely, viz (formal and written)
to wit (formal, especially legal)
in other words
or, or rather, or better
and
as follows
for example, for instance, eg (formal and written), *say, including, included, such as*
especially, particularly, in particular, notably, chiefly, mainly, mostly
of

Some of these indicators either precede or (less commonly) follow the second appositive:

The President of the United States, *in other words* Richard Nixon, was on television last night.

The President of the United States, Richard Nixon *in other words*, was on television last night.

But others can only precede the second appositive: *namely, and, or (rather/better), as follows, including, such as, of,* and the abbreviated forms *ie, viz,* and *eg:*

Many people, *including* my sister, won't forgive him for that.

Included can only follow the second appositive:

Many people, my sister *included*, won't forgive him for that.

Note

It might appear plausible to include among indicators the *wh*-relative pronoun followed by BE, as in

Paul Jones, who was *the distinguished art critic,* died in his sleep last night.

However, the insertion of *who was* alters the syntactic relationship, making *the distinguished art critic* a subject complement. But see 9.180. For the non-restrictive relative clause, see 13.14.

Strict non-restrictive apposition: noun phrases
9.139

Apposition is typically exemplified by noun phrases in full strict non-restrictive apposition. Since within strict non-restrictive apposition, similar semantic relationships are found for both full and partial apposition, we treat the two types together. The semantic relationships

EQUIVALENCE
(ie, in other words)

- appellation (*namely, or; who* +BE)
- identification (*namely*)
- designation (*who/which*+BE)
- reformulation (*or*)

ATTRIBUTION
(who/which+BE)

INCLUSION

- exemplification (*for example*)
- particularization (*especially*)

Fig 9:2 Semantic relationships in strict non-restrictive noun-phrase apposition

between the appositives are displayed in *Fig* 9:2. The figure gives common indicators for each relationship, mentioning only one example from indicators grouped together in 9.138. It also notes the possibility of replacing the second appositive by a corresponding nonrestrictive relative clause.

Equivalence
9.140

Appositives in an equivalence relationship allow the insertion of *that is to say* (and other indicators in the same group), and, less commonly, of *in other words*. As *Fig* 9:2 shows, there are four types of equivalence relationship. The types can be differentiated by the different indicators they admit.

9.141
Appellation

With appellation, both appositive noun phrases are definite and the second is typically a proper noun:

> *The company commander*, (that is to say) *Captain Madison*,
>   assembled his men and announced their mission.   [139]
> *My best friend*, (in other words) *Peter*, was here last night.   [140]

But the second appositive can be a common noun phrase:

> *The passenger plane of the 1980s*, (namely) *the supersonic jet*,
>   will transform relations between peoples of the world.

An example of partial apposition:

> *My best friend* was here last night – *Peter*.

There is unique reference between the two appositives with appellation. The second appositive can be replaced by a corresponding relative clause (*cf* 9.151):

> The *company commander, who is Captain Madison*, assembled
>   his men and announced their mission.   [139a]

The second appositive is more specific than the first, and hence the use of *namely*, an indicator that introduces a more specific appositive. *Or* is less commonly used than the other indicators.

9.142
Identification

With identification, the first appositive is typically an indefinite noun phrase and the second appositive is more specific, and hence the possible use of *namely*. If we make the first appositive of [139] indefinite, we now have identification:

> *A company commander*, (namely) *Captain Madison*, assembled
>   his men and announced their mission.   [139b]

There is no longer unique equivalence, as there was with [139]. The second appositive identifies what is given in the first appositive. A similar relationship obtains if the first appositive is, or contains, a pro-form referring to the second appositive:

> *We* – (that is to say) *John and I* – intend to resign.
> He still enjoys *such books: science fiction, detective stories,*
>   *historical novels.*
> We have *everything we need: land, brains, wealth, technology.*   [141]

An example of partial apposition:

> *An unusual present* was given to him for his birthday, *a book on*
>   *ethics.*

9.143
Designation

Designation is the converse of appellation and identification. The second appositive is less specific than the first and hence we cannot insert the indicator *namely*. Both appositives are commonly definite noun phrases:

> *Captain Madison*, (that is to say) *the company commander*,
>   assembled his men and announced their mission.   [139c]
> *Peter* (that is to say), *my best friend*, was here last night.   [140a]
> *Land, brains, wealth, technology* – (in other words) *everything*
>   *we need* – is plentiful in our country.   [141a]
> He sent ahead *the sergeant*, (in other words) *the most*
>   *experienced scout in the company*.   [142]

Replacement of the second appositive by a corresponding relative clause is possible:

> He sent ahead *the sergeant, who was the most experienced*
>   *scout in the company*.   [142a]

Examples of partial apposition:

> *Peter* was here last night, *my best friend*.
> Have *some Harveys* with your Christmas – *the most*
>   *distinguished sherries you can buy*.   [140b]

Reformulation
9.144
Reformulation is a rewording in the second appositive of the lexical content of the first. Three types of reformulation may be distinguished:

(1) Reformulation based on linguistic knowledge.
(2) Reformulation based on factual knowledge.
(3) More precise formulation.

9.145
In reformulation based on linguistic knowledge, the second appositive is a synonymous expression:

these lifts, or rather elevators
a terminological inexactitude, in other words a lie
sound units of the language, technically phonemes
oculists, that is to say eye-doctors

A synonymous word or phrase may replace the first formulation in order to avoid misinterpretation or provide a more familiar or a more technical term. *Lifts* in our example is restricted in the relevant sense to British English and the reformulation would be appropriate in an American context. On the other hand, in a British context, the order would be reversed if these two expressions were in reformulation apposition, since *elevators* is less commonly used than *lifts*.

In addition to the markers it shares with other types of reformulation, this type admits a large range of expressions that specifically mark linguistic reformulation, *eg*:

(more) simply	in more difficult language
in simple(r) words	in scientific terminology
in simple(r) terms	in more technical terms
put (more) simply	technically (speaking)
to put it simply	in words of one syllable

Partial apposition involving linguistic reformulation includes translations from foreign languages:

savoir (*know* in English)

9.146
With the second type, the reformulation is based less on linguistic knowledge than on knowledge about the external world:

Fred – or Ginger as he is usually called – ...
The United Arab Republic, or Egypt, ...
The United States of America, or America for short, ...

However, the distinction between the two types is not absolute. For example, in

> alligator pears, or avocados as they are usually called, ...

it can be argued that it is our knowledge of the external world that is responsible for our awareness of the greater frequency of the word *avocados*.

9.147

With the third type we have a correction of what was said. In addition to the other indicators for reformulation, *namely* can be used for this type. The correction may be due to an attempt at greater accuracy and precision in formulation:

> His party controls *London, Greater London* that is to say.
> They started going to *the church, the Catholic Church.*

But the intention may be rhetorical (as indeed in the last example) to provide a climactic effect by repetition and expansion of the first noun phrase:

> You could cut the atmosphere with *a knife, a blunt knife* at that.

At that attached to the end of the second appositive is an explicit marker of rhetorical intention. When it is present, *and* can be inserted:

> You could cut the atmosphere with *a knife, and a blunt knife at that.*

Perhaps under this form of reformulation we should include other instances of more precise formulation, some of which do not involve repetition:

> this and just this
> these and these alone
> the women and only the women
> those and no others
> then and not before

Substitution
9.148

A special type of equivalence involves placing a pro-form earlier in the sentence while the noun phrase to which it refers is placed finally. This construction is restricted to informal spoken English, and is considered by some as substandard, though it is in fact very common (*cf* 14.50):

> *He*'s a complete idiot, *that brother of yours.*
> *It* went on far too long, *your game.*

Sometimes the operator is included, occasionally with subject-operator inversion:

He's a complete idiot, $\begin{cases} \textit{John is.} \\ \textit{is John.} \end{cases}$

It went on far too long, *your game did.*

9.149

If the pro-form is substituting for a clause that is positioned finally, the construction (known as extraposition, 14.36 *ff*) is normal in both spoken and written English, including formal varieties of the language, and there is no intonation or punctuation break before the final clause. The pro-form is anticipatory *it:*

> *It* surprises me *that they don't write*
> *It* was good *to see you after such a long time*
> *It* was pleasant *meeting you in London that day*

The form without the substitution is less common for finite and infinitive clauses:

> That they don't write surprises me
> To see you after such a long time was good

though for participle clauses it seems to be perfectly normal:

> Meeting you in London that day was pleasant

With participle and infinitive clauses, *that* is sometimes used as the pro-form, but an intonation or punctuation break is then usual:

> *That*'s a mistake, *letting him go free.*
> *That*'s a shame – *to leave him without any money.*

9.150

In informal spoken English we sometimes have the reverse process: a noun phrase is positioned initially and a pro-form substitutes for it in the relevant position in the sentence. This construction is also considered by some to be substandard:

> *Your friend John*, I saw *him* here last night.
> *That play*, *it* was terrible.

Analogous constructions with clauses are rarer, though they seem more likely with *that* as pro-form:

> *Whether they'll write or not* – *that*'s what worries me.
> *To see you after such a long time, that* was good.
> *Meeting you in London that day, that* was pleasant.

All such constructions, however, seem to be anacolutha, that is to say, they appear to involve an abandonment of the originally intended construction and a fresh start in mid-sentence.

Note
Standard English has a number of expressions for introducing the topic of the sentence initially and substituting a pro-form later in the sentence (see 6.48):

> Talking of (informal) ⎫
> To turn now to   ⎪
> Regarding   ⎬ your friend John, I saw *him* here last night.
> With respect to (formal) ⎪
> As for   ⎭

Attribution
9.151
Attribution involves predication rather than equivalence, and the equivalence indicators *that is to say* and *in other words* are not admitted. On the other hand, we can replace the second appositive by a corresponding relative clause. The second appositive is commonly an indefinite noun phrase:

> *Captain Madison, a company commander,* assembled his men
>   and announced their mission.   [139d]
> *The house, an imposing building,* dominated the street.
> *Ron Pall, a blatant liar,* used to be in my class at school.
> *The captain, a man of considerable courage,* led the soldiers
>   into battle.

But it can be definite, with cataphoric *the* referring forward to a post-modification (*cf* 4.36):

> He introduced me to *the young man, the heir to a fortune.*
> *Many students, the cream of the school,* died in the fire.
> 'I don't know what I would have done if I had seen him,'
>   exclaimed *Mary, the prey of violent and obscure emotions.*

9.152
There are several types of partial strict apposition that express an attribution relationship:

(1) A comparatively trivial distinction from full apposition is when the second appositive is not juxtaposed to the first:

> *Many students* died in the fire, *the cream of the school.*

9.153

(2) An article is absent from the second appositive:

> *Robinson, leader of the Democratic group on the committee,*
> refused to answer questions.
> *Mary Cordwell, 25-year-old singer on television shows,* is being
> invited to the reception.

If the first appositive is in the singular and is deleted from the
first sentence the resultant sentence is unacceptable:

> *Leader of the Democratic group on the committee
> refused to answer questions.

This type of partial apposition is common in newspapers and
magazines. The effect of the omission of the article is to make the
second appositive in each sentence more clearly felt as a reduced
relative clause:

> Robinson, *who was leader of the Democratic group on the
> committee,* refused to answer questions.
> Mary Cordwell, *who is a 25-year-old singer on television
> shows,* is being invited to the reception.

Note

[a] The omission of the article is one of the devices used in headlines, where a sentence such as *Democratic leader refuses to answer questions* would not be
unusual.

[b] If the second appositive is short enough, it can be preposed in restrictive apposition (9.160):

> *Democratic leader* Robinson refused to answer questions.
> *25-year-old television singer* Mary Cordwell is being invited to the reception.

This usage is generally restricted to newspapers and magazines.

9.154

(3) An adverbial that is a clause constituent is added to the second
appositive:

> *Norman Jones, then a student,* wrote several best-sellers.
> *Your brother, obviously an expert on English grammar,* is
> highly praised in the book I am reading.
> *Maureen, normally a timid girl,* spoke rudely to them at the
> party.
> They elected as chairman *Martin Jones, also a Cambridge
> graduate.*

9.155

(4) A somewhat different construction is where the second appositive

has an internal structure of subject and either complement or adjunct (*cf* 9.159):

> *The two men, one a Norwegian and the other a Dane*, were awarded medals.
> *Jones and Peters, both of unknown address*, were charged with the murder of Williamson.
> At the entrance there are *two pillars, one on each side*.

In each case the participle *being* can be inserted between the two internal constituents of the second appositive:

> The two men, *one being a Norwegian and the other being a Dane* . . .
> Jones and Peters, *both being of unknown address*, . . .
> . . . *two pillars, one being on each side*.

They can also be seen as reduced relative clauses:

> The two men, *one of whom was a Norwegian and the other of whom was a Dane,* . . .
> Jones and Peters, *both of whom were of unknown address,* . . .
> . . . *two pillars, one of which is on each side*.

9.156

An attribution appositive is to be distinguished from a verbless adverbial clause. Verbless adverbial clauses (11.44 *ff*) often occur initially and are characteristically interpreted as concessive or causal:

> *An even-tempered man, Paul* nevertheless became extremely angry when he heard what had happened.   [143]
> *The heir to a fortune, his friend* did not need to pass examinations.   [144]

The verbless clause in [143] is interpreted as concessive ('Though he was an even-tempered man') and in [144] as causal ('Since he was the heir to a fortune'). These constructions differ from identification apposition (9.142) in that when they occur initially the subject of the sentence is not marked off from the predicate by intonation or punctuation separation. However, the verbless adverbial clause can occur after the subject:

> *His friend, the heir to a fortune*, did not need to pass examinations.   [144a]
> *Bob Rand, a notorious burglar*, found it easy to force open the lock.

In such cases, the lexical content of the sentence suggests the more probable interpretation. For example in

> *Ron Pall, a blatant liar,* was expelled from the group

a blatant liar can be interpreted as an adverbial causal clause, since it is reasonable to ascribe the expulsion to Pall's being a blatant liar. Whereas in

> *Ron Pall, a blatant liar,* used to be in my class at school

there would normally be no motivation for assuming that Pall's presence in the class had anything to do with his being a blatant liar.

Note
Notice that in [143] *nevertheless* refers back to the content of the initial clause (= in spite of his being an even-tempered man).

Inclusion
9.157
Inclusion applies to cases of apposition where the reference of the first appositive is not identical with that of the second, but rather includes it. Some grammarians might entirely exclude this type of relationship from apposition on those grounds. In any case, the inclusion relationship applies only in partial apposition since the omission of the first appositive brings about a radical semantic change.

There are two types of inclusion:

(1) exemplification
(2) particularization

Exemplification need not have explicit indicators, while particularization must have them.

9.158
Exemplification
In exemplification, the second appositive exemplifies the reference of the more general term in the first appositive:

> They visited *several cities, for example Rome and Athens.*
> *His excuses, say the breakdown of his car,* never seemed plausible.
> *Many people, including my sister,* won't forgive him for that.

The explicit indicators of exemplification apposition are those in the group headed by *for example* in 9.138.

Sometimes there may be ambiguity between exemplification and identification (9.142) if no indicator is present:

> *Famous men (De Gaulle, Churchill, Roosevelt)* have visited this
> university.

Presumably the three men referred to in the second appositive are not the only famous men to visit the university, but are mentioned as examples of such visitors. On the other hand, it is not impossible for the relationship to be interpreted as one of identification. The two types of relationship are distinguished by the explicit indicators: if one of the indicators for identification (*namely, that is to say, in other words*) is inserted, the apposition must be indentification, while if the exemplification indicators *for example, for instance, eg, say,* or *including* are used, then we have an unambiguous case of exemplification.

9.159
Particularization
Particularization is really the marked form of exemplification, and requires an explicit indicator to show that the exemplification has been chosen because it is in some way prominent:

> The book contains *some fascinating passages,* NOTABLY *an account of their trip to North Africa.*
> The children liked the *animals,* PARTICULARLY *the monkeys.*
> We want to invite *a number of friends,* ESPECIALLY *John and Peter.*

The explicit indicators of particularization apposition are those in the group headed by *especially* in 9.138.

We should perhaps include here instances like the following, where a numeral or quantifier in the second appositive indicates the particularization (*cf* 9.155):

> *The two men,* ONE *a Dane,* were awarded medals.
> *The soldiers,* SOME *drunk,* started fighting each other.
> *Several sailors,* ONE *looking like a chap I know,* stepped up to the bar.

Strict restrictive apposition: noun phrases
9.160
Strict restrictive apposition of noun phrases can take three forms:

(1) The first appositive is preceded by a definite determiner (and possibly premodifier) and is more general than the second appositive:

that famous critic Paul Jones	the number three
the singer Robeson	the year 1970
the novel 'Great Expectations'	your brother George
the River Thames	my good friend Bob

(2) The reverse of (1), the second appositive is preceded by a determiner, always *the*, and is more general than the first:

Paul Jones the critic	Thompson the plumber
Robeson the singer	Wright the lawyer

(3) Type 3 is like (1) but with omission of the determiner (*cf* 9.153):

Critic Paul Jones	Lawyer Wright
Singer Robeson	Farmer Brown
(My) Brother George	Democratic leader Robinson
Friend Bob	25-year-old television singer Mary Cordwell

9.161
The first form is the most common. Omission of the determiner in the third form produces partial apposition, with the first appositive becoming premodifier and resembling a title (4.42). Generally, the reduction from the first form is allowed only when the second appositive is the name of a person. Hence we do not find

*novel 'Great Expectations'
*year 1970

Operation and *Hurricane* regularly omit determiners when they are used as proper nouns:

Operation Abolition
Hurricane Edna

Pronouns followed by noun phrases, such as *you boys* (7.40), *you British* (5.21 Note *d*), *we men*, can also be analysed as restrictive apposition.

9.162
Geographical names (4.44 *ff*) merit separate treatment. Certain names of individual mountains and lakes take *Mount* and *Lake* respectively as a title:

Mount Everest	Lake Michigan
Mount Vesuvius	Lake Windermere

We do not prefix them with a determiner. Most other such geographical names take a determiner, the general term being preceded by the proper noun as premodifier:

the Atlantic Ocean	the Rocky Mountains
the Mediterranean Sea	the Nile Valley

Some rivers allow either premodification or the appositive form:

{the River Mississippi   {the River Euphrates
{the Mississippi River   {the Euphrates River

Some districts and a few cities and villages require the general term to come second:

Washington State   Quebec Province
Milwaukee County   Kansas City
New York City   Dulwich Village

In other cases both orders are possible:

County Cork ~ Cork County (and other Irish counties)
County Durham ~ Durham County

Note
City in *Kansas City* is in fact part of the name and can hardly be omitted.

9.163
Instead of the first form of strict restrictive apposition (9.160) the two appositives are more commonly linked by *of* for the names of months and for the names of villages, cities, districts, countries, and regions (*cf* 13.27):

the month of December   the state of Guatemala
the borough of Westminster   the Republic of France
the City of London   the island of Cyprus
the county of Yorkshire   the Rock of Gibraltar
the District of Columbia   the continent of Africa
the state of Washington

In some cases we have a choice between the forms exemplified in *Washington State* and *the state of Washington*. But in many cases the former option is not available:

*London City   *Africa Continent (but *the
Columbia District   African Continent is
*December month   acceptable)
                               *France Republic (but *the
                                   French Republic* is
                                   acceptable)

Note
Books of the Bible can be used in this type of construction:

the book Genesis ~ the book of Genesis
the book Job ~ the book of Job

For other uses of the appositive indicator *of*, see 9.178, 13.27, 13.31.

9.164

An important use of the first form of restrictive apposition (9.160) is found with citations and names of books, films, etc (7.23 Note *c*):

the word 'if'   the expression 'do your own
the noun 'butter'   thing'
the term 'heavy water'   the novel *Crime and Punishment*

The first appositive is often absent:

'If' is a conjunction
'Men' is an irregular plural in English
'Hiss' expresses by its very sound the meaning it conveys
'John and Mary' is a coordinated noun phrase
I'm reading *Crime and Punishment*

We may assume a weak form of ellipsis (9.7) in such cases, an ellipsis of some general phrase such as 'the expression' or 'the citation form', or of an appropriate term in the case of titles, such as 'the book', 'the film', 'the play'. Notice the singular number concord with 'men' and 'John and Mary', which can only be explained if we assume the ellipsis of a singular first appositive (for further examples, see 7.23 Note *c*).

9.165

The second form of restrictive apposition (9.160) is restricted to cases where the first appositive is the name of a person and the second is the designation of an occupation. Hence we do not have

*George the brother
*Bob the friend

Appositives and titles
9.166

In the third form of restrictive apposition (9.160) the first appositive is used as if it were a title. Compare such examples of this type of apposition:

Singer Robeson   Farmer Brown
Critic Paul Jones   Plumber Thompson (especially
(My) Brother George   AmE)
                                 Democratic leader Robinson

with institutionalized titles:

Queen Elizabeth   Lord Harper
President Nixon   Dr Smith (medical doctor or
Judge Harris   doctor of philosophy (PH D))

Professor Brown	Sir John Cartwright
Brother Robert (brother in religious order)	Mr Porter

(1) With appositives a preposed determiner is normal:

the singer Robeson	the farmer Brown
the critic Paul Jones	the plumber Thompson
my brother George	the Democratic leader Robinson

but not with titles:

*the Queen Elizabeth
*the President Nixon
*the Judge Harris

unless the noun phrases are modified restrictively:

the present Queen Elizabeth
the older Professor Brown
the Mr Porter *who lives next door to you*

Title-like adjectives such as *honourable* and *reverend* are commonly used with determiners, but only with the latter can the determiner be omitted:

the honourable Mr Johnson
(the) reverend Jones

Note

[a] The stressed definite article /ðiː/ can be used as in

You are not *the* Judge Harris, are you?

where *the* identifies but has no anaphoric reference (*ie* 'the Judge Harris that everyone knows').

[b] With *Emperor*, the definite article seems to be part of the title, since it is normally retained:

the Emperor Vespasian

9.167

(2) With appositives postposition with *the* is more normal than pre-position without *the*:

Robeson the singer	Thompson the plumber
Paul Jones the critic	Robinson the Democratic
Brown the farmer	leader

Brown the farmer is perhaps on the borderline in this respect, and **George the brother* and analogous constructions with family relationships are ruled out, unless *the* is cataphoric: *George the* *brother of James.* On the other hand, pre-position is more normal for titles, while those phrases that are nearest to being exclusively titles do not allow postposition at all:

*Smith the doctor (PH D)	*Porter the mister
*John Cartwright the sir	*Robert the Brother
*Harper the lord	(in a religious order)

Possessive pronouns are commonly used in this construction with words for family relationship: *George my brother.*

9.168

(3) Appositives and most titles can be used without the proper nouns and with determiners:

the singer	the judge
the farmer	the President
the doctor (when used for	the brother
a medical doctor)	the lord (also *His Lordship*)

But some are not used in this way:

*the doctor (when used for **anybody** except a medical doctor)
*the sir
*the mister

9.169

(4) Most titles can be used as vocatives and so can some appositives such as *Farmer* and *Brother*. For vocatives see 7.39 *f.*

The title *Miss*, for unmarried women, is used in the vocative (especially AmE and substandard BrE), but otherwise is generally followed by a name. The accompanying name must be the last name, *eg: Miss Jones* and not *Miss Alice*, except in archaic or minority (especially British upper social class) use. On the other hand, *sir* when used as a title is followed by the first name: *Sir John* and not *Sir Jones*. The vocative *sir* is an alternative to the substandard vocative *mister* and is not the title found in *Sir John.*

The appositive *Esq* ('Esquire') is used in BrE virtually only in writing (chiefly in addressing letters) and is postposed to a name consisting of a family name with either a first name or initials:

John Porter, Esq
J. Porter, Esq

This is a more formal alternative to

Mr (J.) Porter

Mr and *Esq* are not combined:

*Mr J. Porter, Esq

9.170

We can now show the gradience from apposition in *critic Paul Jones* to full title in *Mr Porter* with the following examples:

(1) critic Paul Jones	(2) Farmer Brown	(3) Brother George
the critic Paul Jones	the farmer Brown	(family)
Paul Jones the critic	?Brown the farmer	my brother George/
the critic	the farmer	?the brother George
?critic (vocative)	farmer (voc)	*George the brother
		the brother
		brother (voc)

(4) Professor Brown	(5) Dr Smith (PH D)	(6) Mr Porter
*the professor Brown	*the doctor Smith	*the Mr Porter
?Brown the professor	*Smith the doctor	*Porter the mister
the professor	*the doctor	*the mister
professor (voc)	doctor (voc)	*mister (voc) (in
		substandard use)

9.171

In certain titles the proper noun is followed by an article and adjective or numeral:

Napoleon the Great
Pitt the Younger
Henry VIII ('the eighth')

In such designations there is occasionally a reordering with the modification preposed in the equivalent

the Great Napoleon
the Younger Pitt
the eighth Henry

9.172

Postposed numbers and letters, as in

paragraph 12   room 10A
equation 4   room B14
Hill 25   Ward C

perhaps imply the ellipsis of the words *number* or *letter*:

paragraph number 12   room number 10A
equation number 4   room number B14
Hill number 25   Ward letter C

If that is so, the postmodifying phrases contain appositional constructions, with the number or letter being in apposition to the ellipted word *number* or *letter* (*number 10A – the number is 10A*).
We also find premodifying numbers and letters:

No 2 Platform
G Block

Strict non-restrictive apposition: units other than noun phrases
9.173
Strict non-restrictive apposition is probably far less common with other units than with noun phrases, while strict restrictive apposition does not apply at all. Clauses, predicates, and predications that are in apposition display an equivalence relationship. The indicators are *that is to say* and *in other words*, and – if the second appositive is more specific – *namely*.

(1) CLAUSES
    I explained the whole document to him, (that is to say) *I went through it word for word with him.*
    All human languages are equally complete as instruments of communication: that is, *every language appears to be as well equipped as any other to say the things the speakers want to say.*
    They put it *where it was light*, (in other words) *where everybody could see it.*

(2) PREDICATES
    They *summoned help – called the police and fire brigade.*
    They *surrendered*, (that is) *threw out their weapons and walked out with their hands above their heads.*

(3) PREDICATIONS
    They had *never anticipated an air assault – never imagined bombers would attack them.*
    They will *summon help – call the police and fire brigade.*

9.174
Adjectives are occasionally in equivalence apposition (*cf* 9.140):

She is *better, very much better*, than he is.
She was *homely, that is to say, plain.*
He drew a *triacontahedral, ie thirty-sided*, figure.

The above three examples involve reformulation (9.144–147). The first is a correction (9.147), while the other two are linguistic reformulations (9.145): AmE *homely* is glossed as *plain* and the more difficult *triacontahedral* is explained by the more familiar *thirty-sided*. In

He is *good* or (to be more specific) *friendly and helpful.*

the second appositive is analogous to the appellation type in noun phrases (9.141).

Note
Compare the rare reformulation with determiners:

the or rather *a* book.

9.175
Adverbs are occasionally in equivalence apposition:

He always wrote *so* – (namely) *childishly but legibly.*
Thirdly and *lastly*, they would not accept his promise.
Secondly and *most importantly*, he is resigning from his job next month.

That is to say, *in other words*, and *namely* are possible indicators after the pro-form *so*. The conjuncts in the second and third sentences (8.89 *ff*) are always linked by *and*.

9.176
Prepositional phrases can be in equivalence apposition:

The President's support is strongest *in the Midwest*, (that is) *in the heart of the U.S.A.*
They handed it *to Bob Pitt*, *to a man of integrity.*
He explained the situation *to his class*, especially *to the older students.*

If the preposition introducing the second appositive is omitted, we then have appositive noun phrases.

Weak apposition
9.177
Weak apposition, where the appositives come from different classes (9.132), is exemplified by a noun phrase in apposition to a clause. The indicator *namely* is used if the second appositive is more specific, which is the case when the second appositive is a clause. Normally the noun phrase comes first, as in these instances of full apposition:

He told them *the news:* (namely) *that the troops would be leaving.*

He has *a problem:* (namely) *should he charge them for the damage or should he forget about it?*

Their solution, (namely) *to appoint a committee,* is deplorable.

His only interest in life, (namely) *playing football,* has brought him many friends.

But the clause, particularly if it is a non-finite clause, can come first:

For them to pay him a commission, his suggestion, seemed an excellent idea.

She enjoyed *teaching English, her job.*

The second appositive, whether a noun phrase or a clause, can be regarded as a reduced relative clause:

He told them the news, *which was that the troops would be leaving.*

His only interest in life, *which was playing football,* has brought him many friends.

In partial weak apposition between noun phrase and clause, the noun phrase appears first:

His explanation, (that is to say) *that he couldn't see it,* is unsatisfactory

He gave them *the news:* (namely) *that the troops would be leaving.*

The first appositive cannot be omitted without producing an unacceptable sentence (9.131). *That is to say* and *namely* are the indicators for this type of apposition. The clause can be regarded as a reduced relative clause.

The first appositive may be part of the clause:

If the government had known what was going to happen, *they* would not *have increased credit facilities – a move that accelerated inflation.*

A move that accelerated inflation is appositive to *they have increased credit facilities.*

9.178

Restrictive apposition is common with such general noun phrases as *the fact, the idea, the view:*

The fact that he wouldn't betray his friends is very much to his credit.

I don't agree with *the view that there is no advantage in being patient.*

The question whether to confess or not troubled him.

Your duty to report the accident takes precedence over everything else.

With participle clauses, and sometimes with *wh*-clauses, *of* is used as an indicator (9.163):

> *The thought of playing against them* arouses all my aggressive instincts.
> He didn't accept *the idea of working while he was studying.*
> *His account of what he had done that year* did not satisfy his colleague.

9.179

Adverbials of different syntactic classes are sometimes placed in apposition:

> He explained it *simply, that is to say in words they could understand.*
> They bought it *cheaply, for three dollars.*
> She wrote it *yesterday, namely (on) Monday.*
> He walked *slowly, (in) the way he always does.*
> She played it *afterwards, I mean when they had left.*
> John stood *in front, where he could see more clearly.*

9.180
Non-restrictive relative clause

Some grammarians have included among appositional constructions non-restrictive relative clauses:

> *His explanation, which we read yesterday,* is unsatisfactory.

Presumably this assignment is motivated by the loose attachment of the non-restrictive relative clause to the sentence and the requirement for co-reference between the *wh*-word in the clause and an antecedent noun phrase. It is also motivated by the frequent possibility of expanding a second appositive into a relative clause:

> *Peter, (who is) my best friend,* was here last night.

(See 9.141, 9.143, 9.151–155, 9.177). Under this interpretation, the non-restrictive relative clause with the previous clause as its antecedent is then said to be appositive to that previous clause:

> He sold his shop, *which surprised me.*

See further 13.14 *f*.

Bibliographical note
Some recent contributions to coordination in general: Dik (1968); Gleitman (1965); Hudson (1970); Karlsen (1959); Lakoff and Peters (1966); Lakoff, R. (1971); Stockwell, Schachter and Partee (1968) *pp* 319–444.

On the distinctions between coordinators, subordinators, and conjuncts, see Greenbaum (1969a). On the conjunction *but*, see Greenbaum (1969b).

On the order of nouns and coordinated adjectives, see Malkiel (1959).

On the order of coordinated adjectives, see 13.65 *ff*; Bolinger (1965) *pp* 129–138.

On apposition, see Haugen (1953); Hockett (1955); Lee (1952); Norwood (1954).

TEN
SENTENCE CONNECTION

10.1

Introduction

The compound sentence is dealt with in Chapter 9 and the complex sentence in Chapter 11. In this chapter we are concerned with devices that cross boundaries of units that it is pointless to regard as anything but sentences, though this is not to deny that many such devices occur also within the sentence. We sometimes have the option in the written language of marking conjoined or juxtaposed clauses as one sentence or as two separate sentences:

> John has loved Alice for a long time, *but* he told her so only last
> night.   [1a]
> John has loved Alice for a long time. *But* he told her so only last
> night.   [1b]

While pairs of sentences as short as [1b] can occur, the justification for the separate treatment of sentence linkage lies in instances when it would be unlikely for the sentences to be written as one sentence or when that possibility is ruled out:

> It was a convention where the expected things were said, the
> predictable things were done. It was a convention where the
> middle class and middle aged sat. It was a convention where
> there were few blacks and fewer beards. *And* that remains
> the Republican problem.   [2]

In [2] *and* links the final sentence to a unit comprising the three preceding sentences. The final sentence contains a comment on what precedes, and cannot be attached merely to the preceding sentence. Similarly, *but* links the final sentence equally to each of the two preceding sentences in

> A paper-boy, a college freshman, and a new graduate may be equally
> skilful in teasing, shouting instructions on the football-field,
> grumbling – or even swearing. They may be as skilful as each
> other or as a professor in English language in any of these uses.
> *But* their skill will probably be unequal when it comes to drafting
> a letter, writing a report, or making a formal speech.   [3]

Note
The isolation of a unit as an independent orthographic sentence may be intended to convey the effect of a dramatic pause in speech:

> He won because what he had to say about the United Nations and the need to
> prevent the spread of nuclear weapons conforms faithfully to the Labour
> Party's proper desires and instincts. *And to Mr Wilson's.*

A dash before the unit can serve the same purpose.

Factors in sentence connection
10.2

In this chapter we shall be dealing primarily with syntactic devices that enter into sentence connection. But there are other factors that may be present as well as syntactic devices, all of which interact in pointing to links between sentences. We illustrate this by examining a lengthy paragraph. For ease of reference, the sentences are numbered.

(i) We sometimes rather thoughtlessly criticize an announcement or a government form which refers to 'male persons over the age of twenty-one years'. (ii) What ridiculous jargon, we think; why couldn't this pompous official have used the word 'man'! (iii) But the official may be forced into a jargon that he likes no more than we do, by the imprecision of the ordinary words that we may prefer. (iv) In the present instance, 'man' may well sound perfectly obvious as the right gloss upon 'male person over the age of twenty-one years', but would the latter be equally our automatic interpretation if the word 'man' had been used? (v) The word 'man' is applied regularly to hundreds of thousands of students, only a minority of whom have reached the age of twenty-one. (vi) We often use it of still younger males of sixteen or seventeen, and it can be applied to a school-boy of ten ('the team is a man short'). (vii) It may simply mean 'brave person', as when we tell a little boy of four to 'stop crying and be a man'. (viii) Or it may mean 'human being', without regard to sex, as in a phrase like 'not fit for man or beast'. (ix) It may even mean a wooden disc – as in the game of draughts.

The factors that we exemplify as entering into sentence connection in the above paragraph are:

[A] implication in the semantic content
[B] lexical equivalence
[C] syntactic devices.

Cutting across but endorsing these three factors are prosodic features of connection (App II.12 *ff*, II.21) which have yet to be fully described and which must consequently be ignored in the present treatment. A reading-aloud of sentences (v–ix), however, would give them close linkage (a) by unity of pitch-range, such that (vi–ix) nested within the wider range set by (v); (b) by parallelism in intonation and rhythm patterns, such that although a reader would have considerable choice of pattern, he would tend to repeat for (vi–ix) the pattern he decided was most suitable for (v); (c) by giving comparable prosodic prominence to *students* in (v), *younger males* in (vi), *brave person* in (vii), *human being* in (viii), and *wooden disc* in (ix), quite possibly arranging them in a series with respect to degrees of emphasis or pitch-height.

10.3
[A] IMPLICATION IN THE SEMANTIC CONTENT
A reader normally expects coherence and takes it for granted that there is a connection between sentences that occur sequentially in speech or in writing. He searches for relationships implied by the juxtaposition of sentences with their semantic interpretation. For example, sentences (vii), (viii), and (ix) present a series of alternatives linked to the joint content of (v) and (vi), but only in (viii) do we find the coordinator *or* marking the alternatives. We could, of course, make the relationship between these sentences explicit by adding *or* to the beginning of (vii) and (ix) as well. On the other hand, sentence (ii) is an exemplification of the content of (i) and it is possible to make this relationship explicit by attaching (say) *for instance* to (ii).

10.4
[B] LEXICAL EQUIVALENCE
We can expect successive sentences to exhibit some relationship through their vocabulary, some equivalence in the lexical items. The simplest form for such lexical equivalence is through the repetition of words or phrases. For example *we* is found in (i), (ii), (iii), (vi),(vii), and its genitive form *our* in (iv); *it may . . . mean* appears in three consecutive sentences – (vii), (viii), and (ix); *jargon* of (ii) is repeated in (iii); and *man*, which first appears in (ii), recurs twice in (iv), and once in (v), (vi), (vii), and (viii).

However, lexical equivalents are often synonyms or near-synonyms. Of course, the whole point of the paragraph is the degree of closeness in meaning between 'male persons over the age of twenty-one years' – (i) and (iv) – and 'man'. For further treatment of lexical equivalents we must find examples outside our cited paragraph.

10.5
The equivalent may be the generic term for the lexical set (the relationship between the two terms being one of inclusion, or *hyponymy* as it has been recently termed):

> The monkey's most extraordinary accomplishment was learning to operate a *tractor*. By the age of nine, the monkey had learned to solo on the *vehicle*.

However, it is often the case that the equivalence is not given in the language but may instead be established by the speaker or writer, and may then result in a chain of equivalences being set up through several sentences:

> The Senate last week refused to confirm the nomination of Judge *Palmer*, a *Californian* of slender reputation, to the Supreme Court. The defeat of the *Californian* was a rebuke to the President, who resented it deeply. *Palmer* fell because of suspicions that he is a racist.

The equivalence of *Palmer* and *Californian* in the first sentence derives from the identification of the two in an appositional construction (*cf* 9.140 *ff*). Other syntactic devices may be used for this purpose, in particular the identification or attribution relationships of subject complement to subject and of object complement to object (*cf* 7.14).

The equivalence may not be given overtly, but may depend on factual knowledge or presuppositions that the speaker feels he can assume on the part of his audience:

> Last week *Paul McCartney* announced that he was separating from the quartet. The *27-year-old Beatle* gave several reasons for the break-up.
> *The radical students* were prominent in this week's session of the national conference. *The nation's subversive elements* put forward a series of resolutions demanding violent action.

In the first example the speaker expects his audience to know that Paul McCartney is a Beatle (a lexical equivalence reinforced by his use of anaphoric *the* in *the 27-year-old Beatle*, *cf* 10.65), while in the second example the speaker assumes that his audience will agree with him in identifying the radical students as the nation's subversive elements. The assumptions that a speaker feels he can make will of course vary considerably according to the audience he is addressing.

Repetition of lexical items is normally avoided, but 'elegant variation' can become as disconcerting as repetition when the variation is obtrusive. Hence we more usually resort to the syntactic device of substitution by pro-forms, such as pronouns.

10.6

From the examples of lexical equivalences that have been cited, it is clear that the equivalents need not have the same syntactic function in the two sentences nor need they consist of the same number of lexical units. As the next example shows, they can also be realized by different parts of speech:

> His initial remarks were *flattering*. The *flattery* made his audience listen more attentively than they would have done otherwise.

10.7

Lexical connection between sentences may depend on relationships between lexical items other than those we have illustrated in 10.4–6. We might mention the various types of oppositeness of meaning that can be exemplified by such pairs as *man : woman; beautiful : ugly; father : son.* For example, the connection between the following two sentences is largely dependent on the antithesis between *men* and *women:*

> Discrimination is undoubtedly practised against *women* in the field of scientific research. We don't find *men* complaining that they are not being interviewed for positions that they are clearly qualified to fill.

Finally, there are co-occurrence expectancies between lexical items, though the lexical sets cannot be established with precision, nor can generalizations be made easily with respect to semantic relations holding between items in the set: *birth: baby; road : car; heat : sun.* For example:

> We heard that the *birth* was easy. The *baby* is smaller than expected, but is in good health.

10.8

[C] SYNTACTIC DEVICES

Syntactic devices, the topic of this chapter, interact with the other factors in the connection between sentences in our cited paragraph. We have said that the word *man* appears in six of the sentences. But the citation form *man* is also referred to by the pronoun *it* – twice in (vi) and once in each of (vii), (viii), and (ix). Thus *man* and its equivalents, lexical or syntactic, form a motif running through the paragraph. *This* in *this pompous official* (ii) refers back to the assumed agent of *an announcement or a government form* (i), and the identity of *this pompous official* with the subject of the next sentence is assured by the use of *the* in *the official* (iii). The concessive relation between (iii) and the two preceding sentences is made explicit by the use of the coordinator *but* in (iii), while one of the alternatives that the sentences in the latter half of the paragraph represent is marked explicitly in one sentence (viii) by *or.* One final example. A comparative form entails a basis for comparison (5.69, 10.72). We do not know from (vi) what the basis for comparison is and are therefore forced to look back for the missing information. From the juxtaposition of the sentences we can infer that *younger* denotes 'younger than twenty-one'.

10.9

Features of the situation may also be relevant: (1) the visible scene – persons and objects, and their activity – though ordinarily this has relevance only to the spoken language or written forms attempting to imitate its effects; (2) the medium of communication; (3) the relationship between the participants in the communication; and (4) the specific purposes of the communication.

(1) The scene is relevant, for example, in comments by a speaker on an action in progress. We can imagine someone watching a game of football and exclaiming *They're far too slow!* and then *He missed it!* The connection between the sentences derives from the sequence of actions that the speaker sees. However, the sequence of sentences need not be motivated by any change in the scene; it may instead derive from the speaker's scanning of the scene. Notice that there need be no previous mention of linguistic units for which the pronouns *they*, *he* and *it* substitute. They can refer directly to visible persons and objects. The 'visible scene' may also be relevant in written material containing illustrations or diagrams. In literature, particularly in poetry, a 'visible scene' is often presupposed.

(2) A simple example of the effect of the medium is the frequent use of *yes* or its equivalents which punctuate a telephone conversation to reassure the speaker that the listener is still on the line. We can also contrast the possibility in a television commentary of relying on references to the visible situation with the necessity for explicit links in a radio commentary.

(3) The social relationship between the participants may affect the type of links and the extent of their use. For example, a couple who have been married for a long time can often assume that references will be understood and can suppress intermediate stages of logical connections between sentences. Moreover, explicit connecters vary in the degree of their formality, a scale which depends on the relationship between the participants.

(4) The purpose of the communication will in part dictate its form. For example, we can expect differences in sentence connection to be exhibited between an official government report and a memorandum sent from one office to another within a government department.

10.10

Syntactic devices used for connecting sentences can be grouped under the following headings:

[A] Time and place relaters (10.11–16)
[B] Logical connecters (10.17–38)
[C] Substitution (10.39–62)

Time and place relaters
Time relaters
10.11

Sentence connection can be established by time-relationships signalled by adjectives or adverbials with temporal significance or by tense, aspect and modality in verbs. Once a time-reference has been established, certain temporal adjectives and adverbs may order subsequent information in relation to the time-reference. Three major divisions of time-relationship may be set up, and examples are given of adjectives and adverbials that signal the relationships:

(1) temporal ordering previous to given time-reference:

ADJECTIVES
earlier, former, preceding, previous, prior

> *eg* He handed in a good essay. His *previous* essays were all poor.

The implication of *previous* is 'previous to the good essay just mentioned'.

ADVERBIALS
already, as yet, before, beforehand, earlier, first, formerly, hitherto (formal), *previously, so far, yet;* and phrases with pro-forms: *before that, before this, before now, before then, by now, by then, until now, until then, up to now, up to then*

> *eg* I shall explain to you what happened. But *first* I must give you a cup of tea.

First is to be interpreted here as 'before I explain to you what happened'.

10.12

(2) temporal ordering simultaneous with given time-reference:

ADJECTIVES
coexisting (formal), *coinciding* (formal), *concurrent* (formal), *contemporary, contemporaneous* (formal), *simultaneous*

eg The death of the president was reported this afternoon on Cairo radio. A *simultaneous* announcement was broadcast from Baghdad.

Simultaneous is 'simultaneous with the report of the death of the president on Cairo radio'.

ADVERBIALS

at present, at this point, concurrently (formal), *contemporaneously* (formal), *here, in the interim* (formal), *meantime, meanwhile, in the meantime, in the meanwhile, now, presently, simultaneously, then, throughout,* and the relative *when*

eg Several of the conspirators have been arrested but their leader is as yet unknown. *Meanwhile* the police are continuing their investigations into the political sympathies of the group.

Meanwhile means 'at the same time as the arrests are being made'.

Note

[*a*] The use of *presently* for time-relationship (2), with the meaning 'at present', has become more common in AmE than it used to be. In BrE *presently* is more commonly synonymous with *soon*. See 8.57 Note *b*.

[*b*] An example of *here* as time-indicator:

I've now been lecturing for over an hour. I'll stop *here* since you all look tired.

10.13

(3)   temporal ordering subsequent to given time-reference:

ADJECTIVES

ensuing (formal), *following, later, next, subsequent* (formal), *succeeding* (formal), *supervening* (formal)

eg I saw him on Friday and he seemed to be in perfect health. The *following* day he died.

Following implies 'following the Friday mentioned in the previous sentence'.

ADVERBIALS

after, afterwards, (all) at once, finally, immediately, last, later, next, since, subsequently (formal), *suddenly, then;* and the phrases *after that, after this*

eg The manager went to a board meeting this morning. He was *then* due to catch a train to London.

Then here means 'after the board meeting'.

The temporal adjunct *again* could be fitted into this category. It is equivalent to 'another time', *ie* a time additional to one previously mentioned:

He told her what he thought of her. He didn't speak to her *again*.

Words with temporal significance do not always have a connective function. Often the time-reference is not explicitly mentioned in preceding sentences. Thus, if somebody says

John's *previous* wife died last year

there need not have been any prior mention of John's subsequent or present wife. The fact that John had been married before may be assumed as known to the hearer.

Note

[a] *Anew* and *afresh* are synonyms of *again* and *once more*, but are rare and formal.

[b] Several adverb compounds that can be classed in (3) are only found in certain formal varieties of contemporary English: *henceforth, henceforward, hereupon, thenceforward, thereafter, thereupon, whereupon*.

10.14

The ordinals constitute a temporal series of adjectives *first, second, third* . . ., with *next* as a substitute for any of the middle terms when moving up the series, and *final* or *last* as a substitute for the term for the end of the series. There is a corresponding series of adjuncts with *first* (also *at first* and, less commonly, *firstly*) as the beginning of the set; *next, then, later, afterwards*, as interchangeable middle terms; and *finally, lastly*, or *eventually* as markers of the end of the set.

10.15

Tense, aspect, and modality are discussed in detail elsewhere (3.23–53). Here we merely illustrate a few of the more obvious time-relationships signalled by these components of the verb phrase:

He *telephoned* the police. There *had been* an explosion.   [4]

Alice *turned on* the radio to full volume. John *was taking* a
  shower.   [5]

Mary *complained* bitterly about the state of the house. Peter
  poured himself a drink.   [6]

The use of the past perfect of the verb in one sentence and of the simple past in the other fixes the temporal sequence of the information conveyed in the two sentences of [4]. The past perfect form allows the two sentences to appear in an order departing from chronological sequence without resultant ambiguity or misinterpretation. In [5] the verb forms indicate that the action described in the first sentence took place during the action described in the second sentence, while in [6] the actions described in the sentences follow the chronological sequence corresponding to the order of the sentences.

Note

The semantic content of the sentences in [4] and [5] is such that we tend to interpret the juxtaposed sentences in each pair as having a cause-effect relationship, and perhaps this is true of [6] too.

10.16
Place relaters

Some words denoting place-relationship can play a part in sentence connection. Ellipsis is then usually involved (*cf* 10.79):

He examined the car. The *front* was slightly damaged.   [7]
The building was heavily guarded by police. The windows on
  the *top* story were covered with boards.   [8]

The ellipted items in [7] and [8] are *of the car* and *of the building* respectively. Often the ellipted items are not in the previous context, but are understood from the context of situation (either accompanying the communication or established by the communication):

The traffic lights soon changed. He walked *across* quickly.   [9]

Across in [9] implies *the road* or some similar noun phrase (*cf* 6.10).

A few place adverbs do not involve ellipsis: *here, there, elsewhere*, the relative *where* and (in formal contexts) *hence, thence, hither* and *thither*. They are pro-forms:

The school laboratory reeked of ammonia. *Here,* during the first
  week of the term, an experiment was conducted.   [10]
All my friends have been to Paris at least once. I am going *there*
  next summer for the first time.   [11]

Here in [10] substitutes for *in the school laboratory* and *there* in [11] for *to Paris*.

Note

[*a*] *Elsewhere* differs from the other substitutes in indicating that the places under consideration are other than those previously mentioned.

[*b*] In sentences like *Stand over there* and *Here it is* the pro-forms may refer directly to the situational context without any linguistic mention of location.

Logical connecters
10.17
Despite a tradition of prescriptive teaching against the practice, it is not uncommon in written English to find sentences (and sometimes even paragraphs) beginning with the coordinating conjunctions *and, or, but.* Most of the other types of logical connecters can be grouped under these coordinators in as much as a similar interpretation could obtain if the coordinator alone is used. Some types could come under more than one coordinator. For example, sentences that are being contrasted can be linked by either *but* or *and* (9.43, 9.54), but logical connecters denoting a contrast have been put under *but*, because that coordinator is used more commonly with contrasted sentences. *Fig* 10:1 displays the logical relationships for which there are explicit connecters, and these are grouped with the three coordinators. The conjunction *for*, also a sentence connecter, is appended, though it has a restricted use.

$$
\begin{array}{ll}
and & \left\{
\begin{array}{l}
listing \left\{
\begin{array}{l}
enumeration \\
addition \left\{
\begin{array}{l}
reinforcement \\
equation
\end{array}\right.
\end{array}\right. \\
transition \\
summation \\
apposition \\
result \\
inference
\end{array}\right. \\
or & \left\{
\begin{array}{l}
reformulation \\
replacement
\end{array}\right. \\
but & \left\{
\begin{array}{l}
contrast \\
concession
\end{array}\right. \\
for & \ cause
\end{array}
$$

Fig 10:1 Logical relationships

10.18
And
The possible relationships between sentences linked by *and* are in general the same as those between clauses linked by *and* (9.40–48). We have referred earlier (10.1) to the use of *and* to link its sentence with a unit comprising several preceding sentences, and, in the example we gave, *and* introduced a comment on the content of the preceding sentences. *And* also links a sentence with a preceding one that has internal co-ordination of clauses, the coordinations being on different levels (*cf* 9.36):

Then, with his boots clean, he can go over to the coffee shop down

the hall and have lunch, and talk with his friends about the
business of hauling and handling and making a living and how
to solve the problems of the world. *And* when he pays his check
he will see the sign on the wall that says, 'Cows may come and
cows may go, but the bull in this place goes on forever.'
The heroine hungers to be more than herself. 'If I have to be just
one person,' she tells her husband, 'I'll kill myself.' She does, and
her husband is left to reflect on her not as a woman he loved
without tenderness but as a natural element that he needed for his
own survival. *And* the reader is left to reflect too. About the
emptiness and boredom that addicts some people to the idea of
leading serial lives, about the consumer culture that feeds the
idea with fantasies, and about the society that provides the
opportunities to realize those fantasies – for better or worse.

Neither and *nor*, semantically often the negative equivalents of *and*
(9.55), also link sentences:

During his long meeting with the representatives of the party he
was unable to secure any discussion of the delegation's aims.
Neither was he able to arrange any meeting with government
officials.
He never quite forgave his parents for their neglect of him when
he was a young child. There were frequent fits of rage and
nightmares. *Nor* could he wholly rid himself of feelings of guilt for
his dreams of revenge on them.

Neither leaves the series open for further additions, whereas *nor* con-
cludes it.

Enumeration
10.19
Enumerative conjuncts (8.89) indicate a cataloguing of what is being
said. Most of them belong to well-defined sets, though a member of one
set may sometimes replace a member of another set in the appropriate
position. Indeed, other listing conjuncts (8.89) are also used in the set,
as *furthermore* in

He attacked the senator viciously, but he was never called before
the committee, though he was prepared for such an occurrence.
First, he was not an important enough figure. *Furthermore*, his
criticism of the senator and his advocacy of the civil rights of
dissenters was completely open. *Finally*, since there was no case
for suggesting he was secretly infiltrating the government, the
elements necessary to a good witch hunt were missing.

The enumerative conjuncts may be introduced by a statement of intention to list:

> I want to give just two pieces of advice. *One*, there is no reason why he should know about your decision. *Two*, it would be better if you acted before he finds out.   [12]

But there is often no previous indication of such an intention:

> Tom Brown is well known in this city. He has been a member of the city council for many years. *Secondly, and far more importantly*, he is a football player of national reputation.   [13]

The addition of *far more importantly* indicates that the statements are listed in ascending order of importance. There are several climactic additive conjuncts (8.89) that mark the end of an ascending order: *above all, on top of it all, to top it (all), to cap it (all)*, and the alliterative expression *last but not least*.

Instead of an ascending order of importance, there can be a descending order, which we can indicate at the beginning of the series by such expressions as *first and foremost*, and *first and most important(ly)*:

> Several reasons can be given for the change in the attitude of many students. *To begin with (and most important of all)*, they fear the outbreak of a nuclear war. Such a prospect had not been thought likely before. *In the second place*, they are concerned over the continuing pollution of the environment. *Moreover*, not enough progress has been made in reducing poverty or racial strife. *And to conclude*, they feel frustrated in their attempts to influence political decisions.   [14]

Most important(ly) and *most important(ly) of all* can occur either at the beginning or at the end of a series; they mark by their position whether the series is in ascending or descending order of importance.

Several other conjuncts are restricted as to the positions they can occupy in a series. It is obvious that *first(ly)*, *second(ly)*, *third(ly)*, etc mark particular positions in a series. *Next* and *then* cannot occur initially in the series, while *last, lastly*, and *finally* can only occur in final position. Reasons for what has been said in the preceding sentence or sentences may be linked by the correlatives *for one thing* ... *(and) for another (thing)*, though the first of the pair may be used alone if the intention is to offer only one reason. The infinitive clauses *to begin with* and *to start with* appear only as the first of a series, while *to conclude* marks the final sentence of a series. The prepositional phrase *for a start* is a more informal variant of *to start with*.

Note

And seems to provide a smoother transition between the last two sentences of [14].

10.20

Apart from the conjuncts, the enumeration may be expressed in ways that are more integrated within the structure of the sentence, as in the following formulaic expressions:

$\begin{cases} \text{I want to begin by saying ...} \\ \text{The first thing I want to say is ...} \end{cases}$

$\begin{cases} \text{The next point I must make is ...} \\ \text{Another thing is ...} \end{cases}$

$\begin{cases} \text{I will conclude by saying ...} \\ \text{The final point is ...} \end{cases}$

However, the introductory expression may be related more closely to the preceding lexical content. For example, in [12] *one* might be replaced by *one piece of advice is*, and *two* by *the other piece of advice is* or *the second piece of advice is*, and in [13] *secondly, and far more importantly*, by *the second reason, which is far more important, is*. We might even have a main clause that serves as a link in the enumeration:

The first point I want to make is this: ...

$\begin{cases} \text{Another thing is this: ...} \\ \text{There is still another thing: ...} \end{cases}$

I want to make one$\begin{cases} \text{more} \\ \text{final} \end{cases}$point: ...

The final thing I want to say is this: ...

What follows these main clauses can be regarded as appositive to a complement or direct object in the clauses.

Noun phrases can be used for enumeration as well as the fuller forms:

the first thing
the next point
another thing
one piece of advice
the second reason

Addition
10.21

The relationship of addition comprises both reinforcement (which includes confirmation) and equation, where there is an indication of the similarity with what has preceded. Since it is sometimes difficult to distinguish between the two types of addition, we treat them together.

The addition relationship is often conveyed by the two subclasses of additive conjuncts, reinforcing and equative conjuncts (8.89):

This food is very good and it's probably something that people
wouldn't get at home. *Also*, it's not difficult to cook and it's
quick to prepare.

There has been a sharp decline in the death rate for babies. And
then, medical science is keeping people alive longer.

People do not think they need to take precautions, but always
consider the other driver to be the cause of road accidents.
Moreover, the wearing of safety belts is thought to be a sign of
fear.

The public can see the paintings the whole of next week. *What is
more*, they can buy them for as little as ten dollars upwards.

There has been no progress in the negotiations between the union
and the employers. The union is determined to get a better offer.
Equally, the employers have absolutely no intention of increasing
their final offer.

Again, *also*, and *then* have less force than the other reinforcing conjuncts
in conveying an incremental effect.

10.22

Additive adjuncts (8.13) specify that part of the sentence is an addition
to what has been previously mentioned or implied:

He asked the Governor for troops but was refused. He then
approached the Justice Department, but there *again*, he found
no support.   [15]

The children read the play. They acted it *too*.   [16]

The Mayor was unaware of the contents of the pamphlet. The
police were *equally* unaware of what appeared in it.   [17]

They owned a large mansion in the country with a lake in the
grounds. They had a farm *besides*.   [18]

He didn't explain what the letter signified. She didn't explain it
either.   [19]

He didn't explain what the letter signified.$\left\{{Neither \atop Nor}\right\}$did she.   [20]

In [15] *again* specifies that in the case of the Justice Department (*there*)
as well as in the previously-mentioned case of the Governor he found no
support. Whereas in [15] the additive is focused on the adjunct *there*, in
[16] it is focused on the verb: *too* indicates the acting was in addition to
the previously-mentioned reading of the play. Similarly, in [17] the focus
is on the subject complement, and in the remaining examples it is on the
direct object [18], and on the subject [19] and [20].

Either, *neither*, and *nor* differ from the others in requiring the two sentences they link to be negative (but *cf* 9.55 Note), and when *neither* or *nor* is used, no other negative appears. In this respect they are the converse of *too*, which generally requires both to be positive. Thus if we negate the sentences in [16] *either*, *neither*, and *nor* are admissible (as are other additive adjuncts, such as *also*), but not *too*:

A: The children didn't read the play.   B: *They didn't act it *too*.
A: The children didn't read the play.   B: They *also* didn't act it.
A: The children didn't read the play.   B: They didn't act it *either*.

A: The children didn't read the play.   B: $\begin{Bmatrix} Neither \\ Nor \end{Bmatrix}$ did they act it.

However, for some people *too* is acceptable in a negative clause when it immediately follows an initial sentence element on which it is focused:

A: The children didn't read the play.
B: Their parents *too* didn't read it.

This has the same interpretation as

A: The children didn't read the play.
B: Their parents didn't read it *either*.

A common correlative set containing an additive adjunct is *not only* . . . (*but*) *also*, usually with subject-operator inversion (*cf* 9.59):

Not only was the Mayor unaware of the pamphlet. The police were *also* unaware of it.

Note

A sentence with the additive adjuncts *either*, *neither*, *nor* can be linked to a preceding sentence by *and* or *but*. For *either* and *neither* as the first of a pair of correlatives with *or* and *nor* respectively, see 9.56.

10.23

Certain attitudinal disjuncts (8.82) express conviction on the truth of what is being said and at the same time may confirm the truth of a previous assertion. Perhaps the most common is *indeed* which can often be paraphrased 'I might go so far as to say':

He did not object to our proposal. *InDĚED*, he gave several reasons for supPÔRting it.

Other attitudinal disjuncts that may be used in the same way are *actually*, *in fact*, and *in actual fact*.

They are not invariably used to confirm what has already been said. They are often used to contradict:

A: You must have spoken to him today.   B: *Actually*, I haven't.

10.24
Transition

And and *now* are both transitional, but whereas *and* seems to link, *now* leads to a new stage in the sequence of thought:

> We have settled that at last. *Now*, what was the other thing we
> wanted to discuss?

The complex preposition *as for* introduces a topic related to what was being discussed:

> Mary has several close friends. *As for* John, he is always surrounded
> by friends.

Certain other complex prepositions may mark a transition, but they can also begin discussion: *with reference to, with respect to, with regard to.* These are commonly used in official language, for instance at the beginning of official letters immediately after the conventional vocative to the reader. For other ways of introducing the topic of the sentence, see 9.150.

Incidentally adds explicitly that what is being said is a digression, if only slight, and an afterthought:

> The airlines charge half-price for students. *Incidentally*, I have
> already bought my ticket to New York.

With *by the way*, the digression is usually drastic.

Certain clauses are commonly used for marking a transition to a new stage:

> Let us now turn to . . . (formal)
> To turn now to . . .
> I want now to turn to another subject.

or to introduce a digression:

> Talking ⎫
> Speaking ⎬ of . . . (informal)
> Apropos (of) . . . (formal)
> That reminds me . . .

Note

[a] In BrE some use *as to* synonymously with *as for*.

[b] *By the by* (also spelled *by the bye*) is a synonym of *by the way*, but is used more rarely.

10.25
Summation

The final part of a unit may consist of a generalization or summing-up based on what preceded. Summative conjuncts (8.89) are specialized for indicating this:

> The techniques discussed are valuable. Sensible stress is laid upon preparatory and follow-up work. Each chapter is supported by a well-selected bibliography. *In all*, this is an interesting and clearly-written textbook that should prove extremely useful to geography teachers.
>
> His plan for a British literary jury, fifty strong, sitting six times annually to choose the Serious Minority Writer of the Year and other dignitaries seems to be bearing rapid fruit. Already about thirty-five eminent people have expressed interest. Both BBC and commercial television have made encouraging noises about televising sessions. *In sum*, against every expectation, the literary show is about to be launched.

The style disjuncts *in a word, briefly, in brief, to be brief,* and *in short* may also be used to mark a summation.

The indication of summation may be integrated within the structure of the sentence constituting the summation or within the first sentence of the concluding unit:

> My conclusion is . . .
> I will sum up by saying . . .
> I shall conclude by saying . . .

Note
The summation may cover more than one sentence. In a long written piece the concluding paragraph is often a summation of the rest of the text.

10.26
Apposition

Indicators of an apposition are discussed in detail elsewhere (9.138). They can be used to refer back to previous sentences:

> He is a scholar who is devoted to his research to a reprehensible extent. *That is to say*, he neglects his family and does not fulfil his responsibilities as a citizen.
>
> It is important that young children should see things and not merely read about them. *For example*, it is a valuable educational experience to take them on a trip to a farm.

The relationships between sentences that can be subsumed under apposition are principally reformulation, exemplification, and particularization.

Integrated indications of certain types of apposition include:

Another way of putting it is . . .
Another instance is . . .
An example would be . . .

See also 10.30.

10.27
Result

We have several result conjuncts (8.89) to introduce a sentence expressing the consequence or result of what was said before.

> They don't often use it over the weekend. *So* you can borrow it, if
> you want to.
> They argue that continued full employment in the major industrial
> countries will bring a great expansion of world trade. They
> *therefore* anticipate an increasing demand for shipping.
> They refused to pay the higher rent when an increase was
> announced. *As a result*, they were evicted from their apartment.
> The committee rejected the idea that consumers could be
> adequately protected by local consumer protection societies.
> *Accordingly*, the report recommended that legislation should be
> introduced as soon as possible to give minimum protection.
> The violent emotions aroused by the horrible crime make it
> impossible to find a local jury of people who have not made up
> their minds against the defendants. *Hence*, it is probable that the
> trial will be held in another area.

The indication that what is being said is a result may be integrated
within the structure of the sentence:

The result is . . .
The consequence was . . .

Anaphoric pro-forms may be additionally used:

The result of that is . . .
The consequence of that was . . .
For that (very) reason . . .

Note

[a] *So* is felt to be informal, while *hence* and (to a lesser extent) *thus* are more appropriate to formal contexts.

[b] Sometimes *so* seems to have lost all result force and introduces a summing-up or
even links sentences that are chronologically related, *eg: She went and asked for
some apples. So he said to her, 'Which kind do you want?'*

10.28
Inference
An inference from what is implicit in the preceding sentence or sentences can be indicated by an inferential conjunct (8.89):

> A: The economic crisis is likely to become worse in the next few
>   months.
>   B: Does it seem to you, *then*, that the Prime Minister is taking a
>   big risk in calling for an election this year?
> A: I'm afraid there isn't much I can help you with.
>   B: *In other words*, you don't want to be bothered.
> A: He says he wants to marry Susan.
>   B: *In that case*, he shouldn't be quarrelling with her all the time.

The inferential conjuncts *else* and *otherwise* are equivalent to a negative condition:

> Agriculture will have to undergo a drastic change to meet the needs
> of the new situation. *Otherwise*, the country will starve.

Otherwise in the above sentence can be interpreted as 'If agriculture does not undergo a drastic change to meet the needs of the new situation'.
Integrated markers of inference include:

$$\text{If}\begin{Bmatrix} \text{so} \\ \text{not} \end{Bmatrix}, \ldots$$

$$\text{I}\begin{Bmatrix} \text{infer} \\ \text{deduce} \end{Bmatrix}\text{from that} \ldots$$

My conclusion is . . .
You can conclude from that . . .
That implies . . .

Note
Inferences are sometimes introduced by a range of style disjuncts that express the speaker's assertion that he is being frank in what he is saying, *eg: frankly, flatly, to be candid, to put it bluntly, frankly speaking, if I may be blunt*. However, these style disjuncts are not restricted to this connective function, and can co-occur with inferential conjuncts.

10.29
Or
The relationships between sentences linked by *or* are generally the same as those between clauses linked by *or* (9.49–53). Of the following three sentences, the first involves reformulation (10.30) and the other two involve replacement (10.31):

> They are enjòying themselves. *Or* (at least) they appÈar to be
> enjoying themselves.

I might stay late at the office tonight, because I'm very much behind
with my work. *Or* I might decide to relax for a change, and go to
a concert.

Women's fashions are very much uglier than they were two years
ago. *Or* don't you notice such things?

Note

Or is probably less common as a linker of sentences than *and* or *but*.

10.30
Reformulation

A reformulation can be introduced by reformulatory conjuncts (8.89):

They are enjÒYing themselves. (Or) *Rather*, they apPÈAR to be
enjoying themselves.

You say you took the book without his permission. *In other words*,
you stole it.

This relationship is a type of apposition (9.144–147, *cf* 10.26).

Integrated markers of reformulation include:

I'll put it more simply: ...
I would rather say ...
A better way of putting it is ...
It would be better to say ...

10.31
Replacement

An alternative to what has preceded can be indicated by replacive
conjuncts (8.89):

I might do it. *Or again* I might not.

Are the Prime Minister's proposals adequate? Is the economy
strong enough to expand? *Alternatively*, are we heading for
another crisis?

You can walk home, if you wish. *Or rather*, I can give you a lift in
my car.

In order to buy the car, I may draw on my savings, though I am
reluctant to do so. *On the other hand*, I might approach my
parents for a loan.

It is possible that Britain might condone the terrorists' activity.
Worse still, she might agree to give way to their demands.

Again and *rather* in this use normally co-occur with an immediately
preceding *or*. *Rather* and *better* indicate that the proposed alternative

is preferable. *Worse,* on the other hand, indicates an unfavourable alternative.

Integrated markers of replacement include:

The alternative is ...
Another possibility would be ...
What is worse is ...
It might be better if ...

Note

[a] *Better* and *worse* are probably elliptical for *what is better* and *what is worse* respectively.

[b] *Instead* might be included here, since it could be used in place of (for example) *rather* in the cited sentence. But *instead* more strongly implies a contrast (10.33).

10.32
But

The relationships between sentences linked by *but* are the same as those between clauses linked by *but* (9.54). *But* indicates a contrast between the sentences, including in many instances the concession that the sentence it introduces is surprising in view of what is given in the previous sentence or sentences:

More than one marriage had its beginnings in the Princess Theatre; more than one courtship was extended and perpetuated there. And it would be fair to say that a number of lives were shaped, to a degree, by the figures and fashions and personalities that flashed upon the screen. *But* years have a way of doing strange things to people, times and events and now the old Princess is nothing much more than a musty, misty memory.

The fate and future of our university are considerably at stake in this election. Blake's determination to bring security and harmony to the campuses is beyond doubt; his program is forceful without being repressive. *But* he excels in his awareness that budget slashing 'makes no sense' as a reaction to campus violence; it only penalizes the whole community of earnest, committed students and teachers, and undermines the strength of a great institution.

Like other cities, Milwaukee is becoming less distinctive as the influence of television and travel homogenize us all into one bland national mixture. *But* the typical Milwaukeean still differs from the typical New Yorker or San Franciscan and Milwaukee has an air of its own.

A normal person is depressed when given cause for depression. *But* a normal person will become elated when he experiences something pleasant.

10.33
Contrast

A contrast with what has preceded can be indicated by antithetic conjuncts (8.89).

On the contrary emphasizes that the opposite is true:

> I didn't ask her to leave. *On the contrary*, I tried to persuade her to stay.
> A: He's very foolish.   B: *On the contrary*, he's very clever.

In the first of the above pairs of sentences, *on the contrary* introduces a restatement in affirmative terms of what has been said in the previous sentence, with an implicit denial of the truth of 'I asked her to leave'. (For a similar use of *but*, see 9.54.)

The other conjuncts introduce a comparison or contrast without entailing a denial of the validity of what preceded:

> He's rather foolish, I'm afraid. *By comparison*, she's a genius.
> Even the largest of whales, the Blue Whale, with a maximum length of about 100 feet and a weight of up to 130 tons, can attain 20 knots for about 10 minutes. *By way of contrast*, the common dolphin can keep up a speed of 20–22 knots for hours.
> A cut of one quarter in the total wages bill would bring only a five per cent saving in the ship's final cost. *By contrast*, the price difference between British and Japanese tankers is now as much as 25 per cent.

On the other hand often indicates contrast, especially when it is the second of a correlative pair with *on the one hand*:

> *On the one hand*, you don't want to be too aggressive. *On the other hand*, you shouldn't be too timid.

Instead involves a contrast, though it also indicates a replacement (10.31). The conjunct is illustrated in

> He doesn't study at all. *Instead*, he sits and day-dreams.

The adjunct *instead* also has a connective function, but specifies that part of the sentence is a replacement for what has been said previously:

> He wanted a fishing-rod for his birthday. His father bought him a book *instead*.

Instead here can be expanded to *instead of a fishing-rod*.

Note

On the other can be used instead of *on the other hand* when it is a correlative. *On the other hand* can also be replacive (10.31) and concessive (10.34).

Concession
10.34

Concessive conjuncts (8.89) signal the unexpected, surprising nature of what is being said in view of what was said before that:

> In 1960, 471 people were tried in this country for murder.
> *Yet* out of that total only seven were hanged.   [21]
> I didn't invite your friend Bill to the party. *Besides*, he wouldn't have come.
> What he wants will ruin the business. *Or else*, it will reduce its effectiveness considerably.
> They want to help her. *Only* [informal spoken English], she refuses to accept help.
> He has been in office for only a few months. He has, *however*, achieved more than any of his predecessors.
> Their term papers were very brief. *Still*, they were better than I expected.

Most of the concessive conjuncts can be paraphrased by a concessive subordinate clause introduced by *though* or *although*. Thus *yet* in [21] is interpreted as *though in 1960 471 people were tried in this country for murder*. *Besides, anyhow*, and *anyway* and the prepositional phrases *at any rate, in any case, in any event*, and *after all* are closer to clauses introduced by *even if* and related to the content of the previous sentence by a reversal of the positive/negative polarity. *Besides, anyhow, anyway* indicate that an addition is being made to a process of reasoning, but are at the same time concessive. With *besides* the additive implication is particularly prominent: it could be paraphrased: 'if you don't find that point convincing, here's another point'. *At any rate* may be roughly paraphrased as 'whatever happens' or 'regardless', and *after all* as 'this at least must be conceded'. The concessive conjunct *else*, which always immediately follows the conjunction *or*, is equivalent to 'even if not'.

Note

When *however* is positioned initially, it is sometimes used in the spoken language to indicate that the speaker wishes to dismiss the topic he is dealing with as one that he does not want to pursue any further:

> I think you had no right to speak to him in that way. *However*, I really wanted to let you know what I think about your recent letters to me.

10.35

Certain attitudinal disjuncts that assert the truth of their sentence (8.82) are often used to express some notion of concession in what is being asserted. They are then roughly equivalent to 'this at least is true':

> actually   to be sure

admittedly	in (actual) fact
certainly	in reality
really	of course

The style disjuncts *strictly* and *strictly speaking* are often used in the same way. Sometimes, there is some reservation about a preceding assertion:

> They played better than they had done for a long time. *Certainly* Bob played splendidly.
> They invited her to the party. *Really*, she should not have been there, since she was far too young.
> I wasn't called up by the army. *Actually*, I volunteered.

But the reservation may relate to what follows, and in such a case *but* or a concessive conjunct is often found in the following sentence:

> *Of course*, the book has some entertaining passages about the private lives of film stars. *But* on the whole it is extremely boring.
> *To be sure*, nobody suspected him of being behind the plot. *Yet* there was clear evidence implicating him.

True is used similarly:

> *True*, there are some cool insights into politicians that are currently active. *However*, much of the book is smug and prejudiced.

In contrast to the concessive conjuncts, *sure enough* introduces a confirmation of the expected:

> Bob is a dreadful bore. I was at a party last night, enjoying a good conversation and trying to avoid him noticing me. *Sure enough*, he came up to me and spent the next hour telling me about his troubles.

Integrated markers of this relationship include:

> It is true . . . (normally reservation is about a following assertion)
> There is little doubt . . .
> I admit . . .
> It cannot be denied . . .
> The truth is . . . (normally reservation is about a preceding assertion)

These markers can also be used in contexts where no reservation is intended:

> A: Did you have anything to do with the theft?
> B: Yes, I admit that I took the money.

10.36
Several attitudinal disjuncts (8.82) suggest that the content of the sentence

to which they are related may not be true in reality: *formally, nominally, officially, ostensibly, outwardly, superficially, technically, theoretically*. The following sentence, which may then indicate what is said to be the the real truth, may be marked for this purpose by *actually, really, in (actual) fact*, or *in reality*:

> OfFÍcially, he is in charge. Áctually, his secretary does all the work.
> TĔCHnically I was without a job and could have drawn unemployment benefit if I had wanted to. *In actual FÁCT* I was busy writing a book commissioned by one of the biggest publishers in the country.

Integrated markers of this relationship include:

> The official position was . . .
> The theory was . . .

There can be further internalization:

> *Officially,*
> The *official* position ⎱she was the secretary. → She was the *official*
>   was that⎰   secretary.

Note
See 8.11 for forms like *officially speaking, in a technical sense, from an official point of view*.

10.37
Even is a concessive adjunct. It implies that part of the sentence is un-expected and surprising, but it is also additive:

> *Even* John was there
> John will *even* sing a song if you ask him

The speaker implies in the first sentence that John was there in addition to others and also that it is surprising that John was there, while in the second sentence what is considered surprising is that in addition to other actions John is prepared to sing a song. In negative sentences the addition is to what has been actually or implicitly negated previously:

> The Johnson boys weren't there. *Even* John wasn't there. (*ie* 'John wasn't there in addition to the others not being there').

10.38
For
The conjunction *for* (formal and usually literary) indicates that what is said is the cause, including reason or motive, for mentioning what has been said previously:

The men's and the women's shops are indistinguishable from each
other. *For* the girls' shop windows display masculine shirts,
while the men's windows are full of scarlet mini-underpants.

The vast majority of the competitors will be well content just to
walk round at their own pace, stopping for rest or refreshment as
required, and finishing in good order. *For* it's a long day's walk by
anybody's standards, and there is much to be said for enjoying
the scenery at the same time.

Substitution
Introduction
10.39
Like ellipsis (9.4), substitution is a device for abbreviating and for
avoiding repetition. In this second respect it is similar to the use of lexical
equivalents that are not identical repetition. Across sentences, substitution seems to be optional, and for stylistic reasons. Within sentences,
it is sometimes obligatory (9.69). Most of the substitutes or PRO-FORMS
within sentences are also used across sentences. Even the reflexive pro-
forms are occasionally used across sentences:

> *John* bought a car. It was for *himself*.

10.40
Most pro-forms are anaphoric, referring back to an earlier unit. The
unit that the pro-form replaces need not be identical with the earlier
unit:

> *A large beautiful vase* fell on *Bob's* head. *It* was very heavy and
> hurt *him*. [22a]
>
> *A large beautiful vase* fell on Bob's head. *The (large beautiful)*
> *vase* was very heavy and hurt *Bob*. [22b]

One pro-form in [22a] is *it*, but the form that would occur if there were
no substitution would normally be *the vase* [22b]. The change of the
article to *the* results, of course, from the need to signal the co-reference of
the two noun phrases (10.65). With this signal, it would not be normal to
repeat the modification.

10.41
Pro-forms are normally unstressed. Hence, though a nucleus is commonly
on the last word of a clause it would not be usual to have a nucleus on

a pro-form (App II.8). The final nucleus in [22a] would normally be on *hurt*:

It was very heavy and HÙRT him.

10.42
Pro-forms will be considered according to the units they replace:

noun phrases and their constituents (10.43–48)
adverbials (10.49–51)
predicate and predication (10.52–62)
clause and sentence (10.62, *cf* 10.64)

Pro-forms for noun phrases and their constituents
10.43
The most obvious pro-forms for noun phrases are the 3rd person pronouns in their various cases (4.106 *ff*). The four plural forms of the 3rd person pronouns substitute for the appropriate forms of *John and Mary* in

John and Mary stole a toy from my son. *Their* mother told *them* to return the toy, but *they* said it was *theirs*.

And similarly we have singular forms in

Dr Solway took *the student's* blood pressure that day. *He* also examined *his* lungs and heart.   [23]
The young girl stared at him and said nothing. *She* seemed to be offended.
There are several reasons for *the movie's* success. *It*'s a spectacular visual treat, is incredibly detailed and scientifically authentic, and deals with a profound subject – the place of man in the cosmos.

It will be noticed that in [23] *he* substitutes for *Dr Solway* and *his* for *the student's*. We interpret the appropriate substitutions from the content of the sentences. For example, we can change the second sentence of [23] to transfer the substitutions:

Dr Solway took *the student's* blood pressure that day. *He* had felt sick during the night and came for *his* help as soon as the clinic opened.   [23a]

The content of the second sentence in [23a] suggests that *he* substitutes for *the student* and *his* for *Dr Solway's*. Where the reference of the pronoun is felt to be ambiguous, the full form or a lexical equivalent can, of course, be used.

10.44

The plurals of the 1st and 2nd person pronouns sometimes have as their antecedent a noun phrase and can therefore be considered in such cases as pro-forms:

> *You and John* can stop work now. *You* can both eat *your* lunch
>   in the kitchen.   [24a]
> *John and I* have finished our work. Can *we* start *our* lunch now?
>   [24b]

A somewhat different situation applies when the 'antecedent' noun phrase does not include the pronoun appearing in the next sentence:

> *Mary and John* will be at the station. *You* can then go together
>   to the party.   [24c]
> *You and John* seem to be finished. Shall *we* have lunch now? [24d]

In [24c] *you* substitutes for an implied *Mary and John and you*, and in [24d] *we* substitutes for an implied *you and John and I*.

10.45

The singulars of the 1st and 2nd person pronouns are never pro-forms for noun phrases: they do not substitute for other items but merely replace themselves.

Even the 3rd person pronouns need not be substitutes. They sometimes refer directly to objects or events in the situational context (10.9). Moreover, *you* and *they* can be indefinites and not substitutes, as in one interpretation of

> *You* can always tell what he's thinking
> *They* don't make such furniture nowadays.

10.46

There are two kinds of pro-forms realized by *one* that are relevant to sentence connection. Both can substitute only for count nouns, and not for mass nouns or proper nouns (4.2):

(1) pro-form for an indefinite noun phrase
      one – plural *some*

> A: Can you give me a few nails? I need *one*.
> B: I'll get you *some* soon.

Compare:

I need $\begin{cases} \text{a nail} \\ \text{one} \end{cases}$ I need $\begin{cases} \text{some nails} \\ \text{some} \end{cases}$

In written English *one* in the above example could be interpreted as elliptical for *one nail*, in which case *one* would be the cardinal numeral. In speech the numeral is differentiated from the pro-nominal because it would have stress.

> (2) pro-form for a noun-phrase head (4.126)
>   *one* – plural *ones*

>> A: Have you any knives? I need *a sharp ONE.*
>>> B: I can get you *several very sharp ONES,* but this is *the best ONE.*
>> A: Where are the books I left on the table?
>>> B: Do you mean *the ONES that have torn covers?*
>> A: No. *Those ONES* I wanted to throw away. I mean *the ONES covered in brown paper.*
>> A: Do you like those plates?
>>> B: No, I prefer *plain ONES* or *ONES with a very simple pattern.*

These pro-forms need not be co-referential with their antecedent (*cf* 10.48):

> A: I bought *a new hat* today.   B: I bought *one* last week.
> A: Sit in *this chair.*   B: No, I want *a more comfortable one.*

One as pro-form for a noun phrase does not take determiners or modification, while *one* as pro-form for a noun-phrase head must have an overt determiner or modifier.

Indefinite *one* (4.126) is not a pro-form:

One should always give people a chance to prove themselves.

10.47

Certain other items – all except *none* functioning as determiner (4.13 *ff*) – can be pro-forms for noun phrases (4.122, 4.127 *f*), though *none* and *neither* are a combination of pro-form and negation: *each* (*cf* 9.123), *none, either, neither, all.*

> *John and Bill* applied for a scholarship. *Each* was able to present
>   excellent references.   [25]
> *Susan, Joan, and Barbara* were invited to the party. However,
>   *none* arrived while I was there.   [26]
> *Bob, George, and Geoffrey* go to the same school as I do. *All*
>   want to be doctors.   [27]

These can be expanded by *of them* or *of* with some other appropriate prepositional complement:

... Each of the boys ...	[25]
... None of the girls ...	[26]
... All of those ...	[27]

Since more than one expanded form is available, there is no reason to posit ellipsis in those cases. It is, however, possible to analyse such cases as ellipsis where the antecedent is not a noun phrase consisting of coordinated proper names:

The boys applied for a scholarship. *Each (of the boys) ...* [25a]
Some *girls* were invited to the party. However, *none (of the girls) ...* [26a]
All *my friends* go to the same school as I do. *All ((of) my friends) ...* [27a]

When *some* and *any* are not determiners, it is usually possible to regard the construction as elliptical:

The boys applied for a scholarship. *Some (of the boys) ...* [25b]
All *my friends* go to the same school as I do. I don't know *any (of my friends)* that want to be doctors. [27b]

Some and *any* (4.127) do not usually refer back to a noun phrase with coordinated proper names. They can do so if they are postmodified by an *of* prepositional phrase:

John, Bob, and Susan were at the party last night. I don't know *any of them* well.

There are restrictions on the type of referents for the antecedents of these pro-forms:

either, neither   – two only }
each   – any number } must be countable
some, any, all, none – uncountable or more than two

With other determiners (*eg: both, half, few, enough*) it is always possible to regard the constructions as elliptical:

John and Bill applied for a scholarship. *Both (John and Bill) ...*
Many *girls* were invited to the party. However, *few ((of the) girls) ...*

Note
One might see *each* as elliptical even with coordinated noun phrases:
John and Bill applied for a scholarship. *(John and Bill) Each ...*

10.48
The same is a pro-form for a noun phrase. The phrase it substitutes for

must be identical with the antecedent, but the two phrases are usually not co-referential (*cf* 10.46):

> A: Can I have *a cup of black coffee with sugar*, please?
> B: Give me *the same*, please.

In the language of official regulations, *the same* is sometimes co-referential with its antecedent:

> The society shall keep minutes of its proceedings, which shall be available for public inspection. From time to time it shall publish *the same*.

Even so, this is more likely to occur within the same sentence.

For DO *the same*, see 10.55 Note *c*. For *the same* as a substitute for a direct object clause, see 10.62.

Pro-forms for adverbials
10.49
Some time relaters (10.11–15) can be pro-forms for time adjuncts (8.56 *ff*), principally *then* (= at that time):

> We saw John *at eight on Monday evening*. We told him *then* that we would be coming to the party.

That (= *that time*) is used as a pro-form for time adjuncts when it functions as subject and the verb is intensive:

> A: He'll arrive here *just before six*.
> B: *That* $\begin{Bmatrix} \text{should be} \\ \text{seems} \end{Bmatrix}$ early enough.

Then and some other time adjuncts can be predicative adjuncts with BE (8.73). The pro-forms *that* and *then* can be used interchangeably in a context such as

> A: I'm meeting George for a drink *this evening*.
> B: $\begin{Bmatrix} That \\ Then \end{Bmatrix}$ would be the best time to discuss the matter with him.

With *that* as subject, BE is intensive ('constitute'), and *the best time . . .* is subject complement. On the other hand, if we select *then* as predicative adjunct, BE is existential ('occur', 'take place'), and *the best time . . .* is subject. With *then* there is subject-verb inversion (14.15), so that we can change the sentence back to the more normal

> The best time to discuss the matter with him would be *then*.

10.50

Some place relaters (10.16) can be pro-forms for place adjuncts (8.45 *ff*), principally *here* (= at this place), and *there* (= at that place, to that place):

> Between London and Oxford there is *a famous inn, where the beer is better than average and the meals are excellent. Here* we stopped for lunch.
> Look *in the top drawer.* You'll probably find it *there.*
> I was in *New York* last November for business reasons. My wife and I hope to go *there* in April for a friend's wedding.

That (= that place) and *it* (= that place) are sometimes used as pro-forms when they function as subject and the verb is intensive:

I noticed *where he put it.* $\begin{Bmatrix} That \\ It \end{Bmatrix}$ seemed a good place.

Like other place adjuncts, *there* can be a predicative adjunct with BE (8.46). *There* can be used interchangeably with *that* or *it* in contexts analogous to those in which *that* and predicative adjunct *then* can be used interchangeably (10.49):

They sat *right in front of the stage.* $\begin{Bmatrix} That \\ It \\ There \end{Bmatrix}$ was where the noise was greatest.

Here and *there* can often be used interchangeably as pro-forms for a place adjunct. However, *here* denotes closeness to the speaker.

10.51

The most common pro-forms for process adjuncts (8.34 *ff*) are (*in*) *that way* and *like that:*

> *Always be frank and open to your colleagues. That way* you'll win their trust and confidence.   [28]
> She plays the piano *with great concentration and with great energy.* I'm afraid she doesn't study *like that.*   [29]

That way in [28] substitutes for 'by always being frank and open to your colleagues', and *like that* in [29] for 'with great concentration and with great energy'.

Note

In formal style, *so* and *thus* are sometimes used as pro-forms for process adjuncts:

> He had expected that his luggage would be handled with due care when it was removed from the plane. However, the porters did not handle it *so.*
> Professor Sands was checking the temperature in the cages where the rats were quartered. While he was *thus* engaged, he observed that one of the rats was behaving very oddly.

Pro-forms for predicate and predication
10.52
Pro-form *do*
DO is a pro-form for the predicate and carries the tense and person distinctions of the operator (3.17):

A: John drives a car.   B: I think BÒB *does* TÒO.   [30]
Some people like a shower after they have played tennis. PÈter
does, for example.   [31]
A: Do they buy their drinks at the local supermarket?
B: No, but WÈ *DÓ*.   [32]
Bill damaged his father's car. At least he TÒLD us that he *DÍD*.   [33]

In [30–33] DO substitutes for the predicate:

... Bob *drives a car* too.   [30a]
... Peter, for example, *likes a shower after he has played tennis*. [31a]
... we *buy our drinks at the local supermarket*.   [32a]
... he told us that he *damaged his father's car*.   [33a]

There is no ellipsis in these cases, since we cannot retain unemphatic DO and supply missing items, *eg:*

~ ... he told us that he did damage his father's car.   [33b]

DO can also substitute for the predicate excluding a time or place adjunct in the antecedent:

A: John paid for the theatre tickets tonight.
B: Yes, he *did* LÀST week TÒO.   [34]
A: Did Peter take a plane to New York today?
B: No, I don't think so. But his WÌFE *did* to ChicÃgo.   [35]

The substitutions are italicized in

... he *paid for the theatre tickets* last week too.   [34a]
... his wife *took a plane today* to Chicago.   [35a]

In replacing a predication, the DO-substitute will exclude an accompanying conjunct or disjunct (8.2 *ff*). We can contrast in this respect the adjunct *usually* with the disjunct *wisely:*

A: Bob *usually* walks to work.
B: Yes, he *does*. (=he *usually walks to work*.)
A: Bob *wisely* walks to work.
B: Yes, he *does*. (=he *walks to work*.)

The DO pro-form does not include within its substitution another auxiliary:

A: Some people *might* like a shower.   B: Perhaps Peter *does*.

In this example, *does* substitutes for *likes a shower* and not for *might like a shower*.

Note
Some speakers can exclude the object in the antecedent, including the object of a prepositional verb:

> A: Peter likes New York.   B: Yes, but he *does* London too.
> A: He spoke rudely to your sister.   B: And he *did* to me too.

However, the existence of the transitive lexical verb DO inhibits this use for many speakers, since it often allows other interpretations. For example, DO *London* can be interpreted in informal spoken English as 'make a quick tour of the important sights of London'.

10.53

Ellipsis with *do* and other operators (and auxiliaries)
Strictly speaking, DO is not a pro-form when it is anyway functioning as operator for negation, interrogation, or emphasis (3.17), since in such cases we can posit ellipsis:

> A: John drives a car.   B: *Does* Bob (drive a car)?   [30b]
> A: Some people like a shower after they have played tennis.
>
> B: Peter *doesn't* (like a shower after he has played tennis).   [31b]
> A: Bill didn't damage his father's car.
>
> B: Oh, but he *did* (damage his father's car).   [33c]

However, it is obviously convenient to treat these cases of ellipsis together with the pro-form DO.

It is similarly convenient to handle at the same time the other operators and auxiliaries, though they too can be regarded as involving ellipsis rather than substitution, even when they occur in positive unemphatic declarative sentences:

> A: John can drive a car.
>
> B: I think Bob *can* (drive a car) too.   [30c]
> A: Some people like a shower after they have played tennis.
>
> B: Perhaps Peter *would* (like a shower after he has played tennis).   [31c]
> A: Will they buy their drinks at the local supermarket?
>
> B: No, but we *will* (buy our drinks at the local supermarket). [32b]
> I was late in applying for the job. Do you think he *was* (late in applying for the job)?
> A: Was the entire building destroyed?
>
> B: Yes, it *was* (destroyed).
> I've left my car just outside the building. I think John *has* (left his car just outside the building) too.
> I have a cold. *Have* you (a cold)? [BrE].

There can also be combinations of operator and auxiliaries with such ellipsis:

> I wonder if the room has been cleaned yet. It certainly ought to
> *have been* (cleaned).
> A: Has the show started? B: It *may have* (started).
> I once thought that John Hallin might be a good man for mayor
> of this city, but I'm very disappointed with his recent irresponsible
> speeches. It's perfectly clear now that he *would not be* (a good
> man for mayor of this city).
> A: Should she have been taking that medicine?
> B: Yes, she *should* (*have* (*been* (taking that medicine))).

In Chapter 9 we discussed ellipsis in such cases in relation to coordinated clauses (9.71 *ff*). The rules of co-occurrence of auxiliaries are the same for both coordinated clauses and sentences. Ellipsis of the predication in the first clause (9.82), as in

> George will (take the course), and Bob might, take the course

does not occur across sentence boundaries.

There is ellipsis with imperative *do* and *don't*:

> A: Can I have a piece of cake?
> B: Please *do* (have a piece of cake).
> A: Shall I start the engine now?
> B: No, *don't* (start the engine now).

Note

The modal auxiliary *need* (3.21) allows ellipsis:

> A: You needn't take the course. B: *Need* he (take the course)?
> A: I'm taking the course. B: I think I *needn't*.

However, there is some restriction with transferred negation:

> A: I'm taking the course. B: I don't think I *need take the course*.

The full form in the previous example is more acceptable than ellipsis:

> A: I'm taking the course. B: ?I don't think I *need*.

Compare the fully acceptable sentence with the lexical verb *need* and ellipsis of the infinitive clause (9.81, 10.58):

> A: I'm taking the course. B: I don't think I *need to* (take the course).

10.54

Complex pro-forms

Substitution can also be effected by a combination of operator (and auxiliaries) with another pro-form, producing a complex pro-form. For DO the complex pro-form is the operator plus the other pro-form and the same is true for passive BE (3.19) and for lexical BE (and lexical HAVE in

BrE). For the modal auxiliaries (3.20–22), progressive BE (3.19, 3.39–42) and perfect HAVE (3.18, 3.37–8), DO sometimes enters into the complex pro-form too. The most common complex pro-forms are shown in *Table* 10:1, where the columns present the possibilities for various operators:

    I: DO
    II: lexical BE
    III: passive BE
    IV: WILL, representing modal auxiliaries
    V: progressive BE
    VI: MIGHT HAVE, demonstrating perfect HAVE and also the
        possibility of a combination of auxiliaries.

The patterns are exemplified by sentences with the various complex pro-forms for DO (Column I) and WILL (Column IV):

ii { A: John drives a car.   B: *So does* BÒB.
    { A: Mary will enter the competition.   B: *So will* JÒAN.

iii { A: John drives a car.   B: *So* he DÒES.
    { A: Mary will win the prize.   B: *So* she WÌLL.

iv { Bob promised to send a donation. I know GÈORGE DÍD *so*.
    { Peter is joining our group. I'm not sure whether DÀvid *will* DÓ
       so.

v { A: Do you know who broke the television set?
    {   B: I heard JÒHN *did* THÁT.
    { A: Sam is supposed to call the meeting.
    {   B: No, PÈter *will do* THÁT.

vi { My brother said he was going to send a letter of protest to the
    {   President. Ì *did it* last week.
    { They say that the Prime Minister will soon dissolve Parliament
    {   and call for new elections. Knowing him, I doubt very much
    {   if he *will* DÒ *it*.

In BrE many allow also the possibility of adding DO alone to (a) DO (not common), or (b) a modal, or (c) perfect HAVE:

(a) Bob says he is going to join the Labour Party. It will be interesting to see whether JÒHN *does do* TÓO.

(b) The Americans are reducing their defence expenditure this year. I wonder if the RÙssians *will do* TÓO.
    A: Will you be attending the meeting this evening?
    B: I MÀY DÓ.

(c) I didn't touch the television set. You can ask Bob. He was here all evening. But PÈRcy *might have* DÓNE.

Phrases with initial *so* and subject-operator inversion allow ellipsis and therefore, strictly speaking, they are not pro-forms:

A: John drives a car.   B: *So does* BÒB (drive a car).

Phrases with initial *so* without inversion are not elliptical since an expansion gives a very different sense. For example, in

A: John drives a car.   B: So he *does*.

the response expresses agreement. But for those who accept the expansion of this response:

A: John drives a car.   B: So he *does drive a car*.

this last *so* is equivalent to *so what if*. Similar reasons militate against considering tag questions as elliptical, since the tag question is not an independent question but an expression of the speaker's expectation (7.59 *f*):

John drives a car, *doesn't he?*

A less common alternative to the *so* ... DO type is the *that* ... DÒ type:

A: I'm told that John won the first prize.   B: $\left\{\begin{array}{l}So\\That\end{array}\right\}$he *DÌD*.

A: Bob promised to be here on time.   B: $\left\{\begin{array}{l}So\\That\end{array}\right\}$he *WÌLL be*.

A variant of the *that* ... DÒ type is the DO *THÁT* type:

A: He was merely a carpenter during the war. Now he owns a fortune.   B: Yes, he *does* THÂT.

These *that* ... DÒ and DO *THÁT* types require the subject to be co-referential with that of the antecedent clause. If the subjects are not co-referential, we have a stylistic variant of the DO *that* shown in Level v of *Table* 10:1 and Column v of *Table* 10:2

A: I'm told that John won the first prize.   B: No, $\left\{\begin{array}{l}\text{BÒB } did\ THÁT.\\that\text{ BÒB } did.\end{array}\right.$

Like DO *that* this stylistic variant does not substitute for lexical verbs from several classes (10.55). For example, it cannot substitute for a relational verb such as *own*:

*A: Tom owns a farm.   B: No, that BÒB *does*.

A less common alternative for DO *it* is DO *this*:

Table 10:1
COMPLEX PRO-FORMS

	I	II	III	IV	V	VI
	DO	BE (lexical)	BE (passive)	WILL (modal)	BE (progressive)	MIGHT HAVE (modal + perfect)
i	DO	BE	BE	WILL	BE	MIGHT HAVE
ii	SO DO	SO BE	SO BE	SO WILL	SO BE	SO MIGHT HAVE
iii	SO … DO	SO … BE	SO … BE	SO … WILL	SO … BE	SO … MIGHT HAVE
iv	DO SO	BE SO	BE SO	WILL do so	BE doing so	MIGHT have done so
v	DO that	BE that	BE that	WILL do that	BE doing that	MIGHT have done that
vi	DO it			WILL do it	BE doing it	MIGHT have done it

They said that the Prime Minister will soon dissolve Parliament and call for new elections. Knowing him, I doubt very much if he will $DO\begin{cases} it. \\ this. \end{cases}$

Note

[a] BE *so* and BE *that* in Column II are not used by some speakers:

A: I consider Peter to be very clever.   B: He certainly $ls\begin{cases} so. \\ that. \end{cases}$

[b] The additional *do* is avoided in BrE DO *do* for stylistic reasons:

Bob says he is going to join the Labour Party. *It will be interesting to see whether John and PÈter *do do* TÒO.

[c] Lexical HAVE admits the two pro-form phrases *so* HAVE and *so* . . . HAVE in addition to HAVE alone:

A: John has a cold.   B: $\begin{cases} \text{Yes, and ì } have \text{ TÒO.} \\ \text{Yes, and } so \ have \text{ ì.} \\ \text{Yes, } so \text{ he } HÀS. \end{cases}$

This use of HAVE as operator is much more common in BrE than in AmE, where it is formal as well as restricted in use (*cf* 3.18 Note). The pro-forms DO, *so* DO, and *so* . . . DO are also used in BrE, but are more common in AmE:

A: John has a cold.   B: $\begin{cases} \text{Yes, and ì } do \text{ TÒO.} \\ \text{Yes, and } so \ do \text{ ì.} \\ \text{Yes, } so \text{ he } DÒES. \end{cases}$

10.55
Pro-forms in relation to verb classes

Not all lexical verbs allow the full range of substitutions displayed in *Table* 10:1. We earlier established seven verb classes (3.41). *Table* 10:2 shows the substitution possibilities for these seven classes. They are shown in relation to DO, WILL (representing modal auxiliaries), and MIGHT HAVE (demonstrating a combination of auxiliary and perfect HAVE), *cf Table* 10:1. The possibilities for lexical BE are given in Column II of *Table* 10:1. The possible pro-forms of passive BE (Column III of *Table* 10:1) are used for all verbs, and those of progressive BE are restricted to verbs or uses of verbs that admit progressive aspect (3.40–41).

From *Table* 10:2 we see that the groupings by substitution possibilities do not wholly coincide with the distinction between stative and dynamic verbs. The division of the entry in Column iv for verbs of inert perception and cognition reflects the fact that for some speakers attitudinal verbs do not allow these substitutions.

?*A: Peter likes work.   B: I think BÒB *does so* TÒO.

?*A: She will hate the way he goes on about his prizes.

   B: PÈter *will do so* TÒO.

?*A: David might have wanted his food now.

   B: MÀRY *might have done so* TÒO.

Table 10:2

PRO-FORMS IN RELATION TO VERB CLASSES

		i DO WILL MIGHT HAVE	ii SO DO SO WILL SO MIGHT HAVE	iii SO … DO SO … WILL SO … MIGHT HAVE	iv DO SO WILL DO SO MIGHT HAVE DONE SO	v DO THAT WILL DO THAT MIGHT HAVE DONE THAT	vi DO IT WILL DO IT MIGHT HAVE DONE IT
DYNAMIC VERBS	*activity verbs*	✓	✓	✓	✓	✓	✓
	momentary verbs	✓	✓	✓	✓	✓	✓
	transitional event verbs	✓	✓	✓	✓	✓	
	process verbs	✓	✓	✓	✓	✓	
	verbs of bodily sensation	✓	✓	✓	✓		
STATIVE VERBS	*verbs of inert perception and cognition*		✓		✓ / ?		
	relational verbs		✓				

Other verbs in this class seem to allow the substitutions without difficulty in British English, but they are odd to varying degrees in American English:

A: They think he is mad.　B: WÈ *do so* TÒO.
A: I can smell perfume.　B: Ì *can do so* TÒO.
A: Bob might have heard the strange noises.
　B: He *might* WÈLL *have done so*.

Below, one example is given for each of the seven classes of verbs with their DO pro-forms, and similar examples could have been given for the analogues of the DO pro-forms, *ie* pro-forms with operators other than DO. Expansions of DO are given in parentheses when they follow DO. Since we have already mentioned the subdivision within verbs of inert perception and cognition, the class is represented by a verb that also allows the DO *so* phrase.

ACTIVITY VERB
　A: John *abandoned* his car during the last snowstorm we had.

B:
I wonder WHÝ he *did* ($\left\{\begin{matrix} so \\ that \\ it \end{matrix}\right\}$).
Yes, and *so did* Ì.
Yes, *so* he DÌD.

MOMENTARY VERB
　A: Bob *kicked* the door several times.

B:
He ÀLways *does* ($\left\{\begin{matrix} so \\ that \\ it \end{matrix}\right\}$) when he wants to attract attention.
Yes, and *so did* PÈter.
Yes, *so* he DÌD.

TRANSITIONAL EVENT VERB
　A: The old man *fell* on his way to church.

B:
I'm sorry to hear that he DÌD ($\left\{\begin{matrix} so \\ that \end{matrix}\right\}$).
Yes, and *so did* his WÌFE.
Yes, *so* he DÌD.

PROCESS VERB
　A: That Ford *slowed down* as we passed.

B:
It's very ÒDD that it *did* ($\left\{\begin{matrix} so \\ that \end{matrix}\right\}$).
Yes, and *so did* the car that FÒLLOwed.
Yes, *so* it DÌD.

VERB OF BODILY SENSATION

A: John *feels* much better.

B: $\begin{cases} \text{I KNÒW he } \textit{does.} \\ \text{Yes, and } \textit{so do } \grave{\textrm{i}}. \\ \text{Yes, } \textit{so} \text{ he } \textsc{dòes}. \end{cases}$

VERB OF INERT PERCEPTION AND COGNITION

A: They *think* he is mad.

B: $\begin{cases} \text{WÈ } \textit{do (so)} \text{ too.} \\ \text{Yes, and } \textit{so do } \grave{\textrm{i}}. \\ \text{Yes, } \textit{so} \text{ they } \textsc{dò}. \end{cases}$

RELATIONAL VERB

A: He *owns* a Cadillac.

B: $\begin{cases} \text{Yes, he } \textsc{dòes} \text{ (so), because the firm bought it for him.} \\ \text{Yes, and } \textit{so does} \text{ his } \textsc{bròther}. \\ \text{Yes, } \textit{so} \text{ he } \textsc{dòes}. \end{cases}$

Note

[a] It is curious that if the action is involuntary and the reason for the action is asked, DO *it* pro-forms are excluded even for a momentary verb such as *kick* that normally allows them:

A: When you chop off a chicken's head and it's already dead, it still *kicks* a few times.

B: Why does it $\left(do \begin{Bmatrix} so \\ that \\ *it \end{Bmatrix} \right)$?

But the DO *it* pro-forms are acceptable in contexts where the reason is not asked:

A: When you chop off a chicken's head and it's already dead, it still *kicks* a few times.

B: I wonder how it *does it*.

The DO *it* pro-forms appear to require that there be volition in the action. In the last example, speaker B talks as if the chicken were still alive and had control over its movements.

[b] For some people, DO *so* pro-forms are unacceptable with relational verbs:

*A: He owned a Cadillac.

B: If he *hadn't done so*, we would not have asked him for a lift.

[c] DO *the same*, DO *similarly*, DO *likewise*, DO *the identical thing*, are alternatives to DO *that* when a comparison is involved, but the subject of the clause is normally not co-referential with that of the antecedent clause:

A: The old man fell on his way to church.

B: $\begin{cases} \text{*I'm sorry to hear that } \textit{he did the same.} \\ \text{I'm sorry to hear that } \textit{his wife did the same.} \end{cases}$

The exception is when the predicate contains more than DO *the same*:

A: The old man fell on his way to church.

B: Yes, and I'm afraid *he did the same* last Sunday.

10.56
Co-referentiality of subjects

The *so* DO type – *so* DO and its analogues (*eg: so* WILL, *so* HAVE) – is used only if the subject of the clause is *not* co-referential with that of the antecedent clause:

A: *John* buys his drinks at the local supermarket.
B: *So do* WÈ.

Hence, *he* cannot be co-referential with *John* in

A: *John* buys his drinks at the local supermarket.
B: *So does* HÈ.

On the other hand, the *so* . . . DO type is used regardless of whether the subjects of the clauses are co-referential or not, though it is more common for them to be co-referential:

A: *John* buys his drinks at the local supermarket.

B: {
So he DOÈS.
So lots of òther people DÓ, I imagine.
So even BÒB DÓES.
}

The other substitution types are used whether or not the subject is co-referential with that of the antecedent clause.

Note
In clause connection, *so* . . . DO may be said by the same speaker when he is reporting what has been said or thought:

I said she would hit him, and *so she* DÌD

In some contexts, *so* may be ambiguous between the pro-form *so* and the result conjunct *so* (= therefore). For the latter, see 8.89, 10.27.

10.57
Operator for negation, interrogation, and emphasis

In Types i, ii, and iii on *Tables* 10:1 and 10:2 – DO, *so* DO, *so* . . . DO and their analogues, *eg:* WILL, *so* WILL, *so* . . . WILL – an operator is present which can be used in negation, interrogation, and emphasis (though in fact there are restrictions on the use of the *so* DO and *so* . . . DO types in negation and they are excluded from questions, *cf* 10.59 *f*):

A: John can drive a car.   B: But *can* BÓB (drive a car)?
A: Some people like a shower after they have played tennis.
   B: PÈter DÓESn't (like a shower after he has played tennis).
A: David wasn't given a prize.   B: Oh, but he WÀS (given a prize).
A: John can drive a car.
   B: Yes, but *so can* many other boys of his age.
A: David wasn't given a prize.   B: *So* he *wasn't*. What a shame!

Similarly, with the complex DO *so*, DO *that*, and DO *it* types, an operator is present when the first member is a modal auxiliary, progressive BE, or perfect HAVE:

A: John can drive a car.   B: Yes, but *can* BÓB *do so?*
A: Mary is paying for her own ticket.
  B: Yes, but JOÀN *isn't doing* THÁT.
A: Arnold won't make a mess.   B: Oh, but he *HÀS done so* alRÈAdy.

On the other hand, the DO *so*, DO *that*, and DO *it* pro-forms with DO as first member (iv–vi in Column I on *Table* 10:1) require an additional DO as operator:

A: John swims a lot.   B: *Does* BÓB *do that?*
A: Do they buy their drinks at the local supermarket?
  B: Yes, but WÈ *don't* DÓ *so.*
A: Bill didn't damage his father's car.   B: Oh, but he DÌD *do it.*

10.58
Exclusion of pro-form types from certain clauses

The modal auxiliaries cannot occur in non-finite clauses (3.15) and hence they cannot function as pro-forms in such constructions. Likewise, the pro-form DO cannot function in non-finite clauses. While we have the pro-form DO in the finite clause:

A: Peter hunts rabbits.   B: Yes, I have noticed that he *does.*

we cannot have it in the non-finite clauses:

A: Peter hunts rabbits.   B: { *Yes, I have noticed him *doing.*
*Yes, I have watched him *do.*
*I know. He wanted me *to do* too. }

We must instead use one of the pro-forms DO *so*, DO *that*, and DO *it*, insofar as all or some of them are allowed by the particular verbs:

A: Peter hunts rabbits.   B: { Yes, I have noticed him *doing so.*
Yes, I have watched him *do that.*
I know. He wanted me *to do it*, too. }

The *so* DO and *so* . . . DO pro-forms occasionally occur in non-finite clauses, but this use would be considered odd by some people:

Newspapers should not include editorial comment in their news columns. { *To so do* / *So to do* } is to betray the confidence of their readers.

To so do would be avoided by some for another reason: the prescriptive objection to the splitting of the infinitive (more effective in BrE than in AmE).

The *so . . .* DO type normally cannot function in a dependent clause:

A: Martin knows French.   B: *I was told that *so he does*.

Contrast:

A: Martin knows French.   B: {I was told that he *does so*.
I was told that *so does* Bill.

However, if the antecedent subject is not co-referential with the subject of the *so . . .* DO clause (*cf* 10.56), the use of *so . . .* DO is possible for some people though very unusual:

A: John buys his drinks at the local supermarket.
B: I was told that *so everybody does*.

Neither the *so . . .* DO nor the *so* DO type can function in an imperative clause:

A: It's time to wash the dishes.   B: {*So (you) do*.
So do (you).
(You) *Do so*.

An alternative to the pro-forms with the *to*-infinitive clause is ellipsis of the infinitive clause, *to* alone being retained (9.81):

A: Peter hunts rabbits.   B: I know. He wanted me *to*, also.

For *so* in *He told me so*, see 10.62.

10.59
Negative clauses
The *so* DO and *so . . .* DO types are sometimes used in a negative clause:

A: Bob can't drive a car.
B: *So can't a lot of other people*, but that doesn't stop them from trying.
A: Mary won't talk to you.
B: I know. *So won't the other girls*, but it's really my own fault.
A: Peter doesn't hunt rabbits.   B: *So he doesn't*. What a pity!
A: Your other daughter isn't here.   B: *So she isn't*. That's surprising.

However, there are restrictions on their use in negative clauses, though the extent of these restrictions is not clear. For example the *so . . .* DO type seems unacceptable if the subject of the clause is a proper name:

A: Bob can't drive a car.   B: *So can't John*.

The other pro-form types are more common in negative clauses. If the second sentence indicates an addition to what has been negated previously, *either* is commonly appended (*cf* 8.17, 10.22):

A: Peter doesn't hunt rabbits. B: No, {
he DÒEsn't.
PÀUL *doesn't* Èither.
PÀUL *doesn't do so* Èither.
PÀUL *doesn't do that* Èither.
PÀUL *doesn't do it* Èither.
}

A: Bob can't drive a car. B: No, {
he CÀN't.
JÒHN *can't* Èither.
JÒHN *can't do so* Èither.
JÒHN *can't do that* Èither.
JÒHN *can't do it* Èither.
}

Nor or *neither* can be used instead of *either*, with obligatory subject-operator inversion (*cf* 9.55):

A: Peter doesn't hunt rabbits. B: No, {nor / neither} {
does PÀUL.
does PÀUL *do so.*
does PÀUL *do that.*
does PÀUL *do it.*
}

A: Bob can't drive a car. B: No, {nor / neither} {
can JÒHN.
can JÒHN *do so.*
can JÒHN *do that.*
can JÒHN *do it.*
}

The DO-phrases with DO as first member require the addition of the operator DO (*cf* 10.57).

10.60
Questions

The *so* DO and *so . . .* DO types cannot be used in questions. All other types occur in questions. As in negation (10.57, 10.59), the DO *so*, DO *that*, and DO *it* types with DO as first member require the operator DO:

A: Does Mary sing folk songs? B: {Yes, / No,} {
does JÓAN?
does JÓAN *do so?*
does JÓAN *do that?*
does JÓAN *do it?*
}

A: Will Susan play the piano? B: {Yes, / No,} {
will ÁNN?
will ÁNN *do so?*
will ÁNN *do that?*
will ÁNN *do it?*
}

Note

The *so* DO type freely co-occurs with tag questions, but the co-occurrence of *so* . . . DO type and tag question seems odd:

> A: Peter collects stamps.   B: And *so does* Paul, doesn't he?
> A: Mary can sing well.   B: ?*So* she *can*, can't she?

10.61
Not as negative pro-form for predicate

Not can be a negative pro-form for the predicate (9.80):

> A: John is a coward.   B: Yes, but *not* BÒB.
> A: David owns a Cadillac.   B: Yes, but *not* JÒE.
> A: Bill might have taken the book.   B: Yes, but *not* TÒM.

It substitutes for the equivalent of the whole of the predicate of the antecedent, but there may be changes, *eg* in person and number of verb and number of noun:

> A: John is a coward.
> B: Yes, {but *not* Bob and JÒE. (=Bob and Joe *are* not *cowards*)
>   {but *not* MÈ. (=I *am* not a coward)
> A: Bob will take it for you.
> B: No, *not* HÌM. (=He will not take it for *me*)

In very formal speech the subjective case of the pronoun would be used instead of the objective case if the pronoun is the subject in the clause that is being replaced:

> A: John is a coward.   B: Yes, but not I. (=I am not a coward)

Not can also be a pro-form for the subject and part of the predicate, including the verb phrase:

> A: Susan invited everybody to her party.
> B: Perhaps, but *not* me. (=Susan did not invite me to her party)
> A: John wanted to pay for the tickets.
> B: True, but *not* for the dinner. (=but John did not want to pay for the dinner)

Not in *why not* and *if not* is a negative pro-form for the equivalent of the whole of the antecedent clause, again with changes sometimes when there is a change of speaker. *So* is the pro-form for the equivalent of the whole clause in the case of *if so*, and (less commonly) *why so*:

> The best way of resolving the dispute seems to be by calling in arbitrators. *If so*, let's agree now on a panel of arbitrators.
> A: I don't want to go in.
> B: Why *not*? (=Why don't you want to go in?)

Note
Instead of treating *not* as a pro-form, we could analyse these instances as ellipsis with an obligatory shift of *not* when the subject is present:

A: John is a coward.
    B: Yes, but *not* Bob. (= but Bob is *not* a coward)

There would also need to be a case change in some instances:

A: Bob will take it for you.
    B: No, *not him*. (= *he* will *not* take it for you)

Such an analysis extends the concept of ellipsis beyond its normal use in this book (*cf* 9.2 *f*).

10.62
Pro-forms for direct object clause
So is used as a pro-form for a direct object clause:

> Oxford is likely to win the next boat race. All my friends say *so*.
> (= that Oxford is likely to win the next boat race)
> John hasn't found a job yet. He told me *so* yesterday. (= that he hasn't found a job yet)

Not can often serve as the negative of *so* in this use:

> Many people believe that there will be another world war before the end of the century. My father thinks *so*, but I believe *not*.
> (My father thinks *that there will be another* . . ., but I believe *that there will not be another* . . .)

This use of *not* is restricted mainly to verbs of belief or assumption (*cf* 11.79), while this use of *so* extends also to some verbs of speaking. Verbs that commonly allow both *so* and *not* as pro-forms for the direct object clause include:

appear	guess	seem
assume	hope	suppose
believe	imagine	think
expect	presume	understand
fancy		

The pro-form *not* is occasionally used with the verbs *claim, say, state*, and *tell*, but the use of the pro-form *so* with these verbs is much more frequent.

Not all verbs of saying allow even *so*. For example, we cannot say
He asked so.

So in this use can take initial position:

> *So* all my friends say

though subject-verb inversion is possible with verbs of saying and is common with the verb *say* itself (14.15):

> *So say* all my friends

The same can also be used as a pro-form for a direct object clause with a similar range of verbs to those that allow *so:*

> A: (I say) Oxford is likely to win the next boat race.
> B: I say *the same.* (= that Oxford is likely to win the next boat race)

But it seems that *the same* requires that the subjects of the verb of speaking or of belief be different in the two sentences, whether this difference is explicit (for example, by retaining the parenthesized *I say* in the first sentence above) or implicit (by omitting the parenthesized *I say*).

That and *it* are used as pro-forms for direct object clauses in direct or indirect speech when the reference is primarily to the actual words used:

> A: $\begin{cases}\text{Who said 'Shakespeare'?}\\\text{Who said that I was crazy?}\end{cases}$. B: I said $\begin{cases}\textit{that.}\\\textit{it.}\end{cases}$

Note

There is no negative pro-form that includes direct statements. *Not* in

> A: Who said 'Shakespeare'? B: *Not me.*

is a pro-form for the predicate (= I did not say 'Shakespeare').

Discourse reference
10.63

There are a number of signals marking the identity between what is being said and what has been said before. Some of these might well have been handled under substitution processes. They have been brought together here because they seem to have in common a 'deictic' reference, that is to say, they seem to be pointing back (ANAPHORIC) or forward (CATAPHORIC) in discourse. The signals can be divided into two groups, distinguished by the type of unit they refer to:

(1) sentence or clause reference signals
(2) noun phrase reference signals

Many of them are adapted from their primary function of denoting temporal or spatial succession, *eg: former, above, here, the following.* Some signal both sentence/clause reference and noun phrase reference.

10.64

Sentence/clause reference

Common signals for sentence or clause reference:

anaphoric and cataphoric: *here*, *it*, *this*

anaphoric only: *that*, *the foregoing* (formal)

cataphoric only: *as follows*, *the following*, *thus*

ANAPHORIC EXAMPLES

Many years ago their wives quarrelled over some trivial matter,
now long forgotten. But one word led to another and the
quarrel developed into a permanent rupture between them.
That's why the two men never visit each other's houses.   [36]

Many students never improve. They get no advice and therefore
they keep repeating the same mistakes. *It*'s a terrible
shame.   [37]

Students want to be shown connections between facts instead
of spending their time memorizing dates and formulas.
Reflecting *this*, the university is moving away from large
survey courses and breaking down academic fences in order
to show subjects relating to one another.

CATAPHORIC EXAMPLES

This should interest you, if you're still keen on boxing. The world
heavyweight championship is going to be held in Chicago
next June, so you should be able to watch it live.

Here is the news. A diplomat was kidnapped last night in
London . . . (radio announcement)   [38]

It never should have happened. She went out and left the baby
unattended.

My arguments are *as follows* . . .

In some instances we can replace the reference signal by a corresponding *that*-clause. For example *that* in [36] could be said to substitute for a
that-clause that corresponds to the immediately preceding clause:

. . . That the quarrel developed into a permanent rupture between
them is why . . .   [36a]

In [37], on the other hand, *it* could be said to substitute for the whole of
the two preceding sentences. With cataphoric signals, the substitution
might be inordinately long in practice. Certainly, *here* in [38] could
refer forward in discourse to an indeterminate length.

The pro-form may refer back to most, rather than all, of the sentence
or clause:

They will probably win the match. *That* will please my brother.

The more likely interpretation of *that* is *their winning the match* with the omission of auxiliary and disjunct, but *that they will probably win the match* is also a possible interpretation.

Above and *below* are used for discourse reference to refer to units of varying length, and even to illustrations:

> the arguments given *below* (perhaps referring to several sentences)
> the question mentioned *above*
> the picture *above*
> The diagrams *below* illustrate . . .

They need not refer to a unit of discourse that precedes immediately or that follows immediately. The furthest possible distance in the discourse between the unit referred to, on the one hand, and *above* or *below*, on the other hand, cannot be determined. *The above* but not **the below* can be used as a noun phrase:

> *The above* illustrates what we mean by . . .

Note

[a] The non-restrictive relative clause with a previous clause or sentence as the antecedent of introductory *which* is sometimes made into a separate orthographic sentence (*cf* 13.15). *Which* is then an anaphoric signal equivalent to *and that:*

> *She borrowed a history book. Which* suggests that her teacher was having some influence on her.

[b] In an ironic context *that* can be used cataphorically:

> I like THÀT. Bob smashes up my car and then expects me to pay for the repairs.

Otherwise, *that* is used anaphorically.

[c] In informal spoken English *what* can have cataphoric reference when it is the direct object of *know* in a question or *guess* in an imperative:

> (Do you) Know WHÁT?
>   Guess WHÀT. }He won't pay up.

[d] In written texts discourse reference can be made, of course, to page numbers, section numbers, or chapters. In some texts it is possible to refer to line numbers.

[e] In legal English *the (a)forementioned, the said,* and *the aforesaid* are used for anaphoric reference both as a premodifier ('the aforementioned provisions') and as a noun phrase. In the latter case they would normally refer to a previous noun phrase with personal reference.

Noun phrase reference
10.65

Certain determiners are used to signal that a noun phrase is referentially equivalent to a previous noun phrase (*cf* 4.13 *f*, 4.28 *ff*, 4.121):

> the
> this – these
> that – those

The noun phrases may have identical heads:

> *A student* was arrested last night for an alleged traffic offence. The police released *the student* after a brief investigation.
> He bought *a battered, old black van* in 1960. What a lot of changes have happened to *that van*.

But, as we have shown in 10.5, the noun phrases may be co-referential though the heads are not identical:

> *His wife* walked slowly by his side. *The old woman* stooped slightly.
> *The chap with a wart on his nose* is in my class. *That boy* is extremely clever.
> Students are free to select *optional courses from any field that touches on American studies. These options* are very popular.

Note

The determiners need not be anaphoric: they can refer directly to the situational context. For example, *that* and *those* in

> *That man* is Bill Jones
> *Those apples* are rotten

can point to visible objects (*cf* 4.121).

10.66

The co-reference of two noun phrases may be emphasized by use of *identical, same, selfsame* (formal), *very*, when the identity is felt to be surprising:

> He spoke to a meeting of *striking workers* that evening. *Those same workers* had previously refused to listen to his speeches.
> He wrote *a short grammar* in 1970. *That very book* was to bring him fame some years later.

10.67

The determiners listed in 10.65 and the adjectives listed in 10.66 can be used to indicate identity of type rather than co-reference:

> He bought *a Jaguar XJ6*. I ordered *that same car* the previous year.
> *Students who know several languages* are at an advantage. *Those very students* are more likely to be accepted.

Such (5.57) is used specifically to indicate identity of type:

> They regularly get *The Daily Courier*. I wouldn't read *such a paper*.

There may not be a previous noun phrase with which there is identity of type, but rather some implication of identity:

> We visited the Browns yesterday and saw the miserable conditions

under which they live. The authorities should demolish *such houses*.

There is no mention of buildings in the previous sentence, but we interpret the previous sentence as implying something like

... the house with the miserable conditions under which they live

or perhaps

... the miserable conditions under which they live in the house

Like plus *that* or *those* is also used anaphorically for identity of type, and postmodifies the noun head:

They regularly take *The Daily Courier*. I wouldn't read *a paper like that*.

Like this and *this way* are used cataphorically:

He told it $\begin{Bmatrix} like\ this \\ this\ way \end{Bmatrix}$: George was running down the road and ...

Note
Such a(n) is used in place of *such* if the head of the noun phrase is a singular countable noun, unless *such* is itself premodified (*some such, any such*).

10.68
The demonstratives (4.121) can be used as noun phrases. They can then be regarded as pro-forms for noun phrases.

I hear that you dislike his latest novel. I read *his first novel. That* was very boring, too.   [39]
He asked for *his brown raincoat*. He insisted that *this* was his usual coat during the cold winter months.   [40]

As when they are used as determiners (10.67), demonstratives can signal identity of type:

These theatres he took me to tired me out. He then made me go with him to a couple of museums. *Those* certainly don't interest me.   [41]

Normally, demonstratives replace noun phrases with a human referent only in intensive clauses with a nominal complement:

Will you try and help me find *Peter Williams? That*'s the man I was telling you about.
You can have two tickets for the middle of the tenth row in the theatre. *Those* are the best seats in the house.

In the second citation *those* is substituting in part for what is implied in the first sentence: *the seats in the middle of the tenth row in the theatre.*

Note

[a] Outside intensive clauses, *that* can be used as an expression of contempt for a human referent:

A: That's my brother.   B: You mean THÂT?

[b] It is possible to regard the demonstratives in [39] and [40] as elliptical, but this would not be true for *those* in [41] or for the two demonstratives cited in Note [a] above. In the more probable interpretation of [41], *those* would be taken as a pro-form for generic *museums* and not *couple of museums*. See also 9.103 *ff*.

10.69

Former and *latter* are used anaphorically to single out one of two previous noun phrases:

> Bob and John were at the meeting. *The former* brought his wife
> with him.

The former points back to *Bob*, the first of the noun phrases in the previous sentence. If *the latter* were used instead, the reference would be to *John*. These two terms can also be used as reference signals when they premodify:

> Bill Singer and Tom Patterson were charged with being drunk and
> disorderly. *The latter student* had two previous convictions on
> such charges.

The former and *the latter* occur mainly in the written language and in formal contexts.

Similarly, when there are more than two previous noun phrases that might be referred to, the ordinals *first*, *second*, etc, and *last* can be used anaphorically to single out one of several phrases.

Although noun-phrase reference is their characteristic function, *former* and *latter* and also the ordinals can refer back to units larger than noun phrases:

> the former reason
> the first proof
> the last suggestion

10.70

So and *that* can have anaphoric reference when they are intensifiers premodifying an adjective:

> There were two thousand people in the theatre. I didn't expect it
> to be $\left\{ \begin{matrix} so \\ that \end{matrix} \right\}$ full.

I had a terrible headache yesterday and had to take some aspirins. I'm not feeling $\left\{\begin{array}{c} so \\ that \end{array}\right\}$ bad today.

We took them to a circus and then to a zoo and gave them lots of ice-cream and chocolate. They haven't had $\left\{\begin{array}{c} so \\ that \end{array}\right\}$ good a time for years.

Such is used more commonly than *so* or *that* when the adjective is in a noun phrase (*cf* 10.67), but then with the word order:

> ... They haven't had *such a good time* for years

This is used as an intensifier, but with reference to what is present to the speaker. *So* and *that* can be used in the same way:

> I didn't expect it to be $\left\{\begin{array}{c} this \\ so \\ that \end{array}\right\}$ full. (= as full as this)

Comparison
10.71
We bring together signals of similarity and difference. In fact, there is not a sharp distinction between signals of similarity and reference signals indicating identity of type (10.67–68). Most signals of similarity and difference can be regarded as involving ellipsis.

10.72
The most obvious comparison signal is found in adjectives and adverbs, whether in the inflected forms or in the periphrastic forms with *more, most, as, less, least* (5.68). If the basis of comparison (5.69) is not made explicit in the clause, it can often be inferred from the previous context:

> John took four hours to reach London. Bill, on the other hand,
>   was driving *more slowly*.   [42]
> Mary used to listen to records most of the time. Sally was a
>   *more enthusiastic* student.   [43]
> There were ten boys in the class. Bob was by far the *best*.   [44]
> Barbara dances beautifully. Joan dances *no less* well.   [45]
> Peter always hands in a well-constructed and intelligent paper.
>   I'm afraid John doesn't expend *as* much effort and time on his
>   papers.   [46]

We can demonstrate the anaphoric reference by supplying the basis of comparison:

... more slowly *than John* (*drove*)   [42a]
... a more enthusiastic student *than Mary* (*was*)   [43a]
... the best (*of the ten boys*) (*in the class*)   [44a]
... no less well *than Barbara* (*dances*)   [45a]
... as much effort and time on his papers *as Peter* (*expends on his papers*)   [46a]

On comparative clauses, see 11.53 *ff.*

10.73

When we find expressions signalling similarity or difference, we must often look at the previous context for the basis of the similarity or difference:

John was the victim of a confidence trick. Bill was tricked *in the same way*.   [47]
Tom gets two dollars a week for pocket money. Bob receives a *similar* amount.   [48]
Mary complained that the roof leaked and the windows fitted badly, so that the place was freezing cold. Her husband complained *likewise*.   [49]
Tom behaved himself at the party. However, the *other* boy had to be sent home.   [50]
John didn't like the car. He asked to see a *different* one.   [51]

We can display the basis of similarity or difference:

... in the same way *as John* (*was* (*tricked*))   [47a]
... an amount similar *to what Tom receives*   [48a]
... complained *about the same thing as Mary* (*complained about*) [49a]
... the boy other *than Tom* ...   [50a]
... see one different *from the car he didn't like*.   [51a]

Ellipsis
10.74

Ellipsis plays an important part in sentence connection. If we find what seems to be an elliptical construction, we are usually forced to look back to what was said previously in order to interpret the sentence. We interpret the sentence by reference to what has been ellipted. And we can only know what has been ellipted on the basis of what is present in the preceding context. (For ellipsis not dependent on linguistic context, see 9.18 *ff.*)

Ellipsis in coordinated clauses is dealt with in detail in Chapter 9 (9.62 *ff*). Much of what is discussed there applies to ellipsis across sentences, with the exceptions noted in 10.53. We also found it convenient to handle earlier in this chapter (10.52 *ff*) the ellipsis of predicate and predication at the same time as the substitution of predicate and predication. Moreover, other instances of what could be considered ellipsis have been referred to in the course of this chapter, *eg* 10.16, 10.47, 10.72. Here we consider ellipsis that is more typical of sentence connection than of clause coordination.

Ellipsis in dialogue
10.75

We first look at the connection between sentences said by different speakers. A sentence said by a second speaker may have the repetition ellipted of the whole or part of what was said by the first speaker. (Strictly speaking, what is ellipted need not be an identical repetition of what was said, since a change of speaker would often introduce consequent changes.) Ellipsis may take place under three conditions, which can, of course, occur in various combinations:

(1) REPETITION: the second speaker repeats what is said by the first.
(2) EXPANSION: the second speaker adds to what is said by the first.
(3) REPLACEMENT: the second speaker replaces what is said by the first with new material.

These conditions will be considered in the light of three patterns of sentences with change of speaker:

(a) question and response (10.76).
(b) statement and question, *ie* a question stimulated by what was said by the previous speaker (10.77).
(c) statement and statement, where the second statement can relate to the first in a number of possible ways, *eg* it can be a comment or a correction or a denial (10.78).

There is usually a choice in repetition between ellipsis, substitution, and the full form. We show the choice, giving optional items in parentheses and alternatives in braces. The categorization is not intended to be exhaustive, but to give typical examples of ellipsis.

10.76

Question and response

The usual function of a question in discourse is to request the listener to respond verbally with information that the questioner seeks (7.54). Hence, question and response constitute a unit with respect to sentence connection. The link between question and response is often reinforced by the ellipsis in the response of material that can be inferred from the question. In that way repetition of material from the question is avoided and attention is focused on what is new (9.4).

(1) REPETITION

A: Did John take the medicine?

B: (Yes,) $\left\{ \begin{matrix} John \\ He \end{matrix} \right\}$ did $\left(\left\{ \begin{matrix} take \left\{ \begin{matrix} the\ medicine \\ it \end{matrix} \right\} \\ so \end{matrix} \right\} \right)$.

A: Have you spoken to the doctor?

B: (Yes,) I have $\left(\left\{ \begin{matrix} spoken\ to \left\{ \begin{matrix} the\ doctor \\ him \end{matrix} \right\} \\ done\ so \end{matrix} \right\} \right)$.

(2) EXPANSION

(a) *by an adverbial*

A: Will they lose the game?

B: *Probably* (they will (lose (the game))).

(b) *by a modifier*

A: Are you angry?   B: (Yes,) (I am) *Very* (angry).

A: Did you buy an apartment?

B: Yes, $\left\{ \begin{matrix} furnished \\ (I\ bought\ a\ furnished \left\{ \begin{matrix} apartment \\ one \end{matrix} \right\}) \end{matrix} \right\}$.

(3) REPLACEMENT

A: Did you speak to John about it?

B: No, $\left\{ \begin{matrix} to\ Peter \\ I\ spoke\ to\ Peter\ (about\ it) \\ I\ did\ (so)\ to\ Peter \end{matrix} \right\}$.

This most commonly occurs with *wh*-questions, where the Q-element (7.63 *f*) is normally replaced in the response:

A: Who told your father?   B: *Mary* $\left(\left\{ \begin{matrix} did\ (so) \\ told \left\{ \begin{matrix} my\ father \\ him \end{matrix} \right\} \end{matrix} \right\} \right)$.

A: Which suit did Peter buy?

B: $\left(\left\{ \begin{matrix} Peter \\ He \end{matrix} \right\} bought \right) The \left\{ \begin{matrix} suit \\ one \end{matrix} \right\} with\ the\ gold\ buttons.$

A: When did he lose the key?

B: $\left(\text{He} \left\{ \begin{array}{l} \text{lost} \left\{ \begin{array}{l} \text{the key} \\ \text{it} \end{array} \right\} \\ \text{did so} \end{array} \right\} \right)$ *Last night.*

A. What did you hit John for?

B: $\left(\text{I} \left\{ \begin{array}{l} \text{hit} \left\{ \begin{array}{l} \text{John} \\ \text{him} \end{array} \right\} \\ \text{did so} \end{array} \right\} \right)$ *Because he hit me first.*

---

(4) COMBINATIONS

(a) *expansion and replacement*

A: When did he lose the key?

B: *Probably* $\left(\text{he} \left\{ \begin{array}{l} \text{lost} \left\{ \begin{array}{l} \text{the key} \\ \text{it} \end{array} \right\} \\ \text{did so} \end{array} \right\} \right)$ *last night.*

(b) *expansion and repetition*

A: Will they lose the game?

B: (Yes,) *I think* $\left\{ \begin{array}{l} \text{(that)} \; \textit{they will} \left(\left\{ \begin{array}{l} \text{lose} \left(\left\{ \begin{array}{l} \text{the game} \\ \text{it} \end{array} \right\} \right) \\ \text{do so} \end{array} \right\} \right) \\ \textit{so} \end{array} \right\}.$

(c) *replacement and repetition*

A: Did you speak to John about it?
B: (No,) *I spoke to Peter* (about it).

(d) *expansion, replacement, and repetition*

A: Would you like some coffee now?
B: (No, thank you, but) *I would like some black coffee after the meal* (if I may).

Where the response is merely repetition, *yes* alone can be used as a substitute for repetition. *No* alone is a substitute for the negation of repetition. The full negative form would of course be an expansion, with the negative particle as the added item.

Neither ellipsis nor substitution need be factors in the connection between a question and the response to it.

To take an example:

A: Can I help you, madam?
B: Well, I'm looking for a pair of white gloves that will fit me,

The second speaker obviously implies that she wants the help offered in the question, but the implication springs from the sequential relationship rather than from any matching of the linguistic items in the question and answer (*cf* 10.3).

Note
Other complex pro-forms can often be used in place of DO *so* (10.54 *ff*).

10.77
Statement and question
Questions are usually stimulated by what was said before, though they may be stimulated also by the situational context.

(1) REPETITION
A question may repeat a preceding utterance, the intention of the speaker being to express polite interest or (with a wider pitch range, *cf* App II.17) incredulity or great surprise:

A: I'm very angry.   B: *ÁRE you* (very angry)?
A: I'm studying grammar.   B: *ÁRE you* (studying grammar)?

This type of question is similar to a *yes-no* echo question (7.81).

(2) EXPANSION
(a) *by a superordinate clause*
A: Peter will be there.

B: *Are you SÚRE* $\left(\left\{ \begin{array}{l} \text{of that} \\ \text{(that)} \left\{ \begin{array}{l} \text{Peter} \\ \text{he} \end{array} \right\} \text{will (be (there))} \end{array} \right\} \right)$?

A: Mary failed her driving test.
B: *Did she TÉLL you*

$\left(\left\{ \begin{array}{l} \text{(that) she} \left\{ \begin{array}{l} \text{failed} \left(\left\{ \left\{ \begin{array}{l} \text{her} \\ \text{the} \end{array} \right\} \text{(driving) test} \\ \text{it} \end{array} \right\} \right) \\ \text{did (so)} \end{array} \right\} \\ \text{that} \\ \text{so} \end{array} \right\} \right)$?

(b) *by a wh-element*

A: Peter has bought a new car.

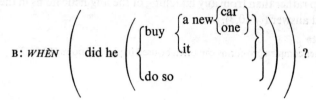

B: *WHÈN* (did he ([buy / do so] { a new {car / one} / it })) ?

A: I went to the theatre this evening.
B: *With WHÓM*

(did you [go / do so] ({to the theatre / there}) } ({this evening / then})) ?

(3) REPLACEMENT

The clearest example of replacement is the *wh*-echo question (7.81):

A: It cost me twenty-five dollars.
B: *HÓW much* (did it cost (you))?
A: I'm studying grammar.   B: *WHÁT* (are you studying)?

(4) COMBINATIONS

(a) *expansion and replacement*

A: Mary failed her driving test.
B: *Didn't she tell you that Bob passed*

({ his / {his / the} (driving) test }) ?

(b) *expansion and repetition*

A: They will lose the game.

B: *How do you know they will* ({ lose / do so } ({the game / it})) ?

(c) *replacement and repetition*

A: John told me what you did.
B: *WHÓ told you* ({what I did / that}) ?

(d) *expansion, replacement, and repetition*

   A: They paid fifty dollars for it.
   B: *Are you SÚRE (that) they didn't pay more*

$$\left(\left(\text{than}\begin{Bmatrix}\text{fifty dollars}\\\text{that}\end{Bmatrix}\right)(\text{for it})\right)?$$

10.78
Statement and statement

(1) REPETITION

   A: They've got a LÒVEly little BĂby.
   B: (Yes,) (they've got) *A ↑ LÒVEly little baby.*

(For the use of the arrow, see App II.17.)

Echo exclamations (7.84) involve repetition:

   A: He's studying Latin.
   B: (He's studying) *LÂTin!* He doesn't know his ÒWN language.

(2) EXPANSION

(a) *by a superordinate clause* (plus *wh*-element or one of the subordinators *after, before, since*)

   A: They didn't want him in their group.
   B: (Yes,) *He understood*

$$\left(\begin{Bmatrix}\text{(that) they didn't (want him (in their group))}\\\text{that}\\\text{it}\end{Bmatrix}\right).$$

   A: He won't play.
   B: *I'd like to know why* $\left(\begin{Bmatrix}\text{he won't (play)}\\\text{not}\end{Bmatrix}\right).$

   A: John was here this morning.
   B: (I know,) (but) *I've seen him since* (he was here (this morning)).

(b) *by an adverbial*

   A: They will like the show.
   B: (Yes,) $\left(\text{they will }\left(\text{like}\begin{Bmatrix}\text{the show}\\\text{it}\end{Bmatrix}\right)\right)$ *Except for the last part.*

   A: He is cleverer than you.
   B: (Yes,) *Unfortunately* $\left(\text{he is}\left(\begin{Bmatrix}\text{cleverer (than me)}\\\text{so}\end{Bmatrix}\right)\right).$

(c) *by a modifier*

A: He owns a cottage on the beach.

B: (Indeed,) (he owns) *A very* BÈA*Utiful* $\left\{\begin{array}{l}cottage\\one\end{array}\right\}$ *(on the beach).*

A: You should put it on the shelf.

B: *O.K.,* ((I'll put it) on) *the top* $\left\{\begin{array}{l}shelf\\one\end{array}\right\}$.

(3) REPLACEMENT

A: Let's have a steak for dinner.

B: *No,* (let's have) *hamburgers* (for dinner).

A: They want the key now.

B: *No,* $\left(\text{they want} \left\{\begin{array}{l}\text{the key}\\\text{it}\end{array}\right\}\right)$ *tonight.*

(4) COMBINATION

(a) *expansion and replacement*

A: He lives in New York.

B: *Well, actually* ((he lives) in) *Washington when Congress is in session.*

(b) *expansion and repetition*

A: John can play billiards.

B: (Yes,) $\left\{\begin{array}{l}John\\He\end{array}\right\} can \left(\left\{\begin{array}{l}\text{play billiards}\\\text{do so}\end{array}\right\}\right) ex$TRÈM*Ely well.*

(c) *replacement and repetition*

A: They want an increase of five pounds a month.

B: (No,) (they want) *An increase of two pounds a* WÊEK.

(d) *expansion, replacement, and repetition*

A: They paid fifty dollars for it.

B: *They certainly paid more* $\left(\left(than\left\{\begin{array}{l}\text{fifty dollars}\\\text{that}\end{array}\right\}\right)(for it)\right)$.

Note

Some *wh*-interrogative expressions are typically used as comments on a previous statement:

How come (that . . .)? $\left.\begin{array}{l}\\\end{array}\right\}$ (informal and especially AmE)
So what (if . . .)?
Why not?

Why not? includes the pro-form *not*. It can be followed by predication with *you* or *we* as implied subject:

Why not take a chance?

10.79
Ellipsis with same speaker
We have illustrated ellipsis in dialogue. But some of the examples could equally well occur in sentences spoken or written by the same person. We give now some illustrations of ellipsis in sentence connection where there is only one speaker or writer. Other examples can be found in the references given earlier (10.74). Although the references to Chapter 9 deal with ellipsis within the sentence and across coordinated clauses, what is said in that chapter generally applies to sentence coordination with the same speaker. As always, the parentheses in the citations represent the elliptled part.

> The drugs have changed very little but the climate and acceptability and hunger of a society for these kinds of products have changed radically and dramatically. Why (have the climate and acceptability and hunger of a society for these kinds of products changed radically and dramatically) now?
> A Soviet newspaper carried out an experiment the other day to see if Moscow's telephone service was as bad as most people here think it is. It was (as bad as most people here think it is).
> A call was made to the information desk of the Hotel Rossiya, the largest in Europe, located in Red Square, but the line was constantly busy. A correspondent was sent by car to the hotel to find out why (the line was constantly busy).
> 'Moratorium' was scarcely known last year. I doubt if you will find the definition (of 'Moratorium') in any of the smaller dictionaries.
> I spoke to workers at the factory. Many ((of the) workers) complained bitterly about the terrible conditions (in the factory).
> The presidential craft will comfortably carry 16 persons besides the crew. Usually aboard (the presidential craft) are the President and his family, his doctor, two Secret Service agents, and his secretary.

10.80
Structural parallelism
If two or more sentences have identical or very similar structure, this connects the sentences, the connection being further reinforced by lexical equivalences and implications of semantic relationship:

> Have you ever seen a pig fly? Have you ever seen a shark walk?
> Everybody thinks Joyce is stupid. Nobody thinks she is clever.

The parallelism between sentences is more transparent, and hence the connection between the sentences is more strongly indicated, if the word order is not the normal one (*cf* 14.11). The effect of a non-normal order in such cases is to point to a contrast between the sentences:

My paintings the visitors admired. *My sculptures* they disliked.   [52]
In New York it is hot and humid during the summer. *In Los
Angeles* it is hot and dry.   [53]
From the ceiling hung a huge lamp. *Along the wall* were pikes.   [54]

The direct objects and the place adjuncts in [52] and [53] respectively are in initial position instead of their normal final position. In [54] the non-normal position is reinforced by the verb-subject inversion.

When constituents are in non-normal position, it suggests a connection between the sentences even if there is no or little structural similarity otherwise:

Proudly, the captain hoisted the flag. *Softly*, a bugle sounded.

An apparent similarity in structure is sufficient to suggest parallelism between sentences:

My paintings the visitors admired. *My sculptures* irritated them.

Our impression of a link between the two initial noun phrases is given impetus by the non-normality of the position of the direct object *my paintings* in the first sentence and the expectation that we are encountering a similar inversion when we reach *my sculptures*, though in fact the former is direct object and the latter is subject. The impression of a link between the two initial noun phrases is reinforced by the internal structure of the two phrases and the lexical set to which both *painting* and *sculpture* belong. The two sentences are further linked by a semantic parallelism, realized syntactically in two ways: a person has a feeling towards an object, an object arouses a feeling in a person. They are also linked, of course, by the use of the pro-form *them* in the second sentence, which substitutes for *the visitors* in the first sentence.

That last example of sentence connection illustrates a combination of several devices: syntactic parallelism, semantic parallelism, lexical relationships, and substitution by a pro-form. The example serves to remind us of a point which we emphasized at the beginning of the chapter (10.2 *ff*), but which may have been obscured by our attention to devices in isolation: several devices – some of them perhaps syntactic – may be interacting to point to links between sentences.

Bibliographical Note

Some recent contributions on sentence connection in general: Crymes (1968), Harris (1963), Hasan (1968), Karlsen (1959).
   On conjuncts and disjuncts, see Greenbaum (1969a).

Coordination and subordination
11.1
The simple sentence, which we studied in Chapter 7, is a sentence which can be analysed as a single clause, in terms of subject, verb, complement, adverbial, etc. Our task now is to examine the structure of the complex sentence, or sentence containing more than one clause.

11.2
One of the two main devices for linking clauses together within the same sentence is that of coordination, already discussed in 9.39 *ff*. The second major device, that of subordination, has been carefully distinguished from coordination (9.25 *ff*), but has not yet been discussed in detail. It will be the main concern of this chapter.

While coordination is a linking together of two or more elements of equivalent status and function, subordination is a non-symmetrical relation, holding between two clauses X and Y in such a way that Y is a constituent or part of X. Diagrammatically, the difference is as in *Fig* 11:1.

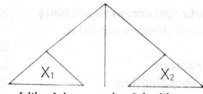

I like John   and   John likes me
COORDINATION

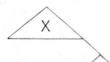

I like John because John likes me
SUBORDINATION

Fig 11:1 Coordination and subordination

A second difference is that a coordinate relationship may have more than two members, while only two clauses enter into the relationship of subordination: we may call them the subordinate clause (Y in the diagram) and the superordinate clause (X in the diagram), the former being a constituent part (subject, object, adverbial, etc) of the latter.

In this respect, one may see subordination as the 'downgrading' of a clause to the status of a subclausal unit, such as a prepositional phrase. Compare:

I like John$\left\{\begin{array}{l}\text{because}\\\text{for this reason: } viz \text{ that}\end{array}\right\}$John likes me

The device of subordination enables us to organize multiple clause structures. Each subordinate clause may itself be superordinate to one or more other clauses, so that a hierarchy of clauses, one within another, may be built up, sometimes resulting in sentences of great complexity: cf 11.80 ff.

If, as in the second example of *Fig* 11:1, there are only two clauses in the sentence and one of them is subordinate, the superordinate clause (of which the other is a constituent part) is also the main clause: cf 7.1. There can of course be more than one main clause in a sentence. If two or more independent clauses are coordinated, each of them can be made superordinate and thus 'main' in relation to other clauses.

11.3
Independent and dependent clauses
The question of degrees and kinds of sentence complexity, whether through coordination, subordination, or a combination of both, will be resumed towards the end of this chapter (11.80–85). First, however, it is as well to begin with the units of which these complex structures are composed. It is useful here to have a further terminological distinction: that between an *independent* clause, that is, a clause capable of constituting a simple sentence; and a *dependent* clause, or a clause which makes up a grammatical sentence only if subordinate to a further clause:

Grammatical: It is late. (independent)
Ungrammatical: *Because it is late. (dependent)
Grammatical: I am going home because it is late. (independent with dependent)

In other words, a dependent clause is one that is subordinate to another clause (and may in turn be superordinate to other clauses as well):

X- Y-   Z-   -Z-Y-X
(I think [that you can do it { if you try }]).

Here the clause beginning at Z- is subordinate to the clause beginning at Y-, which in turn is subordinate to the clause beginning at X-. Both Y and Z are dependent clauses, while X is the independent clause, and is identical with the sentence as a whole. An independent clause may be defined negatively as a clause which is not subordinate to any other clause. Dependent, as well as independent, clauses may be coordinated. Dependent clauses may be classified either by STRUCTURAL TYPE, *ie* in terms of the elements they themselves contain, or by FUNCTION, *ie* the structural position they have in the superordinate clause.

Finite, non-finite, and verbless clauses
11.4
Analysing by structural type, we arrive at three main classes:

> FINITE CLAUSE: a clause containing a finite verb (such as *gave, can work, has worked, is working, is seen:* 3.10)

> *eg* because John is working

> NON-FINITE CLAUSE: a clause containing a non-finite verb (such as *to work, having worked, given:* 3.10)

> *eg* (John) having seen the pictures

> VERBLESS CLAUSE: a clause containing no verbal element at all (but nevertheless capable of being analysed in terms of subject, object, complement, or adverbial)

> *eg* although always helpful

> (analysable as subordinator (see 11.9)+adverbial+complement)

We now describe these types further.

11.5
Finite and non-finite clauses
The finite clause always contains a subject as well as a predicate, except in the case of commands (7.72 *ff*) and subject ellipsis in coordinate clauses (9.65 *ff*). As nearly all independent clauses (in discursive English, though not in 'block language' – 7.90) are finite clauses, this is the type that is most clearly related to the clauses dealt with in Chapter 7. In contrast, the non-finite clause always has the ability to do without a subject, although in many kinds of non-finite clause a subject is optional. The four classes of non-finite verbal construction (3.10) serve to distinguish four classes of non-finite clause:

> [I] INFINITIVE WITH *to*
>> without subject: The best thing would be *to tell everybody*
>> with subject: The best thing would be *for you to tell everybody*

It should be noted that the infinitive clause with *to* and with a subject is found characteristically in anticipatory *it* constructions (14.36): *It would be better (for you) to tell everybody;* the use of *for* to introduce the subject should also be noted.

[II] INFINITIVE WITHOUT *to*
　　　without subject: All I did was *hit him on the head*
　　　with subject: Rather than *John do it*, I'd prefer to give the job to Mary

[III] *-ing* PARTICIPLE
　　　without subject: *Leaving the room*, he tripped over the mat
　　　with subject: *Her aunt having left the room*, I declared my passionate love for Celia

[IV] *-ed* PARTICIPLE
　　　without subject: *Covered with confusion*, I left the room
　　　with subject: We left the room and went home, *the job finished*

When the subject of participial clauses is expressed, it is often introduced by *with* (6.46):

$$\textit{With the tree} \begin{Bmatrix} \textit{growing} \\ \textit{grown} \end{Bmatrix} \textit{tall, we get more shade}$$

Category II (to a lesser extent also Category IV) is rare in comparison with the other three.

Leaving aside the fact that there is usually no subject in a non-finite clause, the normal range of clause types (7.2) is available:

It's great $\begin{cases} \text{(for a man) to be free. Type } (S)VC \\ \text{(for everybody) to be here. Type } (S)VA \\ \text{(for us all) to have arrived. Type } (S)V \end{cases}$

It's unusual $\begin{cases} \text{(for you) to be having a rest. Type } (S)VO \\ \text{(for John) to have made himself ill. Type } (S)VOC \end{cases}$

It's best $\begin{cases} \text{(for us) to get the country out of debt. Type } (S)VOA \\ \text{(for you) to buy yourself a car. Type } (S)VOO \end{cases}$

There is, however, a restriction on the *-ed* participial clause, which is both syntactically and semantically passive, and therefore admits only the four passive clause types SV_{pass}, $SV_{\text{pass}}C$, $SV_{\text{pass}}A$, and $SV_{\text{pass}}O$:

Defeated, he slunk from the room
　　Type $(S)V_{\text{pass}}$ (=active Type SVO)　　　　　　　　　　　　　　　[1]
(Once) appointed supreme commander, he took the stern
　　measures expected of him
　　Type $(S)V_{\text{pass}}C$ (=active Type $SVOC$)　　　　　　　　　　　　　[2]

During emergencies, feelings (*normally*) *kept in check* are
  apt to flourish
  Type $(S)V_{pass}A$ (=active Type $SVOA$)   [3]
The royal prisoner, *allowed unusual privileges*, seemed to
  enjoy his captivity
  Type $(S)V_{pass}O$ (=active Type $SVOO$)   [4]

11.6
Structural 'deficiencies' of non-finite clauses

The absence of the finite verb from non-finite clauses means that they
have no distinctions of person, number, or modal auxiliary. Together
with the frequent absence of a subject, this suggests their value as a means
of syntactic compression. Certain kinds of non-finite clause are particularly favoured in the studied style of written prose, where the writer has
the leisure to make a virtue out of compactness. That subject and finite-
verb form can be omitted is a hint that their meaning should be recoverable from the context. It is, indeed, often possible to postulate certain
missing forms, normally a form of the verb BE, and a pronoun subject
having the same reference as a noun or pronoun in the same sentence.
For examples [1–4] above, one might insert the following:

[*Since/when he was*] defeated   [1a]
Once [*he had been*] appointed supreme commander   [2a]
...feelings [*which are*] normally kept in check   [3a]
...[*since he was*] allowed unusual privileges   [4a]

On the other hand, [5] shows how the advantage of compactness must
be balanced against the stumbling block of ambiguity; for the absence
of a subject leaves doubt as to which nearby nominal element is *notionally* the subject:

We met you [*when you?/we? were*] leaving the room   [5]

It is not always possible to postulate a direct ellipsis of subject and finite-
verb form, but elsewhere a semantically parallel finite construction at
least enables one to identify an 'understood' subject:

I asked *to go* (*cf* I asked *if I could go*)
I asked *him to go* (*cf* I asked *him if he would go*)

When no referential link at all can be discovered with a nominal in the
linguistic context, an indefinite subject 'somebody/something' may be
supplied, or else some definite subject 'I/you/he' may be provided by
the situation:

To be an administrator is to have the worst job in the world.
  ('For someone to be . . .')

The prospects are not very good, *to be honest.*

('. . . if I am to be honest')

A non-finite clause, such as [2a], in which the subordinating conjunction is retained, will be called an *abbreviated clause.*

Note

[a] In negative non-finite clauses, the negative particle is placed immediately before the verb:

It's his fault for *not* doing anything about it

The wisest policy is (for us) *not* to interfere

From the second example, we notice that the *not* precedes the *to* as well as the infinitive, *to* being regarded, for this purpose, as part of the verb.

[b] The inseparability of *to* from the infinitive is also asserted in the widely held opinion that it is bad style to 'split the infinitive' by interposing (let us say) an adverb. For example, the 'bad English' of

He was wrong to *suddenly* leave the country

will be 'corrected' to

He was wrong *suddenly* to leave the country

or

He was wrong to leave the country *suddenly*

It must be acknowledged, however, that in some cases the 'split infinitive' is the only tolerable ordering, or at least that avoiding the 'split infinitive' is only possible at the cost of clumsiness or ambiguity. Examples for which there is no satisfactory alternative ordering to the 'split infinitive' are:

I have tried to *consciously* stop worrying about it

Part of your job, as a teacher, is to *really* understand your pupils' personal problems.

11.7
Verbless clauses

The verbless clause, apart from being verbless, is also (like the non-finite clause) commonly subjectless; it therefore takes the ellipsis of clause elements one stage further than the non-finite clause. Once again, the omitted finite verb can generally be assumed to be a form of the verb BE, and the subject, when omitted, can be treated as recoverable from context:

Whether right or wrong, he always comes off worst in argument
(whether *he is* right or wrong)

One should avoid taking a trip abroad in August *where possible*
(where *it is* possible)

Verbless clauses can also, on occasion, be treated as reductions of non-finite clauses:

Too nervous to reply, he stared at the floor
(*being* too nervous to reply . . .)

(Here the verbless clause itself contains a non-finite clause, *to reply.*)

When the subject is already there, it is the verb alone that has to be supplied:

73 people have been drowned in the area, *many of them children*
(many of them *being* children)

But, as with participle clauses (11.5), the subject is often introduced by *with:*

With the tree now tall, we get more shade

As the verbless clause is basically an elliptical intensive verb clause (Type *SVC* or *SVA*, see 7.2), the variations of its structure are somewhat limited. The following, however, are among possible combinations (*sub* = 'subordinating conjunction', see 11.9):

Suddenly the creature reared up on its hind legs behind the bars, teeth bared, *jaws wide open*, and started to scratch. S [V_{intens}] C_s
She marched briskly up the slope, *the blanket across her shoulder.*
   S [V_{intens}] A
When ripe, these apples will be delicious. *sub* [S V_{intens}] C_s
While at college, he was a prominent member of the dramatic society. *sub* [S V_{intens}] A
His gaze travelled round, *irresolute*. [S V_{intens}] C_s

Optional adverbials may also be added, either initially or finally:

She looked with disgust at the dog, *quiet now in Dinah's grasp.*
   [S V_{intens}] C_s A_{time} A_{place}
Maureen, *normally a timid girl*, snapped back at the others.
   $A_{frequency}$ [S V_{intens}] C_s
They toured the college, *at one time an institution of high repute.*
   A_{time} [S V_{intens}] C_s

When the verbless clause becomes reduced to its bare minimum of a single complement or adverbial, however, it may not be easy to distinguish from an appositional construction, non-restrictive relative clause, or an adverbial which is a direct constituent of the main clause:

The river lay in its crescent loop entirely without movement, *an artifice of green-black liquescent marble*

If the final noun phrase had been placed next to the subject here, there would have been no barrier to its classification as a case of full apposition (9.131). Similarly, although the initial prepositional phrase below is apparently an adverbial of the main clause:

Of humble parentage, he began his working life in a shoe factory it might be better regarded as a verbless clause consisting of adverbial complementation, and therefore as directly parallel to nominal or adjectival verbless clauses like

A man of humble parentage, . . .
Born of humble parents, . . .

Formal indicators of subordination
11.8
Let us now consider the various ways in which the subordination of one clause to another is indicated. On the whole, subordination is marked by some signal contained in the subordinate rather than superordinate clause. Such a signal may be of a number of different kinds: it can be a subordinating conjunction; a *wh*-element; the item *that;* inversion; or (negatively) the absence of a finite verb form.

11.9
Subordinators
Subordinators (or more fully SUBORDINATING CONJUNCTIONS) are perhaps the most important formal device of subordination. Like prepositions (*cf* 6.4*f*), which they resemble in having a relating or connecting function, subordinators forming the 'core' of the class consist of a single word; and again, as with prepositions, there is a larger 'penumbra' of compound items which act, to various degrees, like a single conjunction. In addition, there is a small class of correlative subordinators, *ie* combinations of two markers, one (a conjunction) occurring in the subordinate clause, and the other (normally an adverb) occurring in the superordinate clause.

SIMPLE SUBORDINATORS
> *after, (al)though, as, because, before, but (that), if, how(ever), like* (familiar), *once, since, that, till, unless, until, when(ever), where(ver), whereas, whereby, whereupon, while, whilst* (especially BrE)

COMPOUND SUBORDINATORS
ending with *that:*
> *in that, so that, in order that*†, *such that, except that, for all that, save that* (literary)

† *In order to* (without the *that*) introduces infinitival clauses.

ending with optional *that:*
> *now (that), providing (that), provided (that), supposing (that), considering (that), given (that), granting (that), granted (that),*

> *admitting* (*that*), *assuming* (*that*), *presuming* (*that*), *seeing* (*that*),
> *immediately* (*that*), *directly* (*that*)

ending with *as:*

> *as far as, as long as, as soon as, so long as, insofar as, so far as,*
> *inasmuch as* (formal), *according as, so as* (+ *to* + infinitive)

ending with *than:*

> *sooner than* (+ infinitive), *rather than* (+ infinitive)

other:

> *as if, as though, in case*

CORRELATIVE SUBORDINATORS

> [A] *if . . . then, (al)though . . . yet/nevertheless, as . . . so*
> [B] *more/-er/less . . . than, as . . . as, so . . . as, so . . .* (*that*),
>   *such . . . as, such . . .* (*that*), *no sooner . . . than*
> [C] *whether . . . or*
> [D] *the . . . the*

Note

[a] Some subordinators (*as, like, since, until, till, after, before, but*) also function
as prepositions: *since the war*, etc.

[b] *For, with*, and *without*, elsewhere prepositions, might be added to the list of subordinators when they introduce the subject of a non-finite or verbless clause:

> *for* him to interfere (11.5); *with* so many people there (6.46).

[c] Some of the above-listed subordinators introduce non-finite and verbless clauses
('abbreviated clauses') (*eg: if a nuisance*), others do not (**since a nuisance*). Details
are given under relevant sections (11.27, 11.28, 11.30, 11.33, 11.37).

[d] The following additional archaic subordinators still have a limited currency:
albeit, lest, whence, whither.

11.10
Correlative subordinators

The correlatives are divided into four lists (11.9), of which [A] contains
combinations in which a subordinate adverbial clause comes first, the
main clause being marked by an optional adverb (*cf* 8.92) which merely
emphasizes the relationship indicated by the subordinator:

> *If* all else fails, (*then*) we must resort to force
>   (CONDITIONAL CLAUSE: 11.29 *ff*)
> *Though* all efforts fail, (*yet*) we shall never surrender
>   (CONCESSIVE CLAUSE: 11.33 *ff*)
> *As* the strength of the defenders failed, (*so*) their courage grew
>   (PROPORTIONAL CLAUSE: 11.42)

Such correlatives (especially the latter two) belong to a formal and
deliberative style of writing or oratory.

The second group, [B], contains comparative correlatives, of which

the second element introduces the subordinate clause, while the first
functions as a degree modifier in the main clause:

$$I \text{ was } \begin{Bmatrix} more \text{ ashamed} \\ \text{angri}er \end{Bmatrix} than \text{ } I \text{ have ever been}$$

Type [C] consists of the unique alternative conditional correlative
whether . . . or, and Type [D] of the unique proportional correlative *the
. . . the*.

Note

The range of correlative subordinators can be extended somewhat in literary style
to include, for example, *where . . . there* and *when . . . then*:

When night falls, *then* is the time to explore nature's wonderful variety.

The following occur with inversion (14.16) in the first clause:

no sooner . . . than; hardly/scarcely . . . when/before.

11.11
Borderline subordinators

It is difficult (as with prepositions, 6.6) to be categorical as to what is a
compound subordinator, as opposed to a free syntactic combination.
Three borderline categories may be mentioned: (a) habitual combinations of a subordinator with a preceding or following intensifying adverb (*even if, just as, if only*); (b) participial forms (*supposing that*)
bearing a resemblance to participial-clause disjuncts like *judging from . . .,
speaking frankly*, etc; (c) expressions of time which, although adverbial
in form, act like a single temporal conjunction (*eg: directly/immediately/
the moment (that) I had spoken*). In case (a), a useful test is whether the
adverbial element can be omitted without altering the meaning of the
subordinator; if it can (as in *just as*), it may be regarded as a detachable
intensifier. In case (b), *-ing* forms which can be supplemented by adverbials, *eg:*

supposing *for the sake of argument* that

show themselves to be more like the verb element of a clause than like a
conjunction (contrast **provided for the sake of argument that*). In case
(c), a distinction can be drawn between *immediately (that)* on the one
hand and *the moment (that)* on the other. The relation between *moment*
and the following clause is explicable as the head and relative clause relation in a noun phrase acting as an adverbial of time, and permits something of the range of structural variations that one would expect from
that analysis:

$$\text{The (very)} \begin{Bmatrix} \text{moment} \\ \text{minute} \\ \text{instant} \\ \dots \end{Bmatrix} \text{(that) I saw him, I recognized a friend}$$

Immediately (*that*), however, has only one close structural analogue – *directly* (*that*), and so, since the relation between the adverb and the following clause is virtually anomalous, it is as well to acknowledge this anomalousness by treating *immediately* and *that* as making up a single conjunction and saying that *immediately* no longer has an adverbial function in this context.

11.12
Other indicators of subordination

Now we give a brief preliminary survey of other indicators of subordination, apart from subordinating conjunctions.

(a) *Wh*-ELEMENTS are initial markers of subordination in interrogative *wh*-clauses (11.18), in relative *wh*-clauses (11.20, 11.52, 13.8 *ff*), and in conditional-concessive *wh*-clauses (11.35 *f*). The subordinating *wh*-words are: *who/whom/whose*, *which*, *where*, *when*, *whether*, *how*, *what*, and *why*, together with the compound words *whoever*, *whomever* (rare), *whichever*, *wherever*, *whenever*, *whatever* and *however*. These *wh*-words function as or within one of the clause elements subject, object, complement, or adverbial. They are not conjunctions. There is, however, some overlap between *wh*-elements and subordinators, *where*, for example, appearing in both lists.

(b) The relative pronoun *that* (to be distinguished from the subordinating conjunction *that*) is a subordination marker in relative clauses:

The bus *that took me there* was late (13.8)

(c) Subject-operator inversion (14.16) is a marker of subordination in some conditional clauses, where the operator is *had*, *were*, or *should* (11.32):

Had I known more, I would have refused the job

Other unusual syntactic orderings also play a role in distinguishing a subordinate clause: for example,

Sad though I was (11.34)

(d) The absence of a finite verb form is effectively an indication of subordinate status, since non-finite and verbless clauses (subject to the exception of 7.90) occur only in dependent clauses:

The match will take place tomorrow, *weather permitting*

There are only two types of subordinate clause that contain no marker within themselves of subordinate status: these are

[I] Nominal *that*-clauses from which *that* has been omitted (11.17):

I suppose *you're right* (*cf* I suppose *that* you're right.)

[II] Comment clauses of a kind relatable to the *main* clause in the previous example (11.65):

You're right, *I suppose*

Note

[a] Another clause introducer of conditional-concessive meaning is the combination of *no matter* with a *wh*-element:

No matter what I say or how I say it, he always thinks I'm wrong.

[b] Although the relative pronoun is omissible in certain cases, in its absence, the role of marking subordination is assumed by unusual clause order, since the antecedent, which comes first, cannot have the notional role of subject with respect to the relative clause. The theoretically possible case of a relative clause which has no relative pronoun and where the omitted pronoun is subject is ungrammatical (13.8):

That's the man *that saw me* ↔ *That's the man *saw me*

Contrast:

That's the man *that I saw* ↔ That's the man *I saw*

A functional classification of dependent clauses
11.13
List of functions

Dependent clauses may function as subject, object, complement, or adverbial in the superordinate clause:

subject: *That we need more equipment* is obvious
direct object: I know *that she is pretty*
subject complement: The point is *that we're leaving*
indirect object: I gave *whoever it was* a cup of tea
object complement: I imagined him *overcome with grief*
adjunct: *When we meet*, I shall explain everything
disjunct: *To be honest*, I've never liked him
conjunct: *What is more*, he has lost the friends he had

In addition, they may function *within* these elements, as postmodifier, prepositional complement, etc:

postmodifier in noun phrase: The friend *who remains a friend*
prepositional complement: It depends on *what we decide*
adjectival complement (12.38): Ready *to act promptly*

Note

Dependent clauses rarely act as conjuncts, as object complements, or as indirect objects. The object complement function is limited to non-finite clauses in complex-transitive complementation (12.67 *ff*). On the indirect object function, which is restricted to nominal relative clauses, see 11.14 below.

11.14
Nominal clauses

On the basis of these functions, there emerges a classification similar in some ways to the functional classification of smaller units (words and phrases) as adverbs, noun phrases, etc. The classes of clause we shall distinguish in this way are: NOMINAL, ADVERBIAL, RELATIVE, COMPARATIVE, COMPLEMENTARY, and COMMENT CLAUSES.

The principles of the functional classification are most clearly exhibited by the category of nominal clauses (11.16–25), or clauses having a function approximating to that of a noun phrase. Just as noun phrases may occur as subject, object, complement, appositive, and prepositional complement, so every nominal clause may occur in some or all of these roles:

subject: *Whether we need it* is a different matter
object: I don't know *whether we need it*
complement: The problem is *whether we need it*
appositive: That question, *whether we need it*, has not yet been considered
prepositional complement: The decision must depend on *whether we need it*

The privilege of occurrence of nominal clauses is limited, however, by the fact that in terms of the semantic classification of noun phrases, they are normally abstract; *ie* they refer to events, facts, states, ideas, etc, rather than to objects. The one exception to this generalization is the nominal relative clause (11.20), which may refer to objects, people, substances, etc, and may in fact be analysed, on one level, as a noun phrase consisting of head and postmodifying relative clause, the head and relative pronoun coalescing to form a single *wh*-element (*cf* 13.5 *ff*): We may compare the equivalent sentences:

What pleases one party infuriates the other
That which pleases one party infuriates the other (formal)

Since abstract noun phrases cannot normally be indirect objects, this explains why the nominal relative clause is the only type of clause that can function as indirect object.

Note

The following is a highly exceptional case where the indirect object is a dependent interrogative clause: *We've simply got to give whether to accept his offer some thought.*

11.15
Other functional classes

We turn now to the other functional classes, apart from nominal clauses. ADVERBIAL CLAUSES (11.26–51) operate as adjuncts or disjuncts. In this respect, they are like adverbs, and are often commutable with prepositional phrases. Compare:

Because the soloist was ill, they cancelled the concert
Because of the soloist's illness, they cancelled the concert

RELATIVE CLAUSES as generally understood act as non-restrictive or restrictive modifiers of noun phrases. They are therefore functionally parallel to attributive adjectives or phrases. Compare:

people *who speak Spanish*
Spanish-speaking people

Relative clauses are discussed at length in 13.8–15. However, in addition to the nominal relative clause discussed in 11.14 above, one type of clause which does not have the postmodifying function but which we call 'relative', is discussed in this chapter. This is the 'sentential relative' (11.52), a clause which non-restrictively modifies not a noun phrase, but a whole clause, sentence, or even series of sentences:

After that things improved – *which astonished me.*

What distinguishes a relative clause, in the present account, is not a particular syntactic function, but rather its cross-referring or binding role. The grammatical unit or segment to which it cross-refers is called the ANTECEDENT. In the case of the sentential relative clause, generally the whole of the sentence except for the relative clause itself is the antecedent.

COMPARATIVE CLAUSES (11.53–64), like sentential relatives, are difficult to fit into any of the major functional categories. They often have the appearance of adverbial or adjectival modifiers:

I love you *more* deeply *than I can say*
He's not *as* clever a man *as I thought*

They also have some features in common with adverbial clauses, however. Semantically, we may consider them, together with their correlative element (*more, as, -er*, etc) in the main clause, as equivalent to a degree adverb.

COMPLEMENTARY CLAUSES are non-finite clauses which are equivalent to complements in function, and therefore parallel to adjectival or noun phrases:

I found him *reading the paper.*

They are given no further treatment in this chapter, falling within the subject matter of Chapter 12 (12.52 *ff*, 12.67 *ff*).

COMMENT CLAUSES (11.65–66) perform the function of disjunct or (occasionally) conjunct, and often express the speaker's attitude to the main clause, or his manner of asserting it:

Food is cheap in England, *I believe*

Each of these major functional types (except for postmodifying relative and complementary clauses) will now be examined in greater detail.

Nominal clauses
11.16
Four major categories
Nominal clauses (or clauses equivalent in function to noun phrases) fall into five major categories:

The *that*-clause, or dependent declarative clause (11.17)
The dependent interrogative clause (11.18–19)
The nominal relative clause (11.20)
The *to*-infinitive clause (11.21–22)
The *-ing* clause (11.23–24)

11.17
That-clauses
The *that*-clause can occur as:

subject: *That she is still alive* is a consolation

direct object: $\begin{Bmatrix} \text{I told him} \\ \text{I knew} \end{Bmatrix}$ *that he was wrong*

subject complement: The assumption is *that things will improve*
appositive: Your assumption, *that things will improve*, is unfounded
   (13.16 *f*, 9.177)
adjectival complement: I'm sure *that things will improve*

It cannot, however, occur as prepositional complement (6.2) or as object complement.

When the *that*-clause is object or complement (or delayed subject – 14.36), the conjunction *that* is frequently omitted in informal use, leaving a 'zero *that*-clause':

$\left.\begin{array}{l} \text{I knew} \\ \text{I told him} \\ \text{I'm sure} \end{array}\right\}$ *he was wrong*

When the clause is subject, *that* (which cannot be omitted) can be paraphrased by *the fact that* . . . :

(*The fact*) *that she is still alive* consoles me

Apart from this 'factual' meaning, however, *that*-clauses can express 'putative' (11.72) and 'hypothetical' meaning.

Note

[a] The zero *that*-clause is particularly common when the clause is brief and uncomplicated. In contrast, the need for clarity discourages or even forbids the omission of *that* in complex sentences loaded with adverbials and modifications. Any parenthetical material between the verb of the superordinate clause and the subject of the *that*-clause is especially likely to inhibit deletion:

> We had hoped, in a moment of optimism, *that* the Government would look favourably on our case.

The position of *that* after the second comma, rather than before the first comma, in this sentence, is decisive in assigning the parenthetical adverbial to the main clause and not the *that*-clause. The omission of *that* would leave the structure of the sentence unclear.

[b] Direct passive transforms of clauses with a *that*-clause object are rare, for reasons to be discussed in 14.8. Instead, the version with extraposition (14.36) is preferred: *It is thought that he will come*. The same point applies to other nominal clauses.

[c] While *that*-clauses, like most other nominal clauses, cannot be object complements, an alternative *to*-infinitive construction is available with some verbs. Contrast:

> I thought his argument absurd ↔ I thought his argument *to be* absurd

with:

*I thought his argument that we should pay	↔	I thought his argument *to be* that we should pay

11.18

Wh-interrogative clauses

The dependent *wh*-interrogative clause occurs in the whole range of functions available to the *that*-clause, and in addition can act as prepositional complement:

subject: *How the book will sell* depends on its author.
direct object: I can't imagine *what made him do it*.
subject complement: The problem is not *who will go* but *who will stay*.
appositive: My original question, *why he did it at all*, has not been answered.
adjectival complement: I wasn't certain *whose house I was in*.
prepositional complement: No one was consulted on *who should have the prize*.

As regards meaning, these clauses resemble *wh*-questions (7.63–65) in that they leave a gap of unknown information, represented by the *wh*-element. There is, in fact, a significant contrast to be drawn, in some constructions, between a positive sentence which goes with the certainty of the *that*-clause, and a negative sentence, associated with the uncertainty of the *wh*-clause:

$$\left.\begin{array}{l}\text{I'm sure}\\\text{I know}\end{array}\right\}\textit{that} \text{ they're coming}$$

$$\left.\begin{array}{l}\text{I'm not sure}\\\text{I don't know}\end{array}\right\}\textit{whether} \text{ they're coming}$$

There is also a grammatical similarity to *wh*-questions in that the *wh*-element is placed first; indeed, apart from the absence of subject-verb inversion in the dependent clause, the structures of the two types of clause are in all respects parallel. We have, in the *wh*-interrogative clause, the same choice between initial and final preposition where the prepositional complement is the *wh*-element:

$$\text{He couldn't remember}\left\{\begin{array}{l}\textit{on which shelf} \text{ he kept it (formal)}\\\textit{which shelf} \text{ he kept it } \textit{on} \text{ (informal)}\end{array}\right.$$

Again, within the limitations set out in 7.66, the *wh*-element can be fronted from a position in a clause subordinate to the *wh*-clause (a pushdown *wh*-element); for example the informal:

I don't remember *which shelf* he told me I was to fetch it from

An infinitive *wh*-clause can be formed with all *wh*-words except *why:*

He was explaining *how to start the motor*. ('. . . how one should . . .')
I never know *where to put my coat*. ('. . . where I ought to . . .')

Note

[a] There is no construction with an initial preposition corresponding to

   I can imagine *what it is like/what it is for* (**for/like what it is*)

   ie cases in which the final preposition follows the verb BE. Another case in which there is no preposed alternative is:

   I don't know *what you do it for* (**for what you do it*).

[b] In literary style, there is an occasional subject-verb or subject-operator inversion when the *wh*-element is the A of an *SVA* type clause, or the C of an *SVC* type clause:

   I told them *how strong was my desire* to visit the famous temple.

[c] The preposition preceding a *wh*-clause is optional in certain circumstances:

   I was not certain (*of*) *what to do*.
   We have not solved the problem (*of*) *who was at fault*.

11.19
Yes-no interrogative clauses

The dependent *yes-no* interrogative clause (*cf* 7.56 *ff*) is formed with *if* or *whether*:

> Do you know *if/whether the shops are open?*

The dependent *alternative* question (*cf* 7.68) is formed with *if/whether . . . or*:

> I don't know *whether it will rain or be sunny*
> I don't care *if your car breaks down or not*

Only *whether* can be directly followed by *or not*:

> I don't care $\begin{Bmatrix} whether\ or\ not \\ *if\ or\ not \end{Bmatrix}$ your car breaks down

Except in the second part of an alternative question, a *wh*-clause beginning with *whether* cannot be made negative, whereas an *if* interrogative can:

> I don't care $\begin{cases} \text{if it doesn't rain} \\ \text{*whether it doesn't rain} \end{cases}$

On the other hand, *if* cannot occur in subject position:

> $\begin{Bmatrix} \text{Whether} \\ \text{*If} \end{Bmatrix}$ it rains or not doesn't concern me

Note

With certain introductory verbs or adjectives a negative *whether*-clause is acceptable:

> I wonder whether he doesn't think too much of himself   [i]
> I'm not sure whether he doesn't expect too much from her   [ii]

But by implication, such sentences have a positive rather than negative meaning. Sentence [i], for example, means roughly: 'I think he *does* think too much of himself'.

11.20
Nominal relative clauses

The nominal relative clause, also introduced by a *wh*-element, can act as:

> subject: *What he is looking for* is a wife
> direct object: I want to see *whoever deals with complaints*
> indirect object: He gave *whoever came to the door* a winning smile
> subject complement: Home is *where your friends and family are*
> object complement: You can call me *what(ever) you like*
> appositive: Let us know your college address (that is, *where you live in term time*)

> prepositional complement: You should vote for *which(ever)*
> *candidate you think best*

The nominal relative clause is much closer to noun phrase status than other nominal clauses are. It can normally be paraphrased by a noun phrase containing a postmodifying relative clause:

> *Whoever breaks this law* deserves a fine ('Anyone who . . .')
> I'll give you *however much tobacco you need* ('. . . any amount . . .
>   that you need')
> Quality is *what counts most* ('Quality is that which . . .')
> Tomorrow is *when it would be most convenient* ('. . . the time
>   when . . .')

As pointed out in 11.14, one aspect of this closeness to noun phrases is that nominal relative clauses can be, like noun phrases in general, both concrete and abstract, whereas other categories of nominal clause are invariably abstract.

There is a difference between UNIVERSAL and DEFINITE meaning as expressed by the *wh*-form of a relative clause. We see this in the paraphrases of the four examples above: the first two are paraphrased in 'universal' terms (*anyone, any amount*), while the second two are paraphrased in 'definite' terms (*that which, the time when*). The contrast is highlighted in:

> Quality is *what counts most*   [6]
> Quality is *whatever counts most*   [7]

[6] has the definite meaning 'that which', and states that 'quality is supremely important'; [7] has the universal 'indifferent' meaning 'anything that counts most is "quality"'; that is, it purports to be a definition of 'quality'.

The form *who* is rarely used in present-day English in this nominal relative function (**Who told you that was lying*); consequently the compound form *whoever* has taken over, in many contexts, both universal and definite meanings:

> *Whoever told you that* was lying$\left\{\begin{array}{l}\text{'The person who . . .'}\\ \text{'Anyone who . . .'}\end{array}\right\}$

See further 13.5 Note *a*.

The formation of nominal relative *wh*-clauses follows the same pattern as that of the interrogative kind, except that the list of introductory *wh*-elements used is slightly different. *Whether, if,* and (as we have just seen) *who* are not used for the relative type, while the compounds with *-ever* are not used with the interrogative type.

Where the *wh*-word chosen is available for both nominal relative and interrogative clauses, an ambiguity arises:

> They asked me *what I didn't know*
> ('They asked me that which I didn't know' *or* 'They asked me "What don't you know?"')

On the other hand, there is a wide range of instances where, because of selection restrictions peculiar to abstract nominals (7.37–38), only the relative interpretation is present:

> I gave him *what he needed.*

Note

[a] In subject complement position, nominal relative clauses with *who* are occasionally found: *You're not who I thought you were.*

[b] We distinguish the compound *wh*-words *whatever*, etc, from the informal intensificatory combinations *what ever*, etc (normally spelled as two words), which do occasionally occur in dependent interrogative clauses: *I asked him what ever he was up to* (= ... *what on earth* ...).

To-infinitive nominal clauses
11.21

The *to*-infinitive nominal clause can occur as:

subject: *For a bridge to collapse like that* is unbelievable   [8]

direct object: He likes *everyone to be happy*   [9]

subject complement: To be a member of the Space Club is
    to be one of the most privileged citizens in the world   [10]

appositive: His ambition, *to be a straight actor*, was never
    fulfilled   [11]

adjectival complement: I'm glad *to help you* (see 12.38 *ff*)   [12]

As [8] shows, the presence of the subject of a *to*-infinitive clause normally requires the presence also of the preceding *for* (which is perhaps acting here more as a conjunction, or clause introducer, than as a preposition). The subject, when a pronoun, is in the objective case:

> The idea is for *us* to meet on Thursday

When the clause is a direct object, however, the *for* is omitted:

> He wants me to leave (*rather than:* *He wants for me to leave)

Note

[a] *He wants for me to leave* does, in fact, occur in dialectal AmE.

[b] That the infinitive clause is acting as an object here is shown by the possibility of transforming *He wants me to leave* into the 'pseudo-cleft' sentence (14.21 *f*): *What he wants is for me to leave;* in which case, as the infinitive clause now acts as

complement, the *for* reappears. On the other hand, the infinitive as direct object cannot be easily transferred to the subject role by a passive transformation:

*(For) me to leave is wanted by everyone in the road.

11.22

We have seen that the infinitive resembles the *that*-clause in being unable to function as complement of a preposition, yet its ability to follow directly an item which normally requires a prepositional phrase as complementation suggests that here (as, again, in the case of the *that*-clause – 6.2) there is an 'understood' preposition:

I'm delighted *at what I saw, at having succeeded*
*I'm delighted *at to have succeeded*
I'm delighted *to have succeeded*

(Similarly *I am glad/sorry/pleased/*etc *to have gone; I decided/asked/*etc *to see him;* 12.38, 12.49).

The meaning of the infinitive clause is 'putative' (11.72) rather than factual, as we see when we paraphrase it (where complementation restrictions permit) by a *that*-clause with putative *should:*

To rob one's parents is unforgivable ↔
That one should rob one's parents is unforgivable
The plan is *to blow up the factory* ↔
The plan is *that we should blow up the factory*

Note

Confusion may result from the apparent coalescence of *for* as a preposition and *for* as an infinitive clause introducer when the infinitive clause contains a subject:

I'm longing for the vacation	[i]
*I'm longing for for everyone to go home	[ii]
I'm longing for everyone to go home	[iii]

[i] represents the ordinary case of *long for* with a noun phrase as prepositional complement. The plain addition of the infinitive clause as prepositional complement would result in the ungrammatical repetition of *for* in [ii]; but the rule for the deletion of the preposition turns [ii] into the correct version [iii], in which only one *for* is retained.

Nominal -*ing* clauses
11.23

The nominal -*ing* clause, which may be called, following traditional terminology, a PARTICIPIAL CLAUSE, occurs in the following positions:

subject: *Eating people* is wrong
  direct object: No one enjoys *deceiving his own family*
  subject complement: His favourite pastime is *playing practical jokes*

appositive: His one claim to fame, *being secretary of the local tennis club*, is the recurrent theme of his conversation
prepositional complement: I'm tired of *being treated like a child*
adjectival complement: The children were busy *building sandcastles*

It is the most common type of participial clause, that which has no subject, that is illustrated above. When a subject does occur, the form it assumes is broadly as follows:

GENITIVE CASE in formal style:

I'm surprised at *his/John's* making that mistake

OBJECTIVE CASE (for pronouns) or COMMON CASE (for other

noun phrases) in informal style:

I'm surprised at *him/John* making that mistake

The choice between the two constructions has been confused by the common but groundless assumption that the verb in such clauses is a verbal noun, and that accordingly the genitive is the only 'correct' form. In fact, the genitive frequently has a stilted effect, and is particularly unsuitable when the subject is an inanimate or abstract noun phrase which would not normally take the genitive case; a long noun phrase with a 'group' genitive (13.64) is also avoided:

? The crisis has arisen as a result of *recent uncontrolled inflation's* having outweighed the benefits of devaluation

The genitive ending is exceedingly awkward in this context, and would most probably be omitted, even in formal style. On the other hand, the objective case has an air of infelicity in subject position, where it otherwise seldom occurs; such a sentence as

Him being a Jesuit alters everything

would therefore only occur in very informal speech. Both constructions give trouble and many writers prefer to avoid both of them where ready alternatives are available. In this instance, one could say

(The fact) that he is a Jesuit alters everything.

11.24
Although, as the last example in the above paragraph shows, there is a semantic equivalence between a *that*-clause and a nominal *-ing* clause, the most obvious structural parallel to draw with this construction is that of the *-ing* 'nominalization', or noun phrase with a verbal noun in *-ing* as head (see 4.9 *ff*, 13.34 *f*). One may compare *His dancing of the tango* (noun phrase consisting of possessive pronoun + head + prepositional phrase postmodifier) with *His dancing the tango* (genitive

subject + V-*ing* + object), where only the presence of the preposition *of* in the former distinguishes the two constructions. The addition of an adjective to the former (*eg: His skilful dancing of the tango*) or of the perfect aspect and an adverb to the latter (*eg: His having danced the tango skilfully*) emphasizes the different potentialities of the two constructions. On the other hand, there are many cases which are completely ambiguous as between the two constructions, *eg* where there is just a genitive pronoun followed by an -*ing* form:

> *His dancing* was unexpected

There is equally nothing to distinguish them when the -*ing* form occurs alone:

> I like *dancing;* I hate *singing*

The ambiguity here is that the -*ing* clause specifically links the activity to the subject of the sentence: 'I like it when I dance' as opposed to 'I like it when people in general dance'. When an object is added, the construction is bound to be an -*ing* clause, and only the first meaning is present: *I like dancing the tango* ('I like it when I dance the tango').

Note

[a]   A plan of *his friend's devising*

is an anomalous construction, presumably containing a noun phrase rather than an -*ing* clause. If an -*ing* clause were present, it would be possible to replace the genitive *friend's* by the objective *friend*, something impossible in this case:

*A plan of his *friend* devising.

[b]   Another anomalous construction manifests itself in *There's no telling what they will do*. This must be regarded as a blend of noun phrase and -*ing* clause, since *telling* is marked as a verbal noun by the preceding determiner *no*, and yet is marked as a participle by the following clausal object. The existence of this construction (which occasionally occurs in other contexts, such as *No dancing the tango here!*) reminds us that the genitive pronoun as subject of an -*ing* clause may itself be regarded as the outcome of a blend of the nominal and verbal functions of V-*ing*.

11.25
Bare infinitive and verbless clauses

Two minor types of nominal clause that we must briefly consider are the bare infinitive clause (without *to*) and the nominal verbless clause.

The *to* of the infinitive is optionally omitted in a clause which, as complement, expands the meaning of the verb DO:

> All I did was (*to*) *turn off the gas*
> What the plan does is (*to*) *ensure a fair pension for all*

When the infinitive clause is initial, *to* has to be omitted: *Turn off the tap was all I did.*

The category of a verbless nominal clause is required to account for a type of subject which, although superficially a noun phrase, has some of the structural as well as semantic characteristics of a clause:

A friend in need is a friend indeed (proverb)	[13]
Wall-to-wall carpets in every room is the housewife's dream	[14]
Are *fast cars* wise in cities?	[15]

These may be paraphrased with the aid of non-finite clauses:

To be a friend in need is to be a friend indeed
Having wall-to-wall carpets in every room is the housewife's dream
Is *allowing fast cars in cities* wise?

Moreover, the prepositional phrases are not of the kind which would postmodify the head in a noun phrase. *A friend in need*, for example, as noun phrase, would mean 'a friend who is in need', whereas the appropriate meaning in [13] is '(to have) a friend when one is in need' (*ie* 'Friendship in a time of need is indeed friendship'). A further point in favour of clausal analysis is the singular verb in [14], otherwise difficult to explain. However, in other cases (*eg* [15]) the verb is plural.

Adverbial clauses
11.26
Adverbial clauses, or clauses serving primarily as adjuncts or disjuncts in the main clause, may be placed in various semantic categories, such as time (8.56 *ff*), place (8.45 *ff*), and manner (8.35). These categories may be related to those for adverbials in general (Chapter 8) and for prepositional phrases (6.11–54).

Adverbial clauses, like adverbials in general, are capable of occurring in a final, initial, or medial position within the main clause (generally in that order of frequency). Attention will be drawn, in the paragraphs that follow, to modifications of this general statement.

Our plan will be to begin, under each category, by discussing finite clauses, which are generally introduced by subordinators; then to move to non-finite and verbless clauses, where they are possible. We shall use the term 'abbreviated clause' for non-finite and verbless clauses beginning with a subordinator. After listing and discussing the semantic categories, we shall conclude (in 11.44–51) with a general consideration of non-finite and verbless adverbial clauses.

Note
Medial position is on the whole very rare for adverbial clauses, except possibly in the position (if it is considered medial) immediately following the subordinator in a dependent clause:

I was told that *if I applied early* my case would be given special consideration.

11.27
Clauses of time
Adverbial clauses of time, if finite, are introduced by one of the following subordinators: *after, as, before, once, since, till, until, when(ever), while, whilst* (especially BrE), *now (that), as long as, as soon as, immediately (that), directly (that)*:

Buy your tickets *as soon as you reach the station*
When I last saw you, you lived in Washington
Our hostess, *once everyone had arrived*, was full of good humour

Temporal clauses are common in initial position. In addition, *-ing* clauses without a subject are also used to express time relationship:

Nearing the entrance, I shook hands with my acquaintances ('when/as I neared . . .')
The stranger, *having discarded his jacket*, moved threateningly towards me ('after he had discarded . . .')

Abbreviated *-ing* clauses may follow *after, before, since, when(ever)*, and *while:*

He wrote his greatest novel *while working on a freighter*

Abbreviated *-ed* clauses follow *once, until, when(ever)*, and *while:*

Once published, the book caused a remarkable stir

Abbreviated verbless clauses may follow *as soon as, once, when(ever)*, and *while:*

When in difficulty, consult the manual.

Note
[a] With *until* and its variant *till*, a dynamic verb (3.40 *f*) in the main clause often has to be accompanied by a negative:

*He started to read *until he was ten years old*
He didn't start to read *until he was ten years old*

In the negative sentence, *not* (. . .) *until* means the same as *not* (. . .) *before.*
[b] A complete reversal of the normal relation between subordinate and superordinate clauses takes place with a type of *when*-clause which occurs finally in sentences in formal narrative style:

The last man was emerging from the escape tunnel *when a distant shout signalled its discovery by the guards*

It is usual for the temporal clause to indicate a happening that is given or assumed in the context; but this type of *when*-clause introduces a new piece of information not prepared for by the preceding narrative. It gives dramatic emphasis and climax to the event so described (see 'resolution', 11.80).

[c] Infinitival clauses of 'outcome' may be placed among temporal clauses:

> He rushed to the door, *only to discover that it was locked and barred*
> I awoke one morning *to find the house in an uproar*
> She grew up *to be a successful actress*

These clauses, like all adverbial infinitival clauses (except those introduced by *with*) have no subject. They always follow the rest of the main clause. The sentences could be paraphrased by switching the relationship of subordination, and using a *when*-clause:

> When I awoke one morning, I found the house in an uproar

Their restriction to final position suggests an analogy between these clauses and result clauses (11.40), which they resemble in meaning.

[d] Observations on tense and aspect in temporal clauses are to be found in 11.68 and 11.70.

11.28
Clauses of place

Adverbial clauses of place are introduced by *where* or *wherever*:

> They went *wherever they could find work*
> *Where the fire had been*, we saw nothing but blackened ruins

Abbreviated clauses occur with both the subordinators:

> *Where(ver) known*, such facts have been reported
> *Where(ver) possible*, all moving parts should be tested

Often (as in this last example), place conjunctions take on the more abstract meaning of 'in cases where . . .'.

Clauses of condition and concession
11.29
Overlap of condition and concession

Two classes of adverbial clause between which there is considerable overlap are those of condition and concession. Whereas conditional clauses state the dependence of one circumstance or set of circumstances on another:

> *If you treat her kindly*, she'll do anything for you

concessive clauses imply a contrast between two circumstances; *ie* that in the light of the circumstance in the dependent clause, that in the main clause is surprising:

> *Although he hadn't eaten for days*, he looked strong and healthy

From this, we see that *although* as a subordinator is the approximate equivalent of *but* as a coordinator (9.54):

He hadn't eaten for days, *but* he looked strong and healthy

The overlap between conditional and concessive clauses comes with such subordinators as *even if*, which expresses both the contingent dependence of one circumstance upon another and the surprising nature of this dependence:

Even if he went down on bended knees, I wouldn't forgive him

Such clauses as this will be handled under the independent heading of conditional-concessive clauses.

Both conditional and concessive clauses tend to assume initial position in the superordinate clause.

11.30
If and *unless*
Finite adverbial clauses of condition are introduced chiefly by the subordinators *if* (positive condition) and *unless* (negative condition):

If you don't believe me, what can I do?
He must be lying *if he told you that*
Unless the strike has been called off, there will be no trains tomorrow

The last sentence has roughly the same meaning as 'If the strike has not been called off...'; there is, however, a slight difference between an *unless*-clause and a negative *if*-clause, in that *unless* has the more exclusive meaning of 'only if ... not' or 'except on condition that...'. In this, it is more precisely the opposite of the compound conjunction *provided* (*that*) or *providing* (*that*), which means 'if and only if...':

Provided that no objection is raised, we shall hold the meeting here

Other compound conditional conjunctions approximately synonymous with *provided* (*that*) are *as long as, so long as*, and *on condition that*.

If and *unless* often introduce abbreviated clauses: *if ready; unless expressly forbidden*, etc. Also to be noted are the residual positive and negative conditional pro-clauses *if so* and *if not*.

Note
[a] *If*-clauses are used sometimes as style disjuncts (8.80 *f*): *if you please; if you don't mind; if you follow me; if I may say so;* etc:

She and I are just friends, if you follow me.

[b] *In case* is a subordinator referring to possible future conditions: *Do this in case a fire breaks out* means 'Do this in the event of a fire breaking out'. However, in BrE *in case* in this sentence could also have the meaning of negative purpose: 'Do this to prevent fire breaking out'.

[c] Conditional *if*-clauses have to be distinguished from interrogative *if*-clauses (11.19), which are nominal rather than adverbial. Something like a merger of the two functions is found, however, in a sentence like *I wouldn't object if you took a rest* ('If you took a rest, I wouldn't object to your taking a rest').

11.31
Open and hypothetical condition
Conditional clauses can express either an open condition, as do all the examples so far, or else a hypothetical condition. The open condition leaves unresolved the question of the fulfilment or non-fulfilment of the condition, and hence also the truth of the proposition expressed by the main clause. A hypothetical condition, on the other hand, conveys the expectation that the condition will *not* be fulfilled:

If he changed his opinions,
    he'd be a more likeable person
We could get married today, ⎱ ('but I don't suppose
    if you really wanted to ⎰   he will/you do/etc')
If you listened to me,
    you wouldn't make mistakes

As these examples show, present or future hypothetical meanings are expressed by *would/should* (or another past-tense modal) plus the infinitive in the main (conditioned) clause, and by the past tense in the subordinate clause (see further 11.69).

If-clauses (especially those expressing open conditions) are like questions in that they imply uncertainty about the actual existence of the circumstance referred to. Therefore they tend to contain non-assertive forms such as *any, ever* (see 7.44):

If you *ever* have *any* trouble, let me know

Clauses beginning with *unless*, on the other hand, lay stress on the excluded positive option, and so normally contain assertive forms:

I won't phone you, unless *something* unforeseen happens

For the same reason, *unless*-clauses rarely have hypothetical meaning. Hence the negative conditional clause *If I had not arrived* has no equivalent *unless*-clause, **Unless I had arrived.*

Note
The combination *if only* is an intensified equivalent of *if*, typically used in hypothetical clauses to express what the speaker wishes had happened or would happen:

If only somebody had told us, we could have warned you

The *if only* clause contains (when positive) assertive forms, and nearly always precedes the main clause. Sometimes, however, there is no main clause at all, and the conditional clause stands on its own as a hypothetical wish (7.86): *If only I hadn't lost it!*

11.32

Special types of conditional clause

Apart from the types of conditional clauses outlined above, there are some less usual types involving special verb forms and syntactic orderings.

To express an open condition, the present subjunctive is sometimes used in the conditional clause, instead of the normal present tense:

> If any person *be found* guilty, he shall have the right of appeal

This usage is mainly confined to very formal, legal or quasi-legal contexts.

There are also alternative ways of expressing hypothetical conditions. They are:

(1) *was/were to* followed by the infinitive:

$$\text{If it} \begin{Bmatrix} was \\ were \end{Bmatrix} to\ rain, \text{we should get wet}$$

(2) *should* followed by the infinitive (*cf* putative *should*, 11.72):

> If a serious crisis *should arise*, the public would have to be informed of its full implications

Both constructions are formal, and have overtones of tentativeness.

It will be noticed that in the example of (1) above, the singular past subjunctive form of the verb BE is used rather than the ordinary past tense form; that is, *were* is used for the singular as well as for the plural (3.16). In fact, both the indicative and the subjunctive forms are possible for hypothetical conditions, the subjunctive being preferred in formal written English:

$$\text{If John} \begin{Bmatrix} was \\ were \end{Bmatrix} \text{here, we would learn the truth}$$

The idiom *if I were you*, however, by convention usually contains the subjunctive.

A device which may replace the subordinator *if* in signalling a conditional clause is the inversion of subject and operator, particularly with the operator *had* in hypothetical clauses:

> *Had I known*, I would have written before

Subjunctive *were* and hypothetical or putative *should* can also undergo inversion in somewhat literary style:

> *Were it to reveal its secrets*, that house would collapse in shame
> *Should you change your mind*, no one would blame you.

Note
A further construction occasionally used for expressing a condition is the infinitival clause:

> You have to be strong *to lift a table like that*
> He'd be stupid *not to accept that offer*

These clauses also contain an element of purposive meaning (11.39).

11.33
Clauses of concession
Clauses of concession are introduced chiefly by *although* or its more colloquial variant *though* (which, as seen in 8.91 Note *b*, is a conjunct of concession as well as a conjunction of concession):

> No goals were scored, *though it was an exciting game*
> *Although Britain considers itself an advanced country*, it has a very old-fashioned system of measurements

While and *whereas* are sometimes used to point a contrast between comparable things:

> The USA has immense mineral wealth, *while/whereas* Britain has comparatively little

Even if and *even though* are also concessive in meaning:

> He borrowed my mower, *even though I told him not to*
> *Even if you dislike ancient monuments*, Warwick Castle is worth a visit

Conditional *if* is, in meaning, the opposite of *although* (implying a positive rather than a negative connection between the two clauses); yet occasionally *if* is used concessively (= 'even if'):

> *If he's poor*, at least he's honest

Abbreviated clauses of concession are common and of all three structural types (-*ing*, -*ed*, and verbless): *though a young man; although often despairing of rescue; even if still operating; even though given every attention;* etc:

> *Though well over eighty*, he can walk a mile faster than I can.

11.34
Special types of concessive clause
Like conditional clauses, concessive clauses sometimes have unusual syntactic orderings. The subordinators *as, though,* and *that* occur in non-initial position after the subject complement in:

> *Naked as/that I was*, I braved the storm
> ('Even though I was naked . . .')

> *Miraculous though their survival seemed*, it was nothing to what
> lay ahead ('Even though their survival seemed miraculous . . .')

That and *as*, in this position, can also have the non-concessive meaning
of cause or circumstance (11.37 *f*):

> Michael, *fool as/that he was*, completely ruined the dinner
> ('. . . since he was a fool, being a fool . . .')

The rule which permits this construction applies more generally to *as*
and *though*, such that a whole predication (consisting, *eg*, of lexical
verb, or lexical verb plus object) may be placed in front of the conjunction: *object as you may; fail though I did; change your mind as
you will.* In *much as I would like to help*, on the other hand, it is an adverb
alone that is fronted. Such clauses, rather formal in style, may be
compared with conditional-concessive clauses such as *come what may*
(11.36 Note *b*).

11.35
Alternative conditional-concessive clauses
The overlap between condition and concession, already noted with
even if and *even though*, is particularly marked in two classes of adverbial
clause that we may call ALTERNATIVE CONDITIONAL-CONCESSIVE
and UNIVERSAL CONDITIONAL-CONCESSIVE.

The correlative sequence *whether* (. . .) *or* . . . may be entitled 'alternative conditional' in that logically it combines the conditional meaning of *if* with the disjunctive meaning of *either* . . . *or*. It thus is a means
of coordinating two subordinate clauses:

> *Whether they beat us or we beat them*, the result will be the
> same   [16]
> You will have to face the publicity, *whether you want to or not*   [17]

The concessive element of meaning comes in secondarily, through the
implication that if the same thing takes place in two contrasting conditions, there must be something surprising about at least one of them.
Thus the adverbial clause in [17] could be paraphrased '. . . even if
you don't want to . . .'.

Example [17] has the variant ordering . . . *whether or not you want to*
(*cf* alternative questions, 7.68 *f*).

11.36
Universal conditional-concessive clauses
While the alternative conditional-concessive clause gives a choice
between two possible conditions, the universal conditional-concessive

clause, introduced by one of the *wh*-compound words *whatever, whoever*, etc, indicates a free choice from any number of conditions. One may compare

She looks pretty *whether she wears blue or green* [18]

(two alternatives) with

She looks pretty *whatever she wears* [19]

(any number of alternatives). The concessive implication comes in again, insofar as one might infer from [19] that, for example, she would look pretty *even if* she wore overalls or a spacesuit.

These clauses share with other *wh*-clauses the initial placement of the *wh*-element, and the consequent shift from normal syntactic order:

Come here, *wherever you are* (A S V)
However much advice you give him, he does exactly what he wants
   (O_d S V O_i)
Whatever your opinions are, you are welcome to join our society
   (C S V)

There is a subtle semantic difference between such conditional clauses and the apparently identical time and place clauses beginning *whenever* and *wherever*. The contrast is best shown in the ambiguity of a sentence like:

Wherever you live, you can keep a horse

The locative meaning is 'You can keep a horse at any place where you may live'; the conditional-concessive meaning (more applicable to the city-dweller) is 'It doesn't matter where you live, you can keep a horse – not necessarily in that same place'. The longer constructions *no matter wh-* and *it doesn't matter wh-* may be added to the list of universal conditional-concessive clause introducers:

$\begin{Bmatrix} \textit{No matter} \\ \textit{It doesn't matter} \end{Bmatrix}$ *how hard I try*, I can never catch up with him.

Note

[a] In restricted circumstances (*viz* with an abstract noun phrase subject of an *SVC* clause), the verb BE can be omitted from a universal conditional-concessive clause:

Whatever your problems (are), they can't be worse than mine
However great the pitfalls (are), we must do our best to succeed.

[b] An otherwise obsolete universal conditional-concessive construction involves the front-placing of the main verb in *Come what may* ('Whatever may happen'); *Be that as it may* ('However that may be'); *Do what you will* ('Whatever you do'). On a different interpretation, the initial verbs may be considered optative subjunctives (*cf: Suffice it to say* . . ., 7.86), to be associated with a similar alternative conditional-concessive construction involving the use of subjunctive *be: Be he*

friend or enemy, the law regards him as a criminal. Both constructions are rare and somewhat literary.

11.37
Clauses of reason or cause

Clauses of reason or cause are most commonly introduced by the conjunctions *because*, *as*, or *since*. *Because* has a tendency to follow the main clause, while *as* and *since* have a tendency to precede it:

I lent him the money *because he needed it*
As Jane was the eldest, she looked after the others
Since we live near the sea, we enjoy a healthy climate

These different positional tendencies reflect a different syntactic status: *because*-clauses are close to adjuncts, whereas *as*- and *since*-clauses are more like disjuncts. This is evident in the ability of *because*-clauses, but not of the others, to be the focus of cleft sentences and (more relevantly) of alternative questions (8.3 *ff*):

⎧It's *because he helped you* that I'm prepared to help him
⎩*It's *as he helped you* that I'm prepared to help him
⎧Did they retreat out of panic or *because they wanted to save lives?*
⎩?*Did they retreat out of panic or *since they wanted to save lives?*

In colloquial English, however, a final *because*-clause sometimes functions as a disjunct of reason (*cf* 9.23):

Are you going to the post office? – *because I have some letters to send* (*ie* 'I ask this because . . .')
They've lit a fire, *because I can see the smoke rising*

It is a testimony of the close and obvious connection between cause and temporal sequence that *as* and *since* are conjunctions of time, as well as of cause. This dual function can give rise to ambiguity:

As Dalrymple designed the engine, he must have realized its great capabilities (*ie* 'Because Dalrymple designed the engine . . .' OR 'While Dalrymple designed the engine . . .')

There are no abbreviated clauses of reason (**because a man of ingenuity*), but non-finite and verbless clauses can be used equivalently (see 11.47 *ff*):

Being a man of ingenuity, he had soon repaired the machine.

11.38
Clauses of circumstance

Semantically half-way between conditional clauses and clauses of reason are clauses of circumstance, which express what one might call a 'closed condition', in opposition to either the 'open' or the 'hypothetical' condition expressed by *if*-clauses. That is, they express a condition which is assumed to be fulfilled, or (to put it otherwise) they express a relation between a premise (in the subordinate clause) and the conclusion drawn from it (in the main clause). *Because, since,* and *as* can convey this meaning as well as that of cause/reason; but in addition, there is a special circumstantial compound conjunction *seeing (that)*:

Seeing that the weather has improved, we shall be able to enjoy our game

Non-finite clauses and verbless clauses often have, by implication, this meaning (see further 11.47 *ff*):

The weather having improved, we enjoyed the remainder of the game

The conjunction *now (that)* combines circumstantial with temporal meaning.

11.39
Clauses of purpose

Clauses of purpose are more often infinitival than finite:

To improve the garden, we shall plant shrubs
I left early *to catch the train*

Such infinitival clauses, like most adverbial infinitival clauses, have no subject.

More explicit indicators of purpose are the combinations *in order to* and *so as to:*

In order (for the police) to catch the culprits, elaborate plans were made
Students should take notes *so as to make revision easier*

Finite clauses of purpose may be introduced (in formal style) by the compound subordinators *in order that* (very formal) or *so that*, or (more rarely) simply *that:*

The decision was made $\left\{\begin{array}{l}\text{in order that} \\ \text{so that} \\ \text{that}\end{array}\right\}$ peace should prevail

In the purpose clause, which has 'putative' meaning (11.72), the modal auxiliaries *should* and *may* (past tense *might*) are used.

Note

Negative purpose is expressed by the now rather archaic and very formal conjunction *lest*, or (in informal BrE) by *in case:*

$\left\{\begin{array}{l}\text{Lest} \\ \text{In case}\end{array}\right\}$ the wall should collapse, they evacuated the building

Both conjunctions have the meaning 'for fear that' or 'in order that . . . not', but *cf* 11.68, 11.30 Note *b*.

11.40

Clauses of result

Clauses of result overlap with those of purpose both in meaning and in form. The chief difference is that result clauses are factual rather than 'putative' (see 11.72); hence they may contain an ordinary verb form without a modal auxiliary:

> We planted hundreds of shrubs, *so that by August the garden had improved out of all recognition*

So that, as we see from this example, serves to express result as well as purpose. Result clauses introduced by this conjunction, however, can only appear in final position (9.31).

A syntactic difference between purpose and result clauses is that whereas purpose clauses are adjuncts, result clauses are disjuncts; thus only the former can form the focus of a cleft sentence (14.18):

> It was $\begin{Bmatrix} to \\ so\ that\ we\ might \end{Bmatrix}$ *reach safety by nightfall* that we travelled all day

> *It was *so that we reached safety by nightfall* that we travelled all day

Informally, the *that* of *so that* is omitted:

> I took no notice of him, *so* he flew into a rage

It is interesting that the 'result' relation is the converse of that of 'cause', so that the same meaning can be expressed by reversing the subordinate and superordinate clause relation and using a conjunction such as *because:*

> He flew into a rage *because* I took no notice of him.

11.41

Clauses of manner and comparison

Amongst minor kinds of adverbial clause, four may be mentioned: those of manner, comparison, proportion and preference.

Clauses of manner are introduced by *as* (or often, in substandard English, by *how*):

> She cooks a turkey exactly *as my mother did*
> ('... in the way that ...')

As also introduces a manner clause which involves comparison:

> They hunted him *as a tiger stalks his prey*
> ('... in a manner similar to ...')

If this type of *as*-clause is placed initially, the correlative form *so*, in formal literary English, may introduce the main clause:

As a tiger stalks his prey, (so) they hunted him

Such examples provide a transition to adverbial clauses of comparison, which must not be confused with the major type of comparative clause as discussed in 11.53–64. *As if* and *as though* introduce adverbial clauses indicating comparison with some hypothetical circumstance:

He treats me $\begin{Bmatrix} \text{as if} \\ \text{as though} \end{Bmatrix} \begin{Bmatrix} \text{I'm} \\ \text{I were} \end{Bmatrix}$ a stranger

The use of the hypothetical past makes little difference here, since both the present and past forms imply the unreality of what is expressed in the subordinate clause; *ie* it is assumed from both sentences that 'I am not a stranger'. In other cases, *as if* or *as though* with the present expresses factual meaning:

He looks as if he's sick: fetch the doctor.

Note

[a] *Like,* elsewhere a preposition, is sometimes used as a subordinator replacing *as* in manner clauses or *as if* in clauses of comparison: *It's just like I imagined; He talks to me like I was his dog.* These usages (particularly the second one) are felt to be somewhat substandard, especially in BrE.

[b] Clauses of comparison sometimes show subject-operator inversion:

Klemperer's conducting of the third movement shows the extreme strength of his interpretation, *as does his earlier recording of the Mass in C.*
The present owner is a keen art collector, *as were several of his ancestors.*

11.42

Clauses of proportion

Proportional clauses are an extension of the category of adverbial clauses of comparison; they express a 'proportionality' or equivalence of tendency or degree between two circumstances, and like other clauses of comparison just illustrated, they may be introduced by *as* (with or without the formal matching correlative form *so*):

As time went on, (so) their hopes began to wane
As the lane got narrower, (so) the overhanging branches made it more difficult for us to keep sight of our quarry

The second proportionality could also be expressed in another form, in which the clauses are introduced by the correlative items *the . . . the* followed by the comparative forms:

The narrower the lane got, *the more difficult* the overhanging branches made it for us to keep sight of our quarry

This restructuring can only take place, however, if both clauses contain comparative forms. The fronting of the comparatives in both clauses here results in the kind of syntactic orderings one finds in relative and *wh*-interrogative clauses:

The later you arrive (A S V), the better the food is (. . . C S V).
The more you tell him (O_d S V O_i), the less notice he takes (. . . O S V).

In each case the initial proportional clause is regarded as an adverbial within the main clause. Since both clauses in a proportional sentence are of the same general pattern, however, it is not obvious why the first part of the sentence, and not the second, should be treated as the subordinate clause. Apart from the parallel with *as . . . (so)* sentences, the reason for this analysis lies in the general principle that subordination by means of correlative conjunctions (except for comparative correlatives and the *whether . . . or* construction) entails placing the subordinate clause first. There is also a similarity between the first part and an *if*-clause.

Note
Some aphoristic sentences (7.87), such as *The more the merrier*, take the form of reduced proportional sentences, in which the exact nature of the proportionality is left unspecified (presumably, in the cited example, something like 'The more people there are, the merrier things become').

11.43
Clauses of preference
The conjunctions of preference *rather than* and *sooner than* deserve mention as the only subordinators introducing a bare infinitive clause:

$\begin{cases} Rather\ than \\ Sooner\ than \end{cases}$*travel by air*, I'd prefer a week on a big liner.

Non-finite and verbless adverbial clauses
11.44
Identifying the subject: 'attachment rule'
After the foregoing survey of adverbial clause functions, it will be useful to conclude with some general remarks on the interpretation of non-finite and verbless adverbial clauses, which, as we have seen, have a considerable range of different uses.

One problem is that of identifying the 'understood' subject of a non-finite or verbless clause. The normal rule, which may be called the 'attachment rule', is that if the subject is 'understood' rather than actually present, it is assumed to be identical in reference to the subject of the superordinate clause:

The oranges, *when [they are] ripe*, are picked and sorted

In abbreviated clauses (*ie* non-finite clauses or verbless clauses introduced by a conjunction) such as the above, a direct ellipsis of the subject and operator may be postulated. In other cases, a paraphrase by a finite clause will reveal the identity of the subordinate clause subject with that of the superordinate clause:

> Persuaded by our optimism, he gladly contributed time and
>> money to the scheme
>> ('since he was persuaded . . .')
> Three years later Matthews was released, a changed man
>> ('Matthews was a changed man when he was released')
> Agatha, having been consoled by a large inheritance, wept few
>> tears of remorse over her father's grave
>> ('since she had been consoled . . .')

11.45
'Unattached' or 'unrelated' participle
A so-called 'fault of style', traditionally termed the unattached or unrelated participle, arises when the noun phrase with which the understood subject of the non-finite clause should be identified does not appear as subject of the main clause, and perhaps does not occur in the main clause at all:

> Flying through the air at the speed of sound, a sudden thought
>> struck me
> Since leaving her, the whole of life has seemed pointless

Notionally, the subordinate clause of both examples has *I* as its subject, but the first person pronoun does not actually occur as the subject of either sentence.

The rule of attachment is not, however, always applied so strictly as to exclude all cases of an 'unattached participle'. In particular, mention may be made of three factors which are inclined to render the 'unattached participle' acceptable.

(1) If the noun phrase 'understood' to be subject of the participial clause is present in a function other than subject within the main clause, or if it has an implied agentive role within the main clause, the sentence is less objectionable than if the noun phrase is absent altogether. On this basis, we may present a scale of acceptability running from example [20] to example [23] below:

> Using similar techniques, one can present the topic in
>> different lights. (Participial clause 'subject' = main
>> clause subject)   [20]

?Using similar techniques, the topic can be presented in
    different lights. (Participial clause 'subject' has implied
    agentive role in main clause)   [21]
?Using different techniques, one's results might have
    been less satisfactory. (Participial clause 'subject' is
    present in non-subject function in the main clause)   [22]
*Using similar techniques, the topic can appear in very
    different lights. (Participial clause 'subject' entirely
    lacking from main clause)   [23]

(2) In scientific literature (as the choice of examples above already
suggests) the use of 'unattached participles' is such a convenient
solecism as to be almost accepted as an institution. The following
is a textual example, in which the noun phrase required by the
participial clause does not occur in the main clause:

*When treating patients with language retardation and
    deviation of language development*, the therapy will
    consist, in part, of discussions of the patient's problems
    with parents and teachers, with subsequent language
    teaching being carried out by them.   [24]

(3) Abbreviated clauses with an 'unattached participle' appear to
be more acceptable than similar clauses without the introductory
subordinator. Thus [24], after due allowance has been made
for its occurrence in scientific English, is more acceptable than
the equivalent example without the initial *when*.

Note

[a] Normally considered exempt from the rule of attachment are participial forms
which have assumed the non-verbal functions of disjunct, conjunction, or preposition:

    Putting it mildly, you have caused us some inconvenience (8.80)
    Provided that a film entertains, few people care about its other merits (11.9)
    Considering how much it costs, this machine is a failure (6.4)

[b] Though regarded as unacceptable, examples like [23] are not infrequent since even
in these the subject is implied in the main clause somewhat as in [21] ('. . . can
appear in different lights to the person using the techniques'). Contrast the more
obvious unacceptability of:

    *Using these techniques, a wheel fell off
    *Reading the evening paper, a dog started barking.

11.46

The 'attachment rule' in infinitival and verbless clauses

Although the attachment rule is traditionally stated with reference to
participles, it applies just as much to infinitival and verbless clauses as

to participial clauses. The following are sentences of graded acceptability, paralleling the participial clause examples [20–23]:

To climb the rock face, we had to take various precautions
?To climb the rock face, various precautions had to be taken
?Though very ill, the medicine cured him in no time
*A result of the rise in prices, our economy is suffering
*To climb the rock face, certain precautions are set out below.

Note
Again, there are exemptions to the rule of attachment where the infinitival clause is a
disjunct (8.80):

His moral principles, *to be frank*, begin and end with his own interests

Also where the assumed subject of a verbless clause is an impersonal *it* referring to
the main clause as a whole:

I'll help you, *if necessary* (*ie* 'if it is necessary')
Unknown to his closest advisers, he had made approaches to the enemy, with a
view to a peace settlement (*ie* 'It was unknown to his closest advisers
that . . .')

11.47
Semantic versatility
A second problem about non-finite and verbless clauses is the difficulty
of defining the range of semantic connections they may bear to the main
clause when no subordinator is present. The following examples show
something of the wide range of meanings possible for participial and
verbless clauses (infinitival clauses, although they have a number of
adverbial functions, present no particular problem in this respect):

Being a farmer, he is suspicious of all governmental interference
(*ie* '*As* he is a farmer . . .')
Cleared, this site will be very valuable (*ie* '*When* cleared . . .')
Cleared, this site would be very valuable (*ie* '*If* cleared . . .')
A case in both hands, Mabel stalked out of the house
(*ie* '*With* a case in both hands')
Using a sharp axe, he fought his way into the building
(*ie* '*By* using a sharp axe . . .')

In this, adverbial participial and verbless clauses resemble non-restrictive clauses (13.14), implying the broad and versatile connective function of the coordinator *and* (see 9.40 *ff*). The point about non-restrictive
relative clauses (and for that matter about clauses introduced by *and*) is
that they are capable of assuming, according to context, a more precise
semantic role:

The girl, who was upset by the activities of the ghost, decided to
leave

The girl was upset by the activities of the ghost, and decided to
leave

Although the mode of clause connection does not say so, we infer that
the girl's emotional state, as described in the relative clause and the
initial clause of the coordinate sentence, was the REASON for her departure. Exactly the same point could be made about the equivalent
non-finite clause:

The girl, *upset by the activities of the ghost*, decided to leave

Unlike relative clauses, however, non-finite and verbless clauses can
occur freely in initial, medial, or final positions:

Upset by the activities of the ghost, the girl decided to leave
The girl decided to leave, *upset by the activities of the ghost*

We may illustrate the same point with *ing*-clauses and verbless clauses:

Scratching his head, the clerk confessed himself puzzled
   ('The clerk scratched his head and confessed himself puzzled')
The climbers returned, *hungry and exhausted*
   ('. . . who were hungry and exhausted . . .')

11.48
Supplementive clauses
Because, like non-restrictive relative clauses and *and*-clauses, they have
the chameleon-like semantic quality of adapting to context, these
adverbial participial and verbless clauses may be designated simply
adverbial SUPPLEMENTIVE clauses. Those which have no overt subject
are similar in effect to non-restrictive relative clauses, since the 'understood subject' in such cases provides a link with the main clause, rather
as the relative pronoun provides such a link in postmodifying relative clauses. Those which have an overt subject, such as

No further discussion arising, the meeting was brought to a close

may be designated ABSOLUTE clauses, since they are not overtly bound
to the main clause, even on a semantic level, by any shared element.

11.49
Subjectless supplementive clauses
The formal characteristics of supplementive clauses without a subject
are:

(1) They are participial or verbless clauses.
(2) Their most typical positions in the clause are (a) initial, (b) final,
    and (c) immediately after their 'antecedent' (*ie* the noun phrase
    in the main clause which is their assumed subject).

In position (c), supplementive clauses without a subject may be indistinguishable from participial postmodifying clauses (13.23) or from noun phrases in apposition (9.156); thus it is difficult (and semantically unimportant) to decide whether the participial clause in

> The substance, *discovered almost by accident,* has revolutionized
>   medicine   [25]

is to be regarded as functionally equivalent to

> The substance, *which was (incidentally) discovered almost*
>   *by accident, . . .*   [25a]

or to

> *Discovered almost by accident,* the substance . . .   [25b]

There are, however, various types which may be unambiguously labelled supplementive. They include:

(a) *-ing* clauses containing auxiliary verbs or the verb BE (forms which do not occur in a postmodifying non-finite clause):

> The children, *having eaten their fill,* were allowed to leave the table

(b) *-ing* clauses with a stative verb:

> The teacher, *not knowing who was to blame,* resorted to collective punishment

(c) Most adjectival verbless clauses:

> Lawson, *implacable,* contented himself with a glare of defiance.

The classification of (a) and (b) as supplementive clauses is connected with the fact that these clauses cannot be regarded as reductions of relative clauses, since the equivalent finite relative clauses would be unacceptable: **who were having eaten their fill* and **who was not knowing who was to blame. Cf* also 13.18, 23. We regard (c) as a supplementive clause because adjectival constructions can act as non-restrictive postmodification of a noun phrase only in very special circumstances.
  Hence the unacceptability of [27] in contrast to [26]:

> John welcomed Margaret, *glad of her company*   [26]
> *John welcomed Margaret, *glad of his company*   [27]

Only the supplementive clause, which has as its 'antecedent' the subject of the main clause, is possible here.

11.50
Contingency

Despite what has been said about the semantic affinity between the two types of clause, supplementive clauses are less inclined to be semantically neutral than relative clauses. In fact, it is often implied that what they describe is a 'contingency' or 'accompanying circumstance' to what is described in the main clause. 'Contingency' may be interpreted, according to context, as a causal or temporal connection, or perhaps most commonly of all, a 'circumstantial' one (11.38). In *-ing* clauses, dynamic verbs typically suggest a temporal link, and stative verbs a causal link:

> *Reaching the river*, we pitched camp for the night
> ('When we reached . . .')
> *Living in the country*, we had few social engagements
> ('Because we lived . . .')

This same implication of contingency is typically present with absolute clauses (those with an overt subject).

In some sentences, the absolute clause could easily be replaced by a clause introduced by *and:*

> Members of the family occupied the spare bedrooms, *the remaining guests having been booked in at neighbouring hotels*

But in most cases, a causal, temporal, or circumstantial connection is suggested:

> *All our savings gone*, we started looking for jobs
> A small boy, *his satchel trailing behind him*, ran past

In the second of these sentences, the nature of the assumed connection with the main clause could have been expressed by a relative clause with *have:* 'A small boy, who had his satchel . . .', or else by *with:* 'A small boy, with his satchel . . .'. Here, *have* and *with* can be given the fairly precise meaning of physical possession, but more generally, a *with* can be optionally placed at the head of an absolute clause introducing the 'subject' but otherwise conveying little more than the vague notion of contingency or 'accompanying circumstance':

> (*With*) *the whole meeting in uproar*, the chairman abandoned the attempt to take a vote

The equivalent negative clauses may be introduced by *without:*

> *Without a tear on her face*, the girl watched him led away
> The war was over *without a shot being fired*
> *Without anyone noticing*, I slipped through the window
> I wouldn't dare go home *without the job finished*

Notice that the *without* clause, being negative, normally requires non-assertive forms like *anyone*.

Note

With and *without* also introduce infinitival clauses: *with so much to do; without a thing to worry about.*

11.51
Supplementive clauses in final position
In spite of their resemblance to non-restrictive relative clauses, supplementive clauses need not be separated from the rest of the clause intonationally when they occur in final position. The following are therefore alternative renderings of the same sentence, different only in that [28] has two focuses of information (see 14.2 *ff*), whereas [29] has only one:

The manager apPRÒACHED us, SMÌLing   [28]
The manager approached us SMÌLing   [29]

One result of this is the possible neutralization of the formal difference between non-finite clauses acting as supplementive clauses and those acting as complementation of the verb. Thus [30] is ambiguous:

I saw him going home   [30]

On one interpretation (that of the supplementive clause), *I* is the notional subject of *going*, whereas on the other (that of verb complementation), *him* is.

Further, a sentence such as the following is ambiguous in more than one way:

I caught the boy smoking a cigar

In addition to the two possible structures of [30], this has a third interpretation, in which the non-finite clause is a postmodifying clause. The three interpretations are:

'I caught the boy while I was smoking a cigar'
   (SUPPLEMENTIVE CLAUSE)
'I caught the boy in the act of smoking a cigar'
   (VERB COMPLEMENTATION)
'I caught the boy who was smoking a cigar'
   (POSTMODIFICATION)

On the analogy of [29], we may identify the final adjectival or nominal element of the following examples as a verbless supplementive clause:

The manager approached us *full of apologies*   [31]
He drove the damaged car home *undismayed*   [32]
He came out of prison *a changed man*   [33]

In each, the adjectival or noun phrase is in an 'intensive relationship' (7.6) with the subject of the main clause, and is thus distinct from an object complement, which would be 'intensive' towards the direct object. Also, an object complement could not normally be placed at the front of the sentence, while this manoeuvre is perfectly natural in the three sentences [31–33]; *eg:*

> *Full of apologies*, the manager approached us.

Note
In some sentences in other ways like [31–33], however, the fronting of the final adjectival or nominal element is far from natural:

> He began life *a Protestant*
> They ended the season *bottom of the league*

*A Protestant, he began life would be, to say the least, a vacuous sentence; yet the same would apply to elements of undisputed adverbial status, as in:

> He began life as a miner's son ~
> **As a miner's son*, he began life
> They ended the season with a victory ~
> **With a victory*, they ended the season

The unlikelihood of fronting, in these examples, seems to be due to the low information-content of the remainder of the sentence, which, after the removal of the final adverbial element, is left to bear the main information focus (14.2 *ff*). One cannot therefore argue that immobility here is a reason for not classifying *a Protestant* and *bottom of the league* as verbless supplementive clauses.

11.52
Sentential relative clauses

From the supplementive clause, it is only a short step to the type of relative clause which operates directly within sentences rather than as part of a noun phrase. This is the sentential relative clause, which is so called because unlike other relative clauses, which have a noun phrase as antecedent (13.8 *ff*), it refers back to a whole clause or sentence, or even to a whole series of sentences:

> After that things improved, *which surprised me*   [34]

In this case, that which caused the surprise, the antecedent, is the whole of the event described in the main clause. One might equally imagine a story-teller coming to the end of his story with the words:

> – which is how the kangaroo came to have a pouch   [35]

The *which* here could refer back over the whole length of the story.

Sentential relative clauses are introduced by the relative word *which*, and are closely parallel to non-restrictive postmodifying clauses in noun phrases. Quite frequently, *which* is not a pronoun, but a determiner, preceding an abstract noun such as *fact, case*, etc which could function in apposition to a clause:

> The train may have been held up by repairs to the line,
> *in which case, we may soon hear when it is expected to*
> *arrive*   [36]

Which may also occur as prepositional complement: *as a result of which, instead of which*, etc.

Regarding its function within the sentence, the sentential relative clause is somewhat anomalous. Despite its fixed position at the end of the clause to which it relates, its status is more like that of a disjunct than anything else, as may be gathered from its semantic similarity to comment clauses such as *what is more* (11.65); compare *which surprised me* in [34] above with *what surprised me* as a comment clause. On the other hand, like other non-restrictive relative clauses, it can be most nearly paraphrased by a coordinate clause; for example, [35] could be replaced by *and that's how the kangaroo came to have a pouch*, and [36] by *. . . and in that case . . .* See further 13.15.

Note
The temporal phrases *by which time* and *at which point* also introduce sentential relative clauses.

Comparative clauses
11.53
The essential feature of a comparative construction, in broad grammatical terms, is that two propositions, one expressed by the main clause and one by the comparative clause, are compared with respect to something they have in common. Thus the sentence

> His name is the same *as his father's* (*name is*)

contains the requisites of a comparative clause. More narrowly considered, however, comparison concerns a property measurable in terms of degree, and more specifically still, by means of the comparative items *-er, more, less, worse*, etc (5.68 *ff*), together with the correlative clause-introducer *than*.

11.54
The comparative element
The clause element of the main clause which contains the comparative item will be called the comparative element (comp-element); it acts

as a 'hinge', specifying the common denominator or STANDARD on the basis of which the comparison between the clauses takes place. To understand the semantics of a comparative sentence, we may imagine it arising from two questions introduced by *how* as follows:

$$\begin{cases} \text{How old is Mary (compared with Jane)?} & [37] \\ \text{How old is Jane (compared with Mary)?} & [38] \end{cases}$$

answers to [37]:

$$\begin{cases} \text{Mary is } older \text{ than Jane (is)} & [37a] \\ \text{Mary is } younger \text{ than Jane (is)} & [37b] \end{cases}$$

answers to [38]:

$$\begin{cases} \text{Jane is } younger \text{ than Mary (is)} & [38a] \\ \text{Jane is } older \text{ than Mary (is)} & [38b] \end{cases}$$

Of these four answers, [37a] and [38a] are synonymous, expressing the same relationship in a different order; likewise [37b] and [38b]. Less frequently, comparison is expressed by the item *less*, which indicates tendency to the 'negative' pole of the standard or range of comparison.

Further answers to [37]:

$$\begin{cases} \text{Mary is } less\ old \text{ than Jane (is)} & [37c] \\ \text{Mary is } less\ young \text{ than Jane (is)} & [37d] \end{cases}$$

Again, paraphrase relationships arise, [37c] being synonymous with [37b] and [38b], and [37d] with [37a] and [38a]. Sentences like [37d], in which the 'marked' member of the pair of adjectives is combined with *less*, are rare.

It is seen above that the comp-element (italicized) together with *than* forms a 'hinge' by which the two *wh*-elements of the questions [37] and [38] could be said to be combined. This coalescence, which is central to the comparative process, accounts for an appearance of defective structure in the comparative clause; for example, in [37a] above, the comparative clause *than Jane (is)* contains (optionally) a form of the verb BE, but not a complement or adjunct such as the verb BE normally requires for complementation. One might postulate an omitted repetition of the standard of comparison in the comparative clause: *Mary is older than Jane is [old]*. In fact, however, a comparative clause element corresponding to the comp-element in the main clause can occur only when the standards of comparison are different: *Mary is cleverer than Jane is pretty*. Further structural 'gaps' arise through the optional ellipsis of other elements in the comparative clause, as discussed in 11.56 below.

Note

[a] Constructions with *more . . . than* and *less . . . than* do not necessarily introduce comparative clauses. There is a type of non-clausal comparison in which *than* is followed by an explicit standard or yardstick of comparison, normally a noun phrase of measure, or a noun phrase implying degree:

> I weigh *more than 200 pounds*
> It goes fast*er than 100 miles per hour*
> The strike was nothing *less than a national catastrophe*

Here *than* is best considered a preposition, and the phrase which follows it a prepositional complement, since there is no possibility of expanding the *than*-phrase into a clause:

> *It goes faster than 100 miles per hour goes.

[b] There is a second type of *more . . . than* construction not introducing a comparative clause. This is the quasi-coordinative type of construction illustrated by

> I was more angry than frightened
> (*cf* I was angry rather than frightened)

A distinguishing characteristic of this construction is the non-occurrence of the suffixal form of comparison:

> *I was angrier than frightened.

[c] A comparative clause cannot normally be negative:

> *I worked harder *than Michael didn't*

This observation can be related to the oddity of negative *how*-questions:

> *How hard didn't Michael work?

11.55
The comp-element in various functions

Like the Q-element of a question, the comp-element of a comparative sentence can be any of the main elements of the clause (apart from the verb). We may therefore go on to illustrate it in various clause functions:

> comp-element = S: *More people* use this brand than (use) any
>   other window-cleaning fluid
> comp-element = C_s: I'm *happier* about it than my husband (is)
> comp-element = O_d: He knows *more* than most people (know)
> comp-element = O_i (rare): That man has given *more children*
>   happiness than anyone else (has)
> comp-element = A: You've been working *much harder* than I
>   (have)

Again like *wh*-elements of various kinds, the comp-element is not limited to such clause functions, but may represent a pushdown element within a nominal clause subordinate to the comparative clause:

> Derek caught *more fish* than I expected ((that) he would (catch))
> I felt *more miserable* than I can say ((that) I felt)

In such cases, it is usual to omit the whole of the *that*-clause. The comp-element may also be a prepositional complement:

She's applied for more jobs than Joyce ((has) applied for)

11.56
Ellipsis in comparative clauses

Ellipsis of a part of the comparative clause is likely to occur whenever that part is a repetition of something in the main clause. Since it is normal for the two clauses to be closely parallel both in structure and content, ellipsis is the rule rather than the exception in comparative construc-tions. It is worth while pointing out, however, that there is no necessary parallelism between the main and comparative clauses, and that the comparative clause, so long as it overlaps with the content of the main clause in respect of the comp-element, can be of independent structure. Thus we may take two *how*-questions of disparate clause types (*SV* and *SVO*):

{How quickly does he speak?
{How quickly can his secretary take dictation?

and use them to construct the comparative sentence:

He speaks more quickly than his secretary can take dictation.

Here is a second example in which the comparative clause ends with a preposition that cannot be ellipted:

He's a better man than I took him for

The most characteristic type of comparative clause, on the other hand, is one which imitates the structure of the main clause, and repeats its whole content, with the exception of one element, which provides a contrast:

con-trast		comp-ele-ment		con-trast		
James	enjoys the theatre	more	than	Susan	enjoys the theatre	[39a]
James	enjoys the theatre	more	than	Susan	enjoys it	[39b]
James	enjoys the theatre	more	than	Susan	does	[39c]
James	enjoys the theatre	more	than	Susan		[39d]

This type of clause, as we see in [39a–39d] may be reduced, through the stage-by-stage elimination of repeated matter, to a single element. The reduction process may involve substitution (the use of pronouns and the pro-predication DO) as well as ellipsis. Ellipsis of the object cannot take place unless the verb too is ellipted or replaced by DO; thus [39e] is unacceptable:

*James enjoys the theatre more than Susan enjoys   [39e]

On the other hand, if the object is the comp-element itself, the verb may remain:

James knows more about the theatre than Susan (knows).

Note

[a] In clauses with a pushdown comp-element, as we saw in 11.55, the whole of the nominal clause within the comparative clause may be eliminated through ellipsis:

You spent more money than we intended ((that) you should (spend))

Further, when the comparative clause contains an anticipatory *it* construction, not only is the whole nominal clause removed, but the *it* as well:

You spent more money than was intended

Almost the ultimate in reduction of the comparative construction is reached with phrases like *than usual, than necessary*, the fullest form of which may be reconstructed as follows:

You arrived earlier than (it was) usual/necessary (for you to arrive)

[b] Infinitival clauses with a pushdown comp-element can only be partially ellipted, the front portion of the clause up to and including the *to* remaining intact:

He gets more orders than we ever manage to
She enjoyed it much more than I expected her to

The verb BE cannot be so easily ellipted in this context, however:

She was more beautiful than I imagined her *to be*.

11.57
Ambiguity of *than me*, etc

We have seen that if ellipsis is taken to its furthest extent, we are often left with no more than the subject or object of the original clause:

I speak Greek better than *you* (speak Greek)
The photographs disappointed my parents more than (they
   disappointed) *me*

In this situation, ambiguity can arise according to whether the remaining noun phrase is judged to be the subject or the object of the original clause:

He loves the dog more than his wife

could mean either (a) '... than his wife loves the dog' or (b) '... than he loves his wife'.

If a pronoun is all that remains of the comparative clause, there is a difference between informal English and formal English, in that the former prefers the objective for both constructions (a) and (b) above, whereas the latter prefers the subjective case of the pronoun for construction (a):

He loves the dog more than *her* (informal)
He loves the dog more than *she* (formal)

Prescriptive grammar upholds the second construction, both on grammatical grounds (that *she* is the subject of the clause) and on grounds of clarity, since in formal English, one can distinguish between the following:

He attacked the Government more than we
    ('... than we attacked the Government')
He attacked the Government more than us
    ('... than he attacked us')

whereas in informal English the two meanings are often expressed identically.

On the other hand, one may account for the use of the objective pronoun in informal style by pointing out that, as *than* in this construction has the appearance of a preposition (*cf* 11.54 Note *a*), the pronoun falls within 'object territory' (4.112). Since objections can be raised against both (stiffness or overfamiliarity), writers sometimes steer a middle course using additional pro-forms (*than we did, than he did us*).

11.58
Single-, two-, and three-variable comparisons
The foregoing discussion has revolved around sentences in which the main clause and the comparative clause have differed only in one clause element. We now have to consider whether this type of comparative sentence, which may be called the 'single-variable' type, is the only one possible where the two clauses are of parallel structure; or if not, what alternatives are available.

It is clear that there must be some contrasting element within a comparative sentence, otherwise the whole idea of a comparison would be meaningless. Hence the absurdity of a sentence like:

*More people speak Spanish than speak Spanish

On the other hand, while the single-variable comparison is the most common type, there is no reason why more than one clause element should not contrast:

con-trast 1		comp-ele-ment	contrast 2		con-trast 1		contrast 2
James	knows	more	about films	than	Susan	does	about music

This sentence has two contrasting elements, as marked; and even a three-variable comparative construction is possible:

> Ogden played the piano more skilfully than his fellow-countryman conducted the orchestra.

11.59
Partial contrasts between comparative and main clauses
A second point is that elements of structure may contrast in part rather than as a whole: for example, an auxiliary verb may be newly introduced in the comparative clause, while the lexical verb is carried over from the main clause, so that the two verb phrases are only partially identical:

> I *like* him better than I *did* (*like him*)
> I *get up* later than I *ought to* (*get up*)

It may also be noted that the comp-element itself may contain a partial contrast:

> Her husband is a *better psychologist* than ((he is) *a*) *pathologist*
> The house is much *taller* than it is *wide*

and – yet a further point – the contrast may be purely or chiefly in the form of an addition which the comparative clause makes to the content of the main clause, the only difference otherwise being in the tense or aspect or modality of the verb. Of this type are those already illustrated with the pushdown comp-element in a subordinate nominal clause:

> He is a greater painter than people suppose (he is)   [40]
> You'll enjoy it more than (you did) last year   [41]

A further example is the reduced comparative clause *than ever:*

> He's lazier now than$\begin{cases} \text{ever} \\ \text{he ever was} \end{cases}$ [42]

Examples [41] and [42] make it clear that the verb phrase of the second clause can be ellipted even if it contrasts in terms of tense, modality, etc, so long as it is lexically identical with the verb phrase of the main clause. This accounts for the complete ellipsis of the comparative clause in sentences like:

> You're getting slimmer (than you were)
> You're looking better (than you were (looking))

Here, from the comp-element on its own we infer a comparison with an earlier state of the same person. The whole comparative clause can be omitted, and ellipsis reaches its furthest extent.

Note

There is a second type of circumstance in which the comparative clause is omitted, the comp-element being left on its own. This is where there is anaphoric reference to an implied or actual preceding clause or sentence (*cf* 10.71 *ff*), as in:

I caught the last bus from town; but Harry came home even *later*
(*ie* 'later than that', 'later than I came home').

11.60
Six functions of the comparative item *more*

In addition to classifying comp-elements by their function in the clause, we can consider the comparative item (which, for present purposes, we shall identify with the word *more*) in terms of its function within the comp-element. There are six such functions:

(i) *more* as quantifier: Jack has *more girl-friends* than his brother (has)

(ii) *more* as head of a noun phrase: *More (of them)* are at home than (are) abroad

(iii) *more* as adjunct: I agree with you *more* than ((I agree) with) Robert

(iv) *more* as modifier of adjective head: His speech was *more interesting* than I expected (it would be)

(v) *more* as modifier of adjective premodifier: It was *a more lively discussion* than I expected (it would be)

(vi) *more* as modifier of adverb: The time passed *more quickly* than (it passed) last year

In each of the above examples, the whole comp-element is in italics. It will be noticed that in some cases the word *more* constitutes the whole of the comp-element.

Function types (i) and (ii) refer to quantity (in either a 'countable' or a 'mass' sense); thus in both the sentences illustrating these types, we could replace *more* by *a greater number of*.

Function types (iv) and (v) have to be separated from one another because of the special semantic implications of (v). If we say

There are more intelligent monkeys than Herbert

we make it clear that Herbert is a monkey; that is, by placing the comparative adjective in front of the noun, we transfer the meaning of the noun to the noun phrase in the comparative clause. On the other hand, we could use an alternative construction in which the comparative adjective is placed after the head in a relative clause or reduced relative clause:

There are monkeys (who are) more intelligent than Herbert

In this case, we do not know whether Herbert is a monkey or not; he may be a man whom the speaker wishes to insult. This difference of meaning accounts for the absurdity of:

*There are more intelligent monkeys than the mayor of this town

The same observation can be made about *more* as a modifier of a pre-modifying adverb; the meaning of the construction alters according to whether the head of the phrase in which *more* appears is a noun:

I've never met a man more outstandingly courageous than
    Miss Ada Pennyfeather
*I've never met a more outstandingly courageous man than
    Miss Ada Pennyfeather

The absurdity of the second sentence may be explained by imagining, as a starting point for the sentence, the two *how*-questions:

How outstandingly courageous a man have I ever met?
*How outstandingly courageous a man is Miss Ada
    Pennyfeather?

Both the starred sentences are unacceptable because they imply that Miss Pennyfeather is a man.

Note

[a] In addition to the six functions listed above, the comparative item may have certain anomalous functions in non-clausal comparative constructions (see 11.54 Note *a*):

It's hotter than just warm
He went farther than beyond Chicago
I am more than sad about it
He more than complained: he threw the whole book of rules at me
He was more than slightly hurt

What is in common formally between these constructions is that the comparative item is followed by *than*, which in turn is followed by one of a range of syntactic elements, including adjectives, verbs, adverbs, and prepositional phrases. Semantically, the sentences amount to comments on the inadequacy of linguistic expressions. For example, the first sentence could be rephrased: '*Warm' is an inadequate word to describe the present temperature.*

[b] The modifying sequence $\left\{ \begin{array}{c} less \\ more \end{array} \right\}$ *of a* . . . occurs with gradable noun heads:

He's more of a fool than I thought (he was)

Cf the *How*-question, *How much of a fool is he?*

11.61
As . . . as

Widening the discussion of comparison, we may take into account not only comparisons based on lack of equivalence (on some scale of value), such as that expressed by *more* and *less*, but comparisons based on other relationships, notably those of equivalence, excess, sufficiency, etc, as expressed by *as . . . as, so . . . that, such . . . that, too*, and *enough*.

The *as . . . as* construction is grammatically parallel to the *more . . . than* construction, except that *as* lacks the ordinator, pronoun, and adverb functions of *more*; these gaps are filled by *as much* and *as many*, as the following examples (parallel to (i)–(iv) in 11.60) show:

Jack has *as many girl-friends* as his brother (has)	[43]
As many (of them) are at home as (are) abroad	[44]
I agree with you *as much* as ((I agree) with) Robert	[45]
She may be *as lucky* as she hopes (she will (be))	[46]

Paraphrase relationships exist between sentences with *as . . . as* and negative sentences with *more . . . than:*

⎧ Attila was not more ruthless than Caesar
⎨ Caesar was not less ruthless than Attila
⎩ Caesar was as ruthless as Attila.

Note

[a] The construction corresponding to *more of a . . .* (11.60 Note *b*) is *as much of a . . .:*

It was *as much of a success* as I had hoped.

[b] In a negative sentence, *so . . . as* may be substituted (in more formal style) for *as . . . as:*

He's *not so/as young* as I thought.

11.62

Enough and *too*

A further pair of comparative expressions related through negation are *enough* and *too*, which convey the contrasting notions of 'sufficiency' and 'excess'. Paraphrase pairs may be constructed, using antonymous adjectives or adverbs, as follows:

⎧ The grass is too short (to cut)
⎩ The grass isn't long enough (to cut)
⎧ He's not too poor (to own a car)
⎩ He's rich enough (to own a car)

The infinitive clause which follows the comp-element may be omitted if context allows.

The negative force of *too* is shown in the use of non-assertive forms like *any* or *anything;* compare:

She's *old enough* to do *some* work
She's *too old* to do *any* work

The infinitive clause may or may not contain a subject:

It moves too quickly *for most people to see* (*it*)
I've been alive long enough *to understand that*

As the second of these examples indicates, a pronoun in the infinitive clause may be omitted if it substitutes for the subject of the main clause. When there is no subject in the infinitive clause, the understood subject is often the subject of the main clause. The infinitive may also be passive in meaning:

It moves too quickly *to see* (*ie* 'to be seen' 'for anyone to see it')

An ambiguity accordingly arises when either active or passive meaning would be plausible. *Cf:*

He is friendly enough *to help*
('. . . for him to help others' or '. . . for others to help him')   [47]
He's too good a man *to kill*
('. . . for him to kill others' or '. . . for others to kill him')   [48]

As we see in [48], when *too* modifies an adjective which in turn modifies a singular countable noun, the indefinite article is inserted after the adjective. There is no plural or uncountable equivalent for this construction: instead of **It's too good food to throw away* we have to say *It's food (which is) too good to throw away*. The same problem does not arise with *enough*, which always follows the word it modifies (except when used as a quantifier, when the premodifying position is more usual: *We have enough money to last*).

Note
[a] The threefold ambiguity of *It's too hot to eat* has often been commented on. Apart from the two meanings corresponding to those of [48] above, there is a third interpretation in which *it* is the empty 'climatic' *it* (see 7.18):

The weather is too hot for anyone to eat anything.

[b] The constructions *enough of a . . .*, *too much of a . . .* (*cf* 13.50 Note) should be compared with those mentioned in 11.60 Note *b* and 11.61 Note *a:*

He's $\begin{Bmatrix} \text{enough} \\ \text{too much} \end{Bmatrix}$ of a coward to do that.

11.63
So . . . (that) and *such . . . (that)*
The pair of correlatives *so . . . (that)* and *such . . . (that)* are linked to the two words just considered, *too* and *enough*, by paraphrase relations. For example:

$\begin{cases} \text{It flies fast enough to beat the speed record} \\ \text{It flies so fast that it can beat the speed record} \end{cases}$

$\begin{cases} \text{It's too good a chance to miss} \\ \text{It's such a good chance that we mustn't miss it} \end{cases}$

In each pair, the first sentence is the more idiomatic. It will be observed that in these paraphrases, the verb in the *that*-clause contains a modal auxiliary; when the modal auxiliary is absent, the *so/such* ... (*that*) construction has the more definitive meaning of result or outcome:

He was so wild *that we let him escape*
I so enjoyed it (*or* I enjoyed it so much) *that I'm determined to go again*

The alternation between *so* and *such* depends on grammatical function: *so* is an adverb, whereas *such* is a determiner. The *that* which introduces the comparative clause is sometimes omitted in informal English:

He polished the floor so hard *you could see your face in it*

The construction *so/such ... as to* plus infinitive clause is sometimes used in place of *so* or *such* followed by a *that*-clause:

His satires were *so* brilliant *as to make even his victims laugh*   [49]
The brilliance of his satires was *such as to make even his victims laugh*   [50]

The clauses discussed in this and in the preceding section differ from clauses introduced by *more/less/-er ... than* and *as ... as* in that they do not match the main clause in terms of constant and variable elements, and so do not lend themselves to ellipsis. Their structure is relatively independent of the structure of the main clause.

Note

[a] Apart from the construction illustrated by [50], in formal (perhaps archaic) usage there is one in which *such ... as* is followed by a finite verb clause:

They were fed with *such* sumptuous fare *as kings dream of*

The paraphrase of *such ... as* by 'of a kind which' here suggests the classification of such clauses as relative rather than as comparative (see further 13.11, 13.68).

[b] An emphatic fronting of the comp-element, accompanied by inversion of subject and operator, is sometimes found in formal (especially literary) English:

To such lengths *did she go* in rehearsal that two actors walked out
So strange *was his appearance* that no one recognized him.

[c] When *so* or *such* appears without its correlative *that*, the *so/such* clause may follow the result clause, and assume the character of an afterthought:

I could have punched him on the nose, I felt so wild (informal)
He had no need to make speeches, so impregnable was his position in the party

This construction is often emotive.

11.64

Syntactic function of comparative clauses

The question of the function of the comparative clause within the sentence is problematic, and for that reason has been avoided up to this point. Its frequent inseparability from the comp-element suggests that the comparative clause may be regarded as a postmodifier, in which case what has hitherto been called the 'comp-element' is not in itself an element of clause structure, but makes up an element of structure (adjective, noun, or adverb phrase) when the comparative clause is added to it:

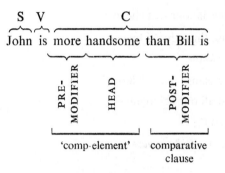

This way of looking at comparative structure has its limitations, however, since if the 'comp-element' occurs in non-final position (particularly in subject position), the comparative clause is usually separated from it and placed at the end of the clause:

More accidents occur in the home *than on the roads*

Indeed, final position of a *than*-clause may be, as in the above sentence, almost obligatory; and is definitely obligatory with the *so/such . . . that* constructions. Contrast:

So many people came to the party *that we ran out of liquor*
*So many people that we ran out of liquor came to the party

Another solution, in keeping with this last observation, would be to regard comparative clauses as of adverbial function within the main clause, and more precisely, of the type of adverbial clause which, like result clauses (11.40), occurs normally only in final position.

One must admit, however, that comparative clauses do not fit easily into any constituent-structure account of the sentence. In semantic terms, the whole clause together with the comparative item *more* etc may be regarded as equivalent to a degree adverb.

Comment clauses

11.65

Comment clauses are somewhat loosely related to the rest of the clause they belong to, and may be classed as disjuncts or conjuncts. In general, they may occur initially, finally, or medially, and have a separate tone unit (App II.12).

The SMĬTHS, | *as you probably KNÓW*, | are going to AMÈRICA |

As the following list of types shows, comment clauses vary in form:

(1) Like a main clause:

At that time, *I believe*, labour was cheap

(2) Like an adverbial clause (introduced by *as*):

I'm a pacifist, *as you know*

(3) Like a nominal relative clause (8.82, 8.89):

What's more, we lost all our belongings

(4) *To*-infinitive clause (8.80 *f*):

I'm not sure what to do, *to be honest*

(5) *-ing* clause (8.80 *f*):

I doubt, *speaking as a layman*, whether television is the right medium

Further examples of each type are:

(1) *I know, I see, I suppose, I'm afraid, you know, remember, one hears, they tell me, God knows, it is claimed*, etc. (Note also imperative clauses with a final subject: *mind you, mark you*, etc)

(2) *as I understand (it), as you say, as is common knowledge, as is generally assumed*. (Note the omission of *it* as subject; *cf* 13.15); on the use of the present tense in *as you say*, etc, see 3.25 (4).)

(3) *what's more surprising/serious/*etc, *what annoys me*, etc.

(4) *to be fair/frank/*etc, *to be serious for a minute, to speak candidly, to put it bluntly*, etc.

(5) *generally speaking, roughly speaking, speaking frankly, speaking off the record, putting it mildly*, etc.

Types 3, 4 and 5 tend to have a rather restricted and idiomatic membership, while Types 1 and 2 are larger and more productive. In each category, however, there are idiomatic or cliché expressions: *you see, as I say, what's more, to be honest, generally speaking*. Similarly, in each category there is at least some freedom to coin new expressions.

11.66

In the first type of clause, which is perhaps the most important, the verb or adjective is of the transitive class which requires an indirect statement as object (11.17, 11.76, 12.47). We may therefore set up a one-to-one relationship between sentences containing such clauses, and indirect statements:

⌠At that time, I believe, labour was cheap	[51]
⌡I believe that, at that time, labour was cheap	[52]

To convert an indirect statement into a sentence such as [51], one has to reverse the relation of subordination between the two clauses, making the *that*-clause into the main clause and the main clause into the comment clause. Because of this reversal of syntactic roles, the two sentences [51] and [52] are not quite paraphrases; but the relationship between them illuminates the function of the comment clause.

Since the *that* of a *that*-clause is normally deletable (11.17), cases arise in which only the intonation (reflected by comma separation in writing) distinguishes which is the superordinate and which the subordinate clause:

⌠You KNOW, | I | think you're WRONG |\ (COMMENT CLAUSE,
⌡You know, I | think you're WRONG | ∫ MAIN CLAUSE)
　You | know (that) I think you're WRONG | (MAIN CLAUSE,
　　THAT-CLAUSE)

(On the use of the onset and tone-unit boundary symbols | and |, see App II.12.)

Quite a number of Type 1 comment clauses introduced by 1st person or 2nd person subjects are stereotyped conversation fillers (*you know*, *I see*, etc). Outside this group, however, clauses can be fairly freely constructed, and variations of tense and aspect, additions of adjuncts, etc, are permitted:

The Indian railways (*my uncle was telling me some time ago*) have
　always made a profit

The subordinator *as* may be added to convert such clauses to Type 2 comment clauses, with virtually no change of meaning:

The Indian railways (*as my uncle was telling me some time ago*)
　have always made a profit

But to add *as* to one of the short stereotyped phrases *you know*, *I see*, *God knows*, etc is to alter the meaning (*as you know* ≠ *you know*) or to make the sentence unacceptable.

Note

[a] There are also comment clauses which may be related to a main clause introducing an indirect question:

> What's he doing, *I wonder?*
>
> (*cf* I wonder what he's doing)

Sometimes a comment clause is itself in the form of a direct question:

> What's he doing, *do you think?*

[b] Clauses which introduce direct speech (11.73) may be considered comment clauses of Type 1:

> 'It's time we went,' *I said.*

The verb phrase in dependent clauses
11.67

Although in general the rules for the uses of tenses, aspects, modal auxiliaries, etc, apply both to dependent and independent clauses, we have to discuss a number of cases in which the nature of a verb phrase is bound up with the particular type of subordinate clause it belongs to. The five main topics to be considered are: the present tense; the hypothetical past; the perfect aspect; the subjunctive; and the 'quasi-subjunctive' use of auxiliaries *should, may*, etc.

11.68
The present tense with *if,* etc

To express future meaning, the present tense is used in preference to the auxiliary *will/shall* in certain types of adverbial clauses:

$$not \begin{cases} \text{*When} \\ \text{*Before} \\ \text{*If} \\ \text{*As long as} \end{cases} \text{he will arrive, the band will play the National Anthem}$$

$$but \begin{cases} \text{When} \\ \text{Before} \\ \text{If} \\ \text{As long as} \end{cases} \text{he arrives, the band will play the National Anthem}$$

The subordinators chiefly involved belong to the temporal and conditional (in part also, concessive) categories:

> TEMPORAL: *after, as, before, once, till, until, when(ever), as soon as*
> CONDITIONAL: *if, unless, as long as, provided* (*that*), *given* (*that*), *assuming* (*that*), *presuming* (*that*), *whatever, whoever*, etc.

Also with a conditional element of meaning, though not exclusively of that category, the conjunctions *even if* and *in case* can be added to the list:

Even if tomorrow's match is cancelled, Lancashire will still be
top of the league
He will come *in case* he's wanted

(In AmE this could mean 'He will come *only if* he is wanted, in the event of his being wanted', but in BrE 'He will come because he may be wanted'.)

In manner clauses also, future events are indicated by the present tense:

Next time I'll do as he *says*

Nominal *that-* and *wh-*clauses tend to contain present tense verbs when the main clause (as well as the subordinate clause) refers to the future; but when the main clause refers to the present, the future *will* is likely to be used in the subordinate clause. Contrast:

I shall ask him what he *wants* tomorrow
The question is what he *will want* tomorrow

However, there are exceptional verbs like *hope, suppose* (in the imperative), and *assume*, after which the simple present can often be used as readily as *will:*

I hope that the parcel *comes* in time
Suppose he *loses* his way
Let's assume our opponents *win* the election

Note
There are two exceptions to the rule that *will/won't* cannot appear in *if*-clauses (and in some of the other types of clause mentioned above):

(i) Where *will/won't* has a volitional or habitual meaning, rather than a pure future meaning:

If you *won't* (='refuse to') help us, all our plans will be ruined.

(ii) Where even though the *if*-clause refers to the future, the condition expressed by the whole sentence obtains in the present:

If he *won't* arrive before nine, there's no point in ordering dinner for him
If it *will* make any difference, I'll gladly lend you some money

In both these sentences, the future contingency expressed in the *if*-clause determines a present decision.

11.69

The hypothetical past tense
The past tense is used, as already explained (11.31), for hypothetical meaning in conditional clauses:

If we *had* enough money, I wouldn't have to work so hard

The corresponding main clause construction is *would/should*+infinitive, except when the past of another modal auxiliary is used:

If we had enough money, we *could* buy a tape-recorder

Other, less important, constructions in which the hypothetical past tense is used are illustrated below (on the subjunctive *were*, see 3.16):

It's time you *were* in bed [53]

He behaves as though he$\begin{Bmatrix} was \\ were \end{Bmatrix}$a millionaire [54]

It's not as though we *were* poor [55]

Just suppose/imagine someone$\begin{Bmatrix} was \\ were \end{Bmatrix}$following us [56]

I'd rather we *had* dinner now [57]

If only I *had* listened to my parents! [58]

From each of these sentences a negative inference can be drawn: for example, from [53] '. . . but you're not in bed'. Hypothetical meaning in past time is indicated by *had* plus the *-ed* participle:

We could have got married today, if you'*d* really *wanted* to
If you *had listened* to me, you wouldn't have made mistakes

In the past, the hypothetical meaning is more absolute than in the present, and amounts to an implied rejection of the condition: 'but in fact you didn't want to'; 'but in fact you didn't listen'. With present and future reference, the meaning may be merely one of negative expectation:

If you *listened* to me, you wouldn't make mistakes
  ('. . . but I don't suppose you will listen to me')

11.70
The perfect aspect with *since*, etc
When *since* is used in a temporal sense, the present perfect is used in the main clause, also sometimes in the subordinate clause, in referring to a stretch of time up to (and potentially including) the present:

Since we have owned a car, we *have gone* camping every year
  (*not:* . . . we *go* camping)
She *has been drinking* Martinis ever since the party started
  (*not:* She *is drinking* . . .)

The same applies to *since* as a preposition:

Scholars *have been writing* English grammars since the sixteenth
  century

After and *when*, in referring to a sequence of past events, can be followed either by a past perfect or simple past tense verb:

$$\left.\begin{array}{l}\text{After} \\ \text{When}\end{array}\right\}\text{he}\left\{\begin{array}{l}\text{had returned} \\ \text{returned}\end{array}\right\}\text{from work, his wife cooked dinner}$$

All four of these are acceptable, and mean roughly the same. The only difference is that *when* and the simple past tense (probably the most popular choices) suggest that the one event followed *immediately* on the other.

Note

If the verb phrase of the main clause is progressive in aspect, or contains a stative verb, *when* indicates the simultaneity, rather than successivity of the events:

When he returned from work, his wife was (cooking dinner) in the kitchen.

11.71
The present subjunctive in conditional clauses, etc

The present subjunctive (3.16) is used very occasionally and in rather formal use, as we have seen, in open conditional clauses and concessive clauses:

Whatever be the reasons for it, we cannot tolerate this disloyalty
  (*cf* Whatever *may be* the reasons . . .)

Clauses of concession and purpose may also very occasionally contain a verb in the subjunctive mood to express 'putative' not factual meaning (see 11.72):

$$\text{Though he}\left\{\begin{array}{l}is \\ be\end{array}\right\}\text{the President himself, he shall hear us}$$

The subjunctive is also possible in *that*-clauses expressing wish, hope, or intention, for the future:

Congress has voted/decided/decreed/insisted/that the present law
  (*should*) *be* maintained

The present subjunctive is more common in AmE than in BrE, where it is little more than an archaism of legalistic style.

 The past subjunctive, which is distinguishable from the past indicative only in the singular form *were* of the copula, is used in formal style to express hypothetical meaning in clauses introduced by conditional conjunctions:

If it *were* real . . .

and also by *as if, as though, though,* and the imperative verbs *suppose* and *imagine:*

Suppose he *were* here . . .

11.72
Putative *should,* etc

Modal auxiliaries, especially *should*, sometimes appear in subordinate clauses in contexts where, historically speaking, a present subjunctive might be expected. We have already noted (11.32) the use of *should* to express a tentative condition in *if*-clauses.

Elsewhere, *should* is used quite extensively in *that*-clauses to express not a subordinate statement of fact, but a 'putative' idea. One may contrast in this connection:

$$\left\{\begin{array}{l}\text{The } idea \text{ is} \\ \text{Someone is suggesting}\end{array}\right\}\text{that education for the over-sixteens}$$
$$\qquad\qquad\qquad\qquad\qquad should\ be \text{ improved}$$

$$\left\{\begin{array}{l}\text{The } fact \text{ is} \\ \text{We know}\end{array}\right\}\text{that education for the over-sixteens } will\ be \text{ improved}$$

The first sentence puts forward an idea or plan which may not be fulfilled, while the second (with the *that*-clause without *should*) asserts the improvement as a fact, and assumes that the plan will be carried out. Contrary to what might be thought, *should* in such clauses does not necessarily carry any sense of obligation, although it is possible to interpret it in the 'obligatory' sense of 'ought to'. A *that*-clause with *should* is frequently replaceable by an infinitive clause:

The idea is *for education for the over-sixteens to be improved*

Also, when a plan or hope for the future is at issue, it is possible to substitute the subjunctive:

The idea is that education for the over-sixteens *be improved*

Examples of main clause constructions which introduce a *that*-clause with *should* are these:

$$\left.\begin{array}{l}\text{It's a pity} \\ \text{I'm surprised} \\ \text{It's disgraceful} \\ \text{It's unthinkable} \\ \text{It worries me}\end{array}\right\}\text{that he should resign}$$

Most of these are constructions in which the *that*-clause is an extraposed subject (14.36, 12.35 *ff*). Notice that in the first two cases, despite the *should*, the event is assumed to have taken place already. This is because the 'factual' bias of the main clause construction overrides the doubt otherwise implicit in the *should* construction. Nonetheless, there is still a difference of feeling between *I'm surprised that he should resign* and *I'm surprised that he is resigning:* in the first, it is the 'very idea' of resignation that surprises; in the second, it is the resignation itself, as an assumed fact.

Note

[a] Putative *should* also occurs in some idiomatic questions and exclamations:

> How *should* I know?
> Why *should* he be resigning?
> That he *should* dare to attack me!
> Who *should* come in but the mayor himself!

[b] *May* and *might* could be regarded as 'subjunctive substitutes' when they occur in formal style in concessive and purpose clauses:

> Poor as you *might* be, you cannot live all your life on charity.
> Let us fight on, that the light of justice and freedom *may* not die in our land.

Direct and indirect speech
11.73
Indirect speech

The difference between direct speech and indirect (or reported) speech is shown in:

> He said: 'I am very angry' (DIRECT SPEECH)
> He said that he was very angry (INDIRECT SPEECH)

In the case of indirect speech, the words of the speaker are subordinated, in the form of a *that*-clause, within the reporting sentence. In the case of direct speech, his speech is rather 'incorporated' within the reporting sentence by means of quotation marks, and retains its status as a main clause. Nevertheless, notionally, the 'incorporated' speech has the function of an element in the clause structure of the reporting sentence. In the above case, for example, it is the notional direct object of *said*. Cf:

> *What* he said was '*I am very angry*'.

Structurally, the reporting clause, in direct speech, may be classed with comment clauses (11.65–66). It may occur before, within, or after the speech itself. Except when it occurs in initial position, there is likely to be an inversion of the subject and a reporting verb in the simple present or past tense:

> 'I am your friend,' $\begin{cases} \textit{John said} \\ \textit{he said} \\ \textit{said John} \end{cases}$

Inversion is unusual and archaic, however, when the subject of the reporting clause is a pronoun: .... *said he*. The medial placing of the reporting clause is very frequent:

> 'Of course,' said Mr Jones, 'we're very grateful'

The conversion from direct to indirect speech entails various other changes in the form of the clause, including the shift from 1st person and 2nd person to 3rd person pronouns:

> '*I*'ll behave *myself*,' he promised
> → He promised that *he*'d behave *himself*

also (sometimes) the change from *this/these* to *that/those*, and from *here* to *there*:

> '*I* live *here*,' he explained → He explained that *he* lived *there*

The most important alteration takes place, however, in the verb phrase: this is the change of tense that is referred to as BACK-SHIFT and is discussed in detail in 11.74 below. These changes collectively represent the DISTANCING effect of indirect speech.

Note
[a] In popular narrative style, the substandard inversion *says I* is sometimes heard.
[b] In journalistic writing, a reporting clause with inversion sometimes occurs even in initial position: *Declared tall, nineteen-year-old Napier: 'The show will go on.'*

11.74
Back-shift
Back-shift takes place when any reported matter is introduced by a reporting verb in the past tense. In these circumstances, the shift from direct to reported speech is accompanied by a back-shift of verb as follows:

	DIRECT		BACK-SHIFTED
(1)	present		→ past
(2)	past	⎫	
(3)	present perfect	⎬	→ past perfect
(4)	past perfect	⎭	

The explanation of the term 'back-shift' should now become clear: if there is (semantically) a shift into the past in the reporting clause, there is a corresponding shift into the past (or if necessary, further into the past) in the reported clause. Examples of each part of the rule are:

(1) 'I *am* tired,' she complained
   → She complained that she *was* tired
(2) 'The exhibition *finished* last week,' explained Ann
   → Ann explained that the exhibition *had finished* the preceding week
(3) 'I*'ve won* the match already!' exclaimed our friend
   → Our friend exclaimed that he *had won* the match already
(4) 'The whole house *had been ruined*,' said the storyteller
   → The storyteller said that the whole house *had been ruined*

The lack of change in case (4) is explained by the observation that if a verb is already in the past perfect form, it already expresses 'past in the past', and no further back-shift to 'past in the past in the past' can be expressed through the grammar of the English verb.

11.75
Exceptions to back-shift
Bearing in mind that back-shift is part of the natural temporal 'distancing' that takes place when we report what was said in the past, we should not be surprised that the rule of back-shift can be ignored in cases where the validity of the statement reported holds for the present time as much as for the time of utterance:

'I *am* a citizen, not of Athens, but of the world,' said Socrates
→ Socrates said that he *was* a citizen, not of Athens, but of the world
'Nothing *can* harm a good man,' said Socrates
→ { (a) Socrates said that nothing *could* harm a good man
     (b) Socrates said that nothing *can* harm a good man

The first statement uttered by Socrates applied only in Socrates' own lifetime, and since from the vantage point of a modern reporter, it deals with what is now past, it has to be reported by application of the back-shift rule. The second statement, on the other hand, is a universal assertion which, if it was true for Socrates' lifetime, should also be true today. We can therefore report it either by (a) applying or (b) ignoring the back-shift rule.

Note
Just as 'distancing' can be avoided, in some circumstances, by not back-shifting the verb, so with pronouns and other forms, the change to the more 'distant' meaning (*eg* to 3rd person pronouns) does not always take place, in that the use of forms appropriate to the reporting situation must take precedence over those appropriate to the reported speech situation. Thus 'I am your friend, Bob' will be reported by Bob, the person addressed, as *He said that he was* my *friend*, rather than as *He said that he was* his *friend*, which would be the expected indirect speech version. So also:

'*You* are very kind,' she said to *me* → She told me that *I* was very kind.

11.76
Indirect statements, questions, commands, and exclamations
Our examples have so far been of indirect statements; but all the main utterance-types (questions, exclamations, commands, as well as statements) may be converted into indirect speech. The constructions are as follows:

INDIRECT STATEMENT: *that*-clause

INDIRECT QUESTION: dependent *wh*-clause
INDIRECT EXCLAMATION: dependent *wh*-clause
INDIRECT COMMAND: *to*-infinitive clause (without subject)

Here are examples of the last three categories:

'Are you ready yet?' asked Joan
→ Joan asked (me) *whether I was ready yet* (*yes-no* QUESTION)
'When will the plane leave?' I wondered
→ I wondered *when the plane would leave* (*wh*-QUESTION)
'How brave you are!' Margaret told him
→ Margaret told him *how brave he was* (EXCLAMATION)
'Be quiet!' I told him
→ I told him *to be quiet* (COMMAND)

What has been said about back-shift applies to questions and exclamations as well as to statements. Indirect commands, in contrast, cannot incorporate back-shift, as they contain no finite verb. The reporting verb, in the case of indirect commands, has to be followed by an indirect object or prepositional object: for the indirect speech version of '*Sit down,*' *I snapped*, one would write not **I snapped to sit down*, but *I snapped at him to sit down*. Alternatively one could render a verb like *sneer* in an indirect command by *tell* with an appropriate adverbial:

$$I \text{ told him} \begin{cases} \text{sneeringly} \\ \text{with a sneer} \end{cases} \text{to sit down}$$

Note

There is no indirect speech construction for echo questions or echo exclamations. Alternative questions are formed with *whether . . . or* on a model similar to *yes-no* questions:

Are you satisfied or not?
→ I asked him *whether or not he was satisfied.*

11.77
The modal auxiliaries and indirect speech

In reported clauses, the back-shift of a modal auxiliary results in the use of past tense forms *would, could*, etc, even if the past tense form does not normally indicate the past of the present tense meaning in direct speech. For example:

'You may be wrong!' → He said (*that*) *they might be wrong*

If a modal auxiliary in direct speech has no past tense equivalent (this includes auxiliaries which are already past, such as *could, might*, as well as *must, ought to, need*, and *had better*), then the same form remains in indirect speech:

'You must be hungry' → He said (*that*) *they must be hungry*

The element of 'involvement of the speaker' which is often present in the meaning of some modal auxiliaries (*eg: may*='permission', 3.45; *must*='obligation', 3.48) is naturally assigned, in indirect speech, to the speaker of the indirect statement. Thus '*You must go, John,' said Jenkins* (='I oblige you . . .') becomes:

Jenkins said that *John must go* (='Jenkins obliged John . . .')

Note
If they are followed by a perfect infinitive, modal auxiliaries in the main or *reporting* clause are counted, for purposes of the back-shift rule, as past tense forms:

'What are you doing?' –→ I ought *to have asked* what he *was* doing.

11.78
Free indirect speech
Free indirect speech is a half-way stage between direct and indirect speech, and is used extensively in modern narrative writing. It is basically a form of indirect speech, but (1) the reporting clause is omitted (except when retained as a parenthetical comment clause), and (2) the potentialities of direct-speech sentence structure (direct question forms, vocatives, tag questions, etc) are retained. It is therefore only the back-shift of the verb, together with equivalent shifts in pronouns, determiners and adverbs, that signals the fact that the words are being reported, rather than being in direct speech:

So that *was* their plan, *was* it? He well *knew* their tricks, and
   would show them a thing or two before he *was* finished. Thank
   goodness he *had* been alerted, and that there *were* still a few
   honest people in the world!

The italicized verbs show back-shift to the past tense. Very often, in fiction, free indirect speech represents a person's stream of thought rather than actual speech. It is quite possible, therefore, that *he thought* would be the appropriate reporting clause to supply for the above passage, rather than *he said*.

11.79
Transferred negation
A strange feature of the syntax of subordination in colloquial English is the transfer of the negative from a subordinate *that*-clause, where semantically it belongs, to the main clause. Thus *I didn't think he was happy* can have two meanings, one in which the negation applies to the main clause, and one in which it applies, through transferred negation,

to the subordinate clause: *I thought he wasn't happy.* It is the un-likelihood of the first meaning, and the difficulty of distinguishing it from the second, that partially accounts for this phenomenon. Trans-ferred negation is limited to verbs of belief or assumption, such as *think, believe, suppose, fancy, expect, imagine, reckon*:

$$I\ don't \begin{cases} think \\ believe \\ suppose \end{cases} (that)\ you've\ paid\ for\ it\ yet$$

$$He\ doesn't \begin{cases} imagine \\ expect \\ reckon \end{cases} (that)\ we\ need\ worry$$

The negative status of the *that*-clauses is shown by the occurrence of *need* (which could not occur in a positive sentence **We need worry*) and the non-assertive form *yet*. Another indication is the form of the tag question in:

I don't suppose (that) he CÀRES, DÒES he?

(*cf* He doesn't CÀRE, DÒES he?)

The tag question in this sort of sentence is attached to the *that*-clause rather than to the independent clause (7.59 Note), as is clear from the tag subject, *he*. Since a tag question with a falling tone contrasts in positive/negative terms with its main clause, however, we would expect DÒESn't *he?* in this context. That in fact a positive tag question occurs is thus evidence of the negativeness of the *that*-clause.

Not all verbs in the semantic field of belief, uncertainty, etc, take transferred negation. It is notable, for example, that *assume, surmise,* and *presume* are not included in the list above:

I don't assume that he came

is not equivalent to:

I assume that he didn't come.

Note

The condensed sentence *I don't think so* contains transferred negation, and is thus synonymous with *I think not*.

Sentence complexity and comprehensibility
11.80
Combining subordination devices within a sentence

We finally return to the concept of the complex sentence with which this chapter started.

The complex sentence is a unit which can be broken down into immediately smaller units, which are clauses. We have examined in Chapter 9 one of the ways in which these units are linked – that of coordination; and in this chapter a second way – that of subordination. All that remains is to consider how these two methods of clause combination interact in the total structure of a sentence.

For simplicity of illustration, our examples up to this point have been almost exclusively of two-clause sentences. If this has misled by building up a false picture of simplicity, it is time to remedy the matter with an example such as this, from a newspaper:

[A]   [Arguments in favour of [suppressing the facts,] [said Mr Harken,] included suggestions [that [if the conditions at the prison were made public,] North Vietnam would retaliate against American prisoners of war.]]

(The Guardian, London, 8 July 1970)

Although quite brief and not unduly complex, this sentence illustrates how several devices of subordination can be simultaneously combined in a piece of everyday written English.

One of the factors which determine the order in which the constituent clauses of a sentence are arranged is the principle that the final clause is felt to be the point of maximum emphasis: the principle (as we may term it) of RESOLUTION. In reading aloud, the 'resolutory' effect of the final clause is often pointed by intonation. A typical reading of the above sentence would put rising or falling-rising tones on all points of information focus (14.2) except the last, approximately as follows:

... FÁCTS ... HÁRKen ... suggĔstions ... PŬBlic ... reTĂLiate ... WÀR

As rising and falling-rising tones have implications of non-finality (App II.13), the effect of this sort of pattern is to build up a continuing sense of anticipation, which is at last 'resolved' by the finality of the falling tone. This principle of resolution is the counterpart, on the sentence level, of the principle of end-focus (14.3) on the clause level.

'Right-tending' structure
11.81

Ignoring for a moment *types* of subordination, we may concentrate on factors of order, particularly on the initial, medial, and final placement of subordinate clauses. Each clause may be visually represented as a triangle, and three main types of subordination distinguished as in *Fig* 11:2.

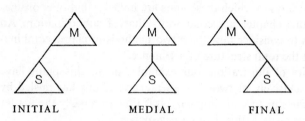

INITIAL   MEDIAL   FINAL

Fig 11:2 Placement of subordinate clauses
[M = main; S = subordinate]

Examples:

INITIAL: If you agree, we shall leave tonight
MEDIAL: We shall leave, if you agree, tonight
FINAL: We shall leave tonight, if you agree

The structure of the sentence [A] in 11.80 above may therefore be pictured as in *Fig* 11:3.

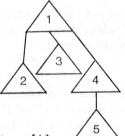

Fig 11:3 Structure of sentence [A]

It is significant that the preponderance of triangles in this diagram is towards the right: in fact, it is a dominant tendency of syntactic structure that the greatest depth of subordination or embedding is reached in the final part of the sentence. A rather extreme instance of this tendency is the following sentence, also from a newspaper report:

   1   2
[B] [He accused the non-partisan commission [headed by Earl
                                     2   3
Warren, Chief Justice of the United States], of [being unfair
        4   5
to the F.B.I. for [criticising the police agency for its failure [to
alert the Secret Service to the presence in Dallas of Lee Harvey
                                5 4 3 1
Oswald, the President's assassin.]]]]

(*Evening News*, London, 19 November 1964)

which, in diagram terms, looks like *Fig* 11:4.

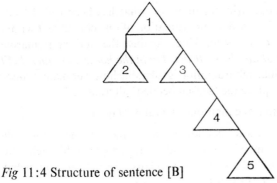

Fig 11:4 Structure of sentence [B]

Note
We should bear in mind that the diagram, however, does not present an adequate picture, as it represents clauses only, and does not take account of other kinds of complexity contributing to the depth of 'right-branching structure', particularly the 'nominalized' clauses (see 13.34*f*) of *its failure (to alert* . . .) and *the presence in Dallas* . . .

11.82
In studying the pattern of clauses within a sentence, we may note that there are special reasons for the tendency to favour final subordination. It may well be that of the three main types of inclusion relation between constituents, 'left-branching', 'nesting' ('medial branching'), and 'right-branching', it is the second that tends to cause most difficulties of comprehension, especially if the nested element is long and complex. Considerable left-branching is possible in the noun phrase, as can be seen in the following genitive construction (*cf* 13.62):

```
1 2 3 4     4        3          2          1
[ [ [ [Tom's]  sister's]  husband's]  mother]
```

But in clause structure, the left-branching or anticipatory type of structuring is limited to one degree of embedding. This is because no subordinate clause can itself be the first element of another subordinate clause, but must at least be preceded by a subordinator, as *if you could* is in [59] rather than [60]:

```
1 2      3          3                2              1
[ [That [if you could] you would help me] is of small comfort]     [59]
1 2 3          3                2              1
*[ [ [If you could] that you would help us] is of small comfort]    [60]
```

If complex medial subordination hampers comprehension, and initial subordination, except directly within the independent clause, is ruled out, there remains only final subordination as a subordinating device without obvious restrictions.

There are even more stringent limits on what has been called 'self-embedding', that is, the medial subordination of one constituent within another constituent of the same kind. Against the nursery rigmarole *This is the . . . rat that ate the malt that lay in the house that Jack built* (which shows that final subordination is tolerable however many clauses one inserts), we may place the 'self-embedded' alternative:

This is the house that the malt that the rat ate lay in

which is extremely awkward-sounding; and in fact one need add only a third layer of self-embedding to render the sentence, although constructed according to rules for relative clause formation, completely baffling to the intellect of the listener:

?*This is the house that the malt that the rat that the cat killed
    ate lay in

It is important to note, therefore, that the factors we have been considering do not just concern good and bad style, but also the more basic question of what is a possible English sentence.

That final subordination can reduce awkwardness in subordination to a minimum is demonstrated by the rewriting of sentence [59] above, through extraposition of the subject (14.36), in a much more acceptable form as:

1   2   3   3 2 1
[It is of small comfort [that you would help me [if you could]]]   [61]

In terms of diagrams, the change brought about between [59] and [61] is as in *Fig* 11:5.

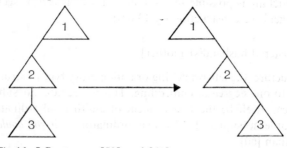

Fig 11:5 Sentences [59] and [61]

Note
It must be noted, however, that despite the overall tendency towards final subordination, certain types of clause, including, for example, temporal clauses and *if*-clauses, favour the initial position (11.27, 11.29). Moreover, adverbial correlative constructions (11.10) not merely favour but require initial placement of the subordinate clause.

11.83

Subordination versus coordination

In discussing comprehensibility, we cannot ignore coordination, which is the kind of link most used for optimum ease of comprehension. It is notable that in spoken English, where immediate ease of syntactic composition and comprehension is at a premium, coordinate structures are often preferred to equivalent structures of subordination:

{ SUBORD: Reaching for the phone, he asked for the operator
{ COORD: He reached for the phone and asked for the operator

{ SUBORD: As it was wet, we decided to stay at home
{ COORD: It was wet, (and) so we decided to stay at home

{ SUBORD: Although it was fine, we decided to stay at home
{ COORD: It was fine, but we decided to stay at home

Further, spoken English, though less complex in structures of subordination, is more inclined than written English to provide the kind of semantic link that can be made by coordination. The following conditional uses of *and* and *or*, for example, are rarely encountered in the language of written prose:

Ask me nicely, and I'll give it to you ('If you ask . . .')
Give it back to me, or I'll tell your mother ('Unless . . .')

It is even arguable that a conjunction like *because*, which occurs almost exclusively in final-position clauses in colloquial language, is, for the purposes of that variety of English, nearer to a coordinator than to a subordinator.

11.84

Constructional ambiguity within sentence structure

When there are more than two clauses in a complex sentence, it is possible for ambiguities to arise through various alternative analyses

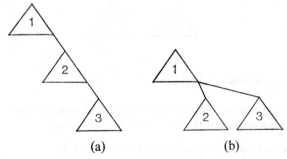

(a)   (b)

Fig 11:6 Ambiguity of sentence [62]

that can be given to the same group of clauses. With reference to sub-ordination only: a sequence of three clauses, the first independent and the other two dependent, could be joined in either of the two ways indicated in *Fig* 11:6. The following is an example of an ambiguous sentence for which either of these readings is possible:

I knew that you had seen him before I met you	[62]
=‘I knew that, before I met you, you had seen him’	[62a]
=‘Before I met you, I knew that you had seen him’	[62b]

A related kind of ambiguity arises with two coordinated clauses followed or preceded by a dependent clause:

He knows and I know that he knows   [63]

The question here is: Does the final subordinate clause belong to the second of the coordinate clauses, or to both together? Punctuation (and in speech, intonation) can distinguish them:

| He knows, and I know that he knows | [63a] |
| He knows, and I know, that he knows | [63b] |

Yet a further type involves a succession of three clauses, in which the first is independent, the second subordinate, and the third coordinate. The ambiguity concerns the status of the last clause: is it coordinated to the main or to the subordinate clause?

Something tells me he's cheating and I can't do anything
about it   [64]

If a relation of coordination is represented as ⟋‾⟍⟋‾⟍, then the difference between these two interpretations is as in *Fig* 11:7.

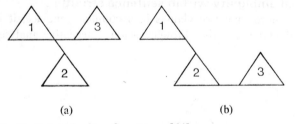

(a)   (b)

Fig 11:7 Ambiguity of sentence [64]

To make it clear that interpretation (b) is intended, we could re-introduce the *that* into the second of the two subordinate clauses:

Something tells me that he's cheating and (that) I can't do
anything about it   [64b]

There is no equally obvious way to insist on interpretation (a), but one can suggest that the major syntactic break of the sentence occurs after *cheating* by using a semi-colon (;), or by exaggerating the tone unit boundary at that point.

11.85
Avoiding ambiguity

From the above three examples of constructional ambiguity, we learn not only what factors cause the ambiguity, but what methods can be used to avoid it. Four devices to be considered are:

(i) *altering the order of the clauses* (*eg* interpretation [62b] is singled out by moving an adverbial clause to initial position).

(ii) *using punctuation* to mark the major (*ie* least embedded) clause boundary, as in [63a].

(iii) *using intonation*, if necessary exaggerated by pause, to indicate the major boundary, as in [64a].

(iv) *supplying ellipted elements* (for example, the subordinator *that* in [64b].

Again, the examples chosen give an unduly simple picture. If we added further clauses to these three-clause sentences, opportunities for ambiguity would increase rapidly.

Bibliographical note

On nominal clauses, see Behre (1955); Lees (1960a); Storms (1966); Vendler (1968), especially Part I.

On comparative clauses, see Hale (1970); Huddleston (1967) and (1971), Chapter 6; Lees (1961); Smith (1961).

On transferred negation (11.79), see Lakoff (1969b); Lindholm (1969).

On sentence complexity and comprehensibility, see Chomsky (1965), especially *pp* 10–14; Huddleston (1965); Rosenbaum (1967b); Yngve (1961).

On indirect speech and 'back-shift', see Jespersen (1909–1949), Vol 4, Chapter 11.

12.1
Introduction

Complementation, which includes the elements of clause structure that are obligatory for the completion of the verb meaning, has already been discussed in various places, notably in 2.3 *ff*, 7.1 *ff* and 11.13 *ff*. This chapter will deal with three aspects of complementation: voice, *ie* the active-passive relation, phrasal and prepositional verbs, and complementation types. The last part includes lists of verbs for some of the more important subtypes.

Voice
12.2
Voice defined

Voice is a grammatical category which makes it possible to view the action of a sentence in two ways, without change in the facts reported:

(a) The butler murdered the detective
(b) The detective was murdered by the butler

Sentence (a) is in the active voice, and sentence (b) in the passive voice.

The active-passive relation involves two grammatical 'levels': the verb phrase and the clause. In the former, which has been treated in 3.12 *ff*, Type D (passive verb phrase) is in contrast with the rest (active verb phrase), for example,

	ACTIVE	PASSIVE
present:	*kisses*	~ *is kissed*
past:	*kissed*	~ *was kissed*
modal:	*may kiss*	~ *may be kissed*
perfective:	*has kissed*	~ *has been kissed*
progressive:	*is kissing*	~ *is being kissed*
modal + perfective:	*may have kissed*	~ *may have been kissed*

In the verb phrase, the difference between the two voice categories is that the passive adds a form of the auxiliary BE and the past participle (the -*ed* form) of the main verb.

At the clause level, passivization involves rearrangement of two clause elements and one addition. (a) The active subject becomes the passive agent, (b) the active object becomes the passive subject, and (c) the preposition *by* is introduced before the agent. The prepositional agent phrase of passive sentences is an optional sentence element. The process of active-passive transformation for a monotransitive sentence with nominal object can be represented diagrammatically (*Fig* 12:1).

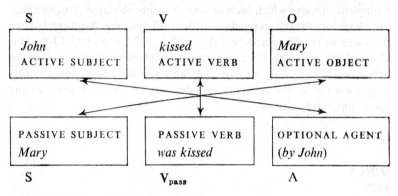

Fig 12:1   The active-passive relation

Alternatively, voice transformation can be expressed in this formula:

noun phrase$_1$ + active verb phrase + noun phrase$_2$
~ noun phrase$_2$ + passive verb phrase + (*by* noun phrase$_1$)

The terms 'subject', 'object', and 'agent' are useful labels for describing phenomena such as subject-verb concord (7.23) or the use of objective pronominal case forms (4.107). But although the structure of a sentence changes under voice transformation, its meaning remains the same. In *John kissed Mary* and *Mary was kissed by John, John* is in both voices the 'performer of the action'. In the sentence structure, however, the active subject corresponds to the passive agent.

12.3

The passive auxiliary

The passive auxiliary is normally BE. Its only serious contender is GET, which however is usually restricted to constructions without an expressed animate agent. Compare the following sentences:

The boy got hurt on his way home from work
*The boy got given a violin by his father

The GET-passive is avoided in formal style. Even in informal English, however, it is far less frequent than the BE-passive:

Our house is getting painted
If they make such criticisms they will get treated with the contempt they deserve
This story eventually got translated into English

GET is much more common as a 'resulting copula' (see 12.32) in sentences which look superficially like the passive but cannot have an agent (*cf* 12.17):

> We are getting bogged down in all sorts of problems (informal)
> I have to get dressed before eight o'clock (='dress')
> I don't want to get mixed up with the police again
> Your argument gets a bit confused here

Compare *He got taught a lesson* ('it served him right') with:

He $\left\{\begin{matrix} \text{was} \\ \text{*got} \end{matrix}\right\}$ taught the lesson on the subjunctive (by our new teacher)

As a resulting copula, GET is often equivalent to BECOME, which is used to express gradual change, often enhanced by modification with *more and more*, *increasingly*, etc:

> Our technique is becoming increasingly specialized
> These four phases became telescoped in a single, coordinated phase of activity.

Voice constraints
12.4
Although it is the general rule that transitive verb sentences can be either active or passive, there are a number of exceptions where there is no simple paraphrase relation. We will distinguish five kinds of 'voice constraint' associated with, respectively, the verb (12.5–7), the object (12.8–10), the agent (12.11), meaning (12.12), and frequency of use (12.13).

Verb constraints
12.5
Active only

There are greater restrictions on verbs occurring in the passive than in the active. In addition to equative and intransitive verbs, which can never take the passive, some transitive verbs (at least in certain uses) do not occur in the passive, for example:

> They *have* a nice house
> He *lacks* confidence
> The auditorium *holds* 5000 people
> This dress *becomes* her
> The coat does not *fit* you
> Will this *suit* you?
> John *resembles* his father.

12.6

Passive only

Conversely, with some verbs only the passive is possible (*cf* 12.56):

John was $\begin{Bmatrix} \text{said} \\ \text{reputed} \end{Bmatrix}$ to be a good teacher

~ *They $\begin{Bmatrix} \text{said} \\ \text{reputed} \end{Bmatrix}$ him to be a good teacher

12.7

Prepositional verbs

In English, prepositional verbs (see further 12.19 *ff*) can often occur in the passive, but not as freely as in the active. Compare the following sentences with prepositional verbs:

The engineers went very carefully into $\begin{Bmatrix} \text{the problem} \\ \text{the tunnel} \end{Bmatrix}$

~ $\begin{Bmatrix} \text{The problem} \\ \text{*The tunnel} \end{Bmatrix}$ was very carefully gone into by the engineers

They arrived at $\begin{Bmatrix} \text{the expected result} \\ \text{the splendid stadium} \end{Bmatrix}$

~ $\begin{Bmatrix} \text{The expected result} \\ \text{*The splendid stadium} \end{Bmatrix}$ was arrived at

In these sentences it is clear that the difference in acceptability can be stated in terms of concrete/abstract passive subjects. It is only in figurative use that GO INTO, ARRIVE AT, LOOK INTO, and many other prepositional verbs accept the passive.

With some ingenuity, one may construct contexts where such verbs will passivize even concretely, especially in a parallel construction:

This private correspondence of mine has been gone into and rummaged so many times that it is totally disarranged

With other prepositional verbs, the non-occurrence in the passive cannot be similarly accounted for:

John $\begin{Bmatrix} \text{cared for} \\ \text{called for} \\ \text{looked at} \\ \text{adjusted to} \\ \text{agreed with} \\ \text{lived with} \end{Bmatrix}$ Mary ~ Mary was $\begin{Bmatrix} \text{cared for} \\ \text{called for} \\ \text{looked at} \\ \text{?adjusted to} \\ \text{*agreed with} \\ \text{*lived with} \end{Bmatrix}$

In 12.19 *ff*, where prepositional verbs are discussed, we set up different degrees of 'cohesion': whereas all such verbs by definition take the pronominal question-form with *who(m)/what*, only some can take the passive. This latter class of highly cohesive prepositional verbs includes most of those listed in 12.27 and, in addition, the following:

> Though something very different from ordinary forest management *is called for*, the trees in the parks do need the forester's skilled consideration.
> This matter *will have to be dealt with* immediately.
> Other possibilities *are talked of* by many of our colleagues.
> If a woman with a university education rejects a career for marriage, her mind *is* not *to be thought of* as thrown away unless we count the family arena of no importance.

Similarly:

ASK FOR	HOPE FOR	TALK ABOUT
BELIEVE IN	LOOK AT	TALK TO
CATER FOR	STARE AT	WONDER AT, etc

Since it adds one element of complexity to the verb phrase, the passive is often felt to be heavier than the corresponding active. In particular, it is the co-occurrence of *be being* that is avoided. Compare the following pairs of sentences:

> The Conservatives won the election
> ~ The election was won by the Conservatives
> The Conservatives have not been winning seats lately
> ~ (?)Seats have not been being won by the Conservatives lately.

Object constraints
12.8
Nominal and clausal objects
Verbs can be followed by both nominal and clausal objects (7.1 *ff*, 11.13 *ff*, and 12.44 *ff*):

nominal object	
noun phrase	John loved Mary
clausal object	
finite clause	John saw that she was pretty
non-finite clause	
infinitive	John hoped to kiss her
participle	John enjoyed seeing her.

12.9
Co-reference between subject and nominal object
Co-reference between subject and nominal object blocks the passive transformation, and occurs with (a) reflexive, (b) reciprocal, and (c)

possessive pronouns in the object. Normally, however, transitive verbs with other nominal objects passivize.

(a) John could see $\left\{\begin{matrix} \text{Paul} \\ \text{himself} \end{matrix}\right\}$ in the mirror

~ $\left\{\begin{matrix} \text{Paul} \\ \text{*Himself} \end{matrix}\right\}$ could be seen in the mirror

(b) We could hardly see each other in the fog
   ~ *Each other could hardly be seen in the fog

(c) The handsome, bald doctor shook $\left\{\begin{matrix} \text{the nurse} \\ \text{her head} \\ \text{his head} \end{matrix}\right\}$

~ $\left\{\begin{matrix} \text{The nurse} \\ \text{Her head} \\ \text{*His head} \end{matrix}\right\}$ was shaken by the handsome, bald doctor.

Note
Since reflexive and reciprocal pronouns are objective case replacements, it would be unexpected anyway to have such a pronoun in the subject position of a passive sentence.

12.10
Clausal objects

Of the clausal objects only those consisting of a finite clause regularly have passive analogues. Compare the active sentences in 12.8 with the following passives:

Mary was loved (by John)
Mary was cared for (by John)
$\left\{\begin{matrix} \text{It was seen (by John) that she was pretty} \\ \text{?That she was pretty was seen (by John)} \end{matrix}\right.$
$\left\{\begin{matrix} \text{*It was hoped (by John) to kiss her} \\ \text{*To kiss her was hoped (by John)} \end{matrix}\right.$
$\left\{\begin{matrix} \text{*It was enjoyed (by John) seeing her} \\ \text{? Seeing her was enjoyed (by John)} \end{matrix}\right.$

Finite clause objects which are introduced by *that, whether,* or *if* normally take passives with *it*-subject and so-called 'extraposition', *ie* the clause remains in post-verbal position in the passive sentence but is introduced by anticipatory *it* as subject. *That* is obligatory in *that*-clauses occurring initially as subject, without anticipatory *it:*

It could hardly be expected (that) Ruth would be on time
   ~ That Ruth would be on time could hardly be expected

The construction with anticipatory *it* never occurs with participles but is sometimes used with infinitives (*cf* 12.49):

It was desired to have the report delivered here.

12.11
Agent constraints

Unlike the active subject, the agent phrase is optional. In fact, approximately four out of five English passive sentences have no expressed (surface) agent. This is the case when it is irrelevant or unknown, as in

The Prime Minister was attacked last night in the debate

The agent is often left out when it is redundant, as in

Jack fought Michael last night and Jack was beaten

An agent phrase *by Michael* would clearly be unnecessary or even impossible in this context.

Since the agent is usually left unexpressed, it may be unrecoverable, which means that change of voice from passive to active is highly restricted:

Order has been restored without bloodshed and without concessions

$\sim \left\{ \begin{array}{l} \text{John (?)} \\ \text{The government (?)} \\ \text{The army (?)} \end{array} \right\}$ has restored order without bloodshed and without concessions.

12.12
Meaning constraints

A shift of meaning may accompany shift of voice in verb phrases containing auxiliaries that have more than one meaning, *eg: shall, will,* and *can* (*cf* 3.43 *ff*):

John cannot do it
It cannot be done (by John)

In the active sentence *can* would normally be interpreted as expressing ability, whereas in the passive sentence it is interpreted as expressing possibility. Even when *can* retains the same lexical meaning in the active and passive, a shift of meaning is possible:

John can't be taught ('He is unable to learn')
He can't teach John ('He is unable to teach John')

12.13
Frequency constraints

To the structural restrictions mentioned in the preceding sections, we may add 'frequency constraints'. There is a notable difference in the frequency with which the active and passive voices are used. The active is generally the more common, but there is considerable variation among individual texts. The passive has been found to be as much as ten times more frequent in one text than another. The major stylistic factor determining its frequency seems to be related to the distinction between informative and imaginative prose rather than to a difference of subject matter or of spoken and written English. The passive is generally more commonly used in informative than in imaginative writing, notably in the objective, non-personal style of scientific articles and news items.

The passive scale
12.14
The formal definition of the passive (12.2 f) is very broad, and will include, for example, all the following sentences:

This violin was made by my father	[1]
This conclusion is hardly justified by the results	[2]
Coal has been replaced by oil	[3]
This difficulty can be avoided in several ways	[4]
We are encouraged to go on with the project	[5]
John was interested in linguistics	[6]
The modern world becomes more highly industrialized and mechanized	[7]

Although they satisfy the formal definition of 'passive', these sentences display a variety of voice relationships.

12.15
Agentive passives
Sentences [1] and [2] have a direct passive-active relation. The difference between the two is that the former has a personal, the latter a non-personal agent (*cf* 6.41):

My father made this violin	[1a]
The results hardly justify this conclusion	[2a]

[3] is a passive with two possible active transforms depending on the interpretation of the *by*-phrase. (Supplied active subjects are given in square brackets.)

Oil has replaced coal	[3a']
[People in many countries] have replaced coal by oil	[3a"]

[3a'] is an active transform like [2a] with a non-personal agent; [3a"] is an active transform where the *by*-phrase has been given an instrumental interpretation ($by = with$). Consequently an active subject must be supplied (*cf* 'agent constraints', 12.11).

Sentence [4] exemplifies the most common type of passive, which has no expressed agent ('agentless passives').

12.16
Quasi-passives

The passive sentences [5] and [6] represent a 'mixed' class whose members have both verbal and adjectival properties (*cf* 5.12 *ff*). They are verbal in having active analogues:

[The results] encourage us to go on with the project	[5a]
Linguistics interested John	[6a']

The adjectival properties are the potentiality for (a) coordination of the participles with adjectives, (b) adjectival modification with *quite, rather, more,* etc, (c) replacement of BE by a lexically 'marked' auxiliary (*cf* 12.31*f*):

We feel rather encouraged and content . . .
John seemed very interested in and keen on linguistics

In such adjectival uses of the past participle, it is rare to have a *by*-agent. However, blends do occur, for example,

I feel rather let down by his indifference

Even passive compounds which are morphologically isolated from the active by not having an infinitive may occasionally have *by*-agents:

We were unimpressed by his attempts
$\sim \begin{cases} \text{*His attempts unimpressed us} \\ \text{His attempts did not impress us} \end{cases}$

The passive sentence [6] can also be seen as related to the following active sentences:

[Someone]$\begin{cases} \text{interested John} \\ \text{made John interested} \end{cases}$ in linguistics	[6a''] [6a''']

As in [3], the prepositional phrase in [6] permits two analyses. The agent interpretation of [6] implies that we recognize *in* as an agent phrase preposition. There are, in fact, several prepositions which can introduce such 'quasi-agents', for example, *about, at, over, to, with* (*cf* 6.42, 12.34). *By* can also be used with similar meaning.

We were all worried about the complication	[8]
$\sim$ The complication worried us all	[8a]

I was a bit surprised at her behaviour   [9]
~ Her behaviour surprised me a bit   [9a]
You won't be bothered with me any more   [10]
~ I won't bother you any more   [10a]
This edition was not known to him   [11]
~ He did not know this edition   [11a]

Clausal complements of such quasi-passive constructions can also be said to have agent function (*cf* 12.42):

I was surprised to hear John failed in the exam   [12]

~ To hear that John failed in the exam $\begin{cases} \text{surprised me} & \text{[12a']} \\ \text{made me surprised} & \text{[12a'']} \end{cases}$

Note

Know is different from the rest in lacking the causative feature of *worry, surprise*, etc. Also, it does not take modifiers like *quite* and *rather*:

Her behaviour made me rather surprised.
*He did not make this edition rather known.

12.17

Non-agentive passives

Sentence [7], finally, has no active transform or possibility of agent addition, since no 'performer' is conceived of. The participles have adjectival values: compare *industrialized ~ industrial* and *mechanized ~ mechanical*. Besides a number of such 'resulting' verbs ending in -*ize* (*organize, americanize*, etc), this class includes 'existing' constructions, as in

The house is already sold   [13]

the corresponding active of which is not [13a'] but [13a'']:

*[The agent] already sells the house   [13a']
[The agent] has already sold the house   [13a'']

In this case, voice transformation involves aspectual shift from present to present perfect (3.36 *ff*).

While it is clear that [7] and [13] are not 'passive' in the sense of the sentences in 12.14, they still satisfy the formal passive requirement and, as in the case of [13], often have an 'indirect' voice relationship. We will therefore call this class 'non-agentive passive/intensive active complement constructions', recognizing that

The house is already sold

is related both to agentive passive

The house has already been sold   [13b] and to the intensive (active) complement construction

The house is $\begin{cases} \text{already gone} \\ \text{no longer available} \end{cases}$

Note
The 'notional passive' with active form as in *The clock winds up at the back* ('can be wound up') is discussed under conversion (App I.41 b).

12.18
Passive classes
Summarizing the discussion of the passive scale, we set up the following classes:

[I] Agentive passives
    (a) With expressed agents (examples [1], [2], [3])
    (b) Without expressed agents (examples [4], [13b])
[II] Quasi-passives (examples [5], [6])
[III] Non-agentive passives/intensive active complement
    constructions ([7], [13])

Phrasal and prepositional verbs
12.19
In considering verb complementation we will have to deal with sentences like the following ('the first set'):

John called the man	[14]
John called up the man	[15]
John called on the man	[16]
John put up with the man	[17]

Verbs can be divided into single-word verbs as in [14] and multi-word verbs, which are PHRASAL VERBS (as in [15]), PREPOSITIONAL VERBS (as in [16]), or PHRASAL-PREPOSITIONAL VERBS (as in [17]). (*Cf* 5.50, 6.9.)

12.20
Leaving aside, for the moment, the internal differences of multi-word verbs, we will first distinguish this set from other, superficially similar sequences consisting of verbs and prepositional phrases ('the second set'):

John called from the office	[18]
John called after lunch	[19]
John called from under the table	[20]

The difference between the first set represented by sentences [15–17], and the second set, represented by sentences [18–20] can be stated in terms of 'cohesion': in the first set, the adverbial or prepositional particle (*up, on, up with*) forms a semantic and syntactic unit with the verb; in the second set, the prepositional particle (*from, after, from under*) is more closely connected with the head of the prepositional phrase.

12.21
Semantic criteria

The semantic unity in phrasal and prepositional verbs (the first set) can often be manifested by substitution with a single-word verb, for example, *visit* for *call on*, *summon* for *call up*, *omit* for *leave out*, *see* for *look at*, etc.

Furthermore, phrasal and prepositional verbs often have composite meanings which are not normally deducible from their parts, for example, *make out* ('understand'), *take in* ('deceive'), *come by* ('obtain'). The terms 'phrasal' and 'prepositional' verbs are not, however, restricted to such idiomatic combinations. We can distinguish three subclasses within the first set (where it will be convenient to refer to both the adverbial and prepositional element as 'particle'):

(a) The verb and the particle keep their individual lexical meanings, as in *look over* ('inspect'), *set up* ('organize'). The individuality of the components appears in possible contrastive substitutions:

    bring ⎫ ⎧in
    take ⎭ ⎩out
    turn ⎫ ⎧on
    switch⎭ ⎩off

(b) The verb alone keeps its basic lexical meaning and the particle has an 'intensifying' function: *find out* ('discover'), *sweep* (*up*) *the crumbs*, *spread* (*out*) *the rug*.

(c) The verb and the particle are fused into a new idiomatic combination, the meaning of which is not deducible from its parts, for example, *bring up* ('educate'), *come by* ('obtain'), *put off* ('postpone'), *turn up* ('appear'), *come in for* ('receive'). In such combinations there is no possibility of contrastive substitution: there are no pairs such as *bring up/down*, *put off/on*, *give up/down*, *give in/out*, etc for this subclass. The adverbial, lexical values of the particles have been lost, and the entire verb-particle combination has acquired a new meaning.

In some cases the same verb-particle combination can belong to more than one subclass with a corresponding difference in meaning (*cf* 12.7):

John went into $\begin{cases}\text{the house (literal meaning)} \\ \text{the problem (figurative meaning)}\end{cases}$

John put up with Mary $\begin{cases}(\text{'stay with'}). \\ (\text{'tolerate'}).\end{cases}$

12.22
Syntactic criteria

(a) PASSIVIZATION

The syntactic similarity of verbs in the first set can be seen in their acceptance of passivization:

first set: The man was $\begin{cases}\text{called up} \\ \text{called on} \\ \text{put up with}\end{cases}$

second set: $\begin{cases}\text{*Lunch was called after} \\ \text{*The table was called from under} \\ \text{?The office was called from}\end{cases}$

In the passive, the verbs of the first set behave identically with single-word transitive verbs (*The man was called*), whereas the verbs of the second set do not admit of the passive. Note that ambiguous combinations like *put up with* take the passive only when they have the figurative meaning:

Mary couldn't easily be put up with
(= 'tolerate' but not = 'stay with')

Combinations of verbs and prepositional phrases which are awkward in minimal sentences can, however, become more acceptable with appropriate contextualization: 'This office has been called from so many times that it was natural to assume that it was the source of the latest call'.

(b) PRONOMINAL QUESTION FORM

The questions of the first set are formed with *who(m)* for personal and with *what* for non-personal objects:

Who(m) did John call up?
What did John look for?

(c) ADVERBIAL QUESTION FORM

The prepositional phrases of the second set have adverbial function, and have question forms with *where, when, how*, etc:

Where did John call from?
When did John call?

There is a certain amount of overlap between the two sets. If we apply the three criteria, (P) passivization, (Q_{pro}) pronominal question form, and (Q_{adv}) adverbial question form, to sentences 21–25, we can state their relations by means of a matrix:

P	Q_{pro}	Q_{adv}		
+	+	−	The police might ask for more details	[21]
−	+	−	John agreed with Mary	[22]
−	+	+	The car stopped beside a wall	[23]
−	−	+	She left before ten o'clock	[24]
−	−	−	His job also comes into the picture	[25]

Sentence [21] has both passive and pronominal question form:

More details might be asked for by the police	[21p]
What might the police ask for?	[21q]

[22] has only the pronominal question form:

Who did John agree with?	[22q]

The passive is highly doubtful:

?Mary was agreed with by John	[22p]

[23] can form no passive, but both types of question are possible; the pronominal one is rather 'recapitulation', whereas the adverbial one is the more natural question:

What did the car stop beside?⎫	
Where did the car stop? ⎬	[23q]

[24] has only the adverbial question form:

When did she leave?	[24q]

[25], finally, shows its idiomatic nature by accepting none of the three criteria, resisting this kind of syntactic manipulation.

Note

[a] In addition to the mentioned pronominal question form, there is an alternative one with an added noun:

What place did the car stop beside?	[23q]
Before what time did she leave?	[24q]

[b] Again, *agreed with* as in [22p] can be acceptable in an extended verb phrase:

Mary is a person who likes to be agreed with (by everybody)

[c] There is considerable overlap between the two question forms:

He built it with these tools	[26]

How did he build it?   ⎫
What did he build it with?⎭   [26q]

She spoke with assurance   [27]

How did she speak?   ⎫
*What did she speak with?⎭   [27q]

The difference between [26q] and [27q] is obviously connected with their respective concrete and abstract meanings (cf 12.7).

12.23
Prepositional verbs defined

What we are faced with here is a number of different and complex relations between verbs and prepositional phrases. We will count as prepositional verbs those which accept the passive and/or the pronominal question form but not the adverbial question form. In the examples of *Table* 12:1, this dichotomy will separate [21] and [22] from [23] and [24], which will be analysed as single-word verbs with prepositional phrases as adverbials. [25] is a lexical idiom that does not obey productive syntactic rules of the kind we have discussed and hence will not be treated in the grammar.

12.24
Phrasal verbs defined

Returning to the first set of 12.19, it now remains to distinguish between phrasal and prepositional verbs. They display certain (a) phonological and (b) syntactic differences:

(a) The particle in phrasal verbs is normally stressed and, in final position, bears the nuclear tone, whereas the particle in the prepositional verb is normally unstressed and has the 'tail' of the nuclear tone on the lexical verb (see App II.12):

He called ˈup the man ∼ The man was called ÙP
He ˈcalled on the man ∼ The man was CÀLLED on

(b) A syntactic difference is that the particle of a phrasal verb can often stand either before or after a noun, whereas it can only stand after a personal pronoun: *Call up the man, call the man up, call him up,* but not **call up him* (unless it has contrastive stress: *call up ˈhim, not his ˈsister*). *Table* 12:1 shows these and other criteria that distinguish the two classes of verbs as having different syntactic patterning with regard to noun object (e), personal pronoun object (b) and (f), position in relative clause (d), and adverb insertion (c). The table shows that prepositional verbs take (b) personal or (d) relative pronouns after the preposition, and admit (c) an inserted adverb; phrasal verbs, on the other hand, have particles which can be separated from the verb by (e) a noun or (f) a pronoun.

Table 12:1

DIAGNOSTIC FRAMES FOR PHRASAL AND PREPOSITIONAL VERBS

	PREPOSITIONAL VERB *call on* = 'visit'	PHRASAL VERB *call up* = 'summon'
(a)	They ׀call on the man	They call ׀up the man
(b)	They ׀call on him	*They call up him
(c)	They call ׀early on the man	*They call early up the man
(d)	The man on whom they call	*The man up whom they call
(e)	*They call the man on	They call the man ׀up
(f)	*They call him on	They call him ׀up

12.25
Verb-adjective combinations

There is a verb-adjective combination that is very similar to phrasal verbs. Compare

He put the cloth straight
He put it out

where only *put out* is considered a phrasal verb. Both combinations form close units but the adjectives in verb-adjective combinations have their individual meaning and grammatical properties:

John didn't put the tablecloth as $\begin{Bmatrix} \text{straight} \\ \text{*out} \end{Bmatrix}$ as Mary

Adjectives in combinations like *cut short, rub dry, scrub clean, set free, dye red, wash clean, work loose,* etc, are however selected from a rather restricted range of adjectives. Thus none of these verbs can have several adjectives, but the adjectives can co-occur with many different verbs, *eg: open: burst open, force open, hold open, kick open, knock open, lay open, pull open, push open, swing open, tear open,* etc (see 5.17). In this respect verb-adjective combinations differ from verb + adjective complements (12.69), which can select complements from a very wide range of adjectives: *He found her pretty/rich/intelligent/fatherless/stubborn,* etc.

12.26
Phrasal-prepositional verbs defined

Phrasal-prepositional verbs are combinations of the two multi-word verb classes that we have discussed in 12.23 and 12.24:

We are all looking forward to your party on Saturday.
He had to put up with a lot of teasing at school.
Why don't you look in on Mrs Johnson on your way back?
He thinks he can get away with everything.

12.27
A sample of multi-word verbs
Multi-word verbs are very numerous, and we can only give a short list
for each verb class (see further 12.46). The words in parenthesis illustrate
or gloss their meanings.

PHRASAL VERBS	PREPOSITIONAL VERBS
BACK UP (somebody)	ADD TO (the bill)
BLOW UP (a ship)	ALLOW FOR (delays)
BREAK OFF (our relations)	APPLY FOR (a post)
BRING ABOUT (a change)	APPROVE OF (an action)
BRING UP (children)	ATTEND TO (the matter)
BURN UP (a house)	CARE FOR (somebody)
CATCH ON ('understand')	COMMENT ON (the results)
DRAW UP (a contract)	CONFORM TO (a standard)
FILL OUT (a form)	CONGRATULATE (someone) ON (his exam)
FIND OUT (a secret)	CONSENT TO (the proposal)
GET OVER (an idea)	CURE (somebody) OF (a disease)
GIVE UP ('surrender')	ENLARGE ON (a topic)
MAKE OUT ('understand')	HINT AT (other possibilities)
MAKE UP (a story)	INSIST ON (coming)
PASS OVER (a question)	LIVE ON (a small salary)
PULL UP ('stop')	OBJECT TO (something)
PUT (an idea) ACROSS	PART WITH (something)
PUT OFF (an answer)	REFER TO (a dictionary)
SEE (somebody) OFF	RESORT TO (violence)
TURN OFF (the light)	RUN FOR (president)
TURN UP (at a meeting)	TAKE TO (drink)

PHRASAL-PREPOSITIONAL VERBS

BREAK IN ON (somebody's conversation)
CATCH UP ON (my reading)
CATCH UP WITH (somebody)
CHECK UP ON ('investigate')
COME DOWN WITH (a cold)
COME UP WITH (the idea)
CUT DOWN ON (expenses)

> DO AWAY WITH (prejudices)
> FACE UP TO (the problems)
> GET AWAY WITH (it, *ie* 'without being punished')
> GET DOWN TO (serious talk)
> KEEP AWAY FROM (somebody's company)
> KEEP UP WITH (the Joneses)
> LOOK DOWN ON (somebody)
> LOOK FORWARD TO ('anticipate')
> LOOK OUT FOR (wet leaves)
> LOOK UP TO (somebody)
> PUT UP WITH (somebody's behaviour)
> RUN AWAY WITH ('become uncontrollable')
> STAND UP FOR (one's ideals)
> TURN OUT FOR (a meeting)
> WALK OUT ON ('abandon')

Note

Some particles, *eg:* *about* and *over*, can serve as a particle of both a phrasal and a prepositional verb:

> I think we'd better pass over these mistakes
>
> ~ I think we'd better pass $\begin{cases} \text{them over} \\ \text{over them} \end{cases}$

Compare:

> He got $\begin{cases} \text{the idea over ('managed to communicate').} \\ \text{over the idea ('managed to forget').} \end{cases}$

12.28
Alternative analyses of strings consisting of a verb + a prepositional phrase

A sentence like *He looked at the girl* can be given two analyses. In one, there is a prepositional phrase (*at the girl*) as adverbial; in the other, *looked at* is a prepositional verb with *girl* as prepositional object. (We will use the shorter term 'prepositional object' for what should properly be termed 'object after a prepositional verb'.)

ANALYSIS 1:   V   A

He looked at the girl

ANALYSIS 2:   prep-V   prep-O

Analysis 1 (verb + adverbial) accounts for the similarity of prepositional phrases with regard to relative clause structure and the positioning of adverbs:

> The girl $\begin{cases} \text{at whom he looked} \\ \text{to whom he came} \end{cases}$

$$\text{He} \begin{cases} \text{looked slyly at the girl} \\ \text{stood quietly near the girl} \end{cases}$$

Analysis 2 (prepositional verb + prepositional object) accounts for the similarity of these structures to that of transitive non-prepositional verbs:

$$\text{The girl was} \begin{cases} \text{looked at} \\ \text{admired} \\ \text{*stood near} \end{cases}$$

Two modes of analysis are also applicable to sentences like

He gave an apple to the girl

where *to the girl* can be considered a prepositional adverbial (Analysis 1), accounting for the similarity between, for example, the following sentences:

$$\text{He} \begin{cases} \text{gave an apple to} \\ \text{found an apple for} \\ \text{aimed an apple at} \end{cases} \text{the girl}$$

Analysis 2, by which *the girl* is a prepositional object, highlights the similarity with the parallel non-prepositional construction:

$$\text{He} \begin{cases} \text{gave} \\ \text{found} \\ \text{*aimed} \end{cases} \text{the girl an apple}$$

The two analyses can be regarded as different, but equally valid and complementary ways of looking at the same structure. The former analysis is that used in Chapter 7; in this chapter, which deals largely with voice, it is natural to adopt the latter analysis.

Types of complementation
12.29
Three types of verb can be distinguished where no complementation occurs:

(i) 'Pure' intransitive verbs, which can never take an object, as in

Our friends *have arrived*

(ii) Verbs which can be transitive or intransitive with little or no difference in meaning or in subject-verb relationship, as in

He *smokes* (cigars) every day

(iii) Verbs which can be transitive or intransitive but with considerable difference in meaning or in subject-verb relationship (*cf* App I.41), as in

> The light *shone* from the far corner
> He *grew* rapidly during that period

beside

> He *shone* the light from the far corner
> He *grew* tomatoes as a hobby.

12.30
Where complementation occurs, there are four main types:

[A] Intensive, *eg: John is only a boy*
[B] Monotransitive, *eg: He caught a big fish yesterday*
[C] Ditransitive, *eg: He gave Mary a doll*
[D] Complex transitive, *eg: She called him a hero*

These complementation types have been discussed in several places, notably in 2.4 *ff* and 7.6. Here, we will consider them all together, paying particular attention to their different subtypes and their active-passive relation (*cf* 12.2 *ff*), and give lists of verbs which occur in the different subtypes of complementation. These lists are of course not exhaustive, but it is hoped that they will be a useful source of reference.

Intensive complementation [Type A]
Copulas
12.31
Intensive complementation obtains in sentences where there is co-reference relation between the subject and the subject complement (see 5.7 *f*, 7.11). The verb in sentences with subject complement is a 'copula' (or 'linking verb'), which of itself has little meaning but functions as a link between the complement and the subject. The dispensability of the copula can be seen in the relation of intensive predication to premodification (*the man who is tall ~ the tall man*) and in object complements of the complex transitive type of complementation: *I found him (to be) unreliable* (12.69).

12.32
The typical, colourless copula is BE, which expresses essence (*Sugar is sweet*) or accident (*John is perplexed*). Other copulas, which have more intrinsic meaning than BE, form two main classes, 'current' and 'resulting' copulas, the most common of which are listed below:

'Current' copulas	'Resulting' copulas
APPEAR (happy)	BECOME (older)
FEEL (annoyed)	COME (true)
LIE (scattered)	GET (ready)
LOOK (dejected)	GO (sour)
REMAIN (uncertain)	GROW (tired)
REST (assured)	FALL (sick)
SEEM (restless)	RUN (wild)
SMELL (sweet)	TURN (sour)
SOUND (surprised)	
STAND (perplexed)	
TASTE (bitter)	

12.33

[A1] Noun phrase complement, as in

John is a nice boy

[A2] Adverbial complement, as in

He is at school today

These complements will not be further discussed here, since they have been dealt with elsewhere: see, respectively, 4.39, 7.2 *ff* and 8.46, 8.73 (where adverbial complements are related to other adjuncts as 'predicative').

Adjective phrase complement
12.34

[A3] Adjective phrase complement without postmodification, *eg*

John is (very) bright

[A4] Adjective phrase with prepositional phrase postmodification (*cf* 5.36 and, for relations to the passive, 12.16).

ABOUT: He was *shocked about* her reaction (*cf* 6.51)

ADJECTIVE	PARTICIPLE
angry	aggrieved
glad	annoyed
happy	frightened
knowledgeable	pleased
mad	worried, etc
reasonable, etc	

AT: She was *bad at* mathematics
She was *annoyed at* his behaviour (*cf* 6.54)

ADJECTIVE	PARTICIPLE
angry	alarmed
clever	amused
good	delighted
hopeless	disgusted
terrible, etc	pleased
	puzzled
	staggered, etc

IN: She was *successful in* her attempts
She is *interested in* languages

ADJECTIVE	PARTICIPLE
efficient	experienced
fortunate	interested
lucky	justified
outstanding	mistaken, etc
persistent	
resolute	
unsuccessful	
zealous, etc	

OF: She was *aware of* his difficulties
She was *convinced of* his brilliance

ADJECTIVE	PARTICIPLE
afraid	convinced
certain	scared
conscious	tired, etc
fond	
glad	
resentful, etc	

ON/UPON: His plan was *based on* co-operation
He is *insistent on* his rights (*cf* 6.51)

ADJECTIVE	PARTICIPLE
contingent	based
dependent	bent
intent	set, etc
keen	
reliant	
severe, etc	

TO: He is *subject to* criticism

ADJECTIVE	PARTICIPLE
answerable	inclined
averse	opposed, etc
liable	
subject, etc	

WITH: This plan is not *compatible with* our principles
He is *concerned with* her behaviour

ADJECTIVE	PARTICIPLE
angry	annoyed
busy	bored
comfortable	delighted
compatible	depressed
content	disappointed
delirious	disgusted
familiar	dismayed
furious	distressed
happy	enchanted
impatient	excited
incompatible	exhausted
jubilant	horrified
sick	intoxicated
uncomfortable	obsessed
uneasy	occupied
unfamiliar	overcome
unhappy, etc	pleased
	satisfied
	upset, etc

[A5] With finite clause postmodification
12.35
That-clauses postmodifying adjective phrase complement may have:

(i) indicative verb: I am sure that he is here now
(ii) subjunctive verb: I am insistent that he be ready (formal)
(iii) putative *should:*   I am sorry that he should come (formal)

Putative *should* occurs after emotive verbs, expressing sorrow, joy, displeasure, surprise, wonder, etc. *Should*-clauses frequently contain words and expressions such as *so, such, like this, like that, ever,* or *at all.* The meaning of putative *should* has been discussed in 11.72 (see also

8.84). For the subjunctive, see 3.16. The following pairs of sentences illustrate possible choices with some subject complements:

I am sorry I have to leave.	I am sorry Mrs Smith should have been so inconvenienced.
I am surprised you haven't called the doctor before.	I am surprised that anyone of your intelligence should be so foolish as to believe this.
It's good the lecture is over.	It's good somebody should have illusions like that.
It was natural for him to go to London after the war.	It was natural that he should like to think that he had so much perspicacity.

That-clauses cannot be preceded by prepositions. Hence adjectives which are constructed with prepositions before noun phrase complements drop them before *that*-clauses (*cf* 12.46). Compare the following:

I am sure $\begin{cases} \text{of his innocence} \\ \text{that he is innocent} \end{cases}$

12.36
Personal subject + copula + adjective phrase + *that*-clause, *eg*

I am *sure* that we'll be late
I am *amazed* that he should get the post

ADJECTIVE	PARTICIPLE
afraid	alarmed
angry	amazed
aware	amused
certain	annoyed
confident	astonished
conscious	depressed
glad	disappointed
grateful	distressed
happy	disturbed
proud	frightened
sad	horrified
sure	irritated
thankful, etc	pleased
	shocked
	upset, etc

12.37

It + copula + adjective phrase + *that*-clause

(i) with indicative verb:

It is *true* that she never came

ADJECTIVE
apparent
certain
evident
implicit
likely
obvious
plain
possible
probable
true
well-known, etc

(ii) with subjunctive verb:

It is *expedient* that he arrive by tomorrow

ADJECTIVE	DEVERBAL ADJECTIVE
appropriate	advisable
compulsory	desirable
crucial	inadvisable
essential	preferable, etc
fitting	
imperative	
important	
necessary	
obligatory	
proper	
vital, etc	

(iii) with putative *should*:

It is *awkward* that he should be late
It is *appropriate* that he should get the post

ADJECTIVE	DEVERBAL ADJECTIVE	PARTICIPLE
appropriate	admirable	alarming
awkward	commendable	annoying
curious	deplorable	depressing
disastrous	despicable	disappointing
dreadful	incomprehensible	disconcerting

ADJECTIVE	DEVERBAL ADJECTIVE	PARTICIPLE
extraordinary	inconceivable	embarrassing
fitting	lamentable	frightening
fortunate	regrettable	irritating
important	remarkable	perplexing
improper	understandable	pleasing
irrational	unjustifiable, etc	shocking
logical		surprising
odd		upsetting, etc
peculiar		
proper		
queer		
sad		
tragic, etc		

[A6] With *to*-infinitive postmodification
12.38
This type contains several superficially similar but basically different constructions. We can distinguish at least the following five classes:

[I] He is splendid to wait (12.39)
[II] He is hard to convince (12.40)
[III] He is slow to react (12.41)
[IV] He is furious to hear about it (12.42)
[V] He is hesitant to agree with you (12.43)

12.39
In constructions of Type I, *He is splendid to wait*, the subject (*he*) of the finite copula (*is*) is also the subject of the non-finite complement clause (*to wait*). These constructions have analogues with anticipatory *it* (*cf* 14.23, 14.35 *ff*):

It is splendid of him to wait

The adjectival complement heads can have alternatives with degree nouns:

He is $\left\{\begin{array}{l}\text{splendid}\\\text{a gentleman}\end{array}\right\}$ to wait

He is $\left\{\begin{array}{l}\text{clever}\\\text{a magician}\end{array}\right\}$ to make so much money

You are $\left\{\begin{array}{l}\text{foolish}\\\text{a fool}\end{array}\right\}$ to spend so much

You are $\left\{\begin{array}{l}\text{wonderful}\\\text{an angel}\end{array}\right\}$ to do this for me

Other nouns than those which denote degree do not accept this construction: *He is a doctor to make so much money. Cf* however: *He must be (quite) a doctor to make so much money.*

12.40

In Type II, *He is hard to convince*, the subject (*he*) of the finite copula (*is*) is the object of the infinitive (*convince*). We may distinguish two subtypes here. In the first of these, there are analogues with the non-finite clause as subject and with extraposition. The adjective is here primarily predicating the infinitive clause.

He is hard to convince
~ To convince him is hard
~ It is hard to convince him

He is difficult to astonish
~ To astonish him is difficult
~ It is difficult to astonish him

He is convenient to send
~ To send him is convenient
~ It is convenient to send him

The second subtype has no analogues with the infinitive clause as subject:

The air is frosty to breathe
~ *To breathe the air is frosty
~ *It is frosty to breathe the air

We can omit the clause more readily with this subtype:

The air is frosty (to breathe)
The food is ready (to eat)
The paper is flimsy (to write on)

With the first subtype there can rarely be an ellipsis:

He is hard ~ He is hard to convince

Since the subject (*he*) is the object of the infinitive (*convince*), no additional direct object is possible:

*He is easy to convince Mary

Indirect and direct object constructions are also odd:

?He is easy to send complaints
?Complaints are easy to send him

Compare, however:

He is easy to send complaints to.

12.41

Type III consists of adjectives which have adverbial transforms. We can distinguish two subtypes. In the first, the subject of the copula is also the subject of the infinitive (*cf* Type I above):

He was $\begin{Bmatrix} \text{prompt} \\ \text{quick} \\ \text{slow} \end{Bmatrix}$ to react

~ He reacted $\begin{Bmatrix} \text{promptly} \\ \text{quickly} \\ \text{slowly} \end{Bmatrix}$

In the second subtype, the subject of the copula is the object of the infinitive (*cf* Type II above and App I.41 b):

The clothes are easy to wash
~ It is easy to wash the clothes
~ The clothes wash easily.

12.42

Type IV consists of 'attitudinal' expressions where the complement head can be either an adjective (*eg: angry*) or an adjectival participle (*eg: annoyed*). In this construction the relation of the infinitive clause to the rest of the sentence is that of a quasi-agent expressing cause (*cf* 12.16):

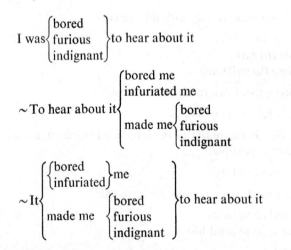

Adjectives like *indignant* without a corresponding verb have only the *make* paraphrase.

ADJECTIVES	PARTICIPLES
angry	annoyed
content	astonished
furious	bored
glad	concerned
happy	delighted
impatient	depressed
indignant	disappointed
jubilant, etc	disgusted
	(dis)satisfied
	embarrassed
	excited
	fascinated
	overwhelmed
	perturbed
	puzzled
	surprised
	worried, etc

12.43

Type V consists of 'volitional' expressions, indicating intention or willingness, or the reverse. The adjectival character of the participles is apparent from the possibility of adjectival premodification and copulas like *feel*, *seem*, etc.

$$ I \begin{Bmatrix} am \\ feel \end{Bmatrix} (rather) \begin{Bmatrix} hesitant \\ prone \\ reluctant \\ willing \\ inclined \\ induced \\ disinclined \\ disposed \end{Bmatrix} \text{to agree with you} $$

As we have found in 12.14 *ff*, there is a passive scale. In relation to such participle-with-infinitive constructions, we can distinguish three subtypes:

(a) I was asked to come
(b) I was forced to come
(c) I was inclined to come

Subtype (a) requires the active with personal subject (12.52 *ff*):

$$ \sim \begin{Bmatrix} [People] \\ [*Circumstances] \end{Bmatrix} \text{asked me to come} $$

Subtype (b) can have actives with either personal or non-personal subjects:

$$\sim \begin{cases} \text{[People]} \\ \text{[Circumstances]} \end{cases} \text{forced me to come}$$

Subtype (c) has only active analogues with the *make* construction:

$$\sim \text{[Circumstances]} \begin{cases} \text{?inclined me} \\ \text{made me inclined} \end{cases} \text{to come.}$$

Monotransitive complementation [Type B]
12.44

Objects have a number of semantic functions (*cf* 7.13 *ff*). It is not possible to consider here all these relations in transitive complementation. The following lists exemplify some of the most common subtypes of complementation. The listing will be particularly unrepresentative in the case of types with numerous verbs, such as monotransitive complementation with noun phrase objects.

12.45
[B1] Noun phrase objects

(a) Animate subject + inanimate, concrete object:

> The boys *caught* the ball
> ~ The ball was *caught* (by the boys)

CARRY	INSPECT	STOP
COVER	LOWER	TEST
EXAMINE	RUIN	WIN
FOLLOW	SEE	etc

(b) Animate subject + inanimate, abstract object:

> Everybody *understood* the problem
> ~ The problem was *understood* (by everybody)

CONSIDER	DESCRIBE	INVESTIGATE
DECIDE	DETECT	RECOGNIZE
DEFINE	DISCUSS	REPORT
DEMONSTRATE	FORMULATE	etc

(c) Animate subject + animate object:

> Everybody *liked* the new neighbours
> ~ The new neighbours were *liked* (by everybody)

ACCEPT	CONVINCE	PAY
ADVISE	FOLLOW	REJECT
APPRECIATE	JOIN	SUPPORT
CALL	MEET	etc

(d) Inanimate, abstract subject + animate object (*cf* 12.16):

The news *shocked* the family
~ The family was *shocked* (by the news)

AFFECT	HELP	SAVE
CONVERT	IMPRESS	SURPRISE
EMBARRASS	INCENSE	TROUBLE
FASCINATE	OVERWHELM	etc

12.46
[B2] Prepositional objects

Sentences with prepositional objects, which should really be termed 'objects after prepositional verbs' (see 12.28), can occur in the passive just like sentences with non-prepositional objects:

John searched $\begin{cases} \text{the room} \sim \text{The room was searched (by John)} \\ \text{for the key} \sim \text{The key was searched for (by John)} \end{cases}$

The prepositional object may be a noun, a pronoun, an *-ing*, or a *wh*-clause (see 6.2):

He concentrated on $\begin{cases} \text{the song} \\ \text{that} \\ \text{singing} \\ \text{what they would sing} \end{cases}$

Infinitives and *that*-clauses cannot be preceded by prepositions. Compare the following two series, (a) with a prepositional verb and (b) with a non-prepositional verb:

(a) He objected $\begin{cases} \text{to the meeting} \\ \text{to it} \\ \text{to meeting her} \\ \text{to what had been decided} \\ \text{(that) they had already met} \end{cases}$

(b) He forgot $\begin{cases} \text{the meeting} \\ \text{it} \\ \text{?meeting her} \\ \text{what had been decided} \\ \text{(that) they had already met} \\ \text{to meet her} \end{cases}$

We *asked for* their assistance
~ Their assistance was *asked for*
(Compare the list in 12.27)

ACCOUNT FOR	CONTRIBUTE TO	PAY FOR
ADJUST TO	DEAL WITH	PRAY FOR
ADMIT TO	DECIDE ON	PREACH ABOUT/ON
AGREE ABOUT/ON/TO	DWELL UPON	PROVIDE FOR
AIM AT/FOR	GET AWAY WITH	QUARREL ABOUT
ARGUE ABOUT	HEAR ABOUT	READ ABOUT
ARRANGE FOR	HOPE FOR	REJOICE AT
ASK FOR	INTERFERE WITH	RELY ON
BELIEVE IN	LEARN ABOUT	SPEAK ABOUT/ON
CALL FOR/ON	LECTURE ABOUT/ON	TALK OF
CALL UPON	LISTEN TO	THINK OF
COMPLAIN ABOUT	LIVE ON	WISH FOR
CONCEIVE OF	LONG FOR	WRITE ABOUT/ON
CONCENTRATE ON	LOOK AFTER/AT/ON/TO	etc

Notes

[a] When *to* precedes an infinitive, it is an infinitive marker (*forgot to meet her*) and not a preposition, in which case *to* (like other prepositions) is regularly followed by the *-ing* form:

> He *admitted* to doing it
> This *amounts* to doing the whole thing over again
> I *confess* to having committed the crime
> We are all *looking forward* to meeting you soon
> He *took* to playing golf

[b] Prepositions may occur with *that*-clauses in the case of the compound conjunction *in that, save that, except that* (11.9), and in passive constructions of the type:

> It *was agreed to* that they would meet again soon.

12.47
[B3] Finite clause objects

Finite clause objects are *that*- and *wh*-clauses (11.66). The conjunction in *that*-clauses may be zero except when it has initial position in passive clauses (and thus obeys the same rules as other nominal clauses as subject, see 11.17). The normal passive analogue has *it* and extraposition. For proforms for direct object clauses (*I believe so, I think not*) see 10.62.

> Everybody hoped (that) he would sing
>
> ~ { That he would sing was hoped by everybody
>   *He would sing was hoped by everybody
>   It was hoped by everybody (that) he would sing

That-clauses may have three types of verb phrase:

(a) indicative verb: I suppose that he $\begin{cases} \text{is coming} \\ \text{will be coming} \\ \text{will come} \\ \text{has come} \end{cases}$

(b) putative *should:*   I regret that he should be so stubborn

(c) subjunctive verb: I request that she go alone

(a) with indicative verb is the unmarked type. (b) with putative *should* has been discussed in connection with intensive complementation (*I am surprised that he should be so stubborn*) where it is more common than with transitive verbs (11.72, 12.35). The subjunctive type (c) seems to be restricted to AmE in cases where BrE favours other means of expression, such as putative *should* (*cf* 3.16).

(a) They *agree* that she is pretty
    ~ It is *agreed* that she is pretty

ACCEPT	DOUBT	OVERLOOK
ADMIT	EXPECT	PROVE
ANNOUNCE	FEEL	REMARK
ANSWER	FIND	REPORT
ASSUME	FORGET	SAY
BELIEVE	GUARANTEE	SEE
CLAIM	HOPE	SHOW
COMPLAIN	IGNORE	SPECIFY
CONTEST	IMPLY	SUPPOSE
DECLARE	INDICATE	THINK
DEMONSTRATE	KNOW	UNDERSTAND
DENY	NOTICE	etc
DISCOVER	OBSERVE	

(b) I *regret* that she should worry about it
    ~ It is *regretted* that she should worry about it

(c) I *request* that she go alone
    ~ It is *requested* that she go alone

Verbs that take putative *should* and subjunctive verb can be given in one list:

ASK	CONSENT (usually *should*)	DESIRE
AUTHORIZE	DECREE	DICTATE

COMMAND	DEMAND	DIRECT
GRANT (usually *should*)	PERMIT	REQUIRE
INSIST	PROPOSE	SUGGEST
MOVE	RECOMMEND	URGE
ORDER	REQUEST	etc

(d) He *asked* $\left\{ {\text{if} \atop \text{whether}} \right\}$ they were coming

~ It was *asked* $\left\{ {\text{if} \atop \text{whether}} \right\}$ they were coming

ASK	DOUBT	KNOW
CONSIDER	EXAMINE	NOTICE
DECIDE	FIND OUT	SAY
DETERMINE	FORGET	TEST
DISCUSS	GUESS	WONDER, etc

(with negative verb) — applies to KNOW, NOTICE, SAY

Non-finite clause objects
12.48
It will be convenient to discuss all non-finite verb clauses together under monotransitive complementation, although some are closely related to other types of complementation. We will distinguish non-finite clause objects with subjects and without subjects, and, within each of these subtypes, between infinitival and participial verb clauses (*Fig* 12:2).

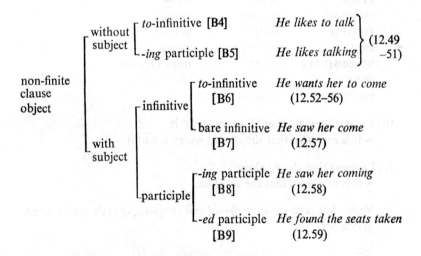

Fig 12:2 Non-finite clause objects

[B4] *To*-infinitive without subject and
[B5] *-ing* participle without subject
12.49
[B4] and [B5] contain several classes of verbs.

(a) Verbs which take only the infinitive:

$$\text{John longed} \begin{Bmatrix} \text{to do} \\ \text{*doing} \end{Bmatrix} \text{his homework}$$

(b) Verbs which take only the participle:

$$\text{John denied} \begin{Bmatrix} \text{having stolen} \\ \text{*to have stolen} \end{Bmatrix} \text{the money}$$

(c) Verbs which take either the infinitive or the participle:

$$\text{John began} \begin{Bmatrix} \text{to sing} \\ \text{singing} \end{Bmatrix} \text{in the shower}$$

(d) Verbs which take either (active) participle or passive infinitive
(*deserve, need, require*, and sometimes *want*):

$$\text{Your shoes need} \begin{Bmatrix} \text{cleaning} \\ \text{to be cleaned} \end{Bmatrix}$$

The passive analogue is rare with these verbs; the infinitive construction
occurs in the passive (with extraposed *it*) only with certain verbs, notably *agree, decide*, and *feel*:

My family decided to go abroad
~It was decided (by my family) to go abroad.

12.50
The infinitive and participle constructions with Class (c) verbs are not in
free variation. There is usually felt to be a difference in meaning between them, although it may be of little practical importance. The participle construction generally implies 'fulfilment', and the infinitive
construction 'potentiality'.

$$\begin{matrix} \text{He enjoys} \begin{Bmatrix} \text{visiting} \\ \text{*to visit} \end{Bmatrix} \\ \text{He expects} \begin{Bmatrix} \text{*visiting} \\ \text{to visit} \end{Bmatrix} \end{matrix} \text{his mother-in-law}$$

The general rule is also apparent in verbs where the choice is not
absolute:

$$\text{He started} \begin{Bmatrix} \text{speaking and kept on for more than an hour} \\ \text{to speak but stopped because she objected} \end{Bmatrix}$$

Another factor governing the choice is aspect (*cf* 3.36 *ff*):

$$\text{I heard the door} \begin{Bmatrix} \text{slamming all night long} \\ \text{slam just after midnight} \end{Bmatrix}$$

Note the present/future verb contrast with REMEMBER:

I remember walking over Westminster Bridge
I'll remember to walk carefully in London.

12.51

For both [B4] and [B5], we may distinguish between (i) an 'emotive' class of verbs, such as FORGET and PREFER, and (ii) a 'process' class of verbs, such as BEGIN, CONTINUE, and CEASE.

(a) verbs with *to*-infinitive	(b) verbs with *-ing* participle	(c) verbs with *to*-infinitive or *-ing* participle
AGREE	ACKNOWLEDGE	(i) *EMOTIVE VERBS*
AIM	ADMIT (TO)	cannot BEAR
ARRANGE	AVOID	DREAD
ASK	CONSIDER	FORGET
ATTEMPT	CONTEMPLATE	HATE
CHOOSE	DEFER	INTEND
CLAIM	DENY	LIKE
CONSENT	DETEST (rarely infinitive)	LOVE
DARE	DISLIKE	NEGLECT
DECIDE	ESCAPE	PREFER
DECLINE	EVADE	REGRET
DEMAND	FACILITATE	REMEMBER
DESERVE	FANCY	etc
DETERMINE	FAVOUR	(ii) *PROCESS VERBS*
EXPECT	FINISH	BEGIN
HOPE	GIVE UP	START
LEARN	cannot HELP	CONTINUE
LONG	INCLUDE	CEASE
MANAGE	KEEP (ON)	DELAY (usually *-ing*)
MEAN	don't MIND	OMIT
OFFER	MISS	PLAN
PRETEND	POSTPONE	TRY
PROMISE	PRACTISE	UNDERTAKE
REFUSE	PUT OFF	
THREATEN	RESENT	
WANT	RESIST	
WISH	RISK	
etc	SHUN	
	cannot STAND	
	STOP	
	SUGGEST	
	etc	

Note

Unlike *eg: cease*, *stop* takes only the participle construction as object:

John stopped $\begin{cases} \text{smoking ('gave up smoking')} \\ \text{to smoke ('stopped in order to smoke', } ie \text{ adverbial)} \end{cases}$

[B6] *To*-infinitive with subject
12.52
The complements consisting of noun phrase + *to*-infinitive in the following two sentences look superficially the same:

(a) I told him to see a doctor
(b) I liked him to see a doctor

However, (a) and (b) differ both in their meaning and in their structural possibilities, as the following examples show.

(i) Pseudo-cleft sentence construction:

What I $\begin{cases} \text{told} \\ \text{*liked} \end{cases}$ him was to see a doctor

(ii) Infinitive replacement by a noun phrase:

I $\begin{cases} \text{told} \\ \text{*liked} \end{cases}$ him something

(iii) Infinitive replacement by a *that*-clause:

I $\begin{cases} \text{told} \\ \text{*liked} \end{cases}$ him that he should see a doctor

(iv) Replacement by the genitive case for the common case of nouns and for the objective case of pronouns:

I $\begin{cases} \text{*told} \\ \text{liked} \end{cases}$ his seeing a doctor

(v) Interchange of object and subject in the non-finite clause:

I told him to see a doctor
~ I told a doctor to see him
I liked him to see a doctor
~ I liked a doctor to see him.

12.53
The two classes of complementation can be analysed in the following way:

(a) I told him to come = S + V + O/S + *to*-infinitive clause
(b) I liked him to come = S + V + O[S + *to*-infinitive clause]

In Class (a) *him* has a double function; it is the object of *told* and the subject of *come:*

I told him that he should come

In Class (b) the whole non-finite clause *him to come* serves as the object of *liked* with *him* as the subject of *come.*

Class (a) can be considered a subtype of ditransitive complementation. Compare:

(a) I asked him $\begin{cases} \text{to answer} \\ \text{a question} \end{cases}$

Class (b) is related both to monotransitive verbs, which have a single object, and to complex transitive verbs, which have an object with intensive relation (see 12.67 *ff*). Compare the following two sets:

(b) I disliked $\begin{cases} \text{his smoking} \\ \text{(the fact) that he smoked} \\ \text{him to be a smoker} \end{cases}$

(c) I found $\begin{cases} \text{him to be a smoker} \\ \text{him a smoker} \\ \text{him smoke} \end{cases}$

Although DISLIKE accepts the infinitive construction with BE, it does not take the intensive relation without the copula: **I disliked him a smoker.* Verbs like FIND, which do so, are called Class (c) verbs. When Class (c) verbs are constructed with an infinitive, it is usually BE:

(b) I urged him $\begin{cases} \text{to take good care of his children} \\ \text{to be a good father} \\ \text{*a good father} \end{cases}$

(c) I found him $\begin{cases} \text{to take good care of his children} \\ \text{to be a good father} \\ \text{a good father} \end{cases}$

The two types are also semantically distinct. The verbs of (b) express cause, intent, etc; the verbs of (c) denote assumption, knowledge, etc.

Note

[a] The two types can be compared with [B3 b/c] and [B3a] (12.47), *ie* verbs taking *that*-clauses as objects where the verbs are subjunctive or putative *should* and indicative, respectively:

(b) I urged that he (should) $\begin{cases} \text{take good care of his children} \\ \text{be a good father} \end{cases}$

(c) I found that he $\begin{cases} \text{took good care of his children} \\ \text{was a good father} \end{cases}$

[b] The causative meaning of (b) verbs also appears in the underlying directional preposition of verbs like FORCE and URGE:

He forced me $\begin{cases} \text{to do it} \\ \text{into doing it} \end{cases}$

He urged me $\begin{cases} \text{to do it} \\ \text{to it} \end{cases}$

He found me $\begin{cases} \text{*to do it} \\ \text{*to it.} \end{cases}$

12.54

The following lists do not take account of all the criteria listed in 12.52, which would entail extensive cross-classification. The classes of verbs have been classified on the following basis:

(a) takes the pseudo-cleft sentence construction:

What I asked him was to come early

(b) does not take the pseudo-cleft sentence construction, except by adding a replacive DO:

*What I expected him was to come early
What I expected him to do was to come early

Class (b) forms two subclasses. The non-finite clause complement of verbs like INTEND, Subclass (I), can have voice transformation without change of meaning; with verbs of Subclass (II), for example URGE, there is a complete change of meaning between the active and the passive:

(I) I intended a doctor to examine him
 ~ I intended him to be examined by a doctor
(II) I urged a doctor to examine him
 ~ I urged him to be examined by a doctor

(c) regularly has BE as infinitive, which is often omissible, thus indicating an intensive relation (12.31 *ff*, 12.67 *ff*):

I believe Brutus $\begin{cases} \text{to be an honest man} \\ \text{an honest man} \\ \text{honest} \end{cases}$

Class (a)	Class (b)	Class (c)
ADVISE	(I) CAUSE	ACKNOWLEDGE
ALLOW	EXPECT	APPOINT
ASK	GET	ASSUME
FORBID	INTEND	BELIEVE
ORDER	LIKE	CHOOSE
PERMIT	MEAN	CLAIM
TEACH	REQUIRE	ELECT

Class (a)	Class (b)	Class (c)	—continued
TELL	WANT	FEEL[b]	
etc	etc	FIND	
	(II) COMPEL	HOLD	
	DARE	IMAGINE	
	ENCOURAGE	KNOW[b]	
	FORCE	OBSERVE[b]	
	HELP[a]	PROCLAIM	
	INCITE	REPORT	
	INDUCE	SUPPOSE	
	PERSUADE	THINK etc	
	PRESS		
	TEMPT		
	URGE etc		

Note

[a] For HELP, see Note in 12.57.

[b] FEEL, KNOW and OBSERVE do not accept omission of the copula:

Everybody observed John to be reliable

~*Everybody observed John reliable

KNOW is rather formal with the copula construction:

We all knew him to be a good man

[c] GIVE can occur with the to-infinitive with certain restricted verbs, especially UNDERSTAND:

He gave me ⎱
I was given ⎰ to understand that . . .

12.55

There is another type with infinitive complement where the verb is constructed with *for:*

He hoped for Mary to come

It includes the following verbs:

APPLY	PLAN	SEND
ARRANGE	PLEAD	TELEPHONE
ASK	PRAY	VOTE
CALL	PREPARE	WAIT
LONG	PROVIDE	etc
MEAN	RING	

12.56

The verbs in [B6] generally have passive analogues (cf 12.2 ff):

They saw him do it ~ He was seen to do it

However, many verbs have no one-to-one voice relation. Some verbs are typically active, such as WANT, ENABLE, and PERSUADE, whereas for example ALLOW, ASK, INTEND, MEAN, OBLIGE commonly occur in the passive. Some verbs, like SAY, CALCULATE, and REPUTE, have in fact no direct active analogue. Consider the following set of verbs:

	PASSIVE	ACTIVE
	seen to do it	~ They saw him do it
	invited to do it	~ They invited him to do it
He was	said to do it	~ { *They said him to do it / They said that he did it }
	calculated to do it	~ { *They calculated him to do it / They calculated that he would do it }
	reputed to do it	~ { *They reputed him to do it / *They reputed that he would do it }

Note
However, REPUTE can be used in the active with BE and HAVE:

> They reputed him to have the means to do it
> They reputed him to be the one who did it

12.57
[B7] Bare infinitive with subject
In the set of sentences given in 12.56, we can note, furthermore, that the passive construction with *to*-infinitive corresponds either to a bare active infinitive (as with SEE) or to a *to*-infinitive (as with INVITE, etc). This is a regular feature in English: there is no verb in the passive that has a bare infinitive (except LET: *The grass was let grow*).

The verbs taking the bare infinitive in the active are the verbs of perception, HEAR, SEE, WATCH, and also HELP, LET, and MAKE.

> They heard him come
> ~ He was heard to come

Note
HELP also takes the *to*-infinitive. The bare infinitive seems to be the more common in AmE than in BrE, but in both varieties the choice is conditioned by the subject's involvement:

> Will you help me clear the table?
> This book helped me to see the truth

In the example with bare infinitive, external help is called in; in the example with *to*-infinitive, assistance is outside the action proper.

12.58
[B8] -*ing* participle with subject
This type contains two classes of verbs. Verbs in (a) permit different con-

structions: either with a genitive instead of the object or a factive clause paraphrase; verbs in (b) have neither of these possibilities.

(a) I dislike $\begin{cases} \text{him} \\ \text{his} \end{cases}$ stealing money
the fact that he steals money

(b) I caught $\begin{cases} \text{him} \\ \text{*his} \end{cases}$ stealing money
*the fact that he steals money

Verbs in Class (a):

DISLIKE	NOTICE	RESENT
HATE	OBSERVE	cannot STAND
LIKE	RECOLLECT	etc
don't MIND	REMEMBER	

Verbs in Class (b) form subsets:

(i) the perception verbs HEAR, SEE, WATCH, which also take the bare infinitive (see B7, 12.57);

(ii) FEEL, FIND, IMAGINE, etc, which also take *to*-infinitive, usually BE (see B6, 12.54);

(iii) CATCH, KEEP, LEAVE, etc, which have no alternative construction with infinitive complement. (The infinitive is adverbial in *I left him to die: cf* 11.44 *ff.*)

12.59
[B9] -*ed* participle with subject

The tourists *found* the chairs occupied
~ The chairs *were found* occupied (by the tourists)

However, some verbs which take the active construction cannot passivize:

I *wanted* two tickets reserved
~ *Two tickets *were wanted* reserved

The verbs form two classes depending on whether they can have an alternative finite *that*-clause for the non-finite construction:

(a) He reported $\begin{cases} \text{the watch stolen} \\ \text{that the watch was stolen} \end{cases}$

(b) He got $\begin{cases} \text{the watch repaired} \\ \text{*that the watch was repaired} \end{cases}$

Class (a) verbs are, for example, FIND, HEAR, REPORT, and SEE. Class (b) verbs are, for example, GET, HAVE, KEEP, LEAVE, and WANT (which, however, admits a finite clause with putative *should: He wanted that everybody should be present*).

Note

Constructions with HAVE + object + *-ed* participle can easily be ambiguous, since HAVE has different meanings: (a) 'cause', (b) 'involvement', or (c) 'possession'. The sentence

John had a book stolen from the library

has at least these three possible interpretations:

   (a) John arranged for a book to be stolen from the library ('cause')
   (b) John suffered the loss of a book from the library ('involvement')
   (c) John had a book that was stolen from the library ('possession').

Ditransitive complementation [Type C]
[C1] Indirect + direct noun phrase object
12.60

Ditransitive complementation involves two objects that are not in a co-referential, intensive relation (see 7.5 *f*, 12.31 *ff*). Type C1 occurs with verbs like GIVE and BUY (for other examples, see 12.63):

He gave the girl a doll
He bought the girl a white hat

  (i) Indirect objects can be omitted without changing the basic meaning:

He gave a doll
~ He gave the girl
He bought a white hat
~ He bought the girl

  (ii) Indirect objects can take prepositional paraphrases (*cf:* C2, 6.37):

He gave a doll to the girl
He bought a white hat for the girl

  (iii) Indirect objects are typically animate, although this is not always the case, as for example in metaphorical use, where the direct object has a verbal analogue:

$$\text{He gave the car} \begin{cases} \text{a wash} \\ \text{a kick} \\ \text{a pat} \end{cases}$$

$$\sim \text{He} \begin{cases} \text{washed} \\ \text{kicked} \\ \text{patted} \end{cases} \text{the car}$$

Compare:

> He gave the girl a doll
> ~ *He dolled the girl

Some ditransitive verbs have two passive analogues:

> ~ A doll was given the girl
> ~ The girl was given a doll

Of these two passives, the second is the more common. The first, with an inanimate subject, normally takes the prepositional paraphrase (*ie* Type C2a in 12.62):

> ~ A doll was given to the girl

In metaphorical use, GIVE has only two passive analogues:

> ~ $\begin{cases} \text{The car was given a wash} \\ \text{A wash was given to the car} \\ \text{*A wash was given the car.} \end{cases}$

12.61

One subset of verbs with ditransitive complementation is distinguished by a different object relation. It includes discourse verbs like ASK, TEACH, TELL, as well as OWE, PAY, and SHOW. With these verbs either object can be omitted without changing the basic meaning; a prepositional paraphrase is also possible:

> I asked John a question

> ~ $\begin{cases} \text{I asked John} \\ \text{I asked a question} \\ \text{I asked a question of John} \end{cases}$

When the direct object is omitted with a verb like ASK, the verb becomes monotransitive (*ie* the indirect object becomes the direct object, *cf* 12.44 *ff*); the verbs like GIVE, however, do not become monotransitive (*ie* the indirect object does not become the direct object).

C1 verbs are listed in 12.63.

[C2] Direct+prepositional object
12.62

This includes two main types of prepositional object:

Inanimate direct + animate prep-phrase object	[C2a]
Animate direct + prep-phrase object	[C2b]

'Animate' should be understood to mean 'typically animate'. Many of the verbs admit either animate or inanimate nouns, for example:

$$\text{We compared} \begin{cases} \text{the boy with his parents} \\ \text{the novel with the short story} \end{cases}$$

Unlike ditransitive verbs with non-prepositional objects (*eg* GIVE, 12.60 *f*), ditransitive verbs with a prepositional object normally have only one passive analogue:

We explained the problem to the children   [C2a]

$\sim \begin{cases} \text{The problem was explained to the children} \\ \text{?The children were explained the problem} \end{cases}$

We reminded him of the agreement   [C2b]

$\sim \begin{cases} \text{He was reminded of the agreement} \\ \text{*The agreement was reminded him} \end{cases}$

Some verbs have all three possibilities of construction, many have two; for others there is only one alternative (in some cases the alternatives are not identical but very similar in meaning):

TELL $(1 + 2a + 2b)$:

> Mary told only John the secret
> Mary told the secret only to John
> Mary told only John about the secret

OFFER $(1 + 2a)$:

> John offered Mary some help
> John offered some help to Mary

ENVY $(1 + 2b)$:

> She envied John the success
> She envied John for his success

PROVIDE $(2a + 2b)$:

> Mary provided funds for him
> Mary provided him with funds

REFUSE (1):

> The bank refused him the loan

SAY $(2a)$:

> Why didn't anybody say this to me?

INTRODUCE $(2b)$:

> Mary introduced John to economics

The different constructional possibilities of certain verbs provide a means of achieving different focus (*cf* 14.2 *ff*). Compare the following pairs of sentences:

{ Mary blamed the broken vase on John
{ Mary blamed John for the broken vase
{ The government supplied blankets for the homeless
{ The government supplied the homeless with blankets.

12.63
The following lists give some of the verbs that occur in Types 1, 2a and 2b.

	Type 1	Type 2a	Type 2b
	SERVE (somebody something)	SERVE (something) to (somebody)	SERVE (somebody) with (something)
(1+2a+2b)	PAY	PAY to	PAY for/with
	SERVE	SERVE to	SERVE with
	TELL	TELL to	TELL about
(1+2a)	BRING	BRING to/on	
	DENY	DENY to	
	DO	DO to/for	
	GIVE	GIVE to	
	GRANT	GRANT to	
	HAND	HAND to	
	LEAVE	LEAVE to/for	
	LEND	LEND to	
	OFFER	OFFER to	
	OWE	OWE to	
	PROMISE	PROMISE to	
	READ	READ to	
	SHOW	SHOW to	
	TEACH	TEACH to	
	THROW	THROW to	
	FIND	FIND for	
	MAKE	MAKE for	
	ORDER	ORDER for	
	RESERVE	RESERVE for	
	SAVE	SAVE for	
	SPARE	SPARE for	
	ASK	ASK of	

	Type 1	Type 2a	Type 2b
(1 + 2b)	ENVY EXCUSE FORGIVE		ENVY for EXCUSE for FORGIVE for
(2a + 2b)		BLAME on PROVIDE for SUPPLY for/to	BLAME for PROVIDE with SUPPLY with
(1)	ALLOW CHARGE FINE REFUSE WISH		
(2a)		ADDRESS to ANNOUNCE to COMMUNICATE to EXPLAIN to SAY to	
(2b)			ADVISE about PUNISH for THANK for PREVENT from PROTECT from INTEREST in ACCUSE of ASSURE of CONVICT of CONVINCE of DEPRIVE of INFORM of PERSUADE of RELIEVE of REMIND of ROB of SUSPECT of WARN of CONGRATULATE on CONSULT on CONFINE to

	Type 1	Type 2a	Type 2b
			INTRODUCE to
			REFER to
			SENTENCE to
			SUBJECT to
			TREAT to
			CHARGE with
			COMPARE with

Note the reflexive verbs (see 4.114) with a prepositional object, *eg*

We pride ourselves on his success.

12.64
[C2c] Verb+noun phrase+prepositional phrase idioms
These constitute a special type of complex object. The verb and the two phrases form a very close, idiomatic unit, which has two passive analogues when either of the noun phrases can become the subject of a passive sentence:

The owner had *made a mess of* the house	[C2c]
~ { *A mess* had been *made of* the house	[2c']
{ The house had been *made a mess of*	[2c"]

Other examples of the latter kind of passive are:

Mary realized she was being *made fun of*
Her beauty was *made much of*
Pretty girls will always be *taken notice of*
The children were *taken good care of*

There is a tendency to use the regular passive if the head of the prepositional phrase is premodified by an open-class adjective (and hence the idiomatic nature of the construction is weakened).

Considerable allowance will be *made for* special cases

rather than

?Special cases will be *made considerable allowance for*

The [2c'] passive is often felt to be more formal than [2c"]. In some cases, it is unacceptable or rare. Compare:

This possibility was hardly ever *made use of*
?*Use* was hardly ever *made of* this possibility

The following list includes some idioms consisting of verb+noun phrase+prep-phrase:

CATCH SIGHT OF	MAKE ALLOWANCE FOR	PUT A STOP TO
GIVE PLACE TO	MAKE FUN OF	SET FIRE TO
GIVE WAY TO	MAKE A FUSS OVER/ABOUT	TAKE ACCOUNT OF
KEEP PACE WITH	MAKE ROOM FOR	TAKE ADVANTAGE OF
LOSE SIGHT OF	MAKE USE OF	TAKE CARE OF
LOSE TOUCH WITH	PAY ATTENTION TO	TAKE NOTE OF
LOSE TRACK OF	PUT AN END TO	TAKE NOTICE OF, etc

12.65
[C3] Noun phrase+finite clause object
With some of the verbs it is not possible to delete the noun phrase object:

John convinced me he was right
~ *John convinced he was right

Other verbs admit object omission:

John showed me that he was honest
~ John showed that he was honest

(a) *That*-clause:

John *assured* her (that) he was honest
~ She was *assured* (that) he was honest

ADVISE	NOTIFY	SHOW
ASSURE	PERSUADE	TEACH
CONVINCE	PROMISE	TELL
INFORM	REMIND	WARN, etc

(b) *Wh*-clause (usually in negative sentences):

John didn't *ask* me whether my wife was coming
~ I wasn't *asked* whether my wife was coming

ASK	REMIND
INFORM	TELL, etc

The difference of meaning between *whether*- and *that*-constructions, as in

John didn't inform me $\begin{Bmatrix} \text{whether} \\ \text{that} \end{Bmatrix}$ his wife was coming

can be stated in terms of different presuppositions. *That* implies that his wife was supposed to come, whereas *whether* is noncommittal on this point.

12.66

[C4] Prepositional phrase+*that*-clause object

All the listed verbs take the preposition *to* and allow omission of the prepositional object.

John *mentioned* to me that they were sick
~ It was *mentioned* to me that they were sick

ACKNOWLEDGE	EXPLAIN	SAY
ADMIT	MENTION	SIGNAL
ANNOUNCE	POINT OUT	STATE
COMPLAIN	PROPOSE	SUGGEST
CONFESS	REMARK	etc
DECLARE	REPORT	

Complex transitive complementation [Type D]

12.67

[D1] Object+noun phrase complement

Complex transitive complementation represents a fusion of the mono-transitive and intensive types of complementation (*cf* 12.44 *ff*, 12.31 *ff*):

We considered Bill a friend
~ {We considered Bill
   {Bill was a friend

The alternative non-finite clause construction with a copula (*We considered Bill to be a friend*) has been discussed in 12.53 *ff*. The D1 type admits the passive thus:

The king *made* him a duke ~ He was *made* a duke (by the king)

Some of the D1 verbs are:

BRING UP	CREATE	MAKE
CONSIDER	DECLARE	THINK, etc

When 'naming verbs' have unique reference (see 4.39), the article is often omitted:

They elected John chairman

Similarly after ANNOUNCE, APPOINT, CALL, CHRISTEN, CROWN, ELECT, NAME, PRONOUNCE, etc.

Many of these verbs have alternative constructions:

We considered him {a genius [D1]
                  {as a genius [D2]
                  {to be a genius [B6]

The intensive relation can obtain, however, not only between the object and the complement as in (a), but also between the subject and the complement as in (b):

(a) She made him a good husband
(b) She made him a good wife

(a) is resulting, 'She made him into a good husband', and has a passive analogue: 'He was made a good husband.' In the entirely different construction (b), there is an intensive relation between the subject and the complement, and hence no passive is possible. The meaning is current: 'She was a good wife for him.'

12.68
[D2] Object+preposition+noun phrase complement

People *recognized* him as a genius
~ He was *recognized* as a genius

ACCEPT AS	DESCRIBE AS	REGARD AS
ACKNOWLEDGE AS	INTEND AS	TAKE AS/FOR
CLASS AS	INTERPRET AS	TREAT AS
CHARACTERIZE AS	KNOW AS	USE AS
CONSIDER AS	MISTAKE FOR	etc
DEFINE AS	RECOGNIZE AS	

The normal preposition is *as*, but *for* also occurs with some verbs. TAKE has both prepositions but with different uses:

He took these words as evidence
He took me for a fool

There is also a different type of prepositional phrase that occurs after certain transitive verbs (such as *put*) which require an adverbial of some kind:

John put the car in the garage
The hostess showed me to the door
Mary placed the vase on the table
Everybody should take this matter into consideration

In such cases there is an adverbial, not an intensive relation between the object and the head of the prepositional phrase:

*The car *was* the garage.

12.69
[D3] Object+adjective phrase complement

We *painted* the house white
~ The house was *painted* white

They *considered* the house beautiful
~ The house was *considered* beautiful

We may distinguish between 'resulting' verbs like PAINT and 'current' verbs like CONSIDER (*cf* 12.32). Many of the latter have alternative constructions with *to be* or *as* + adjective, whereas resulting verbs do not:

~ They considered it $\begin{Bmatrix} \text{to be} \\ \text{as} \end{Bmatrix}$ beautiful

~ *They painted it $\begin{Bmatrix} \text{to be} \\ \text{as} \end{Bmatrix}$ white

Current verbs	Resulting verbs
BELIEVE	GET
CALL	HAVE
CONSIDER	MAKE
DECLARE	PAINT
FIND	RENDER
IMAGINE	SET
KEEP	etc
LEAVE	
LIKE	
PREFER	
REPORT	
THINK	
WANT	
etc	

Note
The resulting verbs can sometimes take (*to*) *be*, but when they do, the object assumes a function of performer in its own right:

Can't you get him to be a little more alert?
Have him be patient a little longer!
They made her be good.

12.70
[D4] Object + prepositional adjective phrase complement

The teacher *described* him as hopeless
~ He was *described* as hopeless

Verbs like DESCRIBE, RECOGNIZE, etc, are likely to have *being* in the active: *They described the boy as being small.*

CLASS AS	REGARD AS
DESCRIBE AS	REPORT AS
RECOGNIZE AS	SEE AS, etc

Bibliographical note

See Jespersen (1909–49), especially Parts III, Chapters 12–18, V, Chapters 1–20; Kruisinga (1931–32), especially Part II.1; Poutsma (1926–29), especially Part II.2; and Huddleston (1971), Chapters 3 and 4.

On voice, see Hatcher (1949), and Svartvik (1966), especially Chapters 5–8, and (1970).

On phrasal and prepositional verbs, see Carvell and Svartvik (1969), especially Chapters 4, 9, 10; Kennedy (1920); Mitchell (1958).

On types of complementation, see Alexander and Kunz (1964); Alexander and Matthews (1964); Allen (1966); Bald and Quirk (1970); Behre (1955); Bladon (1968); Bolinger (1961), (1971b) and (1971c); Chomsky (1965), especially Chapters 1 and 3; Fillmore (1965) and (1968); Halliday (1967–68); Huddleston (1969); Kempson and Quirk (1971); Kiparsky (1970); Lees (1960b); Lyons (1968), especially Chapter 5; Macháček (1965) and (1969); McIntosh (1966); Postal (1971); Quirk (1965); Rosenbaum (1967a and 1967b); Storms (1966); van Ek (1966).

Introduction

13.1

Just as the sentence may be indefinitely complex (11.80 *ff*), so may the noun phrase. This must be so, since subordinate clauses and indeed sentences themselves can readily be subordinated within noun-phrase structure. For example, the following sentences – simple and complex – can become one simple sentence with a very complex noun phrase as subject:

The girl is Mary Smith	[1a]
The girl is pretty	[1b]
The girl was in the corner	[1c]
The girl became angry because you waved to her	[1d]
You waved to the girl when you entered	[1e]
The pretty girl in the corner who became angry because you waved to her when you entered is Mary Smith	[2]

Moreover, starting from [2], we could unhesitatingly reconstruct any of the sentences listed in [1] – and in fact we could not understand the noun-phrase subject of [2] unless we recognized its component parts as they are set out in [1]. Yet [2] has introduced many changes. We have suppressed the verbs in [1b] and [1c] (which have different tenses); we have put the complement *pretty* of [1b] before the noun *girl;* we have replaced *the girl* of [1d] by *who*. The purpose of the present chapter is to state the conditions governing these and other changes that yield complex noun phrases in contrast to the basic noun phrases studied in Chapter 4.

13.2

In describing complex noun phrases, such as the subject of [2], we need to distinguish three component parts:

(a) *The head*, in our example *girl*, around which the other components cluster and which dictates concord and (for the most part) other kinds of congruence with the rest of the sentence outside the noun phrase. Thus

The pretty girl in the corner . . . is . . .

but

The pretty girls in the corner . . . are . . .

Similarly

He frightened *the pretty girl in the corner*

but not

*He frightened *the pretty lampshade in the corner*

That is, there are no constraints affecting *frighten* and *the pretty
. . . in the corner* but only *frighten* and the head *lampshade*. (On
selection restrictions, see 7.37 *f*).

(b) *The premodification*, which comprises all the items placed before
the head – notably adjectives and nouns; for present purposes (but
cf 4.13 *ff*), we may add determiners to these pre-head items. Thus:

> *The pretty* girl
> *Some pretty college* girls

(c) *The postmodification*, comprising all the items placed after the head
– notably prepositional phrases, non-finite clauses, and relative
clauses:

> The girl *in the corner*
> The girl *standing in the corner*
> The girl *who stood in the corner*

13.3
Restrictive and non-restrictive

Modification can be restrictive or non-restrictive. That is, the head can be
viewed as a member of a class which can be linguistically identified only
through the modification that has been supplied (*restrictive*). Or the head
can be viewed as unique or as a member of a class that has been independently identified (for example, in a preceding sentence); any modification
given to such a head is additional information which is not essential for
identifying the head, and we call it *non-restrictive*.

In [2], *the girl* is only identifiable as Mary Smith provided we understand that it is the particular girl who is *pretty*, who was *in the corner*, and
who *became angry*. Such modification would not have been actually
necessary unless there had been other girls present, pretty but not in the
corner, or in the corner but not pretty, or who had not become angry.

By contrast, if a man says

> Come and meet my beautiful wife   [3]

the modification *beautiful* must be understood as non-restrictive unless
we are to imagine that he is distinguishing her from another of his wives
who is not beautiful. Again,

> Mary Smith, who is in the corner, wants to meet you   [4]

has a non-restrictive relative clause since Mary Smith's identity is independent of whether or not she is in the corner, though the information on
her present location may be useful enough. In examples [3] and [4], the
modification was *inherently* non-restrictive, since the heads in question –

being unique – will not normally admit restriction. But any head that can be restrictively modified can also be non-restrictively modified:

> The pretty girl, who is a typist, is Mary Smith   [5]

Here the only information offered to identify the girl as Mary Smith is the allusion to her prettiness; the mention of her work as a typist is not offered as an aid to identification but for additional interest.

We shall draw attention to the distinction in the description of the modification types below, but some general points may be of value here. First, modification at its 'most restrictive' tends to come after the head: that is, our decision to use an item as a premodifier (such as *silly* in *a silly chatterbox*) often reflects our wish that it be taken for granted and not be interpreted as a specific identifier. Secondly, restrictive modification tends to be given more prosodic emphasis than the head; non-restrictive modification, on the other hand, tends to be unstressed in pre-head position, while in post-head position, as in [4], its 'parenthetic' relation is endorsed by being given a separate tone unit (frequently with reduced prominence and narrow pitch range), or – in writing – by being enclosed by commas (App II.12 *ff*, App III.12).

Note
The distinction between restrictive and non-restrictive is valuable but it must not be regarded as rigid or as separating two homogeneous categories of relation. 'Non-restrictive', for example, ranges from the parenthetic, through the appositive afterthought, to the adverbial: *cf* 13.32 *f*.

13.4
Temporary and permanent
There is a second dichotomy that has some affinities with the distinction between restrictive and non-restrictive but rather more with the contrast of non-progressive and progressive in predication (3.39 *ff*) or permanent and temporary in agentials (App I.21 Note *b*). Modification in noun-phrase structure may also be seen as permanent or temporary (5.35 *ff*), such that items placed in premodification position are given the linguistic status of permanent or at any rate characteristic features. Although this does not mean that postmodification position is committed to either temporariness or permanence, those adjectives which have to be postpositive have a notably temporary reference. Thus

> The courteous man

would be understood as

> The man who is courteous (normally and not merely at this moment)

whereas

> The man is ready

would be understood as having reference only to a specific time and this corresponds to the non-occurrence of

*The ready man

(On the relevance of the distinction in determiners between indefinite and definite, see 4.28 *ff.*) On this basis, we see that timidity and fear are contrasted in part according as the first is seen as permanent, the second as temporary:

A man who is timid ~ A timid man
A man who is afraid ~ *An afraid man

Just as some modifiers are too much identified with temporary status to appear in pre-head position, so there can be modification constrained to pre-head position because it indicates permanent status. Thus the toe which is characteristically (and permanently) big in relation to the rest is called 'the big toe', and we cannot say of it '*the toe is big' without destroying this permanent characteristic and making the expression seem to refer only (for example) to a temporary swelling. *Cf* also *the original version* beside *his work is quite original*, which would permit adverbial indication of time span (*now, always, . . .*).

Postmodification
13.5
Explicitness
Such indications of independence as between pre- and postmodification must not however obscure the point made in 13.1 that premodification is in general to be interpreted (and most frequently can only be interpreted) in terms of postmodification and its greater explicitness. That is, *Some pretty college girls* will be interpreted as 'Some girls who are pretty and who are at a college'. It will therefore be best to begin our detailed study of noun phrase structure with the forms of postmodification.

Explicitness in postmodification varies considerably, however. It is greater in the finite relative clause

The girl who stood in the corner

than in the non-finite clause

The girl standing in the corner

from which the explicit tense (*is? was?*) has disappeared, though this in turn is more explicit than the prepositional phrase

The girl in the corner

from which the verb indicating a specific posture has also disappeared.

Part of the relative clause's explicitness lies in the specifying power of the relative pronoun. It is capable (a) of showing agreement with the head and (b) of indicating its status as an element in the relative clause structure.

Agreement is on the basis of a two-term 'gender' system, personal and non-personal (4.85 *ff*, 4.109):

Joan, who . . .	London, which . . .
The boy who . . .	The fox which . . .
The people who . . .	The animals which . . .
The human being who . . .	The human body which . . .
The fairy who . . .	The unicorn which . . .

It will be seen from these examples that 'personality' is ascribed basically to human beings but extends to creatures in the supernatural world (angels, elves, etc) which are thought of as having human characteristics such as speech. It does not extend to the body or character, in part or whole, of a human being, living or dead, when this is considered as separate from the entire person:

Charles is a strange character *who* dislikes parties. (familiar)
Charles has a fine character *which* he inherits from his father.
Smith is now a famous personality *who* is often interviewed on
   television.
Smith has a strange personality *which* repels many people.

Pet animals can be regarded as 'personal' (at least by their owners):

This is the doggie *who* seems ill (familiar)
Rover, *who* was barking, frightened the children

On the other hand human babies can be regarded (though rarely perhaps by their parents) as not having developed personality:

This is the baby *which* needs inoculation

There is some correspondence here with other gender pronouns used of pets and babies (4.90), but ships are different. Though they may take the personal pronoun *she*, the relative pronoun is regularly non-personal:

Is *she* the ship *which* is due to leave for New York tomorrow?

It is noteworthy that collective nouns (4.89) are treated as personal when they have plural concord, non-personal when they have singular:

The $\begin{Bmatrix} \text{committee} \\ \text{group} \end{Bmatrix}$ $\begin{Bmatrix} \textit{who were} \\ \textit{which was} \end{Bmatrix}$ responsible for this decision . . .

Note

[a] Relative clauses with general antecedents preserve the personal/non-personal gender contrast:

indefinite: I am looking for $\left\{\begin{array}{l}\text{a person}\\\text{someone}\end{array}\right\}$ *who* can help me

This is $\left\{\begin{array}{l}\text{a thing}\\\text{something}\end{array}\right\}$ *which* I can't understand

definite: The person *who* helped me has gone
The thing *which* I can't understand is this

A form of relative clause without antecedent is possible in the case of *definite* personal reference (4.35) only with *whoever:*

$\left.\begin{array}{l}\text{*Who}\\\text{Whoever}\end{array}\right\}$ helped me has gone

but is common with definite *non*-personal reference (though with a different pronoun from that formally found in relative clauses):

What I can't understand is this

Replacement of the antecedent by a personal pronoun on the other hand is possible with personal antecedent, but rare and very formal:

?He who helped me has gone

It is more acceptable if *he* corresponds to the generic 'The/A person' (as in 'He who helps the blind deserves support'), while it is impossible with non-personal antecedent:

*It which I can't understand is this (*but, very formal,* That which . . .)

There is a similar constraint on postmodification by other structures:

?He in the corner is my brother
*It in the corner is an antique

except with informal and peremptory vocatives: 'You in the corner: stop chattering!'. *Cf* also 11.20.

[b] Other non-human creatures beside pets may take *who* even in sentences where this involves an apparent clash with the neuter pronoun *it;* thus, from a recent work of non-fiction: 'the chameleon *who* changes *its* colours'. This is less likely however when the relative pronoun is object in its clause, as we see from the following examples on two successive pages of a work on zoology: 'the black rhinoceroses who live in the park', 'the white rhinoceros which we saw in the wilds outside the park'. On the factors involved in this difference, *cf* 13.12 and Note.

13.6
Case in the relative pronoun

Case is used to indicate the status of the relative pronoun in its clause. There are two situations to consider. First, if the pronoun is in a genitive relation to a noun head, the pronoun can have the form *whose:*

The woman *whose* daughter you met is Mrs Brown
(The woman is Mrs Brown; you met *her* daughter),
The house *whose* roof was damaged has now been repaired
(The house has now been repaired; *its* roof was damaged)

In cases like the latter where the antecedent head is non-personal, there is some tendency to avoid the use of *whose* (presumably because many native speakers regard it as the genitive only of the personal *who*), but avoidance involves stylistic difficulty. On the one hand, there is the stiffly formal

The house the roof of which was damaged . . .

and on the other the colloquial and clumsy-sounding

?The house that they damaged the roof of . . .
*The house that the roof was damaged of . . .

Satisfactory alternatives can, however, be found, such as *The house that had its roof damaged* or even *The house with the damaged roof*. In any case, in some fields of discourse, such as mathematics, no evasion is necessary:

Let ABC be a triangle whose sides are of unequal length

Secondly, with a personal antecedent, the relative pronoun can show the distinction between *who* and *whom*, depending on its role as subject of the relative clause or as the object of verb or preposition in it:

The girl who spoke to him	[6a]
The girl to whom he spoke	[6b]
The girl who(m) he spoke to	[6c]
The girl who(m) he met	[6d]

It will be noticed that when the governing preposition precedes its complement (*cf* 6.3) as in the rather formal [6b], the choice of *whom* is obligatory. When it does not, as in the more informal [6c], or when the relative pronoun is the object of the verb, as in [6d], there is some choice between *who* or *whom*, the latter being preferred in written English and by some speakers, the former being widely current in informal conversation (*cf* 13.12).

13.7
Relative pronoun as adverbial
Further, the relative pronoun can have a special form as adjunct of place, time, and cause (*cf* 5.48) in the relative clause:

That is the place *where* he was born	[7a]
That is the period *when* he lived here	[7b]
That is the reason *why* he spoke	[7c]

There are considerable and complicated restrictions on these adjunct forms, however. In the first place, many speakers find their use along with the corresponding antecedent somewhat tautologous – especially [7c] – and would prefer the *wh-* clause without antecedent:

> That is *where* he was born
> That is *when* he lived here
> That is *why* he spoke

No non-restrictive clause is possible with *why* ('*The reason, why he spoke, is . . .'), and in this connection, it is worth noting that the remaining *wh-* adjunct (manner) that would complete the set [7] is totally impossible, restrictively or non-restrictively:

> *That is the way *how* he spoke   [7d]

and if *how* is used, such clauses cannot have an antecedent noun:

> That is *how* he spoke

In the second place, there are restrictions on the antecedent nouns that can occur in [7]. With [7c], *reason* is virtually alone, and with [7a] and [7b], it is also the most general and abstract nouns of place and time that seem to be preferred. Thus while

> The office *where* he works . . .
> The day *when* he was born . . .

are acceptable to most users of English, others would prefer a prepositional phrase in each case:

$$\text{The office} \begin{cases} \text{at which . . . (formal)} \\ \text{which . . . at} \end{cases}$$

$$\text{The day} \begin{cases} \text{on which . . . (formal)} \\ \text{which . . . on} \end{cases}$$

or one of the less explicit forms that we shall now be considering (*The office he works at, The day he was born*).

Note

There is a tendency to favour *when* or *where* if the antecedent is already the head of a prepositional phrase as in *He died on the day when* (rather than *on which*) *his son arrived*.

Restrictive relative clauses
Choice of relative pronoun
13.8

Though most of the examples in 13.5*ff* have been of restrictive clauses, it is in the non-restrictive relative clauses that the most explicit forms of relative pronoun are typically used. In restrictive clauses, frequent use is made of a general pronoun *that* which is independent of the personal or non-personal character of the antecedent and also of the function of the pronoun in the relative clause:

The boy *that* is playing the piano . . . (who)	[8a]
The table *that* stands in the corner . . . (which)	[8b]
The boy *that* we met . . . (who(m))	[8c]
The table *that* we admire . . . (which)	[8d]
The boy *that* the dog ran towards . . . (towards whom)	[8e]
The table *that* the boy crawled under . . . (under which)	[8f]

[8a] would be slightly more usual with informal contraction ('. . . that's playing . . .), but *cf* 13.12. As we saw in [6b] and [6c], some choice exists in placing a preposition which has a *wh*-pronoun as its complement. No such choice exists with *that*, [8e] and [8f] representing the sole pattern.

Provided the relative pronoun is not the subject of the relative clause, as in [8a] and [8b], a further option exists in relative clause structure of having no relative pronoun at all: the clause with 'zero' ($\emptyset$) relative pronoun. The examples [8c–8f] could take this form:

The boy we met . . . (whom, that)
The table we admire . . . (which, that)
The boy the dog ran towards . . . (towards whom, who(m)/that . . . towards)
The table the boy crawled under . . . (under which, which/that . . . under)

Note

While it is important to insist that zero cannot replace the subject in a relative clause

*The table stands in the corner has a broken leg

constructions are encountered that are arguably exceptions; for example, in very informal speech where the antecedent is an indefinite pronoun:

?Anybody does that ought to be locked up

The reason for putting a question mark here is first that most educated native speakers would condemn it as slovenly and secondly that it may result from the subaudibility of a relative pronoun *who* or *that* and thus not be zero at all. A commoner type of example is in the existential sentence (see especially 14.29):

There's a table stands in the corner

This would again be very colloquial, and in any case, although the use of *that* or *which* would be regarded as more acceptable, there are good reasons for distinguishing such clauses from relative clauses.

There's a table $\begin{Bmatrix} \text{that} \\ \text{which} \end{Bmatrix}$ stands in the corner

The obligatory nature of such portions of existential sentences would argue against our equating them with postmodifications in noun phrase structure, and the same applies to similar segments in the cleft sentence (14.19 *f*):

It is John $\begin{Bmatrix} \text{that} \\ \text{who} \end{Bmatrix}$ did it.

13.9

Just as *that* and zero are available when the relative pronoun is dominated
by a preposition as in [8e] and [8f], so they can be used when the relative
pronoun is a place, time or cause adjunct. With place adjuncts, the
preposition must usually be expressed:

That is the garden (that) he sunbathes in
That is the university (that) he works at

though with a general antecedent (especially *place*), zero can be used with
omission of the preposition, suggesting that zero is considered as replacing *where:*

That is the place $\begin{cases} \text{he stays when he's in London} \\ \text{(?)he works} \\ \text{?he studies} \end{cases}$

With time adjuncts, omission of the preposition is usual whether the pronoun is *that* or zero (*cf* 6.32 *f*):

That is the time (that) he arrives (at)
That was the day (that) he left (on)

In many cases, indeed, omission of the preposition is obligatory, especially when the antecedent is itself the head of a time adjunct phrase:

He questioned her the moment (that) he arrived
He worked the whole time (that) he lived there

When (less frequently and more formally) the pronoun is *which*, however,
the preposition must be expressed in all these instances and it would be
usual to make it precede the pronoun (*cf* 13.7):

That is the time *at which* he arrives
That was the day *on which* he left
?He questioned her the moment *at which* he arrived
?He worked the whole time *during which* he lived there

With cause adjuncts, the usual pronoun is *that* or zero, and there is no
preposition:

This is the reason (that) he came

The rare use of *for which* in such a sentence strikes most people as clumsy
or unnatural.

With manner adjuncts, the usual pronoun is again *that* or zero, and
again there is no preposition:

This is the way (that) he did it

It would not be abnormal to find *which* with a preposition in a more formal style:

This is the way *in which* he did it

13.10
The total system of restrictive clauses so far discussed can be summarized as in *Fig* 13:1

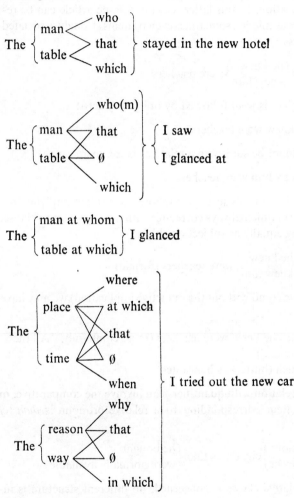

Fig 13:1 Restrictive relative clauses

Note

[a] Even with *stayed* and such a general antecedent as *the place*, zero and *that* are only marginally acceptable and a final *at* would be normal even in familiar usage.

[b] *Way* may be used both of manner and (with an appropriate verb such as *travelled*) direction.

13.11
Quantification and comparison

But there are other types of restrictive clause, concerned with quantification and comparison. As seen in 4.36, the definite article may refer back to something previously specified or forward to something that will constitute the specification. In this latter use, the definite article can be replaced by other determiners, sometimes even by items strongly associated with indefiniteness:

$$\left.\begin{matrix}\text{The}\\\text{Any}\end{matrix}\right\}\text{girls that}\left\{\begin{matrix}\text{he knew}\\\text{knew him}\end{matrix}\right\}\text{were teachers}$$

One such determiner is *what* followed by obligatory zero:

What girls he knew were teachers

but since zero cannot be subject in a relative clause, there is no

*What girls knew him were teachers

A further determiner of this sort is cataphoric *such* (often implying low quantity or quality) which always correlates with *as* in the relative clause, the *as* functioning equally as subject or object:

$$\text{Such girls as}\left\{\begin{matrix}\text{he knew}\\\text{knew him}\end{matrix}\right\}\text{were teachers (formal)}$$

and in place of *such* (and without the reductive implication) we may have *as* + quantifier:

As many girls as he knew were teachers (more commonly: 'All the girls he knew . . .')
He took as much (butter) as he wanted

This type of correlation with quantifiers can involve the comparative, in which case the item corresponding to a relative pronoun is *than* (*cf* 11.53 *ff*):

$$\text{He smoked}\left\{\begin{matrix}\text{more}\\\text{fewer}\end{matrix}\right\}\text{cigarettes than}\left\{\begin{matrix}\text{he bought}\\\text{were normally available}\end{matrix}\right.$$

So far as the relative clause is concerned, no different structure is involved when the comparative quantification relates not to the noun but to the degree of an adjective modifying it:

$$\text{He smokes}\left\{\begin{matrix}\text{more}\\\text{less}\end{matrix}\right\}\text{expensive cigarettes than he can afford}$$

But it should be noted that the *as*-comparative would be difficult with plurals:

?He smokes as expensive cigarettes as he can afford

and is usually replaced by a normal relative clause:

He smokes cigarettes that are as expensive as he can afford

There is no problem with the singular:

He smokes as expensive a cigarette as he can afford
He will marry as pretty a girl as he can find

With the superlative the relative pronoun is normally *that* as subject and *that* or zero as object

$$\text{He eats the finest food} \begin{cases} \text{that is available} \\ \text{(that) he can buy} \end{cases}$$

though normally such postmodification would make intensive relative clauses verbless: *the finest food available*.

Note
Clauses like *What I want* in 'What I want is a drink', where the relative pronoun operates both as an element in the clause and also as head of the noun phrase ('nominal relative clauses'), are described in 11.20.

Stylistic factors
13.12
Occasional comments in 13.5 *ff* have already indicated that the choice of relative clause structure involves stylistic distinctions. In general, it is certainly true that *wh-* pronouns with preceding prepositions are used predominantly in formal English and may be avoided in more informal use as seeming stilted or pompous. Postposition is more generally preferred with prepositional verbs (*This is the book he looked at*). Many prepositions (especially those dealing with temporal and other abstract relations) cannot be postposed, however:

*That was the meeting (that) I kept falling asleep during

and even in familiar speech one might use

That was the meeting during which I kept falling asleep

if not the commoner *when* or *where*. Concrete relations may use postposition even when the preposition is complex (*This is the house he stood in front of*), but clarity of expression would often influence us in the direction of a construction otherwise regarded as formal if postposition leads to clumsiness. Thus, hearing or reading the following sentence,

It was in a book that a former teacher of mine thought of at one time presenting me with some quotations from

we may successively have to reject the interpretations first that the former teacher thought of the book, second that he thought of presenting me with the book, before the belated *from* enables us to achieve the correct interpretation ('. . . from which a former teacher . . .').

When we turn from discussing the preposition-dominated pronoun to the choice of pronoun itself, it is even clearer that a simple polarity of more and less formal will not account for preferred use. In the first place, when the antecedent is personal and the pronoun is the subject of the relative clause, *who* is favoured irrespective of the style and occasion; thus

People who live in glass houses

rather than

People that live in glass houses

though of course there is nothing wrong or odd about the latter. By contrast, with the antecedent still personal but with the pronoun now the object of verb or preposition, there is a converse and much stronger preference for *that* or zero, perhaps to avoid the choice between *who* and *whom*. Thus

People (that) I $\begin{cases}\text{visit} \\ \text{speak to}\end{cases}$

rather than

People who(m) I $\begin{cases}\text{visit} \\ \text{speak to}\end{cases}$

Again there is nothing actually wrong about the latter provided that *whom* is used; but *whom* here would seem pedantic to many people, while *who* as object in relative clauses (as opposed to interrogative sentences: 4.120) is informal and tends to be regarded by some as substandard. Since, therefore, neither *who* nor *whom* is wholly satisfactory, *that* is frequently used despite a personal antecedent.

When the verb in the relative clause is BE, the complement pronoun cannot be *wh-*, whether the antecedent is personal or non-personal:

*John is not the man who he was
*My typewriter is not the machine which it was

In such cases *that* or zero are obligatory.

Note
Avoidance of *whom* may not be the only factor influencing *that* as object with personal antecedent: grammatical objects are more likely to be non-personal or to carry non-personal implication than subjects. Even as subject, *that* can be more acceptably used if the personal antecedent is contextually 'depersonalized' (as not being personally identifiable by name, for example):

The soldiers that captured the post subsequently withdrew.

13.13

There are several other factors influencing the selection of a pronoun that is object in the relative clause, especially when the antecedent is non-personal: one is the proximity of the relative clause to the antecedent, another is the degree of complexity of the subject in the relative clause. When phrases intervene between the antecedent head and the relative pronoun, *which* is generally preferable to *that* and very much preferable to zero:

> I have interests outside my immediate work and its problems which
> I find satisfying

When the subject of the relative clause is more complex than determiner + head, *that* is slightly preferable to *which* and much preferable to zero:

> The building that all elderly university teachers prefer

On the other hand, when the subject is a personal pronoun, zero is preferred to either *which* or *that*, especially if the relative clause itself is fairly short and simple:

> The milk *I bought* has gone sour

In addition, other things being equal, more informal discourse will tend to have a preference for zero.

Non-restrictive relative clauses
13.14

The repertoire of pronouns is much more limited with non-restrictive clauses and only the more 'explicit' of the forms summarized in 13.10 are available. As subject, they are *who* and *which*:

> Here is a letter from John, who wants a job in London
> He got lost on Snowdon, which was enveloped in fog

and, as object of verb or preposition, *whom* and *which*:

> Here is a letter from John, *whom* you've met of course
> He got lost on Snowdon, *which* he was exploring

Objective *who* would be thought by many to be at least as objectionable in non-restrictive as in restrictive clauses. Zero cannot occur and *that* is very rare; it usually shows that a writer has muddled what he has wanted to set down, as in the following example from a serious article:

> One of the most important recent developments in neutral hydrogen studies of our Galaxy has been the discovery of high velocities in the centre and in regions away from the plane, that I have mentioned.

Despite the comma and the corresponding prosodic separation if this is read aloud (a separation that is essential if *plane* were not to be thought the antecedent head), it seems likely that the writer originally wanted the relative clause to be restrictive, as it could readily have been if placed earlier:

> ... has been the discovery that I have mentioned of high velocities ...

Where the relative pronoun is the head of an adjunct phrase, there is again less choice than in restrictive clauses. Expressions with *which* tend to be uncommon except in formally precise writing; the preposition usually precedes *which* and explicitness often extends to completion of the prepositional phrase by a general noun, locative or temporal as the case may be (making *which* a relative determiner):

> In 1960 he came to London, *in which city* he has lived ever since
>
> He came in 1960, $\begin{cases} at\ which\ time \\ in\ which\ year \end{cases}$ there was ...

More commonly, we find *where* or *when* instead of the *which* expression:

> ... to London, where ...
> ... in 1960, when ...

Naturally, this is a point at which the distinction becomes blurred between noun phrase postmodification and adverbial clauses of place and time in complex sentence structure (11.27 *f*).

Note
Non-restrictive clauses are occasionally introduced by *that* when a premodifier or determiner would make a restrictive clause absurd but when *which* on the other hand might imply a too parenthetic relation:

> I looked at Mary's sad face, that I had once so passionately admired.

13.15
With sentential antecedent
There are analogies where the antecedent is a clause or sentence (*cf* 11.52). While a relative clause with *which* is perfectly natural, as in

> He admires Mrs Brown, which $\begin{cases} \text{surprises me} \\ \text{I find strange} \end{cases}$

conversational English, perhaps as a wry affectation of legalistic style, also admits on occasion (in place of the more usual *a fact which, a thing which*):

> He admires Mrs Brown, which fact $\begin{cases} \text{surprises me} \\ \text{I find strange} \end{cases}$

Other general factive nouns are similarly used with *which* ('which allegation', 'which matter', 'which thing', and the like). A merging with adverbial clauses comes through the use of *as*, which we saw as a special type of relative pronoun in restrictive clauses (13.11). In non-restrictive clauses, the use of *as* is twofold. On the one hand, it is used (more commonly than *which*) with sentential antecedent to introduce a relative clause which constitutes a variant of the antecedent and from which the non-variant part is elipted:

He saw the girl, $\begin{Bmatrix} as \\ which \end{Bmatrix}$ he (had) hoped (he would)

In such instances, where the relative pronoun is object, *which* is often somewhat awkward. Where the pronoun is subject, *which* however is fully acceptable while *as* is not:

He saw the girl, $\begin{Bmatrix} *as \\ which \end{Bmatrix}$ delighted him

But with *as* there are important differences which link the clause type with adverbials: it can be expanded to include the elipted part, and it can precede the 'antecedent':

(Just) as he hoped he would (see the girl), he $\begin{Bmatrix} saw\ the\ girl \\ did\ so \end{Bmatrix}$

The other use of *as* to be mentioned is where the item appears to act as subject of the relative clause but where, unlike **as delighted him* above, the *as*-clause shows a link with adverbial clauses in its ability to be preposed:

He married her, $\begin{Bmatrix} as \\ which \end{Bmatrix}$ was natural

$\begin{Bmatrix} As \\ *Which \end{Bmatrix}$ was natural, he married her

Because *which*-clauses must follow their antecedent clauses, they are in fact more usually seen as related to coordinate clauses having *and* with an emphatic demonstrative, often preposed:

He admires Mrs Brown, $\begin{Bmatrix} which \\ and\ this \end{Bmatrix}$ $\begin{Bmatrix} surprises\ me \\ I\ find\ strange \end{Bmatrix}$

Note

[a] Non-restrictive clauses with sentential antecedent are sometimes separated from the antecedent by heavier punctuation than a comma. They may in fact begin a new sentence: *cf* 10.64 Note *a*.

[b] A further point on *as:*

He married her, $\left\{\begin{array}{l}\left\{\begin{array}{l}\text{as}\\\text{which}\end{array}\right\}\text{was natural}\\\left\{\begin{array}{l}\text{*as}\\\text{which}\end{array}\right\}\text{was disgraceful}\end{array}\right.$

The starred variant shows that *as* can fulfil a relative pronoun function when the sentence does not frustrate the semantic role that *as* plays in adverbial clauses.

Appositive clauses
13.16

One remaining type of finite verb clause that plays a part in postmodification needs to be mentioned: the appositive clause (*cf* 9.177 *f*). This resembles the relative clause in being capable of introduction by *that;* in permitting zero, though not commonly and indeed rarely unless the head of the antecedent phrase is the noun *fact;* and in distinguishing between restrictive and non-restrictive. It differs, in that the particle *that* is not an element in the clause structure (subject, object, etc) as it must be in a relative clause. It differs also in that the head of the noun phrase must be a factive abstract noun such as *fact* itself, *proposition, reply, remark, answer,* and the like. For example:

> The fact *that he wrote a letter to her* suggests that he knew her
> The belief *that no one is infallible* is well-founded
> I agree with the old saying *that absence makes the heart grow fonder*
> He heard the news *that his team had won*

As with apposition generally (*cf* 9.130), we can link the apposed units with *be* (where the copula typically has nuclear prominence):

> The fact *is* that he wrote a letter to her (. . . ĭs . . .)
> The belief *is* that no one is infallible
> The old saying *is* that absence makes the heart grow fonder
> The news *was* that his team had won

Or we may replace deverbal nouns like *belief* by the corresponding verb plus object clause: *He believes that no one is infallible.* It will be noticed that these restrictive examples have the definite article before the head noun: this is normal but by no means invariable (except with a few nouns referring to certainty, especially *fact*):

> A message *that he would be late* arrived by special delivery
> Any proposals *that John should be dismissed* must be resisted
> Stories *that the house was haunted* angered the owner

Plural heads, as in the latter examples, are also rare with appositive postmodification and are regarded as unacceptable with *belief, fact, possibility,* etc. We may contrast the following

*The possibilities *that she was lazy and (that she) disliked school*
     worried her mother

with the perfectly acceptable plural head with relative clause postmodification:

     The possibilities that she was now offered seemed very attractive.

13.17

Despite the restriction on the types of noun head that may be postmodified by an appositive clause, it is natural that the superficial similarity to relative clause postmodification can sometimes cause momentary
difficulty. Total ambiguity, however, is rare since so many selectional
factors (7.37 *f*) have to be involved before anything like the following can
occur:

     A report *that he stole* was ultimately sent to the police

The two interpretations ('he stole a report' or 'the report was that he
stole') depend upon the possibility that *a report* can be a physical object
or an abstract (that is, nominalizing the verb *report*); upon *steal* being
permissibly transitive or intransitive; and several other factors (*told* in
place of *sent*, for example, would dismiss the ambiguity though it would
not prevent the hearer or reader from having temporary difficulty).

     Non-restrictive appositive clauses can less easily resemble relative
clauses since irrespective of non-restrictiveness they still involve the
particle *that*, in sharp contrast with non-restrictive relative clauses:

     This last fact, (namely,) that *that* is obligatory, should be easy to
          remember

In illustrating the previous point, this example also illustrates the next,
(namely) that *namely* can be optionally introduced in the non-restrictive
appositions, as can *that is (to say)*. It also illustrates the fact that with this
type of clause, the antecedent head noun may be freely premodified by
adjectives and with a choice of determiners. It will be recalled that with
restrictive appositives *the* was obligatory before *fact*, and it may now be
added that the only adjectives admissible would be non-restrictive in
scope (13.3); contrast:

     The ugly fact that he was holding a gun indicated his guilt

where the restrictive clause permits only the non-restrictive adjective,
with

     A more relevant fact, that the gun had not been fired, was
          curiously ignored

where the non-restrictive clause permits a restrictive adjective.

Note

[a] The non-restrictive apposition is closely related to an ordinary non-restrictive clause in instances like

This last request, which was to come and visit him, was never in fact received.

[b] With both restrictive and non-restrictive appositive clauses, an antecedent noun is often a nominalization (13.34 *f*):

A (police) report that . . . ↔ The (police) reported that . . .

Postmodification by non-finite clauses
13.18
Present (V-*ing*) participle clauses

Postmodification of the noun phrase is possible with all three of the non-finite clause types (11.4 *ff*), and the correspondence between restrictive relative and non-finite clauses can be illustrated as follows.

V-*ing* participle:

$$\text{The man who} \left\{ \begin{array}{l} \text{will} \left\{ \begin{array}{l} \text{write} \\ \text{be writing} \end{array} \right. \\ \text{writes} \\ \text{is writing} \\ \text{wrote} \\ \text{was writing} \end{array} \right\} \text{the obituary is my friend}$$

The man *writing the obituary* is my friend

where the latter will be interpreted, according to the context, as equivalent to one of the former more explicit versions. Other examples:

The dog *barking next door* sounded like a terrier

where the non-finite clause will be interpreted as 'which *was barking* next door';

A tile *falling from a roof* shattered into fragments at his feet

where the postmodification must be interpreted as 'which *fell* from a roof';

Tomorrow you will meet a man *carrying a large umbrella*

where the postmodification will be interpreted as 'who *will be carrying* a large umbrella'. It must be emphasized that not all -*ing* forms in non-finite postmodifiers correspond to progressive forms in relative clauses. Stative verbs, for instance, which cannot have the progressive in the finite verb phrase, can appear in participial form:

He is talking to a girl *resembling Joan* ('who resembles Joan' not '*who is resembling Joan')

It was a mixture *consisting of oil and vinegar* ('that consisted . . .' not '*that was consisting . . .')

In all instances, the antecedent head corresponds to the deleted subject of the non-finite verb clause; there is no non-finite postmodifier, therefore, corresponding directly to the relative clause in

The obituary *that the man is writing* will be published tomorrow

without recourse to the passive (*being written by the man*), thus involving the V-*ed* participle (13.19).

Note

There are sharp constraints upon aspect expression in the participial clauses used in postmodification. We have just seen that *resembling* in 'a girl resembling Joan' obviously could not represent progressive, and the neutralization of the aspectual contrast can further be seen in

$$\text{The girl} \begin{Bmatrix} \text{who works} \\ \text{who is working} \end{Bmatrix} \sim \text{The girl} \begin{Bmatrix} \text{working} \\ \text{*being working} \end{Bmatrix}$$

Similarly the perfective aspect cannot usually be expressed in the non-finite clause:

The girl who has won the race $\sim$?*The girl having won the race
is my sister   is my sister.

Cf, however, with indefinite head: *Any man having witnessed the attack is under suspicion.*

13.19
Past (V-*ed*) participle clauses
Consider now the different versions of the following:

$$\text{The only car that} \begin{Bmatrix} \text{will be repaired} \\ \text{is (being) repaired} \\ \text{was (being) repaired} \end{Bmatrix} \text{by that mechanic is mine}$$

The only car (*being*) *repaired by that mechanic* is mine

where the latter will be interpreted, according to the context, as equivalent to one of the former. Thus:

$$\text{The only car} \begin{bmatrix} \text{repaired} \\ \text{being repaired} \\ \text{repaired} \\ \text{repaired} \end{bmatrix} \text{by that mechanic} \begin{bmatrix} \text{next week} \ldots \\ \text{now} \ldots \\ \text{on Tuesdays} \ldots \\ \text{before he left} \ldots \end{bmatrix}$$

Other examples:

An obituary *written by my friend* appeared last week
('that was written . . .')
Any coins *found on this site* must be handed to the police
('that are found . . .' or, more precisely, 'that may be found . . .')

The antecedent head is identical with the deleted subject of the -*ed* postmodifying clause as it is with the -*ing* construction, but in this case the participle concerned is as firmly linked with the passive voice as that in the *-ing* construction is linked with the active. Since with intransitive verbs the past participles can never be passive, there is no *-ed* postmodifier corresponding exactly to the relative clause in:

> The train *which has arrived at platform one* is from York
> *The train *arrived at platform one* is from York

Limited exceptions occur where the past participle is preceded by certain adverbs (*cf* 8.57), as in

> The train *recently arrived at platform one* is from York
>
> ?A man *just* $\left\{ \begin{array}{l} \textit{returned from India} \\ \textit{come from the meeting} \end{array} \right\}$ told me about it

This phenomenon is related to our ability also to premodify nouns with participles which, unless themselves premodified, can only postmodify (13.53 *f*). It may also however owe something to subaudibility factors: *cf* 13.8 Note.

Note
There are constraints on aspectual expression in V-*ed* postmodifying clauses, though not identical with those for V-*ing* clauses (13.18 Note). A progressive contrast is possible:

> The food which $\left\{ \begin{array}{l} \text{is eaten} \ldots \\ \text{is being eaten} \ldots \end{array} \right\}$ ~ The food $\left\{ \begin{array}{l} \text{eaten} \ldots \\ \text{being eaten} \ldots \end{array} \right\}$

but as with V-*ing* there can be no perfective aspect:

> The food which has been eaten belonged   ?*The food having been eaten
>   to someone else   belonged to someone else

Thus *The food being eaten* may be either a noun phrase or a non-finite clause (11.5), but *The food having been eaten* can be only a non-finite clause.

13.20
Infinitive clauses
The non-finite clause in

> The next train *to arrive* was from York

could, in a suitable context, have precisely the same meaning as the relative clause in

> The next train *that arrived* was from York

But this example gives a misleadingly simple impression in place of the wide range of possibilities that can be left unexplicit in the infinitive postmodifying clause. In the first place, the antecedent need not correspond to the subject in the non-finite clause, which may have its own separate subject introduced by the *for*-device (11.5, 21):

> The man *for John to consult* is Wilson

Or it may have as its subject a deleted indefinite expressed neither in the antecedent nor in the remainder of the sentence:

The man *to consult* is Wilson

where the non-finite clause has neither object (the antecedent) nor subject (indefinite) and could be understood, according to context, as '(The man) that *you* should consult' or 'that *everyone* should consult'. Still more elliptically, the infinitive clause may omit also an entire adjunct phrase, as in

The time *to arrive* is 8 pm
The place (*for you*) *to stay* is the Hilton
A good place *to eat* is Bloom's

where a fairly common alternative is to introduce the relative pronoun and retain the infinitive clause:

... time at which to arrive ...
... place at which to stay ...
... place at which to eat ...

Cf also *the way in which to do it* beside *the way to do it*. Alternatively, we might have fully explicit relative clause constructions:

The time *at which* everyone should arrive is 8 pm
The place *at which* you should stay is the Hilton
A good place *at which* anyone can eat is Bloom's

In the second place, as the examples have now shown, it is by no means only tense that has to be inferred in the infinitive clause: mood is a far more variable factor and the range accounted for in the adverbial infinitive clause (3.12 *ff*) is available for noun phrase postmodification also. Thirdly, the infinitive postmodifier can be active or passive; beside the active examples already given, we may consider the following passive examples which in addition further illustrate the variety of implicit tense and mood:

The case *to be investigated tomorrow* ...
   (*will* or *is to be investigated*)
The animals *to be found in Kenya* ...
   (*can be* or *are found*)
The procedure *to be followed* ...
   (*must* or *should* or *will be followed*)

See also 13.50 Note.

Blurred relationships
13.21

The sharply reduced explicitness in the *-ing, -ed,* and infinitive clauses allows us to blur or neutralize the distinction between noun phrase postmodification and certain other types of construction. It is interesting, for example, that a native English speaker confronted by the sentence

I noticed a man hidden behind the bushes

will be likely to agree that he sees little or no difference in meaning between this and *either* of the following:

I noticed a man *who was hidden behind the bushes*
I noticed *that a man was hidden behind the bushes*

So also with two other sentences of obviously different structure:

(a) He was warned by the fact that a light flashed repeatedly
(b) He was warned by a light that flashed repeatedly

where grammatical rules for nominalization (13.34 *f*) can readily provide for the relation of (a) to

(c) He was warned by the repeated flashing of a light

and for the relation of both (a) and (b) to

(d) He was warned by a light flashing repeatedly

since this last can be a variant of the form with genitive noun (*a light's*) as transformed subject of (a). The fact that (c) and (d) are virtually indistinguishable semantically means that, despite our ability to relate (c) to (a) grammatically and not to (b), it is pointless to speculate on whether (d) is to be grammatically related primarily to (a) or to (b).

13.22

The foregoing examples have illustrated *-ing* and *-ed* in this respect; the infinitive clause occurs in similar merged constructions, but with additional possibilities. For example:

(e) He wants a girl to finish the cleaning

is broadly unambiguous, though it can be related to more than merely noun phrase postmodification:

(f) He wants a girl *who will finish the cleaning*

It can also be related to a complementation type described in 12.52 *ff*; this is the non-finite corresponding to a finite construction that does not exist in English but which can be imagined as

(g) *He wants that a girl will finish the cleaning

There are relations also with two possible adverbial purpose clauses:

(h) He wants a girl in order that she will finish the cleaning
(i) He wants a girl in order that he can finish the cleaning (with her help)

It is doubtless convenient to have a structural type that has such flexibility. The difficulty is to recognize the limits of the flexibility. For example, the indefinite article with *girl* in example (e) is crucially important if we wish to expand such a sentence into the more explicit form (f) rather than (i). The following example makes a non-restrictive analogue to (f) impossible and can be paraphrased only in terms of (h) or 12.54:

He wants Joan to finish the cleaning

So also, although we can reduce

I have a woman who cleans my room daily

to the non-finite form

I have a woman to clean my room daily

without perceptible change or loss of meaning, we must not assume that any sentence of the form

I have X *to do Y*

and still less of the form

I have X *do Y*

can have the non-finite clause expanded as a relative. *Cf* 14.33.

13.23
Non-restrictive postmodification

Non-restrictive postmodification can also be achieved with non-finite clauses:

The apple tree, *swaying gently in the breeze*, had a good crop of fruit
The substance, *discovered almost by accident*, has revolutionized medicine
This scholar, *to be seen daily in the British Museum*, has devoted his life to the history of science

The non-finite clauses here have an obvious correspondence with non-restrictive relative clauses

... which was swaying gently in the breeze ...
... which was discovered almost by accident ...
... who can be seen daily in the British Museum ...

but the correspondence would disappear if we availed ourselves of the opportunity (which is presented with this type) to move the non-finite clauses in front of the related head noun (*cf* 11.44 *ff*):

> *Discovered almost by accident*, the substance has revolutionized medicine

But frequently we find ourselves involved in an implicit relation with widely differing constructions, just as we found with the restrictive non-finite clauses (13.13). For example, the non-finite clause in the following sentence

> The man, *wearing such dark glasses*, obviously could not see clearly

could be a reduction of a relative clause 'who was wearing...', but equally of a causal clause, 'because he was wearing...', or a temporal one, 'whenever he wore....'. So, too, if we decide to make non-finite the relative clause in

> The cost, *which includes meals*, is ninety francs

we must recognize that the result, *including meals*, may be regarded by a reader or hearer as a reduction of a conditional clause, 'if we include meals', or *including* may be regarded as a preposition (6.4).

Note
See the discussion of supplementive clauses, 11.48 *ff*.

13.24
Appositive postmodification
Appositive postmodification is fairly common by means of infinitive clauses. A restrictive example:

> The appeal *to join the movement* was well received

which would correspond to the finite *that people should join the movement*, though such a use of putative *should* (3.46, 11.72, 12.35) is uncommon. There are cases, indeed, of non-finite postmodification where no corresponding finite apposition exists:

> Any attempt *to leave early* is against regulations
> (*... that one should leave early...*)
> He lost the ability *to use his hands*

A corresponding non-restrictive example:

> This last appeal, *to come and visit him*, was never delivered

which leaves the subject of the non-finite clause to be inferred from the context, 'that ? should come and visit him'.

The *-ed* clause has no nominal characteristics and cannot enter into appositive postmodification. The *-ing* clause does so only as head of a prepositional phrase (as in *The problem of learning English*) and thus belongs in the section to follow.

Note

V-*ing* clauses in appositive structures have prepositions which are absent in the corresponding finite clauses (*cf* 6.2):

The hope of winning ∼ X hopes that he will win.

Postmodification by prepositional phrases
Relation to more explicit modifiers
13.25

In 13.1 we saw that the sentence 'The girl was in the corner' had as a noun phrase corresponding to it, *The girl in the corner*. This example, with prepositional phrase, represents by far the commonest type of noun-phrase postmodification in English: it is three or four times more frequent than either finite or non-finite clausal postmodification. The full range of prepositions is involved:

The road *to Lincoln*
A tree *by a stream*
The house *beyond the church*
Two years *before the war*
A man *from the electricity board*
This book *on grammar*

including the complex prepositions (6.5):

Action *in case of fire*
Passengers *on board the ship*

and including those having participial form (6.4):

A delay *pending further inquiry*

though in the case of items related to verbs in current use, postmodifications should probably be regarded as clausal. For example, in

The proposal *concerning child health* was rejected

we should relate the italicized portion to a restrictive relative clause

... which concerned child health ...

rather than to a complement in an equative sentence (itself rather marginal in acceptability)

The proposal was *concerning child health*

since preceded by BE the participle would tend to be interpreted as a part of a complex finite verb.

Among the prepositions less commonly used in postmodification we should mention *like* in the sense 'resembling':

The man *like John* is over there

But it is common and fully acceptable also in the sense 'such as':

A man *like John* would never do that

13.26

It is natural to relate such prepositional postmodifications to BE sentences ('the man in the corner' ~ 'the man *is* in the corner'), though in some instances more seems to be ellipted than the verb BE. For example, we presumably need to regard

The university *as a political forum*

as related to a somewhat fuller predication:

The university is $\begin{Bmatrix} \text{acting} \\ \text{regarded} \end{Bmatrix}$ as a political forum

Again, although there is no problem with

The present *for John* cost a great deal
   (The present is for John)

we cannot interpret so straightforwardly

(a) The man *for the job* is John

where an additional component has to be understood:

The man is $\begin{Bmatrix} \text{right} \\ \text{best} \end{Bmatrix}$ for the job

This is seen still more clearly in a more explicit form of sentence (a):

(b) The right man *for the job* is John

Just as we do not wish to postulate

*The man is for the job

in relation to (a), so we do not wish to postulate

*The right man is for the job

in relation to (b). This problem will be seen in its more general context when we discuss *discontinuous modification* below (13.72 *ff*).

The preposition *with* is another that we cannot fully account for unless we consider more than BE sentences. That is to say, these are adequate to explain

The woman *with the child* is Joan
(The woman *is* with the child)

and even the idiomatic (and old-fashioned)

The woman *with child* is Joan (= 'pregnant')
(The woman *is* with child)

but in general this is true only where *with* can be glossed as 'accompanied by'. No such gloss is possible in

The man *with a red beard*
The girl *with a funny hat*

and here (*cf* 6.11, 6.45–46) we need to connect the prepositional phrase with a HAVE sentence:

The man has a red beard

and hence with a relative clause:

. . . who has a red beard.

Of and the genitive
13.27
The commonest preposition in noun phrase postmodification, *of*, has an even closer correspondence to HAVE sentences: in many cases there is regular commutation with the *-s* genitive (4.94 *f*), as we shall see below. For example:

The ship has a funnel
The ship's funnel is red
The funnel *of the ship* is red

Not all the uses involve comparison with HAVE sentences, however; some are relatable to BE sentences whose subjects are put into *of*-phrases, when an indefinite complement is made definite:

Rome is a city → *The* city (that I mean) is Rome
→ *The* city *of Rome*

Similarly we might postulate such a relation as

The team's victory was (announced as) news
→ *The* news was the team's victory
→ The news *of the team's victory*

We have here a basis for the prepositional postmodification which corresponds directly to the clausal appositive (13.16 and 9.163, 9.178):

That the team had won⎫
The team's having won⎬was (announced as) news

→ The news{that the team had won
          {*of the team('s) having won*

(On *the team* versus *the team's*, see 11.23.)

Because of the obvious relation between 'The city is Rome' (etc) and 'The city of Rome' (etc), it is common to regard such noun phrases as simply nominalizations of BE sentences in which the underlying subject has become the head of the noun phrase, ignoring the relation stressed here between the head and an underlying *complement* in a BE sentence. Few would deny the necessity of the latter interpretation, however, in respect of such examples as:

The fool of a policeman (=The foolish policeman)
   (The policeman is a fool)
The angel of a girl (=The angelic girl)
   (The girl is an angel)

where the postmodifying noun phrase must be indefinite. This would seem to be confirmed by AmE informal variants like

Some fool policeman

where *policeman* becomes the head of a premodified noun phrase.

Objective and subjective
13.28
The variable 'direction' of predications semantically corresponding to *of*-postmodified noun phrases contributes greatly to the complexity of these expressions and has a bearing on the commutation with the *-s* genitive to which reference was made above. Looked at in this way, we have left-to-right predication in the following:

The imprisonment of the murderer	[9a]
((Someone) imprisoned the murderer)	
A man of courage	[9b]
(The man has courage)	

and right-to-left predication in

The arrival of the train	[10a]
(The train arrived)	
The funnel of the ship	[10b]
(The ship has a funnel)	

With the left-to-right examples [9a] and [9b] it seems reasonable to speak of an objective relationship and the right-to-left examples [10a] and [10b] similarly show a subjective relationship. These relations are more obvious in [9a] and [10a] (with their heads being nominalized verbs) than in [9b] and [10b], where the predicational relationship is covert or implicit.

With OBJECTIVE genitive, replacement of the *of*-phrase by a premodifying -*s* genitive 'object' is rather uncommon and unnatural except where the head is a nominalized verb. Thus:

The imprisonment of the murderer ~ The murderer's imprisonment	[9a]

But:

A man of courage ~ *Courage's man	[9b]
The love of power ~ *Power's love	[9c]
((Someone) loves power)	
Reminiscences of the war ~ *The war's reminiscences	[9d]
((Someone) remembers the war)	
Men of science ~ *Science's men	[9e]
(Men (study) science)	

By constrast, replacement of the SUBJECTIVE *of*-phrase by -*s* genitive is common with most types of head, irrespective of whether the subject-predicate relation is overt or not:

The arrival of the train ~ The train's arrival	[10a]
The funnel of the ship ~ The ship's funnel	[10b]
The activity of the students ~ The students' activity	[10c]
(The students are active)	
The *War Requiem* of Britten ~ Britten's *War Requiem*	[10d]
(Britten (composed) the *War Requiem*)	

This is easy enough to understand in relation to [10c] and [10d] where the 'subject' is the type of noun ('animate, especially human') that readily admits the -*s* genitive: *cf* 4.97. For [10a] and other such examples, perhaps, the *of*-phrase acquires by implication some properties of animateness through the very fact that the noun in question has a subject function.

Nevertheless, there are some subjective genitives where replacement by -*s* genitive is impossible. For example:

The joy of his return ~ *His return's joy	[10e]
(His return gives joy)	
An angel of a girl ~ {*The / *A} girl's angel	[10f]
(The girl is an angel)	

This constraint is marked by other restricted and special features in these examples, not least the property 'indefiniteness' in respect of the head noun, which is relevant also in

An opera of Verdi's   [10g]
   (Verdi (composed) this opera – and others)

without, however, blocking a direct commutation with -*s* genitive ('One of Verdi's operas'). We shall return to this example in 13.30.

13.29
Broadly speaking, therefore, the objective relation can be expressed only with the *of*-phrase, the subjective relation with either the *of*-phrase or the -*s* genitive. Where the underlying or implicit verb is intransitive as in [10a], there can be no difficulty in interpreting the *of*-phrase as subjective, but where it is a transitive or prepositional verb problems can arise. *Cf* the ambiguity in phrases like *The shooting of the rebels* ('X shoots the rebels' or 'The rebels shoot X'), which context usually makes clear. The following sentence in a newspaper, however,

The reminiscences of the Prime Minister were very amusing

was actually left ambiguous since the article did not explain whether it was the Prime Minister who had been reminiscing or whether someone had been reminiscing *about* the Prime Minister. But in general it seems that, where an *of*-postmodifier can be interpreted as objective, it will be so interpreted unless there is a counter-indication. Thus

The examination of the man
The scrutiny of the tenants

will tend primarily to suggest that someone is examining the man or scrutinizing the tenants though the converse would be perfectly reasonable. If therefore we wish to make it clear at once that the man and the tenants are subjective in such noun phrases, we must use *by* instead of *of* in each case. Correspondingly, genitive premodification will probably be interpreted as subjective in the absence of counter-indication, as in

The man's examination
The tenants' scrutiny

But a counter-indication in these cases very easily swings interpretation decisively one way or the other:

The man's examination of the student (S V O)
The man's examination by the doctor (O V S)
The tenants' scrutiny of the contract (S V O)
The tenants' scrutiny by the landlord (O V S)

Here, however, we are dealing with transitive 'verbs' which can tolerate deletion of their objects more easily than others. The verb *possess* would scarcely yield a noun phrase in which subject could be expressed without the object:

?*The man's possession* worried me
?*The possession of the man* worried me

If we knew (from the context) that *the man* was subject, we would be inclined to ask 'What does he possess?' as a condition of trying to assimilate either of these sentences. Contrast:

| The pills came into *the possession of some children* | [11a] |
| Some children came into *possession of the pills* | [11b] |

English speakers would be inclined not to interpret the italicized portion of [11a] as a noun phrase because there would not be a sentence having it as subject and preserving the subject-relation in the *of*-phrase:

| *The possession of some children would be dangerous | [11c] |

but the analogous portion of [11b] would be more readily regarded as a unit with noun phrase structure:

| Possession of the pills would be dangerous | [11d] |

In both [11a] and [11b], however, (*the*) *possession* seems to enter into construction with *came* (*into*) rather than with the subsequent part of each sentence: *cf* the construction *take a rest* etc (7.20) and the phrasal verb type *take advantage* (12.64).

13.30
Double genitive

We may return now to example [10g] and consider the peculiarities of this 'double' genitive usage. It will be observed that the postmodifier must be definite and human:

An opera of Verdi's
An opera of my friend's

but not:

*An opera of a violinist's
*A funnel of the ship's

There are conditions which also affect the head of the whole noun phrase. This cannot be a proper noun; thus while we have:

Mrs Brown's Mary

we cannot have:

*Mary of Mrs Brown
*Mary of Mrs Brown's

Further, the head must be essentially indefinite: that is, the head must be seen as one of an unspecified number of items attributed to the postmodifier:

A friend of the doctor's has arrived
*The daughter of Mrs Brown's has arrived
A daughter of Mrs Brown's has arrived
Any daughter of Mrs Brown's is welcome
*The *War Requiem* of Britten's

The double genitive thus involves a partitive (4.7 *f*) as one of its components: 'one of the doctor's friends' (he has more than one) and hence not '*one of Britten's *War Requiem*'. Yet we are able, in apparent defiance of this statement, to use demonstratives as follows:

That wife of mine
This *War Requiem* of Britten's

In these instances, which always presuppose familiarity, the demonstratives are not being used in a directly defining role; rather, one might think of them as having an ellipted generic which allows us to see *wife* and *War Requiem* appositively as members of a class of objects: 'This instance of Britten's works, namely, *War Requiem*'. Even where more than one object exists corresponding to the noun, the double genitive phrase preceded by *this* should be regarded as having a generic partitive; for example

This hand of mine

should be interpreted not as 'This one of my (two) hands' but rather as 'This part of my body that I call "hand"'. Indeed, in earlier English, such an appositive structure was obvious, as in Macbeth's 'this my hand'.

Note
So too when 'A daughter of Mrs Brown's' is already established in the linguistic context, we could refer to 'The/That daughter of Mrs Brown's (that I mentioned)'.

13.31
Restrictive and non-restrictive
Prepositional phrases may be non-appositive or appositive, and in either function, they can be restrictive or non-restrictive:

This book on grammar (non-appositive, restrictive)

This book, on grammar, (non-appositive, non-restrictive)
The issue of student grants (appositive, restrictive)
The issue, of student grants, (appositive, non-restrictive)

But we must mention some limitations. The second example in each case is rare and rather awkward: non-restrictive appositives would more usually be without a preposition as with

The issue, student grants,

and would thus have the primary form described in 9.140 *ff.* On the other hand, if the ambiguous noun phrase

The issue of student grants

had its non-appositive meaning (objective *of:* 'someone issued student grants'), non-restrictive function would be rare and unnatural, plainly suggesting an awkward afterthought:

?The issue, of student grants, was slow because there were so many applicants.

In fact, non-restrictive postmodification with *of*-phrases frequently gives the impression more of accidental afterthought than of well-formed expression:

One man, of around forty years, was convicted of bigamy
?The end, of the world, is at hand
?A party, of children, entered the theatre

and sometimes appears to be quite impossible:

*The man, of property, was Soames Forsyte

By contrast, complex prepositions (6.5) seem to lend themselves less readily to restrictive postmodification than to phrases operating as disjuncts (8.78 *ff*):

?The question *in comparison with others* was difficult
This question, *in comparison with others*, caused resentment.

Position and varied relationship

13.32

As with non-finite postmodifiers when non-restrictive, so with prepositional phrases, the non-restrictive function merges with adverbial expressions; compare

The children {behind the fence / on the bus} jeered at the soldiers which means 'Those children who were . . .'

The children, $\begin{cases} \text{behind the fence} \\ \text{on the bus} \end{cases}$, jeered at the soldiers

which may mean 'The children, who (by the way) were . . .' or, on the other hand, 'The children, now that they were (safely . . .)': cf 9.156 and, on verbless supplementive clauses, 11.48–51. It is rather this latter implication that becomes uppermost if the prepositional phrase is moved into initial position:

$\begin{cases} \text{Behind the fence,} \\ \text{On the bus,} \end{cases}$ the children jeered at the soldiers

Again, the prepositional phrase in the following is poised between interpretation as non-restrictive postmodifier and as adverbial:

Money, in aid of the refugees, was collected from students and staff

In the former interpretation, the money collected was in aid of the refugees, and in the latter, *the act* of collecting money was in aid of the refugees, since in this case the adverbial modifies the whole predication just as it would in initial position:

In aid of the refugees, money was collected . . .

It is important to recognize that, despite the similarity in meaning in the examples discussed here, we do indeed have different constructions and not merely the additional possibility of placing a prepositional postmodifier in front of the noun phrase head. This becomes clear when it is shown that unless a given phrase can be an adjunct it cannot be moved from its postmodifying position. For example, the restrictive postmodification in 'His leap into the water' can be made non-restrictive, if rarely:

His leap, into the water, was wildly cheered

but as the phrase cannot be adjunct in this sentence, it cannot be made initial:

*Into the water, his leap was wildly cheered.

13.33

This naturally applies *a fortiori* to the *of*-postmodifiers that are almost solely restrictive:

*Of children, a party entered the theatre

but there is an apparent exception with partitive expressions. Thus beside

Only a few of the ten reviewers praised his **play**

we may thematically prepose the *of*-phrase (14.12 Note *b*) with no obvious difference in meaning:

Of the ten reviewers, only a few praised his play

This example is misleading however in giving the impression that the preposed phrase of the latter is identical with the postmodifying phrase of the former. They are not, as can be seen when we remove the definite article; this is acceptable in the preposed phrase

Of ten reviewers, only a few praised his play
Of fourteen women, ten were single

but not in postmodification

*Only a few of ten reviewers ...
*Ten of fourteen women ...

The fact that the latter becomes acceptable if the postmodifying phrase is introduced by *out of* (as in 'Ten out of fourteen women', where the phrase can now be preposed) only confirms that the *of*-preposed phrase is functionally different.

Note
Further confirmation comes from the correspondence between the semantically similar

Most of the bus conductors went on strike
Of the bus conductors, most went on strike

where in the second case but not the first we can replace *of* by *as to* or *as for*, preserving the semantic similarity:

*Most as for the bus conductors went on strike
As for the bus conductors, most went on strike

In other words, we should regard the initial prepositional phrase in all these instances as adverbial and not as displaced postmodification; indeed, *as for* and *as to* phrases, when used in the 'aside' sense, must always be initial (6.48, 10.24). Perhaps better, following up the allusion to thematic arrangement made earlier in this paragraph, we should see the preposed phrase as directly related to an existential statement (14.24 *ff*):

Of ten reviewers that there were⎫
                                          ⎬ only a few praised his play.
There were ten reviewers but   ⎭

Nominalization
13.34
We should not, however, exaggerate the difference between the prepositional phrase as adverbial and the prepositional phrase as postmodifier. The second of these should rather be regarded as a special instance of the first, depending for its interpretation on our ability to relate it to a sentence in which it is adjunct. In the following, for instance,

(a) A quarrel broke out *in the morning over pay*

both the prepositional phrases are introduced as adjuncts. If now we wish to refer again to the quarrel, it may suit our purpose to define it in relation to either of these adjuncts, which now become postmodifiers:

(b) The quarrel *in the morning* ruined their friendship
(c) The quarrel *over pay* was the reason for his resignation

The relation of postmodifier to adjunct may be even clearer if instead of (a) we take a sentence in which *quarrel* does not occur as a noun but as a verb:

(d) They quarrelled in the morning over pay

to which we also relate (b) and (c) but in this case through the nominalization of the verb. Such nominalization should be distinguished from the process (11.23) whereby (d) could become a non-finite clause as subject of sentences like (b) and (c):

(b') Their quarrelling in the morning ruined their friendship
(c') Their quarrelling over pay was the reason for his resignation

The subjects of these last two sentences need to be distinguished from noun phrases since the 'head' in these subject phrases will often not admit adjectives in modification while a 'deverbal' head (App I.21, I.31 *f*) like that in (b) and (c) will not admit premodifying adverbs:

The violent quarrel$\begin{cases}\text{over pay}\\\text{in the morning}\end{cases}$

*The violently quarrel$\begin{cases}\text{over pay}\\\text{in the morning}\end{cases}$

*Their safe arriving in Cairo
Their safe arrival in Cairo.

Note
On the relation between deverbal noun, verbal noun and participle, see the discussion of gradience in 4.9 *ff*.

13.35
Some adjuncts however can become postmodifiers more easily than others; compare

$\begin{cases}\text{Their arriving on Thursday (adjunct in non-finite clause)}\\\text{The(ir) arrival on Thursday (postmodifier in noun phrase)}\end{cases}$

where the prepositional phrase is equally acceptable in both, with

$\begin{cases}\text{Their arriving for a month (adjunct)}\\\text{?The(ir) arrival for a month (postmodifier)}\end{cases}$
$\begin{cases}\text{Their behaving with courtesy (adjunct)}\\\text{?The(ir) behaviour with courtesy (postmodifier)}\end{cases}$

$\begin{cases} \text{Their acting in a nasty manner (adjunct)} \\ \text{*The(ir) action in a nasty manner (postmodifier)} \end{cases}$
$\begin{cases} \text{Their contributing out of kindness (adjunct)} \\ \text{*The(ir) contribution out of kindness (postmodifier)} \end{cases}$

It appears that adjuncts relating to cause, manner, or ongoing activity are awkward or inadmissible as postmodifiers. Deverbal nouns (especially from point-action verbs like *arrive*) might be described as mere records of an action having taken place rather than as descriptions of the action itself. Thus the postmodifiers are the adjuncts that can occur in sentences like the following:

The arrival took place *on Thursday*

Contrast:

*The arrival took place *for a month*.

Minor types of postmodification
13.36
We come now to some relatively minor types of postmodification. These are (a) adverbial modification (*cf* 5.61); (b) the postposed adjective (*cf* 5.18 *f*); and (c) the postposed 'mode' qualifier. For example,

(a) *The road back* was dense with traffic
(b) *Something strange* happened last night
(c) *Lobster Newburg* is difficult to prepare

In the first of these, we recognize some such sentence as '*The road* which leads *back* to London' from which all but the subject and an important adjunct have been dropped. Similarly '*The way* (which leads) *in* (to the auditorium)', '*The people* (who are sitting) *behind*'. In some cases, the postmodifying item could be regarded alternatively as a preposition with deleted complement: '*The people* (who are sitting) *behind* (us)'. There are indeed a few cases where prepositional interpretation is forced on us (*cf* 6.9):

The votes for have not yet been counted

where the related explicit structure can only have a prepositional phrase: '*The votes are for the motion*'. But since most examples can be explained as adverbial and few as prepositional, it seems best to regard the few that must be prepositional as being modelled upon the adverbial ones.

13.37
In (b), we have in fact two subtypes. The first has been illustrated. The indefinite pronouns such as *anybody, someone* can be followed but not

preceded by adjective modification. The pronouns concerned are the *any-*, *some-*, *no-* series (4.127 *f*) plus one or two others (*what else, who next*, etc). It is important to realize that one is not free to postpose with indefinites all modifying items that can be preposed with ordinary noun heads; beside

An office girl is waiting

there is no

*Somebody office is waiting

Even adjectives need generally to be 'permanent' and hence eligible for attributive use (13.4); thus

Somebody timid

rather than

?Somebody afraid

We not infrequently come upon noun phrases which defy the conditions here described; for example,

That nasty something has reappeared

It is perhaps enough to say that in such instances (almost always familiar, playful or ironic) the head items are not being used as indefinites but have been given *ad hoc* transfer to the open class of nouns. The motivation for the deviation will vary from one example to another, but a possible explanation for the example just provided would find ready parallels. We might paraphrase it thus: 'You mentioned seeing *something nasty:* well, the thing that you called "something" has reappeared'.

The other subtype in (b) consists chiefly of the sprinkling of noun plus adjective phrases (modelled on French) like *blood royal, heir apparent* (5.18). These are of little importance in themselves, being infrequently used (though our ability to form names like *Hotel Majestic* suggests that they are more than mere fossils) and it is likely that the native speaker feels them to be very similar to compound nouns. He cannot modify such items to show that he conceives of them as comprising an adjective and a noun:

**She has *blood wholly royal* in her veins*
*The heir still apparent was being well educated

In some cases, a sequence has obviously been reanalysed as premodifier plus head; this can be seen in the way *court-martial* is commonly made plural (*cf* 4.63):

No court-martials are held on Christmas Day

Nevertheless, beside this subtype, there is a similar but much more general phenomenon. When a head is non-restrictively modified by a coordinated string of adjectives, it is common to postpose them:

A man, timid and hesitant, approached the official

though the potential mobility of the string allows it to be detached from the noun phrase altogether (*cf* 13.23). Even a restrictively modifying adjective can be postposed if it is itself modified (by an adjunct, not by the intensifier *very: cf* 5.19):

A man always timid is unfit for this task
*A man very timid is unfit for this task

This is particularly common where the modification is of a 'temporary' nature (13.4). Thus beside *The finest available car* we have *The finest car (currently) available.* So too beside the dubiousness of *?Somebody afraid,* complementation of the adjective (*Somebody afraid of the dark*) results in complete acceptability. Comparisons involving nouns of different gender classes require postposition of the adjective as in

A man taller than Mary

where with nouns of the same class, postposition is optional:

A man taller than John
A taller man than John

See further 11.60.

13.38
With (c) in 13.36 we again encounter a French model: *Lobster Newburg.* Though virtually confined to cuisine (rather than mere cooking), it is moderately productive within these limits, perhaps especially in the United States. In Britain one finds *veal paprika* and many others, but there is some resistance to this type of postposition with other than French lexical items, as in *pâté maison, sole bonne femme.* Nevertheless (perhaps because, in examples like the latter, the French and English head nouns are identical), the language has become receptive to hybrids like *baked eggs duchesse.* Though technically a prepositional phrase phenomenon, expressions involving *à la* clearly belong here. This striking type of grammatical hybrid is again perhaps commoner in AmE than in BrE, at any rate in culinary formations like *chicken à la king,* but it is very general in informal or facetious use to designate style, 'in the manner of':

Another play à la Osborne has appeared, though I forget
who wrote it.

Multiple modification
13.39
In section 13.37 above, the example *A man, timid and hesitant* showed a head being simultaneously modified by two items capable themselves of derivation from two sentences, 'X is timid' and 'X is hesitant'. Before we turn to premodification where such multiple modification is achieved with the maximum economy and the minimum explicitness, it will be useful to review noun-phrase structure incorporating this new complication. Multiple modification arises through any or all of the following conditions:

(a) More than one modification is applicable to a single head. Thus

> The girl in the corner
> The girl talking to John

can be brought together as

> The girl in the corner (and) talking to John

Where there is no conjunction, it is often the case that the second postmodifier is modifying the whole of the preceding complex noun phrase:

> {[The girl (in the corner)] talking to John}

(b) A modification is applicable to more than one head. Thus

> The girl in the corner
> The boy in the corner

can be brought together by multiple-head rules which permit the determiner to apply to both heads (*cf* 4.14 Note *b*, 9.110*f*):

> The girl and boy in the corner

By bringing (a) and (b) together, we can produce complexes such as:

The girl and boy in the corner (and) talking to John

(c) A modification contains an item to which in turn a further modification is applicable. We have already seen numerous examples of where such further modification is achieved by means of an adverb; we are here concerned with catenations like

> The girl in the corner nearest the door

from the merging of

> The girl in the corner
> The corner nearest the door.

13.40
Stylistic preference
By bringing (a), (b) and (c) together, we form

The girl and boy in the corner nearest the door talking to John

Although the last postmodifier in this example is so much removed from
the head, ambiguity is impossible: the door could not be talking to John.
Nevertheless, many fastidious users of English would prefer to use a finite
relative clause here ('. . . who are talking to John'), no doubt in response
to an instinct that prompts the periodic introduction of a reassuring explicitness, especially at a point which is relatively distant from the head.
The previous sentence, from *no doubt*, illustrates the principle in question and we may compare a clumsy paraphrase which disregards it:

in response to an instinct in favour of the introduction of explicitness
at intervals for reassurance at points far from the head of the
noun phrase

More is involved than periodic need for explicitness; perhaps formal
repetitiveness (*eg* a sequence of prepositional phrases or relative clauses)
is as objectionable in a lengthy postmodification as is the danger of losing
the thread:

He was the man who wrote the letter which Mary found in the
house which she rented from the man who taught her uncle.

Ambiguity and constraints on multiple modification
13.41
The instances of multiple modification so far considered have raised
problems of style but hardly of actual ambiguity or structural imper-
missibility. Frequently, however, careful ordering of constituents in a
noun phrase is essential to communicate all and only one's intention.
To take an obvious example, the following pair differ in meaning and
are not mere stylistic variants:

The man in black talking to the girl
The man talking to the girl in black

One of the chief reasons for preferring the *of*-phrase to the *-s* genitive is
to avoid discontinuity (with unwanted humour); thus

The ears of the man in the deckchair

and not

*The man's ears in the deckchair

(But *cf*, with group genitive, *The man in the deckchair's ears:* 13.64.)

A special type of multiple modification that requires careful ordering occurs when the modifying clause becomes itself embedded in a clause. Consider the following series:

John will write a poem for you
Tom hopes (that) John will write a poem for you
I will read the poem (*which*) Tom hopes (that) *John will write for you*

In this last sentence, the relative pronoun (*which*) is object in the italicized relative clause. When, however, a relative pronoun is subject under analogous conditions, the conjunctive *that* which remained optional in the foregoing example is obligatorily absent:

A poem will be written for you
Tom hopes (that) a poem will be written for you

I will read the poem (*that*) Tom $\begin{Bmatrix} hopes\ will \\ *hopes\ that\ will \end{Bmatrix}$ *be written for you*

Cf 7.65, 7.78, 11.18.

13.42

Since verbs in the nominal clauses may be made non-finite or may be entirely absent, variations in structure can be very considerable. Related to

We thought $\begin{cases} \text{(that) the boy was honest} \\ \text{the boy honest} \\ \text{?the boy to be honest (rather rare)} \end{cases}$

we have the noun phrases

The boy (that) we thought $\begin{cases} \text{was honest} \\ \text{honest} \\ \text{to be honest} \end{cases}$

Verbless and non-finite postmodification is less acceptable when the adjective is 'temporary' (13.4):

We thought the boy $\begin{cases} \text{?ready} \\ \text{?to be ready} \end{cases}$

Clause embedding in postmodification can sometimes result in *anacoluthon*, especially in speech (*cf* 7.66 Note *a*, on *wh*-questions):

I don't know when the party will end
*I'm going to *a party that I don't know when it will end*

The relative clause here is deviant since it introduces a double pronominalization of the antecedent (*that, it*), but avoidance of the deviance involves rather radical reorganization:

I'm going to a party which will end I don't know when
I'm going to a party and I don't know when it will end

Note
A blend of the finite and non-finite forms of embedded clause produces hypercorrect deviant sentences like

*That is the man whom we thought was not coming

Relative clauses may be complicated more than we have illustrated so far, though one tends to avoid multiple embeddings with successively 'push-down' clauses:

?I have read the book which you thought I had asked John whether he would lend me.

13.43

Even with simpler examples and the most careful ordering, we may find clarity and acceptable grammar difficult to attain in multiple modification. Beginning with

He liked the smiles of delight on all the faces

a noun phrase based on this sentence and having *smiles* as its head may be ambiguous in one ordering:

The smiles of delight on all the faces that he liked

(was it the smiles or the faces that he liked?) or grammatically awkward in another ordering which introduces discontinuity (13.72) to avoid ambiguity:

?The smiles that he liked of delight on all the faces

When we go on from this same sentence to attempt a noun phrase which has *faces* or *delight* as head, the problems increase:

?All the faces that he liked the smiles of delight on

Note
That the objection here is not merely to the final preposition (13.12) is shown by the awkwardness also of

?All the faces on which he liked the smiles of delight

And now the noun phrase with *delight* as head:

?The delight that he liked the smiles of on all the faces
*The delight of which he liked the smiles on all the faces
*The delight on all the faces that he liked the smiles of
*The delight on all the faces $\left\{\begin{array}{l}\text{of which he liked the smiles}\\\text{whose smiles he liked}\end{array}\right.$

All these examples, however, involve discontinuous modification, discussion of which we must defer until later, 13.72 *f.*

Premodification
Types of premodifying item
13.44
In addition to the closed-system items that co-occur with the head of a noun phrase (4.13 *ff*), lexical and grammatical items of a wide range and indefinite complexity and interrelationship can precede a noun head to form a noun phrase whose modification is minimally explicit. From examples [1] and [2] in 13.1, a relationship has already been inferred between the predicative adjective and premodification ('The girl is pretty', 'The pretty girl . . .'), and in 13.3 it was shown that such premodification can be restrictive or non-restrictive. It may be useful to begin the study of premodification by glancing at the range of premodifying items, holding constant a lexical frame (*his . . . cottage*) and non-restrictive function:

(a) ADJECTIVE
   I visited *his delightful cottage*
   (His cottage is delightful)
(b) PARTICIPLE
   I visited *his crumbling cottage*
   (His cottage is crumbling)
   I visited *his completed cottage*
   (His cottage has been completed)
(c) -*s* GENITIVE
   I visited *his fisherman's cottage*
   (The cottage belonged to a fisherman)

It should be noticed that if we had used a more normal example in this instance (*his uncle's cottage*) we would have departed from the constant non-restrictive function and – more importantly – changed the relationship of *his:* in *his uncle's cottage*, *his* forms a noun phrase with *uncle* and it is this noun phrase that then premodifies *cottage*.

13.45
(d) NOUN
   I visited *his country cottage*
   (His cottage is in the country)
(e) ADVERBIAL PHRASE (*cf* 5.63)
   I visited *his far-away cottage*
   (His cottage is far away)
   (?) I visited *his out-in-the-wilds cottage*
   (His cottage is out in the wilds)

Apart from a few institutionalized examples ('an away match' – 'the match is being played away from the home ground'), the flexibility of this type of premodification tends to be exploited only colloquially, and most examples have (and seem deliberately to have) a flavour of originality, convention-flouting, and provisional or nonce awkwardness:

She's wearing *a with-it dress*
That is *the in thing* at present

(f) SENTENCE

(?) I visited *his what-do-you-call-it cottage*
     (*cf* What do you call it when a cottage has walls made from overlapping pieces of timber? Clapboard)
(?) I visited *his pop-down-for-the-weekend cottage*
     (*cf* His cottage is ideal for him to pop down for the week-end)

What was said of (e) applies at least equally here. The few institutionalized examples seem to retain a colloquial or slang flavour: *a do-it-yourself job* is a task for which you need no help; *a who-dun-it story* is one about crime, and the substandard grammar and spelling are preserved as part of the ironic slang. Somewhat more widely acceptable are noun phrases which can be interpreted either as having sentence premodifiers or as being objects (usually of *know*) in an embedded noun clause:

He asked *I don't know* HÒW *many people*

where the intonation might alternatively be '. . . KNÒW . . .'. The meaning is little changed if the sentence is reordered enforcing a different grammatical structure:

I don't know *how many people* he asked

For the most part, however, sentence premodifiers have an air of the outrageous and improvised. Part of a political leader's election campaign was described by a journalist as

today's meet the people (if they can find you) tour
(*The Times*, 1 June 1970)

Far more remarkable is the following quotation from a literary comment in which the sentence premodification itself has highly irregular punctuation to convey highly irregular coordination devices:

His other comments ignore . . . the obvious fallacies inherent in
the "But the poem (play, novel) was meant to be tedious/
pretentious/pointless" line of critical argument.
(*Times Lit Sup*, 21 May 1970)

13.46
Restrictive and non-restrictive

Before looking in more detail at the individual categories (a), (b), (c), and (d) of the two previous paragraphs, there are certain generalizations to be made.

First with respect to restrictiveness. Although there are few formal cues as to whether a premodification is restrictive or not, it may be noted that, by their improvised nature itself, types (e) and (f) tend to be restrictive and to be given more prosodic prominence (App II.7 *ff*) than the head of the noun phrase. Now, it is a general rule that, where there is no postmodification, it is the head of a noun phrase that is given prosodic prominence. Although restrictive premodifiers need not affect this rule, it is interesting to note that where prominence is given to a premodifier (as it normally is to a postmodifier), the item concerned must be restrictive. Thus

> my ugly NÒSE

is not nonsensical, but

> *my ÙGly nose

normally is, unless in the special context of, for example, drawing attention to someone else's unkind allusion. In this connection it should be noted that, although proper names cannot normally be given restrictive modification (13.3), this can occur when a distinction is being made between more entities bearing the same name:

> Do you mean *the KenTÚCKy Richmond* or *the VirGÌNia* $\begin{cases} Richmond? \\ one? \end{cases}$

Secondly, some further discussion of the distinction between temporary and permanent. Generally speaking, nouns and adjectives are stative and verbs are dynamic (2.16, 3.40). It follows that, as modifiers, most adjectives and nouns describe permanent characteristics while most participles describe temporary ones. Since, as we saw in 13.4, pre-head position in the noun phrase is strongly associated with relatively permanent characteristics, it further follows that premodification by adjectives and nouns is rarely subject to constraints, while premodification by participles is frequently constrained.

(a) Premodification by adjectives
13.47

A premodifying adjective, especially when it is the first item after the determiner, can itself be premodified in the same way as it can in predicative position (5.51 *ff*):

> His *really quite unbelievably* delightful cottage

Some intensifiers tend however to be avoided with premodifying adjectives. Thus the predicative phrase in

His cottage which is so beautiful

would not normally be retained in premodification:

His so beautiful cottage (rather affected)

With indefinite determiners, *so* would be replaced by *such:*

A cottage which is so beautiful
Such a beautiful cottage

Or else *so* plus adjective would be placed before the determiner:

So beautiful a cottage

There is resistance also to transferring clause negation to a structure of premodification, and this is possible only in limited circumstances (usually *not* plus intensifier or negative affix):

His behaviour was not $\begin{cases} \text{very courteous} \\ \text{unpleasant} \end{cases}$

allows the formation of

His not $\begin{cases} \text{very courteous} \\ \text{unpleasant} \end{cases}$ behaviour

This gives a slight impression of improvisation so that many might prefer to reformulate as:

His $\begin{cases} \text{rather discourteous} \\ \text{quite pleasant} \end{cases}$ behaviour

even though we have now changed the meaning in the direction of making the behaviour less courteous and more pleasant respectively, as well as removing the hinted negative presupposition.

Non-predicative adjectives
13.48
We saw in 5.35 *f* and 13.4 that there were a few adjectives that could not premodify. So also there are some that cannot be predicative. First, consider the small group exemplified as follows (5.31 *f*):

The mere mention ~ *The mention is mere
Pure nonsense ~ *The nonsense is pure
The only trouble ~ *The trouble is only
The $\begin{cases} \text{sheer} \\ \text{utter} \end{cases}$ disgrace ~ *The disgrace is $\begin{cases} \text{sheer} \\ \text{utter} \end{cases}$

These adjectives, it will be noted, behave irregularly also in disallowing intensification by *very* (5.5), for the good reason that they are *restrictives* (5.31 *f*), most of them clearly related to adverbial intensifiers:

The mention was merely of . . .
It was utterly disgraceful

Some items in this class, however, have homonyms that are regular:

The air is (very) pure
The cliff was (quite) sheer

Secondly, there is a group posing a difficult problem. While adjectives normally refer to quality or to resemblance with substance, some refer to the possessing of substance (*cf* 5.34). Thus *poetic* can mean 'having the qualities of poetry' or 'consisting of poetry'; in the latter sense it cannot be predicative or be intensified or graded:

This very poetic image ~ This image is very poetic
His poetic output ~ His output *of poetry*

So too with *nasal:*

His rather nasal pronunciation ~ His pronunciation is rather nasal

His nasal cavity ~ $\begin{cases} \text{The cavity of his nose} \\ \text{*The cavity is (rather) nasal} \end{cases}$

Predicative usage with *nasal, oral, mathematical*, etc is however possible in technical discourse.

13.49
But there can be other reasons inhibiting the predicative use of an adjective, and one is undoubtedly a deleted constituent. Consider *topless* as in

The topless dress ~ The dress is topless

Note, to begin with, that this adjective already constitutes an exception in being potentially predicative and yet also of the 'consisting' class that will not admit intensification with *very*. But when we speak of 'a topless bar' or 'a topless waitress', where *topless* refers to the deleted noun *dress*, the adjective is no longer predicable unless we wish to state that the bar (or waitress!) has no top. Predication of the adjective is also blocked when the noun head is agential and the adjective refers to the activity (5.33):

A kind writer ~ The writer is kind

A hard worker ~ $\begin{cases} \text{He works hard} \\ \text{*The worker is hard} \end{cases}$

Where the noun can only refer to activity, there is of course no difficulty:

His good writing ~ His writing is good

Compare also *An old friend* – 'He has been a friend for a long time'.

Something similar is involved in the ambiguous sentence

You've got a lovely daughter, Mr Brown

Said by an admiring young man, the adjective is predicable:

Your daughter is lovely

Said by a maternity nurse outside the labour ward, it might be understood as 'You have become the father of a lovely (specimen of) baby girl(ness)' and *lovely* could not be predicated. Alternatively, it might be viewed as 'Here is a lovely situation: you have a daughter'. In either of these interpretations, the non-predicability is analogous to the situation in Romance languages which permit the preposing of adjectives having only a weak logical connection with the grammatical head of the noun phrase.

13.50

Other conditions of non-predicability (at any rate, without introducing some difference of connotation) are to be seen in formulaic expressions such as *grateful* (*thanks*) (*'his (thanks) are grateful'), *humble* (*apologies*), *grave* (*crisis*), *serious* (*hazard*), *intrepid* (*explorer*), *new* (*invention*), *nice* (*girl*), *poor* (*fellow*). Cf 8.44 on formulaic adjuncts. For completeness, one should mention items which fall both outside the closed-system premodifiers discussed in 4.13 *ff* and also outside the class of adjectives as normally understood. Numerals, for example, cannot be freely predicated: beside

the twenty men

the predicative

the men are twenty

would normally mean that they were *aged* twenty (though 'How many are you? – 'We are three' is a possible if unusual sequence). Again relational words like *latter* and *upper* must be in premodification position, as also the quantifiers *little, much, enough;* postmodifying instances of the last mentioned can be somewhat archaic or dialectal:

Have you $\begin{cases} \text{enough beer?} \\ \text{?beer enough?} \end{cases}$

It needs to be emphasized, however, that on the whole we are speaking of strong tendencies rather than immutable rules. Even the adjectives which are most firmly restricted to predicative position can be used exceptionally. In C. P. Snow's novel *The New Men*, we find

But, like many ill men, they resented the well

The author subsequently defended his premodifying use of *ill* as follows:

This is becoming increasingly common, particularly among educated people. It is just a shade more emphatic than, say, 'he is not a healthy man'.
(*Moderna Språk* 55 (1961), *p* 247)

Note
When nouns are used as predicative degree indicators (*cf* 11.60 *ff*), they can be readily postmodified by *enough* plus infinitive clause:

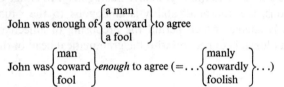

(b) Premodification by participles (*cf* 5.12 *ff*)
Present participles
13.51
Everything here depends on the potentiality of the participle to indicate a permanent or characteristic feature. To a lesser extent, gradability (especially as indicated through intensification by *very*) is concomitant.

She has a very interesting mind

shows *interesting* as fully adjectival despite the direct relation to the verb *interest:*

Her mind *interests* me *very much*

But an item can be a premodifier and yet disallow *very:*

A roaring bull (*very roaring)

And the converse can be true:

The man was very ⎰reassuring / shocked / surprised⎱

?He was a ⎰reassuring / shocked / surprised⎱ man

This last example will illustrate the crucial significance of the 'permanence' characteristic; such participles can freely premodify nouns such as *look, smile:*

He greeted me with a very $\left\{\begin{array}{l}\text{reassuring}\\\text{shocked}\\\text{surprised}\end{array}\right\}$ expression

The man himself cannot have shock or surprise attributed permanently to him, but a particular look can of course be permanently associated with such a value. So too we may speak of *a smiling face* rather than of *a smiling person.* It is thus necessary to realize that we are not here concerned with particular participles so much as with their contextual meaning. *A wandering minstrel* is one habitually given to wandering, but if we saw a man wandering down the street, we could not say

*Who is the wandering man?

Again, someone who told good stories could be *a (very) entertaining person* but one could not say this of someone who happened at the moment of speaking to be entertaining his friends with a good story.

Note
Cf also the acceptability of *giggling girls, a working man,* and see the discussion of aspect in 3.36 *ff.*

13.52
As we have noted before (13.4), the indefinite article favours the habitual or permanent, the definite article the specific or temporary. Thus

?The approaching train is from Liverpool

is strange (especially in BrE) but not

He was frightened by an approaching train

where we are concerned perhaps with what is characteristic in 'approaching trains'. Similarly

?The barking dog is my neighbour's

but

I was wakened by a barking dog

On the other hand, after indefiniteness has been used while a quality was being specified in the postmodification, a participle can in a specific context be moved into premodification with the definite article:

A proposal offending many members . . .
    (The offending proposal . . .)

In addition, the definite article may be used generically (4.28) and hence evoke the same generality and permanence as the indefinite:

The beginning student should be given every encouragement

This last example represents what may be a current trend in journalism and in technical writing (especially in the social sciences) to admit present participles rather more freely in premodification: *the developing* (or *emerging*) *countries, the* (*partially*) *hearing child, a continuing* (or *ongoing*) *commitment, a voting member.*

Past participles

13.53

Much of what has been said of present participles applies to past participles also, but there are additional complications. In the first place, the past participle can be active or passive but as with postmodification (13.19) the active is rarely used in premodification. Contrast

The immigrant who has arrived

with

*The arrived immigrant

The vanished treasure ('The treasure which has vanished') and *A retired teacher* are exceptional, but exceptions are somewhat more general when an active participle is adverbially modified:

The newly-arrived immigrant
Our recently-departed friend
?A recently-arisen problem

Within the passive we must distinguish the predicative and the agential or true passive; a non-agential, predicative example:

Some complicated machinery
  (The machinery is complicated $\sim$
  *The machinery was complicated by the designer)

Here belong also *born* and some uses of *hidden, married, troubled, darkened*, etc, but in premodification they must either have 'permanent' reference or be adverbially modified:

A born musician (=a natural musician)
A newly-born child
A married man
The carefully-hidden spy

The last example illustrates a noteworthy general contrast between present and past participles. Beside the similarity in postmodification

The spy, carefully hidden in the bushes, watched ...
The spy, carefully hiding in the bushes, watched ...

the latter unlike the former resists premodification

*The carefully-hiding spy

Note
With *The newly-arrived immigrant*, we may compare *A well-read woman, A soft-spoken person*, etc.

13.54
Most past participles are of the agential type and naturally only a few will easily admit the permanent reference that will permit premodifying use. We may contrast

The wanted man was last seen in Cambridge
  (The man goes on being wanted by the police)
*The found purse was returned to its owner
  (The purse was found at a particular moment)

But *a lost purse* is grammatical, because although a purse is no longer regarded as 'found' after it has been retrieved, a purse will be regarded as 'lost' throughout the period of its disappearance. So too:

The defeated army
A broken vase
The done thing (familiar BrE, 'The fashionable thing to do')
A damaged car
Its relieved owner

But not (except in special contexts which we must here ignore):

*A sold car
*The mentioned article
*A built house
*A described man

There are apparent exceptions which suggest that the semantic and aspectual factors are more complicated than here described. Although a sum of money can go on being needed, one does not normally say *The needed money*, and although a car is stolen at a moment of time, one can speak of *The stolen car* as one can of *A lost purse*. In *A muttered reply*, however, the participle characterizes a type of reply rather than an instance, and this is no more exceptional, therefore, than the equally typical posture denoted in *A drawn sword.* With *An organized tour* we may perhaps explain the premodification through the continuing and professional nature of the organization (as distinct from a tour privately organized on a specific occasion); or perhaps we should supply a deleted adverb 'an (officially- *or* specially-) organized tour', since we must remember that all of the starred agential participial phrases become acceptable under these conditions:

> A recently sold car
> The above-mentioned article
> A well-built house
> A carefully-described man

(On the tendency to hyphenate such premodifiers, see App III.5 Note *a*.)

Finally, modifiers in *-ed* may be directly denominal and not participles at all (see App I.29): *the vaulted roof, a fluted pillar, a wooded hillside.* But constraints occur (perhaps dictated merely by semantic redundancy), such that there is no

> *A powered engine
> *A haired girl
> *A legged man

though we have

> A diesel-powered engine
> A red-haired girl
> A long-legged man

Since, as we have seen, intransitive verbs rarely yield premodifying past participles, we should perhaps interpret *A (much-) travelled man* as having a denominal rather than a participle. But *cf* 13.53 Note.

(c) Premodification by genitives
13.55

It can be deduced from 13.44 that a noun phrase like *a fisherman's cottage* is ambiguous: the cottage belongs to a fisherman or belonged to a fisherman (or resembles the cottage of a fisherman). This type of premodification is thus sharply different from (a) *a delightful cottage* and (b) *a completed cottage* in that the determiner may as with (a) and (b), refer forward to the head or (more usually) refer only to the genitive. If the latter, then any intermediate modifiers between the determiner and the genitive must modify only the genitive. Thus

> These nasty women's clothing

where *these* must predetermine the plural *women's* and the phrase must mean 'the clothing of these nasty women' and not 'the nasty clothing of these women' which would require the order *These women's nasty clothing*. If the former ('the clothing of . . .'), then an intermediate modifier will be interpreted as referring to the head. Thus

This nasty women's clothing

would mean 'this nasty clothing belonging to (or designed for) women'. Ambiguous instances are however common:

An old man's bicycle (contrast: 'a man's old bicycle')

could mean 'The bicycle belonging to an old man' or 'An old bicycle designed for a man' (or even 'A bicycle designed for an old man').

13.56
Without head
A notable feature of genitive premodification is the deletion of the head especially when this denotes premises or establishment:

I shall be at *Bill's*

where *Bill's* would normally mean 'where Bill lives', even though the hearer might not know whether the appropriate head would be *house, apartment, flat, digs* (BrE); 'lives' is important, however, and *hotel room* (where Bill could only be 'staying') would be excluded. By contrast

I shall be at *the dentist's*

would refer to the dentist's professional establishment and the same applies to proper names where these refer to commercial firms. It would not be absurd to write:

I shall be at Harrod's/Foyle's/Macy's

This usage is normal also in relation to small 'one-man' businesses: 'I buy my meat at *Johnson's*'. With proper names used in this way, however, the connection with the genitive becomes rapidly weakened, the essential plurality of large organizations causes the *s* to be reinterpreted as plural, the apostrophe tends to be moved to suggest a genitive plural (*at Macys'*) or to be dropped altogether as though the name ended in -*s* like *Phillips* or *Rogers* or were a plural:

Harrods is/are very good for clothes

Other commercial organizations move boldly in the other direction. Barclays Bank, founded by the Barclay family, have not merely dropped the apostrophe but encourage singular interpretation with the slogan 'Barclays *is* the friendly bank'.

(d) Premodification by nouns
13.57
While certain postmodifying *of*-phrases correspond, as we have seen, to premodifying genitives, others, in common with prepositional phrase postmodifiers generally, correspond to noun premodifiers, often becoming so closely associated with the head as to be regarded as part of a compound noun (App I.44 *ff*):

> The question of partition ~ The par'tition question
> A rod of iron ~ An iron 'rod
> The door of the cupboard ~ The cupboard 'door
> The shooting of tigers ~ 'Tiger shooting
> The story of his life ~ His 'life story
> A story about the war ~ A 'war story
> A chair with arms ~ An 'arm chair *or* An arm 'chair
> A cloth for dishes ~ A 'dish cloth
> A village in Sussex ~ A Sussex 'village
> A man from Sussex ~ A 'Sussex man

Prepositional phrases will not serve, however, to explain all premodification by nouns. There are coordinations and appositions also:

> The plane is both a fighter and a bomber ~ A fighter-'bomber
> Bernard Miles was both actor and producer ~ The actor-pro'ducer
> Smith is a sergeant ~ Sergeant 'Smith

However, the kind of apposition found in titles of this kind (9.166 *ff*) is severely restricted by convention and style.

13.58
Attention must be drawn to three notable features in the various noun premodifications illustrated above. One is that plural nouns usually become singular (*cf* 4.52d):

> A chair with arms ~ An 'arm chair

This holds even for nouns that otherwise have no singular form:

> A sharpener for scissors ~ A 'scissor sharpener
> The leg of the trousers ~ The 'trouser leg

But while singularization is normal it is by no means universal, especially with noun premodification that is not hardening into a fixed phrase or compound:

> The committee on promotions ~ The pro'motions committee

Cf also *the arms race*. The second important point is the relationship of the determiner. It will be observed that the normal situation is for the determiner to be related to the head identically in the post- and premodified noun phrases. Two exceptions are illustrated:

> *The shooting* of tigers ~ ¹Tiger *shooting*
> *The story* of his life ~ *His* ¹life *story*

The second of these examples conceals a difference in assumption of the sentential context: the postmodified form is neutral as to the subject of a narrating verb, the premodified form is biased towards a subject coreferential with *his*. Thus

> He ⎫
> She ⎬told the story of his life
> I ⎭
>
> He ⎫
> ?She ⎬told his life story
> ?I ⎭

The third significant point concerns accentuation: according to the relationship between the two nouns, the accent will fall on the premodifier or the head; for example, *An iron* ¹*rod* but *A* ¹*war story*. The conditions under which the latter stress pattern is adopted are by no means wholly clear but are connected with the conventionalizing of a sequence in the direction of compounding. See further App I.44 *ff* and App II.6.

13.59
Although we have said that prepositional phrases 'generally' can yield noun premodifiers, this applies in fact only to the most central prepositions:

> *Work in the docks* is arduous ~ ¹*Dock work* . . .

but

> *Work near the docks* is arduous ~ *Dock work . . .

Indeed precisely this point was an issue in the London law courts in 1970, and the Court of Appeal rightly upheld the linguistic statement made above and *The Times* law report had the following headline (7 May 1970):

> Work near docks is not dock work

A further noteworthy constraint against using nouns from postmodifying phrases as premodifiers is the relative impermanence of the modification in question. Thus while

> *The table in the corner* was laid for dinner

will readily yield

The corner table . . .

we cannot do the same with

The girl in the corner spoke to me
*The corner girl . . .

We must insist again that this is not a property of the lexical item (in this instance, *corner*) but of the semantic relation. It is no doubt only because a table is not free to move of itself that we can premodify this word but not *girl* by *corner*.

Multiple premodification
13.60
With single head

The three types of multiple modification specified in 13.39 apply to premodification also. More than one modification may be related to a single head:

His brilliant book ⎫
His last book   ⎬ ~ His last brilliant (. . .) book
His (. . .) book ⎭

Though long sequences are uncommon, the dots should remind us that there is no grammatical limit to the number of premodifiers. This formulation is however misleading in giving the impression that the multiple modifiers constitute an unordered string. In fact there is good evidence that multiple modification follows a recursive process:

His book→His brilliant book→His [last (brilliant book)]

This then means that of several brilliant books we are speaking only of his last one, and we are able to contrast

His book→His last book→His [brilliant (last book)]

where we are saying that his last book was brilliant without commitment to whether any of his other books were. In some instances, however, we do indeed have multiple modifications in which no priority among modifiers need be assumed, and where one modifier plus the head would hardly form a class susceptible to subclassification by means of a second modifier. In such instances we sometimes give separate prosodic treatment to the modifiers (introducing commas in writing):

His LÁST BRÍLLiant BÒOK

or formally coordinate them. Thus

His forceful, lucid remarks

would not be noticeably different in meaning from

His forceful and lucid remarks
His lucid, forceful remarks

When however such coordinated modifiers relate to properties that are normally thought to be mutually exclusive, the coordinator will probably not be *and:*

?His handsome and dirty face
(?)His handsome, dirty face
His handsome but dirty face
His dirty but handsome face

13.61
With multiple head
Modification may apply to more than one head (*cf* 9.108 *ff*):

The new table ⎱
The new chairs⎰ ~ The new table and chairs

The multiple head thus produced can now be subject to recursive or coordinate modification:

The new table and chairs→The beautiful new table and chairs
The new, ugly table and chairs
The new but ugly table and chairs

The reduced explicitness naturally makes ambiguity possible. Since we can coordinate two noun phrases only one of which is premodified, as in:

He wrote *long articles*⎱
He wrote *books*   ⎰ ~ He wrote *long articles and books*

the resulting string will suggest that the modifier applies to both heads if it comes first. In these circumstances, we may disambiguate by reordering or by introducing separate determiners:

He wrote *books and long articles*
He wrote *some long articles and some books*

Noun phrases with separate premodification can however be jointly premodified, as in:

books and long articles→excellent books and long articles

where with one tone unit the latter can be interpreted as having the structure:

{excellent [(books) and (long ÀRTICLES)]}

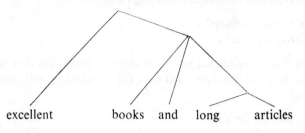

Fig 13:2

This interpretation would be almost inescapable if a determiner such as *some* preceded *excellent*. It follows that if we wish to coordinate noun phrases both of which are premodified, we must introduce either prosodic or punctuation separators, or separate determiners:

excellent books, and long articles
some excellent books and some long articles

With modified modifier
13.62

We have already seen two types of modification with modified modifier:

His really quite unbelievably delightful cottage

where the premodifying adjective *delightful* is itself premodified by the adverbial *really quite unbelievably;* and

These nasty women's clothing

where the genitive premodifier *women's* is itself premodified by *these nasty*, and where the whole genitive phrase could premodify another genitive:

⟨{[These (nasty women's)] employer's} clothing⟩

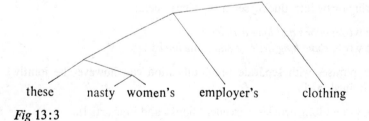

Fig 13:3

(see tree diagram, *Fig* 13:3). Although there is no theoretical limit to such sequences of genitives, there seems to be a practical limit of two, anything more being stylistically objectionable, comic, and difficult to comprehend:

?These nasty women's employer's wife's clothing

A third type of modified modifier has no such limitations. The noun premodifier can be itself premodified by either an adjective or a noun and, if the latter, this can in turn be similarly premodified:

The office furniture→ { The *small office* furniture
                        { The *tax office* furniture ——

—The *property tax* office furniture ←——

——→The *house property* tax office furniture

It should be noted, however, that if we were to introduce an adjective in this last noun phrase, already clumsy and improbable, (i) it would have to come immediately after the determiner, and (ii) it would normally be interpreted as relating directly to the head *furniture* rather than to *house*, the only other possibility:

The pleasant house property tax office furniture

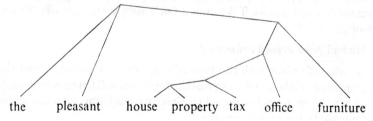

the   pleasant   house   property   tax   office   furniture

Fig 13:4

In the case of 'The small office furniture', it was possible to have the adjective premodifying the premodifier only by selecting an adjective that would hardly refer to furniture (5.41). Compare the following two examples which appeared in the same news item:

The food price rise warning system
The voluntary price rise warning system
    (*The Times*, 7 May 1970)

The identical positioning of *food* and *voluntary* must not obscure the fact that the former modifies *price* and the latter *system*.

13.63

This is not to say however that obscurity cannot exist or that noun premodifiers can modify only the next following noun, as in the instances so far illustrated. Consider

A new giant size cardboard detergent carton

where *size* does not premodify *cardboard* and *cardboard* does not premodify *detergent* but where the linear structure is rather as follows (see *Fig* 13:5 for tree diagram):

A ⟨new {(giant size) [cardboard (detergent carton)]}⟩

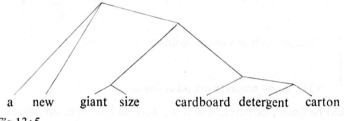

Fig 13:5

Such an example is not, of course, obscure, and indeed it is generally the case that obscurity in premodification exists only for the hearer or reader who is unfamiliar with the subject matter being treated and who is not therefore equipped to tolerate the radical reduction in explicitness that premodification entails. Take even a fairly simple example like the following:

He had *some French onion soup*

If we are unfamiliar with this type of soup, there is nothing about the grammatical, orthographic or prosodic form that will tell us whether it is soup made from French onions, French soup made from onions, or onion soup made in the French manner.

13.64

'Group genitive'

One important type of multiple premodification is the 'group genitive'. While the affixing to a noun of the genitive inflection and the plural inflection follows similar rules for regular nouns (4.61 *f*) in general, the rules for the two inflections are different if the noun is postmodified:

singular {
The teacher   The teacher's (room)
The teacher of music   The teacher of music's (room)
}

plural {
The teachers   The teachers' (room)
The teachers of music The teachers of music's (room)
}

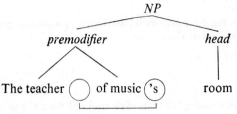

Fig 13:6

(see the tree diagram, *Fig* 13:6). Other examples involve coordinations: *an hour and a half's discussion, a week or so's sunshine.* The group genitive is not normally acceptable when the postmodification is a clause, though in colloquial use one sometimes hears examples like:

Old man what-do-you-call-him's house has been painted
?I like the man standing in the corner's hat
?Someone has stolen a man I know's car

In normal use, especially in writing, such - *s* genitives would be replaced by *of*-genitives:

I like the hat of the man standing in the corner
Someone has stolen the car of a man I know

There are other special types of group premodification that should be mentioned. A friendship between a boy and girl becomes *A boy and girl friendship*. A committee dealing with appointments and promotions can readily be described as

The appointments and promotions committee

while one whose business is the allocation of finance can be

The allocation of finance committee

A noun phrase in which there is noun premodification can be given the denominal affix which puts it into the 'consisting of' class of adjectives (5.34, 13.48) while retaining the noun premodifier; hence, from *party politics* we have

A party political broadcast

Similarly, a noun phrase having a denominal adjective may itself take a denominal affix to become a premodifier in a noun phrase. For example, beside *cerebral palsy* (= 'palsy' of the cerebrum), we have *cerebral palsied children* which has the structure

{[(cerebral palsy)ed] children}

and not

*[cerebral (palsied children)]

cf 13.54, App I.29.

Note

Even with prepositional phrases, the group genitive is tolerable only provided no unwanted interpretation becomes obtrusive. Thus

> The man in the car's ears

might pass muster, but

> The man with the cat's ears

would obviously be avoided if the meaning 'The ears of the man with the cat' was intended.

Relative sequence of premodifiers
13.65
Denominal and nominal

In 13.60, several observations were made on the disposition of premodifying items relative to one another, with particular reference to the contrasts of meaning available through choice of position. We come now to influences upon relative ordering that depend on the class membership or underlying sentential function of the items concerned (*cf* 5.41).

The item that must come next before the head is the type of denominal adjective often meaning 'consisting of', 'involving', or 'relating to', and this can be preceded by a wide range of premodifying items:

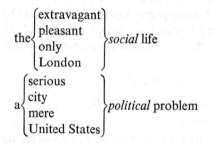

Thus while *dirty British books* could be understood as books that had become grimy, *British dirty books* could only mean books that 'consisted of' or 'were characterized by' dirt (*ie* obscenity).

Next closest to the head is the noun premodifier, already exemplified with *London* and *city* in the foregoing examples. When two nouns premodify, one which corresponds to the head as object to verb will follow one relating to material or agency:

a ⎰*detergent* ⎱ ⎰container
　 ⎱*cardboard*⎰ ⎱carton

a *cardboard detergent*⎰container
　　　　　　　　　　　⎱carton

*a detergent *cardboard*⎰container
　　　　　　　　　　　⎱carton

$$my \begin{Bmatrix} ciga^{\rvert}rette \\ {}^{\rvert}gas \end{Bmatrix} lighter$$

my ₗgas cigaˈrette lighter

*my cigarette gas lighter

Note

Exceptions to the *agent – object – verb* order are common enough where an *agent – verb* sequence has prior institutionalized status, as with *pressure cooker*, which may then as a unit be premodified by an object such as *vegetable*.

Classes of adjectives
13.66
Next before a noun modifier the most important class of items to mention is the adjective of provenance or style:

a *Russian* trade delegation
Gothic church architecture

and preceding this type is the participle:

a *carved* Gothic doorway
some *interlocking* Chinese designs

Preceding the participle, we have adjectives of colour:

a *black* dividing line
a *green* carved idol

And these in turn are preceded by adjectives of age, together with the pre- and postmodifiers that these and other freely gradable adjectives may have:

an *old* blue dress
a *very young* examination candidate
a *really very elderly* trained nurse
a *large enough* lecture room

Next comes the large class that can be rather unsatisfactorily designated 'general', except that between 'general' and colour (and usually all other modifiers to the right) comes the diminutive unstressed use of *little*:

$$a \begin{Bmatrix} gracious \\ typical \\ beautiful \\ peculiar \\ handsome \\ hideous \\ splendid \end{Bmatrix} little \begin{Bmatrix} old\ carved\ Gothic\ doorway \\ old\ blue\ dress \end{Bmatrix}$$

*an old little blue dress

But the situation is more complicated than this would allow. We commonly use *little* after participial premodifiers ('his injured *little* hand'), and the general adjectives comprise several subclasses the relative placing of which is by no means random. For example, we would prefer *beautiful long hair* to *long beautiful hair*, but *long straight hair* to *straight long hair*; we would have *a small round table* rather than ?*a round small table*; *several thick even slices* rather than *several even thick slices*; *a fierce shaggy dog* rather than *a shaggy fierce dog*; *a tall angry man* rather than *an angry tall man*; perhaps *a brief hostile glance* rather than *a hostile brief glance*. It will be noticed that there is little suggestion that the less preferred order is actually unacceptable, and this is doubtless reflected in the fact that subcategorization of the general adjectives is controversial and that grammarians are far from being agreed on the generalizations that underlie the native speaker's preferences. In any case, when coordinated (13.60), most of these adjectives can appear in almost any relative order.

13.67
In part, the preferences seem clearly to correspond to the 'natural' order of recursive qualification (13.60). Thus

the two *typical large* country houses

would be more usual than

the two large typical country houses

In order to be typical, country houses must be large; but it would scarcely be true that in order to be large, they must be typical. This is factual not linguistic information. The preferred order in the two noun phrases above thus reflects reality in showing that the speaker had been obliged to specify the houses as country houses and the country houses as large before it became meaningful to specify the large country houses as typical. Again, the preferred orders *beautiful long hair* and *long straight hair* perhaps reflect the non-linguistic world: length of hair may be a condition of its being adjudged beautiful, and the straightness of hair would tend to be a condition of its seeming long.

Evaluative or subjective adjectives frequently precede those relating to size, while these in turn frequently precede those expressing shape; within size, expressions of height tend to precede those of girth (*a tall fat man* rather than *a fat tall man*). Attempts to explain preferences have invoked rhythm; short items before longer ones; common items before rare ones; restrictive before non-restrictive. One is tempted to suggest one principle accounting not only for all general adjectives but all premodifiers: a subjective/objective polarity. That is, modifiers relating to

determiners etc	general	age	colour	participle	provenance	noun	denominal	head
the	hectic						social	life
the	extravagant					London	social	life
a				crumbling		church		tower
a			grey	crumbling	Gothic	church		tower
some	intricate	old		interlocking	Chinese			designs
a	small		green	carved		jade		idol
his	heavy	new					moral	responsibilities

Fig 13:7 Premodification

properties which are (relatively) inherent in the head of the noun phrase, visually observable, objectively recognizable or assessible, will tend to be placed nearer to the head and be preceded by modifiers concerned with what is relatively a matter of opinion, imposed on the head by the observer, not visually observed and only subjectively assessible. One need hardly add that, with criteria that are themselves so subjective, there is plenty of room for difference of opinion.

It may clarify matters if, ignoring the suggested distinctions within the general class of adjectives, we recapitulate the observations made on the sequence of premodifiers. *Fig* 13:7 gives examples showing the relative positions taken up in a selection of noun phrases.

Note

Though there are many exceptions and few firm constraints, it seems that, to some extent, the order of premodifying adjectives is the inverse of predicative order:

beautiful long hair ~ hair that is long and beautiful
long straight hair ~ hair that is straight and long

With this we may compare the 'agent-object-head' order in premodification (13.65) with the inverse order of clause elements:

a gas cigarette lighter ~ it lights cigarettes by gas

So too with 'adjunct-subject-head':

Euston train arrivals ~ the trains arrive at Euston

and the sequence of modifiers with subjective and objective genitive (13.29):

the men's examination of the student ~ the men examined the student
the men's examination by the doctor ~ the men were examined by the doctor
the examination of them by him ~ they were examined by him

where, although inversion is not always involved, the same principle of ordered clustering in relation to the head is maintained.

13.68

General adjectives are themselves preceded by the semantically weak (formulaic) items such as *nice* (13.50); by non-predicable items like *mere* (though these general adjectives are not in fact usually so modified); by quantifiers; numerals; determiners and associated closed-system items (4.13 *ff*). One subset of determiners has to co-occur with gradable (usually 'general') adjectives but also involves subclassification of the head as singular/plural/mass (*cf* 5.57 *f*):

He told *such* $\begin{cases} a \ (funny) \ story \\ (funny) \ stories \end{cases}$

He bought *such hard wood*

He told $\begin{bmatrix} so \\ as \end{bmatrix}$ *funny a story* $\begin{bmatrix} that \ldots \\ as \ldots \end{bmatrix}$

He told $\begin{bmatrix} ^{*}so \\ ?as \end{bmatrix}$ funny stories $\begin{bmatrix} that \ldots \\ as \ldots \end{bmatrix}$

He bought $\begin{bmatrix} ^{*}so \\ ?as \end{bmatrix}$ hard wood $\begin{bmatrix} that \ldots \\ as \ldots \end{bmatrix}$

There are close parallels in interrogative and exclamatory forms, but with additional complications:

What (funny) stories did he tell?

*What a (funny) story did he tell?

What $\begin{Bmatrix} a \ (funny) \ story \\ (funny) \ stories \end{Bmatrix}$ *he told!*

What hard wood $\begin{cases} did \ he \ buy? \\ he \ bought! \end{cases}$

How tall a man $\begin{cases} is \ he? \\ he \ is! \end{cases}$

*How tall men $\begin{cases} are \ they? \\ they \ are! \end{cases}$

*How $\begin{cases} a \ man \ldots \\ men \ldots \end{cases}$

*How hard wood $\begin{cases} did \ he \ buy? \\ he \ bought! \end{cases}$

It will be seen that, in contrast with *such* and *what*, *so* and *how* share a restriction to singular countable nouns and cause the adjective to move in front of the article; *such* and *what* are also alone in permitting the adjective to be omitted though with some such general sense as 'magnificent' or 'outrageous' understood. The relationship of the four items can be summarized thus, the horizontal pairs being respectively demonstrative (upper) and interrogative (lower), the vertical pairs determiner (left hand) and pronoun (right hand):

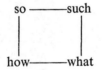

Some problems of coordination
13.69
Coordination gives rise to some points of interest in multiple modification. 'Children who have speech that is impaired' can be reduced to 'Children who have impaired speech' or 'Children with impaired speech'. The normal premodified form (*cf* App I.8) is then

speech-impaired children

But if the impairment is in *speech and language* (a conventional conjoining recognized in speech therapy), the premodification form becomes

> speech and language impaired children

The hyphen is omitted after *language* since this would entail one after *speech* as well, a type of ellipsis indication reserved for rather stiff and technical writing (App III.5 Note *b*):

> Speech- and language-impaired children

Ellipsis provides difficulties in noun phrases involving comparison also; while the following is unobjectionable:

> An equally serious or more serious situation

this is not so when postmodifying complementation is added:

> ?An equally serious or more serious situation than before

which wrongly suggests that we have a possible sequence '*An equally serious situation than before'. A somewhat similar difficulty arising through coordination and rather careless ellipsis is as follows:

> ?The similarity of his house in New York and Connecticut

A more fully explicit form without ellipses will help to show what has gone wrong:

> ... his house[1] in New York *to his house*[2] *in* Connecticut

As explained in 9.101 *f*, the rules for ellipsis have to distinguish between identity of lexical item and identity of reference; if we have only the first without the second, there are constraints on ellipsis. These are not sufficient, however, to block ellipses like the following which retain complete acceptability:

> more than one lecturer
> some book or other
> one or two books

Expressions of approximation
13.70
Coordinate expressions of approximation like 'one or two books' become still more difficult to explain in terms of ellipsis when the numeral following *or* is replaced by *so:*

> ten or so years

The *or so* more usually follows the head (though *or* plus numeral usually cannot do this without a change in prosodic pattern and so ceasing to be an expression of approximation):

  a YÈAR or so
  a YÈAR or two
  one YÈAR or so
  ÒNE year or TWÒ

There is a further approximatory expression making a set of three, all of which specify numbers but differ interestingly in meaning:

  about ten years
  ten or eleven years
  ten years or so

The first will freely allow the actual time to be less than ten as well as more than ten. The second will not normally allow the actual time to go beyond the specified range (though it could err slightly upwards). The third can range appreciably (but especially upwards), so that the actual time might be twelve years as easily as eleven.

13.71
The post-head type of approximation imposes limitations as to what can be estimated:

$$
\text{I liked}
\begin{cases}
\text{the year or} \begin{Bmatrix} two \\ so \end{Bmatrix} \text{I spent there} \\
\text{*the man or} \begin{Bmatrix} two \\ so \end{Bmatrix} \text{I saw there}
\end{cases}
$$

The limitations become clearer with additional examples; thus although we can speak of

  a dollar or so to spend
  a pound or so of butter
  a glass $\begin{cases} \text{of beer or so} \\ \text{or so of beer} \end{cases}$

we cannot speak of

  *a chair or so
  *a child or so

and still less of

  *the chair or so

though '*another* chair or so' is acceptable. In other words, the items preceding the *or so* approximation must be units of measurement (*year*, *pound*) or items contextually rendered units of measurement (*another N*). It may be worth mentioning that 'a glass of beer or so' has the structure

a {glass (of beer)} or so

and not

*a glass {of (beer or so)}

Note

Thus, unlike German, where *oder so* corresponds to all the English uses of *or so* but in addition extends to the equivalent of English 'or something of that sort', there can be no

*He drank brandy or so
*He was eating chocolates or so.

Discontinuous modification
13.72

It is not uncommon for the noun phrase to be interrupted by other items of clause structure. Note for instance the placing of the time adjunct in the following between the head and postmodifier of the italicized noun phrase:

You'll meet *a man* tomorrow *carrying a heavy parcel*

There are more striking examples:

I had *a nice glass of beer* but in *an ugly glass*

This is not as contradictory as it at first seems since it is only in the second noun phrase that *glass* is premodified by an adjective; in the first, *nice* might instead be interpreted as modifying *beer* ('a glass of nice beer'), but it is better to regard *glass of beer* as a complex unit modified as a whole (like *the teacher of music* in '*the teacher of music*'s room': 13.64), but with *glass* having less its concrete meaning than that of a unit of measure. So too with *a weak cup of tea*, and phrases of the form *kind/sort of N* which take premodifiers plainly related to *N* rather than *sort*, both in semantics and in concord:

A big awkward sort of *carton*
?*These big awkward* kind of *cartons*

13.73

Discontinuous modification more aptly applies to examples like the following (*cf* 5.19):

Comparable facilities to ours
Different production figures from those given earlier

The prepositional phrases here do not directly relate to the head (as they do in *roads to London, people from the village*) but to the premodifying adjective:

. . . facilities comparable to ours
. . . figures different from those

Compare now the following pairs

1 { The pretty girl that I kissed
    The first girl that I kissed

2 { The worst discovery that I made
    The earliest discovery that I made

3 { The most recent play I know well is *The Caretaker*
    The most recent play I've seen is *Hamlet*

The superficial resemblance within each pair must not prevent us from seeing that the premodifier in the second member has in each case an adverbial relation in what is plausibly a corresponding sentence:

1 The girl that I kissed *first*
2 The discovery that I made *earliest*
3 The play I've seen *most recently* is *Hamlet*

Nothing corresponds to this discontinuous modification (such as 'The girl that I kissed prettily') in the first noun phrase of each pair.

Compare also 'An *attractive* scheme *financially*' (= 'A scheme which is *financially attractive*'); *cf* 5.59.

13.74

Most discontinuities, however, are brought about by interpolating a parenthesis or the finite verb of the sentence (where the noun phrase is subject) between the head and the postmodifier; and the usual motive is to correct a structural imbalance (*cf* 14.41) or achieve a more immediate clarity:

The story is told *that he was once a wrestler*
The box was by the door *which had contained the papers and other valuables*

Without the discontinuity, we should have had here two sentences with subjects much longer than predicates, and in the second, discontinuity has also permitted the end of the sentence to form a climax. A textual example can perhaps show more clearly the noteworthy facility that discontinuity provides in technical writing, as well as illustrating the sort of awkwardness in style that may in turn be the result:

The . . . question . . . is whether indeed *learning* can take place *of the relationship between two groups of words*, when the particular

words tested have never concretely been associated with each
other in experience
(*Bulletin Brit. Psych. Soc.* 23, 1970)

Where the postmodification is by a prepositional phrase (especially an
of-phrase), this type of discontinuity is difficult to achieve acceptably,
as we see also in the following:

?*Several gallons* are sour *of the milk that was delivered yesterday*

and interruption is least unwelcome when the postmodifier is clausal, as
it is in the following (formal and rather literary) examples:

None can be found $\left\{\begin{array}{l}who\ speak\\speaking\end{array}\right\}$ *well of him*

He had seen *such horrors* when a boy *as he could not describe.*

Conclusion
13.75
The noun phrase, then, is potentially very complex indeed. It is hoped
that by now enough has been said to give some clear indication of the
relationship that exists between types of noun-phrase structure and the
forms of predication to which they appear to have an essential if often
indirect correspondence. By means of the structures that have been
developed in the noun phrase, we can take an indefinitely wide range of
grammatical and semantic data which have either been previously established in the discourse or which can be assumed as knowledge held in
common between speaker/writer and hearer/reader, and then express
them or refer to them with greatly reduced explicitness and consequently
increased economy. For example:

(a) At the mouth of the respiratory tube is *a series of velar tentacles,
corresponding exactly in position to those of amphioxus, and serving
to separate the mouth and oesophagus from the respiratory tube
while the lamprey is feeding.*

(b) It was *the beginning of an operation in which the power of the Holy
Spirit was fulfilled in the person and words and actions of a human
character, Jesus of Nazareth.*

(c) *Subsequent work by Huisgen (1951) and Hey, Stuart-Webb and
Williams (1951, 1952) on the dependence of the rate of rearrangement on both the aryl and acyl groups of the acylarylnitrosamine,
and on the catalysis of the reaction by bases such as piperidine,*
has led to *the formulation of the rearrangement as an intramole-
cular process, as indicated in equation (6), involving nucleophilic
attack, by an internal S_N2 mechanism, of the oxygen of the . . .
nitrosyl group on the carbonyl carbon atom.*

Thus, in the italicized noun phrase of example (a), we are expected to understand that the tentacles form a series and that they correspond to the tentacles found in the species amphioxus. More interestingly, we are expected to relate the tentacles to the velum without prejudice as to whether they are appended to it (a partitive relationship) or actually constitute it (an appositive relationship), on which distinction some biologists would not wish to commit themselves.

13.76
Types of noun-phrase structure in relation to style
But it must be emphasized that anything approaching full exploitation of the potentiality existing in noun-phrase structure is relatively rare and relatively confined to specific styles of discourse. Examining a sample of some 17,000 noun phrases in the Survey of English Usage files yielded the striking contrasts that are summarized in the accompanying table.

Table 13:1

NOUN-PHRASE STRUCTURE AND DISTRIBUTION

		(*pronouns and names*)	SIMPLE	COMPLEX	(*multiple modification*)
whole sample	subject	(5821)	6749	1149	(456)
	not subject	(2193)	4753	4310	(1777)
informal speech	subject	(1941)	2064	148	(62)
	not subject	(677)	1169	811	(327)
fiction	subject	(1943)	2220	211	(92)
	not subject	(754)	1682	1121	(434)
serious talk and writing	subject	(1478)	1745	343	(127)
	not subject	(599)	1273	1238	(492)
scientific writing	subject	(459)	720	447	(175)
	not subject	(163)	629	1140	(524)

'Simple' is here defined as embracing pronouns, names, and nouns having no heavier modification than closed-system items: *she, John, (the) butter*. In view of their numerical and distributional importance, pronouns and names are distinguished as a subclass of 'simple'. 'Complex' embraces all other noun phrases, but a subclass is distinguished comprising those having multiple modification (more than merely a single adjective premodifier or prepositional phrase postmodifier). The table shows that:

(a) Less than one-third of the 17,000 noun phrases in the sample are 'complex', even within these modest limits of 'complexity';

(b) Less than one-eighth have multiple modification;

(c) Nearly one half of the sample are pronouns or names;

(d) The majority of simple noun phrases – and the overwhelming majority of names and pronouns – are subjects of clauses or sentences, but only rather less than a quarter of complex noun phrases are subjects;

(e) When the whole sample is broken down into four types of text, one such type ('serious talk and writing') very closely follows the pattern of distribution for the sample as a whole;

(f) *In respect of these particular noun-phrase parameters*, prose fiction and informal spoken English agree closely and are sharply distinct from the other two styles represented in the sample; they have a much higher proportion of simple to complex and a much stronger association of simple with subject, and complex with non-subject, than the other styles;

(g) Scientific writing differs greatly from the other styles in having a distinctly higher proportion of noun phrases with complexity (and multiple complexity); a distinctly lower proportion of names and pronouns among its simple noun phrases; and the weakest association of simple with subject and complex with non-subject.

Even so coarse-grained a comparison makes clear how sensitive the noun phrase is as an index of style and how responsive it can be to the basic purpose and subject matter of any discourse.

Bibliographical note

On adjectives and other premodifiers, see Bolinger (1967b); Goyvaerts (1968); Mutt (1967). On modification in relation to function, see Aarts (1971).

On nominalization, see Chomsky (1970); Fraser (1970); Vendler (1968), especially Part I.

On relative clauses, see Jacobsson (1963) and (1970); Quirk (1968); and Huddleston (1971), Chapter 5.

On the choice of relative pronouns, see Roggero (1967); Taglicht (1972).

For some recent transformational studies in this area, see Fraser (1970); Kuroda (1969); Schwartz (1968).

For treatment of the noun phrase as a whole, see also Bourquin (1964); Strang (1968), Chapters 7 and 8.

14.1
Introduction

In previous chapters, particularly Chapter 7, we have seen how English sentences are built up from various phrase types which serve a range of CONSTRUCTIONAL functions within the grammar (subject, verb, adverbial, etc). We have also seen (7.13–22) how the elements which have these functions may also have a different kind of function (a participant role) describable in terms such as 'agentive', 'recipient', 'attribute'. In this final chapter, we come to a third way in which one may view these parts of the sentence: as items which can be manipulated within the structure of sentences for different kinds of prominence, serving the total sequential organization of the message. There are three different kinds of prominence to be considered: focus, theme, and emotive emphasis. Studying these aspects of linguistic structure makes one aware of language as a linearly organized communication system, in which judicious ordering and placing of emphasis may be important for the proper understanding of the message. It is an area which has been comparatively neglected by the grammars of the past, and in which modern linguistics has made a clear contribution to the understanding of how language (in particular the English language) works.

Information focus
14.2
Focus and units of information

We start by considering how the English language organizes a spoken message into units of information, as signalled by intonation. (In this section, close reference to Appendix II, especially II.12–15, is advisable.)

Each tone unit represents a unit of information, and the place where the nucleus falls is the focus of information. A sentence has at least one tone unit, and it is common for a tone unit to extend over a single (non-superordinate) clause. A few general (and fallible) rules concerning the relation of grammatical units and tone units may be stated here:

A sentence corresponds to a single tone unit (*eg: We spent our last holiday in* WÀLES) unless

(a) It begins with an optional phrasal or clausal adverbial element, *in which case* the adverbial generally has a separate tone unit:

The year before LÁST, | we spent our holiday in WÀLES|

or (b) It contains a non-restrictive relative clause, or any medial phrase or clause, *in which case* the phrase or clause has a separate tone unit:

> The JapanĔSE, | whose industry is well KNÓWN, | have recently broken all ÈXPORT records|

or (c) It contains a vocative or a disjunct or a polysyllabic conjunct, *in which case* the vocative or other unit generally has a separate tone unit, or at least ends with a tone unit division:

> MĂRY, | are you CÓMing? |

or (d) It has a clause or long noun phrase (especially one with post-modification) as subject, *in which case* the subject generally has a separate tone unit:

> What we WÁNT | is plenty of RÀIN |

or (e) It contains clausal coordination (9.39 *ff*), *in which case* the elements of the coordinate structure may have separate tone units:

> He opened the DǑOR | and walked straight ÌN|

These rules provide some guide lines; but the important point is that no rigid generalization can be made about the division of discourse into information units, which are by their very nature variable stretches of language to be adjusted to the required degree of emphasis, complexity of grammatical units, speed of utterance, and other factors. For example, a sentence with a clausal object will generally have one tone unit so long as all the elements are relatively simple. But if the length of the sentence goes beyond a certain point (very roughly, ten words) it is difficult to avoid splitting the clause into two, or even more, information units:

> The man told us we could park it HÈRE|
> The man TÓLD us | we could park it at the RÀILway station |
> The man TÓLD us | we could PÁRK it | in the street over THÈRE|

14.3
End-focus and contrastive focus

As the clause is the unit of grammar that most closely corresponds to the tone unit, or unit of information, the best way to consider the positioning of the information focus is to relate it to clause structure, taking examples in which clause and tone unit correspond in extent. (For illustrative purposes, the clause is equated with the simple sentence – *cf* 7.1 *f*.)

The neutral position of focus is what we may call END-FOCUS, that is (generally speaking) chief prominence on the last open-class item or proper noun in the clause (App II.8, II.10, II.12):

> Dylan Thomas was born in SWÀNsea.

Special or contrastive focus, however, may be placed at earlier points, and so may fall on any of the non-final elements of the clause. For example:

Focus at S:

> [Who was born in Swansea?] Dylan THÒMAS was (born in Swansea)   [1]

Focus at V:

> [Dylan Thomas was married in Swansea, wasn't he?] NÒ, he was BÒRN in Swansea   [2]

Focus at O_d:

> [I hear you're painting the bathroom blue.] NÒ, I'm painting the LÌVING-room blue   [3]

Focus at A:

> [Have you ever driven a Cadillac?] YÈS, I've ÒFTEN driven one   [4]

Contrastive focus can also be signalled by placing the nucleus on an item subsequent to the one on which it would fall according to the rule of end-focus; for instance, on closed-class items like pronouns and prepositions:

> Who are you working FÒR? (not *with*)
> He was speaking to MÈ. (not to *you*)

Note

The principle that focus normally comes at the end of a tone unit explains why a parenthesis (which is normally bordered by tone-unit boundaries) can be used rhetorically to throw emphasis on a word immediately preceding it:

> And THÌS, | in SHÓRT, | is why I refÙSED.

14.4
Contrastive focus on words and syllables

The above examples show that whichever element is contrastive receives nuclear prominence on its last fully stressed syllable. Intonation can also focus more narrowly on a particular word of a phrase, rather than phrase of a clause:

> DÝLAN Thomas was born in 1914 (not *EDWARD Thomas*)
> We live in THÌS house (not *THAT one*)
> I put them ÒN the bed (not *UNDER it*)

or even on PART of a word, with a contrastive shift from normal word-stress:

> I'm afraid that BÙreaucracy can be worse than AÙtocracy.

Normally word-stress, and hence nuclear prominence, would fall on the second syllable: *au'tocracy* and *bu'reaucracy*.

Note

Noun compounds and phrases with 'compound' stress (App II.6) are exceptional in that end-focus does not fall on the last open-class word: *He's an insùrance agent*. But in accordance with 14.3, nuclear prominence can be transferred to the final noun for contrastive purposes: *He's an insurance àGent* (*not an insurance BRÓKer*).

14.5
Given and new information

Focus is related to the difference between GIVEN and NEW information; that is to say, between information already supplied by context (perhaps by a preceding part of the discourse) and information which has not been prepared for in this way. The focus, signalled by the nucleus, indicates where the new information lies. The rule is that *in any unit marked as new, the nucleus assumes (subject to stress rules) final position.*

This rule has been stated in a vague way intentionally, the whole point being that the 'unit' can be anything from a syllable to the whole clause. If the nucleus falls on the last stressed syllable of the clause (according to the end-focus principle), the new element could, for example, be the entire clause, or the last element (*eg* complement) of the clause, or the predication of the clause. In the following sentence, we mark the extent of the new information for three possible interpretations of the same sentence:

Whole clause is 'new':

NEW

[What's on today?] We're going to the RÀces. [5]

Predication is 'new':

NEW

[What are we doing today?] We're going to the RÀces. [6]

Final adverbial is 'new':

NEW

[Where are we going today?] We're going to the RÀces. [7]

Each of the three questions indicates how much is already assumed by speaker and audience before the reply is made. Example [5] is the true case of 'neutral information focus', where there are no specific prior assumptions at all.

When the nucleus is shifted to an earlier clause element, however, the same ambiguity does not arise: the only interpretation of the three is the contrastive one, in which the new element is a single phrase:

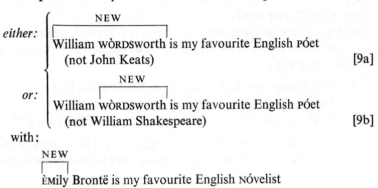

NEW

[Who's going to the races?] WÈ'RE going to the races.   [8]

14.6
Variation in the scope of new information
Some ambiguity may still be present when the nucleus occupies the terminal part of a complex non-final element. Compare:

either:
NEW
William WÒRDSworth is my favourite English PÓet
(not John Keats)   [9a]

or:
NEW
William WÒRDSworth is my favourite English PÓet
(not William Shakespeare)   [9b]

with:

NEW
ÈMily Brontë is my favourite English NÓvelist
(not Charlotte Brontë)   [10]

If the nucleus comes on a non-terminal word within the phrase, as in [10], the narrower scope of 'new' information is the only one possible; but if it comes on the final word, as in [9a] and [9b], either the whole phrase or only the final part of it may be 'new'. 'New', therefore, may be varied in scope right from a whole clause down to a single word, or even to a single syllable.

Note
[a] The subsidiary half of the complex fall-plus-rise nucleus (App II.15) represents 'semi-given' information: *eg: Pass me my CÒAT, JÉEVES* (where Jeeves is assumed to be present, although he has not been actually mentioned). Compare also *I went to FRÀNCE in nineteen-FÌFty* with *I went to FRÀNCE last WÉEK* (especially BrE) where 'last week' is not far from our minds, being recent history, and therefore need not bear the whole weight of new information. In AmE, *last week* in this sentence is likely to be treated as given information, and to receive no nuclear prominence at all:

  I went to FRÀNCE last week

[b] Pre-final focus is habitual in some colloquial sentences, where the assumed 'givenness' (or 'semi-givenness') of the final item is supplied not directly by the context, but by general cultural norms; *eg*

  The KÈTtle's boiling
  The MÌLKman called
  Is your FÁTHer at home? (*Contrast* Is your father OÚT?)

In a domestic context, the one thing to announce about kettles is that they are boiling, just as the milkman's activities are limited to calling, etc. The point, with all three examples, is that given the subject and given the situation, the predicate follows as a foregone conclusion.

[c] There may be more than one contrasted element in the same clause. In the following there are three:

> DÝLan Thomas was born in nineteen-fourTĚEN in SWÀNsea, but
> HŬGH Thomas was born in eighteen-eighty-THRĚE in ÀNGlesey.

14.7
Focus on the operator

One type of focus so far ignored is focus on the operator, which often has the particular function of signalling contrast between positive and negative meaning:

> [A: Why haven't you had a bath?]   B: I HÀVE had a bath.
> [A: Look for your shoes.]   B: I ÀM looking for them.
> [A: Surely he can't drive a bus?]   B: NÒ, but he CÀN drive a CAR.

When the operator is positive, the meaning is 'Yes in contrast to No'; when the operator is negative, the meaning is contrastive in the opposite direction:

> So you HÀVEn't lost it | after ÀLL! ('I thought you had')

It is not surprising that focus on the operator has this function, when we consider that the operator (in *yes-no* questions and in negatives) is the item most concerned in signalling the positive/negative polarity. Also, we may notice that the operator emphasizes positiveness or negativeness when it bears the focus (as it normally does) in elliptical replies:

> [A: Have you seen my books?]   B: No, I HÀVEn't.
> [A: Would you like black coffee?]   B: Yes, I WÒULD.
> [A: Does this bell work?]   B: Yes, it DÒES.

This last example leads us on to the most significant point about focus on the operator, which is that when the finite verb phrase is in the simple present or past tense, and so would not otherwise have an auxiliary verb to function as operator, the 'dummy' operator DO is introduced to bear the nuclear stress. This, then, is a further example of DO-periphrasis (3.17):

> So you DÌD go to the concert this evening? ('I thought you might, but ...')
> But I DÒ think you're a good cook. ('... even if you imagine I don't')

With a rise or fall-rise intonation, focus on past and future auxiliaries

often puts contrastive emphasis on the tense rather than on the positive/
negative polarity:

> He owns – or DĬD own – a Rolls RÒYCE
> We've sold OÙT, but we WĬLL be getting some

Similarly, the nucleus on auxiliaries such as *may* and *ought to* often
signals a contrast between the supposed real state of affairs, and a state
of affairs thought desirable or likely:

> The opinion polls MĂY be right ('but I suspect they're not')
> My purse OŬGHT to be HÈRE ('but it probably isn't')

Thus focus on the operator can indicate contrast of tense, aspect, or
modality, as well as contrast of positive and negative.

Note
A purely emotive emphasis achieved by focus on the operator is discussed below in
14.47.

Voice and reversibility
14.8
Voice, end-focus, and end-weight
Two factors already noted contribute to the presentation of the content
of a clause in one particular order rather than another. One is the tendency to place new information towards the end of the clause, and
another is the tendency to reserve the final position for the more complex
parts of a clause or sentence. The first of these we have called the principle
of end-focus (14.3), and the other may be called the principle of end-
weight. Since it is natural to express given information in few words
(*eg* by pronoun substitution), these principles work together, rather than
against one another. A third factor, which might be thought too obvious
to mention, is the limitation of possible clause structures to those outlined in 2.10 and 7.2, with their associated sets of participant roles
(7.13–22). These restrictions determine, for example, that an 'agentive'
role cannot be expressed by an object or complement, but only by the
subject, or by the agent of a passive clause. From this, one sees the
importance of the passive voice as a means of reversing the normal order
of 'agentive' and 'affected' elements, and thus of adjusting clause
structure to end-focus and end-weight:

> A: *Who* makes these chairs? B: They're made by *Ercol*.

The preference for terminal focus and terminal weight can even override an aversion to somewhat awkward passives (12.64) such as that in

> The regulations *were taken advantage of* by all the tramps and
> down-and-outs in the country

A complex clause as subject is also readily avoided by switching from the active to the passive voice:

> { *That he was prepared to go to such lengths* astounded me
> { I was astounded *that he was prepared to go to such lengths.*

Note
Turning from the clause to the sentence as a unit of discourse, we may be reminded (11.81–82) that the principle of end-weight applies just as much to the ordering of clauses within a sentence as to the ordering of elements within a clause. The principle of end-focus also has its analogue at sentence level in the principle of RESOLUTION (11.80).

14.9
Converses
Quite apart from the grammatical contrast between active and passive, the language possesses other grammatical or lexical means for reversing the order of roles:

> { An uncle, three cousins, and two brothers *benefited from*
> {   the will
> { The will *benefited* an uncle, three cousins, and two brothers
> { An unidentified blue liquid *was in* the bottle
> { The bottle *contained* an unidentified blue liquid
> { A red sports car was *behind* the bus
> { The bus was *in front of* a red sports car

The items or sequences in italics are converses; *ie* they express the same meaning, but with a reversal of the order of participants. The second sentence in each case is generally preferable, since the element with the 'definite' meaning, containing given information, would normally not take terminal focus.

Note
A special case of converseness is the relation of reciprocity expressed by certain terms such as *similar to, different from, near (to), far from, opposite, married to,* where reversing the order of the participants preserves the essential meaning without any other change in the construction:

> My house is opposite the hotel = The hotel is opposite my house

A more complex relation of converseness is illustrated by:

> { The dealer *sold* the car *to* my friend
> { My friend *bought* the car *from* the dealer.

Theme and inversion
14.10
Theme

The initial element of a clause (with the exception of initial adverbials discussed in 14.13 below) may be called its THEME. Apart from the last stressed element of clause structure (that which most naturally bears information focus), the theme is the most important part of a clause from the point of view of its presentation of a message in sequence. Again, for illustrative purposes, we use independent clauses which constitute simple sentences.

The expected or 'unmarked' theme of a main clause is

(1) Subject in a statement (7.53): *He* bought a new house
(2) Operator in a *yes-no* question (7.56): *Did* he buy a new house?
(3) *Wh*-element in a *wh*-question (7.63): *Which* house did he buy?
(4) Main verb in a command (7.72): *Buy* a new house

A scrutiny of this list will show that the theme is somehow an element semantically crucial to the clause; for example, in the case of the *yes-no* question, we have noticed above (14.7) the special role of the operator in signalling the positive/negative polarity. The theme may, indeed, be characterized as the communicative point of departure for the rest of the clause.

The two communicatively prominent elements of the clause, the theme and the focus, are typically as distinct as they can be: one is the point of initiation, and the other the point of completion. The theme of a clause, coming first, is more often given information than any other part of it. Yet the two can coincide; for instance, when the focus falls on the subject of a statement:

[Who gave you that magazine?] BÌLL gave it to me.

Thematic fronting or 'marked theme'
14.11

One may take as theme of a clause some element not usually assuming that function, and it is through this possibility that theme becomes a variable factor of some importance in the total sequential organization of the message. Elements placed at the front of a clause for thematic prominence vary in style and effect.

In informal speech, it is quite common for an element to be fronted with nuclear stress, and thus to be 'marked' (or given special emphasis) both thematically and informationally:

C_s as theme:

JÒE his NÁME is
An utter FÒOL I felt TÒO

C_o as theme:

> RelaxÀtion you call it!

O_d as theme:

> Really good còcktails they made at that hotÉl

It is as if the thematic element is the first thing that strikes the speaker, and the rest is added as an afterthought. The possible insertion of a comma suggests that the non-thematic part is almost an amplificatory tag (14.50) in status: *Joe, his name is.*

A second type of marked theme is found in rhetorical or heightened language, and helps to point a parallelism between two elements in the clause concerned and two related elements in some neighbouring clause of contrasting meaning:

Prepositional complement as theme:

> His fÀce I'm not fŏnd of

O_d as theme:

> but his chăracter I despìse

C_s as theme:

> Hìgginbottom I was bŏrn

C_o as theme:

> so Hĭgginbottom you might as well cÀll me

C_s as theme:

> rĪch I mày be (but that doesn't mean I'm happy)

Predication as theme:

> lĕave him I còuldn't (but at least I could make his life a misery)
> (I've promised to do it,) so 'do it I shÀll

A as theme (but see 14.13 below):

> wĪllingly he'll nèver do it (he'll have to be forced)

Such clauses often have double information focus, one nucleus coming on the theme, and the other on a later (most likely terminal) element of the clause.

14.12
One may thirdly distinguish examples characteristic of written English, and in which the marked theme seems to have the negative function of

arranging clause order so that end-focus falls on the most important
part of the message:

> *Most of these problems* a computer could take in its stride   [11]
>
> *This latter topic* we have examined in Chapter 3, and need
>   not reconsider   [12]
>
> *To this list* may be added ten further items of importance   [13]

The definite items *this* and *these* in [11] to [13] suggest that the marked
theme in such cases most often expresses given information.

Note

[a] A fronted thematic element, like a fronted pushdown *wh*-element (7.66), is sometimes an element from a subordinate clause:

> *Everything – or nearly everything – that the Labour movement exists to stop the
> Tories from doing* Labour will be asked to support the Cabinet in doing.

The whole of the italicized part of this extract (from *The Times*, 11 March 1968)
is the object of a non-finite clause acting as a prepositional object within an infinitival clause within the main clause.

[b] Exceptionally, a theme may be a part rather than the whole of a clause element.
Yes-no questions, for instance, (as we have seen in 14.10) have part of the verb
phrase only as their thematic component. In the following case, a prepositional
phrase equivalent to a postmodifier of the subject complement (but see 13.33)
acts as theme: *Of all the early examples of science fiction, the fantastic stories
of Jules Verne are the most remarkable.*

[c] Sentences containing direct speech quotations seem to provide an example of a
construction in which thematic fronting of the direct object is exceptionally easy
(see 14.15):

> I said: 'That's a pity' ~ 'That's a pity,' I said

But one may propose an alternative analysis, in which the reporting subject and
verb (here *I said*) constitute a dependent comment clause (11.65–66) rather than
the subject and verb of the sentence. This analysis is urged by the possibility of
placing them in the middle of the direct speech, as a parenthesis: 'That,' I said,
'is a pity.'

14.13
Theme with initial adverbials

It is not clear, on first consideration, whether the notion of 'marked
theme' should be extended to include initial adverbials. Some adverbials
(mainly disjuncts and conjuncts) appear characteristically in initial
position, and so should be considered 'unmarked themes' if they are to
be accorded thematic status at all. However, this would mean over-
ruling the unmarked status of other elements (*eg* initial subject in statements) or alternatively acknowledging the possibility of two coexisting
thematic elements in the same clause. That more than one adverbial can
occur initially is a further demonstration that regarding initial adverbials
as thematic is incompatible with a unitary concept of theme: *Often in
summer we would go boating . . .*

On the other hand, initial adverbials may enter into the type of rhetorical parallelism illustrated in 14.11 above:

In LÒNdon I was BÓRN, and in LŌNdon I'll DÌE

And there are certain adjuncts (especially place adjuncts) bound to the post-verbal position closely enough to behave, with respect to thematic fronting, more like complements or objects than like disjuncts or conjuncts. The 'complementary' status of these adjuncts is shown by their association with subject-verb inversion when the subject is a noun phrase heavier than a pronoun (see 14.15):

Into the thick of the smoke we plunged (A S V)
Into the thick of the smoke plunged the intrepid cavalry (A V S)

The conclusion of this argument is, therefore, that certain adjuncts, especially those which would otherwise immediately follow an intransitive or intensive verb, may be treated as 'marked theme' when placed initially; but that otherwise, initial adverbials are disregarded in considering what is the theme of a clause. For adjustment of end-focus (14.3), on the other hand, the initial placing of adverbials is important.

Inversion
14.14
The thematic fronting of an element is often associated with inversion, of which we distinguish two types, consisting respectively in the reversal of SUBJECT and VERB, and the reversal of SUBJECT and OPERATOR.

Note
Since the verb BE in intensive clauses can be simultaneously regarded as verb and operator, we have a choice of classifying its placement before the subject as an instance either of subject-verb or subject-operator inversion. As the lists in 14.15 and 14.16 show, the decision is made according to whether BE, in the given construction, is commutable with another main verb or with another operator.

14.15
Subject-verb inversion
(See also 8.52)

Here's the milkman (A V S)	[14a]
Here comes the bus (A V S)	[14b]
There are our friends (A V S)	[15a]
There, at the summit, stood the castle in its medieval splendour (A A V S A)	[15b]
Away went the car like a whirlwind (A V S A)	[16a]
In went the sun and down came the rain (A V S, A V S)	[16b]
Slowly out of its hangar rolled the gigantic aircraft (A A V S)	[17]
Equally inexplicable was his behaviour towards his son (C V S)	[18]

So say the rest of us (O V S)   [19]

'Go away!' said one child; 'And don't come back!' growled
    another. (... V S, ... V S)   [20]

As examples [14–18] suggest, this type of inversion is mainly found in
clauses of Types *SVA* and *SVC* where a normally post-verbal element
is so tied to the verb that when that element is 'marked' theme the
verb is 'attracted' into pre-subject position. Examples [19] and [20]
illustrate a different type of inversion, with verbs of saying. Some of the
types, those of [14–16], are well established in informal English; others,
such as [17], are more dramatic or literary in tone. The inversions shown
in [14–17] are virtually limited to simple present and past tense verbs
(contrast ¹*There stood our friend* with *¹*There was standing our friend*),
and to certain stative verbs of position (*be, stand, lie,* etc) or dynamic
verbs of motion (*come, go, fall,* etc).

    Subject-verb inversion does not take place in a clause with a personal
pronoun alone as subject; hence corresponding to [14a], [15a], [16a],
etc we have *Here he is, There they are, Away it went,* rather than **Here
is he,* etc.

Note

[a] Adverbial *there* is marked with stress in [15a] as elsewhere, and so is distinguished
from the unstressed existential *there* (14.24 *ff*), which can also appear in pre-
verbal position.

[b] Inversion in a clause reporting direct speech, as in [20], is discussed in 11.73 and
in 14.12 Note *c.*

[c] There is inversion with a pronoun subject followed by postmodification in
archaic English: *Happy is he who is reconciled with his lot.*

14.16
Subject-operator inversion

So absurd was his manner that everyone stared at him
    (11.63 Note *b*)   [21]

Far be it from me to condemn him (7.86)   [22]

Not a finger did I lay on him   [23]

Under no circumstances must the switch be left on $\Big\}$(7.46)   [24]

Hardly had I left before the quarrelling started   [25]

Only by this means is it possible to explain his $\Big\}$(7.48)

    failure to act decisively   [26]

So are we all. So have I. So did the others (10.54 *ff*)   [27]

Often had I intended to speak of it (formal)   [28]

Well do I remember the day when it happened (formal)   [29]

Throwing the hammer is champion William Anderson, who,
    when he's not winning trophies, is a hard-working
    shepherd in the Highlands of Scotland.   [30]

Inversion in examples [21–26] has already been discussed in the sections specified. In [27], *so* as a predication-substitute induces subject-operator inversion, whereas *so* as an object-substitute (10.62) is followed by subject-verb inversion, as we have seen:

    So say the rest of us   [19]

As before, a pronoun as subject following *so* may restore the normal statement order: *So he has, So you say*. But subject-operator inversion may persist, even with a pronoun subject, when focus is required on the pronoun. Hence there is a contrast between:

    You asked me to leave, and ǀso I DÌD ('and I DÌD so, TÒO')
    My friends enjoyed it, and ǀso did ì ('and ì did so, TÒO')

The inversions of [28] and [29] are decidedly literary in tone, and unlike the preceding examples, are optional. Normal subject-operator order, with a medial placing of the adverb, would usually be preferred. Example [30] is a journalistic type of inversion, in which the predication is fronted in order to bring end-focus on a complex subject. The ordering is doubly irregular, predication preceding operator as well as operator preceding subject.

Note
The subject-operator inversions in questions (*Didn't you know? Where has it gone?*) are associated with unmarked theme (14.10), and so are marginal to the present discussion.

14.17
Theme in subordinate clauses
In subordinate clauses, the usual thematic elements are subordinators, *wh*-elements, and the relative pronoun *that*. Special frontings of other elements as theme occur only in idiomatic or literary constructions of minor importance:

$$
\left. \begin{array}{l} \text{Were he alive} \ldots \\ \text{Had I known} \ldots \\ \text{Should you change your plan} \ldots \end{array} \right\} (11.32) \qquad [31]
$$

$$
\left. \begin{array}{l} \text{Keen though I am} \ldots \\ \text{Criticize him as one might} \ldots \\ \text{Genius that he was} \ldots \end{array} \right\} (11.34) \qquad [32]
$$

$$
\left. \begin{array}{l} \text{Do what one may} \ldots \\ \text{Say what you will of him} \ldots \end{array} \right\} (11.36 \text{ Note } b) \qquad [33]
$$

Examples [31] are conditional clauses, and examples [32] and [33] are conditional-concessive clauses. As these minor clause types have already been noted under their appropriate headings in Chapter 11, no further discussion of them is necessary here.

Cleft and pseudo-cleft sentences
14.18
Cleft sentences

A special construction which gives both thematic and focal prominence to a particular element of the clause is the cleft sentence, so called because it divides a single clause into two separate sections, each with its own verb.

Most cleft sentence statements begin with the empty pronoun *it* followed by the verb BE, which in turn is followed by the element on which the focus falls. From a single clause such as *John wore his best suit to the dance last night*, it is possible to derive four cleft sentences, each highlighting a particular element of the clause:

S as focus:

It was JÒHN $\begin{Bmatrix} \text{who} \\ \text{that} \end{Bmatrix}$ wore his best suit to the DÁNCE last night   [34]

O_d as focus:

It was his best sÙIT (that) John wore to the DÁNCE last night   [35]

A_{time} as focus:

It was last NÌGHT (that) John wore his best suit to the DÁNCE   [36]

A_{place} as focus:

$\begin{cases} \text{It was to the DÀNCE that John wore his best sÚIT last night} \\ \text{(formal)} \\ \text{It was the DÀNCE (that) John wore his best sÚIT to last night} \\ \text{(informal)} \end{cases}$

Other kinds of adverbial might also be focus of a cleft sentence (see Chapter 8).

The usefulness of the cleft sentence partly resides in its unambiguous marking of the focus of information in written English, where the clue of intonation is absent. The highlighted element has the full implication of contrastive focus: the rest of the clause is taken as given, and a contrast is inferred with other items which might have filled the focal or 'hinge' position in the sentence. Thus to each of the above, one could add an implied negative, *eg*

It wasn't Jim, but John, $\begin{Bmatrix} \text{who} \\ \text{that} \end{Bmatrix}$ ...   [34a]

It wasn't his night-shirt, but his best suit (that) ...   [35a]

Apart from S, O_d, and A, the two less common clause elements O_i and C_o can marginally act as the focal element of a cleft sentence:

O_i as focus:

> It's *me* (that) he gave the book
> (but *It's me he gave the book to*, with focus on *me* as prepositional complement, is more likely.)

C_o as focus:

> It's *dark green* that we've painted the kitchen

But there are severe restrictions, in Standard English, on the use of C_s in this function, especially with the verb BE following:

> ?*It's a genius that he is. ?It's a lecturer that I am now.   [37]

And V does not occur at all as focus, just as it does not occur as a Q-element (2.18):

> *It's wore that John his best suit to the dance   [38]

One can circumvent the restriction on V as focus by rendering the verb in a non-finite form, either as an infinitive or as a participle:

> It's teach(ing) that he does for a living   [39]

In this case the substitute verb DO comes into use.

Example [37] can be contrasted with the perfectly acceptable

> It's he/him that is a genius   [37a]

Note

[a] In the terms 'cleft sentence' and 'existential sentence' (see 14.24 *ff*), we follow established practice in using the term 'sentence' rather than 'clause', although in fact these structures belong to the clause rather than to the sentence, as we see from their occurrence in dependent clauses (14.20, 14.25 Note *c*). But as almost all our examples are of simple sentences, no practical difficulties arise with this terminology.

[b] *That* or *those* sometimes occurs, instead of *it*, as subject of a cleft sentence:

> That was a fire bomb they let off last night
> Those are my feet that you're stepping on.

[c] The focal element, if a pronoun, can take either the subjective or objective case (4.107). Thus *he* and *him* are alternatives in [37a], *him* being informal.

The 'relative clause' in cleft sentences
14.19

The introductory part of a cleft sentence is largely restricted to *It is, It's,* or *It was;* other forms of BE, such as *It might be,* are less usual:

> It *must have been* his brother that you saw
> It *might be* his father that you're thinking of

The final part of the clause, after the focal element, is obviously close in structure to a restrictive relative clause; and yet (as we shall see below) there are considerable differences. Examples above show that pronouns used in relative clauses (*who, that*, 'zero' pronoun) are also used to introduce cleft sentences. Also reminiscent of the relative clause is the fronting of the pronoun; moreover, as in relative clauses, the pronoun can be fronted from a position in a prepositional phrase, or from a pushdown (7.66) position in a nominal clause as object:

It's *the girl* that I was complaining about (not the boy)
It's *next week's match* that he's hoping to attend (not this week's)
It's *this watch* I said I would let you have (not that)

There are differences, however, in the use of relative pronouns, in that the *wh*-forms are rare in comparison with *that* and zero. Although *whose* is allowed in cleft sentences (*It's Uncle Bill whose address I lost*), *whom* and *which* are only marginally possible, and it is virtually impossible to use *whom* or *which* preceded by a preposition. Thus

It was the dog to which I gave the water

has to be read as a sentence containing a straightforward postmodifying relative clause (compare *She was the woman to whom I gave the water*) rather than as a cleft sentence. Characteristic intonation is also different:

It was the DòG I gave the wÁTer to (cleft sentence)
$\begin{Bmatrix} \text{It} \\ \text{That} \end{Bmatrix}$ was the dog I gave the wÀTer to (SVC sentence with
relative clause)

Note
The focusing function of the cleft sentence may be compared with that of the additive and restrictive adverbs *too, only*, etc (8.13 *ff*).

14.20
A further difference between the postmodifying relative clause and the clause following the focused element in cleft sentences is the ability of the latter to have as its antecedent (*ie* the focused element) not only a nominal element, but an adjunct:

It was *because he was ill* (that) we decided to return
It was *in September* (that) I first noticed it

Indeed, such a construction, where there is no noun phrase antecedent, makes the use of the term 'pronoun' for the linking word *that* misleading; and it is notable that a *wh*-pronoun cannot be used in cleft sentences where the focus element is an adjunct, and where consequently it does not have a strict 'pronominal' status:

*It was because he was ill which we decided to return

The cleft sentence structure can be used in questions, exclamations, and subordinate clauses:

> Was it for this that we suffered and toiled?
> Who was it who interviewed you?
> What a glorious bonfire it was you made!
> He told me that it was because he was ill that they decided to return.

Note

[a] Another contrast between relative clauses and 'cleaving' clauses lies in the possibility, in familiar English, of omitting *that* as subject in a cleft sentence, but not as subject of a relative clause:

> It was the President himself *spoke to me.*

[b] And yet another contrast is that cleft sentences may have a proper noun as a focus element, whereas restrictive relative clauses cannot have a proper noun as an antecedent. Thus *It's Chelsea he lives in* is unambiguously a cleft sentence.

Pseudo-cleft sentences
14.21

The pseudo-cleft sentence is another construction which, like the cleft sentence proper, makes explicit the division between given and new parts of the communication. It is an *SVC* sentence with a *wh*-relative nominal clause as subject or complement, and so differs from the cleft sentences in being completely accountable in terms of the categories of main clause and subordinate clause discussed in Chapter 11. The following are virtually synonymous:

> {It's a good rest that you need most
> {A good rest is what you need most

The pseudo-cleft sentence occurs more often, however, in an inverted form, with the *wh*-clause as subject:

> *What you need most* is a good rest

And it is less restricted than the cleft sentence in that through use of the substitute verb DO, it permits marked focus to fall on the verb or predication:

What he's done is (to) spoil the whole thing	[40]
What John did to his suit was (to) ruin it	[41]
What I'm going to do to him is (to) teach him a lesson	[42]

The complement or 'focus' of these sentences is normally in the form of an infinitival clause (with or without *to*). When the verb in the *wh*-clause has progressive aspect, however, the complement matches it with an *-ing* clause:

What I'*m doing* is *teaching him a lesson*	[42a]

Occasionally, this matching of the two verbs is extended to verbs in the perfect aspect, which can have as their focal counterpart an *-ed* clause:

What he*'s done* is *spoilt the whole thing*.   [40a]

14.22
In other respects, the pseudo-cleft sentence is more limited than the cleft sentence. Only with *what*-clauses does it freely commute with the cleft sentence construction. Clauses with *who*, *where*, and *when* are sometimes acceptable, but mainly only when the *wh*-clause is subject complement:

The police chief was *who I meant*
Here is *where the accident took place*
(In) Autumn is *when the countryside is most beautiful*

But *whose*, *why*, and *how*, for example, do not easily enter into the pseudo-cleft sentence construction:

*With a Scottish accent is how he talked
?*Why we decided to return was because he was ill

In many cases, too, a clause beginning *the person who* or *the one who* is a more acceptable alternative to a *who*-clause:

⎧It must have been the manager who spoke to you
⎨
⎩The person/one who spoke to you must have been the manager.

14.23
Sentences of the pattern *She's a pleasure to teach*
Before leaving the subject of theme, we must examine a construction which gives the emphasis of initial thematic position in the main clause to the object or prepositional object of a nominal clause. The item so fronted replaces anticipatory *it* as subject of the main clause (on the anticipatory *it* construction with extraposition, see 14.35–38):

It's a pleasure to teach her → She's a pleasure to teach
It's impossible to deal with him → He's impossible to deal with
It's easy/difficult to beat them → They're easy/difficult to beat
It's fun for us to be with Margaret → Margaret is fun for us to be with

There is a similar construction for *be sure* and *be certain*, *seem* and *appear*, *be said*, *be known*, etc, except that in these cases the corresponding construction with anticipatory *it* requires a *that*-clause, not a *to*-infinitive clause, and except that it is now the subject of the nominal clause that is fronted:

It's certain that we'll forget the address
→We're certain to forget the address

It seems that you've made a mistake
  →You seem to have made a mistake
It is known that he's a coward
  →He's known to be a coward

This thematic fronting does not apply to all constructions of the same kind. For instance, from *It's odd to lose them*, we cannot arrive at: *They are odd to lose*. See further 12.38 *ff*.

Existential sentences
14.24
Existential sentences are principally those beginning with the unstressed word *there*, and are so called because when unstressed *there* is followed by a form of the verb BE, the clause expresses the notion of existence:

> There is nothing more healthy than a cold shower
>   ('Nothing more healthy exists than a cold shower')

Note
On the use of the term 'sentence' in the expression 'existential sentence', see 14.18 Note *a*.

14.25
Transformational relation to basic clause patterns
There is a regular transformational relation of equivalence between existential clauses with *there* + BE and clauses of the standard clause types outlined in 7.2. The equivalence only applies, however, if the clause of the normal pattern

(1) has an indefinite subject; and
(2) has a form of the verb BE in its verb phrase.

Allowing for these two requirements, we may derive existential clauses from the regular clause types by means of a general rule:

subject + (auxiliaries) + BE + predication→*there* + (auxiliaries) + BE + subject + predication

The subject of the original clause may be called the 'notional' subject of the *there*-sentence, so as to distinguish it from *there* itself, which for most purposes is the 'grammatical' subject (see 14.26 below). Examples of the seven clause types (7.2) are:

Type *SVC*

  Something must be wrong → There must be something wrong

Type *SVA*

Was anyone around? → Was there anyone around?

Type *SV*

No one was waiting → There was no one waiting

Type *SVO*

Plenty of people are getting promotion → There are plenty of people getting promotion

Type *SVOC*

Two bulldozers have been knocking the place flat → There have been two bulldozers knocking the place flat

Type *SVOA*

A girl is putting the kettle on → There's a girl putting the kettle on

Type *SVOO*

Something is causing her distress → There's something causing her distress

Passive versions of the transformation are also to be noted:

Type SV_{pass}

A whole box has been stolen → There has been a whole box stolen

Type $SV_{pass}C$

No shops will be left open → There'll be no shops left open

Note

[a] The rule that existential sentences should have an indefinite noun phrase as 'notional subject' prevents the derivation of sentences like *There's the money in the box* from *The money is in the box*. This limitation can be waived, however, in answers to existential questions (actual or implied):

A: Is there anyone coming to dinner?
B: Yes, there's Harry and there's also Mrs Jones

Also acceptable is the indefinite exclamatory *the* followed by the superlative in:

There's the oddest-looking man standing at the front door!

[b] One may perhaps include under 'indefinite noun phrases' those phrases containing the 'universal' terms *all* or *every;* such noun phrases are not so easily made 'notional subjects' of existential clauses, however, as are other types of indefinite expression. They act as such mostly in answers to existential questions:

A: What is there to be afraid of?
B: There's everything to be afraid of!

[c] Existential *there* occurs widely in dependent clauses:

> Let me know if there's anyone waiting

It is also fronted as subject in a type of sentence discussed in 14.23:

> There appears to be something wrong with the engine

In such sentences the semi-auxiliary verb (3.8) often agrees with the notional subject in number:

$$\text{There} \begin{bmatrix} \text{happens} \\ \text{happen} \end{bmatrix} \text{to be} \begin{bmatrix} \text{only one apple} \\ \text{only two apples} \end{bmatrix} \text{left.}$$

14.26
Existential *there* as subject

The *there* of existential sentences differs from *there* as an introductory adverb both in lacking stress, and in behaving in most ways like the subject of the clause:

(a) It often determines concord, governing a singular form of the verb (see 7.23 Note *a*) even when the following 'notional subject' is plural:

> *There's* some people in the waiting room (informal)

occurs alongside:

> *There are* some people in the waiting room

(b) It can act as subject in *yes-no* and tag questions:

> *Is there* any more soup?
> There's nothing wrong, *is there?*

(c) It can act as subject in *to*+infinitive and *-ing* clauses:

> I don't want *there to be any misunderstanding*
> He was disappointed at *there being so little to do.*

14.27
Existential *there* as 'empty' theme

In the foregoing cases, one may see a common function for the existential *there*, which is as a device for leaving the subject position (which is also generally the theme position) vacant of content; *there*, that is, may be regarded as an empty 'slot-filler'. The point of this device becomes clearer when it is recalled that the initial element or theme of a clause typically contains given information, and is the point of departure for the introduction of new information later in the clause. However, when the subject of a sentence is an indefinite noun phrase, this means that, contrary to general practice, the subject introduces new information, an indefinite expression being by definition a reference to something that has not been previously mentioned or specified. Hence in sentences like *Plenty of us are going* or *Some books are in the cupboard*, there is sensed a certain awkwardness, which may be avoided by the introduction of *there*, and the consequent postponement of the 'notional subject' to a later, non-thematic position.

14.28
'Bare existential' sentences
Apart from sentences related to basic clause types in the manner described in 14.25, we have to consider various other types of sentence introduced by existential *there*. Among them is the 'bare existential' sentence, which simply postulates the existence of some entity or entities. It has a simple clause structure *there* + BE + indefinite noun phrase:

Undoubtedly, there is a God ('God exists')
There have always been wars ('Wars have always existed/taken place')

Note
Other sentences superficially like these are better explained as cases of the kind of existential sentence derived from basic clause types (14.25), in which one of the elements is omitted as understood. For example, the sentence *There'll be trouble*, occurring on its own, implies a definite context: 'There'll be trouble at the match/at the party,' etc.

14.29
Existential sentences with relative and infinitive clauses
A more important additional type of existential sentence is that which consists of *there* + BE + noun phrase + relative clause. Such sentences can be related to sentences of orthodox clause types without the two restrictions mentioned in 14.25: the verb need not be a form of the verb BE, and although there must be an indefinite element, it need not be subject:

Something keeps upsetting him
→ There's something (that) keeps upsetting him   [43]
I'd like you to meet some people
→ There's some people (that) I'd like you to meet   [44]

It is interesting that the relative pronoun *that* in [43] can be omitted even when it is subject of the relative clause; something not permissible according to the normal rule for relative clause formation:

{ There's a man lives in China
{ *I know a man lives in China (see 13.8 Note)

This omissibility is a sign of the special status within the main clause of the relative clause here, as in cleft sentences (14.20 Note *a*).

One may also mention a common existential sentence pattern *there* + BE + noun phrase + *to*-infinitive clause, which is problematic to the extent that it cannot be directly related to the basic clause types of 7.2:

> There was no one for us to talk to
> There's (always) plenty of housework to do

Such infinitive clauses are allied to relative clauses (*cf* 13.20), as we see on comparing

> At last there was something to write home about

with the (stiffly formal) relative clause construction

> At last there was something about which to write home

This type of existential sentence sometimes has a definite noun phrase as notional subject:

> There's the man next door to consider.

Note
Also there is a restricted idiomatic construction consisting of *there* + BE + negative + participial -*ing* clause:

> There's no telling what he'll do
> There isn't any getting away from it

On the peculiarities of this construction, see 11.24 Note *b*.

14.30
Existential sentences with verbs other than *be*
We have finally to consider a less common, more literary type of existential clause in which *there* is followed by a verb other than BE:

> There rose in his imagination gross visions of a world empire
> There exist a number of similar medieval crosses in different parts
>   of the country
> There may come a time when the Western Nations will be less
>   fortunate
> Not long after this, there occurred a sudden revolution in public
>   taste

This construction, which may be accounted for by a simple rule $S + V \rightarrow there + V + S$ (where S is indefinite), is equivalent in effect and style to subject-verb inversion after an initial adverbial. One may notice that the *there* can be freely omitted in sentences of the structure $A_{place} + there + V + S$:

> In front of the carriage (there) rode two men in magnificent
>   uniforms

There in this construction may in fact be regarded as a 'dummy element', which, placed before the subject and verb, provides the necessary condition for inversion to take place; if an initial locative adverbial is also present, of course such a condition already obtains, and so there is nothing to prevent the omission of *there*. Grammatically, *there* is a subject, as we see from the inversion that takes place when the statement pattern is turned into a question: *Will there come a time...?* The notional subject of the sentence, again, usually has indefinite meaning, and the verb is selected from verbs of existence, position and movement (*lie, stand, come,* etc).

The construction is also found with passive verb phrases:

On the following day, *there was held* a splendid banquet.

Existential sentences with *have*
14.31
Corresponding to the type of existential sentence originally discussed in 14.25 (*there*+BE+S+predication) there is a type in which the thematic position is not 'empty', but is filled by a noun phrase subject preceding the verb HAVE (or especially in BrE, HAVE GOT):

The porter had a taxi ready
    (*cf: There was a taxi ready; A taxi was ready* – Type *SVC*)   [45]

He has several friends in China
    (*cf: There are several friends (of his) in China; Several friends*
    (*of his) are in China* – Type *SVA*)   [46]

I have two buttons missing (on my jacket)
    (*cf: There are two buttons missing . . ., Two buttons are*
    missing . . . – Type *SV*)   [47]

They had a few supporters helping them
    (*cf: There were a few supporters helping them; A few supporters*
    were helping them – Type *SVO*)   [48]

As before, these clauses can be related to (and imply) simple clauses of the basic clause types; [45] implies *A taxi was ready,* etc. But an extra participant is introduced as theme: the subject of the verb HAVE. This refers to a person, thing, etc indirectly involved in the existential proposition. Often the subject's role is that of 'recipient' (7.14, 7.16); but the nature of the 'recipient's' involvement in the sentence can be very vague, and the more specific meanings of HAVE (*eg* possession) are not necessarily implied. A sentence such as *My friend had his watch stolen,* in fact, indicates not possession, but lack of possession.

The relation of the subject to the rest of the clause can often be expressed by other means, *eg* by a genitive:

He has a brother in the navy
(= *There is a brother of his in the navy; A brother of his is in the navy*)

Note

[a] With a passive basic clause type, the verb generally has dynamic rather than stative (perfective) meaning: *My friend had his watch stolen* relates to *His watch was stolen* in the sense of 'Someone stole his watch' rather than of 'Someone had stolen his watch'.

[b] In a further use of this construction (especially, but not necessarily, with the passive) the subject of HAVE gives up its 'recipient' role for one of indirect agency: *He had all his enemies imprisoned* is most likely to mean 'He caused all his enemies to be imprisoned'.

14.32

Unlike the *there*-existential clause, the HAVE-existential clause can have a 'notional subject' with definite meaning:

He has his eldest son in boarding school
The car had its roof damaged
(contrast *There was its roof damaged)

A further aspect of this construction not paralleled by the *there* construction is that sentences with an underlying clause structure S V A often have a pronoun prepositional complement which refers back to the subject of HAVE:

He had his wife working for *him*
The trees had loads of apples on *them*
(*cf* There were loads of apples on the trees.)

14.33

Have-existential sentences with relative and
infinitive clauses

Corresponding to *there*-sentences of the same character (14.29), the following illustrate HAVE-sentences containing relative and infinitive clauses:

I've something I've been meaning to say to you   [49]
He has a great deal to be thankful for   [50]

The infinitival clause cannot have a subject introduced by *for* in this construction, as the semantic function of the subject has already been appropriated by the subject of HAVE: [50] above is synonymous with *There's a great deal for him to be thankful for.*

14.34
Clauses introduced by *with* and *without*

Equivalent in construction to HAVE-existential clauses are the non-finite or verbless postmodifying clauses introduced by *with* (or in the negative by *without*) (6.46):

> a man *with a tall hat on* ('. . . who has/had a tall hat on')
> the table *with one leg shorter than the others*
> a job *with plenty to do*

The corresponding adverbial clause has been discussed in 11.50:

> *Without a gardener to keep it tidy throughout the year*, the garden soon deteriorated.

Postponement
14.35
Extraposition

After dealing with the shifting of elements to initial position in 14.11–23, we now consider devices which have the opposite effect of removing an element from its normal position, and placing it towards or at the rear of the sentence. These devices of postponement serve the two principles of end-focus (14.3) and end-weight (14.8).

We reserve the term EXTRAPOSITION for postponement which involves the replacement of the postponed element by a substitute form. Extraposition operates almost exclusively on subordinate nominal clauses.

14.36
Extraposition of a clausal subject

The most important type of extraposition is the extraposition of a clausal subject. The clausal subject is placed at the end of the sentence, and the nominal subject position is filled by the anticipatory pronoun *it*. The resulting sentence thus contains two subjects, which we may identify as the POSTPONED SUBJECT (the clause which is notionally the subject of the sentence) and the ANTICIPATORY SUBJECT (*it*). A simple rule for deriving a sentence with subject extraposition from one of more orthodox ordering is:

> subject + predicate → *it* + predicate + subject

But it is worth emphasizing that for clausal subjects, the postponed position is more usual than the orthodox position before the verb. Examples are:

Type *SVC:*   It's a pity *to make a fool of yourself*
               (*cf: To make a fool of yourself is a pity*)
Type *SVA:*   It's on the cards *that income tax will be abolished*
Type *SV:*   It doesn't matter *what you do*
Type *SVO:*   It surprised me *to hear him say that*
Type *SVOC:*   It makes her happy *to see others enjoying themselves*
Type *SV*~pass~*:* It is said *that she slipped arsenic into his tea*
Type *SV*~pass~*C:* It was considered impossible *for anyone to escape*

14.37
Extraposition of participle and other clauses

The extraposed clause may be any kind of nominal clause, except a nominal relative clause (for example, *Whoever said that was wrong* cannot be rendered **It was wrong whoever said that*). Extraposition of a participial clause is possible:

It was easy *getting the equipment loaded*
    (*cf* Getting the equipment loaded was easy)

but is not very common outside informal speech. Familiar informal examples are:

It's no use *telling him that*
It wouldn't be any good *trying to catch the bus*

However, the participial clause often shows itself incompletely adapted to the extraposition construction, by being incapable of bearing the main information focus. Rather than

It's fun being a HÒSTESS

we hear

It's FÙN being a HÓSTESS

with main focus on the final element of the predicate. (And we might even punctuate *It's fun, being a hostess.*) It might be concluded from this that the participial clause has just as much affinity with a noun phrase tag (14.50; as in *He's a friend of mine, that man*) as with a genuine extraposed subject.

Note

[a] For certain constructions which have all the appearance of clausal extraposition (*It seems/appears/happened/chanced*/etc), the corresponding non-extraposed version does not occur. For example, there is no sentence **That everything is fine seems* to correspond with *It seems that everything is fine.* In such cases, we may say that

the extraposition is obligatory. Other characteristics of the verbs entering into this category are presented in 14.23.

[b] Clauses with extraposed subject must be distinguished from superficially similar clauses in which *it* is a personal pronoun or empty 'prop' subject: *It's good to eat* (ie 'This fish etc is good to eat'); *It's lovely weather to go fishing.*

[c] *If-* and *when-*clauses behave very much like extraposed subjects in sentences like:

> It would be a pity if we missed the show
>> (*cf* It is a pity that we missed the show)
> It'll be a great day when you win the sweepstake

It is doubtful in both cases, however, whether the clause could act as subject, although it could act as initial adverbial clause: *If we missed the show, it would be a pity.* On balance, therefore, these appear to be adverbials rather than extraposed subjects.

[d] Another marginal case is the 'phrasal extraposition' of *It's two hundred miles from Boston to New York*, where the compound prepositional phrase, if fronted, could act either as subject or as adverbial: *From Boston to New York (it) is two hundred miles. Cf* also: *It's Wednesday today ↔ Today (it) is Wednesday* (7.17).

14.38
Extraposition of a clausal object
In *SVOC* and *SVOA* clause types, nominal clauses can undergo extraposition from the position of object:

$$SVOC \begin{cases} \text{You must find } \textit{it} \text{ exciting } \textit{working here} \\ \quad (\textit{cf} \text{ You must find working here exciting; Working here} \\ \quad \quad \text{is exciting)} \\ \text{I made } \textit{it} \text{ my business } \textit{to settle the matter} \end{cases}$$

$$SVOA \begin{cases} \text{I owe } \textit{it} \text{ to you } \textit{that the jury acquitted me} \\ \quad (\textit{cf} \text{ I owe my acquittal to you)} \\ \text{Something put } \textit{it} \text{ into his head } \textit{that she was a spy.} \end{cases}$$

14.39
Postponement of object in *SVOC* and *SVOA* clauses
When the object is a long and complex phrase, final placement for end-focus or end-weight is possible in *SVOC* and *SVOA* clause-types. This time there is no substitution of *it:*

[A] Shift from S V O_d C_o order to S V C_o O_d order (see 7.2 Note *b*):

> They pronounced guilty every one of the accused except the man who had raised the alarm.

[B] Shift from S V O_d A to S V A O_d:

> I confessed to him the difficulties I had found myself in.
> We heard from his own lips the story of how he had been stranded for days without food.

14.40

Order of direct objects, indirect objects, and prepositional adverbs

There is a freer interchange, where there are no pronouns involved, between the two orderings

(a) $O_i + O_d \leftrightarrow O_d +$ prepositional phrase (7.6)
(b) particle $+ O_d \leftrightarrow O_d +$ particle (12.19 *ff*)

The choice between the two is generally determined by the principles of end-focus and end-weight:

(a) { The twins told mother all their sὲcrets
{ The twins told all their secrets to mὸther

(b) { He gave all his heirlooms awὰy
{ He gave away all his hὲirlooms.

14.41

Discontinuous noun phrases

Sometimes only part of an element is postponed. The most commonly affected element is the postmodification of a noun phrase. As elsewhere, the units most readily postponed are nominal (in this case appositive) clauses:

A rumour circulated *that he was secretly engaged to the Marchioness*
   (*cf* A rumour that . . . circulated)
The problem arose (of) *what contribution the public should pay*
   (*cf* The problem (of) . . . arose)

However, other postmodifying clauses, and even phrases, can be so postponed:

The time had come *to decorate the house for Christmas*
That loaf was stale *that you sold me*
A steering committee has been formed, *consisting of Messrs Smith, Brown and Robinson*

The postponement results in a discontinuous noun phrase (13.74) which is italicized in the examples. The noun phrase can be a complement or object, as well as subject:

What business is it *of yours?* (*cf* What business of yours is it?)
We heard *the story* from his own lips *of how he was stranded for days without food*

Discontinuity often results, too, from the postponement of postmodifying phrases of exception (6.49):

All of us were frightened $\begin{Bmatrix} but \\ except \end{Bmatrix}$ *the captain.*

14.42
Pronouns in apposition

In many cases, the postponed elements no doubt undergo postponement because their length and complexity would otherwise lead to an awkwardly unbalanced sentence. With another type of noun phrase, however, it is clearly to give end-focus rather than end-weight that the postponement takes place. This is the noun phrase with an emphatic reflexive pronoun (*himself*, etc) in apposition:

He himsÈLF told me → He told me himsÈLF
Did you yoursÉLF paint the portrait? → Did you paint the portrait yoursÉLF?

As the emphatic reflexive pronoun habitually bears nuclear stress, the postponement is necessary here if the sentence is to have end-focus. The postponement is possible, however, only if the noun phrase in apposition with the pronoun is the subject:

I showed Ian the letter *myself*
**I showed *Ian* the letter *himself*
  (but *cf: I showed Ian himself the letter*.)

Note
With some other cases of pronominal apposition, it is customary to postpone the second element to a position immediately following the operator rather than to the end of the sentence:

They're *none of them* experts
They don't *either of them* eat enough
  (*cf: We*'ve *all* made up our minds)

Similarly *both* and *each* (see 9.123).

14.43
Other discontinuities

Less often, elements other than noun phrases are rendered discontinuous as a result of postponement. Here, for example, it is an adjectival phrase:

I was *afraid*, after that, $\left\{ \begin{array}{l} \textit{to leave} \\ \textit{of leaving} \end{array} \right\}$ *the children alone.*

14.44
Postponement of comparative clauses

Comparative constructions of various types are frequently discontinuous. If we think of a comparative clause functionally as forming the

postmodification of the comp-element (11.64), then there is often a need
to separate it from its head for end-focus or end-weight:

> He showed less pity to his victims than any other blackmailer in
> the history of crime (*cf* 5.19)

The equivalent sentence without postponement would be extremely
awkward: ?**He showed less pity than any other blackmailer in the history
of crime to his victims.* In other cases, the comparative clause, unless postponed, would anticipate the parallel structure in the main clause, making
ellipsis virtually impossible:

> *More people* own houses *than used to years ago*

(rather than

> ?**More people than used to years ago own houses*)

Final position for comparative clauses following *too, so/much,* and
enough is normal, and therefore discontinuity is bound to arise whenever
the comp-element is not in final position:

> I was *so thrilled* by the present *that I forgot to thank you*
> He was *foolish enough*, despite warnings, *to sail the boat alone.*

14.45
Structural compensation

As part of the principle of end-weight in English, there is a feeling that
the predicate of a clause should where possible be longer than the subject;
thus a principle of structural compensation comes into force. With the
SV pattern, one-word predicates are shunned, and there is a preference
for expressing simple present or past actions or states by some other,
circumlocutory means. For example, the verb *sang* is very rarely used as
a predicate in itself, although semantically complete. We may easily say
He sang well or *He was singing*, but would rarely say simply *He sang.*

A common means of 'stretching' the predicate into a multi-word
structure is the construction consisting of a verb of general meaning
(*have, take, give,* etc) followed by an 'effected object'. The bald *He ate,
He smoked*, or *He swam* can be replaced by *He had a meal, He had a
smoke, He had a swim*, etc. (Other examples are supplied in 7.20.) Again,
it may be noted that the progressive forms *He was eating*, etc are less
objectionable than the simple past.

Emotive emphasis
14.46
Apart from the emphasis given by information focus and theme, the language provides means of giving a unit purely emotive emphasis. We have noted, in various sections of the grammar, a number of features of this type. They include exclamations (7.78–79), the persuasive DO in commands (7.77), interjections (7.89), expletives (7.88), and intensifiers (5.31, 5.51 f, 5.54 ff, 8.19 ff), including the general clause emphasizers such as *actually*, *really*, and *indeed*. A thorough study of emotive expressions would take us into the realms of figures of speech such as simile, hyperbole, and irony. Here we confine ourselves to two devices which fall squarely within the province of grammar.

14.47
Stress on operators
If normally unstressed operators receive stress (especially nuclear stress), the effect is often to add exclamatory emphasis to the whole sentence:

> That wìLL be nice! What áRE you dòING? We hÀVE enjoyed ourselves!

DO-periphrasis is introduced where there would otherwise be no operator to bear the emphatic stress:

> You dò look a wreck. He ˈdoes look p̌ALE. You ˈdid give me a frÏGHT.

This device is distinct from that of placing information focus on the operator (14.7). In the first place, emotive emphasis on the operator is not necessarily signalled by pitch prominence: ordinary sentence stress can have a similar effect. Secondly, emotive emphasis has no contrastive meaning; by saying *That wìLL be nice*, for example, we do not imply that now or in the past things have been the opposite of nice. Further intensification, if desired, can be achieved by placing an emphasizer such as *really* or *certainly* in front of the operator: *It really does taste nice*.

Note
Despite its similar emotive connotations, the 'persuasive' *do* in imperatives (7.77) is again distinct from the above use of *do*. The imperative *do* does not obey the rule of DO-periphrasis: one can say *Do be quiet!* in imperatives, but there is no corresponding statement *He dòES be quiet!*

14.48
Non-correlative *so* and *such*
In familiar speech, and especially perhaps in the speech of older women,

stress is also applied to the determiner *such* and to the adverb *so*, to give exclamatory force to a statement, question, or command:

> He's sùCH a nice man!
> I'm ‖so afraid they'll get LÒST
> Why are you |such a BÀBY?
> Don't upsÈT yourself |so!

Again, for extra emphasis, the exclamatory word *so* or *such* may be given nuclear stress: *I'm sò PLÉASED*. *So* and *such* in statements are almost equivalent to *how* and *what* in exclamations (7.78–79):

> They're ‖such delightful children!
> What delightful children they are!

But *so* and *such* can also occur, as the earlier examples show, in questions and commands.

Note
Other words of strong emotive import may take a nuclear tone for special emotive force:

> I wìsH you'd LÍsten!
> I ‖love that MÙsic!
> I'm TÈRribly sÓRry!

Reinforcement
14.49
Reinforcement by repetition and pronoun 'proxy' forms
Reinforcement is a feature of colloquial style whereby some item is repeated (either *in toto* or by pronoun substitution) for purposes of emphasis, focus, or thematic arrangement. Its simplest form is merely the reiteration of a word or phrase for emphasis or clarity:

> It's *far, far* too expensive (*cf* 5.77)
> I agree with *every word* you've said – *every single word*

A reinforcing or recapitulatory pronoun is sometimes inserted, in informal speech, within a clause where it stands 'proxy' for an initial noun phrase (*cf* 9.150):

> This man I was telling you about – he used to live next door to me
> The book I lent you – have you finished it yet?

As a result, the noun phrase is not connected syntactically to the clause to which, in meaning, it belongs. Thematically, it is the 'point of depart-ure' for the sentence, but it may be too long and unwieldy to form the subject of the sentence without awkwardness or danger of confusion. It is probably for this reason, or because he cannot in the act of speaking think of any way of continuing without restructuring the sentence, that the speaker decides to make a fresh start.

14.50
Noun phrase tags

The opposite case arises when an amplificatory noun phrase tag (*cf* 9.148) is added to the end of a sentence, repeating and clarifying the meaning of a pronoun within it:

> They're all the SÀME, these politÍcians
> I KNÒW them, MÉN
> I wouldn't trust him for a MÒMent, ˡthat LÁD

The tag generally occurs in a separate tone unit, with a rising tone. It can be inserted parenthetically, as well as placed finally:

> He's got a good future, your brother, if he perseveres

A repetitive operator (or the substitute operator DO) is sometimes added to the noun phrase for greater explicitness. We have therefore an amplificatory TAG STATEMENT rather than a tag noun phrase:

> That was a lark, *that was!*
> He likes a drink now and then, *Jim does* ⎱ (familiar)
> She's a lovely girl, *is Ann*

All of these have some familiar dialectal flavour, and the last (with the inversion of subject and operator in the tag) is a dialectism especially associated with northern BrE.

Note

The amplificatory noun phrase tag should not be confused with either vocatives (7.39) or what may be called 'tag exclamations', such as *He ran away from* SCHÒOL, *the idiot* (*cf* 9.133 Note). Both these constructions are distinguished from it intonationally, in that they may form the 'tail' of a preceding nucleus, instead of having their own tone unit (usually with a rising nucleus). The intonation marks the following as respectively noun phrase tag and vocative:

He's CÒMing, ǀ JÓHN. ǀ He's CÒMing, John. ǀ

The exclamatory tag is further distinguished by being capable of (a) referring back to a noun phrase other than a pronoun:

That brother of mine ran away from school, the idiot.

and (b) occurring initially as well as finally:

The idiot, he ran away from school.

Bibliographical note
Theme, focus, emphasis, and related matters are treated in Bolinger (1961); Charleston (1960); Firbas (1964) and (1966); Halliday (1967), (1967–8), (1970a); Huddleston (1971), Chapter 8; Jacobsson (1951); Lees (1960b) and (1963); Rosenbaum (1967a), especially §4.1 with reference to extraposition; Svartvik (1966).

Introduction

I.1

Relevance of word-formation to grammar

The rules by which words are constructed are important to the study of grammar for two reasons. Firstly, they help us to recognize the grammatical class of a word by its structure; we are able to tell (to take a particularly clear example) that the word *organization* is a noun from the fact that it ends in the suffix *-ation*. Secondly, they teach us that there is a flexibility in the application of grammatical rules, whereby the native speaker may transfer words, with or without the addition of affixes or other words, to a new grammatical class. If one draws the limits of what is 'grammatical' too fine, one excludes the creative licence of, for example:

> Before following Bean on board, Conrad *singsonged:* 'Dum-
> de-de-dum-de-dum'
> (*Time*, 28 November 1969)

where *singsong* (itself a compound noun based on the verb *sing*) is converted *ad hoc* into a verb.

I.2

Productiveness

For these reasons, therefore, the grammatical rules of sentence formation considered in this book need to be supplemented by some account of lexical rules of word-formation.

A rule of word-formation usually differs from a syntactic rule in one important respect: it is of limited productivity, in the sense that not all words which result from the application of the rule are acceptable; they are freely acceptable only when they have gained an institutional currency in the language. Thus there is a line to be drawn between 'actual English words' (*eg: sandstone, unwise*) and 'potential English words' (*eg:* (*)*lemonstone,* (*)*unexcellent*), both of these being distinct from 'non-English' words like **selfishless* which, because it shows the suffix *-less* added to an adjective rather than to a noun, does not even obey the rules of word-formation.

Rules of word-formation are therefore at the intersection of the historical and contemporary (synchronic) study of the language, providing a constant set of 'models' from which new words, ephemeral or permanent, are created from day to day. Yet on a larger scale, the rules themselves (like grammatical rules) undergo change: affixes and compounding processes can become productive or lose their productivity; can increase or decrease their range of meaning or grammatical applicability. In line with aims elsewhere in the book, we concentrate in this Appendix on productive or on marginally productive rules of word-formation, leaving aside 'dead' processes, even though they may have a fossilized existence in a number of words in the language. For example, the Old English affix *-th*, no longer used to form new words, survives in *length, depth, width* (*cf: long, deep, wide*). A corollary of this approach is that the historical study of a word is irrelevant to its status as an illustration of present-day rules; the fact that the word *unripe* has existed in the English language since Anglo-Saxon times does not prevent us from using it as an example of a regular process of word-formation still available in the language.

Note

[a] New formations, invented casually for a particular occasion (as in the example *singsonged* in App I.1), are normally comprehensible, but are used 'at a certain cost to acceptability'. They are often referred to as NONCE FORMATIONS.

[b] History provides quite a number of examples where a derived form has preceded the word from which (formally speaking) it is derived. Thus *editor* entered the language before *edit, lazy* before *laze*, and *television* before *televise*. The process by which the shorter word is created by the deletion of a supposed affix is known as BACK-FORMATION, since it reverses the normal trend of word-formation, which is to add rather than to subtract elements. It is important, however, to realize that 'back-formation' so described is a purely historical concept, of little relevance to the contemporary study of word-formation. To the present-day speaker of English, the relationship between *laze* and *lazy* need be no different from that between *sleep* and *sleepy, choose* and *choosy*, etc.

I.3
Borrowing and neo-classical formations

A second restriction of this account is that it takes only passing notice of word-formation according to Latin and Greek, rather than English models. From the Renaissance to the early twentieth century, English word-formation, like English (or for that matter European) architecture, was dominated by neo-classicism. The vocabulary was augmented by borrowing and adaptation of Latin and Greek words, or, as time went on, by the formation of words in English-speaking countries according to the Latin and Greek models. The habit of neo-classical formation still flourishes in certain learned areas of vocabulary, particularly in the natural sciences. However, English has adapted to her own purposes a large number of Latin and Greek word-elements, and these, being productive in the 'common core' of the language, we must take into account. Moreover, some purely neo-classical affixes (*-ic, -ous*, etc) are so common that it would be perverse to exclude them from any account of English word-formation.

So great indeed has been the foreign or neo-classical influence on the English language, that the majority of prefixes (as distinct from suffixes) in the language are of Latin, Greek, or French origin. To give an illustration of the difference between native and neo-classical formation: *com-* (*col-/con-/cor-/co-*) is a Latin prefix in *collect, communication, conduct, coagulate;* but *co-*, one of its variants, has been appropriated by the English language and has developed a function of its own in such words as *co-author, co-chairman, co-education.* For our purposes, therefore, *co-* is an English rather than a classical or neo-classical prefix.

I.4
Affixation, conversion, and compounding

A form to which a rule of word-formation is applied is called a BASE (as distinct from STEM: see App I.5 Note), and the chief processes of English word-formation by which the base may be modified are:

(1) AFFIXATION
- (a) adding a prefix to the base, with or without a change of word-class (*eg: author* → *co-author*) (App I.10 *ff*)
- (b) adding a suffix to the base, with or without a change of word-class (*eg: drive* → *driver*) (App I.21 *ff*)

(2) CONVERSION, *ie* assigning the base to a different word-class without changing its form ('zero affixation', *eg: drive* v → *drive* n) (App I.31 *ff*)

(3) COMPOUNDING, *ie* adding one base to another (*eg: tea+ pot*→*teapot*) (App I.44 *ff*)

Affixation and compounding are not always easy to distinguish. For example, we have to decide whether *in-group* is a compound with a prepositional adverb as its first element, or whether the *in-* is a prefix comparable to the *pre-* of *pre-war.* In fact, the meaning (clearly relatable to that of the adverb) and the initial stress suggest that it is a compound. Another borderline example is *policeman*, which is a compound of *police* and *man* as far as writing goes, but in speech, the peculiarity that -*man* is normally pronounced /mǝn/ shows that this element has progressed part of the way to becoming an affix, and cannot be straightforwardly identified with the personal noun *man* (/mæn/). Meaning, spelling, and pronunciation (including compound stress, or main stress on the first element) all help to mark the divergence between a word-element and the separate word from which, historically, it may have been derived; we shall not attempt to assign priority to any of these criteria, or to prescribe a particular point beyond which compounding becomes affixation.

I.5
Reapplication and combination of word-formation processes

Once a base has undergone a rule of word-formation, the derived word itself may become the base for another derivation; and so, by reapplication, it is possible to derive words of considerable morphological and semantic complexity. A moderately complex example is the word *unfriendliness*, the derivation of which we set out as follows:

(1) *friend*   NOUN
(2) *(friend)-ly*   NOUN → ADJECTIVE
(3) *un-[(friend)-ly]*   ADJECTIVE → ADJECTIVE
(4) *{un-[(friend)-li]}-ness*   ADJECTIVE → NOUN

That the bracketing of (3) above correctly shows *un-* and *friendly* to be its major constituents is confirmed by the non-existence of **unfriend*, which would have been the base if the alternative derivation **unfriend+ -ly* had been attempted. Similarly, the alternative analysis of stage (4) as *un-+friendliness* is barred by the non-occurrence of *un-* with noun bases. Sometimes two analyses are possible, and reflect an ambiguity of interpretation; *unmasked*, for example, may be read:

the *un-+masked* intruder ('the intruder who was not masked')
the *unmask+-ed* intruder ('the intruder from whom the mask had been removed')

But there are also many cases in which the choice between two analyses cannot be reasonably made, so little difference does it make: *preselection* might be read indifferently as *pre-+selection* or as *preselect+-(t)ion*.

There are possibilities for mixing processes of derivation in the same word; for instance, compounding and affixation are both found in *colour-blindness*, a word derived from the compound adjective *colour-blind* by the same rule which derives *happiness* from *happy*.

Note
We distinguish the base of a derived word from the STEM, which is the part of the word remaining after every affix has been removed: *friend* in the above example. In a word which has only one affix, such as *friendly*, the stem (*friend*) is also the base.

I.6
Word-formation, spelling, and hyphenation
Two points of orthography may be taken up from the preceding paragraph. The spelling of a word may undergo change, according to the spelling rules of English, when a suffix is added and consequently the final part of the word assumes medial position in the derived word: *unfriendly → unfriendliness; happy → happily; red → reddish; panic → panicky; cause → causation* (but *change → changeable*). The same spelling conventions apply here as in the addition of inflectional suffixes for verbs, etc (see 3.58 *ff*).

Secondly, the hyphen of *colour-blindness* appears to indicate that the main constituent break in the word is between *colour* and *blindness*. This is because of the spelling convention that suffixes, even when added to a compound, are generally attached without a break to the end of the word, while compound elements are frequently hyphenated.

Prefixes are more like compound elements in that they are often joined to the base by a hyphen, especially if they are 'strong' prefixes which normally receive full stress (*non-*, *pseudo-*, *ultra-*, *anti-*, etc). However, a compound, unlike a prefixed word, is often spelled with a gap between the constituents, as if they were separate grammatical items: *army officer*. Hence an even more striking case where orthography fails to reveal the structure of a word is that of *ex-army officer*, where the compound *army officer* is spelled as if it were two separate words, and the prefix *ex-*, which structurally applies to the whole compound, appears to apply to the first half only. Further remarks on hyphenation are given in the section on compounds below (App I.45), and in App III.4 *f*.

Note
Apart from spelling variations, there can be variations in pronunciation such as *nation* /-eɪʃ-/ ~ *nation+al* /-æʃ-/; or variations in both spelling and pronunciation: *deceive* ~ *decep+tion*.

I.7
Lexical items
The above observations make clear that the GRAMMATICAL WORD (item functioning as noun, verb, adjective, etc) is not necessarily identical with the ORTHOGRAPHIC WORD (*ie* a sequence of symbols bounded by spaces on the page). This leads us on to note that there is a similar discrepancy between the 'grammatical word' and the 'lexical word' (or, as it is often called, the 'lexical item'), which is the unit involved in word-formation. It is well known that combinations of grammatical words, called 'idioms', often constitute a single unit as far as the vocabulary is concerned; *ie* constitute a single lexical item. Moreover, in the case of verb+particle constructions (phrasal verbs: 12.19 *ff*), such combinations are subject to the limited productivity of lexical rule; for example, *up* with certain verbs, as in *eat up*, *cut up*, *use up*, *break up*, etc, adds the sense of 'completion' to the verb; *out* in *draw out*, *last out*, *eke out*, *hold out*, etc, conveys the meaning of 'continuation'. These are closely parallel, as far as word-formation is concerned, to a set such as *reclaim*, *retake*, *rebuild* (where *re-* = 'again').

Note
When the particle is placed before the verb and is orthographically joined to it, as in *upset*, *offset*, etc, we have a single word, which is structurally speaking a compound rather than a phrasal verb. This preposing of the particle often takes place when phrasal verbs are the base for derived nouns: (*inlet*, *income*, *outbreak*, *onlooker*, etc) or participial adjectives (*outgoing*, *offputting* [BrE], etc). In the case of the derived nouns, compound status is reinforced by initial compound stress: 'inlet, etc. There

is still the possibility of keeping the particle in second position, however, and so deriving 'phrasal nouns' such as *passer-by, cutter-up, blast-off, touch-down*, etc. In such cases, the particle is hyphenated to the deverbal noun.

I.8
Phrasal derivation

Although rules of word-formation normally operate upon grammatical words, there are occasions when they operate on idioms or lexical items which are grammatical phrases. The agent noun *passer-by* (from the verb *pass by:* see App 1.7 Note) illustrates this process, which may be called PHRASAL DERIVATION. Thus a noun phrase can become the base of a derived word, by affixation or compounding: *old-maidish* (from *old maid*+*-ish*); *short-sighted* (from *short sight*+*-ed*); *veteran car collector* (from *veteran car* [BrE]+*collector*). It is to be noted that a word like *old-maidish*, although it looks like a compound, is in fact formed from a phrase by a process of affixation, and so does not actually involve the compounding process at all.

I.9
Minor word-formation processes

Apart from the major word-formation processes defined in App I.4, English calls upon a number of minor devices (including blending, clipping, and acronymy) as means of forming new words on the basis of old. These minor processes, a number of which have attained some importance in modern times, will be exemplified in App I.58–61. First, however, we attend to the major processes of affixation (prefixation and suffixation), conversion, and compounding, in that order.

Prefixation
I.10

Prefixes do not generally alter the word-class of the base. Productive prefixes normally have a light stress on their first (or only) syllable, the main stress of the word coming on the base: ˌpreˈfabricated. This stress pattern will be assumed in the examples in the following tables, unless words are marked to the contrary. (The noun ˈprefix itself is one of the numerous exceptions to the stress rule: *cf* App I.43.)

So that the relation between competing and contrasting prefixes can be better understood, major living prefixes are classified below according to meaning. Inevitable semantic overlaps between the categories will be signalled by cross-reference, and where an affix has two or more separate semantic or syntactic functions, it will be given two or more separate entries.

I.11
Negative prefixes

	meaning	added to:	examples	comments
UN- (also App I.12)	'the opposite of', 'not'	adjectives; -ed or -ing participles	*unfair, unwise, unforgettable;* *unassuming, unexpected*	Very common. Often unstressed when preceding a stressed syllable.
NON-	'not'	adjectives; nouns; verbs; etc	*non-conformist;* *non-smoker, non-politician;* *non-drip (paint)* (adj)	Can normally be regarded as derivable from clause-negation: *non-smoker* ('one who does not smoke'), etc. Frequently contrasts with *un-* in expressing binary (non-gradable) contrast, rather than the opposite end of a scale: *non-scientific* vs *unscientific*, etc.
IN- (IL- before/l/, IM- before labials, IR- before /r/)	(same as for *un-*)	adjectives	*insane,* *illogical,* *improper, immovable,* *irrelevant*	Generally preferred to *un-* in learned words of Latin or French origin; but its use, against that of *un-*, has declined. Unstressed before a stressed syllable.
DIS- (also App I.12)	(same as for *un-*)	adjectives; verbs; hence abstract nouns	*disloyal, discourteous; disobey,* *dislike; disfavour*	Unstressed before a stressed syllable.

	meaning	added to:	examples	comments
A- /eɪ/ or /æ/ (AN-)	'lacking in', 'lack of'	adjectives; nouns	amoral, asexual; asymmetry	Mostly found in borrowed or neo-classical words: 'atheist, 'anarchy, amorphous, 'atrophied.

Note

[a] *Un-* often confers acceptability on a participial or other deverbal adjective form: contrast *a heeded problem with an unheeded problem, *a speakable condition with an unspeakable condition.

[b] *Non-person* and *non-event* illustrate a pejorative type of noun-formation which has recently acquired popularity. The meaning here is 'a person who is not (ie does not count as) a person'; 'a complete nonentity', etc.

[c] Other prefixes apart from those above have negative implications: notably, the reversative prefixes discussed below (App I.12), and the prefixes of opposition *anti-* and *counter-*, discussed in App I.15.

I.12
Reversative or privative prefixes

	meaning	added to:	examples	comments
UN- (also App I.11)	(a) 'to reverse the action'; (b) 'deprive of', 'release from'	(a) verbs; (b) nouns	(a) undo, untie, unzip, unpack, unwrap; (b) unleash, unhorse	
DE- /diː/	'to reverse the action', 'to get rid of'	verbs; hence abstract nouns	decode, decentralize, defrost, desegregate, de-escalate; deforestation	Contrast borrowed words with the unstressed prefix /dɪ/: depend, etc. However, the longer vowel of /diː/ can also be reduced to /ɪ/ in connected speech.

	meaning	added to:	examples	comments
DIS- (also App I.11)	(as for *un-*)	verbs; hence participles; nouns	*disconnect, disinfect, disown, dishearten; discoloured; discontent*	Often unstressed when preceding a stressed syllable. Contrast borrowed words with unstressed prefix: *dispose of*, etc.

I.13
Pejorative prefixes

	meaning	added to:	examples	comments
MIS-	'wrongly', 'astray'	verbs; hence abstract nouns; participles	*miscalculate, mishear, misfire, misinform, mislead; mis- conduct; misleading*	Normally unstressed if next syllable is stressed.
MAL-	'badly', 'bad'	verbs; hence abstract nouns; participles; adjectives	*maltreat; malfunction; malformed; malodorous*	
PSEUDO-	'false', 'imitation'	nouns; adjectives	*pseudo-Christianity, pseudo-classicism, pseudo-intellectual* (n or adj); *pseudo-scientific*	

Note
For other prefixes with pejorative overtones, see NON- (App I.11 Note *b*); ARCH- (App I.14); OVER-, UNDER-, and HYPER- (App I.14).

I.14

Prefixes of degree or size

	meaning	added to:	examples	comments
ARCH- /ɑ(r)tʃ-/	'supreme', 'highest', 'worst'	mainly human nouns	archduke, arch-enemy, archbishop, arch-fascist	archangel is pronounced /ɑ(r)k-/ and generally has initial main stress. New formations in ARCH- are normally pejorative.
SUPER- (also App I.16)	'above', 'more than', 'better'	nouns; adjectives	ˈsuperˌman, ˈsuperˌmarket; supernatural, supersensitive, superluxury (adj) (airliner, etc)	Nouns usually have initial main stress. Found also in borrowed words, sometimes with shifted stress: suˈperfluous, etc.
OUT-	'(to do something) better, faster, longer, etc than . . .'	mainly intrans verbs (to form transitive verbs)	outgrow, outlive, outrun, outweigh	Very productive. Example: He outran me (ie 'He ran faster than I did').
SUR-	'over and above'	nouns	ˈsurcharge, ˈsurtax	Rare except in borrowed words, where the distinctive meaning of sur- is difficult to recover: survey, surmount, surname, etc.
SUB- /sʌb-/ (also App I.16)	'under', 'lower than', 'less than'	adjectives	subhuman, substandard, subnormal	Borrowed words with unstressed prefix /səb/: subjection, etc.

	meaning	added to:	examples	comments
OVER-	'too much'	verbs; -*ed* participles etc; adjectives	*overdo, overeat,* **over***simplify*; *over*dressed; *overconscientious, overconfident*	Contrast noun compounds with *over* as a particle: ˈ*over*ˌ*spill*, etc.
UNDER-	'too little'	verbs; -*ed* participles etc	*undercook, underfeed, undercharge; underworked, underprivileged*	Contrast noun compounds with *under* as a particle: ˈ*under*ˌ*pass*, etc.
HYPER- /ˈhaɪpə(r)-/	'extra specially'	adjectives	*hypercritical, hyperactive hypersensitive*	Contrast borrowed words with stress shift: *hy*ˈ*perbole*, etc.
ULTRA-	'beyond', 'extremely'	adjectives	*ultra-violet, ultra-modern, ultra-conservative*	Also borrowed and neo-Latin words: *ultramarine, ultramontane.*
MINI-	'little'	nouns	ˈ*mini*-ˌ*car*, ˈ*mini*-ˌ*skirt*, ˈ*mini*-ˌ*cab*	A recent prefix, often used for humorous coinages: ˈ*mini*-ˌ*budget*, etc. The contrasting prefix *maxi*- ('large', 'long') and even *midi*- ('medium') are also fashionable: ˈ*maxi*-ˌ*skirt*, etc.

I.15
Prefixes of attitude

	meaning	added to:	examples	comments
CO- /kou-/	'accompanying', 'with', 'joint'	verbs; human and abstract nouns	*cooperate, coexist; co-heir,* ˈco-ˌdriver, co-education	*Co-operate* and (especially AmE) *cooperate* are alternative spellings. *Co-* is used of mutual relationships; *eg: Smith is Brown's co-director* (director with Brown). *Cf* the use of the compound element *fellow* in *fellow-student,* etc.
COUNTER-	'against', 'in opposition to'	verbs; hence abstract nouns, etc	ˈcounteract (also counterˈact); counter-revolution, counter-espionage, ˈcountersink	Some nouns have compound stress: ˈcounter-aˌttraction, ˈcounterˌmovement. See ANTI-.
ANTI-	'against'	nouns (mainly to form adjectives: *the anti-war campaign*); denominal adjectives: adverbs	ˈantibody, anti-missile, anti-war; anti-social, anti-clerical; anti-clockwise	*Anti-* suggests simply an attitude of opposition, while *counter-* suggests action in opposition to or in response to a previous action. A *counterattack* can take place only if there has already been an *attack.*
PRO- /prou-/	'for', 'on the side of' (antonymous to *anti-*)	nouns (mainly to form adjectives: *the pro-Common Market lobby*); denominal adjectives	*pro-Common Market, pro-Castro; pro-American, pro-communist*	Contrast numerous borrowed and neo-Latin words with unstressed /prə-/: *provide,* etc.

I.16

Locative prefixes

These, like locative prepositions (6.26), may extend their meaning metaphorically to abstract spheres.

	meaning	added to:	examples	comments
SUPER- (also App I.14)	'over', 'above'	nouns	ˈsuperˌstructure	Uncommon except in borrowed or neo-Latin words: *supernumerary*, etc. Compound stress is usual.
SUB- (also App I.14)	'under', 'beneath', 'lesser in rank'	nouns; adjectives; verbs	ˈsubˌway, ˈsubˌsection; *subconscious*; *sublet*, *subdivide*, *subcontract*	Nouns frequently have compound stress. Contrast Latin and neo-Latin words: ˈsubmarˌine, *subliminal*.
INTER-	'between', 'among'	denominal adjectives; verbs; nouns	*international, inter-continental*; *intertwine* (v), *intermarry*, *interweave*; ˈinterˌplay (n)	Also occasionally used of time: (*the*) *inter-war* (*years*). Contrast Latin and neo-Latin words: *intermittent, interfere*.
TRANS-	'across', 'from one place to another'	denominal adjectives; verbs	*transatlantic, trans-Siberian*; *transplant, transship*	Contrast Latin and neo-Latin words: *transfer, translate*, etc.

Note

In 'overspill, 'underpass, etc, over and under are locative particles rather than locative prefixes. (See App I.7 Note.)

I.17
Prefixes of time and order

	meaning	added to:	examples	comments
FORE-	'before'	mainly verbs; hence abstract nouns, etc	*foretell, forewarn, foreshadow; foreknowledge*	Also used with the locative meaning 'front': '*foreleg*, etc. Usually has compound stress with nouns.
PRE- /priː-/	'before'	nouns (mainly to form adjectives); adjectives	*pre-war, pre-school (children), pre-19th century; pre-marital*	The more learned competing prefix *ante-* 'before' is found almost entirely in borrowed and neo-Latin words *antediluvian, antenatal*, etc. *Cf* /prɪ/ in borrowed words: *prevent*, etc.
POST- /poʊst-/	'after'	nouns (mainly to form adjectives); adjectives	*post-war, post-election (boom); post-classical*	*Cf* borrowed words: *postpone*, etc.
EX-	'former'	human nouns	*ex-president, ex-serviceman, ex-film-star, ex-husband*	*Cf* the more general use of *ex-* in borrowed words with unstressed *ex-* (*expect*) and voicing before a vowel (*examine* /əgz-/, /ɪgz-/).

	meaning	added to:	examples	comments
RE- /ri-/	'again', 'back'	verbs; hence abstract nouns, etc	*rebuild, reclaim, reuse, resell, re-evaluate; resettlement*	One of the most common prefixes of the language, occurring in many words borrowed from Latin and French. Note the contrast between unstressed /rɪ/ found in borrowed words, and the /riː/ (reducible to /rɪ/) of a newer formation in *recover*: /rɪ/ = 'get better' and /riː/ = 'cover again'. Contrast also older borrowings with initial voicing of the base (*resound* /rɪz-/) and newer formations *re'sound* /riːˈs-/ (= 'sound again'). There is a similar alternation with DE- (App I.12).

I.18
Number prefixes

English uses a mixture of Latin and Greek prefixes to express number. Although these prefixes generally form words on neo-classical patterns, they are productive and important enough in general English to be worth illustrating here.

	meaning	examples
UNI- MONO-	'one'	¹uni₁cycle, unilateral, ¹unisex; monotheism, ¹mono₁plane, ¹mono₁rail
BI- /baɪ/ DI- /daɪ/	'two'	bifocal, bi-partisan, bilingual, ¹biceps, bimonthly, ¹bicycle; ¹dimeter, dichotomy
TRI- /traɪ-/	'three'	tripartite, ¹tripod, ¹trident, ¹tricycle
MULTI- POLY-	'many'	multi-national, multi-racial; polysyllabic, po¹lygamy, ¹poly₁glot

Note

Bimonthly is deplorably ambiguous, in that it can mean either 'every two months' or 'twice every month'. *Biweekly* has the same ambiguity. *Biennial*, according to some authoritative accounts, has only the meaning 'every two years' (in contrast with *biannual* 'twice a year'), but many speakers in practice find it as ambiguous as *bimonthly*.

I.19
auto-, neo-, pan-, proto-, semi-, vice-

A number of other prefixes on the border between English and neo-classical derivation may be mentioned:

	meaning	examples	comments
AUTO-	'self'	¹autocrat, autosuggestion, autobiography, automation	*Cf* compounds in *self-*: *self-denial.*
NEO-	'new', 'revived'	neo-classicism, neo-Gothic, neo-Nazi	Used for political, artistic, etc, movements.
PAN-	'all', 'world-wide'	pan-African, pan-Anglican, pan-American	Used especially with proper nouns for world-wide or continent-wide movements.
PROTO-	'first', 'original'	Proto-Germanic, ¹proto₁type	

	meaning	*examples*	*comments*
SEMI-	'half'	*'semi,circle, semi-darkness, semi-humorous*	*Hemi-* and *demi-* are less common prefixes with this meaning: *hemisphere, demigod.*
VICE-	'deputy'	*vice-admiral, vice-president, 'viceroy*	Compare *deputy-mayor, under-secretary, sub-manager, assistant director,* etc.

I.20
Conversion prefixes

Finally, we turn to three old and only mildly productive prefixes which may be called 'conversion prefixes', since a major part of their function, in contrast to that of other prefixes, is to convert the base into a different grammatical class. In their role, they are thus more like suffixes than like prefixes.

	added to → to form	*examples*	*comments*
BE-	(a) nouns → participial adjectives (b) { verbs; adjectives; nouns } → { transitive verbs }	(a) *bewigged, bespectacled, bedevilled* (b) *becalm, bedazzle, bewitch*	(a) has various meanings: 'equipped with', 'covered with', 'beset with'. Often there are pejorative or facetious overtones.
EN- (EM- before /p/ and /b/)	nouns → verbs	*enmesh, empower, endanger, entrain, enslave*	Various meanings: 'to make into . . .', 'to put into . . .', 'to get into . . .'.
A-/ə/	verbs → predicative adjectives	*astride, awash, aglimmer, atremble*	The meaning is similar to that of the progressive aspect: *afloat* ='floating'. It is doubtful whether this prefix is still productive.

Suffixation

I.21

Classification of suffixes

Unlike prefixes, suffixes frequently alter the word-class of the base; for example, the adjective *kind*, by the addition of the suffix *-ness*, is changed into an abstract noun *kindness*.

Although suffixes are by no means always limited to a particular class of base, it is convenient on the whole to group them not only by the class of word they form (as NOUN SUFFIXES, VERB SUFFIXES, etc) but also by the class of base they are typically added to (DENOMINAL, *ie* from nouns, DE-ADJECTIVAL, DEVERBAL SUFFIXES, etc). More usefully, we may extend this latter terminology, where convenient, to the derived words themselves, and talk of *worker* as a DEVERBAL NOUN, *hopeful* as a DENOMINAL ADJECTIVE, etc.

The clarity which might result from the treatment of suffixes in such terms is marred by the difficulty of disentangling the neo-classical use of foreign suffixes from their acclimatized use as formatives in the English language. In many cases we can recognize a word as a noun by its ending (*eg: duration*); but there is no verb *DURE in English. In other cases, there is an alternation between two words derived from the same foreign source: for example, between *invade ~ invasion; evade ~ evasion; persuade ~ persuasion*. Such alternations, if frequent, may be worth stating as among the regular features of English word-structure. At the same time, variations in stress (and vowel quality) sometimes occur when a suffix is added to a word of borrowed or neo-classical origin: witness ˈphotograph, photoˈgraphic, phoˈtographer. As a general rule, however, English suffixes are unstressed; the only exceptions are one or two endings of foreign origin, notably -ˈation.

The tables of suffixes set out below are intended only to capture the major generalizations that can be made about suffixation in English.

Note

[a] Inflectional suffixes, if any, always follow derivational suffixes: *kindnesses*.

[b] Deverbal nouns do not include the 'gerund' class of nouns ending in *-ing* (*waiting*, etc) which are designated VERBAL NOUNS (4.11). Because of the complete productivity of the verbal noun category, the relation between verbal nouns and the corresponding verbs is considered to be purely grammatical rather than derivational. Another class of words having arguably the same status of full productivity (see 1.14) is that of AGENTIAL NOUNS (App I.24): *worker*, etc. Notice that although not all verbs have a corresponding institutionalized agential noun (*trick ~ *tricker, flout ~ *flouter*), it is always possible to use an agential noun in a frame such as *a (big) . . . -er of N:*

John flouts authority ~ *John is a flouter
        John is a (big) flouter of authority

I.22

Noun→noun suffixes

The main denominal noun suffixes are given below.

	added to → to form	meaning	examples	comments
[A] *occupational*, etc				
-STER -EER }	nouns→ personal nouns	'person engaged in an occupation or activity'	*gangster, gamester, trickster; engi'neer, profi'teer, racke'teer, pamphle'teer*	Except *engineer*, often pejorative; rather infrequent.
-ER (also App I.24 for *baker*, etc)	nouns → personal and inanimate nouns	varied meanings, eg 'something having X', 'inhabitant of X', 'maker of X'	*glover, teenager, Londoner, three-wheeler*	
[B] *diminutive* and *feminine*				
-LET	countable nouns → countable nouns	'small, unimportant'	*booklet, piglet, leaflet, starlet*	English is poor in feminine or diminutive suffixes, and those listed are used with decreasing frequency. A further diminutive suffix, *-ling*, is added to other word-classes as well as nouns, usually with a mildly contemptuous flavour: *princeling, weakling, underling, hireling*. The base of *waitress, murderess*, etc appears in a reduced or truncated form: *wait[e]r, murder[er]-*. Certain *-ess* words are felt to be old-maidish (*authoress, poetess*) or indelicate (*Jewess, negress*), and are best replaced by periphrases (*Jewish*
-ETTE	nouns → nouns	(a) 'small, compact'	*kitche'nette, ciga'rette*	
		(b) 'imitation' (material)	*leathe'rette, flanne'lette*	
		(c) 'female'	*ushe'rette, suffra'gette*	
-ESS	animate nouns → animate nouns	'female'	*waitress, actress, lioness, authoress, manager-less*	

	added to → to form	meaning	examples	comments
-Y (less frequently spelled -IE) (also App I.27)	nouns → nouns		*daddy, auntie, Johnny,* *pussy, nighty* ('nightgown')	This suffix, largely restricted to familiar contexts, has no meaning apart from that of indicating endearment or familiarity. It is frequently added to a clipped form of the base, *eg: undies* 'underclothes', *movies* [esp. AmE] 'moving pictures'.

[C] status, domain, etc

	added to → to form	meaning	examples	comments
-HOOD	nouns → abstract nouns	'status', etc	*boyhood, brotherhood,* *widowhood*	Only mildly productive; occasionally with adjective bases: *falsehood, hardship.* -DOM can add a pejorative flavour in modern formations, *eg: officialdom.*
-SHIP	(as for -HOOD)	'status', 'condition', etc	*friendship, membership,* *lectureship, dictatorship*	
-DOM /dəm/	(as for -HOOD)	'domain', 'realm', 'condition', etc	*kingdom, officialdom,* *stardom*	
-IOCRACY	(as for -HOOD)	'system of government'	*de'mocracy, plu'tocracy,* *meri'tocracy*	Chiefly neo-classical formations; they alternate with personal nouns in -*crat*, with stress shift: *'democrat*, etc.
-ERY (-RY often after *d, t, l, n* except in sense (b))	chiefly nouns → (a) abstract nouns (b) concrete count nouns (c) mass nouns	(a) 'behaviour' etc (b) 'place of activity or abode' (c) 'collectivity'	(a) *devilry, drudgery,* *pageantry, slavery* (b) *nunnery, rookery,* *refinery* (c) *crockery, machinery,* *gadgetry, rocketry*	Borrowed words such as *chivalry, surgery* are common. A few words have adjective bases: *snuggery, bravery.* Type (a) is frequently used in nonce-formations: *nitwittery, take-over-biddery*, etc.

	added to → to form	meaning	examples	comments
[D] Other				
-ING	countable nouns → mass nouns	'the substance of which N is composed'	*matting, tubing, panelling*	
-FUL usually /fʊl/ (contrast App I.27)	countable nouns → countable nouns	'the amount which N contains'	*mouthful, spoonful, plateful*	

I.23
Noun/adjective → noun/adjective suffixes

	added to → to form	meaning	examples	comments
-ITE	chiefly names → personal nouns (and occasionally non-gradable adjectives)	(a) 'member of a tribe or community' (b) 'member of a faction, sect, or type'	(a) *Israelite, Brooklynite* (b) *Benthamite, Stalinite, laborite* (BrE *Labourite*), *socialite*	Except in biblical connections, the suffix tends to be familiar in style, and nouns of Type (b) are often used derogatorily. An example of the adjectival use of *-ite* is: *His outlook is rather Luddite.*
-(i)AN	chiefly proper nouns → personal nouns and non-gradable adjectives	'belonging to . . .', 'pertaining to . . .', etc	*Indo'nesian, Pa'risian, Eliza'bethan, re'publican, Dar'winian*	Often corresponding to place nouns in -(i)a: *Persia/Persian*, etc. Stress shift to the final syllable of the stem is common: '*Shakespeare/Shakes'pearean*, etc.

	added to → to form	meaning	examples	comments
-ˈESE	chiefly proper nouns → personal nouns and non-gradable adjectives	'nationality', etc.	Chiˈnese, Portuˈguese, Japaˈnese	Used normally for language and dialect names: Cantoˈnese, etc. Extended (usually pejoratively) to linguistic styles: Johnsoˈnese, journaˈlese, etc. In attributive use, the stress generally shifts to initial position: ˈJapanese art.
-IST	nouns/adjectives → personal nouns/adjectives	'member of a party, occupation', etc	masochist, racialist, Buddhist, violinist, stylist, loyalist	Also with verbs (typist, etc). Many nouns with this suffix are borrowed, and consequently the base may not exist as an English noun. A final vowel is generally omitted from the base: cello → cellist. Words ending in -ist and -ite are frequently used attributively: a Fascist government; the McCarthyite view.
-ISM	nouns/adjectives → abstract nouns	'doctrine', 'point of view', 'political or artistic movement', etc	Calvinism, idealism, impressionism, fanaticism, dualism, absenteeism	Many nouns in -ism correspond to a noun in -ist which denotes an adherent of the principle, etc concerned: communist/communism.

I.24
Verb→noun suffixes

	added to → to form	meaning	examples	comments
-ER (-OR) (also see App I.22)	mainly dynamic verbs→mainly personal nouns	agetinal suffix, *eg: singer* 'one who sings (by profession)'	ANIMATE NOUNS: *worker, writer, driver, employer* INANIMATE NOUNS: *receiver, silencer, thriller* (BrE) COMPOUNDS (see further App I.50): *washer-up* (BrE), *window-cleaner, high-flier, eye-opener*	An extremely productive affix, potentially affixable to any verb in the language. The spelling of the affix is often *-or* in borrowed and neo-classical words: *inspector, actor, survivor*. There is no English verb-base for many such words: *author, doctor*, etc. Note the spelling of *liar, beggar*. -ER has 'passive' meaning in a few nouns: *cooker* (BrE) 'an apple for cooking', etc.
-ANT	verbs → personal or impersonal nouns	a less common and more learned agential suffix	*inhabitant, contestant, informant, lubricant, disinfectant*	Often corresponds to verbs in *-ate: lubricant ~ lubricate; participant ~ participate*, etc.
-EE	verbs → personal nouns	passive suffix; *eg: draftee* 'one who is drafted'	*payee, appointee, trainee, employee*	Often the noun, while retaining its passive meaning, is not directly derived from a verb base: *nominee, refugee*. Some examples do not have passive meaning at all: *absentee*.

	added to → → to form	meaning	examples	comments
-ATION /ˈeɪʃn/	verbs → (a) abstract nouns (b) collective nouns	(a) 'state', 'action', etc (b) 'institution', etc	(a) fiˈxation, exploˈration, victimiˈzation, ratifiˈcation, starˈvation (b) founˈdation, organiˈzation	Note stress shift to the penultimate syllable: ˈjustiˌfy (/-faɪ/) → ˌjustifiˈcation (/-fɪˈkeɪʃn/), etc. A very common affix, regularly added to verbs in -fy and -ize and corresponding with -ate in educate ∼ education, etc. Cf borrowed and neo-classical nouns in -tion, -sion, and -xion: section, occasion, connexion (alternative: connection).
-MENT /mənt/	verbs → chiefly abstract nouns	'state', 'action', etc	arrangement, amazement, embodiment, puzzlement	Cf borrowed and neo-classical words: detriment, etc. Also used sometimes to form concrete nouns: equipment, sediment, etc.
-AL /əl/	dynamic verbs → chiefly countable abstract nouns	'action', etc	refusal, revival, dismissal, upheaval	
-ING	verbs → (a) abstract nouns (b) concrete nouns	(a) 'activity', 'state', etc (b) 'that which results from the activity of the verb', etc	(a) bathing, driving, betting (b) painting, building, opening, earnings, shavings	Type (a) is the verbal noun (see App I.21 Note b), mentioned here for completeness, although it is strictly outside word-formation processes. Words of Type (b) may be mass as well as count: stuffing, blacking, etc.

	added to → to form	meaning	examples	comments
-AGE /ɪdʒ/	verbs → mass abstract nouns	'extent', 'amount', etc	coverage, shrinkage, leverage, drainage, wastage	Cf denominal nouns frontage, baggage, etc.

I.25
Adjective→noun suffixes

	added to → to form	meaning	examples	comments
-NESS /nɪs/, /nəs/	adjectives → abstract nouns	'state', 'quality', etc	meanness, happiness, cleverness, usefulness, selfishness, stoutheartedness, up-to-dateness	Very productive. The normal way of forming an abstract noun from an adjective except where some borrowed or neo-classical form already exists, or in cases where -ity is preferred (see below). Note the pronunciation of business /bɪznɪs/, /bɪznəs/.
-ITY	adjectives → abstract nouns	'state', 'quality', etc	ˈsanity, diˈversity, raˈpidity, reˌspectaˈbility, baˈnality, elaˈsticity	Added to many adjectives of classical or French origin, and regularly to those with the suffixes -able/-ible (with consequent change to -aˈbil-/-iˈbil-), -al, and -ic (App I.28). The main stress is shifted (unless already in that position) to the last syllable of the stem: ˈsimilar, ˌsimiˈlarity, etc. A long vowel in the last syllable of the base is often replaced by the corresponding short vowel: chaste /eɪ/ → ˈchastity /æ/; seˈrene /iː/ → seˈrenity /e/; verˈbose /oʊ/ → verˈbosity /ɒ/, etc.

I.26
Verb suffixes

Verb-forming suffixes are very few in English, and we may conveniently deal with them under one heading.

	added to → to form	meaning	examples	comments
-IFY /ɪfaɪ/	nouns, adjectives, etc → chiefly transitive verbs	causative	*beautify* ('to make beautiful'), *diversify, codify, amplify, simplify*	Usually in borrowed and neo-classical formations: *certify, identify,* etc. Note change of stem in *electrify* (← *electric*), *liquify* (← *liquid*). Coinages outside the neo-classical sphere tend to be facetious and pejorative: *dandify, speechify.*
-IZE (-ISE is an alternative spelling in BrE)	nouns, adjectives, etc → chiefly transitive verbs	causative	*decimalize* ('to convert currency to a decimal system'), *symbolize, hospitalize, publicize, popularize, legalize, modernize*	Widespread in borrowed and neo-classical words: *epitomize, organize,* etc. Very productive, especially in association with abstract nouns in *-ization: rationalization,* etc. Overuse of such nouns is often condemned as 'jargon'.
-EN	adjectives → (a) transitive and (b) intransitive verbs	(a) 'make (more) X' (causative) (b) 'become X' (where X is the base adjective)	*ripen, widen, deafen, sadden, quicken, tauten*	Now scarcely productive. All of these verbs (added principally to monosyllabic native adjectives) can be used in sense (a), and most in sense (b) as well.

I.27
Noun→adjective suffixes

	added to → to form	meaning	examples	comments
-FUL often /fəl/ (contrast App I.22)	Chiefly abstract nouns → gradable adjectives	'full of . . .', 'having . . .', 'giving . . .', etc	*useful, delightful, pitiful, successful, hopeful, helpful*	Also with verb bases: *forgetful*.
-LESS	nouns → adjectives	'without . . .', 'not giving . . .'	*speechless, childless, harmless, restless, careless*	There are some antonym pairs with -ful: *harmful/harmless*, etc.
-LY (also App I.30)	chiefly concrete nouns → gradable adjectives	'having the qualities of . . .' etc	*beastly, manly, soldierly, brotherly, worldly, cowardly*	Also with adjectives: *deadly*, etc. A special group of -ly adjectives consists of those derived from nouns of time: *daily* ('every day'), *weekly*, etc.
-LIKE	(as for -LY)	'having the qualities of . . .'	*childlike, cowlike, statesmanlike*	-like is now more productive than -ly, and is more predictable in its meaning.
-Y (also App I.22)	chiefly concrete mass nouns → gradable adjectives	'like . . .', 'full of . . .', 'covered with . . .', etc	*meaty, sandy, creamy, hairy, silky, mangy*	A common mode of formation, especially in familiar speech. Also with verb bases: *crunchy, poppy* (eyes), etc.
-ISH (also App I.29)	chiefly proper and countable nouns → (a) non-gradable and (b) gradable adjectives	(a) 'belonging to . . .' (b) 'having the character of . . .', etc	(a) *Swedish, Turkish, Cornish* (b) *foolish, churlish, selfish, snobbish, roguish, modish*	Type (a) adjectives correspond to national and regional names: *Sweden, Turkey, Cornwall*, etc (4.33). Type (b) adjectives are often pejorative.

	added to → to form	meaning	examples	comments
-ESQUE /lesk/	chiefly proper nouns → adjectives of . . .'	'in the style	Dan'esque, Rembrand'esque	Originally in borrowed words: pictu'resque, bur'lesque, etc.

Note
The following are three less important suffixes which usually form adjectives from noun bases:

-SOME: burdensome, frolicsome, bothersome
-WORTHY: praiseworthy, seaworthy
-ARIAN: authoritarian, Parliamentarian (also used to form nouns: a vegetarian, an octogenarian, etc)

I.28

Some adjective suffixes common in borrowed and neo-classical words

The four endings *-al, -ic, -ive,* and *-ous* are among the most common adjective suffixes in the language, and yet have remained almost wholly in the borrowed and neo-classical sphere of English vocabulary. That they have never become fully 'naturalized' is shown by the paucity of formations from native bases: *tidal, Mil'tonic, talkative,* and *thunderous* are among the exceptions. They frequently alternate with (or, in the case of *-al,* are added to) noun suffixes of classical origin; *-ive* is primarily a deverbal suffix, whereas *-al, -ic,* and *-ous* are primarily denominal. It is impossible to specify a particular meaning for these suffixes: their semantic functions are extremely varied.

suffix	used to form:	examples with corresponding abstract nouns	comments
-AL (also *-ial, -ical*)	primarily non-gradable adjectives	¹*criminal* (*crime*), ¹*cultural* (¹*culture*), *edi*¹*torial* (¹*editor*), ¹*musical* (¹*music*), *philo*¹*sophical* (*phi*¹*losophy*), *prefe*¹*rential* (¹*preference*)	Stress usually on the penultimate syllable of the base.
-IC	gradable or non-gradable adjectives	*a*¹*tomic* (¹*atom*), *em*¹*phatic* (¹*emphasis*), *he*¹*roic* (¹*heroism*), *proble*¹*matic* (¹*problem*), *spe*¹*cific* (*speci*¹*ficity, specifi*¹*cation*)	Stress usually on the last syllable of the base. Often used for language names: ¹*Celtic,* ¹*Arabic* (*cf* the nationality adjectives ¹*Arab, A*¹*rabian*).
-IVE (also *-ative, -itive*)	gradable or non-gradable adjectives	*at*¹*tractive* (*at*¹*traction*), *ex*¹*pansive* (*ex*¹*pansion*), *ex*¹*plosive* (*ex*¹*plosion*), *pro*¹*ductive* (*pro*¹*duction*), ¹*sensitive* (*sensi*¹*tivity*)	Stress usually on the last syllable of the base. The corresponding noun suffix is in most cases *-ion.*
-OUS (also *-eous, -ious*)	primarily gradable adjectives	*am*¹*bitious* (*am*¹*bition*), ¹*courteous* (¹*courtesy*), *er*¹*roneous* (¹*error*), ¹*grievous* (*grief*), ¹*virtuous* (¹*virtue*), *vi*¹*vacious* (*vi*¹*vacity*)	Stress usually on the last syllable of the base.

Note

[a] The noun suffix *-ity* (App I.25) can be attached to all the above four suffixes; but its addition entails certain changes. The suffix *-al* receives the stressed pronunciation /-ˈæl-/ in place of /-əl/ (*neutral ~ neu*¹*trality*); *-ic* changes its pronunciation from

/-ɪk/ to /-'ɪs-/ (*e'lectric ~ elec'tricity*); *-ous* changes its spelling to *-os-*, and receives
the stressed pronunciation /-'ɒs-/ instead of /-əs/ ('*curious ~ curi'osity*); *-ive* is un-
altered, except that it becomes stressed: '*active ~ ac'tivity*.

[b] In some adjectives, *-ic* alternates with *-ical*, with a difference of meaning:

a *classic* performance	~ *classical* languages
('great', 'memorable')	('Latin and Greek')
a *comic* masterpiece	~ his *comical* behaviour
('of comedy')	('funny') (less usual)
an *economic* miracle	~ the car is *economical* to run
('in the economy')	('money-saving')
an *electric* light	~ an *electrical* fault
('powered by e.')	('of electricity')
a *historic* building	~ *historical* research
('with a history')	('pertaining to history')
his '*politic* behaviour	~ po'*litical* parties
('tactful') (unusual)	('concerned with politics')

[c] There are several less common neo-classical affixes, among which *-ary*, *-ate*, and
-ory are particularly notable: *revolutionary, affectionate, obligatory*. Nouns in *-ory*
alternate (with or without stress shift) with nouns in *-tion: o'bligatory ~ oblig'ation,
satis'factory ~ satis'faction*. Both *-ary* and *-ory* are reduced in BrE to /-ərɪ/ or /-rɪ/;
in AmE they are given a secondary stress, and are distinguished in pronunciation
as /-ˌeri/ and /-ˌɒri/.

I.29
Other adjective suffixes

	added to → to form	meaning	examples	comments
-ABLE (-IBLE)	chiefly transitive verbs → adjectives	generally the meaning is passive: 'able to be V-*ed₂*'; 'worthy of being V-*ed₂*'; 'that ought to be V-*ed₂*'	*acceptable, readable, drinkable, commendable, liveable with, (un)get-at-able*	Sometimes the preposition of a prepositional verb is omitted: *accountable* 'able to be accounted for', *unspeakable* 'unfit to be spoken of'. *Cf* borrowed or neo-classical words: *navigable* (~ *navigate*); *edible* (~ *eat*). The variant spelling -*ible* is used in some borrowed and neo-classical words in obedience to the Latin rules of suffixation: *perfectible*, etc. The more usual -*able* is sometimes added to nouns: *fashionable, reasonable,* etc. The suffix may also be added to intransitive verbs, with an active meaning: *variable* 'able to vary'.
-ISH (also App I.27)	gradable adjectives → gradable adjectives	'somewhat . . .' (a downtoning suffix)	*reddish, latish, tallish, poorish, youngish*	Chiefly informal and mainly used with simple, monosyllabic bases. With ages, it has the meaning 'approximately': *seventyish* 'approximately seventy years old'.

	added to → to form	meaning	examples	comments
-ED (on participial -ed in adjectives, see 5.12 ff)	nouns or noun phrases → adjectives	'having . . .', etc	walled, wooded, pointed, blue-eyed, simple-minded, fuller-flavoured, odd-shaped, giant-sized	More restricted with the noun base than with the phrasal base. In a few cases (as well as when /t/ or /d/ precedes: cf 3.57) the -ed suffix is given a syllabic pronunciation /-ɪd/: dogged, wretched, ragged, three-legged. (The present-day meaning of the suffix is absent from the first two of these examples.) This type of formation has to be distinguished from compounds of the pattern much-travelled, self-styled, etc in which the second element is a verb (App I.55).

I.30
Adverb suffixes

	added to → to form	meaning	examples	comments
-LY (also App I.27)	adjectives → adverbs of manner, viewpoint, etc	'in a . . . manner', etc	happily, strangely, comically, oddly, etc	Very productive. Following -ic, the suffix generally takes the form -ally: scenically, etc. On the functions of -ly adverbs other than manner, see Chapter 8.
-WARD(s)	prepositional adverbs, nouns → adverbs of manner or direction	manner and direction of movement	onward(s), backward(s), earthward(s), homeward(s), eastward(s)	In BrE backward as adverb is used in a purely directional sense; backwards means, in addition, movement 'back first'; likewise frontwards. In AmE, forms without -s are general.

added to → to form	meaning	examples	comments
-WISE nouns → (a) adverbs of manner (b) viewpoint adverbs	(a) 'in the manner of . . .' (b) 'as far as . . . is concerned'	(a) *crabwise, clockwise, corkscrew-wise* (b) *weather-wise, education-wise*	Type (b) is especially productive in informal AmE.

Note

Also -STYLE and -FASHION ('in the manner/style of') are sometimes used as adverbial suffixes: They ate *American-style* (*cf* 8.35).

Conversion
I.31
Conversion and suffixation
Conversion is the derivational process whereby an item is adapted or converted to a new word-class without the addition of an affix. For example, the verb *release* (as in *They released him*) corresponds to a noun *release* (as in *They ordered his release*), and this relationship may be seen as parallel to that between the verb *acquit* (as in *They acquitted him*) and the noun *acquittal* (as in *They ordered his acquittal*):

	verb	deverbal noun
SUFFIXATION:	acquit	→ acquittal
CONVERSION:	release	→ release

In the English language conversion is unusually prominent as a word-formation process, through both the variety of conversion rules and their productiveness.

Note
[a] Other, lengthier terms for conversion are 'functional conversion', 'functional shift', and 'zero derivation'.
[b] Conversion includes, in this treatment, cases where the word undergoes some slight phonological or orthographic change, *eg: shelf* → *shelve* (see App I.43).

I.32
Direction of conversion
It should be noted that conversion, like other types of word-formation discussed in this Appendix, is not treated as a historical process, but rather as a process now available for extending the lexical resources of the language. Thus it is irrelevant, from one point of view, whether the verb *release* preceded the noun *release* as an acquisition of English vocabulary. Certainly difficulties arise in explaining conversion, in that one does not have the addition of a suffix as a guide when deciding which item should be treated as the base and which as the derived form. Nevertheless, it is convenient to attempt to make such a distinction, and often the semantic dependence of one item upon another is sufficient grounds for arguing its derivational dependence. For example, the verb *net* can be paraphrased in terms of the noun as 'put into a net', but no comparable paraphrase could be constructed for the noun; that is, to define *net* in some such terms as 'an instrument for *netting*' would be to limit the meaning of the noun quite arbitrarily to exclude (for example) strawberry nets, mosquito nets, and hair nets.

This criterion cannot be easily applied to *release* above, but one may note that *release* as a noun is parallel to other nouns derived from dynamic verbs as regards selection restrictions; that is, one may say *His release was sudden/on Tuesday/etc* just as one may say *His discovery/promotion/etc was sudden/on Tuesday/etc.* Moreover, *release* behaves as a deverbal noun in structures of 'nominalization' (13.34–35): *His release by the government; The government's release of the prisoners.* On these grounds, we treat abstract and agential nouns (*eg: love,* ˈrebel) as derived.

In the survey of types of conversion that follows, we resume the principle of classification that was adopted for suffixation: this means we group words according to the class of the base and the class of the word derived. Thus *release* is to be classed as a deverbal noun under the heading of verb → noun conversion (App I.34).

I.33
Full conversion and 'partial conversion'

Some grammars make a distinction between 'full conversion' (*ie*, conversion as already discussed) and 'partial conversion', where a word of one class appears in a function which is characteristic of another word-class. One may argue, for instance, that in such structures as *the wealthy* (='wealthy people'), *the ignorant, the wicked,* the adjective is 'partially converted' to noun status, in that it is syntactically in a position (head of noun phrase) characteristic of nouns rather than adjectives (5.20–23). That there is not full conversion in such cases is demonstrated by the inability of *wealthy* as it occurs in sentences like *The wealthy are always with us* to behave inflectionally like a noun, that is, to vary in terms of number and case. One cannot say **I met a wealthy; *Those wealthies are my friends;* etc. On the other hand, it is doubtful whether this rather restricted use of adjectives should be treated as a word-formation process at all; not only is there no inflectional evidence of the word's status as a noun, but there is inflectional evidence of its unchanged status as adjective: *the wealthier,* etc. Moreover, there does not appear to be any of the partial productivity, of the distinction between actual and potential English words, that we have seen as one of the hall-marks of a word-formation process (App I.2). Rather, we can claim that any adjective of a permitted class (*ie* applicable to human beings or to abstractions) might be used in such a structure, with no constraints of productivity:

The $\begin{cases} \text{wealthy} \\ \text{kind} \\ \text{well-dressed} \\ \text{foolish} \\ \text{ill-behaved} \\ \text{etc} \end{cases}$ are always with us

The position adopted in this grammar, therefore, has been to treat such cases in purely syntactic terms, as 'adjective functioning as head of noun phrase', rather than to postulate that conversion, or the transfer of an item from one word-class to another, has taken place.

We now present the types of conversion, starting with the three major word-classes chiefly involved: nouns, verbs, and adjectives. As will be evident from the lists, conversions from noun to verb and from verb to noun are the most productive categories. Only the major semantic types are noted under each heading. It is to be understood that a word can be converted with more than one meaning: *run*, in different contexts, can mean 'that which is run', 'the act of running', or 'where (animals) can run'.

I.34
Verb → noun conversion

[A] 'State' (generally 'state of mind' or 'state of sensation') (from stative verbs to count or mass nouns):

desire, dismay, doubt, love, smell, taste, want

[B] 'Event/activity' (from dynamic verbs):

attempt, fall, hit, laugh, release, search, shut-down, swim, walk-out

[C] 'Object of V':

answer ('that which is answered'), *bet, catch, find, hand-out*

[D] 'Subject of V':

bore ('someone who bores/is boring'), *cheat, coach, show-off, stand-in*

[E] 'Instrument of V':

cover ('something with which to cover things'), *wrap, wrench*

[F] 'Manner of V-*ing*':

walk ('manner of walking'), *throw, lie* (eg in *the lie of the land*)

[G] 'Place of V':

divide, retreat, rise, turn

Note
The type of informal deverbal coinage represented by *teach-in* belongs to Category B rather than to any other, but unlike *show-down* cannot be derived from a phrasal verb (there is no *We taught in last night*). The vogue for such formations has produced *sit-in, love-in, swim-in*, and others. They signify an activity (that denoted by the verb) being carried on corporately (typically within an institution and with overtones of social protest).

I.35
Adjective → noun conversion

There is no very productive pattern of adjective → noun conversion. Miscellaneous examples are:

I'd like two pints of *bitter*, please (=type of beer, BrE)
As a footballer, he's a *natural* (=a naturally skilled player)
They're running in the *final* (=the final race)

Also *daily* ('daily newspaper'), *comic* ('comic actor'), *regulars* ('regular customers'), *roast* ('roast beef'), (*young*) *marrieds* ('young married people'; informal). From these examples, it is seen that adjective → noun conversion can usually be explained in terms of a fixed adjective + noun phrase from which the noun has been ellipted.

I.36
Noun → verb conversion

[A] 'To put in/on N':

> *bottle* ('to put into a bottle'), *corner, catalogue, floor, garage, position*

[B] 'To give N, to provide with N':

> *coat* ('to give a coat [of paint, etc] to'), *commission, grease, mask, muzzle, plaster*

[C] 'To deprive of N':

> *core* ('remove the core from'), *gut, peel, skin, top-and-tail* (BrE)

[D] 'To . . . with N' (More precisely the meaning of the verb is 'to use the referent of the noun as an instrument for whatever activity is particularly associated with it'):

> *brake* ('to stop by means of a brake'), *elbow, fiddle, finger, glue, knife*

[E] 'To $\begin{Bmatrix} \text{be} \\ \text{act as} \end{Bmatrix}$ N with respect to . . .':

> *chaperon* ('to act as chaperon to'), *father, nurse, parrot, pilot, referee*

[F] 'To $\begin{Bmatrix} \text{make} \\ \text{change} \end{Bmatrix}$ . . . into N':

> *cash* ('to change into cash'), *cripple, group*

[G] 'To $\begin{cases} \text{(a) send} \\ \text{(b) go} \end{cases}$ by N':

(a) *mail* ('to send by mail'), *ship, telegraph*
(b) *bicycle* ('to go by bicycle'), *boat, canoe, motor*

Most of the verbs in this category are transitive, with the exception of Type G(b), and a few members of Type D.

I.37
Adjective → verb conversion

[A] (transitive verbs) 'to make adj' or 'to make more adj':

calm ('to make calm'), *dirty, humble, lower, soundproof*

[B] (intransitive verbs) 'to become adj' (generally adjectives in Type A can also have this function):

dry ('to become dry'), *empty, narrow, weary* (*of*), *yellow*

Sometimes a phrasal verb is derived from an adjective by the addition of a particle: *smooth out* ('make smooth'); *sober up* ('to become sober'); *calm down* ('to become calm').

This category of conversion competes with suffixation with *-en* (see App I.26), and sometimes both derivations are available for the same adjective:

He $\begin{cases} blacked \\ blackened \end{cases}$ his face with soot.

I.38
Noun → adjective conversion
Membership of this category can be postulated only when the noun form occurs in predicative as well as in attributive positions (5.3):

a *brick* garage ~ The garage is *brick*
reproduction furniture ~ This furniture is *reproduction*
Worcester porcelain ~ This porcelain is *Worcester*
a very *Oxbridge* accent ~ His accent is very *Oxbridge* (BrE)

(The last example, which is the kind of improvised form one sometimes hears in speech, is a case of a noun converted to a gradable adjective.)

It is arguable, however, that in such cases the noun remains a noun even in predicative position (5.11). Other instances of nouns occurring in premodifying position (13.57–59) are definitely best treated as outside the domain of word-formation, for reasons applied to the 'partial conversion' of adjectives in App I.33 above. It is worth noting, however, that a noun often functions as a premodifier in cases where the language happens to possess no adjective to perform that function. The contrast between the adjective modifier of *the Zambian government* and the noun modifier of *the Malawi government* seems to result from the accident that English has no established derivative adjective from the noun *Malawi*.

I.39
Minor categories of conversion
There are several anomalous and less productive types of conversion, chiefly used informally; among them the following are noteworthy:

[I] *Conversion from closed-system words to nouns:*

It is often said that any word can be converted to noun status in English. It is true that there are no limits on the ability of words when cited or named to occur as nouns, as in '*And*' (*ie* the word *and*) *contains three letters*. But apart from such cases, it is only occasionally that items from minor word-classes can undergo this conversion. Examples are:

His argument contains too many *ifs* and *buts*
This book is a *must* for the student of aerodynamics
It tells you about the *how* and the *why* of flight

[II] *Conversion from phrases to nouns:*

Phrases, or sequences of more than one word, are sometimes reduced to noun status by conversion rather than by any of the normal patterns of compounding (App I.44 *ff*):

Whenever I gamble, my horse is one of the *also-rans*
(*ie* one of the horses which 'also ran' but was not among the winners)

[III] *Conversion from phrases to adjectives:*

Similarly, phrases may occasionally be converted to adjectives:

an *under-the-weather* feeling ~ I feel very *under-the-weather*
(lacking in health)
an *upper-class* manner ~ His manner is intolerably *upper-class*

[IV] *Conversion from affixes to nouns:*

Very occasionally, an affix may be converted into a noun:

Patriotism, nationalism, and any other *isms* you'd like to name.

I.40

Change of secondary word-class: nouns

The notion of conversion may be extended to changes of secondary word-class, within the same major word category: for example, when mass nouns are reclassified as count nouns or vice versa (4.2). Such transfers are only partially productive, and yet can be explained systematically in terms of derivation. They are therefore parallel to the major conversion processes already discussed. Types of conversion (or reclassification) within the noun category are:

(a) *Mass noun → count noun*

    (i) 'A unit of N':

        two *coffees* ('cups of coffee'); two *cheeses*

    (ii) 'A kind of N':

        Some *paints* are more lasting than others
        This is a better *bread* than the one I bought last

    (iii) 'An instance of N' (with abstract nouns):

        a *difficulty;* small *kindnesses;* a miserable *failure;*
        home *truths*

(b) *Count noun → mass noun*

'N viewed in terms of a measurable extent' (normally only after expressions of amount):

    An inch of *pencil;* a few square feet of *floor*

(c) *Proper noun → common noun*

    (i) 'A member of the class typified by N':

        a *Jeremiah* ('a gloomy prophet who denounces his age')
        a latter-day *Plutarch* ('... chronicler of great men')
        Edinburgh is the *Athens* of the north
        He wore *wellingtons*

    (ii) 'A person, place, etc called N':

        There are several *Cambridges* ('places called Cambridge')
        in the world

    (iii) 'A specimen of the product $\left\{ \begin{array}{l} \text{made by} \\ \text{called} \end{array} \right\}$ N':

        a *Rolls Royce* ('a car manufactured by Rolls Royce')
        ten *Players* ('ten cigarettes made by Players')

(d) *Stative noun → dynamic noun*

Nouns are characteristically stative, but they can assume the dynamic meaning of 'temporary role or activity' as subject complement following the progressive aspect of BE:

He's being a $\begin{cases} fool \\ nuisance \\ hero \\ etc \end{cases}$ ('He's behaving like a fool', etc).

I.41
Change of secondary word-class: verbs
Similar categories exist for verbs:

(a) *Intransitive → transitive*

'Cause to V':

run the water ('cause the water to run'); *march* the prisoners; *dive* one's hand into the water; *slide* the bolt back

Likewise *budge, fly, slither, stop, turn, twist*

(b) *Transitive → intransitive*

(i) 'Can be V-*ed₂*' (often followed by an intensifying adverb such as *well* or *badly*):

The clock *winds up* at the back ('can be wound up'); Your book *reads* well; The table *polishes up* badly

Likewise: *divide, drive, sail, screw up, steer, undo, unlock, wash*

(ii) 'To V oneself':

Have you *washed* yet? ('washed yourself')

Likewise: *bath, behave, dress, make up, shave*

(iii) 'To V someone/something/etc':

We have *eaten* already ('eaten something, had a meal')

Likewise: *cook, drink, hunt, kill, knit, sew, write*

(c) *Intransitive → intensive*

(i) Current meaning (see 7.14, 7.22):

He *lay* flat; We *stood* motionless

Likewise: *float* (free); *ride* (high); *arrive* (hungry); etc

(ii) Resulting meaning (see 7.14, 7.22):

He *fell* flat; The sun was *sinking* low

Likewise: *run* (cold); *boil* (dry); *wash* (clean); etc

(d) *Intensive → intransitive*

> What must *be*, must *be* ('exist')

(e) *Monotransitive → complex transitive*

> (i) Current meaning:
>
>> We *catch* them young ('... when they are young')
>> Likewise: *can't bear, buy, find, hate, like, sell*
>
> (ii) Resulting meaning:
>
>> I *wiped* it clean ('made it clean by wiping it')
>> Likewise: *knock* (... unconscious); *lock* (... fast); *tease*
>> (... mad)
>
> Note reflexive objects: *I laughed myself silly*, etc.

I.42
Change of secondary word-class: adjectives

(a) *Non-gradable → gradable* (5.39, 5.70)

> He's more *English* than the English; Some people's behaviour
> is rather *incredible;* I have a very *legal* turn of mind

(b) *Stative → dynamic* (5.38)

> As in App I.40 (d) above, dynamic meaning is signalled by the
> progressive aspect of BE.
>
> He's just being *friendly* ('acting in a friendly manner');
> Your uncle is being *bigoted*, as usual; He's being *awkward*
> about it; Martha is being *desirable* this evening.

I.43
Approximate conversion: voicing and stress shift

In some cases conversion is approximate rather than complete; that is, a
word, in the course of changing its grammatical function, may undergo a
slight change of pronunciation or spelling. The most important kinds of
alteration are (1) voicing of final consonants, and (2) shift of stress. Both
kinds (like most phenomena of word-formation) are unpredictable and
idiosyncratic in respect of the particular instances that occur.

(1) VOICING OF FINAL CONSONANTS

The unvoiced fricative consonants /s/, /f/, and /θ/ in the following examples of noun-verb conversion are voiced to /z/, /v/ and /ð/ respectively:

NOUN	VERB	NOUN	VERB
house /-s/	house /-z/	thief /-f/	thieve /-v/
advice /-s/	advise /-z/	belief /-f/	believe /-v/
use /-s/	use /-z/	relief /-f/	relieve /-v/
abuse /-s/	abuse /-z/	mouth /-θ/	mouth /-ð/
grief /-f/	grieve /-v/	sheath /-θ/	sheathe /-ð/
shelf /-f/	shelve /-v/	teeth (pl.) /-θ/	teethe /-ð/
half /-f/	halve /-v/	wreath /-θ/	wreathe /-ð/

It should be noted that in BrE, the difference between *licence* (n) and *license* (v), like that between *practice* (n) and *practise* (v), is one of spelling only: both noun and verb are pronounced with a final /s/. In AmE, the conversion is complete, both noun and verb having the spellings *license*, *practice*.

A substantial change of pronunciation, including modification of the final vowel, is observed in pairs such as: *breath* (/-e-/) ~ *breathe* (/-i-/); *glass* (/-æ-/ in AmE, /-ɑ-/ in southern BrE) ~ *glaze* (/-eɪ-/); *emphasis* (/-ɪ-/) ~ *emphasize* (/-aɪ-/). In other pairs, such as *blood* ~ *bleed*, *food* ~ *feed*, it is the vowel alone that changes.

(2) SHIFT OF STRESS (see App II.5)

When verbs of two syllables are converted into nouns, the stress is sometimes shifted from the second to the first syllable. The first syllable, typically a Latin prefix, often varies its vowel from /ə/ (in the verb) to some other vowel (in the noun):

He was con'victed (/kən-/) of theft, and so became a 'convict (/kɒn-/)

The following is a fairly full list of words undergoing this stress shift:

abstract, compound, compress, conduct, confine (noun plural only), *conflict, conscript, consort, construct, contest, contrast, convert, convict, digest, discard, discount, discourse, escort, export, extract, ferment, import, impress, incline, increase, insult, misprint, perfume, permit, pervert, present, produce, progress, protest, rebel, record, refill, refit, refund, regress, reject, resit, segment, survey, suspect, torment, transfer, transform, transplant, transport, upset*

Occasionally, a word of more than two syllables varies in this way: *over'flow* (v) → '*overflow* (n). There are many examples of disyllabic noun-verb pairs which do not differ in stress; for example, 'contact (v) and 'contact (n) both have forestress (as is usual where the verb is derived from the noun), and de'bate (v) and de'bate (n) both have end-stress.

Compounds
I.44
Definition

A compound is a unit consisting of two or more bases (see App I.4). Such 'compound words' can be nouns (*eg: blood+test=bloodtest*), adjectives (*eg: tax+free=tax-free*), or verbs (*eg: spring+clean=spring-clean*). There is no one formal criterion that can be used for a general definition of compounds in English (*cf* 13.57 *ff*).

I.45
Orthographic criteria

Orthographically, compounds are written

- (a) solid, *eg: bedroom*
- (b) hyphenated, *eg: tax-free*
- (c) open, *eg: reading material*

There are no safe rules-of-thumb that will help in the choice between these three possibilities. Practice varies in many words, and some may even occur in three different compound forms, for example, *flowerpot, flower-pot, flower pot.* In AmE there seems to be a trend away from the use of hyphens: compounds are usually written solid as soon as they have gained some permanent status; otherwise they are written open. In BrE, however, there tends to be more extensive use of the hyphen. The following examples found in two standard dictionaries can serve as illustrations of different practice in this respect in the two varieties of English:

(BrE) *air-brake, call-girl, dry-dock, letter-writer*
(AmE) *air brake, call girl, dry dock, letter writer*

For the use of hyphens, see further App III.4 *f*.

I.46
Phonological criteria

Phonologically, compounds can often be identified as having a main stress on the first element and a secondary stress on the second element.

Hence the compound *blackbird* ('a species of bird') has the stress ˈ— ˌ— in contrast with ˌ— ˈ— for *black bird* ('a bird which is black'), which is the normal stress-pattern for noun phrases consisting of a premodifying adjective and a noun head. On the other hand, many speakers have a secondary stress on the first element in, for example, *headmaster*, *sociolinguistics*. For the stressing of compounds, see further App II.6 *ff*.

I.47
Semantic criteria

Semantically, compounds can be seen to be isolated from ordinary syntactic constructions by having a meaning which may be related to but can not simply be inferred from the meaning of its parts. For example, *a darkroom* ('a room used for photographic processing') is not just 'a dark room', since most dark rooms are not *darkrooms*. A *hothouse* ('a heated glass building for growing plants') is a type of building with a special use, but its last element has enough in common with uses of the word *house* for us to recognize the resemblance. On the other hand, it is difficult to see anything in common between the ordinary noun *dog* and the second element in the compound *hot dog* ('a sausage in a sandwich').

I.48
The treatment of compounds

Since the term 'compound' covers a wide range of different relations between bases, none of these three markers (orthographic, phonological, or semantic) can be used as strict defining criteria. We will have to be content with a broad definition of compounds as isolated multi-base units which function as single words and reflect certain grammatical processes.

It is in keeping with the approach of a grammar to concentrate on the productive or creative types of compounding, and to indicate the relations of the compounding elements by syntactic paraphrases. As an example of this approach, we may take the two compounds *playboy* and *call-girl*, which are superficially similar, consisting of verb + noun. Yet the relations of their elements, and hence the 'grammatical' meanings of the two compounds, are different:

playboy ~ *the boy plays, ie* verb + subject, but
call-girl ~ *X calls the girl, ie* verb + object

Similarly, *daydreaming* and *sightseeing* can be analysed in terms of their sentential analogues:

X dreams during the day, ie verb + adverbial, but
X sees sights, ie verb + object.

Noun compounds
I.49
Subject and verb compounds

SUNRISE	
subject + deverbal noun	bee-sting
~ *the sun rises*	catcall
Very productive type.	daybreak
	earthquake
	frostbite
	headache
	heartbeat
	landslide
	nightfall
	rainfall
	sound change
	toothache, etc

RATTLESNAKE	
verb + subject	crybaby
~ *the snake rattles*	driftwood
Only weakly productive type.	drip coffee
	flashlight
	glowworm
	hangman
	playboy
	popcorn
	stinkweed
	tugboat
	turntable
	watchdog, etc

DANCING GIRL	
verbal noun in -*ing* + subject	cleaning woman
~ *the girl dances*	firing squad
	flying machine
	investigating committee
	wading bird
	washing machine
	working party, etc

I.50
Verb and object compounds

BLOODTEST	*count nouns*	(*primarily*)
object + deverbal noun	book review	*mass nouns*
~ *X tests blood*	crime report	birth-control
~ *the testing of blood;*	haircut	dress-design

suicide attempt
~ an attempt at suicide
Moderately productive type.
Self is a frequent first element.

handshake
suicide attempt
tax cut, etc

meat delivery
office management
steel production
self-control
self-destruction
self-determination,
    etc

SIGHTSEEING
object + verbal noun in *-ing*
(*cf* App I.54, *man-eating*)
~ X sees sights
~ the seeing of sights
(Number is neutralized in
    the compound.)
This type is very productive.
It consists of abstract compounds
    referring to human activity.

air-conditioning
book-keeping
book-reviewing
brainwashing
dressmaking
faultfinding
housekeeping
letter-writing
oath-taking
story-telling
town-planning, etc

TAXPAYER
object + agential noun in *-er*
~ X pays tax(es)
Very productive type, which designates
    concrete (usually human) agents. Note
    however *dishwasher, lawn-mower,*
    penholder, record-player. Neutralization
    of number is normal; *cf: cigar smoker*
    ~ X smokes cigars, etc

cigar smoker
computer-designer
crime reporter
gamekeeper
gate-crasher
hair-splitter
language teacher
matchmaker
radio-operator
songwriter
stockholder
window-cleaner, etc

CALL-GIRL
verb + object
~ X calls the girl
(*~ the girl is on call*)

drawbridge
knitwear
mincemeat
pin-up girl
punchcard
push-button
scarecrow
treadmill, etc

CHEWING GUM
verbal noun in *-ing* + object
~ X chews gum
~ gum for chewing

cooking apple
drinking-water
eating apple
reading material
spending money, etc

I.51
Verb and adverbial compounds

SWIMMING POOL	PLACE
verbal noun in -*ing* + adverbial (consisting of a prepositional phrase)	diving board (dive from a board)
	drinking cup (drink out of a cup)
	freezing point (freeze at a point)
~ *X swims in the pool*	frying pan (BrE: fry in a pan)
~ *a pool for swimming*	hiding-place (hide in a place)
A very productive type.	living room (live in a room)
	typing paper (type on paper)
	waiting room (wait in a room)
	writing desk (write at a desk)
	OTHER
	adding machine (add with a machine)
	baking powder (bake with powder)
	carving knife (carve with a knife)
	sewing machine (sew with a machine)
	walking stick (walk with a stick)
	washing machine (wash with a machine), etc

DAYDREAMING	PLACE
adverbial + abstract verbal noun in -*ing*	churchgoing (go to church)
	horse riding (ride on a horse)
~ $\left\{\begin{array}{l} X\ dreams \\ dreaming \end{array}\right\}$ *during the day*	rope-dancing (dance on a rope)
	sun-bathing (bathe in the sun)
Moderately productive type (*cf* App I.55, *ocean-going*).	TIME
	sleepwalking (walk in one's sleep)
	OTHER
	fly-fishing (fish with a fly)
	handwriting (write by hand)
	shadow-boxing (box against a shadow), etc

BABY-SITTER	PLACE
adverbial + agential noun in -*er*	backswimmer (swim on the back)
~ *X sits with the baby*	city-dweller (dwell in the city)
Moderately productive type.	factory-worker (work in a factory)
	housebreaker (break into a house)
	playgoer (go to a play)
	rope-dancer (dance on a rope)
	sun-bather (bathe in the sun)
	theatre-goer (go to the theatre)
	TIME
	daydreamer (dream during the day), etc

HOMEWORK
adverbial + deverbal noun
~ *X works at home*
Moderately productive type.
Most examples are countables:
  boat-rides, etc. Compare
  gunfight here with
  gunfighting, which is of the
  daydreaming type.

PLACE
boat-ride (ride in a boat)
field-work (work in the field)
homework (work at home)
table talk (talk at the table)
moon walk (walk on the moon)

TIME
daydream (dream during the day)
night flight (fly during the night)

OTHER
gunfight (fight with a gun)
smallpox vaccination (vaccinate against
  smallpox)
tax-exemption (exempt from tax)
telephone call (call on the telephone), etc

SEARCHLIGHT
verb + adverbial
~ *X searches with a light*

PLACE
dance hall (dance in a hall)
springboard (spring from a board)
workbench (work at a bench)

OTHER
grindstone (grind with a stone)
plaything (play with a thing), etc

I.52
Verbless compounds

WINDMILL
$noun_1 + noun_2$
~ $noun_1$ [*powers/operates*] $noun_2$
~ *the wind powers the mill*

air-brake
air rifle
cable car
hydrogen bomb
motorcycle
steam engine, etc

TOY FACTORY
$noun_1 + noun_2$
~ $noun_2$ [*produces/yields*] $noun_1$
~ *the factory produces toys*

honey-bee
oil well
power plant
silkworm
tear gas
textile mill
water pistol, etc

BLOODSTAIN noun$_1$ + noun$_2$ ~ noun$_1$ [*produces/yields*] noun$_2$ ~ *the blood produces stains*	bloodstain cane ˈsugar eiderdown food poisoning gaslight hay fever sawdust tortoise-shell water spot whalebone, etc	

DOORKNOB
noun$_1$ + noun$_2$
~ noun$_1$ [*has*] noun$_2$
~ *the door has a knob*
A very productive type.
Noun$_1$ is inanimate. Animate
  nouns have the *-s* genitive:
  compare *the table leg* with
  the boy's leg.
	arrowhead
	bedpost
	bottleneck (metaphorical)
	cartwheel
	piano keys
	shirt-sleeves
	table leg
	telephone receiver
	television screen
	window-pane, etc	

GIRL-FRIEND
noun$_1$ + noun$_2$
~ noun$_2$ [*is*] noun$_1$
~ *the friend is a girl*
Noun$_1$ refers to a subspecies of
  the species denoted by noun$_2$.
	animate nouns
	drummer boy
	killer shark
	manservant
	pussy-cat
	woman writer,
	    etc
		inanimate nouns
		blinker light
		feeder bus
		oak tree
		pine tree
		tape measure,
		    etc

DARKROOM adjective + noun ~ noun [*is*] adjective ~ *the room is dark*	blackboard blueprint double-talk dry-dock handyman hothouse longboat madman, etc	
FROGMAN noun$_1$ + noun$_2$ ~ noun$_1$ [*is like*] noun$_2$ ~ *the man is like a frog* A very productive type.	butter-bean catfish dragonfly goldfish kettledrum	

sandwich-man
tissue paper
T-square, etc

SNOWFLAKE
noun₁ + noun₂
~ noun₂ [*consisting of*] noun₁
~ *a flake of snow*

bread-crumb
chocolate bar
dustheap
raindrop
sand dune
soap flake, etc

ASHTRAY
noun₁ + noun₂
~ noun₂ [*is for*] noun₁
~ *the tray is for ash*
This highly productive type
  expresses purpose. It is similar
  to the *swimming pool* and
  searchlight types, which
  however have sentential
  analogues with verbs.

birdcage
breakfast time
coffee time
cough drops
cowshed
doghouse
facecloth
fire engine
fish-pond
flowerbed
flypaper
safety belt
tearoom, etc

Note

The difference between *teacup* (~ 'cup for tea') and *cup of tea* (~ 'cup containing tea') is paralleled in *flowerpot*, *matchbox*, *winebottle*, and *soup plate*, etc.

I.53
Bahuvrihi compounds

PAPERBACK
is a 'bahuvrihi compound' in that
  it names an entire thing by
  specifying some feature of it.
  Thus *a paperback* is 'a book
  which has a paper back', *an
  egghead* is 'a person who has a
  head like an egg', *ie*, 'an
  intellectual'.

noun + noun
birdbrain
blockhead
butterfingers
featherbrain
featherweight
hunchback
pot-belly, etc

adjective + noun
bluebell
fathead
hardhat
  ('construction
  worker')
hardtop
heavyweight
highbrow
loudmouth
paleface
redcap, etc

Adjective compounds
I.54
Verb and object compounds

MAN-EATING object + *-ing* participle ~ *X eats men* (*cf* App I.50, *sightseeing*) Productive type. *Self* is a frequent first element.	breathtaking fact-finding heart-breaking life-giving record-breaking self-defeating self-justifying, etc

---

I.55
Verb and adverbial compounds

OCEAN-GOING adverbial + *-ing* participle ~ *X goes across oceans* (*cf* App I.51, *daydreaming*)	fist-fighting law-abiding lip-sucking mouth-watering, etc

---

HEART-FELT adverbial + *-ed* participle ~ *X feels it in the heart* The type is particularly productive when the noun has agential meaning and consists of *self-: self-employed*, *self-taught*.	airborne custom-built handmade home-brewed home-made suntanned thunder-struck town-bred weather-beaten, etc

---

HARD-WORKING adjective/adverb + *-ing* participle ~ *X works hard*	easy-going everlasting far-reaching good-looking high-sounding well-meaning, etc

---

QUICK-FROZEN adjective/adverb + *-ed* participle ~ *X is frozen quickly*	far-fetched new-laid true-born well-meant widespread, etc

---

Note

[a] The idiomatic isolation of some compounds of this type is evident in the replacement of lexical items in sentential analogues, *eg: NEW-laid* (*eggs*) ~ *X has laid* (*the eggs*) *RECENTLY*.

[b] The superficially similar adjective compounds *well-meant* and *well-behaved* differ in respect of voice: *a well-meant remark* ~ *a remark that is meant well* (passive), but *a well-behaved person* ~ *a person that behaves well* (active).

I.56
Verbless compounds

CLASS-CONSCIOUS
noun (denoting respect) +
  adjective
~ *conscious with respect to class*
Very productive type with certain
  adjectives that are frequently
  complemented by prep + noun (5.36),
  eg: free, proof, sick, tight, weary.

duty-free
tax-free
dustproof
fireproof
foolproof
airsick
carsick
homesick
air-tight
watertight
foot-weary
war-weary, etc

GRASS-GREEN
noun + adjective
~ { *as* adjective *as* noun
   adjective *like* noun

ash-blonde
bottle-green
brick red
midnight blue
ocean green
sea-green, etc

SWEDISH-AMERICAN (*contacts*)
adjective₁ + adjective₂ in a coordinating
  relationship
~ (*contacts between*) *Swedish and*
  American (*people*)
In many such compounds, the first
  element is not a separate word and has
  a linking -*o*-. The main stress is on the
  second element.

bitter-sweet
deaf-mute
phonetic-syntactic
Anglo-American
Franco-German
socio-economic
psycholinguistic, etc

Note

In compounds used as premodifiers of the word *dictionary*, the first adjective indicates the language used as the basis for the dictionary. For example, an *English-French dictionary* translates words from English into French.

I.57
Verb compounds

Verb compounds include a BACK-FORMATION like *baby-sit*, which is formed from *baby-sitting* and *baby-sitter*. This process is a reversal of the normal trend of word-formation, by which a new word is formed by adding rather than subtracting elements; *ie* the verbal nouns *singer* and *singing* are taken to be formed from the verb *sing*. But the name 'back-formation' draws attention to a purely historical order of development (*cf* App I.2 Note *b*).

There are two types of syntactic relation in verb compounds formed by back-formation.

SIGHTSEE object + verb ~ *X sees sights*	brain-wash fire-watch house-hunt housekeep lip-read, etc
SPRING-CLEAN adverbial + verb ~ *X cleans in the spring*	baby-sit bottle-feed chain-smoke day-dream sleep-walk spring-clean whip-lash window-shop, etc

Note
Some difficulty is felt with forms like *sightsee* and *baby-sit* which have irregular inflections of the verb. Speakers are inclined to avoid both forms like *babysat* and **baby-sitted* and to use only infinitive forms: *She might babysit for us.*

I.58
Reduplicatives

Some compounds have two or more elements which are either identical or only slightly different, *eg: goody-goody* ('affectedly good', informal). The difference between the two elements may be in the initial consonants, as in *walkie-talkie*, or in the medial vowels, *eg: criss-cross*. Most of the reduplicatives are highly informal or familiar, and many derive from the nursery, *eg: din-din* ('dinner'). The most common uses of reduplicatives are

(a) to imitate sounds, *eg: rat-a-tat* (knocking on door), *tick-tock* (of clock), *ha ha* (of laughter), *bow-wow* (of dog)

(b) to suggest alternating movements, *eg: seesaw, flip-flop, ping-pong*

(c) to disparage by suggesting instability, nonsense, insincerity, vacillation, etc: *higgledy-piggledy, hocus-pocus, wishy-washy, dilly-dally, shilly-shally*

(d) to intensify, *eg: teeny-weeny, tip-top*

I.59

Clipping

The term 'clipping' denotes the subtraction of one or more syllables from a word, which is also available in its full form. The clipped form is normally felt to be informal. The shortening may occur at

(a) the beginning of the word:

phone	telephone
plane	airplane, aeroplane
bus	omnibus (full form now rare)

(b) the end of the word (more commonly):

ad	advert(isement)
photo	photograph
exam	examination
mike	microphone
mini	mini-skirt
memo	memorandum
taxi	taxicab

(c) at both ends of the word (not a common type of clipping):

flu	influenza
fridge	refrigerator
(esp. BrE)	

I.60

Blends

In a blend at least one of the elements is fragmentary when compared with its corresponding uncompounded word form. For example *brunch* (especially AmE, 'a meal subsuming breakfast and lunch') is derived from *br(eakfast)+(l)unch*. Many blends have only a very short life and are very informal, *eg: swimsation ~ swim + sensation.* They are often conscious and deliberate formations, and hence perhaps particularly common in commercial language, *eg: lubritection ~ lubrication + protection.* Quite a few blends, however, have become more or less fully accepted in the language, *eg:*

bit	~	binary digit
breathalyser	~	breath analyser
electrocute	~	electro + execute
Eurovision	~	European television
heliport	~	helicopter + (air)port
Interpol	~	international police
moped	~	motor + pedal (cycle)
motel	~	motor hotel
newscast	~	news broadcast
paratroops	~	parachute troops
smog	~	smoke + fog
telecast	~	television broadcast
transistor	~	transfer + resistor
travelogue	~	travel catalogue

I.61
Acronyms

Acronyms are words formed from the initial letters (or larger parts) of words that make up a descriptive phrase or a proper name. New acronyms are freely produced in Modern English, particularly for names of organizations. There are two main types:

(1) Acronyms which are pronounced as sequences of letters can be called 'alphabetisms', *eg* C.O.D./si ou di/. In writing, the more institutionalized formations have no periods between the letters.

(a) The letters represent full words:

C.O.D.	cash on delivery
EEC	European Economic Community
FBI	Federal Bureau of Investigation
MIT	Massachusetts Institute of Technology
UN	the United Nations

(b) The letters represent elements in a compound or just parts of a word:

TV	television
GHQ	General Headquarters

ID   identification card (AmE)

TB   tuberculosis

(2) Acronyms which are pronounced as a word, *eg* NATO /ˈneɪtoʊ/, and are often used without knowing what the letters stand for:

NATO   the North Atlantic Treaty Organization

UNESCO the United Nations Educational, Scientific and Cultural Organization

WASP   White Anglo-Saxon Protestant (AmE, informal)

laser   lightwave amplification by stimulated emission of radiation

radar   radio detecting and ranging

Bibliographical note

Marchand (1969) is the most up-to-date and compendious reference work on English word-formation. Jespersen (1909–49), Vol vɪ, and Koziol (1937), although less recent, are also valuable for detailed documentation. Seymour (1968) may be consulted for bibliography.

Other books of general coverage are Adams (1973); Ginzburg *et al* (1966).

The periodical *American Speech* frequently publishes articles on new words and trends in AmE word-formation.

Some other contributions to the study of English word-formation are Biese (1941); Brown (1927); Brown (1954); Danielsson (1948); Harder (1968); Hatcher (1960); Lees (1960a); Lindelöf (1937); Ljung (1970); McDavid-Mencken (1963), especially Part V, 'The Language Today'; Reifer (1955); Thun (1963); Zimmer (1964).

APPENDIX II
STRESS, RHYTHM, AND INTONATION

General
II.1
It should be made clear at the outset that the study of stress, rhythm, and intonation is an extremely complex and controversial area of linguistics to which it is impossible to give adequate attention within the space of this Appendix. Our aim must here be strictly limited to presenting an outline of the part these features play in English grammar, to explaining the allusions that have been made to them in this book, and to guiding the reader to the selective reading list with which the Appendix ends.

The three phenomena are less distinct from each other than their separate names might imply, since all are concerned with the perception of relative PROMINENCE. We speak of STRESS when we are considering the prominence with which one part of a word or of a longer utterance is distinguished from other parts. Thus we will say that *indignant* has stress on the second syllable or that the word *like* is stressed in 'Does he like it?', and we can show this with the notation explained in App II.3:

In⎪dignant
Does he ⎪like it?

We speak of RHYTHM when we are considering the pattern formed by the stresses being perceived as peaks of prominence or beats, occurring at somewhat regular intervals of time, the recurring beats being regarded as completing a cycle or 'measure'. Thus, as a language with a tendency for 'stress-timed' rhythm, English often shows an identity of rhythm in sentences like the following, provided that the number of syllables does not vary too widely:

⎪John's at ⎪home ⎪⎪to⎪night
⎪John's ⎪here ⎪now
The pro⎪fessor's in ⎪London this ⎪evening

We speak of INTONATION when we associate relative prominence with PITCH, the aspect of sound which we perceive in terms of 'high' or 'low'; thus we will say that the 'intonation nucleus' in the following sentence (using a notation explained in App II.12) has a 'falling tone':

The ⎪man has GÒNE

and that it would have the value of a question if this nucleus had a rising tone:

The ⎪man has GÓNE

II.2
Physical properties

The physics of these phenomena cannot here concern us, though we must utter a warning against simple equations such as regarding stress as identical with loudness. Stress is closely associated with loudness or amplitude on the one hand and articulatory force on the other, but other factors are or can be involved – notably duration and pitch. This last seems to be the most important factor when a stress is final in a phrase (or when a word is spoken in isolation): the stress is then associated with (or realized by) pitch prominence and often with pitch movement. But what matters is that the hearer expects sharp contrasts of prominence and expects peaks of prominence at particular places in a word or phrase; and that his understanding is severely handicapped if such expectations are frustrated.

Again, we can agree on discriminations between various kinds (and even degrees) of 'rhythmicality' without achieving agreement over the nature of English rhythm itself. The stresses are regarded by speaker and hearer as *beats* at more or less regular intervals of time, thus creating an accentual sequence analogous to the quasi-isochronous *feet* in a poetic metre, each foot consisting of a stressed syllable, usually with one or more unstressed syllables. Perception of the rhythmic base may involve observing variations in loudness or pitch, or measuring intervals of time – or a combination of these, but these are matters of controversial debate and current experiment, to which we cannot turn our attention.

So far as pitch is concerned, we should recognize that, although 'fundamental frequency' is doubtless a more predominant component than anything else in providing cues to our perception, nevertheless loudness or intensity is a significant co-occurrent factor and can readily, in fact, replace fundamental frequency: largely, through amplitude variation (though doubtless other factors are involved), whispered speech is perceived as having the same intonation as normal voiced speech. We need also to distinguish intonation from musical melody. As distinct from music, there is no absolute pitch and there are no fixed intervals to be observed in intonation; one cannot speak 'out of tune', and all pitch distinctions are acoustically relative, however linguistically absolute they may be.

Lastly, it should be noted that the three interrelated factors here discussed are not the only distinctions that are observed in the stream of speech modifying an utterance while the grammar and vocabulary are held constant. Other *prosodic systems*, as they are called, include for example tempo, the relative speed of utterance. It is widely agreed, however, that stress, rhythm and intonation are the most pervasively important and we shall virtually exclude the others from consideration in this sketch.

Note
It will be observed that the linguists' use of *prosodic* is based upon the use of this term in traditional rhetoric but with considerable difference in emphasis and specialization.

Stress and rhythm
Stress within the word
Patterns
II.3

As soon as an utterance is longer than a single syllable, the syllables are arranged in rhythmic patterns comprising a succession of strong-weak-strong-weak, etc; this is true whether the polysyllabic stretch is a sentence, a phrase or a single word. It is possible to distinguish (with more or less difficulty) four or five degrees of stress in a sequence of as many syllables; but it would seem that what is most linguistically relevant is a simple binary opposition – stress versus no stress – though it is often relevant to distinguish an intermediate or secondary stress. As is customary, we shall mark stress with a high vertical stroke before the syllable carrying the stress, leaving lack of stress unmarked. When a stronger stress needs to be indicated, a double vertical mark is used, and where it is desirable to indicate secondary stress, this will be marked by a low vertical stroke before the syllable concerned. For example:

ˈseveral ˈpretty ˈˈwomen
ˌcontriˈbution

We shall first discuss normal stressing, leaving the special features of 'contrastive stress' to App II.9.

Although, as we shall see, we have a good deal of freedom in assigning stresses in utterances longer than a word, the placing of the stress within English words is – save for relatively minor exceptions – so rigorously invariant that it is often difficult for us to understand a word where the accentuation is deviant. If instead of the correct

ˌpalataliˈzation

one were to say

*paˌlataliˈzation

the moving merely of the secondary stress one syllable to the 'right' could be enough (along with the vowel changes that regularly accompany stress shift) to make the word incomprehensible. Deviant stress would have at least as great an effect with a shorter and commoner word such as

*eˈnergy (*in place of* ˈenergy)

In numerous words, on the other hand, interchange of primary and secondary stress would produce a comprehensible pronunciation. This is especially so with words where native speakers themselves show variation, as in

ˌmagaˈzine *or* ˈmagaˌzine

But although the stresses are normally in a fixed position in a word, their position is unpredictable in the sense that – in contrast with some languages – there is no single position where the main stress of a word can be expected to fall. For example, to count from left to right, it may be on the

first syllable:	ˈanswer
second syllable:	aˈbove
third syllable:	manaˈgerial
fourth syllable:	incompreˈhensible
fifth syllable:	palataliˈzation

Thus, to a large extent, the accentual pattern of each word has to be learnt separately, though we shall see that with some classes of words it is helpful and relevant to count syllables from the end rather than from the beginning.

II.4

For there are some noteworthy generalizations, though they are complicated by the mixed nature of English vocabulary – the basic core of Germanic words surrounded by a much larger number of words from foreign languages (notably French, Latin and Greek). Native words and early French adoptions tend to have the main stress on the root syllable and to keep it there, regardless of the affixes that word-formation may add:

ˈkingly	ˈstand(ing)	ˈpassion
ˈkingliness	underˈstand(ing)	ˈpassionately
unˈkingliness	misunderˈstand(ing)	disˈpassionate

By contrast, with the more recent adoptions and coinages, especially those based on words from the classical languages (*cf* App I.3), the place of the stress varies according to the affixation:

	antepenultimate	*penultimate*
ˈtelegraph	teˈlegraphy	teleˈgraphic
	teˈlepathy	teleˈpathic

'photo(graph)	pho'tography	photo'graphic
'transport	trans'portable	transpor'tation
'argument	argu'mentative	argumen'tation

The last two items exemplify a particularly valuable generalization: all abstract nouns ending in *-ion* are stressed on the syllable preceding this ending. Other examples: *sus'picion, tabu'lation, petri'faction, re'vision.*

II.5

But there are numerous other comparable generalizations which help us to predict the placing of English stress. Thus it falls on the syllable before adjectival *-ic* (App I.28):

	penultimate
'phoneme	pho'nemic
e'conomy	eco'nomic
'emblem	emble'matic
'sympathy	sympa'thetic

and on the syllable before nominal *-ity* (App I.25):

	antepenultimate
u'nanimous	una'nimity
'curious	curi'osity
pro'miscuous	promis'cuity

as also on the syllable before nominal or adjectival *-ian*

	antepenultimate
'library	lib'rarian
'grammar	gram'marian
u'tility	utili'tarian
'Cromwell	Crom'wellian

We may contrast the rather similarly used affix *-ite* which leaves the place of the accent unchanged:

| 'Trotsky | 'Trotskyite |
| 'Jefferson | 'Jeffersonite |

cf App I.23.

A fairly numerous set of words that can operate without affixal change as noun or adjective on the one hand, and as verb on the other, have an accentual difference in the two functions (App I.43); for example:

noun or adjective	*verb*
'conduct	con'duct
'contrast	con'trast

ˈconvict	conˈvict
ˈpresent	preˈsent
ˈperfect	perˈfect
ˈattribute	atˈtribute

In one of these (*contrast*) and in several of the other examples that might have been cited (*eg: export*), there is a tendency to discontinue a separate verb form and to use in all functions the form as stressed for the noun.

II.6
Compounds

Compound nouns (App I.44 *ff*) are generally stressed on the first element but with a strong secondary stress on the second element:

ˈblackˌbird   ˈblackˌboard   ˈgreenˌfly

(contrast the complex noun phrases: *a ˌblack ˈbird, a ˌblack ˈboard, a ˌgreen ˈfly*)

ˈearthˌquake   ˈlifeˌboat   ˈwaitingˌroom   ˈfire-exˌtinguisher

When such a compound is made part of another compound, the stress and secondary stress are re-distributed to give the same rhythm:

ˈlightˌhouse   *but*   ˈlighthouse-ˌkeeper

A somewhat smaller number of compounds consisting of free morphemes preserve the stress pattern of the phrases from which they are derived, with main stress on the final component:

ˌarchˈbishop	ˌviceˈchancellor
ˌappleˈsauce	ˌfirstˈrate

Many of these compounds are not nouns, but verbs (ˌback-ˈfire), adverbs (ˌhenceˈforth), and especially adjectives (ˌknee-ˈdeep, ˌflat-ˈfooted). In some cases we may be in doubt as to whether we should regard sequences with this stress pattern as compounds or free syntactic phrases, and we vacillate in writing between hyphenation and leaving as separate words (for example, ˌlawn(-)ˈtennis, ˌcountry(-)ˈhouse); *cf* App I.45, App III.5. On the other hand, we vacillate in our stressing of some examples which are apparently in the process of becoming recognized as compounds of the ˈblackˌbird type; for example:

ˌfield ˈmarshal   *or*   ˈfield ˌmarshal
ˌoverˈseas   *or*   ˈoverˌseas

In any case, the stress often shifts from second component to first when the compound is being used attributively in a noun phrase:

The room is ˌdownˈstairs   *but*   A ˈdownˌstairs ˈroom
His work is ˌfirstˈclass   *but*   His ˈfirstˌclass ˈwork

Note

In AmE there is a strong tendency to give initial stress to many compounds, and in normal AmE use we have, for example, *'apple₁sauce, 'lawn₁tennis, 'back₁fire.* This stress distribution occurs quite often in BrE also.

Stress in phrases and other syntactic units
Phrases compared with compounds
II.7

The examples and the discussion have already taken us outside the limits of the word and into the distribution of stresses in phrases and other syntactic units. It is usual to emphasize the distinction between *the word,* where convention and semantic integration fix a stress and rhythm which the individual cannot alter, and *connected speech,* where the disposition of stresses is subject to the speaker's will and the meaning he wishes to convey. There is much validity in this but it must not be pressed too far, since it depends on a much sharper distinction between phrases and (compound) words than English grammar and lexicology in fact warrant. It will not do to say that initial stressing (as in *'black₁bird*) indicates compounds, and final stressing (as in *₁New 'Deal*) the syntactic phrases of connected speech. We have seen compounds like *₁down'stairs* which (despite similarity with phrases like *₁down the 'street*) we would not wish to analyse as phrases. And *₁still 'life* (in painting), which is usually stressed in BrE as though it was a phrase, shows that it is a compound in having a different plural (*still lifes*) from the simplex noun (*lives*): *cf* 4.65. So too there are initial-stressed phrases that linguists do not normally regard as compounds, since (as is not general in word-formation: *cf* App I.2) we are as free to form such sequences as we are to form any other kind of syntactic unit:

> The 'strawberry ₁picking⎱
> The 'cabbage ₁weeding ⎰has gone well.

II.8

Moreover the stress distribution provides a firm basis for distinguishing not between compound and phrase but different underlying relations between the juxtaposed items:

A 'toy ₁factory (a factory that produces toys)
A 'bull ₁fight (a fight that involves bulls)
A 'French ₁teacher (one who teaches French)
A 'slate ₁quarry (where slate is quarried)

beside

A ₁toy ˈfactory (a factory that is a toy)
A ₁bull ˈcalf (a calf that is a bull)
A ₁French ˈteacher (a teacher who is French)
A ₁slate ˈroof (a roof that is of slate)

Thus the distribution of stresses in units higher than the word is interestingly subject to rule just as it is within the word. Apart from 'object' premodifiers (as in ˈFrench ₁teacher), there is a main stress on the head of a noun phrase where the head is the last item in the phrase:

A reaˈlistic ₁little ₁toy ‖factory
ˈSeveral ˈstale ₁half-ˈeaten ˈcurrant ‖buns

Postmodified noun phrases have the main stress on the last stressable item in the postmodification:

The ₁toy ˈfactory he ˈgot for his ‖birthday
The ˈcurrant ˈbuns that I ˈtried to ‖eat

With equal regularity (and subject to the special factors explored in Chapter 14), a non-contrastive main stress falls on the head of a verb phrase, or on the subsequent particle if the head is a phrasal verb (such as *wash up*: 12.24), or on the operator in an elliptical verb phrase:

ˈWill he have ‖gone?
ˈYes, he ‖will.
He ˈmust be ‖working.   Yes, he ‖must ₁be.
She ˈcan't have been ˈwashing ‖up.

In these last examples, the verb phrases have each come at the end of sentences. This is a point where in any case a climax of prominence is expected and this normally occurs on the last word unless this is a pronoun or (frequently) a preposition:

He ˈtold his ‖mother
It's the adˈdress he ˈsent the ‖letter ₁to.

Note

[a] Even so, final position in this last example has given the preposition a secondary stress although in a syntactically analogous non-final use the preposition would be unstressed:

He ˈsent the ˈletter to the adˈdress he'd been ‖given.

[b] Peaks of prominence in syntactic units of the kinds discussed in this and later paragraphs would in actual speech be normally associated with pitch, and we shall shortly (App II.12) reinterpret these points in terms of intonation. For the present purpose, however, this fact may be ignored without undue distortion.

II.9
Contrastive stress

It is clear, then, that the language determines stress location almost as rigidly in phrases and sentences as it does in individual words, and we should not attempt to impose too sharp a distinction between 'words' and 'connected speech' on these grounds. Let us look now at the individual's ability to place stress freely in units larger than the word. Contrastive stress is capable of highlighting any word in a sentence. This is particularly striking in the case of the closed-system words (2.14) which are normally unstressed, making widespread use of the 'schwa' vowel: [ənd] or [ən] *and*, [bət] *but*, [əv] *of*, [wəz] *was*, etc. Under contrastive stress, they assume the form that they have as dictionary items: [ænd], [bʌt], [ɒv], [wɒz], etc:

ᶦJohn ‖and his ᶦmother ᶦwent (=it is not true that only one of them went)
ᵢWill ‖he have ᶦgone? (=granted that others have gone, is it true of him also?)

This focus device (*cf* 14.3) involves pitch prominence and we shall therefore return to it when we are dealing with intonation. For the present we must observe, however, that it is not limited to sequences longer than the word: the normal accentuation within the word can also be distorted at the speaker's will if he wants to make a contrastive point. Thus instead of *un*ᶦ*happy* one might say ᶦ*unhappy* in a context such as

A: She was looking happy tonight
B: You thought so? She seemed ᶦunhappy to me.

Note
Contrastive stress can also override the distinctions made in App II.8: in *I* ᶦ*said she was a* ‖*French* ₌*teacher, not a* ‖*fresh* ₌*teacher*, we could be referring to nationality.

Rhythm
II.10

In all the phrases and sentences given as examples in App II.4 *f*, one single point of prominence was indicated, because we were looking at analogies to word-stress in syntactic units. In fact, of course, this ignores entirely the rhythm that each of these sentences must possess by virtue of the alternation of stressed and unstressed portions throughout. Broadly speaking, and in the absence of contrastive stress, English connected speech has stresses on the (stressed syllables of) open-class items, and absence of stress upon the closed-system words accompanying them:

He ᶦtold his ‖mother
He ᶦsent it to his ‖mother

It's the ad⎮dress he ⎮sent the ‖letter ⎮to
She was ⎮looking ‖happy to⎮night

The natural rhythm of English, when unaffected by other factors such as hesitation which may slow down the speaker or excitement which may speed him up, provides roughly equal intervals of time between the stresses. This means that if the first two examples above were spoken by the same person under similar conditions, they would take approximately the same time, would have the same rhythmic pattern, and would oblige the speaker to utter the sequence *sent it to his* more rapidly than the sequence *told his* which occupies the same rhythmic unit.

II.11
Regularity of rhythm
It is necessary to emphasize that absolute regularity of rhythm is the exception rather than the rule, and that when the intervals between stresses cease to be merely 'roughly equal' and achieve something like metronomic equality, the stylistic effect is oppressive. One exception is in counting: when we have to count a fairly large number of items, it seems easier to prevent ourselves from getting lost if we adopt a strict isochronous rhythm:

⎮one ⎮two ⎮three ⎮four . . . ⎮seventeen ⎮eighteen ⎮nineteen . . .
   seventy-⎮four seventy-⎮five seventy-⎮six . . . a hundred-and-⎮three
   a hundred-and-⎮four . . .

So too when we are compiling an inventory, giving a list of names, or the like. By contrast, an insistent regularity may also be introduced for emphasis, especially when one is implying repetition of something which ought to be accepted without argument, and especially again perhaps when the speaker is expressing irritation or sarcasm:

You should ⎮never ⎮move the ⎮papers ⎮on my ‖desk

It is the requirements of rhythm rather than of the message which here causes the normally unstressed *on* to be emphasized, and we commonly find that the special use of regular rhythm distorts the normal stress patterns in this way. An earlier example was *a hundred-and-⎮three* in a counting rhythm where this number in isolation would have two stresses: *a ⎮hundred-and-⎮three*. So too ⎮*seventeen*, etc, but in isolation, *seven*⎮*teen*.

But, for the most part, approximations to strictly regular rhythm are rare, brief and rhetorical: in public emotive address, for example, such as appeals, sermons, political speeches. More prolonged use, of course, occurs with the listener's full sanction in the reading of poetry and in forms of religious discourse (especially prayer).

Intonation
II.12
Tone unit, nucleus, and the falling tone

Intonation is normally realized in tone units consisting of a sequence of stressed and unstressed syllables but on occasion the unit may consist of a single pitch-prominent syllable. The peak of greatest prominence is called the NUCLEUS of the tone unit and it is indicated in this book by being printed in small capitals. We shall now review some of the examples quoted earlier reclassifying as nuclei certain peaks of prominence previously marked as stresses. Others will be reclassed as 'onsets'. The ONSET is the first prominent syllable in a tone unit, and it is commonly preceded by one or more syllables with light stress and on a low pitch. Its position will be indicated by a preceding thin vertical (|) and the end of the tone unit will be marked by a thick vertical (|). Between these two points, each tone unit has one of the nuclear patterns outlined in App II.12–15. Examples of tone units:

- (a) He |told his MOTHer|
- (b) It's the ad|dress he ˈsent the LETter ₁to|
- (c) She was |looking HAPpy toˈnight|
- (d) You |THOUGHT ˈso|
- (e) She |seemed UNhappy to ME|

Usually, pitch prominence is associated with pitch change – and the commonest change is a FALL in pitch. We would expect a fall on the nuclear syllable in both (a) and (b) above, for example, and we expect it likewise on that of most sentences and most questions beginning with a *wh*-word, as in (f) and (h), on one-word answers to questions, on words or names or even letters uttered in isolation, as in (g) and (i). It might be said that a tone unit has a falling nucleus unless there is some specific reason why it should not:

- (f) |What's his NÀME|
- (g) Phy|LÀKtis|
- (h) |What's the first LÈTter|
- (i) |P̀|

II.13
The rising tone

When there is such a reason, the falling nucleus is more frequently replaced by a rising one than by any other. Broadly speaking, this is when we wish to indicate that our utterance is non-final or that we are leaving it open and inconclusive. This may be because we are counting or listing and have not come to the last item; or because another clause is going to follow; or because we seek a response from someone (but not by means of a *wh*-question):

... |TWÉLVE| |THÍRteen| |FÓURteen| |FÌFteen|
There are |fifTÈEN|

(Notice again the difference between 'teens' in sequence and in isolation)

|When he CÁME| I |GRÈETed him|
I |saw him this MÓRNing| and in|vited him to DÌNner|
You're |going alRÉADY| |MÚST you|

Some of the examples in App II.12 might well have a rising nucleus, especially (c) perhaps, not so much in order to make it a question as to suggest politely that a (confirmatory) comment would be welcome. Alternatively, one might add a tag question (7.59), with a falling nucleus:

She was |looking HÁPpy to|night| |WÀsn't she|

The absence of dogmatic finality in the rise enables us to make an imperative gentle and persuasive:

|Don't be unPLÉAsant|

Other nuclear tones
II.14
There are no nuclear tones anything like so common as the fall and the rise, but four other tone contours are nevertheless important. The FALL-RISE occurs in many 'contingency' environments (for example as the nucleus of a doubtful condition), but it is perhaps especially common with initial adverbials (8.7):

I'll |see him if he CŎMES|
|FĬNally| we de|cided not to GÒ|

The converse of this, the RISE-FALL, must be sharply distinguished from it since it is really a rather persuasive variant of the falling tone, used to express a genuine or sarcastic warmth or on the other hand a feeling of surprise or shock:

|That's wÔNderful|
He's a com|plete FÔOL|

Rarest of all, the LEVEL tone seems to be a variant of the rise (see App II.17 Note), and it is used to suggest (often somewhat pompously) the exact predictability of what is to follow:

He |DRĀNK| he |STŌLE| he was |soon desPĪsed|

II.15

The remaining tone pattern is by no means rare: it is probably used more often than any other except fall and rise, but we have left it till the end because, unlike the others, this pattern has two nuclei. It is the FALL-PLUS-RISE and (especially in BrE) it would be expected in example (e) of App II.12 above:

She |seemed ÙNhappy to MÉ|

The nucleus is always a peak of semantic or 'information' content in the tone unit; with the fall-plus-rise we have two such peaks of information interest, and they are related, the first being superordinate (*cf* 14.6 Note *a*). That is, when we introduced this example in the first place (App II.9), it was in order to illustrate 'contrastive stress'. Now contrastive stress usually involves moving a tonal nucleus from its normal, unmarked position on to the contrasted item. But it by no means necessarily requires the tone unit concerned to have two nuclei:

Are you |HÁPpy|
|No I'm ÙNhappy|

Compare also the distinction between first and subsequent mention, as in

|This book cost |five DÓLlars| and |this one THRÈE |dollars|
    (*. . . |three DÒLlars|)

beside

|This book cost |five DÓLlars| and |this one |three PÒUNDS|
    (*. . . THRÈE |pounds|)

What the fall-plus-rise does is this: it allows the speaker to express a *double* contrast. In the example contrasting *happy* and *unhappy* ('She seemed UNhappy to ME'), the two nuclei enable us to say (a) that she is *un*happy as opposed to happy, and (b) that this is *my* view as opposed to yours.

In addition to contradictions of this kind, the fall-plus-rise is commonly used with marked focus (*cf* 14.3 *ff*), with the fall placed on the displaced and focused item, the rise on the final lexical item in the tone unit. For example:

It's his |WÌFE that I don't LÍKE| = The |one that I don't LÍKE| is
    his |WÌFE|
It's his |WÌFE that's always NÁsty|

beside the unmarked

I |don't like his WÌFE|
His |wife is always NÀsty|

Intonation in relation to other features
II.16
Tone of voice, pitch, and music

'Intonation' must be distinguished from 'tone of voice' on the one hand and from 'intoning', chanting or singing on the other. One's tone of voice may be warm or cold, kind or harsh, happy or sad, irrespective of the intonation pattern, the length of the tone unit, the location of the nucleus, or the direction of the pitch movement. Indeed, while there can be no doubt that intonation is linguistically relevant (it can distinguish interrogative from declarative, after all), there must be considerable doubt as to whether tone of voice involves linguistic parameters at all. True, on hearing someone say

I've |bought a CÀR|

we can add to our understanding of this statement the inference that the speaker sounded happy or proud or perhaps nervous, but merely because we deduced this from the way he spoke we need not go to the lengths of regarding the deduction as springing from the linguistic form. We might equally have deduced that he had a cold – or food in his mouth.

As to the distinction between intonation and intoning, something has already been said in App II.2. One cannot 'speak out of tune' because the movements in linguistic pitch are purely relative, in sharp contrast to the specific intervals of a musical scale. A person speaking with a high-pitched voice may end a fall at a point far higher than the point at which a fall began as uttered by a low-pitched voice: yet despite total dissimilarity in frequency or acoustic quality both falls would be instantly recognized as linguistically identical. Again, even where they begin at the same point in pitch, two speakers will differ very considerably in the amount of pitch movement that may constitute a rise, yet both rises may be received by hearers as linguistically identical. Nor indeed is it necessary for a speaker to be consistent in his width (App II.17) of pitch movement, even in consecutive tone units.

Note
The part played by musical tone in English is very slight, but it may be of interest to mention that calls (including taunting 'cat-calls') make considerable use of descending minor thirds. A wife may call jocularly to her husband down the garden when supper is ready:

'Come and get it!'

The second bar would be the tune also in trying to attract the attention of a person some distance away: 'Ro-bert!' 'Ma-ry!' It appears also in the ending of the long-standing children's taunt, the words of course being freely varied:

'Johnnie's torn his trousers!'

II.17
Pitch height and pitch range

In the previous section reference was made to the fact that it is possible to make what is linguistically the same nuclear tone with considerable variety in actual pitch and pitch movement. Without diminishing the validity of this, and without suggesting further comparison with the specific tonal intervals of music, we must note the existence of other relative systems in intonation which will allow certain broad differences in pitch height and pitch range to assume linguistic significance.

By PITCH HEIGHT we are referring to the point on the pitch scale at which a stressed syllable occurs in relation to the previous syllable. Most commonly, there is a gentle stepping down in pitch level from syllable to syllable, and against this expected pattern, variations stand out clearly. A step upwards in pitch (↑) or a marked step downwards (↓) can add considerably to the feeling that is being conveyed; thus

His |wife is ↓ always ↑ NÀSTY|

would be one way of emphasizing both the adverbial and the complement of this sentence, and, at the same time, of indicating that the nastiness has not been mentioned by either speaker before or is perhaps alleged as a matter of potential dispute between the speakers. A variant form

His |wife is always ↓ NÀSTY|

might suggest that while the nastiness needs emphasis, it is of a familiar kind. In conjunction with a pointedly regular rhythm, a regularly ascending or descending pitch height can be very effective in achieving climax:

And |all the ↑ people of ↑ this ↑ great ↑ cóUNtry|...
|Why on ↓ earth don't you ↓ do some ↓ wòRK|

By PITCH RANGE we are referring to the amount of pitch movement on the nucleus or from stress to stress in the course of the tone unit, irrespective of whether the starting-point is high or low. An ingratiating, warmly interested or excited attitude can be indicated by a *wide* range, while a *narrow* range, as well as being used to indicate boredom for example, is frequent on the nucleus of subordinate clauses. But these are by no means the only contrasts we can imply by altering our pitch range. As for notation, to use (as elsewhere in this Appendix) that of Crystal and Davy 1969, contrasts in pitch range can be indicated by enclosing the words affected in quotation marks and stating 'wide' or 'narrow' in the margin.

Note

It is through the prosodic property of pitch range that we should relate the association of level nuclei to rising ones (App II.14). That is, level nuclei occur most frequently where rising ones might be expected, and we could thus regard the level as a very narrow rise. We need to be aware, however, that the nuclei in pre-final subordinate syntactic units may be not only narrow rises or levels but not infrequently narrow falls.

II.18

Pause and tempo

It will have become clear that, little by little, we are developing a notation for expressing on paper the more important linguistic distinctions that are made not by words but by sound patterns affecting syllables and syllable sequences. There is one further parameter that we must not ignore. The PAUSE in speech is by no means of random occurrence: together with the tone unit, it tends to divide up the stream of speech into grammatically and lexically relevant sections, and although it is by no means essential to pause at the end of the spoken 'sentence', lengthy pauses are more usual at such points than elsewhere. Speech is however more flexible than writing in allowing us to introduce a 'space', to suit speaker's or hearer's needs, before (or perhaps after) a difficult or specially significant lexical item, even if this occurs in the middle of a noun phrase. Pauses are most relevantly measured in terms of a speaker's own rhythm and tempo, and we take the unit of pausing (–) as equivalent in time to one rhythmic measure or cycle (see App II.1*f*):

She is un|HÀPpy| – |vÈRy un¹happy|

As for TEMPO, to which reference has just been made, we quite often find it valuable to contrast with a given speaker's normal speed of utterance the relatively slow (*lento*) or fast (*allegro*) stretches that occur from time to time, as he displays – for example – special care or seriousness at one point, or an off-handed dismissal or cheerful levity at another point. Here, as with height and range or with tone of voice (App II.17*f*), we can easily slip beyond the normal bounds of linguistic description.

Prosodic marking compared with punctuation

II.19

Even ignoring, as we must, several other features of oral English, we now have a system of conventions capable of expressing on paper for spoken English what the system of punctuation marks does (on the whole, much less well) for written English. There are numerous respects in which conventional punctuation is inadequate (see, for example, App III.5), but we need mention here only one or two such points to show how our prosodic notation both explains and transcends the difficulty. Since the early nineteenth century, institutionalized usage has disallowed any punctuation (except correlative or self-cancelling punctuation: App III.21 *ff*) between subject and predicate. Yet (as student essays show) ordinary users of English are still strongly motivated to put a comma between a long noun phrase subject and the verb, just as they were in Napoleonic times:

> . . . the pretensions of any composition to be regarded as Poetry,
> will depend upon . . .
> (George Crabbe, Preface to *Tales*, 1812)

There is a very good reason for this. After a long noun phrase the coherence of the structure just completed is regularly marked in speech by a prosodic break, usually realized by the end of a tone unit, often by a pause as well. Thus a normal reading of the Crabbe example would be as follows:

> . . . the pre|tensions of ˈany ˌcompoˈsition to be reˈgarded as
> ↓ PÓETry| will de|pend u₁pon . . .

II.20

Again, although in rather informal punctuation we can indicate emphasis (usually by means of italics) we cannot distinguish emphases of radically different sound and value:

> (a) You shouldn't give her *any* flowers
>   (= You must give her no flowers at all)
> (b) You shouldn't give her *any* flowers
>   (= You must give her only certain flowers)

Our prosodic notation, however, adequately represents the difference we hear:

> (a) You |shouldn't give her ↑ ÀNY flowers|
> (b) You |shouldn't give her ̌ANY flowers|

Consider now the prosodic realizations which give sharply different meanings to the various members within each of the following sets of sentences; in each case we begin with the 'unmarked' and most neutral form the sentence might have.

(1) I should |GÒ|
    I should |GÓ| (Is that your advice?)
    |Ì should go| (Not you!)
    I |SHÒULD go| (And I defy you to deny it)
    I |SHŎULD go| (But I don't think I will)

(2) |Somebody must have TÀKen it|
    |Somebody must have ↑TÀKen it| (Surprising as it may seem)
    |Somebody ↑MÙST have ¹taken it| (It's no use your arguing)
    |SŎMEbody must have ¹taken it| (Even if you didn't)

(3) You |said he would CÒME|
    |You said he would CÒME| (I was personally doubtful)
    You |said HĚ would come| (You didn't say that his wife
                               was coming as well)
    You |SÀID he would come| (But that doesn't mean he really
                               will)
    You |SÀID he would CÓME| (And, my goodness, there he is!)

II.21
Combined prosodic systems illustrated

All the examples so far have been of isolated tone units or very short sequences. The systems of stress, rhythm and intonation operate significantly, however, over considerably longer stretches of speech, indicating degrees of connection (*cf* 10.2) and providing significant cues to interrelationship of sentences and parts of sentences. This is of course particularly vital in natural, unprepared discourse, but illustration from such material would necessitate far more explanation of specifically oral aspects of English than we have been concerned with in this book. It may be more relevant instead to quote from the transcription of a radio talk which will show how a speaker, beginning from sentences on paper, can bring his language to oral life with the aid of a complex selection from the repertoire of prosodic devices. Notice, for example, the way in which *training* and *purpose* are prosodically coordinated. The passage is quoted (with some simplification) from Crystal and Davy 1969, *p* 249, and their conventions are followed of using capital letters only in tonal nuclei and of using marginal glosses to characterise other prosodically marked stretches

'rhythmic' his |work as a ↑ CĂRicaturist| – 'is |that in ᴵwhich he
ᴵmost deLÌGHTed|' – it was |NÈver| a |matter of ᴵformal
↑ TRĂINing| or |set ↑ PŬRPose with ᴵhim| – it be|gan with
ᴵmarginal SKÈTCHes| in his |school and ᴵcollege NÒTE-
books| – – |when william ↑ RŎTHenᴵstein| e|rupted into
↑ ŎXford| to |do a ↑ series of ↑ portrait ↑ DRÁWings| –
he |gave enᴵcouragement and ↑ HÈLP| – – it was |HÈ|

'narrow' 'who |taught MÁX to |make his ↑ DRĂWings|' – |not
ᴵmere ᴵpersonal ↑ CĂRicatures| – but |decorative desíGNS|

'allegro' with an aes|thetic exᴵistence of their ↑ ÒWN| – – 'and we
can |easily ↑ TRÀCE this ᴵprocess|'

Bibliographical note

On stress, see Arnold (1957); Gimson (1970), especially Part III; Chomsky and
Halle (1968), especially Chapter 3; Halle and Keyser (1971).

On rhythm, see Abercrombie (1967), Chapter 6; Chatman (1965), especially
Chapters 2 and 5; Leech (1969b), Chapter 7; and Uldall (1971).

On intonation, see O'Connor and Arnold (1961); Kingdon (1958); Bolinger (1963)
and (1965), especially Part I; Halliday (1970b); and (for AmE) Pike (1945).

On grammar and intonation, see Quirk (1968), especially Chapters 12, 13; and
Halliday (1967).

A detailed account of all prosodic systems is given in Crystal (1969), especially
Chapters 4 *ff*, and these are related to style in Crystal and Davy (1969).

Introduction

III.1

In App II we surveyed a set of prosodic devices whereby differentiations of various kinds could modify the stream of speech, thus endorsing and helping us to communicate the grammatical and other distinctions in the English we speak. The purpose of the present Appendix is to examine the visual devices that perform a similar role for the English we write. Our task in App II was more difficult, for although the prosodic devices are acquired naturally by the native speaker (he does not have to be taught them formally), our ordinary educational tradition has largely – for this reason – ignored them and so we had to begin by isolating, describing and labelling them. With punctuation, the array of devices is well recognized; there are established names for the individual items; and their use is (to some considerable extent, at any rate) equally institutionalized, through education and the insistently regular practice of the printing organizations.

There are three stretches of written language formally recognized by name whose bounds are indicated visually: the PARAGRAPH, the SENTENCE, and the WORD. The limits of the PARAGRAPH are indicated by beginning it on a new line (usually 'indented' like the present paragraph which began with the previous sentence) and by beginning the next likewise even if this means leaving part of a line blank (but see App III.18). The paragraph consists of one or more SENTENCES each of which must begin with a CAPITAL (or 'upper case') letter and will normally end with a PERIOD ('full stop' or 'full point' or – informally – 'dot') like the present one. If the sentence is a question it will however end with a 'question mark' and there are several other, less frequent termination points, as we shall see presently. Each sentence consists of one or more WORDS and these are delimited as orthographic units (App 1.6) by being preceded by a space and by being followed either by a space or by a punctuation mark and a space. This laborious statement is necessary to admit as 'words' the italicized parts of the following:

> . . . the *grammar* of . . .
> . . . in *scorn*, when . . .
> . . . the *co-authors* are . . .
> . . . the *reader's* aim . . .

The remaining punctuation marks – by far the majority – perform functions within the sentence (and a very few within the word) but do not mark off clearly defined or well-established units analogous to the sentence or the word. Their functions however are for the most part clear and readily describable.

III.2

In considering the individual punctuation marks, it will be useful to see them in relation to principles underlying the punctuation system as a whole. Two broad purposes are served, *separation* and *specification*, the former of these itself inviting a twofold division:

SEPARATION

(a) *Successive units:* that is, the orthographic symbol separates units which can be regarded as being in a simple linear relation to each other, as when a space separates two successive words.

(b) *Included units:* that is, the unit which is separated is in the position of interrupting some larger unit and the orthographic symbol must therefore be *correlative*, marking both the beginning and the ending of the included unit. For example, the commas which mark off the parenthetic clause in

He is, *I think*, a teacher.

SPECIFICATION

It is convenient to treat as a class those punctuation marks which (often in addition to marking the point at which one unit is separated from another) have a clear role in specifying a function. Thus the apostrophe in *the reader's* specifies the ending as genitive in contrast to the phonologically identical plural in *the readers*.

In respect of these purposes, punctuation practice is governed primarily by grammatical considerations and is related to grammatical distinctions. Sometimes it is linked to intonation, stress, rhythm, pause, or any other of the prosodic features which convey distinctions in speech, but this is neither simple nor systematic, and traditional attempts to relate punctuation directly to (in particular) pauses are misguided. Nor, except to a minor and peripheral extent, is punctuation concerned with expressing emotive or rhetorical overtones, as prosodic features frequently are (see App II.17, for example). It follows that there is much less room in punctuation than in prosody for personal decision in the use of the various devices: necessarily so, since in writing, the originator of the message is not usually present to clear up any difficulty that may arise. Punctuation marks tend, therefore, to be used according to fairly strict conventions and even in the peripheral areas where universal convention does not obtain, each individual publishing house imposes one for all materials that it puts forth in print.

There are two important qualifications to make to the foregoing generalizations. In the first place, there is, as we shall see, a great deal of flexibility possible in the use of the comma, and this punctuation mark does in fact provide considerable opportunity for personal taste and for implying fine degrees of cohesion and separation. Secondly, the conventions as a whole are observed with a variety and low level of consistency in manuscript use (especially personal material, such as private letters) which could not be inferred from the rigour that obtains in the majority of printed material.

We shall now examine the punctuation system according to the major purposes outlined above.

Separation
Separation of successive units
III.3
Hierarchy of punctuation marks
Here we have a well-defined hierarchy of signs reaching (as we have already seen to some extent) from the word to the paragraph. The full hierarchy can be illustrated from the following passage:

> ... and the chairman was careful to point out the help he had had from the secretary and from the members recently elected to the committee. He mentioned two other men, since co-opted: Smith and Fox; they had been very useful. Votes of thanks were proposed and unanimously carried.
>
> Before the meeting closed, some further business was transacted. A motion proposed by Johnson sought to raise money by ...   [1]

Thus we have:

unseparated letters	... opted ...
hyphen (-)	... co-opted ...
word-space	... since co-opted ...
comma (,)	... men, since co-opted ...
colon (:)	... men, since co-opted: Smith ...
semi-colon (;)	... men, since co-opted: Smith and Fox; they ...
period (.)	... men, since co-opted: Smith and Fox; they had been very useful. Votes of thanks ...
paragraph	... had been very useful. Votes of thanks were proposed and unanimously carried. Before the meeting closed, some further business was transacted ...

III.4
The hyphen
The hyphen's function in the above hierarchy is twofold. First, it is

used to separate a word into two parts between the end of one line of text and the beginning of the next. Since the printer can vary the space between words, he uses his skill and ingenuity to avoid dividing words in this way (especially in books), more than is absolutely necessary. When division is unavoidable, it is made at a natural point in the structure of a word. That is, one would not leave *str-* at the end of a line and begin the next with *ucture*. But there can of course be much difference of opinion as to what constitutes a 'natural' point. AmE practice is to respect the phonologically natural points – in other words, syllable division; this would divide *structure* at *struc-*. BrE practice is to give more weight to morphological and etymological considerations, being thus more inclined to make a break in the word at *struct-*. With many words the different criteria give the same result, however, so the net divergence in usage is slight.

Secondly, the hyphen is used to separate the prefix of a newly (or temporarily) formed word such as *psycho-mechanics*, and especially where the second part has a capital letter as in *un-French*. *Cf* App I.45. It may also separate the prefix where juxtaposition would suggest a misleading pronunciation as in *co-opt* or *pre-eminent*. In such cases AmE practice (which in general shows fewer hyphens than BrE) occasionally favours the DIAERESIS as in *coöperate*, but more generally it ignores the problem and prints such words 'solid': *cooperate, preeminent* (but, it so happens, *co-opt*).

Note
The diaeresis is also occasionally used to indicate separate syllables in words where juxtaposed vowels do not result from affixation and where the hyphen could not be used; for example, *naïve*. More commonly, however, such words are spelled without indication of the separate syllabification: *naive*.

III.5
The word in speech and writing
We shall mention other and related uses of the hyphen below (App III.31 *f*), but there is one general point we should make at this stage concerning visual indicators of word limits. It was pointed out in App II.19 that there were numerous respects in which we could not reproduce in writing distinctions made prosodically in speech. Here we have the converse. In speech, we do not normally attempt to make a difference in pronunciation between *a nice drink* and *an ice(d) drink* or (especially in BrE) between the phrases *by far the best* and *by Father Best*. In writing, such distinctions are absolute and must be regularly made. Similarly, irrespective of the sound we make in speech, we must often decide in writing between total separation, hyphenation, and total juxtaposition: *tax payer*, *tax-payer*, and *taxpayer*. Examples like these are an important

reminder (a) that, while the rules of punctuation are related to grammar and lexicology, they are by no means necessarily so related through an intermediate connection with speech; (b) that there is an element of arbitrariness in punctuation, and hesitation is especially unavoidable in relation to the hyphen, with the ultimate decision poised uneasily between the lexicographer, the school-teacher and the publishing house; and (c) that consistency and regularity assume an importance in punctuation (as in spelling) quite unparalleled in the analogous signalling function of prosodic systems in speech.

Note

[a] Phrases written as a sequence of single words when predicative are frequently hyphenated when they are made to premodify. Thus

John's reputation is well established

beside

John's well-established reputation

So also *a do-it-yourself job.* See further 13.45.

[b] Coordination of hyphenated items, especially in formal or technical writing, frequently involves ellipsis with word-space following a hyphen, as in *pro- and anti-government opinion* or *those who are speech- and language-impaired. Cf* 13.69. For additional information on the use of the hyphen, see App III.31 *f.*

The comma

III.6

Although the hierarchy in App III.3 gives three signs for making distinction between the unit 'word' and the unit 'sentence', the comma is the only sign that is truly used for separating parts of the sentence. The other two, the colon and semicolon, are chiefly used to separate closely associated units within a sentence which are so constituted that each part has the elements necessary to operate as a sentence in its own right.

I have some news for you: John has arrived. [2]

The house badly needed painting; the garden was overgrown with weeds. [3]

The comma has no such restrictions. Indeed, it is the most flexible of all punctuation marks in the range of its use and it has eluded grammarians' attempts to categorize its uses satisfactorily. Clearly it is also the most important of the punctuation marks apart from the period, having a frequency of use almost identical with that of the period and being about ten times as frequent as the next most heavily used punctuation mark.

Note

The frequency reported in Summey's description of American punctuation (1949, *p* 161) is confirmed for BrE by the Survey of English Usage files.

The comma with coordinated clauses
III.7
One dominant use of the comma can be described in the precise terms just used to denote the use of the colon and semicolon: 'to separate closely associated units within a sentence which are so constituted that each part has the elements necessary to operate as a sentence in its own right'. Yet different kinds of close association are involved, and we could not substitute a comma in either [2] or [3]. In the case of [2], this is because the second part is in an appositive relation (9.177) to an element in the first part and so provides the classic condition in which the colon is appropriate (App III.14). In [3] we should need to connect the two parts with *and*, thus exemplifying the point made above that the comma essentially separates parts of a sentence, and in this case a coordinate sentence:

> The house badly needed painting, and the garden was overgrown
> with weeds.   [4]

This sentence now in fact admirably illustrates the conditions under which a comma is used in compound sentences:

  (a) the parts are semantically related (both dealing in the present instance with the bad physical condition of premises);

  (b) they are conjoined (in this case by *and*);

  (c) they are grammatically similar (determiner and number of subject, tense of verb);

  (d) there is no ellipsis in the second part.

If condition (a) did not obtain, the two parts could scarcely be brought within one sentence unit at all. If condition (a) obtained but not (b), a comma could not be used, though a semicolon would be appropriate enough, as in [3]. The effect of condition (c) is normally to render a comma merely optional and even where desirable for clarity's sake, it would be by no means essential. Finally, frustration of condition (d) would make a comma both unnecessary and frequently undesirable as well:

> The house badly needed painting and looked deserted.   [5]

Note
Despite condition (b), it is not uncommon to find coordinate clauses separated only by commas, especially when the clauses are short, aphoristic, and (often) three in number:

> I must, I can, I will.

III.8
There are important refinements of these conditions that influence our decision over punctuation. For example, under (c), one important vari-

able is whether or not the subject of the second part is co-referential with that of the first: *The house* . . . *it* . . . as opposed to *The house* . . . *the garden* . . . If it is, a comma is less desirable than if it is not. But our decision in this respect very much depends upon condition (a): if, despite close semantic connection, there is a contrast prompting the use of *but* (or *and yet*) rather than *and* as the appropriate conjunction, a comma will be preferred even where the subjects are referentially identical:

> The house badly needed painting, but it looked comfortable.   [6]

Thus in a recent examination of materials in the Survey of English Usage it was found that three-quarters of the sentences coordinated with *but* had a comma ('+,' in *Fig* III:1), whereas only about a half of the compound sentences using *and* contained a comma. The latter does not however imply random use of the comma: within the *and* sentences it was found relevant to make a further distinction according as the subject of the second part was expressed ('*and* +S' in *Fig* III:2) or ellipted ('*and* −S'). Where subject ellipsis took place, as in [5], the comma appeared in only a third of the sentences while a comma was used in three-quarters of the sentences which had an expressed subject in both parts.

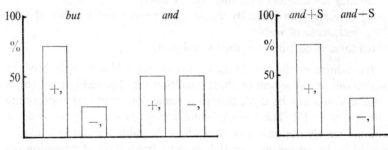

Fig III:1   *Fig* III:2

These results show that we are dealing with tendencies which, while clear enough, are by no means rules. There are plenty of sentences where despite coordination with *and* and despite subject ellipsis, a comma is nevertheless preferred. In such cases, it is probable that the general truth that punctuation conforms to grammatical rather than rhetorical considerations is in fact overridden. If we compare the following two sentences, the extent to which we prefer a comma in the second is a measure of our wish that the punctuation should endorse the meaning – the separation of the second part matching the moment's pause that is mentioned:

He put on his spectacles and then picked up the phone.
He paused for a moment, and then began to speak.

It is fair, however, to summarize the position by saying that the closer the relation between the parts of a sentence, the less need there is for punctuation.

The comma with adverbial units
III.9
The same principle can be applied when we consider the use of the comma to mark off certain adverbials within the simple sentence. It would seem that 'closeness of relation' in this case is linked to adverbial mobility: just as the least mobile are normally those with closest and most indispensable connection with the rest of the sentence, so the least mobile are those least requiring separation by a comma:

He put the chair between you and me.	[7a]
?Between you and me he put the chair.	[7b]
He failed the exam, between you and me.	[8a]
Between you and me, he failed the exam.	[8b]

On the distinction between adjuncts and other adverbials, see 8.2 *ff*. Even those adverbial elements that are so closely related to the rest of the sentence as not to need a comma in final position, however, often need to be thus separated when they are preposed:

You'll succeed if you try.	[9a]
If you try(,) you'll succeed.	[9b]
He lived in India $\left\{ \begin{array}{l} \text{subsequently.} \\ \text{after the war.} \end{array} \right.$	[10a]
$\left. \begin{array}{l} \text{Subsequently(,)} \\ \text{After the war(,)} \end{array} \right\}$he lived in India.	[10b]

A somewhat analogous principle dictates the use of the comma in index entries; *cf: John Quincy Adams* but *Adams, John Quincy* when the surname is moved from its normal end-position. As the parentheses in [9b] and [10b] show, the comma is optional even with many such preposed adverbials, but becomes especially desirable with non-finite and verbless clauses having more than one element:

To visit his mother, he drove through thick fog.	[11a]
Out of breath, he slumped down in a chair.	[11b]

It is also desirable on occasion where its absence might cause the reader to stumble. Thus, although the adverbial has identical function in [12a] and [12b], it is necessary in the latter to avoid misleading the reader into thinking at first that the prepositional phrase is longer than it is:

| After dark(,) I strolled around the square. | [12a] |
| After dark, men and women strolled around the square. | [12b] |

For a comparable reason, a comma would be preferable in

| He tried in vain to find her, in his underclothes. | [12c] |

since it would help to avoid suggesting that she was in his underclothes. And although no ambiguity or comic overtones could affect the following example, the sequence 'in in' would seem less confusing with the separation provided by a comma:

| They hurried on in, in great excitement. | [12d] |

III.10

In general, the length of an adverbial is irrelevant in determining punctuation as is also its structure, whether a single word, a phrase, or an entire clause. Indeed a full clause may often need marking off less than an elliptical or, as in [11b], a verbless one:

| Though he was suffering great pain(,) he walked home alone. | [13a] |
| Though suffering great pain, he walked home alone. | [13b] |

Often, however, mere length of an adverbial will make it seem less closely linked to the rest of the sentence than a short one and so seem to need marking off by a comma; and mere length may also make punctuation desirable for sheer clarity's sake:

It was difficult to decide precisely why he had written at such inordinate length, since it was clear that he could have made the point more succinctly.

Function, however, is usually more important than length. Thus even where an initial adjunct needs no comma, as in [14a], the same adverb as disjunct (8.3 Note *b*) requires one, as in [14b]:

| Again he felt hesitant (='Once more...') | [14a] |
| Again, he felt hesitant (='It should be added that...') | [14b] |

Here indeed is another case where punctuation somewhat mirrors the prosodic difference, since [14a] would usually constitute one tone unit in speech (App II.12) while there would be two for [14b]:

| a|GÀIN he felt ¹hesitant| | [14a] |
| a|GǍIN| he |felt HÈsitant| | [14b] |

Note

The need for easy recognition of structure determines the convention of using commas between thousands in numerals: 41,396,728. Sometimes, spaces are used instead of commas for this purpose: 41 396 728.

III.11
Where separation by comma is disallowed

So far, only adverbials have been considered in relation to the comma. With the main clause constituents, S, V, O and C, there is a strict rule that they cannot be interrupted by punctuation except where 'inclusion' (App III.21) or 'specification' (App III.28) is involved, and with one or two additional but minor exceptions that we shall outline presently. Thus whether such a sentence element consists of a phrase or a clause, it cannot be separated from the verb by a comma:

> *The man over there in the corner, is obviously drunk.   [15]
> *I know, that you are tired.   [16]
> *It is perfectly natural, that men should grow bald.   [17]
> *He gave the leading lady, a bouquet.   [18]

In speech, [15] and possibly [17] and [18] might have a tone unit break where the unacceptable comma has been inserted and (as pointed out in App II.19) we are sometimes tempted to match this with a comma in writing, though the rule is clear enough and is strictly observed in print. Equally clear (and this time generally observed unhesitatingly even in manuscript) is the rule that phrases constituting any of the elements S, V, O, C or A cannot be interrupted by successive-unit commas:

> *The old, man died.
> *He may, go there.
> *They emigrated after, the war.

The comma with relative clauses, appositives, and lists
III.12

The exceptions to these rules are threefold. First, a comma may come between S and V when there might otherwise be momentary confusion, as for instance through two occurrences of the same word (*cf* the similar problem in example [12d]):

> What his name is, is of no interest to me.
> Whatever he does, does not concern me.

Rarely, a comma may also come between S and O or C where V is ellipted:

> The schools must change their examination methods, and the universities, their selection procedures.

And a comma is placed (as we shall see: App III.26) between a subject-verb sequence and direct speech.

Secondly, a comma occurs before the relative pronoun in a non-restrictive relative clause (13.14), matching the commencement of a new tone unit:

He sent for Edward Fenton, who lived in a nearby street.

Similarly, with non-restrictive apposition (9.139 *ff*):

He sent for an old friend, Edward Fenton.

as distinct from the restrictive analogues (13.8, 9.160):

He sent for someone who lived nearby.
He sent for his friend Edward.

The third exception concerns coordination of adjectives, adverbs, verbs, and prepositions, though in fact we should make a distinction between these. With the first, we have the choice of putting either a comma or *and* between adjectives as coordinate premodifiers (13.60):

His long, slow strides	[19a]
His long and slow strides	[19b]

Or, if we wish to indicate not that the strides were both long and slow but that they were slow strides which were (of course) long (13.60), we may ignore punctuation and conjunction:

His long slow strides	[19c]

We may however wish to add to [19a] yet further coordinate adjectives, and if so we would place a comma after each except the last adjective of the string, or if we put *and* before the last adjective, we might omit the previous comma:

His long, slow, steady, deliberate strides	[19d]
His long, slow, steady(,) and deliberate strides	[19e]

Adverbs are coordinated with similar punctuation possibilities:

He slowly, carefully moved the chair.	[19f]
He slowly and carefully moved the chair.	[19g]
He slowly, carefully(,) and deliberately moved the chair.	[19h]

But there is no adverbial analogue to [19c] unless the adverbs belong to different subclasses (8.10 and *Fig* 8:2), as in *He often carefully moved the chair.*

By contrast with [19a] and [19f], we cannot choose between a comma and *and* in coordinating two verbs or two auxiliaries in a verb phrase:

*He can, should do it.	[20a]
*He eats, drinks too much.	[20b]

but must use *and* without punctuation:

He can and should do it. [20c]

He eats and drinks too much. [20d]

With additional items, however, commas would be used in the same way as in [19e]:

He can, may, should(,) and will do it. [20e]

He eats, drinks(,) and talks too much. [20f]

In prepositional phrases, coordinated prepositions follow the same rule:

Government of, by(,) and for the people. [21]

III.13

In [19e], [20e] and [21] we see, in fact, examples of the last separation function of the comma that we need to mention: its use in listing, irrespective of the linguistic status of the items listed. Again the comma before the last item is optional, provided that this is preceded by *and*:

She bought eggs, butter, cheese, bread, rice(,) and coffee.

He wrote down 73, 12, 41, 9, 7(,) and 13, and added them up.

Note
What has been said of the inclusive conjunction *and* applies also to the exclusive conjunction *or* (as in *to or from town; by, with(,) or to a person; butter, eggs(,) or fruit*), except that when *or* connects appositives (9.145) a preceding comma is almost obligatory: *He became an oculist, or eye-doctor.*

The colon
III.14

The colon was placed between the comma and the semicolon in App III.3 not because it makes a stronger separation than the one and a weaker separation than the other, but because it indicates a closer interdependence between the units separated than does the semicolon. Indeed, it indicates as close a relation as the comma does, but it is a different relation. The functions of the colon, a rather infrequent punctuation mark, can be summed up as follows: what follows (as in this sentence) is an explication of what precedes it or a fulfilment of the expectation raised (even if raised only by its own use). Thus,

I have some news for you: John has arrived. [22]

Those who lead must be considerate: those who follow must
be responsive. [23a]

In the former example, [22], it will be noticed that the explication is a clause which can be viewed as being in apposition to a noun phrase in the preceding clause; compare:

The news is that *John has arrived*

and such an appositive relation is typical between units separated by a colon. A further example:

> The man had been drinking heavily: this, not age, explained his
> unsteady walk.   [23b]

Here the pronoun *this* refers back to the whole of the preceding clause ('the fact that the man . . .'). Sometimes the relation is more indirect and subtle, however, as in

> Joan and Mary were obviously weary: I got up to go.   [23c]

where the colon helps to indicate that it was my observation of their weariness that made me decide to go.

It should be noted that in the foregoing examples, a semicolon could replace the colon, and with examples [23a–23c] a semicolon would be more usual, the colon appearing only in the work of the more discerning writers. On the other hand, provided that a coordinating conjunction were introduced between the clauses, the colon could also be replaced in [23a–c] by a comma or by no punctuation. In this respect, too, the [23] set are thus distinguished from [22], in which we have the more central colon situation with its 'as follows' or 'namely' implication. This use is considered more closely in the next paragraph.

III.15
So far, the illustrations have shown the colon separating only clauses. But it commonly separates smaller units such as phrases, and it was its potentiality to do so that justified its place between comma and semicolon in the hierarchy in App III.3.

> There remained one thing he desired above all else: a country
> cottage.

The use of the colon in examples like this resembles most closely the purpose it serves when introducing a quotation or (especially in technical or specialized writing) when it precedes a formal list of items, often preceded by its verbal equivalents *for example, eg, namely* (sometimes written *viz*), *ie, as follows*, or the like (*cf* 9.138). For example:

> Please send the stipulated items, namely:
>   (i) birth certificate
>   (ii) passport
>   (iii) correct fee   [24]

When it appears in such a formal or official use as [24] implies, it is sometimes followed by a short dash (:–), but this is generally regarded as

rather 'heavy' punctuation (App III.20). Certainly, when it is introducing lists in non-technical writing, as in the illustration of the hierarchy
in App III.3, it would never be followed by a dash.

On the contrary in fact: one will find the colon replaced by a comma
at many points where a list is clearly to follow. This hierarchically
'lower' form of punctuation could well be found following 'namely' in
such cases as [24]. In this connection – one of the few in which the colon
and the comma seem to be interchangeable – it is of interest to note that,
whereas the vocative formula at the beginning of letters is normally
separated by a new line and sentence capitalization, it is additionally
marked by a comma or (in AmE formal use) by a colon:

> Dear John,
>   Thank you ...
> Dear Mr Wilson:
>   Thank you ...   (AmE, formal)

Note
On the special conditions for the use of colon in introducing direct speech, see
App III.27.

The semicolon
III.16
The semicolon is next below the period in importance and it is best
regarded as the *coordinating* mark of punctuation, corresponding most
nearly in value to the linguistic coordinating conjunction *and*. That is,
when two independent clauses are regarded as being sufficiently related
to belong to one sentence, this may be shown by prosody in speech
(App II.13) – for example, narrow pitch range or a rising nucleus at the
end of the first clause, with or without a coordinating conjunction.
In writing, it may be shown by a comma followed by a coordinating
conjunction as in [6],

> The house badly needed painting, but it looked comfortable.

or by a semicolon without such a conjunction as in [3],

> The house badly needed painting; the garden was overgrown with
> weeds.

Thus if we represent an independent clause as SVOA, we can compare the
use of commas and semicolons connecting such clauses as follows:

> SVOA, and (then) (S)VOA

is equivalent to

> SVOA; (and) (then) SVOA

where *and* represents the coordinators *and, but, or*, while *then* represents any appropriate way of additionally linking the clauses (10.11 *ff*). It is notable that while the adverb is optional in either case, a coordinator is obligatory with the comma; and that ellipsis of the subject, though frequently found with the comma (App III.7), scarcely occurs after a semicolon.

III.17

As the last sentence of App III.16 shows, however, the use of the semicolon is wider than has so far been stated: here we see it (a) being followed by a coordinator, as is quite common in fact, and (b) coming between two coordinate clauses which are not independent but functioning as nominal clauses related to anticipatory *it*. Such a use (in effect, replacing a comma) is chiefly found in rather formal writing and in sentences whose complexity already involves the use of one or more commas and whose major divisions call for a hierarchically superior punctuation mark if the reader is not to be momentarily puzzled or misled. A simple but convenient application of this principle occurs in lists, where it is often desirable to show subgroupings:

> The chief commodities are butter, cheese, milk, eggs; lamb,
> beef, veal, pork; oats, barley, rye, and wheat.   [25]

Somewhat related is the chief point at which the semicolon shows affinity of use with the colon; namely, the convention (as in this sentence and in [26a]), of preceding such apposition indicators as *namely* or *that is* by a semicolon. Without such an indicator, as in [26b], a colon would usually be appropriate:

> In one respect, government policy has been firmly decided;
> that is, there will be no conscription.   [26a]
> In one respect, government policy has been firmly decided:
> there will be no conscription.   [26b]

Punctuating for sentence and paragraph
III.18

The two highest separators constitute combinations of symbols. We mark off one orthographic sentence from the next by terminating it with a period or (as it is usually called in BrE) a full stop, and by beginning the next with a capital letter; between the period and the capital, there will usually be a somewhat wider space than we normally have between words. The paragraph is also marked off by a complex of symbols in most writing: leaving blank the remainder of the line in which it ends; indention of the line beginning the new one; and (sometimes) a slightly larger space between lines at this point. At the beginning of a chapter or section, new paragraphs normally (as in this book), begin without indention, and in some styles of writing this practice is followed with all paragraphs; as a result, if the end of the previous paragraph happens to coincide with the end of a line, the new one may not in effect be marked at all.

Note
Numbered sections of a chapter, as in this book, are sometimes called 'paragraphs', even where they comprise more than one 'punctuation' paragraph.

III.19
It was stressed in App III.2 that punctuation was linked primarily to grammar rather than to prosody. This does not mean that the sentence and the paragraph, as punctuated, are obvious grammatical units – except to the extent that they are co-terminous with one or more grammatical units and that hence no grammatical units extend beyond their limits. The decision to coordinate several independent clauses within one sentence or to separate them as different sentences, with or without formal sign of their logical connection, is dependent largely upon the style of material one is handling or indeed upon the personal preference of the writer. Guidance on sentence limits which invokes criteria such as 'completeness', 'independence', 'intelligibility as a single whole' is essentially circular, since (a) the writer will necessarily have to decide for himself how 'complete' to make any part of his argument, and (b) punctuation of itself imposes the impression of completeness and independence on units marked off as sentences and conversely helps to show connection between units grouped within sentence limits.

Such points apply, of course, even more obviously in the case of paragraph limits. Rather than attempting to recommend an ideal size of paragraph or models for its ideal identity, we should note that the paragraph enables a writer to show that a particular set of sentences should be considered as more closely related to each other, and that those grouped within one paragraph are to be seen as a whole in relation to those that are grouped in the paragraphs preceding and following.

III.20
Light and heavy punctuation
One further point on punctuation style may be added. It was shown in App III.9 that an initial adverbial was one obvious part of a sentence that could be separated from the rest by a comma. If however we do so in the following,

?Slowly, he strolled over and she smiled gaily at him. [27a]

the punctuation may suggest that *slowly* applies (almost nonsensically) to both clauses in the remaining part of the sentence. Alternatively, the punctuation may seem illogical in making a break *within* the first clause (in effect, *He strolled over slowly*) where there is none *between* the first and second. So, given the constituents of [27a], we may feel obliged to add more punctuation to counteract these objections:

Slowly, he strolled over, and she smiled gaily at him.   [27b]

This is a simple example of how punctuation marks can enforce proliferation, so that once a little punctuation is admitted, much more is necessary in order to preserve a consistent and logical ordering of hierarchical relationships. In preference to rather heavily punctuated sentences like [27b], writers often move in the opposite direction towards a 'light' punctuation, just sufficient to make their sentences quickly and easily understood.

Separation of included units
Correlative punctuation marks, typical included units, and the comma
III.21
An adverbial element such as that which opens [26] need not, of course, be placed initially but may occur medially, like *of course* in the present sentence. In such cases the decision to mark it off by punctuation involves not one comma but two:

Government policy has, *in one respect*, been firmly decided . . .   [26c]

The convention is especially appropriate for conjuncts (8.89 *ff*) such as *of course, however, moreover* or parenthesized clauses such as *I think, you know*, or *that is*. Consider this further (and clumsy) alteration of [26a]:

Government policy has, *in one respect*, been firmly decided; there
    will be, *that is*, no conscription.   [26d]

The effect of the punctuation is to indicate appropriately that the italicized items are not part of the clauses in which they are located: that they are not integrated with these clauses but merely *included* parenthetically within them. For this reason, as well as for clarity and to comply with the rule about separating S, V and C (App III.7), commas must precede as well as follow the included items. Thus we cannot have:

*Government policy has in one respect, been firmly decided; there
    will be, that is no conscription.   [26e]

In other words, punctuation marks used for inclusion must be *correlative:* two instances of the same sign must occur, the first indicating the beginning and the second the end of the included item.

Note
The separation by punctuation at the beginning and end of included units reflects to some extent the distinguishing of such included units in speech by frequently giving them a separate tone unit with perhaps also a change in pitch range or other prosodic feature. *Cf* App II.12 *ff*.

III.22
Adverbial elements and parenthetic clauses are not, however, the only common types of included items. Others are appositions (9.130 *ff*), ellipses (9.91), and analogous parallel structures, as in:

The other man, David Johnson, refused to make a statement.   [28]
The man we need, the man we have been waiting for, is someone adequately trained in business management.   [29]
He is a close friend to, and supporter of, the Republican candidate.   [30]
He should, or rather must, attend better to his studies.   [31]
Her masculine, indeed ungainly, strides made her unattractive.   [32]

So also with vocatives:

I think, John, that you would be wiser not to go.   [33]
But how, ladies and gentlemen, are we to proceed to a freer society?   [34]

III.23
Dashes and parentheses
Although commas are the only items so far illustrated, two other common sets of correlative punctuation marks can be used to mark the separation of such included units as those illustrated in App III.21 *f*. They are dashes and parentheses, the latter known in BrE also as 'brackets' (*cf* App III.24 Note *a*):

The other man – David Johnson – refused to make a statement. [28a]
The other man (David Johnson) refused to make a statement.   [28b]

But this is far from meaning that these three types of inclusion mark are interchangeable. The comma is the least obtrusive and for that reason is preferred unless there is a strong counter-reason, such as the danger of confusion with other neighbouring commas or of failure to mark adequately a rather lengthy inclusion. In these cases dashes or parentheses are preferable, except that dashes tend to give a somewhat more dramatic and informal impression, suggesting an impromptu aside, rather than a planned inclusion:

At that time, the students – goodness knows for what reason – reversed their earlier, more moderate decision, and a big demonstration was planned.   [35]

In this sentence, three commas are used for separation purposes and if commas were to be used for the included clause also, the reader would experience unnecessary difficulty. At the same time, the inclusion is sufficiently informal and violent an interruption to justify dashes rather than parentheses.

Under certain circumstances, even short included items tend to be enclosed by parentheses. In formal writing, for example, they are used for cross-references and the figures denoting life span:

> We shall see below (*p* 63) that Eleanor's first love was William
> Bevan (1812–73).   [36]

III.24
Inclusion approximating to succession

At the opening point of an inclusion, none of the correlative punctuation marks can co-occur with any other separation mark, and the following is therefore inadmissible:

> *I spoke to Mr Wilson, (my neighbour) when I next saw him.

At the close of an inclusion, this is also true so far as the comma and dash are concerned:

> *I spoke to Mr Wilson – my neighbour –, when I next saw him.

But a closing parenthesis can co-occur with other separation items, as in:

> I spoke to Mr Wilson (my neighbour), when I next saw him.   [37]

An important indication that parentheses are hierarchically superior to comma and dash is that parentheses alone can be used to show the 'included' status of a whole sentence and even (though rarely) a whole paragraph:

> He married Mary in 1968. (His father had forbidden him to
> do so earlier.) She was then twenty-four ...   [38]

But they otherwise show their hierarchical status only by the degree to which the included unit is grammatically distinct from the including unit. That is, their 'superiority' does not mean that they must be given priority when there is an inclusion within an inclusion. In this situation any of the paired marks may enclose any other, but care has to be taken (a) to match the enclosing pairs so that the 'inner' inclusion is clearly complete before the 'outer' one is closed, and (b) to use different including marks for the two (or more) included units:

> He had, I was (by then) quite sure, become utterly depraved.
> He had (I was, by then, quite sure) become utterly depraved.
> He had, I was – by then – quite sure, become utterly depraved.

*He had – I was, by then – quite sure, become utterly depraved.
?He had, I was, by then, quite sure, become utterly depraved.

Note

[a] In popular BrE usage parentheses are called 'brackets', a term reserved in AmE for what are in BrE called 'square brackets', sometimes used when inclusions have to be made within inclusions:

The other man (David Johnson [*alias* Wilson]).

[b] These 'square brackets' are used in serious writing also to include the author's or editor's comment upon the form rather than on the content:

He said that *Thursday* was his normal visiting day [italics mine].
It was stated that the heir to the property was Jon [*sic*] Roberts.

[c] It is noteworthy that all forms of bracket, including the braces used in mathematics and other technical writing, {}, differ from other inclusion marks in clearly distinguishing the opening (left-hand) and closing (right-hand) items in the correlative pair. The fact that each item thus indicates independently its correlative status makes parentheses the clearest of the inclusion signs and especially appropriate for lengthy inclusions.

III.25
Included units in relation to lightness of punctuation

Inclusion marks can necessitate the use of additional punctuation that would not otherwise have been desirable and so (as we saw in App III.20) we can be forced from light to unfortunately heavy punctuation. Consider the effect of including the participial clause *seeing this* in the following example:

He smiled at Joan and Mary was cross.   [39a]
*He smiled at Joan and Mary, seeing this, was cross.   [39b]

The latter is unacceptable in seriously misrepresenting the hierarchy of grammatical relations: it would make the reader think at first that *and* was coordinating the two names rather than the two clauses, and so we must have:

He smiled at Joan, and Mary, seeing this, was cross.   [39c]

So also, although a comma is optional in [40a], it is obligatory when *in short* has been included, as in [40b]:

If this is what he seems to want(,) he can have it.   [40a]
If this, in short, is what he seems to want, he can have it.   [40b]

Quotation and quotation marks
III.26

There is one further correlative pair of inclusion marks that is of great importance and in frequent use: the 'quotation marks', informally 'quotes', or (especially BrE) 'inverted commas'. Like parentheses, they can co-occur with other marks of punctuation, and like parentheses too their shape distinguishes between opening and closing item:

The words 'Keep out' were shouted in a loud voice. [41]

Hearing the words 'Keep out', he stopped. [42]

In [41] and [42], the included item begins with a capital letter because it represents a spoken sentence. The logic of this does not, however, extend to terminating the quoted sentence with a period unless the quotation ends the including sentence; otherwise, the end of the quoted 'sentence' is overridden by the fact that the including sentence is not complete:

'I am delighted to see you,' he said. [43]

He said, 'I am delighted to see you.' [44]

In [43] in fact, the 'illogical' comma coinciding with the end of quotation is placed within the quotation marks, according to the dictates of punctuation convention (especially in print). In addition, both [43] and [44] infringe a rule given in App III.11, and we must now state the exception that when the object in a clause or sentence is a piece of direct speech it may be (and usually is) separated by punctuation from the verb and subject elements.

Note
On the punctuation of quoted questions and exclamations, see App III.28 f.

III.27
Quotation marks may be single '. . .' or double ". . .". The latter are more usual in handwritten material and in American printing; the former are more usual in British printing, but the choice lies primarily with individual printing houses. Whichever form is not used for ordinary quotation is then used for quotation within quotation:

'I heard "Keep out" being shouted,' he said. (especially BrE)

"I heard 'Keep out' being shouted," he said. (especially AmE)

Quoted matter does not always require quotation marks. In dramatic dialogue and in newspaper reports of speeches or court proceedings, a series of speakers' names will usually be followed by a colon and the quotation:

Judge Harlan: If you do not answer frankly, the jury will draw its own conclusions.

And only short quotations from other writers will be put in quotation marks in serious writing; longer quotations will be indented and given without quotation marks.

Note

In some writing, an extensive quotation will have an opening quotation mark at the beginning of each new paragraph though a closing mark will occur only at the end of the entire quotation.

Specification

III.28

Question and exclamation marks

Although in App III.2, specification was exemplified with the use of the apostrophe to mark the genitive, in many ways a more obvious example is the question mark. This indicates that the sentence it terminates is a question, whether it is interrogative or (less frequently) declarative in form:

What can be done to help these people?	[45]
You are leaving already?	[46]

In the case of [46] the question mark matches in writing the prosodic contrast between this sentence as question and the same sentence as statement (App II.13). In [45], as with other *wh*-questions, there is no necessary prosodic distinction from declarative sentences to match the punctuation contrast between period and question mark.

The exclamation mark is more rarely used and indeed its excessive use is often taken as a sign of frivolous or immature writing. It is however quite normal in representing an exclamatory sentence, whether or not this has interrogative form:

How silly she is!

Isn't she silly!

Both question and exclamation mark exclude the use of other separation punctuation and have the value of a period inasmuch as what follows begins with the capitalization of a new sentence. But when they co-occur with the end of quotation, they come within the quotation marks and if more of the including sentence follows, no capital letter is used:

'How silly she is!' he thought.

Note

Imperative sentences do not terminate with an exclamation mark unless they represent very peremptory orders:

'Get outside!' he shouted angrily.

For rather different reasons, not all sentences which are interrogative in form end in a question mark. A period is often preferred if the question is lengthy and ends with subordinate clauses, or if the interrogative form is operating as a request:

Would the gentleman who left a silk scarf on the manager's desk care to retrieve it from the porter's office.

III.29

Specification of included units

The use of punctuation in the following illustrates important features of practice in relation to included material:

Did you see the words $\left\{\begin{array}{l}\text{`Are you happy?'}\\\text{`You fools!'}\end{array}\right\}$ on the wall?   [47a]

I saw the words $\left\{\begin{array}{l}\text{`Are you happy?'}\\\text{`You fools!'}\end{array}\right\}$ Did you see them?   [47b]

Did you see the words $\left\{\begin{array}{l}\text{`Are you happy?'}\\\text{`You fools!'?}\end{array}\right\}$ [47c]

Did you see the words `Are you happy'?   [47d]

?Did you see the words `Are you happy?'?   [47e]

*I saw the words `Are you happy?'.   [47f]

These words (`Are you happy?') were on the wall.   [47g]

?These words, `Are you happy?', were on the wall.   [47h]

Though logically correct, [47e] is less acceptable than either [47d] or the corresponding part of [47c] as a means of handling the same problem. It will be noted that in any event a period or other separation mark cannot follow either of these specificatory signs, question or exclamation.

Although they are primarily used at the end of interrogative or exclamatory sentences, question and exclamation marks may also be used, especially in formal or technical writing, to specify doubt or surprise about individual parts of a sentence; in such use, they are often enclosed in parentheses, following the relevant item, though the question mark may sometimes precede (our practice in this book when indicating doubtfully acceptable sentences):

A further semantic (?) problem may be formulated as follows.

The old woman insisted that her name was Shirley Temple (!) and muttered something about being born in what sounded like Abbis (?) Ababa.

Note

[a] The use of ?? or !! and the like to suggest extreme doubt or surprise is confined to very informal writing such as stories for children.

[b] As well as expressing doubt or surprise at individual items in a sentence, we can indicate that individual items have been introduced from a different style (usually by quotation marks, as with the colloquialism in [48a]) or from a foreign language (usually by italics – underlining in manuscript – as in [48b] and [49]). We can further use quotation marks to give the meaning of an expression, as in [48b].

The stranded colonel was obliged to `hitch' a ride from a passing motorist.   [48a]

The word *schadenfreude*, which means `malicious enjoyment', is quite fashionable in English.   [48b]

His slightest *jeu d'esprit* was impressive.   [49]

[c] Quotation marks as in [48a] may indicate a hesitant or apologetic introduction of a doubtful or discordant item. But elsewhere they may equally imply that the item is of doubtful validity because merely alleged; in this usage they may be sly or sarcastic and match a heavy prosodic marking in speech:

> I told him that his 'wife' had come and let him know by the way I said it that I didn't think she really *was* his wife.

[d] As in this last example, italics (ie underlining in manuscript) can be used informally to indicate emphasis.

III.30
The apostrophe

While the apostrophe is most frequently used in serious writing to denote genitive singular and plural as in *the girl's* and *the girls'* (where speech treats these the same as each other and as the non-genitive plural, *the girls:* 4.96), in ordinary use it also marks the colloquial contractions in the verb phrase: *I'm, he's, we're, can't, won't*, etc (3.17*ff*). It is still occasionally found marking such well-established shortened forms as *'phone, 'cello, 'flu,* and in light fiction or other casual writing it is sometimes used to indicate colloquial pronunciation in such forms as *goin'*, *'cos* (= 'because'), and the like. It is similarly used informally for contraction of year numbers, especially in figures; thus for *1974* we have *'74.*

The apostrophe is frequently used before the plural *s* with items which lack institutionalized spelling:

> There are three i's in that word   [50]
> The late 1970's   [51]

But more often the *s* is affixed without an apostrophe (*1970s*) if there is no danger of misreading (as there would be in example [50]).

III.31
Dashes and other specifiers of breaks

A break or anacoluthon is indicated by a dash, but naturally this rather crude device belongs largely to informal or melodramatic writing:

> They gave him a prize for getting top marks – and a certificate
> as well.   [52]
> 'I hoped that you –' His voice broke.   [53]
> John wasn't altogether – I thought he seemed a little unhappy.   [54]

An analogous use of the dash is made to suppress (now rarely) a name or obscenity ('Mr B—'; 'F— off'). A more formal analogy is the short dash used to abbreviate a sequence of numbers: '*pp* 14–23'.

Note

[a] Anacoluthon is also frequently expressed by means of dots (normally three), which could replace the dash in [53] though perhaps giving the impression of trailing away rather than an abrupt break. In formal writing, the dots can indicate 'that which it is unnecessary to specify':

Take a sequence of prime numbers (1, 3, 7, 11, 13, 17, . . .) and consider . . .

[b] Stammering is sometimes informally indicated by hyphens and reduplication of letters:

'P-p-p-please t-t-try;' his teeth chattered through fear and cold.

III.32
Abbreviations and the use of special signs

Abbreviation is marked most generally by a single period following an initial letter or shortened form of a word, as in *Prof. Smith, i.e., e.g., etc.* When the abbreviation includes the final letter of the word abbreviated, there is a widespread convention (especially in BrE) of ignoring the need for a period: *Dr, Mr,* for example. Indeed, in much modern practice, abbreviation is carried out by means of word shortening without the use of periods: *etc* or *&c, cf,* UN, USA, PTO, for example. Such abbreviations as *etc* are used sparingly in formal writing, though RSVP with or without periods is found almost only in formal use (on invitation cards).

Note

In numerals, the period (often raised above the line) marks the point at which integers cease and decimal fractions begin:

71.53 (where the period is read as 'point')

It is similarly used in currency statements, where, however the period is ignored in reading:

$3.40 – read as 'three dollars and forty cents' or 'three forty'
£1.20 – read as 'one pound twenty (pence)'

Small numerals are usually spelled out and it is not usual to introduce mathematical symbols into ordinary writing; such symbols as the following are normally flanked only by numerals, not words:

$=$ read as 'equals'
$+$ read as 'plus' or 'and'
$-$ read as 'minus' or 'take away'
$\times$ read as 'times' or 'multiplied by'
$\div$ read as 'over' or 'divided by'
$\sqrt{}$ read as 'the (square) root of'

Thus: $(17 - \sqrt{9} + \frac{65}{5}) - (4 \times 3) = 15$ would be read as 'Seventeen minus the square root of nine, plus sixty-five over five, minus four times three, equals fifteen.'

Numerals in word form between 20 and 100 (except the multiples of ten) are hyphenated: *twenty-one, eighty-six,* etc; written fractions likewise: *four-fifths, seven-twelfths,* etc. *Cf* 4.129.

In date abbreviations, numerals are separated by solidus (App III.34), colon or period. Thus

7/2/72

7.2.72

7:2:72 (less commonly)

could all be used for '7th February 1972' (BrE) or 'July 2nd, 1972' (AmE). Numerals in abbreviations for time of day use colon (especially AmE) or period (especially BrE), as in:

6:30⎫
6.30⎭(read as 'six-thirty' or 'half past six')

III.33
Use of capitals

In addition to specifying proper names (for example, persons, places, works of literature, days of the week, the names of the months – but not usually the seasons; the planets – but not the earth, the sun or the moon), initial capitals are used for accompanying appositive titles; thus:

John Mills is a colonel   *but*   He is Colonel John Mills
Edinburgh is a city in Scotland   *but*   The City of Edinburgh is in Scotland

So also

Those present included Mr Jones, Miss Graham, Dr Rabin, Mrs Willis, Professor Maisky, and Mrs McDonald.

Occasionally, initial capitals are used to mark key words in formal discourse, especially at the point where such words are introduced for the first time.

The next problem, that of Ultraviolet Radiation, is one on which considerable progress has been made.

Capitals for key words are a particular feature of legal usage:

The Company's Registrars must receive a copy of the Letter together with the Form of Renunciation.

At the opposite extreme, capitals are sometimes used in light or facetious writing to indicate spoken prominence for the words so specified:

'I must certainly see the Man of the House,' she announced, pompously.
'And what do YOU want?' he growled.

Capital letters also appear in the specification of many abbreviations as we saw in App III.32, whether the items abbreviated are proper names (where the use of capitals is normal) or not, as usually in PTO, RSVP. In the latter instances, we seem to have an extension of the use of capitals in block language (7.90), notices, and the like ('No Exit').

Note

In the Middle Ages, the letters *i*, *j*, and *y* were used to some extent interchangeably and it is for complicated reasons of paleographical preference (rather than the egocentric immodesty it might suggest) that capital *I*, itself an alternant of *j*, emerged as the regular spelling of the 1st-person singular pronoun.

III.34

The solidus and miscellaneous conventions

Lesser punctuation conventions may be grouped as (a) chiefly technical, and (b) formulaic:

(a) Parenthesized figures or letters commonly distinguish parts of an exposition, like the (a) and (b) in this section; *a*) and *b*) are common variants.

The solidus (*alias* 'slant', 'slash', 'oblique') is used to indicate abbreviation and also to specify alternatives and subsectioning:

the academic year 1975/6
c/o (in postal addresses, read as 'care of')
students and/or staff
Rule A/32

Bold face draws special attention to an item. Prefixing a name by a cross may indicate a church dignitary, and suffixing a name by an obelisk (†) may indicate that the person is dead.

(b) In App III.18 it was pointed out that beginning a new line was part of the complex symbol separating one paragraph from another. A new line may also specify the formulaic termination of a letter before the signature on a further new line. This convention requires a capital at the beginning of the formula and a comma at the end:

Yours sincerely, (especially BrE)
Sincerely yours, (especially AmE)

A new line (often indented) is also used to specify each major item in the structure of postal addresses, except that city and state appear as one line in AmE practice; again each line may terminate with a comma, but a 'light punctuation' variant is also possible and is especially common in AmE use:

26 Park Drive	43, College Green,
Portsmouth, RI 02840	Dublin,
USA	Ireland.

Note

A new line is commonly used also for each item in a formal list such as an index.

Bibliographical note

Accounts of AmE practice are given in Summey (1949); and University of Chicago Press (1969), *pp* 103–146; and of BrE practice in Carey (1957); Hart (1948); and Vallins (1952), *pp* 81–107, and (1953), *pp* 121–141. AmE and BrE conventions are compared in the alphabetized articles on each of the main punctuation marks in Nicholson (1957). Some aspects of punctuation theory are treated in Firbas (1955).

BIBLIOGRAPHY

AARTS, F. G. A. M. (1971) 'On the Distribution of Noun-Phrase Types in
English Clause-Structure', *Lingua* 26, 281–93
ABERCROMBIE, D. (1967) *Elements of General Phonetics*, Edinburgh
ADAMS, V. (1973) *Introduction to Modern English Word-Formation*, London
AKSENENKO, B. N. (1956) *Predlogi Angliiskogo Yazyka*, Moscow
ALEXANDER, D. and KUNZ, W. J. (1964) 'Some Classes of Verbs in
English', *Linguistic Research Project*, Indiana University
ALEXANDER, D. and MATTHEWS, P. H. (1964) 'Adjectives before
That-Clauses in English', *Linguistic Research Project*, Indiana University
ALLEN, R. L. (1966) *The Verb System of Present-Day American English*, The
Hague
ANDERSON, J. (1968) 'Ergative and Nominative in English', *Journal of
Linguistics* 4, 1–32
ARNOLD, G. F. (1957) *Stress in English Words*, Amsterdam
AVIS, W. S. (1967) *A Dictionary of Canadianisms on Historical Principles*,
Toronto
BACH, E. (1967) '*Have* and *Be* in English Syntax', *Language* 43, 462–85
BALD, W-D. and QUIRK, R. (1970) 'A Case Study of Multiple Meaning',
Essays and Studies 23, London, 101–19
BEHRE, F. (1955) *Meditative-Polemic SHOULD in Modern English THAT-Clauses*,
Göteborg
BENNETT, D. C. (1968) 'English Prepositions: a Stratificational Approach',
Journal of Linguistics 4, 153–72
BIESE, Y. M. (1941) *Origin and Development of Conversions in English*,
Helsinki
BLADON, R. A. W. (1968) 'Selecting the *to-* or *-ing* Nominal after *like, love,
hate, dislike* and *prefer*', *English Studies* 44, 203–14
BLOOMFIELD, L. (1933) *Language*, New York
BOLINGER, D. L. (1957) *Interrogative Structures of American English*,
Birmingham, Alabama
   (1961) 'Syntactic Blends and Other Matters', *Language* 37, 366–81
   (1963) 'Length, Vowel, Juncture', *Linguistics* 1, 5–29
   (1965) *Forms of English*, Cambridge, Mass
   (1967a) 'The Imperative in English', *To Honor Roman Jakobson* Vol I,
   The Hague, 335–63
   (1967b) 'Adjectives in English: Attribution and Predication', *Lingua* 18,
   1–34
   (1967c) 'Adjective Comparison: a Semantic Scale', *Journal of English
   Linguistics* 1, 2–10
   (1969) 'Categories, Features, Attributes', *Brno Studies in English* 8, 37–41
   (1971a) *Degree Words*, The Hague
   (1971b) *The Phrasal Verb in English*, Cambridge, Mass
   (1971c) 'Semantic Overloading: A Restudy of the Verb *Remind*',
   Language 47, 522–47

BOURQUIN, G. (1964) *Le Groupement nominal en Anglais écrit*, Publications Linguistiques de la Faculté des Lettres 3, Nancy

BOYD, J. C. and THORNE, J. P. (1969) 'The Semantics of Modal Verbs', *Journal of Linguistics* 5, 57–74

BRANFORD, W. (1970) *Reports* 1 and 2 on the Dictionary of South African English project (mimeo), Grahamstown

BRITISH COUNCIL (1969) *Annual Report 1968–69*, London

BROWN, R. W. (1927) *Materials for Word Study: a Manual of Roots, Prefixes, Suffixes, and Derivatives in the English Language*, New Haven (1954) *Composition of Scientific Words*, Washington DC

BRYANT, M. (1962) (ed) *Current American Usage*, New York

BUGARSKI, R. (1969) 'Symmetry and Asymmetry in Prepositional Systems', in *Papers to Mark the Fortieth Anniversary of the Department of English*, University of Belgrade, 57–69

CAREY, G. V. (1957) *Punctuation*, Cambridge

CARVELL, H. T. and SVARTVIK, J. (1969) *Computational Experiments in Grammatical Classification*, The Hague

CHARLESTON, B. M. (1960) *Studies on the Emotional and Affective Means of Expression in Modern English*, Bern

CHATMAN, S. (1965) *A Theory of Meter*, The Hague

CHOMSKY, N. (1957) *Syntactic Structures*, The Hague (1965) *Aspects of the Theory of Syntax*, Cambridge, Mass (1970) 'Remarks on Nominalisation', in Jacobs and Rosenbaum (1970)

CHOMSKY, N. and HALLE, M. (1968) *The Sound Pattern of English*, New York

CHRISTOPHERSEN, P. (1939) *The Articles: A Study of Their Theory and Use in English*, Copenhagen

CHRISTOPHERSEN, P. and SANDVED, A. O. (1969) *An Advanced English Grammar*, London

CLOSE, R. A. (1970) 'Problems of the Future Tense', *English Language Teaching* 24, 225–32; 25, 43–9

CLOSS, E. T. and WATERHOUSE, J. (1969) '"Already" and "yet": A Suppletive Set of Aspect Markers?', *Journal of Linguistics* 5, 287–304

CRYMES, R. (1968) *Some Systems of Substitution Correlations in Modern American English*, The Hague

CRYSTAL, D. (1966) 'Specification and English Tenses', *Journal of Linguistics* 2, 1–34 (1969) *Prosodic Systems and Intonation in English*, Cambridge

CRYSTAL, D. and DAVY, D. (1969) *Investigating English Style*, London

CURME, G. O. (1931) *Syntax*, Boston

DANIELSSON, B. (1948) *Studies on the Accentuation of Polysyllabic Latin, Greek, and Romance Loanwords in English*, Stockholm Studies in English 3, Stockholm

DIK, S. C. (1968) *Coordination: Its Implications for the Theory of General Linguistics*, Amsterdam

DIVER, W. (1963) 'The Chronological System of the English Verb', *Word* 19, 141–81

DUŠKOVÁ, L. (1965) 'On Some Disputed Points in the Use of Pronouns in Present-Day English', *Philologica Pragensia* 2–3, 163–70

EHRMAN, M. (1966) *The Meanings of the Modals in Present-Day American English*, The Hague

FILLMORE, C. (1965) *Indirect Object Constructions in English*, The Hague
(1966) 'A Proposal concerning English Prepositions', *Report of the Seventeenth Annual Round Table Meeting on Linguistics and Language Studies*, Georgetown University, Washington DC, 19–33
(1968) 'The Case for Case', in *Universals in Linguistic Theory*, edd E. Bach and R. T. Harms, New York
(1969) 'Toward a Modern Theory of Case', in Reibel and Schane (1969), 361–75

FILLMORE, C. and LANGENDOEN, D. T. (1971) (edd) *Studies in Linguistic Semantics*, New York

FIRBAS, J. (1955) 'On the Problem of the Main Principle in English Sentence Punctuation', *Časopis pro Moderni Filologii* 37, 266–77
(1964) 'On Defining Theme in Functional Sentence Analysis', *Travaux Linguistiques de Prague* 1, 267–80
(1966) 'Non-Thematic Subjects in Contemporary English', *Travaux Linguistiques de Prague* 2, 239–56

FOWLER, H. W. (1965) *A Dictionary of Modern English Usage*, 2nd edn revised by Sir Ernest Gowers, Oxford

FRANCIS, W. N. (1958) *The Structure of American English*, New York

FRASER, B. (1970) 'Some Remarks on the Action Nominalization in English', in Jacobs and Rosenbaum (1970)
(1971) 'An Analysis of "Even" in English', in Fillmore and Langendoen (1971)

FRIES, C. C. (1940) *American English Grammar*, New York

GIMSON, A. C. (1970) *An Introduction to the Pronunciation of English*, 2nd edn, London

GINZBURG, R. S., KHIDEKEL, S. S., KNYAZEVA, G. Y. and SANKIN, A. A. (1966) *A Course in Modern English Lexicology*, Moscow

GIRARD, D. (1970) 'The Special Demands on English in Europe Today', *Incorporated Linguist* 9

GLEASON, H. A. Jr (1965) *Linguistics and English Grammar*, New York

GLEITMAN, L. R. (1965) 'Coordinating Conjunctions in English', *Language* 41, 260–93

GOYVAERTS, D. L. (1968) 'An Introductory Study on the Ordering of a String of Adjectives in Present-Day English', *Philologia Pragensia* 11, 12–28

GREENBAUM, S. (1969a) *Studies in English Adverbial Usage*, London
(1969b) 'The Question of *But*', *Folia Linguistica* 3, 245–54
(1970) *Verb-Intensifier Collocations in English: An Experimental Approach*, The Hague

HALE, A. (1970) 'Conditions on English Comparative Clause Pairings', in Jacobs and Rosenbaum (1970)

HALL, R. A. Jr (1966) *Pidgin and Creole Languages*, Ithaca

HALLE, M. and KEYSER, S. J. (1971), *English Stress*, New York

HALLIDAY, M. A. K. (1967) *Intonation and Grammar in British English*, The Hague

(1967–68) 'Notes on Transitivity and Theme in English', *Journal of Linguistics* 3, 37–81, 199–244; 4, 179–215

(1970a) 'Functional Diversity in Language as seen from a Consideration of Modality and Mood in English', *Foundations of Language* 6, 322–61

(1970b) *A Course in Spoken English: Intonation*, London

HALLIDAY, M. A. K., MCINTOSH, A. and STREVENS, P. (1964) *The Linguistic Sciences and Language Teaching*, London

HALLS, W. D. (1969) 'Report on Modern Languages at the Upper Academic Secondary Level', *Oxford Council of Europe Study*, Oxford

HARDER, K. B. (1968) 'Coinages of the Type "Sit-in"', *American Speech* 43, 58–64

HARRIS, Z. S. (1963) *Discourse Analysis Reprints, Papers on Formal Linguistics* 2, The Hague

HART, H. C. (1948) *Rules for Compositors and Readers*, Oxford

HASAN, R. (1968) *Grammatical Cohesion in Spoken and Written English: Part 1, Programme in Linguistics and English Teaching* Paper 7, London

HATCHER, A. G. (1949) 'To Get/Be Invited', *Modern Language Notes* 64, 433–46

(1960) 'An Introduction to the Analysis of English Noun Compounds', *Word* 16, 356–73

HAUGEN, E. (1953) 'On Resolving the Close Apposition', *American Speech* 28, 165–70

HILL, A. A. (1958) *Introduction to Linguistic Structures*, New York

HILL, L. A. (1968) *Prepositions and Adverbial Particles: An Interim Classification Semantic, Structural, and Graded*, Oxford

HOCKETT, C. F. (1955) 'Attribution and Apposition', *American Speech* 30, 99–102

HORNBY, A. S. *et al* (1963) *The Advanced Learner's Dictionary of Current English*, London

HUDDLESTON, R. D. (1965) 'Rank and Depth', *Language* 41, 574–86

(1967) 'More on the English Comparative', *Journal of Linguistics* 3, 91–102

(1969) 'Predicate Complement Constructions in English', *Lingua* 23, 241–73

(1971) *The Sentence in Written English: A Syntactic Study Based on an Analysis of Scientific Texts*, Cambridge

HUDSON, R. A. (1970) 'On Clauses Containing Conjoined and Plural Noun-Phrases in English', *Lingua* 24, 205–53

JACKENDOFF, R. S. (1969) 'An Interpretive Theory of Negation', *Foundations of Language* 5, 218–41

JACOBS, R. A. and ROSENBAUM, P. S. (1968) *English Transformational Grammar*, New York

(1970) (edd) *Readings in English Transformational Grammar*, Waltham, Mass

JACOBSON, S. (1964) *Adverbial Positions in English*, Stockholm

JACOBSSON, B. (1951) *Inversion in English, with Special Reference to the Early Modern English Period*, Uppsala
(1961) 'An Unexpected Usage: *ahead, alive*, and the like, before nouns', *Moderna Språk* 55, 240–47
(1963) 'On the Use of *that* in Non-Restrictive Relative Clauses', *Moderna Språk* 57, 406–16
(1968a) 'Simple Personal Pronouns and Compound Pronouns in *-self/-selves*', *Moderna Språk* 62, 24–37
(1968b) 'A Note on Common-Number *they/them/their* and *who*', *Studia Neophilologica* 40, 141–45
(1970) 'English Pronouns and Feature Analysis', *Moderna Språk* 64, 346–59
JESPERSEN, O. (1909–49) *A Modern English Grammar on Historical Principles* I–VII, London and Copenhagen
(1917) *Negation in English and Other Languages*, Copenhagen, reprinted in *Selected Writings of Otto Jespersen*, London 1962
(1933) *Essentials of English Grammar*, London
JONES, D. (1969) *English Pronouncing Dictionary*, ed A. C. Gimson, London
JOOS, M. (1967) *The Five Clocks*, New York
KAJITA, M. (1968) *A Generative-Transformational Study of Semi-Auxiliaries in Present-Day American English*, Tokyo
KANEKIYO, T. (1965) 'Notes on Gender in English', *Philologica Pragensia* 8
KARLSEN, R. (1959) *Studies in the Connection of Clauses in Current English: Zero Ellipsis and Explicit Forms*, Bergen
KATZ, J. J. (1968) 'The Logic of Questions', *Logic, Methodology, and Philosophy of Science* 3, edd B. Van Rootselaar and J. F. Staal, Amsterdam
KATZ, J. J. and POSTAL, P. (1964) *An Integrated Theory of Linguistic Descriptions*, Cambridge, Mass
KEMPSON, R. M. and QUIRK, R. (1971) 'Controlled Activation of Latent Contrast', *Language* 47, 548–72
KENNEDY, A. G. (1920) *The Modern English Verb-Adverb Combination*, Stanford University Publications, University Series, Language and Literature 1:1, Stanford
KENYON, J. S. and KNOTT, T. A. (1953) *A Pronouncing Dictionary of American English*, Springfield, Mass
KHLEBNIKOVA, I. B. (1965) 'Homonymy and the Subjunctive Mood in English', *Philologica Pragensia* 2–3, 238–45
KINGDON, R. (1957) 'The Irregular Verbs', *English Language Teaching* 11, 123–33
(1958) *The Groundwork of English Intonation*, London
KIPARSKY, P. and C. (1970) 'Fact', in *Recent Advances in Linguistics*, edd M. Bierwisch and K. E. Heidolph, The Hague
KLIMA, E. S. (1964) 'Negation in English', in *The Structure of Language: Readings in the Philosophy of Language*, edd J. A. Fodor and J. J. Katz, Englewood Cliffs, NJ, 246–323
KOZIOL, H. (1937) *Handbuch der Englischen Wortbildungslehre*, Heidelberg
KRUISINGA, E. (1931–32) *A Handbook of Present-Day English*, Groningen

KURODA, S-Y. (1969) 'English Relativization and Certain Related Problems', in Reibel and Schane (1969)

LAKOFF, G. (1966) 'Stative Adjectives and Verbs in English', *Mathematical Linguistics and Automatic Translation*, Report No NSF-17, Section I, Harvard Computation Laboratory, Cambridge, Mass

LAKOFF, G. and PETERS, S. (1966) 'Phrasal Conjunction and Symmetric Predicates', in Reibel and Schane (1969)

LAKOFF, R. (1969a) 'Some Reasons why there can't be any *some-any* Rules in English', *Language* 45, 608–15

(1969b) 'A Syntactic Argument for Negative Transportation', in *Papers from the Fifth Regional Meeting, Chicago Linguistic Society*, Department of Linguistics, University of Chicago

(1971) 'If's, and's and but's about Conjunction', in Fillmore and Langendoen (1971)

LANGACKER, R. W. (1969) 'On Pronominalisation and the Chain of Command', in Reibel and Schane (1969)

LANGENDOEN, D. T. (1970) *Essentials of English Grammar*, New York

LEE, D. W. (1952) 'Close Apposition: An Unresolved Pattern', *American Speech* 27, 268–75

LEECH, G. N. (1963) 'Disjunctive Grammar in British Television Advertising', *Studia Neophilologica* 35, 256–64

(1969a) *Towards a Semantic Description of English*, London

(1969b) *A Linguistic Guide to English Poetry*, London

(1972) *Meaning and the English Verb*, London

LEES, R. B. (1960a) *The Grammar of English Nominalizations*, Indiana University Research Center in Anthropology, Folklore and Linguistics 12, Bloomington, Indiana

(1960b) 'A Multiply Ambiguous Adjectival Construction in English', *Language* 36, 207–21

(1961) 'Grammatical Analysis of the English Comparative Construction', *Word* 17, 171–85

(1963) 'An Analysis of the "Cleft Sentence" in English', *Zeitschrift für Phonetik* 16, 371–88

LINDELÖF, U. (1937) *English Verb-Adverb Groups Converted into Nouns*, Helsingfors

LINDHOLM, J. (1969) 'Negative Raising and Sentence Pronominalization', in *Papers from the Fifth Regional Meeting, Chicago Linguistic Society*, Department of Linguistics, University of Chicago

LINDKVIST, K. G. (1950) *Studies on the Local Sense of the Prepositions IN, AT, ON, and TO in Modern English*, Lund

LJUNG, M. (1970) *English Denominal Adjectives*, Gothenburg Studies in English 2, Göteborg

LONG, R. B. (1961) *The Sentence and its Parts*, Chicago

LYONS, J. (1968) *Introduction to Theoretical Linguistics*, Cambridge

MACHÁČEK, J. (1965) *Complementation of the English Verb by the Accusative-with-Infinitive and the Content Clause*, Prague

(1969) 'Historical Aspect of the Accusative with Infinitive and the
Content Clause in English', *Brno Studies in English* 8, 123–32

MALONE, J. H. (1967) 'A Transformational Re-examination of English
Questions', *Language* 43, 686–702

MALKIEL, Y. (1959) 'Studies in Irreversible Binomials', *Lingua* 8, 113–60,
reprinted in *Essays on Linguistic Themes*, Y. Malkiel, Berkeley 1968, 311–55

MARCHAND, H. (1969) *The Categories and Types of Present-Day English
Word-Formation*, 2nd edn, Munich

MCCAWLEY, J. D. (1970) 'Tense and Time Reference in English', in
Fillmore and Langendoen (1970)

MCDAVID, R. I. Jr (1963) (ed) *The American Language by H. L. Mencken*,
New York

MCINTOSH, A. (1966) 'Predictive Statements', in *In Memory of J. R. Firth*,
edd C. E. Bazell *et al*, London

MENCKEN, *see* MCDAVID

MITCHELL, T. F. (1958) 'Syntagmatic Relations in Linguistic Analysis',
Transactions of the Philological Society 101–18, Oxford

MULLER, S. H. (1964) *The World's Living Languages*, New York

MUTT, O. (1967) 'Some Recent Developments in the Use of Nouns as
Premodifiers in English', *Zeitschrift für Anglistik und Amerikanistik* 15,
401–08

NICHOLSON, M. (1957) *A Dictionary of American-English Usage*, New York

NICKEL, G. (1968) 'Complex Verbal Structures in English', *IRAL* 6, 1–21
(1971) *Papers in Contrastive Linguistics*, Cambridge

NORWOOD, J. E. (1954) 'The Loose Appositive in Present-Day English',
American Speech 29, 267–71

O'CONNOR, J. D. and ARNOLD, G. F. (1961) *Intonation of Colloquial English*,
London

OLSSON, Y. (1961) *On the Syntax of the English Verb*, Gothenburg Studies in
English 12, Göteborg

OTA, A. (1963) *Tense and Aspect of Present-Day American English*, Tokyo

PALMER, F. R. (1965) *A Linguistic Study of the English Verb*, London

PALMER, H. E. and BLANDFORD, F. G. (1969) *A Grammar of Spoken
English*, 3rd edn revised by R. Kingdon, Cambridge

PERRIN, P. G. (1965) *An Index to English*, 4th edn, New York

PIKE, K. L. (1945) *The Intonation of American English*, Ann Arbor

POSTAL, P. M. (1966) 'On So-Called "Pronouns" in English', in Reibel and
Schane (1969)
(1971) 'On the Surface Verb "Remind"', in Fillmore and Langendoen
(1971)

POUTSMA, H. (1926–29) *A Grammar of Late Modern English*, Groningen

POWELL, A. F. (1967) 'Forms and Uses of Nouns of Nationality', *English
Language Teaching* 21, 159–65

QUIRK, R. (1965) 'Descriptive Statement and Serial Relationship', *Language*
41, 205–17
(1968) *Essays on the English Language: Medieval and Modern*, London

(1970) 'Aspect and Variant Inflection in English Verbs', *Language* 46, 300–11

(1972) *The English Language and Images of Matter*, London

QUIRK, R. and MULHOLLAND, J. (1964) 'Complex Prepositions and Related Sequences', *English Studies* 44, 64–73

REIBEL, D. A. and SCHANE, S. A. (1969) (edd) *Modern Studies in English*, Englewood Cliffs, NJ

REIFER, M. (1955) *Dictionary of New Words*, New York

ROBBINS, B. L. (1968) *The Definite Article in English Transformations*, The Hague

ROGGERO, J. (1967) '*Whose* et *of which*', *Langues Modernes* 61, 405–15

ROSENBAUM, P. S. (1967a) *The Grammar of English Predicate Complement Constructions*, Cambridge, Mass

(1967b) 'Phrase Structure Principles of English Complex Sentence Formation', *Journal of Linguistics* 3, 103–18

SAPIR, E. (1921) *Language: An Introduction to the Study of Speech*, New York

SCHEURWEGHS, G. (1959) *Present-Day English Syntax*, London

(1963–68) *Analytical Bibliography of Writings on Modern English Morphology and Syntax, 1877–1960*, Louvain

SCHOPF, A. (1969) *Untersuchungen zur Wechselbeziehung zwischen Grammatik und Lexik im Englischen*, Berlin

SCHWARTZ, A. (1968) 'Derivative Functions in Syntax', *Language* 44, 747–83

SEYMOUR, R. K. (1968) *A Bibliography of Word-Formation in the Germanic Languages*, Durham, NC

SLOAT, C. (1969) 'Proper Nouns in English', *Language* 45, 26–30

SMITH, C. S. (1961) 'A Class of Complex Modifiers in English', *Language* 37, 342–65

(1964) 'Determiners and Relative Clauses in a Generative Grammar of English', *Language* 40, 37–52

SØRENSEN, H. S. (1958a) *Word-Classes in Modern English with Special Reference to Proper Names, with an Introductory Theory of Grammar, Meaning and Reference*, Copenhagen

(1958b) 'The Function of the Definite Article in Modern English', *English Studies* 40, 401–20

SPENCER, J. (1971) (ed) *The English Language in West Africa*, London

STOCKWELL, R. P., SCHACHTER, P. and PARTEE, B. H. (1968) *Integration of Transformational Theories on English Syntax*, University of California, Los Angeles

STORMS, G. (1966) '*That*-Clauses in Modern English', *English Studies* 47, 249–70

STRANG, B. M. H. (1968) *Modern English Structure*, 2nd edn, London

STRAUMANN, H. (1935) *Newspaper Headlines*, London

SVARTVIK, J. (1966) *On Voice in the English Verb*, The Hague

(1970) 'A New Generation of Passives', *Actes du Xe Congrès International des Linguistes* II, 1137–44, Bucharest

SWEET, H. (1891–98) *A New English Grammar*, Oxford

SUMMEY, G. (1949) *American Punctuation*, New York

TAGLICHT, J. (1972) 'The Choice of Relative Pronouns in Written English: Grammatical and Stylistic Factors', *Scripta Hierosolymitana* 24

TEYSSIER, J. (1968) 'Notes on the Syntax of the Adjective in Modern English', *Lingua* 20, 225–49

THORNE, J. P. (1969) 'English Imperative Sentences', *Journal of Linguistics* 5, 205–14

THUN, N. (1963) *Reduplicative Words in English. A Study of Formations of the Types* tick-tick, hurly-burly, *and* shilly-shally, Uppsala

TURNER, G. W. (1966) *The English Language in Australia and New Zealand*, London

TWADDELL, W. F. (1960) *The English Verb Auxiliaries*, Providence, RI

ULDALL, E. (1971) 'Isochronous Stresses in RP', in *Form and Substance*, Eli Fischer-Jørgensen Festschrift, edd L. L. Hammerich, R. Jakobson and E. Zwirner, Copenhagen

UNIVERSITY OF CHICAGO PRESS (1969) *A Manual of Style*, Chicago

VALLINS, G. H. (1952) *Good English*, London, 81–107

(1953) *Better English*, London, 121–41

VAN EK, J. A. (1966) *Four Complementary Structures of Predication in Contemporary British English*, Groningen

VENDLER, Z. (1968) *Adjectives and Nominalizations*, The Hague

VISSER, F. T. (1963–) *An Historical Syntax of the English Language*, Leiden

WEBSTER'S THIRD NEW INTERNATIONAL DICTIONARY (1961) ed P. Gove, Springfield, Mass

YNGVE, V. (1961) 'The Depth Hypothesis', in *The Structure of Language and its Mathematical Aspects*, ed R. Jakobson, Providence, RI

ZANDVOORT, R. W. (1957) *A Handbook of English Grammar*, London

ZIMMER, K. E. (1964) *Affixal Negation in English and Other Languages*, Supplement to *Word* 20, Monograph 5, New York

INDEX

References are to chapter (or appendix) and section number